Second Edition

Industrial market structure and economic performance

F. M. Scherer

Department of Economics
Swarthmore College

Houghton Mifflin Company • Boston
Dallas • Geneva, Ill.
Hopewell, N.J. • Palo Alto

Preface

The first edition (1970) of this book was written when I was three to five years out of graduate school, not quite dry behind the ears. It was not entirely in jest that I sometimes remarked, "Half the material is wrong, but I don't know which half." Since 1970 I have enjoyed rich opportunities to learn and unlearn. Among other things, a major research project entailing extensive company interviews helped me discern how certain things really work in manufacturing industry. Two years in Washington as a bureaucrat with antitrust enforcement responsibilities were equally educational. Meanwhile, the literature on industrial organization economics grew by leaps and bounds, and I have done my best to keep up. These and other developments provide the background for this major revision, which I now believe is three-fourths correct. To those who misread this fraction as an admission of defeat, I recommend a good course in the intellectual history of macroeconomics.

Although the book's basic approach and organization remain largely intact, there have been substantial changes in the detailed treatment of many topics. Somewhere between half and two-thirds of the original text has been rewritten completely; the rest has been honed and polished. Among the broader organizational changes, a new Chapter 9 surveys what has been learned through statistical structure–performance studies; the two macroeconomic performance chapters have been condensed into one; and the chapter on public regulation has been compressed and integrated into Chapter 18. Despite diligent efforts, it has been impossible to avoid a modest increase in the book's length. There is simply more that is worth saying. As in the first edition, I have tried to say it in tolerably straightforward English, making the material accessible to well-motivated undergraduates and others with no more training than a basic price theory course. (Those who know the first edition well may perceive that I have given up on Supreme Court clerks.) An abundance of footnotes provides counterpoint for the more advanced or ambitious reader.

As before, my intent has been to make the work serve as a state of the art survey—a treatise, if you will. As a textbook, it can be used for a two-term sequence progressing from theory to policy, or for a more breathless dash through both domains. It can also be employed, as it has in the past, by those who disagree with my approach and who tell their students, "Read this so I can talk about other more important things in class." Applications outside the classroom are self-evident. Indeed, it seems a pity my publisher has been unable to devise a pricing scheme that skims off the consumers' surplus from graduate students cramming for industrial organization preliminary examinations and attorneys preparing briefs for cases with a heavy industrial economics content.

Although much has been altered, my debt continues to colleagues and students who provided criticisms and research assistance on the first edition manuscript. They include William Comanor, Shorey Peterson, Jesse Markham, Thomas Kauper, W. G. Shepherd, Darius Gaskins, Ben Branch, John Cross, Saul Hymans, Harold Levinson, Sidney Winter, Ronald Teigen, Michael Klass, Erich Kaufer,

James Denny, Louis Hawkins, Lowell Seyburn, and Thomas Schick. In preparing this revised edition, I have benefited from critical comments by Richard Schmalensee, Ronald Braeutigam, William Comanor, James Rahl, Erich Kaufer, Martin Howe, Frederic Jenny, David Qualls, Bradley Gale, John Kwoka, and Stephen Sosnick. Leonard Weiss kindly supplied data for certain sections. My son Tom compiled data and ran the analyses for parts of Chapters 3, 4, and 13. Joel Mokyr's assistance was so valuable that I risk a lawsuit by not making him coauthor and letting the book be cited as Mokyr et al. Catherine Conrad and Ed Klotz assisted in chasing footnotes and compiling the index. Much of the manuscript was ably typed by Virginia Bostrom, Bonny Stevensen, and Ann Roth.

It is the author's lot to shoulder responsibility for all errors. I do so this time with less than the usual aplomb. For a variety of reasons, moving from manuscript to pressroom was abnormally susceptible to the workings of Murphy's Law. The most I can do now is hope that readers will help call remediable errors to my attention.

As usual, writing such an ambitious work has taken a heavy toll on family life. In small compensation, this edition is dedicated to my children.

F. M. Scherer
August 1979

Table of contents

Chapter 20 Antitrust policy: the control of market structures 527

Monopoly and monopolization
Proposals to reform Sherman Act Section 2
Merger policy
Structural antitrust abroad: a comparison

Chapter 21 Antitrust policy: other restrictions on conduct 571

Price discrimination
Tying contracts, requirements contracts, and exclusive dealing
Resale price maintenance

List of figures

List of tables

1 Introduction

This book explores systematically the field of economics known as *industrial organization*. The name is a curious one, distinctive mainly in its inability to communicate to outsiders what the subject is all about. It has little or nothing to say about how one organizes and directs a particular industrial enterprise, although there are industrial organization courses in business and engineering schools that deal with such matters. Rather, the field is concerned with how productive activities are brought into harmony with society's demands for goods and services through some organizing mechanism such as a free market, and how variations and imperfections in the organizing mechanism affect the degree of success achieved by producers in satisfying society's wants.

Any economy, whatever its cultural and political traditions may be, must decide what end products to produce and how much of each to produce, how scarce resources shall be apportioned in producing each, and how the end products shall be divided up or distributed among the various members of society. There are three main alternative ways to solve this bundle of problems. First, decisions can be made to conform with *tradition*. The economic organization of manors in Europe during feudal times and the caste system of occupational choice in India are prominent examples. Second, the problem can be solved through *central planning*. Illustrations include output and input planning for most indus-

tries in the Soviet Union and China and the elaborate controls the U.S. Department of Defense imposes over its contractors. Finally, there is the *market system* approach, under which consumers and producers act in response to price signals generated by the interplay of supply and demand forces in more or less freely operating markets, each participant seeking to make the best of the market conditions he or she faces, i.e., by maximizing profit or subjective utility.

The field of industrial organization is concerned primarily with the third of these approaches—the market system approach. This is not to deny the existence of a substantial overlap with other fields, such as the field of comparative economic systems, which specializes in analyzing the operation of centrally planned, hybrid socialist, and traditional economies. Many of the structural features we shall examine are of equal concern to the central planner. Likewise, our understanding of free market processes can be sharpened by studying the resource allocation methods of socialist and centrally planned economies. Still, to remain within manageable scope, this book respects the traditional division of intellectual labor, confining its coverage to market processes.

On similar grounds of manageability and convenience, our focus must be narrowed even further. We shall have little to say about the operation of labor markets, whose study is the domain of the labor specialist, and even less about the banking, finance, and insurance industries, which belong conventionally to the field of money and banking. Primary emphasis will be placed on the manufacturing and mineral extraction sectors of industrialized economies, with secondary emphasis on wholesale and retail distribution, services, transportation, and the electric power and related sectors. Manufacturing will occupy the center ring, partly because of further division of labor traditions (e.g., public utility and transportation economics are often considered separate specialties) and partly because of its sheer size and strategic position in the economy. Finally, the empirical analyses in this volume will for the sake of manageability relate mainly to the United States economy, although comparisons with other nations will be drawn frequently. Indeed, there is reason to believe that the theories we developed in this book can be applied equally well in explaining the operation of other industrialized economies.

The scope and method of industrial organization analysis

In the field of industrial organization, we try to ascertain how market processes direct the activities of producers in meeting consumer demands, how these processes may break down, and how they can be adjusted (e.g., through government intervention) to make actual performance conform more closely to the ideal. Many of these questions are also the concern of microeconomic theory or, at least, of the market theory and welfare economics branches of microeconomic theory. How does industrial organization analysis differ from microeconomic theory? In fact, there is a fair amount of overlap, but there are also significant differences in goals and methodology.

Both fields are concerned with explaining why things happen—why, for instance, prices are lower under one set of conditions than under another, or how some variable such as price will change in response to changes in other (independent) variables. Both view the type of market organization linking producers with consumers as an important variable. They differ mainly in the richness of the variables they attempt to subsume and in their concern for applying predictions and explanations to concrete real-world cases. Microeconomic theorists thrive on simplicity and rigor; they are happiest when they can strip their models to the barest few essential assumptions and variables. Industrial organization economists are more inclined toward explanations rich in both quantitative and institutional detail. To be sure, they should prefer a simpler theory over a more complex one when the two have equal explanatory power. But when a tradeoff must be made, the pure theorist will sacrifice some explanatory power for elegance, while the industrial organization specialist bends in the opposite direction.

Another useful perspective on the differences between industrial organization economics and microeconomic theory is provided by Joseph A. Schumpeter's concept of "economic analysis." A science, wrote Schumpeter, is any field of knowledge that has developed specialized techniques of fact finding and interpretation or analysis.[1] What distinguishes the scientific economic analyst from other people who think, talk, and write about economic topics, according to Schumpeter, is a command of three main techniques: history, statistics, and theory—theory being defined as a "box of tools" or a set of models that permits one to deal analytically with broad classes of cases by focusing on certain properties or aspects they have in common.[2] As we shall see repeatedly in later chapters, industrial organization economists must have a command of all three techniques to make the most of their trade. They must be at home in microeconomic theory to forge rigorous predictive links between fundamental assumptions and their behavioral consequences. They must use modern statistical methods to extract appropriate generalizations from data on industrial structure and performance without plunging into the many pitfalls lining the quantitative analyst's path. And they need some familiarity with the methods and results of historical research, both to put their findings in broader perspective and to extract from a tangle of institutional detail the causes of departures from the norm. In short, all three horses in Schumpeter's methodological troika are required to pull the industrial organization cart; pure theory is only one member of the team.

Why should economists be interested in industrial organization problems? There seem to be two main reasons. First, studies in the field have a direct and continuing influence on the formulation and implementation of public policies in such areas as the choice between private and public enterprise, the regulation and coordination of transportation systems and public utilities, the promotion of competition through antitrust, the stimulation of technological progress through patent grants and subsidies, and the like. The field's attraction to policy-oriented economists was especially strong between 1887 and 1915, when the antitrust laws and the first federal regulatory agencies were in their infancy, and between 1933 and 1940, when new developments in economic theory interacted with depression psychosis to stimulate a reassessment of the proper role for competition. After World War II the excitement abated somewhat as economists turned their attention toward such new issues as macroeconomic stabilization and the problems of underdeveloped nations. In the 1970s, however, interest revived sharply. This renaissance appears to have four main roots—spreading governmental regulation of market processes despite mounting skepticism about the effectiveness of time-honored regulatory solutions, the recognition that market organization significantly affects international relations (e.g., through the working of commodity cartels), growing doubts over the adaptability and responsiveness of modern industrial enterprises, and an intensified debate regarding the nature of structure-performance links and their implications for antitrust policy.

A second reason for toiling in the industrial organization vineyard is that it is intellectually exciting. One thing that will become evident as this volume unfolds is our considerable ignorance concerning many facets of an industrialized market economy's functioning. The theory, data, and methodology needed to explore these voids are gradually becoming available. It is likely therefore that an able person doing research on industrial organization problems will advance the frontiers of knowledge, and lucky ones may achieve or trigger major breakthroughs. To those who relish the quest for knowledge, this is an attractive prospect.

An introductory paradigm

Before turning to the tasks at hand, it is useful to have a simple model of our overall approach to industrial organization analysis. We begin from the fundamental assumption that what society wants from producers of goods and services is good performance. Good performance is a multidimensional attribute. It embodies at least the following goals, not necessarily listed in order of social importance or priority:

a. Decisions as to what, how much, and how to produce should be efficient in two respects: Scarce resources should not be wasted outright, and production decisions should be responsive qualitatively and quantitatively to consumer demands.

b. The operations of producers should be progressive, taking advantage of opportunities opened up by science and technology to increase output per unit of input and to provide consumers with superior new products, in both ways contributing to the long-run growth of real income per capita.

c. The operations of producers should facilitate stable full employment of resources, especially human resources. Or at minimum, they should not make maintenance of full employment through the use of macroeconomic policy instruments excessively difficult.

d. The distribution of income should be equitable. Equity is a notoriously slippery concept,

1. Joseph A. Schumpeter, *History of Economic Analysis* (New York: Oxford University Press, 1954), p. 7.

2. Schumpeter, *History of Economic Analysis*, pp. 12–16. See also Joan Robinson, *The Economics of Imperfect Competition* (London: Macmillan, 1933), p. 1.

but it implies at least that producers do not secure rewards far in excess of what is needed to call forth the amount of services supplied. A subfacet of this goal is the desire to achieve reasonable price stability, for rampant inflation distorts the distribution of income in ways widely disapproved.

These goals may not always be completely consistent with one another; later chapters will identify conflicts that cannot be resolved without invoking basic value judgments. Still, to the extent possible, good industrial performance implies maximum satisfaction of all four goals. Measuring the degree to which the goals have been satisfied is also not easy, but operational approximations can be achieved by using data on price-cost margins, the relationship of actual costs to technologically feasible minima, rates of change in prices and output per man-hour, variability of employment over the business cycle, and so forth.

With this ultimate focus, we seek to identify sets of attributes or variables that influence economic performance and to build theories detailing the nature of the links between those attributes and end performance. The broad descriptive model of these relationships used in most industrial organization studies was conceived by Edward S. Mason at Harvard during the 1930s and extended by numerous scholars.[3] It is illustrated schematically in Figure 1.1. *Performance* in particular industries or markets is said to depend upon the *conduct* of sellers and buyers in such matters as pricing policies and practices, overt and tacit interfirm cooperation, product line and advertising strategies, research and development commitments, investment in production facilities, legal tactics (e.g., in enforcing patent rights), and so on. Conduct depends in turn upon the *structure* of the relevant market, embracing such features as the number and size distribution of sellers and buyers, the degree of physical or subjective differentiation prevailing among competing sellers' products, the presence or absence of barriers to the entry of new firms, the ratio of fixed to total costs in the short run for a typical firm, the degree to which firms are vertically integrated from raw material production to retail

distribution, and the amount of diversity or conglomerateness characterizing individual firm's product lines.

Market structure and conduct are also influenced by various *basic conditions*. For example, on the supply side, basic conditions include the

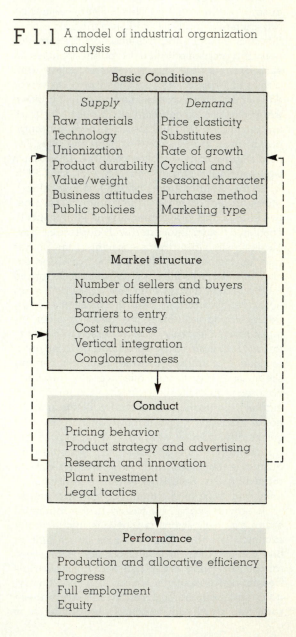

F 1.1 A model of industrial organization analysis

Basic Conditions	
Supply	*Demand*
Raw materials	Price elasticity
Technology	Substitutes
Unionization	Rate of growth
Product durability	Cyclical and
Value/weight	seasonal character
Business attitudes	Purchase method
Public policies	Marketing type

Market structure

Number of sellers and buyers
Product differentiation
Barriers to entry
Cost structures
Vertical integration
Conglomerateness

Conduct

Pricing behavior
Product strategy and advertising
Research and innovation
Plant investment
Legal tactics

Performance

Production and allocative efficiency
Progress
Full employment
Equity

location and ownership of essential raw materials; the character of the available technology (e.g., batch versus continuous process production, or high versus low elasticity of input substitution); the degree of work force unionization; the durability of the product; the time pattern of production (e.g., whether goods are produced to order or delivered from inventory); the value/weight characteristics of the product; and so on. A list of significant basic conditions on the demand side must include at least the price elasticity of demand at various prices; the availability of (and cross elasticity of demand for) substitute products; the rate of growth and variability over time of demand; the methods employed by buyers in purchasing (e.g., acceptance of list prices as given versus solicitation of sealed bids versus haggling); and the marketing characteristics of the product sold (e.g., specialty versus convenience versus shopping goods).[4] Other germane basic conditions are the environment of laws and government policies within which industries operate and the dominant socioeconomic values of the business community, e.g., whether sympathies run toward aggressive individualism or cooperation.

As the heavy arrows in Figure 1.1 suggest, we shall be concerned primarily with relationships or tendencies involving a causal flow from market structure and/or basic conditions to conduct and performance. That is, we seek theories that permit us to predict ultimate market performance from the observation of structure, basic conditions, and conduct. To cite an example pursued further in Chapter 7, we may find that the current technology calls for a capital-intensive production process, which implies a short-run cost structure with high fixed and low variable costs, which encourages aggressive pricing conduct even in oligopolistic industries when demand is price inelastic and cyclically volatile, which in turn has important ramifications in terms of price-cost margins and other performance indicators. Or for a less complex illustration to be elaborated in Chapter 6, durability of an industry's product may have an impact on price-cost margins, other things being equal, because it affects the ability of firms to deal with demand uncertainties by taking inventory positions.

To be sure, not all influences flow from basic conditions or market structure toward performance. There are also feedback effects (broken lines in Figure 1.1). For example, vigorous research and development efforts may alter an industry's technology, and hence its cost conditions and/or the degree of product differentiation. Or the policies pursued by sellers in coordinating their mutual price interactions may either raise or lower barriers to entry, affecting market structure.

This basic conditions - market structure – conduct-performance paradigm provides both theme and counterpoint for the analysis that follows. The book's organizational thrust centers on a structure-conduct-performance trichotomy. After Chapter 2 lays some preliminary groundwork, Chapters 3 and 4 examine the existing structure of American industry and its determinants. Chapters 5 through 16 then undertake an extended analysis of conduct in the pricing, product policy, and technological innovation spheres. Only Chapter 9 deviates from this sequence, offering a survey of statistical evidence on structure-performance relationships anticipated by the core pricing behavior analysis. Chapter 17 provides an integrated appraisal of the extent to which U.S. market structure and conduct yield satisfactory economic performance. Chapters 18 through 21 conclude the work with a survey of public policy measures designed to improve per-

3. Mason's seminal works are "Price and Production Policies of Large-Scale Enterprise," *American Economic Review*, Supplement 29 (March 1939): 61–74; and "The Current State of the Monopoly Problem in the United States," *Harvard Law Review* 62 (June 1949): 1265–85.

4. Convenience goods, such as toothpaste, razor blades, and cigarettes, are items purchased with little shopping around because the costs of obtaining price comparisons outweigh the benefits. Shopping goods, such as furniture, major items of clothing, and mortgages, are items whose purchase is infrequent and whose value is high, so that price and quality comparison shopping trips are warranted. Specialty goods are high-value items on which the buyer has been presold, so that he or she will go to considerable trouble to obtain the particular brand desired. Cf. Richard B. Heflebower, "Toward a Theory of Industrial Markets and Prices," *American Economic Review* 44 (May 1954): 128–29; and R. H. Holton, "The Distinctions Between Convenience Goods, Shopping Goods, and Specialty Goods," *Journal of Marketing* 23 (July 1958): 53–56.

formance by manipulating structure or conduct. As counterpoint to this sequence of themes, we shall be concerned continuously with the detailed interactions among basic conditions, market structure, conduct, and performance.

A note on methodology

Readers already acquainted with the literature of industrial organization will recognize in this conceptual scheme a heavy intellectual debt to the pioneering work of Joe S. Bain. Yet a major difference in approach should be noted. Bain stresses the formulation of direct empirical links between market structure and economic performance, deemphasizing intermediate conduct. Only one chapter out of fifteen in his 1959 text was devoted explicitly to the analysis of conduct. In this volume, by contrast, much of the analysis in Chapters 5 through 16 attacks the question of structure-performance associations by focusing intensely on the business conduct spanning those phenomena. If the difference in approaches had to be characterized by means of labels, it could be said that Bain is predominantly a structuralist, while this author is a behaviorist.

Bain's case for his approach can be summarized in three main propositions.[5] First, the inclusion of conduct variables is not essential to the development of an operational theory of industrial organization. Acceptable predictions of actual performance can be generated by using only structural indices as independent variables. Second, a priori theory based upon structure-conduct and conduct-performance links yields ambiguous predictions. Widely divergent conduct may follow from given structural conditions, or varying qualities of performance may result from presumably similar conduct patterns. Third, even if satisfactory a priori structure-conduct-performance hypotheses could be formulated, the scholar attempting to test those hypotheses would encounter serious obstacles. Much published information on business conduct is incomplete and unreliable, and many business firms have been less than hospitable in allowing well-trained students of industrial organization access to the requisite internal information. Even if this last hurdle could be surmounted, research penetrating the decision-making processes of firms is so costly and time consuming that few company studies could be accomplished. One might be placed in the unhappy position of generalizing from an inadequate sample of special cases.

All three arguments have merit, but none is unassailable. On the first, it is true that much progress has been made in explaining industrial performance using only structural variables. We shall honor these contributions through frequent reference in coming chapters, and we can expect even better results in the future as improved data become available and as students of industrial organization grow in methodological sophistication. But it might be possible to make still better predictions and eliminate some statistical variance that would otherwise go unexplained by probing intermediate structure-conduct and conduct-performance associations. To this claim, the structuralist might reply that predictions using only structure variables are already 'good enough' or, on a more sophisticated plane, that the cost of introducing explicit conduct hypotheses would exceed the value of the increases in predictive accuracy. Such an objection cannot be proved or disproved in the present state of knowledge. But even if it were valid, it would overlook an important point. Although science may be construed narrowly as nothing more than systematically verified prediction, surely the joy of science involves something more: finding out *why* things happen, and not just that they do happen when certain levers are pulled. To stop short of learning what we can about conduct linkages would be to deny our urge to know.

The second argument can be disposed of more brusquely. Bain's observation that traditional a priori theories yield ambiguous predictions is largely correct. The problem lies in the naiveté of the theories, not in theorizing per se. The predictions are ambiguous because significant variables have been excluded from the models. By introducing a much richer complement of independent variables, we should be able to predict conduct from structure, and performance from conduct, with greater precision and confidence.

Bain's third proposition can also be contested. With a large and still growing population of economists and related social scientists, it should be possible to carry out sufficiently many in-depth studies of firms' pricing, product policy, and innovative responses to alternative market environments. To be sure, some business firms have been reluctant to cooperate in research of this nature, partly through fear of investigative bias and partly through fear of what the studies may disclose. But in the author's experience, many companies cooperate gladly when the investigator enters without preconceived conclusions, and the more recalcitrant organizations can then be pulled in through a kind of band-wagon effect. Perhaps a more serious obstacle is the characteristic indolence of economists. It is hard work to plow through file after file of company documents and to interview dozens of executives, cross-checking each observation to guard against bias and misinterpretation. It is much easier to work with census data punched into IBM cards that can be interrogated in the comfort of one's home, that answer all questions without evasion, and that will never complain when bent or spindled. Yet despite these difficulties the job can be done, and there are undoubtedly scholars willing to rise to the challenge—given a little encouragement and financial support.

In any event, we sum up the defense for the methodological tack taken in this book as follows: Industrial organization economists have done well using Bain's structure-performance dichotomy. But we can do still better with a richer model that includes intermediate behavioral links. Opportunities for progress exist, and there are substantial benefits to be attained, if not from improved public policies, then at least from the joy of knowing.

5. See the first edition of Joe S. Bain, *Industrial Organization* (New York: Wiley, 1959), pp. 36–38, 295–301, 310–15. I have also benefited from a discussion of this problem with Professor Bain.

2 The welfare economics of competition and monopoly

Competition has long been viewed as a force that leads to an optimal solution of the economic performance problem, just as monopoly has been condemned throughout recorded history for frustrating attainment of the competitive ideal. To Adam Smith, the vital principle underlying a market economy's successful functioning was the pursuit of individual self-interest, channelled and controlled by competition. As each individual strives to maximize the value of his own capital, said Smith, he

> necessarily labours to render the annual revenue of the society as great as he can. He generally, indeed, neither intends to promote the public interest, nor knows how much he is promoting it. . . . [H]e intends only his own gain, and he is in this, as in many other cases, led by an invisible hand to promote an end which was no part of his intention.[1]

Smith's "invisible hand" is the set of market prices emerging in response to competitive forces. When these forces are thwarted by "the great engine of . . . monopoly," the tendency for resources to be allocated "as nearly as possible in the proportion which is most agreeable to the interest of the whole society" is frustrated.[2]

Much of Smith's detailed analysis is obsolete. Yet his arguments on the efficacy of free competition remain intact, a philosophical foundation stone to nations relying upon a market system of economic organization. Economists have, to be sure, amended their view of competition since the time of Smith, and they have developed more elegant models of how competitive markets do their job of allocating resources and distributing income. One objective of this chapter is to survey these modern views on the nature of and rationale for a competitive market system. In addition, we shall examine some of the qualifications and doubts that have led to the partial or complete rejection of Smith's gospel in many parts of the world.

Competition defined

Let us begin by making clear what is meant by *competition* in economic analysis. Two broad conceptions, one emphasizing the conduct of sellers and buyers and the other emphasizing market structure, can be distinguished. Adam Smith's widely scattered comments, dealing with both conduct and structural features, typify the

1. Adam Smith, *An Inquiry into the Nature and Causes of the Wealth of Nations* (New York: Modern Library, 1937), p. 423.

2. Smith, *Wealth of Nations*, pp. 594–95. See also pp. 61, 147, 712.

dominant strain of economic thought during the 18th and 19th centuries.[3] On the conduct side, Smith considered competition to be essentially an *independent striving* for patronage by the various sellers in a market. The short-run structural prerequisites for competitive conduct were left ambiguous. Smith observed that independent action might emerge with only two sellers, but it was more likely (i.e., collusion among the sellers was less likely) with 20 or more sellers.[4] However, competition in Smith's schema also had a long-run dimension that could be satisfied, despite short-run aberrations, as long as it was possible for resources to move from industries in which their returns were low to those in which they could earn comparatively high returns. This in turn depended upon a structural condition: the absence of barriers to resource transfers. Recognizing that resources were often fairly immobile in the short run, Smith and his followers conceded that the full benefit of competitive market processes might be realized only in a long-run context.

As mathematical reasoning began to penetrate economics during the 19th century, a different, essentially structural, concept of competition came to the forefront. In modern economic theory, an industry is said to be competitive (or more precisely, purely competitive) only when the number of firms selling a homogeneous commodity is so large, and each individual firm's share of the market is so small, that no individual firm finds itself able to influence appreciably the commodity's price by varying the quantity of output it sells. In mathematical jargon, price is a *parameter* to the competitive seller—it is determined by market forces, and not subject to the individual seller's conscious control. The parametric character of price to the competitive firm is

fundamentally a subjective phenomenon. If industry demand curves are smooth and continuous, it is not strictly true that a small seller's output changes have *no* effect on the market price. They simply have such a minute effect that the influence is *imperceptible* to the seller, who can therefore act as if the effect were in fact zero.[5]

This technical definition of competition differs markedly from the usage adopted by businesspeople who, following Adam Smith's lead, are apt to perceive competition as a conscious striving against other business firms for patronage, perhaps on a price basis but possibly also (or alternatively) on nonprice grounds. Failure to recognize these implied semantic distinctions has often led to confusion in policy discussions. To keep such confusion at a minimum, we adopt the term 'rivalry' to characterize much of the activity businesspeople commonly call 'competition.' The essence of rivalry is a striving for potentially incompatible positions (e.g., if Firm A sells 100 units of output to Mr. X, Firm B cannot satisfy that part of X's demand) combined with a clear *awareness* by the parties involved that the positions they seek to attain may be incompatible.[6] Under this dichotomy, it is possible for there to be vigorous rivalry that cannot be called pure competition. The jockeying for position in the automobile market among General Motors, Ford, and Chrysler is an obvious example. At the same time, there can be pure competition without rivalry. For instance, two Iowans growing corn on adjacent farms are pure competitors but not rivals in the sense implied here. Since the market for corn is so large relative to the two farmers' potential supply, it can readily absorb their offerings with scarcely a ripple in the Chicago Board of Trade price. As a result, neither farmer can sensibly consider the neighbor's output decisions as hav-

T 2.1 Principal seller's market structure types

	One	A few	Many
Homogeneous product	Pure monopoly	Homogeneous oligopoly	Pure competition
Differentiated product	Pure monopoly	Differentiated oligopoly	Monopolistic competition

ing any perceptible adverse impact on his own economic position.

Violations of the principal structural preconditions for pure competition give rise to a rich variety of sellers' market types. For present purposes it suffices to identify the five most important types, using the two-way classification based upon the number of sellers and the nature of the product presented in Table 2.1. The distinction between homogeneity and differentiation in this classification hinges on the degree of substitutability among competing sellers' products. Homogeneity prevails when, in the minds of buyers, products are perfect substitutes. Products are differentiated when, owing to differences in physical attributes, ancillary service, geographic location, information, and/or subjective image, one firm's products are clearly preferred by at least some buyers over rival products at a given price. The distinguishing trait of a differentiated product is the ability of its seller to raise the product's price without sacrificing the entire sales volume. Obviously, infinite gradations in the degree of product differentiation may exist, and it is difficult in practice to draw a precise line where homogeneity ends and differentiation begins. Similarly, although pure monopoly ends and oligopoly begins when the number of sellers rises from one to two, it is difficult to specify on a priori grounds exactly where oligopoly shades into a competitive market structure. The key to the distinction is subjective—whether or not the sellers consider themselves conscious rivals in the sense defined earlier. If the sellers are sufficiently few in number to have each believe (a) that its economic fortunes are perceptibly influenced by the market actions of other individual firms, and (b) that those firms are in turn affected significantly by its own actions, then the market can be said to be oligopolistic.

Pure monopolists, oligopolists, and monopolistic competitors share a common characteristic: Each recognizes that its output decisions have a perceptible influence on price or, in other words, each can increase the quantity of output it sells under given demand conditions only by reducing its price. All three types of firms possess some degree of power over price, and so we say that they possess *monopoly power* or *market power*.

Homogeneity of the product and insignificant size of individual sellers and buyers relative to their market (i.e., *atomistic* market structure) are sufficient conditions for the existence of pure competition—the only basic structural type under which sellers possess no monopoly power. It is conventional, however, to add several additional characteristics in describing the 'ideal' competitive market of economic theory. When these are present, competition is said to be not only *pure* but also *perfect*.[7] The most important is the absence of barriers to the entry of new firms, combined with mobility of resources employed or potentially employable in an industry. Conversely, significant entry barriers are the *sine qua non* of monopoly and oligopoly, for as we shall see in later chapters, sellers have little or no enduring power over price when entry barriers are nonexistent. Other conditions sometimes associated with perfect competition include continuous divisibility of inputs and outputs and perfect knowledge of both present and future market conditions. These are less important, as well as less realistic, for their violation does not necessarily alter the main conclusions generated by

3. For admirable surveys of the development of economic thought on the nature of competition, see George J. Stigler, "Perfect Competition, Historically Contemplated," *Journal of Political Economy* 65 (February 1957): 1–17; J. M. Clark, *Competition as a Dynamic Process* (Washington, D.C.: Brookings Institution, 1961), Chapters 2 and 3; Paul J. McNulty, "A Note on the History of Perfect Competition," *Journal of Political Economy* 75, Part 1 (August 1967), pp. 395–99; and *idem*, "Economic Theory and the Meaning of Competition," *Quarterly Journal of Economics* 82 (November 1968): 639–56.

4. Smith, *Wealth of Nations*, p. 342.

5. This definition is given for the sellers' side of an industry. The definition of buyers' competition is symmetric. Pure competition exists among buyers when the number of entities buying a homogeneous product is so large, and each buyer's share of the market so small, that each buyer believes variations in the quantity he buys have an imperceptible effect on the market price. When some buyer can perceptibly influence price, *monopsony* is said to exist.

6. For a more extended analysis using different terminology, see Kenneth E. Boulding, *Conflict and Defense* (New York: Harper & Row, 1962), Chapter 1.

7. This distinction is essentially that adopted by E. H. Chamberlin in *The Theory of Monopolistic Competition* (Cambridge, Mass.: Harvard University Press, 1933), Chapter 1.

The welfare economics of competition and monopoly

the theoretical model of a purely and perfectly competitive market system's operation.

One final terminological point deserves mention, because it is a common source of confusion. The power over price possessed by a monopolist or oligopolist depends upon the firm's size *relative to* the market in which it is operating. It is entirely possible for a firm to be very small in absolute terms, but nonetheless to have considerable monopoly power. The physician in an isolated one-doctor town is an excellent example. So is the Besser Manufacturing Co., which was found guilty in 1951 of illegally monopolizing the concrete block machinery industry, even though it employed only 465 persons at the time and had sales of less than $15 million.[8] On the other hand, a firm may be enormous in absolute terms, but possess little monopoly power in its principal markets. A good illustration is the Cities Service Oil Company, which had sales of $3.2 billion in 1975, but accounted for less than 3 percent of U.S. crude petroleum refining. Monopoly power depends upon size relative to the market, not on absolute size, although relative and absolute bigness may of course coexist. To postulate a 1 to 1 relationship between monopoly power and absolute size is like confusing pregnancy with obesity. Some superficial manifestations may be similar, but the underlying phenomena could hardly differ more.

The case for competition

We proceed now to the principal questions on our agenda. Why is a competitive market system held in such high esteem by statesmen and economists alike? Why is competition the ideal in a market economy, and what is wrong with monopoly?

Political arguments We begin with the political arguments for competition, not merely because they are sufficiently obvious to be treated briefly, but also because, when all is said and done, they and not the economists' abstruse models have tipped the balance of social consensus toward competition. One of the most important arguments is that the atomistic structure of buyers and sellers required for competition decentralizes and disperses power. The resource allocation and income distribution problem is solved through the almost mechanical interaction of supply and demand forces on the market, and not through the conscious exercise of power held in private hands (e.g., under monopoly) or government hands (i.e., under state enterprise or government

F 2.1   Equilibrium under pure competition

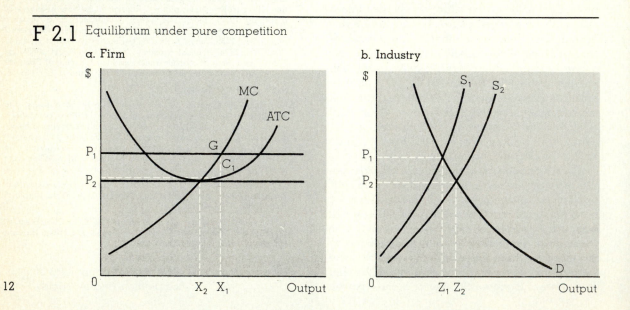

a. Firm

b. Industry

regulation). Limiting the power of both government bodies and private individuals to make decisions shaping people's lives and fortunes is one of the oldest and most fundamental goals in the liberal ideology, which in turn was the guiding spirit underlying the design of the American governmental system. Carl Kaysen has observed:

> If the regime of competition and the arguments of *laissez faire* ever commended themselves widely, it has been primarily on political rather than economic grounds. The replacement of the all-too-visible hand of the state by the invisible hand of the marketplace, which guided each to act for the common good while pursuing his own interests and aims without an overt show of constraint, was what attracted general ideological support to the liberal cause.[9]

A closely related benefit is the fact that competitive market processes solve the economic problem *impersonally*, and not through the personal control of entrepreneurs or bureaucrats. There is nothing more galling than to have the achievement of some desired objective frustrated by the decision of an identifiable individual or group. On the other hand, who can work up much outrage about a setback administered by the impersonal interplay of competitive market forces?

A third political merit of a competitive market system is its freedom of opportunity. When the no-barriers-to-entry condition of perfect competition is satisfied, individuals are free to choose whatever trade or profession they prefer, limited only by their own talent and skill and by their ability to raise the (presumably modest) amount of capital required.

The efficiency of competitive markets Admitting the salience of these political benefits, our main concern nonetheless will be with the economic case for competitive market processes. Figure 2.1(b) reviews the conventional textbook analysis of equilibrium in a competitive industry and Figure 2.1(a) portrays it for a representative firm belonging to that industry. Suppose we begin observing the industry when the short-run industry supply curve is S_1, which in turn em-

bodies the horizontal summation of all member firms' marginal cost curves. The short-run market equilibrium price is OP_1, which is viewed as a parameter or 'given' by our representative firm, so the firm's subjectively perceived demand curve is a horizontal line at the level OP_1. The firm maximizes its profits by expanding output until marginal cost (MC) rises into equality with the price OP_1. It produces OX_1 units of output and earns economic profits—that is, profits above the minimum return required to call forth its capital investment—equal to the per-unit profit GC_1 times the number of units OX_1. Because economic profits are positive for the representative firm, this cannot be a long-run equilibrium position. New firms attracted by the profit lure will enter the industry, adding their new marginal cost functions to the industry's supply curve and thereby shifting the supply curve to the right. Entry will continue, expanding industry output and driving the price down, until price has fallen into equality with average total cost (ATC) for the representative firm.[10] In the figures shown, this zero-profit condition emerges with the short-run supply curve S_2, yielding the market price OP_2. The representative firm maximizes its profits by equating marginal cost with price OP_2, barely covering its total unit costs (including the minimum necessary return on its capital) at the output OX_2.

The long-run equilibrium state of a competitive industry has three general properties with important normative implications:

a. The cost of producing the last unit of output—

---

8. *U.S.* v. *Besser Mfg. Co.*, 96 F. Supp. 304 (1951); affirmed, 343 U.S. 444 (1952).

9. Carl Kaysen, "The Corporation: How Much Power? What Scope?" in E. S. Mason, ed., *The Corporation in Modern Society* (Cambridge, Mass.: Harvard University Press, 1960), pp. 98–99. See also Carl Kaysen and Donald F. Turner, *Antitrust Policy* (Cambridge, Mass.: Harvard University Press, 1959), pp. 14–18.

10. We assume perfect imputation of all factor scarcity rents here. If the imputation process is imperfect, only the marginal firm—the firm just on the borderline between entering and not entering—will realize zero economic profits.

the marginal cost—is equal to the price paid by consumers for that unit. This is a necessary condition for profit maximization, given the competitive firm's perception that price is unaffected by its output decisions. It implies efficiency of resource allocation in a sense to be explored momentarily.

b. With price equal to average total cost for the representative firm, economic (i.e., *supranormal*) profits are absent. Investors receive a return just sufficient to induce them to maintain their investment at the level required to produce the industry's equilibrium output efficiently. Avoiding a surplus return to capital is generally considered desirable in terms of the equity of income distribution

c. In long-run equilibrium, each firm is producing its output at the minimum point on its average total cost curve. Firms that fail to operate at the lowest unit cost will incur losses and be driven from the industry. Thus, resources are employed at maximum production efficiency under competition.[11]

One further benefit is sometimes attributed to the working of pure competition, although with

less logical compulsion. Because of the pressure of prices on costs, entrepreneurs may have especially strong incentives to seek and adopt cost-saving technological innovations. Indeed, if industry capacity is correctly geared to demand at all times, the *only* way competitive firms can earn positive economic profits is through leadership in innovation. We might expect therefore that technological progress will be more rapid in competitive industries. However, some doubts concerning the correctness of this hypothesis will be raised in a moment.

The inefficiency of monopoly pricing Monopolists and monopolistic competitors differ from purely competitive firms in only one essential respect: They face a downward-sloping demand curve for their product. Given this fact of its economic life, the firm with monopoly power knows that to sell an additional unit (or block) of output, it must reduce its price to the customer(s) for that unit; and if it is unable to practice price discrimination (as we shall generally assume, unless otherwise indicated) the firm must also reduce the price to all customers who would have made their purchases even without the price reduction.

F 2.2 Equilibrium under monopoly

a. Pure monopolist

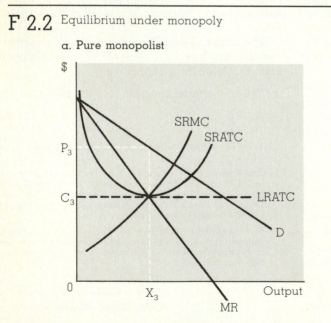

b. Monopolistic competitor

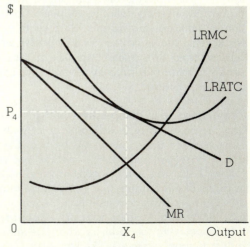

The net addition to the nondiscriminating monopolist's revenue from selling one more unit of output, or its *marginal revenue*, is equal to the price paid by the marginal customer, minus the change in price required to secure the marginal customer's patronage multiplied by the number of units that would have been sold without the price reduction in question.[12] Except at prices so high as to choke off all demand, the monopolist always sacrifices something to gain the benefits of increased patronage: the higher price it could have extracted had it limited its sales to more eager customers. Marginal revenue must therefore be less than the price paid by the marginal customer. Or, to state this critical condition more generally, when demand functions are continuous and smooth, *marginal revenue under monopoly is necessarily less than price* for finite quantities sold. When the monopolist's demand function can be represented by a straight line, marginal revenue for any desired output is given by the ordinate of a straight line intersecting the demand curve where the latter intersects the vertical axis, and with twice the slope of the demand curve, as illustrated in Figures 2.2(a) and 2.2(b).[13] We will normally use straight-line demand curves in subsequent illustrations because they greatly simplify derivation of the associated marginal revenue curves.

Now the profit-maximizing firm with monopoly power will expand its output only as long as the net addition to revenue from selling an additional unit (marginal revenue) exceeds the addition to cost from producing that unit (the marginal cost). At the monopolist's profit-maximizing output, marginal revenue equals marginal cost. But as long as output is positive, marginal revenue is less than the monopoly price. Price therefore exceeds marginal cost. This equilibrium condition for firms with monopoly power differs from the competitive firm's equilibrium position. For the competitor, price equals marginal cost; for the monopolist, price exceeds marginal cost. This behavioral difference has important implications to which we shall return in a moment, after considering some other possible differences between monopoly and competition.

The competitive enterprise earns zero economic profit in long-run equilibrium. Is the firm

with monopoly power different? Perhaps, but not necessarily. Figure 2.2(a) illustrates one out of the many possible cases in which positive monopoly profits are reaped: specifically, the per-unit profit margin P_3C_3 times the number of units OX_3 sold. As long as entry into the monopolist's market is barred, there is no reason why this profitable equilibrium cannot continue indefinitely. Figure 2.2(b), on the other hand, illustrates the standard long-run equilibrium position of a monopolistic competitor.[14] The crucial distinguishing assumptions are that monopolistic competitors are small relative to the market for their general class of differentiated products and that entry into the market is free. Then, if positive economic profits are earned, new firms will squeeze into the industry, shifting the typical firm's demand curve to the left until, in long-run equilibrium, it is tangent to the firm's long-run unit cost function $LRATC$. The best option left for the firm then is to produce output OX_4, where marginal revenue equals marginal cost (as in any monopolistic situation) and the average revenue or price OP_4 is barely sufficient to cover unit cost. Thus, while firms with market power *may* earn monopoly profits, they need not, especially under the plausible conditions of monopolistic competition.

We found earlier that in long-run equilibrium the purely and perfectly competitive firm produces at minimum average total cost. Is this true

---

11. For a more skeptical view, see David Schwartzman, "Competition and Efficiency: A Comment," *Journal of Political Economy* 81 (May/June 1973): 756–64.

12. Generally, for the monopolist price is a function $P = f(X)$ of the quantity X sold. Total sales revenue $R = P \cdot X$. Marginal revenue is the change in total revenue associated with a unit change in quantity sold, thus, $MR = dR/dX = P + X(dP/dX)$. P here is the price paid by marginal consumers; dP/dX is the change in price necessary to attract them (usually with a negative sign); and X corresponds approximately to the quantity that would be sold without the price reduction.

13. Proof: Let the demand curve have the equation $P = a - bX$, where X is the quantity demanded. Total revenue $R = P \cdot X = aX - bX^2$. Marginal revenue $dR/dX = a - 2bX$. At $X = 0$, $P = MR$. The slope $(-2b)$ of the marginal revenue function is twice the slope $(-b)$ of the demand curve.

14. Cf. Chamberlin, *Monopolistic Competition*, Chapter 5.

also of monopoly? Many textbooks imply that it is not, or that it will be true only by accident. Again consider Figure 2.2(a). It assumes that the monopolist operates under constant long-run cost conditions, i.e., that plants (or plant complexes) designed to produce at high outputs give rise to roughly the same cost per unit as those designed to produce at low outputs. We shall see in Chapter 4 that many real-world cost functions exhibit this property over substantial output ranges. If so, the firm will invest in a plant or plant complex characterized by the short-run cost function $SRATC$, with minimum short-run unit costs identical to the minimum long-run cost OC_3 at the profit-maximizing output OX_3. We conclude that it is perfectly conceivable theoretically and empirically that monopolists, like their competitive brethren, will operate in such a way as to minimize average total cost. This is also not necessary, however. Figure 2.2(b) presents the most widely discussed exception. Since the monopolistic competitor in Chamberlinian equilibrium operates with its demand curve tangent to its $LRATC$ curve, and since the demand curve is downward sloping, the $LRATC$ curve must also

have a negative slope at the equilibrium output. It follows that average total cost is *not* minimized, for lower unit costs could be realized by expanding the firm's output. The monopolistic competitor does not do so because price (read off the demand curve) falls more rapidly than unit cost beyond the Chamberlinian equilibrium output, so that a higher output would spell negative profits.

In sum, firms with monopoly power may deviate from the zero-profit and minimum-cost conditions associated with purely and perfectly competitive equilibrium, but they need not do so.[15] The only distinction necessarily implied by the theories of pure competition and pure monopoly is that the monopolist's price exceeds marginal cost, while the competitor's price equals it. This seeming technicality, so trivial at first glance, is the basis of the economist's most general condemnation of monopoly: It leads to an allocation of resources that is inefficient in the sense of satisfying consumer wants with less than maximum effectiveness.

To see this, we must think more deeply about the meaning of price as it affects the decisions of

F 2.3 Resource allocation with competition and monopoly

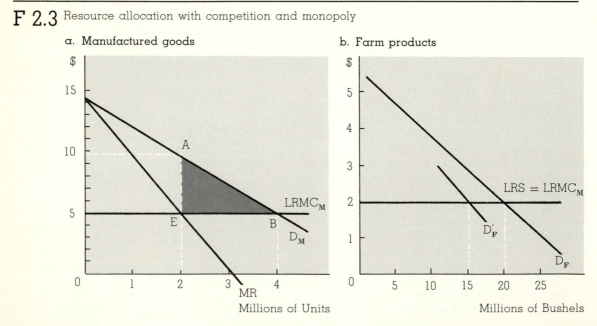

a. Manufactured goods

b. Farm products

Millions of Units

Millions of Bushels

a consumer just on the margin between buying one more unit of a product and not buying it. A numerical illustration is especially helpful, so let us consider Figure 2.3(a). It assumes that the production of a composite commodity 'manufactured goods' with the demand curve D_M is monopolized. The industry is assumed (for simplicity) to produce under constant cost conditions, with long-run average total cost and marginal cost equal to $5.00 per unit at any output level chosen. The manufactured goods monopolist maximizes its profits by setting marginal cost equal to marginal revenue, which for the assumed cost and demand conditions requires producing 2 million units and setting a market-clearing price of about $9.70 per unit.

Now in setting this price, the monopolist chokes off the demand of consumers who would have been willing to purchase units (or additional units) at prices below $9.70. Consider some consumer who would purchase an extra unit at $9.60, but not at $9.70. We say that $9.60 is her *reservation price*—the price just low enough to overcome her reservations about purchasing an extra unit. She buys the extra unit at $9.60 because it is worth that much to her; she refrains from purchasing at $9.70 because she considers the unit not worth the higher price. The consumer's reservation price for any incremental unit of consumption indicates in monetary terms how much that unit is worth to her; it is an index of the value of an extra unit of consumption from the consumer's viewpoint and hence, in a social system honoring consumer sovereignty, from the viewpoint of society.[16]

The extra unit of manufactured goods required to satisfy the demand of this marginal consumer can be produced with resources costing $5.00. The marginal social value of the extra unit is $9.60. Marginal value exceeds marginal cost, so it would appear eminently worthwhile to produce that unit. The same can be said for all other units of manufactured goods that would be demanded at prices from $9.60 down to $5.00; their value to the marginal consumers exceeds their marginal cost, so they ought to be produced. They are not produced—that is, output is unduly restricted—because the monopolist is unwilling to sacrifice the profits it can secure by charging the higher price ($9.70) and selling fewer units.

For virtually all units of manufactured goods the monopolist does supply, the value to consumers of those units (measured as the demand curve ordinate for any given unit consumed) exceeds the monopolist's $9.70 price. On all but the 2 millionth (i.e., marginal) unit supplied and demanded, therefore, there is a surplus of value to consumers over the price paid. This is called *consumers' surplus.*[17] With a monopoly price of $9.70, the total consumers' surplus realized is defined by the triangular area in Figure 2.3(a) bounded by the vertical axis, the horizontal line at the $9.70 level, and the demand function from its vertical intercept to point A. By analogy, the monopolist's profit is called a producer's surplus. It is measured as quantity sold times unit profit, or in Figure 2.3(a) as the rectangular area between 0 and 2 million units and between the $9.70 price and the $5.00 cost. If, contrary to its profit-maximizing instincts, the monopolist reduced its price to $5.00, its profit or producer's surplus would be converted into consumers' surplus on the 2 million units that would have been consumed even at the $9.70 price. This is essentially a redistribution of income. But in addition, 2 million more units will be demanded, virtually all (given the demand function's slope) at reservation prices exceeding $5.00. Satisfying that demand would add consumers' surplus equal to the triangular area ABE between the demand curve and the $5.00 price line. At the $9.70 monopoly price, this surplus is realized neither by the monopolist nor by consumers. It is in effect lost, and therefore it is called

15. But firms with monopoly power cannot normally be free of both deviations simultaneously. If they earn zero or negative profits, they will necessarily find it optimal to operate at higher than minimum average total cost. And (ignoring some dynamic complications to be introduced in Chapter 8) if they find it optimal to operate at minimum average cost, they will earn positive monopoly profits.

16. Indirectly, the reservation price measures the utility of a marginal unit to consumers, for when utility-maximizing consumers are in equilibrium, the price of each commodity included in their market baskets equals the marginal utility of that commodity divided by the marginal utility of money.

17. The terminology used here follows Alfred Marshall, *Principles of Economics*, 8th ed. (London: Macmillan, 1920), pp. 124 ff., 467 ff.

a *dead-weight welfare loss*. It provides a first indication of the inefficiencies associated with monopolistic output restriction. Only through an expansion of manufactured goods output to 4 million units, where price equals marginal cost, does some segment of society realize the surplus *ABE*.

Of course, the resources needed to expand production of manufactured goods must come from somewhere, which (assuming full employment) means that consumption of some other end product must be reduced. The problem of efficient resource allocation is a general equilibrium problem, involving the balance of all sectors in the economy. Unfortunately, the analysis of general equilibrium takes us between Scylla and Charybdis: The rigorous models lack intuitive appeal and the intuitive models lack rigor. Because it is so important to understand the common sense of monopoly resource allocation, we opt for an intuitive approach here. A more rigorous approach is pursued in the mathematical appendix to this chapter.[18]

Suppose the economy consists of only two industries, a monopolized manufactured goods industry and a competitive farm products industry. Figure 2.3 shows these two industries in general equilibrium, given the assumed demand functions D_M and D_F, constant-cost production conditions in each industry, and the assumed market structures. (Note that the diagrams are not drawn to the same scale.) The output of manufactured goods is (as before) 2 million units per year; the output of farm products is 20 million bushels per year. Now suppose we could arrange to transfer resources valued at $100 from the farm products industry to the manufactured goods industry. Since the marginal cost of manufactured goods is $5.00 per unit, it will be possible to produce 20 extra units with these resources. To sell this extra production, price will have to be reduced infinitesimally—e.g., to $9.699. The value of the extra manufactured output from the viewpoint of marginal consumers barely willing to pay this new, lower price is 20 units × $9.699 ≅ $194. However, the loss of farm products owing to the resource transfer must be weighed against this gain. Since the marginal cost of a bushel of farm produce is $2.00, the

transfer of $100 in resources forces society to sacrifice 50 bushels of output. To choke off the demand for this output (at least as a first approximation), the price of farm products must be raised slightly—e.g., to $2.001 per bushel. This reduction in quantity demanded comes at the expense of consumers who were willing to buy an extra bushel at $2.00 but not at $2.001. Since they would rather abstain from consuming that bushel than pay $2.001, the value of the farm products forgone at the margin must be about $2.00 per bushel. The total value of farm products sacrificed as a result of the resource transfer is approximately $2.00 × 50 bushels = $100.00. Recapitulating, society (consumers) has benefited from the resource reallocation by a net increase in output value of approximately $194 − $100 = $94.

If it is possible through such a reallocation to increase the value of the overall output bundle, it must follow that the value of output was not maximized in the original (monopoly) equilibrium. Too few resources were allocated to the monopolized sector, and too many to the competitive sector, relative to that allocation which maximizes the value of output to society. Because it leads to an allocation of resources that fails to maximize the value of the overall output bundle, we say that monopoly misallocates resources, or that it leads to an inefficient allocation of resources.

The same point can be shown in terms of consumers' and producers' surplus. The value of the farm output transferred here is less than $2.001 per bushel. Since before the transfer farm output was sold at a price of $2.00 per bushel, consumers' surplus from its consumption must have been virtually nil. Because price equals marginal cost in a competitive industry, producers' surplus must also have been nil. But after reallocation, the $100 of resources yield additional manufactured goods valued at $194, so either producers' or consumers' surplus of approximately $94 must be generated by the transfer. If it is possible through reallocation to increase surplus in this way, it must follow that the sum of consumers' plus producers' surpluses was not maximized in the original (monopoly) equilibrium. Failure to maximize the value of the output bundle and failure to maximize the sum of consumers' plus producers' surpluses are conceptually identical manifestations of monopolistic resource misallocation.[19] Although we shall use the consumers' surplus concept again later, the output bundle value maximization approach is somewhat more convenient in illustrating the relatively drastic changes implied by our two-sector example, so we emphasize the latter here.

Obviously, if significant value gains can be made by reallocating $100 worth of resources, additional gains can be achieved by carrying the process further. Let us go all the way, breaking up the manufactured goods monopoly into numerous independent production units and eliminating any barriers to the entry of new resources. With the manufactured goods price initially well above the cost of production, resources will flow (or be drawn) into manufacturing, where the lure of positive profits beckons, and out of farming, where a zero-profit competitive equilibrium prevailed. It might seem that the price of farm products must rise above marginal cost as resources are pulled away and output contracts. This is true as a first approximation, but not as a second, for two reasons. First, a competitive industry simply cannot be in long-run equilibrium if price exceeds marginal cost. Something must give to restore the equality between price and cost. Second, as the price of manufactured goods is reduced to sell an expanding output, a substitution effect in favor of manufactured goods and adverse to farm products is induced. Assuming for the moment that the price of farm products hovers near the marginal cost of $2.00, the *ceteris paribus* (i.e., other prices equal) assumption on which the manufactured goods sector's demand function was constructed remains valid, so there will be no shift in D_M. But because of the fall in the manufactured goods price there must be a leftward shift in the farm products demand curve—e.g., to D_F'. Temporarily ignoring some complications, let us assume that D_F' represents the final farm products demand curve after all adjustments have taken place, and D_M the manufactured products demand curve. To be in final equilibrium, each competitive industry must have price equal to long-run marginal cost. This implies an output of 4 million units of manufactured goods with a price of $5.00 per unit and an output of 15 million bushels of farm products at a price of $2.00 per bushel. Resources originally valued at $10 million have been transferred from farm products to manufactured goods production, increasing the value of the aggregate output to society by a substantial amount—specifically, by the triangular area ABE in Figure 2.3(a).

Now let us attempt a further reallocation of resources. If we transfer resources valued at $100 from farm products to manufactured goods production, we sacrifice 50 bushels of farm output. These would have been bought by consumers with reservation prices of $2.00 or slightly higher, so the value of farm output sacrificed is at least $100 and perhaps a bit more. We gain 20 extra units of manufactured goods saleable only at prices slightly less than $5.00, so the value of the additional manufactured output is less than $100. The value of the output gained is less than the value of the output sacrificed, and thus the transfer reduces the overall value of output to society. If we transfer $100 in resources in the opposite direction, we obtain 50 more bushels of farm output, saleable only at prices slightly less than $2.00, for a gain of less than $100. We give up 20 units of manufactured goods that would have been bought by consumers with reservation prices of $5.00 or higher, implying a value sacrifice exceeding $100. The value of the output added in the farm sector is less than the value of the manufactured goods sacrificed, and so this transfer too reduces the total value of output. Thus, a transfer of resources in either direction away from the competitive equilibrium allocation

18. For diverse approaches to the problem, see M. W. Reder, *Studies in the Theory of Welfare Economics* (New York: Columbia University Press, 1947), Chapters 1–4; William J. Baumol, *Welfare Economics and the Theory of the State* (London: Bell, 1952), Chapters 1–6; Francis Bator, "The Simple Analytics of Welfare Maximization," *American Economic Review* 47 (March 1957): 22–59; and Tjalling Koopmans, *Three Essays on the State of Economic Science* (New York: McGraw-Hill, 1957), pp. 4–104.

19. Cf. Arnold C. Harberger, "Three Basic Postulates for Applied Welfare Economics: An Interpretive Essay," *Journal of Economic Literature* 9 (September 1971): 785–97; and Robert D. Willig, "Consumer's Surplus without Apology," *American Economic Review* 66 (September 1976): 589–97.

reduces the total value of output. It follows that the value of output must have been at a (local) maximum in competitive equilibrium. Quite generally, when all sectors of an economy are in competitive equilibrium, with price equal to marginal cost for each firm, the total value of the output, measured in terms of each commodity's equilibrium price, is at a maximum. It is impossible to make any small resource reallocations that yield a higher output value. Because it maximizes the social value of output, a fully competitive market system is said to allocate resources efficiently.[20] Conversely, a system shot through with monopoly elements is inefficient because it fails to do so. This, in a nutshell, is the heart of the economic theorist's case for competition and against monopoly.

The analysis thus far has ignored a few complications. To describe the final equilibrium we need a third approximation. One loose end is that the fall in manufactured goods prices increases the real income of consumers. This income effect will shift both sector demand curves to the right (unless one of the commodities happens to be an inferior good). Monopoly profits are also wiped out, freeing part of the money supply to support these increases in demand.[21] The increased demand for products will be transmitted into increased demand for productive inputs, whose wages will be bid up.[22] This leads to an upward shift in the industry cost functions. With the present model, it is not possible to specify exactly where the final equilibrium will occur after all these effects have worked their way through the system, and therefore the shifted curves are not shown in Figure 2.3. One thing is certain, however. In each sector price will be equal to marginal cost for every producer, and so no further resource transfers can increase the aggregate value of output. Efficiency in the allocation of resources will have been achieved.

While this end result of eliminating monopoly is clearly desirable, another effect is more difficult to assess. Income will have been redistributed, with former monopoly profit recipients losing and other claimants (such as workers) gaining. Whether this is good or bad cannot be decided without a value judgment over which reasonable persons may disagree. There are at least two reasons for thinking that the competitive equilibrium may be preferred to the monopolistic one on equitable grounds, but the case is not airtight.[23] First, society may object to monopoly profits as unearned gains and place a high ethical value on seeing them eliminated. The trouble with this objection is that the monopoly's original builders may already have reaped their gains by selling out their ownership interests at high capitalized values, leaving secondary and tertiary stockbuyers, who are receiving no more than a normal return on their money investment, holding the bag if the monopoly is atomized. Second, the ownership of industrial enterprises is concentrated among a few hundred thousand wealthy individuals. If all persons have similar income utility functions, the marginal utility of income must be higher for the multitudes who supply only their labor services to industry than for the wealthy few with monopoly shareholdings. A redistribution of income away from monopolists and toward labor suppliers will therefore add to total societywide utility. Still, however appealing this may appear intuitively, there is no scientific way of making the interpersonal utility comparisons required to support the assertion. Therefore, we tread warily when we say that competition is beneficial not only because it allocates resources efficiently, but also in terms of income distribution equity.

This completes the case based upon orthodox economic theory against monopoly and for competition. Some other more institutional criticisms of monopoly can be mentioned briefly. Monopolists' price-raising propensities may stimulate imports and complicate individual nations' balance of payment problems.[24] In the absence of competitive pressure, firms may not exercise diligence in controlling their costs and therefore waste resources. As Adam Smith observed, "Monopoly . . . is a great enemy to good management."[25] For similar reasons, monopolists may display a lethargic attitude toward technological innovation, although contrary suggestions will be considered shortly. And finally, enterprises with monopoly power may sustain superfluous advertising, excess production capacity, or other types of waste; or they may maintain pricing systems that encourage inefficient geographic locations and unnecessarily high transportation costs. These alleged flaws, we shall find, may be even more serious than the resource misallocation problem. It is only for reasons of orderly presentation that we defer a more detailed examination until later.

Qualifications and doubts

General equilibrium analysis reveals the superiority of a competitive market system in solving society's resource allocation and income distribution problems under certain assumptions. But can we expect real-world economies to conform to the assumptions of the theorist's abstract model? Might there be violations of assumptions stated explicitly or implicitly, or additional considerations not taken into account that would cause us to modify our judgment? Several qualifications and doubts come to mind.

For one, the whole concept of efficient resource allocation is built upon the fundamental belief that the consumer is sovereign—that individual preferences are what count in the ledger of social values.[20] If, for example, consumers freely choosing in the market demonstrate that they would prefer at the margin to give up 50 bushels of grain to get an additional 20 hair shirts, we conclude that society is really better off because of the transfer. Yet in practice our respect for consumer sovereignty is by no means universal—not, in any event, for infants, convicted criminals, dope addicts, the insane, and others whose preferences cannot be trusted to lead to rational choices. And in this age of widespread neurosis and psychosis, the line between rationality and irrationality is not at all easy to draw. One might even entertain doubts about the soundness of consumption decisions made by presumably normal, rational adults whose tastes (assumed in the conventional theory of consumer behavior to be stable) have been remolded under a barrage of advertising messages. Further qualms intrude when we recognize that there are external diseconomies in consumption, e.g., that the purchase of a new hair shirt by Mr. Willoughby may not only increase his utility, but simultaneously reduce the utility of envious neighbors. All this warns us that the theorems of welfare economics are erected upon shaky foundations. This does not mean that their conclusions are wrong. The demonstration of a competitive system's allocative efficiency makes considerable sense even when complications related to advertising, ignorance, and the like are introduced. But blind faith in the system is also uncalled for.

A second assault on the economist's conventional wisdom holds that only through monopoly can firms be large enough to realize all economies of scale. Under monopolistic (or oligopolistic) organization, then, costs are lower than they would be if an industry includes many small-scale producers. The consequences are illustrated in Figure 2.4. A monopolist's long-run average total cost curve is assumed to be $LRATC_M$, with associated marginal costs $LRMC_M$. If, on the other hand, the industry were atomistically struc-

20. It is remarkable how acute Adam Smith's insight was on this point, when he observed that the individual producer in a competitive economy necessarily labors to render "the exchangeable value of the whole annual produce . . . as great as possible." *Wealth of Nations*, p. 423.

21. Under the previous (second) approximation, payments to all income claimants were $50 million, compared to $59.4 million when the manufacturing sector was monopolized. For monetary equilibrium to be restored, there must either be an input and output price increase or a contraction of the money supply.

22. Unless supply functions are perfectly inelastic, the rise in wages will also call forth increased input supplies, which in turn will permit a general expansion of output, *ceteris paribus*.

23. For another rather involved set of income distribution considerations, see Joan Robinson, *The Economics of Imperfect Competition* (London: Macmillan, 1934), p. 319.

24. See Lawrence J. White, "Industrial Organization and International Trade: Some Theoretical Considerations," *American Economic Review* 64 (December 1974): 1013–20.

25. Smith, *Wealth of Nations*, p. 147.

26. On the consumer sovereignty issue in welfare economics, see Tibor Scitovsky, "On the Principle of Consumers' Sovereignty," and Jerome Rothenberg, "Consumers' Sovereignty Revisited and the Hospitality of Freedom of Choice," both in the *American Economic Review* 52 (May 1962): 262–90; Scitovsky, *The Joyless Economy* (New York: Oxford University Press, 1976); and the debate among G. L. Bach, Steven Hymer, Frank Roosevelt, Paul Sweezy, and Assar Lindbeck in the *Quarterly Journal of Economics* 86 (November 1972): 635–36, 648–50, 661–64, 672–74.

tured, with each member firm operating a plant designed to produce OF units of output at a unit cost of OP_c, the long-run supply curve would be P_cS_c. Given these assumptions, the profit-maximizing monopolist produces output OX_M, which is higher than the competitive supply OX_c. Clearly, it cannot be said that consumer demands are satisfied less fully under monopoly in this case than they would be under competition (although resource allocation would be still better if the monopolist could be induced to expand its production to OX_o, where marginal cost is equal to price). Furthermore, on the output OX_c supplied by the competitively organized industry, unit costs exceed the monopolist's by RP_c, and the rectangular area $RGFP_c$ represents a dead-weight loss of resources that could otherwise be employed in alternative production.[27] Even if the competitive producers' cost disadvantage were less—e.g., with unit costs of OT and hence a competitive output of OX_o—the rectangular excess cost area defined by RT times OX_o exceeds in magnitude the consumers' surplus loss triangle ABC attributable to the low-cost monopolist's output restriction. Excess costs reduce combined consumers' plus producers' surplus just as monopolistic resource misallocation does, and a relatively small unit cost elevation might deplete

the surplus even more than a monopolistic price elevation of appreciable proportions.[28] Still, the applicable conclusion depends upon the relative positions of the monopoly and competitive cost curves. Whether monopolists enjoy such a decided cost advantage as in Figure 2.4 (or indeed any at all) is an empirical question. We shall deal with it thoroughly in Chapter 4.

Previously it was suggested that monopolists, sheltered from the stiff gale of competition, might be sluggish about developing and introducing technological innovations that increase productivity (reducing costs) or enhance product quality. Yet some economists, led by the late Professor Joseph A. Schumpeter, have argued exactly the opposite: Firms need protection from competition before they will bear the risks and costs of invention and innovation, and a monopoly affords an ideal platform for shooting at the rapidly and jerkily moving targets of new technology.[29] If this is true, then progress will be more rapid under monopoly than under competition. And it is the rate of technical progress, not the efficiency of resource allocation at any particular moment in time, that in the long run determines whether per capita real incomes will be high or low. Suppose, as a hypothetical illustration, that real gross national product this year could be $2 trillion under pure and perfect competition, but that the misallocation caused by monopoly elements reduces it at any moment in time by 10 percent—i.e., to $1.8 trillion this year. Suppose, furthermore, that a purely competitive economy can sustain real growth of 3 percent per annum, so that in five years the GNP under competition will be $2.32 trillion. How much more rapid must growth be under monopoly to catch up to the competitive potential in five years, starting from the lower monopoly base of $1.8 trillion? The answer is, a monopolistic economy growing at 5 percent will catch up in five years, and it will surpass the competitive system by an increasing margin from then on. Or if a monopolistic economy starting from a 10 percent static allocation disadvantage could grow at the rate of 3.5 percent per annum, it would overtake the competitive system in 20 years. If in fact growth is more rapid under monopoly than competition, sooner or later the powerful leverage of compound interest will put the

F 2.4   Monopoly with scale economies

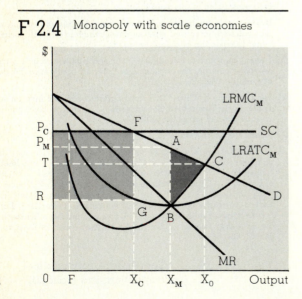

monopolistic system in the lead, despite any plausible starting handicap owing to static misallocation. The basic empirical question is, of course, was Schumpeter right? Is progress really more rapid under monopoly? Orderly presentation demands that we leave the issue unsettled here, returning to it in Chapters 15 and 16.

Whether a high rate of economic growth is indeed desirable has in recent years come increasingly into question.[30] We cannot resolve that value conflict here, but two related observations are warranted. First, for given levels of population, available resources will be stretched further and real income per capita will almost surely be higher with more rather than less (nonmilitary) technical progress. Thus, if one believes that the growth problem mainly entails a clash between burgeoning population and finite resources, Schumpeter's stress on technical progress is not patently inappropriate. Second, the logic of monopoly resource misallocation has special twists when applied to natural resources available only in fixed amounts. In certain cases (e.g., with zero extraction cost and unchanging demand elasticities over time), the profit-maximizing prices, and hence rates of resource depletion, are the same under monopoly as under pure and perfect competition.[31] In other more plausible cases, monopolies tend to charge higher prices than a competitive industry in the early years, but this means that there will be more of the resource and hence lower prices in later years.[32] Thus, if one believes that society is excessively myopic in its rate of natural resource use (which is tantamount to rejecting market-determined interest rates as a guide to dynamic resource allocation), the conservationist bias of monopolists may be applauded. Of course, a similar slowdown of natural resource depletion with arguably less objectionable income distribution ramifications could be achieved through the intervention (e.g., through taxation or public-land leasing policy[33]) of a conservation-minded government.

Another dynamic performance question is whether monopolistic industry organization might be more conducive to the macroeconomic stability of employment, listed in Chapter 1 as an important performance goal. It is conceivable that the hair-trigger price adjustments of purely and perfectly competitive markets could intensify tendencies toward instability, making it more difficult to combat the waste and human misery of cyclical unemployment through fiscal and monetary policy measures. If so, a tradeoff between static efficiency and dynamic stability might be required. The economic arguments are too complex to be summarized here, but they will be investigated in Chapters 7 and 13.

The discussion of allocative efficiency has thus far emphasized the monopoly and monopolistic competition cases, studiously ignoring oligopolistic market structures. We now ask, how much competition is necessary to bring prices into rough equality with marginal cost? Will rivalry among the few, or oligopoly, suffice? This turns out to be an extraordinarily difficult question, for the theory of oligopoly pricing does not yield the neat, confident generalizations about price-cost relationships provided by the pure theories of monopoly and monopolistic competition. We shall spend several chapters exploring

27. For the low-cost monopolist, that rectangle is profit rather than cost. Oversimplifying somewhat, the monopolist's profit provides the purchasing power with which this additional output (presumably from other sectors of the economy) can be purchased for the monopolist's stockholders' consumption.

28. See Oliver E. Williamson, "Economies as an Antitrust Defense: The Welfare Tradeoffs," *American Economic Review* 68 (March 1968): 18–34; with a correction in the *American Economic Review* 69 (December 1969): 954–59.

29. Joseph A. Schumpeter, *Capitalism, Socialism, and Democracy* (New York: Harper, 1942), especially pp. 88, 103.

30. For various views see E. J. Mishan, *Technology and Growth: The Price We Pay* (New York: Praeger, 1969); D. H. Meadows et al., *The Limits to Growth* (New York: Universe, 1972); and Mancur Olson and Hans H. Landsberg, eds., *The No-Growth Society* (New York: Norton, 1973).

31. See Joseph E. Stiglitz, "Monopoly and the Rate of Extraction of Exhaustible Resources," *American Economic Review* 66 (September 1976): 655–61.

32. For simulation analysis evidence on petroleum, bauxite, and copper, see Robert S. Pindyck, "Gains to Producers from the Cartelization of Exhaustible Resources," *Review of Economics and Statistics* 60 (May 1978): 238–51.

33. See the Federal Trade Commission Staff report, *Federal Energy Land Policy: Efficiency, Revenue, and Competition*, Senate Committee on Interior and Insular Affairs print (Washington, D.C.: Government Printing Office, 1976), especially Chapters 3, 5, and 12.

The welfare economics of competition and monopoly 23

the theory and evidence on oligopoly pricing before answers can be ventured. In a similar vein is Professor Galbraith's contention that countervailing power—the power of a few large buyers dealing with monopolistic sellers—offers an effective substitute for competition.[34] Market power on the buyer's side and its effects on economic performance will be the subject matter of Chapter 10.

Of all the qualifications to the purely competitive model, perhaps the most important arises from the theory of monopolistic competition. Because its product is differentiated physically or through service, advertising, location, and so on from the products of other sellers, the monopolistic competitor faces a downward-sloping demand curve, and therefore maximizes its profits at an output that leaves marginal cost below price. Our earlier analysis told us that this departure of price from marginal cost is bad in terms of allocative efficiency, and when entry is free, monopolistic competitors also end up producing at higher than minimum average cost per unit. But the consumer gets something in exchange: greater variety in the available bundle of goods and services. This poses a dilemma. To satisfy the desire for variety, we may have to sacrifice homogeneity of products; but in sacrificing homogeneity, we find each firm facing demand conditions that contribute to resource misallocation. Professor Chamberlin's reaction is devastatingly unambiguous:

> The explicit recognition that product is differentiated brings into the open the problem of variety and makes it clear that *pure competition may no longer be regarded as in any sense an "ideal" for purposes of welfare economics.* In many cases it would be quite impossible to establish it, even supposing it to be desirable. Retail shops, for example, could not all be located on the same spot, and personal differences between actors, singers, professional men, and business men could not be eliminated. But even where possible, it would not be desirable to standardize products beyond a certain point. Differences in tastes, desires, incomes, and locations of buyers, and differences in the uses which they make of commodities all indicate the need for variety and the necessity of substituting for

the concept of a "competitive ideal" an ideal involving both monopoly and competition. How much and what kinds of monopoly, and with what measure of social control, become the questions.[35]

Chamberlin was right. Consumers *are* willing to sacrifice some allocative nicety for variety, and so the social ideal must be not pure competition but some alloy of pure and monopolistic competition. The question of market organization then becomes a quantitative one: how much purity to sacrifice in order to maximize social welfare? On this question, economic theory has only recently begun to provide some answers.[36] We shall examine the relevant analyses in Chapter 14, discovering that monopolistic competition and oligopoly may provide too much variety under certain conditions and too little under others.

The problem of second best Having heaped doubt upon doubt, let us advance to the summit of Mount Agnostica—the problem of second best. Its underlying motivation is as follows: There are many reasons why, in the real world, it is impossible or undesirable to satisfy all the assumptions of the purely competitive general equilibrium model. The desire for variety, and hence the emergence of monopolistic competition, is one. Economies of scale may necessitate monopolistic or oligopolistic industry organization. External diseconomies, such as the air pollution effects of coal-fired electrical generating plants, or external economies, such as the knowledge spillover from individual firm's basic research discoveries, cause divergences between private and social costs or benefits, leading the invisible hand astray. Given the fact that competition cannot be pure and perfect in all sectors, what should be the policy toward the remaining sectors? With the best economic organization out of reach, is the second-best solution to encourage maximum conformity to the competitive model, whenever and wherever we can? The answer suggested by the theory of second best is: Quite possibly not, but it is difficult to say on a priori grounds, since the answer depends upon circumstances peculiar to each case.

To put the problem in perspective, we return to

Figure 2.3. We assume an economy consisting of two sectors, manufactured goods and farm products. The manufactured goods sector is monopolized; there is misallocation of resources, and we want to improve matters. Suppose, however, that there is no feasible way to break up the monopoly, e.g., because of scale economies or a chary Supreme Court. If something is to be done, it must be done in the farm products sector. What to do? Let us, out of desperation, organize the farmers into a monopoly. The farm price will be raised. This will set off a chain of repercussions. Owing to the change in relative prices, a substitution effect will shift the manufactured goods demand curve to the right, drawing resources out of the farming sector. Income effects may induce further shifts and price changes; monopoly profits will rise; wages of some productive inputs will probably fall, shifting marginal cost curves downward; and so on. Suppose, after all the necessary adjustments have been made, the economy settles down into the equilibrium illustrated in Figure 2.5. The price of manufactured goods is $7.00, with 4.25 million units supplied at a cost of $4.00 per unit; and the price of farm products is $2.80, with 11 million bushels supplied at a cost of $1.60 per unit.[37]

Now let us try, as before, to increase the aggregate value of the economy's output by further resource transfers. Suppose we transfer resources valued at $160 out of the farm monopoly into manufacturing. This entails a sacrifice of 100 bushels of farm produce (since the marginal cost is $1.60) and a gain of 40 manufactured good units. The additional manufactured goods can be sold only to consumers with reservation prices below $7.00, and so the value gain must be slightly less than $280. So far, so good. But the farm produce given up has a value to consumers of $2.80 or slightly more per unit, implying a total value sacrifice exceeding $280. The value sacrifice exceeds the gain, and hence the transfer is not worthwhile. It can be seen by similar reasoning that a transfer of resources from manufacturing into farming will reduce the value of output slightly. It follows that the aggregate value of output must be at a (local) maximum in the equilibrium attained by monopolizing both sectors! By abandoning our effort to maintain a world of competition and moving instead to a world of monopolies, we have apparently secured an equilibrium that, like the ideal competitive equilibrium, maximizes the aggregate value of the economy's output.[38]

This happens to be a special case. The curves in Figure 2.5 were constructed so that the ratio of the equilibrium price to marginal cost in the manufactured goods sector (7 to 4) equals the price/marginal cost ratio in the farming sector (2.80 to 1.60). Quite generally, when the supply of productive inputs is fixed, and when all producers sell their end products directly and only to consumers, it is possible to arrive at a completely efficient (first-best) allocation of resources by equalizing the ratio of price to marginal cost for each and every producer. This *rule of proportionality* was proposed by some economists during the 1930s as a possible solution to the monopoly problem, to be enforced by direct government intervention in pricing decisions.[39] Adherence to the rule will follow automatically, even without government intervention, if (as assumed in Figure 2.5) all producers happen to have identical price elasticities of demand at their equilibrium prices.

34. John Kenneth Galbraith, *American Capitalism: The Concept of Countervailing Power* (Boston: Houghton Mifflin, 1952), Chapter 9.

35. Chamberlin, *The Theory of Monopolistic Competition*, 6th ed. (1948), pp. 214–15 (italics in original); reprinted by permission of Harvard University Press. Copyright © 1948 by the President and Fellows of Harvard College. See also his "Product Heterogeneity and Public Policy," *American Economic Review* 40 (May 1950): 85–92; and Lawrence Abbott, *Quality and Competition* (New York: Columbia University Press, 1955).

36. See especially Kelvin Lancaster, "Socially Optimal Product Differentiation," *American Economic Review* 65 (September 1975): 567–85; Michael Spence, "Product Selection, Fixed Costs, and Monopolistic Competition," *Review of Economic Studies* 43 (June 1976): 217–35; and Avinash K. Dixit and Joseph E. Stiglitz, "Monopolistic Competition and Optimum Product Diversity," *American Economic Review* 67 (June 1977): 297–308.

37. Marginal costs have fallen by 20 percent, reflecting a commensurate decline in input wages. The diagrams assume a 13 percent average decline in the quantity of inputs supplied.

38. Cf. Robinson, *The Economics of Imperfect Competition*, Chapter 27.

39. See R. F. Kahn, "Some Notes on Ideal Output," *Economic Journal* 45 (March 1935): 1–35; and Abba P. Lerner, "The Concept of Monopoly Power," *Review of Economic Studies* 1 (June 1934): 157–75.

The welfare economics of competition and monopoly

F 2.5 Resource allocation in a world of monopolies

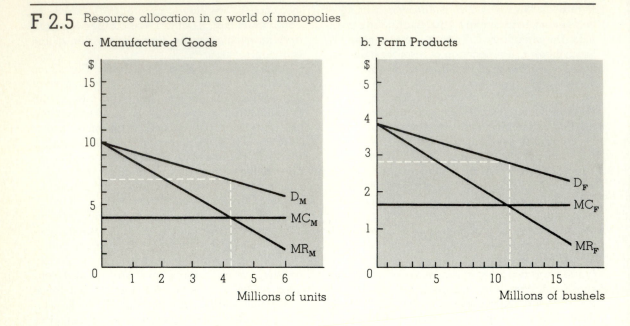

a. Manufactured Goods

b. Farm Products

The odds against such an equal elasticities happenstance are so high that the possibility is unworthy of serious attention. Moreover, enforcing the equal P/MC rule through public authority will not lead to an efficient allocation of resources under certain highly probable conditions. For one, there are always some commodities that almost necessarily are sold under competitive conditions, frustrating attainment of a true world of monopolies. The most prominent example is leisure. The price of leisure to typical consumers is the opportunity cost they incur by not supplying additional labor services—that is, the wage they receive for additional hours of work. From the viewpoint of firms, the marginal cost of labor is the wage paid, unless the labor market is imperfect, in which case it exceeds the wage paid. For the world-of-monopolies solution to be achieved, the price of leisure must be raised above the marginal cost of labor services to firms in the same proportion as all other commodity prices exceed their marginal costs. It is extremely difficult to find a practical way of doing this; direct per-hour subsidy payments by the government to each and every worker obviously fail to meet the practicality test. But unless the price of

leisure is raised relative to the wage paid by producers, or unless all workers' labor supply curves are completely inelastic, workers will consume too much leisure and supply too little labor relative to the quantities required for an efficient allocation of resources. In other words, the total quantity of labor supplied, and hence the size of the output bundle available to society, will be smaller under a world-of-monopolies approach to product pricing than it would be if all products were supplied under competitive conditions.

Another complication stems from the elaborate vertical and horizontal interrelationships characterizing any modern economy. Many products are not sold exclusively to final consumers; they are also used in whole or in part as intermediates by other firms. Consider the case of common salt, and assume (merely to simplify matters) that the only scarce basic resource is labor, which receives an equilibrium wage of $2.00 per hour. Suppose that a hundredweight of salt can be produced using one hour of labor, and that monopolistic salt producers sell their product at $4.00 per CWT, so that the ratio of price to marginal cost is 2. Suppose in addition that the production of a barrel of pickles requires one CWT of salt (for which $4.00 is paid) and one hour of labor (for which the pickle-maker pays $2.00). The combined marginal cost, from the viewpoint of the pickle producer, is $6.00 per barrel. If the rule of proportionality is enforced, the pickles will be sold at a price twice their marginal cost, that is, at $12.00 per barrel. But since both salt and pickles enter directly into the market baskets of final consumers, a distortion emerges. Two hours of labor will produce salt valued at $8.00 by the marginal consumer, or pickles valued at $12.00. A reallocation of resources (labor) from the production of salt for final consumption to the production of pickles (requiring, of course, more intermediate salt) will raise the aggregate value of output. Thus, applying the 'rule of proportionality' fails to maximize the value of output when the products of individual firms serve as both final consumption goods and intermediates. Analogous difficulties arise when a particular intermediate good enters into the various end products' manufacturing processes at different stages, or when the intermediate good accounts for varying proportions of the total cost of different end products.[40]

These and similar problems are assaulted head on in the general theory of second best.[41] Since the theory does not lend itself readily to geometric presentation, we shall summarize the overall approach and its implications here, saving a full mathematical treatment for the appendix.

The starting point of any second-best analysis is recognition that one or more of the conditions necessary for a first-best optimum simply cannot be satisfied, e.g., because one sector of the economy is unavoidably monopolistic. In the monopoly case, it is necessary to assume in addition that one or more other sectors must remain competitive, or at least less monopolistic, so that the world-of-monopolies solution is unattainable. These violations of the first-best optimum conditions are formulated and introduced as additional constraints upon the problem of maximizing the relevant criterion function—i.e., of maximizing social welfare or the aggregate value of output. The second-best problem then is to find for those sectors one *can* control new decision rules that maximize the value of the criterion function,

given as constraints the violations barring attainment of the first-best value.

The typical result is a set of formidably complex decision rules in place of the simple 'price-equals-marginal-cost' conditions customary in first-best problems. Indeed, the general solutions are so complex that it may be impossible to deduce unambiguously even the direction in which particular controlled prices should be adjusted in order to improve resource allocation. The main positive generalization reached by Lipsey and Lancaster in their pioneering article is that when some first-best optimum condition cannot be attained, it is no longer desirable in general to fulfill the other first-best optimum conditions. But the departures called for in any particular case depend upon the detailed cost and demand relations peculiar to that case.

An important subsequent contribution by Professor Bergson provides insight into the directions a second-best policy might take under certain circumstances.[42] He assumes a competitive labor supply sector, one or more uncontrollable industries that elevate price above marginal cost, and one or more industries controlled by the government in which prices are to be set so as to achieve an economy-wide, second-best optimum. When the government-controlled output is a substitute in consumption for the output of uncontrolled and distorted industries, the second-best solution typically entails raising the controlled output's price above marginal cost. The magnitude of the ele-

40. See Lionel McKenzie, "Ideal Output and the Interdependence of Firms," *Economic Journal* 61 (December 1951): 785–803.

41. The standard reference is R. G. Lipsey and Kelvin Lancaster, "The General Theory of Second Best," *Review of Economic Studies* 24, No. 1 (1956): 11–32. An almost simultaneous and similar formulation is found in Marcel Boiteux, "Sur la gestion des monopoles publics astreints à l'équilibre budgétaire," *Econometrica* 24 (January 1956): 22–40, translated into English in the *Journal of Economic Theory* 3 (September 1971): 219–40. For an elegant generalization, see Edward Foster and Hugo Sonnenschein, "Price Distortion and Economic Welfare," *Econometrica* 38 (March 1970): 281–97; extended by Kunio Kawamata in "Price Distortion and Potential Welfare," *Econometrica* 42 (May 1974): 435–60.

42. Abram Bergson, "Optimal Pricing for a Public Enterprise," *Quarterly Journal of Economics* 86 (November 1972): 519–44.

The welfare economics of competition and monopoly 27

vation—i.e., the ratio of the controlled output's price to marginal cost—turns out to be the weighted harmonic mean of price/cost ratios in the uncontrolled sectors (including labor supply), with the weights being the equilibrium quantity of each uncontrolled industry's output times its elasticity with respect to the controlled output's price/cost ratio. The greater the price/cost distortion for any given uncontrolled industry, the more important that industry is in the overall economy, and the more that industry's output expands as the substitute-controlled output's price is raised,[43] the higher will be the second-best controlled price/cost markup, *ceteris paribus*. When the controlled output is a complement in consumption to the uncontrolled output, the controlled output's price may be depressed below its marginal cost in the second-best solution. In a world of mixed substitutes and complements, the direction of second-best price adjustments depends upon the magnitudes of the uncontrolled industries' price distortions, outputs, and demand cross elasticities.

Matters are greatly simplified when the various sectors' outputs are independent in the sense that they are neither substitutes nor complements. Then the second-best solution in the controlled sector is identical to the first-best rule: Price is equated to marginal cost.[44] Yet such a case is undoubtedly rare in a modern economy characterized by rich substitution possibilities in consumption and intricate vertical interdependence in production.

It is difficult to say what should be done as a practical matter when sectoral interdependence renders such simplified piecemeal solutions non-optimal. No central authority could conceivably obtain the masses of information on demand elasticities, cross elasticities, cost functions, and prices needed to devise fully articulated, second-best pricing policies for even a single major industry richly interconnected with other sectors. Even if such data were available, it is doubtful whether second-best actions in that industry alone would do much to offset distortions pervading the rest of the economy. Alternatively, government-imposed price adjustments might be extended to numerous industries that would otherwise follow competitive pricing rules, but the

information requirements would be still more formidable. Because it indicates that maintaining competitive pricing whenever possible is not necessarily optimal but offers no guidance toward improved policies in the absence of information seldom if ever obtainable, the theory of second best is a counsel of despair.

A possible 'third best' might be to choose among alternative *general* policies, trying to adopt the policy that *on the average* has the most favorable resource allocation implications. In the framework of our present concern, the main practical alternatives boil down to letting monopoly increase in sectors not already monopolized versus attempting to enforce as much competition as one can consistent with economies of scale, product differentiation, and so on. When the issue is put this way, the case for competition gains renewed strength. On the positive side, if one has little or no prior information concerning the direction in which second-best solutions lie, eliminating avoidable monopoly power seems at least as likely to improve welfare as does encouraging new monopoly distortions where none existed previously. And on the negative side, it is easy for a policy that is permissive toward monopoly to get out of hand. Too much monopoly distortion may emerge in formerly competitive sectors, especially in view of the fact that some important sectors (such as the labor-leisure market) will by nature remain competitive. Weighing the possible gains from success in approximating a second-best solution against the risks of overshooting the desired degree of monopoly, I believe society will find itself in a superior third-best position on the average under a generally procompetitive policy.[45]

Nevertheless, one may decide that the whole question of allocative efficiency is so confused and uncertain, once second-best considerations are introduced, that policymakers should give up trying to achieve the best possible allocation of resources. Instead, they should base their choices on other criteria such as equity of income distribution, compatibility with political beliefs, conduciveness to production efficiency, and speed of technological progress. It is worth repeating that if this view is adopted, the first two alternate criteria generally favor a procompetitive policy.

Judgment is reserved on the production efficiency and progress issues until the relevant evidence can be examined.

Doubts concerning the profit maximization hypothesis

The conclusions of economic theory regarding the allocation of resources and distribution of income under competition and monopoly are based, among other things, upon the assumption that consumers strive to maximize their subjective satisfaction and firms seek to maximize profits. During the past four decades the profit maximization assumption has been attacked vigorously on several fronts.[46] The argument, in brief, is that profit maximization is at best unappealing and at worst meaningless to business decision makers operating in an environment of dynamic uncertainty, organizational complexity, and conflicting goals. Since these charges may require modifications in both performance predictions based upon orthodox price theory and value judgments on the desirability of competition as opposed to monopoly, we must pay them careful heed.

The effects of uncertainty Nearly all the interesting economic decisions made by business firms require predictions about future events. These predictions are inherently uncertain. Decision makers simply cannot know precisely how strong and how elastic demand will be in the next period, let alone ten years hence, or how far labor unions will carry their struggle for higher wages in forthcoming negotiations, or how rival sellers will react to a price increase, or what the prime interest rate will be next June. How should they behave in the face of these uncertainties? Economic theory usually assumes that business managers formulate definite expectations about the future values of relevant variables and then proceed to plug these expectations into their profit-maximizing decision rules. The expectations presumably include at least an estimate of the most likely or best-guess value and perhaps also some notion about the probability of various departures from the anticipated central tendency. This is already assuming a lot. Critics have noted that many businesspeople are poorly informed about business conditions in general, know almost nothing about the concept of probability, and understand only crudely the logic of

43. This last relationship is probably a special case stemming from Bergson's assumption that price/cost markups in the uncontrolled sectors are invariant. The elasticity effect might be attenuated if an increase in the controlled output's price caused a demand shift in favor of some uncontrolled product, which in turn induced an increase in the uncontrolled product's price/cost markup.

44. See Bergson, "Optimal Pricing," pp. 537–38. Others stressing the independence of sectors as a way out of the second-best dilemma include Otto A. Davis and A. B. Whinston, "Welfare Economics and the Theory of Second Best," *Review of Economic Studies* 32 (January 1965): 1–13; E. J. Mishan, "Second Thoughts on Second Best," *Oxford Economic Papers* 14 n.s. (October 1962): 205–17; and William J. Baumol, "Informed Judgment, Rigorous Theory, and Public Policy," *Southern Economic Journal* 32 (October 1965): 137–45; and R. Dusansky and J. Walsh, "Separability, Welfare Economics and the Theory of Second Best," *Review of Economic Studies* 43 (February 1976): 49–51.

Another special class of second-best problems arises when a violation of first-best pricing rules occurs, not in uncontrollable sectors for which some central authority is attempting to compensate, but rather within a sector over which control can be exercised. An example is a multiproduct public utility that must, because of unexhausted scale economies, set its prices above marginal costs in order to break even and avoid government subsidies financed through taxes that would otherwise distort private sector choices. Then, it can be shown, the optimal second-best strategy is to elevate prices above costs more for products with low price elasticities of demand, whose output is therefore relatively insensitive to the elevation, than for products of high elasticity. See William J. Baumol and David F. Bradford, "Optimal Departures from Marginal Cost Pricing," *American Economic Review* 60 (June 1970): 265–83.

45. For arguments along similar lines, see L. Athanasiou, "Some Notes on the Theory of Second Best," *Oxford Economic Papers* 18 n.s. (March 1966): 83–87; and Y. K. Ng, "Towards a Theory of Third Best," *Public Finance* 32, No. 1: 1–15.

46. The literature is enormous. Seminal contributions include K. E. Boulding, "The Theory of the Firm in the Last Ten Years," *American Economic Review* 32 (December 1942): 791–802; Fritz Machlup, "Marginal Analysis and Empirical Research," *American Economic Review* 36 (September 1946): 519–54; Andreas G. Papandreou, "Some Basic Problems in the Theory of the Firm," in B. F. Haley, ed., *A Survey of Contemporary Economics*, vol. 2 (Homewood, Ill.: Irwin, 1952), pp. 183–222; Herbert Simon, "Theories of Decision-Making in Economics and Behavioral Science," *American Economic Review* 49 (June 1959): 253–83; Robin Marris, "A Model of the 'Managerial' Enterprise," *Quarterly Journal of Economics* 77 (May 1963): 185–209; Oliver E. Williamson, *The Economics of Discretionary Behavior* (Englewood Cliffs, N.J.: Prentice-Hall, 1964); R. M. Cyert and J. G. March, *A Behavioral Theory of the Firm* (Englewood Cliffs, N.J.: Prentice-Hall, 1963); and R. J. Monsen and Anthony Downs, "A Theory of Large Managerial Firms," *Journal of Political Economy* 73 (June 1965): 221–36.

profit maximization, i.e., what variables must be taken into account, such as marginal cost and marginal revenue, and how they must be related to maximize profits. It is hardly realistic to expect that profit-maximizing decisions will sprout magically from such barren soil, the skeptics continue. In defense of orthodoxy, Fritz Machlup has argued that business managers have an intuitive understanding of what is required to maximize profits, even though they cannot articulate rules resembling the economist's price-equals-marginal-cost condition, just as automobile drivers who have never taken a course in differential equations are able intuitively to solve the problem of passing another car on a two-lane highway. He goes on to stress a subjective interpretation of the variables manipulated by entrepreneurs:

> It should hardly be necessary to mention that all the relevant magnitudes involved—costs, revenue, profit—are subjective—that is, perceived or fancied by the men whose decisions or actions are to be explained . . . rather than ''objective''. . . . Marginal analysis of the firm should not be understood to imply anything but subjective estimates, guesses and hunches.[47]

This defense comes close to saying that whatever managers choose to do can be called profit maximization, however remotely it resembles the policies an omniscient maximizer would select. Carried so far, the theory of profit maximization becomes little more than tautology.

Yet even if we assume a close correspondence between business expectations and objective reality, further dilemmas appear. Imagine a decision maker weighing two alternative policies, one offering a best-guess profit expectation of $1 million with a 5 percent chance of bankrupting the firm (whose net worth is currently $4 million), the other an expected profit of $2 million with a 15 percent chance of disaster. Which is the rational choice? It is impossible to say without further information on the attitudes of the firm's owners toward increases in wealth versus total loss of their equity.[48] Rational behavior under uncertainty requires some tradeoff between average payoffs and variability of payoffs or, in the statistician's terms, between means and variances. Only the decision maker who attaches no significance whatsoever to avoiding risk will always choose alternatives with the highest best-guess payoffs. And such managers, empirical studies suggest, are rare.

Further complications are posed by the interactions among uncertainty, risk aversion, and the time horizon of the decision maker. Long-run profit maximization implies maximizing the present value of an enterprise's current and future profit stream. But how far into the future? And at what rate shall future profits be discounted? Should distant profits be discounted more heavily than next year's profits because the distant future is so much more uncertain? How these questions are resolved in practice—and unanimous agreement is lacking even in normative treatises on managerial economics—can have a substantial impact on conduct and performance in particular markets.

Consider, for example, the following problem. A firm with monopoly power must decide upon its pricing strategy. Because the future is uncertain, it may choose virtually to ignore the future repercussions of its current decisions and reap the highest possible profits it can today. This high-discount rate, short-horizon policy dictates a high price today. Alternatively, the firm may choose not to exploit its monopoly power fully today, hoping that a low current price will cement customer loyalties, increasing the probability that the firm will weather whatever storms the uncertain future holds. Either policy might be defended as the correct path to profit maximization under identical supply, demand, and market structural conditions. The only course open to analysts confronted by such ambiguities is to amass as much evidence as they can on the attitudes of real-world managers toward risk and the future and on how these attitudes are correlated with market structure. We shall return to this problem in Chapter 8 when we study the dynamics of industrial pricing behavior.

Other ambiguities or departures from the predictions of traditional theory arise because of uncertainty and firms' adaptation to it. Cyert and March, for instance, suggest that firms avoid uncertainty by using decision rules featuring short-run reactions to short-run feedbacks, circumventing the need to anticipate future events.[49] The use of such rules is almost certain to alter pricing behavior. Investment decisions cannot be made in this way, however, because of the long time spans involved in implementing the investments and realizing the subsequent returns. Here risk aversion may lead to the rejection of some capital expenditure proposals, retarding the expansion of industry capacity and preventing price from falling to its long-run equilibrium level. But on the other hand, and especially under oligopoly conditions, entrepreneurs may consider a vigorous investment program the best possible hedge against unforeseeable future challenges, perhaps even carrying their investment beyond the level compatible with long-run competitive equilibrium. Once again, performance hinges on how decision makers react to uncertainty. Or to add one more example that by no means exhausts the list of possibilities, uncertainty about future business conditions may induce firms with market power to hedge by keeping their costs as low as possible (i.e., staying at fighting weight) when they would not be so inclined if the future could be predicted more confidently. Whereas reactions to uncertainty in the previous cases imply departures from strict profit maximization, in this last case risk aversion drives the firm closer to the profit maximization norm.

Organizational complexity Another feature of the modern business enterprise that may prevent it from behaving in strict conformity to the profit maximization hypothesis is its organizational complexity. Responsibility is typically divided among functional components specializing in production, sales, materials procurement, finance, accounting, research and development, and so forth. In a large firm, an elaborate vertical chain of command extends from workers at the operating level to top management and the board of directors, who in turn represent stockholder interests. This whole structure must be tied together by a communications network so that decisions taken at various levels and in the diverse functional components mesh. It is here that breakdowns occur. Conflicts among functional

groups or hierarchical levels are bound to arise, demanding top management resolution. But the information transmission process is subject to attenuation. Top managers cannot possibly digest all the knowledge possessed by every operating-level employee, and so some grasp of special circumstances affecting particular cases must be sacrificed. Furthermore, the content of messages tends to become distorted to suit the prejudices and fears of both senders and receivers. The more hierarchical filters through which information passes, the more distorted the information is likely to become, and the greater is the chance that incorrect decisions will be made. Or in the reverse flow from top management to operating levels, the more filters there are, the more likely instructions will be misinterpreted or deliberately ignored.

Given this organizational complexity, it may prove very difficult for top management to arrive at and enforce choices that maximize profits. Complicating matters is the fact that operating-level personnel often care little about profit maximization. Even the best-designed employee bonus and profit-sharing systems seldom succeed in instilling much zeal for profit maximization below the middle management level. Operating-level employees see little correlation between their individual actions and the size of the profit pie in which they will share, just as firms in a competitive industry consider their output decisions to have an imperceptible effect on the market price. At the same time, such employees have many goals that conflict with profit maximization. Division chiefs fearing dismissal conceal or gloss over operating problems until the situation has deteriorated beyond repair. Research and development engineers seek technical sophistication and product refinement for their own sake,

47. Machlup, "Marginal Analysis and Empirical Research," pp. 521–22.

48. For theoretical analyses of possible stockholder conflicts, see the "Symposium on the Optimality of Competitive Capital Markets," *Bell Journal of Economics and Management Science* 5 (Spring 1974): 125–84.

49. Cyert and March, *A Behavioral Theory of the Firm*, p. 119.

The welfare economics of
competition and monopoly   31

even when these add more to costs than to revenues. Production foremen find make-work jobs for redundant personnel to maintain a nice-guy reputation. And so on.

It is the classic responsibility of top management to ferret out these deviations and to establish a system of controls and incentives that ensures internal conformity with the firm's profit maximization goal. Organizational complexity, as we have seen, can cause the attempt to fall short of its mark. But an equally significant obstacle might arise out of the very character of the modern business corporation. Like the divisional and functional specialists they command, top managers may pursue the profit goal with less than complete diligence.

One reason for this is said to be the increasing separation between ownership and control of industrial enterprises—a phenomenon alluded to by Lenin[50] and first studied seriously in the early 1930s by Berle and Means.[51] There was a time more than a century ago when individuals managing even the largest U.S. companies held, if not a majority, at least a substantial minority interest in those companies. Gradually this has changed. Big business has become bigger; the lion's share of all industrial output is produced by corporations big under any plausible definition of the word. The ownership of large corporations has been dispersed among thousands of stockholders, no one of whom may own a sufficiently large proportion of the outstanding shares to exercise a dominant controlling role. American Telephone and Telegraph had 2.9 million common stockholders in 1976; Exxon 686,000; and General Motors 1.3 million. The median (250th) firm in terms of stockholder numbers on *Fortune*'s list of the 500 largest U.S. industrial corporations for 1956 recorded more than 9,000 shareholders. In their pioneering study, Berle and Means found 88 of the 200 largest American nonfinancial corporations to be "management controlled" in 1929 because no individual, family, corporation, or group of business associates owned more than a 20 percent share of all outstanding voting stock, and because evidence of control by a smaller ownership group was lacking.[52] Only 22 of the corporations were judged to be privately owned or controlled by a group of stockholders with a majority interest.

Updating the Berle and Means analysis, Robert Larner estimated that 161 of the 200 largest nonfinancial corporations had come to be management controlled by 1963, with no single ownership group holding 10 percent or more of the voting stock.[53] Only eight were controlled by a majority ownership group. This led Larner to conclude that the "managerial revolution" observed in 1932 by Berle and Means was "close to complete."[54]

Larner's finding has been challenged in a still more recent study by Philip Burch.[55] Burch's main point of departure is the argument that families or groups might exercise effective control with less than the 10 percent ownership share taken as a cutoff by Larner. He notes too that the data on U.S. corporate stock ownership are fragmentary and inaccurate, causing Berle and Means

---

T 2.2 Control characteristics of leading U.S. corporations

	Industrial corporations		Merchandising corporations
	Top 50	Top 300	Top 50
Probably family controlled	20.0%	42.7%	58.0%
Possibly family controlled	22.0	16.0	14.0
Probably management controlled	58.0	41.3	28.0

Reprinted by permission of the publisher, from Philip H. Burch, Jr., *The Managerial Revolution Reassessed: Family Control In America's Large Corporations* (Lexington, Mass.: Lexington Books, D. C. Heath and Company, Copyright 1972, D. C. Heath and Company) pp. 68, 96.

and Larner, among others, to overlook significant ownership positions. Following an impressive amount of detective work to determine whether in 1965 some identifiable group held at least 4 to 5 percent of voting stock and whether family representation on a board of directors continued for an extended period of time, he classified the top 300 of *Fortune*'s 500 leading industrial corporations and the top 50 merchandising corporations, as shown in Table 2.2. By his criteria, only 41 percent of the top 300 industrials were management controlled. Furthermore, Burch found that in 93 percent of the companies classified as "probably family controlled" among the 300 largest industrials, family members had served in major executive capacities, i.e., vice presidential or higher.[56] Clearly, there are rather large differences between the Larner and Burch views of how far the managerial revolution has progressed, although both support an inference that it has in fact advanced since the time of Berle and Means.

In a more qualitative study, Professor Myles Mace shed light on how vigorous a role stock-owning family members play on boards of directors and how directors function in family- as compared to management-controlled enterprises.[57] Sometimes, Mace found, family members ceased exercising active control in the boardroom when their stock ownership dropped below 50 percent; in other cases, they continued to exercise de facto control with only a small proportion of the stock. Much evidently depends upon such idiosyncracies as the business ability and interest of family stockholders. When family members did elect to take an active part, this was manifested among other things in seeking guidance from outside board of directors members and bringing family influence to bear on new director choices. In management-controlled boards, on the other hand, new outside board members are typically selected by the 'inside' chief executive officer. Such nominations are normally validated by an overwhelming margin as stockholders docilely assign their proxies. The board of directors in turn approves management's recommendations on new managerial appointments and replacements. Through this process of reciprocal self-selection, the management group maintains its control. Mace's study also demonstrates that out-

side directors tend to be ill-informed about their corporations' operations and that conventional boardroom ethics discourage independent action, or even the posing of embarrassing questions, by outside directors except in crisis situations.[58] Thus, there is reason to believe that, at least in management-controlled corporations, the board of directors does not impose much restraint on management's operating discretion.

As always, we must be wary of oversimplifying. There are organizational constraints on managerial autonomy even in corporations with widely dispersed ownership. As we shall elaborate in the next chapter, substantial blocks of stock have come into the hands of mutual investment funds and banks serving as trustees for diverse individ-

50. V. I. Lenin, *Imperialism: The Highest Stage of Capitalism* (New York: International Publishers, 1939), p. 59.

51. Adolf A. Berle and Gardiner Means, *The Modern Corporation and Private Property* (New York: Macmillan, 1932).

52. Berle and Means, *The Modern Corporation*, pp. 90–118. Other early studies reaching similar conclusions include Raymond W. Goldsmith, *The Distribution of Ownership in the Largest 200 Nonfinancial Corporations*, Temporary National Economic Committee, Monograph no. 29 (Washington, D.C.: Government Printing Office, 1940); and Robert Aaron Gordon, *Business Leadership in the Large Corporation* (Washington, D.C.: Brookings Institution, 1945).

53. Robert J. Larner, *Management Control and the Large Corporation* (Cambridge, Mass.: Dunellen, 1970), pp. 9–24.

54. Larner, *Management Control*, p. 22.

55. Philip H. Burch, Jr., *The Managerial Revolution Reassessed* (Lexington, Mass.: Heath, 1972). Other studies inferring more owner control than Larner did include Jean-Marie Chevalier, "The Problem of Control in Large American Corporations," *Antitrust Bulletin* 14 (Spring, 1969): 163–80; and Lawrence Pedersen and William K. Tabb, "Ownership and Control of Large Corporations Revisited," *Antitrust Bulletin* 21 (Spring 1976): 53–66.

56. Burch, *The Managerial Revolution*, pp. 101–102. Understandably, Burch has no systematic evidence on the proportion of vice presidencies that are mere sinecures—e.g., for sons-in-law. Casual observation suggests that they are not uncommon.

57. Myles L. Mace, *Directors: Myth and Reality* (Boston: Harvard Business School Division of Research, 1971), pp. 154–74.

58. Mace, *Directors*, pp. 43–71, 94–101. See also Ben W. Heineman, "What Does and Doesn't Go on in the Boardroom," in *Fortune*, February 1972, pp. 157–59. For indications of a possible change toward more active board member involvement, see Jeremy Bacon and James K. Brown, *The Board of Directors: Perspective and Practices in Nine Countries* (New York: Conference Board, 1977), Chapters 1 and 8.

The welfare economics of competition and monopoly   33

ual stockholders or pension funds. When crises or proxy contests materialize, these financial intermediaries may wield decisive voting power. In more normal times they may quietly take the initiative in prodding management to change its ways. A tradition of reticence and legal restrictions have limited the control banks and other financial institutions exercise over internal corporate decision making; but as the volume of their holdings increases, their influence cannot help but rise accordingly. It is uncertain, however, whether this additional element of control divorced from any conventional ownership role will necessarily channel managerial energies more consistently in profit-maximizing directions, or whether it might tolerate or even encourage some departures from profit maximization.

The multitude of managerial goals Within certain imprecisely defined bounds, then, management may be free to pursue goals not necessarily consistent with maximizing stockholder earnings. What are these goals? How seriously do they conflict with profit maximization? These are key issues in the debate on the separation of ownership and control.

First, however, we must inquire whether firms as organizations can be said to have unambiguously defined goals at all. It is not clear in theory whether individuals with divergent preferences can somehow fuse those preferences into a consistent set of organizational goals.[59] Students of organizational behavior have suggested two ways out of this problem. For one, it has been proposed that firms as organizations do not maximize the attainment of some well-defined objective function but instead 'satisfice'—i.e., seek choices that satisfy at least minimum levels of aspiration with respect to their several objectives.[60] For example, management may set a target rate of return on invested capital as its profit objective; if that target is achieved, it turns to the satisfaction of other (nonprofit) objectives.[61] This satisficing hypothesis is far from universally accepted, mainly because it is not evident how the targets are set initially and how they are modified dynamically in response to over-fulfillment or under-fulfillment. A second, related conjecture is that firms avoid facing up to goal conflicts by proceeding sequentially, satisfying one objective at a time before considering the fulfillment of others.[62] It is questionable whether the hard choices necessitated by a multitude of wants and a scarcity of means can be persistently dodged through any such technique. At this point we can only conclude that we know far too little about the methods of goal formation and conflict resolution within large organizations. What *is* clear is that business managers are pulled in many directions and that they must and do make choices among alternative objectives.

One possible departure from profit maximization is to seek a placid, comfortable, risk-free business existence. As J. R. Hicks put it in a much-quoted quip, "The best of all monopoly profits is a quiet life."[63] Such a characterization does considerable justice to the archetypal European business leader of past generations. Whether it reflects the psychology of American counterparts or the new European generation is dubious.

Much closer to the mark is the assertion that managers without a significant ownership interest seek security of tenure in their jobs. The security motive does not necessarily conflict with profit maximization; a manager who keeps the profits rolling in is, after all, a good person to have around. Yet conflicts do arise, especially in decision making under uncertainty. As Professor William Fellner has pointed out, there tends to be an asymmetry in the rewards to managers.[64] If risky decisions turn out badly, stockholders lose their assets and managers their jobs.[65] If they turn out well, the manager may be promoted or receive a bonus, but the rewards are seldom commensurate with the stockholders' gains. Faced with this asymmetry, the hired manager is more apt to sacrifice higher expected profits for lower risk than an owner-manager under otherwise identical circumstances. Also, because the stock market reacts sensitively (and perhaps over-reacts) to changes, managers concerned about their tenure exhibit an apparent preference for lower but more stably growing earnings over high but fluctuating earnings. One manifestation is the use of accounting discretion to "smooth" reported earnings—e.g., by shifting the reporting of certain deferrable costs from bad to good years.[66] This bookkeeping hocus-pocus is most likely innocuous, but migration of the stability objective to an organization's operating levels can have more serious *real* resource utilization implications. To protect themselves against attention-drawing setbacks, managers tend to accumulate *organizational slack*—inessential resources that are eliminated only when operating unit profits are under severe pressure. From a study of three divisions of large corporations, Schiff and Lewin estimated that the amount of slack built into divisional budgets averaged 20 to 25 percent of the units' operating expenses.[67] Top management was said to be aware that such slack existed; however, they were unable to eliminate it because they lacked the detailed knowledge needed to set cost and profit budgets tight enough to maximize profits but not so tight as to jeopardize operations.

Being human, most hired managers derive considerable satisfaction from achieving personal prestige and power. Both seem to be correlated more closely with the volume of a firm's sales than with the size or rate of profits it earns. There have also been indications that the compensation of top executives is more closely associated with sales than with total profits. In view of this, it is often argued that hired managers are more concerned with enhancing sales or the growth of sales than increasing profits.[68] In the static theory of the monopolistic or oligopolistic firm, maximizing sales revenue is incompatible with maximizing profits except under improbable circumstances (e.g., when marginal cost is zero). In a dynamic context the conflict between sales growth and profitability is much less sharp. However, increases in growth beyond some point must impose profit sacrifices as management's ability to control is over-strained, low payoff investment projects are approved, and high-cost sources of capital funds are tapped.

Whether managerial compensation systems actually encourage such departures from profit maximization has been the subject of considerable quantitative research.[69] When the methodological deficiencies marring much of this work are circumvented, four main conclusions stand out. First, executive salaries and bonuses do tend to be more closely correlated with sales than with

59. See Kenneth J. Arrow, *Social Choice and Individual Values* (New York: Wiley, 1951), for an analysis of paradoxes in democratic group decision making; and Cyert and March, *A Behavioral Theory*, pp. 26–44, for a more general discussion of organizational goal formation.

60. See Simon, "Theories of Decision-Making," pp. 262–65; Cyert and March, *A Behavioral Theory*, pp. 26–44; and Roy Radner, "A Behavioral Model of Cost Reduction," *Bell Journal of Economics* 6 (Spring 1975): 196–215.

61. R. F. Lanzillotti, "Pricing Objectives in Large Companies," *American Economic Review* 48 (December 1958): 921–40; Jesse Markham's review of A. D. H. Kaplan et al., *Pricing in Big Business, American Economic Review* 49 (June 1959): 473–75; and Alfred E. Kahn, "Pricing Objectives in Large Companies: Comment," *American Economic Review* 49 (September 1959): 671–76.

62. Cyert and March, *A Behavioral Theory*, pp. 35–36, 118.

63. Hicks, "Annual Survey of Economic Theory: The Theory of Monopoly," *Econometrica* 3 (January 1935): 8.

64. William Fellner, *Competition Among the Few* (New York: Knopf, 1949), pp. 172–73.

65. For evidence that adverse deviations from trend profitability lead to a shortening of corporate presidents' tenure, see W. M. Crain, Thomas Deaton, and Robert Tollison, "On the Survival of Corporate Executives," *Southern Economic Journal* 43 (January 1977): 1372–75.

66. See Jacob Y. Kamin and Joshua Ronen, "The Effects of Corporate Control on Apparent Profit Performance," *Southern Economic Journal* 45 (July 1978): 181–91.

67. Michael Schiff and Arie W. Lewin, "Where Traditional Budgeting Fails," *Financial Executive* 36 (May 1968): 50–62; and *idem*, "The Impact of People on Budgets," *Accounting Review* 45 (1970): 259–68. See also Oliver Williamson, *The Economics of Discretionary Behavior*, pp. 85–126. Two of the slack-laden companies studied by Williamson, it is worth noting, were controlled by dominant family ownership groups.

68. For various approaches, see Edith T. Penrose, *The Theory of Growth of the Firm* (Oxford: Blackwell, 1959); William J. Baumol, *Business Behavior, Value, and Growth*, rev. ed. (New York: Harcourt, Brace and World, 1967), Chapters 5–10; Marris, "A Model of the 'Managerial' Enterprise"; J. Williamson, "Profit, Growth and Sales Maximization," *Economica* 34 (February 1966): 1–16; John Lintner, "Optimum or Maximum Corporate Growth under Uncertainty," in Robin Marris and Adrian Wood, eds., *The Corporate Economy* (Cambridge, Mass.: Harvard University Press, 1971), pp. 172–241; Robert M. Solow, "Some Implications of Alternative Criteria for the Firm," in Marris and Wood, *The Corporate Economy*, pp. 318–42; Hayne E. Leland, "The Dynamics of a Revenue Maximizing Firm," *International Economic Review* 13 (June 1972): 376–85; Conway L. Lackman and Joseph L. Craycraft, "Sales Maximization and Oligopoly: A Case Study," *Journal of Industrial Economics* 23 (December 1974): 81–95; Richard Schramm, "Profit Risk Management and the Theory of the Firm," *Southern Economic Journal* 40 (January 1974): 353–63; George K. Yarrow, "Growth Maximization and the Firm's Investment Function," *Southern Economic Journal* 41 (April 1975): 580–92; and Robert E. Wong, "Profit Maximization and Alternative Theories: A Dynamic Reconciliation," *American Economic Review* 65 (September 1975): 689–94.

The welfare economics of competition and monopoly   35

the volume of profits in any given year. But they are even more closely correlated with assets, suggesting that firm size as such is a critical compensation-determining variable, which in turn may reflect a need for greater managerial ability in large enterprises than in smaller firms. It is worth noting that the size-compensation relationship is strongly nonlinear; that is, a doubling of firm size does not lead to a doubling of top executives' pay. Second, when the nonlinear effect of firm size is held constant, increases in executive compensation appear in most studies to be associated systematically with increased profitability. Third, even though there are substantial differences in compensation between large and small corporations, top managers can rarely expect to exploit the full range of those differences, radically increasing their firm's size and hence their salary, within their own foreseeable job tenure. Analyzing the range of sales and profitability growth normally observed over moderate time intervals, Meeks and Whittington found for a large sample of British companies that chief executive compensation tended to increase by a larger absolute amount with profit performance improvements than with sales increases of temporally comparable magnitude.[70] Fourth, for a sample of 48 firms in three industries (chemicals, drugs, and petroleum refining), McEachern discovered that the locus of company control influenced top management compensation structures. Specifically, he found that in companies controlled by an owner group *not* participating actively in management, compensation was positively linked more strongly to profitability or common stock values, and less strongly to sales revenue, than in either owner/manager-controlled or management-controlled companies.[71] All in all, the weight of evidence favors a conclusion that profitability does have a significant positive impact on managers' pay. That compensation schemes may also induce some sacrifice of profits in favor of sales, however, cannot be ruled out, especially (if McEachern's results can be generalized) in management-controlled corporations.

It is also important to recognize that salaries, bonuses, and other cash payments are not the only financial rewards realized by top managers.

Many hired managers own stock and/or hold options to buy stock in the corporations they manage. Even though their stockholdings may be much too small to afford any significant element of owner control, they often comprise the bulk of the executive's personal wealth. Moreover, given an income tax structure preferential to capital gains, the executive's best chance to amass a fortune may lie in seeing the value of his stocks appreciate. This link could provide definite profit maximization incentive effects, especially for executives at the top of the management hierarchy, where the connection between individual action and stockholder gain is most immediate. Wilbur Lewellen found that the average value of their own companies' stock owned by the top five executives of 50 leading U.S. manufacturing corporations ranged from a minimum of $202,000 per capita to a high of $3.0 million between 1940 and 1963.[72] In 1963, dividends, capital gains from company stockholdings, and changes in the value of stock options amounted to 2.29 times the top five executives' average after-tax fixed-dollar remuneration, i.e., salary plus bonuses plus noncontributory pension benefits.[73] In only one year out of 24 did this ratio fall below 0.43, and the simple average over 24 years was 1.36 times fixed-dollar remuneration. The wealth enhancement opportunities presented by these holdings cannot help but engender a healthy respect for company profitability (and also for the advantages of stock purchases and sales exploiting insider information). Whether this incentive effect is the same in manager-controlled as compared to owner-controlled enterprises is not completely clear. By Burch's conservative criteria, 28 of the 50 large manufacturing companies studied by Lewellen were manager controlled. However, for his sample of 48 companies in three industries, McEachern reported that hired managers of firms with an identifiable outside control group owned more than twice as much stock as did the executives of management-controlled companies.[74] To the extent that such differences hold more generally, there may be somewhat less incentive in manager-controlled corporations to avoid straying in the direction of sales or sales growth maximization.

Finally, managers may be motivated by the

simple desire to do good—to pay their employees handsome salaries, to provide pleasant working conditions, to give consumers a square deal on price and product quality, to support worthwhile philanthropic and community causes, and so on. All this is perfectly respectable, even if it does involve some sacrifice of profits, and it is clear that many closely held corporations without an ownership-control separation problem have moved in the same direction. But if carried too far, corporate altruism can sabotage the market mechanism's functioning. Resources may be misallocated when price and wage signals are generated by managerial fiat rather than through the interplay of genuine market forces.[75]

How much discretion do firms have? In sum, there is no shortage of ways in which business decision makers *may* deviate from the behavioral norm assumed in the economist's theory of the profit-maximizing firm. Still, several questions remain to be answered. How serious are the deviations induced by nonprofit goals? How much discretion do owner-controlled and manager-controlled firms have to pursue objectives other than profit maximization? And what are the implications of nonmaximization for the policy choice between competition and monopoly?

One possible check on managerial autonomy is the threat of takeover. According to hypotheses advanced by Professors Marris and Manne,[76] failure to maximize profits will depress company stock prices below their potential value; this will induce some outside entrepreneur to bid for a controlling interest, remove the old management, and redirect the company's energies toward increasing profits and hence stock values. During the 1960s and 1970s, such unfriendly takeovers evolved from rare to commonplace events in the United States.[77]

The Marris-Manne thesis has inspired considerable quantitative research. Much of it has focused on the relationship between frequency of acquisition bids and either profitability or the *valuation ratio*—that is, the ratio of the market value of a company's common stock to its book or accounting value. The characteristic finding has been that relatively unprofitable and/or undervalued corporations do run a somewhat greater

risk of being taken over.[78] But the relationships are statistically weak so that, for example, the probability of takeover in any given year for firms in the second- or third-lowest profitability deciles

(69) The studies on which heaviest reliance has been placed here include Robert T. Masson, "Executive Motivations, Earnings, and Consequent Equity Performance," *Journal of Political Economy* 79 (November/December 1971): 1278–92; George K. Yarrow, "Executive Compensation and the Objectives of the Firm," in Keith Cowling, ed., *Market Structure and Corporate Behaviour* (London: Gray-Mills, 1972), pp. 149–73; Geoffrey Meeks and Geoffrey Whittington, "Directors' Pay, Growth and Profitability," *Journal of Industrial Economics* 24 (September 1975): 1–14; and William A. McEachern, *Managerial Control and Performance* (Lexington, Mass.: Heath, 1975). Yarrow and McEachern provide good critical surveys of the earlier literature. See also David J. Smyth, W. J. Boyes, and D. E. Peseau, *Size, Growth, Profits and Executive Compensation in the Large Corporation* (New York: Holmes and Meier, 1975), pp. 71–79; and Andrew Cosh, "The Remuneration of Chief Executives in the United Kingdom," *Economic Journal* 85 (March 1975): 75–94.

70. Meeks and Whittington, "Directors' Pay," pp. 5–8.

71. McEachern, *Managerial Control*, pp. 77–84. It is not entirely clear whether McEachern's analysis controls adequately for nonlinearity of the size relationship, though he shows awareness of the problem.

72. Wilbur G. Lewellen, *The Ownership Income of Management* (New York: Columbia University Press, 1971), p. 79. If a few extreme values are deleted, the range of averages falls to between $117,000 (for 1949) and $1.0 million. *Idem.*, p. 98. With extreme values omitted, the five top executives' combined stockholdings amounted to 0.21 percent of all the outstanding stock in their companies. *Idem.*, p. 105.

73. Lewellen, *The Ownership Income*, p. 103. For an updating to 1969 with similar conclusions, see W. G. Lewellen, "Managerial Pay and the Tax Changes of the 1960's," *National Tax Journal* 25 (June 1972): 111–31. See also Larner, *Management Control*, pp. 34–43; and (on more recent developments) "Tax Reform Remodels the Pay Package," *Business Week*, 28 February 1977, p. 48.

74. McEachern, *Managerial Control*, pp. 82–83.

75. See Eugene V. Rostow, "To Whom and for What Ends Is Corporate Management Responsible?" in Edward S. Mason, ed., *The Corporation in Modern Society* (Cambridge, Mass.: Harvard University Press, 1960), pp. 59–69; Milton Friedman, *Capitalism and Freedom* (Chicago: University of Chicago Press, 1962), pp. 133–36; and Fritz Machlup, "Corporate Management, National Interests, and Behavioral Theory," *Journal of Political Economy* 75 (October 1967): 772–74. Also apropos is Adam Smith's cynical comment, "I have never known much good done by those who affected to trade for the public interest." *Wealth of Nations*, p. 423.

76. Marris, "A Model of the 'Managerial' Enterprise"; Marris, *The Economic Theory of "Managerial" Capitalism* (London: Macmillan, 1974), especially Chapter 1; and Henry G. Manne, "Mergers and the Market for Corporate Control," *Journal of Political Economy* 73 (April 1965): 110–20.

77. See Patrick J. Davey, *Defense Against Unnegotiated Cash Tender Offers* (New York: Conference Board, 1977).

is both low (e.g., from .03 to .11) and only about twice that of firms in the second- or third-*highest* profitability deciles.[79] Furthermore, the transactions costs of a takeover are sufficiently high that, according to Smiley's estimates, the market value of a company's stock can fall by approximately 13 percent below its potential (i.e., maximum profits) value before the risk of takeover becomes appreciable.[80] There is also evidence that the probability of takeover is inversely related to firm size, which may lead relatively unprofitable and hence vulnerable companies to defend themselves by emphasizing growth (e.g., through an active acquisition campaign) rather than profit enhancement.[81] One can observe numerous hastily brokered "friendly" mergers to avoid imminent takeover by a "raider" likely to remove existing management. Other defense mechanisms include staggering the expiration dates of directors' terms so that sudden changes in voting control are precluded and assiduously cultivating a favorable image among stock analysts. Seen as a whole, the available evidence provides at best only weak support for the hypothesis that takeovers generate an effective disciplinary mechanism against departures from profit maximization.

When forced into the trenches on the question of whether firms maximize profits, economists resort to the ultimate weapon in their arsenal: a variant of Darwin's natural selection theory.[82] Over the long pull, there is one simple criterion for the survival of a business enterprise: Profits must be nonnegative. No matter how strongly managers prefer to pursue other objectives, and no matter how difficult it is to find profit-maximizing strategies in a world of uncertainty and high information costs, failure to satisfy this criterion means ultimately that a firm will disappear from the economic scene. Profit maximization is therefore promoted in two ways. First, firms departing too far from the optimum, either deliberately or by mistake, will disappear. Only those that do conform, knowingly or unknowingly, will survive. If the process of economic selection is allowed to continue long enough, the only survivors will be firms that did a tolerably good job of profit maximization. The economic environment adopts the profit maximizers and discards the rest. Second, knowledge that only the fit will survive provides a potent incentive for all firms to *adapt* their behavior in profit-maximizing directions, learning whatever skills they need and emulating organizations that succeed in the survival game.

To be sure, the selection process operates a good deal less than perfectly. The environment is constantly changing, altering the behavior required for survival, so that adaptations learned today may not serve tomorrow. On the other hand, adaptation by industry members may be sufficiently slow to permit firms performing less than optimally to keep their heads above water for a long time. Winter has demonstrated that even under conditions of pure competition, behavior that conforms only in special cases to the profit-maximizing norm may be consistent with survival.[83] Companies that satisfice, searching for optimal actions only when competitive pressures are unusually intense, are apt to be especially viable. And, of course, if no firms in the industry happen to conform to the optimal pattern, the selection process can bog down altogether, for there will be no 'fit' to expand, multiply, and drive out the less fit.

Despite these qualifications, it seems reasonable to believe that the natural selection process is a stern master in a competitive environment. That it will work equally well under monopoly does not follow. If natural selection is to function in the economic sphere, its activating mechanism must be the competitive challenge of enterprises better adapted to their environment and opportunities. But when firms with monopoly power are shielded by entry barriers, product differentiation, government favoritism, and the like, threats to their survival may be sufficiently blunted that they can survive for decades without ever maximizing profits or minimizing costs. The crucial question is, how much protection from the forces of natural selection does monopoly power confer? How far from profit-maximizing norms can firms possessing such power depart and still remain viable?[84] We shall encounter this issue frequently in the chapters that follow. For the sake of orderly presentation, we must be content to explore here only one further strand of the relevant evidence: how owner versus manager control interacts with varying degrees of monopoly power to affect reported corporate profitability.

There have been numerous statistical investigations. They vary widely in coverage, control measurement assumptions, and in the degree to which account is taken of other plausible profit-influencing variables such as monopoly power, capital structure, and corporations' home-base industries. No doubt because of this, the reported results also vary. The prevalent conclusion of studies without explicit monopoly power variables is that profit returns tend to be slightly, but seldom significantly, higher in owner- than in manager-controlled firms.[85] The food processing industries appear to be an exception.[86]

Yet, as we have seen, there is reason to expect greater leeway for departures from profit maximization when firms enjoy appreciable monopoly power than when competition is intense. Four studies have tried to take this into account. Two with deficient specifications of the monopoly-control-form interaction also yielded a conclusion that owner-controlled enterprises tend to be more profitable.[87] The first to approach the problem in an interaction framework was John Palmer.[88] He divided *Fortune*'s 500 largest industrial corporations into two three-part classes: those with high, medium, and low estimated monopoly power; and those with strong owner, weak owner (i.e., 10 to 29 percent stock ownership), and management control. For firms with medium or low monopoly power, he found no significant relationship between control form and profitability. But for the high monopoly power enterprises, average 1961–69 after-tax profit returns on stockholders' equity were 14.8 percent with strong owner control, 14.5 percent with weak owner control, and 11.4 percent with management control. However, this apparent difference in returns faded in a still more carefully specified analysis by P. David Qualls.[89] Using a 205-firm subset of Palmer's sample for which structural variable measurement problems were least severe and accepting Palmer's three-way classification by control form, Qualls further classified the sample firms according to two different measures of monopoly power—one emphasizing estimated barriers to entry and a second average concentration in the markets served.[90] With this richer breakdown,

(78) See Douglas A. Kuehn, "Stock Market Valuation and Acquisitions," *Journal of Industrial Economics* 17 (April 1969): 132–44; Brian Hindley, "Separation of Ownership and Control in the Modern Corporation," *Journal of Law and Economics* 13 (April 1970): 185–221; Ajit Singh, *Take-overs: Their Relevance to the Stock Market and the Theory of the Firm* (Cambridge, England: Cambridge University Press, 1971); Singh, "Take-overs, Economic Natural Selection, and the Theory of the Firm," *Economic Journal* 85 (September 1975): 497–515; and Douglas Kuehn, *Takeovers and the Theory of the Firm* (London: Macmillan, 1975).

79. See Singh, "Take-overs, Economic Natural Selection," p. 506.

80. Robert Smiley, "Tender Offers, Transactions Costs and the Theory of the Firm," *Review of Economics and Statistics* 58 (February 1976): 22–32. See also A. R. Appleyard and G. K. Yarrow, "The Relationship between Take-over Activity and Share Valuation," *Journal of Finance* 30 (December 1975): 1239–49.

81. See Singh, *Take-overs*, pp. 139–44; and Singh's review of Kuehn's book in the *Journal of Economic Literature* 14 (June 1976): 505–506.

82. The leading theoretical discussions are in Armen A. Alchian, "Uncertainty, Evolution, and Economic Theory," *Journal of Political Economy* 58 (June 1950): 211–21; Sidney G. Winter, "Economic 'Natural Selection' and the Theory of the Firm," *Yale Economic Essays* 4 (Spring 1964): 225–72; and Winter, "Satisficing, Selection, and the Innovating Remnant," *Quarterly Journal of Economics* 85 (May 1971): 237–61. For evidence from simulation studies that natural selection models yield outcomes strikingly similar to those implied by profit maximization, see R. R. Nelson, Sidney Winter, and H. L. Schuette, "Technical Change in an Evolutionary Economy," *Quarterly Journal of Economics* 90 (February 1976): 90–118.

83. Winter, "Economic 'Natural Selection' and the Theory of the Firm," pp. 256–64.

84. For contrasting views on this point, see Shorey Peterson, "Corporate Control and Capitalism," *Quarterly Journal of Economics* 79 (February 1965): 1–24; and Carl Kaysen, "Another View of Corporate Capitalism," *Quarterly Journal of Economics* 79 (February 1965): 41–51.

85. See R. J. Monsen, J. S. Chiu, and D. E. Cooley, "The Effects of Separation of Ownership and Control on the Performance of the Large Firm," *Quarterly Journal of Economics* 82 (August 1968): 435–51; H. K. Radice, "Control Type, Profitability and Growth in Large Firms," *Economic Journal* 81 (September 1971): 547–62; J. W. Elliott, "Control, Size, Growth, and Financial Performance in the Firm," *Journal of Financial and Quantitative Analysis* 7 (January 1972): 1309–20; Robert Sorenson, "The Separation of Ownership and Control and Firm Performance," *Southern Economic Journal* 41 (July 1974): 145–48; and Peter Holl, "Effect of Control Type on the Performance of the Firm in the U.K.," *Journal of Industrial Economics* 23 (June 1975): 257–71.

86. See Radice, "Control Type"; and Robert F. Ware, "Performance of Manager- versus Owner-Controlled Firms in the Food and Beverage Industry," *Quarterly Review of Economics and Business* 15 (Summer 1975): 81–92. The picture for restaurants is still different. In a study of one large chain, John P. Shelton found that branch units were much more profitable when run by franchisee-owners than by hired managers, and profits almost always increased with a shift from hired manager to owner operation and fell with a change in the opposite direction. "Allocative Efficiency vs. 'X-Efficiency': Comment," *American Economic Review* 57 (December 1967): 1252–58. More recent

variations in control form no longer exhibited any significant impact on profitability among the high monopoly power industries. The difference between Palmer's and Qualls's results evidently stems partly from differing sample coverage and partly from Qualls's more ambitious attempt to control for gradations in monopoly power. Which set of results better describes the true state of the world is uncertain. The most that can be said is that the discretion accompanying the juxtaposition of monopoly power with managerial control *may* be exploited to satisfy goals conflicting with profit maximization, but it is not yet clear that it actually *is* so exploited. More careful research with better data continues to be needed.

None of the owner- versus manager-control profitability studies to date has investigated the plausible hypothesis advanced by McEachern that profit performance differs between firms with an owner group actively participating in management and those in which an identifiable owner group delegates operating responsibilities to hired managers. McEachern argues that non-manager owners are more apt to push for profit maximization than owner-managers, who may choose to take what would otherwise be their (and others') profits in the form of nonpecuniary benefits such as lavish office accommodations, "business" travel to watering spots, and the sense of power that comes from managing a vast empire.[91] For statistical samples of modest size, McEachern found that owner-managed firms tended to retain more earnings and accept greater stock market risk than either manager-controlled or outside owner-controlled companies. He also observed that returns on common stock investments between 1963 and 1972 were higher in externally controlled than in manager-controlled corporations and still higher in owner-managed firms.[92] This last finding is of doubtful generality, however, since such stock return analyses tend to be highly sensitive to the specific time interval for which they are calculated.

A companion to the hypothesis that managers sacrifice profits to enhance sales growth is the assertion that company earnings may be plowed back' into growth-oriented investments yielding a lower return than stockholders could attain investing more generous dividends in the stock market. In a pioneering statistical study covering several hundred U.S. corporations, Baumol and associates estimated that the average rate of return on such internal funds plowback investment ranged between 3.0 and 4.6 percent, compared to returns of 14 to 21 percent on new equity capital.[93] In subsequent clarifications, it was discovered that the subset of companies issuing new equity capital realized substantial average returns on their plowback too, and that the main locus of depressed plowback returns was firms issuing no new common stock.[94] Further light on the matter was shed by Grabowski and Mueller.[95] They argued that most corporations experience a kind of life cycle. In the early years lucrative investment opportunities call for external financing; but as the firm and its products mature, cash flows increase while investment opportunities dwindle. Investment of internally generated funds may be maintained at high levels despite falling profitability in the period of maturity because managers seek to expand in accustomed ways and because earnings reinvested internally are taxed more lightly than earnings paid out as dividends and then reinvested. To test this hypothesis, Grabowski and Mueller classified 759 U.S. corporations into mature (e.g., with the majority of their sales in pre-World War II products) and nonmature categories. They found that the nonmature companies realized significantly higher returns on invested capital in each of three periods from 1957 to 1970. From this they concluded that "managers of mature corporations in technologically unprogressive industries re-invest too large a percentage of their internal funds. Their shareholders would apparently be better off with higher payouts . . ."[96] Attempting to integrate this conclusion with what they perceived to be the superior profitability of owner-controlled firms, they suggested that owner-controlled enterprises tend to be younger and to have more profitable investment opportunities than the more mature companies whose stockholdings have become so dispersed that management is in control. However, they attempted no direct test by distinguishing between control modes. Closing that empirical link remains on the agenda for future research.

Implications The last word has surely not been spoken on how assiduously modern industrial corporations strive to maximize their profits. Much remains to be learned. After examining the voluminous published evidence and interviewing many managers, the author believes that assuming profit maximization provides a good first approximation in describing business behavior. Deviations, both intended and inadvertent, undoubtedly exist in abundance, but they are kept within more or less narrow bounds by competitive forces, the self-interest of stock-owning managers, and the threat of managerial displacement by important outside stockholders and takeover raiders. To the extent that deviations do occur, they are likely to be larger when competition is weak and perhaps also when there is sharp separation of ownership from control. From this conclusion two further implications follow. First, to the extent that enterprises possessing monopoly power tolerate extensive organizational slack, pay princely managerial salaries, and the like, economic inefficiency is apt to be higher than one would predict under the theory of profit-maximizing behavior. Income may also be redistributed away from stockholders and toward the managerial class—i.e., from one high income group to another. But, second, to the extent that managers expand sales beyond the profit-maximizing level in order to enhance their own salaries, prestige, and power, the dead-weight losses associated with monopolistic output restriction are mitigated. How these various tendencies balance out remains uncertain.

Workable competition

We return now to our original question: How valid is the competitive ideal as a prescription for economic policy? Given all the qualifications and doubts unearthed in the foregoing pages, extreme confidence in the purely and perfectly competitive model as a blueprint for utopia is hardly in order. We may even experience an impulse to return to the womb—to Adam Smith's crude vision of how the market-economy does its job. Smith was wrong in numerous details, but

(86) developments suggest, however, that company-owned, hired manager-operated units of fast-food chains achieve greater sales volume and are more profitable than franchisee-owner operated units. "Fast-Food Franchisers Squeeze out the Little Guy," *Business Week*, 31 May 1976, pp. 42–48. Whether higher volume flows causally from chain ownership or whether the chains are more likely to buy and operate through hired managers units with locations especially conducive to high volume is unclear.

(87) David R. Kamerschen, "The Influence of Ownership and Control on Profit Rates," *American Economic Review* 58 (June 1968): 432–47; and Larner, *Management Control*, pp. 25–32.

(88) John Palmer, "The Profit-Performance Effects of the Separation of Ownership from Control in Large U.S. Industrial Corporations," *Bell Journal of Economics and Management Science* 4 (Spring 1973): 293–303. For contrary results from an analysis of West German enterprises, see Peter J. Thonet, "Managerialismus und Unternehmenserfolg" (Ph.D. diss., Universität des Saarlandes, 1977).

(89) P. David Qualls, "Market Structure and Managerial Behavior," in Robert Masson and P. D. Qualls, eds., *Essays on Industrial Organization in Honor of Joe S. Bain* (Cambridge, Mass.: Ballinger, 1976), pp. 89–104.

(90) On measures of market concentration, see Chapter 3 *infra*.

91. McEachern, *Managerial Control*, pp. 58–67. See also his "Corporate Control and Growth: An Alternative Approach," *Journal of Industrial Economics* 26 (March 1978): 257–66.

92. McEachern, *Managerial Control*, pp. 89–107. Similar common stock return results for the same time period but a much larger sample are reported by Miron Stano in "Monopoly Power, Ownership Control, and Corporate Performance," *Bell Journal of Economics* 7 (Autumn 1976): 672–79. However, Stano finds stock market risk to be lower, not higher, in owner-controlled firms. He also discovered that management-controlled corporations were significantly more merger-prone between 1962 and 1972.

93. William J. Baumol, Peggy Heim, Burton Malkiel, and Richard Quandt, "Earnings Retention, New Capital and the Growth of the Firm," *Review of Economics and Statistics* 52 (November 1970): 345–55.

94. Irwin Friend and Frank Husic, "Efficiency of Corporate Investment," *Review of Economics and Statistics* 55 (February 1973): 122–27; with a reply by Baumol et al., pp. 128–31. See also Geoffrey Whittington, "The Profitability of Retained Earnings," *Review of Economics and Statistics* 54 (May 1972): 152–60; R. A. Brealey, S. D. Hodges, and D. Capron, "The Return on Alternate Sources of Finance," *Review of Economics and Statistics* 58 (November 1976): 469–77; Donald G. McFetridge, "The Efficiency Implications of Earnings Retentions," *Review of Economics and Statistics* 60 (May 1978): 218–24; and Whittington, "The Profitability of Alternative Sources of Finance," *Review of Economics and Statistics* 60 (November 1978): 632–34.

95. Henry G. Grabowski and Dennis C. Mueller, "Life-Cycle Effects on Corporate Returns on Retentions," *Review of Economics and Statistics* 57 (November 1975): 400–16.

96. Grabowski and Mueller, "Life-Cycle Effects," p. 408.

details of the system may be much less important than the broad scheme of operation. If one stands back and gazes astigmatically at the competitive model without worrying about the fine points, one sees that it does display generally greater responsiveness of product supplies to consumer demands and generates a more potent set of incentives for the frugal use of resources than does the monopoly model. This, rather than the satisfaction of all optimal conditions in a general equilibrium system of 43 quadrillion equations, may be the core of the case for competition.

Comparable doubts concerning the competitive model's utility as a policy guide prompted a search during the 1940s and 1950s for more operational norms of "workable competition." This phrase was coined by J. M. Clark, who observed in his seminal article that perfect competition "does not and cannot exist and has presumably never existed" and that the competitive model of theory affords no reliable standard for judging real-world conditions.[97] Clark went on to argue that some departures from the purely and perfectly competitive norm are not as harmful in a long-run context as was commonly supposed, and he formulated certain minimal criteria for judging the workability of competition. The criteria he chose were influenced by the depression psychosis of the times and are less important than the impact Clark's work had in stimulating other economists.

The result was an explosion of articles on workable competition, many in substantial disagreement with one another. We shall not attempt to review the literature here, since the job has been done admirably by Stephen Sosnick.[98] It suffices to outline some criteria of workability suggested especially frequently by diverse writers. Using Sosnick's general scheme, these can be divided into structural, conduct, and performance categories.

Structural norms include the following:

1. The number of traders should be at least as large as scale economies permit.
2. There should be no artificial inhibitions on mobility and entry.
3. There should be moderate and price-sensitive quality differentials in the products offered.

Conduct criteria include:

4. Some uncertainty should exist in the minds of rivals as to whether price initiatives will be followed.
5. Firms should strive to achieve their goals independently, without collusion.
6. There should be no unfair, exclusionary, predatory, or coercive tactics.
7. Inefficient suppliers and customers should not be shielded permanently.
8. Sales promotion should be informative, or at least not be misleading.
9. Persistent, harmful price discrimination should be absent.

Last, we have a number of *performance criteria:*

10. Firms' production and distribution operations should be efficient and not wasteful of resources.
11. Output levels and product quality (i.e., variety, durability, safety, reliability, and so on) should be responsive to consumer demands.
12. Profits should be at levels just sufficient to reward investment, efficiency, and innovation.
13. Prices should encourage rational choice, guide markets toward equilibrium, and not intensify cyclical instability.
14. Opportunities for introducing technically superior new products and processes should be exploited.
15. Promotional expenses should not be excessive.
16. Success should accrue to sellers who best serve consumer wants.

While the items in this list are not objectionable, the list as a whole may be criticized for redundancy. In particular, the first two criteria might be considered a watered-down statement of the requisites for pure competition which, if satisfied, will lead almost automatically to satisfying many of the other criteria.

More fundamentally, critics of the workable competition concept have questioned whether the approach is as operational as its proponents intended.[99] On many of the variables, a line must be drawn separating enough from not enough or too much. How moderate should quality differentials be? When are promotional expenses excessive, and when not? How long must price discrimination persist before it is persistent? And so on. Value judgments can hardly fail to enter such determinations. Furthermore, fulfillment of many criteria is difficult to measure. For instance, to determine whether firms' production operations have been efficient, one needs a yardstick calibrated against what is possible. Finally and most important, how should the workability of competition be evaluated when some, but not all, of the criteria are satisfied? If, for example, performance but not structure conforms to the norms, should we conclude that competition is workable, since it is performance that in the end really counts? Perhaps not, because with an 'unworkable' market structure there is always a danger that future performance will deteriorate. If stress *is* placed on performance, what conclusion can be drawn when performance is good on some dimensions but not on others? Here a decision cannot be reached without introducing subjective value judgments about the importance of the various performance dimensions. And as Professor George Stigler warns with characteristic cynicism, embarrassing disagreements may result:

> To determine whether any industry is workably competitive, therefore, simply have a good graduate student write his dissertation on the industry and render a verdict. It is crucial to this test, of course, that no second graduate student be allowed to study the industry.[100]

To investigate these weighting and consensus issues more rigorously, Steven Cox obtained from 42 economists, marketing professors, and business writers responses to questionnaires eliciting evaluations of the quality of 14 major industries' 1960–69 performance, both overall and on four subdimensions—product pricing (defined to approximate the criteria of allocative efficiency), technological progressiveness, cost minimization, and wage-price inflation.[101] There was a moderately high level of agreement among the panelists in their overall performance judgments, with the strongest consensus emerging among the panelists indicating greatest knowledge of the 14 industries. In evaluations of overall performance, it was clear that panelists placed by far the greatest weight on whether an industry was technically progressive: The more progressive it was, the higher its overall performance was ranked. Among the academic economist panelists, high scores on the product-pricing subdimension and low advertising expenditures as a percentage of sales (the latter calculated from nonquestionnaire data) also led to significantly higher overall performance rankings. But among the business specialists (i.e., business journal writers and marketing professors) the opposite propensity held: Industries that spent a *large* fraction of their sales dollar on advertising were ranked more favorably, as were industries charging prices yielding profits greater than necessary to call forth their productive effort. Thus, although panelists of divergent backgrounds placed uniformly high and positive weight on the technical performance subdimension, they disagreed on the signs attached to items 12 and 15 in our list of workable competition criteria. This shows that the most difficult stumbling block in evaluating the quality of industries' performance is likely to be securing agreement on what society in fact considers good or bad attributes of performance. Conflicting value judgments concerning certain performance attributes and their weights undoubtedly underlie many disputes as to the proper public policy toward monopolistic enterprises.

97. J. M. Clark, "Toward a Concept of Workable Competition," *American Economic Review* 30 (June 1940): 241–56. Extensions by Clark include "Competition: Static Models and Dynamic Aspects," *American Economic Review* 45 (May 1955): 450–62; and *Competition as a Dynamic Process*, especially Chapters 2–4.

98. Stephen Sosnick, "A Critique of Concepts of Workable Competition," *Quarterly Journal of Economics* 72 (August 1958): 380–423.

99. See Sosnick, "A Critique," pp. 391–415; the substantially modified approach proposed by Sosnick in "Toward a Concrete Concept of Effective Competition," *American Journal of Agricultural Economics* 50 (November 1968): 827–53; and Carl Kaysen and Donald F. Turner, *Antitrust Policy* (Cambridge, Mass.: Harvard University Press, 1959), pp. 53–56.

100. See the comment by Stigler, "Report on Antitrust Policy—Discussion," *American Economic Review* 46 (May 1956): 505.

101. Steven R. Cox, "An Industrial Performance Evaluation Experiment," *Journal of Industrial Economics* 22 (March 1974): 199–214.

One other approach to assessing the workability of competition should be mentioned. As an alternative to evaluating industry structure and performance against predetermined norms, some of which may be unattainable and some insusceptible to direct modification through external action, Jesse Markham has proposed that:

> [a]n industry may be judged to be workably competitive when, after the structural characteristics of its market and the dynamic forces that shaped them have been thoroughly examined, there is no clearly indicated change that can be effected through public policy measures that would result in greater social gains than social losses.[102]

Although this approach encounters the same measurement and value judgment difficulties as the more conventional methods, it does have the merit of focusing attention constructively on the policy problem of prescribing appropriate remedial actions.

Conclusion

Readers seeking a precise, certain guide to public policy are bound to be disappointed by this survey, for we have found none. The competitive norm does seem to serve as a good first approximation, but it is difficult to state a priori how much competition is needed to achieve desirable economic performance, nor can we formulate hard and fast rules for identifying cases in which a departure from competition is desirable. We therefore begin our journey into the following chapters with only a primitive map to guide us. Let us hope that we can avoid going too far astray, and end with experience useful in drawing a better map.

102. "An Alternative Approach to the Concept of Workable Competition," *American Economic Review* 40 (June 1950): 349–61.

3 The structure of U.S. industry

We begin our exploration of structure-conduct-performance links by surveying some structural features of modern industrial economies, with emphasis on the United States. In this chapter we cover four main facets of industry structure: the extent to which the economy as a whole is dominated by large enterprises, the extent to which particular markets are dominated by one or a few sellers, the extent to which firms are diversified across numerous product lines, and the degree to which firms are vertically integrated. Our main concern in this volume is with monopoly power, to which the second (market domination) dimension of structure is most closely related. In the present chapter we nevertheless take a more sweeping view that encompasses structural dimensions possibly interacting with the orthodox bases of monopoly power. At the same time we shall neglect certain important aspects of market structure—notably, the height of entry barriers, the extent of product differentiation, and the degree of buyer concentration. These are handled more conveniently in later chapters.

The position of the largest corporations

Sheer enterprise size and monopoly power are, as we have stated previously, not necessarily synonymous. Nevertheless, there are hypotheses that link variations in economic performance to interactions between overall corporate size and power within particular markets. One may also be apprehensive on social and political grounds about the share of economic activity controlled by large corporations. It repays some labor therefore to examine the impressive position of the largest industrial enterprises.

Impressive it is. In 1977, there were approximately 2 million incorporated business enterprises operating in the United States, along with roughly 12 million partnerships and sole proprietorships. Yet a very few firms towered over all the rest. The biggest of the big in terms of both assets and employment was the American Telephone and Telegraph Company. Its 1977 assets of $94 billion represented nearly 4 percent of the assets of all nonfinancial corporations; its work force of 1.1 million (including subsidiaries) exceeded the populations of 13 states of the Union and was about as large as the industrial labor force of Austria, Switzerland, or Denmark. Among manufacturing and natural resource corporations, General Motors was the largest in terms of sales ($55 billion in 1977) and employment (797,000), while Exxon led the field in assets ($38 billion).

In 1972, there were 660 U.S. nonfinancial corporations with assets valued at $250 million or more. Those 660 controlled 55 percent of the assets of all U.S. nonfinancial corporations. A further breakdown of the distribution of asset holdings by industrial sector is given in Table 3.1. In the communications-electric-gas, transportation, manufacturing, and banking[1] sectors, more than half of all corporate assets are controlled by enterprises with assets of $250 million or more. On the other hand, the agriculture, real estate, construction, and services sectors are the domain of enterprises relatively small as bigness in business goes.[2]

Any analysis of this sort is affected by the choice of a size measure, since some measures show considerably more concentration than others. For example, Table 3.2 shows the share of domestic manufacturing activity for the largest U.S. manufacturing corporations, ranked on the basis of value added in manufacture[3] for the year 1977. Although exactly comparable data for total assets are not available, there is reason to believe the top 100 figure would be approximately 38 percent, reflecting the longer-term behavior of new capital expenditures.[4] Employment is much less concentrated in the hands of the largest manufacturing corporations than value added and sales, which in turn are less concentrated than total assets. This seems to be so for three main reasons. First, as a comparison of payroll and employment shares reveals, the largest corporations tend to pay higher salaries and/or wages. Second, the leading producers in particular industries use more capital-intensive production processes on the average than their smaller compatriots. And third, the list of the 100 largest manufacturing corporations includes a

T 3.1 The percentage of corporate assets accounted for in 1972 by large corporations

Sector	Number of active corporations (all sizes)	Sector share of 1972 GNP*	Corporations with assets of $250 million or more	
			Number	Share of all sector assets
All nonfinancial corporations	1,660,854	—	660	54.6%
Agriculture, forestry, and fisheries	42,974	3.0%	0	0.0
Mining	14,211	1.6	22	47.4
Construction	154,418	4.8	9	6.0
Manufacturing	203,238	24.7	355	67.8
Transportation	55,364	3.9	53	69.0
Communications, electric, sanitary and gas services	17,186	4.9	128	91.3
Wholesale and retail trade	568,228	17.2	60	21.7
Services	314,795	11.5	18	13.1
Real estate	273,182	14.4	15	5.3
Banking, finance, and insurance	151,906		839	66.4

*Includes contributions of unincorporated businesses and government.
Adapted from U.S. Internal Revenue Service, *Statistics of Income: 1972,* "Corporation Income Tax Returns" (Washington, D.C.: Government Printing Office, 1977), Table 6.

T 3.2 Aggregate concentration shares for five different measures

Size measures	100 lgst. corps.	200 lgst. corps.
Domestic employees	25%	33%
Domestic payroll	33	42
Sales of domestic plants	35	45
Value added in manufacture	33	44
New capital expenditures	39	49

Source: U.S., Bureau of the Census, "Concentration Ratios in Manufacturing," *1977 Census of Manufactures* MC77(SR)–9 (Washington, D.C.: Government Printing Office, 1981), Table 4.

disproportionate number of large petroleum refining firms, which are much more capital-intensive than the typical manufacturing enterprise.

Given these divergences, the analyst must choose with care indices of corporate size[5] and *aggregate concentration*—that is, a measure of how large a share of economic activity the largest enterprises control. Value added is probably the best all-around indicator, taking into account the contributions of both labor and capital. Unfortunately, value added data are seldom available for comprehensive collections of individual companies, and in the United States, aggregate value added concentration statistics carefully compiled by the Census Bureau exist only for the manufacturing sector and, even then, only back to 1947. Sales data serve as a tolerable substitute, especially for intercompany comparisons, as long as the degree of vertical integration does not vary too widely. However, the most common criterion is pragmatic: one uses the variable on which one can obtain the highest quality data, or maximum comparability, relevant to one's hypotheses.

Changes in aggregate concentration over time The data problem becomes especially acute when we tackle the interesting question of

trends over time in the aggregate concentration of manufacturing activity. Just after the American Civil War, manufacturing was still predominantly the province of the relatively small firm serving local markets, and manufacturing industry was much less concentrated in the aggregate than it is today. (Transportation, on the other hand, already showed signs of growing dominance by large corporations.) At the time, Karl Marx stood alone among well-known economists in predicting that big business would come to dominate the industrial scene. This development Marx attributed to the corporate form of organization, then acquiring its modern trappings, and to the interaction of scale economies and bitter competition. "One capitalist always kills many," said Marx, leading to a "constantly diminishing number of the magnates of capital, who usurp and monopolise all advantages of this process of transformation."[6] The limit to the process was a state in which "the entire social capital would be united, either in the hands of one single capitalist, or in those of one single corporation," although Marx

1. Asset sizes in banking and finance are not comparable with those in other sectors, since it is easier to put together and manage a large portfolio of financial assets than a large aggregation of physical assets. Also, financial enterprises must be segregated from nonfinancial corporations to lessen double counting, since a high fraction of financial firms' assets consists of claims against the assets of nonfinancial corporations.

2. The fractions of total corporate assets accounted for by corporations with assets of $100 million or more in agriculture, real estate, construction, and services were 7.6, 10.0, 12.1, and 21.6 percent respectively. For all nonfinancial corporations the proportion was 61.3 percent.

3. Value added is defined, ignoring some details on the handling of inventory adjustments, as sales less outside purchases of materials (including energy and certain specialized services).

4. The 100 largest manufacturers' share of new capital expenditures was 38 percent in 1963, 40 percent in 1967, and 35 percent (abnormally low) in 1972.

5. On the important analytic differences the choice of a firm size measure can make, see David J. Smyth, William J. Boyes, and Dennis E. Peseau, "The Measurement of Firm Size: Theory and Evidence for the United States and the United Kingdom," *Review of Economics and Statistics* 59 (August 1977): 290–98.

6. Karl Marx, *Capital*, trans. Ernest Untermann, vol. 1 (Chicago: Kerr, 1912), p. 836.

did not explicitly assert that the ultimate limit would ever be attained.[7]

During the next 60 years, the industrialized economies of the world evidently moved a considerable distance toward fulfilling Marx's prediction. The first systematic attempt to study trends in aggregate concentration was by Adolf Berle and Gardiner Means.[8] Using the rather limited statistics then available, they estimated the 200 largest U.S. nonfinancial corporations' share of all nonfinancial corporation assets to be 49 percent at the end of 1929. They also found

that the 200 leading firms' assets were growing considerably more rapidly than the assets of all corporations between 1909 and 1929. Without committing themselves to a prediction of what actually would happen, they observed that *if* the observed disparity in growth rates continued, the 200 largest would account for 70 percent of all industrial corporations' assets by 1950 and nearly 100 percent by 1972.[9]

Obviously, this did not happen. There is reason to believe Berle and Means overestimated the relative growth of the largest enterprises be-

F 3.1 Trends in aggregate concentration: U.S. manufacturing corporations

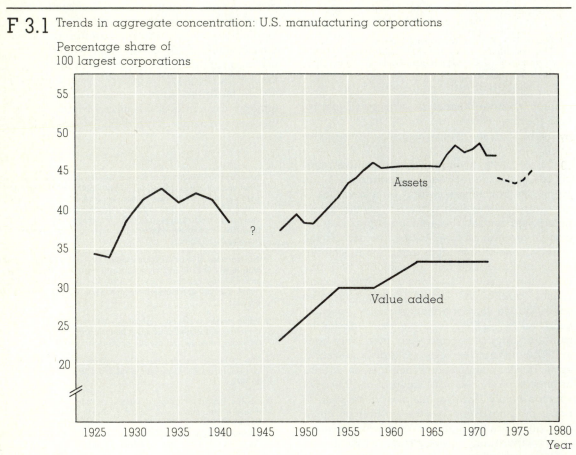

Percentage share of
100 largest corporations

Sources: Federal Trade Commission staff report, *Economic Report on Corporate Mergers*, printed as Part 8A of the U.S., Congress, Senate, Committee on the Judiciary, Subcommittee on Antitrust and Monopoly hearings, *Economic Concentration*, 91st Cong., 1st sess., 1969, pp. 169–78, 716–29; David W. Penn, "Aggregate Concentration: A Statistical Note," *Antitrust Bulletin* 21 (Spring 1976): 91–98; various issues of the *Statistical Abstract of the United States*; and U.S., Bureau of the Census, *1977 Census of Manufactures*, "Concentration Ratios in Manufacturing," MC77(SR)-9 (Washington, D.C.: Government Printing Office, 1981), Tables 1 and 4.

tween 1909 and 1929 and hence extrapolated too steep a trend.[10] Moreover, aggregate concentration appears to have increased only by fits and starts since 1929. The most solidly grounded long-term series, from quarterly surveys of corporate financial accounts since 1947 and a painstaking reconstruction of diverse data sets for earlier years, has been compiled and is periodically updated by the Federal Trade Commission.[11] Its estimates of the 100 largest manufacturing corporations' share of all manufacturing enterprise assets (i.e., incorporated plus unincorporated) are charted in Figure 3.1. Evidently, there was a sharp upsurge in aggregate concentration among manufacturers during the late 1920s and into the early years of the Great Depression, a decline associated with the World War II mobilization and postwar boom, another sustained increase as the wartime boom faded into normalcy, and after a period of stability, a more modest rise during the late 1960s. The long-run trend has clearly been one of increasing aggregate concentration, but at nothing like the pace implied by the projections of Berle and Means.

Similar patterns are seen with respect to the 100 largest manufacturers' share of value added in manufacturing, with the size ranking set on the basis of value added rather than the asset values presented in the Federal Trade Commission series. Consistent data from the quinquennial Census of Manufactures, also plotted in Figure 3.1, exist only since 1947. An analogous but more extended post-World War II upward trend is apparent, followed by a period of stability.

Aggregate concentration measured in terms of value added is much lower than asset concentration for all periods on which comparable figures exist. There are several apparent reasons for this and for the somewhat divergent time patterns. As noted already, the largest corporations tend to be more capital-intensive than smaller manufacturers. Perhaps more important, the value added series charted in Figure 3.1 covers only the domestic manufacturing activity of firms included in the 100-largest numerator and the all-manufacturing denominator. The asset concentration series, on the other hand, is based upon consolidated corporate financial reports and includes for any corporation classified as a

manufacturer virtually all assets, manufacturing and nonmanufacturing, domestic and foreign. The largest manufacturers are probably diversified relatively more into mining, retailing, transportation, and finance than their smaller counterparts, and so an analysis of consolidated assets shows more concentration than a narrower focus on value added in manufacturing only.[12] By the same token, the largest manufacturers have been more active in establishing foreign subsidiaries. In 1970, a sample of 223 typically large U.S. manufacturing companies had majority-owned foreign subsidiaries whose assets amounted to 21 percent of the companies' total assets.[13] The in-

7. Marx, *Capital*, p. 688. In a footnote to the fourth German edition (1890), Frederich Engels called explicit attention to the English and American "trusts" as an attempt to attain single-firm domination of particular industries. See also the more general discussion in Paul M. Sweezy, *The Theory of Capitalist Development* (New York: Monthly Review Press, 1942), pp. 254–69.

8. Adolf Berle and Gardiner Means, *The Modern Corporation and Private Property* (New York: Macmillan, 1932), especially pp. 28–40.

9. Berle and Means, *The Modern Corporation and Private Property*, p. 40.

10. See S. J. Prais, *The Evolution of Giant Firms in Britain* (Cambridge, England: Cambridge University Press, 1976), pp. 211–12.

11. See the source references accompanying Figure 3.1. For other attempts to develop historically comparable series, see Morris Adelman, "The Measurement of Industrial Concentration," *Review of Economics and Statistics* 33 (November 1951): 285–90; testimony of Adelman, U.S., Congress, Senate, Subcommittee on Antitrust and Monopoly hearings, *Economic Concentration*, Part 1, 89th Cong., 1st sess., 1964, pp. 225–40, 339–41; the testimony of Gardiner Means, U.S., Congress, Senate, Subcommittee on Antitrust and Monopoly hearings, *Economic Concentration*, Part 1, 89th Cong., 1st sess., 1964, pp. 15–19, 281–324; and the first edition of *Industrial Market Structure and Economic Performance* (Chicago: Rand McNally, 1970), pp. 42–44. Means's aggregate concentration estimates are several percentage points higher than those of the Federal Trade Commission series because Means consolidated the accounts of jointly controlled corporations publishing unconsolidated financial statements. Adelman's estimates err in the opposite direction of even less consolidation than the FTC. See the Federal Trade Commission staff report, *Economic Report on Corporate Mergers* (Washington, D.C.: Government Printing Office, 1969), pp. 730–35.

12. This bias is partly offset by the exclusion from both numerator and denominator of asset compilations the manufacturing activities of such companies as Sears Roebuck, Safeway, and General Telephone, whose consolidated assets are assigned to sectors other than manufacturing.

13. U.S., Department of Commerce, Bureau of Economic Analysis, *Special Survey of U.S. Multinational Companies: 1970* (Washington, D.C.: National Technical Information Service, 1972), pp. 18–23.

The structure of U.S. industry   **49**

clusion of these overseas asset values in surveys of aggregate asset concentration leads to higher top 100 or top 200 share estimates than emerge for value added data pertaining to domestic manufacturing activity only.

Changes in the accounting treatment of subsidiaries, and especially overseas subsidiaries, underlie the 1973 break in the aggregate asset concentration series shown in Figure 3.1 by a downward shift and a broken line thereafter.[14] Prior to 1973, companies were allowed by the Federal Trade Commission to submit accounting reports on their subsidiaries however they pleased. Many overseas branches were fully consolidated—that is, the total value of their assets was included with the U.S. parent's assets. In 1973, however, the FTC required that U.S. corporations report only their net equity interest in overseas subsidiaries, which was less than the value of overseas assets by the amount of overseas accounts payable and similar liabilities, debt, and minority equity interests. Largely but not entirely because of this change, $72 billion in assets, or about 10 percent of the prechange total, were no longer reported. One impact was a fall in computed aggregate asset concentration from 47.2 to 44.3 percent for the 100 largest U.S. manufacturing corporations and from 59.9 to 56.5 percent for the 200 largest.[15] However, this change still does not reveal the full influence of overseas asset holdings, since the 200 largest enterprises continued to report $81 billion in an asset category, much but not all of which reflected equity interests in foreign subsidiaries. If all such assets are purged from the FTC's data base—an assumption that overstates the magnitude of foreign operations—the fraction of all manufacturing corporations' assets controlled by the top 200 is found to fall by an additional 3 percentage points to 53.5 percent. Thus, at maximum, the inclusion of overseas holdings in analyses of aggregate asset concentration appears to inflate computed concentration figures by about 6 percentage points under the accounting conventions accepted prior to 1973 and 3 points thereafter.

In the first edition of this book, the author speculated that the observed increase in aggregate asset concentration for manufacturing enterprises might in part reflect the relative growth of U.S. corporations' overseas operations. That is, not only was the *level* of computed aggregate concentration influenced, but also the trend. Although this may still be possible, two items of information raise doubts. For one, Mira Wilkins has shown that although U.S. firms' overseas activities have grown dramatically in absolute terms, they were evidently no larger in 1970 relative to domestic GNP than they were in 1914 or 1929.[16] Second, comparison of the two series in Figure 3.1 reveals that both the domestic value added share and the total (domestic plus foreign) asset share of the 100 largest manufacturers rose by about 10 percentage points between 1947 and 1972. It seems unlikely therefore that the rapid absolute growth of overseas subsidiaries could have explained much of the observed rise in asset concentration. Rather, domestic structural changes must have been primarily responsible for this increase.

Aggregate concentration in other nations Is the role of big business in the United States typical or atypical compared to other industrialized nations stressing private enterprise? Sufficient evidence is available to support a number of comparisons.

One salient point is that the United States, with a larger industrial base than other market economy nations, has both bigger industrial enterprises and more of them. No private manufacturing enterprise overseas approaches the size of General Motors; the largest in terms of employment (Philips of Holland) was only half as large in 1976. Below this extreme the comparison is more even. However, the United States harbors a disproportionate fraction of the largest industrial firms. In 1976, 87 U.S. industrial corporations reported sales of $2.5 billion or more. On *Fortune's* 1976 list of the 500 largest industrial corporations outside the United States, there were 86 enterprises, private- and government-owned, surpassing that sales threshold—18 in West Germany, 15 each in the United Kingdom and Japan, 13 in France, and 6 in Canada. In terms of employment, the United States' lead is slightly diminished. *Fortune's* tabulations for 1976 show 66 U.S. industrial corporations with 50,000 or more employees, compared to 93 in the rest of the more or less capitalist world.

With both smaller industrial sectors and a smaller number of large industrial enterprises in nations outside the United States, how does aggregate concentration compare? For several important nations, tolerably comparable analyses have been published. The 100 largest British manufacturers accounted for 22 percent of value added in U.K. manufacturing in 1949—only a percentage point less than the comparable U.S. figure for 1947.[17] Largely as a result of mergers, aggregate concentration subsequently rose more rapidly in Britain than in the U.S. so that by 1968, the 100 largest U.K. enterprises generated 41 percent of value added. In Canada, the 100 largest manufacturers' 1965 value added share was 43.5 percent—10.5 points higher than the contemporary U.S. figure.[18] Data on asset holdings by the 100 largest Canadian nonfinancial corporations suggest, in contrast to the pattern observed for most other nations, a decline in aggregate concentration since the 1920s and 1930s.[19] The hundred largest West German industrial corporations accounted for 52 percent of total 1971 industrial corporation sales, including export sales, and 47 percent when export sales were excluded.[20] Although the ranking methods and measurements are not exactly comparable, these estimates are clearly higher than the 32 percent sales concentration figure for the 100 largest U.S. manufacturers in 1972. Top 100 aggregate sales concentration in West Germany has been estimated at 34 percent for 1954 and 37 percent for 1962, although the upward trend from then to 1971 is probably overstated owing to the less than complete consolidation of affiliated firms' sales for the earlier years. In Japan, the hundred largest manufacturers are reported to have generated 29 percent of all manufacturers' sales in 1967.[21] This appears to be less than the contemporary U.S. value of 33 percent, but extensive affiliations among separately reporting Japanese firms are not consolidated. When appropriate consolidations are effected, the 100 largest *nonfinancial* corporations are found to have controlled 50 percent of all Japanese nonfinancial corporation assets in 1970. Reference to Table 3.1 shows that *660* U.S. nonfinancial corporations ac-

counted for 54.6 percent of all nonfinancial corporation assets in 1972, suggesting that aggregate concentration is probably higher in Japan than in America. Thus, it would appear that in the major industrialized nations on which adequate information is available, the difference in overall industrial activity volume relative to the United States is greater than the difference in leading firm sizes. Consequently, aggregate concentration levels abroad tend to be higher than comparable values for the United States.

Concentration of control through interlocking financial ties Interlocking financial and managerial ties among corporations complicate assessments of how concentrated the control of corporations is. Japan, as we have already intimated, offers a significant example. Many Japanese firms are linked together in complex modifications of what were once called *Zaibatsu* (literally, money clique) ties.[22] Before World War II, four Zaibatsu family holding companies with ownership interests in hundreds of operating enterprises controlled a fourth of all paid-in capital

14. See David W. Penn, "Aggregate Concentration: A Statistical Note," *Antitrust Bulletin* 21 (Spring 1976): 91–98.

15. Penn, "Aggregate Concentration," p. 94. The figures reported by Penn have been adjusted downward by 0.4 percentage points to include within the denominator the assets of unincorporated manufacturing businesses.

16. Mira Wilkins, *The Maturing of Multinational Enterprise: American Business Abroad from 1914 to 1970* (Cambridge, Mass.: Harvard University Press, 1974), pp. 29–32, 55, 436–37.

17. Prais, *The Evolution of Giant Firms in Britain*, pp. 2–7.

18. Department of Consumer and Corporate Affairs, *Concentration in the Manufacturing Industries of Canada* (Ottawa: Information Canada, 1971), p. 15.

19. See the *Report of the Royal Commission on Corporate Concentration* (Ottawa: March 1978), pp. 18–23.

20. Jürgen Müller and Rolf Hochreiter, *Stand und Entwicklungstendenzen der Unternehmenskonzentration in der Bundesrepublik* (Göttingen: Schwartz, 1976), Tabelle 9.

21. Richard E. Caves and Masu Uekusa, *Industrial Organization in Japan* (Washington, D.C.: Brookings Institution, 1976), pp. 16–18. See also Uekusa, "Effects of the Deconcentration Measures in Japan," *Antitrust Bulletin* 22 (Fall 1977): 687–715.

22. See Caves and Uekusa, *Industrial Organization in Japan*, pp. 59–68, for a survey of the literature.

(i.e., equity less retained earnings) in Japanese industry and finance. The American occupation authorities carried out a Zaibatsu dissolution program after the war, but the old Zaibatsu companies subsequently regrouped in looser form through intercorporate stockholdings, ties to trading (i.e., wholesaling and import-export) companies and Zaibatsu successor banks, and regular "club" meetings among their executives. By 1960, the three leading Zaibatsu successor groups controlled 7.4 percent of the paid-in capital of all Japanese corporations if only firms with very close interrelations were counted, or 17.3 percent if firms with weak and uncertain Zaibatsu links were included.[23] A government study showed that in 1972 the pivotal trading companies of six groups held stock in a total of 4,104 companies, including 506 majority ownership positions and 1,057 leading ownership positions.[24] Distinctions drawn to categorize the degree of control exercised through these links are necessarily arbitrary, and as a result even the most carefully researched aggregate concentration estimates are inherently imprecise. Still it is clear that aggregate concentration figures failing to consolidate for Zaibatsu successor ties seriously underestimate the extent to which control over Japanese business activity is concentrated.

A smaller nation, Sweden, provides an even more striking example. Unconsolidated tabulations show the 100 largest private companies to have originated 46 percent of manufacturing value added in 1963. Yet through stockholdings and family banking connections, a single family wielded effective control over 32 ostensibly separate manufacturing companies, including eight of the ten largest privately owned manufacturers, during the 1960s.[25] Value added by firms in which the Wallenberg family had at least a strong minority interest amounted to 14.8 percent of total manufacturing value added in 1963. Twelve other family groups had a combined 21 percent control share in additional Swedish manufacturers.

Intricate ties among seemingly independent corporations are also found in the United States, although typically in more subtle form and on a less spectacular scale. Three main types of intercorporate linkage are of interest: control by family groups, control by financial intermediaries, and interlocking directorates.

A survey conducted during the 1930s turned up several prominent examples of multicorporation control by family groups possessing either majority or substantial minority stockholdings.[26] The du Pont family, through its various holding companies, owned roughly 25 percent of the stock of the du Pont Company and about 20 percent of the United States Rubber Company's stock. The du Pont Company in turn held a 23 percent common stock interest in General Motors. To the Rockefeller family and its philanthropic institutions could be traced stock interests ranging between 7 and 24 percent in six of the largest petroleum refining companies, along with the largest single share interest in the Chase National (now Chase Manhattan) Bank. The Mellon family had dominant ownership positions in the Gulf Oil Corporation, Alcoa, the Mellon National Bank, the Koppers Co., and the Pittsburgh Coal Co., as well as weaker affiliations with several other major corporations (including Westinghouse Electric). Since the 1930s, the control of these groups has been gradually attenuated as stock was distributed among multiplying heirs, as the heirs sold some of their shares to pay inheritance taxes, and as the corporations issued additional common stock to meet growing capital needs. The Mellon family's one-time majority interest in Gulf and Alcoa, for instance, has apparently eroded into a minority position.[27] Another important change came when a 1962 antitrust judgment required the du Pont family to eliminate its dominant ownership position in General Motors. As a result, the concentration of corporate control is surely not as extensive as it was five decades ago, although the evidence on current ownership patterns is fragmentary and no comprehensive statistical assessment is available.

An increasingly important source of concentrated control is the stockholdings of financial intermediaries. In 1966, mutual stock funds, insurance companies, corporate pension funds, and other institutional investors owned approximately 20 percent of the common stock shares listed on the New York Stock Exchange. By 1972, the proportion had climbed to 30 percent and was rising swiftly.[28] Banks manage most pension fund assets, and their duties include exercising voting rights. They also manage extensive trust account stockholdings. In 1977, it was estimated that banks, trust companies, investment companies, insurance companies, and pension funds had voting authority over 39 percent of all outstanding common stock in U.S. corporations.[29] Although there are legal and prudential bars to very high control fractions by any given institution in a particular company's stock, banks and other institutional investors nevertheless occupy strategic positions. A study of voting control over the stock of 122 large corporations revealed that 21 institutional investors held one of the five largest voting positions in 325 of the 610 possible cases.[30] For 75 of the 122 corporations they were the largest single voter. The Morgan Guaranty Trust Co. of New York alone was the largest holder of voting rights—with up to 6.6 percent of outstanding shares—for 27 of the 122 corporations, and one of the next four voteholders for 29 more. Whether this concentration of voting control has noteworthy implications, ominous or beneficial, is arguable. Trust, mutual, and pension fund managers evidently exercise genuine voting discretion in some cases and in others pass voting questions back to the ultimate stock owners or passively ratify the decisions of stock-issuing companies' management. Almost nothing is known about how the possession of such power by financial institutions affects the strategy and operating decisions of U.S. corporations or how it affects the competitors' conduct toward one another when an institution has important voting positions in competing corporations. In Germany, where the fraction of outstanding stock controlled by a few key banks tends to be much larger and banks' willingness to exercise power overtly is evidently greater, it is clear that the banks do have a significant behavioral impact.[31]

Interlocking directorates provide still another way of establishing ties where no direct financial connections exist. The simplest type of interlocking directorate occurs when one person sits on the boards of two or more corporations. Although there has apparently been a decline in the number and richness of interlocks since the early years of this century,[32] such multiple directorships continue to be widespread. A House of Representatives study found that the 463 directors of 29 large industrial corporations held directorates in more than 1,200 different corporations during 1962.[33] Interlocking directorates among competing firms were outlawed by the Clayton Act of 1914, and most of the interlocks revealed by the study undoubtedly had little or no effect on competition. However, the law was not vigorously enforced until 1968, and the study produced a long list of cases in which a single individual acted as director for two or more companies operating in similar product lines (typically, it would appear, representing only a small share of the implicated firms' total business).[34] The race by a few individuals from boardroom to boardroom also contributes to the maintenance of an

23. Eugene Rotwein, "Economic Concentration and Monopoly in Japan," *Journal of Political Economy* 72 (June 1964): 268.

24. See the translation of the Japanese Fair Trade Commission's "Report on the Investigation of General Trading Companies," *Antitrust Bulletin* 20 (Spring 1975), especially p. 182.

25. Alf Carling, *Industrins Struktur och Konkurrensförhållanden* (Stockholm: Statens Offentliga Utredningar, 1968), pp. 128–37; and "The 'Wallenberg Boys'—and How They Grew," *Business Week*, 25 February 1967, pp. 116–22.

26. U.S., National Resources Committee, *The Structure of the American Economy*, Part 1 (Washington, D.C.: Government Printing Office, 1939), pp. 160–63, 306–17.

27. See "The Mellons of Pittsburgh," *Fortune*, October 1967, pp. 121–22.

28. See "Big-Block Buyers May Speak Up," *Business Week*, 26 November 1966, p. 139; and "Can U.S. Industry Find the Money It Needs?," *Business Week*, 22 September 1973, p. 45.

29. U.S., Congress, Senate, Committee on Governmental Affairs, Subcommittee on Reports, Accounting and Management staff study, *Voting Rights in Major Corporations*, 95th Cong., 1st sess., 1978, pp. 13–14.

30. U.S., Congress, Senate, Committee on Governmental Affairs, *Voting Rights*, pp. 258–59. See also U.S., Congress, House, Subcommittee on Domestic Finance, reports, *Bank Stock Ownership and Control*, 89th Cong., 2nd sess., 1966, and *Commercial Banks and Their Trust Activities*, 2 vols., 90th Cong., 2nd sess., 1968; as well as David M. Kotz, *Bank Control of Large Corporations in the United States* (Berkeley: University of California Press, 1978).

31. See "Germany Catches Its Second Wind," *Fortune*, April 1969, pp. 147–48; and "Three Rich, Powerful Banks Dominate the Economy," *Business Week*, 19 April 1976, pp. 89–98. On the conflicts within a bank between trust and lending activities, see "Conflicts Worry French Banker," *New York Times*, 10 March 1972, p. 52.

32. See David Bunting and Jeffery Barbour, "Interlocking Directorates in Large American Corporations, 1896–1964," *Business History Review* 45 (Autumn 1971): 317–35.

33. U.S., Congress, House, Committee on the Judiciary, Antitrust Subcommittee, staff report, *Interlocks in Corporate Management*, 89th Cong., 1st sess., 1965, pp. 115–16.

34. *Interlocks in Corporate Management*, pp. 159–64, 234–55. See also Peter C. Dooley, "The Interlocking Directorate," *American Economic Review* 59 (June 1969): 314–23.

industrial and commercial elite, to which one might object on political and social grounds.

An indirect interlock exists when directors of some firm (often a financial institution) individually hold seats on competing firms' boards. For example, the chairman of the board of Morgan Trust Company served in 1962 on the board of General Motors, while directors of both Ford Motor Company and Chrysler sat on the Morgan Trust board. The chairmen of both the New Jersey and California Standard Oil companies sat on the board of the First National Bank of New York, as did a director of Mobil Oil. Banks supposedly take pains to ensure that their directors who also sit on competing clients' boards preserve confidences and engage in no unethical practices, and it is conceivable that the persons involved in these interlocks never discuss matters of mutual competitive interest when they meet. Nevertheless, the potential for abuse definitely exists. Whether or how frequently it blossoms from possibility into actuality, we simply do not know.

In sum, there are many formal and informal ties that, if exploited fully, could render domination of American industry by a few groups more monolithic than it appears in the bare statistics describing aggregate concentration. It is unlikely that a serious breakdown of corporate independence can be traced to these ties, partly because groups with weak minority voting positions may be unable to pull reluctant managers along and partly because the officers of financial intermediaries have a tradition of reticence in exercising the power they possess. Yet our ignorance on this subject is great, and we can scarcely afford a complacent assumption that interlocking directorates and other intercorporate affiliations have no significant behavioral effects.

Turnover among the largest corporations We have seen that a relatively few very large enterprises account for a considerable share of all industrial activity, whatever measure of size is used. Is membership in this select group a stable phenomenon or something that slips readily from the grasp of those whose attention and zeal waver? In other words, is turnover among the ranks of the largest corporations relatively high or low?

Several studies of turnover among the largest U.S. corporations have been published.[35] In one of the most comprehensive efforts, Collins and Preston compiled lists of the 100 largest manufacturing, mining, and distribution companies, ranked by assets, for the years 1909, 1919, 1929, 1935, 1948, and 1958. They found that a total of 209 identifiable corporations appeared on these six lists at one time or another. Thirty-six of the top hundred in 1909 remained among the 100 leaders of 1958. On the average, 2.5 firms per year disappeared from the list.

Why did some drop off the list, while others ascended? A first impression can be gained by considering what happened to the leading ten corporations on the 1909 list. They are ranked in order of 1909 assets, and the figure in parentheses indicates the company's rank or status in 1977, as determined from an updating of the Collins-Preston analysis by the author:

1. United States Steel (14)
2. Standard Oil of New Jersey (1)
3. American Tobacco (63)
4. International Mercantile Marine (dropped)
5. International Harvester (45)
6. Anaconda Copper (dropped)
7. United States Leather (dropped)
8. Armour (dropped)
9. American Sugar Refining (dropped)
10. Pullman Inc. (dropped)

Only one of the top ten in 1909 remained among the top ten of 1977, and six dropped from the list of the leading 100. Of these six, only one disappeared altogether.[36] After nearly succumbing in the 1921 recession and then struggling along for three more decades, United States Leather was liquidated in 1953. International Mercantile Marine, renamed United States Lines, was still plying the oceans as a subsidiary of Walter Kidde and Co. in 1977. At the time it was acquired by Kidde, its assets were too modest to warrant inclusion among the top 100. Anaconda Copper, though still large enough on its own to remain on the 100-largest list, was acquired in 1977 by the Atlantic Richfield Company. Having grown too slowly to remain among the top 100 by an asset measure, Armour merged in 1968 with the General Host Company, which in turn was acquired in 1969 by Greyhound of bus fame. American Sugar Refining, renamed Amstar, ranked 307th in terms of assets on *Fortune's* list of the 500 largest industrials. Pullman Inc. continued to be America's largest railroad car manufacturer and had diversified into other lines, but its assets were sufficient only to place it near the 200 mark by the Collins-Preston criteria.

These disappearances and declines primarily reflect the transition of the American economy into the age of automobiles, aircraft, and electronics from an era in which food and basic clothing were the principal items in the average consumer's budget. Both Armour and American Sugar Refining were directly involved in the food processing industry, and International Harvester's indirect dependence on agriculture was heavy. Pullman and United States Lines were obvious victims of technological change. Other 1909 pacesetters who disappeared from the list of 100 leaders (and, in some cases, from the business scene altogether) for similar reasons include American Agricultural Chemical, American Cotton Oil, American Hide and Leather, American Ice, American Linseed Oil, Baldwin Locomotive Works, Cudahy Packing, General Cigar, Harbison-Walker Refractories, International Salt, U.S. Cast Iron Pipe and Foundry, United Shoe Machinery, Wilson Meat Packing, and Wells Fargo.

A similar picture emerges when we trace the ten largest firms of 1977 back to 1909:

1. Exxon (formerly Standard Oil of N.J.) (2)
2. General Motors (not listed in 1909)
3. Mobil Oil (not listed)
4. Ford Motor Co. (not listed)
5. IBM (not listed)
6. Texaco (91)
7. Standard Oil of California (not listed)
8. Sears Roebuck (45)
9. Gulf Oil (not listed)
10. General Electric (16)

The ascendance of General Motors and Ford (already listed among the top ten in 1919) is explained, of course, by the automotive revolution. It in turn propelled four additional petroleum refiners to the top by 1977—two of them fragments of the original New Jersey Standard

Oil Company, broken off after a 1911 antitrust judgment. The only real newcomer to the top ranks was IBM, which occupied only 68th place on the list for 1948.

Movement up and down on lists of the largest corporations over time depends in part upon broad shifts in the pattern of demand. In a statistical analysis, Seymour Friedland found a positive correlation between the rate of growth of 44 leading corporations' total assets and the rate of change of their home industry group's share of all manufacturing activity.[37] The simple correlation coefficient was 0.87 for the 1906–28 time period and 0.80 for the 1928–50 period.[38]

Since there are no unambiguous criteria for judging, it is difficult to say whether the observed rate of turnover is high or low in some absolute sense. Whatever one's value judgments may be on this point, it is clear that the rate of turnover has declined over time. This is shown in Table 3.3

35. A. D. H. Kaplan, *Big Enterprise in a Competitive System* (Washington, D.C.: Brookings Institution, 1954; rev. ed., 1964), Chapter 7; Seymour Friedland, "Turnover and Growth of the Largest Industrial Firms, 1906–1950," *Review of Economics and Statistics* 39 (February 1957): 79–83; N. R. Collins and L. E. Preston, "The Size Structure of the Largest Industrial Firms," *American Economic Review* 51 (December 1961): 986–1011; the testimony by John Blair in *Economic Concentration*, pp. 86–88, 207–10; David Mermelstein, "Large Industrial Corporations and Asset Shares," *American Economic Review* 59 (September 1969): 531–41; Stanley E. Boyle and Joseph P. McKenna, "The Mobility of the 100 and 200 Largest U.S. Manufacturing Corporations: 1919–1964," *Antitrust Bulletin* 15 (Fall 1970): 505–19; Ronald S. Bond, "Mergers and Mobility Among the Largest Manufacturing Corporations," *Antitrust Bulletin* 20 (Fall 1975): 505–19; and R. C. Edwards, "Stages in Corporate Stability and the Risks of Corporate Failure," *Journal of Economic History* 35 (June 1975): 428–57. See also the exchange between Mermelstein, Boyle, and David Kamerschen in the *American Economic Review* 61 (March 1971): 160–74. For a similar analysis of the British scene, see Geoffrey Whittington, "Changes in the Top 100 Quoted Manufacturing Companies in the United Kingdom, 1948 to 1968," *Journal of Industrial Economics* 21 (November 1972): 17–34.

36. For an account of the problems of these and other "dropout" firms, see "The Dropouts," *Forbes*, 15 September 1967, pp. 149–72.

37. Friedland, "Turnover and Growth of the Largest Industrial Firms," pp. 79–80. See also Stanley E. Boyle and Robert L. Sorenson, "Concentration and Mobility: Alternative Measures of Industry Structure," *Journal of Industrial Economics* 19 (April 1971): especially pp. 119–21.

38. We shall use correlation analysis and its cousin, regression analysis, repeatedly in subsequent pages. For those whose path has not been crossed by that star, an elementary exposition of the central concepts is provided in the Appendix to Chapter 3.

The structure of U.S. industry   55

through a tabulation of the average number of firms disappearing per year from the Collins and Preston lists, augmented by this author's extension of the data to 1977. Two measures are given: one showing the rate of exit for all reasons; and the second counting only "natural" exits, excluding primary and secondary effects of mergers and government antitrust actions.[39] By either measure, a decline in the rate of turnover, at least up to the 1940s, is apparent. Four possible reasons for this change can be postulated. First, the largest firms might somehow have become more entrenched by virtue of the power their increased size confers, although it is difficult to think of a mechanism by which this entrenchment process could work. Second, the rate of technological change, or the rate of change in demand patterns, might have slowed. This too seems implausible in view of the enormous scientific and technological advances made since the end of World War II. Third, the management of large corporations may have become more professionalized, taking a longer term view of its role and identifying its function not as the sale of certain products but preservation of the firm *qua* organization. This implies among other things a willingness to adopt new product lines when the demand for traditional items declines. Such a change has probably occurred. Finally, as a by-product of their more professional managerial outlook and

increased size, large corporations may have become more diversified, hedging against shifts in demand. This, we shall find later, has in fact happened.

Concentration in particular markets

We turn now to the dimension of structure most closely related to the main concern of this volume: the possession of monopoly power. Let us begin by considering alternative means of measuring the phenomenon.[40]

Alternative monopoly measures Some are performance-oriented, such as the well-known *Lerner Index*, defined as $M = (Price - Marginal Cost)/Price$.[41] Its merit is that it directly reflects the allocatively inefficient departure of price from marginal cost associated with monopoly. Under pure competition, $M = 0$. The more a firm's pricing departs from the competitive norm, the higher is the associated Lerner index value. A related performance-oriented approach focuses on the *net profits* realized by firms or industries. We shall make abundant use of these measures in subsequent chapters, particularly in Chapter 9.

The other main approach is to focus on observable dimensions of industry structure. Economic theory suggests that the vigor of competition is related positively to the *number of firms* in the relevant industry, other things (such as the height of entry barriers) being equal. However, the degree of inequality can also matter. In an industry with 100 sellers, does each firm control 1 percent of the industry's output or do four firms control 80 percent while the remaining 96 produce only 20 percent? A simple measure that copes with the inequality dimension by stressing the position of the largest firm is the *market concentration ratio C*, defined as the percentage of total industry sales (or capacity, or employment, or value added, or physical output) contributed by the largest few firms, ranked in order of market shares. The most common variant in American studies (referred to as the four-firm sales concentration ratio and often as *the* concentration ratio)

T 3.3 Exits from the top 100 industrial corporations, 1909–77

	Ave. no. of exits per year for all causes	Ave. no of natural exits per year
1909–19	4.0	2.6
1919–29	3.1	2.1
1929–35	2.7	2.0
1935–48	1.5	1.5
1948–58	1.6	1.7
1958–77	1.7	1.6

Source: N. R. Collins and L. E. Preston, "The Size Structure of the Largest Industrial Firms," *American Economic Review* 51 (December 1961): 986–1011; supplemented by the author's own research.

is the percentage of total industry sales originated by the leading four firms. Concentration ratios are also published for U.S. manufacturing industries with respect to the leading 8, 20 and 50 firms.[42] Obviously, concentration data for several different numbers of firms provide more information on industry structure than the ratio for only one set (i.e., the top four), and it is often useful to present a *concentration table*, as in Table 3.4, which provides a breakdown on the U.S. phonograph record and tape industry for 1972. A drawback to the concentration table approach is the awkwardness, both in verbal discourse and statistical analyses, of working with several sets of numbers.

A graphic technique for summarizing the information in a concentration table is the *Lorenz curve*, which shows as a continuous function the percentage of total industry sales (or some other variable) accounted for by any given fraction of the total company population, with the firms ranked in order of market share or size. Lorenz curves can be characterized numerically by means of the *Gini coefficient*, which measures the departure between the Lorenz curve actually observed and the curve that would appear if all firms had equal market shares or sales.[43] A Gini coefficient of zero indicates perfect equality of firm shares; a coefficient of 1.0 reveals total inequality (with the leading firm producing the entire output). The Lorenz-Gini approach has two main disadvantages. As an index solely of in-

equality, the Gini coefficient may suggest paradoxical inferences when an industry is occupied by a small number of evenly matched firms. The Gini coefficient for duopolists or triopolists with equal market shares is zero, but one could hardly conclude that monopoly power is absent in such cases. Second, the shape of the Lorenz curve and the value of the Gini coefficient are quite sensitive to errors in defining the number of firms in the industry. The more borderline firms one includes, the higher the indicated degree of inequality tends to be.

39. On the methodology, see Collins and Preston, "The Size Structure of the Largest Industrial Firms," pp. 996–99. In extending the analysis to 1977, it was discovered that Collins and Preston counted as separate two oil companies clearly controlled by the Getty interests. They also included a Canadian corporation, International Nickel. At least two distribution firms, Safeway and Anderson Clayton, were improperly omitted. Whether or not these oversights are corrected has no material impact on the 1958–77 results. No attempt was made to trace back the implications for earlier years. The effect is likely at most to be a one-unit change in the first digit after the decimal point in the annual exit rate. The decline of United Fruit might arguably be considered a nonnatural exit, but it was not so classified because United's antitrust divestiture alone was not of sufficient magnitude to explain United's exit from the top 100.

40. For perceptive early methodological discussions, see John Perry Miller, "Measures of Monopoly Power and Concentration: Their Economic Significance," and Tibor Scitovsky, "Economic Theory and the Measurement of Concentration," both in the National Bureau of Economic Research conference report, *Business Concentration and Price Policy* (Princeton: Princeton University Press, 1955), pp. 101–40. More recently, an axiomatic approach to the choice of measures has been advocated. See Marshall Hall and Nicolaus Tideman, "Measures of Concentration," *Journal of the American Statistical Association* (March 1967): 162–68; Christian Marfels, "The Consistency of Concentration Measures: A Mathematical Evaluation," *Zeitschrift für die gesamte Staatswissenschaft* 128 (June 1972): 196–215; and Leslie Hannah and J. A. Key, *Concentration in Modern Industry* (London: Macmillan, 1977), pp. 41–63.

41. A. P. Lerner, "The Concept of Monopoly and the Measurement of Monopoly Power," *Review of Economic Studies* 1 (June 1934): 157–75.

42. Concentration ratios are now published in a special section in the first summary volume of the quinquennial U.S. *Census of Manufactures.* More complete tabulations appear in a special report, the most recent of which is "Concentration Ratios in Manufacturing," *1972 Census of Manufactures,* MC72(SR)-2 (Washington, D.C.: Government Printing Office, 1975). The report for the 1977 Census is scheduled for publication in 1980. For a summary of earlier U.S. concentration ratio sources, see Ralph L. Nelson, *Concentration in the Manufacturing Industries of the United States* (New Haven, Conn.: Yale University Press, 1963), pp. 17–19.

43. On computational techniques, see Horst Mendershausen, *Changes in Income Distribution During the Great Depression* (New York: National Bureau of Economic Research, 1946), pp. 160–67.

T 3.4 Concentration table for the record industry

Group of firms	Percentage of total industry sales
Largest 4	48
Largest 8	61
Largest 20	76
Largest 50	85

Source: U.S., Bureau of the Census, "Concentration Ratios in Manufacturing," *1972 Census of Manufactures,* MC72(SR)-2 (Washington, D.C.: Government Printing Office, 1975), p. SR2–39, Table 4.

The structure of U.S. industry 57

A summary measure in the same spirit as the Gini coefficient, but without its serious flaws, is the so-called *Herfindahl-Hirschman Index*, given by the formula:[44]

$$H = \sum_{i=1}^{N} S_i^2$$

where S_i is the market share of the ith firm. When an industry is occupied by only one firm (a pure monopolist), the index attains its maximum value of 1.0. The value declines with increases in the number of firms N and increases with rising inequality among any given number of firms.[45] By squaring market shares, the H index weights more heavily the values for large firms than for small.[46] How desirable or undesirable this weighting scheme is depends upon the relevant theory as to how market structure, conduct, and performance are related. Operationally, the H weighting scheme makes it unimportant whether one has precise data on the market shares of very small firms. But by the same token, it is crucial that the largest sellers' market shares be measured accurately. Unfortunately, such market share data have in the past been difficult to obtain.[47] A similar measure favored by some economists is the *entropy coefficient*, defined as:[48]

$$E = \sum_{i=1}^{N} S_i \log_2 (1/S_i)$$

When market shares are equal, its value reduces to $\log_2 N$, being zero under pure monopoly and rising nonlinearly as the number of firms increases. For a given number of firms, it rises with increased equality of market shares. To add only one more of the numerous candidates jostling for use as indices of structure, the variance of the logarithms of industry members' sales or employment V has also been advocated.[49] V relates well to certain theories seeking to explain striking uniformities in the shapes of observed firm size distributions, as we shall see in Chapter 4. However, like the Gini coefficient, V emphasizes inequality to the exclusion of differences in the number of firms. And in contrast to the H and E indices, V places relatively heavy weight on the sizes of smaller firms.

With such a rich menu of alternative market structure measures, which one should the analyst use? Ideally, the choice should be based upon how well an index accords with relevant underlying economic theory. Certain theories do support a definite preference.[50] Nevertheless, theory provides conflicting guidance. As we shall see, there are hypotheses suggesting that, for a given number of sellers, greater equality of market shares is conducive to coordinated monopolistic behavior, but other hypotheses imply that inequality fosters leadership and hence monopolistic behavior. A degree of open-mindedness seems appropriate, especially in view of the fact that the nonlinear properties of the often-preferred H index can be emulated by transformations of simple indices such as the four-firm concentration ratio. Pragmatism must also enter in for, in many instances, concentration ratio data are available in greater abundance, or at a higher level of accuracy than, say, H indices or the information needed to compute them.

Except when fine distinctions must be made, which market structure measure one uses may not be a matter of great moment, since the leading contenders tend to yield similar industry rankings and have highly correlated numerical values. To illustrate, four structural indices—the four-firm sales concentration ratio, the eight-firm sales concentration ratio, the four-firm employment concentration ratio, and the H index—were correlated for a sample of 91 industries on which comparable data were available.[51] For the six two-way comparisons of these four measures, the average correlation coefficient was 0.921, and the lowest of the six correlations was 0.859. The correlation between the four-firm sales concentration ratio (the most commonly used of all measures) and the H index was 0.936. Analogous results have been obtained in other studies of alternative market structure measures.[52] Thus, if an industry has a high four-firm concentration ratio, it is likely also to have a high Herfindahl-Hirschman index, a high eight-firm concentration ratio, and a small number of sellers. And although asset concentration ratios tend to be higher than sales concentration ratios, which in turn are somewhat higher than employment ratios, all tend to be *relatively* high for a given industry if any one ratio is high. The choice of a measure could nonetheless make an appreciable difference when one is using concentration indices to predict performance or other variables and the underlying relationships are fragile statistically.[53] Concern for this possibility is clearly warranted. Nevertheless, a much more serious danger is the possibility that any structural index chosen, while suggesting the same inferences as alternate measures, will convey a false impression about the actual degree of structural monopoly.

The limitations of concentration ratios

To see this, we must consider more carefully some of the assumptions and limitations of the concentration index approach. The most widely used concentration ratio tells the percentage of all industry sales made by the leading four firms. When concentration ratios are computed, some difficulties may be encountered disentangling the four industry leaders' sales in the desired industry from their sales in other fields, for diverse activities may be housed together under a single roof. But these problems are seldom serious, and in the United States they can be avoided easily.[54] A much more vexing problem arises in defining the industry meaningfully—that is, so that all firms which are competitors, and only those firms, are included.

Most studies of market concentration use data collected by national census bureaus. Each census agency has developed or adapted an elaborate system for categorizing by industry or product line the output of business establishments. In the United States, the basic system is called the Standard Industrial Classification, or S.I.C. From it, the Census Bureau has developed an even more intricately subdivided system organized around a series of seven-digit numbers, each successive digit reflecting a finer degree of classification.[55] Consider, for example, the seven-digit product line 2844515 (suntan oils). The first digit (2) indicates that this set of commodities is produced in the manufacturing sector of the economy (as opposed to, say, 5 for trade or 0 for agriculture and forestry). The first two digits together (28) reveal that the commodity is produced in the "chemicals and allied products" group of the manufacturing sector. There are 20

44. On its history, see A. O. Hirschman, "The Paternity of an Index," *American Economic Review* 54 (September 1964): 761.

45. See I. M. Grossack, "Toward an Integration of Static and Dynamic Measures of Industry Concentration," *Review of Economics and Statistics* 47 (August 1965): 301–308; and M. A. Adelman, "Comment on the 'H' Concentration Measure as a Numbers Equivalent," *Review of Economics and Statistics* 51 (February 1969): 99–101. Note that when s_i is defined as the deviation of the ith firm's market share from the industry mean, the variance of market shares is given by $\Sigma_{i=1}^{N} s_i^2/(N-1)$. A standard formula of statistics is that $\Sigma s_i^2 = \Sigma S_i^2 - (\Sigma S_i)^2/N$. But when the S_i are market shares, $\Sigma S_i = 1$ and so $(\Sigma S_i)^2 = 1$. Substituting, we have $\Sigma s_i^2 = \Sigma S_i^2 - 1/N$. Rearranging according to the formula in the text, we obtain:

$$H = \Sigma S_i^2 = \Sigma s_i^2 + 1/N$$

The first term on the right-hand side is the *variance equivalent*, the second term the inverse of a *numbers equivalent*. Note that if all firms had equal market shares, $\Sigma s_i^2 = 0$ and the H index falls monotonically but nonlinearly with an increasing number of firms.

46. There is no a priori reason why the weighting scheme need be quadratic, as with the H index. For an approach emphasizing variable exponent weights, see Hannah and Key, *Concentration in Modern Industry*, pp. 41–63. Note that in the limiting case of a zero exponent (in place of the H index's 2), one gets a concentration index that merely counts the number of firms.

47. The only source of H indices computed directly from U.S. census data is Nelson, *Concentration in the Manufacturing Industries*, Appendix A. For Canada, see Department of Consumer and Corporate Affairs, *Concentration in the Manufacturing Industries of Canada*, Table A–1. Comprehensive estimates from which one can compute U.S. manufacturing firm market shares, sometimes subject to large errors, can be obtained from Economic Information Systems, Inc., or Dun and Bradstreet. Precise, finely subdivided data for 1950 are available in the Federal Trade Commission Statistical Report, *Value of Shipments Data by Product Class for the 1,000 Largest Manufacturing Companies of 1950* (Washington, D.C.: Government Printing Office, 1972). Similar data for 1972 may be published if the FTC overcomes organized opposition by several hundred corporations to such disclosure.

48. See Marfels, "The Consistency of Concentration Measures," pp. 203–208; and Ira Horowitz, "Numbers-Equivalents in U.S. Manufacturing Industries," *Southern Economic Journal* 37 (April 1971): 396–408.

49. P. E. Hart and S. J. Prais, "The Analysis of Business Concentration: A Statistical Approach," *Journal of the Royal Statistical Society*, Series A, vol. 119, part 2 (1956): 150–81. Compare Irwin H. Silberman, "On Lognormality as a Summary Measure of Concentration," *American Economic Review* 57 (September 1967): 807–31; and Hannah and Key, *Concentration in Modern Industry*, pp. 51–52.

50. See George J. Stigler, "A Theory of Oligopoly," *Journal of Political Economy* 72 (February 1964): 55–59; Thomas R. Saving, "Concentration Ratios and the Degree of Monopoly," *International Economic Review* 11 (February 1970): 139–46; Keith Cowling and Michael Waterson, "Price-Cost Margins and Market Structure," *Economica* 43 (August 1976): 267–74; John C. Hause, "The Measurement of Concentrated Industrial Structure and the Size Distribution of Firms," *Annals of Economic and Social Measurement* 6 (Winter 1977): 79–90; and David Encaoua and Alexis P. Jacquemin, "Degree of Monopoly, Indices of Concentration and Threat of Entry," Working Paper no. 7802 (Universite Catholique de Louvain, September 1978).

51. The data are from Nelson, *Concentration in Manufacturing Industries*.

such two-digit groups altogether in manufacturing, numbering 20 through 39. The first three digits together (284) place our commodity in the "cleaning and toilet products" field. Adding the fourth digit locates it more finely in *S.I.C. industry* 2844, covering "toilet preparations." Drawing upon the 1972 Census of Manufactures, concentration ratios for some 450 manufacturing industries have been published. At a still finer level of detail is the five-digit *product class* 28445—in this case, a catch-all category covering "other cosmetics and toilet preparations" (shaving preparations, perfumes, dentifrices, and the like, having received separate five-digit codes). The 1972 Census of Manufactures covered 1,293 such five-digit product classes, for most of which concentration ratios are available. Finally, one jumps to the seven-digit *product* or *commodity* level. Examples in the five-digit class 28445 include suntan oils, cleansing creams, lipsticks, aerosol deodorants, nail lacquer, and cosmetic and baby oil. At this level of detail the Census of Manufactures identifies some 11,500 products. No concentration ratios are published at the seven-digit level.[56]

Census Bureau industry and product class definitions do not always conform to the criteria economists would like to apply. To get its difficult job done at all, the Bureau must use definitions facilitating accurate reporting by business firms, which usually means that they must follow the way firms have grouped or segregated their production operations. Emphasis is often on similarity of production processes, which may not reflect competitive interrelationships. Consequently, four-digit census industries and even five-digit product classes are sometimes too broad relative to the economist's ideal industry definition, and sometimes they are too narrow.

The ideal definition of a market must take into account substitution possibilities in both consumption and production. On the demand side, firms are competitors or rivals if the products they offer are good substitutes for one another in the eyes of buyers. But how, exactly, does one draw the line between "good" and "not good enough" substitutes? The essence of the matter is what happens when price relationships change. If the price of product A is raised by a small percentage and as a result consumers substitute product B for product A in significant quantities, then A and B are good substitutes and ought to be included under a common market definition. Pinning a numerical value on the phrase "in significant quantities" here can be problematic.[57] However, a more fundamental difficulty is the fact that extensive substitution may occur only within certain relative price ranges and not in others. When the delivered price of coal is $40 per ton, an increase in the price of petroleum from $7 to $12 per barrel may not prompt much substitution of coal for petroleum because petroleum is more economical as a boiler fuel over the entire $7 to $12 price range. As the price of petroleum is pushed even higher, however, a point must be reached at which it becomes attractive to substitute coal for oil. In judging whether or not products are substitutes, then, one must make assumptions about the plausible range of prices. In this there are risks of circularity if markets are being defined for purposes of measuring structural monopoly power, for a rational oil monopolist would raise its price until it comes near, without overstepping, the point at which coal begins making substantial inroads. To avoid this measurement pitfall, one must ask whether a given percentage change in price *above the competitive price* would induce significant substitution of coal for oil. This, of course, is very difficult. As a result, economists are often forced to fall back on commonsense devices such as searching for a marked qualitative gap in the chain of substitutes, as Joan Robinson recommended.[58]

Substitution on the production side must also be considered. Groups of firms making completely nonsubstitutable products may nevertheless be meaningful competitors if they employ essentially similar skills and equipment and if they can quickly move into each others' product lines should the profit lure beckon. The four-digit Census industry "screw machine products" is a good example of a definition satisfying these criteria, for screw machine shops turn out everything from ball bearing races to lamp couplings with equipment readily shifted from one product to another quite different one. Again, however, the application of such criteria poses practical judgmental problems. How quickly must firms be able to shift over between products to be classified in the same industry? Given a long enough period and sufficient investment, shifts in production activity more accurately described as "new entry" than as "substitution" can take place. A distinction between substitutability in production and ease of entry (i.e., where barriers to new entry are minimal) must be drawn. At the risk of being somewhat arbitrary, we should probably draw the line to include as substitutes on the production side only existing capacity that can be shifted in the short run, i.e., without significant new investment in plant, equipment, and worker training.

In view of these broad principles, how good are the Census Bureau's industry definitions for purposes of identifying structural monopoly conditions? What problems arise from the system? Are there consistent biases in the definitions and, if so, in what direction? And how can they be combatted operationally? As a backdrop for exploring these questions, Table 3.5 presents 1972 sales concentration data for a sample of 46 U.S. manufacturing industries. All but two of the industries are defined at the four-digit level. The sample is fairly representative except for excluding vaguely defined catch-all categories and favoring the larger, more prominent industries and a few of the most highly concentrated industries that will reappear frequently in later chapters.

The most important single source of problems is a definition excessively broad or narrow relative to the possibilities for substitution in consumption. Several of the industries in Table 3.5 are clearly too broad. The worst offender is pharmaceutical preparations, which lumps together dozens of drugs or classes of drugs for which there are no adequate substitutes (except perhaps greatly extended medical care). Economically meaningful market definitions must generally be found in this case at the seven-digit level of detail, given that substitution in production is often blocked by patent barriers. Other industries defined too broadly include aircraft (involving a wide diversity of aircraft types requiring special production tooling and skills), motors and generators (with similar diversity of products and required equipment), and soap and detergents (with several functionally distinct product lines,

and with strong product differentiation segmenting markets for functionally identical offerings). Industries defined too narrowly include the separate metal cans and glass container groups

(52) High correlations are reported in Gideon Rosenbluth, "Measures of Concentration," in *Business Concentration and Price Policy*, pp. 63–69, 89–92; Hall and Tideman, "Measures of Concentration," pp. 166–67; R. W. Kilpatrick, "The Choice Among Alternative Measures of Industrial Concentration," *Review of Economics and Statistics* 49 (May 1967): 258–60; Alexis P. Jacquemin and Henry W. de Jong, *European Industrial Organisation* (London: Macmillan, 1977), pp. 49–50; and (for a factor-theoretic approach) E. Vanlommel, B. de Brabander, and D. Liebaers, "Industrial Concentration in Belgium: Empirical Comparison of Alternative Seller Concentration Measures," *Journal of Industrial Economics* 26 (September 1977): 1–20. But compare Hause, "The Measurement of Concentrated Industrial Structure," pp. 93–99, who focuses only on the most highly concentrated tail of the distribution; and Richard Schmalensee, "Using the H-Index of Concentration with Published Data," *Review of Economics and Statistics* 59 (May 1977): 186–93.

(53) See John E. Kwoka, Jr., Federal Trade Commission staff paper, "Does the Choice of Concentration Ratio Really Matter?," (Washington, D.C.: Federal Trade Commission, 1978).

(54) Specifically, the *product class* concentration ratios published by the U.S. Census are freer of "contamination" than the *industry* ratios.

(55) On the Census classification system, see M. R. Conklin and H. T. Goldstein, "Census Principles and Product Classification, Manufacturing Industries," in *Business Concentration and Price Policy*, pp. 15–36.

56. But see Dean A. Worcester, Jr., *Monopoly, Big Business and Welfare in the Postwar United States* (Seattle: University of Washington Press, 1967), pp. 70–81, who summarizes an analysis of concentration in selected seven-digit lines.

57. Sometimes this substitutability relationship may be reflected in high values of the *cross elasticity of demand*, defined as the percentage change in the quantity sold, say, of product B associated with a given percentage change in the price of product A, holding product B's price constant. But cross elasticities are not without interpretational difficulties. Suppose, for example, initial sales of product A = 1,000 units and initial sales of product B = 100 units. Now let the price of A be raised by 10 percent and assume that 30 units of demand shift from A to B. The cross elasticity $(\triangle Q_B/Q_B)/(\triangle P_A/P_A)$ is 3.0, suggesting high substitutability. But if we assume instead that B reduces its price by a comparable 10 percent and that the same 30 units of demand shift from A to B, the computed cross elasticity $(\triangle Q_A/Q_A)/(\triangle P_B/P_B)$ is 0.3. In this case, the producer of A is not likely to consider B a very good substitute for its product.

On these and other difficulties encountered in using cross elasticities to delineate market boundaries, see Charles E. Ferguson, *A Macroeconomic Theory of Workable Competition* (Durham, N.C.: Duke University Press, 1964), pp. 32–43; Klaus Stegemann, "Cross Elasticity and the Relevant Market," *Zeitschrift für Wirtschafts-und Sozialwissenschaften*, no. 2, (1974): 151–65; and Kenneth D. Boyer, "Degrees of Differentiation and Industry Boundaries," in Terry Calvani and John Siegfried, eds., *Economic Analysis of Antitrust Law* (Boston: Little Brown, 1979), pp. 88–106.

58. Joan Robinson, *The Economics of Imperfect Competition* (London: Macmillan, 1934), p. 5.

T 3.5 1972 concentration ratios for representative industries

S.I.C. code	Industry description	4-firm ratio	8-firm ratio	Number of firms
37111	Passenger cars (five-digit)	99	100	n.a.
3211	Flat glass	92	n.a.	11
2043	Cereal breakfast foods	90	98	34
3511	Turbines and turbine generators	90	96	59
3641	Electric lamps	90	94	103
3632	Household refrigerators and freezers	85	98	30
2111	Cigarettes	84	n.a.	13
3672	Cathode ray television picture tubes	83	97	69
3334	Primary aluminum	79	92	12
3011	Tires and inner tubes	73	90	136
3331	Primary copper	72	n.a.	11
36512	Household television receivers (five-digit)	66	93	n.a.
3721	Aircraft	66	86	141
3411	Metal cans	66	79	134
2822	Synthetic rubber	62	81	50
2284	Thread mills	62	77	61
2841	Soap and detergents	62	74	577
3691	Storage batteries	57	85	138
3221	Glass containers	55	76	27
3873	Watches, clocks, and watch cases	55	67	183
2082	Beer and malt beverages	52	70	108
3562	Ball and roller bearings	53	73	99
3523	Farm machinery and equipment	47	61	1465
3621	Motors and generators	47	59	325
3312	Blast furnaces and steel mills	45	65	241
2873	Nitrogenous fertilizers	35	53	47
3143	Men's footwear, except athletic	34	51	118
2041	Flour and other grain mill products	33	53	340
2911	Petroleum refining	31	56	152
2211	Cotton-weaving mills	31	48	190
3552	Textile machinery	31	46	535
2051	Bread, cake, and related products	29	39	2800
3241	Cement	26	46	75
2834	Pharmaceutical preparations	26	44	680
2651	Folding paperboard boxes	23	35	443
2851	Paints and allied products	22	34	1318
3541	Metal-cutting machine tools	22	33	857
2026	Fluid milk	18	26	2026
2421	Sawmills and planing mills	18	23	7664
2711	Newspapers	17	28	7461
2512	Upholstered household furniture	14	23	1201
2086	Bottled and canned soft drinks	14	21	2271
3494	Valves and pipe fittings	11	21	643
2335	Women's and misses' dresses	9	13	5294
3273	Ready-mixed concrete	6	10	3978
3451	Screw machine products	6	9	1780

n.a. = not available.
Source: U.S., Bureau of the Census, *1972 Census of Manufactures*, "Concentration Ratios in Manufacturing," MC72(SR)–2 (Washington, D.C.: Government Printing Office, 1975).

(since cans and bottles are readily substitutable in many applications); cotton-weaving mills (since synthetic fabrics and wool compete in many uses and looms are often readily interchangeable between cotton and synthetic blend yarns); and synthetic rubber (for which natural and reclaimed rubber, accounting for about a fourth of total rubber consumed in 1972, can sometimes be substituted). Concentration ratios in the primary copper and aluminum (and, to a lesser degree, steel) industries also tend to overstate monopoly power, other things being equal, partly because these metals compete with one another in numerous applications and partly because the output of domestic scrap reprocessors is omitted from consideration. In 1972, resmelted copper scrap constituted about a third of all domestic copper production and reprocessed aluminum 17 percent of all aluminum production.

Concentration ratios can also overstate monopoly power by failing to take into account the import competition of foreign suppliers. For members of the European Common Market and for other nations (like Sweden and Switzerland) with largely open economies, this problem is so serious that it renders national concentration ratios virtually meaningless for industries in which international trade thrives. Import competition is less significant overall but growing in importance in the United States, which during the mid-1970s experienced manufactured goods imports amounting to approximately 6 percent of domestic manufacturers' sales. Import competition, both potential and actual, is nevertheless a major consideration for some Table 3.5 industries, such as textile machinery (with imports amounting to 40 percent of domestic output in 1971); shoes (with imports of 16 percent in 1971, growing to 58 percent for women's shoes in 1977); watches and clocks (with 19 percent imports); television sets (with 17 percent imports, including 43 percent of domestic black and white set output); steel (with imports at 17 percent of 1972 domestic consumption); and automobiles (with imports accounting for one of every seven cars purchased in the United States during 1972).[59]

While failure to consider import competition causes concentration ratios to exaggerate the degree of structural monopoly, the implicit census assumption that all markets are nationwide in scope errs in the opposite direction. Certain bulky, low-value commodities cannot economically be transported far from the site of production, and so the market definition must be regional or local to be meaningful. Cement is a classic example. Table 3.5 shows that the leading four firms accounted for 26 percent of all nationwide sales in 1972. Yet it costs something on the order of 45 cents to ship a dollar's worth of cement 350 miles, and largely for that reason 90 percent of all cement is shipped 200 miles or less. When the United States is divided into 51 regions (essentially on a statewide basis), one finds that in only three of the regions did the leading four producers account for less than 50 percent of 1964 cement sales.[60] Newspapers and ready-mixed concrete are even more extreme, since relevant markets are seldom much larger than a single metropolitan area, so one finds near-monopoly conditions in many local newspaper markets and tight oligopoly in all but the most densely populated ready-mixed concrete markets. Because of the centripetal pull of transportation costs, national concentration ratios also tend to overstate concentration for more meaningfully defined markets in glass containers, beer, nitrogenous fertilizers, paperboard boxes, fluid milk, and petroleum refining. The same would be true for metal cans were it not for the fact that the leading producers have a strong presence in nearly all important geographic markets.

Finally, published concentration ratios may misrepresent the extent of structural monopoly power for various institutional reasons. The bot-

59. See *inter alia* U.S., Bureau of the Census, *U.S. Commodity Exports and Imports as Related to Output, 1971 and 1970* (Washington, D.C.: Government Printing Office, 1974). For a survey of U.S. executives' subjective perception of the foreign competition threat, see Werner Sichel, "The Foreign Competition Omission in Census Concentration Ratios: An Empirical Evaluation," *Antitrust Bulletin* 20 (Spring 1975): 89–105.

60. Federal Trade Commission, *Economic Report on Mergers and Vertical Integration in the Cement Industry* (Washington, D.C.: Government Printing Office, 1966), pp. 29–31. State market boundaries are probably too narrow on average, but they approximate a correct definition much more closely than nationwide figures.

tled and canned soft drinks industry, with a four-firm concentration ratio of 14, is an especially good illustration. Its ostensibly low concentration reflects the organization of the industry into numerous local bottling companies. But most bottlers operate under franchises from nationwide firms like Coca-Cola and Pepsi-Cola. A more meaningful index of concentration would be the proportion of the nationwide market commanded by products tied to the leading national firms. Some indication is provided by the fact that product class 20873—flavoring syrups for use by soft drink bottlers—had a four-firm concentration ratio of 89 in 1972.

To sum up, concentration ratios understate the true quantum of monopoly power when markets are defined to include nonsubstitutes, when meaningful markets are local or regional rather than nationwide, when sellers enjoy strong product differentiation advantages within relevant product lines, and when special institutional features (like the soft drink franchise pattern) intrude. The degree of monopoly power is overstated when substitutes are excluded from the industry definition and when import competition is significant.

How do these influences balance out? In an attempt to assess the average bias, the author carefully reviewed each of the industries in Table 3.5, determining whether the concentration ratios tended on balance either to understate or overstate the true extent of concentration by 10 percentage points or more. The judgments were necessarily subjective, and the reader may wish to try his or her own hand at the game. But for what they are worth, true concentration was found to be understated in 19 industries and overstated in only eight. This conclusion cannot be extended directly to the entire population of census industries, since the Table 3.5 sample is not random. Very broadly defined industries like "toilet preparations" and catch-all industries like "industrial organic chemicals, not elsewhere classified," whose concentration ratios typically understate substantially the actual degree of structural monopoly, were deliberately excluded. Thus, it appears probable that the total population of four-digit manufacturing industries as classified for census purposes errs on the side of

excessive breadth even more than the sample of industries in Table 3.5. However, five-digit definitions may be biased slightly in the opposite direction.

Given these deficiencies, what practical steps can be taken to avoid mistakes in the use and interpretation of concentration ratios? The most important is to recognize that pitfalls exist: Concentration indices are at best only a rough one-dimensional indicator of monopoly power, and their use must be governed by common sense. However, it is difficult to inject common sense into an electronic computer. Consequently, in statistical studies it is desirable to adjust misleading concentration ratios—e.g., by consolidating industries that have been defined too narrowly and by employing five-digit or regional concentration ratios when the four-digit national industry is defined too broadly.[61] We shall have more to say on this in Chapter 9.

Another problem encountered in statistical work is a divergence in the degree of industry detail for which different variables are available. Concentration ratios are generally published at the four- and five-digit levels, while, for instance, profit and advertising data may be available only for three-digit groups and research and development expenditures data only at the two-digit level. A standard practice in such cases is to compute weighted average concentration ratios for the broader groups, weighting each appropriately defined narrow industry's concentration index by employment or sales in that industry. We shall encounter this convention frequently in subsequent chapters.

The overall extent of market concentration in the American economy Forewarned and forearmed, we turn to the task of assessing how concentrated markets are in the American economy. For many sectors, we can do no more than hazard impressionistic guesses, since adequate quantitative data are totally lacking. Perspective on the relative sizes of the various sectors is provided by the 1972 gross national product share figures given in the second numerical column of Table 3.1.

In the agriculture, forestry, and fisheries sectors, industry structures are overwhelmingly atomistic. However, competition is moderated by a heavy overlay of government price supports, marketing orders, acreage restrictions, and other interventions. Also, in logging, the cost of transporting trees to sawmills or pulp mills is so high that there are few mills purchasing timber in any given forest area. Thus, the structure is characterized by oligopsony (few buyers).[62]

Mining presents a mixed picture. Some mining industries, such as limestone and common sand and gravel, are atomistic nationally, although product values are sufficiently low in relation to transportation cost that oligopoly prevails in appropriately defined regional and local markets. Others, such as copper, iron ore, uranium, lead, zinc, sulphur, gold, and phosphate are moderately to highly concentrated even at the national level. For the higher-value minerals, imports could be a significant check on monopoly power, but for many of the rarer minerals (such as chromium, molybdenum, nickel, and diamonds) concentration is also high in world markets, and international cartels are not uncommon. Crude oil production in the United States is loosely oligopolistic, with the four leading producers originating 34 percent of domestic output in 1973. However, interpretation of concentration ratios is complicated by the existence of many joint ventures among the leading petroleum firms. Also, since 1973 the price of crude oil in the United States and most other industrialized nations has been determined, except to the extent that government controls have been imposed, by the cost of supplementing limited domestic reserves through importation from the OPEC (Organization of Petroleum Exporting Countries) cartel. In that sense, price setting for petroleum is subject to substantial monopoly power. The four leading soft coal mining firms accounted for 30 percent of U.S. production in 1972, and the eight leaders accounted for 40 percent. Higher concentration ratios prevail in specific coal mining regions, but with coal prices pulled up by cartel-dominated oil prices and with pollution laws encouraging long-distance shipment of low-sulphur western United States coal, markets became increasingly nationwide in scope during the 1970s. Thus, loose oligopoly is probably the best characterization of the coal industry's structure. Working with limited evidence, Kaysen and Turner estimated that roughly two-thirds of all value added in mining originated from atomistically structured industries and one-third from oligopolistic industries.[63] This judgment probably errs on the low side, since both coal and petroleum were viewed as atomistic.

Contract construction is characterized by large numbers of small firms and can be termed generally competitive in structure, despite pockets of localized oligopoly.

Competition in the transportation, communications, and electrical and gas utilities sectors is controlled and restrained by formal public regulation. Peering behind the regulatory veil, one would find that oligopoly is the predominant market structure in railroading, air transport, intercity bus lines, parts of water transportation, and highway freight carriage between less densely travelled points, while large numbers of sellers operate on the high-volume trucking routes and in inland water transportation. Intermodal competition is strong and would be even more vigorous in the absence of regulation. In telephone communications and the electricity and gas distribution industries, natural monopoly is the rule. Radio communication is best described as monopolistically competitive except in isolated low population areas, while television broadcasting is oligopolistic. The growth of cable tele-

61. For methodological guidance, see George J. Stigler, *Capital and Rates of Return in Manufacturing Industries* (Princeton: Princeton University Press, 1963), pp. 206–11; Leonard Weiss, "Average Concentration Ratios and Industrial Performance," *Journal of Industrial Economics* 11 (July 1963): 237–54; and Carl Kaysen and Donald F. Turner, *Antitrust Policy* (Cambridge, Mass.: Harvard University Press, 1959), pp. 295–99. Weighted average regional and local concentration ratios for U.S. manufacturing industries in 1963 are presented in David Schwartzman and Joan Bodoff, "Concentration in Regional and Local Industries," *Southern Economic Journal* 37 (January 1971): 343–48. A complete set of subjectively adjusted manufacturing industry concentration ratios for 1966, with the benefit of the doubt resolved almost uniformly on the side of making upward adjustments, can be found in William G. Shepherd, *Market Power and Economic Welfare* (New York: Random House, 1970), pp. 263–67.

62. See Walter J. Mead, *Competition and Oligopsony in the Douglas Fir Lumber Industry* (Berkeley: University of California Press, 1966).

63. Kaysen and Turner, *Antitrust Policy*, pp. 37–39, 286–88. Unfortunately, the U.S. *Census of Mineral Industries* normally publishes only concentration data for individual establishments (i.e., mines) and not for firms, some of which operate multiple mines.

vision systems will make it possible to have sufficient channels for a monopolistically competitive broadcasting structure, but installation and operation of the cables tends toward single-firm monopoly or very tight oligopoly.

Wholesale and retail trade are more difficult to categorize. In metropolitan areas of substantial size (i.e., with population exceeding 100,000), market structures are characteristically atomistic or very loosely oligopolistic. Despite the rise of the chain store, single-unit ventures continue to thrive. Some 1.6 million single-unit retailing firms accounted for 53 percent of all U.S. retail sales in 1972. Chains with 101 or more units made 25 percent of total 1972 sales—an increase from 12 percent in 1948 and 16 percent in 1963.[64] In food retailing, where chain-store operation has had a particularly long history, oligopoly is prevalent in metropolitan area markets. Among 263 U.S. metropolitan areas, four-firm concentration ratios in grocery retailing for 1972 ranged from 26 (for Charleston, South Carolina) to 81 (for Cedar Rapids, Iowa), with a median value of 52.[65] Elements of spatial and subjective product differentiation often fragment metropolitan area retail markets into smaller segments. The urban consumer without an automobile may find it necessary to pay appreciable taxi fares or shop for groceries in a smaller, relatively high-priced neighborhood store. And there are few stores where one can find freshly made German bratwurst, a good-quality violin, or a serious book on some arcane subject such as the economics of industrial market structure. If a simple verdict must be rendered, however, it would be that high concentration is more the exception than the rule in retailing.

The pattern in banking is one of loose oligopoly in nationwide credit markets and large cities, with very tight oligopoly or even monopoly confronting individuals in smaller cities and towns. Competition in banking is regulated, as it is also in the insurance industries of many states, which exhibit high to moderate concentration in the health and life insurance fields and low concentration in other fields. The real estate brokerage trades are atomistically structured except in very small towns.

The service industries, including hotels and motels, laundry services, funeral parlors, barber and beauty shops, repair services, pest control firms, legal and medical services, and the like tend toward large numbers of sellers except in small towns.[66] Nevertheless, the amount of monopoly power present is much greater than a superficial analysis of market structure implies. This is so in part because of very strong product differentiation and in some fields (such as medicine and surveying) cartel-like restrictions on new entry. The extensive repair service trades pose special problems: Once the customer has left his amplifier or automobile or watch with a particular shop, a bilateral monopoly condition exists, and the customer typically lacks bargaining power because of his technical ignorance. Also included in the services sector are the various amusement and recreational industries, where concentration is high except in the largest cities.

The government sector, accounting for 13 percent of gross national product in 1972 (including only activities directly carried out by government bodies, not work contracted for by private industry) is much too complex for any blanket statement. Many government services (such as law enforcement and defense) are provided outside the market framework, and it makes little sense to discuss them in terms of a competition-monopoly structural spectrum. In other areas, such as the Postal Service, the Government Printing Office, the Navy's shipyards, and the vast array of schools, government activities coexist with more or less parallel private functions.

The manufacturing sector has been reserved for more thorough analysis in the next section, but one preliminary note is appropriate. During the mid-1970s, the federal government was spending approximately $26 billion annually for the development and production of advanced weapon systems, space vehicles, and other technologically sophisticated military and civilian equipment. Because of the technological uncertainties, complexity, and unique applications associated with these defense and space projects, administrative supervision and controls were substituted for the price system as a directing mechanism. It should be recognized therefore that between 4 and 6 percent of all manufacturing sector activity, spread over numerous four-digit industries, occurred outside the market system. These nonmarket operations pose fascinating analytic problems that we will not be able to examine in the present volume.[67]

It is futile to attempt a quantitative summary of how much structural monopoly power exists in the whole of the American economy. Suffice it to say that there is a modest amount of activity (not more than 5 or 6 percent of gross national product) approaching pure monopoly, most of which is subject to government regulation or control, somewhat more activity approximating pure competition, and liberal quantities of oligopoly and monopolistic competition.[68]

Manufacturing industry concentration levels and trends

Manufacturing is the largest single sector in the U.S. economy. It is also the only sector for which comprehensive data on industry concentration exist, permitting detailed structural analyses.

Although it is possible to find examples for very narrowly defined chemical, drug, and other product categories, monopoly in the sense of a single seller is virtually nonexistent in nationwide U.S. manufacturing industries of appreciable size.[69] The principal instances of companies that in recent years have maintained positions even approaching monopoly for any significant length of time are Western Electric (with about 85 percent of the domestic telephone equipment market); General Motors (with a diesel locomotive market share averaging 77 percent between 1956 and 1971); IBM (whose general-purpose digital computer systems market share ranged between 72 and 82 percent during the 1960s and early 1970s); Eastman Kodak (with about 90 percent of domestic amateur film production and roughly 65 percent of all film sales, including instant photo packs); Dow Chemical (with 90 percent of U.S. magnesium production until new entry took place in 1969); Xerox (with 75 to 80 percent of electrostatic copier revenues during the 1960s, declining to 55 percent by 1978 after key patents expired); and Campbell (with approximately 85 percent of canned soup sales, ignoring such substitutes as dehydrated soups and the homemade alternative).

Oligopoly, on the other hand, is abundant. Table 3.6 shows the distribution of 449 four-digit manufacturing industries in 1977 by four-firm sales concentration ranges. When the leading four firms control 40 percent or more of the total market, it is fair to assume that oligopoly is beginning to rear its head. Inspection shows that 199 industries, comprising 44 percent of all industries by number and also in terms of value added, had four-firm concentration ratios of at least this magnitude. Given the tendency for four-firm census industry definitions to be somewhat too broad on the average, these figures suggest that something in excess of half of all American manufacturing industry can be categorized as oligopolistic.

Has this always been the case? And is there an observable trend toward increasing or decreasing concentration? Very long-run analyses plunge us into the realm of incommensurables. During the first half of the 19th century, nationwide concentration of manufactured goods output was undoubtedly much lower than it is now.

64. U.S., Bureau of the Census, "Summary and Subject Statistics," *1972 Census of Retail Trade*, vol. 1, sec. 1 (Washington, D.C.: Government Printing Office, 1976).

65. See Bruce W. Marion, Willard F. Mueller et al., *The Profit and Price Performance of Leading Food Chains, 1970–74*, U.S., Congress, Joint Economic Committee, 91st Cong., 1st sess., 1977, pp. 126–32.

66. See U.S., Bureau of the Census, *1972 Census of Selected Services*, vol. 1, "Summary and Subject Statistics" (Washington, D.C.: Government Printing Office, 1976).

67. But see M. J. Peck and F. M. Scherer, *The Weapons Acquisition Process: An Economic Analysis* (Boston: Harvard Business School Division of Research, 1962); and F. M. Scherer, *The Weapons Acquisition Process: Economic Incentives* (Boston: Harvard Business School Division of Research, 1964).

68. For other views on the overall incidence of competition and monopoly in the U.S. economy, see Kaysen and Turner, *Antitrust Policy*, pp. 26–43; George J. Stigler, *Five Lectures on Economic Problems* (London: Longman, Green, 1949), pp. 46–62; Clair Wilcox, "On the Alleged Ubiquity of Oligopoly," *American Economic Review* 40 (May 1950): 67–73; and Shepherd, *Market Power and Economic Welfare*, Chapters 5–10 and Appendix Table 14.

69. A study of 314 four-digit manufacturing industries revealed the average estimated leading firm market share to be 17.5 percent, with a range from 68.7 to 1.1 percent. The average market shares for the second, third, and fourth sellers were 10.0, 7.0, and 5.3 percent respectively. John E. Kwoka, Jr. "The Diversity of Firm Size Distributions in Manufacturing Industries," forthcoming in *Industrial Organization Review*, 1979.

But markets were predominantly local then. The railroads had not been built on any significant scale; wagon roads were primitive; and the waterways system was circuitous, slow, and blocked in winter. As a result, competitive contact among geographically scattered manufacturers was modest, and the amount of monopoly power they possessed must have been high. As the railroads expanded their coverage from 9,000 miles of road operated in 1850 to 167,000 miles in 1890, and as the spread of telegraph and then telephone service greatly facilitated communications, something resembling a true national market emerged for the first time.[70] Firms interpenetrated each others' former home territories and competition flourished. Indeed, if we could measure monopoly power in manufacturing directly, we might well find it to have been at an all-time low between 1870 and 1890, for there was a sharp increase in concentration following 1880. This was attributable to the rapid internal growth of those enterprises that proved themselves fit for the competitive struggle, and even more to an enormous number of mergers among previously independent firms. We shall discuss this merger movement more fully in the next chapter. The main point for present purposes is that it ran its course shortly after the turn of the century, so that the economy of 1904 was structurally quite different from the economy of 1830 or 1870. Whether there was more or less monopoly power in 1904 than in 1830 no one can say with confidence, because the whole economic environment had been transformed so radically.[71]

The gap between 1904 and the present can be bridged in less vague terms, thanks to the painstaking labors of G. Warren Nutter.[72] Utilizing numerous published sources and a good deal of guesswork, Nutter estimated that 32.9 percent of all national income originating in the manufacturing sector came from industries in which the four largest enterprises accounted for 50 percent or more of output at one time or another between 1895 and 1904.[73]

Similar figures can be derived from the various post-World War II censuses of manufactures. The proportions of manufacturing value added originating in industries with four-firm sales concentration ratios of 50 or higher were as follows:[74]

1947	24.4 percent
1954	29.9 percent
1958	30.2 percent
1963	33.1 percent
1972	29.0 percent
1977	26.8 percent

Were it not for Nutter's original benchmark, one might be inclined to infer that a strong upward trend was operating, at least up to 1963. But since the 1963 high-water mark barely exceeded Nutter's concentration estimate for 1895–1904, it seems more reasonable to assume that some sort of cyclical movement occurred, with industry concentration falling to unusually low levels during the sellers' market immediately following

---

T 3.6 Distribution of manufacturing industries by four-firm sales concentration ratios, 1977

Four-firm concentration ratio range	Number of industries	Percentage of all industries	Percentage of total value added
0–19	87	19.4	22.8
20–39	163	36.3	33.2
40–59	125	27.8	24.9
60–79	49	10.9	12.4
80–100	25	5.6	6.6

Adapted from U.S., Bureau of the Census, *1971 Census of Manufactures*, "Concentration Ratios in Manufacturing," MC77(SR)-9 (Washington, D.C.: Government Printing Office, 1981).

World War II—a pattern analogous to the one observed for aggregate concentration.

Further analysis discloses that much of the postwar increase was the result of events in a few of the largest industries. Thus, about half the gain from 1947 to 1954 was due to a recorded rise in the steel industry's four-firm concentration ratio from 45 to 54, nudging steel into the "concentrated" group. A modification in Census Bureau classification assumptions was partly responsible for this change. The relative stability from 1954 to 1958 is explained in part by two offsetting sets of influences. The recession of 1958 significantly reduced the value added shares of large, concentrated industries like automobiles and steel. But the aircraft industry, which had expanded its value added share from 0.8 percent in 1947 to 2.4 percent in 1958 as a result of booming Cold War defense contracts, reentered the concentrated group when its four-firm ratio rose from 47 to 59. Then, of the 3 percentage point increase between 1958 and 1963, 2 points can be traced to the boom experienced by the automobile industry in 1963, although this gain was partly offset by a 0.5 percentage point decline in the aircraft industry's value added contribution. Of the 6.3 point decline from 1963 to 1977, 4.2 points came from decreases in steel and computing equipment industry ratios to 45 and 44 percent respectively.[75]

From these few observations it should be clear that the Nutter approach to identifying trends in concentration is quite sensitive to relatively small concentration changes in key oligopolistic industries. An alternative view of the post-World War II experience is obtained by computing weighted average concentration ratios for all manufacturing industry, letting each individual industry's four-firm ratio be weighted by the value added originating in that industry.[76] The resulting concentration indices are as follows:

1947	35.3
1954	36.9
1958	37.0
1963	38.9
1972	39.2
1977	38.5

This approach suggests a much more modest rise in concentration on the average between 1947 and 1963, with a weak reversal of the trend by 1977.

Additional insight is provided by an analysis of 154 four-digit industries whose definitions re-

70. For a more skeptical view of the railroads' impact, see Robert W. Fogel, *Railroads and American Economic Growth: Essays in Econometric History* (Baltimore: Johns Hopkins, 1964).

71. Another broader development deserves mention. Manufacturing has always been more concentrated than farming. From 1840 to 1900, value added in the farming sector fell from about 70 percent of total agriculture, mining, manufacturing, and construction output to roughly 33 percent, and since then it has fallen further to 9 percent in 1975. This represents a long-run structural shift away from more competitively structured economic activity. For the early figures, see U.S., Bureau of the Census, *Historical Statistics of the United States, Colonial Times to 1957* (Washington, D.C.: Government Printing Office, 1960), p. 139.

72. G. Warren Nutter, *The Extent of Enterprise Monopoly in the United States: 1899–1939* (Chicago: University of Chicago Press, 1951), especially pp. 35–48, 112–50. Nutter's aim was to determine whether the amount of monopoly in the *overall* economy was increasing. He concluded that it might or might not be, depending upon the quantitative assumptions taken. See also H. A. Einhorn, "Competition in American Industry, 1939–58," *Journal of Political Economy* 74 (October 1966): 506–11.

73. Nutter, *The Extent of Enterprise Monopoly*, p. 147. Note that one is likely to find more industries with a four-firm concentration ratio exceeding 50 at some time during a ten-year period than in any single year. But there are so many other possibilities for error in a reconstruction job as difficult as Nutter's that it makes little sense to dwell heavily on this particular bias. See, for example, the comment by Stanley Lebergott and the rejoinder by Nutter in the *Review of Economics and Statistics* 35 (November 1953): 349–53.

74. Industries in the ordnance group (formerly set aside under S.I.C. 19) were excluded from both numerator and denominator of the 1947–63 calculations, since no concentration data were published for them. Data did become available for 1972, but six such industries (five of them above the 50 percent threshold) were excluded to maintain consistency.

75. The basic four-digit steel industry was subjected to further redefinitions over time, and the Census Bureau has recomputed old concentration ratios for the new definitions, so the ratio given for 1963 in the 1972 tabulation is 48, not 50, as drawn from the 1963 tabulation and utilized here.

76. The 1947, 1954, and 1958 figures are drawn from a table presented by Professor Adelman in the Senate Antitrust and Monopoly Subcommittee hearings, *Economic Concentration*, Part 1, 89th Cong., 1st sess., p. 355. Since the calculations for earlier years were based upon all available information, six ordnance industries whose concentration ratios were first published for 1972 were included in the 1972 weighted average. If they are excluded, the average falls to 38.9, showing no change from 1963. Because the Census industry classification was somewhat more finely subdivided in 1972—i.e., with 444 nonordnance industries on which useable data were published, as compared to 417 in 1963—average indicated concentration would probably have fallen slightly in the absence of classification changes. For 1977, there are 449 industries, including the six ordnance segments.

mained sufficiently constant to permit a comparison over a period extending from the 1947 census to the 1972 census.[77] The sample in Table 3.7 covers 34 percent of all manufacturing industries by number as of 1972 and 32 percent of 1972 manufacturing value added. However, it is not perfectly representative, since the industries not redefined were generally less dynamic technologically than those requiring redefinition. Four different average four-firm sales concentration ratios were computed for each year. All four series exhibit a rise in average concentration between 1947 and 1972. The indicated increase is greater when industry ratios are weighted by own-year value added (+2.2) than for unweighted indices (+1.8), suggesting that the rise in concentration was associated more with the larger industries. Most of the weighted average change took place by 1954. When constant base-year value added weights are employed, the 25-year increase is found to be much smaller: 0.7 points with 1947 weights and 0.5 points for 1972 weights. This reveals that most of the weighted average concentration increase stemmed from relatively more rapid growth of the more highly concentrated industries.

If attention is shifted to the shorter 1963–72 interval, over which fewer industry definition changes occurred, comparisons can be made for a total of 323 industries. The simple average concentration index rose by 0.9 points from 39.4 to 40.3. However, the own-year value added weighted index moved only from 37.6 to 37.7. The indicated changes were no larger in indices weighted consistently with either 1963 or 1972 value added magnitudes.

To sum up, average industry concentration levels in U.S. manufacturing apparently increased quite modestly during the quarter century following World War II. Less solid evidence suggests that the increase was slight even when compared to the levels prevailing at the turn of the century. As Professor Adelman concluded in an earlier study of concentration trends, "Any tendency either way, if it does exist, must be at the pace of a glacial drift."[78]

Comparisons with other nations Let us broaden our perspective. Three questions concerning the structure of industry in other nations are of special interest. Are there consistent patterns in the degree of concentration observed in similar industries for other nations? Is concentration higher or lower on average in manufacturing industries outside the United States? And are there discernible trends in market concentration overseas?

Because there are substantial differences among nations in industrial classification systems and in the extent to which data are reported for the more finely subdivided classes, formidable problems are encountered in making the inter-

---

T 3.7 Concentration changes under alternate weighting schemes

	1947	1954	1963	1972
Simple (unweighted) average	39.7%	39.5%	40.7%	41.5%
Average (own-year's value added weights)	36.3	38.1	37.8	38.5
Average (1947 value added weights)	36.3	36.6	36.4	37.0
Average (1972 value added weights)	38.0	38.1	37.9	38.5

Adapted from U.S., Bureau of the Census, *1972 Census of Manufactures*, "Concentration Ratios in Manufacturing," MC72(SR)–2 (Washington, D.C.: Government Printing Office, 1975).

national comparisons needed to answer the first two questions.[79] Inevitably, many industries must be excluded as noncomparable. Even when one attempts to analyze only comparably defined industries, there are pitfalls. For example, it is hardly obvious from inspection that the British industry, "aluminium and aluminium alloys and manufactures thereof" covered almost solely fabrication activity up to 1970, since until then Britain had only one primary aluminum smelter, which could supply less than 10 percent of domestic ingot demands, the balance being imported. Without such knowledge, one can only be puzzled at the five-firm concentration ratio of 51 for the British industry in 1968 when the aluminum industries of most other major nations are found to be highly concentrated.

Such comparability problems were minimized in a study of 12 industries across six nations done by the author and several colleagues. The usual national census and trade publication sources were supplemented by some 125 company interviews in the six nations. The standardized three-firm national concentration ratios compiled in this way are arrayed in Table 3.8. A considerable amount of variation among nations is apparent, but one can also see that certain industries—e.g., cigarettes, bottles, refrigerators, and batteries—tend to be relatively highly concentrated in every nation, while others, such as weaving, paints, and shoes, tend to be relatively unconcentrated. This qualitative impression is verified quantitatively by correlating the concentration ratios for each nation pair. Using international automobile identification letters to designate the nations, the relevant matrix of intercorrelations is as follows:

	USA	CAN	GB	S	F	D
USA	1.00	.73	.48	.44	.75	.77
CAN		1.00	.59	.50	.76	.62
GB			1.00	.90	.77	.79
S				1.00	.62	.73
F					1.00	.81
D						1.00

All the off-diagonal correlation coefficients are positive, and 12 of the 15 are statistically significant at the 95 percent confidence level or better. Thus, if concentration in some industry is relatively high in one nation, it tends also to be relatively high for the same industry in other nations. The proportion of variance in sets of concentration ratios explained by another nation's ratios (i.e., the square of the correlation coefficient) ranges from 19 to 81 percent.

A danger in any such study is that the small industry sample may not be representative. Indeed, the present sample clearly is not in at least one respect: The leading U.S. companies in the industries selected tended to operate more plants each than the comparable average for all American manufacturing industries. However, there is reason to believe that the observed international concentration ratio correlations are not atypical. Professor Frederic Pryor carried out similar correlation analyses covering larger samples of industries for the six nations in Table 3.8 and six others. A comparison of his U.S.-other nation correlation coefficients is presented in Table 3.9, with the size of Pryor's sample given in subscripted parentheses. Except for Sweden, the values are extremely close. Similarly, the correlation between sets of four-firm sales concentration ratios for 73 carefully matched U.S. industries (for 1966) and Canadian industries (for 1965) was 0.79—quite close to the values for Pryor's smaller sample and the author's 12-industry sample.[80]

77. Excluded from the analysis were four industries with missing concentration ratios for some years and eight "not elsewhere classified" industries with continuous coverage of at least the 1963–72 interval, along with 284 industries whose definitions changed significantly. For a similar analysis of 166 industries reaching generally similar findings, see Willard F. Mueller and Larry G. Hamm, "Trends in Industrial Concentration, 1947 to 1970," *Review of Economics and Statistics* 56 (November 1974): 511–13.

78. Adelman, "The Measurement of Industrial Concentration," pp. 295–96.

79. Beginning in 1963, the European Common Market Commission began collecting concentration data for standardized market definitions. However, those data have another very serious deficiency. All the sales or employment of a reporting enterprise are lumped together in the enterprise's "primary" industry, and as a result large amounts of irrelevant or "contaminating" activity are included in the figures for industries to which highly diversified firms have been assigned. The U.S. Census avoids this problem by collecting data on an individual plant basis. See also note 54 *supra*.

80. The data are from *Concentration in the Manufacturing Industries of Canada*, Table A-13. Industries with missing four-firm concentration ratios or ratios with more than a 10-point range of uncertainty were excluded. Where ranges were published in the table, the midpoint was entered into the correlation analysis.

T 3.8 Three-firm concentration ratios for twelve identically defined industries in six nations, 1970

Industry	United States	Canada	United Kingdom	Sweden	France	West Germany
Brewing	39	89	47	70	63	17
Cigarettes	68	90	94	100	100	94
Fabric weaving	30	67	28	50	23	16
Paints	26	40	40	92	14	32
Petroleum refining	25	64	79	100	60	47
Shoes (except rubber)	17	18	17	37	13	20
Glass bottles	65	100	73	100	84	93
Cement	20	65	86	100	81	54
Ordinary steel	42	80	39*	63	84	56
Antifriction bearings	43	89	82	100	80	90
Refrigerators	64	75	65	89	100	72
Storage batteries	54	73	75	100	94	82
Simple average	41	71	60	83	66	56

*Prenationalization value

Source: F. M. Scherer, Alan Beckenstein, Erich Kaufer, and R. D. Murphy, *The Economics of Multi-Plant Operation: An International Comparisons Study* (Cambridge, Mass.: Harvard University Press, 1975), pp. 218–19, 426–28. Reprinted by permission of Harvard University Press. Copyright © 1975 by the President and Fellows of Harvard College.

Other analyses of this genre all point to the same conclusion:[81] Sufficient similarity in concentration patterns exists among nations to suspect that some common cluster of concentration-determining forces is at work. We shall take up the search for those common elements in Chapter 4.

T 3.9 Comparison of Pryor's international concentration correlations with those for a smaller sample

	Pryor	Table 3.8 sample
Canada	.77$_{(37)}$	.73
Great Britain	.51$_{(72)}$	.48
Sweden	.68$_{(74)}$	.44
France	.74$_{(47)}$	.75
West Germany	.73$_{(67)}$	.77

Source: Frederic L. Pryor, "An International Comparison of Concentration Ratios," *Review of Economics and Statistics* 54 (May 1972): 136.

Table 3.8 shows a considerably lower *average* level of industry concentration in the United States than in the five other nations. How representative these results are is open to some doubt. It appears established beyond question that in small industrialized nations like Sweden (with a 1975 population of 8.3 million), Canada, Belgium, and Switzerland, industry concentration levels are distinctly higher on average than in large nations like the United States, Germany, and Japan.[82] Frequently, the markets of small nations are simply too small to accommodate many viable competitors. Whether this inverse nation size-concentration relationship persists all the way out to a nation the size of the United States, the largest capitalist industrial country, is less certain. The weight of the evidence from several comparisons between the United Kingdom and the United States supports a conclusion that U.K. industries are on average more concentrated.[83] Pryor's study shows a slightly lower average level of concentration in West Germany and France than in the United States during the early 1960s, but there is conflicting evidence too, and the data comparability problems are sufficiently acute that an open verdict must be returned.[84] For Japan, the most comprehensive set of data suggests marginally lower average concentration than in the United States, but it is unclear whether taking into account Zaibatsu successors' intercorporate ties would alter the picture.[85]

Much more confident conclusions can be reached on concentration *trends* within nations. Since the 1950s the United Kingdom, West Germany, Sweden, and France, unlike the United States, all experienced substantial upward trends in average manufacturing industry concentration levels.[86] Kenneth George's study of 157 U.K. product lines whose definitions remained constant reveals a 10 percentage point average increase in five-firm sales concentration ratios between 1958 and 1968. However, the formation and extension of the European Common Market poses problems for the interpretation of such national industry trends similar to those engendered by the spread of American railroads and communication systems in the 19th century. In Canada, there was apparently an upsurge during the 1950s followed, as in the United States, by a decade with little or no clear concentration trend.[87] The best evidence for Japan suggests declining average concentration from 1937 into the 1960s, with a reversal in the trend since then.[88] The historical record among nations is clearly not uniform. Why concentration trends might differ among industries and nations is a question we will return to in Chapter 4.

The stability of leading positions The concentration ratio is a static index, characterizing market structure for a single typically short interval in time. We should not be surprised that the identity of the leading sellers in an industry changes occasionally. When turnover among the top firms is rapid, high concentration ratios may conceal or belie the intensity of competition for two reasons. First, the shares of industry leaders, and hence the concentration ratio, will be lower when computed on, say, a five-year basis than the shares of leaders identified for any shorter interval, since momentary leaders will tend to be firms enjoying market shares exceeding long-run average values. Second, the very rapidity of turn-

81. See, for example, Gideon Rosenbluth, *Concentration in Canadian Manufacturing Industries* (Princeton: Princeton University Press, 1957), pp. 89–92; Kenneth D. George and T. S. Ward, *The Structure of Industry in the EEC* (Cambridge, England: Cambridge University Press, 1975), pp. 15–21; Caves and Uekusa, *Industrial Organization in Japan*, pp. 23–24; and Ira Horowitz, "Employment Concentration in the Common Market: An Entropy Approach," *Journal of the Royal Statistical Society*, Series A, vol. 133, part 3 (1970): 475–78.

82. See Pryor, "An International Comparison," pp. 133–34; *Concentration in the Manufacturing Industries of Canada*, pp. 49–50; Rosenbluth, *Concentration in Canadian Manufacturing Industries*, pp. 75–87; and Jacquemin and de Jong, *European Industrial Organisation*, p. 59.

83. See P. Sargant Florence, *The Logic of British and American Industry* (London: Routledge and Kegan Paul, 1953), pp. 130–35; B. Peter Pashigian, "Market Concentration in the United States and Great Britain," *Journal of Law and Economics* 11 (October 1968): 299–319; and Malcolm C. Sawyer, "Concentration in British Manufacturing Industry," *Oxford Economic Papers* 23 n.s. (November 1971): 371–74. Compare W. G. Shepherd, "Structure and Behavior in British Industries, with U.S. Comparisons," *Journal of Industrial Economics* 21 (November 1972): 40–44, who subjectively adjusted both U.S. and U.K. concentration ratios to allow for regional markets, excessively broad industry definitions, and the like and found the adjusted U.S. ratios to be higher on average.

84. Pryor, "An International Comparison," pp. 133–34. See also George and Ward, *The Structure of Industry in the EEC*, p. 17, who conclude from an analysis of questionable data on 41 industries that average 1963 concentration was substantially higher in the U.K. than in West Germany and France. Compare Frederic Jenny and André-Paul Weber, "The Determinants of Concentration Trends in the French Manufacturing Sector," *Journal of Industrial Economics* 26 (March 1978): 193–96, revealing "strikingly close" average concentration levels in France and the United States.

85. Caves and Uekusa, *Industrial Organization in Japan*, pp. 19–26.

86. See Kenneth D. George, "A Note on Changes in Industrial Concentration in the United Kingdom," *Economic Journal* 85 (March 1975): 124–28; Prais, *The Evolution of Giant Firms in Britain*, pp. 16–20; Sawyer, "Concentration in British Manufacturing Industry," pp. 352–57; Jacquemin and de Jong, *European Industrial Organisation*, pp. 55–58; Müller and Hochreiter, *Stand und Entwicklungstendenzen der Unternehmenskonzentration in der Bundesrepublik*, Chapter 4; Monopolkommission, *Mehr Wettbewerb Ist Möglich* (Baden Baden: Nomos, 1976), especially pp. 638–47; Statens Pris och Kartellnämnd, *Storföretag och Koncentrationstendenser* (Stockholm: 1971); and Jenny and Weber, "The Determinants of Concentration Trends," pp. 194–96. For Holland, the only known study suggests no upward trend. H. Booij and W. Pelupessy, "De Ontwikkeling van de Concentratie in de Nederlandse Nijverheid in de Periode 1930–1963," *De Economist* 119 (March-April 1971): 137–64. Similarly, for Yugoslavia, see Stephen R. Sacks, "Changes in Industrial Structure in Yugoslavia, 1959–1968," *Journal of Political Economy* 80 (May/June 1972): 561–74.

87. See *Concentration in the Manufacturing Industries of Canada*, pp. 43–44; and *Report of the Royal Commission on Corporate Concentration*, pp. 34–37.

88. Caves and Uekusa, *Industrial Organization in Japan*, pp. 26–28.

over suggests a competitive struggle for position. High turnover is said by some economists to be an indicator of dynamic competition, which may be present even when concentration ratios imply the absence of much competition in a static structural sense.[89]

A first look at the available statistics on leading firm turnover lends some support to the claim that dynamic competition is vigorous. One early study of 262 product lines revealed that all four sales leaders of 1935 maintained their leadership positions during 1937 in only 19 percent of the fields covered. In 40 percent of the product lines, two or more of the 1935 leaders were replaced by other firms in 1937, and in 13 percent, three or more of the 1935 leaders had been displaced.[90] An analysis of more recent data covering 204 four-digit industries yields the same magic number 19 as the percentage of all cases in which the four industry leaders of 1947 continued to be the leaders during 1958. In only 6 percent of the 204 cases did the rank order of the four enterprises leading their industries in 1947 remain identical in 1958.[91]

However, these statistics may be misleading. Most of the market share changes causing some firms to drop out of the top four and others to enter are small. If, for instance, the firms ranked third and fourth in an industry at some moment in time have market shares of 7.0 and 5.3 percent, while the firms ranked fifth and sixth have shares of 4.2 and 3.4 percent,[92] it does not take a shakeup of dramatic proportions to displace the third and fourth ranked firms. And most market shares, Michael Gort found in an analysis spanning the years 1947 through 1954, do not change drastically over such a seven-year interval.[93] He obtained confidential census data on the market shares of all firms among the 15 sales leaders in 205 four-digit industries in 1947, 1954, or both. He then correlated, industry by industry, the market shares of those firms in 1954 with their 1947 market shares. In 74 percent of the 205 cases, the intertemporal correlation coefficient was 0.80 or higher. In only 10 percent was the correlation coefficient less than 0.50. Thus, if a firm's market share was low relative to the pack in 1947, it was likely to be low also in 1954; if it was high in 1947, it was likely to remain high in 1954.

Moreover, there is evidence that stability of market positions and concentration in the static sense are positively associated. The correlation between the intertemporal correlation coefficients (serving as an index of relative stability) and 1947 four-firm concentration ratios for the 205 industries in Gort's sample was 0.52.[94] In another study, L. E. Preston found that industries with no change in the identity of their leading firms between 1947 and 1958 were on the average more concentrated than the industries in which at least one company was displaced.[95] These results might have a trivial statistical explanation—e.g., because there is greater inequality of market shares in more concentrated industries, so that larger absolute and relative deviations are needed to effect a change in rank. However, in an analysis that controlled for concentration class biases and a large number of other variables, Caves and Porter found that annual relative (i.e., percentage) changes in sellers' market shares tended to fall with rising concentration.[96]

It is also possible that high market share instability—to some economists a manifestation of competitive vigor—has the paradoxical long-run effect of increasing the level of static concentration. We shall examine this hypothesis in the next chapter.

The diversification of American corporations

Product line diversification is interesting for several reasons: as an increasingly prominent structural attribute; as a condition that might affect firms' pricing behavior (explored in Chapter 12) and research and development decisions (Chapter 15); as a potential focus of the government's antimerger policy (Chapter 20); and as a possible cause of the largest corporations' increasing share of all manufacturing activity.

Although reliable information on individual company structure is difficult to obtain, there have been many attempts to assess the extent and pattern of diversification among large manufacturing enterprises.[97] A possibly incomplete count of the three-digit industries occupied by corporations on *Fortune*'s industrials list for 1974 showed General Electric to be the most diversified, with identifiable operations in 32 three-digit manufacturing and mining industries (out of a maximum possible 163). Runners-up were International Telephone and Telegraph (ITT) (31), Gulf and Western Industries (27), Litton Industries (founded only in 1953) (26), and Textron (25). As one might expect, the largest industrial corporations tend to be more diversified than their smaller counterparts. This is seen *inter alia* by examining the number of three-digit manufacturing and mining industries covered by the 100 largest industrial corporations alongside the corporations ranked 501 to 600 on *Fortune*'s 1974 list (Table 3.10). None of the corporations ranked 501 to 600 was found to operate in more than ten three-digit industries, whereas a third of the largest 100 had attained at least that level of diversification.

Merely counting product lines exaggerates in some respects the overall significance of diversification, since most firms' product volume distributions are highly skewed, with a few product lines accounting for the bulk of sales or employment while numerous other lines are relatively small. However, company activities outside primary product lines are far from inconsequential. Under its *Enterprise Statistics* program, the U.S. Census Bureau assigns each reporting company to that single category among 207 different manufacturing, mining, construction, trade, and service industry categories in which the firm has its largest sales volume—that is, to its primary industry. It then splits the company's operating establishment (i.e., plant, mine, or store) employment into two classes: establishments specializing in the primary industry and those specializing in

---

T 3.10 Comparative diversification of large and medium-sized industrial corporations

Number of three-digit industries	Number of corporations in grouping	
	Corporations 1–100	Corporations 501–600
1–3	10	64
4–6	17	24
7–10	40	7
11–15	18	0
16–20	7	0
21–25	4	0
26 or more	4	0
Total	100	95*

*Comparable information was available on only 95 of corporations 501–600.
Source: F. M. Scherer, "Segmental Financial Reporting: Needs and Tradeoffs," in Harvey Goldschmid, ed., *Business Disclosure: Government's Need to Know* (New York: McGraw-Hill, 1979), p. 17.

89. For reviews of the various hypotheses, see Jonathan D. Ogur, Federal Trade Commission staff report, *Competition and Market Share Instability*, (Washington, D.C.: Government Printing Office, 1976); and Richard E. Caves and Michael E. Porter, "Market Structure, Oligopoly, and Stability of Market Shares," *Journal of Industrial Economics* 26 (June 1978): 289–313.

90. See Rosenbluth, "Measures of Concentration," p. 93, citing and correcting errors in findings by Willard Thorp and Walter Crowder.

91. See the testimony of Jules Backman, U.S., Congress, Senate, Subcommittee on Antitrust and Monopoly hearings, *Economic Concentration*, Part 2, 89th Cong., 1st sess., 1964, pp. 562–63.

92. Cf. note 69 *supra*.

93. Michael Gort, "Analysis of Stability and Change in Market Shares," *Journal of Political Economy* (February 1963): 51–61.

94. Gort, "Analysis of Stability and Change in Market Shares," p. 56. See also Grossack, "Toward an Integration of Static and Dynamic Measures," pp. 307–308; and Arnold A. Heggestad and Stephen A. Rhoades, "Competition and Firm Stability in Banking," *Review of Economics and Statistics* (November 1976): 443–52.

95. Testimony of L. E. Preston, U.S., Congress, Senate, Subcommittee on Antitrust and Monopoly hearings, *Economic Concentration*, Part 1, 89th Cong., 1st sess., 1964, pp. 68–69.

96. Caves and Porter, "Market Structure, Oligopoly, and Stability," pp. 306–307.

97. See, for example, Michael Gort, *Diversification and Integration in American Industry* (Princeton: Princeton University Press, 1962); the Federal Trade Commission staff report, *Conglomerate Merger Performance: An Empirical Analysis of Nine Corporations* (Washington: Federal Trade Commission, 1972); Richard P. Rumelt, *Strategy, Structure, and Economic Performance* (Boston: Harvard Business School Division of Research, 1974); Charles H. Berry, *Corporate Growth and Diversification* (Princeton: Princeton University Press, 1975); (on the United Kingdom) M. A. Utton, "Large Firm Diversification in British Manufacturing Industry," *Economic Journal* 87 (March 1977): 96–113; and J. Hassid, "Diversification and the Firm's Rate of Growth," *Manchester School of Economics and Social Studies* 45 (March 1977): 16–28.

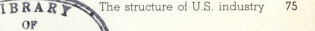

any of the other industries.[98] In 1972, all companies (including the very smallest) whose primary field was manufacturing had an aggregate "specialization ratio" of 66.9 percent. That is, 66.9 percent of their total operating establishment employment was in their primary industry category and 33.1 percent in other, or diversified, categories. Retail trade companies were much less diversified; 91.8 percent of their operating establishment employment was in their primary line. For mineral industry companies, the specialization ratio was 80.0 percent. Within manufacturing, industry categories that were home base to highly specialized enterprises included women's dresses and blouses (93 percent); newspapers (91 percent); and upholstered furniture (92 percent). Categories with relatively diversified companies included pulp and paper products (with 36 percent specialization); industrial chemicals and synthetics (53 percent); and radio, television, and communications equipment manufacture (52 percent).

Diversification can be viewed statically as an element of market structure at some moment in time or as a dynamic process of movement by companies into new and different lines. In neither respect is diversification an entirely new phenomenon. However, both the amount and rate of diversification have apparently increased since World War II. Using confidential Census data for a particularly thorough study of 111 large U.S. manufacturing corporations' diversification histories, Professor Gort found that the 111 firms collectively added 48 new four-digit product lines per year between 1929 and 1939, 43 new lines per year between 1939 and 1950, and 108 new lines per year between 1950 and 1954.[99] A Federal Trade Commission staff study picks up the thread from 1950. Table 3.11 shows the distribution of the largest 200 U.S. manufacturing corporations as of 1950 and 1968 according to the number of four-digit manufacturing industries they occupied. The fraction of the 200 largest manufacturing corporations operating in more than 20 four-digit industries rose from 19 to 38 percent, while operation in five or fewer industries became increasingly rare. Rumelt traced the histories of some 183 to 207 large industrial corporations and found that in 1949, 35 percent realized 95 percent or

T 3.11 Changes over time in the number of four-digit industries occupied by the 200 largest U.S. manufacturing companies

Number of four-digit industries in which the companies operated	Number of companies	
	1950	1968
5 or fewer	56	16
6–10	55	38
11–20	51	70
21–30	28	37
31–40	6	19
41–50	3	11
More than 50	1	9
Total	200	200

Adapted from Federal Trade Commission staff report, *Conglomerate Merger Performance: An Empirical Analysis of Nine Corporations* (Washington, D.C.: Government Printing Office, 1972), p. 64.

more of their sales in a single line of business.[100] By 1959, the incidence of such single-business companies had declined to 16 percent, and by 1969 it had fallen further to 6 percent.

Another perspective is provided by the Census Bureau's tabulation of specialization ratios for companies whose primary line of activity was a manufacturing industry category.[101] The total number of categories to which companies were assigned changed from one census to the next; therefore, the comparison is necessarily inexact, since a more richly subdivided set of categories will tend to show lower primary industry special-

T 3.12 Splice of company specialization ratios from four censuses

Year	Specialization ratio		
1958	$80.8_{(179)}$		
1963	$76.2_{(179)}$	$76.4_{(202)}$	
1967		$71.0_{(202)}$	
1972			$66.9_{(207)}$

ization, all else equal. The computed specialization ratios by census year for all manufacturing companies are shown in Table 3.12, with the number of categories used being indicated in subscripted parentheses. For 1963, specialization ratio estimates are available under both the old 179 and new 202 category breakdowns. We see that the classification's fineness had only a small impact (and in an unexpected direction) on the computed ratios. This permits us to conclude that manufacturers' primary industry specialization ratio declined by about 13 percentage points between 1958 and 1972. The rate of decline appears to have been especially rapid—1.35 points per year—between 1963 and 1967.

The movement into new lines of activity was accomplished to a considerable extent by merger. As we shall see in the next chapter, 1968 was the peak year in a massive merger wave that was preponderantly conglomerate, or diversification-oriented, in emphasis. Diversification was also achieved to some extent by the development of new products in companies' own research and development laboratories. Unfortunately, there is little solid quantitative evidence on the relative importance of mergers versus internal development as paths toward increasing corporate diversification.

The very notion of diversification—movement into new fields—implies a breaking with past product specialization patterns. Still for most companies this movement has not been totally unstructured. Much diversification effort has been related in one way or another to existing product lines. Companies like du Pont, which initially specialized in explosives, have spread out into other chemical products such as dyestuffs, synthetic fibers, plastics, and paints. General Electric expanded its coverage of the electrical product spectrum and drew upon its expertise in steam turbine technology to become a leading manufacturer of turbojet aircraft engines. Armour developed soaps and other chemical products to utilize meat-packing by-products more fully, and soap maker Procter and Gamble diversified into food and paper product lines calling for similar marketing skills and retail distribution channels. The trend, however, has been toward increasingly unrelated or "pure conglomerate" diversifi-

cation. Rumelt found that among the 183 to 207 industrial corporations he studied in detail, the fraction whose product line strategies could best be said to entail "related business" diversification increased from 27 percent in 1949 to 40 percent in 1959 and 45 percent in 1969.[102] The share pursuing an essentially "unrelated business" diversification strategy rose from 3.4 percent to 6.5 percent between 1949 and 1959 and then surged to 19.4 percent in 1969.

Certain additional patterns deserve notice. The new product lines entered by established firms typically have grown rapidly, often as a result of technological advances. Studying pre-1955 behavior, Gort discovered that diversification activity was correlated more closely with the ratio of engineers and chemists to total employment in the industries entered by diversifying firms than in the home-base industries of those firms. He also found that diversification was positively associated with the four-firm concentration ratio in diversifying firms' primary industries—apparently because high concentration made it difficult to expand in traditional product lines without disrupting pricing relationships, causing oligopolistic sellers to turn outward in search of growth opportunities.[103] Analyzing more recent developments, Berry found only weak statistical relationships between the prior growth and profitability experience of large U.S. corporations and whether they tended to diversify into closely or distantly related industries.[104]

98. U.S., Bureau of the Census, "General Report on Industrial Organization," *1972 Enterprise Statistics*, part 1, (Washington, D.C.: Government Printing Office, 1977), Table 2. Excluded from the analysis here is employment in central offices, research and development laboratories, warehouses, and other auxiliary establishments. Such employment amounted to 9.2 percent of total manufacturing company employment in 1972.

99. Gort, *Diversification and Integration*, pp. 44–48.

100. Rumelt, *Strategy, Structure, and Economic Performance*, pp. 50–53.

101. Drawn from Table 2 of the *Enterprise Statistics* reports, part 1, for 1972, 1967, and 1963.

102. Rumelt, *Strategy, Structure, and Economic Performance*, p. 51.

103. Gort, *Diversification and Integration*, pp. 135–43.

104. Berry, *Corporate Growth and Diversification*, pp. 91–108.

Is the movement toward diversification responsible for observed increases in the share of all U.S. industrial activity controlled by the largest manufacturing corporations? The only available direct quantitative evidence comes from Gort's study of 111 companies. He found that their payrolls in nonprimary (i.e., diversified) product lines rose from 31 percent in 1947 to 36 percent in 1954. Over the same interval, the share of the 100 largest manufacturers in all manufacturing value added rose from 23 percent to 30 percent. If we assume that the diversification pattern displayed by Gort's sample is representative of the 100 largest corporations, then the 100 largest in 1954 originated 19.2 percent of all manufacturing value added through operations in their primary product line ($30 \times .64$) and 10.8 percent through their diversification lines. Had their primary product share remained unaltered at 19.2 percent, but their diversified product share been maintained at only 45 percent of primary products ($100 \times 31/69$), as in 1947, the diversified product share would have been 8.6 percent and their total share of 1954 value added 27.8 percent, instead of 30 percent. These calculations suggest that increased diversification accounted for only about a third of the value added share growth of the 100 largest manufacturing enterprises between 1947 and 1954. And this estimate, Gort argues, is generous, since his sample was apparently more diversification-prone than the 100 largest manufacturers, and since companies might have grown more in their primary product lines had they grown less through diversification.[105] The remaining two-thirds of value added share growth, Nelson's analysis suggests, was attributable mainly to the extraordinarily rapid growth of the leading aircraft and automobile producers between 1947 and 1954.[106]

Gort and Nelson were able to develop these insights by being given access to confidential Census Bureau records. Since their work was completed, the Census Bureau has ceased granting such access to outside scholars. We therefore remain in the dark as to what role diversification played in subsequent aggregate concentration changes (and on many other questions as well). The data, collected at an expense of tens of millions of dollars, lie unanalyzed in Census Bureau files. Though less apt to draw headlines than Congressional junkets and the overpayment of welfare recipients, this state of affairs is equally wasteful.

Vertical integration in American industry

Vertical integration, like diversification, can be viewed both as a static dimension of market structure and as a process of altering market structures. Dynamically, firms integrating "upstream" or backward undertake to produce raw materials and semifabricated inputs that might otherwise be purchased from independent producers. Firms integrating "downstream" or forward move toward further finishing of semifabricated products and the wholesaling and retailing operations that put manufactured goods in the hands of consumers. Vertical integration in the static sense, of course, describes the extent to which firms in fact cover the entire spectrum of production and distribution stages.

One motive for vertical integration is to reduce costs. A classic example is found in the steel industry: Integration of blast furnaces, converters, and primary reduction mills reduces handling and the need for reheating. Vertical integration may also give producers enhanced control over their economic environment. Upstream integration, for example, can help ensure that supplies of raw materials will be available in time of shortage and protect the user from a price squeeze by monopolistic suppliers. Downstream integration gives the firm greater control over its markets, lessening the probability, among other thngs, of foreclosure (being shut out from the market) by powerful middlemen. With increased control over the market through integration may come the opportunity to abuse that control. We shall consider the potential pricing consequences of vertical integration at length in Chapter 10.

Although there is little solid evidence on the extent of vertical integration in the American economy, we can gain rough qualitative impressions. We know, for example, that the major petroleum refiners are highly integrated, commanding extensive crude oil reserves, refining facilities, the pipelines through which crude oil and refined products are transported, and in many instances networks of company-owned retail gasoline stations. Glass bottle manufacturers, on the other hand, exhibit very little integration. Most of them buy their sand, natural gas or oil, machinery, and (less consistently) shipping cartons from other companies and sell their output to packers and bottlers, who in turn utilize independent retailers to convey the end products to consumers. Problems arise, however, when we try to develop quantitative measures of vertical integration that permit systematic comparisons across industry lines and between firms within industries.

At first glance, the ratio of value added to sales, which averages about 0.47 for manufacturing industries when measured at the plant level, might seem an appropriate measure. However, it gives misleading comparisons when firms or industries are located at varying stages in the stream of economic activity. Suppose, to use an example coined by Adelman, an economy consists of three disintegrated firms—a raw materials producer, a fabricator, and a distributor—and suppose each contributes one-third of total value added.[107] Assuming further that the raw materials producer buys nothing from outside suppliers, its value added/sales ratio is 1.0, giving the misleading impression that it is totally integrated vertically. The fabricator (buying raw material valued at one-third and adding its own labor, etc. valued at one-third) has a value added/sales ratio of 0.5, while the distributor will have a ratio of 0.33. The nearer the raw materials end of the production stream a specialist firm's (or industry's) operations are located, the higher its value added/sales ratio tends to be, ceteris paribus. Because of this bias, attempts to measure the degree of vertical integration in particular enterprises or industries using only the statistical data readily available to researchers give results which at best must be viewed with caution, and which at worst may be nonsensical.[108]

Gort attempted to circumvent the conventional measurement problems in his study of 111 large corporations. Through qualitative analysis, he identified for each company those four-digit product activities that were "auxiliary" to the firm's primary (largest) product class, namely, activities that either supplied inputs into the primary production operation or contributed to further downstream fabrication or distribution of the primary product. His index of integration was then defined as the percentage of employment in auxiliary industries to total company employment. Not surprisingly, he found petroleum industry members to have by far the highest integration index—67 percent. Distant runners-up were machinery, with 30.5 percent of employment in auxiliary activities, and food products, with 30.3 percent. The least integrated manufacturers were found in the transportation equipment group (9.7 percent), electrical equipment (12.8 percent), and fabricated metal products (15.0 percent).[109]

An attempt to characterize quantitatively the dynamics of vertical integration has been made by Livesay and Porter.[110] They consulted numerous historical sources to determine whether the largest U.S. manufacturing companies in six reference years had moved upstream into raw materials production and downstream into transportation, wholesaling, and retailing. Thirty-eight percent of the companies in their sample had integrated into raw materials production by 1899. The fraction increased to 51 percent in 1909, then grew very slowly to 55 percent by 1948. The proportion of sample companies integrated into retailing rose from 11 percent in 1899 to 26 percent

105. See Gort's testimony in the Senate Antitrust Subcommittee hearings, *Economic Concentration*, Part 2 (1965), pp. 673–76.

106. *Concentration in the Manufacturing Industries of the United States*, pp. 99–108.

107. M. A. Adelman, "Concept and Statistical Measurement of Vertical Integration," in *Business Concentration and Price Policy*, pp. 281–83.

108. For an alternate measurement proposal, see Werner Sichel, "Vertical Integration as a Dynamic Industry Concept," *Antitrust Bulletin* 18 (Fall 1973): 463–82.

109. *Diversification and Integration*, pp. 80–82.

110. Harold C. Livesay and Patrick C. Porter, "Vertical Integration in American Manufacturing, 1899–1948," *Journal of Economic History* 29 (September 1969): 494–500.

in 1919 and 36 percent in 1929, showing no clear
trend thereafter. Thus, it would appear that manufacturers' most important moves toward vertical
integration into other stages occurred rather
early in the century. A limitation of the Livesay-
Porter approach is its inability, at least without
access to data seldom publicly available, to determine how intensive companies' involvement in
nonmanufacturing stages is. Thus, General Electric was evidently considered integrated into retail distribution even though only its major appliances, and indeed only a fraction of them, have
ever been sold and serviced directly through
GE-owned outlets. The auto manufacturers were
also counted as active in retailing despite the
fact that most of their outlets are independently
owned franchised dealerships.

Economists seeking to measure changes over
time in the intensity of integration have had to
accept the limitations of value added/sales ratios. Adelman examined such ratios for the manufacturing industry as a whole from 1849 to 1939
and for selected steel companies from 1902 to
1952, and found no clear trend toward either
increased or reduced vertical integration.[111]
Laffer computed similar ratios for all corporations
in ten broad sectors of the economy from 1929 to
1965, and concluded that there was no discernible time trend in the degree of integration.[112] In
this respect, as with respect to market concentration, the structure of American industry has
changed surprisingly little since early in the century.

111. "Concept and Statistical Measurement of Vertical Integra-
     tion," pp. 308–11. See also Irvin B. Tucker and Ronald P.
     Wilder, "Trends in Vertical Integration in the U.S. Manufac-
     turing Sector," *Journal of Industrial Economics* 26 (September
     1977): 81–94. Some upward drift in the ratio for all manufac-
     turing is evident since 1939, but not to a level appreciably
     higher than the values attained in 1889 and 1931.

112. Arthur B. Laffer, "Vertical Integration by Corporations,
     1929–1965," *Review of Economics and Statistics* 51 (February
     1969): 91–93.

4 The determinants of market structure

What accounts for the widespread differences in market structure found in diverse industries? Is it necessary for concentration to be as high as it is in many manufacturing industries? These questions are our concern in the present chapter. We shall explore several determinants of market structure, including economies of scale, mergers, various government policies, growth, and chance.

Economies of scale

One condition that could lead to concentrated market structures is the existence of substantial scale economies, permitting relatively large producers to manufacture and market their products at lower average cost per unit than relatively small producers. Economies of scale are best analyzed in terms of three categories: product-specific economies, associated with the volume of any single *product* made and sold; plant-specific economies, associated with the total output (possibly encompassing many products[1]) of an entire plant or plant complex; and multi-plant economies, associated with an individual firm's operation of multiple plants. Each deserves extended consideration.

Ball bearing manufacturing provides a good illustration of several product-specific economies. If only a few bearings are to be custom-made, the ring machining will be done on general-purpose lathes by a skilled operator who hand-positions the stock and tools and makes measurements for each cut. With this method, machining a single ring requires from five minutes to more than an hour, depending upon the part's size and complexity and the operator's skill. If a sizeable batch is to be produced, a more specialized automatic screw machine will be used instead. Once it is loaded with a steel tube, it automatically feeds the tube, sets the tools and adjusts its speed to make the necessary cuts, and spits out machined parts into a hopper at a rate of from 80 to 140 parts per hour. A substantial saving of machine running and operator attendance time per unit is achieved, but setting up the screw machine to perform these operations takes about eight hours. If only 100 bearing rings are to be made, setup time greatly exceeds total running time, and it may be cheaper to do the job on an ordinary lathe. As the number of parts made increases, setup time per unit of running time falls—e.g., to 88 percent of running time with 1,000 rings and 9

---

1. On the theory of scale economies associated with the interaction between individual product volume and the agglomeration of multiple products, see William J. Baumol, "On the Proper Tests for Natural Monopoly in a Multiproduct Industry," *American Economic Review* 67 (December 1977): 809–22; and John C. Panzar and Robert D. Willig, "Economies of Scale in Multi-Output Production," *Quarterly Journal of Economics* 91 (August 1977): 481–93.

percent with 10,000 rings. The larger the batch, the lower the average cost (i.e., setup *plus* running time per unit) will be. Analogous savings come with higher volume at other stages of the bearing-making process—e.g., in grinding, groove honing, cage stamping, and assembly. If very large quantities (i.e., a million per year) of a single bearing design can be sold, a still different production approach is likely to be chosen. Even more specialized higher speed machines are used, and parts are transferred automatically to the next processing stage in a continuous straight-line flow. Computer-guided devices then match completed inner and outer rings with balls to attain the desired tolerances; and the parts are assembled, greased, and packaged without any human intervention. With such an automated straight-line bearing production approach, unit costs may be 30 to 50 percent lower than with medium-volume batch methods. But in order to realize these savings, the production line must be kept running without change-over two shifts per day, and this requires a large and continuous volume.

When individual products are manufactured in large quantities, it also pays to devote more effort to working out the bugs in their production processes. Reporting that output per worker increased by 167 percent when average rayon cloth-weaving runs increased in length from 3,800 to 31,000 yards, the British Textile Council observed that:

> When staff at all levels can concentrate on the production of a very limited number of products, the smallest details can receive attention and be brought to near perfection. Time and effort which would be wildly uneconomic in normal circumstances can be justified if the volume of production is sufficiently great.[2]

Product-specific economies of scale also have an important dynamic dimension.[3] When intricate labor operations must be performed, as in shoe stitching and aircraft or computer assembly, workers tend to gain proficiency in their jobs with experience—that is, they learn by doing. Output per hour of work rises, the number of errors tends to fall, and unit costs decline along a so-called learning curve with increases in the cumulative volume of a specific product manufactured. Studies of World War II aircraft production show that labor costs per unit fell by approximately 20 percent with each doubling of cumulative output. As experience accumulates, production engineers and workers also discover new ways to improve productivity. Nowhere is this seen more graphically than in the manufacture of large-scale integrated circuits—thumbnail-sized electronic calculator and computer components embodying the functions of thousands of transistors, diodes, resistors, and the like. It is extremely difficult to deposit precisely the right (microscopic) amounts of material in the various LSI strata, and so at first one is lucky if one or two components out of 100 function properly. The rest must be discarded. But as production experience accumulates, the staff gradually learn how to control the processes, and yields rise to as much as 50 or 80 percent, with a corresponding 25- to 80-fold decrease in cost per properly functioning component.

At the plant-specific level, the most important economies of scale come from expanding the size of individual processing units. This is especially apparent in the process industries such as petroleum refining, iron ore reduction and steel conversion, chemical transformation, cement making, and steam generation. The output of a processing unit tends within certain physical limits to be roughly proportional to the volume of the unit, other things being equal, while the amount of materials and fabrication effort (and hence investment cost) required to construct the unit is more apt to be proportional to the surface area of the unit's reaction chambers, storage tanks, connecting pipes, and the like. Since the area of a sphere or cylinder of constant proportions varies as the two-thirds power of volume, the cost of constructing process industry plant units can be expected to rise as the two-thirds power of their output capacity, at least up to the point where they become so large that extra structural reinforcement and special fabrication techniques are required. There is considerable empirical support for the existence of this *two-thirds rule*, which is applied by engineers in estimating the cost of new process equipment.[4] Energy usage also tends to rise less than proportionately with increases in processing vessel size up to certain limits. The scale-up of machines such as compressors, turbines, conveyors, rolling mills, furnaces and air conditioners, packaging machines, and the like appears to follow similar though less mathematically exact laws: Within limits, increases in capacity come at a less than proportionate rise in equipment cost. Moreover, the crew required to operate a large processing unit or machine is often little or no larger than what is needed for a unit of smaller capacity, so labor costs per unit of output fall sharply with scale-up.[5]

Another advantage of increased plant size arises from what E. A. G. Robinson calls "the economies of massed reserves."[6] A plant large enough to use only one specialized machine may have to hold another machine in reserve if it insists upon hedging against occasional, essentially random breakdowns in order to sustain production. For a larger plant with numerous machines, a single extra machine may provide almost the same degree of protection at much lower cost relative to total capacity carrying costs. Similarly, the number of repairmen a company must employ to maintain any stipulated level of service in the event of random machine failures rises less than proportionately with the number of machines in operation, all else being equal.[7] Massed reserves economies can also be realized when unit shutdowns occur regularly and predictably. For example, the violent reactions occurring in a basic oxygen steel-making furnace (BOF) necessitate relining the furnace with new refractory brick every 25 to 40 days. It is important to maintain a fairly steady flow of steel to keep subsequent equipment busy. Therefore, in a two-furnace shop, one furnace is usually shut down for relining while the other is working. Adding a third BOF and augmenting the relining crew so that two furnaces are being operated while a third is relined doubles sustainable output with an investment increase of only about 50 percent.

Other plant-specific scale economies stem from increases in work force specialization. With a larger output of a given product mix, workers can specialize more narrowly and build up greater proficiency in their tasks. An automobile assembly line is the classic illustration. Special-

ization economies may also be achieved in plant overhead functions. Thus, a large plant can have one or more specialized cost accountants, production schedulers, stockkeepers, nurses, plant guards, and so on. A small plant must often double up such functions, with possible skill losses (but gains in perspective); or if individual capabilities or union rules prevent such doubling up, it may utilize certain specialized workers to less than full capacity; or it may have to make do with more costly part-time help or contracting-out expedients. Any plant must also have a manager, and in a large plant, the manager's salary can be spread over a larger output volume, permitting lower costs per unit; or a higher salary can be paid, which presumably will attract managers of superior ability.

2. The Textile Council, *Cotton and Allied Textiles*, vol. I (Manchester: Textile Council, 1969), pp. 72–73.

3. See Armen Alchian, "Costs and Output," in Moses Abromovitz et al., *The Allocation of Economic Resources: Essays in Honor of B. F. Haley* (Stanford: Stanford University Press, 1959), pp. 23–40; Jack Hirshleifer, "The Firm's Cost Function: A Successful Reconstruction?" *Journal of Business* 35 (July 1962): 235–55; L. E. Preston and E. C. Keachie, "Cost Functions and Progress Functions: An Integration," *American Economic Review* 54 (March 1964): 100–106; Sherwin Rosen, "Learning by Experience as Joint Production," *Quarterly Journal of Economics* 86 (August 1972): 366–82; Leonard Dudley, "Learning and Productivity Changes in Metal Products," *American Economic Review* 62 (September 1972): 662–69; and (for an exaggerated view) *Perspectives on Experience* (Boston: Boston Consulting Group, Inc., 1972).

4. See F. T. Moore, "Economies of Scale: Some Statistical Evidence," *Quarterly Journal of Economics* 73 (May 1959): 232–45; John Haldi and David Whitcomb, "Economies of Scale in Industrial Plants," *Journal of Political Economy* 75 (August 1967): 373–85; Lawrence J. Lau and Shuji Tamura, "Economies of Scale, Technical Progress, and the Nonhomothetic Leontief Production Function," *Journal of Political Economy* 80 (November/December 1972): 1167–87; and Richard C. Levin, "Technical Change and Optimal Scale: Some Evidence and Implications," *Southern Economic Journal* 44 (October 1977): 208–21.

5. See especially Lau and Tamura, "Economies of Scale," pp. 1180–85, who find no increase in labor usage in larger Japanese petrochemical plants.

6. E. A. G. Robinson, *The Structure of Competitive Industry*, rev. ed. (Chicago: University of Chicago Press, 1958), pp. 26–27. Robinson's work continues to be the classic reference on the logic of scale economies.

7. Compare T. M. Whitin and M. H. Peston, "Random Variations, Risk, and Returns to Scale," *Quarterly Journal of Economics* 68 (November 1954): 603–12; and David Levhari and Eytan Sheshinski, "A Microeconomic Production Function," *Econometrica* 38 (May 1970): 559–73.

Specialization and massed reserves economies may also extend to the operation of multiple plants by a single firm. The multi-plant enterprise can employ a more richly specialized array of accounting, finance, marketing, production process trouble-shooting, research, and legal talent than a single-plant firm, all else being equal. This may be reflected in lower administrative costs and/or higher productivity. It can achieve more specialization within individual plants for a given product line breadth. It can mass its cash balance reserves[8] and spread production, market, and financial risks over a larger volume of activity. It may be able to get more mileage out of its expenditures on a field sales force and other marketing instruments. Determining how important such multi-plant economies are must be deferred to a later stage of our analysis.

What checks the realization of scale economies? It is clear that economies of scale exist and that unit costs fall with increases in product volume, plant size, and firm size, at least within limits. Does this decline in costs continue indefinitely? There are many reasons for believing that it does not.

In nearly all production and distribution operations, the realization of scale economies appears to be subject to diminishing returns. With a large enough volume, setup costs dwindle to insignificance. Learning curves flatten out as very large cumulative output volumes are attained.[9] Cement kilns experience unstable internal aerodynamics above 7 million barrels per year capacity. Other scaled-up process vessels and machines become unwieldy or require special structural reinforcement beyond some point, increasing unit costs rather than reducing them. Massed reserves advantages peter out. Workers and machines become so specialized that they cannot adapt or be adapted to change. And so on.

Sooner or later a point is reached at which all opportunities for making further cost reductions through increased size or volume are exhausted. This point is associated, though not necessarily in a simple way, with the scale at which the largest or most specialized machine or other input can be utilized fully. What complicates matters is that other large-scale processes may not dovetail perfectly with the largest scale process at its own optimal size. For example, in the mid-1970s a basic oxygen shop with three 250-ton furnaces could turn out 6 million tons of raw steel per year. Its scale set a floor for the size of a least-cost inland steel works. Individual blast furnaces large enough to supply such a BOF shop had been built, but at mid-1970s energy cost levels they probably had higher unit costs than blast furnaces with capacity equivalent to 4 million tons of steel output—i.e., about 2.8 million tons of pig iron output.[10] One such least-cost blast furnace was insufficient to keep a least-cost BOF shop supplied; two were too much; and building a half-size blast furnace to supplement the least-cost unit entailed clear unit cost increases. The *least common multiple* at which the principal iron- and steel-making processes dovetailed exactly was an output of 12 million tons of steel per year, achieved with two BOF shops and three blast furnaces. Barring other complications, this scale constituted the *minimum optimal scale* (MOS) for an integrated steelworks—that is, the smallest scale at which minimum unit costs were attained. Equally low unit costs might be enjoyed at capacities representing an integral multiple of the minimum optimal scale—i.e., in the present case, at annual capacities of 24 million tons, 36 million tons, and so on. As a first approximation, these higher capacities could be obtained if a firm built additional 12-million-ton plants in other locations or, less plausibly, by multiplying a single plant's scale. Between these least common multiple values, unit costs were slightly above their minimum value owing to the imperfect dovetailing of processes; and the long-run cost curve of the firm had a generally horizontal but scalloped shape beyond 12 million tons' annual capacity.

Other considerations may render the doubling and redoubling of least common multiples at a single plant site uneconomic. Psychological surveys show that for reasons still imperfectly understood, workers express less satisfaction with their jobs, and especially with the challenge their jobs offer, in large plants than in small plants.[11] To attract a work force in the face of such alienating job conditions, large plants must in effect buy off their workers with a wage premium—one that has apparently been growing over time. The superior productivity associated with realizing scale economies provides the wherewithal to pay this premium, but as the least common multiple plant size is exceeded, *further* productivity gains are nil and therefore unavailable to sustain still larger wage premia. Second, especially in smaller cities and towns, increasing the size of a plant's work force may require expanding the geographic radius from which workers are drawn, which in turn implies higher worker commutation costs and higher offsetting wages. Third, materials flows lengthen and become more complex as plant scales increase, and handling costs rise commensurately, discouraging continued expansion at a given plant site. Fourth, the risks of fire, explosion, and wildcat strikes are at a maximum when all production is concentrated at a single plant site, and so firms enjoying sufficient sales volume generally prefer to expand at other locations once they have achieved the minimum optimal scale (and sometimes even before) at one site. Finally, it is much harder to manage a big plant than a small one, all else being equal. To keep their operations taut and under control, companies characteristically avoid expanding individual plants beyond the size required by equipment scale-up and work force specialization imperatives.

This last point is more general, being applicable at the firm level as well as at the plant level.[12] Any enterprise must have a single individual who assumes ultimate authority and responsibility. Classical economists referred to this person as the entrepreneur; or as in President Truman's homelier simile, he or she is the person on whose desk rests the sign, "The buck stops here." The entrepreneur or chief executive is a fixed, indivisible input. And as every sophomore economics student has learned by heart, whenever increasing doses of variable inputs (workers, middle managers, technicians, rolling mills, and so forth) are used in combination with some fixed input, sooner or later diminishing marginal returns take hold. Concretely, as enterprises increase in size, their chief executives are confronted with more and more decisions, and they are removed farther and farther from the reality of front-line production and marketing operations. Their ability to make sound decisions is attenuated, with a consequent rise in costs and/

or fall in revenues. The problem is aggravated when the firm operates in a rapidly changing and uncertain environment, for it is the nonroutine decisions associated with change that press most heavily upon top managers' capacities.[13]

A related hypothesis asserts that as the enterprise increases in size, it becomes more and more difficult to keep each branch's operations in harmony with those of every other part. Hordes of middle managers, coordinators, and expediters[14] proliferate. Not only is the money cost of this bureaucracy far from inconsequential, but organizational sluggishness also tends to rise with complexity. As Robinson puts it, a mistake by a platoon commander demands only an instantaneous "As you were!" A mistake by an army commander may require days of labor to set right.[15] The result of these management and co-

8. See William J. Baumol, "The Transactions Demand for Cash: An Inventory Theoretic Approach," *Quarterly Journal of Economics* 66 (November 1952): 545–56; and Karl Brunner and Allan H. Meltzer, "Economies of Scale in Cash Balances Reconsidered," *Quarterly Journal of Economics* 81 (August 1967): 422–36.

9. See Harold Asher, *Cost-Quantity Relationships in the Airframe Industry*, R-291 (Santa Monica: RAND Corporation, 1956), especially Chapters 4 and 7; and Gerald W. Brock, *The U.S. Computer Industry* (Cambridge, Mass.: Ballinger, 1975), p. 29.

10. See David G. Tarr, "The Minimum Optimal Scale Steel Plant in the Mid-1970's," Working paper no. 3 (Washington, D.C.: Federal Trade Commission Bureau of Economics, 1977).

11. F. M. Scherer, "Industrial Structure, Scale Economies, and Worker Alienation," in Robert T. Masson and P. D. Qualls, eds., *Essays on Industrial Organization in Honor of Joe S. Bain* (Cambridge, Mass.: Ballinger, 1976), pp. 105–21.

12. See Robinson, *The Structure of Competitive Industry*, Chapter 3; Nicholas Kaldor, "The Equilibrium of the Firm," *Economic Journal* 44 (March 1934): 60–76; R. H. Coase, "The Nature of the Firm," *Economica* 4 (November 1937): 386–405; E. H. Chamberlin, "Proportionality, Divisibility, and Economies of Scale," *Quarterly Journal of Economics* 62 (February 1948): 229–62; and Oliver E. Williamson, "Hierarchical Control and Optimum Firm Size," *Journal of Political Economy* 75 (April 1967): 123–38.

13. For an ingenious attempt to test statistically the relationship between uncertainty and optimal firm size, see David Schartzman, "Uncertainty and the Size of the Firm," *Economica* 30 (August 1963): 287–96. Schwartzman finds that the more uncertain the market environment is, as exemplified by the frequency and magnitude of price markdowns at the retail level, the smaller the largest manufacturing firms in the industry tend to be.

14. For readers untutored in the ways of bureaucracy, an expediter is a person whose desk is between the desks of two coordinators.

15. Robinson, *The Structure of Competitive Industry*, p. 41.

ordination problems is upward pressure on costs that becomes increasingly intense as firm scales rise. At some critical point, the diseconomies of large-scale management overpower the economies of scale and unit costs begin rising with output, giving the long-run average total cost curve its U-shape familiar to readers of microeconomic theory texts. The downward segment of the U is governed by orthodox scale economies, the upward thrust by managerial diseconomies.

The concept of the U-shaped cost curve simplifies many problems of economic theory. But is it valid? Quite possibly not. Some extremely able persons have turned their inventive talents to overcoming the problem of large-scale management diseconomies. Staff functions have been designed to supply decision-making information to the chief executive in its most useful form and to round out a system of checks and balances reducing the probability that important aspects of decisions will be overlooked. Communication has been simplified and accelerated by such technological innovations as the telephone, the teletype, and most recently, computerized information systems. Techniques of cost accounting and budgetary control have been brought to a high state of perfection, giving the chief executive a clearer view of the organization's past performance and future plans. Perhaps most important of all, ways have been devised to make the management of large organizations manageable through the decentralization of operating authority and financial responsibility to product line or territorial divisions. The decentralized multidivisional form of corporate organization, Professor Oliver Williamson suggests, may well have been "American capitalism's most important single innovation of the 20th century."[16]

The classic model of a giant corporation that has tried hard to stave off the managerial diseconomies of scale through decentralization is General Motors.[17] In a series of reorganizations during the 1920s, substantial authority and responsibility were delegated to operating divisions, while a strong central staff was established to provide analysis and advice (but in principle, not direction) on matters of policy. Whenever feasible, operating entities are set up as semiautonomous profit centers, with the stern calculus of profit and loss simultaneously guiding the decisions of operating-level executives and providing top management with an indicator of good or bad performance. To charge the system with incentive, key managers are paid bonuses that vary to reflect supervisors' evaluations of how well performance objectives have been satisfied. Granted, the principle of central management nonintervention in detailed operating decisions has been much honored in the breach. There also have been important divisional structure reorganizations—most recently, shifting authority away from its traditional car division locus and toward unified component and assembly divisions, evidently to secure the manufacturing scale economies associated with maximum standardization.[18] This new organizational pattern could aggravate a well-known problem of decentralization: Profit and loss calculations often can send false signals to executives selling or buying component parts whose prices are set by interdivisional negotiation, and not in the market.[19] It also remains to be seen whether General Motors' leaders will free themselves from chronic blind spots inhibiting adaptation to a changing environment.[20] Yet for more than half a century, the GM organizational system has passed the acid test of restraining managerial scale diseconomies. General Motors has been not only the world's largest private manufacturing corporation (at least, as measured by the number of employees), but also one of the most profitable. For it, the long-run unit cost curve has not turned perceptibly upward.

The General Motors strategy of decentralization has been emulated, subject to numerous detailed variations, by many other corporations both in the United States and abroad. Few if any have succeeded completely in overcoming the problems of large-scale bureaucracy. Interviews with 125 North American and European companies revealed a virtually unanimous consensus that decision making in the large multi-plant firm is slower and that top executives are farther removed from the personalities and problems of operating levels, with a possible (but less certain) degradation in the quality of decisions.[21] How well companies cope with the managerial problems of size appears to depend upon the complexity of marketing and production challenges and the abilities of a firm's guiding individuals. A few firms muster sufficient organizational genius to sustain superior profitability despite what would otherwise be debilitating scale. Others achieve average profits only because scale economies of an orthodox character are persistent enough to offset significant managerial diseconomies. Still others, such as the United States Steel Corporation, have experimented with myriad organizational forms but remain less efficient than smaller rivals.[22] And in such volatile industries as fashion handbag manufacturing or on-site home building, where rapid adaptation to changing conditions is vital and orthodox scale economies are quickly exhausted, managerial diseconomies severely restrict the sizes firms can attain without experiencing rising unit costs.

We conclude then that the long-run cost function of industrial firms has a shape something like that shown in Figure 4.1. Up to some minimum optimal scale OA, economies of scale facilitate reductions in unit cost as capacity is increased. Through decentralization and other management techniques, it is possible to increase the firm's size considerably beyond OA at more or less constant costs per unit. But if the enterprise expands too far—i.e., beyond scale OB—managerial

diseconomies of scale may take hold, leading to operation at higher-than-minimum cost per unit.

This analysis of the managerial cost-scale problem has been largely static. In a more dynamically oriented analysis, Mrs. Edith Penrose has shown that the relationship may be more complex, for one must take into account not only the choice of a particular size on the long-run cost curve, but also the process of moving from one scale to another.[23] Specifically, she argues that expansion during any short interval of time is constrained by the inability of the firm's management to cope with all the planning and leadership problems created by greatly increased size. Over the medium run of a few years, then, the firm's cost curve bends upward at a scale only slightly larger than its present scale. But as time passes, management digests the problems con-

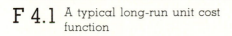

F 4.1 A typical long-run unit cost function

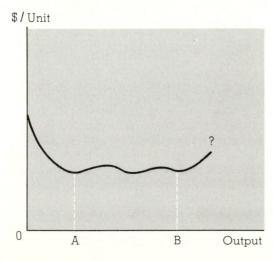

16. Oliver E. Williamson, *Corporate Control and Business Behavior* (Englewood Cliffs, N.J.: Prentice-Hall, 1970), p. 175. See also Alfred D. Chandler, Jr., *Strategy and Structure: Chapters in the History of the Industrial Enterprise* (Cambridge, Mass.: MIT Press, 1962).

17. See Chandler, *Strategy and Structure*, Chapter 3; and Peter F. Drucker, *The Concept of the Corporation* (New York: Day, 1946), especially Part II.

18. See "GM Moves To Centralize All Operations," *Automotive News*, 20 September 1971, pp. 1, 36; and "Project Center: GM Management System's New Aid," *Chicago Tribune*, 27 February 1977. Similarly, Sears Roebuck, characterized by Chandler as having attained its "final" decentralized structure in 1948, has apparently moved more recently toward greater centralization of merchandising decision making. See "What Sears' New Look Means to Sears," *Business Week*, 26 January 1976, p. 27.

19. On this "transfer pricing" problem, see Richard Heflebower, "Observations on Decentralization in Large Enterprises," *Journal of Industrial Economics* 9 (November 1960): 14–15; Jack Hirshleifer, "On the Economics of Transfer Pricing," *Journal of Business* 30 (July 1956): 172–84; and John A. Menge, "The Backward Art of Interdivisional Pricing," *Journal of Industrial Economics* 23 (July 1961): 215–32.

20. See Drucker, *The Concept*, pp. 85–97; Dan Cordtz, "The Face in the Mirror at General Motors," *Fortune*, August 1966, pp. 117 ff.; and "A Swinger Tries To Cure Chevrolet's Blues," *Business Week*, 18 September 1971, pp. 60–61.

21. F. M. Scherer, Alan Beckenstein, Erich Kaufer, and R. D. Murphy, *The Economics of Multi-Plant Operation: An International Comparisons Study* (Cambridge, Mass.: Harvard University Press, 1975), p. 324.

22. See "A New Boss at the Corporation," *Business Week*, 8 July 1967, p. 140.

23. Edith Tilton Penrose, *The Theory of Growth of the Firm* (Oxford, England: Basil Blackwell, 1959).

ferred by past growth and adapts its capabilities for dealing with new problems, making it possible to grow further without driving up unit costs. The managerial limit to efficient expansion recedes over time, and as a result, Penrose argues, there is no single optimal firm size in the long run. This view of the firm's cost-scale relationships and the static model are not incompatible. Figure 4.1 merely ignores the transitional problems of growth in assuming that the firm can operate anywhere within the output range AB at roughly constant cost per unit. Given sufficient time for managerial adaptation, the locus of cost-volume points within AB is indeed accessible.

Transportation costs Another major influence that can prevent scale economies from being realized indefinitely is the cost of delivering output to customers. Transportation costs affect cost-scale relationships primarily at the level of a single plant or geographically clustered plant complex. If more output is produced in a plant complex, more must be sold. To sell more, it may be necessary to reach out to more distant customers. This in turn can lead to increased transportation costs per unit sold. The magnitude of the increase depends in a complex way upon a number of variables. One is the size of the plant in relation to the size of the market served. If the plant supplies only a small fraction of market demand, it may be able to increase sales substantially without expanding its geographic penetration. In this case transportation costs will be an insignificant constraint on plant size. A second factor is the nature of the pricing system. Transportation costs borne by the producer rise with output only if they cannot be passed along to buyers in the form of higher prices. This will occur when prices are uniform in all markets, or when the price in more distant markets is set by more advantageously located rival producers. As we shall observe in Chapter 11, such situations, which require the producer to absorb freight in supplying more distant markets, are fairly commonplace. The third variable is the geographic structure of transportation costs. Usually the cost of transporting a given volume of freight rises less than proportionately with the distance shipped. The smaller the percentage increase in cost as-

sociated with shipping freight an extra 100 miles, the less will transportation costs constrain plant size. Fourth, the geographic distribution of potential customers matters. If buyers are distributed evenly over the map, transportation costs will rise less than proportionately with the number of customers served, *ceteris paribus*, since shipping cost is related to the radius of shipment while volume of patronage is related to the square of the radius. If, on the other hand, customer density declines sharply away from the home market, transportation costs may rise more than proportionately with the volume of output sold. Finally, the relationship of the commodity's production cost to its bulk is relevant. For bulky, low-value commodities like sand or beer bottles, unit transportation costs rise relatively rapidly with distance shipped. For compact, high-value items like transistors and machine tools, they rise slowly.

The combined effect of these influences is illustrated in Figures 4.2(a) and 4.2(b). We assume that increased output must be sold at greater distances by absorbing freight charges. For each diagram, an identical production cost-scale curve UPC is assumed. The minimum optimal scale in terms of production costs occurs at output OX. In Figure 4.2(a), unit shipping costs USC rise slowly with increased output. Total cost per unit LRATC is the vertical sum of unit production costs and unit shipping costs. The least-cost scale, taking into account both production and transportation costs, occurs in Figure 4.2(a) at output OY. In Figure 4.2(b), unit shipping costs rise much more rapidly, and this causes a reduction in the least-cost scale to OZ.

Dynamic changes in transportation costs affect market structures in similar ways. For instance, the expansion of railroad networks during the second half of the 19th century induced a fall in unit transportation costs, moving many producers from a position like that of Figure 4.2(b) to one like 4.2(a). The least-cost scale of production thereupon rose, and firms took advantage by building new plants of unprecedented size.

Scale economies and vertical integration
One further conceptual issue must be explored. The typical large manufacturing corporation

F 4.2 The effect of transportation costs on the scale optimum

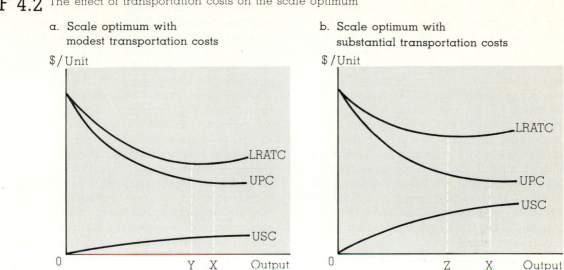

a. Scale optimum with
   modest transportation costs

b. Scale optimum with
   substantial transportation costs

carries out a bewilderingly complex array of activities. Yet, as we have seen in the preceding chapter, it spends more than half of its sales dollar purchasing raw materials, components, machines, special services, and the like from other firms. What determines which operations a firm will perform internally and which it will farm out to others?

Of particular interest here are activities entailing minimum optimal scales large in relation to other facets of the firm's operations. For example, the most costly component of a refrigerator or windowsill air conditioner is its compressor. Economies of scale in compressor manufacturing persist to outputs of 2 to 3 million units per year, not necessarily all of the same design. Scale economies in refrigerator box fabrication and assembly, on the other hand, are exhausted at a plant output of 800,000 units per year.[24] Must the refrigerator assembler be large enough to produce its own compressors at minimum unit cost, or can it buy its compressors from outside specialists and operate efficiently at the smaller assembly-only MOS? Similarly, a minimum-cost automobile assembly plant produces about 200,000 vehicles per year on double shift operation. But stamping body parts and machining automatic transmis-

sions or carburetors require larger annual volumes—i.e., from 250,000 to 400,000 units per year for each line.[25] Is an auto firm of optimal size one that merely assembles other firms' high-scale-economy parts efficiently, or must it be large enough to span the full range of component manufacturing activities at minimum unit cost? In other words, how vertically integrated must a firm of efficient size be, and to what extent can it satisfy its needs through vertical disintegration of high-scale-economy activities, perhaps avoiding some diseconomies of managing a large organization?[26]

There are several related answers to this set of questions. In a seminal article, R. H. Coase ob-

24. Scherer et al., *The Economics of Multi-Plant Operation*, pp. 80, 269.

25. See Lawrence J. White, *The Automobile Industry Since 1945* (Cambridge, Mass.: Harvard University Press, 1971), Chapters 3 and 4; and C. F. Pratten, *Economies of Scale in Manufacturing Industry* (Cambridge, England: Cambridge University Press, 1971), pp. 132–49.

26. On the economics of vertical disintegration, see Robinson, *The Structure of Competitive Industry*, p. 20.

The determinants of market structure   **89**

served that the distinguishing mark of a firm is the "supersession of the price mechanism."[27] Resource allocation in the market is normally guided through prices, but within the firm the job is done through the conscious decisions and commands of management. Activities are collected in what we call a firm, Coase argues, when transaction costs incurred in using the price mechanism exceed the cost of organizing those activities through direct managerial controls. One reason why market transaction costs may be appreciable is that price shopping, the communication of work specifications, and contract negotiation take time and effort. Especially when goods or services would have to be contracted for repeatedly in small quantities, it may be cheaper to bring them under the firm's direct span of managerial control.

The benefits from integration also increase with the complexity of product component interrelationships. It is easier to make the various parts of an automobile body fit together when all parties to the coordination effort work for the same boss than when design changes must be processed through a purchasing office. Also, periodic changes in automobile body designs (and hence in metal stampings) are a significant dimension of interfirm rivalry. Rapid adaptation to competitive developments (as well as maintaining secrecy of one's own designs) is facilitated under an integrated production approach.

For components, materials, and services whose provision involves compelling scale economies, the choice between integration and disintegration entails an important additional dimension. By the logic of specialization and division of labor, one might expect the rewards from vertical disintegration to be especially great, since then, as Professor Robinson argues, "The specialist firm, working for a number of the smaller firms, is on a larger scale than any of the individual firms could have achieved for that particular process or product."[28] But precisely because scale economies are so compelling, the number of disintegrated product sellers is likely to be small. For example, the total U.S. market for household and analogous refrigerators, freezers, and air conditioners in 1972 was large enough to support only five or six least-cost compressor manufacturers.

Similar conditions hold with respect to the supply of automobile transmissions, Diesel truck and bus engines, specialized paint pigments, and many other intermediate goods. From fewness of supply sources may follow monopolistic pricing of components bought outside. Even if the monopolistic supplier chooses not to exercise fully its power to elevate prices, buyers recognize their dependence upon the supplier's restraint, and fear, naturally enough, that they may not always be so fortunate. To avoid actual or feared monopolistic exploitation, users of high-scale-economy materials or components often decide to commence internal production, even though they may incur a cost penalty in doing so. In effect, they view the higher cost of vertically integrated production, sacrificing some scale economies, as a less onerous burden than the risk of being gouged by a more efficient but monopolistic outside supplier.

Nor does the story end there. If several firms reason in this way and integrate vertically, the independent supply market will sooner, i.e., if integration occurs through merger, or later be even thinner. For example, in the United States during the 1970s there was only one independent producer (Tecumseh Products) of refrigerator compressors; in Western Europe there were three (Danfoss, Stern, and Necchi). The dependence of nonintegrated buyers is therefore heightened. To be sure, integrated firms may offer to sell some of their own production, among other things to take fuller advantage of unrealized scale economy opportunities. But although being dependent upon a single independent supply source for some critical raw material or component is unnerving, it is even worse when the supplier is also one's main-line competitor. The situation in such instances is unstable. When vertical integration induced by fewness of supply sources thins the market further, other buyers may be stampeded into integrating as well despite appreciable scale economy sacrifices. Dynamics of this sort can be observed in the histories of the U.S. and European refrigerator-freezer industries, the U.S. automobile industry, and the movement by American steel makers into iron ore mining.[29] "Upstream" integration may also be induced by market failures stemming from causes other than compelling scale economies. Petroleum before

1973 provides an example. Crude oil prices in the United States were artificially elevated as a result of state-sanctioned cartelization, import controls, and a depletion tax structure that encouraged integrated firms to take as much of their profit as possible at the crude oil production stage. This spurred integration, which in turn constricted the noncaptive supply available to nonintegrated refiners, intensifying refiners' fear of being squeezed or cut off, and hence their incentives to integrate.[30]

Quite generally, the more prone markets are to a breakdown of competitive supply conditions, the stronger are individual buyers' incentives to protect themselves by integrating upstream. An extreme illustration of this generalization can be seen by comparing the shoe industries of the United States and the Soviet Union. In the United States, more or less workably competitive sources of supply exist for glues, shoe-finishing chemicals, sole rubber compounds, paperboard containers, lasts, and special shoe-making machines. U.S. shoe manufacturers are therefore willing to rely upon independent specialists to meet their needs. In the Soviet Union, markets are virtually nonexistent and independent suppliers frequently fail to meet plan requirements, thereby disrupting "downstream" operations. To avoid such supply difficulties, Soviet shoe-making firms have undertaken extensive vertical integration to satisfy their own requirements. And because glue-making, rubber-compounding, or machine-building operations of minimum optimal scale can satisfy numerous efficiently sized shoe plants' needs, the compulsion toward such integration increases the least common multiple. As a result, shoe manufacturing firms grow to sizes unnecessary in the U.S. industry, with its greater opportunity to disintegrate vertically.[31]

We shall return to other aspects of this issue in Chapters 10 and 20. The main point for present purposes is that the breakdown of competition in vertical price relationships may lead some firms to integrate operations that would otherwise be vertically disintegrated. And when a few firms do so, fear of even worse market failure induces others to follow suit, if they can. If they are too small to do so, they may find it difficult to survive. The result is an increase in the size of an optimal production complex and hence upward pressure on market concentration.

The measurement of cost-scale relationships

We have proposed viewing economies of scale in terms of the minimum optimal scale of production (such as OA in Figure 4.1 or OX in Figure 4.2) at which all attainable unit cost savings are realized. The crucial question remains: Is the MOS large or small in relation to the demand for an industry's output? Whether there is room for many firms in the market, each large enough to enjoy all scale economies, for only one firm (a *natural monopoly* situation), or for just a few (*natural oligopoly*) depends upon two key variables: the relevant technology, and the size of the market (i.e., the output that would be demanded at a price just sufficient to cover minimum unit cost).

27. Coase, "The Nature of the Firm," p. 389. See also Oliver E. Williamson, "The Vertical Integration of Production: Market Failure Considerations," *American Economic Review* 61 (May 1971): 112–23; and Kenneth J. Arrow, "Vertical Integration and Communications," *Bell Journal of Economics* 6 (Spring 1975): 173–83.

28. Robinson, *The Structure of Competitive Industry*, p. 20. See also George J. Stigler, "The Division of Labor Is Limited by the Extent of the Market," *Journal of Political Economy* 59 (June 1951): 185–93.

29. On refrigerators and iron ore, compare Scherer et al., *The Economics of Multi-Plant Operation*, pp. 264–65; Daniel R. Fusfeld, "Joint Subsidiaries in the Iron and Steel Industry," *American Economic Review* 48 (May 1958): 578–87; Richard B. Mancke, "Iron Ore and Steel: A Case Study of the Economic Causes and Consequences of Vertical Integration," *Journal of Industrial Economics* 20 (July 1972): 220–29; and Donald O. Parsons and Edward J. Ray, "The United States Steel Consolidation: The Creation of Market Control," *Journal of Law and Economics* 18 (April 1975): 194–206.

30. See testimony of Alfred E. Kahn, U.S., Congress, Senate, Subcommittee on Antitrust and Monopoly hearings, *Governmental Intervention in the Market Mechanism: The Petroleum Industry*, Part 1, 91st Cong., 1st sess., March 1969, pp. 132–42; and U.S., Congress, Senate, Committee on Government Operations, Permanent Subcommittee on Investigations, *Preliminary Federal Trade Commission Staff Report on Its Investigations of the Petroleum Industry*, 93rd Cong., 1st sess., July 1973, pp. 25–27, 60–62. Since percentage depletion for large crude oil producers and import quotas have been eliminated, the structure of incentives has changed. See Federal Trade Commission staff report, "The Effects of Decontrol on Competition in the Petroleum Industry," in U.S., Congress, Senate, Committee on Interior and Insular Affairs Hearings, *Oil Price Decontrol*, 94th Cong., 1st sess., 1975, pp. 359–94.

31. See Alice C. Gorlin, "Soviet Firms and the Rationalization of the Shoe Industry of the USSR," Ph.D. dissertation, University of Michigan, 1972, especially pp. 214–16; and Scherer et al., *The Economics of Multi-Plant Operation*, p. 270.

The determinants of market structure   91

There are several techniques for measuring cost-scale relationships. Some are suitable mainly for ascertaining the minimum optimal *plant* size, some the minimum optimal *firm* size, and some for both.

One approach is to analyze profitability as a function of size. At the firm level there are abundant data. However, several pitfalls exist. For one, profitability is not necessarily related in any simple way to scale economies, as conventionally defined. Large firms may realize higher profit returns not only because of superior efficiency, but because they possess more monopoly power. Or they may be less profitable because they bear a disproportionate share of the monopoly output restriction burden. Also, profit figures may be quite sensitive to variations in accounting conventions governing depreciation, the valuation of assets acquired through mergers, and the like. A special accounting problem affecting comparative firm size analyses is a possible tendency of smaller corporations' owner-managers to pay themselves salaries including a generous dose of what would otherwise be called profit. This is done to avoid double taxation. As a result, small firms' reported profits may be biased downward.[32] Finally, the comparative profitability of small versus large corporations appears to vary with the business cycle, with smaller enterprises doing relatively well in boom periods and poorly in recessions.[33] This presumably reflects larger firms' greater monopoly power, their use of accounting discretion to smooth reported earnings, and/or their stronger tendency to accumulate organizational slack in prosperous times and reduce it in downturns.[34]

In Chapter 9 we shall make extensive use of profitability data. Here a preliminary glimpse of broad relationships observed among manufacturing corporations must suffice. Table 4.1 arrays the average after-tax rates of return on stockholders' equity for all manufacturing corporations in six size classes during four time intervals—the nearly normal 1963–65 period, the Vietnam War boom of 1966–69, the generally sluggish 1969–71 period, and the unprecedented 1975–77 years of unusually high unemployment accompanied by inflation. The 1972–74 interval is omitted because comprehensive wage and price controls distorted market relationships. Data for corporations with assets of less than $10 million are omitted to minimize owner-manager compensation biases. In all periods the largest corporations exhibit higher returns. The differential is most prominent during the normal 1963–65 period and the 1969–71 recession; it is least pronounced during the late 1960s boom and, contrary to historical precedent, the mid-1970s.

A second empirical approach to the optimal scale question is the so-called "survivor test," developed in its modern form by Professor George Stigler.[35] The logic is simple: Firm or plant sizes that survive and contribute increasing proportions of an industry's output are assumed to

T 4.1 Average after-tax returns on stockholders' equity for manufacturing corporations in various asset size classes, 1963–77

Corporations with assets of:	1963–65	1966–69	1969–71	1975–77
Over $1 billion	13.5%	12.7%	10.3%	13.2%
$250–1000 million	11.0	12.1	10.4	13.0
$100–250 million	11.2	12.0	9.7	12.1
$50–100 million	10.4	11.2	8.6	12.0
$25–50 million	10.0	11.4	8.2	11.9
$10–25 million	9.9	11.0	7.9	12.4

Derived from Federal Trade Commission, *Quarterly Financial Report for Manufacturing Corporations* (Washington, D.C.: Government Printing Office), various issues. The averages are unweighted averages of quarterly rates of return. Reflecting the midyear change in business conditions, the 1966–69 period includes the first two quarters of 1969; the 1969–71 period includes the last two quarters of 1969.

be optimal; those that supply a declining share of output are deemed too large or too small. This test of optimality clearly covers a much broader range of variables than mere production scale economies. As Stigler states, under the survivor test an efficient firm size "is one that meets any and all problems the entrepreneur actually faces: strained labor relations, rapid innovation, government regulation, unstable foreign markets, and what not"; and survival may reflect monopoly power or discriminatory legislation as well as conventional scale economies.[36] With this caveat more or less firmly in mind, several investigators have applied the survivor test to more than a hundred different industries.[37] The most prominent result has been the wide range of firm and plant sizes that seem to pass the test. This has been interpreted (somewhat misleadingly) by Stigler as evidence that "the long run marginal and average cost curves of the firm are customarily horizontal over a large range of sizes." Applications of the test also suggest that the minimum optimal plant or firm size is small relative to market size in most industries. This, for instance, was the conclusion of T. R. Saving, who found that 64 of the 91 industries for which he was able to make 1947–54 survivorship estimates had minimum optimal plant sizes requiring the production of 1 percent or less of industry value added.[38] Nevertheless, the survivor test is not free of ambiguities. Survival patterns are not always stable over time; curious patterns appear (such as survival of only the largest and smallest plants); and the criteria for distinguishing surviving from nonsurviving size groups entail a certain element of arbitrariness. Tests on the same industries by different analysts have sometimes yielded quite different estimates.[39] Because of these problems, the survivor method is better employed as a supplement to and check on other techniques than as one's sole or primary approach to analyzing optimal scale patterns.

Another more direct approach, appropriate mainly for plant studies, is statistical cost analysis. To determine the shape of the long-run plant cost curve, the analyst relates average production cost observations for a broad cross section of plants to statistics reflecting the output of those plants, taking into account such additional variables as the percentage of capacity utilization, differences in the age of the capital stock (and hence in the state of the technological art embodied), differences in input prices, differences in output mixes, cumulative volume produced, and so forth. All this is easier said than done. Complete, reliable data sufficient for statistical generalization are hard to come by. When the data are obtained, comparability between plants may be impaired by differences in cost accounting conventions. One of the most serious problems relates to the imputation of rents attributable to specialized resources. If there are systematic differences in rent imputation between small plants and large, 'true' cost variations associated with scale differences may be either masked or exaggerated.

Despite these difficulties, there have been several dozen attempts to measure statistically the relationship between plant size and long-run unit cost of various industries, some executed at a

32. Cf. Herman O. Stekler, *Profitability and Size of Firm* (Berkeley: University of California Institute of Business and Economic Research, 1963), pp. 20, 36–46; and George J. Stigler, *Capital and Rates of Return in Manufacturing Industries* (Princeton: Princeton University Press, 1963), pp. 59–61. See also the discussion of economic and accounting profits in Chapter 9 *infra*.

33. See especially J. L. McConnell, "Corporate Earnings by Size of Firm," *Survey of Current Business* 25 (May 1945): 6–12; and Stekler, *Profitability and Size*.

34. Cf. Chapter 2, p. 35 *supra*.

35. George J. Stigler, "The Economies of Scale," *Journal of Law and Economics* 1 (October 1958): 54–71.

36. Stigler, "The Economies of Scale," p. 56.

37. See especially T. R. Saving, "Estimation of Optimum Size of Plant by the Survivor Technique," *Quarterly Journal of Economics* 75 (November 1961): 569–607; Leonard W. Weiss, "The Survival Technique and the Extent of Suboptimal Capacity," *Journal of Political Economy* 72 (June 1964): 246–61, with a correction, *Journal of Political Economy* 73 (June 1965): 300–301; and R. D. Rees, "Optimum Plant Size in United Kingdom Industries: Some Survivors Estimates," *Economica* 40 (November 1973): 394–401.

38. Saving, "Estimation of Optimum Size of Plant," p. 580.

39. See William G. Shepherd, "What Does the Survivor Technique Show About Economies of Scale?" *Southern Economic Journal* 34 (July 1967): 113–22.

high level of competence, others not.[40] If any single typical result can be identified, it has been a cost curve similar to Figure 4.1, showing definite economies of scale at relatively small plant sizes, a range of intermediate sizes over which unit costs did not vary perceptibly, and (in a minority of cases) diseconomies of scale for very large plants. With few exceptions, the minimum optimal plant scale revealed in studies of American manufacturing industries has been small relative to industry size. It would be hazardous to generalize from this last result, however, since industries with sufficiently numerous plants to permit a statistical approach to cost analysis should (assuming cost-minimizing behavior) be those with relatively small minimum optimal scales.

Finally, there is the *engineering approach* to scale economies measurement. Most larger companies employ engineers who specialize in planning and designing new production units and plants. In smaller enterprises, the same job is done by generalist senior engineers or other executives. Both small companies and large also draw upon the special expertise of outside machinery and plant design firms. The persons or groups performing these functions accumulate much information on alternative equipment and plant designs and the associated investment and operating costs. This expert knowledge can be tapped through interviews and questionnaires to estimate cost-scale relationships and minimum optimal scales. Scale economies studies using the engineering approach span a wide range of detail, from those that estimate cost relationships for each individual machine or process and integrate them through a statistical or mathematical model[41] to questionnaires asking little more than the best overall scale of operations and its advantage over plants of some stipulated smaller scale. With the simple questionnaire approach, important complications may be overlooked, leading to unwarranted generalizations. Considerable on-site interviewing is usually necessary to support confident conclusions—a costly process both for the investigator and informants. The best engineering information for process and plant alternatives will reflect firms' most recent choices, so answers are likely to vary between static and fast-growing companies, and perhaps also with informants' technical progressiveness. Therefore, substantial effort is required to enforce uniformity of technological assumptions. As with statistical cost function studies, cost and scale relationships may be complicated by product mix variations. Despite these difficulties, carefully executed engineering estimates undoubtedly provide the best single source of information on the cost-scale question.

There have been several studies using the engineering approach to develop plant scale economies estimates for a substantial sample of industries.[42] Partly from pride of authorship but mainly because the evidence resulted from an unusually ambitious interviewing program in seven industrialized nations, we focus initially here on estimates for 12 fairly representative major industries compiled by the author and several colleagues.[43] Table 4.2 summarizes the findings in terms of three measures: (1) the capacity, output, or employment of a minimum optimal scale plant, assuming mid-1960s best-practice technology; (2) how large a share of total 1967 U.S. output, capacity, or employment such an MOS plant would contribute; and (3) the percentage elevation of long-run unit costs as a consequence of building and operating plants only one-third the MOS instead of the full MOS. Two implications stand out. First, with the exception of the refrigerator-freezer industry, the optimal plant sizes tend to be quite small relative to the national market—too small to warrant high levels of concentration, assuming that each leading firm is large enough to operate only one MOS plant. By this assumption, the four-firm concentration ratio in brewing would be 14, in cigarettes 26, and in fabric weaving less than 1. Second, the long-run cost curves in most industries are much less steep at suboptimal plant scales than one is led to believe by typical textbook illustrations. Only in cement are unit costs elevated at one-third MOS by anything like the magnitudes suggested earlier in Figure 2.4 or 4.1. In half the industries, the elevation is 5 percent or less. In refrigerators, where realizing all intraplant scale economies requires the highest level of concentration, one could have an industry of 21 separate plants if one were willing to accept excess production costs of 6.5 percent.

Two almost concurrent studies cover 23 additional industries, for which the data are summarized in Table 4.3. One set of estimates, by C. F. Pratten and colleagues, was based upon apparently extensive interviewing in the United Kingdom; the other, by Leonard Weiss, came from more limited interviews and mail questionnaires in the United States. The incidence of industries in which minimum optimal scales are found to contribute 10 percent of total U.S. demand or more is considerably higher than in Table 4.2—seven cases out of 23, compared to one in 12 for Table 4.2. However, six of the seven originated in Pratten's sample, which, according to his co-worker, was intentionally biased toward industries in which economies of scale were believed to be significant.[44]

That such a bias is present in Table 4.3 is suggested by other evidence. Because engineering approach studies are so costly, less expensive surrogate measures of the minimum optimal plant scale have been sought. One such surrogate is the average size of plants comprising the upper half of the sales or employment size distribution, as revealed in U.S. Census reports. The ratios of such "top 50 percent" plant size averages to total industry size tend to be closely associated with engineering approach share estimates like those in Tables 4.2 and 4.3. The simple correlation coefficients for comparable industries range from 0.59 to 0.89.[45] Average "top 50 percent" plant size shares were computed for 155 four-digit U.S. manufacturing industries with value added of $75 million or more in 1963. In only 14 industries did the average sales of the largest plants amount to 10 percent or more of total industry sales.[46]

We conclude then that economies of scale at the plant level do not in the vast majority of instances necessitate high national concentration levels for U.S. manufacturing industries. There are exceptions, to be sure. Middling levels of oligopoly are required in such industries as refrigerators, passenger autos, cellulosic fibers (i.e., rayon), and tractor manufacturing; and tight oligopoly is probably mandated in a few industries such as turbogenerators, Diesel engines, typewriters, and civilian airliner production.

A less sanguine conclusion emerges when we recognize that transportation costs often lead to geographic markets considerably smaller than the nationwide expanse assumed in Tables 4.2 and 4.3. Shipping a dollar's worth of beer 350 miles from the brewery, for example, cost approximately 7.8 cents on a representative 1963 haul.[47] This level of transportation cost is sufficient to fragment the continental United States into five to seven meaningful geographic markets, within which an MOS brewery contributes a sufficient share of output to make oligopoly probable. Seven of the 12 industries in Table 4.2 experience shipping costs high enough to induce regionalization. Table 4.4 attempts to take this into account by estimating the number of regional markets into which the lower 48 states might properly have been subdivided during the 1960s. These estimates are then used to indicate (in the last column) the share of 1967 output an MOS plant would have contributed in the average regional market. A considerably stronger tendency toward oligopoly—i.e., with mean four-firm regional market concentration ratios of 40 or more in five of the

40. Literature surveys and discussions of the analytic hazards include Caleb A. Smith, "Survey of the Empirical Evidence on Economies of Scale," with a comment by Milton Friedman, in *Business Concentration and Price Policy* (Princeton: Princeton University Press, 1955), pp. 213–38; J. Johnston, *Statistical Cost Analysis* (New York: McGraw-Hill, 1960); A. A. Walters, "Production and Cost Functions: An Econometric Survey," *Econometrica* 31 (January–April 1963): 1–66; and John S. McGee, "Efficiency and Economies of Size," in Harvey Goldschmid, H. Michael Mann, and J. Fred Weston, eds., *Industrial Concentration: The New Learning* (Boston: Little, Brown, 1975), pp. 55–97.

41. See for example Hollis B. Chenery, "Engineering Production Functions," *Quarterly Journal of Economics* 63 (November 1949): 507–31 (on natural gas pipelines); and Myles G. Boylan, Jr., *Economic Effects of Scale Increases in the Steel Industry* (New York: Praeger, 1975).

42. The pioneering study of this genre, covering 20 industries, was Joe S. Bain, *Barriers to New Competition* (Cambridge, Mass.: Harvard University Press, 1956), especially pp. 71–83, 227–49.

43. Scherer et al., *The Economics of Multi-Plant Operation*.

44. Aubrey Silberston, "Economies of Scale in Theory and Practice," *Economic Journal* 82 (March 1972) supplement, p. 379.

45. Scherer et al., *The Economics of Multi-Plant Operation*, pp. 182–83; and Leonard W. Weiss, "Optimal Plant Size and the Extent of Suboptimal Capacity," in Masson and Qualls, eds., *Essays on Industrial Organization*, pp. 132–33.

46. See Scherer et al., *The Economics of Multi-Plant Operation*, pp. 434–39.

47. Scherer et al., *The Economics of Multi-Plant Operation*, p. 90.

The determinants of market structure   95

T 4.2 Minimum optimal plant scales as a percentage of 1967 U.S. demand, and the cost disadvantage of suboptimal scale plants

Industry	Minimum optimal scale	Percentage of 1967 U.S. demand	Percentage by which unit cost rises at one-third MOS
Beer brewing	4.5 million (31 U.S. gallon) barrels per year capacity	3.4	5.0
Cigarettes	36 billion cigarettes per year; 2,275 employees	6.6	2.2
Cotton and synthetic broad-woven fabrics	37.5 million square yards per year; 600 employees in modern integrated plants	0.2	7.6
Paints	10 million U.S. gallons per year; 450 employees	1.4	4.4
Petroleum refining	200,000 (42 U.S. gallon) barrels per day crude oil processing capacity	1.9	4.8
Nonrubber shoes	1 million pairs per year; 250 employees on single shift operation	0.2	1.5
Glass bottles	133,000 tons per year; 1,000 employees	1.5	11.0
Portland cement	7 million 376-pound barrels per year capacity	1.7	26.0
Integrated steel	4 million tons per year capacity	2.6	11.0
Antifriction bearings	800 employees	1.4	8.0
Refrigerators	800,000 units per year	14.1	6.5
Automobile storage batteries	1 million units per year; 300 employees	1.9	4.6

Source: F. M. Scherer, Alan Beckenstein, Erich Kaufer, and R. D. Murphy, *The Economics of Multi-Plant Operation: An International Comparisons Study* (Cambridge, Mass.: Harvard University Press, 1975), pp. 80, 94. Reprinted by permission of Harvard University Press. Copyright © 1975 by the President and Fellows of Harvard College.

seven industries—is revealed. These are, it must be stressed, crude averages. In the densely populated Northeast and North Central states, MOS plant market shares would have been lower, while in the sparsely populated Plains states, much higher concentration levels are implied. Since the Table 4.2 sample was deliberately biased toward industries with relatively high transportation costs, the Table 4.4 analysis probably overstates the average impact of regionalization

T 4.3 Minimum optimal scale plant output shares and cost gradients, as estimated by Pratten and Weiss: 23 industries

Industry	MOS as % of U.S. demand, circa 1967	% incr. in unit cost at ½ MOS
Flour mills	0.7	3
Soybean mills	2.4	2
Bread baking	0.3	7.5
Tufted rugs	0.7	10
Printing paper	4.4	9
Linerboard	4.4	8
Sulphuric acid	3.7	1
Synthetic rubber	4.7	15
Cellulosic synthetic fibers	11.1	5
Nylon, acrylic, and polyester fibers	6.0	7–11
Detergents	2.4	2.5
Passenger auto tires	3.8	5
Bricks	0.3	25
Iron foundries: lg. castings	0.3	10
Turbogenerators	23	n.a.
Diesel engines, up to 100 hp	21–30	4–28
Machine tools	0.3	5
Electronic computers	15	8
Electric motors	15	15
Transformers (mix. of types)	4.9	8
Integrated passenger auto production	11.0	6
Commercial transport aircraft	10	20
Bicycles	2.1	n.a.

Source: Leonard W. Weiss, "Optimal Plant Size and the Extent of Suboptimal Capacity," in Robert T. Masson and P. D. Qualls, eds., *Essays on Industrial Organization in Honor of Joe S. Bain* (Cambridge, Mass.: Ballinger, 1975), pp. 128–31; adapted in part from C. F. Pratten, *Economies of Scale in Manufacturing Industry* (Cambridge, England: Cambridge University Press, 1971). Reprinted with permission from *Essays on Industrial Organization,* copyright 1976, Ballinger Publishing Company.

on concentration. In a survey of 283 manufacturing industries, Weiss found only 96 in which three or more probable regional markets existed.[48] Still, we cannot overlook the interaction between shipping costs and scale economies in setting a floor for concentration levels consistent with production and distributional efficiency.

We turn briefly now to product-specific scale economies. Not much can be said on the subject because there have been no systematic quantitative studies like those reviewed thus far for plant-specific economies. A preliminary grasp of the problem can be had by invoking the "80–20 rule"—a rough empirical generalization indicating that the best-selling 20 percent of a firm's products by number account for 80 percent of total sales, while the more numerous "cats and dogs" items contribute the remaining 20 percent. Observation suggests that the typical sizeable U.S. manufacturer manages to exploit most if not all product-specific economies on the best-selling 20 percent of its products, but falls short, and often far short, of realizing minimum costs on the remaining "cats and dogs." For the latter, demand is insufficient to sustain long, low-cost production runs but sufficient to cover the higher costs of low-volume production. In a limited sense, the production of special Bock beers, navy blue acrylic blend cloth printed with camelia designs, 36-inch steel I-beams, or roller bearings designed for a particular tractor tends toward natural monopoly.[49] This 80–20 generalization is extremely rough. In smaller nations like Canada and Sweden, a considerably larger fraction of all output is manufactured in suboptimal volumes.[50] And in the United States, the ratio varies from industry to industry, depending upon demand and production process characteristics. Thus, in continuous process industries such as cement making and petroleum refining, product-specific

48. Leonard W. Weiss, "The Geographic Size of Markets in Manufacturing," *Review of Economics and Statistics* 54 (August 1972): 245–66.

49. The power that goes with monopoly is limited in most such cases (but not for 36-inch I-beams) because competitive production may be commenced quickly and easily by resetting equipment used on other products.

50. See Scherer et al., *The Economics of Multi-Plant Operation,* p. 51, and the references cited there.

The determinants of market structure   97

scale-economy sacrifices are miniscule. But for most if not all individual electronic computers and military or civilian aircraft, learning curve economies probably continue out to the total quantity demanded at any price covering cost. Research delineating more precisely the distribution of production volumes by the extent to which product-specific economies are realized, and the cost implications thereof, is sorely needed.

The impact of technological change and market growth How high concentration must be to secure production efficiency depends, as we have seen, upon the balance between technology and market size. Thus far our view of this balance has been static—i.e., a snapshot at one moment in time. But conditions change. In the early 1950s, Professor Bain found, an MOS flat-rolled steel products plant had a capacity of from 1.0 to 2.5 million tons per year.[51] By 1965 the MOS capacity had increased to 4.0 million tons. As noted earlier, scale-up advances in blast furnace and basic oxygen furnace technology raised the optimum further by 1975—most likely to a capacity

T 4.4 The impact of regionalization on MOS plant market shares

Industry	Approx. no. of regional mkts. in cont. U.S.	MOS plant share per ave. regional mkt.
Beer brewing	6	20.4
Paints	5	7.0
Petroleum refining	5	9.5
Glass bottles	9	13.5
Cement	24	40.8
Steel works	4	10.4
Storage batteries	6	11.4

Source: F. M. Scherer, "Economies of Scale and Industrial Concentration," in Harvey J. Goldschmid, H. Michael Mann, and J. Fred Weston, eds., *Industrial Concentration: The New Learning* (Boston: Little, Brown, 1974), pp. 28–31; adapted in part from Leonard W. Weiss, "The Geographic Size of Markets in Manufacturing," *Review of Economics and Statistics* 54 (August 1972): 245–66. Reprinted with permission.

of about 12 million tons per year. This trend toward larger optimal scales will be reversed if newer direct iron ore reduction techniques come to dominate the traditional blast furnace method;[52] however, at least up to the late 1970s, what one observed was an unbroken history of optimal scale increases.

This pattern has been repeated again and again during the 20th century. There has been a general movement toward larger minimum optimal plant sizes. Saul Sands analyzed 46 industries for which comparable data on physical output and the number of plants were available, and found that average physical output per plant increased between 1904 and 1947 by about 3 percent per annum.[53] But while plants have been getting larger, so have the markets for their output. According to estimates by the National Bureau of Economic Research, physical output of all manufacturing industries increased by nearly 4 percent per year between 1904 and 1947. If Sands' sample were representative of all manufacturing industries, this comparison would suggest a *decline* in average plant size relative to market size. The comparison is apparently not perfect, however, since Sands found in a related study that the largest 20 plants in 47 four-digit industries originated an (unweighted) average of 42 percent of industry shipments by value in 1904 and 47 percent in 1947.[54] This might be interpreted to mean that, at least for his sample, the long-run balance between increasing plant size and increasing market size ran slightly in favor of the former.

There is reason to believe that in the period immediately following World War II, the growth of plant scale was generally slower than the growth of markets. A study of 125 four-digit industries for which comparable data were available revealed that the share of industry sales originating in the eight largest plants declined between 1947 and 1958 in 67 cases, while it increased in only 48.[55] According to John M. Blair, this seeming reversal of past trends was attributable to fundamental changes in the direction of technological advance away from centralizing innovations and toward decentralizing techniques.[56] Examples include the replacement of central motive power units by individual electric motors; the rise to prominence of easily fabricated plastics and light metals; the replacement of highly specialized machines by more flexible and adaptable units, such as computer or tape-controlled contour milling machines; and the displacement of water and rail transportation by trucks, with greater flexibility and more economical accommodation of less-than-carload shipments. Also, the growing breadth of product lines in some industries and rising demand volatility associated with fashion consciousness have complicated the job of managing plants, inducing plant size declines.[57] So have wage increases in urban centers, precipitating a flight to smaller towns where plant sizes are constrained by local labor availability.

Thus, some developments have contributed to rising optimal plant scales while others have worked in the opposite direction. Of the 12 industries covered by Table 4.2, minimum optimal scales rose between 1958 and 1970 in 6—steel, cement, brewing, paints, refrigerators, and batteries. They fell, usually modestly, in only 3—bearings, shoes, and (less clearly) weaving. This suggests that the net bias was toward continued MOS growth. Yet, according to Blair, an analysis of individual industry trends might not tell the whole story, since demand may have been shifting away from industries with large-scale plants and toward those with small optima. On this point, the evidence is fragmentary. Census statistics reveal that plants with 1,000 or more employees accounted for 32.8 percent of total manufacturing establishment employees in 1947, 30.5 percent in 1958, 30.5 percent in 1963, 32.8 percent in 1967, and 28.7 percent in 1972. Unless one is willing to infer a trend from the 1972 drop, no systematic shift toward smaller plants is apparent.

To the extent that industry concentration is influenced by the efficiency imperatives associated with plant scale economies, one would expect concentration to be higher, the smaller markets are, and especially, the smaller they are in relation to minimum optimal plant scales. Also, the more rapidly demand grows, the more likely it is that rising plant scale requirements will be outstripped, all else being equal,[58] and hence the stronger any trend toward declining concentration, or the weaker any trend toward rising

concentration. These hypotheses are at least crudely testable.

On the first, Ralph Nelson reported a strong and persistent negative correlation between the 1954 sales of U.S. manufacturing industries and their four-firm concentration ratios, both before and after adjusting for the tendency of relatively large industries to be defined too broadly.[59] Updating the analysis to 1963 for a sample of 101 four-digit industries, all large enough to have value added of at least $75 million, R. D. Murphy found negative but weak correlations (i.e., of from -0.12 to -0.17) between value added and the

51. Bain, *Barriers to New Competition*, p. 236.

52. See "Mexico Promotes Steel Process," *New York Times*, 2 April 1979, p. D7.

53. Saul S. Sands, "Changes in Scale of Production in United States Manufacturing Industry, 1904–1947," *Review of Economics and Statistics* 43 (November 1961): 365–68. It is important in such an analysis to use some measure of physical output, as Sands did, and not employment, as others have occasionally done. Plant sizes often increase in real terms while employment declines because of capital-labor substitution and productivity increases.

54. Saul S. Sands, "Concentration in United States Manufacturing Industry, 1904–1947," *International Economic Review* 3 (January 1962): 79–92.

55. See testimony of John M. Blair, U.S., Congress, Senate, Subcommittee on Antitrust and Monopoly hearings, *Economic Concentration*, Part 4, 89th Cong., 1st sess., p. 1550. Unfortunately, the Census Bureau has not published similar data for later years.

56. *Economic Concentration*, Part 4, 89th Cong., 1st sess., pp. 1536–37; his article, "Technology and Size," *American Economic Review* 38 (May 1948): 121–52; and his comments in Goldschmid et al., *Industrial Concentration*, pp. 109–10.

57. Scherer et al., *The Economics of Multi-Plant Operation*, pp. 31–34, 82–83.

58. Technological changes are in part induced by market growth, and therefore the variables treated here cannot be considered entirely independent. See Jacob Schmookler, *Invention and Economic Growth* (Cambridge, Mass.: Harvard University Press, 1967), especially Chapters 6–9. However, there is no clear evidence that changes in the minimum optimal scale of production are related systematically and causally to changes in market size.

   It should be noted also that rapid market growth may lead to concentration decreases not only by outstripping the growth of optimal plant and firm sizes, but also by encouraging and facilitating the entry of new competitors. We shall discuss this point further in Chapter 8.

59. Ralph L. Nelson, *Concentration in the Manufacturing Industries of the United States* (New Haven, Conn.: Yale University Press, 1963), pp. 46–48.

The determinants of market structure   99

four-firm concentration ratios.[60] To relate *relative* market size to concentration, he calculated the ratio of average "top 50 percent" plant sales to total industry sales as a surrogate measure of the national market share required by an MOS plant. The "top 50 percent" ratio and four-firm concentration were strongly correlated, with r values of +0.68 to +0.76. The larger the size of industry-leading plants was relative to industry sales, the higher concentration was.[61] This result persists when relative market size statistics derived through the engineering method are employed to analyze concentration in 12 industries and six different national markets—Canada, the United States, France, the United Kingdom, West Germany, and Sweden.[62] The larger the number of MOS plants a particular national market could hold, the lower the three-firm concentration ratio was. The correlation coefficient for variables in logarithmic form was −0.67. It seems clear that large market size, absolute or (especially) relative, is a significant inhibitor of high concentration.

Several statistical studies have disclosed an analogous dynamic relationship between *changes* in market size and changes in concentration. Nelson, for example, observed that each 100 percentage point increase in an industry's value added between 1935 and 1954 (i.e., from a 1935 index of 100 to a 1954 index of 200, and again from 200 to 300, and so on) was accompanied on the average by a 1.45 percentage point incremental decline in the four-firm concentration ratio.[63] A multiple regression analysis of 154 U.S. manufacturing industries showed that, taking into account also the initial 1947 concentration level, industry size, and consumer versus producer goods orientation, the four-firm concentration ratio tended to fall between 1947 and 1972 by 0.44 percentage points for each percentage point increase in the continuously compounded annual rate of value added growth over that interval. For a larger sample of 323 industries comparable over the 1963–72 interval, a similar analysis showed concentration declining on average by 0.2 percentage points for each percentage point increase in the annual 1963–72 growth rate.[64] The changes in concentration associated with market expansion were modest, and one may choose to

conclude with Shepherd that "it would take a thumping amount of growth to reduce concentration by even a sliver."[65] Yet it is equally true that without the thumping amounts of growth actually experienced, there would have been a stronger upward trend in concentration.

Economies of multi-plant operation Our analysis up to this point has been concerned primarily with economies at the plant level or lower—that is, with plant-specific and product-specific economies. Although we have seen that concentration increases with the need to operate plants large relative to the market, this is not the only, or perhaps even the main, cause of high concentration. That other influences are at work is shown by the fact that the leading firms in most industries operate multiple plants supplying a similar array of products. The most complete data on multi-plant operation patterns in manufacturing come from the 1963 Census of Manufactures.[66] There is reason to believe that no material changes have occurred since then.[67] Table 4.5 presents the distribution of 417 four-digit industries according to the average number of industry-specific plants per Big Four seller (excluding warehouses, R&D laboratories, headquarters and sales offices, and the like). The leading four sellers operated a single plant each in only 22 industries.

T 4.5 Extent of multi-plant operation in 417 manufacturing industries

Plants per Big Four Member	Number of industries	Percent of industries
1.00 to 1.5 plants	78	18.7
1.75 to 2.5 plants	89	21.3
2.75 to 4.0 plants	87	20.9
4.25 to 7.0 plants	87	20.9
7.25 to 10 plants	28	6.7
10.25 to 20 plants	35	8.4
More than 20 plants	13	3.1
All industries	417	100.0

Source: U.S., Congress, Senate, Subcommittee on Antitrust and Monopoly report, *Concentration Ratios in Manufacturing Industry: 1963*, Part 2, 89th Cong., 1st sess., Table 27.

Evidently, the preeminent position of most leading firms can be attributed not merely to maintaining large plants, but to operating *many* of them.[68] From this it does not necessarily follow that high concentration and extensive multi-plant operation are uniquely associated.[69] Indeed, there is little systematic difference in the extent of multi-plant operation between leading firms in highly concentrated as compared to much less concentrated industries, as shown by the tabulation of 1963 U.S. nationwide data in Table 4.6. The most that can be said is that if the industry leaders in *both* concentrated and atomistically structured industries operated fewer plants, all else being equal, there would be less concentration across the board.[70]

The crucial remaining question is, does this multi-plant operation by leading firms confer economies above and beyond those associated with operating a single plant of optimal scale? And, if so, how significant are they? Or to reverse the focus, how seriously disadvantaged are firms operating only a single MOS plant, compared to the largest multi-plant enterprises?

We shall organize our analysis into three main categories—economies of multi-plant production, investment, and physical distribution; economies of risk spreading and finance; and advantages of sales promotion on a multi-plant scale. As we shall see, these have varying performance implications, some entailing clear-cut efficiency gains, some redistributions of income, and some a blend of efficiency, redistributive, and monopolistic effects. Two other sets of possible consequences must be dealt with summarily. For one, there may be economies of scale in conducting research and development that persist as the firm expands into a size range embracing multiple MOS plants. This possibility is so important that much of a chapter (Chapter 15) will be devoted to it. We therefore defer further discussion until then. Second, a multi-plant enterprise may be able to economize on management services by having a common central pool of financial planners, accountants, market researchers, labor relations specialists, purchasing agents, lawyers, and the like. The problem here is that while economies of specialization undoubtedly exist in such functions, there may be diseconomies in coordinating a multi-plant enterprise. The best available evidence on this point, derived from interviews with 125 manufacturing firms, suggests that the managerial and central staff economies of multi-plant operation are at most slight, and that in many instances, especially beyond some modest threshold, multi-plant size is disadvantageous.[71]

60. Scherer et al., *The Economics of Multi-Plant Operation*, pp. 193–94.

61. See also Peter Pashigian, "The Effect of Market Size on Concentration," *International Economic Review* 10 (October 1969): 291–314, who obtains similar results using minimum optimal *firm* size estimates derived through the survivor method. Cf. S. I. Ornstein, J. Fred Weston, M. D. Intriligator, and R. E. Shrieves, "Determinants of Market Structure," *Southern Economic Journal* 40 (April 1974): 612–25.

62. Scherer et al., *The Economics of Multi-Plant Operation*, pp. 222–23.

63. Nelson, *Concentration*, pp. 52–56.

64. The regression results are reported more fully in Table 4.8. Except in classifying industries on the basis of new data and using continuously compounded growth rates, they are similar in both approach and findings to Willard F. Mueller and Larry G. Hamm, "Trends in Industrial Market Concentration, 1947 to 1970," *Review of Economics and Statistics* 56 (November 1974): 511–20. See also James A. Dalton and Stephen A. Rhoades, "Growth and Product Differentiability as Factors Influencing Changes in Concentration," *Journal of Industrial Economics* 22 (March 1974): 235–40.

65. Testimony of W. G. Shepherd, U.S., Congress, Senate, Subcommittee on Antitrust and Monopoly hearings, *Economic Concentration*, Part 2, 89th Cong., 1st sess., p. 639.

66. U.S., Congress, Senate, Subcommittee on Antitrust and Monopoly report, *Concentration Ratios in Manufacturing Industry: 1963*, Part 2, 89th Cong., 1st sess., Table 27.

67. See Edward Miller, "Size of Firm and Size of Plant," *Southern Economic Journal* 44 (April 1978): 863–64.

68. However, the four industry leaders do operate larger plants than their followers—in 1972, 14 times as large on the average as all non-Big Four firms and 2.4 times those of the fifth through eighth largest sellers. See Miller, "Size of Firm and Size of Plant," pp. 867–69.

69. As we saw a page earlier, logarithms of the three-firm concentration ratios for 12 industries in six nations were inversely correlated with logarithms of the number of MOS plants a national market could hold. The coefficient of determination r^2 (expanded to three significant digits) was 0.444. Adding as a further explanatory variable the logarithms of the number of plants operated per Big Three member raises the multiple R^2 only to 0.450.

70. Needless to say, multiunit operation is also extensive among the leading firms in the retail trades. In 1972, the leading four companies operated an average of 2,012 stores each in food retailing, 621 in the department store field, 667 in apparel and accessories, and 401 in drugs. U.S., Bureau of the Census, *1972 Census of Retail Trade*, vol. I (Washington, D.C.: Government Printing Office, 1976), Table 2C.

71. See Scherer et al., *The Economics of Multi-Plant Operation*, pp. 321–25, 335, 339–40.

T 4.6 The relationship between seller concentration and the extent of multi-plant operation

Four-firm concentration ratio	Number of industries	Average number of plants per company		
		Four leaders	Next four	Rest of industry
1–19	90	4.4	2.7	1.03
20–39	162	6.1	3.5	1.07
40–64	103	4.7	2.4	1.08
65–100	62	5.9	2.2	1.09

Source: U.S., Congress, Senate, Subcommittee on Antitrust and Monopoly report, *Concentration Ratios in Manufacturing Industry: 1963*, Part 2, 89th Cong., 1st sess., Table 27.

If multi-plant operation yields economies in production, investment, and physical distribution, real resource savings generally result, and society is almost surely better off, all else (such as the degree of monopolistic resource misallocation) being held equal. To begin analyzing such economies, it is useful to divide firms operating multiple plants in an industry into three categories (recognizing of course that hybrid cases also exist). First is the case in which a market of considerable geographic expanse is served and outbound transportation costs are appreciable.[72] Then the firm's least-cost strategy is likely to involve operating multiple geographically dispersed plants, each supplying for the most part only the customers nearest its location. The operating patterns of sizeable firms in the cement, beer, petroleum refining, and glass bottle industries provide relatively pure examples. Second is the case of firms with low shipping costs (e.g., less than 1.5 percent of ex-plant sales revenue on 350-mile deliveries) but complex product lines. Then each plant of a multi-plant enterprise may specialize in some narrow segment of the product array—e.g., one plant in women's cemented-sole fashion shoes, another in women's casuals, a third in men's Goodyear welts, a fourth in work shoes, and so on. The third case is a catch-all to cover enterprises with multiple plants joined together more or less randomly, usually by merger, without any attempt to enforce either geographic or product specialization. Such combinations are not likely to provide production or distribution economies and can therefore be ignored.

Now, if delivery costs are substantial, as they are for beer or cement or steel reinforcing rods, it is obviously more economical, if one is to serve the entire continental United States market, to have multiple dispersed plants than to ship everything from one giant centrally located installation. But this begs the fundamental question: Why does a firm have to serve the entire continental market? Are there any production, investment, and/or distribution cost differences between the case in which a single enterprise operates five optimal-sized, geographically dispersed plants and the one in which five independent geographically dispersed firms operate a single MOS plant each?

There may be. It can be shown that when demand is fixed at any moment in time but grows over time and when scale economies can be realized by expanding capacity in large indivisible chunks, excess capacity carrying costs can be reduced, and the scale economy opportunities exploited more fully, by playing a kind of investment whipsaw game.[73] First a large investment is made at location A, with other plants reducing their shipping radii to satisfy growing nearby demand more fully and letting plant A serve what would normally be their peripherally located customers. Later plant B expands and territories are readjusted to utilize its new capacity, and so on. Transportation costs are higher under this coordinated investment staging scheme than with autarkic expansion by each individual plant, jointly or independently owned, but investment carrying costs may be lower by a more than offsetting amount. However, such a scheme will not yield net savings if the individual plants can cover temporary capacity deficits by buying from recently expanded *nearby* competitors at prices approximating marginal cost and if they can sell excess supplies to such competitors, or if *local* supply and demand (no longer assumed fixed) can be equilibrated by market price adjustments before and after major expansions. The more smoothly local markets work in facilitating adjustment to capacity jumps, the smaller are the benefits from coordinated multi-plant, multi-region investment staging. In other words, such investment coordination economies are of a second-best character, realizable when and because local markets fail to balance demand and supply.

Economies may also result from the operation of multiple geographically dispersed plants as an integrated system. For instance, the demand for automobile batteries peaks during the winter months in the northern United States and during the summer in the South. A firm with plants in both areas might be able to maintain less peak-load capacity by shipping north in the winter and south in the summer. In practice, however, this is not normally done, largely because the costs of carrying additional capacity are less than cross-shipping costs.[74] Similarly, it can be shown that under certain cost curve conditions, production cutbacks in response to a general demand slump can be accomplished more economically by shutting down one or more whole plants in an integrated network than by reducing output at each of many independent plants.[75] Again, this is infrequently observed, in part because cost curves fail to have the requisite shapes and in part because the retention of skilled workers argues for spreading the impact of cutbacks rather than concentrating it geographically.[76] As a third illustration, an integrated truck or barge fleet may be used to fuller capacity by coordinating backhauls among several plants or, when shipping costs are not so high as to require plant dispersion, by consolidating the output of several plants to secure lower full truckload or carload rates from common carriers. Numerous cases of this sort were uncovered in interviews with 125 companies. For the most part, however, the observed savings were small.[77]

The other main interesting mode of multi-plant operation occurs when plants specialize in some narrow slice of a product array—e.g., small mass-produced ball bearings at one plant, other small ball bearings at a second, large ball bearings at a third, tapered bearings at a fourth, and so on. Plants with a narrow line of products are easier to manage. For a plant of given size, production run lengths will be greater, and hence product-specific economies will be realized more fully, the narrower the line manufactured is. The key interpretive questions are, can't the same degree of plant specialization be achieved by single-plant firms that choose to offer only a narrow line of products? And are the plants of multi-plant sellers in fact more narrowly specialized than those of single-plant firms?

In answer to the first question, it appears that at least in some industries, there are marketing advantages to being a broad-line supplier. This in turn argues for multi-plant operation unless one's product line can be rounded out through purchases from other competing manufacturers. Among 12 industries studied in depth by the author, the compulsions toward broad-line marketing were strongest in refrigerators, bearings, and fabrics.

72. A variant involves plants tied to geographically dispersed raw material sources of modest size by high input shipping costs or weight losses in processing. Uranium milling, pulp mills, and tomato canning are examples.

73. See Scherer et al., *The Economics of Multi-Plant Operation*, pp. 40–48, 143–47, 290–95, drawing upon the theory developed in Alan S. Manne, ed., *Investments for Capacity Expansion* (Cambridge, Mass.: MIT Press, 1967).

74. Scherer et al., *The Economics of Multi-Plant Operation*, p. 277.

75. See Don Patinkin, "Multi-Plant Firms, Cartels, and Imperfect Competition," *Quarterly Journal of Economics* 61 (February 1947): 173–205.

76. Scherer et al., *The Economics of Multi-Plant Operation*, pp. 280–82.

77. Scherer et al., *The Economics of Multi-Plant Operation*, pp. 271–74.

The second question in effect asks whether single-plant producers in multi-product industries incur only a marketing disadvantage by not offering a broad line, or whether they also tend to cram relatively more low-volume products into the production schedules of their only plant and therefore sacrifice product-specific economies as well. The evidence on this point is weak and mixed.[78] There does appear to be a tendency in some industries for single-plant firms to experience shorter production runs than their multi-plant rivals. However, many exceptions exist, and the shorter runs of some relatively small firms may signify nothing more than specialization on low-volume items in which the larger companies have no interest—e.g., because their management structures may be too hierarchical to cope with the challenges of small-lot production. Also, multi-plant size and the attainment of product-specific economies do not appear to be closely correlated. Many large multi-plant firms are large because they produce commensurately more products than single-plant rivals, not because they produce a given array of products in higher volume. The overall picture is quite complex, and we must conclude that there is far too little hard evidence on this important dimension of multi-plant scale economies.

Capital-raising and other pecuniary economies

Economies of scale are also encountered when firms raise capital through common stock issues and borrowing. Indeed, this appears to be one of the most persistent advantages of corporate size, with small incremental capital cost savings being enjoyed out to very large scales. Thus, a study of debt costs in the 1960s revealed that, on the average, corporations with assets of $200 million borrowed funds at an average interest rate 0.74 percentage points lower than firms with assets of $5 million. Billion-dollar corporations enjoyed a 0.34 point incremental advantage over their $200 million asset counterparts.[79] This advantage, it should be noted, can stem from multi-plant size in a broader sense than what we have considered thus far. That is, it may derive from operating a multiplicity of plants in different industries as well as in the same industry.

The evaluation of such savings poses special problems. By way of analogy, consider the case of a large firm obtaining price concessions from the suppliers of some important input such as steel sheets or synthetic resins. (Such size-correlated concessions are quite common despite the existence of laws against price discrimination. However, they appear to be linked more frequently to large-scale purchasing at a *single* plant, rather than the aggregation of multiple plant purchases.[80]) If the concessions are the result of differential bargaining power and not of any differences in the way production or distribution takes place, we say that the economies achieved are *pecuniary*—that is, reflecting no physical resource savings but only a redistribution of income from sellers to buyers. *Real* economies of scale on the other hand are those resulting from size-correlated differences in supply arrangements that confer real resource savings—e.g., through longer production runs, less administrative effort per unit of output sold, or more efficient truck loading. The problem is, to which category do capital input cost savings belong?

It seems clear that the capital-raising economies of scale are partly associated with real resource savings. Negotiating a loan or new stock issue or obtaining the necessary regulatory agency clearances entails transaction costs that are nearly fixed, whether the amount of funds raised is small or large. The larger the issue is, the lower those costs are per dollar of capital raised. In a statistical analysis of 238 common stock issues floated between 1960 and 1962 by corporations of widely varying sizes, Archer and Faerber found that flotation costs ranged from 5 to 44 percent of the total value of the shares sold. Flotation cost as a percentage of total share value was inversely correlated with both size of the issue and size of the issuing firm.[81]

The other main basis for firm size-correlated capital cost differences is risk. Investments in large corporations are less risky in the sense that earnings tend to be more stable and defaults or bankruptcy rarer. Statistical investigations reveal that profitability varies less over time for individual large corporations than for smaller concerns. Thus, the average standard deviation of the ratio of annual earnings before tax plus interest to assets over the 1960–68 time period varied as follows with respect to the size of 768 U.S. corporations for which a continuous data set was available:[82]

Asset Size	Standard Deviation
$10 million	.068
$100 million	.041
$1 billion	.014

The greater intertemporal stability of large corporations' earnings has at least three possible explanations. First, large multi-plant firms tend to possess more monopoly power than smaller enterprises, all else being equal. One manifestation of this tendency, as we shall see in subsequent chapters, may be the ability to pursue an earnings-stabilizing pricing policy. Second, large firms appear more prone to smooth reported earnings through various accounting manipulations.[83] Third, the ability to spread risks increases with size. The effect of a major fire, explosion, or localized wildcat strike is apt to be less devastating for a company with numerous plants than for the single-plant producer. Large multi-plant enterprises are likely to offer more distinct products and/or serve more geographic markets, and this makes them better able to weather a price war or the loss of an important customer in any single market or product segment.

The risk-spreading and monopolistic advantages of size are to some extent antithetical, for with a given volume of sales, one's share in any given narrowly defined market must be inversely correlated with the number of markets or product lines one supplies. Moreover, the less closely related those markets are, the less monopoly power the firm is likely to have, but the greater the stabilization effect may be. To see this, we note that the standard deviation of total profits for a firm operating in two markets is given by:

$$\sigma_F = \sqrt{\sigma_1^2 + \sigma_2^2 + 2r\sigma_1\sigma_2}$$

where σ_1 is the standard deviation of profits in market 1, σ_2 the standard deviation of profits in market 2, and r is the coefficient of correlation between profit movements over time in the two markets. Suppose each market is served by a distinct plant, and for each market the expected

(i.e., mean or best-guess) value of profits is $1 million per year, with a standard deviation of $400,000. If the plants are organized as independent firms, each finds the standard deviation of its profits to be 40 percent of the mean. If the two markets are influenced so similarly by demand and cost conditions that profit fluctuations between them are perfectly correlated over time, with $r = +1.0$, combining the two plants into a single multi-plant firm will leave the standard

78. In Canada, where the extent of multi-plant operation is considerably less than in the United States, plants are also smaller on average and tend to produce a broader diversity of products than in the U.S. See Richard E. Caves, *Diversification, Foreign Investment, and Scale in North American Manufacturing Industries* (Ottawa: Economic Council of Canada, 1975), especially Chapters 5 and 6. It is not clear from Caves's results whether the scale economy sacrifices associated with high product diversity are mitigated by multi-plant operation in Canada.

79. Scherer et al., *The Economics of Multi-Plant Operation*, p. 287.

80. Scherer et al., *The Economics of Multi-Plant Operation*, pp. 260–62.

81. S. H. Archer and L. G. Faerber, "Firm Size and the Cost of Externally Secured Capital," *Journal of Finance* 21 (March 1966): 69–83.

82. These figures were computed using data kindly supplied by Daryl N. Winn and originally analyzed in his article, "On the Relations Between Rates of Return, Risk, and Market Structure," *Quarterly Journal of Economics* 91 (February 1977): 157–63. They are derived from bivariate regression equations relating the standard deviation of pretax earnings *plus* interest *divided by* assets to the base ten logarithm of assets. The simple correlation (r) between the two variables was −0.51. The relationship is probably not precisely log linear as assumed, since the regression predicts a negative standard deviation of earnings for corporations with assets exceeding $3.3 billion. For all sampled corporations, the mean standard deviation of the earnings variable was 0.046.

   For other evidence on the negative relationship between firm size and the intertemporal variability of earnings, see Geoffrey Whittington, *The Prediction of Profitability* (Cambridge, England: Cambridge University Press, 1971), pp. 66–73; Gloria J. Hurdle, "Leverage, Risk, Market Structure and Profitability," *Review of Economics and Statistics* 56 (November 1974): 481–82; Alex Jacquemin and Wistano Saëz, "A Comparison of the Performance of the Largest European and Japanese Industrial Firms," *Oxford Economic Papers* 28 (July 1976): 271–83; and (for evidence suggesting no significant variability-size relationship) David J. Smyth, William J. Boyes, and Dennis E. Peseau, *Size, Growth, Profits, and Executive Compensation in the Large Corporation* (New York: Holmes & Meier, 1975), pp. 60–66. On the variability of profitability for corporations of differing size at a given moment in time, see Stekler, *Profitability and Size of Firm*, p. 92.

83. Cf. Chapter 2, pp. 34–35 *supra*.

deviation at 40 percent of mean profits.[84] But the more different or conglomerate the markets are, the lower their intertemporal correlation r will tend to be. When there is a completely random relationship between profit changes across the two markets, $r = 0$ and $\sigma_F \cong \$566,000$, or roughly 28 percent of combined mean profits. The more markets with randomly related demand and cost movements the firm serves, *ceteris paribus*, the more its risks will be spread, and the smaller will be the standard deviation of profits as a percentage of mean profits.[85]

The variability of profits affects firms' capital cost because investors in the capital markets are risk-averse. They will invest their capital at lower effective interest rates or dividend payouts—and hence a lower cost of capital to the firm—if they expect the profits stream from which they will draw to be stable than if they expect it to be highly variable over time. This is so for at least two reasons. First, with an extremely variable profits pattern, there is a greater chance that one or two particularly bad years will plunge the firm into bankruptcy, perhaps wiping out investors' equity.

The second reason is more subtle and complex. An important development in corporate finance theory is the so-called "capital asset pricing model" (CAPM), which works out the logic of risk-averse investors' attempts to maximize their utility by acquiring a portfolio with the optimal mix of risky and risk-free assets.[86] "Risk" in the model's operational sense is generally measured in terms of the variability of returns on financial investments—e.g., returns on common stock purchases and holdings. Those returns depend upon macroeconomic and investor psychology variables affecting all stock prices and also upon individual companies' profitability. In a world of perfect knowledge, a truly random deviation in some company's profits for one year should not cause investors to modify their expectations concerning the firm's long-run profitability. But given imperfect knowledge, investors are apt to interpret profit deviations as forerunners of a trend, so they will bid the stock's price up or down accordingly. Under CAPM, investors are assumed to acquire portfolios that spread risks to the optimal degree. The extent to which they will require a risk pre-

mium before buying any particular security depends upon how that security's risk profile affects the riskiness and mean return of their overall portfolio. The size of the risk premium $E(P_i)$ for the ith company's security is expressed by the formula:

$$E(P_i) = \beta_i[E(R_m) - R_F]$$

where $E(R_m)$ is the expected return from a portfolio including all assets traded in the market, R_F is the rate of interest on riskless securities, the difference between them is the overall market risk premium, and β_i is a coefficient reflecting the so-called *systematic* or *undiversifiable* risk associated with security i. The value of β_i is given by:

$$\beta_i = r_{im}\left(\frac{\sigma_i}{\sigma_m}\right)$$

where r_{im} is the intertemporal correlation between the returns of security i and the market portfolio, σ_i is the standard deviation of security i's returns, and σ_m is the standard deviation of market portfolio returns. The larger r_{im} is, the more closely ups and downs in security i's returns are synchronized with those of the broader market portfolio, and so the more difficult it is to combine security i with the market portfolio and achieve a reduction in *combined* variability through risk pooling. In other words, one cannot readily diversify against risk correlated with the market's aggregate risks. Therefore, the higher r_{im} is, the higher will be the risk premium on security i, and hence the higher cost of capital to company i, all else being equal. Also, for a given r_{im}, the higher the ratio σ_i/σ_m is, the higher the risk coefficient β_i will be.

There is statistical evidence that the β values associated with the stocks of U.S. corporations during the 1960s were systematically lower, the larger a company was and the more concentrated the industry in which it operated.[87] Exactly how investors' stock price evaluations are influenced by the apparently greater stability of powerful corporations' earnings is unclear, since the β values of individual common stocks have been correlated only moderately with such operating indices as the variability or covariance of companies' reported earnings and growth over time.[88] Nevertheless, it seems established that size and monopoly power, either separately or in tandem, do lead to cost advantages in raising equity capital. This in turn evidently reflects investors' subjective aversion to risk plus their inability—e.g., because of transaction costs, ignorance, or the unavailability of appropriately diversified mutual fund shares—to diversify their portfolios sufficiently to avoid the greater risk of buying smaller companies' stock. Bearing risks to which one is averse is presumably a real cost in the same sense that doing manual labor to which one is averse is a cost. It is probably wrong, therefore, to say that the capital cost savings enjoyed by low-β corporations are a strictly pecuniary economy. Yet if such savings constitute real savings, they are economies with unique income distribution implications, given the fact that between 1962 and 1972, the wealthiest 1 percent of all individuals in the United States owned from 50 to 75 percent of the outstanding personally held corporate stock by dollar value.[89] It is unclear also whether the advantages enjoyed by powerful corporations need to be as large as they are, or whether they might be mitigated by the development of capital market institutions such as no-load mutual funds that apply modern CAPM theory to select optimally diversified stock portfolios. On this issue, as on so many others, the last word has not yet been said.

Thus far it has been implicitly assumed for simplicity's sake that a firm of any given size and degree of diversification faces a uniquely determined cost of capital invariant no matter how much capital the firm raises. This is not entirely true. A corporation with assets of $500 million might be able to borrow $25 million at very close to the prime rate, but if it tries to double its assets in a short time frame by borrowing, it will have to pay a steep interest premium, and it may not be able to find any willing lenders.[90] Such capital market imperfections may contribute to concentration in industries like steel, automobiles, petroleum refining, and general-purpose digital computers requiring a very high capital investment for minimum optimal scale operation, since small competitors or new entrants may experience considerable difficulty financing a great leap forward to MOS operation.

In a variation on this theme, Lance Davis has argued that the rapid growth of industrial concentration in the United States during the late 19th century was partly the result of capital market imperfections, giving rise to an environment in which only a few entrepreneurs with especially good banking connections (like Carnegie, Rockefeller, and Swift) could mobilize the capital sums required to exploit opportunities opened up by market growth and technological change.[91] British industry experienced less concentration during the same period, Davis continues, because capital was more widely accessible. The trend toward rising U.S. concentration ebbed in the early 20th century as capital markets were perfected. Although his handling of the evidence leaves something to be desired, there is probably more than a grain of truth in Davis's conjectures.

One final point must be mentioned. Because of its superior access to capital, the large firm may have greater staying power in periods of

---

84. The firms' combined

$$\sigma_F = \sqrt{400,000^2 + 400,000^2 + (2 \times 1 \times 400,000^2)}$$
$$= \sqrt{4 \times 400,000^2} = 2 \times \$400,000$$

Combining the two markets leads not only to doubled profit expectations but also a doubled standard deviation.

85. Concretely, when $r = 0$ and the individual markets are of identical size, the ratio of the σ_F to the expected value of total firm profits declines by the ratio $1/\sqrt{N}$ with increases in N, the number of markets served.

86. For a particularly good survey, see Michael C. Jensen, "Capital Markets: Theory and Evidence," *Bell Journal of Economics and Management Science* 31 (Autumn 1972): 357–98.

87. See Timothy G. Sullivan, "The Cost of Capital and the Market Power of Firms," *Review of Economics and Statistics* 60 (May 1978): 209–17.

88. See for example Donald J. Thompson II, "Sources of Systematic Risk in Common Stocks," *Journal of Business* 49 (April 1976): 173–88.

89. U.S., Bureau of the Census, *Statistical Abstract of the United States: 1976* (Washington, D.C.: Government Printing Office, 1976), p. 427, citing studies by and unpublished data from James D. Smith and Stephen D. Franklin.

90. This partly reflects the "principle of increasing risk" articulated by Michal Kalecki in an article with the same name, *Economica* 4 (November 1937): 440–47.

91. Lance Davis, "The Capital Markets and Industrial Concentration: The U.S. and U.K., a Comparative Study," *Economic History Review* 19 (August 1966): 255–72.

unusually sharp competition. This advantage includes the ability to weather a severe business recession successfully and to finance predatory ventures such as price wars and lengthy court battles over patent rights. We shall have more to say about such activities in later chapters.

Economies of large-scale promotion Economies of large-scale promotion and marketing also raise analytic difficulties. For one, they may show up not only in the form of lower costs, but also in the ability of firms to charge prices higher than those of smaller rivals for comparable products, or in some combination of price premiums and cost savings. Thus, both cost curves and demand curves are affected. A second complication is the element of chance associated with sales promotion. A massive advertising campaign may be a spectacular success or a resounding flop, depending upon the ingenuity and luck of the Madison Avenue people in charge. And most important of all, the private benefits realized through large-scale promotion may not be mirrored by benefits to the public. It is not clear that society gains when one firm's monopoly power is bolstered by a successful promotional campaign, or whether bleary-eyed television viewers are better off from the barrage of messages to which

they are subjected. These are matters of considerable controversy, and we shall progress best by dodging them for the present and scheduling a fuller debate for Chapter 14. Here we confine ourselves to the narrower question, to what extent is market concentration encouraged or entrenched by the private advantages of large-scale promotion?

Even there, no simple answer can be provided. In his pioneering study of 20 American industries, Professor Bain concluded that product differentiation was "of at least the same general order of importance . . . as economies of large-scale production and distribution" in giving established market leaders a price or cost advantage over rivals, and especially over new entrants.[92] However, a later 12-industry study found that although product differentiation was very important, firms with only a single plant of efficient scale were by no means barred from success.[93] In several industries, single-plant enterprises were able to promote their products on virtually equal terms, realizing all or most scale economies; and in others they could find sizeable market segments in which to operate profitably despite a promotional handicap.

To explore further the reasons for these somewhat disparate conclusions, let us begin by

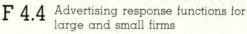

F 4.3 Advertising response function

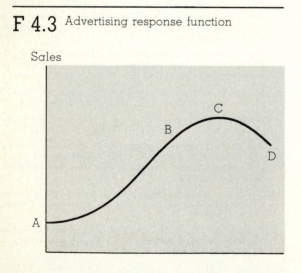

Number of advertising messages

F 4.4 Advertising response functions for large and small firms

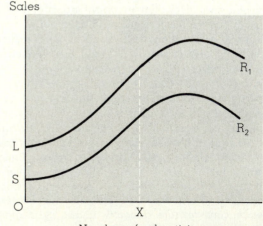

Number of advertising messages

focusing on advertising, which Bain found to be the single most important basis of large-firm advantages.

One possible source of scale economies is the need to attain a certain threshold level of advertising messages before reaching maximum effectiveness. There are two main reasons why this might be so. First, the average consumer's behavior may not be influenced by a single message, whereas five or six delivered messages (out of a possibly larger number sent) are likely to induce action, if indeed advertising is able to do so at all.[94] Second, when advertising messages are communicated further by word of mouth and peer influence, conditions analogous to those governing chain reactions or the spread of epidemics may apply.[95] A small impulse soon peters out, but one that affects a sufficiently large initial critical mass spreads rapidly and covers a large segment of the population. To the extent that either of these two models of advertising effectiveness is valid, there must exist an "advertising response function" of the logistic shape illustrated in Figure 4.3. Over the range AB the threshold (no doubt varying for different consumers) is being approached and surmounted, and the average sales generated by an additional message rise. But beyond point B average returns fall, at first slowly and then (if oversaturation can occur) precipitously.

There is debate as to whether the shape assumed in Figure 4.3 in fact reflects real-world conditions or whether diminishing returns set in immediately. The answer may depend upon the specific advertising medium. Julian Simon has brought together a persuasive body of evidence showing continuously diminishing returns for direct-mail and clip-out coupon methods.[96] The studies he cites on other media suffer from methodological shortcomings and therefore are less convincing. Perhaps the most carefully controlled marketing research on which a published account is available, covering beer advertising on television, suggests a relationship like Figure 4.3, but with separate maxima for each of two distinct market segments.[97] When the intensity of Budweiser beer advertising was varied systematically among local markets, increasing returns showed up at lower message levels. But at high intensities, the response function turned downward, as with segment CD. Consumers deluged with Budweiser ads reportedly requested of their liquor dealers, "Give me anything but Bud."

The existence of an increasing returns range AB is not by itself enough to imply an advertising cost advantage for larger firms. If all firms face essentially the same advertising response function, all will find it profitable to carry their advertising to approximately the threshold level B if they advertise at all, and all will thereby enjoy similar sales responses.[98] For economies of scale to exist, there must be some *further* interacting set of circumstances conferring an advantage to larger firms—e.g., by letting them have different

92. Bain, *Barriers to New Competition*, pp. 142–43, 216.

93. Scherer et al., *The Economics of Multi-Plant Operation*, p. 258.

94. See "Advertising: Frequency and Effectiveness," *New York Times*, 22 June 1976, p. 57.

95. See Stephen Glaister, "Advertising Policy and Returns to Scale Where Information Is Passed Between Individuals," *Economica* 41 (May 1974): 139–56.

96. Julian L. Simon, *Issues in the Economics of Advertising* (Urbana, Ill.: University of Illinois Press, 1974), Chapter 1.

97. Russell L. Ackoff and James R. Emshoff, "Advertising Research at Anheuser-Busch, Inc. (1963–68)," *Sloan Management Review* 17 (Winter 1975): 1–15. The response function derived by Ackoff and Emshoff was measured in terms of percentage changes in sales, rather than absolute sales levels, but it can be transformed into one like Figure 4.3.

    For other evidence on response functions and economies of scale in advertising, see William S. Comanor and Thomas A. Wilson, *Advertising and Market Power* (Cambridge, Mass.: Harvard University Press, 1974), pp. 49–53; Jean-Jacques Lambin, *Advertising, Competition and Market Conduct in Oligopoly over Time* (Amsterdam: North-Holland, 1976), pp. 94–98, 127–29; and Randall S. Brown, "Estimating Advantages to Large-Scale Advertising," *Review of Economics and Statistics* 60 (August 1978): 428–37.

98. This is only a heuristic approximation. More exactly, assume that the product price and unit production cost are fixed so that each additional unit of output sold yields a gross margin m, expressed as a ratio of sales. Let A be the number of advertising messages, S the dollar volume of sales [$= s(A)$], and c the cost of an advertising message. Then the firm maximizes $\pi = m \cdot s(A) - cA$. Differentiating, $d\pi/dA = m \cdot ds/dA - c = 0$ at the maximum. Since dS/dA is in effect the marginal sales revenue of advertising, this means that the marginal revenue from advertising net of production costs must be set equal to the cost of the marginal advertising message.

    To illustrate further, let the advertising response function be characterized by the cubic equation $S = 100 + 20A + 4A^2 - .333 A^3$, which has the same shape as Figure 4.3 and a maximum (equivalent to point C) at $A = 10$. If $m = .25$ and $c = 4$, the profit-maximizing level of advertising $A^* = 8.47$.

The determinants of market structure

and more favorably configured response functions than their smaller rivals. This may stem from consumer inertia or from physical barriers to the rapid expansion of sales. For example, one supermarket chain may for a variety of historical reasons operate 50 stores in some metropolitan area, another chain only 15. Most of both chains' customers are apt to be tied by force of habit or other considerations to their regular shopping locales; only a small fraction are movable in any given short period by advertising. And if either chain did attract customers very rapidly through advertising, congestion would build up in its aisles, curbing the patronage gains. The large chain may therefore face a response function like LR_1 in Figure 4.4 while the small chain faces SR_2. If both must send approximately OX advertising messages to achieve a threshold level of awareness, the large chain will cover the population of switchable consumers *and* reinforce the purchasing habits of its (larger) group of regular patrons at a substantially lower advertising cost per sales dollar than the small chain. The response functions facing firms of varying size may also differ because advertising has cumulative as well as current effects. It takes a long time to build an image and get consumers in the habit of requesting Prestone when what they need is ethylene glycol antifreeze. In the short or medium run, the small firm trying to expand its sales of an essentially equivalent product through vigorous advertising runs into sharply diminishing returns long before it has achieved the size of the well-established sellers it is seeking to displace. What this says is that short- or medium-run response functions may differ between small and/or new as compared to large firms, but it does not necessarily imply that over the long run a newcomer cannot gain an equivalent sales volume at comparable advertising cost if it cultivates the market slowly and patiently. Such long-run equivalence may be ruled out as well, however, if more or less permanent marketing advantages accrue to firms that pioneered some product segment, or managed through superior skill or luck to come up with a captivating product image—e.g., as Coors did in the brewing industry during the 1960s. On this general phenomenon we shall have more to say in Chapters 14 through 16.

Economies of scale in marketing can also interact dynamically with production scale economies to magnify the handicap of smaller firms. Beer in the United States provides an example.[99] From the time of their reincarnation after the repeal of Prohibition in 1933, a few brewers—notably, Anheuser-Busch, Schlitz, and Pabst—chose to cultivate a nationwide "premium" image. They set their prices high relative to those of local and regional beers both to sustain that image and to cover the high costs of shipping throughout the nation from Midwestern breweries. But beginning in the 1950s, several things happened. The Big Three built or bought breweries on the East and West coasts, reducing transport costs and (with prices held roughly constant) providing more money to plow into advertising. This, coupled with rising affluence and the desire of consumers to trade up to more prestigious beers, led to rapidly growing sales for the Big Three. That in turn permitted them to build additional new breweries which, by exploiting a combination of technological advances and scale-up economies, had much lower production costs per unit than those of regional brewers lacking premium image brands. With lower costs, the Big Three (joined by Coors and later Miller's) could squeeze the premium-popular price differential, enhancing their market shares even more, which in turn permitted them to advertise as heavily in absolute terms as smaller regional rivals but at appreciably lower average outlays per sales dollar.[100] The upshot of these interacting developments was an increase in the four-firm concentration ratio in brewing from 21 to 1947 to 61 in 1976.

This overview of the advantages of size in advertising has skipped over some potentially important tactical details. For one, with respect to what organizational unit are advertising scale economies realized? For supermarket chains, advertising strives to lure consumers into *stores*, but most advertising by consumer goods manufacturers is focused on individual *brands*, not plants or firms. When threshold effects apply in the latter case, they may have to be attained brand by brand, not at the aggregate firm level. Unless there are multibrand interactions, firm size is largely irrelevant. Partly related questions are, how does the array of feasible media vary with firm size, and how in turn are costs affected by any such variations? Jewel, a Chicago area retail grocery chain with the largest local market share, cannot sensibly advertise on nationwide network television or in national magazines. A&P, with a much smaller Chicago position but broader geographic compass, might.

Multibrand interactions can occur if a favorable reputation from one set of products (e.g., General Electric's refrigerators) spills over to other products (such as hair dryers), or if the media offer discounts for combining a large volume of advertising, perhaps spanning multiple brands, in one place or time period. Discounts do exist. The *New York Times*, for example, offered general contract advertisers volume discounts ranging up to 4.5 percent for buying the equivalent of 40 pages in a year as compared to one page.[101] A 10-second spot television commercial costs half as much as a 30-second announcement, but the discount gained by purchasing longer commercials may be more than offset by diminishing marginal effectiveness as the message lengthens.[102] Whether larger advertisers enjoyed significant *cumulative* volume discounts from the television networks has been the subject of heated controversy.[103] The weight of the evidence favors a conclusion that such discounts in the mid-1960s were at best erratic. Moreover, they were not large enough to induce medium-sized advertisers to concentrate their purchases with a single network more than large firms that maintained an advertising volume sufficient to earn the discounts several times over. After 1967, a shift in emphasis toward straight undiscounted "participation" minutes further weakened whatever correlation there might have been between advertising scale and net cost per thousand viewers.

Potentially more important than such volume-massing advantages might be the savings nationwide advertisers enjoy by purchasing network time, which, depending upon the time of day, costs 15 to 30 percent less than what one would pay buying the same coverage through individual station spot messages.[104] For regional firms, more costly spot messages may be the only practical option. There is, however, an offsetting consideration. Network advertising is less flexible than spots; it cannot be adapted to individual market conditions—e.g., to emphasize local markets where special sales campaigns are planned or to avoid cities where one has no distribution. Spot advertising offers sufficiently compelling flexibility benefits that some nationwide consumer goods makers employ it almost exclusively, while others use the networks for their base-line advertising and adjust to local market conditions through extensive spot purchases.[105] These considerations imply that the advertising cost disadvantage of regional firms is not nearly as serious as one might expect merely from comparing rates paid per thousand viewers. But there are undoubtedly cases in which the advertising rate structures do confer an appreciable advantage on larger national firms.

For industries like brewing with high product transportation costs, the chief advantage of nationwide multi-plant operation may lie not so much in having a more attractive array of advertising options as in capitalizing fully on the nationwide image one enjoys. That is, somehow or

99. Scherer et al., *The Economics of Multi-Plant Operation*, pp. 248–49.

100. See Douglas F. Greer, "Product Differentiation and Concentration in the Brewing Industry," *Journal of Industrial Economics* 19 (July 1971): 214.

101. Simon, *Issues in the Economics of Advertising*, p. 148.

102. Simon, *Issues*, p. 15; and Michael E. Porter, "Interbrand Choice, Media Mix and Market Performance," *American Economic Review* 66 (May 1976): 402.

103. See Harlan Blake and Jack A. Blum, "Network Television Rate Practices: A Case Study in the Failure of Social Control of Price Discrimination," *Yale Law Journal* 74 (July 1965): 1339–1401; David M. Blank, "Television Advertising: The Great Discount Illusion, or Tonypandy Revisited," *Journal of Business* 41 (January 1968): 10–38; the comment by William Leonard with rejoinder by Blank in *idem* (January 1969): 93–112; John L. Peterman, "The Clorox Case and Television Rate Structures," *Journal of Law and Economics* 11 (October 1968): 321–422; Peter C. Riesz, "Size versus Price, or Another Vote for Tonypandy," *Journal of Business* 46 (July 1973): 396–403; the comment by Morton Schnabel and reply by Riesz in *idem*, (January 1976): 68–72; and Comanor and Wilson, *Advertising and Market Power*, pp. 53–61.

104. I am indebted to Robert L. Steiner for obtaining this 1977 cost information through an advertising agency executive. In "Interbrand Choice," p. 403, Porter asserts that the savings from purchasing network time range from 30 to 90 percent of the equivalent spot coverage cost. This appears to be a gross exaggeration.

105. Scherer et al., *The Economics of Multi-Plant Operation*, pp. 247–53.

other, certain products catch on, and once they do, the word spreads. As with Coors beer, this can happen even without any advertising outside one's home territory. Once a product does gain a favorable nationwide image, that image is an asset whose full value is captured only through nationwide distribution. If transportation costs are high, this in turn may require the operation of multiple decentralized plants.

Another quite different advantage of large scale is sometimes enjoyed by the sellers of complex durable goods, especially consumer durables. The automobile industry affords the leading example. Most consumers are unwilling to buy a particular new car unless they are confident they can obtain prompt, reliable service not only at home, but wherever they may travel or migrate. This gives the manufacturer with a far-flung, high-quality dealer network a sales advantage. Establishing such a network is difficult for the smaller manufacturer, since there are economies of scale at the sales and service establishment level.[106] A certain minimum investment in specialized testing equipment, tools, and spare parts is necessary. More important, the most able entrepreneurs are not apt to find the dealership for an auto brand attractive unless they can expect to sell a fairly high annual volume, and in smaller cities and towns, only the more popular brands offer this expectation. This sets up a vicious circle. Low-volume manufacturers cannot attract the most able dealers in smaller cities because of their limited volume potential. But they cannot build up their volume potential because they lack a strong nationwide distribution network and therefore suffer in the eyes of consumers. This particular advantage of large size probably persists out to larger nationwide sales volumes than any other scale economy in the automobile industry. B. P. Pashigian estimated that a manufacturer needs an annual volume of roughly 600,000 units before avoiding serious disadvantages of small-scale distribution through franchised dealers, and additional advantages may accrue at volumes up to three times this level.[107] Inability to overcome its dealership problem broke the back of Studebaker and several earlier postwar automobile industry manufacturers; and it is one of the most serious

handicaps facing American Motors and (to a lesser degree) Chrysler.

Nevertheless, a few foreign car makers—notably, Volkswagen, Toyota, and Datsun—seem to have experienced fair success in surmounting the problem. One reason was probably their special appeal as second cars for the urban motorist, permitting the foreign producers to ignore the small towns and emphasize building high-volume urban dealerships. Also, all three created their dealership networks at what may have been a uniquely propitious time—when there was little small-car competition from domestic manufacturers and the U.S. dollar was pegged at artificially elevated foreign exchange rates, giving German and Japanese manufacturers a cost advantage out of which dealers could be generously compensated. Whether these conditions can be duplicated under floating exchange rates is uncertain but doubtful.

The automobile industry provides the premier example of a further interacting advantage of size associated with product differentiation. Through some perverse quirk of human nature, the average consumer is decidedly unhappy driving around last season's assemblage of metal stampings. Body designs are therefore altered periodically—usually with thoroughgoing changes every three to five years and exterior facelifts of varying extent more frequently. This is expensive. New dies must be made for each new stamped part. During the early 1970s a high-volume die for such parts cost from $20,000 to more than $100,000, and many parts require multiple dies. For an entirely new model, die costs ranged from $16 to $35 million in 1972 for European-size cars, and subsequent inflation has undoubtedly elevated these figures substantially.[108] With appropriate maintenance, such dies can be used to produce many million parts—far more than the market is normally willing to absorb. Assuming updated die costs of $50 million and no facelifts, the average die-making cost per car for various total production volumes over the life of a model is as follows:

100,000 cars	$500
200,000 cars	250
500,000 cars	100

1,000,000 cars	$50
2,500,000 cars	20
5,000,000 cars	10

Clearly, there are important scale economies out to substantial volumes. The critical but frequently overlooked question is, does the volume a manufacturer achieves depend solely upon the size of the market it chooses to serve (e.g., low-volume sports, medium-volume luxury, or high-volume standard) and on the quality of the design, or does the manufacturer's own size matter? If everything depends upon the specific market addressed so that two firms, one large and one small, with identical designs would sell the same number of autos, scale economies are entirely product-specific and not at all firm-specific. One might lament the loss of die utilization economies when only 100,000 replications of some car are produced, but increasing firm size will not remedy the situation. There are, however, at least three reasons why firm size could matter. First, the quality of design affects sales, but may be affected by firm size. Unless one interprets better design to mean "more popular" or "embodying more cost-reducing quality sacrifices," smaller auto manufacturers probably have the edge here. Second, economies of scale in dealer network development and advertising may permit the large firm to sell more of any given design than a small firm. And third, the large multimodel firm may be able to achieve greater commonality of stamped (and also machined) parts than the smaller company—e.g., using the same inner door panel die to make parts for Buicks, Pontiacs, Oldsmobiles, and Chevrolets in the same size class. These second and third advantages of firm size are probably very important in the automobile industry. No quantitative evidence is available on how much these advantages explain General Motors' profitability lead over Ford, and Ford's lead over Chrysler and American Motors.

In summary, in at least some industries, and especially in certain consumer goods industries, there are appreciable economies of scale in many aspects of sales promotion and product differentiation. The implication conveyed thus far is that these advantages of size and their inter-

actions can lead to market concentration exceeding what is required to realize all narrowly construed production and physical distribution economies. This is correct, but it does not tell the whole story. The product differentiation sword can also cut in the opposite direction. Through successful product differentiation, smaller firms may be able to carve out for themselves a small but profitable niche in some special segment of a large market. Their sales volume may be too low to confer all production and promotional scale economies, but the higher costs associated with foregoing these advantages may be more than offset by the price premium consumers pay for the special product features they offer. Product innovation is one tactic by which smaller firms can survive despite conventional scale disadvantages. For example, economists studying the cigarette industry during the late 1940s concluded that the Big Three (then Reynolds, American, and Liggett & Myers) enjoyed a decisive advantage over smaller rivals owing to economies of large-scale promotion. Yet those firms' combined share of the market fell from 85 percent in 1947 to 69 percent in 1959 and 51 percent in 1975 as a consequence of successful king size, filter tip, low tar, and other innovations by initially smaller manufacturers.

Another strategy is to cater to some narrow geographic market segment, or to some special consumer taste with a sales potential too small to interest the leading firms. Even in the automobile industry, where the disadvantages of small-scale production are so formidable, such niches can be found. For example, since 1964 Excalibur, a small company, has been turning out 100 custom-crafted cars per year at a 1977 price of

---

106. On similar scale economies in servicing computers, see Brock, *The U.S. Computer Industry*, pp. 33–37.

107. See B. P. Pashigian, *The Distribution of Automobiles: An Economic Analysis of the Franchise System* (Englewood Cliffs, N.J.: Prentice-Hall, 1961), especially pp. 238–39.

108. See John S. McGee, "Economies of Size in Auto Body Manufacture," *Journal of Law and Economics* 16 (October 1973): 248–53.

The determinants of market structure   113

$22,200 each.[109] Evidently, some automobile buyers are able and willing to pay an impressive premium for the right kind of uniqueness. It is partly for this reason and partly because of more innovative engineering that numerous high-priced European cars are able to penetrate the American market despite their inadequate distribution networks.

Although consumers' demand for variety helps small-scale firms selling differentiated goods survive, the overriding tendency in recent decades has been toward increasing concentration in consumer goods industries, perhaps particularly in those industries whose products are susceptible to strong brand or image differentiation. Early statistical support for this inference came from Mueller and Hamm, who subdivided 166 four-digit U.S. manufacturing industries into four categories—producer goods, consumer goods of low product differentiation, consumer goods of moderate product differentiation, and consumer goods of high product differentiation.[110] The simple average four-firm concentration ratio changes for the four groups between 1947 and 1970 were as follows:

Producer goods	−1.3
Consumer goods:	
Low differentiation	+0.4
Moderate differentiation	+6.4
High differentiation	+12.7

The results obtained by Mueller and Hamm have been criticized for the subjectivity and arbitrariness of the consumer versus producer goods and product differentiation classifications.[111] To overcome those problems to the maximum feasible degree, data on 154 four-digit manufacturing industries whose definitions were comparable between 1947 and 1972 along with 323 industries comparable over 1963 to 1972 were carefully reclassified by the author using information from the 1963 input-output tables.[112] A simple dichotomy between consumer and producer goods industries was rejected because there are many industries (such as detergents and petroleum refining) that sell both to consumers, often with a substantial product differentiation effort, and to industrial users less susceptible to the blandishments of advertising. The industries therefore were divided into three groups: consumer goods, in which personal consumption accounted for at least 60 percent of 1963 sales; producer goods, in which personal consumption was 33 percent or less; and mixed industries with a personal consumption share of 34 to 59 percent. The simple average observed changes in four-firm concentration ratios for the two time intervals and three groups are indicated in Table 4.7. For both time intervals, the more rapid indicated rise in consumer goods as compared to producer goods industry concentration is statistically significant at the 99 percent confidence level.

The consumer goods and mixed industries were then classified further according to the intensity of their 1963 advertising outlays, as deduced from input-output statistics.[113] Industries were assigned to the low differentiation category if they spent less than 1.5 percent of sales on advertising, to the moderate differentiation category if they spent 1.5 to 4.9 percent of sales on advertising, and to the high differentiation category if their expenditures were 5.0 percent or more. However, industries assigned initially to the low or moderate categories were moved up one category if their *total* 1963 advertising outlays exceeded $75 million. The simple average four-firm concentration ratio changes for these more finely subdivided industry categories are presented in Table 4.8. A tendency for concentration to rise (and also to have higher absolute levels) with the degree of product differentiation shows up clearly for consumer goods over the full 1947–72 interval, but not for mixed consumer-producer goods industries and also not for consumer goods over the shorter (and more completely sampled) 1963–72 interval. When the

---

T 4.7 Average observed changes in four-firm concentration ratios

	1947–72	1963–72
All industries	+1.71	+0.86
Producer goods	−1.67	−0.32
Consumer goods	+6.36	+3.51
Mixed industries	+5.29	+1.14

114

T 4.8 Four-firm sales concentration ratio changes, by degree of product differentiation

	154 industries comparable over the 1947–72 interval				323 industries comparable over the 1963–72 interval	
	Total change, 1947–72*	1947–63 change	1963–72 change	Average 1972 concentration level	Total change, 1963–72*	Average 1972 concentration level
All industries	+ 1.71(154)	+0.92	+0.79	41.5	+0.86(323)	40.3
Producer goods	− 1.67(87)	−1.25	−0.41	41.3	−0.32(206)	39.8
Consumer goods						
low differentiation	+ 3.78(18)	0.00	+3.78	25.3	+4.28(40)	28.2
moderate differentiation	+ 7.73(22)	+5.68	+2.05	42.1	+3.28(32)	44.5
high differentiation	+ 8.00(10)	+4.70	+3.30	53.9	+2.12(17)	51.9
Mixed industries						
low differentiation	+11.80(5)	+8.60	+3.20	50.8	+4.50(8)	45.1
moderate differentiation	+ 2.60(10)	+3.70	−1.10	50.5	−0.06(17)	49.2
high differentiation	+ 2.50(2)	−1.00	+3.50	55.0	−1.00(3)	57.3

*Figures in parentheses give the number of industries covered.
Derived from U.S., Bureau of the Census, "Concentration Ratios in Manufacturing," *1972 Census of Manufactures*, MC72(SR)–2 (Washington, D.C.: Government Printing Office, 1975).

154-industry sample is broken down into subperiods, one finds that most of the concentration increase in the consumer goods industries of high and (especially) moderate product differentiation had already taken place by 1963.

Further insight into the role of product differentiation and other variables affecting concentration changes is provided by multiple regression analyses taking as dependent variable the change in an industry's four-firm concentration ratio (in percentage form) from either 1947 to 1972 or 1963 to 1972. Independent variables were the following:

C47 or C63   Four-firm concentration ratio in the initial year (either 1947 or 1963).

Growth   Continuously compounded annual percentage rate of growth in value added over the period covered.

109. "She's a Real Beauty—the '77 Excalibur," *Chicago Tribune*, 27 February 1977. See also "Special Cars for Special People," *Fortune*, February 1968, pp. 136–43.

110. Mueller and Hamm, "Trends in Industrial Market Concentration," pp. 511–20. For similar but weaker results for France, see Frederic Jenny and André-Paul Weber, "The Determinants of Concentration Trends in the French Manufacturing Sector," *Journal of Industrial Economics* 26 (March 1978): 193–207. See also Neil R. Wright, "Product Differentiation, Concentration, and Changes in Concentration," *Review of Economics and Statistics* 60 (November 1978): 628–31.

111. Stanley I. Ornstein, *Industrial Concentration and Advertising Intensity* (Washington, D.C.: American Enterprise Institute for Public Policy Research, 1977), pp. 20–22. In a later paper attempting *inter alia* to avoid the difficulties identified by Ornstein, Mueller and Richard T. Rogers obtained results quite similar to both their original work and my own new research summarized below. "The Role of Advertising in Changing Market Concentration," manuscript, University of Wisconsin, April 1978.

112. Industries were excluded if definition changes occurred affecting more than 3 percent of sales or employment. Also, eight catch-all (i.e., not elsewhere classified) industries and four industries with missing data were excluded.

Size   Mean of the logarithms (to base e) of industry value added for census years of the period covered.

Cons   Dummy variable with value of 1 if consumer goods industry and zero otherwise.

Mixed   Dummy variable with value of 1 if mixed consumer-producer goods industry and zero otherwise.

A/S   1963 advertising outlays as a percentage of sales.

The results are summarized in Table 4.9. By far the strongest and most consistent explanatory variable is initial year concentration. The higher it was, the more concentration tended to decline in subsequent years.[114] Consistent with the discussion in an earlier section, the market size and growth effects are uniformly negative but weak. For both time intervals and samples, concentration shows a strong tendency to rise more rapidly in consumer goods industries—i.e., by 3.5 to 6.3 percentage points more than in producer goods industries, all else being equal. The incremental explanatory role of high advertising intensity, as shown in equations (2) and (4), is erratic. Over the entire 1947–72 period, high advertising intensity had a significantly positive impact on the growth of concentration, and the A/S variable's inclusion gives rise to a small but statistically significant increase in the value of R^2. However, for the later interval and larger sample, its coefficient is negative and insignificant.

The one thing that seems quite clear is that the forces influencing concentration changes in consumer and producer goods industries since World War II were somehow different. Consumers' greater susceptibility to advertising may provide part of the explanation, but the concentration-increasing impact of intense advertising appears to have peaked and perhaps reversed by the early to mid-1960s, perhaps coinciding with both consumers' and advertisers' increased maturity in relating to television as a medium of information and persuasion.

All in all, the evidence points toward a conclusion that economies of large-scale image differentiation and sales promotion are substantial in at least a fair number of industries; and they may have contributed prominently to rising market concentration. We shall return in subsequent chapters to additional facets of the links between product differentiation and changes in market structure. .

T 4.9   Regression analysis results: determinants of concentration change

Dependent variable: concentration change from:	No. of obs.	Constant	Independent variables							R^2
			C47	C63	Growth	Size	Cons	Mixed	A/S	
(1) 1947 to 1972	154	15.6	−.190** (.040)		−.439 (.348)	−1.37 (.91)	+6.34** (2.02)	+7.57** (2.93)		.249
(2) 1947 to 1972	154	17.0	−.200** (.040)		−.543 (.349)	−1.51* (.91)	+4.76* (2.15)	+6.37* (2.96)	+.553* (.273)	.270
(3) 1963 to 1972	323	12.1		−.086** (.019)	−.195* (.109)	−1.36** (.40)	+3.50** (.94)	+2.14 (1.49)		.142
(4) 1963 to 1972	323	11.5		−.079** (.019)	−.163 (.111)	−1.32** (.40)	+4.14** (1.01)	+2.69* (1.52)	−.253 (.154)	.150

*Statistically significant at the .05 level (one-tail test).
**Statistically significant at the .01 level.

Conclusions It is difficult to draw simple generalizations concerning the relationship between multi-plant economies of scale and the necessity of concentration. The possibilities are complicated. A fair amount depends upon luck and the particular market segments individual firms choose to serve. Some aspects (such as pecuniary capital-raising and materials procurement economies and product differentiation advantages) call for value judgments as to whether gains made by large firms are also gains to society. Nevertheless, generalizations do afford a useful perspective, and so Table 4.10 attempts to provide an overview of how important multi-plant economies were in the late 1960s for 12 U.S. industries studied intensively by the author and four colleagues. It focuses on firms operating in the mainstream of their industries, not in offbeat market niches; and it weights the various advantages of size according to their strategic importance in the marketplace without adjustments for social desirability.

Column (1) estimates the overall disadvantage experienced by firms operating only one plant of minimum optimal scale compared to enterprises enjoying all the benefits of multi-plant size. Ranges are given to reflect relevant variations in market conditions and historical legacies. Column (2) then estimates how many MOS plants a firm needed to operate in order to have not more than a "slight" overall handicap vis-à-vis enterprises enjoying all multi-plant economies. "Slight" here implies unit cost handicaps or the loss of price premia (less promotional costs) of not much more than 1 percent. In four or (less confidently) five industries, multi-plant operation conferred no more than slight advantages; in the rest, multi-plant firms enjoyed somewhat greater advantages over single-plant general-line rivals. Column (3) describes briefly the main sources of multi-plant economies both for industries in which they were important and where they were not. Many facets appear, but those relating to product differentiation and the need for sales and production strategies geared to buyers' preferences for broad-line suppliers predominate.

Column (4) translates the column (2) judgments into an estimate of how large a share of the U.S. market an enterprise needed to realize all but slight untapped advantages of multi-plant size. In effect it summarizes the imperatives for high concentration at the nationwide level. In only 3 of the 12 industries—refrigerators, brewing, and perhaps cigarettes—were oligopolistic national industry structures (i.e., with four-firm concentration ratios exceeding 40) required. However, in several of the industries, transportation costs were sufficiently high to confine the sales of any single plant to a regional (i.e., less than nationwide) market. As a result, achieving the main advantages of size required oligopolistic structures in most glass bottle and many petroleum, steel, and cement markets. It should be noted too that the steel market share estimates assume mid-1960s technology, before advances in blast furnace technology doubled or trebled the size of an MOS plant. And in bearings, the estimates assume a firm specializing in ball, roller, or tapered models, not all three. With multi-plant firms thus specialized, there would be middling oligopoly levels in ball and roller bearings and high concentration in such specialty lines as tapered or needle bearings. The overall picture then is one of production or marketing compulsions toward oligopoly, usually loose, in more industries than not. On the other hand, oligopoly was rather clearly not necessary for most production in shoes, batteries, paints, and fabrics.

Column (5) indicates the average market share held by individual firms among the indus-

(113) Advertising/sales ratios for many industries were provided in Ornstein, *Industrial Concentration*, Appendix B. Data for the other industries were derived, typically subject to some aggregation bias, from U.S., Department of Commerce, Office of Business Economics, *Input-Output Structure of the U.S. Economy: 1963*, vol. 1 (Washington, D.C.: Government Printing Office, 1969). In a few cases the input-output data were overridden when it was clear from data for other years and/or the author's personal knowledge that the 1963 figures were either misleading (e.g., as a result of excessive aggregation) or atypical.

114. This no doubt reflects the 'regression effect' first observed by Sir Francis Galton in the tendency for the sons of fathers above average in height to be shorter than their fathers, and the obverse for the sons of especially short fathers. Its roots lie in the possibility that unusually high or low initial values may owe their extreme position to nonsustainable chance events.

T 4.10 Evaluation of firm size required to experience not more than slight price/cost handicaps

Industry	(1) Overall disadvantage of representative general-line single MOS plant firm	(2) Number of MOS plants needed to have not more than "slight" overall handicap	(3) Main bases of multi-plant firm's advantage
Beer brewing	Slight to severe, depending upon inherited brand image	3–4	National brand image and advertising; coordination of new plant investments
Cigarettes	Slight to moderate (borderline)	1–2	Advertising and image differentiation
Fabric weaving	Very slight to moderate, depending upon product line	3–6	Integration into finishing; broad-line sales force and advertising
Paints	Slight	1	Integration into raw materials production
Petroleum refining	Very slight to moderate, depending upon regional market position and crude oil access	2–3	Risk spreading on crude oil ventures; coordination of plant investments; advertising and national image
Shoes	Slight to moderate, depending upon product line	3–6	Broad-line sales force and advertising
Glass bottles	Slight to moderate, depending upon location and products	3–4	Need for central engineering and design staff
Cement	Slight	1	Risk spreading and capital raising
Ordinary steel	Very slight	1	Capital raising; plant expansion coordination
Bearings	Slight to moderate, depending upon product line	3–5	Broad-line customer preferences affecting lot sizes; central engineering
Refrigerators	Moderate	4–8 (incl. other appliances)	Image and market access, affecting production run lengths; warehousing and transportation
Storage batteries	Slight	1	Market access

Source: F. M. Scherer et al., *The Economics of Multi-Plant Operation: An International Comparisons Study* (Cambridge, Mass.: Harvard University Press, 1975), pp. 334–36. Reprinted by permission of Harvard University Press. Copyright © 1975 by the President and Fellows of Harvard College.

tries' three leading producers during 1970. By comparing column (5) with column (4), one gains an impression of the mesh between scale economy-mandated, or required, levels of concentration and actual concentration. For brewing, refrigerators, and petroleum refining, the mesh was fairly close.[115] In weaving and batteries, at the other extreme, Big Three members were roughly ten times as large as they needed to be to enjoy all but slight residual advantages of size. For all 12 industries, the average ratio of actual to required market share is 4.4. Thus, to the extent that the 12-industry sample is representative—and on this little corroborating or conflicting evidence exists[116]—actual concentration in U.S. manufacturing industry appears to be considerably

higher than the imperatives of scale economies require.

Mergers and concentration

Market structure is also affected by mergers, acquisitions, and other legal transformations through which two or more formerly independent firms come under common control. We defer discussion of whether the 'urge to merge' is independent of scale economies. By way of introduction we will belabor the obvious: Any merger among firms competing in the same market is a

(4) Share of U.S. market required in 1967	(5) Average market share per U.S. Big Three member, 1970
10–14%	13%
6–12	23
1	10
1.4	9
4–6	8
1	6
4–6	22
2	7
3	14
4–7	14
14–20	21
2	18

step, however large or small, toward increased concentration.

In assessing the impact of mergers on market structure, it is customary to distinguish three major merger waves that swept the American economy—the first roughly between 1887 and 1904, the second between 1916 and 1929, and the third peaking in 1968. An overview of trends in manufacturing and mining industry mergers is provided by Figure 4.5, which combines tabulations developed by Ralph L. Nelson, Willard Thorp, and the Federal Trade Commission. The series are not completely comparable because of differences in the information sources tapped, the focus (value versus number of acquisitions), and changes in the size cutoff governing inclusion of acquired firms. Still, any imprecision is overwhelmed by the prominence of merger activity fluctuations. Each of the three identifiable merger waves warrants further analysis.

The great merger wave of 1887–1904   The merger wave that began with recovery from the worldwide depression of 1883 and ended with the depression of 1904 was a reaction of epic proportions to the vast changes in transportation, communications, manufacturing technology, competition, and legal institutions that coincided during the closing decades of the 19th century.[117] It involved at least 15 percent of all plants and employees occupied in manufacturing at the turn of the century.[118] Its outstanding characteristic was the simultaneous consolidation of numerous producers into firms dominating the markets they supplied. Nelson found that of the roughly 3,000 merger-related independent firm disappearances he counted for the 1895–1904 period, 75 percent occurred in mergers involving at least five firms and 26 percent in consolidations of ten or more firms. By way of contrast, 14 percent of all 1915–20 disappearances involved mergers of five or more firms, and only 1.4 percent consolidations of ten or more firms.[119] Multifirm consolidations have been extremely rare in the United States since World War II.

115. However, the column (2) and (4) estimates for petroleum refining are significantly affected by the assumption that it was important to be vertically integrated into offshore oil exploration and production. Such integration became less important in the mid-1970s when percentage depletion allowances were abolished for large producers and as imported oil came to cover an increasingly large fraction of domestic refinery inputs.

116. But see Nicholas Owen, "Scale Economies in the EEC," *European Economic Review* 7 (February 1976), who found national advantage in bilateral European trade flows for some 59 to 63 industries to be generally more closely associated with *plant* size (reflecting plant-specific economies) than with *firm* size (reflecting multi-plant economies).

117. There is an extensive literature covering this period. The best single survey and interpretation is Jesse W. Markham, "Survey of the Evidence and Findings on Mergers," in *Business Concentration and Price Policy*, pp. 141–212. Another valuable source is Ralph L. Nelson, *Merger Movements in American Industry, 1895–1956* (Princeton: Princeton University Press, 1959).

118. This is the estimate by Markham in "Survey," p. 157.

119. Nelson, *Merger Movements*, pp. 28–29, 53.

F 4.5 Volume of manufacturing and mining firm acquisitions: 1895–1977

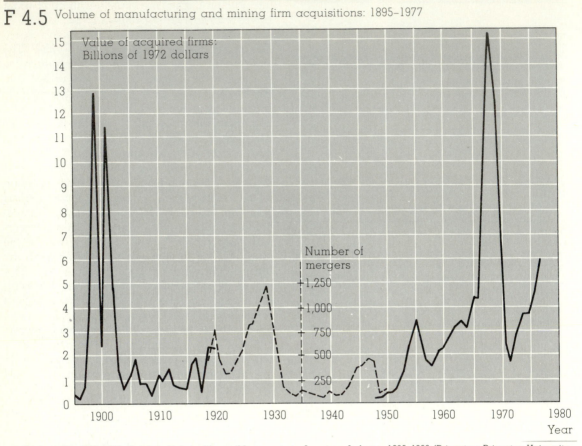

Sources: For 1895–1920, Ralph L. Nelson, *Merger Movements in American Industry, 1895–1956* (Princeton: Princeton University Press, 1959), p. 37; for 1919–1939, Willard L. Thorp, "The Merger Movement," in Temporary National Economic Committee Monograph No. 27, *The Structure of Industry* (Washington, D.C.: Government Printing Office, 1941), p. 233; for 1940–50, U.S., Congress, House, Select Committee on Small Business staff report, *Mergers and Superconcentration*, 87th Cong., sess., 1962; and 1948–77, Federal Trade Commission, *Statistical Report on Mergers and Acquisitions* (Washington, D.C.: Government Printing Office, November 1977), p. 100. The Nelson and FTC series (solid lines) are in terms of the dollar value of assets acquired or merged; the Thorp and Small Business Committee series (dashed lines) are counts (undoubtedly incomplete) of the number of mergers. The dollar series have been converted to constant 1972 dollar values using a composite price deflator with 53 percent weight given to the overall gross national product deflator or (earlier) the all-commodity Wholesale Price Index, 20 percent to nonresidential construction or (earlier) construction materials, and 27 percent to producers' durable equipment or (earlier) industrial machinery. Price indices are from William H. Shaw, *Value of Commodity Output Since 1869* (New York: National Bureau of Economic Research, 1947), pp. 294–95; U.S., Bureau of the Census, *Historical Statistics of the United States, Colonial Times to 1957* (Washington, D.C.: Government Printing Office, 1960), pp. 116–17; the *Survey of Current Business* 33 (July 1953): 26; and the *Survey of Current Business* 56 (January 1976): 86–91. Deflator splice years were 1929–31 and 1948–50. The FTC's series from 1946 covers so-called large mergers, that is, with acquired company assets of $10 million or more. Asset values are for acquired companies only. The Nelson series for 1895–1920 estimates authorized capitalization or (roughly) stock values, which were found to be similar in magnitude to gross asset values—the measure used by the FTC. See Nelson, *Merger Movements*, pp. 19–20. For multifirm consolidations, Nelson estimates the total capitalized value of the resulting enterprise and not just the value of firms that might by some relative size criterion be said to have been acquired. This imparts an unavoidable upward bias in the Nelson series relative to the FTC series.

A pioneer in the "market-dominance-by-merger" game was the Standard Oil Company. Incorporated in 1870, it brought together 20 of the 25 existing Cleveland area petroleum refiners in early 1872. It then embarked upon a sustained program of acquiring competitors in other parts of the nation, adding roughly 100 more affiliations by merger during the next two decades and capturing a 90 percent share of U.S. petroleum refining capacity.

The pinnacle of the 1887–1904 merger wave was reached with the formation in 1901 of the United States Steel Corporation, combining an estimated 785 plants into the first American industrial corporation with a capitalization exceeding $1 billion. Actually, U.S. Steel is better described as a "combination of combinations." During the late 1880s, a series of mergers consolidated more than 200 formerly independent iron and steel makers into 20 much larger rival entities. Most of these new firms were confined to just a few facets of steel making, and after their formation many mapped out programs of integrating vertically to cover the whole spectrum from ore mining through fabrication. Charles Schwab, then president of Carnegie Steel, foresaw that this would lead to excess capacity and sharp price competition. He communicated his views to J. P. Morgan, who organized a merger among 12 of the prior consolidations and for his labor realized promotional profits estimated at $62.5 million. The end product was U.S. Steel, which at the time of its creation controlled roughly 65 percent of all domestic steel-making capacity.

Similar developments reshaped many other industries, large and small. In an early study of 92 large consolidations, John Moody found that 78 gained control of at least 50 percent of total output in their home industry, and 26 secured a market share of 80 percent or more. Although his figures are marred by slight inaccuracies, they have been shown to be substantially correct.[120] The industries affected included copper, lead, railroad cars, explosives, tin cans, tobacco products, electrical equipment, rubber products, paper, farm machinery, brick-making, chemicals, leather, sugar, business machines, photographic equipment, and shoe machinery. Many corporations that continue to dominate the American

industrial scene were formed. General Electric, for instance, was created in 1892 through a merger of Thomson-Houston, which had previously bought out numerous rivals, and Edison General Electric, which had acquired several suppliers and major industrial customers in earlier mergers. The result was a virtual duopoly (with Westinghouse) in many lines of electrical equipment manufacturing. The American Can Company was organized in 1901 through one grand consolidation of some 120 firms with a combined 90 percent share of the national market. American Tobacco, a consolidation of the leading five producers, had 90 percent of the national cigarette market at its inception and added to its control by forcing small competitors to the wall and buying them out. DuPont achieved a virtual monopoly of the explosives industry by acquiring or merging with nearly 100 rivals between 1872 and 1912. When forced in an antitrust action to divest some of its acquisitions, it pursued the merger route into other areas of the chemicals industry. Other firms whose formation or rise to prominence owes much to mergers during this period include National Lead (now NL Industries), U.S. Rubber (now Uniroyal), United Shoe Machinery, Pittsburgh Plate Glass (now PPG Industries), International Paper, United Fruit (now United Brands), Standard Sanitary (now American Standard), Allis-Chalmers, Eastman Kodak, International Salt, Corn Products Refining Company (now CPC International), International Harvester, and U.S. Gypsum. As Markham concluded, "The conversion of approximately 71 important oligopolistic or near-competitive industries into near monopolies by merger between 1890 and 1904 left an imprint on the structure of the American economy that 50 years have not yet erased."[121]

Merger activity declined sharply in 1903 and 1904, coinciding with two major events—a severe

120. Cf. Markham, "Survey," pp. 158–62, commenting on John Moody, *The Truth About Trusts* (New York: Moody, 1904), and later studies. See also Nelson, *Merger Movements*, p. 102.

121. Markham, "Survey," p. 180.

recession, and a set of judicial pronouncements in the *Northern Securities* case revealing for the first time that mergers leading to market dominance could be attacked successfully under the antitrust laws.[122] A period of relative quiet continued for a dozen years, interrupted occasionally by such ripples as the formation of International Business Machines Corporation (in 1911) and General Motors (combining Buick, Cadillac, Oldsmobile, and several other producers to gain a 22 percent share of the market in 1909, and adding Chevrolet a few years later). In hindsight, the most spectacular episode appears to be 'the one that got away.' Twice Henry Ford was willing to sell out to General Motors—for $3 million in 1908 and for $8 million one year later. But GM was unable to raise the required cash, and so the two leading auto producers remained independent.

The 1916–29 merger movement The merger movement showed signs of reviving in 1916 and 1917, but was interrupted by the conversion to war production in 1918 and 1919 and the readjustment recession of 1921 and 1922. Then it rode the stock market boom of the 1920s to heights paralleling, at least in terms of the number of companies acquired, those of 1899. Markham has estimated that roughly 12,000 firms disappeared through mergers between 1919 and 1930.[123] However, this wave differed from its turn-of-the-century predecessor in several respects.

For one, a great deal of the activity, including many of the largest combinations, occurred in the electrical and gas utility sector. According to Markham, approximately 2,750 utilities, comprising 43 percent of all public utility firms operating in 1929, were swallowed up to create the giant holding companies that collapsed so resoundingly during the 1930s. Since these firms typically had a monopoly in their local markets before being acquired, and since most were regulated by state commissions, the public utility merger wave led at most to only peripheral increases in monopoly power.

In the manufacturing and mining sectors, the approximately 8,000 mergers surveyed by Markham had a much less dramatic impact on market structure than a smaller number did in the 1887–

1904 movement. Mergers creating a single dominant firm were evidently discouraged by the antitrust laws, even though the law was not stringently interpreted and enforced at the time. It is also possible that earlier merger activity had exhausted most of the promising opportunities for ascending to nationwide dominance through consolidation. Whatever the reason, simultaneous multifirm consolidations were rarer, and most of the mergers in manufacturing and mining involved relatively small market share accretions by the acquiring firms. Some of the most prominent manufacturing mergers created a relatively large 'number two' firm in an industry previously dominated by one giant—e.g., the rise of Bethlehem Steel by combining with the third, fourth, sixth, and eighth ranking steel producers of 1904; or Continental Can's absorption of 19 smaller companies between 1927 and 1930. The difference between the 1887–1904 and 1916–29 merger waves has been depicted by George Stigler as the difference between "mergers for monopoly" and "mergers for oligopoly."[124]

The wave of the 1920s also appears to have been characterized by a higher incidence of vertical integration and diversification mergers than its predecessor. Roughly 43 percent of the recorded manufacturing sector mergers took place in the food products, chemicals, and metals industries.[125] Typifying developments in food products was the experience of the National Dairy Co., which moved into (and sometimes came to dominate) numerous local areas, each a distinct market in the economic sense, through several hundred acquisitions of small milk and dairy products firms. In copper, mergers of refiners with fabricators were common, leading to an oligopolistic fabricated products market structure parallelling the primary metal-smelting market structure. In chemicals, the formation of Allied Chemical in 1920 through a consolidation of five firms operating in largely noncompetitive lines set a pattern emulated frequently on a smaller scale. Altogether, Carl Eis has estimated, approximately 53 percent of all 1926–30 mergers by either number or asset value were horizontal in character, with the balance falling largely into the product line extension and vertical integration categories.[126]

The merger movement following World War II With the onset of the Great Depression in 1929, merger activity declined sharply and remained at low levels until the end of World War II was in sight. Then followed a revival that gradually accumulated momentum despite the passage of a substantially strengthened antimerger law in 1950. In the late 1960s there was a dramatic acceleration, leading to a peak in 1968. Following an equally dramatic decline, an upturn began again in the mid-1970s.

The dimensions of post-World War II merger activity are charted most accurately using the Federal Trade Commission's large merger statistical series, which covers acquisitions of manufacturing and mining businesses (including both whole firms or parts thereof) with assets of $10 million or more. Unlike related surveys that draw upon newspaper and other accounts to encompass the much larger number of less-than-$10 million asset acquisitions, the FTC large merger series is believed to be comprehensive and historically consistent (except in the sense that a $10 million asset floor falls over time in constant-dollar terms). Data for the peak year 1968 suggest that less-than-$10 million asset acquisitions amounted to approximately 16 to 20 percent of all manufacturing and mining corporation acquisitions by asset value.[127]

Between 1948 and 1966, 974 "large" manufacturing and mining enterprises were acquired. Their assets totalled $32.5 billion. From 1967 through 1975, another 1,094 large firms with assets totalling $61.4 billion were acquired.[128] By way of perspective, the nearly $94 billion of assets acquired between 1948 and 1975 amounted to 18.6 percent of the total value of all manufacturing and mining corporations' assets in the peak merger year 1968. On average, 0.8 percent of manufacturing and mining company assets changed hands through "large" mergers or acquisitions each year. In the peak year 1968, 2.72 percent of total assets were acquired. Had all the companies acquired between 1948 and 1975 survived as viable independent enterprises instead of being acquired, the number of U.S. manufacturing and mining corporations with assets of $10 million or more at the end of 1975 would have been approximately 5,900,

rather than the 3,946 actually in existence.[129]

Despite relatively high absolute levels, the merger movement of the post-World War II period, and especially the activity of the 1960s, was quite different from earlier U.S. merger waves. The Celler-Kefauver antimerger act of 1950 and subsequent judicial interpretations discouraged horizontal and vertical mergers entailing sizeable market share shifts. But while business leaders' "urge to merge" remained strong, it was deflected, perhaps even with little aggregate diminution, toward alternate merger opportunities considered more apt to pass legal muster.[130] These were for the most part conglomerate mergers of diverse types. Table 4.11 classifies large manufacturing and mining firm acquisitions in four postwar subperiods into the five qualitative categories used by the Federal Trade Commission's statistical series. Horizontal mergers are defined as those in which the merging companies sell closely related products in the same geographic market—e.g., when computer maker Minneapolis-Honeywell acquired the loss-plagued

122. *U.S.* v. *Northern Securities Co.*, 120 Fed. 721 (April 1903), 193 U.S. 197 (March 1904).

123. Markham, "Survey," pp. 168–69. See also Carl Eis, "The 1919–1930 Merger Movement in American Industry," *Journal of Law and Economics* 12 (October 1969): 267–96.

124. George J. Stigler, "Monopoly and Oligopoly by Merger," *American Economic Review* 40 (May 1950): 23–34.

125. See Eis, "The 1919–1930 Merger Movement," pp. 274–75. Cf. Markham,, "Survey," pp. 168–71.

126. Eis, "The 1919–1930 Merger Movement," pp. 280–84.

127. Federal Trade Commission staff report, *Economic Report on Corporate Mergers* (Washington, D.C.: Government Printing Office, 1969), pp. 741–42.

128. Federal Trade Commission, *Statistical Report on Mergers and Acquisitions* (Washington, D.C.: Government Printing Office, 1976), pp. 93–103.

129. From the 2,068 reported acquisitions, 91 were subtracted because they involved only parts of the so-called acquired firm and another 23 were taken out to offset possible double counting—e.g., when an entity was acquired and then sold off to still another corporation.

130. On the hypothesis that U.S. firms began seeking acquisitions more aggressively in Canada, see C. J. Maule, "Antitrust and the Takeover Activity of American Firms in Canada," *Journal of Law and Economics* 11 (October 1968): 423–32; with a comment by Grant L. Reuber and reply by Maule in the *Journal of Law and Economics* 12 (October 1969): 405–24.

computer operations of General Electric in 1970. Vertical mergers are those with significant potential or actual buyer-seller relationships—e.g., when a paper manufacturer acquires a timberland holding company. A product extension merger entails the joining of noncompeting products with related marketing channels or production processes—e.g., when leading detergent manufacturer Procter & Gamble acquired bleach maker Clorox. Under market extension mergers, a firm such as Kroger acquires additional supermarkets in a geographic market it previously had not served. Finally, there is an "other" category for mergers too conglomerate to have any clear competitive, buyer-seller, or functional relationships—e.g., when International Telephone & Telegraph (ITT) acquired Continental Baking, the makers of Wonder Bread. Frequently, mergers do not fit neatly into these categories, or functional interrelationships may not be apparent to the outside analyst. Still, the FTC series is believed to be at least reasonably consistent in applying its classification criteria using public and (since 1969) subpoenaed information. If anything, it has probably erred on the side of inferring horizontality in doubtful cases, since mergers were viewed as horizontal when there was *any* significant competitive overlap even though most of the merger partners' sales were noncompeting.

Two historical developments stand out in Table 4.11. One is the marked decline in the fraction of assets acquired through horizontal mergers after the Celler-Kefauver Act took hold. It is worth repeating that Eis found the share of acquired assets falling into the horizontal category during the late 1920s to have been at least 36 percent and probably nearer 56 percent.[131] Even more striking was the rise of "other"—i.e., relatively pure—conglomerate mergers from 3.2 percent of all acquired assets in 1948–55 to 49.2 percent in the mid-1970s. The surge of such conglomerate acquisitions was clearly the most distinctive feature of the 1960s' merger boom. A leading and not atypical example was Litton Industries, which rose from 249th place on *Fortune*'s list of industrial corporations in 1960 to 35th in 1971 through roughly 100 acquisitions. These included such diverse enterprises as the Monroe Calculating Machine Corp., Emertron, Inc. (household appliances), Fitchburg Paper, Hewitt-Robbins (materials handling equipment), Ingalls Shipbuilding, Royal McBee (typewriters), American Book Co., Jefferson Electric Co. (industrial electrical equipment), and Landis Tool Co. (machine tools).

Antitrust constraints precluded 1890s- or 1920s-like mergers that conferred market dominance except in special cases—e.g., involving regulated

---

T 4.11 Distribution of large manufacturing and mining company assets acquired by type of merger, 1948–77

Type of merger	Percentage of all assets acquired			
	1948–53	1956–63	1963–72	1973–77
Horizontal	36.8%	19.2%	12.4%	15.1%
Vertical	12.8	22.2	7.8	5.8
Conglomerate				
Product extension	44.8	36.0	39.3	24.2
Market extension	2.4	6.7	7.3	5.7
Other	3.2	15.9	33.2	49.2
Total	100.0	100.0	100.0	100.0

Adapted from Federal Trade Commission staff report, *Economic Report on Corporate Mergers* (Washington, D.C.: Government Printing Office, 1969), p. 673; and the FTC's annual *Statistical Report on Mergers and Acquisitions*, Table 17, various years. Acquisitions of nonpublic corporations are excluded from the post-1963 analysis.

and mortally ill eastern U.S. railroads such as the New York Central, Pennsylvania, and New Haven; certain regulated local bank markets; and perhaps some special product lines too small to attract the attention of the antitrust agencies. Even before the Celler-Kefauver Act took effect, dramatic concentration-increasing mergers were rare. A fragmentary but probably representative view is provided by Professor Weiss's study of six industries—autos, steel, petroleum refining, cement, flour milling, and beer brewing.[132] He found that for the period between 1929 and 1958, mergers did lead to increases in concentration—on average, roughly 2 percentage points' increase per decade in the four-firm concentration ratio. Although no similar study has been done for later periods, it is likely that even smaller effects would be observed owing to tightened antitrust enforcement. When concentration-increasing mergers did escape antitrust challenge after 1950, it was usually because the level of market concentration was low (as in textiles and bituminous coal[133]) and the market share accretions were small, or because some sizeable entity in a concentrated industry (e.g., Douglas Aircraft or RCA's digital computer division) was on the brink of failure.

In Europe, the post-World War II merger experience has been strikingly different. Most Western European nations have no significant antimerger laws, and those that do (e.g., England since 1965 and West Germany since 1973) have tended to enforce them sparingly. In part because of this, and perhaps even more because the lowering of trade barriers and (in England and Germany) the enforcement of new laws curbing price-fixing agreements precipitated a surge of new competition akin to that experienced during the 1880s in the United States, horizontal merger waves of impressive proportions have occurred.[134] One indication of the differences among nations comes from a comparative analysis of mergers in the 12 industries covered by Tables 4.2 and 4.10. For each industry in each of six nations, an attempt was made to determine whether the leading firm as of 1970 had experienced between 1958 and 1970 a major horizontal merger with a company of roughly equal size, or whether it had acquired between 1958 and 1970

at least as many industry-specific plants as it had operated during 1958. For West Germany and France, mergers meeting one or both of these criteria were observed in 8 of the 12 industries; for Sweden, in 6; for the United Kingdom, in 5; for Canada, in 2; and for the United States, in none.[135] In a partly overlapping study, Müller and Hochreiter estimated the four-firm concentration ratio changes attributable to mergers between 1958 and 1971 in 12 West German manufacturing industries (Table 4.12). The average change over 13 years was 12.7 percentage points, and by 1971, the average four-firm concentration ratio in those 12 industries had risen to 73. Similarly, M. A. Utton found that the ten-firm concentration ratio in 13 broadly defined United Kingdom manufacturing industry sectors (e.g., food, drink, chemicals, and the like) rose by 11.1 percentage points on average between 1954 and 1965.[136] If assets acquired by those ten leading firms during the period studied are subtracted from the firms' terminal year assets, the indicated increase in U.K. industry concentration is completely nullified.

131. Eis, "The 1919–1930 Merger Movement," pp. 282–84.

132. Leonard W. Weiss, "An Evaluation of Mergers in Six Industries," *Review of Economics and Statistics* 47 (May 1965): 172–81.

133. See George E. Hale, "The Case of Coal: Should All Horizontal Mergers Be Held Illegal?" *Journal of Law and Economics* 13 (October 1970): 425–29.

134. The United Kingdom experienced a turn-of-the-century merger wave similar to but less intense than that of the United States. See Leslie Hannah, "Mergers in British Manufacturing Industry, 1880–1918," *Oxford Economic Papers* 26 (March 1974): 1–17. On the stimuli to more recent merger waves in the U.K. and elsewhere, see Kenneth D. George and Aubrey Silberston, "The Causes and Effects of Mergers," *Scottish Journal of Political Economy* 22 (June 1975): 179–93; John J. McGowan, "International Comparisons of Merger Activity," *Journal of Law and Economics* 14 (April 1971), especially pp. 240–48; and Bengt Rydén, *Mergers in Swedish Industry* (Stockholm: Almqvist & Wiksell, 1972).

135. Scherer et al., *The Economics of Multi-Plant Operation*, pp. 161–68, 219, 426–28.

136. M. A. Utton, "Mergers and the Growth of Large Firms," *Bulletin of the Oxford University Institute of Economics & Statistics*, 34, No. 2 (1972); 194–96. See also his "The Effect of Mergers on Concentration: U.K. Manufacturing Industry, 1954–65" *Journal of Industrial Economics* 20 (November 1971): 42–58; and Sam Aaronovitch and Malcolm Sawyer, "Mergers, Growth, and Concentration," *Oxford Economic Papers* 20 n.s. (March 1975): 136–55.

Even though, unlike the European experience, mergers since World War II have not caused substantial concentration increases in individual U.S. manufacturing industries, the wave of predominantly conglomerate mergers did contribute to rising aggregate concentration. Only a crude demonstration of this point is possible. The 200 largest manufacturing corporations accounted for 48.2 percent of all U.S. manufacturing corporation assets in 1948, as measured through Federal Trade Commission surveys, and 60.0 percent in 1972—the last year from which the FTC survey criteria remained sufficiently constant to permit comparisons.[137] In 1972 the top 200 manufacturers reported total assets of $399.0 billion. Had they maintained only their 1948 asset share, their 1972 assets would have been $320.5 billion. Thus, the asset growth associated with their observed share increase was $78.5 billion. Between 1948 and 1972, those same 200 largest manufacturers acquired manufacturing and mining firms with assets valued in the years of acquisition at $44.7 billion.[138] Thus, approximately 6.7 percentage points [i.e., $11.8 \times (44.7/78.5)$] of the 200 largest manufacturers' observed asset share growth appears traceable to mergers. This estimate is biased on the high size because other corporations not on the 1972 top 200 list might have displaced some of the listed concerns had the latter not made sizeable acquisitions, and their displacement would cause measured concentration to fall by less than the amount of the merged assets. But it is also biased downward because foreign company acquisitions, domestic acquisitions outside manufacturing and mining, and acquisitions of manufacturing and mining firms with assets of less than $10 million are not included in the $44.7 billion figure but are counted in the top 200 corporations' total asset base. Downward biases also intrude because the acquisition sum used assumes in effect that the acquired firms ceased to grow following acquisition and therefore contributed *only* $44.7 billion to the acquirers' 1972 size. The two sources of downward bias are in all probability much more important than the upward (displacement) bias. Therefore, it seems reasonable to conclude that post-World War II mergers have caused aggregate asset concentration for the 200 largest manufacturers to be substantially higher than it otherwise would have been.

T 4.12 Concentration changes attributable to mergers in 12 West German industries

	Concentration change, 1958–71	1971 concentration ratio
Beer brewing	+20.9	34
Cigarettes	+ 9.1	88
Petroleum refining	+20.0	57
Leather shoes	+ 6.7	38
Glass containers	+ 5.7	70
Cement	+ 9.8	58
Steel	+18.8	65
Antifriction bearings	0.0	92
Refrigerators & freezers	+16.8	77
Passenger autos	+ 3.4	95
Small trucks	+17.8	100
Large trucks (> four tons)	+23.5	100

Source: Jürgen Müller, "The Impact of Mergers on Concentration: A Study of Eleven West German Industries," *Journal of Industrial Economics* 25 (December 1976): 113–32; augmented for cement from Müller and Rolf Hochreiter, *Stand und Entwicklungstendenzen der Unternehmenskonzentration in der Bundesrepublik* (Göttingen: Schwartz, 1976). Copyright © Verlag Schwartz. Reprinted with permission.

Merger cycles and stock market fluctuations

An enticing byway in the study of mergers is the analysis of relationships between merger activity and the business cycle. Changes in the number of mergers per year appear to be related to the gyrations of the stock market. Careful examination of Figure 4.5 suggests that major declines in merger activity have usually accompanied stock market slumps—e.g., in 1904, 1907, 1921, 1929–31, and 1969–70. In an early statistical assault on the question, Nelson found cyclical deviations in the number of mergers occurring per year between 1895 and 1954 to be positively correlated with deviations in stock prices, the correlation coefficient being 0.47. He obtained a much weaker correlation of 0.08 between trend-adjusted changes in the number of mergers and in the Federal Reserve Board's index of industrial production.[139] However, work by Peter Steiner and Alan Beckenstein suggests that the correlations broke down in the 1970s.[140] Changes in merger activity failed to track the stock market's upsurge in 1971 and 1972, its sharp decline in 1974, and its 1976 recovery. Whether this breakdown resulted from unusual inflation-cum-recession conditions affecting stock prices, pent-up investor disillusionment concerning previously disappointing conglomerate mergers, or some other set of causes is unclear. One unprecedented development that could have stabilized merger activity at moderate levels despite stock price swings might have been the effort of many companies to reverse unsuccessful previous acquisitions. According to one survey of both small and large mergers, more than half the mergers announced in 1976 involved sales of unprofitable or mismatched corporate subsidiaries.[141]

The generally positive correlation between long-term merger movements and stock prices casts doubt upon the hypothesis (first suggested by U.S. and British experience in the late 19th century) that mergers were a means of escaping or suppressing the intense competition prevailing during business slumps. However, it is possible that the desire to mitigate slack period competition led entrepreneurs to seek mergers consummated only when capital market conditions were propitious—i.e., in bullish times. Complex expectational considerations also affect both the timing and intensity of merger activity. On these we shall say more later.

Sellers' motives for merger Let us probe more deeply now into the reasons why mergers have occurred in such impressive but variable quantities. There are many reasons why business leaders might seek to merge. They range from the desire for enhanced wealth to dreams of empire. Except in the case of hostile takeovers, which continue to comprise a small fraction of all mergers,[142] the decision to merge is bilateral, involving the managements of both the acquiring and ac-

quired enterprises. It is useful to begin our exploration of merger motives by examining matters from the acquired firm's perspective.

Seller motives are definitely important. J. K. Butters and his colleagues found in a detailed study of 80 early post-World War II mergers that in more than two-thirds of the cases, the initiative was taken by the acquired firms.[143] Although the proportion of seller-initiated mergers has probably declined since then, there continue to be several reasons why the owners of a corporation might wish to sell out.

137. David W. Penn, "Aggregate Concentration: A Statistical Note," *Antitrust Bulletin* 21 (Spring 1976): 91–98. See also Chapter 3, p. 50.

138. Federal Trade Commission, *Statistical Report on Mergers and Acquisitions* (Washington, D.C.: Government Printing Office, 1974), p. 151. See also William N. Leonard, "Mergers, Industrial Concentration, and Antitrust Policy," *Journal of Economic Issues* 9 (June 1976): 354–61; and John McGowan, "The Effect of Alternative Antimerger Policies on the Size Distribution of Firms," *Yale Economic Essays* 5 (Fall 1965): 465–71.

139. Nelson, *Merger Movements*, p. 118. See also Nelson's "Business Cycle Factors in the Choice Between Internal and External Growth," in William W. Alberts and Joel E. Segall, eds., *The Corporate Merger* (Chicago: University of Chicago Press, 1966), pp. 52–66; Markham, "Survey," pp. 146–54; C. J. Maule, "A Note on Mergers and the Business Cycle," *Journal of Industrial Economics* 16 (April 1968): 99–105; and the comment by Carl Eis, *Journal of Industrial Economics* 19 (November 1970): 89–92. For similar evidence on early British merger movements, see Hannah, "Mergers in British Manufacturing," pp. 8–9.

140. Peter O. Steiner, *Mergers: Motives, Effects, Policies* (Ann Arbor, Mich.: University of Michigan Press, 1975), pp. 208–17, reporting analyses by Alan R. Beckenstein.

141. "Merger Moves Up 3% in Nine Months of '76," *New York Times*, 13 October 1976. See also "Finding Buyers for the Bad Buys," *Business Week*, 13 September 1969, pp. 49–51.

142. The Securities and Exchange Commission listed 90 attempted takeovers through tender offer in 1975, not all of which were necessarily hostile or contested by management. See U.S., Congress, Senate, Committee on Banking, Housing, and Urban Affairs hearings, *Corporate Takeovers*, 94th Cong., 2nd sess., 1976, pp. 138–58. The Federal Trade Commission listed for the same year 1,228 attempted and completed mergers sizeable enough to receive notice in standard business periodicals. See also note 77, Chapter 2, p. 37 *supra*; and Gerald D. Newbould, *Management and Merger Activity* (Liverpool, England: Guthstead, 1970), p. 48, who found that 2.5 percent of all identifiable 1968–69 mergers in the United Kingdom were contested by acquired firm directors. However, for acquisition targets valued at £10 million or more, the hostile takeover rate was 23 percent.

143. John Keith Butters, John M. Lintner, and W. L. Cary, *Effects of Taxation on Corporate Mergers* (Boston: Harvard Business School Division of Research, 1951) p. 309.

First, they may find their ship sinking under them and seek rescue from a company with adequate financial resources, able management, and new ideas. However, an imminent threat of failure appears to be an important consideration in relatively few sizeable mergers. Only 24 of the 515 manufacturing and mining corporations with assets of $10 million or more that were listed by the FTC as having been wholly or partially acquired during the 1966–69 merger boom reported net losses in the year before their acquisition.[144] In the generally less prosperous 1970–75 period, however, the number of acquired companies with prior-year losses rose to 47 out of the 383 firms for which profitability data were available.

Second, company owner-managers may be aging or weary of business pressures and lack heirs or other successors to take their place, so they turn to merger as a means of selling out and perpetuating what they have started. This is one of the most common motives underlying small-firm sales. The decision to sell out may be hastened if the firm has obsolete equipment for whose replacement owners are unable or unwilling to raise the necessary capital. Weiss estimated, using the survivor technique, that from 83 to 91 percent of the capacity acquired through mergers in the steel, auto, petroleum refining, cement, flour, and brewing industries between 1929 and 1958 was of suboptimal scale.[145] A similar contributing element is growth of the firm to a size where new managerial philosophies and methods unattractive to present owner-managers are required.[146]

Third, and interacting with the second motive, income and estate tax ramifications often heighten the desire of individuals owning companies with unlisted or thinly traded stocks to sell out. By retaining earnings in their firms until they sell out, entrepreneurs can take advantage of the relatively low capital gains tax rates to build their fortunes. Inheritance taxes mount to 41 percent on bequests exceeding $1.2 million to heirs other than one's spouse and 70 percent on bequests over $5.2 million. Settlements are risky unless closely held concerns merge with a larger corporation, since lack of a clear-cut market price for the small company's common stock leaves heirs at the not-so-tender mercy of the Internal Revenue Service in estimating their tax liability. A requirement that estate taxes be paid within nine months once bolstered merger incentives, since heirs could be forced to liquidate stock at distress prices on a thin market to raise sufficient cash. However, this provision has gradually been liberalized, most recently in the Tax Reform Act of 1976, to allow extensions of up to ten years for closely held businesses and in other hardship cases. In an interview survey covering 89 mergers completed during the 1940s, Lintner and Butters found tax considerations to have been a major reason for selling out in roughly 40 percent of mergers entailing asset transfers of $15 million or more, but only rarely when the acquired firm had assets of less than $1 million.[147] In a questionnaire survey of 401 firms with unlisted stock that merged between 1955 and 1959, when the nine-month payment rule still applied, Bosland found company officers' concern over estate and gift tax problems to be the most important single incentive for merger, said to be of "substantial significance" in 63 percent of all cases.[148]

Fourth, owners of firms too small or with too limited resources to diversify internally may seek to reduce their risk exposure by trading their stock for the shares of more diversified corporations listed on a major exchange. And last but not least, owners may sell out because some potential acquiring firm makes an offer too attractive to turn down. This leads us into the question of what benefits buyers hope to secure through merger.

Monopoly, promotional, and speculative motives It is usually more difficult to ascertain buyers' than sellers' merger motives, in part because decision makers aware of the legal risks are often less than candid about monopolistic or self-aggrandizing intent. Also, given the complexity of merger decisions, they may be unaware of deep-seated drives affecting their actions. One way out of this problem is to judge the motives for merger by the effects achieved, since rational entrepreneurs presumably intend what they bring about.[149] The main difficulty is that the correlation between achievement and intent is far from perfect. A firm may have tried hard to establish a monopoly but failed. Or power over price might be an incidental and largely unintended consequence of a series of mergers undertaken for quite different reasons. The best strategy is to combine both approaches, supplementing evidence on the effects of merger with whatever direct, credible evidence we have on motives.

Monopoly power was such a striking result of numerous mergers around the turn of the century that one could hardly deny with a straight face that it was intended. Moreover, since monopolization through merger was a relatively new game at the time, it seems reasonable to assume that other consolidations were formed in the hope of achieving market control but failed to fulfill that hope. The first inference is corroborated by statements of individuals involved in some of the better-known mergers. There is little doubt from the extensive historical record that forestalling the competition bound to develop if each of several steel combinations pursued its independent expansion plans was uppermost in the minds of United States Steel organizers, even though they may also have been concerned, as they claimed, with such purported benefits as the power to combat European steel cartels in export markets.[150] Likewise, monopoly power was a significant motivating factor behind the formation of General Electric, as Thomas Edison's remark to a reporter at the time of the merger shows:

Recently there has been sharp rivalry between [Thomson-Houston and Edison General Electric], and prices have been cut so that there has been little profit in the manufacture of electrical machinery for anybody. The consolidation of the companies . . . will do away with a competition which has become so sharp that the product of the factories has been worth little more than ordinary hardware.[151]

Those were days when U.S. businessmen were not yet intimidated by the wrath of trustbusters or public opinion. Now, comparable examples are found more easily overseas where antimerger laws have not yet taken hold.[152]

As we have seen, mergers were a much less prominent concentration-increasing force in recent decades, and from this change in effects it is reasonable to infer that the desire to build mo-

nopoly or oligopoly power has diminished in importance as a motive for merger. Still, it has not disappeared completely. In the cement industry, for example, the president of one firm wrote in 1928 to the president of another concerning the acquisition of several price-cutting independents, "It is proven that the most effective way to cure a bad situation is to buy up the offenders."[153] And in coal, acquisition of the Nashville Coal Co. by the West Kentucky Coal Co. during 1955 not only hastened oligopolization of the midwestern market, but also eliminated the leading price cutter and brought a price war to an end.[154] It is hard to believe that there are not more cases of mergers motivated by the desire to establish pricing tranquility even when market dominance of the 1890s variety is not attained.

Another important motive for merger has been

144. Federal Trade Commission, *Statistical Report on Mergers and Acquisitions* (Washington, D.C.: Government Printing Office, 1976), Table 25. See also Stanley E. Boyle, "Pre-Merger Growth and Profit Characteristics of Large Conglomerate Mergers in the United States: 1948–1969," *St. John's Law Review* 44 (Spring 1970): 152–70; Robert L. Conn, "The Failing Firm/Industry Doctrines in Conglomerate Mergers," *Journal of Industrial Economics* 24 (March 1976): 181–87; and Steiner, *Mergers*, pp. 185–86.

145. Weiss, "An Evaluation of Mergers in Six Industries," pp. 176–77.

146. Cf. Penrose, *The Theory of Growth of the Firm*, p. 161.

147. John Lintner and J. K. Butters, "Effects of Taxes on Concentration," in *Business Concentration and Price Policy*, pp. 272–73; drawing upon Butters, Lintner, and Cary, *Effects of Taxation*, Chapter 8.

148. C. C. Bosland, "Has Estate Taxation Induced Recent Mergers?" *National Tax Journal* 16 (June 1963): 159–68.

149. This is the approach advocated by Markham in his "Survey," pp. 158–62.

150. For a skeptical view of U.S. Steel's success as an exporter and an excellent analysis of how it achieved and exploited its monopoly power, see Parsons and Ray, "The United States Steel Consolidation," pp. 184–93, *et seq.*

151. *New York Times*, 21 February 1892, p. 2, cited in H. C. Passer, *The Electrical Manufacturers: 1875–1900* (Cambridge, Mass.: Harvard University Press, 1953), p. 326. See also p. 54 on the motives for several earlier Thomson-Houston mergers.

152. See Newbould, *Management and Merger Activity*, pp. 136–39; and F. M. Scherer, "Economies of Scale at the Plant and Multi-Plant Level: Detailed Evidence," multilith manuscript, September 1975, p. 49.

153. Quoted in Samuel M. Loescher, *Imperfect Collusion in the Cement Industry* (Cambridge, Mass.: Harvard University Press, 1959), p. 120.

154. Reed Moyer, *Competition in the Midwestern Coal Industry* (Cambridge, Mass.: Harvard University Press, 1964), pp. 82, 157.

The determinants of market structure   129

the desire of parties involved to profit from their promotional efforts. The Morgan syndicate's $62.5 million profit in assembling U.S. Steel was only the most spectacular example of an almost everyday practice at the turn of the century. This motive for merger and the monopolistic motive are related. The value of a company's common stock depends upon investor expectations regarding its future profits. If competition can be eliminated through merger, profits will presumably rise, making the new consolidated firm's shares worth more than the sum of the original competing companies' share values. Promoters sought to achieve such capital value transformations by arranging competition-reducing mergers, retaining a block of the new firm's stock as a reward for their trouble. However, many went farther. Because investors were captivated by the prospect of pursuing this road to fortune, and because there were no effective controls on the quality of information disseminated in connection with new capital stock flotations, unscrupulous promoters arranged mergers with little chance of securing real monopoly power. Simultaneously they issued misleading prospectuses, planted rumors, and primed the market to convince investors otherwise. By exciting false expectations, the promoters were able to sell the stock of newly consolidated firms at prices far exceeding its true economic value—a practice known as *stock watering*.[155] As in honestly monopolistic consolidations, the promoters were paid in newly issued stock for their contribution. Only in this case, they hastened to sell their shares to unwary outsiders before the bubble burst. And burst it did. Shaw Livermore studied 328 mergers consummated between 1888 and 1905 and discovered that at least 141 were financial failures, 53 collapsing shortly after their formation.[156] Analyzing a smaller sample, Markham found that consolidations promoted by outside banks, syndicates, and the like failed much more frequently than those put together by individuals with a continuing commitment to the affected industry.[157] From his survey of this and other evidence, he concludes that the quest for promotional profits was the most important single motive for merger during the frenzied 1897–99 and 1926–29 periods.[158]

Alarm over such abuses led to passage of the Securities Act of 1933 and the Securities Exchange Act of 1934, establishing federal regulation of securities issue information and other promotional practices. They and the antitrust laws made it difficult for promoters to realize the kinds of gains typical of the 1890s. However, investment bankers continue to draw fees in the quarter-million to million-dollar range for their role as merger brokers.[159] And entrepreneurs have invented new ways to reap speculative gains through merger while remaining within (or sometimes merely staying a step ahead of) the law.

One such device is the artful exploitation of accounting loopholes to inflate reported post-merger profitability.[160] For example, under the 'pooling of interest' accounting popular during the 1960s merger boom, acquired assets were recorded at their original book value even though they had been purchased at prices substantially exceeding book. Relative to 'purchase' accounting, under which the acquired assets are valued at something approximating current market value at the time of acquisition, this raises the ratio of reported profits to assets or stockholders' equity. It also provides an opportunity for reporting sizeable (but in a real sense fictitious) profit gains when undervalued assets are resold. In the depressed stock market of the early 1970s, an opposite bias resulted from the then prevalent use of purchase accounting. The assets of companies acquired at bargain prices were revalued downward, permitting reduced depreciation charges and hence higher reported earnings.[161] In principle, investors should not be fooled by such accounting flummery, but some apparently are. Their gullibility provides an opportunity for speculative gain by knowledgeable insiders and merger brokers.

In the same spirit was the 'perpetual growth machine' strategy cultivated by some conglomerate merger impresarios of the late 1960s.[162] To understand its logic, consider the hypothetical Company A with current annual profits of $10 million, one million shares of common stock outstanding, earnings per share of $10, and (because investors are enthusiastic about its growth prospects) the relatively high stock price/earnings ratio of 20. One share of A's common stock sells at $10 × 20 = $200. Company A then sets out to acquire the Z Corporation, with profits of $2 million, 200,000 shares of stock outstanding, earnings per share of $10, and a more conventional price/earnings ratio of 8, yielding a price per share of $80. A offers Z's shareholders 6 A shares for each 10 Z shares. If Z's shareholders expect the A stock price to persist, this is an irresistible offer, since they receive 6 shares valued at a total of $1,200 in exchange for 10 shares valued at $800. To finance the deal, A issues 120,000 new shares. Consolidated profits of the newly expanded Company A are $12 million. With 1,120,000 shares outstanding, earnings per share are $10.71. If the market continues to evaluate A's stock at a price/earnings multiple of 20, the price per share rises to $214.20. Everyone is wealthier than before, even though earnings have not increased at all!

This Midas touch will fail if the A price/earnings ratio falls because the postmerger organization is less attractive after the assimilation of less glamorous Z Corporation. But that need not happen if investors can be kept in the proper frame of mind. As long as A can continue to acquire firms with lower price/earnings ratios and (more importantly) as long as investors believe it will continue to do so, earnings per share will rise and the growth expectations that led investors to pay a high price/earnings multiple will be validated. Should those expectations for any reason be contradicted, however, the A stock price will fall relative to earnings; Company A will find it much more difficult to acquire other firms with lower price/earnings multiples, and the growth on which its stock price depended must slow. The whole process is fueled by self-reinforcing but inherently fragile speculative expectations. When they falter, the bubble bursts, as it did in 1969. Indeed, such speculation inevitably sows the seeds of its own undoing. As the perpetual growth strategy is imitated by others, sooner or later the opportunities for making attractive acquisitions dwindle as candidate firms' price/earnings multiples are bid up competitively, the ranks of acquirable firms are depleted, and/or the acquiring company develops managerial indigestion. Meanwhile, shrewd speculators and company executives with stock options and inside information have made a killing.

This is probably too harsh an explanation of many merger promoters' motives, even at the peak of speculative madness. Some of the most prominent conglomerators were evidently surprised by the 1968–69 stock market slump, and financial setbacks presumably caused them to shed many a bitter tear into their Olympic-sized swimming pools. No doubt, entangled with such entrepreneurs' desire to strike it rich by dangling before investors the lure of perpetual growth was a genuine desire to build a corporate empire. In this quest for empire the James Lings and Harry Figgies et al. may have fooled themselves as well as others. The main point is that, whatever their motivation, sooner or later some investors in the companies they amalgamated had to lose as long as the stock price appreciation realized at the peak of merger activity was rooted in the expectation of a growth rate that could not be sustained.

Speculative motives also energize mergers in a less systematic and more benign way. The stock market is myopic, and the information that drives it is often flimsy. As a result, some companies tend at any moment in time to be undervalued relative

155. Merely selling stock in the new firm at prices exceeding the sum of the old firms' share values is not necessarily stock watering, despite statements to this effect by some commentators. The critical question is whether the new firm's earnings are sufficient to yield a normal return on the new, higher share values.

156. Shaw Livermore, "The Success of Industrial Mergers," *Quarterly Journal of Economics* 49 (November 1935): 68–96.

157. Markham, "Survey," p. 163 note.

158. Markham, "Survey," p. 181.

159. See "How Lazard Became the Merger House," *Business Week*, 18 March 1972, p. 16; "Greenhill: A New Takeover Artist," *Business Week*, 14 December 1974, pp. 55–56; and "Ira Harris: Chicago's Big Dealmaker," *Business Week*, 25 June 1979, pp. 70–72.

160. For an excellent overview of this complex issue, see Steiner, *Mergers*, pp. 109–27.

161. "Gimmick for All Seasons," *Forbes*, 1 October 1975, pp. 60–64. Note that by reducing the acquired enterprise's depreciation tax shield, this strategy leads to higher income tax obligations and lower after-tax cash flow. It is therefore an extremely shortsighted approach to wealth maximization.

162. See Walter J. Mead, "Instantaneous Merger Profit as a Conglomerate Merger Motive," *Western Economic Journal* 7 (December 1969): 295–306; and Steiner, *Mergers*, pp. 103–109, 203–204.

to their long-run earnings potential while others are overvalued. The officers of an overvalued concern wise enough to recognize the market's error know their stock provides uniquely economical currency for making acquisitions. Such companies, as well as those whose stock is 'correctly' valued, have an incentive to seek out acquisition candidates whose stock is undervalued and whose earnings potential can therefore be obtained at a bargain price. To be sure, if stockholders of the target company recognize that their shares are undervalued, they will not sell out except at price premia so high as to eliminate the acquirer's gain. But if holders of a majority of the shares are short sighted, a merger, which most parties to the deal perceive as beneficial to themselves, can take place.[163] The expectations of all parties are of course uncertain, and one might suppose that the kinds of expectational divergences that engender a mutuality of interest arise with special frequency in times of unusual economic turbulence—e.g., when rapid technological changes are occurring or there are rapid movements, especially upward movements, in stock prices.[164] In the end, someone must be right and someone wrong. But because expectational divergences have arisen more or less randomly and because stockholders presumably have chosen democratically to merge without being misled by merger promoters, this sort of merger for speculative gain is generally considered less objectionable than the perpetual growth or tortured-accounting humbugs.

Other stock value effects Investors need not be wrong in their view that a merger is advantageous to stockholders of both the acquired and acquiring entities. The combined enterprise may indeed be worth more than the sum of its parts as a result of complementarities called "synergy" by merger aficionados. One reason, we have seen, is that combination enhances monopoly power. Another plausible merger consequence with a direct impact on stock prices is diversification reducing the variance of combined company earnings and perhaps the correlation of company stock price movements with overall market swings.[165] One might expect the diversification benefits to be especially important for conglom-

erate mergers. However, the reduction in earnings and stock price variability achieved by U.S. conglomerates appears to have been considerably less than what could have been accomplished had a deliberate variance-minimizing acquisition strategy been pursued.[166] This suggests that risk-reducing diversification per se was not a paramount objective. The characteristically high leveraging of conglomerate firm capital structures (i.e., with a relatively high ratio of debt to equity capital) is also inconsistent with risk reduction as a primary motive.

As Chapter 2 indicated, growth-oriented managers in corporations with rich cash flows but stagnant investment opportunities may plow earnings back into projects yielding a lower return than one could obtain in other industries.[167] This type of allocative inefficiency is abetted by the fact that earnings paid out as dividends are taxed once at the corporate level and again as personal income before they become available for reinvestment by stockholders. When such cash-rich, opportunity-poor companies diversify through acquisition (or internal growth) into higher opportunity fields, they can in effect create an internal capital market avoiding double taxation. The result may be more profitable investment of their cash flows, which benefits shareholders *and* (absent the aggravation of other market imperfections) improves the overall allocation of resources. This is essentially a second-best benefit of mergers. *If* managers could be dissuaded from making low-yield investments (e.g., if they would instead exploit the tax advantages of repurchasing their company's own shares), this benefit would be nonexistent. It would also be reduced if not eliminated by a tax structure overhaul ending the double taxation barrier to free capital flows. But to the extent that managers' plowback instincts are taken as a behavioral given, diversification-enhancing mergers can lead to efficiency gains. There is evidence that during the 1960s diversifying companies often, though not consistently, sought out rapidly growing and profitable acquisition candidates, which afforded attractive outlets for the internal reallocation of funds.[168] From this, it seems reasonable to infer that improved capital allocation was in fact a conglomerate merger motive.

Another financial synergy comes from the possibility of carrying forward the losses accumulated by an acquired company as a shield against taxes on the acquiring company's profits. The federal government in such cases confers what amounts to a subsidy on the merged company's shareholders, presumably in the hope of salvaging the less profitable entity's operations.

Operating efficiencies Finally, we must consider at some length the possibility that mergers yield scale economies of a more conventional sort—e.g., in production, marketing, research and development, management, and the like. We address each in turn.

In the first edition of this book the author expressed considerable skepticism concerning the likelihood of production scale economies being realized through merger. The argument began from the premise (which appears still to be much more right than wrong) that plant-specific economies are vastly more important than multi-plant production economies. It continued as follows: "Suppose then that two previously independent plants producing the same product are brought under the same corporate shell. What economies of scale will be realized? The answer must be: little or none. The plants are already built; not much can be done to unbuild them to increase their scale . . ."

Newer evidence suggests that this view is wrong in certain respects. The main problem is that it failed to recognize the difference between product-specific and plant-specific economies. Plant sizes *are* difficult to change, but when two firms manufacture similar and overlapping product lines, production assignments might be rearranged rather quickly to combine and lengthen production runs and minimize duplicating machine setups. An extreme illustration is provided by the 1969 merger of three English antifriction bearing manufacturers—Ransome and Marles, Hoffmann, and Pollard.[169] The first two sold extensively overlapping lines of general-purpose bearings whose dimensions conformed for the most part to international standards. Immediately following the merger, production assignments were revamped to eliminate duplication and lengthen runs. Within three years, output per

employee had been improved by some 40 percent, partly as a direct result of the increase in specialization and partly through simple belt tightening. Substantial further gains were expected from the introduction of six automated

163. Except in the weighting of votes according to shareholdings, the choice problems here are analogous to those faced by voters in municipal referenda. See Howard R. Bowen, "The Interpretation of Voting in the Allocation of Economic Resources," *Quarterly Journal of Economics* 58 (November 1943): 27–48; and Anthony Downs, *An Economic Theory of Democracy* (New York: Harper & Row, 1957), especially Chapters 3 and 8.

164. This view of merger motives was first articulated by Michael Gort in "An Economic Disturbance Theory of Mergers," *Quarterly Journal of Economics* 83 (November 1969): 624–42. See also William W. Alberts, "The Profitability of Growth by Merger," in Alberts and Segall, eds., *The Corporate Merger*, especially pp. 244–47, 272–83. In *Management and Merger Activity*, p. 52, Newbould found for a sample of 223 acquisitions that the mean ratio of stock prices four weeks before a takeover bid to the year's high was significantly lower and more variable for acquired than acquiring firms. This supports an inference that random downward fluctuations in the acquired firm's stock price was a takeover-precipitating factor.

165. Cf. Chapter 4, pp. 104–7 *supra* and Corry Azzi, "Conglomerate Mergers, Default Risk, and Homemade Mutual Funds," *American Economic Review* 68 (March 1978): 161–72. In "A Note on Mergers and Risk," *Antitrust Bulletin* 19 (Fall 1974): 523–29, Harold Bierman, Jr. and J. L. Thomas observe that mergers do not unambiguously lessen the risk of bankruptcy faced by both sets of original stockholders. An extremely large loss in one of the merged entities may drag the entire company into ruin, whereas investors in the nonlosing entity would have been unscathed had they remained independent.

166. See J. Fred Weston, Keith V. Smith, and Ronald E. Shrieves, "Conglomerate Performance Using the Capital Asset Pricing Model," *Review of Economics and Statistics* 54 (November 1972): 357–63; Keith V. Smith and John C. Schreiner, "A Portfolio Analysis of Conglomerate Diversification," *Journal of Finance* 24 (June 1969): 413–27; Oscar J. Holzmann, R. M. Copeland, and Jack Hayya, "Income Measures of Conglomerate Performance," *Quarterly Review of Economics and Business* 15 (Autumn 1975): 67–78; Ronald S. Bond, "A Note on Diversification and Risk," *Southern Economic Journal* 41 (October 1974): 288–89; and Paul M. Gorecki, "An Inter-Industry Analysis of Diversification in the U.K. Manufacturing Sector," *Journal of Industrial Economics* 24 (December 1975): 131–43.

167. Cf. Chapter 2, p. 40 *supra*. See also Williamson, *Corporate Control and Business Behavior*, pp. 138–45; and Dennis C. Mueller, "A Theory of Conglomerate Mergers," *Quarterly Journal of Economics* 84 (November 1969): 643–59.

168. See Michael Gort and Thomas Hogarty, "New Evidence on Mergers," *Journal of Law and Economics* 13 (April 1970): 167–84; Ronald W. Melicher and David F. Rush, "Evidence on the Acquisition-Related Performance of Conglomerate Firms," *Journal of Finance* 29 (March 1974): 141–49; and the Federal Trade Commission staff report, *Conglomerate Merger Performance: An Empirical Analysis of Nine Corporations* (Washington, D.C.: Government Printing Office, 1972), pp. 28–31.

169. Scherer et al., *The Economics of Multi-Plant Operation*, pp. 312–13.

production lines for high-volume bearings—the first such installations in the United Kingdom.

Similar but less dramatic product-specific economy gains were achieved in a merger between Canadian household appliance makers GSW and Moffats in 1971. Each produced a broad line of refrigerators, washing machines, and the like prior to merger. Following the merger, plants were specialized to achieve longer production runs. This pattern was repeated in several German, French, and British white goods producer mergers.[170] Interviews with 125 companies in 12 industries, at least 36 of which had experienced major horizontal mergers, revealed several other cases of post-merger economies, most of which were much less significant than those illustrated here. Table 4.13 summarizes impressionistically the observed differences in postmerger product-specific savings potential and the reasons why such savings might be unattainable. By far the most important constraining factor is the demand of consumers for physically differentiated products requiring separate production setups or lines. In shoes and fabrics, for example, major horizontal mergers were followed by little or no increase in production run lengths because any possible production cost savings were more than outweighed by the sales volume losses that product standardization would cause. The bearings industry represents an opposite extreme in this respect because of the international agreements under which product dimensions have been standardized.

It must be noted too that examples of product-specific economies following merger were far more frequent and involved much greater savings in Europe and Canada than in the United States. This was so for at least four reasons, stated in descending order of importance. First, the much greater size of the United States market made it easier to attain most product-specific economies without merger. Second, price competition was typically more vigorous in U.S. industries, generating greater pressure for U.S. producers to specialize in products on which they could capture most scale economies. For many

T 4.13 Observed potential for product-specific economies through merger in 12 industries

Industry	Savings potential	Limiting factors
Brewing	Slight	Product differentiation; small-batch product orientation
Cigarettes	Negligible	Strong product differentiation
Fabric weaving	Slight	Strong product differentiation
Paints	Slight to moderate	Product differentiation; managerial inertia (in Europe)
Petroleum refining	Negligible	Continuous flow process
Shoes	Negligible	Strong product differentiation
Glass bottles	Slight	Product differentiation (designs to customer order); transport costs
Cement	Negligible	Continuous flow process
Steel	Slight to moderate	Transport costs; restraints on worker layoffs (in Europe)
Bearings	Substantial	Slight product differentiation
Refrigerators	Substantial	Product differentiation
Storage batteries	Slight to moderate	Cost curve gradient not steep

Source: Drawn impressionistically from F. M. Scherer et al., *The Economics of Multi-Plant Operation: An International Comparisons Study* (Cambridge, Mass.: Harvard University Press, 1975), Chapters 4 and 7.

European producers, merger constituted a second-best route to product-specific economies, compensating for the failure of competition to enforce specialization. Third, because of the U.S. market's vast geographic expanse, the transportation costs that would be incurred if merged but distant plants specialized more narrowly frequently outweighed the production cost savings greater specialization might permit. And finally, legal barriers to sizeable horizontal mergers in the United States probably have deterred at least a few mergers that would have yielded product-specific economies, especially in the antifriction bearing and steel industries.

We return now to plant-specific economies. One case in which mergers can confer savings occurs when an industry has substantial chronic excess capacity and when the various industry members have all found it more profitable to continue operating than to shut down—e.g., because short-run variable costs are low relative to total unit costs, because competition has been insufficiently vigorous to drive the price below the minimum variable cost of high-cost producers, and/or because product differentiation ties consumers to individual firms and permits the maintenance of cost-covering prices. The overextended U.S railroad system is probably the paramount example of an industry in which, within limits, mergers and plant abandonments could lead to impressive savings, despite labor union resistance and the intimidating Penn-Central experience.[171] Comparably strong examples in the manufacturing and mining sectors are difficult to find.

Only slightly different from these severe excess capacity cases are situations in which plants are acquired and shut down while another (usually more modern) plant is expanded. One must in all such instances stop and ask: why spend good money acquiring a rival's plant, only to close it? Why not proceed directly to the favored plant's expansion without traversing the merger byway? The answer in almost every case involves some imperfection of competition. Four examples serve to illustrate the spectrum of considerations. Built-up brand preferences made it difficult for smaller American brewers lacking a premium image to increase their sales rapidly and keep pace with rising production scale economy imperatives during the 1960s. A strategy pursued by some was to purchase failing brewing companies, close their outmoded plants, and transfer production of the viable brands to expanded and modernized breweries. The main acquisition target was the set of brands and their goodwill, not the plant, for which no more than scrap value may have been paid. Indeed, in one instance, the G. W. Heileman Co. acquired no production facilities at all, but paid $10.7 million for, as its advertisements later proclaimed, the Blatz trademark, 32 trucks, and the Blatz marching band.[172] In the United Kingdom, most beer is consumed on premises; with the number of pubs fixed by government regulation, virtually the only way to expand was to acquire rival breweries and their tied houses (i.e., captive pubs). Several aggressive companies did this and then closed down the inefficient breweries and built large modern units.[173] Most of the price paid was for the pubs' spatial monopoly franchises and goodwill. In Sweden, localized brewing companies entered into a cartel agreement under which each firm sold only in its home territory. The average brewery was as a consequence only one-fiftieth as large as the minimum optimal scale. A Stockholm firm, Pripps, then merged with or acquired some 40 competitors, closed many of their breweries,

170. Scherer et al., *The Economics of Multi-Plant Operation*, pp. 162–63. On television set production, see also P. E. Hart, M. A. Utton, and G. Walshe, *Mergers and Concentration in British Industry* (Cambridge, England: Cambridge University Press, 1973), pp. 46–48.

171. For a review of the relevant literature, see John F. Due, "A Comment on Recent Contributions to the Economics of the Railway Industry," *Journal of Economic Literature* 13 (December 1975): 1315–20. For an analysis of scale *diseconomies* foreshadowing the Penn-Central disaster, see Robert E. Gallamore, "Railroad Mergers: Costs, Competition and the Future Organization of the American Railroad Industry" (Ph.D. diss., Harvard University, May 1968).

172. Subtracting $300,000 for the trucks, this is equivalent to buying a perpetual annuity of $1.25 million per year discounted at 12 percent. In the year of acquisition Blatz sales were 1.2 million barrels and declining. This implies that Heileman must have valued the Blatz goodwill at somewhat more than $1 per barrel, or about 3 to 5 percent of the beer's wholesale price.

173. This and the next two cases are drawn from Scherer et al., *The Economics of Multi-Plant Operation*, pp. 164–66.

and concentrated production at three modern plants. And in the Westphalian area of Germany, a cartel that had sustained more than two dozen tiny, inefficient cement plants was declared illegal in 1967. After a sharp price war, the largest German cement producer began building a modern plant and bought up survivors of the price war to remove the threat of their capacity from the market. Here the price it paid reflected the value to it of blunted competition.

To persons inculcated in the American pro-competitive ethic, the small U.S. brewers' strategy of expansion through acquisition seems innocuous and perhaps inevitable, the German cement maker's strategy outrageous, and the British tied house system somewhere between the extremes. Most cases of scale economies attainable through merger and plant closure fall along a similar spectrum, calling for more or less difficult value judgments concerning necessity and social desirability.

We consider next situations in which firms expand through merger and leave the acquired plants pretty much as they are. This is probably the most typical case. Clearly, no plant-specific scale economies result from such mergers, at least in the short run. Nor is such "expansion," as seen from the eyes of the acquiring firm, growth from a broader social perspective, for what is added to the acquiring firm's economic activity is offset by the acquired company's disappearance. The crucial question again is, why do firms choose to grow in this way rather than by building new facilities? One possible reason is that another firm's plant becomes available at a price lower than the cost of building afresh. This is most likely to occur when stock prices are depressed and new construction costs are inflated, as they were in the mid-1970s. The other main reason again turns on monopolistic elements. An enterprise desiring to grow may perceive that the output from new capacity will be absorbed in the market only if prices are reduced, and if so, it may prefer buying someone else out, leaving total market supply and prices essentially unchanged.[174]

Mergers leading to no immediate plant expansion might nevertheless affect the realization of scale economies over a longer period. There are two plausible scenarios. First, a company with many older plants is likely to have a larger amount of capacity due for replacement at any interval in time than a smaller firm, all else being equal. This may make it easier to carry out large-scale replacement investments, especially when optimal-sized production units come in large indivisible lumps, as in steel, petroleum refining, and cement making. Second, if all firms in an industry experience more or less equal proportionate demand growth, the company with a large market share, gained *inter alia* through mergers, can expect to enjoy larger *absolute* increments of growth and therefore may be better situated to invest in sizeable new plant units. In both of these cases, the long-run advantage from merger-related size hinges upon the assumption that firms view their sales potential passively and do not strive actively—e.g., through price competition—to gain whatever sales volume they need to utilize new capacity increments of efficient scale. That businesspeople may well behave in this way, especially in Europe, is suggested by evidence that plant sizes are positively and significantly correlated with leading firms' market shares.[175] But one must not overlook the underlying causation. If mergers do contribute to the realization of scale economies in this way, it is because entrepreneurs lack the nerve to compete independently in bringing new efficient-size plants on stream.

We find then a pervasive analytic thread. Plant-specific and product-specific scale economies can and do result from mergers. But for a large fraction of the cases in which they do, it is because competition has failed to stimulate efficient plant investment or product specialization choices. Mergers are a second-best solution, given the failure of competition. It follows obversely that the more effectively competition is working, the less essential mergers are as a source of production scale economies.

The question remains, how frequently *do* mergers yield such benefits? Several surveys shed light on this point. The author and his colleagues interviewed 36 companies, mostly outside the United States, that had effected one or more horizontal mergers increasing their sales or employment by at least a third compared to 1958 levels. In roughly half of those firms, merger was followed by significant enlargement or modernization of acquired plants or closure to permit expansion of other facilities.[176] In an interview study of 38 British mergers, mostly horizontal, Newbould found that 15 were followed by no attempt, or a negligible effort, to reorganize and improve production efficiency. In only two cases was a "high" level of post-merger efficiency-increasing activity observed.[177] John Kitching studied 69 acquisitions, preponderantly of the pure and product extension conglomerate types, carried out by 20 U.S. corporations. He found that high amounts of production synergy were achieved in 6 acquisitions and medium amounts in 5 others.[178] A presumably less reliable mail survey of 1,826 Canadian acquisitions consummated between 1946 and 1961 revealed that economies from the integration of plants and raw materials use were rated as having been the principal result from 6.5 percent of all mergers and 15.2 percent of the horizontal manufacturing industry mergers.[179] In 2.7 percent of the horizontal manufacturing mergers, respondents indicated that it was cheaper to buy than build. The general implication of these four surveys is that production economies do arise in conjunction with many mergers, and especially horizontal mergers, but that for the most part the benefits are not large.

Mergers may also confer advantages in marketing—e.g., through the pooling and streamlining of field sales forces, the ability to offer distributors a broader line, the use of common advertising themes, and (to the extent they exist) the sharing of advertising media quantity discounts. In his survey of U.S. companies, Kitching found the marketing advantages of merger to be much more important than production economies—second only in importance to the kinds of financial advantages we have considered earlier. Marketing synergies were rated high or medium in value for 33 of his 69 acquisitions. However, a survey by the Federal Trade Commission suggests that little was done to reorganize the administration of advertising and promotional functions in 97 companies acquired by nine U.S. conglomerates. In only 17 was there any post-merger administrative change.[180] Some doubt is

also cast on the pervasiveness of merger-induced marketing advantages by the findings of Newbould and the Economic Council of Canada survey, suggesting that such advantages were quite unimportant—indeed, less important than production economies.

Complementarities may also exist in research and development. One firm may have two or three unusually creative engineers but lack the distribution network needed to derive full commercial benefit from the new products they turn out. Another may have superb marketing channels but find its laboratories populated with unimaginative clods. Together they can make beautiful music. Ideas and money also can be brought together through merger. There is reason to believe that such motives have influenced an appreciable number of mergers, especially those in which small research-based enterprises were acquired.[181] R&D and technology synergies were rated high or medium in 15 of the 69 mergers Kitching studied.

Finally, there is the possibility that mergers infuse superior new management into companies suffering from talent or motivational deficiencies.[182] Or they may permit managerial overhead streamlining. After analyzing 28 merger-prone U.S. conglomerates, two of them through detailed

174. See Richard B. Heflebower, "Corporate Mergers: Policy and Economic Analysis," *Quarterly Journal of Economics* 77 (November 1963): 554–57.

175. Scherer et al., *The Economics of Multi-Plant Operation (TEMPO)*, pp. 92–94, 103–15.

176. Scherer et al., *TEMPO*, pp. 166–67.

177. Newbould, *Management and Merger Activity*, especially p. 168.

178. John Kitching, "Why Do Mergers Miscarry?" *Harvard Business Review* 45 (November–December 1967): 87–90.

179. Economic Council of Canada, *Interim Report on Competition Policy* (Ottawa: Queen's Printer, July 1969), pp. 213–18.

180. Federal Trade Commission, *Conglomerate Merger Performance*, pp. 37, 41, 47–49. In contrast, the administration of insurance, legal matters, auditing, and borrowing was changed in at least three-fourths of all cases.

181. See Murray N. Friedman, *The Research and Development Factor in Mergers and Acquisitions*, Study no. 16, U.S., Congress, Senate, Committee on the Judiciary, Subcommittee on Patents, Trademarks, and Copyrights, 85th Cong., 2nd sess., 1958.

182. Cf. Chapter 2, pp. 37–38 *supra*.

on-site case studies, Harry H. Lynch concluded that improved performance following acquisition is "less likely to result from the traditionally discussed economies in the combined use of physical resources than from the more effective use of specialized human resources, specifically managerial and technical resources."[183] Even for the horizontal mergers surveyed by the Economic Council of Canada, economies in administration and management were given top rating in 33.5 percent of all cases—more than twice as frequently as for plant and materials integration. Yet merger is clearly no panacea for management weaknesses. Newbould found that the mergers in his sample of 38 frequently led to significant managerial teething problems—so much so that 18 of the companies said undertaking similar acquisitions was impossible because their managerial resources were insufficient.[184] It is significant too that many of the U.S. conglomerates Lynch studied in the late 1960s—much praised at the time for their reputed managerial virtuosity—were subsequently afflicted by acute cases of acquisition indigestion, with subsidiary losses proliferating out of control, followed by extensive divestiture of mismatched acquisitions to improve matters.[185] The efficiency losses from too thinly stretched managerial resources were plainly substantial. At what cost in human displacement, disillusion, and alienation this inept game of corporate volleyball was played, we shall probably never know.[186]

The financial consequences of mergers

Mergers have many motives. It is clear that they can yield benefits, real and pecuniary. It is equally clear that they can be mismanaged or bring fame and riches to their promoters while unwary stockholders are gulled. One can find numerous examples of mergers exemplifying each of the motives or effects identified here. The important question remains, what is the central tendency? Do mergers on average confer large benefits, small benefits, or net disbenefits? Many studies have addressed this question using diverse financial return variables as an index of merger success.

That merger-prone corporations have generally achieved more rapid sales and asset growth than similar but nonacquisitive firms emerges as a conclusion from virtually every study. The analyses that have attempted to distinguish growth through merger *per se* from internal growth also show that acquisitions made the difference.[187] That is, if one takes as the basis for comparison the initial-year sales of acquiring firms combined with sales for the same year of the companies they acquired, one finds that growth from that base was no more rapid on average than growth from the initial sales base of nonacquisitive corporations. In other words, the more rapid growth resulted from adding the parts, not from any change in the merger components' basic growth rates.

In reviewing the results of comparative profitability analyses, it is useful to separate those that emphasize U.S. conglomerate mergers from studies that encompass many horizontal acquisitions—e.g., covering pre-1960 merger activity in the United States or mergers, including more recent ones, in nations lacking strong antimerger laws. From the preceding scale economy discussion, one might expect horizontal mergers to yield greater operating economies and/or increases in monopoly power, and hence larger profitability gains, than conglomerate mergers. However, a study of 478 large U.S. manufacturers over the 1951–61 period,[188] another encompassing 353 U.S. firms from 1946 to 1965,[189] one of 77 British manufacturers over 1955–60,[190] one covering 78 British firms over 1954–70,[191] another covering 233 U.K. acquisitions over 1964 to 1972,[192] and one involving between 258 and 369 Canadian companies over 1960 to 1970,[193] all reach essentially the same conclusion: that the post-merger profitability experience of merger-prone companies was either less successful, or not significantly more successful, than the experience of otherwise comparable low-merger companies or the average of the merger-prone firms' home-base industries. The observed failure of active acquirers to achieve superior profit returns appears to persist over a wide range of comparison methodologies, company samples, and time frames.

Extraordinarily revealing data on the post-merger profitability of certain businesses acquired by conglomerate corporations were obtained by the Federal Trade Commission and a congressional committee. The FTC study found that the postmerger profit/sales ratio declined relative to its premerger value for 34 acquired entities and rose for 25.[194] However, such changes could reflect general industrywide business conditions as well as the specific effects of merger. When profit rates were related to contemporary averages for the acquired manufacturing firms' home-base industries, an equal split of relative increases and decreases was found in a comparison of year-before and year-after merger figures, but when years immediately contiguous to the acquisition date were excluded, profitability increases were found to outnumber decreases by 20 to 14. None of these observed differences was statistically significant by conventional standards. Analyzing the congressional data on 28 companies acquired by four conglomerates, Robert Conn found that the average postmerger profit/assets ratio declined from 6.7 percent premerger to 4.2 percent postmerger.[195] The comparable ratios for the acquired firms' home-base industries declined concurrently from 6.8 to 6.0 percent. When industry effects were taken into account, the fall in acquired firm profit rates was statistically significant only at the 10 percent level. In view of the partly conflicting implications and the possibility of both sample selection and accounting biases, the most that can be concluded is that there is no clear tendency for an enterprise's profitability to increase following acquisition by a conglomerate.

Other analyses have been forced for want of richer data to compare the overall profitability of conglomerate firms against more or less carefully selected control samples of low-merger enterprises. In the first study of this genre, J. Fred Weston and S. K. Mansinghka found that the average profitability of 63 conglomerates in 1958, before their intensive burst of merger activity, was significantly lower than that of sizeable firms in two randomly selected control samples.[196] By 1968, the conglomerates' reported profitability had become virtually equal to that of the control groups, leading Weston and Mansinghka to conclude that the conglomerates had successfully diversified away from their prior earnings depression. For a 45-company subset of the Weston and Mansinghka sample, R. W. Melicher and

183. Harry H. Lynch, *Financial Performance of Conglomerates* (Boston: Harvard Business School Division of Research, 1971), abstract p. 3. See also pp. 277–83.

184. Newbould, *Management and Merger Activity*, pp. 182–83.

185. See for example "Litton Down to Earth," *Fortune*, April 1968, pp. 139 ff.; "Why Rain Fell on 'Automatic' Sprinkler," *Fortune*, May 1969, pp. 88 ff.; "Trying To Put the Profit Back into U.S. Industries," *Business Week*, 7 July 1975, pp. 38–39; and "Bringing Sanity to a 140-Company Conglomerate," *Business Week*, 15 March 1976, p. 66.

186. For a poignant case history, see Michael Hope, "On Being Taken Over by Slater Walker," *Journal of Industrial Economics* 24 (March 1976):163–79.

187. For a review of this and much other merger performance literature, see Steiner, *Mergers*, pp. 189–95. On sales growth comparisons, see also the first edition of Scherer, *Industrial Market Structure and Economic Performance*, p. 120.

188. Samuel R. Reid, *Mergers, Managers, and the Economy* (New York: McGraw-Hill, 1968), pp. 153–264. See also the methodological criticisms by J. Fred Weston and S. K. Mansinghka and the reply by Reid in the *Journal of Finance* 29 (June 1974): 1011–15.

189. H. Igor Ansoff, Richard G. Brandenburg, Fred E. Portner, and Raymond Radosevich, *Acquisition Behavior of U.S. Manufacturing Firms, 1946–1965* (Nashville: Vanderbilt University Press, 1971), especially pp. 65–77.

190. Ajit Singh, *Take-overs: Their Relevance to the Stock Market and the Theory of the Firm* (Cambridge, England: Cambridge University Press, 1971), pp. 161–65. Singh's control of industry and timing effects is particularly careful.

191. M. A. Utton, "On Measuring the Effects of Industrial Mergers," *Scottish Journal of Political Economy* 21 (February 1974) pp. 13–28. Unlike the other studies, Utton's compares the performance of merger-intensive firms with a randomly selected control group of internal-growth firms.

192. Geoffrey Meeks, *Disappointing Marriage: A Study of the Gains from Merger* (Cambridge, England: Cambridge University Press, 1977), pp. 9–46.

193. S. N. Laiken, "Financial Performance of Merging Firms in a Virtually Unconstrained Legal Environment," *Antitrust Bulletin* 18 (Winter 1973): 827–51. Laiken finds some significant positive correlations between merger intensity and operating income gains, but they fade into insignificance when debt costs are deducted to arrive at net income.

194. Federal Trade Commission, *Conglomerate Merger Performance*, pp. 55–58. See also Jesse W. Markham, *Conglomerate Enterprise and Public Policy* (Boston: Harvard Business School Division of Research, 1973), p. 88, who provides no insight into profit *rates*, but whose data show much more postmerger expansion of capital investment and depreciation charges than of profits.

195. Robert L. Conn, "Acquired Firm Performance After Conglomerate Merger," *Southern Economic Journal* 43 (October 1976): 1170–73. The profit/assets ratio is a rather unsatisfactory measure, especially in view of possible asset revaluations resulting from the mergers. However, similar results appear when profit/sales ratios are analyzed.

196. J. Fred Weston and S. K. Mansinghka, "Tests of the Efficiency Performance of Conglomerate Firms," *Journal of Finance* 26 (September 1971): 919–36.

D. F. Rush carried a similar analysis past the honeymoon era into 1971, when conglomerates' managerial problems became acute.[197] Their control group was also different, being drawn randomly from the sampled conglomerates' 1960 home-base industries. They found that by acquiring companies more profitable than themselves, the conglomerates equalled the control group's return on stockholders' equity by 1965 and surpassed it from 1967 through 1969. But then problems mounted and they fell to rough equality again in 1971. Mason and Goudzwaard pursued a still different tack.[198] Using data obtained from 22 presumably representative conglomerates, they constructed 22 randomized independent firm investment portfolios with an industry distribution similar to the conglomerates' actual 1967 diversification profiles. They found that in terms of accounting profit plus interest returns on assets, the randomized portfolios significantly outperformed the conglomerates.

To the extent that these studies fall into a coherent pattern, they seem to say that the hyperactive conglomerates of the 1960s did well in their heyday by acquiring companies with strong profit histories and prospects. But there is no indication that they did any better with the assets they acquired than the acquired companies would have done if left independent.[199] And after problems began to intrude in the late 1960s, partly for causes traceable to the acquired entities' home-base industries but also because of managerial indigestion and high financial leverage, the overall profitability of the conglomerates may well have been lower than it would have been for the sum of their independent parts. How the conglomerates will fare after their 1970s divestiture and reorganization efforts are completed remains to be seen.

These profitability analyses, and especially the conglomerate comparisons, are rendered hazardous by the artful juggling companies often carried out in their asset and profit accounting for acquired subsidiaries. Another approach to the question is to ask, what return would common stock investors have realized buying the securities of merger-intensive firms, as compared to buying stocks in a comparable portfolio of companies emphasizing internal growth? In an early analysis running only to 1964, Thomas Hogarty found that investors in 43 merger-prone corporations realized lower returns than the average of the firms' home-base industries.[200] Baruch Lev and Gershon Mandelker reached the opposite conclusion with respect to both accounting and stock market returns for a sample of 69 acquiring firms matched with 69 other supposedly nonacquiring companies, but critics demonstrated that many of the latter were in fact as merger-prone as the former and hence constituted an inappropriate control group.[201] Using a more carefully controlled sample, Melicher and Rush found that investors in conglomerates' stock realized significantly higher average returns from 1966 to 1969 but lower returns from 1969 to 1971, with returns over the entire period being insignificantly different.[202] The depressed returns of the later period appear to have persisted. The 21 companies on Lynch's list of "acquisitive conglomerates"[203] and also on *Fortune*'s list of the 1,000 largest industrial corporations for 1977 had an average 1967–77 return to stock market investors of −6.4 percent, compared to +4.2 percent for the full *Fortune* sample. With a preslump terminal date, R. H. Mason and M. B. Goudzwaard found the average 1962–67 return to purchasers of 22 conglomerates' stock to be 7.5 percent, compared to between 11.8 and 14.0 percent for investments in similar but randomized stock portfolios.[204] It seems quite clear that, in general, the stocks of merger-prone corporations have been no magic path to riches for long-term investors.

Numerous studies reveal that acquiring firms have paid the stockholders of acquired companies premia averaging 15 to 25 percent relative to the stock prices prevailing four to eight weeks before the merger announcement.[205] Finding that mergers enhanced the aggregate value of the combined companies' stocks only in exceptional cases, Gort and Hogarty concluded that, on the average, the prior stockholders of acquiring companies lost from their acquisitions.[206] They rationalize the continuation of merger activity as a kind of 'hope springs eternal' phenomenon—the occasional large gains from some mergers lure others who will be much less successful in enhancing their stock values. This conclusion has been challenged in two newer studies. Mandelker found that the stockholders of 241 companies making acquisitions between 1941 and 1962 real-

ized a normal return on their stocks while acquired company stockholders averaged 14 percent premium returns.[207] Halpern concluded that
the absolute stock value increases in 77 mergers
consummated between 1950 and 1965 were distributed equally between acquiring and acquired firm stockholders. The latter exhibited
higher *percentage* gains only because the stock
value base to which the absolute gain was applied was much smaller.[208] Neither finding is
necessarily inconsistent with evidence that, on
average, mergers did not lead to earnings increases during the pre-1965 period.[209] All that is
required is that mergers made the combined
firms' stocks appear more valuable to buyers.
Mandelker and Halpern lean toward a managerial synergy explanation, but the premerger
stock price trends revealed by Mandelker's analysis seem equally consistent with the hypothesis
that acquiring firms moved in to take advantage
of randomly depressed acquired company share
prices. To the extent that this is true, the premia
realized by acquired firm stockholders were genuine gains only if no reversal of stock price trends
would have occurred had the acquired corporations remained independent. On this, as on many
other details of the merger phenomenon, much
remains to be learned.

Conclusion No simple summary can do justice
to the question of mergers' effects and motives.
One can, if one looks hard enough, find facts to
support almost any hypothesis. We must content
ourselves with a few sweeping generalizations.
First, mergers have definitely led to increases in
market concentration, although the magnitude of
this effect has dwindled over time, at least in the
United States. Second, business leaders are motivated in a variety of ways to enter mergers, and
in most instances multiple motives are at work.
The monopoly motive has been declining in relative significance over time; the speculative motive
has been alarmingly constant. Third, the expectations of private gain that inspire mergers are
frequently neither well founded nor accompanied by commensurate benefits to the consuming
public. Mergers may instead merely redistribute
wealth, intensify product differentiation, or provide an illusory growth with no counterpart in the
national income accounts. While many mergers

are clearly beneficial, the balance of social advantage in other cases is sufficiently tenuous to
warrant a skeptical public policy stance. We
shall return to the policy issues in Chapter 20.

The impact of government policies

As framer of the legal environment within which
business operates and as the largest single do-

197. Ronald W. Melicher and David F. Rush, "The Performance of Con-
glomerate Firms: Recent Risk and Return Experience," *Journal of
Finance* 28 (May 1973): 381–88. See also their related article in the
Journal of Finance 29 (March 1974): 141–49.

198. R. H. Mason and M. B. Goudzwaard, "Performance of Conglomerate
Firms: A Portfolio Approach," *Journal of Finance* 31 (March 1976):
39–48.

199. For similar conclusions from a somewhat more broad-ranging survey, see Dennis C. Mueller, "The Effects of Conglomerate Mergers,"
Journal of Banking and Finance 1 (1977): 315–47.

200. Thomas F. Hogarty, "The Profitability of Corporate Mergers," *Journal
of Business* 43 (July 1970): 317–27.

201. Baruch Lev and Gershon Mandelker, "The Microeconomic Consequences of Corporate Mergers," *Journal of Business* 45 (January
1972): 85–104; with comments by T. Crawford Honeycutt and
Samuel R. Reid and a reply by Lev and Mandelker, *Journal of
Business* 48 (April 1975): 267–74.

202. Melicher and Rush, "The Performance of Conglomerate Firms,"
p. 386.

203. Lynch, *Financial Performance of Conglomerates*, p. 73. An analysis of
less closely matched data on the seven acquisitive conglomerates
identified by Lynch but not on the *Fortune* lists revealed similarly
subpar average stock market returns.

204. Melicher and Rush, "The Performance of Conglomerate Firms," p. 47.

205. For a survey, see Paul J. Halpern, "Empirical Estimates of the
Amount and Distribution of Gains to Companies in Mergers," *Journal
of Business* 46 (October 1973): 554–73. During the mid-1970s there
was an apparent escalation in the size of premia. Much higher
average premia also appear to be paid in contested takeovers. See
Newbould, *Management and Merger Activity*, pp. 54–57.

206. Michael Gort and Thomas F. Hogarty, "New Evidence on Mergers,"
Journal of Law and Economics 13 (April 1970): 173–76.

207. Gershon Mandelker, "Risk and Return: The Case of Merging Firms,"
Journal of Financial Economics 1 (December 1974): 303–35.

208. Halpern, "Empirical Estimates," pp. 568–72. See also Robert L. Conn
and James F. Nielsen, "An Empirical Test of the Larson-Gonedes
Exchange Ratio Determination Model," *Journal of Finance* 32 (June
1977): 749–59.

209. Nor are they inconsistent with the rather different historical circumstances of the late 1960s, when hyperactive conglomerates' shareholders took a beating.

mestic customer for goods and services, the federal government cannot help but shape industrial market structure. Here we examine some areas in which its impact is particularly direct and noticeable.

One important policy tool mentioned already is the array of antitrust laws and interpretations. We shall deal with them at length in Chapters 19 through 21, but certain comments are appropriate here. Paradoxically, it is possible passage of the Sherman Act in 1890 actually encouraged the great wave of mergers that followed. After a period of uncertainty, the Supreme Court enunciated a hard line against price-fixing agreements in 1897, but not until 1904 were mergers brought squarely under the law's control. If a group of sellers sought to eliminate competition during this seven-year period, they stood a better chance of avoiding legal difficulties by merging than by engaging in a more loosely structured price-fixing conspiracy. How important this legal imbalance was as a stimulus to the merger movement peaking in 1899 is unknown. We do know that the first industrial (as contrasted to transportation) price-fixing ring struck down by the Supreme Court was united, after an adverse Court of Appeals decision and only weeks before Supreme Court pleadings commenced, in a merger that placed three-fourths of the nation's cast-iron pipe manufacturing capacity in the hands of the surviving firm.[210] A similar but more recent imbalance in the British and German antitrust laws may have contributed to precipitating a wave of mergers.[211] Nevertheless, American entrepreneurs might have preferred mergers to loose price-fixing arrangements even if both paths had been open. And during the 1890s they were generally contemptuous of the Sherman Act, which had not yet demonstrated its sting. So it is difficult to be sure what the incremental effect of the antitrust laws was at the time. Historical research utilizing legal opinions written for business leaders contemplating late 1890s mergers and the minutes of merger planning meetings could yield valuable new insights into this question.

An attempt to assess subsequent trends in the antimerger and other antitrust laws would carry us too far afield. The most widely accepted interpretation is that their impact on market concentration in any short period has been small, but that over the span of several decades they have probably had a substantial cumulative limiting effect. On the other hand, they have done little or nothing to inhibit the growth of aggregate concentration.

Through the grant of patent rights on inventions, the government may facilitate dominance of a market by one or a few firms and make entry by newcomers difficult or impossible. We shall spend a full chapter later analyzing the logic and effects of the patent system. Suffice it to say here that patents contributed significantly at one time or another to concentration in such industries as telephone equipment, electric lamps, synthetic fibers, photographic materials, copying machines, shoe machinery, and certain classes of pharmaceuticals. On the other hand, they have also helped small innovative firms enter and maintain a foothold in numerous industries.

With the advent of World War II, the federal government's purchase of goods and services expanded enormously. Since then the government's voracious consumption has remained at generally high levels as it continued an active (but fluctuating) defense procurement program and moved into such fields as the exploration of space, interstate highway building, railroad operations, and the encouragement of energy technology development. In 1976, for example, the federal government spent more than $50 billion for goods and services supplied by private U.S. business firms.

These expenditures have both direct and indirect effects on the structure of industry. Directly, the government affects industrial concentration by favoring or discriminating against the largest corporations in awarding contracts. In general, orders in the defense sector—generating by far the largest volume of government purchases from industry—tend to be quite concentrated. During World War II, the 100 largest defense prime contractors, ranked by volume of contracts, received nearly 67 percent of all military prime contract awards by dollar volume. For the Korean war (fiscal years 1951 through 1953) the comparable figure was 64 percent, and at the peak of the Vietnam war procurement effort (fiscal years 1966–68) it averaged 66 percent. In the more placid post-Vietnam environment of fiscal years 1974–76, the concentration of awards among the top 100 increased to 68 percent.

It does not necessarily follow that aggregate concentration has been raised by government procurement practices, since the largest government contractors are by no means the largest firms in the private sector, despite the fact that government orders have propelled several defense specialists into the multibillion dollar sales category. It is useful in this respect to see how well the largest industrial corporations, taking both private and government sales into account, fare in the distribution of defense orders. This has been done for the 50 firms leading *Fortune*'s list of the 500 largest industrials in 1973.[212] Those 50 corporations accounted for 25.8 percent of all 1973 manufacturing corporation sales and 36.5 percent of the volume of defense prime contracts during fiscal years 1972 through 1974. This suggests that defense procurement has exerted modest upward pressure on aggregate concentration.

Possibly more important are the indirect effects of government procurement. The pace of technological change has been extremely rapid in the defense, space, and atomic energy fields. Companies winning major government contracts to develop new concepts and equipment could achieve a substantial "know-how" advantage over others in civilian applications of the new technology. Generally, the government has tried to distribute its orders so that at least several firms gain proficiency in new areas. Boeing's rise to leadership in the jet airliner field was based in part upon experience accumulated through the B-47 bomber program, but the Air Force required Boeing to share its B-47 production workload with Douglas (now McDonnell-Douglas) and Lockheed—a decision that helped those companies regain a position in the commercial airliner market after their propeller-driven mainstays fell from favor. The widespread diffusion of government research and development contracts in the transistor, integrated circuit, radar, and similar electronics fields contributed to the formation of numerous viable competitors. However, the government's procompetitive (or at least pro-oligopoly) contracting policy has not always been suc-

cessful. IBM's preeminence in the electronic computer industry was bolstered by its experience under huge SAGE air defense system contracts. Hughes Aircraft Company's leading position in communications satellite technology was based upon know-how built up through a long series of missile and space system contracts. And in the jet engine and atomic reactor fields, the government initially supported research and development by several contractors. However, both industries evolved into near duopolies after some firms dropped out owing to lack of interest and others were denied further support because of unsatisfactory performance.

The federal government has also shaped the structure of important industries through its surplus war plants disposal programs. During World War II rapid expansion of defense production was accomplished partly by the construction of government-owned, contractor-operated plants in key industries. After the war many of these plants, particularly those devoted to raw materials production, were sold to private industry. Some striking inconsistencies materialized. In aluminum, what was once a virtual Alcoa monopoly was transformed into a triopoly through the sale of plants (built at a cost of $300 million and operated during the war mainly by Alcoa) to Kaiser and Reynolds at a total purchase price of $100 million. Alcoa, with an antitrust conviction hanging over its head, was excluded from the bidding.[213] The sale of synthetic nitrogen plants was also arranged in such a way as to increase

210. Almarin Phillips, *Market Structure, Organization and Performance* (Cambridge, Mass.: Harvard University Press, 1962), pp. 115–16.

211. For a suggestion that earlier price-fixing prohibitions in Germany had the same effect, see Fritz Voigt, "German Experience with Cartels and Their Control During Pre-War and Post-War Periods," in John Perry Miller, ed., *Competition, Cartels, and Their Regulation* (Amsterdam: North-Holland, 1962), p. 204.

212. The last year for which this comparison can be made is 1973, because after that the FTC's *Quarterly Financial Report* series was changed so that overseas subsidiaries were no longer reported on a basis comparable to the company financial statements used by *Fortune*.

213. See M. J. Peck, *Competition in the Aluminum Industry: 1945–1958* (Cambridge, Mass.: Harvard University Press, 1961), pp. 11–19.

the number of competing sellers.[214] On the other hand, the wartime synthetic rubber program was run under procedures giving a few large firms a patent and know-how advantage in the postwar development of that new industry, and because no attempt was made to prevent multi-plant purchases, the sale of 25 plants ended with 3 firms controlling 47 percent of industry capacity. For many plants there was only one bidder. In every other case but one, the successful bidder was the firm that had previously operated the plant for the government.[215] Similarly, the sale of a $200 million plant in Geneva, Utah, to its wartime operator, United States Steel, high bidder at $47 million, raised U.S. Steel's share of Pacific coast and mountain states' ingot capacity from 17 percent to 39 percent.

Another significant facet of government involvement has been as guarantor of loans. At first this role was biased in a concentration-decreasing direction—e.g., as the Small Business Administration made direct loans to its clientele and promoted the development of small business investment corporations. More recently, however, the government has stepped in and underwritten loans for large enterprises whose otherwise imminent failure or retrenchment was considered too severe a blow for some geographic region—e.g., with the $250 million loan guarantee for Lockheed Aircraft in 1971 and the $730 million guarantee to support General Dynamics' Quincy, Massachusetts, shipyard operations in 1977.

Federal government policies have also had a complex but appreciable influence on the structure of such mineral-based industries as petroleum, whose members included 10 of the top 25 industrial corporations on *Fortune*'s 1975 list. Three aspects deserve mention. First, Washington's support of the largest petroleum companies' participation in an international cartel dividing up Middle Eastern oil franchises among themselves and the leading European companies retarded (but did not stop) the expansion of smaller producers into world markets.[216] Second, as the nation's premier landlord, the government has shaped industry structure through the policies it pursues in leasing mineral exploration and development rights. By requiring large front-end payments before any drilling is done, the "bonus

bidding" system of awarding Outer Continental Shelf oil and gas rights has increased risks and enhanced the relative advantage of giant companies. Thus, in 1972, the eight largest petroleum producers accounted for 63 percent of all OCS production. Onshore, where different leasing methods give rise to much lower front-end costs and risks, the eight leaders' share of production from federal lands was only 38 percent.[217] Compensating to some extent for these biases was the government's policy of granting to smaller refiners preferential crude oil import quotas up to 1973 and preferential "entitlements" to price-controlled domestic crude oil beginning in 1974.[218]

Shifting our concern to still another tentacle of the federal octopus, tax policies influence market structure in a variety of ways. We have already seen that the inheritance tax laws encourage mergers. The corporate income tax exemption accorded fixed-interest securities was exploited by conglomerate merger promoters of the late 1960s, who bought out the common stock of companies they sought to acquire by issuing tax-deductible debt.[219] According to Professors Lintner and Butters, the corporate income tax laws have also tended to encourage concentration by making it difficult for successful small businesses to retain earnings and attract outside capital to support the rapid growth that would permit them to challenge current industry leaders.[220] This handicap may be partly offset, however, by the favorable treatment given capital gains in the personal income tax structure, making investment in rapidly growing firms attractive to wealthy persons.

The effects of tariffs are more complicated. On one hand, they may foster the development of infant industries to a stage of maturity where they can withstand foreign competition unaided. On the other hand, they may insulate already monopolistic or oligopolistic industries, preserving them in a form that has little or no economic justification and blunting their incentives to adopt efficiency-increasing measures. Since few U.S. industries are in their infancy relative to foreign competitors, the latter effect is undoubtedly more prevalent.

Finally, there is a host of special government

policies affecting particular industries or segments of the business population. The time required to fill out government tax, regulatory, and statistical survey forms is virtually fixed in many cases and rises less than proportionately with organizational size in many others. Even though large firms have to complete more forms than small firms, the burden of governmental paperwork probably falls relatively more heavily on smaller enterprises. The effect of this regressive 'tax' on small firms' ability to survive is undoubtedly small but not trivial. Equipment needed to control smoke pollution from iron foundries and cement works, water pollution from paint plants, and noxious lead particles within automobile battery plants is subject to substantial scale economies. Increasingly stringent antipollution law enforcement has led to the closure of numerous small plants in these and similarly affected industries.[221] And by limiting entry into such regulated industries as air transport, taxi cab operation, trucking, mail services, on-premises airport car rental, and banking, federal and local governmental agencies have often constricted the competitive alternatives available to consumers.

Stochastic determinants of market structure

Up to this point we have assumed that market structures are the more or less determinate result of such variables as technology, the receptiveness of consumers to advertising, the size of the market, the effectiveness of managerial organization, merger decisions, and government policies. A quite different view of the processes by which market structures emerge has been postulated by some economists. Let us begin by stating the hypothesis in its baldest, most radical form: The market structures observed at any moment in time are the result of pure historical chance.

This idea is best introduced by a concrete illustration. Suppose an industry comes into being with 50 member firms, each with first-year sales of $100,000 and hence each with a 2 percent starting share of the market. Now suppose the firms begin growing. Each is assumed to have the

same average growth prospect as every other firm. But this average is subject to statistical variance; in any given year some firms will be lucky, growing more rapidly than the average, while others are unlucky, growing by less than the average. Let the probability distribution of growth rates confronting each firm be normal, with a mean of 6 percent per annum and a standard deviation of 16 percent. These parameters were chosen to reflect the average year-to-year growth actually experienced between 1954 and 1960 by 369 companies on *Fortune*'s list of the 500 largest industrial corporations for 1955. To repeat, each firm faces the same distribution of growth possibilities. Its actual growth is determined by random sampling from the distribution of possibilities. What will the size distribution of firms look like a number of years hence?

By applying a bit of probability theory it is possible to estimate the parameters of the resulting firm size distribution for any future moment in time. However, insight is enriched by employing

214. See Jesse W. Markham, *The Fertilizer Industry: Study of an Imperfect Market* (Nashville: Vanderbilt University Press, 1958), pp. 106–107.

215. See Robert A. Solo, *Synthetic Rubber: A Case Study in Technological Development Under Government Direction*, Study no. 18, U.S., Congress, Senate, Subcommittee on Patents, Trademarks, and Copyrights, 85th Cong., 2nd sess., 1959, pp. 115–24; S. E. Boyle, "Government Promotion of Monopoly Power," *Journal of Industrial Economics* 9 (April 1961): 151–69; and (for a more favorable view) C. F. Phillips, Jr., "Market Performance in the Synthetic Rubber Industry," *Journal of Industrial Economics* 9 (April 1961): 132–50.

216. See John M. Blair, *The Control of Oil* (New York: Pantheon, 1976), especially Chapters 4 and 9.

217. Federal Trade Commission staff report, *Federal Energy Land Policy: Efficiency, Revenue, and Competition*, Senate Committee on Interior and Insular Affairs print (Washington, D.C.: Government Printing Office, 1976), pp. 383, 451A.

218. See testimony of Paul Homan, U.S., Congress, Senate, Subcommittee on Antitrust and Monopoly hearings, *Governmental Intervention in the Market Mechanism*, "The Petroleum Industry," Part 1, 91st Cong., 1st sess., 1969, p. 106; and Calvin T. Roush, Jr., *Effects of Federal Price and Allocation Regulations on the Petroleum Industry*, Federal Trade Commission staff report (Washington, D.C.: Government Printing Office, 1976), pp. 49–56.

219. Steiner, *Mergers*, pp. 83–84.

220. Lintner and Butters, "Effects of Taxes on Concentration," pp. 274–75.

221. See "Foundries Fail on Clean-Air Laws," *Business Week*, 29 August 1970, p. 48; and "The Modest Price of Purging Pollution," *Business Week*, 18 March 1972, pp. 19–20.

a computer to simulate the dynamic properties of the assumed growth process model. Each firm's growth in each year was determined through random sampling from a distribution of growth rates with a mean of 6 percent and standard deviation of 16 percent. The firms' growth histories and the overall size distribution of the industry were then tabulated at 20-year intervals. The results of 16 consecutive simulation runs are summarized in the form of four-firm concentration ratios in Table 4.14.

Contrary to what untutored intuition might advise, the firms do not long remain equal in size and market share, even though their growth prospects are identical *ex ante*. Patterns resembling the concentrated structures of much American manufacturing industry emerge within a few decades. After the growth process has run its course for a century, it is not uncommon to find a single industry leader controlling 25 or 35 percent of the market while its former equals muddle along with 0.1 percent. For the 16 simulation runs at the 100-year mark, the range of leading firm market shares was 10 to 42 percent, with an aver-

age of 21 percent. The four-firm concentration ratios after a century of growth ranged from 33.5 percent to 64.4 percent, with a mean of 46.7 percent.

Why do concentrated firm size distributions arise from initial conditions that seemingly give each firm an equal chance? The answer, in a word, is luck. Some firms will inevitably enjoy a run of luck, experiencing several years of rapid growth in close succession. Once the most fortunate firms climb well ahead of the pack, it is difficult for laggards to rally and rectify the imbalance for, by definition, each firm—large or small—has an equal chance of growing by a given percentage amount.[222] Furthermore, once a firm has, by virtue of early good luck, placed itself among the industry leaders, it can achieve additional market share gains if it should happen again to be luckier than average (as it will be in roughly half of all cases). In 10 of the 16 simulation runs underlying Table 4.14, the leading firm in Year 140 occupied a position among the top four firms in Year 60, and in four cases the Year 140 leader was also first in Year 60. In Run 13, the

---

T 4.14 Four-firm concentration ratios resulting from 16 simulation runs of a stochastic growth model

Simulation	Four-firm concentration ratio at year:							
	1	20	40	60	80	100	120	140
Run 1	8.0	19.5	29.3	36.3	40.7	44.9	38.8	41.3
Run 2	8.0	20.3	21.4	28.1	37.5	41.6	50.8	55.6
Run 3	8.0	18.8	28.9	44.6	43.1	47.1	56.5	45.0
Run 4	8.0	20.9	26.7	31.8	41.9	41.0	64.5	59.8
Run 5	8.0	23.5	33.2	43.8	60.5	60.5	71.9	63.6
Run 6	8.0	21.3	26.6	29.7	35.8	51.2	59.1	72.9
Run 7	8.0	21.1	31.4	29.0	42.8	52.8	50.3	53.1
Run 8	8.0	21.6	23.5	42.2	47.3	64.4	73.1	76.6
Run 9	8.0	18.4	29.3	38.0	45.3	42.5	43.9	52.4
Run 10	8.0	20.0	29.7	43.7	40.1	43.1	42.9	42.9
Run 11	8.0	23.9	29.1	29.5	43.2	50.1	57.1	71.7
Run 12	8.0	15.7	23.3	24.1	34.5	41.1	42.9	53.1
Run 13	8.0	23.8	31.3	44.8	43.5	42.8	57.3	65.2
Run 14	8.0	17.8	23.3	29.3	54.2	51.4	56.0	64.7
Run 15	8.0	21.8	18.3	23.9	31.9	33.5	43.9	65.7
Run 16	8.0	17.5	27.1	28.3	30.7	39.9	37.7	35.3
Average	8.0	20.4	27.0	33.8	42.1	46.7	52.9	57.4

leading firm held its leadership position at every single 20-year benchmark; and in Run 5, the leader led at every 20-year point but one.

The simulation experiment reported here was designed to conform to the assumptions of Gibrat's law of proportionate growth.[223] Specifically, the population of firms was fixed, and the distribution of growth rates confronting each firm was the same, being independent of both firm size and the firm's past growth history.[224] Stochastic growth processes adhering to Gibrat's law generate a log normal size distribution of firms—that is, a distribution highly skewed when sales are plotted by the frequency of their actual values, with one or a few firms realizing high sales while most make low sales, but which is normal and symmetric when the logarithms of firms' sales are plotted.[225] As we have seen in the preceding chapter, the parameters of the log normal distribution have been proposed as indices of market concentration by some economists, and statistical studies reveal that a log normal distribution often (but not always) fits actual firm size data tolerably well.[226] However, the assumptions of Gibrat's law need not be satisfied rigidly to obtain results similar to those of Table 4.14. There is a whole family of stochastic growth processes that lead to the skewed firm size distributions typical of real-world industries.[227] All have the common feature of making a firm's size in, say, year $t + 1$ proportional, subject to random variation, to its size in year t. Other dynamic processes lacking the proportionate growth property exist, but they typically fail to generate firm size distributions resembling those most frequently encountered in the real world.[228] Reasoning backward from observation to hypothesis, Simon and Bonini argue that industry structures must in fact be determined by some such stochastic growth process, since actual size distributions "show such a regular and docile conformity . . . that we would expect some mechanism to be at work to account for the observed regularity."[229]

We are all so thoroughly imbued with the belief that chance favors the well prepared that it is difficult to accept a model making corporate growth as the result of mere chance. Still it is not essential to interpret the stochastic growth models quite so literally. There are certainly

222. For an analogous illustration concerning runs in coin-flipping, see William Feller, *An Introduction to Probability Theory and Its Applications*, 2nd ed., vol. I (New York: Wiley, 1957), pp. 83–85.

223. R. Gibrat, *Les Inegalites Economiques* (Paris: Recueil Sirey, 1931); and Michal Kalecki, "On the Gibrat Distribution," *Econometrica* 13 (April 1945): 161–70.

224. In one sense Gibrat's assumptions were violated. A "bankruptcy rule" was included, causing a firm to drop out of the industry permanently if its sales fell to $30,000 or less. There were only three bankruptcies in the 800 company histories simulated.

225. Proof: Let S_{0j} be the initial sales of the jth firm and ϵ_i the random growth multiplier in the ith year. Then sales in year t are $S_{tj} = S_{0j}\epsilon_1 \cdots \epsilon_i \cdots \epsilon_t$; that is, the cumulative product of initial sales times a string of random growth multipliers. Taking logarithms, we obtain: $\log S_{tj} = \log S_{0j} + \log \epsilon_1 + \cdots + \log \epsilon_i + \cdots + \log \epsilon_t$. By the central limit theorem, the distribution of the sum of T random variables is asymptotically normal when $T \rightarrow \infty$.

226. See P. E. Hart and S. J. Prais, "The Analysis of Business Concentration," *Journal of the Royal Statistical Society*, Part 2, 119 (1956): pp. 150–81; Herbert A. Simon and C. P. Bonini, "The Size Distribution of Business Firms," *American Economic Review* 48 (September 1958): 607–17; and (for results suggesting that the log normal distribution holds in roughly half the industries studied) Irwin H. Silberman, "On Lognormality as a Summary Measure of Concentration," *American Economic Review* 57 (September 1967): 807–31.

227. See especially Herbert A. Simon, "On a Class of Skew Distribution Functions," *Biometrika* 42 (December 1955): 425–40, and Yuji Ijiri and Herbert A. Simon, *Skew Distributions and the Sizes of Business Firms* (Amsterdam: North-Holland, 1977). In fact, the distributions are sufficiently similar that it is difficult to find statistical tests distinguishing which of several alternative stochastic processes generated the observed size distribution. See Richard E. Quandt, "On the Size Distribution of Firms," *American Economic Review* 56 (June 1966): 416–32.

228. Firm size distributions with realistic skewness properties also result from a complex "natural selection" model embodying random innovative search and imitation, with growth linked to the success of those activities. Richard R. Nelson, Sidney G. Winter, and Herbert L. Schuette, "Technical Change in an Evolutionary Model," *Quarterly Journal of Economics* 90 (February 1976), especially pp. 113–16. For a nonstochastic hypothesis attributing log normal firm size distributions to a particular type of monopoly pricing (to be considered tangentially in Chapter 8), see Dean A. Worcester, Jr., *Monopoly, Big Business, and Welfare in the Postwar United States* (Seattle: University of Washington Press, 1967), Chapters 5 and 6. See also Lennart Hjalmarsson, "The Size Distribution of Establishments and Firms Derived from an Optimal Process of Capacity Expansions," *European Economic Review* 5 (August 1974): 123–40, whose model is more suited to plant than firm size distributions and lacks an adequate set of assumptions on how demand is distributed among competing firms. For simulations of several alternative Gibrat-type and non-Gibrat stochastic growth models, see Alan R. Beckenstein and Thomas J. Schriber, "A Simulation Study of the Size Distribution of Firms," *Proceedings of the Fourth Conference on Applications of Simulation* (December 1970).

229. Simon and Bonini, "The Size Distribution of Business Firms," p. 608.

aspects of business enterprise in which luck plays a significant role—e.g., in the hiring of key executives, in research and new product development decisions, in legal disputes involving critical patents, in the choice of an advertising campaign theme, or in a thousand and one other decisions among attractive but uncertain alternative courses of action. Given the operation of chance in these elemental decisions, high or low sales growth follows in a more traditionally deterministic manner.

One implication of this milder restatement is the possibility that growth rates for a given firm from year to year will not be independent, as assumed in the Gibrat model. For example, a lucky chief executive choice may affect growth favorably for a decade or more. Yet this is not a fatal objection. Ijiri and Simon have demonstrated in a simulation study that size distributions similar to those generated by Gibrat models can also be obtained when there is serial correlation in firms' year-to-year growth rates.[230]

The assumptions of the Gibrat model may also be violated if growth rates, or the standard deviations of growth rates, are systematically related to firm size. Independence of size and growth rates implies that small firms operate at neither an advantage nor a disadvantage relative to large firms. If, on the other hand, economies of scale persist out to substantial market shares, large firms would possess an advantage that might be exploited, *inter alia*, in the form of more rapid sales growth rates. Such a state of affairs, combined with stochastic elements, would lead to even more rapid concentration of output in the hands of the largest firms. Conversely, if small firms could grow more rapidly on the average, *ceteris paribus*, or if there were a continuous inflow of small new firms, the tendency toward increasing inequality of firm sizes would be moderated and under certain circumstances checked altogether. Several empirical investigations have sought to determine whether firm growth rates are systematically related to firm size. The results vary widely, depending upon the nation, time period, and size measure observed.[231] At least for the United States, they suggest that assuming growth rates uncorrelated with initial firm size is not a bad first approximation to the real-world facts.

There is less support for the Gibrat assumption that growth rate standard deviations are independent of firm size. With few exceptions, statistical studies have shown that the variability of growth rates for large firms is lower than for small firms; that is, large firms seem to enjoy more stable growth.[232] Still, this qualification is compatible with the hypothesis that the skewed firm size distributions one observes have been generated by some stochastic growth process.[233] Indeed, it strengthens the case. Chance will occasionally permit a small firm facing a highly variable distribution of growth rates to be propelled to large size, and such events increase concentration, *ceteris paribus*. But once a company enters the large size bracket, the variance of its growth rate distribution diminishes, and so the chance that it will fall abruptly to a lower size level is much smaller. Thus, the statistical forces that might cause decreases in concentration, once it has developed, are blunted, while the forces leading to increased concentration remain intact. The conjunction of these phenomena may explain why market share turnover tends to be lower in concentrated industries than in atomistically structured industries.[234]

One final point implicit in the discussion thus far should be made explicit. The more variable firm growth rates are, the more rapidly concentrated industry structures will emerge, other things being equal. Two important implications follow.

First, despite its grounding in actual industry growth data, the simulation model of Table 4.14 probably overstates the length of time required for concentrated market structures to emerge as a consequence of random growth. The growth rate standard deviation of 16 percent was derived from a sample including only the largest corporations. For smaller firms—e.g., companies of the size typical during an industry's infancy—variability of growth rates is likely to be much higher, implying more rapid convergence toward market concentration.

Second, the variability of growth rates is likely to differ from industry to industry, depending upon the nature of the product and the character of competition.[235] We might expect variability to be especially high in industries characterized by a rapid pace of product design change owing to technological or styling innovation and also in markets populated by fickle consumers who respond enthusiastically to clever advertising campaigns.[236] The firm with a good design or promotional idea may leap ahead rapidly; the firm that misgauges market sentiments can suffer spectacular market share declines.

Testing the hypothesis that concentration rises especially rapidly in differentiated durable goods industries because of the chance elements permeating design competition, Weiss divided 87 sizeable four-digit industries into seven product characteristics classes. For the 1947–54 period, but not for 1954–58, he found concentration rising significantly more rapidly on average in consumer durables, consumer semidurables, and durable equipment—industries that presumably experienced the most vigorous design change competition.[237] Extension of his analysis to a broader sample of 154 manufacturing industries whose definitions changed insignificantly between 1947 and 1972 provides only equivocal support for Weiss's conjectures.[238] The simple average four-firm concentration ratio changes between 1947 and 1972 were as follows for industries classified according to Weiss's schema (with the number of industries covered indicated in parentheses):

High hypothesized design change group

Consumer durables (20)	+6.40
Consumer semidurables (33)	+7.00
Durable equipment (19)	−3.95

Low hypothesized design change group

Nondurable materials (20)	+0.25
Semidurable materials (31)	−1.65
Durable materials (17)	−1.41
Consumer nondurables (24)	+4.96

The overall average concentration change for the high design competition group was +3.45 percentage points, compared to +0.53 points for the low design competition group. This appears consistent with Weiss's hypothesis. However, the pattern is not uniform within groups. Changes for the individual product type subgroups exhibit the previously identified propensity for concentration to rise in consumer goods industries and fall in producer goods industries. This could reflect chance elements in consumers' response to advertising and promotional campaigns; but with presently available data, the alternative hypoth-

230. Yuji Ijiri and Herbert A. Simon, "Business Growth and Firm Size," *American Economic Review* 54 (March 1964): 77–89; *idem*, "Interpretations of Departures from the Pareto Curve Firm-Size Distributions," *Journal of Political Economy* 82 (March/April 1974): 315–31; and Daniel R. Vining, Jr., "Autocorrelated Growth Rates and the Pareto Law: A Further Analysis," *Journal of Political Economy* 84 (April 1976): 369–80.

231. See Ajit Singh and Geoffrey Whittington, "The Size and Growth of Firms," *Review of Economic Studies* 42 (January 1975): 15–26; Smyth, Boyes, and Peseau, *Size, Growth, Profits and Executive Compensation*, pp. 28–37; Stephen Hymer and Peter Pashigian, "Firm Size and Rate of Growth," *Journal of Political Economy* 70 (December 1962): 556–69; and Edwin Mansfield, "Entry, Gibrat's Law, Innovation, and the Growth of Firms," *American Economic Review* 52 (December 1962): 1031–34. In "A Note on the Determinants of the Growth of Firms and Gibrat's Law," *Canadian Journal of Economics* 3 (November 1969): 580–89, Matityahu Marcus finds that growth varies positively with profitability and negatively with market share, and these two forces offset each other to give observed growth rates independent of size.

232. See the sources in note 231. In an analysis of cumulative growth for the years 1953 through 1961 covering 352 corporations on *Fortune's* 1955 list, the author found the standard deviation of growth rates for firms in the quartile of largest companies to be persistently lower than the standard deviation for firms in the smallest company quartile. There seemed to be some tendency for the disparity in standard deviations to level off and perhaps to decline over intervals exceeding seven years, which may explain why Hart and Prais found no correlation between size and variability of growth rates in their analysis spanning the exceptionally long 1885–1950 period. The question of very long-run relationships deserves further study.

233. Cf. Simon, "On a Class of Skew Distribution Functions;" and his comment in the *Journal of Political Economy* 72 (February 1964): 81.

234. Cf. Chapter 3, p. 74 *supra*.

235. See Singh and Whittington, "The Size and Growth of Firms," p. 20; and C. J. Aislabie, "Further Evidence on the Size and Growth of Firms," *Economic Record* 47 (June 1971): 230–44.

236. For strong support of the product change hypothesis and ambivalent support of the advertising hypothesis, see Richard E. Caves and Michael E. Porter, "Market Structure, Oligopoly, and Stability of Market Shares," *Journal of Industrial Economics* 26 (June 1978): 289–308. See also Chapter 3, p. 74 *supra*.

237. Leonard W. Weiss, "Factors in Changing Concentration," *Review of Economics and Statistics* 45 (February 1963): 70–77, summarized and updated in U.S., Congress, Senate, Subcommittee on Antitrust and Monopoly hearings, *Economic Concentration*, Part 2, 89th Cong., 1st sess., pp. 731–34.

238. Cf. Chapter 4, pp. 114–16 *supra*.

esis of scale economies in advertising and other forms of sales promotion cannot be ruled out.[239]

To sum up, the random growth hypotheses have considerable appeal, both because chance plainly does play some role in company growth and because firm size distributions observed in the real world often correspond closely to those generated by stochastic process models. It would be unwise, however, to reject more conventional explanations of market structure summarily. Economies of scale, mergers, government policies, and the like are surely influential, and not merely in a random way. Indeed, the fact that many industries remain atomistically structured despite the concentration-increasing forces associated with stochastic growth suggests that static and dynamic managerial diseconomies of large size and rapid growth must frequently retard the rise of firms to dominance. A sophisticated explanation of how industry structures came to be what they are must blend the conventional, more or less static, determinants with the kinds of dynamic considerations introduced by stochastic growth process models. This is where future research on the determinants of market structure is most urgently needed.

239. Cf. Chapter 4, pp. 116–17 *supra*.

5 Economic theories of oligopoly pricing

We turn now from market structure to conduct in the market, keeping in mind that the two cannot be divorced completely. A paramount task of industrial organization theory is to identify links running from market structure to such aspects of conduct as pricing behavior, decisions concerning product variety and quality, and innovation, and from there to economic performance. In this chapter we begin the task.

We have observed that in the manufacturing sector and in parts of mining, finance, and retailing, a few relatively large sellers commonly supply the lion's share of output in the markets they serve. If then we wish to learn how the real-world price system functions, we must understand oligopoly pricing. This will be our principal concern in the next four chapters. Chapters 5 and 6 review the developments in pure theory that came to associate monopolistic performance with oligopolistic market structures and examine institutions that contribute to the maintenance of monopoly prices. Chapters 7 and 8 then analyze conditions that limit the power of oligopolists to hold prices persistently above cost.

Oligopolistic interdependence

Oligopoly pricing is interesting and important not only because it is so prevalent, but also be-cause it poses such difficult problems for the economic theorist. When either pure competition or pure monopoly prevails, there are clear-cut solutions to the firm's price and output decision problem, assuming only that managers seek to maximize expected profits and that they hold definite (though probabilistic) expectations concerning future cost and demand conditions. With rivalry among the few, however, this is not so. Each firm recognizes that its best choice depends upon the choices its rivals make. The firms are interdependent, and they are acutely conscious of it. Their decisions depend then upon the assumptions they make about rival decisions and reactions, and many alternative assumptions might be entertained.

Economists have developed literally dozens of oligopoly pricing theories—some simple, some marvels of mathematical complexity. This proliferation of theories is mirrored by an equally rich array of behavioral patterns actually observed under oligopoly. Casual observation suggests that virtually anything can happen. Some oligopolistic industries appear to maintain prices approximating those a pure monopolist would find most profitable. Others gravitate toward price warfare. To illustrate the latter extreme, in 1964 the entry of a new supermarket into the New London, Connecticut area touched off a price war in which bread sold at five cents per loaf (about one-fifth the usual price) and milk at twenty-nine cents per half gallon (about half the usual price).[1]

Recognizing the wide range of theoretical predictions and actual behavior, some economists have asserted that the oligopoly problem is indeterminate.[2] This is correct, in the narrow sense that one cannot forge unique and compelling mechanistic links from cost and demand conditions to price equilibria. But it would be misleading to conclude that we cannot develop theories predicting oligopolistic conduct and performance with tolerable precision. A more constructive interpretation is this: To make workable predictions we need a theory much richer than the received theories of pure competition and pure monopoly, including variables irrelevant to those polar cases. In our quest for a realistic oligopoly theory we must acquire Professor Mason's "ticket of admission to institutional economics,"[3] at the same time retaining the more sharply honed tools with which economic theorists have traditionally worked. We must not expect too much, however. The most that can be hoped for is a kind of soft determinism: predictions correct on the average, but subject to occasionally substantial errors.

The pure theory of oligopoly pricing

To begin, it is useful to survey briefly a few landmarks in the development of oligopoly theory. The first noteworthy attempt to deal with the oligopoly problem was by Augustin Cournot, whose work was published in 1838, but not really discovered by mainstream economists until 45 years later.[4] Cournot postulated that each firm chooses to market the quantity of output that maximizes its own profits, assuming the quantities marketed by rivals to be fixed. From this simple assumption, Cournot derived two main conclusions. First, for any industry, there exists a determinate and stable price-quantity equilibrium. Second, the equilibrium price depends upon the number of sellers. With a single seller, the monopoly price results. As the number of sellers increases, the

equilibrium price declines until, when there are many firms, price approaches equality with marginal cost. Thus, the Cournot model indicates that competitive equilibrium is more closely approximated as the number of sellers increases—a prediction compatible with ordinary observation.

Cournot's initial premises were nonetheless unrealistic in important respects. For one, he assumed that the quantity of output supplied was the firms' key decision variable. Firms chose their outputs and then offered them on the market, which (through some unarticulated bidding process) established a price just sufficient to equate quantity demanded with the total quantity supplied. This assumption was criticized by later economists, who argued from observation that price typically is the decision variable of primary interest to firms with monopoly power. That is, sellers set a price and then let buyers decide whether and how much to purchase at that price. This objection can be met while preserving the heart of the Cournot model if we assume some degree of product differentiation, so that different producers are able simultaneously to sell in the same market at different prices. To illustrate the modified theory, a numerical example is useful.

We assume an industry with two firms selling differentiated products. Each company chooses the price for its product, and buyers respond by deciding from whom and how much to purchase. Profits depend upon the price charged and the amount sold, as well as on costs. Figure 5.1 summarizes the possible results of this duopolistic rivalry from the viewpoint of Firm 1. The numerical entries give the net profits (in thousands of dollars per month) realized by Firm 1 for any combination of its own price P_1 and rival Firm 2's price P_2. Three simple but plausible assumptions underlie the equations generating these profit values. First, the two firms share the market equally when their prices are identical. When their prices are not equal, the high-price firm's market share is smaller, the greater is the percentage difference between its price and its rival's price. Second, the total quantity demanded from the two firms is an inverse linear function of the two prices, weighted by the firms' market shares. No units will be demanded when both firms charge prices of $200 per unit or more, and at a zero price 10,000 units would be demanded monthly. Third, the firms are assumed to have identical U-shaped short-run average total cost functions, with the minimum attainable cost of $65 per unit occurring at an output of 2,250 units per month.[5]

Firm 1's Cournot-type decision-making problem is to pick the value of its own price that maximizes its profits, assuming that the price of rival Firm 2 remains constant. Suppose, for instance, Firm 2's price is $140 per unit. We read across the row of possible payoffs associated with that price until we find the highest profit (about $141,000) attainable by Firm 1, achieved by setting P_1 at slightly less than $120 per unit. This is Firm 1's Cournot-optimal decision when Firm 2's price is $140. But if Firm 2's price should instead be $120 per unit, the best choice under the Cournot assumption is for Firm 1 to quote $110 per unit, earning profits of $118,000 per month. Similar Cournot-optimal values of P_1 can be found for any other price rival Firm 2 might quote. The locus of all these values is traced out by the line R_1 in Figure 5.1. It is called Firm 1's Cournot *reaction function*, because if rival Firm 2 changes its price from, say, $140 to $120, Firm 1 will react by moving along R_1 from $118 to $110.

A similar profit matrix could be drawn up for Firm 2, although to keep Figure 5.1 legible, it is not shown. Assuming symmetry of cost and demand functions, it would be the transpose of Figure 5.1; that is, the profit to Firm 2 with $P_2 = \$80$ and $P_1 = \$100$ is the same as the profit to Firm 1 with $P_1 = \$80$ and $P_2 = \$100$. From Firm 2's profit matrix we can derive its Cournot reaction function, shown by the line R_2 in Figure 5.1.

Now the stage is set to play through the Cournot drama. Suppose Firm 2 is charging a price of $140 per unit (which would maximize its profits as a pure monopolist) when Firm 1 enters the industry. Firm 1 assumes this price to be fixed and makes the best of it, moving to its reaction function R_1 by quoting a price of $118. But now conditions have changed for Firm 2, which must readjust its price policy. Given Firm 1's price of $118, the best price for Firm 2 is $110. (It is found by drawing a horizontal line to the P_2 axis from Firm 2's reaction function at the point where a vertical line representing Firm 1's price of $118 intersects.) This alters the conditions initially as-

sumed by Firm 1, which therefore moves along its reaction function to a new Cournot-optimal price of $107 per unit. This process of price cutting and counter-cutting continues until the two firms reach the point where their reaction functions intersect. There and only there, where each firm is quoting a price of $103 per unit and selling 2,450 units per month, will the two firms find no alternative price yielding higher profits, assuming the rival's price to remain constant. At this point stable Cournot equilibrium is attained.

Given the stipulated behavioral assumptions, convergence to the Cournot equilibrium point follows almost inexorably.[6] But what has hap-

1. "Bread 5¢ in New London Price War," *New York Times*, 5 December 1964, p. 33. For other examples, see Ralph Cassady, Jr., *Price Warfare in Business Competition* (East Lansing: Michigan State University, 1963).

2. Cf. K. W. Rothschild, "Price Theory and Oligopoly," *Economic Journal* 57 (September 1947): 299–302; and R. B. Heflebower, "Toward a Theory of Industrial Markets and Prices," *American Economic Review* 44 (May 1954): 121–39

3. Edward S. Mason, *Economic Concentration and the Monopoly Problem* (Cambridge, Mass.: Harvard University Press, 1957), p. 60.

4. Augustin Cournot, *Researches Into the Mathematical Principles of the Theory of Wealth*, translated by N. T. Bacon (Homewood, Ill.: Irwin, 1963).

5. In mathematical form, Firm 1's market share S_1 is given by the exponential decay equations:

$$S_1 = .5 \exp^{-3[(P_1 - P_2)/P_2]}$$

when $200 > P_1 > P_2$; and

$$S_1 = 1 - .5 \exp^{-3[(P_2 - P_1)/P_1]}$$

when $P_1 < P_2 < 200$. The total quantity X demanded from *both* firms is given by $X = 10,000 - 50 \, S_1 P_1 - 50 \, S_2 P_2$. The total quantity demanded from Firm 1 is $S_1 X$, and Firm 1's total revenue is $P_1 S_1 X$. Firm 1's total cost function (identical to Firm 2's) is: $C_1 = 50,000 + 20 X_1 + .01 X_1^2$. Firm 1's profit, given in Table 5.1, is $P_1 S_1 X - C_1$, except in cases when Firm 1's price is so much lower than Firm 2's price that Firm 1 is able to sell such a large quantity that marginal cost rises above price. In such cases, it has been assumed that Firm 1 sells only that quantity at which the price equals marginal cost. This might lead to a diversion of sales to high-price Firm 2, requiring a redefinition of the market share equations, but this complication has been ignored.

6. For some dynamic complications, see R. E. Quandt and M. McManus, "Comments on the Stability of the Cournot Oligopoly Model," *Review of Economic Studies* 28 (February 1961): 136–39; J. Hadar, "Stability of Oligopoly with Product Differentiation," *Review of Economic Studies* 33 (January 1966): 57–60; and R. E. Quandt, "On the Stability of Price Adjusting Oligopoly," *Southern Economic Journal* 33 (January 1967): 332–36.

Net profit matrix for firm 1

Price quoted by firm 2

	75	80	85	90	95	100	105	110	115	120	125	130	135	140	145	150	155
$155	25	40	55	72	90	109	129	143	151	154	153	147	139	128	116	102	89
150	25	40	55	72	90	109	128	141	148	150	148	142	133	122	110	96	84
145	25	40	55	72	90	109	127	139	145	146	143	136	126	115	102	90	79
140	25	40	55	72	90	109	126	136	141	141	136	129	119	107	95	84	73
135	25	40	55	72	90	109	124	133	136	135	129	121	110	98	87	77	67
130	25	40	55	72	90	109	122	129	131	128	121	111	100	90	79	70	61
125	25	40	55	72	90	108	119	124	124	120	111	101	91	81	71	62	54
120	25	40	55	72	90	106	115	118	116	110	100	91	81	71	63	54	46
115	25	40	55	72	90	104	110	111	106	98	89	80	71	62	53	45	37
110	25	40	55	72	89	100	104	101	95	87	78	69	60	51	43	36	28
105	25	40	55	72	87	95	95	90	83	75	66	57	49	41	33	26	19
100	25	40	55	72	84	87	84	78	71	62	54	45	37	29	22	15	9
95	25	40	55	76	77	77	72	66	58	50	41	33	25	18	11	5	0
90	25	40	55	66	69	66	60	53	45	36	28	21	13	7	0	−4	−9
85	25	40	54	59	58	53	47	39	31	23	15	8	2	−3	−9	−14	−18
80	25	40	49	50	46	40	33	25	17	10	3	−2	−8	−14	−18	−22	−26
75	25	37	40	38	33	26	18	11	4	−2	−8	−13	−18	−23	−26	−30	−33

R₁ Joint maximum R₂ Cournot equilibrium

75 80 85 90 95 100 105 110 115 120 125 130 135 140 145 150 155

Price quoted by firm 1

pened to the duopolists' profits in the process? At the Cournot equilibrium price, each firm realizes profits of roughly $91,000 per month. This is no bargain for Firm 2, which enjoyed profits of $220,000 as a monopolist before the intrusion of Firm 1. If both firms must remain in the industry, they could do much better by raising their quoted prices, moving diagonally northeast in Figure 5.1 until each is quoting a price of $128 per unit and

realizing profits of $112,000 per month. Such a move would seem clearly advantageous from the two firms' viewpoints. But if each adheres to the Cournot assumption that its rival's price will remain constant (at the Cournot equilibrium value of $103), neither has an incentive to raise its own price. For if, say, Firm 1 were to increase its price while Firm 2 maintained a price of $103, Firm 1's profits will necessarily fall.

The cause of this paradox is the Cournot stipulation that firms assume their rivals' decision variables (in this case price) to be fixed. Yet, as Irving Fisher observed in an early criticism:

> no business man assumes either that his rival's output or price will remain constant any more than a chess player assumes that his opponent will not interfere with his effort to capture a knight. On the contrary, his whole thought is to forecast what move the rival will make in response to his own.[7]

Even if the firms' managers were not chess players, the very process of moving toward Cournot equilibrium would demonstrate that their assumptions had been incorrect. For if Firm 1 altered its price, believing that Firm 2's price would remain constant, it could hardly avoid noticing that its assumption was contradicted by Firm 2's retaliatory action. By failing to recognize that rivals will react to its price initiatives, a firm conforming to the Cournot assumption is guilty of myopia. We shall see in later chapters that decision makers do exhibit myopic tendencies in certain rivalry situations. Nevertheless, economists have come to believe that the Cournot assumption is quite unrealistic when applied to pricing decisions involving only a few firms.

Chamberlin's contribution There have been many efforts to patch up the Cournot theory by devising more complex reaction assumptions, e.g., by postulating that firms expect their rivals to react to price or output changes in a specific way.[8] All suffer from the objection that an intelligent business manager would find his or her assumptions contradicted if they were tested thoroughly. A bolder and more influential step was taken in 1929 by Edward Chamberlin.[9]

Chamberlin asserted that when the number of sellers is small and products are standardized, the oligopolists can scarcely avoid full recognition of their interdependence. Each therefore would be reluctant to take measures which, when countered, would leave all members of the industry worse off. Instead, the firms would set price at the monopoly level:

> If each seeks his maximum profit rationally and intelligently, he will realize that when there are only two or a few sellers his own move has a considerable effect upon his competitors, and that this makes it idle to suppose that they will accept without retaliation the losses he forces upon them. Since the result of a cut by any one is inevitably to decrease his own profits, no one will cut, and although the sellers are entirely independent, the equilibrium result is the same as though there were a monopolistic agreement between them.[10]

When sellers are few in number, Chamberlin emphasized, this result follows from the very structure of the industry. No formal collusion or agreement is necessary. Each firm can make its own price and output decisions without consulting the others. For the monopoly price to emerge, it is essential only that the firms *recognize* their mutual interdependence and their mutual interest in a high price. Indeed, he argued, it would

7. Irving Fisher, "Cournot and Mathematical Economics," *Quarterly Journal of Economics* 12 (January 1898): 126.

8. For surveys of the literature, see J. R. Hicks, "Annual Survey of Economic Theory: The Theory of Monopoly," *Econometrica* 3 (January 1935): 1–20; and William Fellner, *Competition Among the Few* (New York: Knopf, 1949), pp. 55–119. For an extension see J. W. Friedman, "Reaction Functions and the Theory of Duopoly," *Review of Economic Studies* 35 (July 1968): 201–208. See also three papers by Richard M. Cyert and Morris H. DeGroot incorporating adaptive learning and dynamic programming assumptions: "Multiperiod Decision Models with Alternating Choice as a Solution to the Duopoly Problem," *Quarterly Journal of Economics* 84 (August 1970): 410–29; "Bayesian Analysis and Duopoly Theory," *Journal of Political Economy* 78 (September/October 1970): 1168–84; and "An Analysis of Cooperation and Learning in a Duopoly Context," *American Economic Review* 63 (March 1973): 24–37. For an attempted empirical application to the Japanese flat glass duopoly, see Gyoichi Iwata, "Measurement of Conjectural Variations in Oligopoly," *Econometrica* 41 (September 1974): 947–66. A fairly complex computer simulation is found in Julian L. Simon, C. M. Puig, and John Aschoff, "A Duopoly Simulation and Richer Theory: An End to Cournot," *Review of Economic Studies* 40 (July 1973): 353–66.

9. E. H. Chamberlin, "Duopoly: Value Where Sellers Are Few," *Quarterly Journal of Economics* 43 (November 1929): 63–100; incorporated with revisions as Chapter III in *The Theory of Monopolistic Competition* (Cambridge, Mass.: Harvard University Press, 1933). Subsequent references are to the sixth edition of the latter.

10. Chamberlin, *The Theory of Monopolistic Competition*, p. 48. Reprinted by permission of Harvard University Press. Copyright 1933 © by the President and Fellows of Harvard College.

be unreasonable to expect members of a highly concentrated industry to behave otherwise:

> The assumption of independence cannot be construed as requiring the sellers to compete as though their fortunes were independent, for this is to belie the very problem of duopoly itself. It can refer only to independence of action—the absence of agreement or of "tacit" agreement.[11]

This passage, as we shall see much later, had a profound impact on the intellectual foundations of antitrust policy, for it led economists to recognize that monopoly pricing could occur without explicit collusion if the industry structure is conducive, and that the gatherings in smoke-filled rooms traditionally attacked under the antitrust laws were not an essential ingredient of monopoly behavior.

Chamberlin acknowledged that monopoly prices might not be attained or maintained owing to certain complications. Perhaps most obvious, when the number of sellers becomes sufficiently large that individual firms begin to ignore their direct or indirect influence on price, an abrupt break toward the competitive price is apt to occur. Second, when substantial time lags intervene between the initiation and matching of price cuts, some firms might undercut the monopoly price, risking future profits for the sake of short-term gains. And finally, sellers might fail to hold prices at the monopoly level if they are uncertain about the reactions, intelligence, or farsightedness of their rivals. Despite these qualifications, the main impact of Chamberlin's analysis was to show that when sellers are few and products standardized, a monopoly price can be established without formal collusion.

Complications owing to cost and demand asymmetries[12] Chamberlin's formal theory covered only an especially simple and unrealistic case—duopolists producing at zero cost. Once costs enter the picture, difficulties arise. Notably, the firms may come into conflict over the most favorable monopoly price if they produce under differing cost conditions.

We can gain an analytic handle on the problem by assuming that, in equilibrium, all members of an oligopolistic industry charge the same price for their products. This assumption is almost certain to be satisfied when the products are perfect substitutes, since any firm trying to charge more than its rivals' price would sooner or later suffer the erosion of its entire sales volume. For oligopolies with differentiated products, it serves as a useful first approximation, perhaps modifiable to permit constant price differentials in equilibrium. With price matching, each firm should normally expect to supply a more or less fixed share of the overall market, whether the price quoted by all is relatively low or relatively high. If so, each producer can estimate from knowledge of the industry demand curve its own individual demand curve. The quantity it sells is simply some constant fraction of the total quantity demanded from all sellers at the common price.[13] The market shares of the several industry members under this price-matching assumption need not be identical; some firms may sell more than others because of minor product quality advantages, a larger sales force, historical ties built up by serving more customers during periods of shortage, and so on.

In order to focus on the impact of cost asymmetries, let us nevertheless begin by assuming that two firms have identical shares of the market at identical prices. For clarity we shall

F 5.2 Constant-shares pricing with differing costs

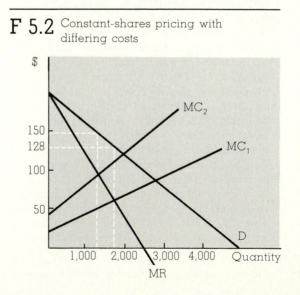

use the same numerical assumptions as those underlying Figure 5.1. The industry demand function is assumed to be $P = 200 - .02 (X_1 + X_2)$, where X_1 and X_2 are the amounts demanded from Firms 1 and 2 respectively. Each duopolist serves half of this demand, so that the demand function of Firm 1 is $P = 200 - .04 X_1$, illustrated by D in Figure 5.2. Its marginal revenue function (identical to Firm 2's) is given by MR in Figure 5.2. We assume initially that each firm operates with the same total cost function: for Firm 1, $TC_1 = 50,000 + 20 X_1 + .01 X_1^2$. Its marginal cost function (shown as MC_1 in Figure 5.2) is $MC_1 = 20 + .02 X_1$. If Firm 1 independently sets marginal cost equal to marginal revenue, it will quote a price of $128 per unit and produce 1,800 units. Firm 2, facing identical cost and demand conditions, will do the same. The $128 price maximizes joint profits, as one can see by referring back to Figure 5.1. Thus, by engaging independently in the conventional calculus of profit maximization, duopolists with identical costs and equal price-matching market shares avoid the Cournot dilemma, each choosing the price-output combination that maximizes their collective profits.

Suppose, however, that Firm 2 has the higher marginal cost function MC_2, derived from the total cost function $TC_2 = \$20,000 + 40 X_2 + .02 X_2^2$. This might happen because Firm 2 is endowed with poorer natural resources, or because it has chosen to build a plant with low initial (and subsequently fixed) capital costs, but with high and more rapidly rising marginal costs. High-cost Firm 2 will find the price of $147 (rounded) per unit associated with an output of 1,333 units optimal from its viewpoint, while low-cost Firm 1 (with marginal cost function MC_1) prefers a price of $128 per unit. There is conflict between the companies in their price and output preferences.

This result is quite general. Whenever producers obtaining equal shares of a market at identical prices have disparate marginal cost functions, their individual price preferences differ, except in a special case.[14] The value of a numerical example is that it allows us to compare the profits each firm would earn charging its own preferred price with the profits earned at its rival's preferred price. For the cost functions assumed, individual and combined profits are presented in Table 5.1. Each firm is worse off at its rival's favored price than at its own, and each therefore would prefer to see its own favored price set on an industrywide basis.[15]

When homogeneity of products precludes any lasting price differential, or when the price differential required for producers of differentiated products to retain their customary market shares is not equal to the difference between favored prices, some means of resolving the conflict must be found. One way is for the firms to strike a compromise among their conflicting preferences, e.g., through meetings and collusive agreements or more subtle tacit bargaining.[16] But this implies a sacrifice of pricing independence, undermining Chamberlin's argument for the emergence of a

11. Chamberlin, *The Theory of Monopolistic Competition*, pp. 46–47. Reprinted by permission of Harvard University Press. Copyright 1933 © by the President and Fellows of Harvard College.

12. For some early approaches to the material in this section, see A. J. Nichol, "Professor Chamberlin's Theory of Limited Competition," *Quarterly Journal of Economics* 48 (February 1934): 317–37; R. H. Coase, "The Problem of Duopoly Reconsidered," *Review of Economic Studies* 2 (February 1935): 137–43; and Fellner, *Competition Among the Few*, pp. 198–229.

13. If, for example, the total quantity demanded from the industry $Q = f(P)$, the quantity demanded from Firm A is $\alpha f(P)$, where α is Firm A's share of the market. At any given price, Firm A's individual demand curve has the same price elasticity as the industry demand curve. Proof: The industry elasticity of demand is $(df/dP)(P/Q)$. Firm A's elasticity is $(d/dP)[\alpha f(P)](P/\alpha Q) = \alpha(df/dP)(P/\alpha Q) = (df/dP)(P/Q)$.

14. I.e., when the two firms' marginal cost functions intersect each other where they mutually intersect the common marginal revenue curve.

15. Combined profits are slightly higher with Firm 2's preferred price of $147 because Firm 2, with more rapidly rising marginal costs, enjoys a greater cost reduction in reducing output from 1,800 to 1,333 units than does Firm 1.

16. Cf. Fellner, *Competition Among the Few*, pp. 23–24.

T 5.1 Price preferences of sellers with differing cost functions

	Firm 1's profits	Firm 2's profits	Joint profits
P = $128	$112,000	$73,600	$185,600
P = $147	$100,950	$86,667	$187,617

monopoly price through purely independent action. An alternative method is for the firm preferring the lowest price arbitrarily to impose its will upon the other producers. Because patronage will flock to the low-price seller, the firm with the lowest price preference will have a distinct advantage over its rivals in this regard. If others attempt to hold the price up at the higher levels they favor, they will suffer a severe erosion of sales and market shares. Still, this mode of price leadership is not always quite so simple. If firms with higher costs do attempt to maintain their prices despite market share losses, the low-price producer may be forced to satisfy more customers and hence supply more than the quantity of output that maximizes its profits. Or if the high-cost firms are dissatisfied with their profits at the low-cost firm's favored price, they may resort to aggressive pricing tactics, either out of desperation or in the hope of threatening and coercing the low-cost firm into adopting a more cooperative stance. The result can be an uncontrolled war in which the price is driven well below the low-cost producer's preferred level.[17] In short, when the members of an oligopolistic industry operate under significantly divergent cost conditions, attaining a price-quantity equilibrium approximating the monopoly solution through independent action is not always easy or certain.

Analogous problems arise when, owing to moderate degrees of product differentiation or differences in capacity, the various members of the industry obtain different shares of the market at identical prices. Figure 5.3 presents the analysis for one case. Two firms are considered, each (for analytic convenience) with the same marginal cost function $MC_{1,2}$. Firm 1, with demand curve D_1 and marginal revenue function MR_1, is assumed normally to sell 60 percent of the duopoly's output. Firm 2 sells the remaining 40 percent, so its demand curve D_2 and marginal revenue curve MR_2 lie to the left of Firm 1's corresponding curves. Equating marginal cost with its own marginal revenue, Firm 1 maximizes its profits by producing output OX_1. Reading up to demand curve D_1, we find its preferred price to be OP_1. Firm 2 maximizes its profits individualistically with output OX_2, which calls for a price of OP_2. Again the sellers' preferences conflict. The

firm with the smaller market share prefers a lower price than its rival with a larger market share.

This conclusion holds only for a situation in which marginal costs rise as output is increased. The high-share firm prefers a higher price in this instance because, in the higher output range where it operates, rising marginal costs discourage expansion more than at lower outputs. More generally, three cases exist for firms with identical marginal cost functions:

1. When marginal costs are rising, the lowest price is preferred by the firm with the smallest market share, *ceteris paribus*.
2. When marginal costs are constant over the relevant range of outputs, differences in market shares do not lead to different price preferences, *ceteris paribus*.
3. When marginal costs fall with higher output, the lowest price is preferred by the firm with the largest market share, which has an incentive to expand and take full advantage of the low costs associated with high outputs.

One implication of these relationships is that the amount of conflict over preferred price levels may depend upon whether firms price to achieve long-run or short-run objectives. As we have seen in Chapter 4, long-run average and marginal

F 5.3 Oligopoly pricing with disparate market shares

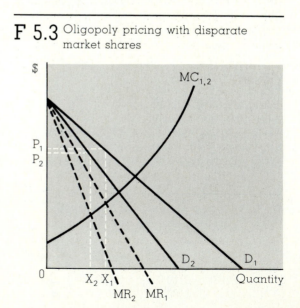

costs tend to be roughly constant over the range of plant sizes and degrees of multi-plant operation observed most frequently in manufacturing industry. This suggests the prevalence of no-conflict case (2) when pricing is oriented toward long-run goals. On the other hand, short-run cost curves are more likely to fit the case (1) mold, except in output ranges substantially below designed plant capacity, and so considerable conflict might be expected among firms of diverse size pricing to maximize short-run profits.

Obviously, both market shares and cost functions may vary simultaneously from firm to firm; the two problems have been kept separate thus far only for analytic convenience. Disparities in both may render the problem of setting a mutually acceptable price even more difficult, although it is also possible (e.g., when firms with small market shares use less capital-intensive production processes, and hence have higher short-run marginal cost functions) that the opposing forces will tend to cancel out. Since market shares and capital intensity do tend to be inversely correlated, there probably is some cancelling out of conflicts. Still, substantial conflicts do exist, as we shall observe repeatedly in later chapters.

A further complication related to cost conditions must be examined. When fixed costs are high and/or when marginal costs vary substantially among firms, it is conceivable that no set of price-quantity choices consistent with independent action by industry members will maximize collective profits. To see this, we return to our numerical example. Firm 1 is assumed to be a capital-intensive, low-marginal-cost producer, with the total cost function $TC_1 = 50,000 + 20 X_1 + .01 X_1^2$. Firm 2 is a high-marginal-cost producer, with $TC_2 = 20,000 + 40 X_2 + .02 X_2^2$. To find the outputs that yield maximum combined profits, we must set up a joint profit equation, consisting of total revenue from sales of both firms' outputs less total costs of the two separate production operations:

$$\pi_{\text{joint}} = (X_1 + X_2) [200 - .02 (X_1 + X_2)] \\ - (50,000 + 20 X_1 + .01 X_1^2) \\ - (20,000 + 40 X_2 + .02 X_2^2)$$

When this function is maximized with respect to

the outputs of Firms 1 and 2, the optimal values of X_1 and X_2 turn out to be 2,500 and 750 units respectively. With total production of 3,250 units per month, the price that equates demand with supply is $135 per unit. Joint profits are $215,000—about 15 percent higher than those attainable if the production burden is shared equally at Firm 2's preferred price of $147. If Firm 1 collects all the revenue from selling its output of 2,500 units and deducts from it the costs of producing that output, its total profits turn out to be $175,000. Firm 2, producing and selling only 750 units per month, realizes profits of only $40,000. Firm 2 could do much better under the equal market shares approach discussed earlier, selling either at its own preferred price of $147 or at Firm 1's preferred price of $128. Firm 2 is therefore not apt to cooperate in this 'rationalization' scheme, despite the higher collective profits, unless a plan for distributing profits on some basis other than individual output is enforced. And obviously, such profit-pooling agreements are several steps removed from the independent action implied in a naive version of Chamberlin's joint profit-maximization theory.

Even higher collective profits could be realized under the stated numerical assumptions if, by shutting down high-cost Firm 2's plant completely, the fixed costs of $20,000 associated with maintaining that plant could be eliminated. Then low-cost Firm 1 would produce and sell the pure monopoly output of 3,000 units at a price of $140 per unit, realizing profits of $220,000. But again, Firm 2 would surely not consent to such a drastic step unless an ironclad agreement were reached assuring that it would receive a substantial share of the enhanced industry profits.

One final point must be made clear. Rationalization measures such as closing down high-cost Firm 2's plant increase collective industry profits by enforcing a more efficient organization of pro-

17. See R. L. Bishop, "Duopoly: Collusion or Warfare?" *American Economic Review* 50 (December 1960): 933–61. For an example from rail freight pricing on the Chicago–New York route during the late 19th century, see Paul W. MacAvoy, *The Economic Effects of Regulation* (Cambridge, Mass.: M.I.T. Press, 1965), pp. 129–35.

duction. But in the example presented, *prices* are higher and quantities sold lower under either rationalization scheme than they would be if the two firms made their output decisions independently, letting Firm 1 pull the price down to its preferred level of $128. In other cases the consumer could conceivably benefit directly through lower prices under rationalization schemes accompanied by a pricing policy that maximizes producers' collective profits. This can occur only when marginal costs are falling continuously over the attainable range of outputs, or when the low-cost firm's marginal cost function is at all relevant outputs below the lowest point on the high-cost firm's marginal cost function.

To sum up, when cost functions and/or market shares vary from firm to firm within an oligopolistic industry, conflicts arise that, unless resolved through formal collusive agreements, interfere with the maximization of collective monopoly profits. And if left unresolved, these conflicts may trigger myopic, aggressive behavior that drives the industry away from the joint profit-maximizing solution of its price-output problem.

The contributions of game theory

Because of these complications, it became clear that the conventional tools of microeconomic theory could not provide a full explanation of oligopoly pricing. New hope for a definitive solution arose with the publication of the *Theory of Games and Economic Behavior* by John von Neumann and Oskar Morgenstern.[18] Or at least, many economists who had not waded through the book's 632 pages of set theoretic proofs added hopeful footnote citations in works applying traditional tools to the oligopoly problem with less than evident success. We shall find that the hopes of the more optimistic were in vain. Nevertheless, game theory is extremely useful as a source of insights into the oligopoly problem, even though it seldom if ever yields completely determinate solutions.

The most compelling contribution by von Neumann and Morgenstern was their theory of

zero-sum games, for which they derived solutions that are indeed determinate, assuming rational but conservative behavior on the part of rivals anxious to make the best of their rivalry. The consequences of alternative choices by each rival are represented through a payoff matrix, as in the following illustrative matrix for Player A in a two-person zero-sum game involving A and Player B:

$$
\begin{array}{cc}
 & B\text{'s strategies} \\
A\text{'s strategies} &
\begin{array}{ccc}
 & b_1 & b_2 & b_3 \\
\alpha_1 & 8 & -5 & -10 \\
\alpha_2 & 0 & -2 & 6 \\
\alpha_3 & 4 & -1 & 5
\end{array}
\end{array}
$$

Each entry in the matrix is the payoff expected by A associated with a particular pair of strategy choices by A and B. For example, if A chooses strategy α_2 and B chooses strategy b_3, A's payoff will be $+6$. Rival B's payoffs are the negative of A's; if A gains 6, B must lose 6. All payoff pairs sum to zero, hence the name *zero-sum*. To determine his best strategy, A examines each row of his payoff matrix to find the worst payoff that can occur if he chooses the strategy associated with that row: -10 for α_1, -2 for α_2, and -1 for α_3. The best of these worst outcomes—the *maximum minimorum*—is -1, associated with strategy α_3. Because it makes the best of the worst that can happen, α_3 is A's optimal (though not very lucrative) choice. Rival B follows the same procedure. Since his payoffs are the negative of those in A's matrix, he looks for the best outcome to A (and hence the worst outcome to himself) in each column (representing a strategy choice by B) of A's payoff matrix. These are $+8$ for b_1, -1 for b_2, and $+6$ for b_3. The worst of these best outcomes (*minimum maximorum*) from A's viewpoint, and hence the best of the worst from B's viewpoint, is -1, associated with strategy b_2. This is B's optimal *minimax* strategy. The set of strategies α_3, b_2 turns out to be a stable solution, or saddle point, to the game, since each participant's expectations about its rival's choices are confirmed. That is, B in fact chooses the strategy b_2 which is least favorable to A, given A's choice of α_3. Not all zero-sum games have such simple solutions, but von Neumann and Morgenstern proved that for all two-person zero-sum games there exists a minimax strategy (or set of strategies) promising each participant higher average payoffs than any alternative set of strategies, assuming that each rival intelligently tries to maximize the expected value of its payoffs.

For our purposes there is only one hitch. As von Neumann and Morgenstern recognized, the kinds of rivalry encountered in oligopoly seldom conform to the zero-sum assumption. Only two exceptions can be found. First, firms might set market share as their sole competitive objective, and one firm's market share gain is necessarily the market share loss of other firms. But to depict oligopolistic rivalry in terms of such simple objectives is undoubtedly to misrepresent reality. The intense interest in market position displayed by many oligopolists probably reflects the belief that higher profits come hand in hand with certain kinds of market share gains, and thus it is profit that the shouting is really about. A second defense of zero-sum oligopoly models is only slightly more plausible: that firms engage in 'games of survival' or 'games of ruin,' the winner enjoying the whole of a profitable market.[19] Although some examples can be found in real life and forced into the zero-sum mold, the task is difficult. And as we shall see much later, the authorities in most nations with antitrust laws take a dim view of business tactics explicitly calculated to ruin one's rival.

For a more realistic example of the payoff structure encountered in business rivalry, we refer again to Figure 5.1. It should be evident now that Figure 5.1 is simply a large payoff matrix. To facilitate the analysis, let us consider only two alternative price strategies for each firm. At the price ($105) nearest the Cournot equilibrium point, each firm receives profits of $95,000, and so joint profits are $190,000. If Firm 1 holds its price at $105 while Firm 2 raises its price to $130 (nearest the joint-maximizing point), total profits will be $122,000 (for Firm 1) plus $57,000 (for Firm 2) = $179,000. If both firms quote prices of $130, joint profits will be $222,000. The payoffs in the matrix clearly do not sum to zero, nor is there any simple mathematical transformation (such as subtracting a fixed amount from every payoff) that will make them sum to zero. Games of this

sort, in which some outcomes are more favorable to the participants jointly than others, are called nonconstant-sum or variable-sum games.

Minimax is an unbeatable strategy in zero-sum games. But it is ill-suited to the typical variable-sum game of oligopolistic rivalry. To see this, let us find the minimax strategy for Firm 1 in Figure 5.1. We scan each column, corresponding to a strategy (price) choice by Firm 1, locating the worst possible outcome if that strategy is chosen. The best of these is a profit of approximately $40,000 resulting when Firm 2 quotes a price of $75 and Firm 1 a price of $85.[20] If Firm 2, with symmetrical cost and demand conditions, reasons similarly, both firms will quote minimax prices of $85. As a result they end up with profits of $54,000 each, instead of the $91,000 each they could earn through supposedly myopic Cournot behavior, or the $112,000 attainable if both quote prices of $128 to maximize joint profits.

The nature of the pricing problem in oligopoly can be seen still more sharply if we limit our focus to two salient strategy alternatives—e.g., as before, $105 and $130. The profits (in thousands of dollars per month) to Firms 1 and 2 resulting from various strategy combinations are set down in abbreviated game matrix form as follows:

		Firm 2's price strategies	
		$130	$105
Firm 1's price strategies	$130	111,111	57,122
	$105	122, 57	95, 95

18. John von Neumann and Oskar Morgenstern, *Theory of Games and Economic Behavior* (Princeton: Princeton University Press, 1944). For a lucid exposition of the central concepts, see Anatol Rapoport, *Fights, Games, and Debates* (Ann Arbor: University of Michigan Press, 1960), pp. 105–242. A more advanced presentation is found in R. D. Luce and Howard Raiffa, *Games and Decisions* (New York: Wiley, 1957). The most ambitious applications to oligopoly theory are Martin Shubik, *Strategy and Market Structure* (New York: Wiley, 1959); Lester G. Telser, *Competition, Collusion, and Game Theory* (Chicago: Aldine-Atherton, 1972); and James W. Friedman, *Oligopoly and the Theory of Games* (Amsterdam: North-Holland, 1977).

19. See Shubik, *Strategy and Market Structure*, pp. 204–222.

20. Actually, because the payoff matrix has been truncated to exclude lower prices, the true minimax strategy involves even lower profits. It should be noted also that a saddle point minimax equilibrium may not exist.

Because Firm 1's gains are not necessarily Firm 2's losses, we must record two profit outcomes for each strategy pair—the first (before the comma) Firm 1's profit, and the second, Firm 2's profit. The worst that can happen from Firm 1's viewpoint if it quotes a price of $130 is a profit of $57,000; the worst if its price is $105 will be $95,000. The lower price is the minimax strategy. Or consider the problem of choice from another perspective. If Firm 2 quotes a price of $130, Firm 1 will be better off quoting $105. If Firm 2 quotes $105, Firm 1 will be better off quoting $105. In the language of game theory, the $105 price *dominates* the $130 price. The low-price strategy seems to have an irresistible magnetism. Yet if both rivals engage in mental processes of this sort, they end up with lower profits than they need to have!

This paradoxical situation is a typical member of the genus called Prisoners' Dilemma games.[21] A digression on the original prisoners' dilemma will provide valuable analogies for subsequent use. Suppose Smith and McAlpin are charged with committing a mail-train robbery. The district attorney is unable to prove his case unless he can obtain a signed confession, but he can make lighter charges (e.g., possessing stolen goods) stick. The two suspects are interrogated in separate rooms (after being informed of their constitutional rights) and are confronted with specific alternatives. If McAlpin doesn't confess, both will get one year in prison on the minor charge if Smith clams up too. If Smith turns state's evidence, McAlpin receives a ten-year sentence and Smith goes free. If McAlpin confesses and Smith does not, Smith gets ten years and McAlpin goes free, while if both confess, both will get six years. In game matrix form, with Smith's time in prison listed first, the payoffs are as follows:

		McAlpin's strategies	
		Don't confess	Confess
Smith's	Don't confess	$-1, -1$	$-10, 0$
strategies	Confess	$0, -10$	$-6, -6$

Assuming that he dislikes prison and that his safety from McAlpin's revenge is assured, Smith is better off confessing, no matter what McAlpin's choice may be. The same holds true from Mc-Alpin's viewpoint. Confessing is a dominant strategy for both prisoners. If they reason in this way, both end up spending six years in jail, instead of the single year they would serve if somehow they could solve the prisoners' dilemma and deny their guilt despite the strained circumstances.

In terms of their static, single-play structure, the oligopoly price game presented earlier and the classic Prisoners' Dilemma game are identical.[22] There is a minimax strategy that, if chosen by both parties, leads to an outcome in which both parties are worse off than they need be. Nor are these the only such examples. In the military field, the deterrence of nuclear attack, decisions whether or not to use poison gas, and arms races also tend to have the structure of Prisoners' Dilemma games. And as we shall see in later chapters, advertising and new product rivalry in oligopoly often fit the Prisoners' Dilemma mold.

With similar structures, these games might be expected to tend toward similar outcomes. But this is not the case. We observe, for example, that nuclear deterrence has been remarkably stable and successful for three decades. There has been no exchange of nuclear weapons leaving all nations worse off, even though successful unilateral attack could lead to military domination and being attacked unilaterally would (at least in the average citizen's judgment) be disastrous. On the other hand, nations large and small have had little success in avoiding mutual and therefore self-defeating steps in quantitative and qualitative arms races. Why is it that in some Prisoners' Dilemmas the participants avoid mutually unfavorable outcomes, while in others they do not?

The answer evidently involves more than the static structure of the payoff matrix. Particularly important are the dynamics of the situation, the amount of information available to participants, and the opportunities for communication.

The problem in the classic Prisoners' Dilemma is one of information and communication. If Smith and McAlpin could get together on their stories and remain constantly in touch so that each knows the other is not confessing, both could get off with light sentences. It is a wise district attorney who places the prisoners in separate interrogation rooms to foment uncertainty and distrust.

One reason why nuclear deterrence has worked is that communication is relatively free and rapid. A hostile move is known at least as soon as the first weapon explodes. In addition, nations have invested vast sums in early warning systems to detect attacks before they damage retaliatory capabilities and in "hot lines" to guarantee that accidents will not be misunderstood. As a result, each nation finds it possible to wait and watch. If all goes well, this process of watchful waiting and abstinence from aggressive (or preemptory defensive) moves will continue indefinitely. We shall find close analogies for oligopoly pricing in Chapter 7. In contrast, nations have been unable to resist the development of new weapons, partly because of the secrecy in which military research and development efforts are enshrouded. Not knowing what is going on in foreign laboratories, military leaders have tended to fear the worst (the minimax assumption) and initiated the development of each new potentially decisive weapon. These actions in turn validate the suspicions of other nations, giving the technological arms race its irresistible momentum.

The existence of lags is a second important determinant. It is possible to retaliate quickly to a massive nuclear attack or to certain kinds of price cuts. In such cases, potential aggressors recognize that they have little to gain and much to lose from aggression, and therefore they refrain. It may take many years, however, to respond fully to a successful new weapon system or the superior new product of an industrial rival. Consequently, aggressive moves may be taken both because initiators believe they can gain an advantage of some duration and because nervous decision makers fear they must begin now to offset secret rival moves which, if not countered, could lead to a painfully long period of inferiority.

A third factor is the dynamics of the rivalry. Some rivalries are continuous; others are discontinuous or perhaps even one-shot affairs. Maximization of joint benefits is more likely when the rivalry is continuous for two main reasons: Repeated experience under stable conditions affords an opportunity for learning to cooperate and trust one another; and when the game will be played continuously or repeatedly, each party can threaten its rivals with damaging retaliation

tomorrow if cooperation is not forthcoming today. Indeed, these two elements interact, for rivals can in time be taught to cooperate by the deft use of threats, rewards, and punishments.[23] Thus, a further reason why nuclear deterrence is stable is that the game is replayed day after day. Conversely, it is difficult to avoid qualitative arms races because each new round is different in many details from the prior round. This experience leads us to predict that oligopolists selling an unchanging product under stable demand conditions are more likely to maximize joint profits than oligopolists selling rapidly changing products under variable demand conditions. Supporting evidence will be marshalled in later chapters.

A final reason why some rivalries are resolved cooperatively while others are not is that even the single-play payoff matrices can differ. Rivals often find it advantageous to manipulate their payoff structures so as to encourage cooperative behavior. Paradoxically, *worsening* some of one's own payoff possibilities may improve the probable outcome.[24] In the Prisoners' Dilemma, for instance, a Mafia-like pact that rat finks will be assassinated eliminates the "Confess" strategy's attractiveness. Likewise, after being convicted and fined for price fixing, in 1963 General Electric announced a "price protection" plan under which it guaranteed that if it gave a discount on any new turbogenerator order, it would retroactively grant the same discount on all orders taken

21. See Luce and Raiffa, *Games and Decisions*, pp. 94–102.

22. This identity no longer holds, and the character of the solution may change, if sequential and contingent strategies are built into the game's structure. See Anatol Rapoport, "Escape from Paradox," *Scientific American*, July 1967, pp. 50–56; James W. Friedman, "A Non-cooperative Equilibrium for Supergames," *Review of Economic Studies* 38 (January 1971): 1–12; and Thomas Marschak and R. Selten, "Restabilizing Responses, Inertia Supergames, and Oligopolistic Equilibria," *Quarterly Journal of Economics* 92 (February 1978): 71–93.

23. For a superb treatment of this problem, see T. C. Schelling, *The Strategy of Conflict* (Cambridge, Mass.: Harvard University Press, 1960), Chapter 5.

24. Schelling, *Strategy of Conflict*, pp. 23–25, 150–61.

within the preceding six months.[25] In the framework of our previous example, if cutting the price from $130 to $105 required rebates totalling $150,000 to customers of the past six months, the payoff matrix is transformed as follows:

		Westinghouse's price strategies	
		$130	$105
GE's price	$130	111,111	57,122
strategies	$105	−28, 57	−55, 95

Keeping the price at $130 is now both the minimax and dominant strategy for GE. To be sure, this leaves GE vulnerable to a price cut by Westinghouse. But if Westinghouse's main incentive previously for price cutting was fear that GE would cut its price, that fear is assuaged. Moreover, even though Westinghouse could gain temporarily under the new payoff structure by setting a $105 price, it must recognize that GE would soon terminate the price protection plan if it took advantage of GE's vulnerability, so the dynamics of the game favor a cooperative (i.e., $130) strategy by Westinghouse. In fact, Westinghouse emulated GE's price protection plan in 1964, transforming its own payoff matrix to encourage cooperation; and both companies maintained the plans until forced in 1977 by the government to abandon them.

Besides yielding insight into the nature of real-world rivalries, game theory makes another important contribution. By reducing oligopoly pricing problems to game payoff matrices, it is possible to conduct controlled experiments testing relevant hypotheses. Several fruitful experimental efforts have been reported.

L. B. Lave administered numerous repetitions of a Prisoners' Dilemma game to subjects isolated and unable to communicate formally. He found that through repeated experience, three-fourths of the players learned to cooperate in choosing the strategy pair that maximized their joint payoff. However, on the last trial (after which punitive retaliation for uncooperative behavior was impossible) double-crossing was common.[26] L. E. Fouraker and S. Siegel observed that repeated bidding served as a means of communication through which participants in bilateral monopoly games were able to reach bargains that were optimal (or, more precisely, Pareto-optimal) in the sense that no further change could be made that increased one player's profits without reducing the other's profits. In another set of experiments, they found that cooperation to maximize joint oligopoly profits is less likely, the larger the number of participants and the less information participants have on rival prices, outputs, and profits.[27] Repeating the Fouraker-Siegel experiments with a slightly different payoff matrix, J. L. Murphy found that prices and profits were higher when both rivals faced a threat of outright losses from mutual price cutting than when they did not.[28] An experiment administered by J. W. Friedman revealed an equilibrium tendency for subjects to reach and adhere to agreements on oligopoly prices roughly 80 percent of the time, despite the possibility of cheating to increase profits once agreements were concluded. Friedman observed in addition that Pareto-optimal agreements were more likely in symmetric duopoly games—i.e., when both cost curves and market shares were the same—than in asymmetric games.[29] This result underscores the hazards to oligopolistic coordination posed by unequal costs and market shares, as revealed through a priori analysis in the preceding section.

In sum, although game theory yields no compelling mechanistic solutions to oligopoly pricing problems, it does help identify certain general structural characteristics of situations involving conflict mixed with incentives for cooperation. Armed with these generalizations, we are better able to understand the conditions facilitating and impeding solution of the pricing problems faced by real-world oligopolists.

The kinked demand curve and price rigidity

The minimax strategy of game theory is a strategy of pessimism: It assumes rivals will take actions least favorable from one's own viewpoint. It is in fact much too pessimistic to describe most oligopoly behavior realistically. But by making an assumption that meets minimax halfway down the road to pessimism, we encounter the kinked demand curve theory, which has been employed to explain why oligopolistic firms shy away from frequent price cutting.[30]

The theory asserts that oligopolists face two different subjectively estimated demand curves: one describing the quantities they will sell at various prices, assuming that rivals maintain their prices at current levels (the Cournot assumption); and the other describing the amount of output sold, assuming that rivals exactly match any price changes away from the present level (the price-matching, constant-market-shares assumption). The latter curve has the same elasticity at any given price as the overall industry demand curve. The first, however, is more elastic. If Firm 1 raises its price while rivals hold their prices constant, the quantity of output demanded from Firm 1 will fall off much more sharply than it would if all sellers matched the price increase. If Firm 1 lowers its price while rivals do not, it will make inroads into their market shares, and the quantity of output it can sell will be greater than it would be if rivals matched the price reduction. The two curves intersect at the current price level, for if Firm 1 (whose kinked demand curve we shall construct) continues to quote its current price, the alternative assumptions of rival price maintenance and price matching imply identical rival prices.

Figure 5.4 illustrates these points, assuming the current price to be OP per unit and the quantity supplied by (and demanded from) Firm 1 to be OX. DEF is Firm 1's demand curve, assuming that rival firms hold their prices at OP per unit no matter what Firm 1 does. GEH is Firm 1's demand curve, assuming that rivals match Firm 1's prices. DS is the marginal revenue curve associated with demand curve DEF, and GR the marginal revenue curve for demand curve GEH.

These curves, to repeat, are defined for two alternative rival reactions to price changes: holding the line, or matching. The key assumption of kinked demand curve theory is that oligopolists expect rivals to choose the less favorable of these alternatives in response to a price change. The theory does not go as far as minimax—that is, assuming that rivals will *take the initiative* in choosing a damaging strategy—but only that they will *react* unfavorably to one's own

price initiatives. Specifically, if Firm 1 raises its price, rivals are expected not to follow the increase, enjoying an increase in market share at Firm 1's expense because of the newly created price differential. If Firm 1 reduces its price, rivals are expected to match the cut promptly in order to ward off incursions into their own market shares. When these pessimistic assumptions are held, only the more elastic demand segment DE is applicable for contemplated increases above the current price by Firm 1, while only the less elastic demand segment EH is applicable for price cuts by Firm 1. The complete demand curve (as visualized by Firm 1) is composed of these two segments DE and EH, with a kink at the current price OP and output OX. The other segments EF and GE are obliterated by Firm 1's pessimistic assumptions, and so in Figure 5.5 we include only the applicable segments of the kinked demand curve DEH.

Eliminating the two demand curve segments EF and GE also requires that we eliminate the associated marginal revenue segments. For the remaining demand curve segment DE, only the

25. *U.S.* v. *General Electric Co. et al.*, "Plaintiff's Memorandum in Support of a Proposed Modification to the Final Judgment Entered on October 1, 1962, Against Each Defendant," December 1976.

26. L. B. Lave, "An Empirical Approach to the Prisoners' Dilemma Game," *Quarterly Journal of Economics* 75 (August 1962): 424–36.

27. L. E. Fouraker and Sidney Siegel, *Bargaining Behavior* (New York: McGraw-Hill, 1963), especially pp. 50–51, 165–66, 199. For supporting results from a more elaborate experimental game, see F. T. Dolbear *et al.*, "Collusion in Oligopoly: An Experiment on the Effect of Numbers and Information," *Quarterly Journal of Economics* 82 (May 1968): 240–59. See also B. Lowes and C. L. Pass, "Price Behaviour in Asymmetrical Duopoly," *Manchester School of Economics and Social Studies* 38 (March 1970): 29–44.

28. "Effects of the Threat of Losses on Duopoly Bargaining," *Quarterly Journal of Economics* 80 (May 1966): 296–313.

29. "An Experimental Study of Cooperative Duopoly," *Econometrica* 35 (July–October 1967): 379–97. See also his survey, "On Experimental Research in Oligopoly," *Review of Economic Studies* 36 (October 1969): 399–415.

30. The kinked demand curve theory was proposed independently and almost simultaneously by R. L. Hall and C. J. Hitch in "Price Theory and Business Behaviour," *Oxford Economic Papers* 2 (May 1939): 12–45; and Paul M. Sweezy in "Demand Under Conditions of Oligopoly," *Journal of Political Economy* 47 (August 1939): 568–73. For a discussion of some antecedents, see J. J. Spengler, "Kinked Demand Curves: By Whom First Used?," *Southern Economic Journal* 32 (July 1965): 81–84.

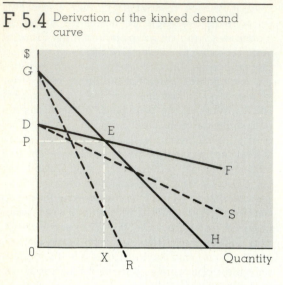

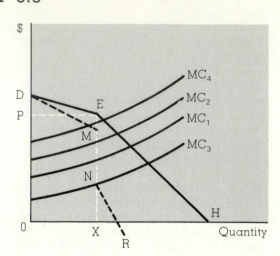

marginal revenue segment *DM* to the left of the current output level is applicable. For the remaining demand segment *EH*, only the segment *NR* to the right of the current output is relevant. Therefore, the marginal revenue function for the kinked demand curve *DEH* in Figure 5.5 is the discontinuous set of curves *DM* and *NR*.[31] We see that whenever there is a kink in the demand curve, there must be a vertical discontinuity in the associated marginal revenue function. The more the demand curve segments differ in elasticity in the neighborhood of the kink, the greater will be the vertical discontinuity or gap between the associated marginal revenue segments.

We know that to maximize its profits, a firm must equate marginal cost with marginal revenue. Let us see what implications the kinked demand curve has for an oligopolist's maximizing decisions in the face of cost and/or demand changes. Suppose initially that Firm 1 faces cost conditions represented by marginal cost function MC_1 in Figure 5.5. Then output *OX* will be optimal, for at a lower output marginal revenue exceeds marginal cost, providing an incentive to expand, while at a higher output marginal revenue is less than marginal cost, so profits could be increased by reducing the quantity supplied. An important implication of the kinked demand curve theory is that the same output *OX* and price *OP* will be optimal even after a change in cost

conditions, as represented by either the higher marginal cost function MC_2 or the lower curve MC_3. In both new situations, the marginal cost function cuts the marginal revenue function in the latter's discontinuity, so there is no incentive either to expand or contract output. Only with a very substantial change in costs—e.g., to MC_4—will there be an incentive to move to a new (in this case lower) output and (higher) price.

The same rigidity of prices (but not outputs) follows for moderate shifts in demand. In Figure 5.6, for example, the original situation is reflected by demand curve *DEH* kinked at the price *OP*, with the corresponding marginal revenue function *DLKR*. Should a recession overtake the industry, the demand curve shifts horizontally to the left to *ABC*, and the corresponding new marginal revenue function is *ATUV*. In both cases marginal cost continues to cut the marginal revenue functions through their gaps, and so there is no incentive to change the price, although output will be reduced to *OY* to clear the market in the face of reduced demand.

In sum, the kinked demand curve theory yields two main predictions: (1) When the constant-shares demand curve is relatively inelastic, oligopolists will refrain from price cutting, since they expect that matching cuts by rivals will nullify any profit gains; and (2) oligopoly prices will tend to be rigid in the face of moderate cost and demand conditions changes. Both predictions are consistent with a fair amount of observed oligopoly behavior. Interviews with business executives and the testimony recorded in numerous antitrust investigations reveal that a paramount consideration deterring price cutting, especially in industries with few sellers and homogeneous products, is the belief that cuts will be matched, forcing all firms onto inelastic segments of their demand curves.[32] There is also evidence (to be considered more fully in Chapter 13) that oligopoly prices are adjusted less frequently than in atomistically structured industries.

There are, however, cases in which the theory's fit with reality is less than satisfactory. A strict interpretation of the theory implies that prices should be more rigid under oligopoly conditions than in pure monopolies or in industries dominated by a single firm, for monopolists or dominant firms need have little or no concern over whether their pricing initiatives are followed by other (insignificant or nonexistent) rivals. But studies of price setting for pharmaceutical products, electric power, magazine advertising space, and selected other products reveal that prices tend to be about as rigid in markets approximating a purely monopolistic structure as with two or more oligopolistic sellers.[33] Evidently, the kinked

demand curve mentality is not the only reason for price inflexibility when sellers enjoy significant monopoly power. When price structures are complex, cost considerations may discourage frequent price revisions, since a certain amount of administrative toil invariably goes into price-setting decisions and since the cost of printing and disseminating new price lists may be appreciable. More importantly, as we shall see in Chapter 8, monopolists as well as oligopolists may set prices at levels satisfying long-run strategy goals and not deviate from their announced price structure when demand or cost changes perceived to be of only temporary duration occur. And although they do not explain the similarity of monopoly and oligopoly price setting, there are clearly reasons other than kinked demand curves for price inflexibility in oligopoly—e.g., the fear that frequent price changes may jeopardize industry discipline.

A second limitation of the kinked demand curve theory is more subtle. Using the theory, suppose we try to explain price rigidity in industries that have experienced fair success in maintaining prices tending to maximize joint oligopoly

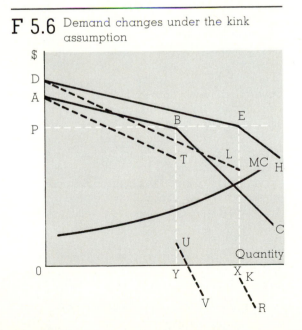

F 5.6 Demand changes under the kink assumption

31. Many students have trouble understanding the kinked demand curve analysis because they fail to remember that *quantity* is the independent variable in defining marginal revenue, and as a result they do not see that each marginal revenue segment is applicable only up to that quantity of output at which the demand curve kink occurs.

32. For examples, see J. W. Markham, *Competition in the Rayon Industry* (Cambridge, Mass.: Harvard University Press, 1952), p. 143; A. D. H. Kaplan, J. B. Dirlam, and R. F. Lanzillotti, *Pricing in Big Business* (Washington, D.C.: Brookings Institution, 1958), p. 174 (steel); R. B. Tennant, "The Cigarette Industry," in Walter Adams, ed., *The Structure of American Industry*, 3rd ed. (New York: Macmillan, 1961), pp. 370–72; Reed Moyer, *Competition in the Midwestern Coal Industry* (Cambridge, Mass.: Harvard University Press, 1964), pp. 53–54; and (for a case in which the kink was not always effective) E. P. Learned and C. C. Ellsworth, *Gasoline Pricing in Ohio* (Boston: Harvard Business School, 1959), pp. 244–52. Other examples can be found in the records of the tetracycline (*F.T.C. v. American Cyanamid et al.*) and breakfast cereal (*F.T.C. v. Kellogg et al.*) antitrust cases.

33. See George J. Stigler, "The Kinky Oligopoly Demand Curve and Rigid Prices," *Journal of Political Economy* 55 (October 1947): 442–44; Walter J. Primeaux, Jr., and Mickey C. Smith, "Pricing Patterns and the Kinky Demand Curve," *Journal of Law and Economics* 19 (April 1976): 189–99; W. J. Primeaux, Jr., and Mark R. Bomball, "A Reexamination of the Kinky Oligopoly Demand Curve," *Journal of Political Economy* 82 (July/August 1974): 851–62; and Julian L. Simon, "A Further Test of the Kinky Oligopoly Demand Curve," *American Economic Review* 59 (December 1969): 971–75.

Economic theories of oligopoly pricing   167

profits. We assume identical cost conditions and market shares for all industry members, although the same analysis can be applied to individual firms whose low price preferences place a ceiling on the industry price. To maximize collective profits, marginal cost must equal marginal revenue (derived from the constant-shares demand curve) for a representative firm. If the price is set so as to satisfy this condition and then a kink appears, the marginal cost curve must cut the marginal revenue curve gap at the very bottom of that gap—e.g., at point N in Figure 5.5. This is so because only the segment NR is marginal to the constant-shares demand curve. It follows that prices will now be rigid against upward shifts in the marginal cost function, but even a slight downward shift will induce a price reduction (since any marginal cost curve lower than MC_3 will no longer cut the gap). Yet observation indicates that prices tend to be at least as rigid downward as they are upward in well-disciplined oligopolies. We are forced to conclude either that the kinked demand curve theory cannot fully explain pricing behavior in industries maximizing joint profits, or that the price must initially have been set below the profit-maximizing level if the subsequent emergence of a kink makes the price rigid against both upward and downward cost curve shifts.

Finally, the kinked demand curve theory is much better at explaining why prices persist at particular levels than how they attained those levels in the first place. To see this, consider Figure 5.5 once again. Suppose there is a substantial increase in costs, so that Firm 1 now operates with MC_4, cutting the marginal revenue function to the left of the gap MN. A price increase by Firm 1 appears warranted, despite the anticipated loss of market share and sales. Assume also that all other firms in the industry experience the same cost increase (e.g., because of pattern bargaining over wages or because all purchase inflation-impacted raw materials in the same markets). Since their position is symmetric to Firm 1's, they too will have an incentive to raise their prices. But if they do, Firm 1's pessimistic assumption that rivals will hold their prices constant—the heart of the kinked demand curve theory—is contradicted. Alternatively, if other firms' cost curves do not shift upward and the rivals

adhere initially to price OP, their demand curves must shift to the right (i.e., they enjoy higher sales at price OP) because of Firm 1's new higher price. If this rightward shift is sufficiently large, it may induce a price increase by the rivals, again contradicting the price maintenance assumption. Similar contradictions arise when exogenous demand curve shifts induce at least one firm to change its price.[34] In short, the assumptions of the kinked demand curve theory are violated when incentives for a price change appear either simultaneously or sequentially for several members of the oligopoly. As a result, the theory cannot explain how prices change or how they settle down at new levels when cost or demand conditions alter, even though it can explain why they remain stable once they do settle down. Other mechanisms must be invoked to explain the dynamics of price changes. We shall consider several in Chapter 6.

Conclusion

Let us try now to tie together the principal lessons emerging from this survey. Any realistic theory of oligopoly must take as a point of departure the fact that when market concentration is high, the pricing decisions of sellers are interdependent, and the firms involved can scarcely avoid recognizing their mutual interdependence. If they are at all perceptive, the managers of oligopolistic enterprises will recognize too that profits will be higher when cooperative policies are pursued than when each firm looks only after its own narrow self-interest. As a consequence, we should expect oligopolistic industries to exhibit a tendency toward the maximization of collective profits, perhaps even approaching the pricing outcome associated with pure monopoly. Still, coordination of pricing policies to maximize joint profits is not easy, especially when cost and market share disparities engender conflicting price and output preferences among industry members. Factors conducive to cooperation include free and rapid interfirm communication, repetitive transactions, and the cultivated expectation that price cuts will be promptly countered.

34. See Stigler, "The Kinky Oligopoly Demand Curve," p. 436.

6 Conditions facilitating oligopolistic coordination

Our first approximation to a theory of oligopolistic pricing predicts a tendency toward the maximization of collective industry profits. Yet adoption of joint profit-maximizing policies is not automatic or easy, especially when industry members have diverse and conflicting opinions about the most favorable price structure. How do oligopolists arrive at mutually satisfactory prices for their products? What processes of coordination and communication operate to resolve conflicts? In this chapter we examine five important institutions facilitating oligopolistic coordination: overt and covert agreements, price leadership, rules of thumb, the use of focal points, and the buffering of demand shocks through inventory and order backlog adjustments.

Overt and covert agreements

Collusion to secure monopolistic prices and profits is a venerable, if not venerated, institution. It was practiced in ancient Babylon, Greece, and Rome. Adam Smith remarked sagely that "people of the same trade seldom meet together, even for merriment and diversion, but the conversation ends in a conspiracy against the public, or in some contrivance to raise prices." In the United States nearly every form of agreement, open or secret, to fix prices or restrict output is illegal; but

dozens of violations are prosecuted each year, and countless others go undetected. As one executive involved in the electrical equipment conspiracy of the 1950s observed, price fixing is "a way of life" for many American businesspeople.[1] Until recently, European laws were more tolerant of price-fixing arrangements, and as a result, cooperative activity on the Continent has been more visible to the naked eye. During the early 1930s, nearly all raw materials and semifinished goods production and at least a fourth of all finished goods manufacturing in Germany were covered by formal restrictive arrangements.[2] A government commission found 136 formal horizontal price-fixing cartels in force during 1953 in tiny Switzerland.[3] And despite a bias toward secrecy inspired by fear of antitrust prosecution under Article 85 of the European Economic Community treaty, firms doing business in the Common Market had by 1967 registered several hun-

---

1. R. A. Smith, "The Incredible Electrical Conspiracy," *Fortune*, May 1961, p. 224.
2. Fritz Voigt, "German Experience with Cartels and Their Control During Pre-War and Post-War Periods," in J. P. Miller, ed., *Competition, Cartels, and Their Regulation* (Amsterdam: North-Holland, 1962), p. 183.
3. Corwin D. Edwards, *Cartelization in Western Europe*, U.S., Department of State (Washington, D.C.: Government Printing Office, 1964), p. 3.

dred horizontal price-fixing cartels with the EEC Commission.

The variety of collusive pricing arrangements in industry is limited only by the bounds of human ingenuity. Some are casual and short lived, e.g., the spontaneous meetings called to terminate price wars. Others endure for decades, held together by an elaborate organizational web and binding written contracts. Here only the most important species can be identified.

Social gatherings are an occasion for one of the least structured, but not ineffective, forms of collusion. A well-known example was the Gary dinners held by Judge Elbert H. Gary, chairman of U.S. Steel's board of directors, during the early years of this century. Judge Gary once explained that the "close communication and contact" developed at these dinners generated such mutual "respect and affectionate regard" among steel industry leaders that all considered the obligation to cooperate and avoid destructive competition "more binding . . . than any written or verbal contract."[4] A modern variant is the trade association convention held in a resort hotel, where members who have been cutting prices are alternately browbeaten, plied with martinis, and cajoled until they promise to adopt a more gentlemanly stance in the future.

Informal gentlemen's agreements are also reached on a wide range of specific issues and practices. The best-known examples are, of course, agreements to set and abide by particular prices. If this is impractical, emphasis may be placed on securing mutual adherence to pricing formulas or lists of "representative" prices published by trade associations. When product lines are very complex, firms often find it advantageous to collude on specific product details and on the handling of extras. Until recently, for instance, American steel producers were fairly successful in abjuring price competition on standard products without resorting to formal collusion. But they found it far more difficult tacitly to coordinate prices for the virtually infinite gradations in finish, temper, gauge, packaging, and the like requested on special order by individual customers. As a result, company representatives held covert meetings to agree on uniform standards, specifications, interpretations, and charges for extras.[5] In the gypsum board industry, price-fixing agreements were supplemented by agreements to use only rail delivery and to charge uniform interest rates to customers granted extended credit.[6] Finally, business executives may meet in smoke-filled rooms to agree on output limitations, market shares, or specific geographic areas or product lines to be regarded as each firm's exclusive sphere of interest. Spheres of interest agreements have been especially popular among giant international chemical producers as a means of restricting competition.[7]

Nearly all these dimensions of collusion were present in the electrical equipment conspiracy of the 1950s.[8] It involved at least 29 different companies selling turbine generators, transformers, switchgear, insulators, industrial controls, condensers, and other electrical equipment with total sales of roughly $1.5 billion annually. Although agreements to limit competition had been a recurrent feature of the electrical industry since the 1880s, the schemes of the 1950s were given specific impetus when repeated episodes of price warfare proved incompatible with top management demands for higher profits. Several collusive systems evolved, each tailored to the peculiar features of the particular product line and selling method.

On standardized products such as insulators, standard transformers, and industrial controls, company representatives met and agreed upon prices each promised to quote in all subsequent transactions until an agreement to change was reached. This was by far the simplest arrangement, but it suffered from the disadvantage of arousing suspicions when all firms submitted identical bids in repeated transactions.[9] A more complex approach was required for products such as turbine generators, since each buyer demands modifications to suit its own special needs, and, as a result, two orders are seldom exactly alike. Collusion in this instance was facilitated by the publication of a pricing formula book half the size of a Sears Roebuck catalogue. By piecing together the prices of each component required to meet a buyer's generator specifications, firms were able to arrive at the book price on which discussions centered.

Some of the most elaborate procedures were

devised to handle switchgear pricing. As in the case of generators, book prices served as the initial departure point. Each seller agreed to quote book prices in sales to private buyers, and meetings were held regularly to compare calculations for forthcoming job quotations. Sealed-bid competitions sponsored by government agencies posed a different set of problems, and new methods were devised to handle them. Through protracted negotiation, each seller was assigned a specified share of all sealed-bid business, e.g., General Electric's share of the high voltage switchgear field was set at 40.3 percent in late 1958, and Allis-Chalmers's at 8.8 percent. Participants then coordinated their bidding so that each firm was low bidder in just enough transactions to gain its predetermined share of the market. In the power switching equipment line, this was achieved for a while by dividing the United States into four quadrants, assigning four sellers to each quadrant, and letting the sellers in a quadrant rotate their bids. A "phases of the moon" system was used to allocate low-bidding privileges in the high voltage switchgear field, with a new seller assuming low-bidding priority every two weeks. The designated bidder subtracted a specified percentage margin from the book price to capture orders during its phase, while others added various margins to the book price. The result was an ostensibly random pattern of quotations, conveying the impression of independent pricing behavior.

It seems indisputable that prices and profits were elevated substantially through the electrical equipment conspiracy when it operated successfully.[10] Yet durable success is by no means assured under informal restrictive arrangements. Indeed, the electrical equipment case illustrates vividly the fragility of nonbinding collusive agreements, for parties to the agreements of the 1950s "chiseled" repeatedly, touching off bitter price wars. As one General Electric executive explained his group's decision to go its own independent way in 1953, "No one was living up to the agreements and we . . . were being made suckers. On every job someone would cut our throat; we lost confidence in the group."[11]

Two problems underlie the tendency for informal price-fixing and output-restricting agreements to break down. First, the parties to the conspiracy may have divergent ideas about appropriate price levels and market shares, making it difficult to reach an understanding all will respect. Second, when the group agrees to fix and abide by a price approaching monopoly levels, strong incentives are created for individual members to chisel—that is, to increase their profits by undercutting the fixed price slightly, gaining additional orders at a price that still exceeds marginal cost. These two problems often interact, for parties dissatisfied with the original agreement may be especially prone to cheat in its subsequent execution.

The first of these difficulties has already been raised in the previous chapter. Hard bargaining lubricated by hard liquor cannot eliminate differences in firms' price and output preferences stemming from cost and market share disparities;

4. From a government antitrust brief cited in Fritz Machlup, *The Political Economy of Monopoly* (Baltimore: Johns Hopkins, 1952), p. 87. See also Donald O. Parsons and E. J. Ray, "The United States Steel Consolidation: The Creation of Market Control," *Journal of Law and Economics* 18 (April 1975): 208–12.

5. "Steel Gets Hit with the Big One," *Business Week*, 11 April 1964, pp. 27–28. Although the accused firms denied their guilt at the time, in July 1965 they pleaded 'no contest', which in a criminal antitrust case involving large firms is tantamount to an admission of guilt.

6. "Gypsum Trial Shows How Price-Fix Plan Supposedly Operated," *Wall Street Journal*, 3 October 1975, pp. 1, 16.

7. See G. W. Stocking and M. W. Watkins, *Cartels in Action* (New York: Twentieth Century Fund, 1946), Chapters 9–11.

8. See Smith, "The Incredible Electrical Conspiracy," *Fortune*, April and May, 1961; J. G. Fuller, *The Gentlemen Conspirators* (New York: Grove, 1962); and John Herling, *The Great Price Conspiracy* (Washington, D.C.: Luce, 1962).

9. On the tradeoff between the greater inflexibility of identical bidding arrangements versus higher coordination costs of bid rotation schemes, see William S. Comanor and Mark Schankerman, "Identical Bids and Cartel Behavior," *Bell Journal of Economics* 7 (Spring 1976): 281–86.

10. Dispute nevertheless exists. See especially Ralph G. M. Sultan, *Pricing in the Electrical Oligopoly*, vol. I (Boston: Harvard Business School Division of Research, 1974), Chapters 6 and 8.

11. Smith, "The Incredible Electrical Conspiracy," *Fortune*, April 1961, p. 172, quoting Clarence Burke. See also Allan T. Demaree, "How Judgment Came for the Plumbing Conspirators," *Fortune*, December 1969, pp. 97–98, observing that the conspirators had to meet repeatedly to reassure themselves and that, as one company official said, "we wouldn't trust each other outside the damn room."

it can only provide a favorable environment for compromise, if compromise is possible at all. Because price-fixing negotiations are usually conducted in secrecy, we have little evidence on the amount of internal stress encountered in establishing agreements. But there are indications that it is considerable. In the electrical equipment conspiracy, for example, there were conflicts over pricing policy between the high- and low-cost producers, and over market shares between the bigger firms and two smaller firms—one a new entrant. Both disputes were resolved only when General Electric and Westinghouse made concessions to save the agreement. In OPEC—without doubt the most lucrative cartel of modern history—sharp divisions of opinion complicated the process of setting crude oil price levels, and in 1976, they led to open disagreement.[12] One source of difficulty was a difference in time horizons. Heavily populated, underdeveloped nations such as Iran and Nigeria sought prices that would generate maximum short-term revenue to support their ambitious economic development programs, while Saudi Arabia, with a much smaller population and a surfeit of cash, was more concerned about long-run considerations. Differing estimates of the elasticity of demand for OPEC's oil also may have contributed. Saudi Arabia in particular appeared more sensitive to the stimulus high prices gave to discovery and use of non-OPEC energy resources and to the possibility that very high prices and their attend-

ant balance of payments dislocations impaired consuming nations' ability to maintain full employment, which in turn reduced the demand for oil.

Given the difficulty of agreeing, there is a tendency for price changes to be avoided once agreements are reached. Fear of upsetting group discipline led OPEC to forgo or delay several price increases advocated by some member states at ministerial meetings. In his study of six cartels operating legally under Danish laws, Bjarke Fog uncovered an extreme case in which a key product's price was left unchanged for a decade despite rising costs and disappearing profits.[13] Parties to the agreement were reluctant to suggest a price increase for fear of appearing weak to their confederates.

Once agreement has been reached, a different set of problems arises. The very act of fixing the price at a monopolistic level creates incentives for sellers to expand output beyond the quantity that will sustain the agreed-upon price. The essence of the matter is illustrated in Figure 6.1. Assume that the price is successfully raised from the competitive level OP_C, as shown in industry diagram (a), to OP_M. To sustain the increase, output must be cut from OQ_C to OQ_M. This leaves the typical party to the agreement in a situation characterized by panel (b). If it sells only a modest fraction of the total output, the individual seller may consider the collectively fixed price to be virtually parametric—that is,

F 6.1 Incentive to undercut a collusively set price

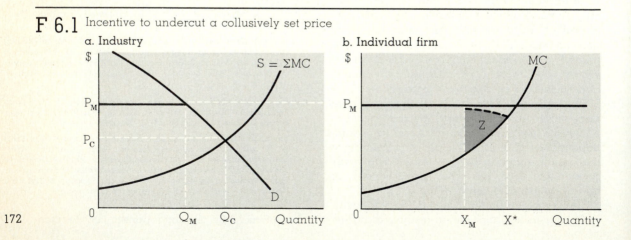

a. Industry

b. Individual firm

insensitive to its own output choices. With its output held at OX_M, its marginal cost is well below the fixed price, and so the firm is tempted to break with the agreement, quote a slightly lower price (broken line), and enjoy additional business $X_M X^*$ at chiseled prices. Its short-run profits are increased by the shaded triangular area Z in (b). Of course, if every seller were to behave in this manner, the industry price will descend from the agreed-upon monopoly value to the level of all producers' marginal cost, where no further incentive for output expansion remains. However shortsighted such undercutting may be, it has been known to topple many a price-fixing scheme.

An additional hazard, to be analyzed further in Chapter 8, is the lure a high price holds for new entrants. The added output contributed by such entrants either drives down the price immediately, or it forces parties to the original agreement to restrict their own outputs further in defending the price, and this in turn can evoke such dissatisfaction that the original members choose to abandon the agreement. In his study of German cartels, Fritz Voigt found that a combination of chiseling, bickering among insiders, and new entry from outside caused numerous price-fixing agreements to be short lived, breaking down after periods of operation as short as a few months.[14]

Despite these difficulties, we cannot conclude that explicit collusion is necessarily ineffective or unsuccessful. Notwithstanding predictions by economists that divisive forces and a 90 percent divergence between price and marginal cost would cause its early demise, OPEC provides a spectacular counterexample. An agreement successful for even a short period may yield monopoly profits sufficient to make the effort worth while. Furthermore, many business managers (and heads of oil-rich nations) are farsighted enough to recognize that their long-run interests are served best by maintaining industry discipline, and this may be enough to inhibit widespread chiseling. Finally, it is often possible (especially in nations with weak antitrust laws, or in international trade) to formalize restrictive agreements in such a way as to reduce greatly the incentives for cheating.

An approach particularly popular because of its effectiveness and compatibility with antitrust policies is the insertion of restrictive provisions into patent licenses. Several types of restriction are possible when one firm or (outside the United States) several firms jointly hold a strong patent position. First, the entry of new sellers can be blocked by refusal to grant licenses. Second, each licensee can be restricted to a specific geographic territory or segment of the market. Third, the price of the patented product can be specified as one of the license terms.[15] And fourth, direct or indirect output restrictions can be incorporated in the licensing agreement. A potent way of damping licensees' incentive to expand output by shading prices is to combine quota restrictions with punitive royalty provisions. For example, during the 1930s Westinghouse's license to use General Electric's incandescent lamp improvement patents stipulated a royalty of 2 percent for sales by Westinghouse up to 25.4421 percent of the two firms' combined sales, but the royalty rate increased to 30 percent for sales exceeding this quota.[16] Similarly, du Pont's moisture-proof cellophane patent license to Sylvania during the 1930s prescribed a punitive royalty rate of 30 percent or more for sales exceeding some predetermined share of the total cellophane market.[17]

When patent protection is lacking, output restrictions may be enforced through various other formal cartel agreements. One approach is the so-called compulsory cartel, under which a government agency imposes binding production and marketing restrictions upon individual firms. The

12. See the several relevant articles in the *New York Times*, 18 December 1976, and "The Implications of the New Oil Price Hike," *Business Week*, 10 January 1977, pp. 60–62. See also "Weaker OPEC Is Worried about Disunity over Prices," *New York Times*, 23 December 1977, p. D1.

13. Bjarke Fog, "How Are Cartel Prices Determined?," *Journal of Industrial Economics* 5 (November 1956): 16–23.

14. Voigt, "German Experience with Cartels," pp. 169–208.

15. Patent license restrictions, and particularly price restrictions, lie in a grey area of American antitrust law. See U.S., Attorney General, *Report of the Attorney General's National Committee to Study the Antitrust Laws* (Washington, D.C.: Government Printing Office, 1955), pp. 231–46.

first true modern cartels (dating back to the late 18th century) were of this type, and governments (including that of the United States) have over the years continued to encourage or sanction output restriction in some industries, particularly for raw materials such as petroleum, sugar, grain products, milk, citrus fruits, and coffee, and for services such as maritime shipping and other modes of transportation. If national laws permit, industry members may enter voluntarily into formal cartel agreements prescribing penalty payments when output quotas are exceeded. Excess production penalties were a prominent feature of the European steel and aluminum cartels following World War I.[18] As a third possibility, workweek limitations written into labor contracts through collective bargaining may be used as a means of restricting output. This approach was successful in the U.S. flat glass industry during the 1920s.[19] The United Mine Workers have been accused of similar attempts in the bituminous coal industry, although the evidence is disputed.[20]

A cartel tightens its control over member prices and outputs if it can require all members to distribute their output through a central industry sales bureau. During the depression of the 1930s, soft coal producers in the Appalachian Mountain region organized an exclusive selling agency with power to apportion sales and outputs among the 137 member firms.[21] European coal producers continue to distribute much of their output through government sales syndicates, and during the late 1960s West German steel makers sold through four privately owned syndicates.[22]

A variant of the central sales bureau method adapted for products purchased under "competitive" bidding is the so-called bidding or tender cartel. The U.S. electrical manufacturers' conspiracy possessed many attributes of a bidding cartel, although it lacked formal, binding agreements and organization. The Water-Tube Boilermakers' Association agreement approved in 1959 by the British antitrust authorities is typical of formally organized bidding cartels.[23] When bids for steam generating boilers were requested by some buyer (such as the nationalized Central Electricity Generating Board), each member firm submitted to the association director a confidential quotation of the price at which it was willing to fill the order. Using a formula that compared recent with historical shares of the market, the director nominated one firm to undertake the job. The firm nominated could then adjust its quotation downward to meet the lowest quotation, and when the revised bids were officially tendered to the buyer, the nominated firm was usually the winner. Since nomination to be low bidder depended upon the past allocation of orders rather than price, there was no incentive for member firms to undercut each other's price quotations.

The ultimate in overt agreement, short of merging all producers into a monopoly, is the rationalization cartel. Rationalization, or integrated planning of production, is profitable when cost functions differ from firm to firm, or when not all plants in the industry can operate at minimum average cost in producing the output that maximizes joint profits.[24] In the former case, profits can be increased by assigning to low-cost firms higher production quotas than high-cost firms. In the latter case it is profitable in the long run to

T 6.1 Profit implications of alternative market division and pricing schemes

	Firm 1's profits	Firm 2's profits	Joint profits
Each firm produces 1,800 units; price = $128 per unit	$112,000	$73,600	$185,600
Each firm produces 1,330 units; price = $147 per unit	$100,950	$86,667	$187,617
Rationalization, with Firm 1 producing 2,500 units and Firm 2 producing 750 units at a price of $135	$175,000	$40,000	$215,000

shut down some plants completely. Both points are illustrated by the example presented in Chapter 5, where Firm 1 is a low-cost producer and Firm 2 a high-cost producer. The outcomes of alternative price-output plans are reconstructed in Table 6.1. Joint profits are higher under a rationalization plan taking advantage of Firm 1's lower costs than they are when the two firms share the market equally, setting either of the prices preferred from their individual myopic viewpoints. Nevertheless, Firm 2 will not go along with the rationalization scheme unless a profit-pooling agreement is reached, for it would be better off under either equal-shares approach than it would be retaining the profits from selling only its own rationalized production. Yet Firm 1 would be well advised to encourage profit pooling, since it could transfer to Firm 2 as much as $63,000 of its profits under rationalization and still be as well off as under the equal-shares approach with its preferred price of $128. As a practical matter, a centralized sales bureau is normally required along with profit pooling to operate a rationalization cartel successfully.

Yet even when joint profits are increased through rationalization and profit pooling is feasible, it is by no means certain that high-cost firms will participate willingly. Agreeing to reduce one's output substantially, or to shut down altogether, has been likened to disarming.[25] One never knows whether firms producing most of the output under rationalization will take advantage of their position in the future, demanding a higher share of total profits. Maintaining production capabilities intact is a good bargaining counter against such demands. As a result, few cartels have gone very far toward the rationalization of production, even when profit pooling is accepted.[26] The elaborately organized ocean shipping cartels afford the most extreme example on which substantial information exists.[27] Even they, however, found their ability to maintain high prices undermined by the emergence of competition from nonmember Soviet Union ships.[28]

Despite their normally illegal status, there have been many price-fixing and other restrictive agreements in the United States. A fair amount of research has been devoted to analyzing the characteristics of agreements sufficiently transparent or careless to be detected and prosecuted successfully by the antitrust authorities. One prominent feature is the typically small number of sellers and the high degree of seller concentration in the relevant product or geographic market.[29] Evidently, agreement is easier to achieve

(16) See Stocking and Watkins, Cartels in Action, pp. 308–10; and H. C. Passer, The Electrical Manufacturers (Cambridge, Mass.: Harvard University Press, 1953), pp. 161–64.

(17) G. W. Stocking and W. F. Mueller, "The Cellophane Case and the New Competition," American Economic Review 45 (March 1955): 43.

18. G. W. Stocking and M. W. Watkins, Cartels or Competition? (New York: Twentieth Century Fund, 1948), pp. 185–86; and R. F. Lanzillotti, "The Aluminum Industry," in Walter Adams, ed., The Structure of American Industry, 3rd ed. (New York: Macmillan, 1961), p. 192. For an analysis of the statics and dynamics of quota systems, see Fritz Machlup, The Economics of Sellers' Competition (Baltimore: Johns Hopkins, 1952), pp. 482–88.

19. G. W. Stocking and M. W. Watkins, Monopoly and Free Enterprise (New York: Twentieth Century Fund, 1951), pp. 123–24.

20. For conflicting views, see Almarin Phillips, Market Structure, Organization and Performance (Cambridge, Mass.: Harvard University Press, 1962), p. 134; and Reed Moyer, Competition in the Midwestern Coal Industry (Cambridge, Mass.: Harvard University Press, 1964), pp. 162–64.

21. Phillips, Market Structure, pp. 125–32.

22. See Voigt, "German Experience with Cartels," p. 189; and Klaus Stegemann, Price Competition and Output Adjustment in the European Steel Market (Tübingen: Mohr, 1977), pp. 244–53.

23. In re Water-Tube Boilermakers' Agreement, L. R., 1 R. P. 285 (1959).

24. See Don Patinkin, "Multiple-Plant Firms, Cartels, and Imperfect Competition," Quarterly Journal of Economics 61 (February 1947): 173–205; and William Fellner, Competition Among the Few (New York: Knopf, 1949), pp. 191–97.

25. Fellner, Competition Among the Few, pp. 218–20, 232.

26. See John A. Howard, "Collusive Behavior," Journal of Business 27 (July 1954): 196–204, for an analysis of the degree to which rationalization was carried in certain British industries. An alternative explanation for the paucity of rationalization is that the benefits are modest, e.g., because cost conditions vary little from firm to firm, because long-run cost curves are flat (as suggested in Chapter 4), and because most firms in normal years run their plants at or near the level that minimizes average cost.

27. See B. M. Deakin and T. Seward, Shipping Conferences (Cambridge, England: Cambridge University Press, 1973); and (on the relevant theory, with applications to shipping cartels) Esra Bennathan and A. A. Walters, "Revenue Pooling and Cartels," Oxford Economic Papers 21 n.s. (July 1969): 159–76.

28. See "The Rate War with Russia," Business Week, 30 June 1975, pp. 111–12; and "Grabbing a Big Share of the Shipping Trade," Business Week, 12 January 1976, p. 46.

Conditions facilitating oligopolistic coordination   175

when the number of sellers is modest—e.g., ten or fewer, as Hay and Kelly found in 79 percent of the cases they studied. When a larger number of sellers were involved, a trade association or central sales agent commonly undertook the more complex task of coordinating the participants' behavior.[30] Homogeneity of products appeared more conducive to agreement than heterogeneity—e.g., associated either with product complexity or heavy advertising.[31] There is evidence that agreements occurred more frequently in slowly growing or stagnating markets with below-average profits, suggesting that dissatisfaction with profit levels may be an important spur to collusion.[32] However, a statistical study of price fixing before it was outlawed in the United Kingdom provides some reason to believe that *effective* agreements (and not all were) had a tendency to *raise* price-cost margins.[33]

To sum up, restrictive agreements are widespread, and they can assume numerous forms. Some approaches are more successful in yielding monopoly profits than others. None is completely free from the risk of breakdown. Yet their central tendency is quite clearly to elevate prices above the level that would be sustained under independent competitive conduct.

Price leadership

The paramount problem for firms trying to make the best of an oligopolistic market structure is to devise and maintain communication systems that permit behavior to be coordinated in the common interest. The conflicts that inevitably arise must be resolved without resorting to price warfare. Adjustments to changes in demand and cost conditions must be made so as to elicit unanimous consent and minimize the risk that actions taken in the group's interest will be misinterpreted as self-serving aggression. Collusion is communication par excellence, but it is generally illegal in the United States, and the tide of antitrust legislation is running against it in other industrialized nations. Business firms have an understandable desire to find alternative means of coordinating their behavior without running

afoul of the law. One such means (which lies in the grey area of American antitrust law) is price leadership.[34]

Price leadership implies a set of industry practices or customs under which list price changes are normally announced by a specific firm accepted as the leader by others, who follow the leader's initiatives. Wide variations are possible in the stability of the price leader's position, the reasons for its acceptance as leader, its influence over other firms, and its effectiveness in leading the industry to prices that maximize group profits. Economists commonly distinguish three main types of price leadership: dominant firm, collusive, and barometric.[35]

Dominant firm price leadership occurs when a single firm dominates an industry in the conventional sense of the word and is surrounded by a fringe of competitors, each too small to view itself as having a perceptible influence on the industry price. The dominant firm sets a price that best serves its own objectives, taking into account the anticipated supply reactions of fringe firms. The latter react as profit-maximizing pure competitors confronted with a parametric price. The dominant firm case entails no significant elements of oligopolistic interdependence, and so further analysis is best deferred to Chapter 8.

The concept of price leadership "in lieu of overt collusion" was formulated by Professor Markham to characterize the kind of leadership especially apt to support a monopolistic solution to oligopolists' pricing coordination problem. According to Markham, collusive price leadership is most likely to emerge when five conditions coexist: The industry is tightly oligopolistic, the sellers' products are close substitutes, the oligopolists' cost curves are similar, there are barriers to the entry of new competitors, and demand for the industry's output is relatively inelastic (so that price raising pays).[36]

Against collusive price leadership is juxtaposed the notion of barometric leadership, under which, as its name suggests, the price leader does no more than act as a barometer of market conditions, setting prices approximating those that would emerge in any event under competition. Distinguishing characteristics are said to include occasional changes in the identity of the price leader (who is likely in any case to be one of the largest sellers); the absence of leader power to coerce others into accepting its price; a tendency for the leader formally to validate price reductions that other sellers have already initiated through off-list concessions; upward leadership only when rising costs or demand warrant price hikes; and occasional lags in following, or outright rejection of, the leader's price initiatives.

In practice, it is difficult to categorize actual cases quite so neatly. This point is best seen by carefully considering how price leadership has operated in several important industries.

Cigarettes The cigarette industry during the 1920s and 1930s affords a classic example of price leadership used to establish a price structure that (barring miscalculations) tended to yield maximum collusive profits.[37] The Big Three, selling from 68 to 90 percent of industry output, mostly through their Camel, Lucky Strike, and Chesterfield brands, clearly recognized their mutual interdependence. The leading brands were quite similar physically; blindfold tests revealed that experienced smokers could not distinguish among them. There is no close substitute for cigarettes in the minds of most consumers, and so the cigarette manufacturers enjoyed considerable discretion in choosing an overall price level.

Between 1911 and 1921, conditions in the cigarette industry were unsettled owing to several radical changes: the dissolution of the old Tobacco Trust in an antitrust action, the introduction of new tobacco blends, and the initiation of nationwide advertising campaigns. In 1918 American Tobacco tried to lead a price rise, but Reynolds (the largest seller) refused to follow. In 1921, American cut its price and Reynolds retaliated with a further cut, which American and the other sellers matched. This experience apparently had a profound educational impact on American and the other major brand sellers, none of whom challenged Reynolds's leadership again for a decade. Between 1923 and 1941, virtual price identity prevailed continuously among the Big Three's standard brands, although certain other cigarettes of similar size and quality sold in smaller quantities at premium prices, and premium-priced Philip Morris grew through heavy

advertising to a 6 percent market share. During this period there were eight standard brand list price changes. Reynolds led six of them, five upward and one downward, and was followed each time, in most cases within 24 hours of its

29. See George A. Hay and Daniel Kelley, "An Empirical Survey of Price Fixing Conspiracies," *Journal of Law and Economics* 17 (April 1974): 13–38; and Arthur G. Fraas and Douglas F. Greer, "Market Structure and Price Collusion: An Empirical Analysis," *Journal of Industrial Economics* 26 (September 1977): 29–33. Compare Peter Asch and Joseph J. Seneca, "Characteristics of Collusive Firms," *Journal of Industrial Economics* 23 (March 1975): 233–35; and James M. Clabault and John F. Burton, Jr., *Sherman Act Indictments: 1955–65* (New York: Federal Legal Publications, 1966), pp. 138–41.

30. Hay and Kelley, "An Empirical Survey," p. 21; and Fraas and Greer, "Market Structure and Price Collusion," pp. 32–39.

31. Hay and Kelley, "An Empirical Survey," pp. 24–25; and Asch and Seneca, "Characteristics," pp. 230–36.

32. Asch and Seneca, "Characteristics," pp. 227–36; *idem*, "Is Collusion Profitable?," *Review of Economics and Statistics* 58 (February 1976): 1–10; and John Palmer, "Some Economic Conditions Conducive to Collusion," *Journal of Economic Issues* 6 (June 1972): 29–38.

33. Almarin Phillips, "An Econometric Study of Price-Fixing, Market Structure and Performance in British Industry in the Early 1950s," in Keith Cowling, ed., *Market Structure and Corporate Behaviour* (London: Gray-Mills, 1972), pp. 177–92.

34. As the legal counsel for the Plumbing Fixture Manufacturers Association is said to have exclaimed after learning of illegal collusion by its members, "I think the industry is stupid. . . . If they only had price leadership, . . . which they don't have . . . that isn't violative of anything." Demaree, "How Judgment Came," p. 170. See also John Q. Lawyer (pseudonym), "How To Conspire To Fix Prices," *Harvard Business Review* 41 (March–April 1963): 97.

35. This schema was proposed by Jesse W. Markham, expanding on an earlier proposal by George J. Stigler. See Stigler, "The Kinky Oligopoly Demand Curve and Rigid Prices," *Journal of Political Economy* 55 (October 1947): 444–46; and Markham, "The Nature and Significance of Price Leadership," *American Economic Review* 41 (December 1951): 891–905. For critical comments, see Alfred Oxenfeldt, "Professor Markham on Price Leadership," *American Economic Review* 42 (June 1952): 380–84; R. F. Lanzillotti, "Competitive Price Leadership: A Critique of Price Leadership Models," *Review of Economics and Statistics* 39 (February 1957): 56–64; and Joe S. Bain, "Price Leaders, Barometers, and Kinks," *Journal of Business* 33 (July 1960): 193–203.

36. Markham "The Nature and Significance of Price Leadership," pp. 901–903.

37. Markham, "The Nature and Significance of Price Leadership," pp. 903–905; William Nicholls, *Price Policies in the Cigarette Industry* (Nashville: Vanderbilt University Press, 1951); and R. B. Tennant, "The Cigarette Industry," in Adams, *The Structure of American Industry*, 3rd ed., pp. 357–92.

Conditions facilitating oligopolistic coordination   177

announcement. The other two changes were downward revisions during 1933 led by American and followed by the other standard brand vendors. American also attempted to lead a price increase in 1941, but Reynolds again refused to follow and the change was rescinded. Throughout this period, the return on invested capital realized by Reynolds, American, and Liggett & Myers averaged 18 percent after taxes—roughly double the rate earned by American manufacturing industry as a whole.

The 1933 departures from Reynolds's leadership illustrate further the high degree of coordination displayed by the Big Three. Even the most astute price leaders make mistakes, and Reynolds made one in 1931. In June, as cigarette consumption was declining because of widespread unemployment and as leaf tobacco prices reached their lowest level since 1905, Reynolds announced an increase in the net wholesale price of Camels from $5.64 to $6.04 per thousand, or $.1208 per pack—ostensibly to generate revenue for the promotion of its new moisture-proof cellophane package. The other leading producers followed immediately—American, allegedly, because it saw "the opportunity to make some money" and Liggett & Myers because its officers concluded that "safety lay in imitation."[38] But this increase, combined with the dire financial straits in which many cigarette smokers found themselves, opened up significant market penetration possibilities for firms selling cigarettes of inferior quality. With the standard brands selling at retail prices of up to $.15 per pack, these so-called ten-cent brands increased their share of the market from 1 percent in early 1931 to 23 percent in late 1932. In response, American cut its Lucky Strikes price from $6.04 to $5.29 per thousand in January 1933, and then to $4.85 per thousand (after wholesale discounts) in February 1933. Reynolds and Liggett followed immediately, this time without undercutting.[39] At the same time the Big Three pressured retailers to keep the price differential between standard brands and the ten-cent brands below three cents, and in some chain outlets the price of standard brands fell to ten cents per pack. The counterattack against the intruding ten-cent brands was largely successful; their share of the market dropped from 23 percent

in November 1932 to 6 percent in May 1933. Having recovered much of the lost ground, American and Liggett followed Reynolds's increase to $5.38 per thousand in January 1934.

Following World War II the pattern changed. Efforts by the smaller firms to lead price increases were rebuffed. But American Tobacco successfully led several increases, in part because it briefly moved into first place in total cigarette sales and in part because the cigarette brand structure became much more complex. For an appreciable period American had the highest sales volume in nonfilter cigarettes and also exercised price leadership there. Reynolds meanwhile led in the price adjustments on filter tips, where most of its volume was concentrated. Then American's market share fell and Philip Morris moved ahead aggressively, asserting price leadership successfully from second place in overall sales soon after its Marlboro brand became the world's best-selling cigarette.[40]

Despite these changes in leadership roles and the proliferation of differentially priced king size, extra long, mentholated, and low-tar brands, there was little indication of intensified price rivalry among the cigarette makers; [41] and profits remained well above all-manufacturing averages notwithstanding stagnant demand.

Steel Largely because of the United States Steel Corporation's initially commanding market share and the cooperative attitudes cultivated at the Gary dinners, a tradition of lock-step followership behind U.S. Steel's price leadership developed during the 1900s. Despite occasional limited *sub rosa* shading from list prices, the industry's pricing discipline for the next half century was little short of remarkable.[42] The first signs of change began to appear in 1958. Even though a recession had reduced the industry to a 61 percent capacity utilization rate, industrywide wage increases precipitated a clamor for higher prices. U.S. Steel, under attack from a congressional committee for inflationary wage and price behavior, failed to exercise the expected leadership. Eventually Armco, with roughly 4.4 percent of industry capacity, announced an increase, which was followed by U.S. Steel and the rest of the industry. For nearly four years no further general list price changes were attempted. Then, in 1962, U.S. Steel's announcement of a list price increase averaging $6 per ton drew withering criticism from President Kennedy and was rescinded. This experience apparently dampened U.S. Steel's zeal for bearing the onus of price leadership. The following year, price increases were announced on a product-by-product (as opposed to across-the-board) basis in numerous product lines by several smaller producers. The typical reaction of U.S. Steel was to follow with a slightly smaller increase in its own list prices, causing the original leaders to revise their quotations downward and fall into line. Price revisions through 1968 continued to be made on a piecemeal basis, with the initiative coming from several different companies. When U.S. Steel did exercise leadership, it announced cuts mixed with increases, displaying a "new diplomacy" that contrasted vividly with the "bludgeon" approach employed up to 1962.[43]

With price leadership being passed from hand to hand and with price changes announced almost monthly in some product line, the danger of coordination breakdowns grew. By 1968 the strains could no longer be suppressed. Lacking strong leadership and under mounting pressure from imports, which had captured nearly 20 percent of the American market, steel producers began to engage in increasingly widespread *sub rosa* price cutting. This was not unprecedented, but another development was. As its domestic market share fell to an all-time low of 21 percent, U.S. Steel abandoned its traditional policy of holding list prices inviolate and joined the 'chiselers,' offering substantial secret concessions to a number of buyers. The once-rigid steel price structure began to crumble.

These developments led headlong into one of the most fascinating episodes in steel industry history.[44] On November 4, 1968, Bethlehem Steel announced a 22 percent cut in the list price of hot-rolled steel sheets, from $113.50 per ton (excluding extra charges) to $88.50 per ton. Its action, covering a product line accounting for 11 percent of total industry output, was evidently provoked by an under-the-counter offer U.S. Steel made to a major Bethlehem customer. In its announcement, Bethlehem asserted that the reduc-

tion was effected "in spite of rising costs to meet current domestic competition." "Prices should go up, not down," the statement continued, but "Bethlehem must be competitive." Within three days all significant producers had joined in the decrease. Three weeks later U.S. Steel in effect sued for peace, quoting a new price of $125 per ton for fully processed hot-rolled steel sheet and simultaneously creating a new semifinished product category, hot-rolled bands, to be priced at $110 per ton.[45] Bethlehem, however, waited nine days before responding. On December 6 it matched U.S. Steel's hot-rolled band price but raised its fully processed product price to only $117 per ton. A week later U.S. Steel revised its price schedules to match the lower response. In February of 1969 Bethlehem then led an increase in prices to $124 per ton for hot-rolled bands and

38. Nicholls, *Price Policies*, pp. 84–85.

39. There is some evidence that outright collusion occurred at this point. The night before American's second price announcement, the A&P Company's national headquarters telegraphed its 15,000 stores to reduce prices of *all* standard brands to ten cents per pack. In subsequent court testimony, A&P officials denied receiving advance notice from the several rival firms, but said their action was based upon "trade rumors." Nicholls, *Price Policies*, pp. 119–20.

40. "Marketing Observer," *Business Week*, 24 February 1973, p. 48.

41. For the closest thing to a possible exception, see "Cigarette Producers Dabble in Dual Pricing," *Business Week*, 29 March 1976, p. 33.

42. See Leonard W. Weiss, *Economics and American Industry* (New York: Wiley, 1961), pp. 293–99; and George J. Stigler and James K. Kindahl, *The Behavior of Industrial Prices* (New York: Columbia University Press, 1970), pp. 71–74.

43. See "U.S. Steel Lifts Prices on Most Types of Plate But Also Trims Quotes on Some Other Items," *Business Week*, 5 March 1966, p. 44; "Did Prices Rise? Steel Users Ask," *New York Times*, 2 September 1965; "Steel Price Step a 3-Prong Attack," *New York Times*, 17 October 1965, Section 3; "U.S. Steel Proves It's the Leader," *Business Week*, 16 December 1967, p. 34; and "Calling the Shots on Steel Prices," *Business Week*, 10 August 1968, pp. 26–27.

44. Accounts of key developments include "Bethlehem Cuts Major Price 22%," *New York Times*, 5 November 1968, p. 67; "Steel Industry Hit By Major Price Cut," *Business Week*, 9 November 1968, p. 35; "U.S. Steel Moves To End Price War," *New York Times*, 28 November 1968, p. 75; "New Split Opens in Steel Pricing," *New York Times*, 7 December 1968, p. 73; "Revolution in Steel Pricing?," *Business Week*, 14 December 1968, p. 41; "Bethlehem Cuts Steel Sheet List," *New York Times*, 5 February 1969, p. 47; and "Steel Heads Up Again," *Business Week*, 8 February 1969, p. 27.

45. The $125.00 price is not directly comparable with the earlier $113.50 price because it included some elements that had previously been priced as "extras." According to the U.S. Steel announcement, the new $125.00 price approximately restored the *status quo ante bellum*.

$129 per ton (or after adjustment for extra charge changes, $125) for fully processed sheets. The price war was over. Bethlehem had communicated its message in the most vivid possible terms, and, at least temporarily, it apparently achieved its intended goal of restoring industry discipline.

During the ensuing decade, the leadership role continued to rotate among industry members, some of them small. A United States Steel price initiative was openly rebuffed on one occasion.[46] Bethlehem, the number two producer, attempted repeatedly to act as a disciplinarian when others deviated quietly from the industry price line.[47] But its efforts were at best only partly successful. *Sub rosa* chiseling was widespread in times of excess capacity and sharp import competition. Steel industry profit returns dropped well below the all-manufacturing average. The old order had changed. What was once a clear example of collusive price leadership had evolved into something more closely matching the barometric model.

This does not mean that the steel industry's price leaders had no impact. Indeed, it seems undeniable that in the absence of what leadership there was, steel prices in the United States, instead of rising, would have fallen sharply between 1974 and 1978, as they did elsewhere in depressed world steel markets.[48]

To make the best of a difficult price-setting situation, the American steel manufacturers have followed several time-tested rules. First, an oligopolist anxious to exercise price leadership will not announce list price changes too frequently. Each move carries a risk that the change will be misinterpreted or opposed, with the further risk of a breakdown in industry discipline. Most oligopolists, including the steel makers, appear willing to forgo the modest gains associated with micrometer-like adjustment of prices to fleeting changes in demand and costs in order to avoid the risk of more serious losses from poorly coordinated pricing policies and price warfare. Second, the leader will announce price changes only in response to changes in cost and demand recognized throughout the industry. Thus, steel price increases have tended to coincide with industrywide wage or energy cost increases, while list price cuts were made in response to particularly potent import threats or significant *sub rosa* price shading. Third, the leader will prepare other firms for its announcement by directing public attention to the changed demand or cost conditions through executive speeches, interviews with trade publications, and the like. The steel industry's use of this technique prior to its 1958 price rise prompted one government official to suggest that a new form of "conspiracy through newspaper announcements" was under way.[49] And fourth, price increases will be announced effective only at some later date, so there is time to rescind the announcement before actual price differentials emerge if others fail to follow suit.

Automobiles Special timing problems affect the working of price leadership in the automobile industry. An important occasion for list price changes is the day on which new models are introduced. General Motors has been the price leader since World War II, but production scheduling considerations often require the other producers to announce their new models and hence their prices before GM does. They then try hard to anticipate GM's decisions and set their prices accordingly, but if GM's subsequent announcement brings surprises, they beat a hasty retreat, raising or lowering their prices into the desired relationship with those of General Motors.[50]

In his seminal article on price leadership, Professor Markham argues that when oligopolists' products are not homogeneous, multiple pricing policies will be pursued and price leadership may even be meaningless.[51] He cites the automobile industry as an example of individualistic pricing owing to product differentiation. This characterization has certainly not been valid since the 1950s, for price leadership-followership has been an unmistakable feature of the leading U.S. auto makers' conduct. Although auto models differ greatly, each company aims specific models toward particular market segments, and each GM rival knows how its models relate to those of GM and therefore how they must be priced. A statistical analysis reveals that the prices quoted by different producers for models of comparable performance and interior space

180

have been quite similar.[52] What product differentiation does is permit modest price differentials to exist without inducing drastic market share shifts. Thus, during the late 1960s, Ford charged $10 to $20 more than Chevrolet for comparable full-sized models and Plymouth $40 to $50 more.[53] Smaller independents such as American Motors experienced considerably greater latitude, e.g., to reduce prices by as much as $200 relative to General Motors models without evoking retaliation.[54] Reductions of similar magnitude on poorly selling Chrysler models were also tolerated. However, when Chrysler offered substantial rebates to combat an industrywide 1975 model year sales slump, Ford and General Motors quickly retaliated in order to protect their market shares.[55] Such deviations from the pattern, it must be stressed, are exceptional; normally, adherence to General Motors' price leadership in autos has been close.

Ready-to-eat-cereals Further evidence on the character of price leadership in industries with differentiated products can be found in the ready-to-eat breakfast cereal industry.[56] Some products, such as the corn flakes and raisin brans of Kellogg and Post, were recognized by many if not most consumers to be close substitutes; and a retail price differential of one or two cents per package could lead quickly to appreciable market share shifts. Consequently, both price changes and package size changes were matched rapidly, and virtual price identity per ounce was the rule. But cereals come in many grain bases, shapes, and flavors, and such children's cereals as Trix and Froot Loops or nutritional cereals like Product 19 and Total could be priced several cents apart on comparable packages before a significant movement toward the lower priced brand became evident. This, plus the fact that certain other cereals such as Grape Nuts and Life were fairly unique, gave the cereal makers a band of discretion within which they could vary prices without experiencing much volume change. Also, cereal consumers react more slowly to price signals than, say, steel or automobile buyers, for whom the stakes are sufficiently high on any single transaction that careful price shopping is stimulated. This meant that failure to match a rival's price increase immediately was seldom a serious threat to the rival.

Nevertheless, the Big Three (controlling 80 percent of total ready-to-eat cereal sales in 1975) were also acutely aware that if one firm raised prices above those of similar rival products by more than some discernible amount—usually by more than three or four cents per package—it moved into a "trouble area" or even "greatly weakened its efforts" to maintain volume.[57] Between 1962 and 1970, the Big Three increased their average wholesale prices per pound by 14 cents—much more than the differential any single company could sustain through individual pricing action. Price leadership facilitated the joint movement to higher prices.

46. "Steel Price-Rise Cancellation: Fight for Orders Called Cause," *New York Times*, 4 September 1976, p. 25.

47. See "Dr. Bethlehem's New Steel Formula," *Business Week*, 15 November 1969, p. 39; "Bethlehem Steel's New Price Gambit," 9 May 1970, p. 21; "Steel Rift Caused Price-Rise Delay," *New York Times*, 13 August 1971, p. 1; and "A Hold on Steel Prices," *Business Week*, 4 November 1972, p. 33.

48. See U.S., Council on Wage and Price Stability report, *Prices and Costs in the United States Steel Industry* (Washington, D.C.: Government Printing Office, October 1977), Chapters II and III; and Federal Trade Commission staff report, *The United States Steel Industry and Its International Rivals* (Washington, D.C.: Government Printing Office, November 1977), Chapter 4.

49. *Washington Post*, 24 February 1963, p. E-1, quoting Victor R. Hansen's testimony before the Kefauver committee.

50. See Lawrence J. White, *The Automobile Industry Since 1945* (Cambridge, Mass.: Harvard University Press, 1971), pp. 109–16, 126–33; and "Detroit's Dilemma on Prices," *Business Week*, 20 January 1975, p. 82.

51. Markham, "The Nature and Significance of Price Leadership," p. 902.

52. Stanley E. Boyle and Thomas F. Hogarty, "Pricing Behavior in the American Automobile Industry, 1957–71," *Journal of Industrial Economics* 24 (December 1975): 81–95.

53. White, *The Automobile Industry*, p. 115.

54. "Rambler Takes a Gamble," *Business Week*, 25 February 1967, p. 39.

55. See "GM Also To Offer Rebates up to $500 on Smaller Models," *Washington Post*, 21 January 1975, p. D-1; and "Auto Rebates: A Financial Disaster for Detroit," *Business Week*, 10 March 1975, pp. 72–73.

56. This analysis is based upon the author's testimony in the Federal Trade Commission's antitrust case, *in re Kellogg Co. et al.*, Docket 8883, especially transcript pp. 27,799–925.

57. From a 1967 General Mills pricing analysis included in the cereal antitrust case record as CX-GM-278.

Conditions facilitating oligopolistic coordination   181

Kellogg was recognized by all as the leader. It normally led increases in rounds covering many but not all the products in its line.[58] Out of 15 unambiguous price increase rounds between 1965 and 1970, Kellogg led 12. It was followed nine times by General Mills and ten times by Post; on only one occasion did neither of the two follow. The median lag between the effective date of Kellogg's price increases and those of General Mills and Post was 22 days. General Mills led once and was followed by the other Big Three members; General Foods led twice and was followed once. Quaker, the fourth largest seller, with a 5 to 7 percent market share, tended to pursue a more independent policy, seldom following Kellogg's lead directly but paying close attention to the relationship of its own prices to those of the Big Three. Unlike cigarettes, steel, and automobiles, the price leader in cereals rarely rescinded its price increase when others failed to follow. Rather, it relied upon its product differentiation to prevent a sudden loss of business, hoped for (and waited until) parity was restored in a subsequent round, and in certain cases intensified its promotional activity to compensate for its high price disadvantage. When General Mills or Post failed to follow Kellogg on some round, they tended to make up for the failure by raising prices on a disproportionate share of their product line in a subsequent round. During the 1960s, General Mills also utilized the discretion product differentiation afforded by moving from a price position somewhat lower than Kellogg's early in the decade to a premium price position by the late '60s. Its internal decision-making memoranda reveal an acute sensitivity as to how far it could push without endangering its market position. All in all, the price leadership pattern in cereals exhibited more flexibility than in well-disciplined industries with more homogeneous products. Yet leadership was sufficiently robust to permit price increases in times of both booming and stagnant demand; and the *sub rosa* price-shading characteristic of barometric leadership was totally absent. In internal memoranda, the Big Three placed considerable stress on the importance of their price leadership institutions. It seems virtually certain that leadership contributed to the coordination of their pricing behavior, permitting *inter alia* ex-

traordinarily high price-manufacturing cost margins and an average 1958–70 profit return on assets roughly twice that for all manufacturing corporations.

Turbogenerators The U.S. turbogenerator industry illustrates a quite different approach to reconciling product heterogeneity and the use of price leadership.[59] In May 1963, two and one-half years after it was convicted for illegal price fixing, General Electric announced a new pricing policy for turbine generators.[60] One facet of the policy was the publication of a new and more simplified pricing book that permitted rival Westinghouse rather easily to compute the "book" price of any generator on which the two firms might be asked to bid. GE also announced a standard multiplier it would apply to the book price on each bid, and it communicated its intent not to deviate from the standard 'book price times announced multiplier' procedure in bidding. The multiplier itself varied over time, but changes were publicly announced by General Electric. Consequently, what might otherwise have been a very complex coordination problem was reduced to a matter of Westinghouse's knowing how to calculate the so-called book price and following GE's price leadership with respect to the multiplier.

During the first year after this policy was implemented, Westinghouse evidently misinterpreted how book prices were to be computed, causing General Electric to suspect deliberate price cutting and in retaliation to reduce its price multiplier. But within two months after the GE reduction, Westinghouse realigned its prices to the earlier GE multiplier. After GE followed suit, the two companies are said to have applied identical multipliers to identical book prices on their turbogenerator bids for the next 12 years—until the practices were challenged by federal antitrust authorities. In sharp contrast to the history of the 1950s and early 1960s, GE and Westinghouse effected *no* generator price decreases during this period. General Electric led a number of increases, with Westinghouse typically following by announcing an identical multiplier increase within four days (although on one occasion the lag was three months). Thus, by linking price leadership to a simplification of the methods for computing bid prices, General Electric successfully avoided the pricing coordination breakdowns that had materialized even with outright collusion in earlier periods.

Gasoline Unusually complete information is available on the pricing of gasoline in Ohio during the 1950s. There, the Standard Oil Company of Ohio was said to be a classic barometric price leader. Especially for price decreases, a barometric leader often merely formalizes through list price announcements changes that have already permeated the market through informal departures from the list price. As an executive of Sohio described the price adjustment process in his territory:

> The major sales executives of all companies watch carefully the number and size of subnormal markets. . . . If the number of local price cuts increases, if the number and amount of secret concessions to commercial consumers increase, if the secret unpublicized concessions to dealers increase, it becomes more and more difficult to maintain the higher prices. . . . Finally, some company, usually the largest marketer in the territory, recognizes that the subnormal price has become the normal price and announces a general price reduction throughout the territory.[61]

For list price increases, the barometric leader must exercise a higher degree of initiative. This is brought out clearly in another Standard Oil of Ohio statement:

> On the other hand, in our own interest we must usually take the lead in attempting higher price levels when we believe that conditions will permit. Having a substantial distribution in our market we are confronted with the fact that few marketers, especially those with a lesser consumer acceptance, can take the lead in increasing prices.[62]

The same statement emphasizes that such initiatives may be rejected by the rest of the industry:

> Upward moves in our market are made by us only when, in our opinion, general prices and the economic pressure from industry costs are such that our competitors in their own interest

will follow. It is notorious that when we guess wrong, or when we advance our market too far, immediate market disintegration sets in.

The interpretation given these leadership patterns—lowering the list price when market conditions are depressed, while raising it successfully only when demand and cost conditions support the higher level—is that the leader merely acts as a barometer of market conditions, and not as an instrument of collusion. As Professor Stigler put it, the barometric firm "commands adherence of rivals to his price only because, and to the extent that, his price reflects market conditions with tolerable promptness."[63]

Evaluation It should be clear from these examples that simple distinctions between barometric and collusive price leadership are not easily drawn. Of the cases examined, gasoline pricing in Ohio and steel pricing after 1965 conform most closely to the barometric model. But although more than one economist has earned a high consulting fee by doing so, it would be misleading to conclude that any leadership pattern displaying barometric characteristics is benign. Consider first the matter of price increases. The price an industry can sustain obviously depends

58. There were very few clear-cut list price decreases. Of 1,122 list price changes between 1950 and 1972 uncomplicated by package or case size changes, only 17 were price decreases.

59. This account is drawn from the complaint in *Appalachian Power Co. et al.* v. *General Electric Co. et al.*, S. D. New York, December 29, 1971; and from the "Plaintiff's Memorandum in Support of a Proposed Modification to the Final Judgment" in *U.S.* v. *General Electric Co. et al.*, Civil No. 28, 228, E. D. Pennsylvania, December 1976. See also Bruce T. Allen, "Tacit Collusion and Market Sharing: The Case of Steam Turbine Generators," *Industrial Organization Review* 4, No. 4 (1976): 48–57.

60. See Chapter 5, pp. 163–64 *supra* for another important component of the new policy.

61. Statement of S. A. Swensrud, quoted by Stigler in "The Kinky Oligopoly Demand Curve," *Journal of Political Economy* 19 (August 1947): 445. Copyright 1947 by the University of Chicago Press.

62. Edmund P. Learned and Catherine C. Ellsworth, *Gasoline Pricing in Ohio* (Boston: Harvard Business School Division of Research, 1959), p. 25, quoting a company policy statement. See also pp. 42, 83 of the same volume.

63. Stigler, "The Kinky Oligopoly Demand Curve," pp. 445–46.

upon market conditions, as suggested in the theory of barometric leadership. But under given supply and demand conditions, alternative institutional arrangements may lead to different price levels. And here the institution of price leadership can be important. As the Standard Oil of Ohio statement quoted previously indicates, even when market conditions are firm, producers with weak market positions might be unable to increase price successfully. An accepted price leader like Sohio can lead the way to prices higher than those attainable if no such firm existed. This price may not be *much* higher, but there is no guarantee that it will not exceed the competitive level by at least a small amount on the average.

Consider too the classic symptom of barometric price leadership: when the price leader reduces its list price only because *sub rosa* departures from the list price are widespread. This is also not necessarily harmless. By making a dramatic list price cut, the price leader can often restore industry discipline and discourage further price cutting. It achieves this result in two ways: by providing a rallying point at which prices can be held, and by raising the implicit threat that further off-list pricing will incite additional list price reductions, constraining even more the opportunities for profitable operation. The latter was no doubt what Bethlehem had in mind with its hot-rolled steel price cut of 1968. If it failed, the failure must be attributed not to the type of leadership exercised, but to underlying structural conditions—i.e., in that particular instance, to the difficulty of holding prices much above those at which numerous foreign steel producers stood willing to sell. This appears to be true more generally for companies described as barometric price leaders. Professor Learned, for example, observed that if Standard Oil of Ohio "had thought it could reasonably get more it would have tried to do so."[64] We are led to conclude that the intent of ostensibly barometric price leadership may be identical to the intent of collusive price leadership: maximization of joint industry profits. What varies is the success the leader has in achieving that goal, which depends in turn upon seller concentration, the height of entry barriers, and a variety of other

conditions to be examined further in Chapters 7 and 8.

In sum, the effect of both collusive and barometric price leadership in oligopoly tends to be the establishment of prices higher than they would otherwise be, other things being held equal. This effect is achieved by sending to other members of the industry clear signals that indicate the way toward the profit-maximizing price in good times and serve as a rallying point in depressed times. Only two important exceptions need to be noted. First, when a price leader in a concentrated industry has lower unit costs than its principal rivals, as is probably true with respect to General Motors in the automobile industry, it may hold the price below levels desired by other sellers. And second, strong price leaders may occasionally resist raising prices to the short-run profit-maximizing level during a boom, partly because long-run profits might be reduced by exploiting temporary conditions to the utmost and partly as an act of economic statesmanship, e.g., to cooperate with the government in combatting inflation.[65] Taking this latter qualification into account, we find that price leadership tends both to increase prices on the average and to reduce the magnitude of price fluctuations.

Price leadership also has implications for the kinked demand curve theory. For a firm whose leadership role is solidly established, the kink is eliminated, since the leader can expect its rivals to follow price increases as well as decreases. The kink remains, however, for sellers (like Liggett & Myers) whose price increase initiatives are consistently rebuffed. They cannot expect to be followed upward, although they can usually expect their price cuts sooner or later to be matched. Finally, for barometric firms whose leadership is sometimes rejected, the kinked demand curve theory becomes an uncertain engine of analysis.

Rule-of-thumb pricing as a coordinating device

Another means of maintaining industry discipline when prices are set or changed is the use of pricing rules of thumb. These typically involve some variant of the full-cost or cost-plus pricing principle, in which a "normal" or desired profit margin or percentage return on invested capital is added to estimated unit costs to calculate the product price. If all firms in an industry have similar costs and adhere to similar full-cost formulas—or if a price leader uses the formula and other sellers accept its leadership—then price cutting below full-cost levels is minimized, the behavior of rivals becomes more predictable than it otherwise would be, and efficient producers are virtually assured of realizing at least "normal" profits.

Business enterprises have apparently been using pricing rules of thumb for a long time, but the concept did not penetrate the mainstream of economic analysis until it was discovered (along with the kinked demand curve) by R. L. Hall and Charles J. Hitch through an interview survey of pricing practices in 38 British firms.[66] Since then an enormous literature on the subject has appeared.[67]

Hall and Hitch and later analysts found several reasons why business managers use cost-based rules of thumb in their pricing decisions. For one, it is a way of coping with (essentially by ignoring) uncertainties in the estimation of demand function shapes and elasticities. Second, many businesspeople defend the practice on typically vague grounds of fairness. Under closer scrutiny, this explanation appears sometimes to reflect the belief that a firm's long-run position will be jeopardized by charging too high a price in the short run, and sometimes the belief that all firms in an oligopolistic market benefit if each refrains from charging prices providing less than a fair margin of profit over cost. Third, calculation and posting of prices are costly, especially for companies selling hundreds or thousands of different products with considerable flux in the items supplied. Adopting rules of thumb greatly simplifies the pricing problem in such businesses, of which department stores, automobile repair shops, and metal-working job shops are representative.

All sorts of full-cost pricing rules are encountered. Here two examples must suffice. In the retail trades, a conventional pricing approach is to seek some standard percentage margin—e.g., 40 percent—of price less cost over price. Knowing the wholesale cost W of an item, the indicated price is simply $W/(1 - .4)$. The 40 percent margin in this case is not pure profit, since all selling and overhead expenses must be covered by the total margin realized from selling a vast array of items priced this way.

A quite different, well-known full-cost pricing rule is the technique used with evident success by General Motors for more than 50 years.[68] GM is said to begin its pricing analysis with an objective of earning, on the average over the years, a return of approximately 15 percent after taxes on total invested capital.[69] Since it does not know how many autos will be sold in a forthcoming year, and hence what the average cost per unit (including prorated fixed costs) will be, it calculates costs on the assumption of *standard volume*—that is, operation at 80 percent of conservatively rated capacity. A *standard price* is next calculated by adding to average cost per unit at standard volume a sufficient profit margin

64. Learned, *Gasoline Pricing in Ohio*, p. 158.

65. See for example A. D. H. Kaplan, Joel B. Dirlam, and R. F. Lanzillotti, *Pricing in Big Business: A Case Approach* (Washington, D.C.: Brookings Institution, 1958), p. 271; and Chapter 13 *infra*.

66. R. L. Hall and C. J. Hitch, "Price Theory and Business Behaviour," *Oxford Economic Papers* 2 (May 1939): 12–45.

67. For excellent surveys of the literature, see Richard B. Heflebower, "Full Costs, Cost Changes, and Prices," in the National Bureau of Economic Research conference report, *Business Concentration and Price Policy* (Princeton: Princeton University Press, 1955), pp. 361–96; and Aubrey Silberston, "Surveys of Applied Economics: Price Behaviour of Firms," *Economic Journal* 80 (September 1970): 511–82.

68. See Donaldson Brown, "Pricing Policy in Relation to Financial Control," *Management and Administration* 7 (February–April 1924): 195–98, 283–86, 417–22; Albert Bradley, "Financial Control Policies of General Motors Corporation and Their Relationship to Cost Accounting," *National Association of Cost Accountants Bulletin* 1 (January 1927): 412–33; H. B. Vanderblue, "Pricing Policies in the Automobile Industry," *Harvard Business Review* 17 (Summer 1939): 385–401; U.S., Congress, Senate, Committee on the Judiciary Report, *Administered Prices: Automobiles*, 85th Cong., 2nd sess., 1958, pp. 104–30; and Kaplan et al., *Pricing in Big Business*, pp. 48–55, 131–35.

69. A 15 percent return on invested capital yields a return of roughly 20 percent on GM's net worth. There is reason to believe that the profit target may have been adjusted downward at some point, since the Bradley article cited above suggests that the target yield on *total* capital during the 1920s was 20 percent.

to yield the desired 15 percent after-tax return on capital. A top level price policy committee then uses the standard price as the initial basis of its price decision, making adjustments upward or downward to take into account actual and potential competition, business conditions, long-run strategic goals, and other factors. During the depressed 1930s, the announced price was reduced below the standard price more frequently than it was raised. No evidence is available on postwar adjustment patterns. It seems plausible that actual prices of smaller cars facing stiff import competition were below standard prices more often than not during the 1960s and 1970s. For luxury cars, the opposite may have been true. The actual amount of profit realized also depends, of course, upon the number of vehicles actually sold. During the 1950s, it is known, unit sales tended to exceed standard volume, and the average return on invested capital actually realized was above the 15 percent target rate.

Case studies reveal that the use of full-cost pricing procedures is widespread. Only 8 of the 38 firms in the Hall-Hitch sample indicated that they used no such rules. Half of the 20 large U.S. corporations studied by Kaplan, Dirlam, and Lanzillotti used some target return on investment approach to pricing major products.[70] In a study of 139 Danish firms, Fog found that most used some kind of full-cost pricing scheme.[71] Applying a simple wholesale cost markup rule, Cyert, March, and Moore were able to predict to the penny the prices actually charged for 188 out of 197 randomly selected items sold by a large department store.[72] At a more aggregative level, empirical studies of corporate income tax shifting provide modest support for the full-cost hypothesis. Gordon, for example, found little shifting incompatible with strict profit maximization in manufacturing industry generally, but there was evidence of considerable shifting in the most concentrated industry sectors.[73] However, his and other tax incidence analyses have suffered from such severe methodological and/or data limitations that the issue remains unsettled.

Much of the economic literature on full-cost pricing has been addressed to the question: Does it contradict the profit maximization assumption of microeconomic theory? Since the time of Alfred Marshall, received doctrine has held that both demand and cost must be taken into account by a firm with monopoly power to set the price that maximizes profits. Full-cost pricing seems to consider only cost, ignoring the demand half of the Marshallian scissors. Early participants in the debate made their heresy explicit, arguing from observation that companies using full-cost rules of thumb consciously abjured profit maximization, at least in any conventionally defined sense. According to Hall and Hitch, if maximum profits result at all from the application of full-cost pricing, they do so "as an accidental (or possibly evolutionary) by-product."[74] Lanzillotti concluded on the basis of his joint research with Kaplan and Dirlam that profit maximization "is not the *dominant* motive of the firm, particularly the large corporate oligopoly."[75] Defenders of the traditional wisdom argued in reply that although full-cost pricing methods appeared superficially to be inconsistent with the profit maximization conditions of economic theory, they were in fact a profit-maximizing response to the complexities and uncertainties of business decision making. Indeed, Kaplan, Dirlam, and Lanzillotti reported in their joint book that the executives they interviewed doubted whether any change in pricing procedures would lead to higher profits.[76] Similarly, General Motors' stated policy in using its full-cost pricing technique is to obtain "over a protracted period of time a margin of profit which represents the highest attainable return commensurate with capital turnover and the enjoyment of wholesale expansion, with adequate regard to the economic consequences of fluctuating volume."[77]

To determine whether full-cost pricing rules are compatible with profit maximization, three questions must be considered. First, does the application of the rules take into account differences in demand conditions between products? Second, is their application to a particular product adapted in the short run to changing demand conditions? And third, does the use of a full-cost approach permit profit maximization in the long run, even though it might not make the most of market conditions at any moment in time?

A perhaps excessively rigid interpretation of the full-cost doctrine implies that the percentage profit margin will be the same whether demand is elastic or relatively inelastic. Is this consistent with economic theory? Suppose a firm plans its capacity so that average total cost ATC (excluding profit) is minimized at the normal or average output. When profits are maximized, marginal cost MC = marginal revenue MR. It is readily shown that, where P is the price and e is the demand elasticity,[78] $MR = P - P/e$. To maximize profits, we must have $MC = MR = P - P/e$. Rearranging, we obtain $(P - MC)/P = 1/e$. Since $MC = ATC$ when ATC is at its minimum, we can substitute ATC into this expression, obtaining the equilibrium condition $(P - ATC)/P = 1/e$. The first term is the profit margin, expressed as a fraction of price.[79] The more elastic demand is, the lower the profit-maximizing profit margin will be. Firms maximizing their profits must apply lower percentage profit margins in pricing products with close substitutes (i.e., with highly elastic demands) than in pricing products whose demand is relatively inelastic, *ceteris paribus*.

Virtually all the recent evidence on full-cost pricing practices shows that firms do not in fact apply rigid profit margins, regardless of demand conditions. They vary the margin to suit the product: the more elastic the demand, the lower the margin.[80] Or in some bizarre cases observed by Fog, they applied fixed margins, but juggled their cost allocations to achieve the same result.[81] In this respect, then, the evidence is consistent qualitatively with the profit maximization assumption.

The problem of short-run price and margin adjustments over the business cycle is more complicated, and fuller analysis must be deferred to Chapter 13. Except under a standard volume rule of the General Motors type, unit *profit margins* will not decline in a recession if full-cost pricing is scrupulously practiced; in fact, they can increase under some full-cost rules. Likewise, under all but a standard volume regime, we should expect full-cost *prices* to rise in a recession, since fixed overhead must be prorated over a smaller unit volume. The evidence related to these predictions is mixed. Twelve of the 38 British business officials interviewed by Hall and Hitch indicated that they would break away from full-cost rules and cut prices in a severe recession, while an equal

70. Kaplan et al., *Pricing in Big Business*, p. 130; and Lanzillotti, "Pricing Objectives in Large Companies," *American Economic Review* 48 (December 1958): 923, 929. Similarly, half of some 88 very small firms interviewed by W. W. Haynes made at least some use of full-cost rules. "Pricing Practices in Small Firms," *Southern Economic Journal* 30 (April 1964): 320. See also R. C. Skinner, "The Determination of Selling Prices," *Journal of Industrial Economics* 18 (July 1970): 201–17.

71. Bjarke Fog, *Industrial Pricing Policies: An Analysis of Pricing Policies of Danish Manufacturers*, trans. I. E. Bailey (Amsterdam: North-Holland, 1960), p. 217.

72. R. M. Cyert and J. G. March, *A Behavioral Theory of the Firm* (Englewood Cliffs, N.J.: Prentice-Hall, 1963), pp. 146–47. Somewhat less success in applying similar rules at a different store during 1968 was reported by William J. Baumol and Maco Stewart. "On the Behavioral Theory of the Firm," in Robin Marris and Adrian Wood, eds., *The Corporate Economy* (Cambridge, Mass.: Harvard University Press, 1971), pp. 118–34.

73. Robert J. Gordon, "The Incidence of the Corporation Income Tax in U.S. Manufacturing, 1925–62," *American Economic Review* 57 (September 1967): 731–58. See also Marian Krzyzaniak and Richard A. Musgrave, *The Shifting of the Corporation Income Tax* (Baltimore: Johns Hopkins Press, 1963); John G. Cragg et al., "Empirical Evidence on the Incidence of the Corporation Income Tax," *Journal of Political Economy* 75 (December 1967): 811–21; and the exchange of views in the *Journal of Political Economy* 78 (July/August 1970): 768–77.

74. Hall and Hitch, "Price Theory and Business Behaviour," pp. 18–19.

75. Lanzillotti, "Pricing Objectives in Large Companies: Reply," *American Economic Review* 49 (September 1959): 685 (his italics).

76. Kaplan et al., *Pricing in Big Business*, p. 130. See also the review by Jesse W. Markham in the *American Economic Review* 49 (June 1959): 474.

77. Brown, "Pricing Policy," p. 197. See also *Administered Prices: Automobiles*, p. 104.

78. Proof: Total revenue $= P \cdot Q$. Marginal revenue $MR = P + Q(dP/dQ) = P[1 + (dP/dQ)(Q/P)]$. Elasticity e is defined as $-[(dQ/dP)(P/Q)] = -1/[(dP/dQ)(Q/P)]$. Substituting this last expression for e into the expression for MR, we obtain $MR = P(1 - 1/e) = P - P/e$.

79. The percentage margin over cost can be derived from this. It is $100\{[e/(e - 1)] - 1\}$. The more elastic demand is, the closer the margin over cost approaches zero.

80. See Fog, *Industrial Pricing Policies*, pp. 101–15, 204–23; Heflebower, "Full Costs," pp. 380–82; Cyert and March, *A Behavioral Theory*, pp. 138–45; Haynes, "Pricing Practices," p. 318; Kaplan et al., *Pricing in Big Business*, p. 173; Skinner, "The Determination of Selling Prices," p. 205; Weiss, *Economics and American Industry*, p. 397; and D. G. McFetridge, "The Determinants of Pricing Behaviour: A Study of the Canadian Cotton Textile Industry," *Journal of Industrial Economics* 22 (December 1973): 141–52. Compare Martin Howe, "A Study of Trade Association Price Fixing," *Journal of Industrial Economics* 21 (July 1973), especially pp. 249–50.

81. Fog, *Industrial Pricing Policies*, pp. 65, 98.

number insisted that they would adhere to the rules.[82] Fog found only 14 out of 67 Danish firms unwilling to cut below calculated full costs when running at less than capacity.[83] Similarly mixed historical evidence on the pricing behavior of 9 U.S. manufacturing industries was compiled by Markham.[84] Evidently, some, but far from all, industrial pricing is consistent with strict interpretations of the full-cost hypothesis.

One might suppose that observed departures from full-cost pricing rules in times of especially weak or strong demand represent a profit-maximizing response. But this may be true only in a narrow sense. Breaks in time of slack demand could instead reflect price rivalry that reduces the profits of all firms (though it is initiated by companies myopically trying hard to increase their individual profits). By adhering rigidly to the rule, a seller no doubt fails to squeeze the most out of its profit-making opportunities at every moment in time.[85] Nor will slavish adherence maximize joint profits for a group of firms enjoying effective methods of coordinating their prices and outputs. But in most real-world oligopolies, and particularly when legal prohibitions inhibit outright collusion, the old Russian adage that "the perfect is the enemy of the good" holds with special force. Poorly coordinated efforts to increase short-run profits under changing and uncertain demand and cost conditions can, through shortsightedness or misinterpretation, deteriorate into moves and countermoves that reduce rather than increase group profits. Faithful application of full-cost rules, by improving coordination and discipline, virtually assures at least satisfactory profits over the long pull, even though gains may not be as high as they would be under impossibly perfect coordination. If by employing rules of thumb an industry does the best it can on the average under less than ideal conditions, we must conclude that the rules constitute an instrument of long-run profit maximization.

This conclusion is now widely accepted. It is supported *inter alia* by case study evidence. Machlup observes that through the application of full-cost pricing rules, cartels may "succeed in the maintenance of a monopolistic level of price in spite of strong temptations for competitive price cutting." He adds that "tacit understandings to observe average-cost rules of pricing sometimes constitute an alternative way of achieving price maintenance in a declining market."[86] Heflebower summarizes several studies revealing the use of full-cost rules as a coordinating device in loose-knit cartels.[87] Hall and Hitch note that full-cost pricing is especially prevalent in oligopoly, where the established price, approximating the full cost of a representative firm, "is reached directly through the community of outlook of business men, rather than indirectly through each firm working at what its most profitable output would be if competitors' reactions are neglected."[88] Cyert and March stress the use of rules of thumb to eliminate oligopolistic uncertainties:

> Our studies . . . lead us to the proposition that firms will devise and negotiate an environment so as to eliminate the uncertainty. . . . In the case of competitors, one of the conspicuous means of control is through the establishment of industry-wide conventional practices. If "good business practice" is standardized . . . we can be reasonably confident that all competitors will follow it. We do not mean to imply that firms necessarily enter into collusive agreements in the legal sense; our impression is that ordinarily they do not, but they need not do so to achieve the same objective of stability in competitive practices.[89]

Kaplan, Dirlam, and Lanzillotti describe how, by the application of well-known costing rules, members of the steel industry were able independently to make fairly good advance estimates of the price increase announced in 1956 by United States Steel.[90] Haynes's interviews with small business managers disclosed that trade associations attempt to restrict cutthroat competition by urging wider adoption of full-cost pricing. He found also that full-cost prices serve as "resistance points" below which prices are not permitted to fall.[91] Fog claims that firms adhered to full-cost pricing rules because they inhibited the inclination to reduce price on myopic grounds and because under standards of "commercial morality" it was considered "unloyal" to deviate from accepted prices.[92] In sum, full-cost pricing facilitates oligopolistic coordination by making rivals' decisions more predictable and by providing common guidelines as to appropriate price levels.

When costs vary widely from firm to firm within an industry, coordination through the use of full-cost rules becomes more difficult. One escape, although not a very plausible one, is the "representative firm" device discussed by Hall and Hitch. Price leadership appears more workable, with followers drawing upon their knowledge of the leader's costs if they must make independent price calculations. Still more effective, and apparently widespread, is the dissemination by a trade association of industrywide average cost data by product line, function, or component. This information then becomes, by overt or tacit consent, the basis of price calculations.[93] Coordination of pricing decisions is also aided when a trade association develops standard cost accounting systems for the benefit of its members.

When pricing decisions are based upon some kind of full-cost rule, we should expect as a corollary that prices will be more responsive to changes in cost than to changes in demand. Industrywide cost changes generate, under the rule, a readily understood signal that price changes are in order. As Heflebower observes, "When factor prices fall, the initiator of a selling price reduction is not suspected of trying to enlarge his share. Or, in reverse, the boldness of the firm which moves to reflect higher factor prices in his selling prices is appreciated, particularly when margins have been squeezed sharply."[94] The adjustment problem is different for demand changes. When demand declines, full-cost pricing may call for price increases to cover higher overhead allocations, but this could be barred by the very weakness of demand. Still, price cutting may at least be avoided because it goes contrary to the rule and because retaliation is feared. In boom times, full-cost rules dictate little or no increase in prices unless marginal costs have risen sharply owing to pressure on capacity, pulling total cost per unit along. Producers may be willing to hold their prices below levels supportable by current demand, Heflebower suggests, because this is a good method of cementing long-run relations with customers.[95] Thus, we expect

prices to be more rigid over the business cycle than they would be if sensitive marginalist adjustments to demand changes were attempted. There is evidence that concentrated industries do display such pricing rigidity, as we shall see in Chapter 13.

One further implication must be mentioned briefly. Setting a price that affords only a moderate profit margin may not maximize profits during the immediate time period. However, unless an industry enjoys substantial barriers to new entry, a higher price and profit margin policy could attract new entrants, whose additional output will have a depressing impact on future prices and profits. Profits over the long pull may therefore be higher if firms use pricing rules that yield less

82. Hall and Hitch, "Price Theory and Business Behaviour," pp. 25–27.

83. Fog, *Industrial Pricing Policies*, p. 120.

84. Jesse W. Markham, "Administered Prices and the Recent Inflation," in the Commission on Money and Credit compendium, *Inflation, Growth, and Employment* (Englewood Cliffs, N.J.: Prentice-Hall, 1964), pp. 144–73.

85. Simulation studies suggest that under at least some plausible conditions, the use of full-cost rules can lead to near-maximum profits. See William J. Baumol and Richard E. Quandt, "Rules of Thumb and Optimally Imperfect Decisions," *American Economic Review* 54 (March 1964): 23–46; Odd Langholm, *Full Cost and Optimal Price: A Study in the Dynamics of Multiple Production* (Oslo: Universitetsforlaget, 1969); and J. Hadar and D. Hillinger, "Imperfect Competition with Unknown Demand," *Review of Economic Studies* 36 (October 1969): 519–25.

86. Machlup, *The Economics of Sellers' Competition*, p. 65. See also Alexander Henderson, "The Theory of Duopoly," *Quarterly Journal of Economics* 69 (November 1954): 576–79.

87. Heflebower, "Full Costs," pp. 376–78.

88. Hall and Hitch, "Price Theory and Business Behaviour," pp. 27–28.

89. Richard M. Cyert and James G. March, *A Behavioral Theory of the Firm*, p. 120. © 1963 by Prentice-Hall, Inc.

90. Kaplan et al., *Pricing in Big Business*, p. 16.

91. Haynes, "Pricing Practices," pp. 317–19.

92. Fog, *Industrial Pricing Policies*, pp. 78–79, 152–53.

93. See Haynes, "Pricing Practices," p. 317; and Cyert and March, *A Behavioral Theory*, p. 120.

94. Richard B. Heflebower, "Toward a Theory of Industrial Markets and Prices," *American Economic Review* 44 (May 1954): 135. See also his "Full Costs, Cost Changes, and Prices," pp. 389–90.

95. Heflebower, "Toward a Theory of Industrial Markets and Prices," p. 137.

than the maximum return attainable in any current period, but at the same time discourage new entry. This important aspect of business pricing strategy will be analyzed further in Chapter 8.

Focal points and tacit coordination[96]

We have emphasized repeatedly that in the Prisoners' Dilemma game of oligopoly pricing, coordinated action is the key to joint profit maximization.' Coordination is only moderately difficult when the oligopolists can communicate freely and openly. But the antitrust laws make overt communication hazardous. Price leadership and adherence to rules of thumb may be adequate substitutes. There are also more subtle ways of coordinating pricing decisions. Insight into these communication methods is provided by Professor Schelling's theory of focal points.[97]

The theory is introduced most conveniently through a noneconomic example. Consider the following problem posed by Schelling:

> You are to meet someone in New York City. You have not been instructed where to meet; you have no prior understanding with the person on where to meet; and you cannot communicate with each other. You are simply told that you will have to guess where to meet and he is being told the same thing and that you will have to try to make your guesses coincide.
>
> You are told the date but not the hour of this meeting; the two of you must guess the exact minute of the day for meeting. At what time will you appear at the chosen meeting place?[98]

Although there are tens of thousands of conceivable meeting places in New York City, a majority of the 36 persons on whom Schelling tried this problem chose the information booth at Grand Central Station, and nearly all chose to meet at 12 noon. The reason is that Grand Central Station (at least for New Yorkers) and noon have a certain compelling prominence; they are focal points. And in a wide variety of problems, when behavior must be coordinated tacitly—that is, without direct communication—there is a tendency for choices to converge on some such focal point. The focal points chosen may owe their prominence to analogy, symmetry, precedent, aesthetic considerations, or even the accident of arrangement; but they must in any event have the property of uniqueness. In economic problems, round numbers tend to be focal points, as do simple rules such as "split the difference."

Focal points also play a role in explicit, across-the-table bargaining when a solution is difficult to reach despite free communication because a concession by one party generates an expectation in the other's mind that further concessions may be extracted. Focal points provide a barrier each recognizes as a natural place for further concessions to be resisted, and thus they facilitate convergence upon a unique solution. As Schelling observed, the automobile salesperson who works out the arithmetic for a rock-bottom price of $2,507.63 is almost pleading to be relieved of $7.63.[99] Labor contract agreements often converge on some round number cent or percentage increase, or on a split-the-difference decision. In international relations, prominent natural features such as rivers or mountain ridges provide the most common basis of boundary adjustments, followed by round number parallels of latitude.

The great merit of Schelling's general focal point theory is that it permits us to integrate into the mainstream of oligopoly theory a number of phenomena that might otherwise be deemed mere curiosities. Several specific ways in which focal points enter into oligopolistic price determination can be identified.

First is the practice of *price lining*, widespread at the retail level. Even dollar amounts serve as one focal point for pricing decisions. More common in retailing is the use of odd pricing points such as $199.95, which owe their acceptance to tradition. By setting its price at some such focal point, a firm tacitly encourages its rivals to follow suit without undercutting. Conversely, if one company announces a price that has no such compulsion, a rival is tempted to set its own price just a cent or two below. This leads to a further small retaliatory cut, precipitating a downward spiral which, in the absence of focal points, has no clear-cut stopping point. In setting price at a focal point, one in effect asks rhetorically, If not here, where?—implicitly warning rivals of the danger of downward spiraling.[100]

Most consumer goods manufacturers are well aware that adherence to accepted pricing points facilitates coordination and discourages price warfare. They go to considerable pains to preserve the system. The problem of passing along to consumers the benefits of the 1965 excise tax reform was complicated by the desire of many sellers to protect their pricing points while making downward adjustments. As a result, the price reductions on some items were less than the tax cut, while on others they were actually greater.[101] Tampering with the accepted pricing point structure threatens industry discipline and may induce price warfare. Nationally branded men's shirt manufacturers apparently experienced several such conflicts when some firms attempted to shift from pricing points like $4.95 to even dollar points, although in prosperous 1966 the transition was made with the aid of price leadership.[102]

Government agencies may inadvertently facilitate price parallelism by setting ceiling prices, e.g., as part of anti-inflation campaigns. For instance, a student of French price controls concluded that official ceiling prices provided a focus for individual quotations that might otherwise have differed.[103] In England it was customary, at least until the last few months before the steel industry was nationalized in 1967, for all producers to quote only the maximum prices announced by the Iron and Steel Board.[104]

Turning to still another class of pricing practices, how does one explain the following experience of the U.S. Veterans Administration? On June 5, 1955, five different companies submitted sealed bids to fill an order for 5,640 100-capsule bottles of the antibiotic tetracycline, each quoting an effective net price of $19.1884 per bottle.[105] The typical purchasing agent's reaction would be that no explanation is needed; the Justice Department should be called in to investigate a clear-cut case of conspiracy. But although one can never be certain, it is probable there was no direct collusion connected with this transaction.

Rather, the bids were influenced by two kinds of focal points. First, there was a past history of price quotations that provided a focal point for the June 5 bids. This facet will be explored more fully in a moment. But second, the curious price of $19.1884 per bottle was arrived at through the application of a series of round number discounts to round number base prices: $19.1884 is the standard trade discount of 2 percent off $19.58, which (after rounding) is 20 percent off the wholesale price of $24.48, which in turn is 20 percent off the $30.60 price charged to retail druggists, which is 40 percent off the prevailing retail list price of $51.00, which in turn reflected an earlier 15 percent cut from the original list price of $60.00 per 100 capsules.

When price reductions were effected by the oligopolistic suppliers of antibiotics, they nearly always took one of three forms: a cut to a new

---

96. A slightly different version of this section appeared as "Focal Point Pricing and Conscious Parallelism" in the *Antitrust Bulletin* 12 (Summer 1967): 495–503. © Federal Legal Publications, Inc., 157 Chambers St., New York.

97. Thomas C. Schelling, *The Strategy of Conflict* (Cambridge, Mass.: Harvard University Press, 1960), especially Chapters 2 and 3. On p. 74, Schelling anticipates the application of his ideas to price theory: "In economics the phenomena of price leadership, various kinds of nonprice competition, and perhaps even price stability itself appear amenable to an analysis that stresses the importance of tacit communication and its dependence on qualitatively identifiable and fairly unambiguous signals that can be read in the situation itself."

98. Schelling, *The Strategy of Conflict*, p. 56.

99. Schelling, *The Strategy of Conflict*, p. 67.

100. Schelling, *The Strategy of Conflict*, pp. 111–12.

101. See "Excise Cut Begins To Trickle Down," *Business Week*, 26 June 1965, p. 36.

102. "Shirt Prices Up 5¢, But Who Cares," *New York Times*, 24 April 1966.

103. John Sheahan, "Problems and Possibilities of Industrial Price Control: Postwar French Experience," *American Economic Review* 51 (June 1961): 352.

104. "Steel Price War Rages in Britain," *New York Times*, 7 April 1966. See also Martin Howe, "The Iron and Steel Board Pricing, 1953–1967," *Scottish Journal of Political Economy* 15 (February 1968): 43–67.

105. From exhibit PX-645 in the Federal Trade Commission antitrust case *in re American Cyanamid Co. et al.*, FTC Docket no. 7211 (1959).

even dollar price, an even percentage reduction in the old price, or rounding off the odd fraction of a cent produced when round number discounts led to a figure like $19.1884. Consider, for instance, the history of prices to retailers and hospitals of American Cyanamid's antibiotic Aureomycin in bottles of 16 capsules. It was introduced in December 1948 at $15.00 per bottle. In response to the introduction of a competing product, the price was cut to $10.00 in March 1949. In February 1950, the price was cut 20 percent to $8.00. In May 1950, a 25 percent reduction to $6.00 followed. In September 1951, the price was cut 15 percent to $5.10, at which level it stabilized for several years.[106]

This sort of round number discounting is apparently not confined to the drug industry, although we have little information on how widespread it is. It was a prominent feature of plate glass mirror pricing, on which some evidence has been assembled. The Mirror Manufacturers Association published a list price booklet for various mirror sizes, and nearly all wholesale transactions were made at round number discounts —e.g., 80 percent and then 10 percent off the list price.[107]

What is the significance of round number discounting and quoting as a coordinating device? When products are sold repeatedly in fairly large quantities to well-informed buyers, sellers are anxious to have some means of changing prices once in a while without precipitating a spiral of retaliatory undercutting. By reducing its price a round percentage amount, the initiator tacitly says to its rivals, "See here, I'm not trying to touch off a war. I think the price should be lower, and I've quoted a good, clean reduction to which we all should now conform." A cut that lacks the prominence of a round number percentage discount or a new round number value is a cut without staying power. There is no magnetic attraction preventing a further change on the next transaction. And since large, well-informed buyers are adept at making prices slide downhill, it is to the interest of sellers to avoid incessant price changes. The way to do so is to ensure that any changes move to a new focal point likely to be respected by rivals.

Focal point pricing may also be used as a

coordinating device by *buyers* anxious to avoid driving up the prices of commodities in an oligoposonistic market (i.e., one with few buyers). Bakken and Mueller found that tobacco leaf buyers' adherence to round number quotations in the Wisconsin market discouraged aggressive outbidding of each others' offers.[108]

The notion of round number discounts as focal point barriers to further cutting applies not only to pricing, but also to certain kinds of nonprice rivalry. For an example, we return to the antibiotic industry. A common trade practice is to avoid price cutting, but to compete for hospital and retail pharmacy orders by giving free goods—that is, additional units of a product for which no bill is rendered. One company's analysis of the New York district situation in 1955 revealed that in 46 out of 47 instances, the percentage of free goods to supplies purchased by hospitals was one of three round numbers: 10, 15, or 20. In the same memorandum, the district sales manager reported that "gradually the [free goods percentage] is at 20 percent. We back away when it goes beyond because once that barrier is broken, our experience has been that there is no bottom."[109] This clearly reflects the spiraling problem encountered once a critical focal point is passed: if not here, where?

The theory of focal points can be extended along dynamic heuristic lines. Even a price that has no particular uniqueness or compulsion in its own right may become a focal point simply by virtue of having been quoted repeatedly. The Veterans Administration tetracycline price history is again illustrative. The first VA order for tetracycline was filled by the Pfizer Company as sole bidder at a price of $19.58 less 2 percent trade discount. In the next transaction (March 1955), five firms bid $19.58, but three omitted the 2 percent discount. When all matched the winning bid of $19.1884 net in the third transaction (on June 5), that price obtained the additional prominence of unanimous acceptance. All five firms then adhered to it in responding to four further VA sealed bid requests during the following year. Extensive antitrust litigation produced no evidence that this pattern of identical bidding was the result of outright collusion, nor were meetings and explicit agreements essential under the circumstances. Given a focal point established through past experience, and given the five tetracycline sellers' reluctance to initiate a movement to lower price levels by departing from that focal point, everything needed for coordinating *tacitly* on identical bids of $19.1884 net per bottle was in place.

Each year the federal and state governments receive thousands of sets of identical bids in the sealed-bid competitions they sponsor.[110] It is probable that many such transactions have a history similar to the tetracycline pricing example. This is not to deny that identical bidding is sometimes attributable to direct collusion; the repeated identical bids submitted by electrical transformer and insulator manufacturers were, for example, the result of an elaborate price-fixing conspiracy. But overt agreement is not a *necessary* condition for identical bidding. If the participants wish to avoid undercutting one another, they can coordinate their behavior tacitly by searching for and respecting focal points.

Order backlogs, inventories, and oligopolistic coordination

In the orthodox static theory of monopoly profit maximization, output and price are determined simultaneously, taking into account observed or predicted demand and cost conditions. But when oligopolists seek more or less successfully to maximize joint profits, the price (or price structure) is the subject of explicit or tacit bargaining. Achieving consensus on prices alone can be difficult; negotiating both price and quantity jointly is much harder in the absence of an elaborate cartel organization. Characteristically, therefore, the coordination process in oligopoly focuses primarily on price—i.e., through explicit collusion, leadership, rules of thumb, or the use of focal points. Given a price or price structure, production decisions must be made. If the oligopoly has been successful in elevating prices above the competitive level, its individual members cannot be guided by the rule of expanding

output until marginal cost rises into equality with the price, for to do so would undermine the jointly accepted price. Uncertainty concerning the position of industry demand functions and how demand is to be shared among the oligopolists under varying circumstances obscures the derivation of individual firm marginal revenue functions.[111] Oligopolists recognizing their common interest in orderly pricing are therefore likely to adopt a passive output determination policy, adjusting production to demand at the accepted price and abjuring attempts to force upon the market (or withhold) output in a way that could upset the price equilibrium.[112]

Since demand functions are constantly shifting, mistakes in setting output undoubtedly will be made. Yet this poses no insuperable problems. If too much is produced relative to the current flow of orders at the established price, the first reaction is a buildup of inventories or the reduction of order backlogs, rather than a cut in price to clear the market. If too little is produced, inventories will be drawn down or delivery times extended. Inventory and order backlog changes provide both *buffers* to compensate for produc-

106. Federal Trade Commission, *Economic Report on Antibiotics Manufacture* (Washington, D.C.: Government Printing Office, June 1958), p. 190.

107. Phillips, *Market Structure, Organization and Performance*, pp. 177–96.

108. H. H. Bakken and Willard F. Mueller, *The Market for Wisconsin Binder Leaf Tobacco*, Research Bulletin 181 (Madison: University of Wisconsin Agricultural Experiment Station, June 1953), pp. 34–38.

109. From exhibit RACX-753A, *in re American Cyanamid Co. et al.*, placing in evidence an American Cyanamid interoffice memorandum dated April 18, 1955.

110. For various views on the identical bidding problem, see Vernon A. Mund, "Identical Bid Prices," *Journal of Political Economy* 68 (April 1960): 150–60; R. A. Bicks, "The Federal Government's Program on Identical Bids," *Antitrust Bulletin* 15 (November–December 1960): 617–26; Paul W. Cook, Jr., "Fact and Fancy on Identical Bids," *Harvard Business Review* 41 (January–February 1963): 67–72; and Comanor and Schankerman, "Identical Bids and Cartel Behavior."

111. For a geometric elaboration on the sharing problem, see the first edition of *Industrial Market Structure and Economic Performance*, pp. 149–52.

112. This passive policy with respect to price may be accompanied by measures to increase one's share of the market through such non-price measures as personal selling, advertising, and innovation. See Chapter 14 *infra*.

tion imbalances and *feedback signals* to guide the meshing of future production to demand. Substituting this simple passive output determination policy for the $MC = P$ or $MC = MR$ rules in no way leads to indeterminacy. The system is supremely operational—so much so that it is hard to understand why it has been overlooked so often by students of inventory behavior.[113]

Inventory and order backlog adjustments play a role along with output level changes in adapting to demand shifts because there are certain natural lags in the production planning process. It takes time to reschedule production. Changes in the production plan are also costly: setup, hiring, and retraining costs increase with frequent production rate alterations; productivity falls with the interruption of routines; and work force morale may suffer. As a result, firms find it undesirable to make hair-trigger changes in production schedules on the basis of only faint demand change signals. They wait for stronger signals. And since the flow of orders is inherently erratic, time is required to distinguish a random short-term aberration from a more persistent demand change. Therefore, decisions to change the level of production tend to lag changes in demand by a sizeable interval. In his pioneering studies of inventory and production cycles, Metzler found the planning period between changes in demand and changes in production to be five months on the average.[114] In the interim, at least as a first approximation, the imbalance is corrected through changes in inventories and/or backlogs.

Of course, when production is imperfectly synchronized with demand, prices might also be manipulated to clear the market. Incentives exist for absorbing at least a part of the adjustment burden through price changes.[115] Theoretical studies suggest that there is some (possibly complex) optimal relationship between inventory levels and sales.[116] Too large an inventory causes excessive capital, storage, and deterioration costs; too small an inventory leads to uneconomic production lot sizes and the loss of sales when items are out of stock. Similarly, too small a backlog reduces production scheduling flexibility; too large a backlog alienates customers.[117]

Thus, when inventory levels climb sharply or order backlogs fall, an incentive to reduce price materializes; while when inventories decline or order backlogs grow, there is an incentive to choke off some of the excess demand through a price increase. These incentives to limit inventory and backlog fluctuations apply more or less uniformly across all industry structures—atomistic, oligopolistic, and monopolized. But as we have seen, the difficulty of coordinating price changes and the threat of changes to industry discipline discourage short-run price adjustments under oligopoly. This motive for avoiding price adjustments is absent in atomistically structured and (rare) purely monopolized markets. Therefore, we should expect oligopolistic industries to rely more heavily than atomistic industries upon inventory and backlog variations in adjusting to demand fluctuations, *ceteris paribus*, and less heavily upon price variations. Concretely, prices should be less variable and inventories and backlogs more variable over time in oligopolistic than in atomistic industries. Inventory and backlog variability should be especially pronounced in concentrated industries lacking formal arrangements (such as cartel agreements) for coordinating prices and outputs, but striving nonetheless to take into account mutual interdependence.[118]

This set of conjectures is quantitatively testable. The limited amount of evidence available at present clearly supports the stated hypotheses.[119]

In an unpublished exploratory study, the author collected quarterly inventory and sales data for 23 broadly defined industry groups, spanning most of the manufacturing sector, for the 1955–61 period.[120] A coefficient measuring the variability over time of seasonally adjusted inventory/sales ratios was computed for each industry. This variability coefficient was found to be positively correlated with the weighted average four-firm concentration ratios of the 23 industry groups, after also taking into account whether the industries produced durable or nondurable goods and consumer or producer goods. The partial correlation between variability and concentration was 0.36, which is statistically significant at the 90 percent confidence level. Thus, the more concentrated the industries were, the more variable over time their inventories were relative to sales, other things being held equal.

As one might expect, the analysis also showed that inventory/sales ratios are more variable in durable goods industries than in nondurables. Basic product characteristics such as perishability and style obsolescence undoubtedly force firms in many nondurable goods industries to avoid large inventory buildups, and consequently make it more difficult to avoid price cuts in response to short-run demand declines. This is an important factor explaining the flexibility of prices and profits in the moderately concentrated meat-packing industry. At least one leading producer—Swift (now renamed Esmark)—consciously attempted to gain more control over prices by integrating into product lines more susceptible to storage.[121]

Using a model neglecting oligopolistic interdependence, E. S. Mills found that production changes could be predicted quite well from inventory behavior, but that the predicted correlations between price and inventory movements failed to emerge. He rationalized the latter result by suggesting that prices were insensitive to short-run changes in demand and inventory levels in the quasi-collusive industries analyzed (cement, rubber tires, shoes, and southern pine lumber)—an explanation consistent with the hypotheses advanced here.[122] In a study of 11 Japanese industries covering the 1950–55 period, S. Fujino discovered that the more consistently firms reacted to inventory buildups or drawdowns by adjusting production, the less prices were adjusted. He postulated that differences in these reactions were related to market structure differences, although no explicit tests were made of the hypothesis.[123]

Order backlogs may also play an important shock absorber role, especially in the durable goods industries, where the value of order backlogs is roughly four times the value of finished goods inventories in a typical year. The only relevant analysis is by Victor Zarnowitz. He observed that the more average delivery periods (i.e., the ratio of order backlogs to sales) varied, the less variable prices were.[124] He found also that changes in price were more closely correlated with changes in order backlogs than with changes in wages in the relatively unconcentrated paper and textile industry groups, while

113. For example, this motive for carrying inventories is not recognized in a leading theoretical and empirical work relating prices and inventories: Edwin S. Mills, *Price, Output, and Inventory Policy* (New York: Wiley, 1962), especially pp. 47–49, 82–84. Mills cites three main reasons for carrying inventories: the speculative motive (producing quantities that will not be sold in the current period in anticipation of subsequent price increases); the desire to reduce production costs by smoothing production; and the desire to avoid rejecting orders when imperfectly predictable demand turns out to be especially strong.

114. Lloyd Metzler, "Factors Governing the Length of Inventory Cycles," *Review of Economics and Statistics* 29 (February 1947): 7. The actual period of production, excluding planning time, appears to be much shorter for most manufactured goods. See John A. Carlson, "The Production Lag," *American Economic Review* 63 (March 1973): 73–86.

115. This point is stressed, and the oligopoly price coordination risk is explicitly taken into account, by George A. Hay in "Production, Price, and Inventory Theory," *American Economic Review* 60 (September 1970): 531–45; and "The Dynamics of Firm Behavior under Alternative Cost Structures," *American Economic Review* 62 (June 1972): 403–13.

116. For an extensive bibliography, see Mills, *Price, Output, and Inventory Policy*, pp. 261–65.

117. See M. D. Steuer, R. J. Ball, and J. R. Eaton, "The Effect of Waiting Times on Foreign Orders for Machine Tools," *Economica* 33 (November 1966): 387–403; and John A. Carlson and T. B. O'Keefe, "Buffer Stocks and Reaction Coefficients: An Experiment with Decision Making under Risk," *Review of Economic Studies* 36 (October 1969): 467–84.

118. We should also expect inventories of firms with monopoly power to be larger, as well as more variable, on the average. Firms with downward-sloping demand curves are generally uncertain how much they can sell at any given price; while in pure competition, a firm can presumably be confident of selling its whole output at the ruling price. The higher price is relative to marginal cost (and hence, implicitly, the more monopoly power a firm has) the more worthwhile it is to carry high inventories to reduce the probability that sales will be lost owing to shortages in periods of peak demand. See Mills, *Price, Output, and Inventory Policy*, pp. 82–83, 96, 116–17.

119. Discussion of studies relating price variability to market structure is deferred to Chapter 13.

120. The source of the inventory and sales data was the Federal Trade Commission-Securities and Exchange Commission series, *Quarterly Financial Reports for Manufacturing Corporations*. Ideally, the analysis should have included only finished goods inventories, which account for only a third of all manufacturing industry inventories. But detailed industry breakdowns for periods shorter than a year continue to be fragmentary. See the U.S., Bureau of the Census report, *Manufacturers' Shipments, Inventories, and Orders: 1958–1976*, M3-1.6 (Washington, D.C.: Government Printing Office, 1976).

121. Kaplan et al., *Pricing in Big Business*, p. 47.

122. Mills, *Price, Output, and Inventory Policy*, pp. 124–25, 258–59. See also M. D. Steuer and A. P. Budd, "Price and Output Decisions of Firms—A Critique of E. S. Mills' Theory," *Manchester School of Economics and Social Studies* 36 (May 1968): 1–25.

123. S. Fujino, "Some Aspects of Inventory Cycles," *Review of Economics and Statistics* 42 (May 1960): 203–209.

124. Victor Zarnowitz, "Unfilled Orders, Price Changes, and Business Fluctuations," *Review of Economics and Statistics* 44 (November 1962): 380–81.

changes in wages were by far the more powerful explanatory variable in the relatively concentrated primary metals, machinery, and fabricated metal products groups.[125] These results lend strong support to the hypothesis that oligopolists rely upon order backlog variations rather than price adjustments to adapt to short-term demand changes.

Industry case studies also reveal that the ability and willingness to absorb short-run demand shocks through inventory variation are important to maintaining stable price structures. In the copper industry, for example, companies operating in the atomistically structured scrap-smelting segment typically refuse to hold large inventories; when scrap supplies are high, the output of smelters exercises a depressing influence on prices. However, primary copper producers Anaconda, Kennecott, and Phelps Dodge, controlling about 75 percent of total U.S. production, have repeatedly shored up the price structure by taking strong inventory positions. In 1949, Kennecott maintained production but discontinued all open market sales until custom smelter supplies had been exhausted and prices had risen 30 percent above earlier depressed levels.[126] During the early 1960s the Anglo-American producers held 100,000 tons of copper off the world market to stabilize prices at $.31 per pound over a two-year period.[127]

Similar inventory behavior is observable in the aluminum industry. When sales fell off sharply because of the Great Depression, Alcoa in 1931 accumulated inventories equal to six months' output before closing down any of its plants. Although other world producers also found themselves holding large stocks, prices remained firm. As Aluminium Ltd. of Canada noted in its 1932 annual report, "World stocks of aluminium are not excessively large. They are in firm hands and do not weigh unduly upon the world market."[128] Following World War II, short-term declines in the demand for aluminum ingot were again absorbed primarily through inventory accumulation rather than price cuts or production shutdowns.[129] As new entry into ingot production occurred, pricing discipline broke down in 1971, but inventory buildups again contributed to the avoidance of price declines during the unusually sharp recession of 1975.[130] The mere desire to avoid disruptive price cutting was not, however, a sufficient explanation for the willingness of aluminum producers to accept enormous inventory fluctuations, M. J. Peck found. High fixed costs and the wide disparity between marginal costs ($.06 per pound in 1948) and price ($.15) made it worthwhile to incur substantial inventory carrying charges in anticipation of future profitable sales when demand recovered.[131] And of course, aluminum ingots are not subject to physical or style deterioration. Inventories of fabricated aluminum products are allowed to vary much less than ingot inventories, partly because of obsolescence risks and partly because the margin between price and variable cost is smaller. It is probable that the palpably weaker pricing discipline in many fabricated aluminum products lines can be traced in part to this inventory policy difference as well as to the larger number of fabricating firms.

Markham's study of the rayon industry prior to 1950 exhibits both similarities and differences.[132] Short-term fluctuations in demand were regularly absorbed through inventory variations and not production adjustments or price changes. Only when sales declines persisted for several months were cutbacks in production initiated, while price changes were resisted even longer. When demand continued to decline, however, industry discipline was not strong enough to ward off downward price revisions, partly because profit margins fell sharply at below-capacity production rates and partly because smaller firms were unwilling to bear the continued burden of high inventory carrying costs. Still, these recession-inspired price cuts were not nearly as detrimental to industry profits as they might have been in other industries, for they permitted rayon producers to win back a more than proportionate volume of business from substitute fibers whose prices were highly flexible downward during recessions.

Other industries have been less successful in avoiding price competition through their inventory policies. The accumulation of especially large stocks of gasoline in local markets has often triggered price wars, despite efforts by the major integrated producers to keep excess supplies out of the hands of firms prone to price cutting.[133] Producers in the relatively unconcentrated textiles industry characteristically accumulate finished goods stocks to smooth out production during slack periods, but when demand continues to be weak and carrying charges mount, they tend to dispose of their inventories at distress prices.[134] And in a large retail department store studied by Cyert and March, price changes are the usual means of keeping inventories in check.[135]

Thus, by letting inventories and order backlogs fluctuate, oligopolistic producers can adjust to short-term demand shifts in a way that minimizes the threat to industry pricing discipline. However, such a strategy carries the concomitant risk that under stress the fainthearted will dump excessive stocks at disruptive prices. Variations in inventories and backlogs also provide a feedback mechanism to guide production decisions under conditions of oligopolistic interdependence. Much more research is needed on this facet of oligopoly behavior.

Conclusion

In sum, there are several means by which oligopolists can coordinate their pricing decisions to approximate the maximization of joint profits. Collusion, although under increasing antitrust fire, has not vanished. Price leadership facilitates monopolistic pricing when follower firms are willing to cooperate with the leader's decisions. Mutual adherence to full-cost pricing rules is not apt to yield profits as high as under ideal collusive conditions, but it helps keep them higher than they would be under a regime of independent competitive conduct. Firms can also reduce the likelihood of competitive price cutting by setting and keeping prices at focal point values. A complement to all of these coordination methods is the substitution of passive output determination behavior for attempts continually to equate marginal cost with price or marginal revenue.

125. Zarnowitz, "Business Fluctuations," pp. 390–91.

126. Kaplan et al., *Pricing in Big Business*, pp. 176–81.

127. Thomas O'Hanlon, "The Perilous Prosperity of Anaconda," *Fortune*, May 1966, pp. 121, 235.

128. M. J. Peck, *Competition in the Aluminum Industry* (Cambridge, Mass.: Harvard University Press, 1961), p. 88, n. 6.

129. Peck, *Competition in the Aluminum Industry*, pp. 83–96.

130. See the U.S., Council on Wage and Price Stability staff report, *Aluminum Prices: 1974–75* (Washington, D.C.: Government Printing Office, September 1976), pp. 132–37, 151–54.

131. Peck, *Competition in the Aluminum Industry*, p. 88. During the 1970s the ratio of marginal to total unit costs rose sharply, making firms more willing to cut back production in the face of a slump. See *Aluminum Prices*, pp. 27–30, 128–30.

132. Jesse W. Markham, *Competition in the Rayon Industry* (Cambridge, Mass.: Harvard University Press, 1952), Chapters 7 and 8.

133. See Ralph Cassady, Jr., *Price Warfare in Business Competition* (East Lansing: Michigan State University, 1963), p. 52; Learned and Ellsworth, *Gasoline Pricing in Ohio*, pp. 33–48; and Robert T. Masson and Fred C. Allvine, "Strategy and Structure: Majors, Independents, and Prices of Gasoline in Local Markets," in Masson and P. D. Qualls, eds., *Essays on Industrial Organization in Honor of Joe S. Bain* (Cambridge, Mass.: Ballinger, 1976), pp. 155–80.

134. See Weiss, *Economics and American Industry*, p. 143.

135. Cyert and March, *A Behavioral Theory of the Firm*, p. 140.

7 Conditions limiting oligopolistic coordination

While oligopolists have incentives to cooperate in maintaining prices above the competitive level, there are also divisive forces. In this chapter we examine several conditions limiting the effectiveness of coordination. They include significant numbers of sellers, heterogeneity of products and distribution channels, the interaction of high overhead costs with adverse business conditions, lumpiness and infrequency of product purchases, opportunities for secret price cutting, and weaknesses in an industry's informal social structure.

The number and size distribution of sellers

One structural dimension with an obvious influence on coordination is the number and size distribution of sellers. Generally, the more sellers a market includes, the more difficult it is to maintain prices above cost, other things being equal. This is so for three main reasons.

First, as the number of sellers increases and the share of industry output supplied by a representative firm decreases, individual producers are increasingly apt to ignore the effect of their price and output decisions on rival actions and the overall level of prices. As a very crude general rule, if evenly matched firms supply homogeneous products in a well-defined market, they are likely to begin ignoring their influence on

price when their number exceeds 10 or 12. It is more difficult to generalize when the size distribution of sellers is highly skewed. Then pricing discipline depends critically upon several variables (to be analyzed subsequently) affecting the rate at which smaller firms can expand their sales through price cutting.

Second, as the number of sellers increases, so also does the probability that at least one will be a maverick, pursuing an independent, aggressive pricing policy. And if market shares are sensitive to price differentials, even one such maverick of appreciable size can make it hard for other firms to hold prices near monopoly levels. As Peck observed, "[O]ne Henry Ford could introduce a new price policy, whereas fifteen sellers with conservative styles of business might produce results akin to the most 'static' of monopolies."[1]

Finally, different sellers are likely to have at least slightly divergent notions about the most advantageous price. Especially with homogeneous products, these conflicting views must be reconciled if joint profits are to be held near the potential maximum. The coordination problem increases with the number of firms. Some economists have suggested that the difficulty of coordi-

1. M. J. Peck, *Competition in the Aluminum Industry: 1945–1958* (Cambridge, Mass.: Harvard University Press, 1961), p. 207.

nation rises nearly exponentially with the number of firms.[2] Their reasoning is as follows. Unless there is a central coordinating agency (such as a cartel sales bureau or a well-accepted price leader), each firm must tacitly or overtly communicate with every other firm over a *modus vivendi* in pricing. The number of two-way communication flows required is given by the combinatorial expression $N(N-1)/2$. With two sellers, the number of channels is one; with six, it rises to 15, and so on. Breakdown of any single channel can touch off independent actions threatening industry discipline. Although oligopolists may escape the implications of the formula by building in redundancies and creating central coordination institutions, the difficulty of coordination undoubtedly does increase more than proportionately with the number of sellers.

One point merits further consideration here. Does the presence of numerous small firms operating on the fringe of an otherwise oligopolistic industry affect pricing behavior and profits? It undoubtedly does, though the strength of the effect depends upon the ability of fringe producers to make inroads into the market shares of industry leaders. Oligopolists who take their interdependence seriously are not apt to counter aggressive moves by fringe firms contributing only a tiny fraction of industry output, since even a doubling of the fringe's sales has a modest proportionate effect on their own sales. They are especially unlikely to respond if the retaliatory cut must apply across the board because of anti-discrimination laws or because all buyers will demand any price reduction offered to selected customers. Recognizing this, fringe producers will not be deterred from initiating independent pricing actions by fear of retaliation. But over the short run of a year or two, the impact of their actions depends upon the relationship between their production capacity and total industry output.

When demand is strong, fringe members will be able to produce at capacity and sell their output at the price preferred by the industry leaders, or at some mutually accepted price differential. But if a recession occurs, they may find themselves operating well below desired levels if they adhere to the high prices the oligopolistic leaders are attempting to maintain. To remedy this, they will bid for additional orders at reduced prices. This pattern has been observed repeatedly in cement, rayon, tin cans, gasoline, steel, and fabricated aluminum products, among others.[3] The reaction of the leading firms depends then upon the magnitude of the fringe's incursions. If the fringe's capacity is small relative to total industry output, so that the shift in market shares is less than approximately 10 percent of total industry output, the leading producers are apt to ignore the incursions and persevere in their efforts to hold the price line. But when larger market share transfers appear imminent, defensive price reductions by the leading firms will normally begin. Whether price cutting will proceed further depends mainly upon three things: the expected duration of the demand slump, the degree to which cost constraints inhibit deeper price shading by the smaller firms, and the responsiveness of fringe producers to the educational message implicit in the leading firms' retaliatory price moves. In general, oligopoly price structure breakdowns are more likely the higher the proportion of industry capacity in the hands of competitive fringe producers and the more industry leaders find themselves departing from desired operating levels at posted prices.

Product heterogeneity

Product homogeneity implies that the offerings of rival sellers are alike in all significant physical and subjective respects, so that they are virtually perfect substitutes in the minds of consumers. With perfect homogeneity, there remains only one dimension along which rivalrous actions and counteractions can take place: price. In such cases, oligopolists have a particularly easy task of coordinating their behavior, for they must coordinate along only the one dimension. When products are heterogeneously differentiated, the terms of rivalry become multidimensional, and the coordination problem grows in complexity by leaps and bounds.

Four broad product heterogeneity classes, arrayed in order of increasing dimensionality, can be identified. First, there may be stable inter-firm differences in real or subjectively imputed product quality sufficient to require price differentials in market equilibrium. The coordination problem here is two dimensional, involving both the price level and the amount of the differential. Judging from the amount of conflict over gasoline price differentials between major brand and independent retailers, it is probably more than twice as difficult to coordinate on these two magnitudes together than it is to reach tacit agreements concerning only a uniform price.[4] Second, when sellers are located at varying distances from buyers (i.e., there is spatial differentiation) and transportation costs are relatively high, a very complex price structure may be required. Further analysis of this problem is deferred to Chapter 11. Third, product qualities may be dynamically unstable, as in fashion goods industries and fields subject to rapid technological change. Each product change alters the relative competitive position of every producer and requires either a new set of pricing decisions or the acceptance of a rigid, historically based price structure not likely to maximize profits. Fourth, complex products such as airplanes, electrical power generators, buildings, and nonstandardized personal services are sold on a custom-made basis. When no two orders are ever exactly alike or when there is leeway for deviations from the buyer's product specifications in hundreds of particulars, tacit coordination on joint profit-maximizing strategies becomes extremely difficult to maintain.

Several examples serve to illustrate the range of coordination difficulties associated with static and dynamic product heterogeneity. Perhaps most extreme is the problem of aerospace firms bidding to secure government contracts for the development of new, technologically advanced weapon systems and space vehicles. The choices of government decision makers are necessarily multidimensional. What is sought is the best combination of qualitative design features, time of availability, and expected development, production, and operating costs. A virtual infinity of potential design feature combinations is open to bidders, and each firm's judgment concerning the quality-cost-time tradeoffs most likely to win

approval from the customer (itself a bureaucratic maze with internally conflicting preferences) invariably differs from that of its rivals. Effective tacit coordination of bid details under these circumstances is literally impossible, and interfirm rivalry to win attractive new development program contracts has been vigorously independent even when only two firms were bidding.[5] Because of this, and given certain other characteristics unique to the environment of advanced weapons and space systems development, competition for new research and development program contracts often has more desirable behavioral effects when the number of rivals is small than when there are numerous bidders.[6]

For nearly a century, the heavy electrical equipment industry has exhibited the pricing patterns associated with complex, multidimensionally differentiated products. During the closing decades of the 19th century, spirited competition prevailed with respect to both product quality and price in the electric traction motor, induction motor, and polyphase generator lines, even though there were only two sellers vying for

2. See Almarin Phillips, *Market Structure, Organization and Performance* (Cambridge, Mass.: Harvard University Press, 1962), pp. 29–30; and Oliver E. Williamson, "A Dynamic Theory of Interfirm Behavior," *Quarterly Journal of Economics* 79 (November 1965): 600.

3. See Samuel M. Loescher, *Imperfect Collusion in the Cement Industry* (Cambridge, Mass.: Harvard University Press: 1959), pp. 120, 293; Jesse W. Markham, *Competition in the Rayon Industry* (Cambridge, Mass.: Harvard University Press, 1952), pp. 78, 127–36; James W. McKie, *Tin Cans and Tin Plate* (Cambridge, Mass.: Harvard University Press, 1959), pp. 217–18; Edmund P. Learned and Catherine C. Ellsworth, *Gasoline Pricing in Ohio* (Boston: Harvard Business School Division of Research, 1959), pp. 108, 149; and Peck, *Competition in the Aluminum Industry*, pp. 66–72.

4. See Learned and Ellsworth, *Gasoline Pricing in Ohio*, pp. 133, 149; and Leonard W. Weiss, *Economics and American Industry* (New York: Wiley, 1961), pp. 411–12.

5. For a fascinating account of the two-firm TFX aircraft competition, see Richard A. Smith, *Corporations in Crisis* (Garden City: Doubleday, 1963), Chapters 9 and 10. On another vigorous two-firm competition, see John M. Mecklin, "Why Boeing Is Missing the Bus," *Fortune*, 1 June 1968, pp. 80 ff.; and "Rolls Royce and G. E. Fighting To Win Airbus Engine Orders," *New York Times*, 6 March 1968, p. 61.

6. See F. M. Scherer, *The Weapons Acquisition Process: Economic Incentives* (Boston: Harvard Business School Division of Research, 1964), pp. 44–49.

Conditions limiting oligopolistic coordination 201

many of the orders. Harold Passer isolated two main reasons for the strenuous duopolistic rivalry in traction motors: complexity of the product and rapid technological change. Regarding the complexity of railway motors, he observed:

> When a product possesses many features and when the possible variations in these features are numerous, it is hard to see how agreement on the product could be tacit. And the process of reaching explicit agreement on the product would have been lengthy and elaborate, if possible at all.[7]

On the other hand, his analysis shows that after an initial period of settling, price competition was mild and stable in the electric arc lamp and incandescent lamp fields, where the products were simpler and more readily standardized.[8]

Contrasting behavioral patterns in static product lines to those in technologically dynamic ones, he observed further:

> It is probable that continuous and unpredictable change in the technology of a product and its manufacture introduces the element of uncertainty which accounts for the competitive rather than the monopolistic behavior of the oligopolists. . . . If technological change proceeded at a slower pace . . . the traditional duopoly case, with a fairly homogeneous product and a recognition of mutual dependence, may have resulted. Product competition based on a static technology, in which product choices are made from a perfectly well-known and unchanging set of alternatives, may have an effect on duopolistic behavior different from that based on a rapidly advancing technology.[9]

Of the two disruptive influences stressed by Passer, complexity of the product seems to have been more important, for in the absence of explicit collusive agreements, there were periods of intense price competition in the electrical generator field despite a maturing of the product technology. We recall from Chapter 6 that to facilitate standardized pricing, General Electric developed and published an elaborate pricing formula book with which industry price analysts

could build up the prices for thousands of generator component parts into an overall book price. Yet because the typical generator order is so complex, there was considerable opportunity for alternative interpretations of customer specifications, and parties to the conspiracies of the 1950s found mere agreement to follow book pricing techniques an insufficient foundation for effective collusion. They felt compelled to meet and compare calculations before submitting bids. When the meetings were suspended because some company refused to participate, the poor coordination of price calculations was one element leading to sharp price reductions, although as we shall see shortly, there were other contributing factors.

Automobile tires present a different set of pricing coordination problems. Tires are fairly simple products and the industry is quite concentrated, with eight firms accounting for 93 percent of shipments in 1972. One might expect a high degree of tacit cooperation. Yet the price structure in tires has been described as "chaotic"; tire manufacturers have been subjected to "an almost uninterrupted series of price buffetings"; and profits have been lower on the average than those of other industries with comparable market structures.[10] One apparent reason is the great variety of manufacturers' and private-label grades, complicated by the welter of conflicting sales claims, labels, guarantees, and prices. Even under uniform grading requirements proposed by a federal government agency during the early 1970s, the array of possibilities confronting consumers would continue to be quite complex.[11] Whether further standardization and simplification will render interdependent pricing more feasible, as one student of the industry has predicted, remains to be seen.[12]

Four brief examples round out the picture. The value of crude petroleum varies with gravity (i.e., the proportion of heavier components), sulfur content, and access to low-cost transportation. The price premium or discount that a particular crude oil can command changes over time—e.g., with heavier crudes selling at less of a discount when unusually cold winter weather stimulates heating oil demand and with advantageously located crudes (such as those from Libya and

Nigeria) selling at a higher premium when the ocean tanker market is tight. Inability to reach and continuously revise their agreement on how large such price differentials should be has been a significant source of discontent among OPEC cartel members—although not enough to undermine their discipline in maintaining a high overall price level after 1973. The traditionally tight pricing discipline of American steel producers was upset during the late 1960s and mid-1970s by disparate handling of extra charges and especially by the propensity of some firms to sell first-quality steel strip at the much lower prices normally charged for secondary or defective output.[13] In railroading, the Grand Trunk Line provided circuitous and hence slower service than its three major rivals between Chicago and New York City during the 1880s and 1890s. It could attract a substantial volume of perishable commodities like dressed meat only by charging lower rates. Disputes over the size of the rate differential led to two rate wars in which rate levels fell by roughly 50 percent.[14] And despite a long record of price uniformity among standard brand cigarettes, the introduction of new king size and filter tip cigarettes by the leading producers during the 1950s was followed by several years of widely varying differentials before all firms came together on a uniform price structure.[15]

In sum, when the offerings of rival producers differ over numerous dimensions, the problem of coordinating on a common price structure is much more complex than it is with homogeneous products. Other things being equal, cooperation to maintain high collective profits is less likely to be successful the more heterogeneous products are. However, some aspects of product differentiation work in the opposite direction. When sellers can build strong brand loyalties or when economies of scale in product differentiation raise barriers to the entry of new competition, profits may be higher than they would be with homogeneous products. The net effect of these opposing forces depends in a complex way upon the specific character of product differentiation and the degree to which other influences conducive to coordinated pricing operate. The type of heterogeneity most likely to disrupt pricing discipline

appears to be multidimensionality of a product's technical features.

The extent of product heterogeneity in concentrated markets How widespread is product heterogeneity as a structural condition limiting interfirm coordination? To gain insight into this question, an analysis was made of the 65 manufacturing industry groups defined by Carl Kaysen and Donald Turner as Type I oligopolies—those in which the leading eight firms made at least 50 percent and the leading 20 firms at least 75 percent of industry shipments.[16] Those 65 industries presumably have structures most conducive to oligopolistic pricing. Each industry was given a score of from 1 to 4 on four attributes: multidimensionality of its products, the rate of change in product technology, the degree to which there are physical differences in the quality of rival products, and the degree to which consumers subjectively impute quality differences to products as a result of such influences as advertising. (No attempt was made to take geographic or

7. Harold C. Passer, *The Electrical Manufacturers: 1875–1900* (Cambridge, Mass.: Harvard University Press, 1953), p. 263.

8. Passer, *Electrical Manufacturers*, pp. 62, 161–62.

9. Passer, *Electrical Manufacturers*, pp. 352–53. See also Ralph G. M. Sultan, *Pricing in the Electrical Oligopoly*, vol. 1 (Boston: Harvard Business School Division of Research, 1974), pp. 28–36; and vol. 2 (1975), Chapter 12.

10. A. D. H. Kaplan et al., *Pricing in Big Business* (Washington, D.C.: Brookings Institution, 1958), p. 280.

11. See "The 324 Ways To Grade a Tire," *Business Week*, 19 February 1972, pp. 22–23. See also "U.S. Agency Unveils Tire Quality Rules," *New York Times*, 15 July 1978, p. 6.

12. Louis P. Bucklin, "The Uniform Grading System for Tires: Its Effect upon Consumers and Industry Competition," *Antitrust Bulletin* 19 (Winter 1974), especially pp. 799–801.

13. Robert Lamb, "The Mystery of Steel Prices," *Fortune*, March 1977, pp. 158–60.

14. Paul W. MacAvoy, *The Economic Effects of Regulation: The Trunkline Railroad Cartels and the ICC Before 1900* (Cambridge, Mass.: M.I.T. Press, 1965), pp. 129–35.

15. R. B. Tennant, "The Cigarette Industry," in Walter Adams, ed., *The Structure of American Industry*, 3rd ed. (New York: Macmillan, 1961), pp. 376–77.

16. Carl Kaysen and Donald F. Turner, *Antitrust Policy* (Cambridge, Mass.: Harvard University Press, 1959), pp. 27–37, 275–313.

spatial differentiation into account.) With respect to product dimensionality, the following system of scores was used:

1. Standardized technical configuration
2. Some configuration options
3. Complex configuration options
4. Very complex configuration options

On the rate of technological change, physical product difference, and subjective product quality difference attributes, the scores varied from 1 for *virtually none* to 4 for *great*, with *modest* and *considerable* categories intervening.

The results were as follows. The mean score was 1.85, suggesting a net tendency more toward homogeneity than heterogeneity. Seven of the 65 industries received a score of 1 on all four attributes, connoting virtually complete product homogeneity both statically and dynamically. Thirty-nine industries, or 60 percent of the total, had no score higher than 2, while 34 percent had at least two scores of 1 and none higher than 2. Forty percent of the industries had at least one score higher than 2, indicating a considerable degree of heterogeneity on at least one attribute. There were 46 scores of either 3 or 4 altogether. Thirteen industries had scores of 3 or 4 on the product dimensionality criterion, which probably affects pricing coordination with special force.

Although the analysis is subject to judgmental errors, it seems reasonable to draw three broad conclusions. First, few manufacturing industries conform tightly to the polar case of perfectly homogeneous oligopoly. Second, somewhere between 20 and 40 percent of the concentrated industries supply products heterogeneous enough to pose fairly difficult obstacles to tacit coordination. Third, the predominant pattern in oligopolistically structured manufacturing industries is a modest degree of product heterogeneity, engendering slight to moderate coordination problems.

Methods of coordinating heterogeneous product pricing Even modest product heterogeneity might undermine pricing discipline were it not for certain devices that facilitate coordination. One considered in Chapter 6 is focal point pricing. Price lining is especially important in consumer goods fields such as clothing, where style changes occur frequently. Faithful adherence to focal points permits sellers to avoid price competition that changes in product design and image would otherwise precipitate. But even when direct price competition is minimized, active quality competition may continue as firms attempt to offer the most attractive qualitative features consistent with a fixed, inflexible price. This phenomenon will be considered in Chapter 14.

Independent pricing behavior may also be headed off through the negotiation of standardization agreements on product features that would seriously complicate tacit collusion if left uncoordinated. In the steel industry, for example, explicit agreements were at one time concluded to secure uniform treatment of extras—i.e., complex differences in finish, temper, packaging, and so on.[17] Although the layman might think that cement is cement, cement trade associations found it necessary to negotiate standardization agreements in order to discourage rivalry based upon claims of superior quality. They also published for the guidance of members standardized terms of sale, cash discounts, package charges, refunds for returned bags, and bin-testing cost rules. Differences in any of these categories could undermine a carefully cultivated system of direct and tacit price agreements.[18] Still another common practice (until it was condemned in a series of antitrust decisions) was the maintenance of basing point pricing systems to overcome the intricate problem of quoting transportation charges in industries where such costs constitute a major fraction of the total delivered product price. The basing point system will be examined at greater length in Chapter 11.

Other aspects of heterogeneity Conflicts over pricing policy may also arise because of interfirm differences in distribution channels, vertical integration, or reliance upon foreign sources of supply.

For instance, the tire industry's pricing problems, vexing enough because of the tangle of conflicting grades and quality claims, are complicated further by the diversity of middlemen and retail outlets through which replacement tires are sold. In 1966, some 120 private label operations purchased tires from the regular manufacturers and marketed them through their own distribution channels under their private brand names. Kaplan and his associates found that the importance of mail-order houses, auto supply chains, and oil companies in imparting fluidity to the tire price structure was "overwhelming." The tires supplied by these outlets

> have undercut the factory brands and necessitated a continuous procession of sales and special discounts, allowances, and so on—some authorized, some not. . . . In addition, private brands have led to a succession of changes in tire quality, innovations that have upset the precarious stability of tire "levels" as a framework for a price structure.[19]

Professor Edward Mason concluded that the tire industry's distribution channels led to a discount structure facilitating price cutting "on the slightest provocation."[20] This experience lends some credence to Clair Wilcox's quip that "the formula for competition is simple: add one part of Sears Roebuck to twenty parts of oligopoly."[21]

The drug industry sells its products directly to all sorts of public and private hospitals and agencies, offering varying discounts off the list price to different customer types. To avoid the confusion that could arise in making quotations to hospitals whose status is ambiguous, firms adhered by mutual tacit consent to published standard hospital classification guides. Even so, errors sometimes occurred, much to the dismay of industry sales executives.[22]

Differences in degrees of vertical integration led to pricing policy conflicts among American copper producers during the 1947–55 period, despite nearly perfect product homogeneity and high market concentration. Anaconda, integrated on a broad scale into fabricated product lines and heavily dependent upon copper supplies from Chile, desired high primary copper prices partly to placate the volatile Chilean government and partly to maintain an advantage over nonintegrated rival fabricators by keeping their input costs high. Kennecott, on the other hand, was much less integrated vertically. It was anxious to hold the primary price at more moderate levels to maintain demand for its ample pri-

mary copper supplies. According to J. L. McCarthy, these conflicts prevented the industry from achieving joint maximization of profits.[23]

Dynamic implications of cost structures

The ability of oligopolists to cooperate with one another is also affected in a variety of ways by cost conditions. In Chapter 5 this problem was examined from a static viewpoint. Generally, the more cost functions differ from firm to firm, the more trouble the companies will have maintaining a common price policy, and the less likely joint maximization of profits will be. Nothing more need be added on this point. Instead, we shall turn to some dynamic implications of industrial cost structure.

A dynamic corollary of the proposition just stated is self-evident and can be treated briefly. The more rapidly producers' cost functions are altered through technological innovation, and the more unevenly these changes are diffused

17. Cf. Chapter 6, p. 170 *supra*.

18. Loescher, *Imperfect Collusion*, pp. 134–35. On similar credit term and delivery method agreements in the gypsum board industry, see "Busting a Trust: Gypsum Case Unravels Alleged Price-Fix Plan," *Wall Street Journal*, 3 October 1975, p. 16.

19. Kaplan et al., *Pricing in Big Business*, p. 203. See also the Federal Trade Commission staff report, *Economic Report on the Manufacture and Distribution of Automotive Tires* (Washington, D.C.: Government Printing Office, March 1966), Chapters 2 and 4.

20. Edward S. Mason, *Economic Concentration and the Monopoly Problem* (Cambridge, Mass.: Harvard University Press, 1957), p. 68. See also "Pricing Strategy in an Inflation Economy," *Business Week*, 6 April 1974, p. 45.

21. Clair Wilcox, "On the Alleged Ubiquity of Oligopoly," *American Economic Review* 40 (May 1950): 71.

22. See exhibit PH-129A in *Federal Trade Commission* v. *American Cyanamid Co. et al.*, FTC Docket no. 7211 (1959), offering in evidence a sales manager's report of a rival's bid, apparently "submitted in error" to a state hospital at the prevailing federal agency price.

23. "The American Copper Industry: 1947–1955," *Yale Economic Essays* 4 (Spring 1964): 64–130. Unfortunately, McCarthy did not attempt to specify the price level at which industry profits would in fact have been maximized.

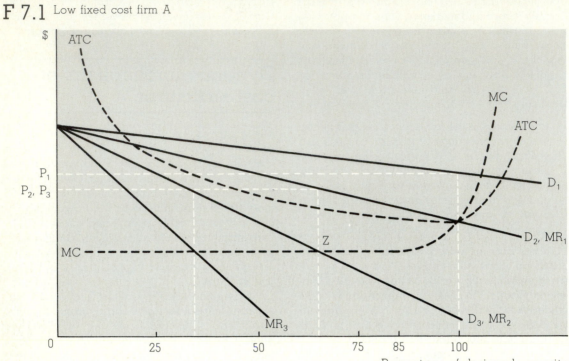

F 7.1 Low fixed cost firm A

throughout the industry, the more likely there will be conflict regarding pricing choices. For example, National Steel, after installing new and more efficient continuous strip mills during the 1930s, became an active price cutter, pulling other steel makers with higher costs along.[24] The introduction of mechanized window glass production techniques around the turn of the century touched off a struggle for survival in which prices were driven below cost even for the new and more efficient machine methods. After stability was restored through cartel agreements, a second episode of price warfare between glass makers using new continuous process techniques and those employing obsolete methods arose during the early 1930s.[25] In the sanitary pottery fixtures industry, conflicts associated with the introduction of tunnel kilns (replacing more costly beehive oven processes) were in part responsible for the failure of producers to eliminate widespread price cutting despite repeated attempts to reach collusive agreements.[26] And in the ocean shipping industry, the introduction of highly efficient containerships during the 1960s undermined long-standing cartel agreements and triggered a wave of price competition.[27]

Our main concern will be with a different issue: the dynamic interaction between cost structures and business conditions. There is evidence that industries characterized by high overhead costs are particularly susceptible to pricing discipline breakdowns when a cyclical or secular decline in demand forces member firms to operate well below designed plant capacity. This tendency appears to be especially marked in industries with heavy investments in developed natural resource deposits (like petroleum extraction and underground coal mining) and those using highly capital-intensive production processes (such as railroading, petroleum refining, chemicals, steel, aluminum, cement, glass, and papermaking).

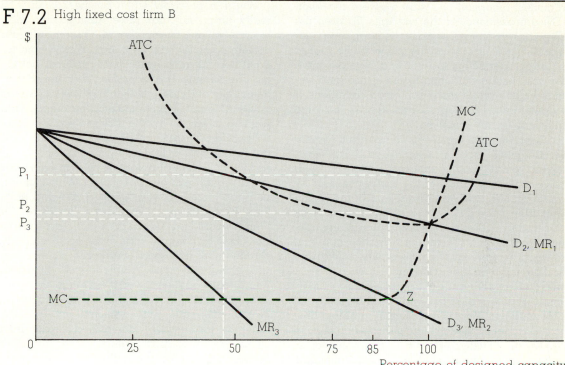

$ ATC MC ATC

P_1 D_1
P_2
P_3 D_2, MR$_1$

MC Z D_3, MR$_2$

MR$_3$

0   25   50   75   85   100

Percentage of designed capacity

To understand this phenomenon, two questions must be answered. First, why do oligopolists with high fixed costs have stronger incentives to cut prices when demand declines than firms with low fixed costs? And second, if price cutting does break out, how does the cost structure affect the extent to which it will be carried?

We proceed, using diagrams comparing two different (not necessarily competing) firms: Firm A, with average fixed costs amounting to 15 percent of average total cost ATC at 85 percent of designed capacity output [Figure 7.1]; and Firm B, with average fixed costs equalling 50 percent of ATC at 85 percent of designed capacity output [Figure 7.2]. Since the shape of the cost curves is crucial, we must strive to be as true to life as possible. For both firms, marginal cost is assumed to be constant up to 85 percent of designed capacity output, after which it rises sharply. This is consistent with most of the statistical evidence on short-run cost functions.[28] To

ensure comparability, average total cost is equal in the two cases at designed capacity output (that is, where ATC is at a minimum). Identical linear constant-shares demand curves reflecting three states of the business cycle—prosperity (D_1),

24. See Weiss, *Economics and American Industry*, pp. 296–97.

25. G. W. Stocking and M. W. Watkins, *Monopoly and Free Enterprise* (New York: Twentieth Century Fund, 1951), pp. 121–26.

26. Cf. Phillips, *Market Structure, Organization and Performance*, pp. 175–76.

27. "Cooling the Rate War on the North Atlantic," *Business Week*, 29 April 1972, pp. 48–52. For background, see Robert Larner, "Public Policy in the Ocean Freight Industry," in Almarin Phillips, ed., *Promoting Competition in Regulated Markets* (Washington, D.C.: Brookings Institution, 1975), pp. 113–30.

28. For surveys of the literature, see J. Johnston, *Statistical Cost Analysis* (New York: McGraw-Hill, 1960), Chapters 4 and 5; and A. A. Walters, "Production and Cost Functions: An Econometric Survey," *Econometrica* 31 (January-April 1963): 39–51.

Conditions limiting oligopolistic coordination   **207**

a modest recession (D_2), and a severe recession (D_3) are assumed for the two firms. To keep the drawings as simple as possible, each lower demand curve has twice the slope of its higher neighbor, permitting the marginal revenue curve for one demand function to serve also as a demand curve under more depressed conditions. It follows that the demand curves all have the same elasticity at any given price.[29]

Suppose each firm is operating at 100 percent of designed capacity with demand D_1, maximizing profits under the assumption of rival price matching (and hence constant shares) by equating MR_1 with MC, and selling at the highly profitable price OP_1. Now a mild recession shifts demand to D_2. For low fixed cost Firm A, the optimal reaction is a substantial reduction in output to about 65 percent of capacity, where MR_2 and MC are equated, and a modest reduction in price to OP_2. A smaller but still appreciable profit margin is attained. High fixed cost Firm B's marginal cost situation dictates a reduction in output only to 90 percent of capacity, but a sharp reduction in the profit-maximizing price to OP_2. The previously substantial profit margin is nearly eliminated. Thus, when demand falls below levels that will sustain capacity output, the profit-maximizing enterprise with high fixed costs cuts prices more sharply and suffers more severe erosion of profits than a similarly inclined firm with low fixed costs. This result is quite general, for marginal costs must fall more steeply with reduced output from the point at which ATC is minimized for a firm with higher fixed and lower marginal costs at below-capacity production levels.

We turn the screw tighter now, letting demand shift from D_2 to D_3. For Firm A, since both MR_2 and MR_3 (derived from demand curves with the same elasticity at given prices) cut MC at the same level, no change in price is induced. For Firm B, with a slight curvature in MC in the neighborhood of its intersection with MR_2, an insignificantly small price reduction is induced. Thus, when marginal costs are roughly constant at below-capacity operation, as statistical studies suggest, and when demand curves shift isoelastically, the intensification of an already depressed situation motivates little or no price reduction by oligopolists pursuing joint profit maximization.[30]

Yet it is precisely when business conditions really turn sour that price cutting runs most rampant among oligopolists with high fixed costs. Something more than the marginal conditions for profit maximization must affect producer behavior. The missing link is profits. With the shift in demand from D_2 to D_3, both firms show losses; P_3 is below ATC at the profit-maximizing output. Firm A's loss is small, by the inflated standards of textbook draftsmanship—about 5 percent of costs. But Firm B, with its high fixed costs spread over a restricted volume of output, shows an enormous deficit—roughly 27 percent of costs. With a milder, perhaps more realistic leftward demand shift, Firm B would incur substantial losses, while Firm A would find itself in the black. These losses are likely to confront Firm B, or some similarly situated high fixed cost operator in B's industry, with a financial crisis. Unable to meet dividends and interest payments out of earnings, the firm's decision-making horizon shortens. Its managers turn all their attention to immediate remedies, ignoring the risks of diminished profits from weakened industry discipline in the uncertain future. They see that if additional business could be secured by quietly undercutting joint profit-maximizing price OP_3 slightly and moving off the constant-shares demand curve along a 'rival price constant' curve, operation at higher capacity levels would be possible, overhead could be spread over more units of output, and losses would be reduced or even (if capacity utilization could be increased to 90 percent) eliminated. Some producers in Firm B's straits will choose to take the chance. As Hall and Hitch summarized their interviews with British businessmen during the depressed 1930s, "Usually one entrepreneur is overcome by panic: 'there is always one fool who cuts'; and the rest must follow."[31] Unless they are imbued with a strong sense of group loyalty, the rest will indeed follow sooner or later as price cutters make inroads into their sales, and the end result will be a general decline in price away from the joint profit-maximizing level OP_3.

Assuming the persistence of depressed demand state D_3, the limit to which proliferating noncooperative price cutting can be carried is where price falls uniformly to the level of marginal cost, at point Z in Figures 7.1 and 7.2.

Here again we find an important difference between industries with high and those with low fixed costs. Price cutting will be checked at higher price levels when marginal costs are high and fixed costs low than when marginal costs are low and fixed costs high. The industry characterized by high fixed costs suffers more when demand is depressed both because of stronger inducements toward price cutting and a lower floor to price declines.

From this analytic conclusion, we are tempted to generalize: The higher fixed costs are relative to total costs, the more prone an industry is to serious pricing discipline breakdowns during recessions. Unfortunately, the problem is more complicated. Recognizing the temptations confronting them, firms in high fixed cost industries seem to exercise extraordinary restraint in their pricing actions; and when tacit restraint fails, they have an unusually high propensity to scurry into formal collusive agreements. According to Alfred Neal, when the number of sellers is small:

> each seller realizes that if every other seller follows his price, all will make smaller profits or greater losses and no permanent cure to depressed demand will be achieved, since only the most ruthless price war will eliminate enough capacity to improve the price situation. Under such circumstances, only the most sanguine or the most foolhardy seller would start an open price war (though none would be averse to making secret concessions up to the point where an open price war threatened to start).[32]

Yet when several firms engage in this sort of brinkmanship, some are likely to lose their footing, pulling the rest along, unless an explicit collusive agreement can be reached quickly to halt the slide. We conclude then that the probability of pricing discipline breakdowns increases with the burden of fixed costs borne by sellers, *ceteris paribus*, but that recognition of this danger may stimulate institutional adaptations nullifying the tendency.

It is hard to predict *a priori* the outcome of this tug-of-war between the incentive to look out only for one's own short-run interests and the incentive to cooperate. Some examples show the range

of observed behavior.

Railroading is the case par excellence of an industry with high fixed costs and an historical propensity toward pricing discipline breakdowns when competition is left unfettered. The capital of railroads in 1914 has been estimated at 574 percent of gross operating revenues, compared to 94 percent for manufacturing companies.[33] Thus, railroading was much more capital-intensive than manufacturing generally, with a heavy component of fixed charges for capital sunk in roadbeds, rails, terminals, and rolling stock. This was accompanied by low short-run marginal cost for adding an extra freight car or two onto an already scheduled train. Because of these cost conditions, rivalry among railroads in the closing decades of the 19th century was often marked by oscillation between price warfare and collusive agreements. This pattern was most striking on the key Chicago–New York routes.[34] During the early 1870s, only the New York Central and the Pennsylvania offered through service between Chicago and New York City. By concluding explicit price-fixing agreements they managed to maintain eastbound grain rates at roughly $.56 per hundredweight. However, when the Baltimore & Ohio completed its route in 1874, it refused to join the agreement, price shading developed, and the grain rate fell to $.40 that year, $.20 in 1876, and $.15 in 1877. Some shipments moved east for as

29. Cf. Chapter 5, p. 157, note 13, *supra.*

30. Or when elasticities change symmetrically with the shift in demand, equiproportional price changes will result. This case is ignored because the change in price follows from demand conditions and not from differences in the cost structure.

31. R. L. Hall and Charles J. Hitch, "Price Theory and Business Behaviour," *Oxford Economic Papers* 2 (May 1939): 25. See also Bjarke Fog, *Industrial Pricing Policies: An Analysis of Pricing Policies of Danish Manufacturers,* trans. I. E. Bailey (Amsterdam: North-Holland, 1960), p. 34; and Alfred C. Neal, *Industrial Concentration and Price Inflexibility* (Washington, D.C.: American Council on Public Affairs, 1942), p. 87.

32. Neal, *Industrial Concentration and Price Inflexibility,* p. 77.

33. Eliot Jones, "Is Competition in Industry Ruinous?," *Quarterly Journal of Economics* 34 (May 1920): 484–85.

34. See MacAvoy, *The Economic Effects of Regulation.*

little as $.075 per hundredweight during the summer of 1879—a rate that may not even have covered immediate marginal costs, although the evidence is inconclusive. Subsequent collusive arrangements between the New York Central, Pennsylvania, B & O, and Grand Trunk lines succeeded in raising rates to $.30 under favorable conditions, but the agreements broke down repeatedly until the whole rate structure was subjected to effective regulation by the Interstate Commerce Commission. The New York–Chicago lines were perhaps extreme in the duration and intensity of their competitive price cutting, since there were four financially independent trunk lines and several rail-water interlines vying for business, but similar price wars of shorter duration occurred on many other segments of the U.S. railroad network.[35]

Turning now to the manufacturing sector, rayon manufacturing is a capital-intensive industry whose pricing behavior before 1950 has been analyzed thoroughly.[36] Producers had short-run cost relationships similar to Figure 7.2, with fixed costs amounting to one-third of total unit cost at capacity output, and with average total cost rising to 125 percent of its minimum value for operation at one-half capacity. [In Figure 7.2, the comparable figure is 138 percent.] The first reaction of producers to a decline in demand was typically to maintain capacity production and build up inventories. If the recession persisted, the larger firms restricted output to maintain the price level, but smaller firms tended to shade prices to keep their plants busy. This approach was successful in preserving a semblance of pricing discipline in mild recessions. But if operations fell much below 75 percent of capacity, profit margins were wiped out completely; after this point, attempts to maintain stable prices proved futile.[37] In the depths of the early 1930s depression, when industry leaders American Viscose and du Pont were operating at only 55 percent of capacity, a formal price-fixing agreement was instituted. Elaborate steps were taken to implement it, but financial pressures on individual firms were so strong that the agreement broke down. Even the largest producers were violating it through off-list selling.[38]

The cement industry has a cost structure similar to rayon's.[39] Though the product is essentially homogeneous and the number of sellers in most markets is relatively small, the industry has experienced repeated pricing discipline breakdowns when demand declined generally or locally. Recognizing their inability to collude tacitly with any great success, U.S. cement makers entered into a series of price-fixing arrangements, but these have tended to collapse under financial stress. From 1930 to 1932, unfettered price cutting drove down the average realized price per barrel by 30 percent while unit overhead costs were rising.[40] An antitrust judgment in 1948 deprived the industry of its principal collusive device—the basing point system. Strong demand kept prices on the upswing during the early 1950s; but excess capacity began to appear after 1956, precipitating price shading and, during the 1960s, a general decline in the price level.[41]

The steel industry is not unlike rayon and cement. Its products are fairly homogeneous, once the extras problem is solved; and the fixed costs associated with its capital-intensive, vertically integrated production processes are relatively high. When account is taken of geographic market bounds, the American steel industry is less concentrated than either cement or rayon. Yet up to 1968 and except for some episodes during the 1929–38 depression, it was more successful than either cement or rayon in avoiding widespread price deterioration, even when operating at less than 65 percent of capacity between 1958 and 1962. The main explanation for this record apparently lies in the extraordinary respect U.S. industry members exhibited for their mutual interdependence. A price structure that permitted producers to avoid outright losses unless output fell below 40 percent of capacity was a contributing factor[42]—at least, until stiff import competition forced a general reduction of price-cost margins during the late 1960s and mid-1970s. Even then, the downward rigidity of its price structure stood in remarkable contrast to that of European steel makers.[43]

High fixed and low marginal costs also played a part in the heavy electrical equipment industry's apparent inability to avoid price warfare without formal collaboration in times of depressed demand. Demand for electrical equipment is cyclical—either feast or famine. In addition to carrying fixed plant and equipment costs, producers maintained staffs of skilled design and production engineers they were reluctant to disperse, and so a significant fraction of labor costs was also viewed as fixed.[44] These conditions contributed to the rivalry that on occasion drove prices as low as 40 percent of book values.

Finally, we consider the petroleum extraction and refining industries, which have their own special fixed cost problems. Much extraction capital is invested in holes in the ground—sunk cost in every sense of the word. Once a well is drilled, the marginal cost of drawing oil from it is for many years practically nil. Refineries are capital-intensive, and to complicate matters, many products emerge from the distillation towers as joint or by-products with a marginal cost that is either low or indeterminate. Tacit collusion in the sale of refined products is complicated by disagreements over retail price differentials between major and independent brands and by the perishability (through physical deterioration) of local gasoline inventories. Frequent gasoline price wars at the retail and wholesale levels have been the result. At the crude oil extraction stage, prices in the United States fell from an average of $1.19 per barrel in 1930 to $.65 per barrel in 1931, descending to $.25 per barrel in some territories during the summer of 1931 as the onset of the Great Depression and the opening up of new fields coincided. However, U.S. crude oil prices exhibited remarkable downward rigidity between 1945 and 1973, mainly because of import restrictions (after 1959) and the cartelized prorationing system, under which Texas producers in particular were required under state and federal laws to restrict their supply when demand fell. Since 1973 Saudi Arabia and Libya, with cash inflows from oil sales exceeding their capacity to spend, have played a similar role in supporting OPEC cartel prices at 10 to 20 times marginal production costs despite episodes of substantial excess capacity.[45]

To summarize, some industries (like American steel up to 1968 and world oil since 1973) have been quite successful in minimizing rivalrous pricing despite high fixed and low variable costs and depressed demand; some have been successful only when the financial pressures on their members were not strong; and some have been unsuccessful even after engaging in collusion. The explanation for these differences appears to lie largely in the presence or absence of other conditions conducive to cooperative pricing. When other factors such as the size distribution of firms, the degree of product homogeneity, the extent of acceptance accorded the price leader, the ability and willingness of producers to carry sizeable inventories, and deftness in avoiding antitrust action are favorable, pricing discipline may be maintained despite substantial fixed costs. When they are unfavorable, a heavy fixed cost burden makes independent pricing during

35. For a skeptical view of the extent of rate warfare, see C. Emery Troxel, *Economics of Transportation* (New York: Rinehart, 1955), pp. 428, 657; and Tom Ulen, "The Interstate Commerce Commission as a Cartel Manager," (Ph.D. diss. chapter, Stanford University, 1977). Although railroading has been studied by dozens of scholars, hard evidence on the incidence of price warfare is remarkably meager.

36. See Markham, *Competition in the Rayon Industry*, pp. 103, 130, 150–53.

37. Markham, *Competition in the Rayon Industry*, p. 161.

38. Markham, *Competition in the Rayon Industry*, pp. 76–77, 135–36. The pricing of other synthetic fibers appears to have been more disciplined in the 1950s and 1960s, but during the 1970s industry discipline deteriorated under a heavy burden of excess capacity. "The Losses Pile Up in Synthetic Fibers," *Business Week*, 6 December 1976, pp. 46–47.

39. Loescher, *Imperfect Collusion*, pp. 59–72.

40. Loescher, *Imperfect Collusion*, Chapters 4 and 5, especially pp. 181–85.

41. Federal Trade Commission, *Economic Report on Mergers and Vertical Integration in the Cement Industry* (Washington, D.C.: Government Printing Office, April 1966), pp. 16–17.

42. See the U.S., Congress, Senate, Subcommittee on Antitrust and Monopoly report no. 1387, *Administered Prices: Steel*, 85th Cong., 2nd sess., 1958, pp. 45–51.

43. See the U.S., Council on Wage and Price Stability staff report, *A Study of Steel Prices* (Washington, D.C.: Government Printing Office, 1975) pp. 39–75. See also note 95 *infra*.

44. See Sultan, *Pricing in the Electrical Oligopoly*, vol. 1, p. 205 n. 8.

45. On the history of foreign and domestic crude oil cartels, see Morris A. Adelman, *The World Petroleum Market* (Baltimore: Johns Hopkins, 1972); U.S., Congress, Senate, Committee on Foreign Relations report, *Multinational Oil Corporations and U.S. Foreign Policy*, 93rd Cong., 2nd sess., 1975; and John M. Blair, *The Control of Oil* (New York: Pantheon, 1976).

business downturns all the more probable. The net balance among these tendencies can only be ascertained through statistical analysis—a task we defer to Chapter 9. To anticipate a fragment of the results, there is evidence that high capital intensity leads on average to lower profit returns, presumably reflecting more fragile pricing discipline. However, the profit-depressing effect of capital intensity is mitigated to some extent when market concentration is particularly high.[46]

To the extent that governments learn how to use the tools of macroeconomic stabilization successfully, the interaction of fixed costs with depressed business conditions may be a less important cause of pricing discipline breakdowns. But when recessions do materialize, or when shifts in demand adverse to particular industries occur, fixed costs will be a more pressing problem to business firms since the trend is for a growing proportion of all costs to fall into the fixed category. This is so partly because the work force composition is shifting away from direct laborers and operatives, whose numbers can be varied with demand, to overhead-type employees like managers, salespeople, clerks, and engineers, who are hired to meet longer term needs and are not laid off as readily in response to short-run production declines. The ratio of production workers to all workers in manufacturing industries declined from 82 percent in 1939 to 76 percent in 1954 and 71 percent in 1972.[47] In addition, unions are increasingly demanding and winning greater job security for direct laborers. This raises the fixed component of cost structures and makes it difficult for producers to absorb demand shocks by maintaining prices and restricting output.[48] On the other hand, the maturing and homogenization of entrepreneurial attitudes—a phenomenon to be discussed in a later section—may exert a countervailing influence in the direction of firmer pricing discipline.

A digression on cutthroat competition

Thus far, we have implicitly assumed that when a fall in demand induces price competition among oligopolists, society is the gainer, since monopolistic profit margins are reduced and prices are brought into closer proximity to marginal cost. Nevertheless, this judgment is not universally accepted. It is sometimes argued that competition among oligopolists burdened with high fixed costs has a tendency to become "cutthroat" or "ruinous," and that it should be restrained through price-fixing agreements or mergers. This view was widespread around the turn of the century, but even in recent years it has been propounded by a few American economists and by many prominent scholars abroad.[49]

The cutthroat competition issue has two principal branches. One pertains to industries with chronic excess capacity because superior substitutes have appeared on the scene, or as the aftermath of some unique episode such as a surge of wartime orders or the abandonment of tariff protection. The other concerns industries subjected to sharp cyclical or random fluctuations, with vigorous price competition breaking out during troughs of the cycle. Each is worth considering carefully, although in so doing we must depart from the main thread of our analysis.

The sick industry problem First we have the case of the secularly declining or "sick" industry, of which railroading, coal (up to the 1950s in America and 1970s in Europe), rayon, hotels in older U.S. cities, Belgian and British steel, better-quality shoes, some branches of agriculture, and (during the 1920s and 1930s in America and through the 1970s in many western European nations) textile manufacturing are well-known examples. As this range of illustrations suggests, it is not necessary that the market structure be oligopolistic; sick industry problems can occur in atomistically structured fields. There are two chief prerequisites: capacity substantially in excess of current and probable future demands, and rigidities that retard the reallocation of capital and/or labor toward growing industries. Then unless there is some artificial restraint such as government price regulation (as in railroading) or tightly knit cartel agreements, competition is likely to drive prices down to levels that yield investors much less than a normal return on their capital. When firms' cost structures include a high proportion of fixed costs, this profitless existence can continue for years or even (as in railroading and coal mining) for decades, since producers find it preferable to continue operation and cover at least their (relatively modest) variable costs than to shut down and have their investments wiped out completely. The burden of stagnating demand may also fall upon the industry's labor force, for if workers are unable or unwilling to acquire new skills and/or migrate to new regions offering more abundant job opportunities, unemployment will be acute and wage rates may fall to low levels. Capitalists almost surely suffer, then, in a sick industry, and laborers may suffer if they lack alternative employment opportunities.

It is standard practice for the afflicted, and frequently also for well-meaning outsiders, to urge that such industries be granted immunity from the rigors of competition to ease the pain of adjustment. Through private- or government-sponsored price-fixing programs, prices can be held at levels that let investors realize a 'fair' return on their capital and permit the payment of 'just' wages to laborers during the adjustment period. These proposals have a certain amount of appeal on equitable grounds. But abandoning the discipline of competition carries a distinct cost. However painful, losses serve the economic function of driving out surplus and inefficient production capacity and compelling the reallocation of resources into more remunerative lines. Monopolistic price-fixing schemes protect the inefficient producers who, under competitive pressure, would exit first from an industry. They almost always retard the adjustment of physical capacity to reduced demand, although it is less clear that labor mobility is necessarily enhanced by downward pressure on wages. In some cases price-fixing agreements, by permitting positive monopoly profits to be gained, have actually caused capacity to be increased in industries confronted with stagnating demand, aggravating the resource misallocation problem.[50] This perverse effect is particularly likely in cartels allocating numerous members' sales and profit shares in proportion to physical capacity, for by building additional redundant capacity, a firm can increase its profits.[51]

The policy maker dealing with such situations faces a value judgment: He or she must weigh the pain associated with competitive pricing against its superior allocative efficiency. It is well known that politicians opt frequently for a narcotic approach. However, there are compelling arguments for the competitive solution. When demand is price elastic, as is often the case for products

46. See Sidney Schoeffler, Robert D. Buzzell, and Donald F. Heany, "Impact of Strategic Planning on Profit Performance," *Harvard Business Review* 52 (March-April 1974): 141–43; and Sidney Schoeffler, "Cross-Sectional Study of Strategy, Structure, and Performance: Aspects of the PIMS Program," in Hans B. Thorelli, ed., *Strategy + Structure = Performance* (Bloomington: Indiana University Press, 1977) pp. 117–20.

47. Computed from the relevant *Censuses of Manufactures*, vol. I. Employees in central offices and other auxiliary establishments are included in the denominator, with the figure for 1939 estimated from the 1954 value.

48. The striking cyclical price flexibility observed in Japanese industries may be due to the fact that workers in the larger Japanese enterprises have virtual lifetime tenure in their jobs. Therefore, most labor costs (with the exception of bonus payments) tend to be fixed. See James C. Abegglen, *The Japanese Factory* (Glencoe, Ill.: Free Press, 1958), pp. 11–25; and Walter Galenson and Konosuke Odaka, "The Japanese Labor Market," in Hugh Patrick and Henry Rosovsky, eds., *Asia's New Giant* (Washington, D.C.: Brookings Institution, 1976), pp. 613–27.

49. For various views, see Spurgeon Bell, "Fixed Costs and Market Price," *Quarterly Journal of Economics* 32 (May 1918): 507–24; Eliot Jones, "Is Competition in Industry Ruinous?," *Quarterly Journal of Economics* 34 (May 1920): 473–519; J. M. Clark, *Studies in the Economics of Overhead Costs* (Chicago: University of Chicago Press, 1923), especially pp. 434–50; L. G. Reynolds, "Cutthroat Competition," *American Economic Review* 30 (December 1940): 736–47; Fritz Machlup, "Monopoly and the Problem of Economic Stability," in E. H. Chamberlin, ed., *Monopoly and Competition and Their Regulation* (London: Macmillan, 1954), pp. 385–97; S. M. Loescher, *Imperfect Collusion*, pp. 191–99; Almarin Phillips, *Market Structure, Organization and Performance*, pp. 16–19, 221–42; Romney Robinson, "The Economics of Disequilibrium Price," *Quarterly Journal of Economics* 75 (May 1961): 199–233; Kojiro Niino, "The Logic of Excessive Competition," *Kobe University Economic Review* 8(1962): 51–62; Edgar Salin, "Kartellverbot und Konzentration," *Kyklos* 16(3) (1963): 177–202; G. B. Richardson, "The Pricing of Heavy Electrical Equipment: Competition or Agreement?," *Bulletin of the Oxford University Institute of Economics and Statistics* 28 (May 1966): 73–92; Sultan, *Pricing in the Electrical Oligopoly*, vol. 1, Chapter II, and vol. 2, pp. 286–98; Alfred E. Kahn, *The Economics of Regulation*, vol. II (New York: Wiley, 1971), pp. 172–220; and Alfred S. Eichner, "Monopoly, the Emergence of Oligopoly and the Case of Sugar Refining: A Reply," *Journal of Law and Economics* 14 (October 1971): 521–27.

50. Cf. Loescher, *Imperfect Collusion*, pp. 192–94.

51. See Kurt Bloch, "On German Cartels," *Journal of Business* 5 (July 1932): 213–22.

whose secular decline stems from the incursion of substitutes, or when machinery can be substituted readily for labor (as in coal mining and textiles), keeping prices and wages up through monopolistic restrictions will substantially increase the number of immobile laborers thrown into the ranks of the unemployed. The higher income enjoyed by those who manage to retain their jobs is not likely to outweigh the losses experienced by those who do not. Moreover, it may be possible to satisfy both goals—equity and efficiency—through programs to retain and subsidize the relocation of workers employed in or displaced from declining industries. Extending subsidies to investors caught by declining demand, on the other hand, seldom commands much political support. Because, therefore, monopolistic price-fixing schemes do not necessarily ease the lot of workers, because economic efficiency is definitely impaired, and because no premium is placed on avoiding occasional capital losses by investors, most economists are inclined to reject the argument that cutthroat competition in declining industries justifies a deviation from the competitive rule.[52]

Cyclical competition The case of temporary cyclical or random demand downturns is more complicated. Here, by definition, capacity is not permanently in excess of demand, and the problem is to avoid the loss or deterioration of capacity needed when demand recovers. Oligopolists operating evenly matched capital-intensive plants in cyclically sensitive, price-inelastic durable goods markets may, in the absence of institutions facilitating collusion, engage in especially bitter competition during recessions. Each company may strive to increase capacity utilization and cover overhead costs by price shading, and none will cease operations, relaxing the pressure of its supply on price, until all are near the brink of collapse.[53] Competition of this character is said to have several potentially undesirable effects.

For one, if the slump persists, some firms can be driven into bankruptcy by their losses. These will not necessarily be the least efficient producers, but those that are weakest financially—e.g., the newer and smaller organizations without well-developed banking connections.[54] This is clearly objectionable on equity grounds, and it might at first glance appear that capacity needed to meet future demands is lost. However, the latter supposition is debatable. The financial reorganization following a bankruptcy plea seldom entails the outright dismantling of technically efficient production facilities. Rather, the plants are normally acquired at bargain prices by another solvent firm, which sooner or later restores them to operation, burdened by much lower capital charges. It must be noted too that major bankruptcies are relatively rare. In 1975, at the trough of an unusually severe general business recession, there were 1,645 recorded manufacturing business failures, out of a total population of 450,000 incorporated and unincorporated manufacturing business enterprises. Nearly half of the failures had liabilities of less than $100,000, and the total liabilities of failing manufacturers approximated $1 billion.

Second, it is claimed that the stop-and-go operation of plants and firms associated with financial reorganization or less drastic intrafirm adjustment to sharp competition causes diverse inefficiencies. The maintenance and replacement of machines may be postponed; workers may be laid off; skills deteriorate during layoffs; organizational continuity is lost; and research and development projects may be slowed down or terminated. While all this is possible, it is an empirical question whether the long-run efficiency sacrifices accepted under pressure from temporarily intense price competition are very great. What evidence we have suggests that serious sacrifices are uncommon in ordinary slumps, showing up only during a depression as deep and protracted as that of the 1930s. Indeed, Mueller found that industrial enterprises adjusted their capital expenditure plans to *favor* long-term research and development projects at the expense of capital replacement and expansion projects during the recession of 1958.[55] Moreover, it is doubtful whether firms would invest more heavily in new equipment and retain more workers on their payrolls under a monopolistic high-price policy (which reduces the quantity of output demanded and capacity utilization rates, *ceteris paribus*) than they would in a competitive milieu. We shall return to this last point in Chapter 13.

An argument heard frequently overseas, but seldom in the United States, is that temporary price-fixing arrangements to control cutthroat competition during recessions prevent permanent increases in market concentration, because otherwise small firms would either fail or head off the inevitable by merging with stronger industry leaders. There is no evidence that small but efficient U.S. firms have been forced in wholesale lots into the arms of their larger rivals during business recessions since the 1930s. However, some reports indicate that a movement toward crisis-induced concentration operated during the relatively mild Japanese recession of 1965 and 1966.[56] The Japanese experience may have differed from that of the United States because of disparate job tenure commitments to workers or because in Japan there was a much larger fringe of inefficiently small enterprises.[57] Yet even if the need of small firms to merge were accepted as inevitable, mergers could be channeled in such a way as to minimize adverse structural effects through a strong antitrust policy (which most nations abroad lack).

One thing is indisputable. When all-out competition does break out during business slumps, driving price below the unit costs of efficient producers, prices *must* rise above full cost during booms if average profits over the complete business cycle are to attract a continuing supply of investment. The more volatile downward prices are in recessions, the more volatile upward they must be in booms. This poses several problems. First, wide fluctuations in prices and profits may have destabilizing macroeconomic effects, making it more difficult to maintain aggregate employment at high levels through fiscal and monetary policy. This is an extremely complex question which we must postpone until Chapter 13. Second, public opinion is often myopic, and attempts by important oligopolistic industries to raise their prices during booms to levels compensating for recession losses could provoke demands for government price controls and other direct intervention. Recognizing the difficulty of controlling such controls once they are imposed, politicians and entrepreneurs alike may prefer some formal price stabilization scheme to a less structured situation in which tacit collusion yields high boom profits but collapses in recessions. Third, some firms may fail under the burden of losses accumulated during hard times, even though long-run profit expectations are favorable. Fear of this contingency can lead risk-averting investors to demand, before committing their capital, a return exceeding the return earned in less volatile industries. If so, an industry subjected to alternating periods of highly profitable operation and price warfare

52. It is also true that the seriousness of the 'sick industry' problem is exaggerated by those who favor monopolistic restrictions on other (typically self-seeking) grounds. As George Stigler suggests, relatively few industries are really "sick," but many are hypochondriacal. *The Theory of Price* (New York: Macmillan, 1952), p. 249.

53. Conversely, an industry whose members operate numerous plants of widely varying efficiency and with a high variable cost component can adapt more smoothly to demand downturns, since less efficient plants will be closed down long before the most efficient plants (and their controlling firms) are threatened with failure.

54. See Phillips, *Market Structure, Organization and Performance*, pp. 104, 116, for some spectacular if ancient examples.

55. Dennis C. Mueller, "The Firm Decision Process: An Econometric Investigation," *Quarterly Journal of Economics* 81 (February 1967): 71–73. In contrast, Sultan argues that in the heavy electrical equipment industry, spending on new product development was linked positively with cash flow, and he attributes an apparent decline in innovation during the 1930s to depressed business conditions. *Pricing in the Electrical Oligopoly*, vol. 1, pp. 34–37, 171–73, and vol. 2, Chapter 12. But see pp. 192–95 in his vol. 2, from which one might infer that especially rapid turbogenerator technology advances in the 1920s left the opportunities for further progress depleted. Sultan also implies that Allis-Chalmers may have reacted to adversity by taking unwarranted technical risks with its "Big Allis" generator, which later experienced repeated serious breakdowns. Vol. 2, pp. 214, 219. Cf. "Out of the Shadow of 'Big Allis,'" *Business Week*, 24 July 1971, p. 22, on Allis-Chalmers's corrective actions. A senior turbogenerator engineer indicated in an interview with me that difficulties like those occurring with Big Allis, the first million-kilowatt capacity generator, were not uncommon. He saw no reason to believe that Allis-Chalmers had cut corners on quality. See also "The Opposites: GE Grows While Westinghouse Shrinks," *Business Week*, 31 January 1977, pp. 63–64, on similar difficulties experienced by Westinghouse with large turbogenerators built when the industry was not experiencing sharp price competition.

56. See "Big Businesses in Japan Are Growing Bigger," *New York Times*, 24 January 1966, p. 37; "MITI May Enforce New Antidepression Cartel," *Japan Times*, 9 February 1966; and Richard E. Caves and Masu Uekusa, *Industrial Organization in Japan* (Washington, D.C.: Brookings Institution, 1976), pp. 26–30, 145–48.

57. Caves and Uekusa, *Industrial Organization in Japan*, pp. 101–15.

might be forced to pay more to attract a given amount of capital than more stable industries, other things being equal. With capital costs lower under a price stabilization scheme, producers might conceivably sell their output at lower average prices.

A theoretical analysis of price stabilization cartels

Nevertheless, this last result is by no means assured. To see why, we must plunge more deeply into the analysis of who gains and who loses from price stabilization cartels.[58]

To keep a complex exposition as simple as possible without sacrificing essential insight, we assume that industry demand fluctuates randomly between two states—boom condition D_{BOOM} and slump condition D_{SLUMP}. Each state occurs half the time, i.e., with probability 0.5.[59] The demand functions are assumed to be linear and to shift in such a way that they remain parallel. The short-run industry supply function S is assumed to be stable and linear over the range of its intersection with D_{BOOM} and D_{SLUMP}. These assumptions are represented graphically in Figure 7.3, with the additional demand function D included to show the mean level of demand, averaging boom and slump.

The white dashed lines in Figure 7.3 are constructed to compare two pricing regimes—Case 1, in which prices and output are competitively determined, and Case 2, in which the price is stabilized at the level that would prevail under pure competition with the mean demand function $\bar{D}$. With competitive Case 1, the price rises to OP_B in the boom, and the quantity supplied and demanded is OQ_B. In the slump the price falls to OP_S and output is OQ_S. Under stabilization cartel Case 2, the price is $O\bar{P}$ at all times. During the boom, producers expand output to $OQ_B^\star$, where marginal cost equals the price $O\bar{P}$. Note that at this price the quantity demanded exceeds $OQ_B^\star$, so nonprice rationing must take place. In the slump, the quantity $OQ_S^\star$ is demanded at the stabilized price $O\bar{P}$, and producers' supply must be restricted through quotas or other devices.

The profitability of the two arrangements can be compared by evaluating producers' surpluses—i.e., the sum of the surpluses of price over

marginal cost (read from the supply curve) for all units produced. Surplus components are designated in Figure 7.3 by capital letters for each relevant area. Listing boom values first and slump values second, the expected value of producers' surplus under freely competitive pricing Case 1 is:

$$(7.1) \quad E(PS_1) = .5\,[E + F + G + H + I + J \\ + K + L + M] + .5\,[L + M]$$

With the price stabilized at $O\bar{P}$, the expected value of producers' surplus for Case 2 is:[60]

$$(7.2) \quad E(PS_2) = .5\,[I + J + K + L + M] \\ + .5\,[I + L]$$

Subtracting, we obtain:

$$(7.3) \quad E(PS_1) - E(PS_2) = .5\,[E + F + G + H \\ + M] - .5\,I$$

Because by assumption D_{BOOM} and D_{SLUMP} are parallel and equidistant from $\bar{D}$, $\bar{P}P_B = P_S\bar{P}$, and so areas $E + F$ together necessarily exceed area I.[61] Therefore, the profits earned by letting prices fluctuate competitively (Case 1) are necessarily larger than those gained under the stabilization cartel. Such profit sacrifices will not be accepted

---

F 7.3 Simple price stabilization cartel

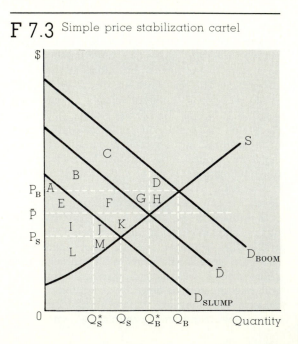

gladly by cartel members unless they place great weight on being relieved of the risk of price fluctuations. It seems almost inevitable that they will try to improve their lot by using their collective monopoly power to stabilize the price at a level exceeding the mean competitive level $O\bar{P}$.

Whether society as a whole benefits from the stabilization cartel can be ascertained by assuming (heroically) that producers' and consumers' surpluses are commensurable. The expected value of consumers' surplus for competitive Case 1 is:

$$(7.4) \quad E(CS_1) = .5\ [A + B + C + D] \\ + .5\ [A + E + I + J]$$

For Case 2, it is:[62]

$$(7.5) \quad E(CS_2) = .5\ [A + B + C + E + F + G] \\ + .5\ [A + E]$$

Subtracting (7.5) from (7.4), we find that consumers' surplus is slightly *higher* under the stabilization cartel:

$$(7.6) \quad E(CS_1) - E(CS_2) = .5\ [I + J + D] \\ - .5\ [E + F + G]$$

since $[E + F + G]$ exceeds $[I + J + D]$ by the area of the triangle K. However, summing (7.3) plus (7.6), we see that the combined producers' plus consumers' surplus under competitive pricing (Case 1) exceeds the surplus under a stabilization cartel by $.5\ [D + H + J + M]$.[63] Economic welfare is clearly higher with competitively fluctuating prices, and without making consumers worse off, there is no way risk-neutral producers can be compensated for the profit sacrifices they incur if they stabilize the price at $O\bar{P}$.

This result is not completely general. It depends in part upon the assumption of parallel demand function shifts, which in turn implies that demand becomes more elastic in the slump. If demand shifts so that its elasticity is the same at any given price during the slump as in the boom, and *a fortiori* if demand becomes less elastic in the slump, the excess of the competitive boom price over the competitive price with mean demand $O\bar{P}$ will be less than the excess of $O\bar{P}$ over the competitive slump price. The slump producers' surplus gain $I - M$ from stabilization might

then exceed the boom profit sacrifice $E + F + G + H$. This is more likely the less elastic the supply function is in the neighborhood of the equilibria.[64] For industries susceptible to purported cutthroat competition, marginal cost (and

58. The most general analyses of the problem are Benton F. Massell, "Price Stabilization and Welfare," *Quarterly Journal of Economics* 83 (May 1969): 284–98; and Stephen J. Turnovsky, "Price Expectations and the Welfare Gains from Price Stabilization," *American Journal of Agricultural Economics* 56 (November 1974): 706–16. Other contributions, some seminal, include F. V. Waugh, "Does the Consumer Benefit from Price Instability?," *Quarterly Journal of Economics* 58 (August 1944): 602–14; Walter Y. Oi, "The Desirability of Price Instability under Perfect Competition," *Econometrica* 29 (January 1961): 58–64; Albert Zucker, "On the Desirability of Price Instability," *Econometrica* 33 (April 1965): 437–41; Clem A. Tisdell, *The Theory of Price Uncertainty, Production and Profit* (Princeton: Princeton University Press, 1968); N. F. Laing, "Price Uncertainty, Production and Profit," *Economic Record* 46 (September 1970): 411–18; the colloquy among Paul A. Samuelson, Oi, and Waugh in the *Quarterly Journal of Economics* 86 (August 1972): 476–503; Richard E. Just and Michael S. Salkin, "Welfare Effects of Stabilization in a Vertical Market Chain," *Southern Economic Journal* 42 (April 1976): 633–43; R. M. Townsend, "The Eventual Failure of Price Fixing Schemes," *Journal of Economic Theory* 14 (February 1977): 190–99; and Peter Helmberger and Rob Weaver, "Welfare Implications of Commodity Storage under Uncertainty," *American Journal of Agricultural Economics* 59 (November 1977): 639–51.

59. Letting the demand curve shift with a continuous probability distribution having mean $\bar{D}$ does not essentially alter the results. See Turnovsky, "Price Expectations," pp. 707–709.

60. We assume an allocation system during the slump that lets output be produced by firms with the lowest marginal cost—i.e., as in the rationalization cartels discussed in Chapter 5. Otherwise, producers' surplus will be smaller.

61. Nonlinearity of the supply function alters this result, but usually in a direction that strengthens the conclusions reached here. Any nonlinearity is likely to entail a supply function convex downward, and if the supply curve is steeper between its intersection with $\bar{D}$ and D_{BOOM} than between $\bar{D}$ and D_{SLUMP}, then $P_B\bar{P} > \bar{P}P_S$.

62. We assume here a rationing system during the boom that puts output only in the hands of consumers realizing the highest consumers' surplus. That is, no output is sold to consumers with demand ordinates to the left of OQ_B^*. If, as is likely, this condition is not satisfied, consumers' surplus under the stabilization cartel will be less than indicated in equation (7.5).

63. Compare Chapter 2, p. 16 *supra*. The dead-weight welfare loss triangle ABE from monopolistic price raising there is analogous to slump welfare loss $J + M$ in Figure 7.3. Triangle $D + H$ in Figure 7.3 has a similar rationale.

64. For a further analysis, see the first edition of *Industrial Market Structure and Economic Performance*, pp. 203–205.

hence supply) functions like the one illustrated in Figure 7.2 are plausible, suggesting fairly inelastic supply. On the crucial question of how demand elasticity varies over the business cycle, one finds only conflicting *a priori* conjectures and virtually no empirical evidence.[65] It seems at least conceivable that a Figure 7.3-type stabilization cartel could under the appropriate conditions be sufficiently profitable that producers, and especially risk-averse producers, would be content not to raise the price above the competitive mean demand level. But the required conditions are sufficiently stringent that one might expect such cases to be rare.

A cartel in which output is rationed during the boom and curbed by producer quotas in the slump is not, however, the only feasible means of stabilizing prices. An alternative is a buffer stock cartel, under which some central authority stabilizes prices by accumulating goods during the slump and disposing of them in boom years. Its operation is characterized in Figure 7.4. As before, the price is assumed to be stabilized at the level $O\bar{P}$ associated with competition and mean demand $\bar{D}$. Confronted with this price, producers supply output OQ_M in both boom and slump.

During the slump, the quantity demanded is only OQ_S^* (compared to OQ_S demanded if the price were allowed to fall competitively), and the cartel authority must buy and stockpile $Q_S^*Q_M$ units per time period. During the boom, the quantity demanded at repressed price $O\bar{P}$ is OQ_B^*, and the cartel authority covers the gap $Q_MQ_B^*$ between production and demand out of its stockpile. If $O\bar{P}$ is indeed the price associated with mean demand, buffer stock accumulations during slumps will over the long run just balance stock drawdowns during booms.

We proceed now to analyze gains and losses. The expected value of producers' surplus under competition with prices fluctuating (i.e., Case 1) is:

$$(7.7) \quad E(PS_1) = .5\,[D + E + F + I + J \\ + K + L + M] + .5\,[L + M]$$

With a buffer stock cartel stabilizing the price at $O\bar{P}$ (Case 3), the comparable surplus is:

$$(7.8) \quad E(PS_3) = .5\,[I + J + K + L + M] \\ + .5\,[I + J + K + L + M]$$

Letting Case 1 be the benchmark for comparison, we find:

$$(7.9) \quad E(PS_1) - E(PS_3) = .5\,[D + E + F] \\ - .5\,[I + J + K]$$

Unless supply is perfectly inelastic, $[D + E + F]$ exceeds $[I + J + K]$, and the buffer stock cartel is less profitable than uninhibited competitive pricing.

Turning to the consumers' side, competitive pricing yields the expected surplus:

$$(7.10) \quad E(CS_1) = .5\,[A + B + C] \\ + .5\,[A + D + I + J]$$

With a buffer stock cartel, it is:

$$(7.11) \quad E(CS_3) = .5\,[A + B + C + D + E + F \\ + G + H] + .5\,[A + D]$$

Subtracting (7.11) from (7.10), we obtain:

$$(7.12) \quad E(CS_1) - E(CS_3) = .5\,[I + J] - .5\,[D \\ + E + F + G + H]$$

Since the negative term is larger than the positive term, consumers are clearly better off under the buffer stock cartel than under freely competitive pricing. Indeed, summing (7.9) and (7.12), we discover that the combined producers' plus con-

---

F 7.4 Buffer stock cartel

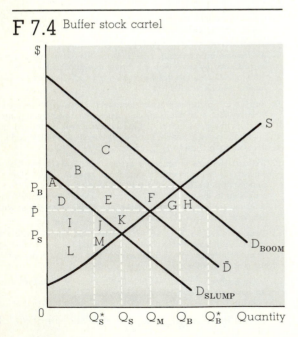

sumers' surplus advantage of competitive pricing Case 1 over the buffer stock cartel Case 3 is $-.5 [G + H + K]$. That is, aggregate welfare is *higher* with the assumed buffer stock cartel than with freely varying competitive prices. This stands in distinct contrast to the results for the more restrictive cartel Case 3. One implication is that it might be possible to compensate producers for their lower profits under the assumed buffer stock cartel—e.g., through lump-sum transfers or (more plausibly) by raising the stabilized price above the level associated with mean demand—without dissipating entirely the surplus consumers derive from price stabilization. This is all the more likely if producers are risk averse and hence willing to supply a given output at a lower price when the risk of price fluctuations is lower. On the other hand, costs of administering the stabilization scheme and storing buffer stocks have not been counted in the analysis, and they might be of sufficient magnitude to deplete an appreciable fraction of the net surplus (i.e., $.5[G + H + K]$) realized through stabilization.

Some broader considerations Several practical complications have been ignored to keep the analysis tractable. For one, producers have been assumed to adjust their supply to the price as it is at any moment in time, rather than making predictions about what it will be. This is probably appropriate for industries whose production cycle is short in relation to the business cycle over which demand changes occur, but not for most farm products and for manufactured items with long gestation periods (such as turbogenerators and airplanes). Turnovsky has shown that producers will gain, not lose, from a Case 3 buffer stock cartel if they base their output decisions on a naive extrapolation of prior period prices and if high demand in one period tends to be followed by low demand in the next, and vice versa.[66] On the other hand, a buffer stock cartel leaves producers worse off if, in adapting their output decisions, they exhibit a sophisticated understanding of the supply and demand conditions governing competitive price fluctuations. With either expectational approach, the sum of producers' plus consumers' surpluses continues to be higher under a buffer stock stabilization cartel of the

Case 3 type than under freely fluctuating competitive prices.

Recognition that output decisions must be based upon predictions of an uncertain future suggests a second important set of qualifications. For the buffer stock cartel to work as contemplated in Figure 7.4, the cartel authority must be able to predict demand fluctuations (and also supply shifts[67]) sufficiently well that accumulations in slump periods balance disposals in boom periods. This, of course, is easier said than done.[68] Unless there are persistent economies of scale in forecasting or stock holding, it is not at all clear that a cartel authority can do a better job than individual producers in predicting the future and hedging against it. If the cartel authority's forecasting ability is only equal to that of individual producers, and given the fact that stabilization at price $O\bar{P}$ is in many (but not necessarily all) cases less profitable for producers than resort to unfettered competitive markets, producers may well choose not to support the cartel unless it offers them an attractive quid pro quo. If demand fluctuations are predictable and if buffering pays, many producers might prefer to hold their own inventories or, if not, to take their chances in the competitive spot market—augmented by futures and options markets, if

65. Cf. R. F. Harrod, "Imperfect Competition and the Trade Cycle," *Review of Economic Statistics* 18 (February 1936): 84–88; R. F. Bretherton, "A Note on the Diminishing Elasticity of Demand," *Economic Journal* 47 (September 1937): 574–77; and Richard B. Heflebower, "The Effect of Dynamic Forces on the Elasticity of Revenue Curves," *Quarterly Journal of Economics* 55 (August 1941): 652–66.

66. Turnovsky, "Price Expectations and the Welfare Gains from Price Stabilization," pp. 710–11.

67. When it is supply rather than demand that is shifting randomly, buffer stock cartels tend to yield *higher* producers' surplus than freely competitive markets whose mean price equals the stabilized price. See Turnovsky, "Price Expectations," pp. 708–709.

68. On the less than sterling record of the international tin, coffee, and cocoa buffer stock cartels, and on proposals for several new stabilization arrangements, see "The Lure of 'Orderly Marketing'," *Business Week*, 9 May 1977, pp. 67–83; G. W. Smith and G. R. Schink, "The International Tin Agreement: A Reassessment," *Economic Journal* 86 (December 1976): 715–28; and "International Tin Agreement Reported Near Collapse," *New York Times*, 20 January 1977, p. 57.

they exist.[69] To win and maintain support in the face of these handicaps, the cartel authority will almost surely slant its decisions toward stabilizing prices at a level higher than the average under free competition.[70] Producers would then enjoy the best of both worlds—risk avoidance *and* average returns at least commensurate with what they would be in the competitive market. And for consumers, the attendant elevation of average prices must make the stabilization cartel a less attractive proposition than the pure theory implies.

Skepticism about the risk avoidance benefits of stabilization cartels is also prompted by evidence that the risks of financial failure are not all that high in cyclical industries prone to alleged excesses of cutthroat competition. Eliot Jones studied the financial records of the steel, harvester, sugar refining, tobacco, whiskey, cordage, wallpaper, malt, bicycle, and other manufacturing industries, which entered into large-scale consolidations around the turn of the century in a purported effort to escape ruinous competition.[71] He found that although many of the firms had experienced some lean years, nearly all managed to remain financially healthy. Loescher concluded that the "quite brutal" competition occasionally breaking out in the American cement industry did not impair the industry's long-run health, and that incentives for price warfare were aggravated by the excessive capacity lured into the industry by earlier attempts to stabilize prices at too high a level.[72] Conduct resembling ruinous competition has been extremely rare in the recessions experienced by the United States since World War II. With the possible exception of the electrical turbogenerator industry, from which Allis-Chalmers exited in 1962, leaving inadequate domestic capacity to serve subsequently booming demands,[73] it is hard to find examples of manufacturing industries not declining secularly whose structural or financial health has been significantly impaired by episodes of sharp price competition. And although members predicted dire consequences from the elimination of cartel-like minimum brokerage commission rules on the New York Stock Exchange, the actual consequence appears to have been more a trimming of manifest inefficiencies (accompanied, to be sure, by the failure of some less efficient firms) than any impairing of the industry's ability to satisfy the demand for its services.[74]

Thus, claims that competition has cutthroat and destructive propensities, and hence that cartelization is warranted, deserve to be taken with several grains of salt. Economic theory nevertheless reveals that certain kinds of price stabilization schemes—notably of the buffer stock variety—could, at least in principle and under favorable conditions, yield attractive net benefits. How often the requisite conditions hold is uncertain, and there is clearly a danger that a stabilization cartel will exploit its power to degrade overall economic welfare instead of enhancing it. A skeptical stance seems appropriate. Yet it must also be admitted that there might conceivably be cases—no doubt exceptional—in which the benefits of stabilization arrangements could outweigh their costs.

Lumpiness and infrequency of orders

We return now to our main theme. The effectiveness of oligopolistic coordination also depends upon the size distribution over time of buyers' orders. Profitable tacit collusion is most likely when orders are small, frequent, and regular. It is least likely when requests for price quotations on large orders are received infrequently and at irregular intervals.[75]

Any decision to undercut a price on which industry members have tacitly concurred requires a balancing of probable gains against costs. The gain is an increased probability of securing a profitable order. The cost involves the likelihood of rival reactions driving down the level of future prices and hence reducing future profits. The gains from price cutting are obviously greater when the order at stake is large relative to total sales than when it is small. Expected costs, on the other hand, probably rise less than proportionately with order size. The amount of information a firm conveys concerning its pricing strategy depends more upon the number of transactions in which it quotes independent prices than upon the size of the transactions. A price cut on a small order transmits as much information as one on a large order. To be sure, rivals may weight more heavily the information on cuts involving substantial revenues. But this needn't be true when opportunities to bid for large orders appear only infrequently and irregularly. More typically, competitors will reason, "Well, this was evidently a special case that can hardly be disregarded, but which is also not necessarily a good indicator of what we have to do to win the next round." Three or four departures in close succession on $10,000 orders are more apt to trigger rival retaliation than undercutting the established price on a single, unusual million-dollar order.[76] Consequently, the gains-cost balance will often be conducive to price cutting when a large order is at stake, while it will seldom be so for a small order, other things being equal.

Occasional large orders are particularly attractive to enterprises with short time horizons or high future discount rates—e.g., those having difficulty covering high overhead costs during a moderate recession. Such a firm will be favorably disposed toward accepting the risk of uncertain future retaliation if the immediate gain is an order sufficiently large to keep operations humming at capacity for several months. Small companies, it should be noted, will have stronger incentives from this standpoint with respect to orders of a given size than large firms.

The history of the cast-iron pipe industry during the 1880s and 1890s illustrates these relationships well. The product, purchased mainly by municipalities and gas utilities through competitive bidding, was homogeneous; and the number of sellers in the Midwestern market, isolated by high freight costs, was at most 15. Phillips describes the problems faced by firms in bidding as follows:

> Jobs for a large city on which a bid was submitted might be of sufficient magnitude to keep a shop operating for weeks or months. The fine adjustments within each firm which would allow variations in output according to revenue and costs so as to maximize profits were impossible. In the absence of agreement among firms, the outcome of the bidding made the difference between operating and

not operating for a substantial period of time. The firm with excess capacity, bidding on a large job, would be prone to submit any price so long as it was in excess of incremental costs of filling the order. And in view of the sporadic and large-sized jobs, some one of the several firms was apt to have the excess capacity created by a few unsuccessful bids.[77]

The result, at least in the absence of formal collusion, was intense price competition, and several bankruptcies occurred. Another consequence

69. See Ronald I. McKinnon, "Futures Markets, Buffer Stocks, and Income Stability for Primary Producers," *Journal of Political Economy* 75 (December 1967): 844–61; Benton F. Massell, "Some Welfare Implications of International Price Stabilization," *Journal of Political Economy* 78 (March/April 1970): 404–407; and Allen B. Paul, ed., "Price Instabilities and Public Policy: Summary of an ERS-University Seminar," U.S., Department of Agriculture Economic Research Service, National Economic Analysis Division working paper (Washington, D.C.: Department of Agriculture, January 1976).

70. See for example "House Documents Link Coffee Groups, U.S. Aides," *New York Times*, 11 November 1977, p. B-10.

71. Jones, "Is Competition in Industry Ruinous?," pp. 473–519.

72. Loescher, *Imperfect Collusion*, pp. 192–94.

73. See "Allis-Chalmers To Stop Making Some Generators," *Wall Street Journal*, 21 December 1962. In 1970 it reentered the business, apparently without great start-up difficulties, through a joint venture with West German generator maker Kraftwerk Union. See "Allis May Resume Building Big Generators," *New York Times*, 10 December 1969, p. 77; "Allis Rejoins the Power Play," *Business Week*, 28 February 1970, p. 40; and the full-page advertisement in the *New York Times*, 25 March 1971, p. 54.

74. For various views before and after, see Kahn, *The Economics of Regulation*, vol. II, pp. 193–209; Richard R. West and Seha M. Tinic, "Minimum Commission Rates on New York Stock Exchange Transactions," *Bell Journal of Economics and Management Science* (Autumn 1971): 577–605; "Excerpts from Report on Securities Markets," *New York Times*, 6 August 1971, p. 47; H. Michael Mann, "The New York Stock Exchange: A Cartel at the End of its Reign," in Almarin Phillips, ed., *Promoting Competition*, pp. 301–27; and "Free Market on the Stock Market," *New York Times*, 22 July 1977, p. A20.

75. When there is a regular flow of orders from large buyers in addition to the flow of small orders, systematic price discrimination may arise. This case will be considered further in Chapters 10 and 11.

76. See also the discussion of learning through repeated bidding in Chapter 5, p. 163 *supra*.

77. Almarin Phillips, *Market Structure, Organization and Performance*, p. 103. Reprinted by permission of Harvard University Press. Copyright © 1962 by the President and Fellows of Harvard College.

was the formation of a bidding cartel to restrain industry members' competitive zeal. This arrangement was the target of a precedent-setting antitrust decision in 1899.[78]

For a second example we return to the 20th century. By far the largest single buyer of the antibiotic tetracycline is the federal government. As we observed in the preceding chapter, during 1955 and 1956 the five tetracycline producers settled down into a pattern of submitting identical $19.1884 bids per 100-capsule bottle in Veterans Administration transactions, the largest of which involved 30,000 bottles. Then, in October of 1956, the Armed Services Medical Procurement Agency (ASMPA) made its first tetracycline purchase, calling for 94,000 bottles. Partly because of the unusually large order volume and partly because pricing precedents for the agency were unclear, industry discipline broke. Two firms held to the established $19.1884 price, but Bristol-Myers undercut to $18.97 and Lederle cut all the way to $11.00.[79] Even at this reduced price, Lederle secured before-tax profits of at least $750,000, since the marginal cost of producing an additional 100 capsules was less than $3.00. This action touched off a series of rival countermoves, although the exact form of the retaliation would have been difficult to predict in advance. In the next VA transaction (two weeks later, for 50,400 bottles), four suppliers (including Lederle and Bristol-Myers) quoted $19.1884, apparently because they considered the VA and ASMPA purchases, which differed in delivery details, to be in different classes. But Pfizer cut to $17.63 (10 percent off the old $19.58 base) less 2 percent trade discount. Nearly a year later, in the next Armed Services purchase (this time for only 14,112 bottles), Pfizer matched Lederle's previous $11.00 price, but Lederle returned to $19.1884. Seven months later, in the third Armed Services transaction, all bidders returned to the $19.1884 level. The overall picture during the two years following Lederle's $11.00 bid was one of considerable disarray in both ASMPA and VA bidding, punctuated by Lederle's persistent adherence to the prebreak price in an apparent effort to signal that it wished to see stability restored at high price levels after it had captured the largest plum.

Lumpiness of orders contributed also to the poor pre-1960s pricing discipline of the electrical equipment industry. In the slump year 1958, only 33 turbogenerators were ordered from U.S. producers; in relatively prosperous 1960, there were 80, some on multiunit contracts. A single order was sufficient to keep General Electric or Westinghouse, the industry leaders, busy for as much as a month. For Allis-Chalmers, whose market share averaged 10 percent in the decade before its 1962 exit, a single order might mean a half year's successful operation. Similarly, in Great Britain, where electrical equipment purchasing is concentrated in the governmental Electricity Generating Board, a single turbogenerator order could keep one of the three producers busy for more than a year, and a transformer order might amount to three months' backlog. There, too, pricing discipline has been fragile because of the struggle for orders to fill capacity voids.[80]

Secrecy and retaliation lags

The tendency for sellers to cut prices to secure orders ensuring capacity operation for a substantial period is a special case of a more general phenomenon. The longer the adverse consequences of rival retaliation can be forestalled, the more attractive undercutting the accepted price structure becomes. A common method of attempting to delay retaliation is to grant price concessions secretly. Whenever price exceeds marginal cost under oligopoly and when it appears feasible to keep special concessions secret, producers experience the temptation to engage in secret price shading. If the practice is confined to a small fraction of industry sales, the price cutters may be able to enjoy, more or less permanently, a larger volume of profitable business than they could by adhering faithfully to list prices. But when secret price cutting spreads to more than 20 or 30 percent of total sales volume, list prices will undoubtedly be reduced openly. If further *sub rosa* shading continues, industry discipline may collapse completely.[81]

Our old friend, the electrical equipment industry, illustrates the latter, more dramatic result.

The propensity of manufacturers to enter into secret deals with major buyers aggravated other disruptive conditions described previously. Thus, the proximate cause of the 1957–58 "white sale" in switchgear, during which prices plunged to 40 percent of book values, was an under-the-counter bargain that turned out not to be secret. In 1956 and early 1957 the conspiracy among switchgear sellers was proceeding swimmingly, and prices had been stabilized at high levels. Then Westinghouse offered a secret 4 percent discount to the president of Florida Power and Light Company on a million-dollar order. General Electric salesmen learned of the deal and offered to match it. When Westinghouse sales officials heard of the leak, they reacted angrily by cutting prices on another buyer's order. Other firms joined in, and the conspiracy broke down in a torrent of price warfare.[82] A key element in turbo-generator manufacturers' subsequent price protection plan, by which they avoided uninhibited price rivalry from 1964 through 1976, was the publication of all orders and price quotations by General Electric and Westinghouse. They also permitted buyers to inspect their records and verify that transactions in fact took place at the prices the sellers had publicly announced.[83]

A different pattern has been observed in the steel, rayon, and aluminum industries. Price shading is usually initiated under adverse business conditions by the smaller firms. They are encouraged to act independently in part by knowledge that the details of their concessions will be kept secret, even though industry leaders typically find out quickly that chiseling is taking place.[84] Thus, it is not so much secrecy per se as the limited scope of the deviations that inhibits retaliation; secrecy is merely a priming element in the process. If the covert concessions become fairly widespread, however, industry leaders react by announcing formal list price reductions. In aluminum extrusions, for instance, where the independent fabricators entering into secret deals controlled about half the market, off-list pricing normally led to a reduction in list prices because the chiselers made serious inroads into primary producer sales. But in aluminum sheet fabrication, the independents accounted for only about 6 percent of total sales, and primary producers were inclined to ignore off-list quotations as a minor irritant.[85] Likewise, the three smallest primary aluminum producers, with a combined 8 percent share of U.S. ingot capacity, managed through small discounts to utilize their capacity fully during the 1974–75 recession. Industry leaders Alcoa, Reynolds, and Kaiser ignored the cuts, adhered to list prices, and cut output back to less than 75 percent of capacity.[86]

Secret price cutting, whether pursued to the

78. U.S. v. Addyston Pipe and Steel Co. et al., 171 U.S. 614 (1899).

79. See Federal Trade Commission, Economic Report on Antibiotics Manufacture (Washington, D.C.: Government Printing Office, 1958), pp. 195–97. The tetracycline producers were subsequently acquitted of antitrust price-fixing charges. Nor is it likely that Lederle would have cut the price as deeply as it did had a prior collusive understanding existed.

80. See Richardson, "The Pricing of Heavy Electrical Equipment," pp. 73–92.

81. A number of works attempt to analyze mathematically the dynamic logic of secret price cutting, detection, and deterrence. Among these, the earliest and most influential was George J. Stigler, "A Theory of Oligopoly," Journal of Political Economy 72 (February 1964): 44–61. See also Ronald I. McKinnon, "Stigler's Theory of Oligopoly: A Comment," Journal of Political Economy 74 (June 1966): 281–85; Daniel Orr and Paul W. MacAvoy, "Price Strategies To Promote Cartel Stability," Economica 32 (May 1965): 186–97; G. Warren Nutter and John H. Moore, "A Theory of Competition," Journal of Law and Economics 19 (April 1976): 39–66; Dale K. Osborne, "Cartel Problems," American Economic Review 66 (December 1976): 835–44; and the exchange of views in the American Economic Review 68 (December 1978): 938–49. All suffer from naive notions of how business firms learn about sub rosa price shading by rivals, asymmetry in their assumptions as to which firms are potential price shaders, and/or neglect of the tensions and institutional complexity inescapable in Prisoners' Dilemma-type situations with mixed incentives for conflict, cooperation, and dynamic learning. For a critique of the earlier models, see Basil S. Yamey, "Notes on Secret Price-cutting in Oligopoly," in Marcelle Kooy, ed., Studies in Economics and Economic History in Honour of Prof. H. M. Robertson (London: Macmillan, 1972), pp. 280–300.

82. See Smith, Corporations in Crisis, pp. 132–33.

83. U.S. v. General Electric Co. et al., "Plaintiff's Memorandum in Support of a Proposed Modification to the Final Judgment Entered on October 1, 1962, Against Each Defendant," December 1976, pp. 7–10, 17–18. See also Chapter 5, pp. 163–64 supra.

84. See Weiss, Economics and American Industry, pp. 295–98; Markham, Competition in the Rayon Industry, p. 128; Peck, Competition in the Aluminum Industry, p. 69; and U.S., Council on Wage and Price Stability, A Study of Steel Prices, pp. 9–15.

85. See Peck, Competition in the Aluminum Industry, pp. 66–68.

86. U.S., Council on Wage and Price Stability Staff report, Aluminum Prices: 1974–75 (Washington, D.C.: Government Printing Office, 1976), especially pp. 73, 121–23.

point of a complete breakdown in industry discipline or merely to across-the-board list price reductions, interferes with the maximization of collective profits. Recognizing this, oligopolists have tried to nip the problem in the bud by making it difficult to conceal concessions. They do this through some variant of the so-called "open price" policy, advocated in 1912 by corporate lawyer Arthur Jerome Eddy.[87] In the typical case, an industry trade association is authorized to collect detailed information on the transactions executed by each member. To ensure full compliance, the association or an independent auditing firm is sometimes empowered to audit company records, and fines may be levied for failure to report sales quickly or accurately.[88] The association then publishes at frequent intervals (e.g., weekly) a report describing each transaction, including the name of the seller, the buyer, the quantity sold, and the price. Thus each member knows shortly after the fact who has been shading prices for whom and can take appropriate retaliatory action. The potential price-cutting firm in turn recognizes that it will be found out quickly, so the incentive for offering concessions in the hope of deferring retaliation through secrecy fades. Maximum knowledge of rival actions provides an exceptionally favorable environment for tacit collusion, as one open price agency, the American Hardwood Manufacturers' Association, boasted to prospective members:

> The theoretical proposition at the basis of the Open Competition plan is that . . . *knowledge regarding prices actually made is all that is necessary to keep prices at reasonably stable and normal levels.* . . . By keeping all members fully and quickly informed of what the others have done, the work of the Plan results in *a certain uniformity of trade practice.* There is no agreement to follow the practice of others, *although members do naturally follow their most intelligent competitors*, if they know what these competitors have been actually doing. . . . The keynote to modern business success is mutual confidence and co-operation. *Co-operative competition, not Cut-throat competition.*[89]

It is worth noting that eliminating opportunities for secret action is an effective cure for chiseling not only in price rivalry, but also in many other conflict situations characterized by a payoff matrix of the Prisoners' Dilemma type. Failure of the United States and Russia to agree on measures for assuring that covert tests were not being conducted was one bottleneck frustrating negotiation of an underground nuclear test ban, just as confidence that atmospheric tests could be detected was vital to the test ban treaty of 1963. The hot line between Washington and Moscow was originally intended to ensure that an accidental nuclear explosion (analogous to a mistaken price cut) was not misinterpreted as the start of real hostilities. And a sense of urgency was instilled into the U.S. atomic and hydrogen bomb development programs by the fear that similar actions were being taken covertly in rival nations' laboratories. Eliminating the secrecy enshrouding new weapons developments is a precondition for slowing down the qualitative arms race.[90]

This message has permeated governmental economic thinking as slowly as it has foreign policy. Except in procuring complex, technologically advanced equipment such as weapon systems and space vehicles, the federal government and most state and local governments require that purchases of supplies, equipment, and the like be made through sealed competitive bidding. That is, the procurement agency issues a request for bids with detailed specifications of the items desired, and would-be suppliers tender sealed price quotations. These are opened publicly on a predetermined date, and the firm submitting the lowest responsible quotation wins the order. (In case of ties, various procedures may be employed, depending upon time pressures. The winner may be chosen by lot, or the order may be split, or negotiations to secure a lower price may be initiated, or all bids may be rejected and new bids requested.) This approach to procurement has the great advantage of minimizing opportunities for bribery and favoritism. But as Paul Cook observes, "It would . . . be hard to find a device less calculated to foster open and aggressive competition among [oligopolistic] sellers."[91] Any firm tempted to cut its price below the prevailing industry level knows its action cannot escape the attention of rivals, and therefore it must fear re-

224

taliation on the next round. It will cut only if the gain appears to outweigh this clear-cut risk. In addition, sellers may be reluctant to cut prices below current levels in a sealed-bid competition because other large *buyers* will find out and demand similar price reductions.[92] Aware that oligopolistic suppliers are more willing to make price concessions in secret than openly, and because they are better able to control internal corruption (or are less apt to be the subject of front-page headlines when it is discovered), large industrial buyers typically rely upon secret negotiations rather than sealed bidding in their procurement operations.

Industry social structure

We turn last to the relationship between an industry's informal and formal social structure and its ability to coordinate pricing behavior.[93] This set of influences lies beyond the reach of conventional economic analysis, and its effects would be difficult to predict even with a very rich multidisciplinary theory. Consequently the economist is forced, without denying their importance, to view variations in industry conduct and performance owing to differences in social structure as an unexplained residual or 'noise.' We can nevertheless at least identify some conditions that appear either to facilitate or impair collusion.

We have noted repeatedly the remarkable discipline of American steel producers, who resisted the urge to break from list prices during the late 1950s even when operating at only 60 percent of capacity. The industry's finely honed esprit de corps can be traced back to the Gary dinners of 1907 through 1911.[94] Differences in social structure undoubtedly have much to do with the contrasting performance observed in the European steel industry. During the 1960s excess steel capacity began to appear in Europe. Although they served overlapping market areas and were separated by only moderate transportation costs and tariffs, the Continental and (prenationalization) British sectors reacted differently. On the Continent prices fell by as much as 25 percent, while British domestic prices held

firm despite an influx of imports from hard-pressed Continental producers. British companies adhered to list prices in part because they shared homogeneous goals and had a close-knit industry organization, and because their directors (many of whom attended the same elite schools and belonged to the same social clubs) held cooperative attitudes.[95] On the other hand, entrepreneurs in the European Coal and Steel Community embodied many diverse back-

87. See Arthur Jerome Eddy, *The New Competition* (Chicago: McClury, 1912). On the steel industry as a forerunner to Eddy's approach, see Donald O. Parsons and E. J. Ray, "The United States Steel Consolidation," *Journal of Law and Economics* 18 (April 1975): 208–209. For a more modern argument in the same spirit as Eddy's, see G. B. Richardson, "Price Notification Schemes," *Oxford Economic Papers* 19 n.s. (November 1967): 355–65.

88. For a summary of several cases, see G. W. Stocking, "The Rule of Reason, Workable Competition, and the Legality of Trade Association Activities," *University of Chicago Law Review* 21 (Summer 1954): 527–619.

89. Phillips, *Market Structure, Organization and Performance*, pp. 147–48, quoting from *U.S. v. American Column and Lumber Co. et al.*, 257 U.S. 377, 393–394 (1921) (italics in original).

90. See F. M. Scherer, "Was the Nuclear Arms Race Inevitable?," *Co-existence* (January 1966): 59–69. For other analogies, see Thomas C. Schelling, *The Strategy of Conflict* (Cambridge, Mass.: Harvard University Press, 1960), especially pp. 20, 33.

91. Paul W. Cook, Jr., "Fact and Fancy on Identical Bids," *Harvard Business Review* 41 (January-February 1963): 67–72. See also Vernon A. Mund, "Identical Bid Prices," *Journal of Political Economy* 68 (April 1960): 150–69.

92. For example, the "most favored nation" clauses in Salk vaccine procurement contracts, requiring that the seller charge no higher price to that buyer than it does to any other buyer, were a significant deterrent to price cutting. See *U.S. v. Eli Lilly & Co. et al.*, CCH 1959 Trade Cases, para. 69,536.

93. For a seminal treatment of this problem, see Phillips, *Market Structure, Organization and Performance*, Chapter 2. See also Richard B. Heflebower, "Stability in Oligopoly," *Manchester School of Economics and Social Studies* 29 (January 1961): 79–93.

94. Cf. Chapter 6, p. 170 *supra*. For a fascinating account of how steel makers bring social and other pressure to bear on nonconformists, see Dan Cordtz, "Antiestablishmentarianism at Wheeling Steel," *Fortune*, July 1967, pp. 105 ff. In "Price Fixing Conspiracies: Their Long-Term Impact," *Journal of Industrial Economics* 42 (March 1976): 201–202, W. Bruce Erickson argues on the basis of three case studies that prolonged explicit collusion creates preconditions favorable to the subsequent development of price leadership or similar oligopolistic coordination methods.

95. See Dennis Swann and D. L. McLachlan, "Steel Pricing in a Recession," *Scottish Journal of Political Economy* 12 (February 1965): 81–104.

grounds, styles of doing business, and national goals; and a permissive bias toward orderly pricing on the part of ECSC's High Authority was not enough to overcome these obstacles to cooperation. Again, during the steel industry recession of the mid-1970s, even nonbinding quotas administered through the European Community Commission were insufficient to quench centrifugal national industry instincts, and vigorous price rivalry persisted despite the stabilization effort.[96]

As time passes and more executive positions are filled by persons emerging from the filter of middle-class upbringing and graduate business school training, the heterogeneity of American business leaders' backgrounds is declining. This change may well lie behind an apparent trend toward greater respect for interdependence, manifested *inter alia* in enhanced willingness to restrict output instead of cutting prices during temporary business slowdowns. However, the phenomenon is difficult to document objectively, but its existence seems apparent.

As suggested in the preceding chapter, informal social contacts made at trade association meetings often lead to bonds of friendship and mutual understanding that facilitate tacit and explicit collusion. This was one basis for the rayon industry's cooperative pricing policies; another was the fact that the two leading firms occupied adjacent home office buildings in Wilmington, Delaware.[97] American rayon producers also participated, directly or through affiliates, in cartel arrangements in nations where they were legal, and this collaboration abroad engendered cooperative attitudes in the domestic market. Nor is the pattern unique to rayon. Stocking and Watkins found that the three firms dominating the U.S. sulfur industry competed vigorously between 1913 and 1922. However, they then formed an export cartel (legal under the American antitrust laws) that apparently fostered the spirit of cooperation necessary to sustain high prices even during the severe depression of the 1930s.[98] Similarly, extensive intertwining of nearly all the U.S. primary aluminum ingot producers in joint bauxite mining and alumina refining ventures overseas was believed by the Council on Wage and Price Stability staff to be a plausible partial explanation for the absence of vigorous price discounting during periods of substantial excess capacity.[99]

Still the existence of an industry association institutionalizing frequent business and social contacts does not guarantee cooperation. Personal antagonisms and distrust arising from all sorts of real and imagined causes can shatter organizational harmony. Ralph Cassady found that emotional behavior resulting from fear, anger, hatred, or desperation plays a major part "in many if not all" price wars.[100] Testimony from an antitrust case involving southern U.S. mirror manufacturers illustrates vividly the problems that can arise. At a trade association meeting in 1954, several producers got together to negotiate an increase in prices.[101] One participant described his experience as follows:

> I had never expressed myself to him, my actual feelings at all times. So when we got in this meeting . . . I just decided to tell him, "John, you are the one that started this price war to begin with." I can't recall just the exact things that took place, but he as much as said I was a damn liar, that I started it. I said, "What do you mean, I started it, Mr. Messer?" He said, "You shipped mirrors into Galax, Virginia. You started it." I said, "I have never shipped a square foot of mirrors into Galax, Virginia, and I want you to retract and quit accusing me of starting this price war, when you are the one that did it." . . . Mr. Messer turned so red I thought he was going to have a stroke.

Another participant recalled:

> I thought they were going to come to blows. The luncheon meeting had been very congenial, but after the first two or three minutes in this meeting . . . it looked like there might be a free-for-all break out at any time.

An agreement was in fact reached by all save Mr. Messer, but during the following month the agreed upon price was undercut on nearly 70 percent of all transactions. In his analysis of this case, Phillips concludes that "in a psychological sense, it is doubtful that these men were capable of agreeing on anything."[102] The uniqueness of the case is shown by the fact that the western and northern branches of the mirror industry, with similar market structures, managed to avoid price warfare without engaging in known collusion.[103] However, the problem of mutual distrust does not seem to be an unusual one. Fog observes that in Denmark, where formal price-fixing agreements were legal:

> cartel agreements are not always the expression of cordial co-operation among firms. In many cases it is rather a deeply rooted distrust that necessitates the signing of binding agreements, as the firms dare not place confidence in a gentleman agreement.[104]

Similar coordination problems arise when an industry includes a maverick of significant size— i.e., a strong-headed, individualistic entrepreneur whose values or business methods differ from those of other industry members. Ernest P. Weir, president of National Steel, was such a figure; and during the 1930s his aggressive pricing policies contributed significantly to some of the industry's rare pricing discipline breakdowns. Henry Ford played the role during the early decades of the auto industry, as did his friend Harvey Firestone in the rubber tire industry. The emergence of a maverick willing and able to disrupt industry tranquility seems to depend more on chance than on identifiable structural or behavioral preconditions, and this imparts an additional element of randomness into predictions of industrial performance. Nonetheless, really striking cases appear to be rare, perhaps in part because large, less aggressive firms will often pay a handsome acquisition price to eliminate small rivals actively promoting price competition. As the president of a cement manufacturing company wrote the head of a rival concern, "The most effective way to cure a bad situation is to buy up the offenders."[105]

Conclusion

To summarize, cooperation to hold prices above the competitive level is less likely to be successful, the less concentrated an industry is; the larger the competitive fringe is, the more heterogeneous, complex, and changing the products supplied are; the higher the ratio of fixed or overhead to total costs is, the more depressed business conditions are; the more dependent the industry is on large, infrequent orders, the more opportunities there are for under-the-counter price shading, and the more relations among company executives are marred by distrust and animosity. None of these links is strictly deterministic; all reflect central tendencies subject to random deviation. It is in part because of this complexity and randomness that oligopoly poses such difficult problems for the economic analyst.

96. See "European Steel Industry Faces Worst Crisis in Memory," *New York Times*, 23 May 1977, pp. 41–42.

97. See Markham, *Competition in the Rayon Industry*, pp. 3, 97–98.

98. Stocking and Watkins, *Monopoly and Free Enterprise*, pp. 126–28.

99. Council on Wage and Price Stability, *Aluminum Prices: 1974–75*, pp. 23–26, 226–27, 232.

100. Ralph Cassady, Jr., *Price Warfare in Business Competition* (East Lansing: Michigan State University Bureau of Business and Economic Research, 1963), pp. 53–55.

101. Phillips, *Market Structure, Organization and Performance*, pp. 183–93, drawing upon the record of *U.S. v. Pittsburgh Plate Glass Co. et al.*, 260 F. 2d 397 (1958), 360 U.S. 395 (1959). Reprinted by permission of Harvard University Press. Copyright © 1962 by the President and Fellows of Harvard College.

102. Phillips, *Market Structure*, p. 193.

103. Phillips, *Market Structure*, p. 192.

104. Fog, *Industrial Pricing Policies*, p. 155.

105. Loescher, *Imperfect Collusion in the Cement Industry*, p. 120, n. 76. See also Reed Moyer, *Competition in the Midwestern Coal Industry* (Cambridge, Mass.: Harvard University Press, 1964), pp. 82, 157.

8 The dynamics of monopoly and oligopoly pricing

To the extent that the profit motive directs business behavior, it is almost surely long-run rather than short-run profits that firms normally seek to maximize. This fact has important performance implications. They are explored in the present chapter.

Before we begin, one hazard must be anticipated. Long-run profit maximization requires that the consequences of today's pricing decisions be weighed far into an uncertain future. Entrepreneurs making such decisions may reach divergent conclusions concerning probabilities and contingencies under identical objective conditions. To avoid framing hypotheses that explain everything but predict nothing, we shall for the most part in this chapter emphasize performance variations linked in a systematic and compelling way to observable structural variables.

Substitution and long-run demand functions

One hypothesis with significant performance implications is that demand for the products of a firm or interacting group of firms possessing monopoly power is much more price elastic over the long run than in the short run. This was first argued persuasively by J. M. Clark, who suggested that long-run demand schedules might "in numerous cases approach the horizontal so closely that the slope would not be a matter of material moment, in the light of all the uncertainties involved."[1]

There are two main reasons for the higher elasticity of long-run demand schedules. First, competition among substitute products is more effective over the long run than during any short period; a given percentage change in price will induce greater shifts in purchases between substitutes over the long pull than in the short. Second, efforts by a particular firm or group of firms

1. J. M. Clark, "Toward a Concept of Workable Competition," *American Economic Review* 30 (June 1940): 248. See also Richard B. Heflebower, "Toward a Theory of Industrial Markets and Prices," *American Economic Review* 44 (May 1954): 126; and P. W. S. Andrews, *On Competition in Economic Theory* (London: Macmillan, 1964), pp. 73–85.

   The very notion of a long-run demand curve poses difficulties that are virtually intractable if one is confined to two-dimensional geometry, since both prices and quantities are likely to vary over the multiple periods taken into account. For a list of early works struggling to cope with the problem, see the first edition of *Industrial Market Structure and Economic Performance*, p. 213, note 1. The only really satisfactory solution is to replace the orthodox geometric apparatus with a calculus of variations approach in which rates of change in the quantity demanded over time take the place of traditional elasticities. This method will be adopted in a different context in the next section. For a precursor with direct applicability to the long-run substitution problem, see Sidney G. Winter and E. S. Phelps, "Optimal Price Policy under Atomistic Competition," in E. S. Phelps, ed., *Microeconomic Foundations of Employment and Inflation Theory* (New York: Norton, 1970), pp. 309–37.

to hold its price persistently above cost may attract new entry, which in the long run makes heavy inroads into sales volume. In this section we focus on long-run competition among substitutes. The entry problem will be studied from several angles in later sections.

Competition among substitutes is one of the most universal economic phenomena. Steel, aluminum, magnesium, copper, titanium, high density polyethylene, fiberglass, western pine, bamboo, and dozens of other raw materials are potential substitutes for one another in thousands of fabricated product applications. Which one wins out in any particular application depends *inter alia* upon relative prices. To be sure, some materials have unique advantages, so the choice is multidimensional, but there is nearly always some combination of price and other features at which custom will shift away from one possibility and toward another. The same is true with respect to virtually every good and service; it is only through failure of imagination that we sometimes consider certain lines to have no substitutes.

Competition among substitutes is more effective in the long run than in the short for several reasons, all related to adjustment lags on both the demand and supply sides of the market.

Consumers, for one thing, are creatures of habit. A sharp rise in butter prices will induce only a moderate shift to oleomargarine in the short run, but as homemakers reconsider their budgets and by experimentation find acceptable new uses for the substitute, the shift will increase in magnitude. Introductory sales are one way through which producers attempt to break the habit barrier. By inducing consumers to try a substitute product at unusually attractive prices, they build up preferences that make it possible to sell more of their product at any given price in the future.

Not all consumer lags stem from subjective inertia, however. Some shifts in consumption can occur only after modifications in complementary durable good stocks are accomplished. When, for example, fuel oil and natural gas prices rose rapidly during the 1970s, the most consumers could do in the short run was turn down the thermostat—e.g., substituting sweaters for fuel. But as the higher prices persisted, additional

home insulation was installed and a search for such substitutes as solar energy was precipitated. And over the very long run, one might expect even more drastic substitution effects, such as a shift away from single-family homes and the construction of coal-fired central heating plants providing steam to a multiplicity of residences. Similarly, the initial impact of rapidly rising gasoline prices was slight, but over the longer run there has been a movement toward smaller and more energy-efficient autos both in the United States (where extensive government intervention complicated the analysis of market responses) and in Europe (where price changes had a more direct effect).

Comparable rigidities constrain industrial purchasers. Products must often be redesigned and production processes retooled to substitute one material input for another. Consequently, once production is geared to use a particular input, the demand for that input is relatively inelastic in the short run. But given time and the appropriate incentives, redesign and retooling will take place. For example, in 1966 the American automobile industry began seeking ways to reduce its consumption of copper after sharp price increases added more than $30 million to annual materials costs.[2] The immediate impact was negligible, but the development of new production processes made it possible to displace copper even from such traditional uses as in radiators.

High prices also induce efforts to invent and develop substitute products which, after sometimes substantial lags, provide a powerful new competitive challenge. For instance, during the 1920s natural rubber prices rose as a result of cartel agreements. This triggered intensified research and experimentaton on synthetic rubber, which ultimately displaced natural rubber in many applications.[3] Likewise, when the Chilean nitrate cartel drove fertilizer nitrogen prices up during the first two decades of the 20th century, a search for synthetic sources began, and from 1913 to 1918 the share of the world's fixed nitrogen output supplied by synthetic producers soared from 8 to 23 percent.[4] During the 1950s the aluminum and container industries developed aluminum cans that ended the sovereignty of costly tin-plated steel in the tin can market. The steel industry fought back with research and development on a steel container stock coated with aluminum (at $.25 per pound at the time) in place of tin (at $1.90 per pound).[5] And when sugar prices rose rapidly during the 1970s, vegetable packers and soft drink bottlers found ways of using corn syrup instead, within three years displacing a million tons of sugar demand per year.[6] More generally, in a comparative analysis of input-output tables for 1947 and 1958, Anne Carter found that rapid developments in technology rendered materials increasingly interchangeable, with steel giving way to aluminum and cement, copper to aluminum, natural fibers to synthetics, wood to paper, and paper to plastics.[7]

The net effect of these influences is to make demand more sensitive to price in the long run than in the short run, and because of this to constrain the prices firms or oligopolistic groups can charge without inviting sales losses through substitution. If then producers strive to maximize long-run profits, prices may depart less from cost than one might expect merely from considering the short-run monopoly power held. The current prices of monopolized products will be kept lower the more rapidly substitution is expected to occur as a result of high prices, and the less heavily firms with monopoly power discount future earnings.

There is evidence that many monopolistic and oligopolistic enterprises do exercise pricing restraint to ward off substitution. During the mid-1960s, for instance, the domestic copper oligopoly held its prices in the neighborhood of $.40 per pound, ostensibly to prevent further inroads by aluminum, while prices of secondary (reprocessed scrap) copper and London Metal Exchange quotations reached $.80 per pound.[8] Peck found that aluminum producers refrained from raising prices to short-run profit-maximizing levels in order to enhance long-term growth. He concluded that the existence of close substitutes made high long-run price elasticity a permanent feature of the aluminum market.[9] Nevertheless, the aluminum firms' exercise of pricing restraint was clearest where the threat of *short-run* substitution was most acute—notably, in container stock. Burdened by rapidly rising input costs, they raised aluminum ingot prices by 95 percent between 1974 and 1976 while holding aluminum

can stock prices constant. Steel makers at the same time *reduced* substitute tin plate prices by 2 percent while the average price of all steel products rose 56 percent.[10] In the rayon industry, according to Jesse Markham, strong competition from other fibers limited the leading producers' control over their prices.[11] And there is reason to believe that in choosing the $10 to $13 range at which world crude oil prices settled after rapid escalation during the mid-1970s, the OPEC cartel placed considerable emphasis on the costs of alternative energy sources such as coal.[12]

It is apparent, however, that fear of long-run

2. See Thomas O'Hanlon, "The Perilous Prosperity of Anaconda," *Fortune*, May 1966, pp. 118–19. On subsequent reactions when aluminum prices rose rapidly, see "Aluminum Gambles on a Higher Price," *Business Week*, 23 August 1976, p. 25.

3. George W. Stocking and Myron W. Watkins, *Cartels in Action* (New York: Twentieth Century Fund, 1964), p. 73.

4. Stocking and Watkins, *Cartels in Action*, p. 127.

5. See "How Steel May Save an Old Market," *Business Week*, 5 December 1964, p. 33.

6. "Sugar's Anguished Plea for More Federal Aid," *Business Week*, 8 August 1977, p. 60.

7. Anne P. Carter, "The Economics of Technological Change," *Scientific American*, April 1966, pp. 25–31.

8. Compare J. L. McCarthy, "The American Copper Industry," *Yale Economic Essays* 4 (Spring 1964): 77–80; and (for a view somewhat more skeptical of the substitution hypothesis) David L. McNicol, "The Two Price System in the Copper Industry," *Bell Journal of Economics* 6 (Spring 1975), especially pp. 59–73.

9. M. J. Peck, *Competition in the Aluminum Industry: 1945–1958* (Cambridge, Mass.: Harvard University Press, 1961), pp. 52–62, 206–207. For other, partly conflicting, estimates of short-run and long-run aluminum price elasticities, see the Council on Wage and Price Stability staff report, *Aluminum Prices: 1974–75* (Washington, D.C.: Government Printing Office, September 1976), pp. 7–8, 115.

10. "New Threats to the $6 Billion Can Industry," *Business Week*, 22 November 1976, p. 78.

11. Jesse W. Markham, *Competition in the Rayon Industry* (Cambridge, Mass.: Harvard University Press, 1952), p. 208. See also "The Losses Pile Up in Synthetic Fibers," *Business Week*, 6 December 1976, p. 46.

12. See "OPEC: The Economics of the Oil Cartel," *Business Week*, 13 January 1975, pp. 80–81. OPEC's prices were, of course, considerably higher than the level that would have prevailed under competition, largely because substitutes for oil became attractive only at relatively high oil prices. Similarly, substitutes for bauxite in aluminum production were sufficiently inferior that cartel prices could be sustained well above the competitive level. See Robert S. Pindyck, "Cartel Pricing and the Structure of the World Bauxite Market," *Bell Journal of Economics* 8 (Autumn 1977): 343–60.

The dynamics of monopoly
and oligopoly pricing   231

substitution has not deterred some firms from setting prices paving the way to competitive inroads by alternative products. Steel is the most prominent example. American producers implemented a series of sharp price increases during the 1950s that led to increasing infringement upon traditional steel markets by substitute metals and plastics. This and pricing policies in other industries that encouraged substitution could have resulted from upward cost pressures on prices, shortsightedness, conscious decisions to sacrifice long-term market position for higher immediate profits or, most probably, a combination of all three.

The steel experience demonstrates that fear of long-run substitution is no surefire guarantee against excessive prices. But even when producers fail to show restraint, the possibility of turning to substitutes at least gives consumers an escape from severe and extended monopolistic exploitation. And as science makes it possible to create substitutes for more and more products, the combination of these two protective mechanisms—the threat of substitution and its actual occurrence—provides an important check on the social losses attributable to monopoly power.

Limiting entry: the dominant firm analysis

Another check on industrial pricing power is the threat of entry by new competitors and expansion by smaller existing rivals. To begin our analysis of this phenomenon we focus on the pricing problem faced by a so-called dominant firm—that is, a firm controlling roughly 40 percent or more of its industry's output, but faced with the actual or potential competition of fringe rivals, each too small to exert an appreciable influence on price through its individual output decisions.[13] If the industry's products are homogeneous, sellers comprising the fringe take the dominant firm's price as given, making the best of it by expanding their output up to the point at which short-run marginal cost rises to equal the price. If products are differentiated, the price at which fringe members sell will be the dominant firm's price minus (or plus) some differential. The dominant firm's problem in either case is to choose the best price from its own viewpoint, taking into account the supply of the competitive fringe at whatever price it sets.

The static solution is illustrated in Figure 8.1(a). The overall market demand function is D. The supply function for all members of the competitive fringe at a moment in time is SS_F (assumed linear only to simplify the construction). At the price OS, no output will be supplied by fringe members (because that price is less than the minimum marginal cost of every fringe producer). As the dominant firm sets prices exceeding OS by increasing amounts, firms in the fringe will find it profitable to produce more—at each possible announced price equating that price with their (rising) marginal costs. Knowing the fringe's supply function SS_F, the dominant firm knows how much of the market will be served by the fringe at any price, and hence how much is left over to be served by itself. At prices of OS and lower, it has the entire market to itself. At price OG, the competitive fringe supplies all the output the market will absorb at that price, with no demand left over for the dominant firm. Intermediate quantities of fringe supply are called forth at prices between OS and OG, so that the dominant firm's own effective or residual demand function is the kinked curve GBD, found by subtracting from the total quantity demanded at any given price the amount supplied by the competitive fringe.

Given its residual demand curve GBD, the dominant firm derives its marginal revenue function GMR. It now maximizes its profits by producing that output OX where its marginal cost (represented by curve MC) equals its marginal revenue, and it announces the price OP that brings the quantity it produces into equilibrium with its demand schedule. That is, at the price OP, the dominant firm will produce and sell $OX = PZ$ units, while the competitive fringe produces and sells ZA units (which, by construction, equals PT units). The overall market will be in equilibrium with $PA = (PZ + ZA)$ units supplied and PA units demanded. In this equilibrium, the dominant firm's profits (defined over the ordinate of its av-

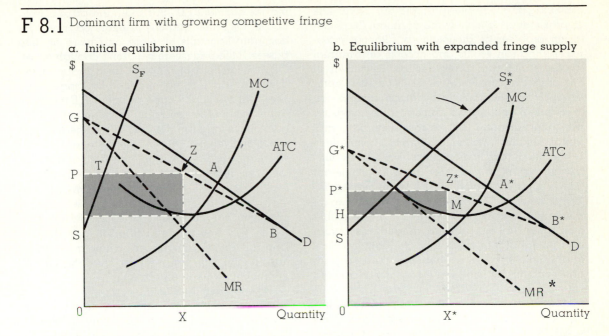

a. Initial equilibrium

b. Equilibrium with expanded fringe supply

erage total cost function *ATC* at output *OX*) are given by the shaded rectangle in Figure 8.1(a).

This solution is perfectly determinate in the short run. But if the price set by the dominant firm is high enough to let fringe producers earn positive economic profits, they will as time passes have an incentive to expand their capacity and/or build new plants. Also, new entrants will be attracted into the fringe. This expansion and new entry cause the competitive fringe's supply function to shift to the right, as shown by $SS_F{}^*$ in Figure 8.1(b). Since its own residual demand curve is found by subtracting the fringe's output from total market demand, the dominant firm's residual demand curve G^*B^* shifts downward and to the left. Given its new, more constrained demand function, the dominant firm reoptimizes, equating marginal revenue with marginal cost and setting the new, lower price OP^*, yielding a new (necessarily smaller) shaded profit rectangle P^*Z^*MH.

Again, this situation will not be stable if price OP^* is sufficient to let fringe firms earn positive economic profits. Further fringe expansion will occur, the dominant firm's residual demand function will shift even more to the left, and its market

share and profits will continue to decline. If it conforms to the classic dominant firm short-run profit maximization logic, the dominant firm in effect encourages and makes room for an expanded competitive fringe. Its high prices and profits today set into motion a chain of repercussions reducing the dominant firm's profits in subsequent years.

A simple limit pricing strategy In many instances there is only one way for the dominant firm to head off this Greek tragedy: It must abandon its attempt to maximize short-run profits, instead reducing its price to a level at which new entry and the expansion of fringe members are

13. The dominant firm theory was originally articulated by Karl Forchheimer in "Theoretisches zum unvollständigen Monopole," *Schmollers Jahrbuch* (1908): 1–12. See also A. J. Nichol, *Partial Monopoly and Price Leadership* (Philadelphia: Smith-Edwards, 1930). An important extension is Dean A. Worcester, "Why 'Dominant Firms' Decline," *Journal of Political Economy* 65 (August 1957): 338–47.

The dynamics of monopoly and oligopoly pricing   233

discouraged.[14] An overly simple but useful first approximation is to view the dominant firm's decision problem as dichotomous: Either it maximizes short-run profits and accepts an eventual market share and profit decline, as shown in Figures 8.1(a) and 8.1(b), or it sets prices to deter *all* entry and expansion by fringe competitors.

Figure 8.2 provides a framework for analyzing the latter strategy. DD' is the dominant firm's initial demand function. (If there is a competitive fringe, its output is assumed to have been subtracted out; if on the other hand the dominant firm is a pure monopolist, DD' is the market demand function. In either case, overall market demand is assumed provisionally to be stable over time.) Now suppose that fringe rivals, actual and potential, are small in scale relative to the total market volume, so they view the dominant firm's price as a parameter essentially unaffected by their output decisions. Suppose too that at their scale of operation, the lowest unit cost (including normal profits) attainable by fringe firms is OP_o. Then if the dominant firm sets and maintains a price even slightly above OP_o, fringe firms can realize supranormal profits. Existing fringe enterprises, if any, will expand, and outsiders will enter. The dominant firm's demand curve—initially DD'—will not remain stable. It will shift to the left and continue shifting to the left owing to the expanding fringe supply as long as the price is held above OP_o. The dominant firm's long-run demand function cannot therefore be DD'. It does include segment ED'. But when the price is held above OP_o, the quantity demanded from the dominant firm falls off more and more as time passes. If the price were held long enough above OP_o, the amount of output demanded from the dominant firm (i.e., not supplied by fringe members) will eventually approach zero. P_oE therefore approximates the remaining segment of the dominant firm's long-run demand curve, the whole of which is given by P_oED'. At the price level above which new entry flows in, the dominant firm's long-run demand function tends to become perfectly elastic. It is this entry phenomenon, more than long-run substitution between different products, that prompted J. M. Clark, Sir Roy Harrod, P. W. S. Andrews, and others to insist that the long-run demand curves confronting monopolists and oligopolistic groups tend to be highly elastic, approaching the horizontal.[15]

Now, to keep the existing competitive fringe in check and deter new entry, the dominant firm must set and maintain a price slightly below OP_o. This price, which we shall for simplicity represent by OP_o, is called the *limit price*—that is, the price that limits to zero the entry and expansion of fringe rivals. The dominant firm must also ensure that the market demand of OX_o at that price is fully satisfied. It must therefore supply output OX_o and maintain capacity suited to supplying that output. Figure 8.2 assumes that the dominant firm has chosen a plant capable of supplying OX_o at minimum unit cost. The profitability of an entry deterrence strategy depends then upon the dominant firm's unit cost at output OX_o. Figure 8.2 assumes that it is lower than OP_o and hence lower than actual or potential fringe firms' costs—e.g., because the dominant firm can realize scale economies that small fringe members cannot.[16] If this is the case, the dominant firm can set the limit price OP_o, hold fringe rivals in check, and continue year after year to rake in profits given by the shaded rectangle P_oEBC_M.

Is this the most profitable strategy for the dominant firm? In moving toward an answer, let us consider the alternative short-run profit maximization strategy. Given the cost functions in Figure 8.2, the short-run profit-maximizing price is OP_M, and the associated output OX_M, with profits equal to the rectangular area P_MHKG. These are

F 8.2 Pricing to deter small-scale entry

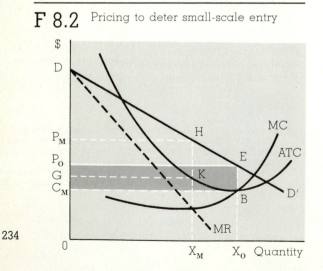

234

necessarily higher than the profits under a limit pricing strategy. But they are also shorter lived. As entry occurs, profits realized under short-run profit maximization will decline as shown in the upper panel of Figure 8.3. Under limit pricing, as illustrated in the lower panel, they will be smaller initially but larger eventually. Which time pattern is preferable? The answer turns upon the discount rate applied to future earnings, the rate at which entry occurs and profits decline under short-run profit maximizaton, and the extent to which the dominant firm is able persistently to maintain a price exceeding unit cost without encouraging fringe expansion. The latter in turn depends (under the assumptions accepted thus far) upon the dominant firm's unit cost advantage over fringe rivals.

If dominant firms discount the future heavily, they may place little weight on the future profits forgone owing to new entry and strive for maximum profits in the short run. According to standard managerial economics texts, high discount rates are especially appropriate when the future is uncertain, as it surely is in planning long-range pricing policy.[17] However, uncertainty might work in the opposite direction. As Harrod observes:

> All entrepreneurs . . . have in mind the vast uncertainties of a relatively distant future. The best method of insuring against them is to attach to oneself by ties of goodwill as large a market as possible as quickly as possible. If one can get a substantially larger market by earning no more than a normal profit than one could get by earning a surplus profit . . . one may well choose to do the former, as an insurance against future uncertainties.[18]

It is well known that some decision makers are more shortsighted or discount the future more heavily than others. Fog found such differences to be the most important single source of internal conflict and disagreement in Danish price-fixing cartels.[19] The psychology of the decision makers involved may therefore be a relevant variable affecting the pricing strategy choice.

Objective variables are also important, however, and prove more amenable to systematic analysis. Consider, contrary to our assumptions

thus far, a situation in which the dominant firm enjoys *no* unit cost advantage relative to fringe rivals, actual or potential. To deter their entry and/or expansion, it must maintain a limit price at which it realizes no supranormal profits. The limit pricing profit rectangles in Figure 8.3 will therefore have zero height. Then short-run profit maximization is unambiguously more profitable

14. Seminal works on this problem of "limit pricing" include Nicholas Kaldor, "Market Imperfection and Excess Capacity," *Economica* 2 (February 1935): 33–50; Clark, "Toward a Concept of Workable Competition," pp. 247–48; Joe S. Bain, "A Note on Pricing in Monopoly and Oligopoly," *American Economic Review* 39 (March 1949): 448–64; P. W. S. Andrews, *Manufacturing Business* (London: Macmillan, 1949); George J. Stigler, *The Theory of Price*, rev. ed. (New York: Macmillan, 1952), pp. 231–34; R. F. Harrod, *Economic Essays* (London: Macmillan, 1952), especially pp. 139–74; H. R. Edwards, "Price Formation in Manufacturing Industry and Excess Capacity," *Oxford Economic Papers* 7 n.s. (February 1955): 194–218; Joe S. Bain, *Barriers to New Competition* (Cambridge, Mass.: Harvard University Press, 1956); Paolo Sylos-Labini, *Oligopoly and Technical Progress*, trans. Elizabeth Henderson (Cambridge, Mass.: Harvard University Press, 1962); Franco Modigliani, "New Developments on the Oligopoly Front," *Journal of Political Economy* 66 (June 1958): 215–32; and B. P. Pashigian, "Limit Price and the Market Share of the Leading Firm," *Journal of Industrial Economics* 16 (July 1968): 165–77. Creative surveys include Dale K. Osborne, "The Role of Entry in Oligopoly Theory," *Journal of Political Economy* 72 (August 1964): 396–402; Jagdish N. Bhagwati, "Oligopoly Theory, Entry-Prevention, and Growth," *Oxford Economic Papers* 22 n.s. (November 1970): 297–310; and Graham Pyatt, "Profit Maximisation and the Threat of New Entry," *Economic Journal* 81 (June 1971): 242–55.

15. See note 1 *supra* and Harrod, *Economic Essays*, pp. 162–63.

16. If it were contemplating a higher price, lower output policy, the dominant firm would probably invest in less capacity than Figure 8.2 assumes, and with lower unit costs at output OX_M, its profits would be somewhat higher than those shown. Note that *ATC* is a short-run average cost function, i.e., one of many on the long-run envelope curve. The assumption that OP_o is the lowest unit cost attainable by entrants can be taken to mean that at the largest output an entrant can achieve, OP_o is the corresponding long-run cost function ordinate.

17. See Joel Dean, *Managerial Economics* (Englewood Cliffs, N.J.: Prentice-Hall, 1951), p. 568; and William J. Baumol, *Economic Theory and Operations Analysis*, 2nd ed. (Englewood Cliffs, N.J.: Prentice-Hall, 1965), pp. 454–55.

18. Harrod, *Economic Essays*, pp. 147, 174.

19. Bjarke Fog, "How Are Cartel Prices Determined?," *Journal of Industrial Economics* 5 (November 1956): 16–23. Fog observes that larger firms typically placed more weight on long-run considerations—an emphasis possibly related more to objective capital market access differences than entrepreneurial psychology.

The dynamics of monopoly and oligopoly pricing   235

over the long run too, and unless (Harrod's suggestion to the contrary notwithstanding) its desire for a secure future is extraordinary, the dominant firm will almost surely prefer to set prices at an entry-attracting level.

A crucial role therefore emerges for *barriers to entry* or to the expansion of fringe rivals. These can take several forms.[20] For one, the dominant firm (or firms) may enjoy absolute unit cost advantages over fringe rivals as a consequence of superior patented production methods or having acquired on favorable terms superior nonreproducible production inputs (such as ore deposits or hydroelectric power generating rights).[21] Second, as suggested already, the dominant firm's unit costs may be lower because of scale economies in production, physical distribution, purchasing, capital raising, or promotion not attainable by smaller fringe rivals. On this we shall have a good deal more to say later. Third, the dominant firm's output may enjoy product differentiation advantages—i.e., a brand "image" or accumulation of goodwill that makes buyers willing to pay a higher price than they would for the otherwise comparable products of new entrants or fringe rivals. Image advantages are analogous to unit cost advantages in their operation as entry barriers—both act as a wedge between the limit price and the dominant firm's own unit costs. As Chapter 4 brought out, the inability of fringe rivals to emulate a dominant firm's image advantages may in turn be related to scale economies in sales promotion efforts.[22] Fourth, capital raising, product differentiation, and information access handicaps might *slow down* the entry and expansion of fringe rivals, thus affecting the time pattern of the dominant firm's profit returns, instead of permitting the dominant firm *persistently* to enjoy supranormal profits without attracting entry. And finally, through its conduct the dominant firm may be able to engender expectations in the minds of rivals that discourage rival entry and expansion. On this too, more must be said later.

A fully dynamic model We have in hand now most of the analytic pieces one needs to study firms' long-run pricing strategy choices. But they are not yet put together properly. One problem is that the simple limit pricing model permits only crude behavioral predictions. Second, it is questionable whether dominant firms face only a dichotomous choice between deterring all fringe entry or raising price to the short-run profit-maximizing level. Intermediate strategies might be even more profitable. A fully dynamic analysis by Gaskins goes far toward eliminating these two problems.[23]

The critical assumption is that the rate at which new entrants enter and fringe rivals expand is neither exogenous nor dichotomous, but varies continuously with the price set by the dominant firm.[24] This is so because potential entrants will perceive the attractiveness of entry

F 8.3 Comparison of profit streams over time

Short-run profit maximization

Limit pricing

Period (1)   (2)   (3)   (4)

more rapidly when the profit stimulus is strong and because higher anticipated profit returns make it more likely that interested investors will choose to commit their funds. If then P_o is the unit cost at which potential entrants or fringe firms can operate, $P(t)$ is the price set by the dominant firm at time t, and $X(t)$ is the amount of output supplied by fringe firms at time t, the dynamics of entry are characterized by the simple differential equation:

$$(8.1) \quad \frac{dX}{dt} = k\,[P(t) - P_o]$$

where dX/dt is the rate of fringe expansion (or, for negative values of $P(t) - P_o$, contraction) per time period and coefficient k reflects the speed at which fringe firms respond to the profit stimulus. Equation (8.1) is then incorporated into the dominant firm's long-run profit maximization problem and, using the mathematical techniques of optimal control theory, that problem can be solved to find the time path of prices yielding the highest discounted present value of profits.[25] In this instance, $P(t)$ is known as a control variable—that is, a behavioral variable manipulated over time by the dominant firm to maximize its profit performance functional. The so-called state variable, $X(t)$, in the present case reflects the structure of the market as it is shaped by the dominant firm's pricing policy. It is worth pointing out that while the value of $X(t)$ influences the dominant firm's pricing policy at any moment in time—i.e., structure affects conduct—the choice of a pricing policy in turn affects dX/dt and hence has important feedback effects on market structure.[26]

From analysis of the basic Gaskins model (as well as more complex variants), a number of strong and plausible conclusions emerge. For one, unless the fringe's unit costs are so high that they exceed the price a monopolist would set to maximize short-run profits—a case Bain previously designated as *blockaded* entry[27]—the monopolist *always* finds its long-run profits enhanced by exercising restraint and holding its price below the short-run profit-maximizing level. Thus, when the rate of new entry varies with the dominant firm's price choice, pricing to exclude *some* entry becomes an interesting option alongside pricing to deter *all* entry. The strategy problem is no longer merely a choice between blocking all entry or maximizing short-run profits.

What price path over time the dominant firm chooses depends *inter alia*, as one might expect, upon its cost advantage vis-à-vis fringe firms, the entry response coefficient k, and the discount rate. For dominant firms not subjected to a "sudden death" threat—e.g., because a key patent is about to expire—and hence with a reasonably long time horizon, three main cases emerge.

20. Cf. Bain, *Barriers to New Competition*, pp. 1–19; and *idem, Industrial Organization*, 2nd ed. (New York: Wiley, 1968), pp. 204–205, 255.

21. Strictly speaking, supranormal profits gained through such possession are rents imputable to the patent's or deposit's superiority. What one calls them is less important than what implications they have for structure and performance.

22. Cf. Chapter 4, pp. 108–10 *supra.*

23. Darius W. Gaskins, Jr., "Dynamic Limit Pricing: Optimal Pricing under Threat of Entry," *Journal of Economic Theory* 3 (September 1971): 306–22. A fuller exposition covering a broader array of cases is found in his Ph.D. dissertation, "Optimal Pricing by Dominant Firms" (University of Michigan, 1970).

24. For early statistical support, see Edwin Mansfield, "Entry, Gibrat's Law, Innovation, and the Growth of Firms," *American Economic Review* 52 (December 1962): 1023–30.

25. Assuming that the quantity demanded from all sellers, dominant and fringe, is $Q[P(t)]$, the quantity sold by the dominant firm is obviously $Q[P(t)] - X(t)$. Assuming furthermore that the dominant firm produces at constant unit cost c, the dominant firm's profits in period t are

$$[P(t) - c]\,\{Q[P(t)] - X(t)\}.$$

If r is the dominant firm's time discount rate, the firm's decision problem is to maximize the functional

$$\int_o^\infty [P(t) - c]\,\{Q[P(t)] - X(t)\}\,e^{-rt}\,dt$$

subject to the fringe behavioral condition

$$dX/dt = k[P(t) - P_o]$$

and subject also to various initial and boundary conditions. For a derivation of the solution conditions, which are rather complex, the reader is referred to Gaskins, "Dynamic Limit Pricing."

26. Cf. Alex P. Jacquemin and Jacques Thisse, "Strategy of the Firm and Market Structure: An Application of Optimal Control Theory," in Keith Cowling, ed., *Market Structure and Corporate Behaviour* (London: Gray-Mills, 1972), pp. 63–75; and Gerald Brock, "Optimal Pricing with Endogenous Barriers to Entry" (manuscript, University of Arizona, 1978).

27. Bain, *Barriers to New Competition*, pp. 21–22. Short-run profit maximization may also occur if the dominant firm's discount rate is infinite or at the moment the dominant firm's life ends—e.g., because its charter expires. Both cases are highly implausible.

Case I: the declining dominant firm When the dominant firm has no cost or image advantage over actual and potential fringe rivals, and *a fortiori* when it operates at a cost or image disadvantage, it will maximize long-run profits by setting its price above the limit price P_o (but below the short-run profit-maximizing price), earning (somewhat constrained) monopoly profits while it can, and letting its market share steadily decline. Its optimal price will gradually converge toward the limit price and eventually equal it as the dominant firm's market share dwindles either to zero or (more plausibly) to a level at which the firm no longer has power over price.[28] A similar strategy is likely to be adopted by dominant firms with only a small unit cost or image advantage. This is more probable as the dominant firm's time discount rate rises. The larger the rival response coefficient k is—that is, the faster entry occurs in response to an above-cost price—the more restraint the dominant firm will exercise in elevating its price and encouraging fringe expansion.[29]

Case II: exclusionary pricing When there is a competitive fringe of appreciable size and when the dominant firm has a significant unit cost or image advantage over fringe members, the dominant firm's long-run profit-maximizing strategy will often be to set its price initially below the level of fringe firms' unit cost and drive the rivals out. This is more likely the larger the dominant firm's price-cost advantage is, the lower its time discount rate is, and the larger k is—that is, the more rapidly fringe firms exit in response to prices below their unit cost. In many instances, given its cost advantage, the dominant firm will continue to earn positive profits as it squeezes rivals out. However, with sufficiently large initial fringe output and k values, the dominant firm may rationally cut the price temporarily below its own unit cost in order to hasten rivals' exit and to enhance its market share.[30] In either event, as the fringe dwindles, the dominant firm gradually raises its price, realizing rising profit margins, while the exit of remaining rivals decelerates. It can be shown[31] that there exists an asymptotically optimal market share toward which the dominant firm aspires. That market share is larger, the greater the dominant firm's cost ad-

vantage, the lower its discount rate, and the higher the fringe response coefficient k are. As the dominant firm's actual market share approaches its asymptotic optimum, the firm raises its price toward the limit price and relaxes its efforts to squeeze out additional competition.

Case III: asymptotic limit pricing Given enough time, the market share of a dominant firm with an appreciable cost advantage over rivals will approach the value at which further market share gains cost more in terms of current profit sacrifices than they add through the generation of profits on a larger future sales volume. From then on, the dominant firm will pursue a classic limit pricing policy, keeping its price $P(t)$ equal to the fringe firms' unit cost P_o. If its cost advantage is slowly eroding over time—e.g., because patents are expiring one by one—it may alternatively begin by driving out rivals but later charge a price *above* the limit price and attract entry. However, Gaskins demonstrates for a range of plausible cases that when this "low-price followed by high-price" strategy maximizes long-run profits, a second-best strategy of maintaining the price consistently at or near the limit price P_o typically entails only modest profit sacrifices compared to the first-best rule.[32] Because of its simplicity and perhaps also because pricing to drive out rivals could invite antitrust sanctions, the constant limit price strategy may well be favored by dominant firms. As we shall see in a later chapter, the risk of an antitrust complaint might also increase sharply as the dominant firm's market share exceeds some threshold value—e.g., on the order of 65 percent. And in any event, it cannot exceed 100 percent. Gaskins demonstrates that when a dominant firm is charging less than the limit price to drive out fringe competitors and when its market share rises to some such boundary value, its optimal policy shifts abruptly to one of maintaining prices persistently at the limit price level.[33]

The basic Gaskins model yields a rich set of predictions about how the pricing behavior and profits of firms with monopoly power will vary both statically and dynamically with cost conditions, factors affecting the speed of entry, and market shares. This analytic power is achieved

238

by accepting some important simplifications of reality—notably, the assumption of a certain, deterministic entry function such as equation (8.1), the assumption that entry and exit occur in small (i.e., infinitesimal) quantities rather than large lumps, and the closely related assumption that fringe firms and potential entrants are mechanistic price takers ignoring the effect of their own actions on the behavior of the dominant firm. Much of our remaining agenda in this chapter involves relaxing these assumptions. However, further consideration of the uncertainty and lumpiness problems is warranted immediately. One means of coping with inevitable deviations from the deterministic entry behavior implied by equation (8.1) is for the dominant firm to follow optimal feedback rules when entry or exit occurs unexpectedly. Gaskins shows that introducing such feedback rules for the case of stochastic entry causes no essential changes in the predictions generated with his simpler "open loop" model.[34] A different approach developed independently by Morton Kamien and Nancy Schwartz is to make uncertainty and lumpiness a central feature of the analysis.[35] They assume that if entry takes place, it occurs in a sizeable lump, and that the probability of its occurrence in any given time period increases, the higher the price charged by the dominant firm. Like Gaskins, they find that the dominant firm reduces price more to retard entry, the lower its time discount rate is and the more probable entry is in response to a given price (which embodies both the cost advantage and speed of entry features of the Gaskins model).

Some illustrations The view of pricing strategy presented thus far is compelling not only because it yields rich predictions, but also because those predictions appear to be consistent with a good deal of what we know about American industrial history. Steel provides an especially well-documented illustration.[36] When the United States Steel Corporation was formed by merger in 1901, it accounted for approximately 65 percent of U.S. steel ingot production. There is reason to believe that its plants had no operating cost advantage over those of efficient rivals, and in subsequent decades it had clearly higher costs

than several rivals. The theory of optimal dynamic pricing predicts that under these circumstances it should have adopted a pricing policy inducing entry and a decline in its market share. This it clearly did. Despite acquiring a sizeable competitor in 1907 and opening in 1911 the world's largest steel works at Gary, its share of domestic steel ingot production fell to 51 percent in 1915, 42 percent in 1925, and 24 percent in 1967. By that time its behavior had changed sufficiently as to raise doubts about whether the dominant

28. In his original work, Gaskins proved this result only for a nongrowing market. He found that market growth nullified the tendency for the dominant firm's market share to approach zero asymptotically and for the price to decline to P_o. However, in "Concentration and the Growth of Market Demand," *Journal of Economic Theory* 5 (October 1972): 303–305, N. J. Ireland shows that this conclusion followed from a special and perhaps implausible assumption of the Gaskins model. When increases in demand are shared between the dominant firm and fringe members in proportion to current market shares, the tendency for the price to converge toward P_o is restored.

29. For some qualifications to this last point, see Raymond De Bondt, "On the Effects of Retarded Entry," *European Economic Review* 8 (August 1977): 361–71.

30. This is much less likely when the rate of entry for values of $P(t)$ exceeding P_o is greater than the rate of exit for equivalent $P(t)$ values below P_o—e.g., when the analogue of equation (8.1) is a quadratic equation of the form $(dX/dT) = k_1[P(t) - P_o] + k_2[P(t) - P_o]^2$, with $[P(t) - P_o] \geq -k_1/2k_2$. See Gaskins, "Optimal Pricing by Dominant Firms," pp. 26–40.

31. Gaskins, "Dynamic Limit Pricing," pp. 311–12.

32. Gaskins, "Optimal Pricing by Dominant Firms," pp. 22–24. The profit sacrifice is particularly small when the dominant firm enjoys only a moderate cost advantage.

33. Gaskins, "Optimal Pricing," pp. 91–104.

34. Gaskins, "Optimal Pricing," pp. 82–90.

35. Morton I. Kamien and Nancy L. Schwartz, "Limit Pricing and Uncertain Entry," *Econometrica* 39 (May 1971): 441–54. Extensions include Kamien and Schwartz, "Uncertain Entry and Excess Capacity," *American Economic Review* 62 (December 1972): 918–27; Kamien and Schwartz, "Cournot Oligopoly with Uncertain Entry," *Review of Economic Studies* 42 (January 1975): 125–31; David P. Baron, "Limit Pricing, Potential Entry, and Barriers to Entry," *American Economic Review* 63 (September 1973): 666–74; and Raymond R. De Bondt, "Limit Pricing, Uncertain Entry, and the Entry Lag," *Econometrica* 44 (September 1976): 939–46.

36. See especially Eliot Jones, *The Trust Problem in the United States* (New York: Macmillan, 1921), Chapter 9 and in particular, on comparative costs, pp. 218–19; and Donald O. Parsons and Edward J. Ray, "The United States Steel Consolidation: The Creation of Market Control," *Journal of Law and Economics* 18 (April 1975): 181–220.

firm analysis continued to be applicable.[37] Stigler shows that at least in the early years of U.S. Steel's history, this high-price, declining market share strategy was quite profitable.[38] In iron ore, on the other hand, United States Steel controlled at the time of its creation a considerable share of the nation's richest deposits; and in the subsequent decade it bought up most of the remaining high-grade reserves so that only low-quality ore remained for nonintegrated rivals (to whom it sold ore) and fringe entrants. With this cost advantage, U.S. Steel evidently pursued an ore pricing policy under which its share of domestic iron ore production remained fairly constant in the 40 to 45 percent range throughout the first three decades of its existence and probably even longer.[39]

There are many other cases of declining dominant firm market shares over time, in at least some of which corroborating evidence of little or no cost advantage exists. One of the more spectacular involved the Reynolds International Pen Corporation, which sold its pioneering ball point pens (costing 80 cents to produce) at retail prices of $12 to $20 in late 1945 and precipitated the entry of some 100 competitors. By 1948 its market share had fallen to zero.[40] In 1919, the American Viscose Company controlled 100 percent of the domestic rayon market. Once key patents expired, new entry and the expansion of entrants caused its share to fall to 42 percent in 1930, after which, according to Markham, it no longer conformed to the dominant firm pricing model.[41] However, it continued to bear the brunt of industry output restriction efforts, and by 1949 its share had fallen further to 26 percent. American Can controlled 90 percent of all tin can output at the time of its organization in 1901. Its high-price policy encouraged new entry, and its market share fell to 63 percent in 1913 and to roughly 40 percent by 1960.[42] Similar histories are observed in corn products refining,[43] farm implements,[44] synthetic fibers,[45] aluminum extrusions,[46] instant mashed potatoes,[47] frozen orange juice,[48] and, when dominance in regional markets is taken into account, the gasoline industry.[49]

A particularly sophisticated entry control strategy was pursued by the Xerox Corporation in leasing its copying machines.[50] When the Xerox 914 copier was introduced in 1959, sales efforts were initially directed toward penetrating the low- and medium-volume market segments— i.e., serving customers making fewer than 5,000 copies per machine per month. In the low-volume segment, where Xerox had no inherent long-run cost advantage over alternate copying processes, prices were set very close to the short-run profit-maximizing level. According to Xerox executives, this decision was taken partly because the company was desperately in need of cash, and therefore discounted the future at a high rate, and partly because they realized that Xerox would eventually have to surrender the market to substitute copiers—notably, to those using the Electrofax process, which is simpler but uses expensive coated paper. Actually, 29 firms entered the low-volume market with Electrofax machines between 1961 and 1967. In the medium- and high-volume ranges, xerography had a modest to substantial cost advantage. Xerox prices were set below the short-run profit-maximizing level, but above the entry-deterring level, in the expectation that a share of the market would gradually be handed over to Electrofax producers. The entry rate was in fact much less than in the low-volume market. In 1967, there were 10 firms offering Electrofax machines designed for medium-volume application and only 4 firms in the high-volume range. Finally, in the very high-volume field (above 100,000 copies per month), Xerox's comparative cost position left entry essentially blockaded until its basic patents expired or would-be rivals succeeded in the formidable task of inventing around its patent portfolio. As it moved into this market with new high-speed machines during the 1960s, it was able for nearly a decade to charge prices exceeding cost by a substantial margin without experiencing appreciable entry.

Cases in which dominant firms retained their dominant positions over an extended period are rarer, perhaps because it is exceptional for a single company to enjoy a persistent and substantial cost or image advantage. One important exception is the computer industry. Estimating the Gaskins optimal dynamic pricing model econometrically, Gerald Brock found that IBM could charge prices roughly 10 to 15 percent higher than its costs without sacrificing market share.[51] His model tracks IBM's pricing trajectory well but underestimates the tendency for IBM's market share to erode (from 75 percent in 1956 to 68 percent in 1967) and fails to cope with details of the strategies IBM adopted in introducing new computer and peripheral equipment models. We shall have more to say about those strategies, including some evidently aimed at driving rivals from the market, in later chapters.

With control of superior domestic bauxite reserves and low-cost hydroelectric power rights, the Aluminum Company of America maintained a 100 percent share of U.S. primary aluminum production from 1893 to 1940. There is reason to believe that Alcoa followed a conscious policy of charging less than the market would bear at any moment in time in order to maintain its long-run market position.[52] The International Nickel Company controlled 75 to 90 percent of the Western world's nickel supply through the first half of the 20th century. Its dominance was based upon the ownership of uniquely rich sulphide ore deposits in the Sudbury, Ontario, area, which afforded it a cost advantage great enough to make a limit pricing strategy highly profitable.[53] However, as Inco's best ore reserves approached exhaustion, it raised nickel prices to a level permitting the profitable mining of inferior but abundant laterite ores, and this encouraged new entry and expansion by existing rivals. As a result, its noncommunist world market share fell to approximately 50 percent in the late 1960s and continued to fall to 30 percent by 1977.

General Motors has managed to maintain its share of domestic auto production in the 45 to 60 percent range since 1950. One reason for its continued dominance has undoubtedly been image and cost advantages over smaller manufacturers, permitting it to earn very high profit returns while Ford's profits exceeded the average for all manufacturers by only a slight margin and firms smaller than Chrysler teetered on the brink of failure.[54] The only competition to which GM yielded market share more than temporarily in the post-World War II period has been importers. Holding other things (such as the range of small car offerings) equal, importers' ability to make gains at GM's expense was greater during peri-

37. Cf. Chapter 6, pp. 178–80 supra.

38. See George J. Stigler, "The Dominant Firm and the Inverted Umbrella," Journal of Law and Economics 8 (October 1965): 167–72.

39. See Parsons and Ray, "The United States Steel Consolidation," pp. 201–202.

40. Thomas Whiteside, "Where Are They Now?," New Yorker, 17 February 1951, pp. 39–58.

41. Markham, Competition in the Rayon Industry, pp. 14–20, 46–47, 103–104.

42. C. H. Hession, "The Metal Container Industry," in Walter Adams, ed., The Structure of American Industry, 3rd ed. (New York: Macmillan, 1961), pp. 432–34; and James W. McKie, Tin Cans and Tin Plate (Cambridge, Mass.: Harvard University Press, 1959), pp. 46, 89.

43. Simon N. Whitney, Antitrust Policies, vol. II (New York: Twentieth Century Fund, 1958), pp. 258–60.

44. A. D. H. Kaplan, Joel B. Dirlam, and R. F. Lanzillotti, Pricing in Big Business (Washington, D.C.: Brookings Institution, 1958), p. 69.

45. See R. W. Shaw and S. A. Shaw, "Patent Expiry and Competition in Synthetic Fibres," Scottish Journal of Political Economy 24 (June 1977): 117–32; and "Sagging du Pont Casts Shadow over the Dow," Business Week, 8 April 1967, p. 120.

46. Peck, Competition in the Aluminum Industry, p. 70.

47. Lester C. Telser, Competition, Collusion, and Game Theory (Chicago: Aldine-Atherton, 1972), pp. 299–304.

48. Telser, Competition, Collusion, and Game Theory, pp. 304–305.

49. Kaplan et al., Pricing in Big Business, pp. 86, 157; Edmund P. Learned and Catherine C. Ellsworth, Gasoline Pricing in Ohio (Boston: Harvard Business School Division of Research, 1959), pp. 23–24, 161; and (on the entry-inducing strategy of British petroleum refiners) R. W. Shaw, "Price Leadership and the Effect of New Entry on the U.K. Retail Petrol Supply Market," Journal of Industrial Economics 23 (September 1974): 65–79.

50. Erwin A. Blackstone, "Limit Pricing and Entry in the Copying Machine Industry," Quarterly Review of Economics and Business 12 (Winter 1972): 57–65.

51. Gerald W. Brock, The U.S. Computer Industry (Cambridge, Mass.: Ballinger, 1975), pp. 71–87.

52. See Leonard W. Weiss, Economics and American Industry (New York: Wiley, 1963), pp. 189–204.

53. See O. W. Main, The Canadian Nickel Industry (Toronto: University of Toronto Press, 1955); "The Beguiling New Economics of Nickel," Fortune, March 1970, pp. 100 ff.; and "With Its Long Sway in Nickel Fading, Inco Gears Up To Fight," Wall Street Journal, 20 April 1978, p. 1. The summary here also relies upon a paper, "The Nickel Industry," written by James M. Kennedy at the University of Michigan in 1972.

For similar analyses of the pricing strategies of depletable resource cartels in crude oil, bauxite, and copper, see Robert S. Pindyck, "Gains to Producers from the Cartelization of Exhaustible Resources," Review of Economics and Statistics 60 (May 1978): 238–51.

54. Cf. Lawrence J. White, The Automobile Industry Since 1945 (Cambridge, Mass.: Harvard University Press, 1971), especially Chapters 4, 8, and 15.

ods when the U.S. dollar was overvalued relative to the Japanese yen and European currencies, lessening the cost advantage of U.S. producers. Again, this history is consistent with the predictions of optimal dynamic limit pricing theory.

Except for the added complication of intragroup coordination, the pricing problem faced by a cartel or a group of oligopolists acting jointly is analogous to that of a single dominant firm. If the group has no significant cost advantage over nonmembers or potential entrants, raising price above the entry-inducing level will be the most profitable but ultimately self-defeating policy. Fritz Voigt found that most of the thousands of German cartels formed between 1873 and 1933 collapsed quickly, often after only a few months of operation. The reason was that "if they succeeded in raising prices, new firms entered the industry, operating as outsiders, which led to a decline in sales by the cartel members; the cartel collapsed and a price war set in. . . ." Only the cartels with strong patent protection or other effective entry barriers were able to hold prices up while retaining their market shares, but they were the exceptions.[55] As Machlup put it, cartel members often "find themselves 'holding the umbrella' over outsiders and getting increasingly wet feet."[56]

The pricing behavior of the U.S. steel industry during the 1960s and 1970s is better described as that of a remarkably well-disciplined oligopolistic group than by the dominant firm model. As Japanese and West European steel producers rebuilt and expanded their industries with modern equipment following World War II, and with the dollar significantly overvalued during the 1960s, U.S. steel makers found themselves at a cost disadvantage relative to importers. Their most profitable strategy was to set U.S. prices above the entry-excluding level. Imports rose from 1.5 percent of U.S. demand in 1957 to nearly 17 percent in 1967, after which government-supported import quotas stemmed the tide. Devaluation of the dollar reversed a renewed trend toward rising imports in 1971. After that, the picture has been sufficiently blurred by price controls, worldwide escalation of energy costs, rapid U.S. price increases following the end of controls, and the imposition of a "trigger price" system when imports soared anew that it is difficult to discern a clear long-run pricing strategy. The evidence is surely not inconsistent with the declining dominant group model's predictions.

The U.S. brewing industry illustrates the opposite case of a leading group pricing to drive out existing rivals. As noted in Chapter 4, the principal nationally advertised brewers enjoyed an image advantage over local and regional beers and, after building large new decentralized breweries during the 1960s, they also gained an appreciable unit cost advantage.[57] Their strategy in view of these conditions was to squeeze the price differential between premium and popular beers. As a result of these developments, the number of companies brewing beer in the United States fell from 404 in 1947 to 108 in 1972, and the combined national market share of the four leading brewers rose from 21 percent in 1947 to 61 percent in 1976.

Further implications Several additional implications of the basic limit pricing analysis merit attention before we turn to more complex extensions.

For one, it is entirely possible that equilibrium will occur at a point where industry demand is price inelastic. This is plainly true in Figure 8.2, if we assume the absence of a competitive fringe. At the entry-deterring output OX_o, dominant firm (and hence industry) short-run marginal revenue is negative. Nearly all A students of economic theory (and a few B students) have at one time or another written into examination booklets that profit-maximizing monopolists never operate in an inelastic segment of the industry demand function. Yet, because *after* entry their private residual demand function would diverge from the industry demand function, this is not necessarily true.

Second, if a group of oligopolists elects to practice limit pricing, marginalist output determination rules are no longer appropriate. The total amount of output to be produced by the group is clear if the group chooses to exclude all new entry—it is the quantity OX_o in Figure 8.2. It can also be determined uniquely, following more laborious mathematical analysis, under a Gaskins-type analysis balancing the benefits of a higher current price against eventual erosion of the group's collective market share. However, there is no compelling calculus telling individual group members how much to produce. If each member sets output at the level where its marginal cost equals marginal revenue (derived under the price-matching, constant-shares assumption), too little will be produced. If each equates marginal cost with the price, too much will usually be produced. Ideally, each firm might produce a predetermined share of the total quantity demanded when the price is set at the optimal entry-limiting level. But this requires explicit agreements on market shares, and even that is insufficient in a world of change and uncertainty. When the industry demand function shifts erratically over time (as most demand functions do), member firms could find themselves in the awkward position of planning to produce a known share of an unknown total quantity demanded. As a result, there is no way of ensuring that the quantities member firms plan to supply, either independently or collusively, will add up to a total that just clears the market at the strategically determined price. That price can be sustained only if production planning errors are absorbed through fluctuations in finished goods inventories and order backlogs. Changes in orders, backlogs, and inventory levels also provide signals to guide member firm production decisions when collusive output determination institutions are lacking. This feedback system, rather than marginalist rules, must be the main basis of output decisions in tacitly collusive oligopolies practicing limit pricing.

In recognizing these problems, we must also be aware that even when oligopolists mutually prefer to adopt an entry-limiting price policy, the desired price may not be attained or maintained. Through miscalculation, the price may be set too high. But more importantly, if the group's discipline is weak, the actual price may fall persistently below the limit price. In this case entry will be deterred, but member firms will realize lower profits than they would under an effectively coordinated deterrence policy.[58]

One further link between marginalist rules and limit pricing must be considered. As Chapter 6 brought out, since 1939 economists have been debating whether the use of full-cost pricing rules, which appear devoid of any attempt to equate marginal revenue with marginal cost, is

consistent with profit maximization. The conflict fades in a limit pricing context. Producers pricing to deter entry must set their price slightly below the entrants' minimum average cost. The application of full-cost pricing rules is an operational method of achieving this result. When prices of labor and raw materials change, they tend to do so more or less uniformly for all industry members, actual or potential. The limit price must therefore change correspondingly, and adjustments based upon a full-cost rule will keep actual prices in fairly close step with the altered conditions of entry deterrence. The 'conventional profit margin' applied to accounting cost need not be invariant across industry lines; it may be adjusted (as case studies have documented) to reflect the cost or image advantage established companies have over potential entrants. Thus, when the most profitable long-run strategy for existing producers is to deter new entry, intelligent application of full-cost pricing rules is apt to bring firms as close to the goal of maximum profits as they can hope to come in a world of change and uncertainty.[59]

Deterring large-scale entry

Thus far we have assumed for the most part that new entrants or existing fringe firms add output on such a small scale relative to total market

---

55. "German Experience with Cartels and Their Control during the Pre-War and Post-War Periods," in John Perry Miller, ed., *Competition, Cartels and Their Regulation* (Amsterdam: North-Holland, 1962), pp. 171–72, 181, 184.

56. Fritz Machlup, *The Economics of Sellers' Competition* (Baltimore: Johns Hopkins, 1952), pp. 527–29.

57. Cf. Chapter 4, p. 110 *supra*.

58. In *The Economics of Sellers' Competition*, p. 537, Machlup suggests that poorly coordinated oligopolists trying to practice limit pricing are caught on the horns of a dilemma. Low prices may induce actual competitors to compete belligerently, while high prices will induce new entry.

59. For an early reconciliation of full-cost pricing with the equalization of long-run marginal revenue and marginal cost, see Harrod, *Economic Essays*, pp. 161–63.

volume that they can reasonably assume their influence on price to be negligible. When impressive economies can be realized by entering or expanding on a large scale, however, this assumption may be violated. To deal with this case we need a more complicated analysis. Although there is a slightly different British tradition following the work of P. W. S. Andrews,[60] we emphasize here the approach pioneered by Joe S. Bain and Paolo Sylos-Labini and extended by Franco Modigliani.[61]

The problem, in essence, is that a firm contemplating entry on a large scale has reason to fear that its incremental output contribution will be absorbed by the market only if the price is reduced. As a result, even though the entrant's costs may be just as low as those of enterprises already in the industry, and even though the preentry price exceeds the entrant's full expected unit cost, the price after entry may fall below cost, and entry will prove to be unprofitable. If this is anticipated, entry will be deterred.

Now the amount by which the price falls following entry depends *inter alia* upon the surplus of postentry over preentry output. This in turn depends not only upon the entrant's output but also upon any output changes effected by the original industry members. Here we run squarely into the problem of oligopolistic interdependence. How will the established sellers react? Conceivably, they could reduce their own outputs to make room for the newcomer. If so, the price might not decline at all. At the other extreme, they could hold their production constant or even increase it to make life as difficult as possible for the interloper. Some assumption has to be made by a potential entrant calculating the profitability of entry. The economist too must build a theory upon assumptions conforming, one hopes, as closely as possible to the thought processes of real-world entrepreneurs.

Both Bain and Sylos-Labini emphasize maintenance of output by established firms as the most likely reaction to new entry. Bain's principal defense of output maintenance is that it is a relatively pessimistic assumption from the standpoint of the new entrant.[62] And of course, a certain amount of pessimism is in order when one is contemplating entering a new industry on a

large scale. According to Sylos-Labini, existing firms maintain their output partly in an effort to discourage entry and partly because cost structure rigidities encourage full utilization of capacity.[63] If we provisionally accept the output maintenance assumption, we can derive from it several testable generalizations. For simplicity we assume in all cases that new entrants can, by building a plant of minimum optimal scale, produce at unit costs just as low as those of existing firms. We also ignore price premia associated with brand image differences, in effect assuming the absence of appreciable product differentiation. The problem is, how much can existing firms elevate prices above their own (minimum) unit costs without attracting new entry?

Suppose initially that the new entrant chooses to enter at minimum optimal scale, i.e., to produce an output volume just sufficient to realize all economies of scale. Then the larger the minimum optimal scale is relative to the overall size of the industry, the more the price will be depressed by a new entrant, other things (such as the elasticity of demand) being equal. Assume, for example, that demand has unit elasticity in the relevant neighborhood. If entry at minimum optimal scale requires the entrant to produce (and hence dispose of) 10 percent of the total quantity demanded at the postentry price, price will be depressed by 9 percent owing to entry. So unless the preentry price exceeds the potential entrant's expected unit costs by more than 10 percent, entry will be unprofitable. A preentry price exceeding minimum unit cost by slightly less than 10 percent will be just sufficient to deter entry. If, alternatively, entry at optimal scale requires the entrant to produce only 5 percent of the total quantity demanded at the postentry price, price will fall by only 4.5 percent upon entry; and existing firms can hold their price no higher than 5 percent above minimum unit cost without encouraging entry. Generalizing, the smaller the minimum optimal scale is relative to the output volume demanded at a price equal to minimum unit cost (i.e., the competitive price), the less price can be held persistently above the competitive level without attracting new entry, *ceteris paribus*.

Suppose now that the scale of entry continues

F 8.4   Deterring large-scale entry with cost functions of varying curvature

(a) The cost curves

(b) Deterrence with cost curve b

(c) Deterrence with cost curve c

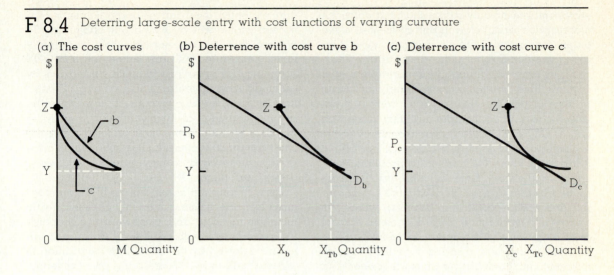

to be 10 percent of total market volume at the competitive price. If the elasticity of demand is 2 instead of 1, price will fall by only about 4.5 percent instead of 9 percent upon entry. If the elasticity is 5, price will fall by only about 2 percent, and a preentry price exceeding minimum unit cost by more than 2 percent will attract entry. Thus, the more elastic market demand is—i.e., the more readily the market will absorb an increment of supply without a large fall in price—the less price can be held persistently above the competitive level without attracting new entry, *ceteris paribus*.

Finally, we relax the assumption that the new entrant must enter at the least-cost scale. By entering at a size smaller than MOS, a newcomer incurs the disadvantage of higher unit costs, but gains the advantage of adding a smaller output increment and thus precipitates a milder price decline. Recognizing this possibility, established output-maintaining sellers must set their output and price at levels such that the market demand curve segment not satisfied by their supply—that is, the segment to the right of their output on a conventional industry demand diagram—lies at no point above the potential entrant's cost curve, whose zero-output point is set to coincide with the existing firms' total output point. To comprehend this notion and its implications, consider Figure 8.4. Panel (a) displays two alternate long-run cost

functions *b* and *c*.[64] Both exhibit economies of scale over their full illustrated range; both reach the minimum optimal scale at the same output *OM* and unit cost *OY*; and both have the same vertical intercept *OZ*. The only difference between them is that curve *c* has unit costs declining at first more rapidly with scale increases than curve *b*. Now let us in effect slide the cost curves horizontally to the right—curve *b* until it just touches the market demand function D_b in panel (b), and curve *c* until it is similarly tangent to market demand curve D_c. Tangency in both cases implies that if the output of established firms ends where the output of the entrant begins [i.e., at OX_b in panel (b) and OX_c in panel (c)] and if the

60. See especially Andrews, *Manufacturing Business;* and Bhagwati, "Oligopoly Theory, Entry-Prevention, and Growth."

61. *Supra* note 14.

62. Bain, *Barriers to New Competition,* p. 105. Bain did explore alternative output behavior assumptions in the course of his analysis.

63. Sylos-Labini, *Oligopoly and Technical Progress,* p. 43.

64. This method of presentation is adapted from Modigliani, "New Developments on the Oligopoly Front."

The dynamics of monopoly
and oligopoly pricing   **245**

entrant makes the only output choice at which the market price is not *below* its unit costs—that is, the output associated with its demand curve tangency position OX_{Tb} or OX_{Tc}—the entrant will just cover its costs (including the opportunity cost of capital). Entry will therefore be barely attractive. In view of this, the insiders must commit themselves to maintaining output at slightly more than OX_b or OX_c and charge (in the absence of entry) a corresponding price just below OP_b or OP_c to leave no room in the market for profitable suboptimal scale entry. Note that this entry-deterring price is higher in case (b), with more slowly falling unit costs, than it is in case (c), where the entrant can realize most of the economies of scale at an output smaller in relation to the MOS. Quite generally, the less disadvantaged by above-minimum unit costs an entrant is when operating at some suboptimal fraction of the minimum optimal scale, the less insiders can hold the price persistently above the competitive level without attracting new entry, *ceteris paribus*.

To sum up, when potential entrants expect existing firms to maintain their output in the face of sizeable new entry, price can be held persistently above the competitive level by a greater percentage margin without attracting entry, (1) the less elastic demand is, (2) the higher the proportion of total industry output a firm of minimum optimal scale must produce, and (3) the more a firm operating at less than minimum optimal scale is disadvantaged by high unit costs. We see then that even when new entrants are physically able to operate just as efficiently as existing firms, the interaction between the necessity of large-scale entry and price effects can be a significant deterrent to new entry. Because of this deterrent effect, existing firms may command supranormal profits more or less permanently.[65]

This conclusion depends heavily upon the assumption that existing sellers maintain their output in the face of new entry. Will they in fact do so? If, despite pricing at a level calculated to deter new entry under the output maintenance assumption, new entry does take place, maintaining output normally will *not* be the most profitable strategy for the original firms. Indeed, if entry occurs at the least-cost scale and established firms maintain their output, price will fall to the competitive level and the original firms' supranormal profits will be wiped out altogether. To enforce this outcome—or the only marginally more profitable outcome following sub-MOS entry—when higher profits could be earned by reducing output would be like cutting off one's nose to spite the face. Sooner or later, it can be argued, the original firms will react to entry by backing off and raising their price to either the short-run profit-maximizing level or the limit price (modified, perhaps, to reflect their prior unsuccessful experience).[66]

Now, if a potential large-scale entrant recognizes that the existing firms have no economic incentive to adopt and maintain an uncooperative price-output policy following its entry, it will not be deterred by the belief that its addition to industry output will depress the price severely. The threat of output maintenance and price cutting by established firms lacks credibility, and threats that are not credible do not deter. This is analogous to the classic problem of nuclear deterrence. If the Soviet Union invaded Western Europe, would the United States retaliate massively with nuclear weapons, knowing that the Soviets would respond in kind against the American homeland? If not, the nuclear deterrent is not credible, and it must be replaced by other barriers to entry such as large conventional forces.

There is more to be learned from the nuclear deterrence analogy. Let us assume that a nuclear response to conventional aggression would be irrational in the normal meaning of the word. If, however, U.S. leaders have committed their reputations to such a response, or if U.S. troops were steamrollered by the aggressor, or if emotional behavior for any other reason displaced sober analysis, escalation might progress to the large-scale use of nuclear weapons. Fear by a potential aggressor of such an *irrational* response contributes to deterrence. Furthermore, the U.S. has something to gain by cultivating the impression that it will act irrationally or that events will get out of control if aggression occurs, for this too contributes to deterrence. By making irrational actions seem more likely in a contingency one seeks to avert, one may move nearer the rational goal of averting the contingency. This is the so-called rationality of irrationality.[67] So also with deterring market entry. There is always a chance that industry discipline will break down when new entry takes place. Oligopolistic coordination is often a fragile thing, and entry may strain it to the breaking point. If a newcomer captures a significant volume of sales from producers burdened by high fixed costs, the latter may undercut the established price to solve their individual short-run financial problems, touching off a price war. Or some entrepreneurs may be carried away by their irrational desires to make life difficult for the interloper, even though the punishment also hurts the executor. There is evidence that such behavior sometimes accompanies entry. Ralph Cassady found that irrational reactions by established sellers to new entry were a common cause of price wars.[68] Even if they hope to avoid irrational pricing, established firms can enhance their deterrent by concealing that hope, conveying the impression that pricing discipline will deteriorate in the event of entry. Or, as we shall consider further in Chapter 12, they may on selected occasions wage a deliberate price war against new entrants with the intent of teaching all others who might be considering entry that the risks are appreciable.

Fear of irrational or avowedly rapacious action, then, rather than the expectation of rational pricing responses, may be what deters the potential new entrant from entering on a large scale, if it is deterred at all. But if this is so, why should existing industry members limit their price to the value calculated under the Bain-Sylos output maintenance theory? Assuming that they retain sufficient fighting capacity in reserve to support an expansion of output,[69] why not hold price at the short-run profit-maximizing level, leaving open the possibility of a sharp decrease if someone tries to enter?[70] Alternatively, given that it often takes two years or longer to build and equip new production facilities in industries characterized by substantial scale economies, why not cut to the Bain-Sylos price on the day a potential new entrant first shows definite interest, thereby 'showing the flag' in the most vivid possible way?

Bain's explanation for adherence to a restrained limit price is that "the entrant is likely to read the current price policies of established firms as some sort of a 'statement of future intentions' regarding their policies after his entry has occurred."[71] This is not entirely convincing, given the role bluff, counterbluff, and irrational response play in deterrence. It seems more reasonable to believe that monopolists and oligopolists anxious to deter new entry exercise restraint because, if they held their price at levels that maximize short-run profits except when the threat of large-scale new entry is imminent, entry at inefficient scales too small to evoke a price response would be encouraged. Recognizing this brings us full circle to our original approach to limit pricing. The synthesis that emerges is a two-pronged strategy of deterrence. Existing sellers hold down the price and increase output just enough to deter inefficiently small entry and fringe rival

65. For variations on this theme, see Donald Dewey, "Industrial Concentration and the Rate of Profit: Some Neglected Theory," *Journal of Law and Economics* 19 (April 1976): 67–78.

66. Predicting how the original firms will react plunges us into the complexities of oligopolistic interdependence. Predictions in the extant literature range from short-run profit maximization jointly with the entrant to equating the postentry price with the original firms' marginal or average total cost. See for instance John T. Wenders, "Collusion and Entry," *Journal of Political Economy* 79 (November/December 1971): 1269–77; Dale K. Osborne, "On the Rationality of Limit Pricing," *Journal of Industrial Economics* 22 (September 1973): 71–80; and Michael Spence, "Entry, Capacity, Investment and Oligopolistic Pricing," *Bell Journal of Economics* 8 (Autumn 1977): 534–44.

67. See Herman Kahn, *On Thermonuclear War* (Princeton: Princeton University Press, 1960), pp. 291–95; and Thomas C. Schelling, *The Strategy of Conflict* (Cambridge, Mass.: Harvard University Press, 1960), Chapter 8.

68. Ralph Cassady, Jr., *Price Warfare in Business Competition* (East Lansing: Michigan State University Bureau of Business and Economic Research, 1963), pp. 51–53.

69. The value of reserve capacity is stressed by John T. Wenders in "Excess Capacity as a Barrier to Entry," *Journal of Industrial Economics* 20 (November 1971): 14–19; and Spence, "Entry, Capacity, Investment and Oligopolistic Pricing."

70. In "Oligopoly Theory, Entry-Prevention, and Growth," p. 310, note 1, Bhagwati suggests that since ample cash reserves provide strength in a price war, maximizing short-run profits before the threat of entry appears might in some circumstances help discourage entry.

71. Bain, *Barriers to New Competition*, p. 95. For a similar view, see Wayne A. Leeman, "The Limitations of Local Price-Cutting as a Barrier to Entry," *Journal of Political Economy* 64 (August 1956), especially p. 331.

The dynamics of monopoly and oligopoly pricing

expansion or to optimize the rate of entry. The more important economies of scale and absolute cost advantages possessed by the leading insiders are, the higher is the margin by which the price can exceed the insiders' unit costs without encouraging such fringe competition. On the other hand, implicit or explicit threats of price warfare are brandished to deter entry at large, relatively efficient scales.

The modes of entry This conclusion is consistent with the systematic evidence available on actual patterns of entry into concentrated industries. Measured by the sheer number of entities making the decision to enter, most new entry involves relatively small firms—too small, as a rule, to achieve all conventional economies of scale.[72] Entry at or near the minimum optimal scale into significant oligopolistic markets is a rarer phenomenon. Indeed, it is sufficiently rare that it usually receives considerable attention in the relevant trade press—a source that has been tapped too little by economists studying the dynamics of entry. Whether the aggregate volume of output contributed by many small entrants equals the contribution of occasional but large entrants is uncertain. What *is* clear is that the sum of many small entries, or expansions by many small firms, can have a significant concentration-reducing effect.[73]

The systematic statistical evidence on variables positively associated with new entry is sparse and somewhat contradictory. Nevertheless, there are indications that the rate of entry is higher when preentry profits are ample, when concentration is high, and perhaps especially when demand is growing rapidly.[74] Growth is conducive to entry partly because it opens up sales opportunities not exploited rapidly enough by established enterprises and partly because capacity constraints and satisfaction with the business already in hand may prevent industry leaders from carrying a retaliatory price war very far.[75]

When entry does occur at a substantial scale, the reactions to it by leading established firms appear to vary widely in ways predictable only if one has rich information on demand and cost conditions, industry traditions, and perhaps even

personalities, if indeed confident predictions are possible at all. At one extreme was the behavior of the Canadian Cement Company, which in 1946 controlled an 80 percent share of the cement trade in Canada.[76] It pursued a consistent price maintenance, give-way policy in the face of repeated entry, on occasion choosing to operate at only 40 to 55 percent of capacity rather than fighting. As a consequence its national market share fell to 34 percent by 1970. Similar propensities to avoid price warfare following large-scale new entry were evident in the nickel industry, the once-monopolized British tin can industry,[77] the magnesium industry,[78] and Bethlehem Steel's invasion of the Chicago area steel market, among others. The aluminum and (before pervasive price controls were imposed) petroleum product industries occupy an intermediate position, with entry of significant size precipitating price shading and instability, but with leading producers making an effort to contain the impact, among other things by curbing their own output.[79] Near the other extreme were IBM's response to inroads by such computer peripheral equipment manufacturers as Telex,[80] the price wars following the startup of large polyethylene and anhydrous ammonia plants,[81] or the localized price war in 1967 and general shift to discount pricing in 1970 that accompanied entry by new grocery chains into the concentrated Washington, D.C., retail food market.[82] The most that can be said with confidence from this and other qualitative evidence is that sizeable new entrants can by no means be certain that existing firms will give ground. Therefore, the need to add a substantial output increment in order to exploit scale economy opportunities does act as a barrier—to be sure, not always an effective one—to large-scale entry.

Potential entrants are well aware of this; and when they consider entering a market, they devote a good deal of thought to finding an entry strategy that strikes the best compromise between securing scale economies and minimizing the risk of price warfare.[83] One common strategy is to enter at a small scale with a plant that can be expanded gradually when and if demand growth permits. This is done more readily in industries with flexible, divisible production processes (such as in textile manufacturing and most retail trades) than in continuous process industries like petroleum refining and cement, where major equipment items may come only in large chunks. When indivisibilities compel large-scale entry, other devices to soften the output expansion blow may be sought. For example, when the Dundee Cement Company opened an unprecedentedly large new plant near St. Louis in 1968, it tried to minimize the price repercussions by barging its cement as far south as Mobile, Alabama, so that no single local market had to absorb more than a 5 percent supply increment.[84] Its luck was bad, however, because a general cement demand slump aggravated the absorption problem, and as a result widespread price cutting followed. In the petroleum industry, companies constructing a new refinery in some market often build up demand in advance by shipping in gasoline and fuel oil from more distant refineries, purchasing supplies from others and selling them as their own, and/or lining up sales contracts in advance of the refinery's startup date. A frequent concomitant of both large- and small-scale entry is seeking out some qualitative or geographic niche in the market where one will have an advantage over existing suppliers. On this we shall have more to say shortly.

How effective entry deterrence is depends also upon the characteristics of the entrant. Like small local entrants, firms importing into a market from abroad may be able to sell in sufficiently small quantities or reduce their supply with sufficient ease in the event of adverse price reactions, that it is reasonable for them to view the import market price as a parameter. Consequently, it is difficult to deter import entry or expansion unless the domestic price is held below importers' home market costs (or, under GATT antidumping rules, prices) plus freight and duties.[85] For importers, unlike local entrants, the realization of production scale economies does not normally hinge upon selling a large quantity of output in any single target market. This observation applies with equal force to firms interpenetrating regional and local markets separated within national boundaries by moderate to high transportation costs. If anhydrous ammonia producers in Iowa set their prices above the level of produc-

72. See Robert McGuckin, "Entry, Concentration Change, and Stability of Market Shares," *Southern Economic Journal* 38 (January 1972): 369; and F. M. Scherer, Alan Beckenstein, Erich Kaufer, and R. D. Murphy, *The Economics of Multi-Plant Operation: An International Comparisons Study* (Cambridge, Mass.: Harvard University Press, 1975), pp. 147–54. A somewhat different picture is suggested by data on 946 narrowly defined "businesses" from the PIMS sample, to be discussed at greater length in Chapter 9. Twenty-nine percent of the reporting businesses experienced new entry into their markets during the preceding five years by rivals with a market share of 5 percent or greater. This figure includes entry by importers. Interpreting it is rendered difficult because many of the companies defined their markets much more narrowly than, say, the four-digit Census industries against which MOS plant sizes are commonly compared. Strategic Planning Institute, *The PIMS Research Data Bases* (Cambridge, Mass.: Strategic Planning Institute, October 1977), p. 163.

73. See McGuckin, "Entry," pp. 363–70; and Roger Sherman, "Entry Barriers and the Growth of Firms," *Southern Economic Journal* 38 (April 1971): 238–47.

74. See Larry L. Duetsch, "Structure, Performance, and the Net Rate of Entry into Manufacturing Industries," *Southern Economic Journal* 41 (January 1975): 450–65; and Paul K. Gorecki, "The Determinants of Entry by New and Diversifying Enterprises in the UK Manufacturing Sector, 1958–1963," *Applied Economics* 7 (June 1975): 139–47; Maury N. Harris, "Entry and Barriers to Entry," *Industrial Organization Review* 4, No. 3 (1976): 165–74; Harris, "Entry and Long-Term Trends in Industry Performance," *Antitrust Bulletin* 21 (Summer 1976): 295–312; and (for more negative results) Dale Orr, "The Determinants of Entry: A Study of the Canadian Manufacturing Industries," *Review of Economics and Statistics* 56 (February 1974): 58–66.

75. Cf. Sylos-Labini, *Oligopoly and Technical Progress*, pp. 61–62; and Bhagwati, "Oligopoly Theory," p. 310.

76. Scherer et al., *The Economics of Multi-Plant Operation*, pp. 151–52.

77. "A U.S. Canmaker Breaks a Stranglehold," *Business Week*, 3 February 1973, p. 37.

78. See "Magnesium Eyes Lightweight Crown," *Business Week*, 31 May 1969, pp. 52–53.

79. See for example the Council on Wage and Price Stability staff report, *Aluminum Prices: 1974–75*, pp. 17–18, 107–62; and Shaw, "Price Leadership and the Effect of New Entry."

80. See Brock, *The U.S. Computer Industry*, pp. 114–34; and Chapters 11 and 12 *infra*.

81. See "Polyethylene Is Up Off the Floor," *Business Week*, 8 November 1969, p. 76; and George C. Sweeny, Jr., "The U.S. Nitrogen Industry," *Agricultural Chemicals*, February 1970.

82. Russell C. Parker, *Discount Food Pricing in Washington, D.C.*, Federal Trade Commission staff report (Washington, D.C.: Government Printing Office, March 1971).

83. Scherer et al., *The Economics of Multi-Plant Operation*, p. 153.

84. Scherer et al., *The Economics of Multi-Plant Operation*, pp. 150–51.

85. For brief case studies of import competition in flat glass, aluminum, typewriters, and tractors, see Peter C. Frederiksen, "Prospects of Competition from Abroad in Major Manufacturing Oligopolies," *Antitrust Bulletin* 20 (Summer 1975): 339–71.

tion costs plus transportation from Louisiana, they risk "import" entry from companies already taking more or less full advantage of scale economy opportunities and who, under more restrained pricing, would not have been viewed as obvious competitors of the Iowa firms.

The threat of price warfare is also not apt to be credible against companies entering through upstream vertical integration. Major food packers and beverage producers, for example, have repeatedly entered or threatened to enter the "tin" can and glass bottle industries. Even if such entry touched off a price war, the integrated entrant would not be adversely affected, since it enjoys a captive market influenced only indirectly by outside price levels.[86] Because of this credible entry threat, the prices of food and beverage containers have undoubtedly been held much lower than one might have anticipated merely from observing the high levels of seller concentration in regional container markets.

Just as entrants seek strategies minimizing the price repercussions of sizeable entry, they commonly attempt to exploit any advantages they might already possess to offset or minimize their absolute cost, scale economies, or product differentiation handicaps vis-à-vis already established sellers. This often means that the most plausible new entrants into some market are companies already well established in another more or less closely related field.[87] Thus, when full-scale entry demands a large investment, corporations with an ample cash flow and/or good links to capital markets are more likely entrants than some totally new enterprise. The company whose salespeople visit supermarkets weekly is more apt to enter a food product line in which it was previously inactive than is a ball bearing or shoe manufacturer. The firm with a plant die-casting and machining refrigerator compressors is a more likely entrant into small gasoline engine production than is a computer assembler. And more generally, a substantial proportion of the new large-scale entry into the markets of many nations since World War II has been by companies well established in the design, production, and marketing of similar products abroad—at first, with United States firms serving as a leading source of entrants but, more recently, with Euro-

pean and Japanese enterprises interpenetrating the U.S. and each others' national markets as well.[88]

All this means, as Professor Bain recognized in his seminal work,[89] that there may in effect be an upward-sloping supply schedule for new entrants, with some potential entrants being deterred only if established firms set prices yielding themselves no more than the opportunity cost of their capital, while other would-be entrants face substantial entry barriers. This complicates the strategy problem of established sellers but does not change it fundamentally.[90] To oversimplify, if there is an abundant supply of potential entrants at prices approximating existing sellers' costs and if the scale of individual entry is likely to be small, there is not much the existing industry leaders can do but take their profits and watch their market shares decline. If only one or a small number of potential entrants are as well situated as the leading insiders, the latter may choose to let them enter the club while pursuing a strategy that deters all others. If every potential entrant faces significant barriers owing to cost or image disadvantages or credible adverse price reactions, deterrence of *all* entry may be attempted. Thus both the height of entry barriers generally and how they vary with respect to different potential entrants are critical.

Limit pricing with learning by doing The height of entry barriers depends in part upon technological conditions and historical legacies such as the possession of a key patent or ore deposit. But as we have seen in our analysis of pricing reactions to large-scale entry, sellers' conduct also matters. An especially interesting interaction among entry barriers, business conduct, and market structure occurs when there are product-specific scale economies associated with "learning by doing."[91]

The essence of the matter is that one learns how to reduce production costs through actual production experience. The more a particular firm has produced, the lower its unit costs tend to be, all else being equal. To the extent that such experience is not readily transferable to other enterprises, this means that the first company into some new product line begins with a natural cost advantage over subsequent rivals, for by the time the latter enter or consider entering, the pioneer has already progressed some distance down its learning curve. More important for our present concerns, the pioneer's pricing policy also affects the magnitude of its advantage.[92] By keeping its price low initially, the pioneer can stimulate rapid expansion of demand for its product and therefore progress farther down its learning curve before others begin competing. Also, with an initial cost advantage, the pioneer may choose to pursue an aggressive low-price policy that higher cost rivals have difficulty emulating. If it can underprice its rivals, it will almost surely maintain a dominant market share, and with a larger market share it will enjoy more of the learning-by-doing economies and hence hold a continuing cost advantage, reinforcing its exclusionary pricing incentive. Only by accepting initial losses can rivals beginning with lower cumulative volume compete their way to a position of approximate equality. Of course, if the pioneer pursues an unaggressive pricing policy and others undercut it, the challengers may expand rapidly enough to seize a cumulative volume advantage, turning the tables on the pioneer and perhaps relegating it to a minor position.

It is conceivable that when learning-by-doing economies are important, the capturing of an initial advantage by some company could set in motion a dynamic process that ends with the relevant product line more or less permanently monopolized. However, several circumstances may mitigate any such tendency. For one, the rate of unit cost reduction with repeated doublings and redoublings of cumulative output does appear to taper off eventually.[93] As the leading firm approaches this learning curve asymptote, its incentive to constrain price in the hope of gaining further cost advantages weakens, and it will be tempted to price less aggressively and reap the profit fruits of its prior pricing restraint. Second, some of the cost reduction benefits associated with cumulative experience are likely to trickle out to other firms as skilled employees are hired away, patents expire, and production techniques become public knowledge. Although rivals with a lower cumulative volume may not catch up completely, their eventual cost

disadvantage may be much less than the assumption of strictly firm-specific learning implies. Third, some of the product lines in which learning by doing is most important (such as semiconductors, aircraft, and computers) are also characterized by rapid technological obsolescence of product designs. The development of a completely new design often permits an initially handicapped producer to jump to a new learning curve in a position of equality or even superiority. And finally, antitrust fears or the desire of industrial buyers to ensure that multiple, competing

86. If outside suppliers' prices fall after upstream integration, one might say that an opportunity cost has been incurred by not taking advantage of the new, lower price. But the opportunity might not have materialized had the packer not integrated vertically.

87. See Howard H. Hines, "Effectiveness of 'Entry' by Already Established Firms," *Quarterly Journal of Economics* 71 (February 1957): 132–50; Frank J. Kottke, "Market Entry and the Character of Competition," *Western Economic Journal* 5 (December 1966): 24–43; and Richard E. Caves and Michael E. Porter, "From Entry Barriers to Mobility Barriers," *Quarterly Journal of Economics* 91 (May 1977): 241–61.

88. For a diversity of views, see John H. Dunning, ed., *Economic Analysis and the Multinational Enterprise* (London: Allen & Unwin, 1974), especially Chapters 1 through 6. See also Richard E. Caves, "Causes of Direct Investment: Foreign Firms' Shares in Canadian and United Kingdom Manufacturing Industries," *Review of Economics and Statistics* 56 (August 1974): 279–93; and Paul K. Gorecki, "The Determinants of Entry by Domestic and Foreign Enterprises in Canadian Manufacturing Industries," *Review of Economics and Statistics* 58 (November 1976): 485–88.

89. Bain, *Barriers to New Competition*, pp. 8–10.

90. Compare Roger Sherman and Thomas D. Willett, "Potential Entrants Discourage Entry," *Journal of Political Economy*, Part 1, 75 (August 1967): 400–403; Victor Goldberg, "Limit Pricing and Potential Competition," *Journal of Political Economy* 81 (November/December 1973): 1460–66; Lionel Kalish, Jerry Hartzog, and Henry Cassidy, "The Threat of Entry with Mutually Aware Potential Entrants: Comment," *Journal of Political Economy* 86 (February 1978): 147–53; and Kalish et al., "Potential Competition: The Probability of Entry with Mutually Aware Potential Entrants," *Southern Economic Journal* 43 (January 1978): 542–55.

91. See Chapter 4, p. 82 *supra*.

92. Again, the proper analytic vehicle is optimal control theory. See R. W. Latham and D. A. Peel, "Profit Maximizing Firms and Inelastic Demands," *Applied Economics* 7 (Spring 1975): 161–65; and Wayne Y. Lee, "Oligopoly and Entry," *Journal of Economic Theory* 13 (August 1975): 35–54.

93. See Harold Asher, *Cost-Quantity Relationships in the Airframe Industry* (Santa Monica: RAND Corporation Study R-291, 1956), pp. 89–109, 129.

The dynamics of monopoly and oligopoly pricing 251

sources of supply survive[94] may lead firms with a cumulative learning advantage to stop short of a pricing strategy yielding an exclusive monopoly position. Nevertheless, when learning-by-doing economies are important, it seems clear that there will be a heightened tendency toward high concentration in narrowly defined product lines.

That such interactions between experience-related cost advantages and pricing policy exist is supported by considerable evidence.[95] Pricing to enhance one's market position and hence gain learning curve advantages has been especially prevalent in the semiconductor industry and some of its offspring, including hand-held electronic calculators, certain computer components, and digital watches.[96] Consumers benefitted during the early years of those industries from relatively low prices charged by producers vigorously striving for a market share advantage. Although concentration in specific product lines tended to be high, sometimes after an intense competitive shakeout, rapid technological progress kept downward pressure on prices even when some firms did achieve a significant advantage in a narrow line. It is questionable whether performance will be as satisfactory when the rate of technological progress ebbs, as it eventually must, and pricing behavior settles into patterns characteristic of more mature tight oligopolies.

Implications The possibility of competitive entry and how established business enterprises react to it have extremely important implications for economic performance. If monopolists or oligopolists strive to hold prices well above unit costs when entry barriers are modest, their efforts will sooner or later be defeated by the entry of new competition and the erosion of their monopoly power. If they choose to defend or extend their market positions, they must restrain the margin between price and cost to a level consistent with their advantage over fringe firms and potential entrants. In the first case, society bears monopoly burdens today but has them relieved in future periods; in the latter case, the burden is mitigated today, perhaps greatly, but continues into the indefinite future. Which pattern of conduct is preferred depends in part upon one's discount rate and, in particular, upon whether consumers

tend to discount future welfare gains more or less heavily than producers discount the future profits they either forgo or enhance through their long-run pricing strategy choices.[97] *Either* behavioral pattern is preferable to a situation in which elevated monopoly prices are maintained indefinitely.

Serious and persistent monopolistic deviations of price from cost are likely only when there are substantial barriers to the entry of new competition and the expansion of fringe rivals. This appears to be more the exception than the rule even in industries characterized by high seller concentration. Subjectively classifying 20 manufacturing industries by entry barrier height after a careful study of barrier-generating conditions, Professor Bain found that only five or six had very high barriers to entry—defined as those sufficient to permit established firms to elevate prices 10 percent or more above minimum unit costs while forestalling new entry.[98] Bain's sample deliberately emphasized relatively concentrated industries, and there is reason to believe that entry barriers are lower on average in less concentrated manufacturing lines and in the trade and services sectors.[99] That *production* cost barriers to entry are generally modest is suggested by the evidence that manufacturing plants characteristically need only small market shares to realize all scale economies[100] and by the modest cost penalties associated with sub-MOS operation. To the extent that entry barriers are not very high in the "typical" industry, a crucial constraint on the exercise of monopoly power exists. In the next chapter we shall devote considerable attention to assessing the implications of diverse entry barrier types and magnitudes for industrial performance.

Entry deterrence through plant location strategy

Up to this point we have focused solely on how established sellers can deter competitive entry by charging low prices and offering correspondingly increased outputs. Price, however, is not the only strategic variable manipulatable to impede entry. We consider now some other possibilities, beginning with the location of plants in geographic space.

As noted earlier, new entrants often try to circumvent entry barriers by seeking market niches where they have an advantage over established producers. Geography offers one set of possible niches. When transportation costs are a significant component of total product costs, either because the goods are of low value in relation to their shipping weight or because consumers must make a special trip to receive the goods or services at their supply origin, markets tend to be localized or regionalized. Potential entrants may then seek out some local market or set of markets inadequately served by existing firms and locate there, where proximity to customers gives the entrant an advantage over incumbents. Recognizing this threat, established producers anxious to maintain their dominance must decide how to cope with it. Preempting the niches by locating plants or other outlets in them may be the answer.

To explore the theory of such preemption, let us consider an extended example kept as simple as possible without sacrificing essential features.[101] Suppose that the commodity with which we are concerned is ready-mix concrete. We assume for mathematical convenience that the market lies along a continuous straight line—e.g., a road in otherwise uninhabited space—of unspecified but considerable length, and that population and hence demand is of uniform density along the road. A fixed price is quoted at each plant and buyers pay the delivery charges, amounting to twenty-five cents for each ton-mile of transportation from the plant to the demand locus.[102] Buyers' demand varies inversely and linearly with the sum of the ex-plant price and transport charges. We assume that if this sum is zero, the total quantity demanded per month over a unit in geographic space (i.e., over one linear mile) is 500 tons. If the sum rises to $40 per ton, the quantity demanded drops to zero. These assumptions permit us to determine the total demand for any monopolist plant's output.[103] Economies of scale will play an important role in the analysis, so we assume a very simple long-run cost function with unit costs falling continuously as output is increased. Specifically, establishing a plant is assumed to entail fixed investment

outlays whose unavoidable monthly carrying cost is $60,000. The marginal cost of output is assumed constant at $10 per ton.[104]

Now suppose Firm A seeks to dominate the

94. On the desire for multiple sources of supply, see Scherer et al., *The Economics of Multi-Plant Operation*, pp. 134–35. There is reason to believe that competition in the production of a given aircraft type accelerated the rate of learning. See F. M. Scherer, *The Weapons Acquisition Process: Economic Incentives* (Boston: Harvard Business School Division of Research, 1964), pp. 119–26.

95. Indeed, a consulting firm has thrived on advising industrial enterprises how to take advantage of learning-by-doing effects in their pricing decisions. See "Selling Business a Theory of Economics," *Business Week*, 8 September 1973, pp. 85–90; and Boston Consulting Group, Inc., *Perspectives on Experience* (Boston: Boston Consulting Group, Inc., January 1972).

96. See Douglas W. Webbink, *The Semiconductor Industry*, Federal Trade Commission staff report (Washington, D.C.: Government Printing Office, January 1977), especially pp. 49–59, 80–82; "The Complexities of Electronics Pricing," *Business Week*, 6 April 1974, pp. 44–45; "New Leaders in Semiconductors," *Business Week*, 1 March 1976, pp. 43–44; and "The Great Digital Watch Shake-out," *Business Week*, 2 May 1977, p. 78.

97. A much-needed extension of dynamic limit pricing theory is a thorough comparison of how alternative pricing strategies affect economic welfare under plausible circumstances. For a first step, see F. M. Scherer, "Predatory Pricing and the Sherman Act: A Comment," *Harvard Law Review* 88 (March 1976), especially pp. 883–89.

98. Bain, *Barriers to New Competition*, p. 170.

99. Bain, *Barriers to New Competition*, pp. 44–46.

100. See Chapter 4, pp. 94–98 *supra*.

101. The analysis here closely follows D. A. Hay, "Sequential Entry and Entry-Deterring Strategies in Spatial Competition," *Oxford Economic Papers* 28 n.s. (July 1976): 240–57. Such models have a tradition dating back to Harold Hotelling, "Stability in Competition," *Economic Journal* 39 (March 1929): 41–57. Newer extensions dealing with important dynamic questions include Edward C. Prescott and Michael Visscher, "Sequential Location among Firms with Foresight," *Bell Journal of Economics* 8 (Autumn 1977): 378–93; B. Curtis Eaton and Richard G. Lipsey, "The Theory of Market Pre-Emption: Barriers to Entry in a Growing Spatial Market" (manuscript, March 1976); and Ram C. Rao and David P. Rutenberg, "Pre-Empting an Alert Rival: Strategic Timing of the First Plant by Analysis of Sophisticated Rivalry" (manuscript, Queens University, Kingston, Ontario, December 1977).

102. This is known as ex-works or F.O.B. pricing, which will be analyzed further from a different perspective in Chapter 11.

103. The price m miles from the plant is the ex-works price P plus 0.25 m. The quantity demanded over a mile's span m miles from the plant is $q_m = 500 - 12.5 P - 3.125 m$. The *total* quantity demanded Q on *both* sides of the plant out to Z miles is

$\int_0^Z q_m \, dm = 1,000 Z - 25 ZP - 3.125 Z^2.$

104. Thus, total cost $TC = 60,000 + 10 Q$. More complex cost functions—e.g., with a U-shape—complicate the mathematics formidably.

The dynamics of monopoly
and oligopoly pricing   253

ready-mix business along our hypothetical linear market or road. Suppose it sets out to do so by building plants at evenly spaced intervals along the road—e.g., every 80 miles, as illustrated by plant locations A_1, A_2, and A_3 in Figure 8.5, with distance calibrated from the location of plant A_2.[105] With this spacing, the monopoly profit-maximizing price at each (identical) plant is $22.50 per ton.[106] As a consumer's distance from the nearest plant increases, the total paid per ton—i.e., the ex-works price plus delivery charges—rises linearly until, at the boundary between plants, it is $32.50. The quantity demanded falls accordingly with greater distance and hence a higher effective price. The total quantity demanded from any plant selling out to 40 miles in both directions is 12,500 tons per month, and the total profit per plant (after the deduction of fixed costs) is $96,250 per month.

The realization that Firm A is making profits amounting to more than a third of its sales is likely to attract the interest of potential entrants. Also, and more important, by locating at the boundary between two of Firm A's plants, an entrant Firm B can take advantage of the high effective prices consumers in that vicinity pay. Suppose entry does occur at locations B_{12}, B_{23}, and similar points not shown. Suppose too that each such entrant quotes the same ex-works price as Firm A—i.e., $22.50 per ton. Then consumers nearer a Firm B plant than a Firm A plant will patronize Firm B, and demand will be di-vided equally between the A and B plants, with the boundary lying 20 miles from each plant. There will also be an overall increase in demand, since the effective price paid by customers near Firm B plants has been reduced because their concrete is now shipped a shorter distance. A typical entrant plant (e.g., at B_{23}) will experience demand of 7,500 tons per month.[107] With an assumed cost function identical to Firm A's, and hence with a gross margin of $12.50 per ton and fixed costs of $60,000, the entrant plant will realize profits of $33,750. Clearly, if matters work out in this way, entry will have proved to be highly profitable, and if they can anticipate such profits, competitors will indeed enter.

This entry is not, of course, advantageous from the original dominant Firm A's perspective. Each of its plants impacted by entry will be restricted to a selling radius of 20 miles, and like an entrant's plant, each will have profits of $33,750 instead of the $96,250 experienced before entry. Firm A might react to entry by cutting its price and trying to maintain a disproportionate territorial share, but this is costly when entrant Firm B has a delivery cost advantage on its own side of the 20-mile boundary. Also, Firm B may well respond with a matching price cut that restores an equal territorial division. Recognizing the futility of such price warfare, Firm A is likely to refrain from initiating it, and if potential entrant Firm B realizes this, the threat of price warfare will not be credible as an entry deterrent. Indeed, if Firm A accepts entry at

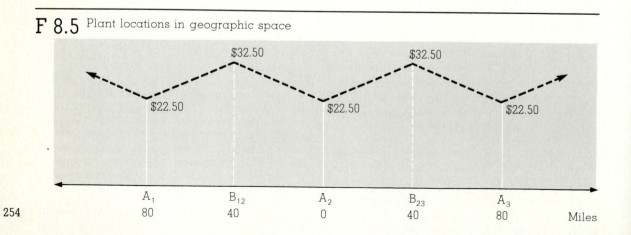

F 8.5 Plant locations in geographic space

	A_1	B_{12}	A_2	B_{23}	A_3
	80	40	0	40	80

Miles

B_{12}, B_{23}, . . . as a *fait accompli*, it will *raise* its price to $23.75, which maximizes joint profits (at $34,531 per plant) with the smaller 20-mile plant shipping radius. In the spirit of collective profit maximization, Firm B plants will presumably follow the price lead.

To avert the loss of profit and market share resulting from competitive entry, Firm A will surely consider preempting the entrants by establishing its own plants at B_{12}, B_{23}, and similar locations. Its profits will be less (by some $27,188 per 80 miles of market supplied) than they would be if a single plant shipped 40 miles in each direction, but they will be twice the $34,531 realized per 80-mile segment if competitive entry occurred at each node. Preemption will indeed be an attractive option.

The question then arises, Will this new 40-mile plant spacing be sufficient to deter entry, or will entry now occur at the boundaries of the more closely spaced Firm A plants—e.g., 20 miles from each? Figure 8.6 reassesses the situation from Firm A's revised perspective. It has plants 40 miles apart at A_2, A_{23}, A_3, and analogous locations along the market road. Its short-run profit-maximizing price at each is $23.75, and the effective price including delivery charges rises to $28.75 at the plants' shipping boundaries. Given the possibility of winning away customers served at relatively high delivered prices by locating at such boundary points as B_{223} and B_{233}, will potential entrant Firm B in fact enter? Let us assume that if it does, Firm A will not try to wage a price war, but will instead raise its price to $24.375, consistent with short-run joint profit maximization when the markets are divided equally and its plants deliver to customers no more distant than 10 miles. The typical entrant plant follows suit. It too will have a shipping radius of 10 miles, and output per plant will be 3,594 tons per month. The entrant plant's profit will be ($24.375 − 10.00)(3,594) − $60,000 = −$8,336. Entry will *not* be profitable, even though each plant of Firm A is realizing profits of $34,531 (i.e., 21 percent of sales) at 40-mile spacing.[108] Supranormal profits persist, and yet entry is deterred.[109]

This happens for reasons analogous to those underlying the more traditional large-scale entry deterrence analysis of Figure 8.4. Economies of scale are the key. If a market niche could be entered on a very small scale at no significant unit cost disadvantage, no deterrence strategy by established sellers would be effective. But economies of scale create a lumpiness problem—the entrant must either add to the market a large lump of output for which insufficient absorption capacity exists, or it must enter on such a small scale that its unit costs are elevated above any feasible price it can charge. In other words, given

105. In "Sequential Entry and Entry-Deterring Strategies," pp. 244–45, 254, Hay implies that profits are maximized by building plants at a spacing that leaves zero demand at the boundary between plants when the profit-maximizing price is set. In the present example, this would entail a distance of 160 miles between plants, which does not in fact maximize Firm A's profits. That is, profits are $280,000 for 320 miles of market covered with 160-mile spacing and $385,000 for the same coverage with 80-mile spacing. Hay's conclusion appears to stem from a misinterpretation of second-order conditions. Spacing of 80 miles comes within a mile of maximizing profits per mile served, assuming no threat of entry.

106. Profits per plant π are (price minus marginal cost) times quantity less fixed costs. Thus, $\pi = (P − 10)(1,000\, Z − 25\, ZP − 3.125\, Z^2) − 60,000$. For a maximum, $d\pi/dP = 1,250\, Z − 50\, ZP − 3.125\, Z^2 = 0$. Solving for the profit-maximizing price P^*, we obtain $P^* = 25 − .0625\, Z$. With $Z = 40$ (i.e., the distance to the plant boundaries), $P^* = $22.50. From the expression in note 103 it can be ascertained that $Q^* = 12,500$ tons. $\pi = (22.50 − 10)(12,500) − 60,000 = $96,250$.

For a more general analysis of cases in which entry leads to price increases, see Dennis R. Capozza and Robert Van Order, "A Generalized Model of Spatial Competition," *American Economic Review* 68 (December 1978): 896–908.

107. From note 103, $Q = 1,000 \times 20 − 25 \times 20 \times 22.50 − 3.125 \times 20^2 = 7,500$ tons.

108. Note that if Firm B did enter, Firm A's plants would experience similar losses owing to the decrease in sales volume.

109. The entrant might alternatively try to enter with an ex-works price higher than the existing firm's, letting Firm A maintain its preentry price and retain more than an equal share of the market between two plants. Although such a strategy might work when demand is relatively price inelastic and shipping costs are very high, it does not make sense at this stage in the present example. Thus, if the entrant charges a price of $26 per ton while Firm A charges $24.375, the entrant's shipping radius is cut to 6.75 miles, output falls to 2,220 tons, and the monthly loss increases to $24,478.

Another possibility is for the entrant to enter immediately adjacent to a Firm A plant—e.g., at location A_{23}—and attempt to share the market from there. But at best this gives the entrant no larger sales volume than with B_{223} or B_{233} entry, and, indeed, sales must be smaller because less will be demanded by customers in the B_{223} or B_{233} vicinity owing to higher delivery charges. Therefore, profits are lower with side-by-side entry.

The dynamics of monopoly
and oligopoly pricing   255

existing Firm A's strategy of packing geographic space with plants, whatever demand curve might be left over for an entrant to capture lies at all points below the entrant's (lumpy) long-run cost curve. There is, however, an important difference between the spatial entry case and the Bain-Sylos-Modigliani case described by Figure 8.4. The latter assumed one common homogeneous product market, so the entrant added its output to the output of *all* existing sellers' plants and hence interacted competitively with all those plants. Under those circumstances, it is not unusual for a minimum optimal scale capacity lump to be small relative to the total output volume of established sellers. Therefore, the percentage by which output can be held below the competitive level without leaving room for a new entrant may be similarly small, all else being equal. But in one-dimensional geographic space with substantial transportation costs, entrants impinge upon the markets of only two plants—one on each side of the entering plant's chosen location. An entering plant's output contribution is almost certain to be large in relation to the market served by those two plants; consequently, the difference in the revenue-cost balance before versus after an entry lump will also be considerable. Or even in the more realistic case of entry into two-dimensional geographic space, the company filling the niche will impinge upon the demand of only a half dozen or so nearby established plants. Its lump will again be sizeable in relation to the volume of established sellers, and

so the latter may be able persistently to restrict output and hold prices above costs by an appreciable margin without leaving sufficient room for the entrant's output to be absorbed profitably.[110]

Would it be possible for established firms to accomplish the same entry deterrence result by more conventional means—notably, by reducing price and expanding output at more widely scattered plants? To do so successfully, they must convince the potential entrant that the demand curve it will secure following entry lies at all points below its cost curve or, in the borderline case, that its demand and cost functions will be tangent. Much depends in this instance upon the assumptions made about the postentry reactions of established sellers. Given the delivery cost advantage a niche-filling entrant enjoys and the corresponding advantage of established sellers near their own plants, the Bain output maintenance assumption seems excessively pessimistic. A more plausible but still conservative assumption is that the established sellers will maintain their (already restrained) price in the face of new entry and that the new entrant, occupying a relatively small niche and recognizing the self-defeating nature of a price war, will charge the higher price that maximizes its profits. Then Firm A, while maintaining 80-mile plant spacing (i.e., as in Figure 8.5) can keep potential entrant Firm B at the zero-profit level, with its postentry demand function tangent to its cost curve, by charging an ex-works price of $20.1625. The best response open to the entrant is to charge a price

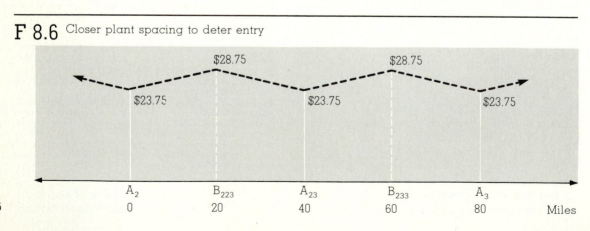

F 8.6 Closer plant spacing to deter entry

of $24.2625 and sell no farther than 11.8 miles from its plant.[111]

If no entry occurs as a consequence of this limit pricing strategy, Firm A's profit per plant with plants 80 miles apart is $90,786. This is considerably more than the total of $69,062 earned from *two* plants spaced 40 miles apart under the geographic space-packing deterrence strategy analyzed previously. However, it is arguable whether the $20.1625 limit pricing strategy is as credible as the plant proliferation strategy. Should entry occur despite the $20.1625 price, Firm A's profits will fall to $56,870—less than under the 40-mile space-packing strategy. They will be even lower if Firm B can expand its selling radius beyond 11.8 miles—e.g., by threatening a price war if Firm A matches its price reductions. Given Firm B's unsought but now unavoidable competition on its flanks, it would be both easy and tempting for Firm A to raise its price and accept a more equal division of the market with Firm B. If Firm B recognizes this, its entry will not be deterred by Firm A's low $20.1625 price. In contrast, once Firm A has packed the market with plants at 40-mile spacing, withdrawing—that is, shutting down the plants—is likely to be quite costly and hence improbable. Because plants have a permanence that prices cannot match, the strategy of entry deterrence by packing geographic space with plants is more credible than a strategy of quoting a low price and offering a correspondingly expanded supply. Even though the latter strategy is more profitable as long as the bluff is not called, the plant proliferation strategy may well be adopted for its superior credibility.

Limit pricing combined with wider spacing of plants is not unambiguously more profitable than entry deterrence through close spacing with prices set at short-run profit-maximizing levels. The 40-mile spacing of Figure 8.6 perpetrates some overkill, imposing upon in-between entrants $8,336 losses rather than the infinitesimal losses assumed sufficient for deterrence under limit pricing with 80-mile spacing. If we change our assumptions to let fixed costs be only $52,000 instead of $60,000, the entrant between plants spaced 40 miles apart loses $340. Two Firm A plants, spaced 40 miles apart, deterring entry

under this lower fixed price variant, realize combined profits of $85,063. A single 80-mile plant practicing optimal limit pricing earns $94,675 covering the same market segment. Thus, even without overkill, limit pricing is somewhat more profitable—if it succeeds. However, analysis of additional entry deterrence scenarios with different parameters revealed that plant proliferation could under some conditions be more profitable than limit pricing. This was more likely, the higher transport costs were in relation to other costs and price.

This last point appears quite important empirically. In an interview study of plant size and location decisions in 12 industries across six nations, the author observed by far the strongest emphasis on geographic space packing as an entry-deterring strategy in the cement industry.[112] Transport costs for cement averaged forty-five cents per dollar of ex-works product value on a representative 350-mile haul.[113] Second but far behind in its emphasis on space packing was the glass bottle industry, with transport costs averaging ten cents per dollar of product value on a 350-mile haul. In none of the other 10 industries, all with lower transport cost indices, was plant proliferation by itself viewed as an effective deterrent strategy.

The question remains, How does entry deterrence through geographic niche filling affect overall economic performance? And in particular, is it more or less desirable than a limit pricing approach? Several considerations are relevant. The proliferation of smaller plants is likely to entail significant scale economy sacrifices and hence higher production costs, but transportation

---

110. See B. C. Eaton and Richard G. Lipsey, "The Non-Uniqueness of Equilibrium in the Löschian Location Model," *American Economic Review* 66 (March 1976): 77–93.

111. This result is obtained by solving simultaneously the entrant's optimal price equation $P^* = 25 - .0625 Z$ and the entrant's profit function set equal to zero. The solution involves a third-degree polynomial.

112. Scherer et al., *The Economics of Multi-Plant Operation*, pp. 152–53.

113. Scherer et al., p. 90.

costs are reduced. In our original (i.e., $60,000 fixed cost) example, combined average production plus delivery costs (the latter borne by customers) are $21.20 per ton with the 40-mile spacing deterrence strategy, compared to $18.60 with 80-mile spacing and a limit price of $20.1625.[114] Second, with the limit pricing strategy, consumers near Firm A's more widely spaced plants benefit from lower delivered prices; and although the most distant customers pay more than they would if entry were deterred by geographic space packing, they cannot be really badly treated under limit pricing, or deterrence will fail. In fact, total consumers' surplus is clearly higher under the 80-mile spacing limit pricing strategy, given the assumptions of our example.[115] Third, to the extent that the limit pricing strategy is less credible as a deterrent, fresh competition is more apt to develop, bringing with it the possibility (although, in view of the oligopolistic interdependence among adjacent sellers, not a certainty) of invigorated price competition. Thus, it is doubtful whether an entry deterrence strategy emphasizing geographic space packing is as beneficial to society as strategies that involve keeping prices low and outputs high.

Entry deterrence through product differentiation

In addition to seeking unfilled niches in geographic space, would-be entrants often look for unfilled product design or image niches to facilitate their entry. Consumers' desire for products of diverse characteristics is in this respect analogous to their desire to buy from geographically proximate suppliers.[116] The buyer of wine, for instance, may be interested in dryness, tartness, fruitiness, alcohol volume, prestige, and diverse other attributes as well as price. Each of these can be mapped as a dimension in N-dimensional product characteristics space, just as the set of possible plant locations is mapped in two-dimensional geographic space. A product with specific characteristics is in effect located at a point in that N-space. Products with similar characteristics are located near one another, while products

with quite different characteristics are located far apart, appealing to different consumers or different facets of a given consumer's tastes. The loss of utility consumers experience from having to consume products located some distance from their ideal bundle of desired characteristics is analogous to the delivery costs consumers must pay buying from geographically distant plants. A firm attempting to gain a product differentiation advantage to facilitate its entry will seek some unfilled or poorly filled locus in product characteristics space, just as companies in industries with high transport costs gravitate toward locations with no nearby competing plant. To deter entrants pursuing this product niche-filling strategy, established sellers may seek to 'pack' product characteristics space with a sufficient diversity of product variants so that no room for profitable new entry remains. The analogy to geographic space packing is quite close, and so the formal logic developed in the previous section can be applied with little modification to analyze what appears to be an important aspect of real-world firms' entry deterrence strategy.

Although economists were slow to recognize this point, entrepreneurs were not. A key 1921 strategy decision of the reorganized General Motors Corporation was to establish a complete spectrum of automobile offerings. As its chairman at the time, Alfred Sloan, later described the move:

> It seemed to me that the intelligent approach would be to have a car at every price position, just the same as a general conducting a campaign wants to have an army at every point he is likely to be attacked. We had too many cars in some places and no cars in other places. One of the first things we did was to develop a line of products that met competition in the various positions in which competition was offered.[117]

An unusually clear illustration of the product space-packing strategy is found in the history of the government-owned Swedish Tobacco Company.[118] Until 1961, the company had a legal monopoly over cigarette production and distribution in Sweden. Then its control over distribution was terminated, and non-Swedish firms began to capture a rapidly growing market share with cigarettes imported duty-free from other European Free Trade Association nations. An important component of Swedish Tobacco's effort to contain this entry threat was to identify through marketing research and then fill in every significant point in the cigarette taste and image spectrum. Between 1961 and 1969 it moved from having 12 brands to 25, redesigned its packages, and increased its advertising roughly twelvefold. The strategy was apparently successful, for Swedish Tobacco managed to maintain a market share on the order of 80 percent.

As in the case of geographic space packing, the lumpiness associated with economies of scale is what makes product variety proliferation a profitable entry deterrence strategy. Developing a new product variety costs a more or less fixed sum, and there may also be product-specific economies of scale in production. Perhaps even more important, threshold effects in advertising and other sales promotional methods mean that a sizeable lump must be invested in launching a new product into a branded consumer goods market.[119] If a new entrant comes in with too small a launching campaign, the effort may be ineffective, or the sales gained insufficient to cover high unit development and production costs. If, on the other hand, established sellers can 'crowd' product characteristics space densely enough, the amount of demand left over for any differentiated new brand will be too small to permit entrants to cover the costs of a full-scale launching campaign. As in geographic space, the number of existing product varieties or brands upon which a new entrant impinges may be small, and so the size of the entry lump is large in relation to the volume of demand with which it interacts competitively. Because of this lumpiness, established products may be able to command continuing supranormal profits while expected profits for an additional new product remain negative.[120]

Assuming a market in which differentiation is sufficiently strong that new products impinge only upon the sales of immediately adjacent brands and assuming also price-matching behavior on the part of entrants, Schmalensee has shown that limit pricing is less profitable than brand proliferation as a deterrence strategy.[121]

114. With more modest scale economies than assumed here, the comparison is apt to be closer. There is reason to believe that combined unit production plus transportation cost curves tend to be rather flat over a broad range. See Figure 4.2, Chapter 4, p. 89 *supra;* and Scherer et al., *The Economics of Multi-Plant Operation,* pp. 368–81.

In a simulation analysis that ignores production costs, J. M. A. Gee finds that sequential entry into imperfectly competitive spatial markets leads to transportation costs substantially above those associated with perfect (but unrealizable) competition. "A Model of Location and Industry Efficiency with Free Entry," *Quarterly Journal of Economics* 90 (November 1976): 557–74.

115. At any given delivery distance m, consumers' surplus with linear demand is one-half the difference between the demand function's delivered price intercept less the sum of F.O.B. price plus delivery cost times the quantity demanded. Thus, let:

(1) $q_m = \alpha - b(P + tm)$

where in our example $\alpha = 500$, $b = 12.5$, and $t = 0.25$. Consumers' surplus at m is:

(2) $CS_m = 1/2\, q_m\, [\alpha/b - (P + tm)]$

Substituting (1) into (2), we obtain:

(3) $CS_m = 1/2\, (b\, t^2 m^2 + b\, P^2 + 2tb\, P\, m$
$- 2\alpha P - 2\alpha t m + \alpha^2/b)$

This is the consumers' surplus at a point in space m. Consumers' surplus for a plant selling Z miles in each direction is $2 \int_0^Z CS_m\, dm$. Integrating by parts, we obtain:

(4) $CS_{2Z} = \dfrac{bt^2 Z^3}{3} + b\, P^2 Z + tb\, P\, Z^2$
$- 2\alpha P Z - \alpha t Z^2 + (\alpha^2/b)\, Z$

which has been known to make strong men weep. However, substituting in $\alpha = 500$, $b = 12.5$, and $t = 0.25$, we have:

(5) $CS_{2Z} = 0.2604\, Z^3 + 12.5\, P^2 Z + 3.125\, P Z^2$
$- 10,000\, PZ - 125\, Z^2 + 20,000$

This is readily solved for the appropriate values of Z and P. Under limit pricing, $Z = 40$ and $P = \$20.1625$. Total consumers' surplus in serving a space 80 miles wide is \$114,240. With entry deterrence through geographic space packing, $Z = 20$ and $P = \$23.75$. Recalling that it takes two plants to cover an 80-mile space, we find consumers' surplus to be \$95,570.

It is uncertain how general this result is. Even though there is a simple linear relationship between P and Z in the short-run profit-maximizing (i.e., nonlimit pricing) case, the mathematics of consumers' surplus comparisons appear intractable, especially when a comparison is to be made with the limit pricing conditions, introducing an additional third-degree polynomial. The most that can be said is that an attempt was made to select parameters representative of situations with fairly high transportation costs. Extensive computer simulation would no doubt yield interesting insights.

116. The pioneer in utilizing the analogy between geographic and product characteristics space was Hotelling, "Stability in Competition." The notion of characteristics space was significantly extended by Kelvin Lancaster in "A New Approach to Consumer Theory," *Journal of Political Economy* 74 (April 1966): 132–57, and in numerous subsequent works by him. For an admirable survey plus extensions of direct relevance to the analysis here, see Richard Schmalensee, "Entry Deterrence in the Ready-To-Eat Breakfast Cereal Industry," *Bell Journal of Economics* 9 (Autumn 1978): 305–27.

The dynamics of monopoly
and oligopoly pricing   259

He observes too that moving products in characteristics space, like moving plants in geographic space, is costly; and with 'backing off' relatively unlikely, the space-packing strategy deters sizeable entry more credibly than limit pricing. Thus, the use of a brand proliferation strategy appears quite plausible, especially in consumer goods lines amenable to strong product differentiation.

Whether society is well served when entry is deterred in this way is arguable. To the extent that tastes are highly varied, the proliferation of product varieties adds to consumers' utility. But if there are persistent product-specific scale economies in production, it also increases production costs. And perhaps more important in consumer goods fields, advertising and other marketing costs are likely to escalate. How these benefits and costs balance out is a difficult question we must defer for more systematic analysis in Chapter 14. To anticipate a part of our conclusions, when most or all sellers forgo price competition and emphasize the proliferation of high-priced product variants, more product variety is apt to materialize than the amount that maximizes social welfare.

Other product differentiation barriers to entry of a less complex nature might also permit established firms to hold prices above their own costs without attracting new entrants or fringe rival expansion.[122] It is sometimes argued that through heavy advertising, established firms can build up consumer loyalty to their products and that the loyalty created in this way makes entry difficult for newcomers. Deferring to Chapter 14 the question of whether advertising actually does on balance cement loyalties, this view is too simple unless it is accompanied by an explanation of why new entrants cannot play the loyalty-winning game on equal terms. There are two main plausible extensions. First, as we have seen in Chapter 4 and reiterated here, it may be necessary to achieve a certain minimum threshold level of advertising or other promotional activity to have much effect on consumer behavior. The firm with a large market share can spread the cost of reaching that threshold over a larger sales volume than a small (possibly new) rival. The smaller enterprise might aspire to reach a size at which it suffers no such unit promotional cost disadvantage. However, the effort may take a long time, or it may not be feasible at all if high unit advertising costs, the failure to realize production scale economies, and capital market access difficulties interact with the pursuit of a limit pricing strategy or space-packing strategy by established firms to retard the entrant's attainable growth. Also, history endows companies with different promotional cost–sales response functions. There may be no practical promotional strategy by which a latecomer can acquire a product image equivalent to the image of the firm that pioneered the field or had the good luck to capture consumers' imagination with a unique advertising campaign that cannot be duplicated. With an inferior image, new entrants and fringe firms may be condemned more or less permanently to receiving prices lower than those of well-established firms and/or spending more on promotion per dollar of sales to cultivate and maintain whatever brand loyalty they enjoy. In a statistical study of 103 large company operating units, Robert Buzzell and Paul Ferris found that having been the pioneer in a consumer goods market permitted an average advertising and sales promotion cost saving amounting to 1.45 percent of sales relative to early nonpioneer suppliers, all else being equal.[123] Late entrants, on the other hand, had to spend 2.12 cents per sales dollar *more* on promotion than early but not first suppliers. With promotional cost and price advantages, well-established sellers may indeed find it profitable to set their prices at levels that impede the entry and growth of fringe rivals.

In his pioneering study of entry barriers, Professor Bain found that product differentiation was "of at least the same general order of importance . . . as economies of large-scale production" in giving established market leaders a price or cost advantage over new entrants.[124] In the next chapter we shall examine the available statistical evidence to see what impact such entry barriers have had on industrial performance.

Pricing to maximize sales growth

Our analysis of dynamic pricing strategy has thus far adhered to the assumption that business firms seek to maximize profits over the long pull. An alternate hypothesis has been advanced by a number of economists. In a seminal statement of the proposition, Professor William Baumol argued that instead of maximizing profits, either short-run or long-run, firms with monopoly power tend to maximize sales revenue, subject only to the condition that profits not fall below some specified minimum value.[125] He was led to this break from orthodoxy by repeated observation of managers' preoccupation with the level and growth of their companies' sales rather than current profits.[126] He postulated several explanations for this apparent emphasis on sales: banks are less willing to finance companies with declining sales; personnel relations problems increase when falling sales necessitate layoffs; and the power to adopt effective competitive tactics is weakened when sales and market position decline. Such considerations might be rationalized in terms of a desire to maximize long-run profits. As Richard Heflebower observed in an earlier work:

> management recognizes good market position to be a valuable asset, whose long-term attributes must condition all short-term decisions. Its value is not merely defensive . . . but also is a basic attribute of the firm's ability to make positive moves; that is, to deal with unanticipated developments when they occur. In that sense, market position becomes a means of long-term profit maximization under conditions of uncertainty.[127]

But in addition, Baumol asserted, executives are interested in increasing sales revenue *for its own sake* because managerial salaries and prestige are more closely correlated with sales than with profits. Thus, sales maximization was said to be an independent goal of managers, quite apart from its connection with long-run profit maximization. Subsequent empirical studies reviewed in Chapter 2 have cast doubt on whether managers' compensation incentives are in fact as closely tied to sales and divorced from profitability as was believed at the time Baumol wrote. Nevertheless, models of firms sacrificing profits to enhance sales revenue have attracted great interest.

No such analysis denies that profitability plays a role in company decision making. In the original version of his theory, Baumol assumed that sufficient profits must be achieved "to pay dividends, and to reinvest in such amounts that the combination of dividend receipts and stock price rises can remunerate stockholders ade-

(117) Quoted in Alfred D. Chandler, Jr., *Strategy and Structure: Chapters in the History of the American Industrial Enterprise* (Cambridge, Mass.: M.I.T. Press, 1962), p. 143.

(118) Cf. Scherer et al., *The Economics of Multi-Plant Operation*, p. 157.

(119) The size of this lump can to some extent be influenced by the conduct of established sellers. By advertising more heavily, they increase "media clutter," above which entrants can be heard only by advertising at a similarly intensified level.

(120) See Schmalensee, "Entry Deterrence," who develops the product space-packing and lumpiness logic to explain the high sustained profitability of ready-to-eat cereal brands; and G. C. Archibald and Gideon Rosenbluth, "The 'New' Theory of Consumer Demand and Monopolistic Competition," *Quarterly Journal of Economics* 89 (November 1975): 584–89.

(121) Schmalensee, "Entry Deterrence," pp. 311–13, 323–24. See also Archibald and Rosenbluth, "The New Theory," p. 589.

122. For an early conceptualization of this view, see Oliver E. Williamson, "Selling Expense as a Barrier to Entry," *Quarterly Journal of Economics* 77 (February 1963): 112–28. The most comprehensive treatment is by William S. Comanor and Thomas A. Wilson, *Advertising and Market Power* (Cambridge, Mass.: Harvard University Press, 1974). For a control-theoretic extension of the Gaskins limit pricing model to include product differentiation investments, see Mark B. Schupack, "Dynamic Limit Pricing with Advertising" (mimeograph, Brown University, August 1972).

123. Robert D. Buzzell and Paul W. Farris, "Marketing Costs in Consumer Goods Industries," in Hans B. Thorelli, ed., *Strategy + Structure = Performance* (Bloomington: Indiana University Press, 1977), pp. 128–29. See also Ronald Bond and David Lean, *Sales, Promotion, and Product Differentiation in Two Prescription Drug Markets*, Federal Trade Commission staff report (Washington, D.C.: Government Printing Office, February 1977).

124. Bain, *Barriers to New Competition*, pp. 142–43. See also Harris, "Entry and Long-Term Trends in Industry Performance," pp. 307–308.

125. William J. Baumol, *Business Behavior, Value, and Growth* (New York: Macmillan, 1959), pp. 45–82; rev. ed. (New York: Harcourt, Brace & World, 1967), pp. 45–82, 86–104.

126. It is worth noting that many of the observations reported by Baumol were made as a consultant for a marketing research firm. Conceivably, executives interested in hiring and working with such a firm may have had a functional bias toward sales maximization. In a study of Danish firms, Bjarke Fog found that sales departments tended to stress maximum sales while production departments held out for higher profit margins. *Industrial Pricing Policies: An Analysis of Pricing Policies of Danish Manufacturers*, trans. I. E. Bailey (Amsterdam: North-Holland, 1960), p. 31.

127. "Toward a Theory of Industrial Markets and Prices," p. 126. See also the Harrod quotation on p. 235 *supra*.

quately."[128] He therefore argued that the firm maximized sales subject to a minimum profits constraint. His analysis is illustrated in Figure 8.7. The Baumol model is represented more conveniently in terms of *total* cost and revenue curves rather than the average and marginal curves used in most of this volume. In Figure 8.7 *TR* is the firm's total revenue or sales curve and *TC* its total cost curve. The shapes assumed are conventional. Profit is the vertical distance between the *TR* and *TC* curves and is shown explicitly by the π curve. Profit is maximized at output OX_1 and sales revenue is maximized at output OX_3. If the firm's managers insist upon earning profits of *OC* before seeking to satisfy other objectives such as sales maximization, they will not be in a position to increase sales beyond the short-run profit-maximizing level, since the profit objective lies out of reach. To come as close as possible to meeting its profit constraint, the firm must produce the profit-maximizing output OX_1. If, however, profits of *OB* will suffice, the firm's profit goal is overfulfilled at OX_1. It can increase output to OX_2 while earning at least *OB* in profits, enjoying higher sales than it would under a (short-run) profit maximization policy. Finally, if its profit constraint is the still lower magnitude *OA*, the firm will increase its output all the way to OX_3, where sales revenue is maximized. It will not expand farther, even though the profit goal is overfulfilled at OX_3, because additional output would be absorbed in the market only at prices reduced so much as to make total sales fall.

A noteworthy implication of the early Baumol analysis is that if firms with monopoly power strive to increase sales revenue for its own sake and if their minimum profits constraint is not too stringent, they will charge lower prices and supply more output than they would under short-run monopoly profit maximization. Thus, tendencies toward monopolistic resource misallocation may be mitigated.[129]

The analysis of Figure 8.7 is strictly static. In a later modification of his theory, Baumol proposed that managers seek to maximize not sales revenue at any moment in time, but the rate at which sales grow.[130] Profits then became an instrumental variable for obtaining the capital to finance expansion. A high-price policy yields enhanced profits to support the investment required for higher future sales, while a low-price policy directly stimulates current sales. In Baumol's amended view, the firm's problem is to maximize its growth subject to making enough profit to support that growth.

Baumol's original contributions precipitated an outpouring of sales and growth maximization models, many of whose results conflict with one another because of differing assumptions. An important influence on this trend of thought was exerted by the work of Robin Marris, as extended by John Williamson.[131] They argued that the critical constraint on the firm's ability to sacrifice profits in favor of sales or sales growth is the reaction of financial markets. If profits are too low, the firm has insufficient internally generated funds to finance its growth, an adverse stock market valuation of its securities and hence inadequate access to external finance and, most important, an increased risk of being taken over by a raider who will implement new policies more palatable to outside investors. Using these and other as-

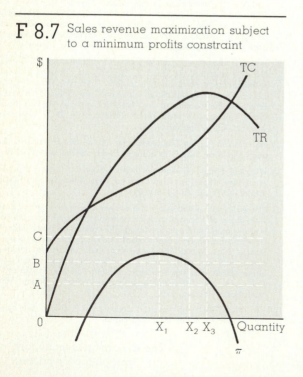

F 8.7 Sales revenue maximization subject to a minimum profits constraint

sumptions, Williamson concluded that the principal difference between growth and long-run profit-maximizing firms is not their choice of output levels (and hence prices at any moment in time), but the fraction of earnings that are paid out as dividends instead of being plowed back internally.[132] In both cases, short-run profit maximization was found to be consistent with the realization of long-term objectives. However, firms maximizing the discounted present value of sales revenues (the long-term analogue of Baumol's short-run sales revenue maximization) were found by Williamson to charge less and produce more than under short-run profit-maximization.

Although they yield many interesting results, models of the Marris-Williamson genre suffer from two serious limitations. First, they assume for simplicity a steady-state equilibrium of growth rates, dividend payout ratios, and the like. In reality, the investment opportunities faced by business enterprises change over time with their progress through some sort of life cycle.[133] Rapid growth with high earnings plowback is optimal under virtually any plausible criterion in periods of high opportunity, whereas slower growth and high dividend payouts may, depending upon managerial objectives, take precedence in periods of diminished opportunity. The neglect of this phenomenon can be, and has been, patched up using the methods of optimal control theory.[134] Second, and more important, the sales growth maximization models assume that a firm's pricing decision at any moment in time is affected primarily by current cost and (monopoly) demand functions along with the impact of current profits on the firm's financial capacity and stock market attractiveness. To the extent that current decisions affect future demand, it is only through the medium of investment in research, advertising, and expanded production capacity. Yet as we have seen throughout this chapter, an absolutely essential consideration in a monopolistic or oligopolistic enterprise's long-run strategy problem is how this year's prices affect the inroads made by substitute products and rival sellers, and hence the position of future period demand functions. None of the works in the Baumol-Marris-Williamson tradition deals squarely with this

problem. They assume in effect that sellers enjoy monopoly positions with blockaded entry. All have left out a good deal of what dynamic pricing strategy is all about.

No one has yet succeeded in showing whether or not business enterprises actually behave in the ways and for the reasons postulated by Baumol and other sales growth theorists. The results of empirical tests have been largely equivocal, and the benchmark against which sales-maximization hypotheses have been compared has typically been short-run profit maximization, which more often than not is a straw man.[135] One obstacle to

128. Baumol, *Business Behavior*, 1st ed., p. 51.

129. However, it is possible for the sales-maximizing firm to overshoot the competitive output, after which resource misallocation again rises. See W. G. Shepherd, "On Sales-Maximising and Oligopoly Behaviour," *Economica* 29 (November 1962): 420–24.

130. Baumol, "On the Theory of Expansion of the Firm," *American Economic Review* 52 (December 1962): 1078–87. In a footnote Baumol acknowledges the influence of work by Marris, cited below.

131. Robin Marris, "A Model of the 'Managerial' Enterprise," *Quarterly Journal of Economics* 77 (May 1963): 185–209 and *The Economic Theory of "Managerial" Capitalism* (London: Macmillan, 1964); and John Williamson, "Profit, Growth and Sales Maximisation," *Economica* 33 (February 1966): 1–16.

132. Williamson, pp. 11–12. See also J. B. Herendeen, "Alternative Models of the Corporate Enterprise," *Quarterly Review of Economics and Business* 14 (Winter 1974): 59–75. For conflicting results from a richer model, see John Lintner, "Optimum or Maximum Corporate Growth under Uncertainty," in Robin Marris and Adrian Wood, eds., *The Corporate Economy* (Cambridge, Mass.: Harvard University Press, 1971), pp. 172–218.

133. Cf. Chapter 2, p. 40 *supra*.

134. See Hayne E. Leland, "The Dynamics of a Revenue-Maximizing Firm," *International Economic Review* 13 (June 1972): 376–85; Robert E. Wong, "Profit Maximization and Alternative Theories: A Dynamic Reconciliation," *American Economic Review* 65 (September 1975): 689–93 (assuming, unlike other papers in the Baumol-Marris tradition, *competitive* product markets); and Jacques Lesourne, "The Optimal Growth of the Firm in a Growing Environment," *Journal of Economic Theory* 14 (August 1976): 118–37.

135. See the summaries of profitability and earnings plowback research in Chapter 2 *supra* and the survey of merger effect studies in Chapter 4 *supra*. See also Marshall Hall, "Sales Revenue Maximization: An Empirical Examination," *Journal of Industrial Economics* 15 (April 1967): 143–54; the comment by Leonard Waverman in the *Journal of Industrial Economics* 17 (November 1968): 73–80; and Conway L. Lackman and Joseph L. Craycroft, "Sales Maximization and Oligopoly: A Case Study," *Journal of Industrial Economics* 23 (December 1974) 81–95.

The dynamics of monopoly
and oligopoly pricing   263

enlightenment is the fact that the behavioral differences between *long-run* profit maximization (e.g., through limit pricing) and various forms of sales revenue or sales growth maximization are sufficiently subtle that econometric tests with available data are not powerful enough to discriminate among the contending hypotheses. There are, to be sure, some cases in which the sales maximization and limit pricing hypotheses generate conflicting predictions. In this sense the limit pricing hypothesis would appear to hold an empirical edge, since (unlike revenue maximization) it can explain expansion by monopolists and well-disciplined oligopolists into ranges of inelastic market demand. However, no final verdict can be rendered given the present state of knowledge. To resolve the impasse, it is probably necessary not only to conduct much more sophisticated econometric research, but also to carry out case studies in greater depth than any heretofore attempted by economists.

Other dynamic influences affecting price

A few further dynamic considerations affecting price decisions must be mentioned to round out the picture. One is the whole set of influences lumped together conveniently under the caption 'public opinion.' Clear and blatant exploitation of monopoly power leads to a bad press, which most business managers prefer to avoid. The executive concerned about a place in the history books can scarcely ignore the fact that William H. Vanderbilt is remembered more for his "the public be damned" outburst than for his substantial entrepreneurial and philanthropic accomplishments. Persistently high prices and profits may also provoke direct government intervention in the form of price controls or antitrust proceedings. The desire to maintain a favorable public image and fear of government intervention undoubtedly induce some companies to avoid squeezing all they can out of a monopolistic market position.

Uncertainty also affects pricing in a variety of ways. Output may be expanded beyond the level at which short-run profits are maximized in order

to cement customer relations and ensure room for maneuvering should some adverse contingency materialize in the future. On such aspects of dynamic strategy economic theory has little to contribute; its significance is an empirical question. However, theoretical analysis provides some interesting insights into the links among demand uncertainty, inventory policy, and pricing behavior.

A firm in a purely competitive market can, by definition, sell as much output as it wishes at the ruling market price. Uncertainty pertains only to the price that will prevail. This is not so for the firm possessing monopoly power. At any given quoted price, the monopolistic firm will be able to sell more if demand turns out to be strong than if it is weak. Unless production to order is practical, the firm must decide how much to produce before it knows how strong demand will be. If it produces too much, it will be left holding a large inventory, incurring higher storage, capital, and possibly obsolescence costs, or else it will have to dispose of its surplus at distress prices. If it produces too little, it will lose sales and perhaps drive disappointed customers permanently into the arms of rival sellers. It must decide then upon an optimal price, production, and inventory policy to make the best of demand uncertainties.

Do price and output decisions differ under these conditions from what they would be in a world of certainty? Pioneering mathematical analyses by Mills, Karlin and Carr suggest that they do, although numerical simulation studies by Nevins show that under plausible assumptions the deviations are not very large.[136]

Unfortunately, few sweeping generalizations are possible. The output of an enterprise with a downward-sloping demand function may be either greater or less under uncertainty than under certainty; it depends upon the amount and character of the uncertainties faced, the shapes of cost and demand functions, the costs and risks of maintaining an inventory position, and whether the firm is risk neutral or risk averse. One fairly general result relates inventory policy to market structure. When errors in predicting demand are symmetrically distributed about their mean, the monopolistic firm will tend to produce and hold more output for inventory (reducing the probability of shortages and dissatisfied customers), the higher the ratio of price to marginal cost.[137] This is so because the more price exceeds marginal cost, the more profitable it is to satisfy an extra unit of demand from inventory in times of peak demand, amply repaying inventory holding costs. This is one sense in which monopoly power confers some compensating benefits. To keep the phenomenon in perspective, it should be noted that monopolistic firms will never find it optimal to produce an output that makes marginal cost exceed price—e.g., more than the competitive output—merely to hedge against demand uncertainties.[138]

The dependence of price upon inventory behavior is even more complex. As we have seen in Chapter 6, the main function of inventory policy in oligopoly may be to support the price at a value chosen for strategic reasons, and not to maximize profits in any narrower sense. But if we limit our attention to profit maximization efforts that ignore oligopolistic interdependence, mathematical studies of optimal inventory policy become relevant. Mills, Karlin and Carr have demonstrated that when demand is uncertain, only by coincidence will firms with monopoly power set their price at the same value as that which maximizes profit under certainty. Nevins clarified this conclusion by showing that the certainty and uncertainty pricing strategies will be identical, ceteris paribus, in the unlikely event of zero time discount rates and inventory carrying costs. Excluding this case, producers must make a complicated tradeoff decision balancing the effects of price changes on expected demand against the effects of price and inventory variations on the probability of costly shortages or surplus production. The price resulting from this tradeoff may be above or below the price that would be set by a monopolist under certainty; it depends mainly upon the shape of the marginal cost function and the character of the demand uncertainties, e.g., whether the error distribution is additive or multiplicative relative to mean expected demand.[139] In the case of rising short-run marginal costs, which is most typical of real-world conditions when production is not greatly below capacity, the optimal price under uncertainty tends to be less than the certainty price. At the same time, how-

ever, production is likely to be restricted so that out-of-stock situations occur more frequently than surpluses.

Much more research on the implications of demand uncertainty for business pricing behavior remains to be done. The theory can still be extended, and perhaps more important, empirical studies of actual inventory and price policies and their effects are needed. Among other things, difficult welfare problems arise when demand is inadequately satisfied, not because of high monopoly prices, but because production and inventory levels are inadequate to meet peak demands at the (possibly restrained) prices set.[140] Much depends then upon the nonprice rationing system adopted—i.e., to what extent supplies go to high as compared to low reservation price

136. Edwin S. Mills, "Uncertainty and Price Theory," *Quarterly Journal of Economics* 59 (February 1959): 116–30, and *Price, Output, and Inventory Policy* (New York: Wiley, 1962), Chapters 5 through 7; Samuel Karlin and Charles Carr, "Prices and Optimal Inventory Policy," in Kenneth Arrow et al., *Studies in Applied Probability and Management Science* (Stanford: Stanford University Press, 1962), pp. 159–72; and Arthur J. Nevins, "Some Effects of Uncertainty: Simulation of a Model of Price," *Quarterly Journal of Economics* 80 (February 1966): 73–87. For extensions raising doubts about the generality of certain earlier results, see E. Zabel, "Monopoly and Uncertainty," *Review of Economic Studies* 37 (April 1970): 205–19.

A substantial literature has also emerged analyzing the optimal pricing decisions of monopolistic firms (such as electric utilities) unable to carry inventory over into subsequent periods as a means of coping with uncertainty. See for example Hayne E. Leland, "Theory of the Firm Facing Uncertain Demand," *American Economic Review* 62 (June 1972): 278–91; Enrique R. Arzac, "Profits and Safety in the Theory of the Firm under Price Uncertainty," *International Economic Review* 17 (February 1976): 163–71; and Donald V. Coes, "Firm Output and Changes in Uncertainty," *American Economic Review* 67 (March 1977): 249–51. The effects of uncertainty on output and price are, as in the inventory analyses emphasized in the text here, quite complex. See Leland, p. 284 note 15, for a case in which the reaction to uncertainty by a firm required to set its price before demand is known is an increase in output *and* a reduction in price relative to the certainty optima.

137. Mills, "Uncertainty and Price Theory," pp. 121–22.

138. Mills, *Price, Output, and Inventory Policy*, p. 90.

139. When inventory carry-overs are infeasible, another critical variable is whether the firm must determine its price, its output, or both before actual demand is known. See Leland, "Theory of the Firm Facing Unknown Demand," p. 289.

140. Cf. Dennis W. Carlton, "Uncertainty, Production Lags, and Pricing," *American Economic Review* 67 (February 1977): 246–47.

The dynamics of monopoly and oligopoly pricing

consumers. The more the latter are favored over the former, the larger resource misallocation losses will be. On what actually happens when rationing of this sort occurs, we know all too little.

Conclusion

It is appropriate now to draw together the main conclusions emerging from Chapters 5 through 8. We have seen that when sellers are few in number, there are incentives for them to recognize their interdependence and to cooperate in policies that lead toward maximum group profits. Institutions such as outright collusion, price leadership, pricing by rules of thumb, and focal point pricing facilitate the maintenance of prices above the competitive level. But there are important limits on the ability of monopolists and oligopolists to hold prices at highly profitable levels. Oligopolistic coordination may break down owing to conflicts over the most suitable price, heterogeneity of products, the pressure of underabsorbed fixed costs, secret price cutting, or simple cussedness on the part of some maverick producer. Long-run substitution and the threat or actuality of entry by new competitors place a ceiling—and sometimes a low one—on producers' pricing discretion.

The performance implications of this complicated picture are themselves complex. It is clear that under conditions favorable to the exercise of monopoly power, prices may be held substantially above competitive levels for extended periods of time. Still this result does not follow automatically from the mere existence of a concentrated market structure. Prices often hover closer to cost than one would predict from an analysis that takes into account only the fewness of sellers, ignoring coordination obstacles and long-run constraints. These more subtle structural and behavioral variables help explain why pricing performance in modern industrial markets has on the whole been fairly satisfactory despite significant departures from the structural ideal of pure economic theory.

9 The price and profit consequences of market structure

The theory of how market structure influences pricing behavior yields numerous testable hypotheses about industries' ultimate economic performance. A fully developed theory, we have seen, is necessarily quite rich. Quantitative tests of the theory should ideally reflect this richness, although, as a practical matter, simplifying assumptions must be made. In this chapter we survey the premises, methodology, results, and unresolved puzzles of economists' attempts to confront theory with the statistical evidence on industrial performance.

A pioneering effort to relate pricing performance to market structure was a 1951 article by Joe S. Bain.[1] His hypothesis was simple: that in view of the pricing behavior expected under monopoly or tight oligopoly, the average profit return realized by firms in highly concentrated industries will tend to be significantly higher than that of firms in less concentrated oligopolies or atomistically structured industries. Bain obtained information on the average 1936–40 after-tax profit returns on stockholders' equity of leading companies in 42 U.S. manufacturing industries screened to satisfy several data quality criteria. He found that in industries with eight-firm sales concentration ratios of 70 or higher, the average profit return was 12.1 percent, compared to 6.9 percent for industries with concentration ratios below 70. The difference was highly significant statistically, providing the first systematic quantitative support for the conjecture that tightly knit oligopolies tend to hold their prices above competitive levels.

This contribution was followed first by a trickle and then, beginning in the 1960s, by a torrent of analogous market structure-profitability studies. In a 1974 survey, Weiss identified 54 such works, and the rate of output was if anything accelerating.[2] Statistical testing of structure-performance hypotheses became the closest thing industrial organization economists had to sausage production. We cannot possibly do fitting justice to all the studies here, and any attempt to do so would be redundant, given the existence of several convenient surveys.[3] What we shall do instead is focus on the main substantive and methodologi-

---

1. Joe S. Bain, "Relation of Profit Rate to Industry Concentration: American Manufacturing, 1936–1940," *Quarterly Journal of Economics* 65 (August 1951): 293–324.

2. Leonard W. Weiss, "The Concentration-Profits Relationship and Antitrust," in Harvey J. Goldschmid et al., eds., *Industrial Concentration: The New Learning* (Boston: Little, Brown, 1974), pp. 201–20.

3. See Weiss, "The Concentration-Profits Relationship"; Weiss, "Quantitative Studies of Industrial Organization," in Michael D. Intriligator, ed., *Frontiers of Quantitative Economics* (Amsterdam: North-Holland, 1971), pp. 362–411; and John M. Vernon, *Market Structure and Industrial Performance: A Review of Statistical Findings* (Boston: Allyn and Bacon, 1972), especially Chapters 3 and 4.

cal issues and attempt to convey what is known and still unknown as a result of the accumulated research.[4]

The basic paradigm

Let us begin with first principles. As we observed in Chapter 1, the paradigm commonly employed by industrial organization economists holds that structure affects conduct, which in turn determines ultimate economic performance. In the realm of pricing, it is hypothesized that certain market structures are conducive to monopolistic conduct—i.e., the raising of prices above costs. This conduct in itself may be difficult to analyze quantitatively, but its consequences are believed to be observable in some performance indicator such as profits. In the original Bain article, profit returns on stockholders' equity were considered to depend statistically upon seller concentration, thus:

$$(9.1) \qquad \pi_i = f_1(C_i, \epsilon_i)$$

where the dependent variable π_i is the profit index for the ith industry, independent variable C_i is the industry's concentration ratio, and ϵ_i is an error term impounding a host of unmeasured and/or random influences. This is much too simple. As Bain recognized already in 1951, other structural variables such as the height of barriers to entry undoubtedly matter; and precision in estimation makes it desirable to take into account explicitly the effect of such nonstructural variables as the state of demand, any special characteristics of buyers, and the nature of an industry's technology. Thus, we have:

$$(9.2) \qquad \pi_i = f_2(C_i, B_i, OS_i, X_i, e_i)$$

where B_i denotes a set of entry barrier measures, OS_i a set of other relevant structural indicators, X_i a set of nonstructural variables believed to affect profitability, and e_i a modified (and presumably smaller) statistical error term. The estimation of particular forms for equations like (9.2) through multiple regression techniques has been the most common approach in statistical research on the structure-performance paradigm.

There are many reasons why this expanded approach may still be too naive. One of the most important follows from our analysis of limit pricing models in Chapter 8. Market structure, as characterized by the concentration ratio C_i, may not be a truly independent variable. It may itself be influenced by the pricing policies sellers choose, taking into account entry barriers, e.g., as prices are either set high with the expectation of inducing substantial new entry or held low to retard entry. With the profit variable π_i reflecting the level at which prices are set, we therefore have:

$$(9.3) \qquad \frac{d\,C_i}{dt} = g(B_i, \pi_i, \gamma_{it})$$

where $d\,C_i/dt$ is the rate of change in concentration over time. Some means of capturing the simultaneous working of relationships (9.2) and (9.3) must be found, especially when the π_i variable is defined, as it was in Bain's original study, over a time interval sufficient for appreciable structural changes to occur.

This overview by no means exhausts the complications appearing when one seeks a statistical method compatible with a rich theoretical conception of industrial reality. Nevertheless, we leave a discussion of additional points until later, turning now to the more mundane problem of finding appropriate measures for performance, structure, and other relevant variables.

Measurement problems

Monopoly power presumably permits sellers to hold prices above the levels that would prevail under competition, all else being equal. One might wish to focus one's statistical analysis directly upon prices. But this is seldom possible. A single firm may set dozens or even thousands of prices on different product variants and to different customers; even if this were not a problem, it is difficult directly to compare the prices of aluminum, turbogenerators, and ice cream cones. Some common denominator is needed. The usual reference point is cost.

Theory reveals that under monopoly (ignoring

certain price discrimination cases) price exceeds marginal cost, while under pure competition, price equals marginal cost. This divergence, we learned in Chapter 2, underlies the tendency for resources to be misallocated when some prices are set monopolistically. A logical candidate for comparative analysis is therefore the Lerner Index, or the ratio of price minus marginal cost to price.[5] Unfortunately, it is difficult to obtain systematic data on business firms' marginal costs or the ratio of marginal costs to prices. As a surrogate, one might use the ratio of price less average production cost per unit to price, or (for short-run analyses) the ratio of price less average variable production cost to price. As we shall see, reasonable approximations to these indices can often be secured. Average production cost, full or variable, will of course exceed marginal cost when a firm is producing less than the output that minimizes average cost and fall below it at greater outputs.

Economic profit is the surplus of revenue over cost, including the cost of attracting capital from alternative uses. It is entirely possible for a purely competitive or monopolistically competitive industry to realize positive economic profits under short-run disequilibrium (e.g., boom) conditions. But in the long run, competitive entry should erode such 'supranormal' profits, leaving nothing more than a 'normal' return on invested capital. A monopoly does not necessarily secure economic profits,[6] but one ordinarily expects the two to coincide, and if there are appreciable barriers to entry, monopoly profits may persist for a long time or even indefinitely. These potential differences lead us to predict that on the average, and especially outside business boom periods, supranormal profits are more apt to be found where industry structures are monopolistic or tightly oligopolistic than where they are more or less atomistic. The essence of this long-run relationship is best characterized by the ratio of supranormal profit to normal unit cost. This is approximated by the ratio:

$$\pi_S = \frac{\text{Sales revenue} - \text{noncapital costs} - \text{depreciation} - (\text{total capital} \times \text{cost per unit of capital under competition})}{\text{Sales revenue}}$$

The cost per unit of capital under competition is not recorded in firms' accounting statements, so it must be imputed, which is difficult to do well.[7] Statistical researchers seeking to avoid that difficulty have usually opted for various second-best surrogates. One is the return (usually computed after the deduction of income taxes) on stockholders' equity:[8]

$$\pi_E = \frac{\text{Accounting profit attributable to stockholders}}{\text{Accounting book value of stockholders' equity}}$$

Another is the total return on capital:

$$\pi_C = \frac{\text{Accounting profits} + \text{interest payments}}{\text{Total assets}}$$

Other profit indices have been used, but they depart more from the theoretical ideal than π_S, π_E, or π_C.

Reconciling the units of analysis An industry or market is the natural unit of analysis in industrial organization studies. It is not, however, the basis from which raw performance data originate except in rare pure undiversified monopoly situations. Profit information comes from the accounting records of whole companies or, more recently, sizeable segments of whole companies. These profit data must somehow be meshed with *industry* structure variables. Several approaches exist.

One is the so-called primary industry method. Any given firm's primary industry—that is, the

---

4. For a survey of methodological hazards, see Almarin Phillips, "A Critique of Empirical Studies of Relations between Market Structure and Profitability," *Journal of Industrial Economics* 24 (June 1976): 241–49.

5. Cf. Chapter 3, p. 56 *supra*.

6. Cf. Chapter 2, p. 15 *supra*.

7. But see the Qualls reference in note 37, p. 277.

8. Stockholders' equity is the residual accounting value obtained when one subtracts from total assets all short-term liabilities, long-term debt, and other nonowner claims. It usually consists of the original or par value of outstanding common and preferred stock plus the value of retained earnings.

industry in which it has the largest single share of its sales or assets—is identified, and all relevant accounting values for the whole firm are added to that industry's totals. Sometimes, as in Bain's pioneering 1951 study, this is done by the analyst. A limitation is the fact that comprehensive sales, profit, and asset data are publicly available only for a very few thousand corporations whose securities are traded on public exchanges. Most of the companies for which data are unavailable are small. However, there are important closely held exceptions such as Deering-Milliken, one of the largest U.S. textile makers; Mars Inc., the largest U.S. candy producer; Hoffmann-LaRoche, a leading pharmaceutical manufacturer; and Cargill, the largest U.S. grain elevator operator. Many analysts have circumvented the data unavailability problem by using industry financial data aggregations compiled by governmental statistical agencies—most often, the U.S. Internal Revenue Service's annual *Statistics of Income: Corporation Income Tax Returns* series. These, however, do not avoid an even more serious problem.

IRS, like individual researchers, assigns whole companies to their primary industry category.[9] But for diversified corporations, this means that vast amounts of irrelevant or "contaminating" activity are loaded into the primary industry totals along with correctly classified primary industry profits, sales, and assets. Thus, General Electric's turbojet engine, refrigerator, synthetic diamond, electron tube, and light bulb activities would probably be lumped together with motors, generators, and switchgear into the "other electrical equipment and supplies" category. General Motors' important gas turbine, diesel locomotive, bus, and missile guidance system activities would be among the contaminating data assigned to the "motor vehicle and equipment" category. As American corporations have become increasingly diversified,[10] the contamination problem has grown more complex. The 1960s, marked by a massive conglomerate merger wave, were a kind of watershed in this regard. By 1966, the problem was already severe. It is hardly an exaggeration to say that any study using subsequent financial data classified by the primary industry method without elaborate quality controls is virtually worthless.

An alternative approach is to refrain from aggregating firms into industries, focusing instead upon individual firms as the unit of analysis and computing weighted market structure indices matched to each firm's particular situation. Suppose, for example, Firm Z has half of its sales in Industry A, whose concentration ratio is 63; 30 percent of its sales in Industry B, with a concentration ratio of 17; and 20 percent of its sales in Industry C, with a concentration ratio of 96. Then the weighted average concentration ratio would be $[(63 \times .50) + (17 \times .30) + (96 \times .20)] = 55.8$. This is used as a structural variable to "explain" the company's profitability in all industries combined. A comparative study of 80 food manufacturers' profitability revealed that the weighted average structural index method was able to bring into sharp relief relationships that appeared much weaker when the primary industry method of assigning structural indices was used.[11] Nevertheless, the weighted average method is far from ideal. As the example shows, it compresses especially high and low structural index values toward the mean for all industries, and this weakens the power of regression analyses in detecting systematic structure-performance relationships. There are also complex statistical problems arising from the tendency for errors due to the omission of relevant industry variables for one firm to be correlated with the errors for all other firms operating in the same industry.[12]

A preferable solution would be to obtain disaggregated performance data—e.g., having Firm Z report separately its profits in industries A, B, and C. The individual firm data can then be analyzed separately,[13] or firm data on particular industry segments can be aggregated by industry. Four possibilities in this vein deserve mention.

Beginning in 1977, U.S. corporations were required by the Financial Accounting Standards Board to report profits, sales, and assets defined in a standardized way broken down by "industry segments" that accounted for 10 percent or more of total company sales or profits.[14] A significant limitation of the FASB approach is that companies have broad discretion to define their segments as they please, and so large diversified corporations like General Electric report their profits for such meaninglessly broad segments as "consumer products and services," "industrial products and components," and "technical systems and materials." This plus the fact that a 10 percent segment for a large corporation is likely to be much more broadly defined than a 10 percent segment for a small corporation also means that the industry segments are not comparable from firm to firm. However, the FASB-mandated segmental data are amenable to analysis using the weighted average structural index method, and in this respect, they are an improvement over whole-company performance statistics.

By far the most richly subdivided data used in industrial organization analyses during the mid-1970s was the so-called PIMS (Profit Impact of Market Strategy) data set.[15] Beginning with 1970, a group of typically large corporations began supplying to a private organization elaborately detailed performance and structure data on certain of their individual "businesses," defined as company units selling a distinct set of products or services in competition with a well-defined set of competitors. By 1978, the PIMS data set had grown to cover some thousand such businesses operated by more than 200 corporations. The principal limitations of the PIMS data are twofold. First, there is an element of self-selection for both the cooperating companies and the businesses on which they choose to report, and in some quantifiable respects the sample is clearly not representative.[16] Second, the data are subjected to stringent confidentiality restrictions so that an analyst cannot ascertain what companies and industries are being studied or what the absolute size of any given business is. Despite these limitations, we shall see that some very important research has been done using the PIMS data.

The Federal Trade Commission's Line of Business (LB) reporting program provides an alternative solution. Beginning with 1974, the FTC sought to have 450 of the largest U.S. manufacturing enterprises report annually sales, various cost elements, profits, and assets broken down into 261 standardized manufacturing and 14 nonmanufacturing industry categories. With an average of nine lines per reporting company, the LB surveys were expected to yield data on approximately 4,000 individual company/industry segments. The data were to be published in the form of industry aggregates and, subject to con-

fidentiality rules, could also be analyzed on an individual company basis by FTC statistical staff. There was bitter industry opposition to the program.[17] Some 180 companies refused to submit reports and joined in a series of suits and countersuits testing the program's legality. The FTC achieved a decisive legal victory in 1978,[18] and despite continuing rear-guard skirmishes, it seems likely that the LB program soon will begin making available industrial performance statistics of unprecedented fineness.

A fourth and quite different approach takes advantage of the fact that the U.S. Census Bureau collects statistics on manufacturing activity at the level of individual plants. Each plant is assigned to its primary industry, and since plants are on average much more specialized than companies, the problem of contamination is

9. There are minor exceptions, e.g., when multiunit corporations file unconsolidated tax returns.

10. Cf. Chapter 3, pp. 74–77 *supra*.

11. James A. Dalton and David W. Penn, *The Quality of Data as a Factor in Analyses of Structure-Performance Relationships,* Federal Trade Commission staff report (Washington, D.C.: Government Printing Office, June 1971).

12. See Blake Imel and Peter Helmberger, "Estimation of Structure-Profit Relationships with Application to the Food Processing Sector," *American Economic Review* 61 (September 1971): 614–27; with the comment by John M. Vernon and Marjorie B. McElroy and reply by Imel and Helmberger in the *American Economic Review* 63 (September 1973): 763–69.

13. The Imel-Helmberger correlated omitted variables problem remains when disaggregated individual firm data are analyzed.

14. Financial Accounting Standards Board, Statement of Financial Accounting Standards no. 14, *Financial Reporting for Segments of a Business Enterprise* (Stamford, Conn.: Financial Accounting Standards Board, December 1976).

15. See Sidney Schoeffler, "Cross-Sectional Study of Strategy, Structure, and Performance: Aspects of the PIMS Program," in Hans B. Thorelli, ed., *Strategy + Structure = Performance* (Bloomington: Indiana University Press, 1977), pp. 108–21.

16. For example, in 57 percent of the sample businesses, the reporting company claimed to be one of the pioneers in its market.

17. For a debate on the substantive issues, see F. M. Scherer, "Segmental Financial Reporting: Needs and Tradeoffs," and George J. Benston, "The Segment Reporting Debate," in Harvey J. Goldschmid, ed., *Business Disclosure: Government's Need To Know* (New York: McGraw-Hill, 1979), pp. 3–118.

18. *In re Federal Trade Commission Line of Business Report Litigation,* CCH 1978-2 Trade Cases paragraph 62,152; *cert. den.* 99 S. Ct. 362 (1978).

The price and profit consequences
of market structure   271

greatly reduced. From the aggregated Census industry statistics, it is possible to compute an average *price-cost margin*, defined approximately as:

$$PCM = \frac{\text{Total plant sales } - \text{ material costs } - \text{ in-plant payroll costs}}{\text{Total plant sales}}$$

The index is a poor measure of net profitability because Census data do not permit one to identify with any precision, and hence deduct, such out-of-plant costs as advertising, central office costs, sales force expenditures, and separate research and development laboratory outlays as well as in-plant depreciation. However, its magnitude usually lies between the ratio of price minus average total manufacturing cost to price (i.e., the gross margin) and the ratio of price minus average variable manufacturing cost to price (sometimes called the variable gross margin). Hence, it serves as a crude approximation to the Lerner Index. A principal attraction of the price-cost margin is its ready availability at a level of aggregation that exactly matches the level at which industry concentration ratios are published.

Economic profit and accounting profit The analyst who has accomplished an acceptable match between performance and structure data is not yet home free. One must also be concerned about biases that might intrude as a result of the diverse accounting conventions companies adopt.

How companies value their assets—the denominator in many profitability indices and a key element in the imputed capital cost component of the π_s index—poses a number of potential problems. Whatever it is that gives the firms in an industry monopoly power is in a sense an asset that might be sold and purchased. If a firm holding or sharing in monopoly power is acquired, or if its acquisition by another enterprise will enhance the power to maintain elevated prices, the acquiring firm is apt to pay a higher price for the acquisition than if no such monopoly potential were present. After the merger, the value of assets may be written up so much that profit returns appear to be only 'normal.' This is more likely if the acquiring firm uses purchase accounting methods, bringing the acquired firm's assets onto its books at market value, than if it uses pooling of interest accounting, incorporating the acquired firm's assets at their book value.[19] The more extensive merger activity has been in an industry, the more likely it is that monopoly profit expectations will have been capitalized, so that accounting figures provide a downward-biased picture of monopoly power. Inflation also complicates matters. If the rate of inflation exceeds the rate at which technological advances raise the productivity of assets, older assets will tend to be undervalued relative to newly acquired assets. This can among other things cause the profitability of slower growing firms or industries to be overstated relative to that of entities with a comparatively young portfolio of assets. This problem became increasingly severe as the rate of inflation escalated beginning in the late 1960s.

Varying or inappropriate depreciation policies also engender difficulties. Most companies keep at least two sets of books—one for the tax collector and another for financial reporting purposes. Profit returns reported in the Internal Revenue Service's *Statistics of Income* series are much more apt to be reduced by accelerated depreciation than those appearing in company annual reports. One must also be wary of bizarre special cases. An extreme example is the petroleum industry, which in fiscal year 1967 showed an after-tax return on stockholders' equity of 5.6 percent according to IRS reports and 12.5 percent according to the Federal Trade Commission's compilation of company financial reports. The difference resulted largely from the use of arbitrary percentage depletion allowances on domestic oil production and massive credits against royalty payments to foreign nations in the petroleum companies' U.S. tax returns. A more general problem is the standard accounting convention of writing off research and development expenditures, exploratory oil well drilling costs, and advertising outlays as a current cost. Such outlays might actually be more in the nature of an investment yielding benefits over an extended time frame. To the extent that this is true, economic reality would be portrayed better by capitalizing the outlays and then depreciating them at an appropriate rate. Current costing tends to understate assets, and it may either overstate or understate annual costs, depending upon the firm's rate of growth. Generally, current costing overstates true economic profit returns when the true rate of profit exceeds the rate of growth of advertising or R & D outlays and understates them when the obverse holds.[20]

Owner-managed corporations pose additional problems. Owner-managers may pay themselves unrealistically high salaries in order to avoid double taxation (i.e., of corporate earnings and then dividends), although they might underpay themselves when corporate profits can be shielded by accelerated depreciation and capital gains are taxed at preferential rates.[21] A smaller proportion of concentrated industries' sales and profits tends to be contributed by small firms, which are more apt to be owner managed. Thus, systematic biases correlated with market structure may intrude unless appropriate exclusions and adjustments are effected.

Finally, when the profits of a corporation are broken out into more narrowly defined industry segments, as for the PIMS data and the Federal Trade Commission's Line of Business reporting program, a certain amount of arbitrariness in allocating common costs—e.g., the cost of maintaining central offices, joint sales forces, and broad-ranging basic research—is inescapable. Distortions may also arise through the setting of arbitrary interdivisional transfer prices. For instance, if the crude oil production division of an integrated petroleum company transfers its output to the company's refineries at prices exceeding those an arm's-length transaction would sustain, the crude oil division's profitability will be overstated and the refining operation's profitability understated.

There are various possible reactions to this formidable array of accounting problems. One is to hope that the errors introduced by varying or inappropriate accounting conventions are not systematically correlated with the industry structure characteristics under investigation, so that estimated structure-performance relationships are only attenuated by statistical noise but not biased in one direction or another. In certain cases, however, such optimism is clearly unwarranted. Thus, capitalization of monopoly returns through merger leads to a systematic underestimation of profit-concentration relationships, while any tendency for excessive owner-manager salaries to be paid on a more widespread scale in unconcentrated industries imparts the opposite bias. Another response is to throw up one's hands and despair of doing any meaningful research using accounting data. This errs on the side of excessive pessimism. A more constructive course is to devise methods of detecting and, if possible, adjusting for systematic biases. For example, the effects of inflation can be compensated by including in one's analysis capital stock vintage and growth variables. Mergers pose more difficult problems, but a crude adjustment is possible by introducing variables measuring their extent and recency or by estimating the values that would obtain if assets were entered into the books at preacquisition figures. Adjustments can be made for owner-manager salary biases, or the effect of excluding very small firms from one's analysis can be tested and reported. Sophisticated techniques have been developed to capitalize and depreciate advertising and R & D outlays improperly charged off as current costs. When profit data for multiple segments of companies are analyzed, the sensitivity of one's conclusions to alternative common cost allocation formulas can be tested. Vertically related segments with substantial transfers can be reintegrated for similar sensitivity tests, or separate variables measuring the relative volume of intersegment sales and purchases can be introduced to detect systematic

19. See Peter O. Steiner, *Mergers* (Ann Arbor: University of Michigan Press, 1975), pp. 109–27. Pooling of interest accounting was used extensively for mergers consummated during the 1960s, but only infrequently thereafter.

20. See Thomas R. Stauffer, "The Measurement of Corporate Rates of Return: A Generalized Formulation," *Bell Journal of Economics and Management Science* 2 (Autumn 1971): 434–69; and Leonard W. Weiss, "Advertising, Profits, and Corporate Taxes," *Review of Economics and Statistics* 51 (November 1969): 421–30.

21. See note 32, Chapter 4, p. 93 *supra*. See also Robert W. Kilpatrick, "Stigler on the Relationship between Industry Profit Rate and Market Concentration," *Journal of Political Economy* 76 (May–June 1968): 479–87.

The price and profit consequences
of market structure   273

transfer pricing biases. In short, much can be done if sufficient care and imagination are exercised. At the very least, the person analyzing structure-performance relationships statistically must be sensitive to the possible intrusion of biases so that their direction and probable magnitude can be acknowledged.

The 'independent' variables Careful attention must also be devoted to measuring the independent variables—that is, the variables whose values are believed to influence profitability. From the time of Bain's 1951 article, some index of seller concentration has played a central role. As we have seen in Chapter 3, there are many possible measures, with the Herfindahl-Hirschman Index and the humble concentration ratio (most commonly for the leading four sellers) being the principal contenders. In choosing among them, theoretical considerations are of course important. However, unless one is partial toward naive Cournot or dominant firm models assuming short-run profit maximization (e.g., because of their mathematical elegance),[22] it must be admitted that the guidance provided by theory is ambiguous. A certain amount of pragmatic empiricism, guarded against spurious inference by retesting across diverse data samples, seems warranted.

Much more important as a rule is getting structural indices reflecting economically meaningful definitions of the relevant markets. As Chapter 3 brought out, the concentration indices based upon Census industry definitions often fall short of satisfying this criterion. Poorly defined industries must be excluded, or adjustments must be made, if sensible analysis is to be done. It is not excessively cynical to observe that economists who believe market structure does not influence prices and profitability—a group that might be loosely identified as the University of Chicago school—tend to spend little time or effort worrying about faulty market definitions. As a result, their research frequently conforms all too closely to the "garbage in, garbage out" principle. We argued in Chapter 3 that more often than not, four-digit Census industries are too broadly defined, and therefore their concentration ratios tend to be too low in the sense that they understate the true level of structural monopoly or oligopoly. Failure

to control for this bias leads to inflated measurement errors and a concomitant tendency not to detect systematic relationships that might, if correctly measured, be statistically significant.[23]

There are also dangers in adjusting concentration ratios to reflect market realities more accurately, for if one knows that profits are high in some industry, one may be tempted to infer that structural monopoly power is present and adjust the concentration ratio upward to reflect that belief. This can lead to correlations that are spurious if the inference is unfounded. Ideally, adjustments should be based upon objective information independent of the performance indicators. Regional and local markets for manufactured products can be identified by a low sales value per unit of weight, a high ratio of transportation cost per dollar of sales over a standardized distance, or a short average shipment radius.[24] A crude adjustment for markets of supra-national scope can be made by introducing an additional variable reflecting imported goods sales as a fraction of total domestic consumption.[25] In compensating for inadequately delineated product markets, subjective judgment is inescapable. Such adjustments should if at all possible be made before the profit data are inspected, although in practice it is difficult to combine sufficient knowledge to make well-founded industry definition judgments with ignorance of industry performance. Here statistical analysis of structure-performance relationships becomes more of an art than a science.

Theory tells us that barriers to entry should also be important in explaining profitability differences. Concentration may be conducive to tacit or explicit collusion, high prices, and high profits, but unless there are appreciable barriers to entry, the profits will attract new entrants and the collusion will be undermined sooner or later. Monopoly returns may be realized despite low concentration if entry has been restricted and individual sellers' output cannot readily be expanded. Medical practice is the classic example.

There are two main approaches to the measurement of entry barriers for statistical analyses. One entails a more or less careful study of an industry's technology, raw material availability, spatial configuration, consumer buying practices, and legal environment followed by subjective judgments as to whether entry barriers are, say, *very high*, *substantial*, or *moderate to low*.[26] As with the adjustment of concentration ratios, there is a danger that these judgments will be colored by awareness of industries' profit records, leading to spurious correlations.

The other approach seeks objectively measurable indices consonant with the theory of entry deterrence. The Bain-Sylos-Modigliani theory suggests, for example, that prices can be held persistently above costs by a greater margin, the larger a minimum optimal scale firm is relative to the size of the market, the steeper cost curves are at less than minimum optimal scale, and the less elastic demand is.[27] Minimum optimal *plant* scales have been estimated by the engineering method for at least 33 industries, and statistical studies reveal that a much more readily accessible index—the ratio of the sales of plants at the midpoint of industry plant size distributions to total industry sales—is significantly correlated with engineering estimates.[28] Attempts have also been made, though with less compelling support, to use plant census data in identifying industries with particularly steep unit cost curves.[29] Since it may be harder to enter an industry requiring a massive capital investment, the product of midpoint plant sales times capital investment per dollar of sales has been used as a proxy for what Professor Bain called absolute capital requirement barriers to entry. And to add a variable that will compel more careful scrutiny later, the ratio of advertising expenditures to sales has been used as a proxy for the height of product differentiation barriers to entry.[30]

Other independent variables with a claim to inclusion in multiple regression equations explaining profitability must be mentioned more briefly. Both Cournot-type short-run profit-maximizing and Bain-Sylos limit pricing theories predict that firms with monopoly power will be able to gain larger supranormal returns when demand is relatively price inelastic in the neighborhood of the competitive price, all else being equal. However, obtaining demand elasticity estimates for a sizeable sample of industries is extremely difficult, and only one study has made a serious effort to do so.[31] Since even atomistically competitive industries can realize supranormal profits under disequilibrium conditions, the struc-

22. See note 50, Chapter 3, p. 59 *supra*.

23. It is well known that coefficient estimates are biased toward zero in a regression analysis when an independent variable is subject to random errors of measurement. See J. Johnston, *Econometric Methods* (New York: McGraw-Hill, 1963), pp. 148–75. Usually, however, the errors in measuring concentration are not random. There is a bias toward underestimation, and "true" concentration values that are large probably tend to be understated by a larger absolute amount than small values. When this occurs, regression coefficient estimates may be inflated relative to their true values, but standard errors will be inflated even more, biasing the test toward a finding of statistical insignificance.

24. See F. M. Scherer, Alan Beckenstein, Erich Kaufer, and R. D. Murphy, *The Economics of Multi-Plant Operation: An International Comparisons Study* (Cambridge, Mass.: Harvard University Press, 1975), pp. 183–87, 201, 408–13, 429–39; Leonard W. Weiss, "The Geographic Size of Markets in Manufacturing," *Review of Economics and Statistics* 54 (August 1972): 245–66; and note 61, Chapter 3, p. 65 *supra*. When the data needed to compute regional market concentration ratios are unavailable, Weiss's market count indices or the Scherer-Murphy transportation cost indices can be used as shift variables interacting multiplicatively with the uncorrected concentration ratios. A commonly used alternative with much less theoretical justification is an index reflecting the degree to which employment or sales in an industry's plants is dispersed geographically in proportion to population. To the extent that it has any logical validity at all, the dispersion index should interact multiplicatively with the unadjusted concentration ratios. This point is uniformly overlooked.

25. See Louis Esposito and Frances F. Esposito, "Foreign Competition and Domestic Industry Profitability," *Review of Economics and Statistics* 53 (November 1971): 343–53. Again, (1 − the import ratio) should interact multiplicatively with the concentration ratio, but there is many a slip between theory and practice.

26. See Joe S. Bain, *Barriers to New Competition* (Cambridge, Mass.: Harvard University Press, 1956), pp. 170–71.

27. See Chapter 8, pp. 244–46 *supra*.

28. See Scherer et al., *The Economics of Multi-Plant Operation*, pp. 182–83; and Leonard W. Weiss, "Optimal Plant Scale and the Extent of Suboptimal Capacity," in Robert T. Masson and P. D. Qualls, eds., *Essays on Industrial Organization in Honor of Joe S. Bain* (Cambridge, Mass.: Ballinger, 1976), pp. 126–34.

29. See Richard E. Caves, J. Khalilzadeh-Shirazi, and M. E. Porter, "Scale Economies in Statistical Analyses of Market Power," *Review of Economics and Statistics* 57 (May 1975): 133–40. For a less than convincing critique, see Brian C. Brush, "On the Large-Scale Measurement of Plant Scale Economies," *Industrial Organization Review* 4, No. 3 (1976): pp. 134–41.

30. For an approach to entry barrier measurement that combines nearly all these variables in a single index, see Dale Orr, "An Index of Entry Barriers and Its Application to the Market Structure Performance Relationship," *Journal of Industrial Economics* 23 (September 1974): 39–49.

31. William S. Comanor and Thomas A. Wilson, *Advertising and Market Power* (Cambridge, Mass.: Harvard University Press, 1974), pp. 82–92, 123–27. For an attempt to circumvent the problem by analyzing changes over time in profitability and concentration, assuming elasticities to be more or less unaltered, see Keith Cowling and Michael Waterson, "Price-Cost Margins and Market Structure," *Economica* 43 (May 1976): 267–74.

tural relationships for boom years should be estimated separately from those for normal or recession periods. Disequilibrium may also be specific to a particular industry. Therefore, a variable measuring industry growth over the past several years is often included in the expectation that profits will be abnormally high in fast-growth industries because investment in additional capacity has not caught up with demand. In periods of rapid inflation, on the other hand, this relationship may be offset by a tendency for rapidly growing industries to have a younger, higher cost plant and equipment mix than slowly growing industries. One might also expect profits to be higher in industries characterized by particularly high risks. Many studies have therefore attempted to include a measure of risk more or less solidly rooted in the theory of corporate finance.[32] We saw in Chapter 7 that the temptation to chisel on price agreements may be especially strong during business slumps in industries bearing a heavy burden of fixed costs. To capture this and other effects, variables measuring capital intensity—e.g., plant and equipment value per dollar of sales—have been introduced. And although other plausible candidates will make their appearance later, we mention only one more here. The typical structure-performance analysis ex-cludes explicit conduct variables, partly because they are so hard to measure and partly because it is believed that performance can be "explained" statistically merely on the basis of variables reflecting market structure and fundamental supply and demand conditions.[33] In a few cases, however, evidence of known price-fixing agreements or participation in trade associations has been incorporated into the explanatory model.[34]

The empirical findings

Continuing his early work, Professor Bain published a more ambitious study in 1956 that sought to take into account the effects of entry barriers as well as seller concentration.[35] Through extensive interviews and a questionnaire survey, he divided his sample of 20 manufacturing industries into three entry barrier height categories, with *very high* barriers defined to imply the ability to hold prices 10 percent or more above minimum unit costs without inducing significant new entry and *substantial* barriers as the ability similarly to hold prices 5 to 9 percent above costs. The mostly oligopolistic industries were also sorted into two

T 9.1 Average profit rates on stockholders' equity in two studies of concentration and entry barriers

Concentration	Very high barriers	Substantial barriers	Moderate to low barriers
1936–40			
High	$19.0_{(5)}$	$10.2_{(5)}$	$10.5_{(2)}$
Moderate	—$_{(0)}$	$7.0_{(3)}$	$5.3_{(5)}$
1947–51			
High	$19.0_{(5)}$	$14.0_{(5)}$	$15.4_{(2)}$
Moderate	—$_{(0)}$	$12.5_{(3)}$	$10.1_{(5)}$
1950–60			
High	$16.4_{(8)}$	$11.1_{(8)}$	$11.9_{(5)}$
Moderate	—$_{(0)}$	$12.2_{(1)}$	$8.6_{(8)}$

Adapted from Joe S. Bain, *Barriers to New Competition* (Cambridge, Mass.: Harvard University Press, 1956), pp. 192–200; and H. Michael Mann, "Seller Concentration, Barriers to Entry, and Rates of Return in Thirty Industries," *Review of Economics and Statistics* 48 (August 1966): 296–307. Subscripts in parentheses indicate the number of industries in each class.

seller concentration categories, with an eight-firm ratio of 70 as the dividing point. Average after-tax profit rates on stockholders' equity for the leading sellers in each industry were computed for the years 1936–40 and 1947–51. His results, along with the results from H. Michael Mann's similar study of 30 industries covering the 1950–60 period, are summarized in Table 9.1.

As hypothesized, the more concentrated industries had generally higher average rates of return than those with eight-firm ratios below 70. But in addition, highly concentrated industries with very high entry barriers (in Bain's sample, automobiles, cigarettes, liquor, typewriters, and quality fountain pens; plus chewing gum, ethical drugs, flat glass, nickel, and sulphur in Mann's augmented sample) had higher rates of return than the other highly concentrated industries categorized as having lower entry barriers.[36] Among the industries with substantial and moderate to low entry barriers, the relationship was mixed. Those with substantial barriers were less profitable if highly concentrated, but more profitable if moderately concentrated. However, none of these differences was statistically significant. Interpretation of the results is complicated to some extent by the not surprising fact that concentration ratios uniformly exceeded 69 in all the very high entry barrier industries. Recasting Mann's data in a form suitable for more discriminating multiple regression analysis, with C being a continuously scaled four-firm concentration ratio and LMB, SB, and VHB being zero-one class variables denoting the low to moderate, substantial, and very high barrier groups respectively, Weiss obtained the following equation:[37]

$$(9.4) \quad \pi_E = 7.8 + \underset{(.033)}{.047}\ C \cdot LMB + \underset{(.027)}{.050}\ C \cdot SB$$
$$+ \underset{(.024)}{.103}\ C \cdot VHB;\ N = 30,\ R^2 = 0.51$$

(Standard errors of the regression coefficients are given in parentheses.) The impact of concentration in raising profits is clearly and significantly greater in the very high barrier industries, where a 10-point rise in the concentration ratio was associated on average with a 1-point increase in the after-tax return on stockholders' equity.

The Bain and Mann studies have been criticized on a variety of grounds. One problem, of course, is the subjective character of the entry barrier classifications and, to a lesser degree, the concentration measurements. By taking a peculiarly broad definition of the automobile industry (including as independent producers the captive parts contractors to the leading assemblers), Singer was able to reclassify it to the moderate concentration group, and when weighted averages were computed, this plus the auto industry's vast size was sufficient to eliminate the difference in profitability between industries of high and moderate concentration.[38] Another problem is the

32. For an interesting attempt to characterize barriers to entry in terms of the risks facing *smaller* firms (as contrasted to all sellers), see Robert J. Stonebraker, "Corporate Profits and the Risk of Entry," *Review of Economics and Statistics* 58 (February 1976): 33–39.

33. See Chapter 1, p. 6 *supra*.

34. See especially Almarin Phillips, "An Econometric Study of Price-Fixing, Market Structure and Performance in British Industry in the Early 1950s," in Keith Cowling, ed., *Market Structure and Corporate Behaviour* (London: Gray-Mills, 1972), pp. 177–92; Peter Asch and Joseph J. Seneca, "Is Collusion Profitable?," *Review of Economics and Statistics* 58 (February 1976): 1–10; and William F. Long, "An Econometric Study of Performance in American Manufacturing Industry" (Ph.D. diss., University of California at Berkeley, 1971).

35. Bain, *Barriers to New Competition*, Chapters 6 and 7.

36. Hindsight reveals the limitations of these subjective classifications and the need for a full-blown dynamic analysis. Many of the very high barrier industries have experienced substantial new entry—e.g., in automobiles, from importers; in fountain pens and typewriters, through technological innovation; in nickel, because International Nickel's sulphide ore deposits become depleted; in sulphur, through by-product sales resulting from natural gas and petroleum desulphurization mandates; and in distilled liquor, because of a shift in consumption toward spirits that are not aged and perhaps also because Bain overestimated the strength of brand loyalties.

37. Weiss, "Quantitative Studies of Industrial Organization," p. 376. See also Stephen A. Rhoades, "Concentration, Barriers and Rates of Return: A Note," *Journal of Industrial Economics* 19 (November 1970): 82–88; and the reply by H. M. Mann and rejoinder by Rhoades in the *Journal of Industrial Economics* 19 (July 1971): 291–93; and *Journal of Industrial Economics* 20 (April 1972): 193–95. See also P. David Qualls, "Concentration, Barriers to Entry, and Long-Run Economic Profit Margins," *Journal of Industrial Economics* 20 (April 1972): 146–58, who reanalyzes the Bain and Mann data in terms of supranormal profit rates (i.e., π_S as defined earlier) and obtains generally similar but slightly stronger results. Cf. also note 89, Chapter 2, p. 41 *supra*.

38. Eugene M. Singer, "Industrial Organization: Price Models and Public Policy," *American Economic Review* 60 (May 1970): 91–97.

small size of the samples analyzed. Bain and Mann attempted to limit their samples to industries that were well defined and for which adequate profitability data could be obtained when companies were assigned to industries according to the primary industry criterion. Brozen has shown, as Bain anticipated in his 1951 article,[39] that when larger and less discriminating industry samples are analyzed using the same approach, the positive association between profitability and concentration deteriorates.[40] This is hardly surprising, for it is much more difficult to detect systematic relationships, if indeed they exist, when one's independent variables are badly measured. Brozen's broader sample suffers from the failure to recognize regional markets for such industries as nonalcoholic beverages and beer, and from excessively broad product line definitions for glass products, flavoring extracts, drugs and medicines, industrial chemicals, cutting tools (including razor blades), and perfumes, cosmetics, and toiletries, among others. Still another Brozen criticism—that Bain and Mann caught their concentrated industries during a period of disequilibrium when profits were abnormally high—will be deferred for fuller consideration later.[41]

The problem of drawing large samples for which performance data are correctly matched to structural data can be overcome, at the cost of accepting other limitations, by analyzing Census price-cost margin (PCM) statistics. Collins and Preston were the first to plow that furrow systematically.[42] Using virtually exhaustive U.S. manufacturing industry samples for 1958 and 1963, and correcting for poorly defined markets only through the inclusion of a geographic dispersion index, they found consistent but typically modest positive associations between price-cost margins and four-firm seller concentration ratios, both with and without the inclusion of a capital intensity variable. The concentration-PCM associations were generally stronger for consumer goods industries than for producer goods industries. They were also stronger for industries in which concentration was stable or increasing than for those in which it was decreasing.[43] There have been many subsequent studies extending the basic Collins-Preston approach by adding further plausible explanatory variables. One by Weiss is among the most comprehensive and serves to illustrate the variables used.[44] Analyzing 1963 data on 399 Census industries, he estimated *inter alia* the following regression equation, with the price-cost margins expressed in percentage terms:

$$(9.5) \quad PCM = 16.3 + \underset{(.024)}{.050} \; C - \underset{(.010)}{.029} \; DISP$$
$$+ \underset{(.016)}{.119} \; CAP/S + \underset{(.18)}{1.30} \; A/S$$
$$- \underset{(4.2)}{1.9} \; CAO + \underset{(.136)}{.023} \; INV/S$$
$$+ \underset{(.09)}{.26} \; GROW + \underset{(.00030)}{.00083} \; CONS \cdot C$$
$$+ \underset{(.130)}{.095} \; MID - \underset{(.020)}{.033} \; PLANTCAP;$$
$$N = 399, \; R^2 = .427$$

Price-cost margins were positively and significantly associated with seller concentration C, the ratio of capital to sales CAP/S, the ratio of advertising outlays to sales A/S, past output growth $GROW$, and a shift variable $CONS \cdot C$, i.e., the product of the concentration ratio times the percentage of industry sales going to consumer goods markets. Margins were significantly lower, the less dispersed production was geographically, as indicated by high values of $DISP$. Variables estimating the ratio of central office employment to total employment CAO and the ratio of inventories to sales INV/S were statistically insignificant. So also were two variables included to account for entry barriers: the ratio of midpoint plant sales to total industry sales MID and the estimated amount of capital $PLANTCAP$ required by a midpoint plant—the latter with an unexpected negative sign.

One could quibble at length about the results of these and the many other studies attempting to relate some index of profitability to concentration, entry barriers, and other variables. To do so would be to lose track of the main message in the jumble of distracting noise. Despite sometimes formidable mismeasurement, there is a rather robust tendency for a positive association to

278

emerge between seller concentration and profitability. No simple statistical summary does justice to the diversity of methods, subsamples, and results, but this conclusion emerges unmistakably from scrutiny of the 54 studies covered in Weiss's survey article.[45]

To be sure, many of the correlations are weak, and deviant results can be found. Exceptions to the general pattern appear to be of three main types. First, the positive concentration-profits relationship definitely broke down during the booming period of readjustment immediately following World War II, and it may have weakened more briefly during subsequent booms. Second, although a few studies yield conflicting evidence, there appears to be a tendency for the concentration-profits association to be stronger in consumer goods industries than in producer goods industries. This might stem from industrial buyers' greater knowledge and their superior ability to play one oligopolistic seller off against another. We shall explore this hypothesis further in the next chapter. Third, concentration indices and such entry barrier measures as the midpoint plant/industry sales ratio and the amount of capital invested in a midpoint plant are often highly correlated with one another. If one is high, the others tend to have high values as well. Because of this, they compete with one another for explanatory power. It is quite common when such collinear variables are entered into a regression equation that one dominates the explanation while the others prove to be statistically insignificant or even, because of a very few deviant observations, take on paradoxical negative signs. Sometimes it is the concentration variable that is overwhelmed, but in equation (9.5) concentration dominates the MID and PLANTCAP variables. It is worth noting that the negative partial correlation between Weiss's *PCM* and *PLANTCAP* variables turns positive when the other entry barrier proxies and concentration are excluded.[46] What this says in effect is that all the variables reflect a closely intertwined constellation of structural attributes, and that they are not measured precisely enough, or there is too little intrinsic structural variation, to disentangle the links. Only by obtaining a larger, more varied, and/or more precisely measured sample can one

avoid the difficulties engendered by collinear explanatory variables.

Assuming then that profit rates in fact tend to rise with market concentration, what is the exact nature of the relationship? Is it linear or nonlinear, continuous or discontinuous? The linearity question is sometimes posed in terms of a choice between the simple concentration ratio and the Herfindahl-Hirschman Index. Despite the difficulty of obtaining well-measured *H* Index data, there have been several comparative tests spanning a variety of industry samples.[47] The results are equivocal. In some cases the *H* Index exhibited superior explanatory power either by itself or, in Kwoka's particularly comprehensive analysis, because it proved to be less collinear with other structural variables. In other instances, the four-firm concentration ratio did better. The dif-

39. "Relation of Profit Rate to Industry Concentration," pp. 314–17.

40. See Yale Brozen, "Bain's Concentration and Rates of Return Revisited," *Journal of Law and Economics* 14 (October 1971): 351–69; and "Concentration and Profits: Does Concentration Matter?," *Antitrust Bulletin* 19 (Summer 1974): 381–99.

41. See Brozen, "The Antitrust Task Force Deconcentration Recommendation," *Journal of Law and Economics* 13 (October 1970): 279–92; and *idem*, "Concentration and Structural and Market Disequilibria," *Antitrust Bulletin* 16 (Summer 1971): 241–48.

42. Norman R. Collins and Lee E. Preston, "Price-Cost Margins and Industry Structure," *Review of Economics and Statistics* 51 (August 1969): 271–86; and *Concentration and Price-Cost Margins in Manufacturing Industries* (Berkeley: University of California Press, 1970). For a precursor that found a similar positive price-cost margin-concentration relationship for the years 1931 and 1933, see Alfred C. Neal, *Industrial Concentration and Price Inflexibility* (Washington, D.C.: American Council on Public Affairs, 1942), pp. 130–34.

43. Similar results are reported for 1963 and 1967 by Stanley I. Ornstein, "Empirical Uses of the Price-Cost Margin," *Journal of Industrial Economics* 24 (December 1975): 105–17. However, the correlations are weakened substantially when the variables are analyzed logarithmically, which, Ornstein argues, is theoretically preferable. His theoretical argument rests on the assumption that price-cost margins are properly interpreted as returns to capital, which is doubtful.

44. Weiss, "The Concentration-Profits Relationship and Antitrust," p. 229. Revised coefficient values were kindly provided by Professor Weiss.

45. Weiss, "The Concentration-Profits Relationship," pp. 201–20.

46. Weiss, "The Concentration-Profits Relationship," pp. 202, 223–25, 230–31. See also Caves et al., "Scale Economies in Statistical Analyses of Market Power," pp. 135–40.

ferences for the most part tended to be small, suggesting that a verdict be deferred until data of greater quality and abundance are tested.

More extensive and sophisticated research has been done on whether the relationship between profitability and concentration is continuous (i.e., with a steady upward progression of profit rates as concentration increases) or discontinuous. The results for a diversity of profitability indices and U.S. industry samples are remarkably uniform: Virtually all show a distinct upsurge in profit rates as the four-firm concentration ratio passes through a range somewhere between 45 and 59 percent.[48] They lend support to Chamberlin's hypothesis that respect for mutual oligopolistic interdependence tends to coalesce at some critical level of seller concentration.[49]

The causal nexus: pricing power or cost differences? We have come as far as we can without raising a fundamental question. Up to this

point it has been assumed that the higher average profitability observed for concentrated industries comes from the power to elevate prices that monopoly confers. There is, however, an alternative hypothesis: that the relationships reflect the superior efficiency of large oligopolistic sellers.[50]

To explore its logic, let us visualize two industries, A and O, each producing an essentially homogeneous product. The industries differ in the first instance in their cost conditions, as illustrated in Figure 9.1. In Industry A the economies of scale are exhausted quickly, after which production occurs at constant long-run unit cost, as shown by the broken cost curve. In Industry O there are persistent scale economies out to an output of 40 units, as shown by the solid cost curve. Let the size distribution of firms in each industry be provisionally characterized by the circled letters $F_1, F_2, \ldots, F_5$ on each cost curve. Now suppose there is sufficient monopoly power in each industry for prices to be raised to $4.50

F 9.1 Economies of scale and price-cost relationships

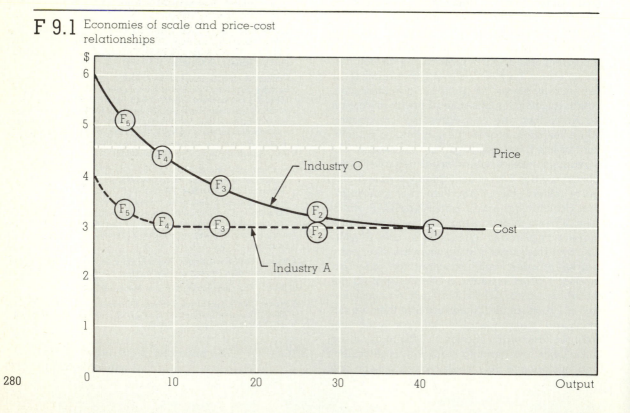

per unit—well above minimum unit cost. In Industry A, firms of all sizes will realize substantial and more or less uniform supranormal profits. In Industry O, on the other hand, the largest seller F_1 will have the highest profit rate and small firms will realize no supranormal profits (e.g., F_4) or even negative returns (like F_5). If the ability to elevate prices stems from concentration, a positive correlation between profitability and concentration will presumably emerge for all sizes of firms if cost conditions are like those of Industry A, whereas it will materialize only for the larger firms if the situation is more like that of Industry O. There is a fair amount of evidence that the correlations are stronger for the four or so largest sellers in an industry than for others, while for quite small fringe sellers, they tend to disappear altogether.[51] This suggests that conditions in oligopolistic industries may more nearly approximate those of Industry O than Industry A. Of course, to some extent this prophesy may be self-fulfilling when there are economies of scale, since the elevation of prices above minimum unit cost both attracts and permits the survival of fringe firms so small that their inefficiently high unit costs leave no margin for economic profits.

Suppose we now reinterpret the numbers on the output axis of Figure 9.1 as market shares. With such compelling scale economies, one would expect Industry O to be, or become, tightly oligopolistic. The pull toward concentration is much weaker in Industry A (although mergers, the operation of Gibrat's law, and other influences could lead to concentration levels higher than those needed for minimum-cost operation). If Industry A firms fail to become much larger than F_4 or F_5, concentration will be modest and it will be difficult to sustain price levels much above the minimum unit cost of $3.00. The type O industries with compelling scale economies will thus gravitate toward concentrated structures and high profit margins, while type A industries are more apt to have atomistic structures and low profit margins. If this is true, it might be argued that the high profits observed in oligopolistic industries are simply the result of the largest sellers' superior efficiency, and hence merit nothing but admiration.[52]

One must nevertheless inquire, Why don't the smaller type O firms expand to attain equally low

(47) See George J. Stigler, "A Theory of Oligopoly," *Journal of Political Economy* 72 (February 1964): 57–58 (reporting stronger rank correlations for the *H* Index in a sample of 17 U.S. manufacturing industries); Weiss, "Quantitative Studies of Industrial Organization," p. 375 (analyzing price-cost margins for 34 industries); John Kwoka, "The Effect of Market Share Distribution on Industry Performance," *Review of Economics and Statistics* 61 (February 1979): 101–109 (studying price-cost margins in 314 manufacturing industries); J. C. H. Jones, Leonard Laudadio, and M. Percy, "Market Structure and Profitability in Canadian Manufacturing Industry," *Canadian Journal of Economics* 6 (August 1973): 356–68 (in which the four-firm concentration ratio explained profit returns better than the *H* Index for a sample of 30 Canadian consumer goods industries); and D. G. McFetridge, "Market Structure and Price-Cost Margins," *Canadian Journal of Economics* 6 (August 1973): 345–55 (giving a slight edge to the square of the *H* Index for 43 Canadian three-digit industries).

48. Robert W. Kilpatrick, "The Choice Among Alternative Measures of Industrial Concentration," *Review of Economics and Statistics* 49 (May 1967): 258–60; Stephen A. Rhoades, "The Concentration-Profitability Relationship," *Antitrust Bulletin* 18 (Summer 1973): 333–54; Rhoades and J. M. Cleaver, "The Nature of the Concentration-Price/Cost Margin Relationship for 353 Manufacturing Industries: 1967," *Southern Economic Journal* 40 (July 1973): 90–102; James W. Meehan, Jr., and Thomas Duchesneau, "The Critical Level of Concentration," *Journal of Industrial Economics* 22 (September 1973): 21–36; James E. Dalton and David W. Penn, "The Concentration-Profitability Relationship: Is There a Critical Concentration Ratio?," *Journal of Industrial Economics* 25 (December 1976): 133–42; Lawrence J. White, "Searching for the Critical Industrial Concentration Ratio," in Stephen Goldfeld and Richard E. Quandt, eds., *Studies in Non-Linear Estimation* (Cambridge, Mass.: Ballinger, 1976), pp. 61–75; and Donald T. Sant, "A Polynomial Approximation for Switching Regressions with Applications to Market Structure-Performance Studies," Federal Trade Commission staff working paper (Washington, D.C.: Federal Trade Commission, February 1978).

In "The Effect of Market Share Distribution," Kwoka observes a significant jump in price-cost margins when the *two-firm* concentration ratio crosses a 35 percent threshold. Continuously scaled two-firm ratios also exhibited more explanatory power than their four-firm counterparts, even though they explained profitability less well than a dichotomous two-firm index. This could reflect the crucial role of industry leaders—e.g., in providing price leadership—as a determinant of industry performance. However, there is reason to believe that statistical biases may also have influenced the results. Monte Carlo studies reveal that even when industries' price-raising propensities depend upon the four-firm concentration ratio alone, the confounding of price-raising and scale economies effects in industry cross-section studies leads to higher observed correlations for two-firm than four-firm concentration ratios. See David Ravenscraft, "Price-Raising and Cost-Reducing Effects in Profit-Concentration Studies: A Monte Carlo Simulation Analysis," (Ph.D. diss., Northwestern University, 1980).

Similar statistical biases may underlie the observed tendency for increases in the market shares of middle-ranked sellers—i.e., the third to eighth largest—to be associated with *falling* profitability. For early discussions of such hypotheses, compare Richard A. Miller, "Marginal Concentration Ratios and Industrial Profit Rates," *Southern Economic Journal* 34 (October 1967): 259–67; Collins and Preston, "Price-Cost Margins and Industry Structure," pp. 274–76; and Miller, "Marginal Concentration Ratios as Market Structure Variables," *Review of Economics and Statistics* 53 (August 1971): 289–93.

49. Cf. Chapter 5, p. 156 *supra*.

unit costs, in the process driving prices down to competitive levels? Some barrier to fringe firm expansion or the entry of new low-cost firms must be present. And even if such barriers exist, why don't large F_1 and F_2 firms expand their own output further, again driving down the price? The most plausible answer is that they recognize their monopoly power, and probably also the barriers to entry; and therefore they refrain from competing away their supranormal profits. A more reasonable interpretation, then, is that in type O situations, society bears the burden of monopolistic pricing to get the benefits of large-scale, low-cost production. If economies of scale are as compelling as the cost function drawn for Industry O implies, the sacrifices in efficiency resulting from an alternative, less oligopolistic industry organization could be prohibitive.

An additional, more subtle, statistical point must be noted. If type O industries gravitate toward high concentration, the largest, most profitable enterprises will produce the lion's share of industry output, and their profits will therefore dominate industry averages. Even if the largest firms in type A industries enjoy scale economies forgone by their smaller rivals, their unit cost advantages will not be as great as in the type O case. And larger firms in less concentrated type A industries will carry less weight in industry profit averages than an equivalent number of leading sellers in concentrated type O industries. Thus, the *average* level of profits will be higher in highly concentrated industries both because of the superior profitability of the largest sellers and the greater weight accorded their profits. Even if the equivalent number of largest firms in less concentrated industries realize equally high profit margins, the differential weight given to leaders in more concentrated industries will lead to positive concentration-profitability correlations in aggregated industry cross-sectional analyses. The correlations should tend to deteriorate when the analysis focuses on subsets of sellers—e.g., the top four, the next four, and so on. Such a pattern is in fact discernible.[53] Moreover, the correlations for aggregated industry data may to some extent be spurious or seriously biased. Through theoretical and Monte Carlo simulation analyses, Ravenscraft has demonstrated that

positive and statistically significant concentration-profitability correlations regularly appear in industry cross-section studies even when there are *no* price-raising effects associated with concentration, but when larger sellers enjoy economies of scale.[54] His work raises doubts whether any confident generalizations about causation can be drawn from studies relating aggregated industry profits to seller concentration.

The general argument here rests in part upon the premise that industries sufficiently oligopolistic to sustain high profit margins have cost structures more like that of Industry O in Figure 9.1 than that of Industry A. Doubts on this point are suggested by the evidence reviewed in Chapter 4 that minimum optimal plant scales, and even minimum optimal multi-plant firm scales, are characteristically small in relation to the size of U.S. markets, and that leading firms tend to be much larger than they need to be to realize all or most of the advantages of size.[55] Yet that evidence, and especially the modest quantity of multi-plant firm evidence, might conceivably be less than fully representative of conditions in tightly oligopolistic, high-profit industries, or it might not sufficiently account for product-specific scale economies and the product varietal segmentation of markets. We would therefore prefer to have a more direct confrontation of the concentration-efficiency-monopoly power question. Toward that ambitious goal we press forward.

Industry concentration vs. individual firm market shares Retaining for the moment our assumption that an industry's products are homogeneous, an industry structure that facilitates the exercise of monopoly power should permit both large and small sellers to enjoy elevated prices. Given the level of prices, the realization of scale economies should lead to a systematic positive association between relative firm size—i.e., as reflected in individual firm market shares—and profit margins. If then one had individual firm performance and structure data sufficiently varied and precisely measured to distinguish structural characteristics underlying industry-wide monopoly power from relative firm size differences, it should be possible statistically to disentangle monopoly from scale economies effects and to tell whether the "typical" industrial case conforms more closely to type O or type A in Figure 9.1. Ravenscraft's simulation studies show that when four-firm industry concentration ratios *and* individual firm market share variables are introduced together into disaggregated regression equations seeking to explain individual sellers' profitability, and when price-raising effects are related solely to four-firm industry concentration while unit costs fall with rising market share, the two structural variables do rather well disentangling price-raising and scale economies effects.[56] There may be slight biases attributable to the misspecification of nonlinearities, but the biases are smaller and of less consistent direction than those intruding when concentration ratios alone are employed to explain profitability in aggregated industry cross sections affected by economies of scale.

Several empirical studies have used whole-company data to examine the relationship between profitability, weighted average industry concentration, and weighted average individual firm market shares.[57] All but Shepherd's effort, which used a peculiarly specified industry structure measure, revealed statistically significant profit increases with *both* higher industry concentration *and* higher firm market shares or an interaction of the two variables. The implication is that both monopoly price raising and scale economy or other effects related to firm size coexist.

Far more suitable for pinpointing the relative roles of industry structure and firm market shares are data disaggregated to the level of individual sellers' lines of business. The PIMS data set was the only such body of data systematically analyzed at the time this book was written.[58] Four-firm concentration ratios were found in PIMS data analyses to be positively associated with businesses' return on investment (ROI), defined as net income before the deduction of taxes and interest charges expressed as a percentage of stockholders' equity plus debt. However, market shares exhibited a considerably more powerful and consistent influence. For some 1,082 businesses, the bivariate correlation between ROI averaged over four-year intervals during the 1970s and the four-firm concentration ratio was +0.09; between

ROI and market share it was +0.32. In contrast to the results earlier investigators obtained with aggregated company data, only the market share variable was statistically significant when both structural indices were introduced together. PIMS data studies reveal that increasing sample businesses' market share from 10 to 50 percent led on average to a doubling of ROI—from 16 to 32 per-

(50) See in particular Harold Demsetz, "Industry Structure, Market Rivalry, and Public Policy," *Journal of Law and Economics* 16 (April 1973): 1–10; Demsetz, "Two Systems of Belief About Monopoly," in Goldschmid, ed., *Industrial Concentration*, pp. 175–81; and Yale Brozen, "Concentration and Structural and Market Disequilibria," pp. 245–48.

(51) In addition to the references in note 50, see Collins and Preston, "Price-Cost Margins and Industry Structure," pp. 280–83; Ronald S. Bond and Warren Greenberg, "Industry Structure, Market Rivalry, and Public Policy: A Comment," with a reply by Harold Demsetz, *Journal of Law and Economics* 19 (December 1976): 201–209; and John R. Carter, "Collusion, Efficiency, and Antitrust," *Journal of Law and Economics* 21 (1978), pp. 435–44. Bond and Greenberg make the important observation that the firms for which the correlations disappear are very much smaller—at least seven times as small on the average—as those for which the correlations persist.

(52) This appears to be the kernel of the Demsetz argument.

53. See for example Demsetz, "Two Systems of Belief," p. 178; Weiss, "The Concentration-Profits Relationship," pp. 228–29; and Edward M. Miller, "Determinants of Profit Margins in Manufacturing," *Antitrust Bulletin*, forthcoming in volume 24 (1979).

54. Ravenscraft, "Price-Raising and Cost-Reducing Effects."

55. See Chapter 4, pp. 117–19 *supra*.

56. Ravenscraft, "Price-Raising and Cost-Reducing Effects."

57. See Dalton and Penn, *The Quality of Data*; Imel and Helmberger, "Estimation of Structure-Profit Relationships," p. 625; W. G. Shepherd, "The Elements of Market Structure," *Review of Economics and Statistics* 54 (February 1972): 25–37; Bradley T. Gale, "Market Share and Rate of Return," *Review of Economics and Statistics* 54 (November 1972): pp. 412–25; and James A. Dalton and Stanford L. Levin, "Market Power: Concentration and Market Share," *Industrial Organization Review* 5, No. 1 (1977): 27–35.

58. The summary of PIMS analyses here relies heavily upon Bradley T. Gale and Ben S. Branch, "Concentration versus Market Share: Which Determines Performance and Why Does It Matter?" (manuscript, Strategic Planning Institute, Cambridge, Mass., February 1979); Gale and Branch, "Scale Economies: The Evidence from a Cross-Sectional Analysis of Business Unit Data," (manuscript, February 1979); Schoeffler, "Cross-Sectional Study"; Sidney Schoeffler, Robert D. Buzzell, and Donald F. Heany, "Impact of Strategic Planning on Profit Performance," *Harvard Business Review* (March–April 1974): 137–45; Buzzell, Gale, and Ralph G. M. Sultan, "Market Share—A Key to Profitability," *Harvard Business Review* 79 (January–February 1975): 97–106; and various issues of the Strategic Planning Institute's *PIMSLETTER on Business Strategy*.

cent. These results suggest that sellers with large market shares enjoy advantages smaller rivals lack and that the elevation of prices above costs by such sellers does no more than reflect those advantages, rather than the effects of seller concentration per se. What the nature of the advantages is, therefore, becomes a question of paramount interest.

In addressing the question, investigators using the PIMS data encounter two special problems. For one, the sample is in important respects not fully representative of all business enterprises or even of all larger companies. The *median* PIMS sample business in 1977 ranked second in its served market, with a market share of 19 percent. Thus, industry leaders were significantly overrepresented. Second, and probably more important, the data are submitted in such a way that it is impossible to cluster individual businesses by industry. As a result, one cannot distinguish type A from type O industries—i.e., those in which the advantages of size peter out quickly from those in which there are continuing advantages out to very large market shares. What is observed is an unknown mixture of strong, weak, and negligible size effects. Ravenscraft's studies indicate that the greater the diversity of industry minimum optimal scales within a sample of individual businesses, the more likely it is that errors-in-variables biases will be impounded in the structural coefficient estimates, and especially in the industry concentration coefficient estimates.[59]

Despite these problems, further analysis of PIMS data provides persuasive evidence that at least some of the observed interfirm profit variations reflect economies of scale.[60] Participating businesses were asked to estimate the level of their unit materials, production, and distribution costs as a percentage of the comparable costs of their three leading rivals. For both homogeneous and differentiated goods producers, this index of "relative direct cost" tended to be lower, the larger a firm's market share was. Entities with high market shares had significantly lower ratios of capital investment and inventories to sales in differentiated goods markets, but not in homogeneous goods fields. In homogeneous goods industries, marketing expenditures tended to consume a smaller fraction of the sales dollar when market shares were high. After controlling for differences in vertical integration, purchases per dollar of sales declined with rising market share, but manufacturing costs did not rise proportionately. This suggests that firms with large market shares may have been able to purchase materials and components on especially favorable terms or to produce them internally at costs lower than outside purchase prices. On this more will be said in Chapter 10. All in all, the early PIMS analyses imply large-firm cost advantages, real and pecuniary, greater than those uncovered through the author's own interview survey of 12 manufacturing industries.[61] Whether the PIMS findings will persist for a larger and more representative cross section of companies can probably be tested only when the Federal Trade Commission's Line of Business data set becomes available.

To advance farther, we must open the gates to an alternative conjecture held in abeyance up to this point. Is it possible that the higher profit margins associated with larger market shares reflect not lower costs (or not *only* lower costs) but higher prices than those of smaller rivals? If products were homogeneous this would be improbable; but product differentiation is widespread in modern industry, and so the homogeneity assumption must be relaxed. Again, the PIMS data provide a number of important clues. If superior ability to differentiate one's products were at work, one might expect market share to have a stronger impact on profits for consumer goods than for producers' goods. This conjecture is supported.[62] Further analysis reveals that the market share relationship for industrial products interacts with the number of customers served. When customers are few, profits increase more with rising market share than when buyers are fragmented, suggesting that sellers with large market shares are better able to withstand downward pressure on price exerted by buyers with countervailing power. On this, too, more will be said in Chapter 10. The lesson for present purposes is that the market share-profit relationship apparently does include some price effects.

Further insight into the relationships can be gained by examining information PIMS companies provided on the relative levels of their product quality and prices. They were asked *inter alia* to estimate the percentage of their sales volume accounted for by products and services *assessed from the perspective of the customer* as superior, equivalent, and inferior in quality to those of the leading three rivals. On average, the PIMS participants rated their products as superior much more often than inferior. However, there was a strong market share effect. Half the businesses with market shares of 27 percent or more reported having superior quality on average, compared to only 23 percent of the businesses with market shares of less than 12 percent. Furthermore, profitability generally varied with differences in perceived quality, holding market share constant, as Table 9.2 shows.[63]

Participants were also asked to estimate the average level of their selling prices as a fraction of their *three largest* competitors' prices. On the average, PIMS firms' prices were about 3.5 percent higher. (Whether larger differentials prevailed with respect to smaller companies is unknown.) For differentiated products, on which one would expect quality and price differentials to be potentially important, a multiple regression relating the reporting businesses' relative price indices (*RPI*) to relative quality (*RQ*) and a market share index *MS* was as follows:[64]

(9.6) $RPI = 1.05 + 3.14\ RQ$
$$(.26)$$
$$+\ 0.51\ MS;\ R^2 = .188,\ N = 761$$
$$(.26)$$

T 9.2 Relationship between profits, market share, and product quality in the PIMS sample

Perceived product quality	Market share		
	Under 12%	12–26%	Over 26%
	ROI	ROI	ROI
Inferior	5%	11%	20%
Average	10	18	22
Superior	17	18	28

Adapted from Sidney Schoeffler, Robert D. Buzzell, and Donald F. Heany, "Impact of Strategic Planning on Profit Performance," *Harvard Business Review* 79 (March-April 1974): p. 141.

Both independent variables are statistically significant, although the relative quality variable has a much higher *t*-ratio and considerably more systematic explanatory power. Evidently, if the PIMS firms generally and the high market share businesses in particular charge higher prices and realize ample profit returns, they also place in the balance products and services of superior perceived quality. But the definition of quality here, it must be emphasized, is a subjective one. It seems certain that the makers of Budweiser beer would have ranked their product as superior in perceived quality to those of the leading three rivals, just as IBM would judge its computer services to be superior in customers' perception, even though 'objective' technical evaluations might lead to a different conclusion. On this we shall have a good deal more to say in Chapter 14. The main point for the moment is that the profit differences associated with market share appear to embody a complex mixture of scale economy, materials cost, selling price, and product differentiation advantages.

Advertising and product differentiation An alternative approach to assessing the role played by product differentiation is to develop variables capturing its effects directly. Typically, this has meant using a variable relating company or industry advertising expenditures to total sales. The results have been both striking and controversial. Comanor and Wilson did the pio-

59. Ravenscraft, "Price-Raising and Cost-Reducing Effects."

60. See especially Gale and Branch, "Concentration versus Market Share"; and Buzzell et al., "Market Share—A Key to Profitability."

61. Scherer et al., *The Economics of Multi-Plant Operation*, especially Chapter 7.

62. Gale and Branch, "Concentration versus Market Share." Compare Schoeffler, "Cross-Sectional Study," p. 113, who found the opposite result using an earlier PIMS sample containing fewer consumer goods businesses.

63. The tendency for profit returns to increase with perceived quality also holds consistently when the businesses are subdivided into consumer durable, consumer nondurable, capital goods, raw materials, components, and supplies groups.

64. Gale and Branch, "Concentration versus Market Share."

The price and profit consequences of market structure **285**

neering research.[65] They hypothesized that in industries with substantial advertising expenditures, product differentiation barriers to entry would be relatively high for several reasons, i.e.: (1) newcomers would have to incur disproportionately high advertising outlays per dollar of sales to win patronage away from established sellers enjoying significant brand preferences; (2) economies of scale in advertising favored firms with sizeable market positions; and (3) the absolute amount of capital needed for successful entry was higher when an entrant had to advertise intensively along with setting up production operations. They therefore introduced an advertising/sales ratio variable into regression equations seeking to explain profitability in 41 consumer goods industries. It was positively and significantly correlated with profitability, holding constant other variables such as concentration, demand growth, and the relative size and capital requirements of a typical plant. On average, an increase in the advertising/sales ratio from 1 to 10 percent was accompanied by an increase of 3.0 to 4.5 percentage points in the after-tax return on stockholders' equity, other variables being equal.

The Comanor-Wilson approach has been replicated many times using diverse profitability measures and firm or industry samples. The results have proved to be quite robust, at least for manufacturing industries.[66] Advertising/sales ratios appear consistently to be positively correlated with indices of profitability. Nevertheless, it is conceivable that these results are affected by subtle biases. Three possibilities deserve attention.

First, as we observed before, advertising spending might properly be viewed as a capital outlay with potentially long-lasting effects. Accounting for it as a current expense, as was done in the original Comanor-Wilson article and many other studies, can lead to upward-biased profitability values when profit rates exceed the growth rate of advertising outlays.[67] This in turn implies upward-biased estimates of the effect advertising has on profitability. Some attempts to correct for this problem by capitalizing and then depreciating advertising outlays show that the early Comanor-Wilson findings remain essentially unaltered.[68] However, the positive correlation between the advertising/sales ratio and profitability fades to insignificance when the effects of advertising are assumed to be very long lived, that is, when the applicable depreciation rate is quite low.[69] The crucial question is whether the effects of advertising depreciate fairly rapidly, e.g., at a rate of 33 to 90 percent per year, or slowly, e.g., at the 5 percent rate favored by Bloch. The higher range of depreciation rates appears more plausible, but the issue is still in dispute.[70]

Second, there is a problem in ascertaining the direction of causation.[71] As the margin between price and unit production cost rises, sellers have a greater incentive to compete for additional business on nonprice bases, e.g., by increasing their advertising outlays. Ample gross profit margins induce high advertising—the reverse of the causal nexus assumed in the hypothesis that high advertising reflects barriers to entry, which in turn lead to high net profits.[72] To untangle these differing chains of causation, one needs a properly specified simultaneous equations model, preferably using data for narrowly defined lines of business spanning a considerable period of time. Simultaneous equation model tests falling appreciably short of this data quality ideal provide consistent but generally weak support for the hypothesis that higher industry profits do *flow from* relatively high advertising/sales ratios.[73] Further insight into this question will no doubt emerge as data on profits and costs in companies' individual lines of business become available.

Third, the positive association between advertising and profitability does not hold up consistently when samples are subdivided into smaller subsets. Porter found that for "nonconvenience goods" industries—that is, those in which retailers' salespersons provide substantial in-store assistance to consumers and thereby influence product choices—the effect of advertising on profits was positive but weak.[74] But for small-ticket "convenience goods" typically purchased on a self-service basis with little shopping around, a powerful positive profits-advertising correlation emerged. Bass and associates broke company data down into clusters of at most a very few industries and observed further attenuation of profits-advertising correlations, concluding from their results that no homogeneous statistical relationship existed.[75] However, this approach loses sight of important theoretical considerations, since if heavy advertising reflects product differentiation barriers to entry, it is the differences *among* industries that primarily matter. The closer one comes to analyzing purely intra-industry differences, the more any positive interindustry effects will be attenuated. Indeed, if there are economies of scale in advertising, as seems plausible, and if firms within an industry have similar markups of price over production cost, one would expect to find a *negative* correlation between profit rates and advertising/sales ratios at the intra-industry level of analysis.

In sum, there is reason to believe that for at least an important group of industries intense advertising is associated with relatively high profits. This relationship presumably reflects the ability of sellers to hold the prices of strongly differentiated products above costs. We shall return for a fuller exploration of the phenomenon in Chapter 14.

Direct evidence on structure-price relationships Through the statistical analysis of profit data, we have found that it may be difficult to disentangle the price-raising effects of concentrated market structure from the cost-depressing effects of scale economies realized by firms with relatively large market shares. An alternative approach to the problem is to analyze structure-price relationships directly.[76] This is seldom possible, largely because of the apples and oranges problem in comparing the prices of diverse industries' products. However, when the same commodity is sold in numerous well-defined regional or local markets, meaningful comparisons can be made.

Money is an unusually homogeneous product and, at least for consumer-type loans, the relevant markets are local. There have been numerous studies of the relationship between local market structure and the prices consumers pay for money (i.e., the interest rate on loans) or for checking account services, taking into account also diverse bank operating cost-influencing

65. William S. Comanor and Thomas A. Wilson, "Advertising Market Structure and Performance," *Review of Economics and Statistics* 49 (November 1967): 423–40; and *Advertising and Market Power*.

66. They have not held up for nonmanufacturing industries, where, it is argued, advertising tends to be more informative than persuasive or brand-image sustaining. See Kenneth D. Boyer, "Informative and Goodwill Advertising," *Review of Economics and Statistics* 56 (November 1974): 541–48; and Franklin R. Edwards, "Advertising and Competition in Banking," *Antitrust Bulletin* 18 (Spring 1973): 23–32. For a comprehensive critical survey of profitability-advertising studies up to 1974, see James M. Ferguson, *Advertising and Competition: Theory, Measurement, Fact* (Cambridge, Mass.: Ballinger, 1974), especially Chapters 6 and 7. Important later works include Michael E. Porter, "Consumer Behavior, Retailer Power and Market Performance in Consumer Goods Industries," *Review of Economics and Statistics* 56 (November 1974): 419–36; Porter, "Interbrand Choice, Media Mix and Market Performance," *American Economic Review* 66 (May 1976): 398–406; Bond and Greenberg, "Industry Structure, Market Rivalry, and Public Policy"; and Allyn D. Strickland and Leonard W. Weiss, "Advertising, Concentration, and Price-Cost Margins," *Journal of Political Economy* 84 (October 1976): 1109–21.

67. See Chapter 9, pp. 272–73 *supra*.

68. See the extension of work by Comanor and Wilson in *Advertising and Market Power*, Chapter 8; Weiss, "Advertising, Profits, and Corporate Taxes"; and John J. Siegfried and Leonard Weiss, "Advertising, Profits, and Corporate Taxes Revisited," *Review of Economics and Statistics* 56 (May 1974): 195–200.

69. See Harry Bloch, "Advertising and Profitability: A Reappraisal," *Journal of Political Economy* 82 (March/April 1974): 267–86; and (for an analysis that is plainly flawed methodologically) Robert Ayanian, "Advertising and the Rate of Return," *Journal of Law and Economics* 18 (October 1975): 479–506. Compare the author's comment in Robert B. Helms, ed., *Drug Development and Marketing* (Washington, D.C.: American Enterprise Institute for Public Policy Research, 1975), pp. 121–22.

70. For a literature survey suggesting that the weight of the evidence favors relatively high depreciation rates, see Darral G. Clarke, "Econometric Measurement of the Duration of Advertising Effect on Sales," *Journal of Marketing Research* 13 (November 1976): 345–57.

71. See John Cable, "Market Structure, Advertising Policy and Intermarket Differences in Advertising Intensity," in Cowling, ed., *Market Structure and Corporate Behaviour*, pp. 108–109; and Richard Schmalensee, "Advertising and Profitability: Further Implications of the Null Hypothesis," *Journal of Industrial Economics* 25 (September 1976): 45–54. See also note 98, Chapter 4, p. 109 *supra*. If there are diminishing marginal returns in the effectiveness of advertising—i.e., if $dS/dA > 0$ and $d^2S/dA^2 < 0$—an increase in the gross margin rate m will lead to an increase in the profit-maximizing amount of advertising A.

72. For powerful confirmation of the gross margin-advertising hypothesis using the PIMS data base, see Robert D. Buzzell and Paul W. Farris, "Marketing Costs in Consumer Goods Industries," in Thorelli, ed., *Strategy + Structure*, pp. 122–44.

73. See Comanor and Wilson, *Advertising and Market Power*, pp. 153–63; Strickland and Weiss, "Advertising, Concentration, and Price-Cost Margins"; and Stephen Martin, "Theoretical Issues in the Specification of Models of Industrial Organization," Working Paper no. 7705, Michigan State University Econometrics Workshop, January 1978.

variables.[77] They reveal quite uniformly that loan interest rates and service charges tend to be higher, the more concentrated local banking markets are.

Retail gasoline prices in 22 cities over the 1964–71 period were analyzed by Howard Marvel.[78] He found that after controlling for transport costs, city size, and local taxes, price levels were positively correlated with the Herfindahl-Hirschman Index of local market concentration. The relationship was much stronger at the low end of the price range than at the high end. This, Marvel infers, implies uniformly high pricing across cities among premium price retailers, whereas differences in market structure had their principal effect on competition among unbranded and maverick branded sellers. Analysis of year-by-year patterns also suggested that adherence to a nationwide price increase led by Texaco in 1965 broke down more quickly in urban markets where concentration was relatively low.

Food retailing offers another opportunity for intermarket price comparisons. The only study controlling for city size, market growth, wage levels, and other relevant variables was by Marion, Mueller, and associates.[79] It dealt with the average October 1974 prices of market baskets including up to 127 products sold by three large chains in 36 metropolitan areas. The authors found that average price levels were significantly higher, the higher the local four-firm concentration ratio was and the higher a reporting firm's local market share was. Holding all other variables constant, a 40 percentage point increase in the four-firm concentration ratio led on average to a market basket price increase of from 6 to 12 percent, depending upon the specific regression equation estimated.

Although one can, as always, quarrel with the particular samples, controls, and methods employed in these studies, their overall thrust is unambiguous. Prices do tend to be higher when markets are highly concentrated than when they are not.

Superiority, luck, strategy, and leading firm profitability That profitability increases systematically with market share, as we saw earlier, seems somewhat at odds with the evidence that, beyond some typically modest size threshold, economies of scale tend to peter out. Let us pursue the search for alternative explanations further. Professor Demsetz has urged that the greater profitability of leading firms may have little or nothing to do with economies of scale in the conventional sense and, indeed, that the scale economies hypothesis may assume the wrong chain of causation.[80] He argues that for reasons possibly unrelated to its initial size, some firm may come up with significant methods of reducing cost or with superior new products that permit it to enjoy unusually high profits. Owing to this element of superiority, which for some reason may be difficult to imitate, the firm grows rapidly to a position of industry leadership. Looking at the situation after this process has been in effect for a while, the statistical analyst sees a correlation between size and profitability. The scale economies hypothesis implies that size has conferred an advantage, but in fact, superior innovativeness or managerial skill has led to size *and* supranormal profits.

Richard Mancke carried this argument in a different direction by recasting it in the spirit of the Gibrat-type processes we considered in Chapter 4.[81] He postulated an initial situation in which all firms start from identical positions and periodically reinvest their profits in lumpy, uncertain business opportunities. Each firm faces the same probability distribution of investment payoffs. Those who are particularly lucky will realize large returns over an extended period, have larger sums to reinvest, and hence will grow more rapidly. After some time, the largest firms will be the luckiest ones who will also have been reporting relatively high profit returns. Again, a positive correlation between market share and profitability will be observed. Its basis is neither economies of scale nor superiority in any conventional sense, but plain luck.

In an ingenious use of PIMS data, Caves and associates have attempted to test the Mancke hypothesis.[82] They reasoned that if above-average size and profitability were the consequence of past chance events, one would expect the positive association between market share and profitability to be stronger, the more uncertain or turbulent is the environment within which firms operate. Distinguishing between high- and low-turbulence situations on the basis of seven qualitative characteristics as well as the observed instability of leading firm market shares, they found support for the random effect hypothesis only in businesses whose products underwent regular model changes. For other characteristics such as newness of the business, the importance of technological change, and being in the early stages of the product life cycle, the evidence was either wholly inconsistent with the Mancke hypothesis or, paradoxically, consistent with it only for industries of low market share instability.

An ambitious test of the Demsetz superiority hypothesis was attempted by Professor Sam Peltzman.[83] He proceeded from the conjecture that certain firms made cost-reducing innovations leading to enhanced profits and rapidly growing market shares. The more this occurred, he reasoned, the more likely it was that over an extended interval one would observe an association between relative *decreases* in unit production costs and *increases* in an industry's four-firm concentration ratio. Using 1947–67 Census data on 165 U.S. manufacturing industries, he found, as hypothesized, a statistically significant negative correlation between concentration changes and unit cost changes, holding other relevant variables constant. However, his interpretation of the results suffers from serious flaws, mostly related to his failure to look behind the numbers and ascertain how they were derived and what was actually happening in the industries analyzed.[84] He made no attempt to see whether the industries experiencing large concentration increases were in any way qualitatively different from other industries. Had he done so, he would have found that they were preponderantly consumer goods industries and, moreover, that many had over the period studied experienced important *product* innovations and/or large-scale advertising campaigns geared to the advent of television. They were not for the most part industries in which the cost-reducing innovations stressed by Peltzman played a prominent role. It is conceivable that relatively rapid cost reductions accompanied product innovation, and this might explain the correlations Peltzman ob-

(74) Porter, "Consumer Behavior, Retailer Power and Market Performance," p. 429.

(75) Frank M. Bass et al., "Market Structure and Industry Influence on Profitability," in Thorelli, ed., *Strategy + Structure*, pp. 181–201.

(76) Still another avenue of approach is to examine the links between concentration and *common stock* values, usually in relation to the accounting value of stockholders' equity. Again, positive structure-performance relationships are manifest. See Stanley I. Ornstein, "Concentration and Profits," *Journal of Business* 45 (October 1972): 519–41; Ronald W. Melicher, David F. Rush, and Daryl N. Winn, "Degree of Industry Concentration and Market Risk-Return Performance," *Journal of Financial and Quantitative Analysis* 11 (November 1976): 627–35; Timothy G. Sullivan, "A Note on Market Power and Returns to Stockholders," *Review of Economics and Statistics* 59 (February 1977): 108–13; and Stavros B. Thomadakis, "A Value-Based Test of Profitability and Market Structure," *Review of Economics and Statistics* 59 (May 1977): 179–85.

77. See Weiss, "The Concentration-Profits Relationship," p. 202n.; Frederick W. Bell and Neil B. Murphy, "Impact of Market Structure on the Price of a Commercial Banking Service," *Review of Economics and Statistics* 51 (May 1969): 210–13; R. C. Aspinwall, "Market Structure and Commercial Bank Mortgage Interest Rates," *Southern Economic Journal* 36 (April 1970): 376–84; Arnold A. Heggestad and John J. Mingo, "Prices, Non Prices, and Concentration in Commercial Banking," *Journal of Money, Credit, and Banking* 8 (February 1976): 107–17; and Heggestad and Mingo, "The Competitive Condition of U.S. Banking Markets and the Impact of Structural Reform," *Journal of Finance* 32 (June 1977): 649–61.

78. Howard P. Marvel, "Competition and Price Levels in the Retail Gasoline Market," *Review of Economics and Statistics* 60 (May 1978): 252–58.

79. Bruce W. Marion, Willard F. Mueller et al., *The Profit and Price Performance of Leading Food Chains, 1970–74*, study for the Joint Economic Committee of the U.S. Congress (Washington, D.C.: Government Printing Office, April 1977). Positive associations between profitability, market share, and a nonlinear (i.e., approximately logistic) concentration variable were also found for 96 divisions of 12 companies. The study was sharply attacked by food industry representatives. For the give and take, see the Joint Economic Committee hearings, *Prices and Profits of Leading Retail Food Chains, 1970–74*, 95th Cong., 1st sess., 1977.

80. Demsetz, "Industry Structure, Market Rivalry, and Public Policy," pp. 1–5. For antecedents, see Brozen, "Concentration and Structural Market Disequilibria," pp. 245–48; and (especially) John S. McGee, *In Defense of Industrial Concentration* (New York: Praeger, 1971).

81. Richard B. Mancke, "Causes of Interfirm Profitability Differences: A New Interpretation of the Evidence," *Quarterly Journal of Economics* 88 (May 1974): 181–93. Cf. Chapter 4, pp. 145–50 *supra*.

82. Richard E. Caves, B. T. Gale, and M. E. Porter, "Interfirm Profitability Differences: A Comment," with a reply by Mancke, *Quarterly Journal of Economics* 91 (November 1977): 667–80.

83. Sam Peltzman, "The Gains and Losses from Industrial Concentration," *Journal of Law and Economics* 20 (October 1977): 229–63. See also Steven Lustgarten, "Gains and Losses from Concentration: A Comment," *Journal of Law and Economics* 22 (April 1979): 191–208.

84. See F. M. Scherer, "The Causes and Consequences of Rising Industrial Concentration," *Journal of Law and Economics* 22 (April 1979): 191–208.

tained. However, the correlations undoubtedly resulted to an unknown extent also from biases generated by the peculiar way output indices (from which unit cost indices were derived) are compiled by the Census authorities for industries experiencing rapid product technology change and changes in product mix. Thus, Peltzman's contribution largely misses the real-world point.

Nevertheless, there is an important real-world point that ought not be missed. Appreciable market share and concentration increases are not merely the result of random Gibrat-like processes. The firms experiencing rapid market share gains are frequently found to have been doing something different with their products, services, promotional or distribution methods, price strategies, production processes, or the like. It is not a difficult leap to infer that if they were successful, they must have been exhibiting superiority of some sort. With the proper amount of faith and another leap, one reaches the further conclusion that if their success was achieved in a marketplace where buyers and sellers could choose freely, any correlation between profitability and market structure that emerges from the ensuing dynamics must reflect superiority and hence, in a broader sense, economic efficiency. One need not question why other firms failed to enter and compete away supranormal profits, whether the industry's structure might have been so transformed that wholly different pricing behavior patterns resulted, or whether the structural transformations that followed were indispensable expectationally to triggering the initial innovation. To quote Professor McGee's extreme view, in freely functioning markets:

> such economies as there are will assert themselves, and no one need be concerned with how large or small they are. . . . [A]part from those industries dominated by State controls, there is the strongest presumption that the existing structure is the efficient structure.[85]

Although there are also factual and interpretational quarrels, whether or not one accepts this view—i.e., that whatever happens in the marketplace must be for the best—is the most fundamental point of disagreement separating the diverse schools of economists debating the meaning of structure-performance relationships. It is doubtful that the disagreements would vanish even if statistics on performance and structure were available in unlimited quantity and impeccable quality. We shall nonetheless have a good deal more to say about the issues when product differentiation and technological innovation are subjected to detailed study in Chapters 14 through 16.

A somewhat different view of the world emerges from the theoretical analysis developed in Chapter 8. It says that market structure and the pricing behavior flowing from it do not occur through chance or simple acts—e.g., of innovation. Rather, they are consciously shaped as firms with a sufficiently dominant position in some market choose business policies that maximize long-run profits. When a dominant seller (or group of sellers acting jointly) obtains for one reason or another a significant cost or price (i.e., product differentiation) advantage over rivals, it can set prices just high enough to realize unit profits commensurate with its advantage while maintaining its market share, or it can temporarily reduce prices and profit margins to enhance its share and ability to earn even higher profits later. When its advantage over actual and potential rivals is slight, it is likely to elevate prices if it can, experience temporarily high profitability, but over the longer run to see its market share and its power to influence prices decline. Which of these (and other more complex) strategies it chooses depends crucially upon the dominant seller's advantages vis-à-vis rivals—that is, upon the barriers to new entry and fringe rival expansion. A statistical analysis that relates profitability to concentration, market share, and various entry barrier proxies without taking into account these dynamic elements is likely to yield biased structural relationship estimates. The impact of concentration on *long-run* profitability will be underestimated for industries in which leading firms are pursuing a market share-enhancing pricing policy; it will be overestimated for declining dominant firms. Other more complex strategies may also be adopted. For example, firms may invest heavily in product space-filling new brands and accompanying or independent large-scale advertising, sacrificing current profitability in the hope of deterring entry and increasing long-run profits. A complete, unbiased statistical analysis must capture the dynamic interdependence among profitability, concentration, market shares, and product differentiation.

Attempts to accomplish such an analysis began only in the 1970s. Early econometric studies of interindustry structure-performance relationships in a simultaneous equations framework do more to whet one's appetite than to provide consistent or conclusive results.[86] The first known effort to estimate a three-equation system with industry profitability (from Census price-cost margin data), concentration, and advertising/sales ratios had difficulty, like many less ambitious studies, disentangling the effects on profitability of concentration and entry barrier proxy variables.[87] This may have stemmed also from violating the conditions for statistical identification.[88] Martin attempted to surmount the identification problem by estimating a similar three-equation system with additional exogenous variables, some motivated by the Gaskins model of optimal dynamic limit pricing.[89] However, his long-run model incorporating entry barrier variables explained price-cost margins less well than a simpler short-run model lacking them. His somewhat implausible interpretation is that entry barriers affect profitability only through their indirect impact on concentration. Robert Masson and Joseph Shaanan also began with the Gaskins model but pursued a different tack, estimating a two-equation system with dominant firms' profit returns and the rate of new entry into 37 U.S. manufacturing industries as endogenous variables.[90] Their results are more consistent with theoretical predictions. They reveal *inter alia* that entry is encouraged by high profits and retarded by large average plant sizes and high advertising/sales ratios, while profitability rises with concentration, industry growth, and the height of entry barriers.

What one should conclude from these early studies is uncertain. They are certainly a step in the right direction. Yet if the estimation of simultaneous equation systems is to add significantly to our knowledge, it is important that they be specified not only to satisfy econometric constraints but also to reflect as closely as possible the underlying economic structure. Whether this occurs when variables are strung out in easily estimable additive arrays is arguable. One might also entertain doubts about how much good a sophisticated econometric structure does when the data suffer, as in the Strickland-Weiss and Martin studies, from the usual Census concentration and price-cost margin measurement difficulties, or in the Masson-Shaanan case, from the mixing of dominant firms' primary industry profits with returns in other industries. If definitive results are to be obtained, they will have to come from joining solid theory, imaginative casting of the theory in statistically estimable form, sophisticated econometric technique, and broadly representative, intertemporally comparable performance and structure data covering individual company lines of business. That objective is still out of reach. Perhaps it will always be so, but optimism is a pardonable folly, even for economists.

Having laid a proper foundation, we return

85. From his commentary in Goldschmid, ed., *Industrial Concentration*, p. 104.

86. More sophisticated work has been done on intra-industry relationships. See Ralph G. M. Sultan, *Pricing in the Electrical Oligopoly*, vol. 2 (Boston: Harvard Business School Division of Research, 1975), especially Chapter 14; and H. Landis Gabel, "A Simultaneous Equation Analysis of Industrial Structure and Performance" (manuscript, University of Virginia, 1978). Gabel purports to test for simultaneous equation bias on profit-concentration coefficient estimates. However, it is questionable whether his data support the conclusions drawn. He pays insufficient attention to regional characteristics of the petroleum products markets, to the changing degree of regionalization over time as pipeline networks were extended, and to such problems as the inconsistency of minimum efficient scale estimate assumptions over time.

87. Strickland and Weiss, "Advertising, Concentration, and Price-Cost Margins."

88. Martin, "Theoretical Issues in the Specification of Models of Industrial Organization," pp. 6–8.

89. Martin, "Theoretical Issues."

90. Robert T. Masson and Joseph Shaanan, "Dynamic/Stochastic Limit Pricing: An Empirical Test," working paper, Cornell University, June 1978.

(91) See note 41 *supra*. See also the exchange among Brozen, John T. Wenders, Paul W. MacAvoy, James McKie, and Lee E. Preston in the *Journal of Law and Economics* 14 (October 1971): 485–512.

now to an issue deferred earlier. In his criticism of early concentration-profitability studies, Professor Brozen showed *inter alia* that there was a tendency for the profits of more or less identical firms assigned to high-concentration, high-profit industries to decline in subsequent time periods.[91] He argues that the studies therefore caught concentrated industry leaders during a period of disequilibrium—e.g., when their industries were adjusting to new scale economy imperatives, and before entry or the expansion of smaller rivals had eroded supranormal returns. There are alternative explanations for his findings, such as the tendency for returns to converge toward the all-manufacturing average as particularly profitable companies diversify into less profitable lines. Nevertheless, a properly formulated dynamic theory indicates that one should indeed expect to see especially profitable firms' returns decline *unless* entry barriers are sufficiently high to warrant a consistent entry deterrent or exclusionary pricing strategy. What the evidence shows on this point is a bit unclear, since mergers and diversification have made the primary industry method of classifying individual companies an unreliable tool of long-run analysis; and the parties to the debate initiated by Brozen appear to have picked and chosen industry and firm samples in ways that arouse suspicion. Qualls's work seems the most careful both theoretically and in terms of sample selection. He took all 30 industries originally analyzed by Mann for the 1950–60 period and, assuming a uniform 6 percent competitive cost of capital, computed comparable supranormal profit margins for 1961–65.[92] He observed a tendency for supranormal margins to fall in all entry barrier and concentration classes. However, in the high entry barrier group the decline was from an average of 8.4 percent in 1950–60 to 7.1 percent in 1961–65, while for industries with lower entry barriers, supranormal margins fell from 2.8 percent to 1.6 percent on average. Evidently, if profit returns in high entry barrier industries regress eventually to normal levels, they do so at an extremely slow pace. That high profit returns tend to persist for long periods is also shown by studies of company data unclassified by market concentration and entry barrier characteristics.[93]

Other results A few other results emerging from the many statistical studies of structure-profitability relationships merit a briefer review.

One would expect profits to be higher in industries that are in some sense risky than in low-risk industries. Is it possible that risk and concentration are correlated, so that correlations between profitability and concentration reflect in part supranormal returns more correctly attributable to the restriction of capacity and output owing to investors' risk aversion? Concentration and risk, as exemplified by the intertemporal variability of profits, could conceivably coincide because of a greater tendency for concentrated industries to oscillate between episodes of collusion and price warfare.[94] The evidence on whether such a relationship exists is ambiguous. Simple bivariate analyses appear preponderantly to show that profit returns are *less* variable over time in more concentrated industries.[95] However, when additional variables such as firm size (which tends to be correlated with seller concentration) are taken into account, the relationship may reverse, showing concentrated industries to be riskier, all else being equal.[96] Whatever the association may be between risk measures and concentration, correlations between the level of profitability and concentration tend to hold up when such indices of risk as the intertemporal variability of profits or the β values of capital asset pricing theory are introduced as additional explanatory variables.[97] Thus, greater riskiness cannot fully explain the higher returns observed in more highly concentrated industries.

The use of profit variability indices as a measure of risk poses problems from whose resolution useful insights can be gleaned. The variability of profits over time depends not only upon demand and cost conditions and how firms relate to one another in a given market structure, but also upon the decisions companies make concerning their financial structures. If sellers in concentrated industries anticipate supranormal returns on their investments, they can enhance returns to common stockholders all the more by building substantial leverage into their capital structures, that is, by relying relatively heavily upon debt as compared to equity financing. This does increase the firm's financial risk, especially if there is high intrinsic variability over time in the stream of returns on total capital. A tradeoff must therefore be made between magnifying returns to common stockholders and the avoidance of risk. Two studies reveal a tendency for companies in concentrated industries to use *less* leverage, in effect sacrificing average returns on equity to reduce risk; but a third study shows no clear leverage-concentration pattern.[98] In view of these equivocal results, it is uncertain whether firms enjoying monopoly power have followed J. R. Hicks's dictum by taking part of their rewards in the form of a quiet life.[99] It is nonetheless clear that financial risk, financial structure, and average profitability can depend upon one another. A correct determination of their effects therefore demands a properly specified simultaneous equations approach. Attempts to estimate such simultaneous equation systems have yielded results generally consistent with theory, among other things showing, contrary to the outcome of more naively estimated regression analyses, that profits tend to be higher for firms with higher leverage and greater intertemporal profit variability.[100]

A related issue concerns the impact of capital intensity on profitability. We saw in Chapter 7 that a business slump can have an especially adverse effect on the profits of capital-intensive enterprises, a relatively large share of whose costs are fixed over the short and intermediate run. This prediction finds no support in two studies of manufacturers' experience during the 1960s, each of which showed a weak negative partial correlation between the *variability* of profits over time and capital/sales ratios.[101] A mitigating factor may have been the unusually steady economic growth achieved by the U.S. economy between 1960 and 1969. From a different perspective, the prediction that capital intensity matters behaviorally receives striking confirmation. Analysis of the PIMS data set shows a strong negative association between profit *levels* during the early 1970s and capital intensity, measured by the ratio of the undepreciated value of plant and equipment to sales. Table 9.3 shows how 1970–72 before-tax returns on invested capital varied with capital intensity for various levels of four-firm seller concentration.[102] Apparently, in capital-intensive industries, producers tended to

92. David Qualls, "Stability and Persistence of Economic Profit Margins in Highly Concentrated Industries," *Southern Economic Journal* 40 (April 1974): 604–12. Qualls's measure of profitability is essentially the π_S index described on p. 269 *supra*.

93. See Geoffrey Whittington, *The Prediction of Profitability and Other Studies of Company Behaviour* (Cambridge, England: Cambridge University Press, 1971), Chapter 4; and Dennis C. Mueller, "The Persistence of Profits above the Norm," *Economica* 44 (November 1977): 369–80.

94. See Richard E. Caves and Basil S. Yamey, "Risk and Corporate Rates of Return: Comment," *Quarterly Journal of Economics* 85 (August 1971): 513–17.

95. See for example Daryl N. Winn, "On the Relations between Rates of Return, Risk, and Market Structure," *Quarterly Journal of Economics* 91 (February 1977): 163; George J. Stigler, *Capital and Rates of Return in Manufacturing Industries* (Princeton: Princeton University Press, 1963), pp. 54–70; and David J. Smyth, G. Briscoe, and J. M. Samuels, "The Variability of Industry Profit Rates," *Applied Economics* 1 (May 1969): 147–48. These studies emphasize intertemporal variability. For any given period in time, there appears to be greater interindustry and intra-industry variability of profits in concentrated and/or high barrier to entry industries. See Richard W. McEnally, "Competition and Dispersion in Rates of Return: A Note," *Journal of Industrial Economics* 25 (September 1976): 69–75.

96. See Winn, "On the Relations," p. 160; and Gloria J. Hurdle, "Leverage, Risk, Market Structure and Profitability," *Review of Economics and Statistics* 56 (November 1974): 478–85 (who finds *inter alia* a negative relationship between market shares and intertemporal profit variability up to shares of 29 to 36 percent, after which a positive association takes over). For banks, Franklin R. Edwards and Arnold Heggestad find a negative relationship even in multivariate analyses. "Uncertainty, Market Structure, and Performance in Banking," *Quarterly Journal of Economics* 87 (August 1973): 455–73.

97. See for example Hurdle, "Leverage, Risk, Market Structure and Profitability"; and James L. Bothwell and Theodore E. Keeler, "Profits, Market Structure, and Portfolio Risk," in Masson and Qualls, ed., *Essays on Industrial Organization in Honor of Joe S. Bain*, pp. 71–88. On the derivation and meaning of β, see Chapter 4, p. 106 *supra*. An exception is I. N. Fisher and G. R. Hall, "Risk and Corporate Rates of Return: Reply," *Quarterly Journal of Economics* 85 (August 1971): 518–22. Their analysis appears to suffer from severe statistical problems, with 11 repetitively used industry concentration ratios and 11 industry intercept dummy variables ensuring singularity or virtual singularity of their covariance matrix.

98. Compare Hurdle, "Leverage, Risk, Market Structure and Profitability"; and Timothy G. Sullivan, "Market Power, Profitability and Financial Leverage," *Journal of Finance* 29 (December 1974): 1407–14; with Ronald W. Melicher, David F. Rush, and Daryl N. Winn, "Industry Concentration, Financial Structure, and Profitability," *Financial Management* (Autumn 1976): 44–49.

99. J. R. Hicks, "Annual Survey of Economic Theory: The Theory of Monopoly," *Economica* 2 (January 1935): 8.

100. See Hurdle, "Leverage, Risk, Market Structure and Profitability," pp. 482–84; Samuel H. Baker, "Risk, Leverage, and Profitability: An Industry Analysis," *Review of Economics and Statistics* 55 (November 1973): 503–507; and William T. Carleton and Irwin H. Silberman, "Joint Determination of Rate of Return and Capital Structure: An Econometric Analysis," *Journal of Finance* 32 (June 1977): 811–21.

compete away profit margins more vigorously, presumably in the hope of keeping their plants operating at high levels. That is, the centrifugal propensities discussed in Chapter 7 evidently outweighed capital-intensive companies' instinct to try all the more vigorously to cooperate and maintain pricing discipline. Relatively high seller concentration seems to help curb price cutting, but not with complete success.

One further plausible constraint on sellers' pricing discretion is a substantial flow of competing imported goods. In a study of 77 U.S. manufacturing industries, Louis and Frances Esposito found 1963–65 profit returns to be lower, the higher the ratio of imports to domestic sales was.[103]

Results for nations other than the United States Structure-performance analyses similar to the United States studies emphasized in this chapter have been carried out for a number of other nations. An exhaustive survey would add little, so an undoubtedly incomplete footnote listing and a terse overview must suffice.[104] Generally, the data problems tend to be more formidable overseas than in the United States. There are greater mismatches between performance and structural data sources; statistics on seller concentration tend to be of lower quality and available only at higher levels of industry aggregation; the problem of defining markets meaningfully is more difficult in nations with more extensive foreign trade than the United States; and

statistics on individual firms' market shares are virtually nonexistent. One finds, as for the United States, results that conflict, even when similar data sets have been tapped, e.g., because of sample size variations and differences in the way concentration ratios were computed in the face of definitional mismatches.[105]

Despite these obstacles, the studies provide a fair amount of support for the hypothesis that market structure and profit performance are related. Virtually all of the studies incorporated some index of seller concentration, and many also included other structural variables such as midpoint or average plant sizes and a measure of how much capital an average plant requires. In the 23 studies sufficiently independent in terms of data or methodology to be counted as distinct, 17 found a positive relationship, statistically significant at the 90 percent confidence level or greater, between profitability and concentration or some (typically collinear) cluster of market structure variables including concentration. Interpretation of the exact causal nexus is complicated by the same collinearity problems experienced with U.S. data: Sometimes the concentration variable was statistically significant standing alone, but fell to insignificance when plant size or capital requirements variables were added. The most consistent positive relationships between concentration and profitability emerged in Canadian and Japanese studies. The most negative results, usually based upon very weak data, were for Italy, Belgium, and Australia. There were a few tests of the hypothesis that profits are higher in industries with sizeable advertising/sales ratios. The results were positive in three British studies, negative in another, and equivocal in a fifth. In three Canadian studies, there were two yielding support for the hypothesis. The only Japanese study directly accessible to a *Gaijin* (i.e., roughly, foreigner) revealed a significantly positive advertising intensity-profitability correlation.

T 9.3 Relationship between profit returns and capital intensity for various concentration classes

Industry concentration	Degree of capital intensity		
	Low	Average	High
Low	21%	18%	2%
Average	23	17	7
High	23	23	14

Adapted from Sidney Schoeffler, "Cross-Sectional Study of Strategy, Structure, and Performance: Aspects of the PIMS Program," in Hans B. Thorelli, ed., *Strategy + Structure = Performance* (Bloomington: Indiana University Press, 1977), pp. 118–19.

Conclusion

How can what is already a summary be summarized? Only with a heroic generalization: that there is considerable statistical support for industrial organization theory's predictions of a relationship among profitability, seller concentration, and barriers to entry. This conclusion must be leavened with appropriate caveats, for the results are not uniform, the data have many shortcomings, the statistical tests leave much more variation in profitability unexplained than they explain, and we are still some distance away from disentangling fully the relative importance of price-raising and cost-reducing linkages. One cannot help recalling the Princeton physics professor who concluded a research report by noting, "The experiments indicate that the negative mesons are absorbed only one billionth as rapidly as calculated by the theoretical physicists. This would be a major error even for an economist."[106] Against that modest standard, at least, industrial organization theory has done well. It must be recognized too that a certain amount of art is unavoidable in statistical studies of structure-performance relationships— e.g., in choosing meaningful indices of market concentration and the difficulty of entry, in devising a proper econometric structure, and even in interpreting what has been observed. This poses risks of conscious or inadvertent bias, or, as Professor Demsetz has warned, that "believing is seeing."[107] Still it seems clear that statistical studies of structure and performance reveal the existence of important relationships whose presence stands out more sharply, the better is the quality of the data analyzed. The research agenda for the future must stress obtaining data of high quality and assaulting them imaginatively with high-powered econometric tools to discriminate among contending behavioral hypotheses.

(101) Hurdle, "Leverage, Risk, Market Structure and Profitability," p. 482; and Winn, "On the Relations," p. 160.

(102) Note that the sample includes a *poor* year (1970), a *middling* year (1971), and a *good* year (1972) averaged together. See also Schoeffler et al., "Impact of Strategic Planning on Profit Performance," p. 143.

103. Louis and Frances Esposito, "Foreign Competition and Domestic Industry Profitability." See also Harry Bloch, "Prices, Costs, and Profits in Canadian Manufacturing: The Influence of Tariffs and Concentration," *Canadian Journal of Economics* 7 (November 1974): 594–610, who finds a tendency for prices to be relatively high when *both* concentration and tariffs are high.

104. For the United Kingdom, see Phillips, "An Econometric Study of Price-Fixing, Market Structure and Performance"; Smyth, Briscoe, and Samuels, "The Variability of Industry Profit Rates," pp. 137–50; W. G. Shepherd, "Structure and Behavior in British Industries," *Journal of Industrial Economics* 21 (November 1972): 47–50; Sally Holterman, "Market Structure and Economic Performance in U.K. Manufacturing Industry," *Journal of Industrial Economics* 22 (December 1973): 119–39; Javad Khalilzadeh-Shirazi, "Market Structure and Price-Cost Margins in United Kingdom Manufacturing Industries," *Review of Economics and Statistics* 56 (February 1974): 67–76; Caves, Khalilzadeh-Shirazi, and Porter, "Scale Economies in Structural Analyses of Market Power"; Cowling and Waterson, "Price-Cost Margins and Market Structure"; P. E. Hart and Eleanor Morgan, "Market Structure and Economic Performance in the United Kingdom," *Journal of Industrial Economics* 25 (March 1977): 177–93; Theodore Hitris, "Effective Protection and Economic Performance in UK Manufacturing Industry, 1963 and 1968," *Economic Journal* 88 (March 1978): 107–20; and Stephen Nickell and David Metcalf, "Monopolistic Industries and Monopoly Profits or, Are Kellogg's Cornflakes Overpriced?," *Economic Journal* 88 (June 1978): 254–56.

For Canada, see Orr, "An Index of Entry Barriers"; Bloch, "Prices, Costs, and Profits in Canadian Manufacturing"; McFetridge, "Market Structure and Price-Cost Margins"; and Jones, Laudadio, and Percy, "Market Structure and Profitability in Canadian Manufacturing Industry."

Studies for other nations include Manfred Neumann, Ingo Böbel, and Alfred Haid, "Profitability, Risk and Market Structure in West German Industries," *Journal of Industrial Economics* 27 (March 1979): 227–42; Frederic Jenny and A. P. Weber, "Profit Rates and Structural Variables in French Manufacturing Industries," *European Economic Review* 7 (February 1976): 187–206; Louis Phlips, *Effects of Industrial Concentration* (Amsterdam: North-Holland, 1971), pp. 59–87 (on Belgium, Italy, and an abandoned French effort); C. M. Guerci, "Tassi di Profitto e Strutture di Mercato nell'Industria Italiana," *L'Industria* (October-December 1970): 503–29; D. K. Round, "Industry Structure, Market Rivalry and Public Policy: Some Australian Evidence," *Journal of Law and Economics* 18 (April 1975): 273–81; Lawrence J. White, *Industrial Concentration and Economic Power in Pakistan* (Princeton: Princeton University Press, 1974), pp. 138–46; and Richard E. Caves and Masu Uekusa, *Industrial Organization in Japan* (Washington, D.C.: Brookings Institution, 1976), pp. 72–82, 92–96. For a listing of other Japanese studies, see Weiss, "The Concentration-Profits Relationship and Antitrust," pp. 214–15.

International comparisons studies of structure-profit relationships include William James Adams, "International Differences in Corporate Profitability," *Economica* 43 (November 1976): 367–79; Khalilzadeh-Shirazi, "Market Structure and Price-Cost Margins: A Comparative Analysis of U.K. and U.S. Manufacturing Industries," *Economic Inquiry* 14 (March 1976): 116–28; and J. C. H. Jones et al., "Profitability and Market Structure: A Cross-Section Comparison of Canadian and American Manufacturing Industry," *Journal of Industrial Economics* 25 (March 1977): 195–211.

105. Compare for example the Shepherd, Holterman, Khalilzadeh-Shirazi, and Hart-Morgan studies, all using price-cost margin data for three-digit British Census industries.

106. Quoted from Jacob Viner, "The Economist in History," *American Economic Review* 53 (May 1963): 16.

107. Demsetz, "Two Systems of Belief about Monopoly," p. 164.

The price and profit consequences
of market structure   295

10 Buyer power and vertical pricing relationships

In this chapter we turn from concern with the power sellers have over prices to the buyers' side of the power ledger. We consider four main topics—the extent of buyer concentration, how monopsony (i.e., buyer) power affects pricing, the links between vertical integration and pricing behavior, and the hypothesis originally associated with Professor Galbraith that countervailing power by strong buyers mitigates the pricing distortions otherwise associated with monopoly.

The extent of buyer concentration

A quantitative picture of how much buyer concentration exists is difficult to secure, for there are no statistical series analogous to the abundant data on seller concentration. An impressionistic view suggests that concentration on the buyers' side is generally more modest than concentration on the sellers' side, although significant pockets of monopsony or oligopsony power (the power associated with fewness of buyers) can be found.

Roughly two-thirds of the gross national product flows ultimately to consumers for personal consumption. Buyer concentration in this vast consumer goods market is obviously low. Yet most goods pass through numerous intermediate transactions before reaching the consumer's hands. Consumers buy from retailers; who some-

times obtain their supplies from wholesalers; who buy from consumer goods manufacturers; who obtain raw materials, equipment, and parts from other manufacturing and mining enterprises; who in turn purchase from still other companies, and so on. Within manufacturing industry alone, each dollar of final product sales at wholesale generates on the average a dollar's worth of additional manufacturers' sales for parts, materials, and the like. At any point in this chain of transactions monopsony power (as well as monopoly power) may intrude.

Although local market definitions are appropriate in measuring retail sellers' concentration, retailers as buyers normally purchase all but perishables and bulky, low-value commodities in something approaching a national market. The largest U.S. retailing firm in 1975 was Sears, Roebuck, with domestic sales of $11.6 billion. Total U.S. retail sales in the fields most closely related to Sears' interests—tires and auto accessories, furniture and appliances, hardware, apparel, and general merchandise—amounted in that year to $162 billion.[1] If Sears' share of sales in each product line were the same as its overall share, it would account for roughly 7 percent of

---

1. U.S., Bureau of the Census, *Statistical Abstract of the United States: 1976* (Washington, D.C.: Government Printing Office, 1976), p. 800.

wholesale purchases in each line. But since it is stronger in some fields than others, its share of purchases no doubt ranges from as little as 1 percent in certain clothing lines to as much as 25 percent on such items as washing machines and auto accessories.

The domestic sales of Safeway, the largest food chain, were $7.9 billion in 1975, or 7 percent of total food store sales. Taking into account restaurant and institutional demands, its share of most food product purchases at wholesale must have been on the order of 5 percent. The four largest food chains together contributed 16 percent of food store sales in 1972 and hence some 10 to 12 percent of food product purchases.[2]

Buyer concentration in other lines of retailing appears to be even lower. The four largest retail shoe chains made 20 percent of such outlets' sales in 1972, but they competed in procuring their stock with the shoe departments of many general-line retailers, including Sears. Walgreen, the largest drug chain, made 6 percent of all drug store sales in 1975; the four largest drug store chains together accounted for 11.4 percent of their trade's 1972 sales. However, hospitals and government agencies are also important wholesale buyers of drug products. The 25 percent of Walgreen's sales accounted for by prescription and proprietary drug products amounted to roughly 2 percent of the drug manufacturing industry's total output.[3] On most of the other products it retailed, Walgreen's competed at wholesale for supplies with food chains, restaurants, and diverse other soft goods and appliance retailers, and so its purchasing share must have been even lower. Similar overlaps lead to low buyer concentration levels in most other major retailing fields.

The degree of buyer concentration among manufacturers purchasing from other manufacturers is harder to assess quantitatively. If each supplying industry specialized in providing inputs to a single buying industry, the concentration of buying power could be estimated directly from seller concentration ratios in the buying industries. This is seldom the case, however. Three complications arise.

First, inspection of input-output tables for the American economy shows that most raw materials and intermediate goods manufacturing industries sell their products to many other using industries and are dependent upon any single class of industrial buyers for only a small fraction of their sales. The steel industry's best customer is typically the automotive (i.e., automobile, truck, and bus) industry, which absorbs from 16 percent of domestic steel output in a weak auto sales year to 22 percent in a strong year.[4] This fact in isolation suggests that because manufacturers' interindustry sales are spread over so many fields, buyer concentration is much lower on the average than end product seller concentration. Such spreading is less extensive at the raw materials extraction or agricultural supply stage, where outputs are often specialized to a single using industry. Thus, virtually all domestic iron ore supplies are used by steel makers, and most of the roughly 60 percent of U.S. grown leaf tobacco not exported is purchased by a very few domestic cigarette manufacturers.

A minor qualification to this first point stems from the diversification of many industrial corporations. Since General Motors accounted for roughly half of domestic auto, truck, and bus output, we might expect its share of all steel purchases directly or indirectly (i.e., through parts suppliers) to have ranged from 8 to 11 percent. However, GM bought steel not only for automotive products, but also for locomotives, construction equipment, Frigidaire appliances, and military equipment. Its total share of steel purchases must therefore have been somewhat higher than the figure for automotive products alone.

The third complication is more compelling. The industry definitions in available input-output tables are often too broad to reflect the true amount of seller dependence. The glass industry (excluding containers) sold 14 percent of its output to motor vehicle producers in 1967.[5] Yet a handful of auto and truck makers purchase most of the output of plants specializing in laminated and tempered glass. Similarly, a few refrigerator and air conditioner firms are the main outlets for small compressors, and until digital watch and automobile electronic control demand soared, the highly concentrated computer industry purchased the lion's share of all large-scale inte-

298

grated electronic circuit devices. When plant and equipment are specialized to meet the needs of a single concentrated buying industry, the buying firms may possess considerable monopsony power. But such narrow specialization in serving a single buying industry appears to be more the exception than the rule among producer's good and intermediate material manufacturers. Thus, average concentration on the buyers' side in manufacturing is undoubtedly lower than seller concentration.

The exercise of buyer power: theory

The student with a Teutonic obsession for classifying things into neat categories can identify at least six main market structure types involving power on the buyer's side, including a single buyer facing a single seller (bilateral monopoly), a single buyer facing many purely competitive sellers (pure monopsony), a few buyers facing a few sellers (bilateral oligopoly), a few buyers facing many sellers (oligopsony), and so on. Only for the first two cases, which are seldom encountered in a pure form in the real world, do we possess much in the way of formal economic theory.

Bilateral monopoly The theory of bilateral monopoly is indeterminate with a vengeance. It embodies all the problems we met in our study of oligopoly theory in Chapter 5: for example, do the parties attempt to maximize their individual profits, ignoring their interdependence, or do they cooperate to maximize joint profits? And unlike oligopoly, even if buyer and seller do collaborate to establish the joint profit-maximizing output, the price is indeterminate within a potentially wide range.

Figure 10.1 presents the standard diagrammatic analysis.[6] The curve marked MC,S_c represents either the marginal cost function of a monopolistic supplier or the supply function of a competitively producing industry. Since end consumers seldom have significant monopsony power, the demand side of the picture must for maximum realism reflect a derived demand, or the average net value of the product (AVP,D_c) produced by the buying firm using the input X, whose quantity is measured on the horizontal axis of Figure 10.1. If both supply and demand were competitive, input purchases would be expanded until supply equals demand at OX_c, with a resulting price of OP_c. However, if the buyer is a monopsonist and if it faces either competitive sellers or a monopolistic supplier accepting the buyer's quoted price as a parameter and making the best of it, the buyer must recognize that the more of X it seeks to buy, the higher its purchase price will be. It therefore reckons the marginal cost of its purchases in terms of the curve MMC marginal to the supply function MC,S_c. Let us provisionally assume that the monopsonist also has monopoly power in its output market, and so it perceives that the more of input X it buys and hence the more output it puts on the market, the lower its output's price must be and hence the lower will be the average value derived from the inputs it purchases. It therefore sees the benefits from purchasing more input in terms of the curve marginal to AVP,D_c—i.e., the marginal revenue product curve MRP. To maximize profits, it equates MMC with MRP, buying OX_B units and quoting the price OP_B sufficient to call forth the desired supply.

If on the other hand the seller is a monopolist and sets a price to which the buyer responds, the seller will recognize that the buyer maximizes

2. U.S., Bureau of the Census, *1972 Census of Retail Trade*, vol. I (Washington, D.C.: Government Printing Office, 1976), p. 1–114.

3. Estimated from company annual reports and the 1972 *Census of Manufactures*.

4. American Iron and Steel Institute, *Annual Statistical Report: 1974* (Washington, D.C.: American Iron and Steel Institute, 1975), p. 32.

5. U.S., Department of Commerce, Bureau of Economic Analysis, *Input-Output Structure of the U.S. Economy: 1967*, vol. 1 (Washington, D.C.: Government Printing Office, 1974), p. 142.

6. The original standard exposition is A. L. Bowley, "Bilateral Monopoly," *Economic Journal* 38 (December 1928): 651–59. The most thorough analysis of complications is James N. Morgan, "Bilateral Monopoly and the Competitive Output," *Quarterly Journal of Economics* 63 (August 1949): 371–91. See also William Fellner, *Competition Among the Few* (New York: Knopf, 1949), Chapter 9.

profit by expanding its purchases of X until its marginal revenue product has fallen into equality with the quoted price. Therefore, MRP is the derived demand function confronting the monopolist supplier to the monopsonist-monopolist buyer. The seller's relevant marginal revenue function is the curve marginal to MRP, or $MMRP$, and it will maximize its own profits by equating its marginal cost with $MMRP$ at output OX_s, quoting the price OP_s that induces the buyer to purchase the desired quantity.

We see then that what happens under bilateral monopoly depends in part upon whether the buyer or the seller exercises price leadership. Neither of these leadership solutions, however, is consistent with joint profit maximization. If maximum profit is to be extracted from a bilateral monopoly situation, the quantity of input supplied and used must be set at the level OX^*, where marginal cost equals marginal revenue product.[7] One way to achieve this result is for the parties to agree through bargaining that OX^* will be transferred. They must then agree on a price. There is no compelling calculus indicating what that price must be. It could conceivably be so high that the buyer derives no profit from the transaction—i.e., when the price equals the buy-

er's average value product at point H in Figure 10.1. Alternatively, it could be so low that it equals the seller's average cost of production—e.g., at point L in Figure 10.1. Within such a range, the price is theoretically indeterminate, depending upon the relative bargaining power and skill of the protagonists, which in turn may hinge upon diverse institutional variables, some of which will be considered later. The joint profit-maximizing quantity might also be achieved if one party can successfully pursue a "take it or leave it" strategy, e.g., with the buyer saying in effect, "I will buy OX^* units from you at a price 5 percent above X^*L, and if you won't go along, I just won't bargain any more and we can both shut down and lose money." Again, if output OX^* can be set through such tactics, combined profits will be higher than they would be if one party quoted a price and the other adjusted its output to make the best of it. Moreover, unlike the case of collusion in duopoly, consumers benefit along with producers from such cooperative behavior. The amount of the relevant input transferred is necessarily higher with joint profit maximization under bilateral monopoly than it would be with either buyer or seller price leadership—i.e., leading to outputs OX_B or OX_s in Figure 10.1. And barring extreme production or cost function assumptions, if the amount of input is higher, the amount of end product will also be higher, and this necessarily means lower prices to consumers.

Vertical integration and efficiency It is clear then that cooperative behavior can be socially desirable when a monopolist deals with a monopsonist. Nevertheless, reaching a cooperative solution may not be easy, especially when the parties find themselves engaging in the brinkmanship of "take it or leave it" threats. Bargaining stalemates can arise, leading to a cessation of trade injurious to both parties' interests (as well as to consumers). Recognizing this, parties to a bilateral monopoly frequently seek to foster a more stable relationship through the vertical integration of successive production stages.[8]

When monopsony and monopoly stages are integrated vertically, decisions regarding how much of an input to use can be guided by the actual marginal cost of the input, rather than by

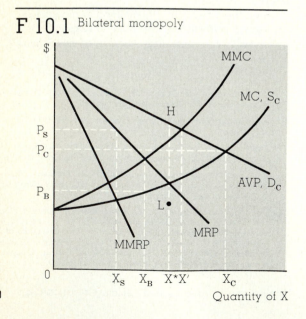

F 10.1 Bilateral monopoly

bargaining stratagems or by the monopsonist's concern for restraining the volume of its purchases in order to avoid driving up the supply price. Consequently, vertical integration facilitates arriving at the input choice that extracts maximum profits from whatever monopoly power exists at either stage—that is, the choice consistent with joint profit maximization under unintegrated bilateral monopoly.[9] For ultimate consumers, this is less satisfactory than competitive behavior at *all* stages. But as we have seen, it is an improvement over the even greater output restrictions and end product price elevations that can occur under imperfect bargaining or a price leadership solution to the bilateral monopoly problem. If then bargaining difficulties preclude joint profit maximization under bilateral monopoly, vertical integration can make everyone—producers *and* consumers—better off. Economic welfare is unambiguously improved.

This point has implications transcending the bilateral monopoly case. Indeed, in our prior analysis of the situation in which a monopolistic input supplier quotes a price to which the buyer reacts, monopsony power on the buyer's side was irrelevant, for in accepting the seller's price lead, the buyer essentially waives the use of its monopsony power. What induced an excessive restriction of output in that case was not monopsony, but the vertical pyramiding of two *sellers' monopolies*—one at the input stage and one at the output stage. Each monopolist's decision is guided by the marginal revenue derived from the demand curve it directly faces, and through cumulated myopic marginalization, a greater restriction of output results than that which maximizes the joint profits of all firms in the vertical chain.[10] If the buyer can exercise monopsony power and break the monopolistic supplier's price leadership, a joint profit maximization solution might be restored. But success is uncertain, and because vertical integration of pyramided sellers' monopolies also helps to avoid the output restrictions from cumulated marginalization, it has been singled out as a compelling welfare-enhancing solution to the 'vertical chain monopoly' problem.[11]

The theoretical propositions established thus far—that piling one monopoly on top of another

7. This is far from obvious intuitively, so a mathematical proof may comfort the skeptical reader. For simplicity, we assume that the supplying firm has a linear marginal cost function $MC_s = a + 2bX_s$, so the total cost function is $TC_s = k + aX + bX^2$. Let one unit of the input X be transformed by the buying firm into one unit of output Q after a processing cost of c per unit is incurred. The inverse demand function for the buying firm's output Q is assumed to be $P(Q) = d - fQ$, where $d > (a + c)$. The buying firm's profits as a supplier of output can be written:

(1) $\quad \pi_B = Q(d - fQ) - cQ - P_x Q$

where P_x is the price charged by the supplier for a unit of X transformed into a unit of Q. Maximum profits for the buying firm occur where:

(2) $\quad \dfrac{\partial \pi_B}{dQ} = d - c - P_x - 2fQ = 0$

Given that $Q \equiv X$, this can be transformed into the derived demand curve MRP confronting a price-announcing supplier, i.e., $P_x = d - c - 2fX$. Henceforth we shall use the 1 to 1 assumed relationship between Q and X to write all functions in terms of input quantities X rather than end product output Q.

Joint profits π_j are the sum of the buying firm's profits $\pi_B = X(d - fX) - cX - P_x X$ plus the supplier's profits $\pi_s = P_x X - k - aX - bX^2$. Thus,

(3) $\quad \pi_j = dX - fX^2 - cX - P_x X + P_x X - k - aX - bX^2$

Setting the derivative of this function equal to zero and solving for the joint profit-maximizing value of X^*, we have:

(4) $\quad X^* = \dfrac{d - c - a}{2(f + b)}$

Let $M = d - c - a$ and $N = f + b$. Then total profits:

(5) $\quad \pi_j^* = d\left(\dfrac{M}{2N}\right) - f\left(\dfrac{M}{2N}\right)^2 - c\left(\dfrac{M}{2N}\right) - k - a\left(\dfrac{M}{2N}\right) - b\left(\dfrac{M}{2N}\right)^2$

$\quad\quad = (d - c - a)\left(\dfrac{M}{2N}\right) - (f + b)\left(\dfrac{M}{2N}\right)^2 - k$

$\quad\quad = M\left(\dfrac{M}{2N}\right) - N\left(\dfrac{M}{2N}\right)^2 - k$

$\quad\quad = \dfrac{M^2}{4N} - k$

Assume now that the buyer is price leader, proposing a price P_x for X to which the supplier reacts by equating its marginal cost with P_x. Its supply function is therefore $P_x = a + 2bX$, which is in turn the *average* input cost function to the buyer. The buyer now chooses a level of input purchase (and a value of P_x consistent with the input supply function) so as to maximize its profits:

(6) $\quad \pi_B = X(d - fX) - cX - X(a + 2bX)$

Differentiating, setting the derivative equal to zero, and solving, we obtain:

(7) $\quad X_B = \dfrac{d - c - a}{2(f + 2b)}$

Comparing this quantity with the joint profit-maximizing X^* in equation (4), note that $(f + 2b) > (f + b)$, and so the amount of X used under buyer price leadership is necessarily less than under joint profit maximization. To determine total profits, let $M = d - c - a$ as before and let $ZN = f + 2b$, with $Z > 1$. Thus,

in a vertical chain can lead to lower total profits, and that integrating such monopolies vertically can enhance both profits and welfare—have an important corollary. It states that if a firm has a monopoly over the supply of some indispensable input (i.e., one without substitutes) at any stage in a vertical chain of markets, the firm's monopoly power cannot be enhanced by vertical integration into other *competitive* stages.[12] For wherever it is in the chain, the monopoly can take full advantage of all output-restricting, profit-enhancing opportunities by correctly deriving its own monopoly demand function from the demand functions and costs of competitive stages nearer the consumer, i.e., downstream.

This corollary does not necessarily hold when downstream firms can substitute other inputs for the monopolist's output, nor is it true, as is sometimes argued, that an upstream monopolist cannot increase its profits by integrating into downstream competitive stages. The second part of this qualification is demonstrated in Figure 10.2.[13] It analyzes the input choice problem of a competitive firm able to substitute along isoquant Q_D between competitively supplied input Y and monopolized input X in producing a given quantity of output. Because X is monopolized, its price will be high in relation to its marginal cost, and the isocost line C_M confronting the buying firm will be relatively steep, leading to the input mix choice M. If, however, the input monopolist integrates vertically downstream, then as a user of X it perceives the cost of X not as its monopoly price, but as the lower real marginal cost of X. Its isocost line will have a less steep slope, as in C_{I1}, leading to the more X-intensive input combination choice V. Since the unintegrated input choice bundle M lies on a higher parallel isocost line C_{I2}, again assuming X to be accounted for at marginal cost, it follows that the elimination of input choice distortions through integration yields real cost savings proportional to the distance between C_{I2} and C_{I1}. As a first approximation, these cost savings accrue as additional profits to the integrating monopolist.

It is conceivable that the integrated monopolist will pass some of these savings on to end product consumers in the form of lower prices. However, it is also possible that, having gained control over the downstream industry's use of *all* inputs, the integrated firm will *raise* prices on its newly monopolized end product.[14] The mathematical relationships are complex and no completely general predictions are possible. Numerical analyses suggest that for plausible assumptions concerning substitution relationships, an end product price increase will be the most likely consequence of integration that permits a substitutable input monopolist also to monopolize previously competitive downstream production.[15] That increase tends to be larger, the less important the once solely monopolized input is in relation to the downstream stage's demand for all inputs, and the less elastic end product demand is. Integration increases the input monopolist's profit both by permitting lower cost production and by broadening its control over prices. Since these two effects have opposite welfare implications, no simple conclusions can be drawn as to whether on balance the vertical extension of monopoly power into a competitive stage makes society better or worse off. The answer, as in many economic problems, depends upon the data of the particular situation.

Vertical integration as a source of monopoly power Excepting only the last paragraph, the

F 10.2 Choice of monopolized and competitive inputs

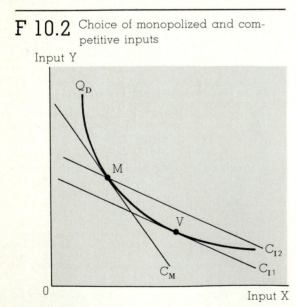

Input Y

preceding subsection provides a capsule view of the 'Chicago School' argument for viewing vertical integration as either socially desirable or innocuous. Vertical integration is perceived as enhancing efficiency by dissolving bilateral monopoly bargaining stalemates, eliminating double marginalization by vertical chain monopolies, and minimizing input substitution distortions. And at least for a special class of cases, it also leads to lower end product prices. Therefore, the argument continues, it should not be discouraged—e.g., by antitrust actions.

The final paragraph shows that exceptions to this sanguine conclusion can arise. Vertical integration leading to the monopolization of once-competitive industries *may* enhance monopoly power, raise prices, and reduce the sum of producers' plus consumers' surplus. That might be demonstration enough that the economic world is complex. But long before the early 1970s, when the articles proving these qualifications were published, there was a school of thought that saw vertical integration as a significant potential source of heightened monopoly power. Something needs to be said about both the theory and evidence underlying those earlier views.

Perhaps the most straightforward hypothesis is that vertical integration increases barriers to new entry and fringe expansion.[16] There are two main steps in the reasoning.

First, it is said that survival as a nonintegrated entity is precarious in a concentrated industry whose principal sellers also have strong positions upstream in input markets and downstream in fabrication and distribution markets. Supplies of needed inputs may be cut off at will or priced to squeeze independent downstream firms' processing margins; and customers who are also competitors may cut back orders sharply and favor their integrated supply units, especially in times of slack demand. To avoid these hazards, entrants may feel compelled to enter on a fully integrated basis, with a considerably larger capital investment.

Second, capital market imperfections may make it impossible or at least more costly to raise the larger sum needed for integrated entry, and thus the supply of potential entrants is depleted, or existing firms can hold prices above costs by a

$$(8) \quad \pi_j^B = M\left(\frac{M}{2ZN}\right) - N\left(\frac{M}{2ZN}\right)^2 - k$$

$$= \left(\frac{2ZM^2}{4Z^2N}\right) - \left(\frac{M^2}{4Z^2N}\right) - k$$

$$= \left(\frac{2Z-1}{Z^2}\right)\left(\frac{M^2}{4N}\right) - k$$

Since $(2Z - 1)/Z^2 < 1$ for $Z > 1$, profits with buyer price leadership [equation (8)] must be less than profits with joint profit maximization [equation (5)].

Now let the monopolist supplier confront the buyer with a price P_x, leading the buyer to maximize its profits according to equation (2). The supplier's perceived demand function is $P_x = d - c - 2fX$. The supplier's profit function is:

$$(9) \quad \pi_S = X(d - c - 2fX) - k - aX - bX^2$$

Setting the derivative equal to zero and solving for X, we obtain:

$$(10) \quad X_S = \frac{d - c - a}{2(2f + b)}$$

Again, this is necessarily less than the joint profit-maximizing X^* in equation (4). And by a proof analogous to equation (8), it is readily shown that joint profits are also lower under seller price leadership.

(8) Cf. also Chapter 4, pp. 89–91 *supra*.

(9) Extending the analysis of note 7, an integrated monopolist views its total revenue as $X(d - fX)$ and its total costs as $cX + k + aX + bX^2$. Its profit function is therefore $\pi_I = dX - fX^2 - cX - k - aX - bX^2$. Since this is identical to equation (3) in note 7, maximizing π_I is the same as maximizing π_j.

For an analysis of the efficiency gains resulting when, through upstream vertical integration, a monopsonist can transform into fixed costs rents that would be variable costs in the absence of integration, see Martin K. Perry, "Vertical Integration: The Monopsony Case," *American Economic Review* 68 (September 1978): 561–70.

(10) This follows directly from equations (2), (9), and (10) in note 7.

(11) See especially Joseph J. Spengler, "Vertical Integration and Antitrust Policy," *Journal of Political Economy* 68 (August 1950): 347–52. See also M. L. Greenhut and H. Ohta, "Related Market Conditions and Interindustrial Mergers," *American Economic Review* 66 (June 1976): 267–77.

12. Proof: Modifying the assumptions of note 7, we assume that the input supplier is a pure monopolist but that the end product market is competitive, with demand function $P(Q) = d - fQ$. No changes are made in cost assumptions. The competitive industry will expand until its end product price $P(Q)$ equals its unit processing cost c plus the input price P_x. Thus, in equilibrium $P(Q) = d - fQ = c + P_x$. Recalling that $Q \equiv X$, it follows that $P_x = d - c - fX$. This is the demand for the monopolist supplier's output. Its profits are:

$$(1) \quad \hat{\pi}_S = X(d - c - fX) - k - aX - bX^2$$

Setting the derivative equal to zero and solving for X, we obtain:

$$(2) \quad \hat{X}_S = \frac{d - c - a}{2(f + b)}$$

which is identical to the joint profit-maximizing output X^* in equation (4) of footnote 7. Moreover, since the competitive stage earns zero profits, the monopolist input supplier realizes all of the industry's profits. It is easily shown that these are equal to the joint maximum profits in equation (5) of note 7.

higher margin before attracting entry. This argument is typically dismissed out of hand by Chicago School economists, who insist that capital market imperfections either do not exist or are of little consequence.[17] On this the Chicagoans are almost surely wrong, since it is definitely more difficult or costly for small new entrants to raise capital than for established firms.[18] However, whether the interaction between vertical integration and capital market imperfections leads to significantly elevated entry barriers depends upon how large the required capital lump is, how much difference integration makes in it, and who the otherwise most favored entrants are—i.e., newcomers or already well-established corporations with abundant access to funds for diversification. Cases in which the interaction of these factors is important as an entry barrier can undoubtedly be found. Yet they may well be rare. On their importance, there is very little evidence.

Integration can also affect the conduct of firms in ways that have feedback effects on structure. As suggested already, integrated enterprises may occasionally or regularly refuse to sell to or buy from nonintegrated rivals; or they may raise input prices while holding prices constant at the next stage downstream, thus subjecting nonintegrated rivals at that stage to a squeeze. Numerous claims of such squeezes or refusals to deal can be found. They have several apparent rationales.

For one, harassment of nonintegrated competitors might, as Comanor observes, be "an investment in entry barriers" aimed at limiting existing rivals' expansion and discouraging new single-stage entry.[19] Second, monopolistic suppliers may squeeze their nonintegrated competitor-customers because the customer's costs are inefficiently high—either because of distorted input prices or causes outside the supplier's control—and the supplier believes it can achieve greater efficiency and earn higher profits by taking over the customer's business, e.g., through mergers consummated at prices depressed owing to the customer's relative unprofitability.[20] Third, a tradition of well-disciplined pricing behavior can add significantly to monopoly power in an oligopolistic industry. Walter Adams and Joel Dirlam argue that price squeezes were employed by the leading U.S. steel producers during the 1950s and early 1960s to discourage price cutting by less integrated wire products makers using a mix of domestic and imported inputs.[21] Major petroleum companies' reluctance to provide pipeline access and product supplies to nonintegrated refiners and marketers may have had similar intent,[22] although such tactics appear to have had at best only transitory success in keeping the independents in line. Fourth, refusals to deal and squeezes might lead over time to market share changes sufficiently large to convert a loose oligopoly into one tight enough to sustain coordinated pricing behavior. This could occur, for example, when there is a linking of three phenomena—difficult entry conditions at a vertical stage whose competitive fringe is large enough to preclude coordinated pricing by the oligopolistic core, entry and exit highly responsive to profit levels at a partly integrated downstream stage,[23] and a distinct preference on the part of nonintegrated downstream firms to buy from nonintegrated (i.e., nonrival) suppliers. Then by charging high upstream product prices and squeezing out and/or acquiring downstream independents, integrated sellers might be able to increase their downstream market share and consequently (by shifting the distribution of supply source preferences) increase their upstream market share without experiencing the new entry and fringe expansion that a high upstream price would encourage in the absence of substantial upstream entry barriers.

A basic problem in evaluating these and similar market power aggrandizement hypotheses is that it is hard to determine whether they, or a more benign causal nexus, better explain observed behavior. Thus, there have been repeated assertions that primary aluminum producers have squeezed independent fabricators by setting high ingot prices and then forcing down fabricated product prices to levels insufficient to cover processing costs.[24] Squeezes have definitely occurred. What is not clear is whether they were deliberate, or the unintended result of strong price discipline at the primary ingot stage combined with vigorous competition at the fabricated product stage. The weight of evidence favors the latter conjecture, but it is difficult to rationalize such anomalies as losses in products like aluminum conductor cable persisting over four decades. A complementary explanation might be that when integrated firms succeed in holding their primary product prices well above marginal costs, they take only those marginal costs, and not arm's-length transaction prices, into account in pricing products processed further internally; and this marginal cost pricing intensifies downstream competition. In the absence of special patterns of price discrimination[25] or predatory intent, however, this is economically irrational, for when a firm sells the same product both externally and to its own internal divisions, the true marginal cost of internal usage is the revenue forgone by not selling additional units to outsiders. Failure to recognize this underlies the common but probably erroneous assertion that integrated petroleum companies with substantial crude oil reserves are likely in an era of artificially elevated crude oil prices to price their refined products so low as to jeopardize the survival of nonintegrated refiners.

The case of petroleum suggests still another explanation for vertical price squeezes. Many of the industries in which allegations of such squeezes have appeared frequently—e.g., petroleum, copper, aluminum, steel, and cement—have mineral extraction stages enjoying special income tax preferences associated with resource depletion. In certain forms, such tax preferences create incentives for integrated producers to shift as much of their reported earnings as possible to the raw material extraction stage, among other things by setting high prices at that stage and accepting low margins downstream. If internal transfer and external sale prices are the same, this can impose a squeeze on nonintegrated raw material buyers.[26] There is compelling evidence that in both the United States and in Europe the integrated petroleum companies have tended to show very low accounting profits in their refining and marketing operations, compensating with high returns at the less heavily taxed crude oil stage. Much less clear is whether this has squeezed independent refiners. Except in periods of severe market disequilibrium (sometimes aggravated by government controls), the independents appear to have thrived despite the dis-

(13) Drawn with minor modifications from John M. Vernon and Daniel A. Graham, "Profitability of Monopolization by Vertical Integration," *Journal of Political Economy* 79 (July/August 1971): 924–25.

(14) In "Vertical Integration Revisited," *Journal of Law and Economics* 19 (April 1976): 28, John S. McGee and Lowell R. Bassett observe correctly that the monopolist could achieve comparable control *inter alia* by monopolizing all substitute inputs instead of integrating downstream. Thus, the critical phenomenon is the breadth of the monopoly achieved rather than vertical integration per se.
   Downstream integration may also permit the monopolist to practice price discrimination with respect to both customers of the downstream industry and other suppliers of inputs to that industry. See J. R. Gould, "Price Discrimination and Vertical Control: A Note," *Journal of Political Economy* 85 (October 1977): 1063–71. Or it may facilitate more profitable adaptation to downstream demand uncertainties. See Roger D. Blair and David L. Kaserman, "Uncertainty and the Incentive for Vertical Integration," *Southern Economic Journal* 26 (July 1978): 266–72.

(15) Frederick R. Warren-Boulton, "Vertical Control with Variable Proportions," *Journal of Political Economy* 82 (July/August 1974): 783–802; and Richard Schmalensee, "A Note on the Theory of Vertical Integration," *Journal of Political Economy* 81 (March/April 1973): 442–49.

(16) See especially William S. Comanor, "Vertical Mergers, Market Power and the Antitrust Laws," *American Economic Review* 57 (May 1967): 259–62.

17. See e.g. John S. McGee's comment on Comanor in the *American Economic Review* 57 (May 1967): 270.

18. See F. M. Scherer, Alan Beckenstein, Erich Kaufer, and R. D. Murphy, *The Economics of Multi-Plant Operation: An International Comparisons Study* (Cambridge, Mass.: Harvard University Press, 1975), pp. 284–90.

19. Comanor, "Vertical Mergers," p. 261.

20. See Schmalensee, "A Note on the Theory of Vertical Integration," pp. 448–49.

21. Walter Adams and Joel Dirlam, "Steel Imports and Vertical Oligopoly Power," *American Economic Review* 54 (September 1964): 640–46.

22. See the Preliminary Federal Trade Commission staff report on its *Investigation of the Petroleum Industry*, print of the Permanent Subcommittee on Investigations, Senate Committee on Government Operations (Washington, D.C.: Government Printing Office, July 1973), pp. 6–11, 25–26.

23. Cf. the Gaskins model analysis in Chapter 8 *supra*.

24. Compare Donald H. Wallace, *Market Control in the Aluminum Industry* (Cambridge, Mass.: Harvard University Press, 1937), pp. 374–95, 449–73; *U.S. v. Aluminum Company of America et al.*, 44 F. Supp. 97, 178–223 (1942); M. J. Peck, *Competition in the Aluminum Industry: 1945–1958* (Cambridge, Mass.: Harvard University Press, 1961), pp. 72–82, 97–119; "Aluminum Frets Over Another Big Glut," *Business Week*, 29 November 1969, pp. 28–29; "Aluminum Prices Head for the Roof," *Business Week*, 18 April 1970, p. 26; and U.S., Council on Wage and Price Stability staff report, *Aluminum Prices: 1974–75* (Washington, D.C.: Government Printing Office, September 1976), pp. 21–23, 142–49.

torted price structure—evidently, either because internal and external prices were not identical, or because the independents were more efficient than their integrated counterparts, or perhaps both. Still, the opportunity for a plausible vertical squeeze plainly existed.

Finally, business concerns may engage in what appears to be exclusionary conduct not to enhance the level of monopoly power in a series of vertically integrated industries but merely to redistribute it. Oligopolies frequently settle down into behavioral patterns in which price competition is shunned even though some or all members suffer from appreciable excess capacity. Nonprice rivalry then becomes crucial to the distribution of sales. One form of nonprice competition is the acquisition of downstream enterprises who, all else (such as prices) being equal, will purchase from their upstream affiliates. If acquisitions of this sort deflect significant amounts of sales, disadvantaged rivals are apt to acquire other potential customers in self-defense; and reciprocal fear of foreclosure may precipitate a bandwagon effect in which remaining independent downstream enterprises are feverishly sought. This seems to be what happened in the late 1950s and early 1960s as cement manufacturers acquired numerous ready-mix concrete companies despite an evident dearth of efficiency-increasing or monopoly-enhancing opportunities and the acknowledged anxiety of cement makers over the course they found themselves pursuing.[27]

These explanations of the motives for vertical integration, some implying the enhancement of monopoly power and some not, are both theoretically and empirically much messier and less satisfying than the hypotheses associated with the Chicago School of thought. Emphasizing oligopoly rather than pure monopoly and dynamics rather than statics, they are less easily hammered into a mathematically tractable mold. Since multiple causes and motives could plausibly be at work, it is harder to obtain a clear picture of what is happening and why. Because both benign and rapacious motives can seldom be ruled out conclusively and because the outcomes of strategic moves in oligopoly often diverge from what was intended, a good deal of skepticism is warranted

in evaluating claims that monopoly power is being aggrandized through vertical integration. Yet dogmatic insistence that it cannot happen is equally unwarranted.

Countervailing power and consumer prices

Let us focus now more closely on the exercise of monopsony power, whose importance was stressed in a well-known 1952 book by J. K. Galbraith.[28] He argued *inter alia* that in modern oligopolistically structured industries, the main force compelling sellers to conform to consumer wants and to hold prices near cost is not competition but countervailing power exercised by strong buyers. As examples, Galbraith cited A&P's deft use of power to extract price reductions from grocery manufacturers; the discounts won from oligopolistic tire makers by Sears, Roebuck; the auto industry's reputed success in curbing the pricing power of steel mills; and (on the other side of the market) the ability of strong unions to win large wage and fringe benefit concessions from powerful employer groups.

The pure theory In the analysis of bilateral monopoly accompanying Figure 10.1, we found that although joint profit maximization by a strong buyer facing a monopolistic seller led to higher output and lower prices than alternate price leadership strategies, output was still substantially restricted compared to the competitive equilibrium. Under what circumstances might countervailing power lead to still better results for the consumer? The answer must involve an asymmetry on the buyer's side: The buyer must be powerful enough to constrain the monopolistic seller's prices, but lack the power as reseller to charge monopoly prices. If in the terms of Figure 10.1 the buyer lacks monopoly power, it will expand its purchases until the perceived marginal cost of input X rises into equality with the average value (not the marginal value, as with downstream monopoly) of X. Thus, it will use OX' units of X—more, as Figure 10.1 is constructed, than the joint profit-maximizing bilateral monopoly quantity OX^*.[29] With more input purchased, more output will presumably be produced and consumers will benefit from lower prices. Should the supply of X be perfectly elastic (i.e., with curve MC,S_c horizontal) because the monopolist producer of X operates at constant unit costs, a buying firm with monopsony power but no monopoly power would expand its purchase all the way out to the level associated with pure competition at both the input and end product producing stages. We see then that countervailing power is likely to benefit consumers most when three conditions hold simultaneously: when upstream supply functions are highly elastic, when buyers can bring substantial power to bear on the pricing of monopolistic suppliers, and when those same buyers face substantial price competition in their end product markets.

Bilateral oligopoly The simultaneous attainment of all three conditions is unlikely under pure bilateral monopoly, which in any event is rare in the real world. However, bilateral oligopoly—with a few powerful buyers facing oligopolistic sellers—is more promising. It is entirely conceivable that a few end product sellers could have sufficient power as buyers to hold the price of intermediate products supplied by upstream oligopolists at or near competitive levels. At the same time, for any of the reasons analyzed in Chapters 7 and 8, they might find themselves unable to depart appreciably from competitive pricing in their end product market.

Strong buyers restrain the pricing power of oligopolistic sellers in several ways. One was identified in Chapter 7, where we saw that oligopolists are prone to cut prices in order to land an unusually large order, especially when they have excess capacity. Large buyers can exploit this weakness by concentrating their orders into big lumps, dangling the temptation before each seller and encouraging a break from the established price structure. Yet it is not always necessary to be one of the largest buyers to play the game, and mere size is insufficient if wielded ineffectively. In the cement industry, for example, the largest buyers were often state governments procuring supplies for their highway construction programs. But during the depressed 1930s, and

even when all requirements of a state were lumped together into a single giant purchase, cement makers refused to undercut each other because when the state purchasing agency announced an aggressive winning bid, as required by law, rival cement makers instituted retaliatory cuts on nongovernmental business. Large construction contractors, who normally purchased less cement than the state governments, were more successful in breaking the producers' pricing discipline because they shopped around and bargained for *secret* concessions before placing their sizeable, irregularly occurring orders. Recognizing this, many states ceased buying cement directly, decentralizing the procurement function to highway contractors.[30]

(25) But see Robert Crandall, "Vertical Integration and the Market for Repair Parts in the United States Automobile Industry," *Journal of Industrial Economics* 35 (July 1968): 212–34; David L. McNicol, "The Two Price System in the Copper Industry," *Bell Journal of Economics* 6 (Spring 1975): 64–72; and Bruce T. Allen, "Vertical Integration and Market Foreclosure: The Case of Cement and Concrete," *Journal of Law and Economics* 14 (April 1971): 255–58 and especially note 21.

(26) On the logic of the squeeze in petroleum pricing, see Melvin G. de Chazeau and Alfred E. Kahn, *Integration and Competition in the Petroleum Industry* (New Haven: Yale University Press, 1959), pp. 221–25; the preliminary FTC staff report on its *Investigation of the Petroleum Industry*, pp. 25–26, 60–62; Richard B. Mancke, *The Future of U.S. Energy Policy* (New York: Columbia University Press, 1974), pp. 102–105, 173–74; and Ben Bolch and William M. Damon, "The Depletion Allowance and Vertical Integration in the Petroleum Industry," *Southern Economic Journal* 26 (July 1978): 241–49.

27. See especially Allen, "Vertical Integration," pp. 251–74; the references cited there; and the comment by James W. Meehan, Jr. and reply by Allen in the *Journal of Law and Economics* 15 (October 1972): 461–71. On apparently similar motives for downstream integration into semiconductor products, see Douglas W. Webbink, *The Semiconductor Industry*, Federal Trade Commission staff report (Washington, D.C.: Government Printing Office, January 1977), pp. 62–66.

28. John Kenneth Galbraith, *American Capitalism: The Concept of Countervailing Power* (Boston: Houghton-Mifflin, 1952). For a critical view, see George J. Stigler, "The Economist Plays with Blocs," *American Economic Review* 44 (May 1954): 7–14.

29. However, this result depends upon the moderately high supply elasticity assumed. With less elastic supply and hence a sharper monopsony restriction, the amount of X purchased could be less than OX^*.

30. Samuel M. Loescher, *Imperfect Collusion in the Cement Industry* (Cambridge, Mass.: Harvard University Press, 1959), pp. 54–55, 112–13, 130–34.

Large buyers also play one seller off against the others to elicit price concessions. For instance, each of the major automobile manufacturers has a principal tire supplier, but each also spreads its business around to other tire makers so that it can threaten to shift, or actually shift, its distribution of orders in favor of the supplier who offers more attractive terms. Similar practices were reported by James McKie in his study of price relationships between the tin can and tin-plated steel manufacturers.[31] A complementary ploy is considered unethical if not illegal in business circles, but it occurs with some frequency.[32] When sellers lack confidence in each other's determination to maintain pricing discipline, they are easy prey to the purchasing agent who fabricates convincing but fictitious claims of concessions offered by unnamed rivals. Once a single supplier is taken in by this ruse, the actual quotation (and the favorable shift in patronage with which it was rewarded) provides a lever to extract lower prices from additional sellers.

These tactics are pursued most successfully when demand is slack, so that producers have excess capacity that can be utilized profitably if an increased share of some major buyer's business can be captured through price cuts, or when the loss of business to a price-cutting rival would leave previously favored sellers with a substantial burden of underabsorbed overhead costs. The balance of power is clearly in the hands of the buyer, and especially the large buyer, during a downturn. One might expect a bargaining power reversal during booms, when demand is outracing capacity. Then oligopolistic sellers may be in a position to compensate for past concessions, playing one eager buyer off against the others to bid prices up. On this symmetry conjecture we have little concrete evidence. Adelman's rough estimates show that A&P won proportionately larger special price concessions from its suppliers during the depressed early 1930s than in prosperous 1929, and there were faint indications of a decline in concessions as the onset of World War II revived demand.[33] McKie, on the other hand, found no evidence that tin-plated steel manufacturers were able to play one large tin can maker off against the others to escalate prices when steel was in short supply following

the war. His explanation was that "sellers hesitate to give buyers their own medicine at such times, fearing the imminent return of a buyer's market. Thus, there tends to be an asymmetry of bargaining power in bilateral oligopoly, other things being equal."[34] As we shall see in a later chapter, oligopolistic industries have tended to show more restraint than competitively structured industries in raising prices during booms, although it is not clear whether this is attributable to countervailing power, a longer run perspective in pricing decisions, or the concentrated industries' greater vulnerability to governmental suasion and anti-inflationary measures. Thus, we must return a Scotch verdict. We simply do not know whether strong buyers in a bilateral oligopoly situation forgo in booms what they gain during slumps.

Large buyers can also issue credible threats to integrate vertically upstream, producing their own requirements of an input unless prices are held close to cost. Unlike potential outside entrants, they have an assured market, and therefore have no reason to fear the pricing reactions of established producers. When the buyer's demand is large enough to permit realization of all scale economies in producing for its own use, it can scarcely lose: Either sellers restrain their prices in response to its threat or, if the threat fails, the buyer displaces them and consumes its own low-cost production. Numerous applications of this dual strategy are recorded in industry studies. Although some scale economies are apparently unattainable to firms integrating vertically, tin-plated steel prices were restrained before aluminum became an important substitute by the ability of can manufacturers to begin plating their own steel. Tin can prices were in turn held in check by the threat (and in some cases the actuality) of upstream integration by large food canners and beer brewers.[35] The auto manufacturers have kept downward pressure on prices for glass windows, electrical components, fabricated parts, and even cold-rolled steel sheet by their demonstrated willingness to produce for their own use whenever the prospect of cost savings becomes attractive.[36]

Surprisingly, Adelman found only one clear instance of a successful vertical integration threat by A&P to win price concessions, despite the giant retailer's extensive entry into food manufacturing operations.[37] Whether this reflects inadequacies in the available evidence or A&P's belief that threats of potential competition would have little effect on food suppliers already under heavy pressure from their many competitors is not certain. The A&P history does demonstrate, however, that the desire to countervail oligopoly pricing power is not the only motive for vertical integration into suppliers' fields. Integration can also confer real economies in transferring goods from one stage to another—e.g., minimization of sales representation and contracting functions, better coordination of production with requirements, streamlining of distribution channels, lower spoilage, and the like.[38]

A further approach to upstream integration merits more extended comment. Some firms, including the automobile and aircraft manufacturers, engage in what is called "tapered integration."[39] That is, they produce a portion of their materials and parts requirements and farm out the remainder to independent specialists. This approach gives the buyer a powerful bargaining position relative to the suppliers, for the buyer can threaten credibly to increase internal production at their expense unless prices are held in check. Internal production also gives the buyer a good feel for costs, which is most useful in bargaining. In addition, the buyer can transfer the risk of demand fluctuations to suppliers. In both good times and bad, internal production lines are kept operating near capacity. Peak requirements are met by loading outside suppliers with orders, while in a slump outside orders are cut back sharply. As a result the outsiders bear nearly all the brunt of output swings, and the percentage variation in their employment over the business cycle is much greater than it would be if they produced the buyer's full requirements. Of course, overflow suppliers will be reluctant to accept this precarious existence without being compensated for their risks, and one might expect them to hold out for high prices in periods of peak demand. The available evidence fails to support this hypothesis, apparently because the suppliers recognize that when the boom ebbs, their ability to keep going at all depends upon the goodwill

of their customer. The main connection between risk and profits in such cases works through the mechanism of entry. New firms will not enter unless buyers are paying prices sufficiently high to compensate for the risks. If buyers desire to maintain a flow of new outside investment to satisfy their needs, they must refrain from frightening would-be entrants by taking full advantage of their bargaining power over companies whose investments are already committed. If on the other hand they believe there is too much investment in supplier capacity—e.g., because demand is secularly declining, as it was in the military manned aircraft field during the 1950s and in guided missiles and spacecraft during the early 1970s—they can extract unusually favorable

31. James W. McKie, *Tin Cans and Tin Plate* (Cambridge, Mass.: Harvard University Press, 1959), pp. 58–63.

32. On the legal difficulties resulting from A&P's use of the tactic, see the Federal Trade Commission's opinion *in re The Great Atlantic & Pacific Tea Co., Inc., et al.,* 87 F.T.C. 962 (1976). See also Chapter 21 *infra.*

33. Morris A. Adelman, *A&P: A Study in Price-Cost Behavior and Public Policy* (Cambridge, Mass.: Harvard University Press, 1959), pp. 237, 242.

34. McKie, *Tin Cans and Tin Plate*, pp. 24–25, 63.

35. McKie, *Tin Cans and Tin Plate*, pp. 50–54, 110–14, 291–92.

36. See Simon N. Whitney, *Antitrust Policies*, vol. I (New York: Twentieth Century Fund, 1958), pp. 496–500; A. D. H. Kaplan, Joel B. Dirlam, and R. F. Lanzillotti, *Pricing Practices in Big Business* (Washington, D.C.: Brookings Institution, 1958), p. 172; and (for an instance in which countervailing power failed) "Move To Sidetrack Steel's Price Rise Dropped by G.M.," *New York Times*, 6 August 1969, p. 47.

37. Adelman, *A&P*, pp. 269–71 and Chapter 12 generally.

38. Adelman, *A&P*, pp. 253–58. For evidence that integration between manufacturing and retailing stages often yields only modest economies, see Scherer et al., *The Economics of Multi-Plant Operation*, pp. 269–71, 319–20.

39. For autos, see Whitney, *Antitrust Policies*, pp. 496–98; and "UAW Mounts Campaign Against 'Monopsony,'" *Business Week*, 24 July 1965, pp. 43–44. For aircraft, see M. J. Peck and F. M. Scherer, *The Weapons Acquisition Process: An Economic Analysis* (Boston: Harvard Business School Division of Research, 1962), pp. 386–404; and John S. Day, *Subcontracting Policy in the Airframe Industry* (Boston: Harvard Business School Division of Research, 1956). On the widespread use of tapered integration in Japan as a means of increasing flexibility when large-company workers have lifetime employment tenure, see Richard E. Caves and Masu Uekusa, *Industrial Organization in Japan* (Washington, D.C.: Brookings Institution, 1976), pp. 112–15.

bargains from their overflow suppliers, whose lot is not a happy one.

Thus, large buyers may find it advantageous to integrate vertically upstream for any of several reasons, of which the desire to hold suppliers' prices near competitive levels is only one. Still, the fact that U.S. retailing giants do relatively little manufacturing for resale and that manufacturers spend on the average half of every sales dollar for materials and parts supplied by independent firms supports either and probably both of two conclusions: (1) that only in a minority of cases does the net financial advantage lie in favor of making rather than buying general-purpose materials and parts; and (2) that supplier prices are often kept near competitive levels, if not by actual competition, then by fear of new competition through vertical entry. Only when barriers to entry into the suppliers' fields are high do these generalizations break down.

Pass-on dynamics It seems clear that countervailing power can and does lead to lower prices, at least in that middle ground of oligopolistic market structure where sellers are few enough to recognize their interdependence, but too weak to maintain a disciplined front against the whipsaw tactics of a strong, shrewd buyer. The question remains—Who benefits, the strong buyer, or the consuming public? Are prices to consumers reduced because retailers and consumer goods manufacturers have struck unusually favorable bargains on the procurement side of their operations?

The answer depends in part upon whether price reductions gained by one large buyer or by a very few spread more widely through the buying industry. Three main cases can be distinguished. First, if the concessions reflect real production and distribution economies associated with large-scale ordering and production, there is no reason to believe that smaller buyers will receive the same opportunities as their sizeable counterparts, at least in the absence of arbitrary legal compulsion.[40] Second, if the concessions are exacted not because of cost differences but because the buyer has bargaining leverage smaller buyers lack, the large buyer may (again in the absence of legal intervention) enjoy a

persistent price advantage over its less powerful rivals. This is the clearest form of price discrimination, to which we shall return in the next chapter. A striking example was the Champion Company's sale of identical spark plugs to Ford Motor Company at $.06 per unit for use in original equipment and $.22 for replacement part use, while independent wholesalers paid $.261 per unit.[41] But third, when several aggressive buyers purchase substantial quantities of an intermediate product, a concession unrelated to cost offered by an oligopolistic supplier to one buyer will sooner or later be found out by other buyers and sellers and, unless discipline in the oligopoly is strong, the concession stands a high probability of spreading. Here what begins as isolated price discrimination touches off a chain of rivalrous reactions that ultimately affects the whole structure of prices.

It is in this last case that contervailing power is most apt to have an effect generally beneficial to consumers. As McKie observes from his study of vertical price relationships in the tin can industry:

> When there is moderate or low concentration among sellers—a "loosely" oligopolistic structure—and there are some large buyers, the result is likely to be a pattern of behavior more effectively competitive than if there were atomistic competition on the buying side.[42]

Similarly, Adelman concluded that

> A limited degree of monopoly ("substantial bargaining power") on one side of the market can be of great service in maintaining competition on the other. A strong, alert buyer, large enough so that the loss of his patronage is not a matter of indifference, constantly on the watch for a break which he can exploit by rolling up the whole price front, able to force concessions first from one and then from all, and followed by the other buyers, can collapse a structure of control or keep it from ever coming into existence.[43]

Whether *all* the benefits of countervailing power are passed on to consumers, or whether some gains are trapped within the vertical price structure, depends upon the absence or presence of power on the selling side of the market. The essential combination of power on the buying side with lack of it on the resale side appears especially compatible with conditions in the retail trades, suggesting that Galbraith's emphasis on retailing to illustrate workable countervailing power was not misguided.[44] As buyers, the large mail-order, food, and drug chains and the major department stores can engage in all the bargaining tactics discussed earlier. These do not always work—e.g., against pharmaceutical manufacturers with strong patent protection, or cereal and detergent companies offering heavily advertised, trademarked brands. But under favorable conditions they can succeed, and the result is a reduction in wholesale prices. The chains in turn are under competitive pressure to pass along their gains. Entry into retailing is not particularly difficult, in part because stores traditionally operating in one field (such as groceries or clothing) can with a minimum of bother add a whole new line (e.g., small appliances or drugs) if the prospects are attractive. Incentives for independent pricing behavior are also strong in retailing, since it is difficult with thousands of different products to play the price-matching game characteristic of oligopolists selling a few homogeneous items.[45] Given these conditions, there is a good chance that gains made through the exercise of buying power will sooner or later be squeezed out and passed along to the consumer.

Still the competitive steamroller does not operate flawlessly even in retailing. Pockets of monopsony profit may persist for extended periods of time. A&P did not, for instance, pass along to consumers all the gains derived from its superior purchasing power and efficiency during the late 1920s and early 1930s. Because of organizational inertia and internal pricing policy disputes, its prices were adjusted downward more slowly than the fall in costs, and profits climbed to new peaks. But A&P's very success created incentives for others to imitate its methods and introduce their own innovations (such as the supermarket). As they did, A&P's volume declined, dragging profits along. By "pursuing a policy of making too much money," A&P "was slowly drowning in its own good fortune."[46] This slow-acting competition forced A&P to reassess its business policies, and one result was a concerted effort to reduce retail price-cost margins and prices. Ultimately then, even if not immediately, consumers were the beneficiaries of A&P's power as a buyer.

Statistical evidence During the 1970s the results of statistical analyses became available to supplement the anecdotal evidence on countervailing power and its effects. They reveal quite uniformly that buyer power does materially affect pricing and profitability.

A key problem in such analyses is devising an appropriate index of buyer power. The approach used most frequently is to compute for any given selling industry the average concentration ratio for the industries to which it sells, weighted by the fraction each buying industry's purchases are of total sales, as indicated in input-output tables.[47] Unless the products sold by a given industry to other industries are specialized (e.g., with the steel industry selling only tin-plated steel to can manufacturers, cold-rolled sheet to auto makers, I-beams to builders, and so on), this index is biased upward, the more so, the more a selling industry's homogeneous output is diffused over

40. Such as the Robinson-Patman Act, which will be studied in Chapter 21.

41. See H. L. Hansen and M. N. Smith, "The Champion Case: What Is Competition?," *Harvard Business Review* 29 (May 1951): 89–103. On the rationale of this practice, which continued into the 1970s, see Allan Zelenitz, "Below-Cost Original Equipment Sales as a Promotional Means," *Review of Economics and Statistics* 59 (November 1977): 438–46.

42. McKie, *Tin Cans and Tin Plate*, pp. 20–21.

43. M. A. Adelman, "Effective Competition and the Antitrust Laws," *Harvard Law Review* 61 (September 1948): 1300.

44. See also Michael E. Porter, *Interbrand Choice, Strategy, and Bilateral Market Power* (Cambridge, Mass.: Harvard University Press, 1976), pp. 11–13, 28–30, 49–53.

45. For evidence of independent pricing of advertised items by Philadelphia retail food chains, see W. J. Baumol, R. E. Quandt, and H. T. Shapiro, "Oligopoly Theory and Retail Food Pricing," *Journal of Business* 38 (October 1965): 346–62.

46. Adelman, *A&P*, pp. 36, 45. The first quotation is from A&P president John Hartford, the second is Adelman's interpretation.

47. For an exception, see L. A. Guth, R. A. Schwartz, and D. K. Whitcomb, "The Use of Buyer Concentration Ratios in Tests of Oligopoly Models," *Review of Economics and Statistics* 58 (November 1976): 488–92; and "Buyer Concentration Ratios," *Journal of Industrial Economics* 25 (June 1977): 241–58. Unfortunately, their index construction assumptions and sample selection are fatally flawed.

many buying industries. In perhaps the most careful and ambitious work published thus far on buyer concentration, Steven Lustgarten attempted to compensate for this bias by including as an additional variable the degree to which a selling industry's sales were dispersed across many buying industry groups.[48]

Lustgarten estimated the following multiple regression equation for 327 manufacturing industries, where *PCM* is the selling industry's price-cost margin in 1963, *CR4* is the four-firm seller concentration ratio, *BCR* is the weighted average buying industry concentration ratio, *DSP* is the index of buying industry dispersion (higher values indicating *less* dispersion), and *KS* is the 1963 ratio of capital to sales:[49]

$$(10.1) \quad PCM = .205 + \underset{(.016)}{.120}\, CR4 - \underset{(.021)}{.111}\, BCR$$

$$- \underset{(.013)}{.051}\, DSP + \underset{(.015)}{.102}\, KS;$$

$$R^2 = .304;\ N = 327$$

Selling industry price-cost margins were significantly higher, the more concentrated and capital-intensive the selling industry was. They were *lower*, the higher average buying industry concentration was and the less dispersed selling industry sales were over many buying sectors, *ceteris paribus*. Similar evidence that buyer power has a restraining effect on sellers comes from analyses of the PIMS data[50] and from more aggregative statistical analyses taking as the dependent variable the ratio of pretax profit plus interest to two-digit manufacturing industry group assets.[51] It is noteworthy that in both the price-cost margin and profitability analyses, buyer concentration variables not only had a significant explanatory role in their own right, but their inclusion also enhanced the observed explanatory power of seller concentration ratios. Thus, taking into account the buyer side of the market appears to be essential for achieving a full, statistically unbiased view of the links between structure and performance.

A different but not inconsistent view of the role of buyer power has been taken by Michael Porter.[52] Unlike the studies surveyed thus far, his work focused on consumer goods manufacturers only. Porter argues that the power of retailers in extracting price and other concessions from these manufacturers depends *inter alia* upon whether products are retailed preponderantly through convenience outlets (such as grocery and book stores), in which the consumer receives little or no advice from salespersons, or through nonconvenience outlets (e.g., for shoes and appliances), in which the salesperson's expertise often influences consumer choices. According to Porter, buyer power is likely to be greater for items sold through nonconvenience outlets. For convenience goods, retailers can exert more pressure on manufacturers' prices when producers do little preselling through advertising than when they do a great deal.

Porter found a considerable amount of statistical support for these conjectures. Thus, multiple regression equations emphasizing *seller* market structure variables explained profitability much better for convenience goods industries than for nonconvenience goods industries. The ratio of manufacturers' advertising outlays to sales had an especially marked differential impact—it was strongly correlated with profitability in convenience goods but insignificantly correlated for producers of nonconvenience goods. Moreover, the addition of variables on the average size, concentration, and diversity of buying retail trades substantially improved regression equation explanations of manufacturers' profitability in nonconvenience goods industries, but not in convenience goods industries.[53] The exercise of countervailing power by retailers therefore appears to be an important check on consumer goods producers' monopoly power when direct personal selling materially affects consumer behavior or when product differentiation is weak. It is ineffective when manufacturers differentiate repetitively purchased convenience goods so successfully that the products "pull" themselves through distribution channels with little "push" from the retailer, who therefore cannot push back on the manufacturers' prices.

Conclusion

Our evidence on the links from buyer concentration and the vertical organization of markets to performance is less solid than the evidence concerning market structure on the sellers' side. It seems clear, however, that vertical structure matters. By bringing their bargaining power to bear, strong buyers are frequently (but not always) able to restrain the price-raising proclivities of monopolistic sellers. If the buyers in turn face significant competition as sellers, consumers benefit. Vertical integration can also alleviate the distortions caused by monopolistic pricing, although there can be special circumstances in which integration bolsters monopoly power rather than taming it. The problem, as always, is to develop bases for predicting which effect will predominate under particular circumstances. Toward that goal we have made at least modest progress.

48. Steven H. Lustgarten, "The Impact of Buyer Concentration in Manufacturing Industries," *Review of Economics and Statistics* 57 (May 1975): 125–32.

49. Lustgarten, "Impact of Buyer Concentration," p. 129. Standard errors of the regression coefficients are given in parentheses. All variable values appear to be scaled in ratio form. For an extension to 1967 with different sample coverage and model structure, see Robert McGuckin and Heng Chen, "Interactions Between Buyer and Seller Concentration and Industry Price-Cost Margins," *Industrial Organization Review* 4, No. 3 (1976): 123–32.

50. See Chapter 9, p. 284 *supra* and Robert D. Buzzell, Bradley T. Gale, and Ralph G. M. Sultan, "Market Share—a Key to Profitability," *Harvard Business Review* 53 (January-February 1975): 102–103.

51. See Douglas R. Brooks, "Buyer Concentration: A Forgotten Element in Market Structure Models," *Industrial Organization Review* 1, No. 3, (1973): 151–63; and Thomas C. Clevenger and Gerald R. Campbell, "Vertical Organization: A Neglected Element in Market Structure-Performance Models," *Industrial Organization Review* 5, No. 1 (1977): 60–66.

52. Michael E. Porter, "Consumer Behavior, Retailer Power and Market Performance in Consumer Goods Industries," *Review of Economics and Statistics* 56 (November 1974): 419–36.

53. Porter, "Consumer Behavior," pp. 434–35; and (for a fuller set of tests) Porter, *Interbrand Choice*, pp. 217–31.

11 Price discrimination

Most of the analysis up to this point has assumed that sellers quote a uniform price to all buyers during any short period of time. This is a tolerable first approximation to most retail product pricing in the United States (but not in the Middle East!) and to much wholesale and intermediate goods pricing. Still, many exceptions are encountered. When a seller charges diverse prices to different buyers of products that are essentially identical (in terms of subsidiary services such as packaging and delivery, as well as in the usual physical sense), the seller is engaging in price discrimination.

No simple, all-inclusive definition of price discrimination is possible. Succinctly, price discrimination is the sale (or purchase) of different units of a good or service at price differentials not directly corresponding to differences in supply cost. Note that this definition includes not only the sale of identical product units to different persons at varying prices, but also the sale of identical units to the same buyer at differing prices (e.g., when electric utilities charge less for additional kilowatt-hour blocks), and the execution of transactions entailing different costs at identical prices (e.g., when an airline provides steak dinners to tourist passengers on evening flights, but nothing more than coffee and a sandwich at mid-afternoon).

For a seller to practice price discrimination profitably, three conditions must be satisfied. First, the seller must have some control over price—some monopoly power. A purely competitive firm cannot discriminate profitably. It can of course sell some units at less than the market price (e.g., for altruistic reasons), but it need not do so to sell as much as it wants, and it sacrifices profit in doing so. Second, the would-be discriminator must be able to segregate its customers into groups with different price elasticities of demand, or into discrete classes with varying reservation prices (the highest prices buyers will pay for any specific unit of output). Third, opportunities for *arbitrage*—resale by low-price customers to high-price customers—must be constrained. Reselling personal services such as medical care and transportation to make an arbitrage profit is virtually impossible, and so the service industries lend themselves particularly well to price discrimination. Because most *goods*, on the other hand, can be stored, transported, and resold, arbitrage is more easily practiced with manufacturing industry outputs. Thus, the possibilities for price discrimination are more limited, although by no means negligible.[1]

Standard theoretical cases

It is customary, following the lead of A. C. Pigou, to speak of three main price discrimination classes: first degree, second degree, and third degree.[2] With first degree, or perfect, discrimination, each unit is sold at its reservation price, so that every consumer is milked of the largest outlay he or she would be willing to commit for the good in question and still consider its purchase worthwhile. In other words, the perfect discriminator leaves no consumers' surplus, but appropriates it all as producer's surplus. Second-degree discrimination is similar, only cruder. It is illustrated in Figure 11.1. The standard demand curve is given by DD', the marginal revenue curve by $D\,MR$, and the marginal cost curve by MC. A simple monopolist would equate marginal cost with marginal revenue, setting the uniform price of OP_M for all buyers and selling OX_M units. A discriminating monopolist, however, is able to partition demand into ten blocks in order of descending reservation prices. There are consumers willing to buy P_1K units at the highest discernible reservation price OP_1; an additional EF units will be taken at the lower price of OP_2, and so on. The seller, charging each block its reservation price, finds it worthwhile to expand output until there are no remaining blocks whose reservation price exceeds marginal cost. Thus, OX_D units will be sold at a total of seven different prices. Total profit is the sum of the declining margins of price over

average unit cost OC_D for all units sold. It is shown by the shaded area. This discriminatory profit is considerably larger than the profit realized under simple nondiscriminatory monopoly (shown by the area of the rectangle with height C_MP_M and width OX_M).

Third-degree discrimination is quite different. It is assumed that the seller can divide customers into two or more independent groups, each of which has its own continuous demand function reflecting quantities sold to that group at alternative prices.[3] If these demand functions have different elasticities at common prices, it will pay to discriminate. To see this, suppose the firm charges the uniform price P^* to each of two groups, at which price the demand elasticity for Group A is 2.0 and for Group B 4.0. This strategy does not maximize profits. We recall from Chapter 6 that marginal revenue is related to price by the formula $MR = P - P/e$, where e is the elasticity of demand.[4] Thus, marginal revenue must be one-half of price P^* in selling to Group A and three-fourths of price P^* in selling to Group B. It pays to reallocate some output away from Group A and toward Group B, for the marginal revenue from selling an extra unit to Group B customers exceeds the marginal revenue lost from selling one unit less to Group A customers. This reallocation can continue profitably until prices in the two markets have changed by a sufficient amount to equalize marginal revenue. Generalizing, a third-degree discriminator maximizes profits by charging the highest price in the market whose demand elasticity at the simple monopoly price is lowest and the lowest price in the market with the highest elasticity at the simple monopoly price.

Figure 11.2 presents the conventional geometric analysis of third-degree discriminating monopoly for two markets, A and B, whose demand and marginal revenue curves are given in panels (a) and (b). The problem is to ensure that the last unit of output sold in Market A adds the same amount to total revenue as the last unit sold in Market B, that is, to equalize the marginal revenues. To accomplish this, the marginal revenue curves of the two markets are summed horizontally, giving the combined marginal revenue function CMR in panel (c). CMR is equated to marginal cost MC, indicating the optimal com-

F 11.1 Second-degree price discrimination

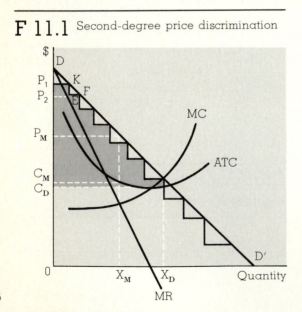

F 11.2 Third-degree price discrimination

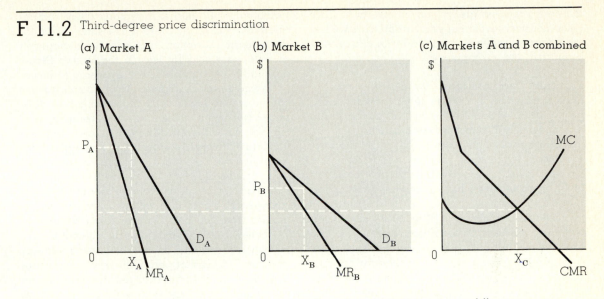

(a) Market A (b) Market B (c) Markets A and B combined

bined output OX_c. To equalize marginal revenue in the separate markets at the profit-maximizing value, we construct a horizontal line from the point where $MC = CMR$. The output in each market is found where this horizontal line intersects a market's MR function, and the profit-maximizing price is found (as usual) by reading off the relevant demand function the price at which the profit-maximizing quantity is demanded. Thus, the higher price OP_A is charged in the less elastic Market A and the lower price OP_B in the more elastic Market B.

Types of discrimination found in practice

So much for the theoretical categories. Although the soporific effect of exhaustive categorization normally outweighs any educational value, a systematic list of ideal types provides useful insight into the tremendous variety of real-world price discrimination practices. We can do no better than follow, with slight modifications, the classification scheme adopted by Professor Machlup.[5] Three main classes are identified: personal discrimination, based upon differences among individual customers; group discrimina-

tion, in which intergroup differences are exploited; and product discrimination, under which

(1) In a classic case, duopolists Röhm & Haas and du Pont charged $.85 per pound to general industrial users of the plastic molding powder methyl methacrylate, while special mixtures of the same compound were offered for use in denture manufacture at $22 per pound. The opportunity for making an arbitrage profit attracted firms who bought at the industrial price, incurred moderate conversion costs, and undercut the duopolists' denture price. To thwart the arbitragers, Röhm & Haas considered mixing some arsenic into the industrial powder so it would be unsuitable for oral use. It ultimately rejected the idea, but did plant rumors that the industrial powder had been adulterated. See G. W. Stocking and M. W. Watkins, *Cartels in Action* (New York: Twentieth Century Fund, 1946), pp. 402–404.

2. A. C. Pigou, *The Economics of Welfare* (London: Macmillan, 1920), pp. 240–56. For additional cases, see Stephen Enke, "Some Notes on Price Discrimination," *Canadian Journal of Economics and Political Science* 30 (February 1964): 95–109.

3. On violations of the independence assumption, see Enke, "Some Notes," pp. 104–109; and Russell G. Thompson and E. O. Olsen, Jr., "A Discrimination Model for the Dynamic Monopoly Firm," *Zeitschrift für Nationalökonomie* 36, No. 1–2 (1975): 77–88.

4. Cf. Chapter 6, p. 187 *supra*.

5. Fritz Machlup, "Characteristics and Types of Price Discrimination," in the National Bureau of Economic Research conference report, *Business Concentration and Price Policy* (Princeton: Princeton University Press, 1955), pp. 400–23. Reprinted by permission of the publisher. Machlup in turn borrowed some of his categories from Ralph Cassady, Jr., "Techniques and Purposes of Price Discrimination," *Journal of Marketing* (October 1946): 135–50.

different products are priced at divergent and discriminatory levels. For each broad class we list the principal types encountered with a brief explanation and example.

Personal discrimination *Haggle-every-time* Each transaction is a separately negotiated bargain. Examples include the typical pricing practice in Middle Eastern bazaars and the sale of used textbooks by students to college bookstores.

Give-in-if-you-must Secret departures are made from list prices when buyers play one seller off against the others. Examples were given in the preceding chapter.

Size-up-their-income Wealthier customers with inelastic demand are charged more than the less affluent, who at high prices would restrict consumption disproportionately. Standard examples are the pricing of legal and medical services.

Measure-the-use Customers who use a good or service more intensively are charged more, even though differences in cost may be negligible. For instance, Xerox machine rental charges are based upon the number of copies made, and the incremental volume-related charge more than compensates for maintenance costs.

Group discrimination *Absorb-the-freight* There are several types of discrimination involving the absorption or overcharging of freight to customers located at varying distances from one's production site. Since these will be analyzed later, we defer a more precise enumeration.

Kill-the-rival Prices are systematically reduced, perhaps below cost, only in the market served by a rival the discriminator is trying to drive out of business. During the 1890s, the American Tobacco Company sold 'fighting brands' of cigarettes at prices well below its production costs and on at least one occasion at a price covering only excise taxes.

Dump-the-surplus Goods in excess supply are offered at reduced prices overseas so as not to depress the domestic price. Although Western nations have signed antidumping agreements, allegations of dumping continue, as in the steel industries during the mid-1970s.

Get-the-most-from-each-region Prices are persistently held higher in regions where competition is weak than where it is strong. Thus, for many years European high-fidelity phonograph records were sold for less in the United States than in the countries where they were produced.

Promote-new-customers New customers are offered prices lower than those paid by established customers in the hope of developing permanent brand loyalty. Magazines are avid practitioners of this art, offering new subscriptions for much less than what old subscribers pay.

Favor-the-big-ones Large buyers are granted systematic price concessions exceeding the cost savings associated with volume transactions. Examples were given in the preceding chapter.

Protect-the-middleman In an attempt to protect wholesalers from competition, large retailers who incur the cost of performing their own warehousing functions are charged the same prices as retailers who buy from wholesalers. As we shall see in Chapter 21, the Robinson-Patman Act was intended to encourage discriminaton of this genre.

Hold-them-in-line Retailers who fail to comply with a manufacturer's list price suggestions are denied special discounts granted to those who conform.

Divide-them-by-elasticity Group discrimination may also be practiced whenever groups readily classifiable by age, sex, occupation, and so on have different reservation prices or demand elasticities. For example, lower prices are charged for children's haircuts (despite the higher labor input in shearing a wiggling subject) because of stronger do-it-yourself competition.

Product discrimination *Appeal-to-the-classes* Differences in price more than proportional to differences in cost are associated with premium quality. For example, much higher margins between price and incremental production cost are realized on clothbound as compared to paperbound books. Cadillacs command higher price markups than Oldsmobiles and Pontiacs of comparable size and mechanical equipment.

Make-them-pay-for-the-label Manufacturers distribute a physically homogeneous product under various brands, charging more for the better-known brands. Examples abound on the shelves of any chain supermarket.

Clear-the-stock Price concessions are granted at special times of the year, or continuously in special sections of a retail store, in order to reduce inventories or increase sales to customers with weak budgets and strong elbows. Filene's basement in Boston is a breathtaking example.

Switch-them-to-off-peak-times Lower prices are charged for services identical except with respect to time of consumption in order to encourage fuller and more balanced utilization of capacity. Resort prices varying with the season and the 60 percent reduction in weekend long-distance telephone rates are examples.[6]

Bundle-the-outputs Diverse goods and services are sold together at a single package price, even though many customers do not consume all components of the bundle. IBM's bundling of programming and maintenance services with computer hardware, even for users able to do their own programming, is illustrative.

Get-the-most-from-each-group In this final catch-all category we include such practices as charging higher railroad freight rates on more valuable commodities; offering additional blocks of electricity at lower rates to encourage homeowners to install electric stoves, water heaters, and heating systems; and the realization by multiproduct firms of higher price-cost margins on items for which demand is relatively inelastic than on those in elastic demand. Also noteworthy is *skimming*—introducing a new and superior product at a high price designed to extract the highest possible revenue from persons with high reservation prices, and then gradually reducing the price to penetrate a broader market.[7]

The implications of discrimination for economic welfare

With such a diversity of types, it is clearly impossible to reach any simple blanket judgment about the social desirability of price discrimina-tion. We can, however, formulate some guidelines for assessing specific types in terms of three criteria: income distribution effects, efficiency effects, and impact on market structure and the intensity of competition.

Income distribution effects Price discrimination causes a redistribution of income toward the discriminator and away from its customers. In the absence of legal quirks, no firm with market power *has* to discriminate. It will do so only if a system of discriminatory prices yields higher expected profits than uniform pricing, *ceteris paribus.*[8]

Whether this is a bad thing or not hinges on value judgments over which reasonable (as well as self-interested) persons may disagree. Most academic economists believe that social welfare would be enhanced if monopoly profits gained through price discrimination were redirected into the hands of the consuming public and away from corporate stockholders, the majority of whom (by dollar holdings) are already well off. But this is a subjective evaluation, and there is no way of demonstrating its correctness. Furthermore, the practitioners of price discrimination are not always the great corporations. Physicians are the most highly paid professional class in the United States, with mean earnings for males of $30,538 in 1970, compared to $14,001 for electrical engineers, $12,537 for professional accountants, and $9,789 for high school teachers.[9] The relative af-

---

6. If there are constant returns to scale in production, price differentials just sufficient to repay the cost of building facilities capable of satisfying peak demands are not strictly discriminatory in a long-run sense. See Peter O. Steiner, "Peak Loads and Efficient Pricing," *Quarterly Journal of Economics* 71 (November 1957): 585–610. Indeed, failure to charge peak-load demanders for the cost of maintaining peaking capacity would be discrimination in favor of such users.

7. See Joel Dean, *Managerial Economics* (Englewood Cliffs, N.J.: Prentice-Hall, 1951), pp. 419–21.

8. An exception may occur when secret discriminatory price cuts by oligopolists made with the intention of raising individual profits induce spreading retaliation that reduces *group* profits.

9. U.S., Bureau of the Census, *1970 Census of Population*, "Earnings by Occupation and Education," PC (2)-8B (Washington, D.C.: Government Printing Office, January 1973), pp. 9–36.

fluence of the medical profession can be attributed in part to unnecessarily high barriers limiting entry into medicine and in part to the exploitation of opportunities for price discrimination, especially before federal medical insurance programs reduced demand elasticities for lower-income citizens.[10] Again, approval or disapproval depends to some extent on one's values and prejudices. Given the apparent excess supply of well-qualified medical school applicants, it is questionable whether such large income distribution differentials are necessary to maintain high health care standards.

Third-degree price discrimination also redistributes income away from consumers in the low price elasticity groups, who normally pay a price higher than under simple monopoly, toward consumers in the high-price elasticity groups, who pay lower prices.[11] As in all income redistribution situations, economic analysis provides no hard and fast criteria for evaluating this result, although economists and policymakers may have strong personal opinions. As Joan Robinson has observed:

> we may have some reason to prefer the interests of one group above those of the other. For instance, members of the more elastic markets (for whom price is reduced) may be poorer than members of the less elastic markets, and we may consider a gain to poorer buyers more important than a loss to richer buyers. In this case price discrimination must always be considered beneficial. On the other hand, the less elastic market may be at home and the more elastic market abroad, so that the interests of the members of the stronger market are considered more important than the interests of the weaker market.[12]

Efficiency effects Price discrimination is sometimes condemned because it is symptomatic of monopoly, and the exploitation of monopoly power implies a misallocation of resources. This is an inappropriate criticism if monopoly power would be present whether or not discrimination were practiced. The correct question is, Are resources allocated more or less efficiently under discriminating monopoly than under simple (uniform price) monopoly? The answer depends

somewhat upon the type of discrimination practiced.

First- and second-degree discrimination usually lead to larger outputs than under simple monopoly, and hence (*ceteris paribus*) to an improved allocation of resources. To see this, consider Figure 11.1 again. The simple monopolist, recognizing that any price reduction made to customers on the margin between buying and not buying must also be offered to customers who would buy even if the price was not reduced, maximizes profits by equating marginal cost with marginal revenue, producing output OX_M. The second-degree discriminating monopolist must offer a price reduction *only* to marginal buyers, and therefore finds it profitable to expand output all the way to OX_D. Indeed, the discriminating monopolist of Figure 11.1 produces as much as a competitive industry with a short-run supply curve identical to the monopolist's marginal cost function, since price to the last block of customers served is equal to the marginal cost of serving those customers. More generally, first- and second-degree discriminators characteristically produce more than the simple monopoly output, and unless adverse income effects associated with their pricing policies are large[13] or their ability to segregate marginal customers by reservation prices is quite imperfect,[14] their output closely approximates the competitive output, *ceteris paribus*. Thus, the inefficiencies of output restriction for which simple monopoly is criticized tend to be reduced and may even disappear altogether under first- or second-degree discrimination.[15]

As indicated earlier, first-degree discrimination is rare in actual practice. But many examples of second-degree discrimination can be found. Much personal discrimination conforms to the second-degree model—e.g., haggle-every-time, size-up-their-income, and measure-the-use. Other cases include super-saver or standby rates offered air travelers who can plan discretionary trips well in advance or who are willing to schedule their trips flexibly to coincide with the availability of unfilled seats. In such instances price discrimination typically permits more output to be supplied than under uniform monopoly pricing.

Third-degree discrimination is probably the

most widely used of the three main theoretical types. It also has the most ambiguous efficiency implications. If the demand functions for both (or all) markets are linear, as in Figure 11.2, total output under discrimination will be identical to output under simple uniform-price monopoly, assuming that the monopolist sells at least some output in the more (most) elastic market and ignoring income effects on the demand curve positions. For third-degree discrimination to increase output above the simple monopoly level, certain conditions involving the geometry of the various demand functions must be satisfied. Briefly, the demand curve in the more elastic market must be less convex from below (i.e., with respect to the quantity axis) than the demand curve in the less elastic market.[16] We have little evidence on whether this condition occurs more frequently than the converse. Joan Robinson has argued on a priori grounds that the most likely impact of third-degree discrimination will be to increase output, since the quantity of output demanded by consumers in the low-elasticity market will remain near the satiety point even after price is raised to the discriminatory level, whereas a small reduction in price to high-elasticity customers will induce a large increase in quantity demanded.[17] But we really do not know, and so it is impossible to determine whether on balance third-degree discrimination increases output and improves the allocation of resources.

Any type of discrimination may have desirable allocative effects in special situations where demand is too weak to permit profitable operation of a service under simple monopoly pricing. It is possible, for instance, that no physician would be attracted to a small town if he or she were required to charge the same fee to rich patients as to poor. Since profits can be increased by discriminating, the added revenue attainable through discrimination may be sufficient to make the difference in whether or not a service is supplied.[18] In the same vein, it is probable that railroad service would not have been provided to remote areas of the American frontier during the 19th century had rate discrimination between high-value and low-value commodities been impossible.

Price discrimination can also provide a way out of an efficiency dilemma encountered in regulated natural monopoly industries, as illustrated in Figures 11.3 and 11.4. If the long-run average total cost curve *LRATC* is continuously falling, the long-run marginal cost curve must lie below it. Efficiency in resource allocation requires that if a uniform price is charged, it must be set at the marginal cost level OP_M in Figure 11.3, with the output OX_M being supplied. But then average

10. See Reuben A. Kessel, "Price Discrimination in Medicine," *Journal of Law and Economics* 1 (October 1958): 20–59; and Elton Rayack, *Professional Power and American Medicine* (Cleveland: World, 1967), especially Chapters 3, 4, and 5.

11. If discrimination facilitates an expansion of output permitting the realization of substantial scale economies, it is possible (although not necessary) that the price to consumers in the less elastic market will also be lower than the simple monopoly price.

12. Joan Robinson, *The Economics of Imperfect Competition* (London: Macmillan, 1933), p. 204.

13. For an implausible example in which this is true but the sum of consumers' plus producer's surpluses is reduced, see Basil Yamey, "Monopolistic Price Discrimination and Economic Welfare," *Journal of Law and Economics* 17 (October 1974): 377–80.

14. See John E. Kwoka, Jr., "Output under Second-Degree Price Discrimination," Federal Trade Commission Bureau of Economics working paper (Washington, D.C.: Federal Trade Commission, 1978).

15. Similar but more attenuated conclusions hold for commodity bundling and for "two-part tariffs"—a form of second-degree discrimination under which consumers are charged a flat entry fee plus a fixed price per unit bought. See W. J. Adams and Janet L. Yellen, "Commodity Bundling and the Burden of Monopoly," *Quarterly Journal of Economics* 90 (August 1976): 475–98; and Walter Y. Oi, "A Disneyland Dilemma: Two-Part Tariffs for a Mickey Mouse Monopoly," *Quarterly Journal of Economics* 85 (February 1971): 77–96. However, in "Monopoly Pricing Structures with Imperfect Discrimination," *Bell Journal of Economics* 7 (Autumn 1976): 449–62, H. E. Leland and R. A. Meyer show that second-degree block pricing discrimination has generally more favorable efficiency implications than two-part tariffs under comparable conditions.

16. Robinson, *Imperfect Competition*, pp. 188–95; E. O. Edwards, "The Analysis of Output under Discrimination," *Econometrica* 18 (April 1950): 163–72; and (for a counterexample) M. L. Greenhut and H. Ohta, "Joan Robinson's Criterion for Deciding Whether Market Discrimination Reduces Output," *Economic Journal* 86 (March 1976): 96–97. Robinson's "concavity from above" is the same as "convexity from below," as used here.

17. Robinson, *Imperfect Competition*, pp. 201–202.

18. For a geometric treatment of the problem, see Pigou, *Economics of Welfare*, pp. 950–51. It should be noted that if price discrimination were not practiced in larger cities, the potential smalltown physician's opportunity cost would be lower, and he or she might settle in the small town at a lower profit expectation.

cost $X_MC = OB$ exceeds the price, and the enterprise incurs a deficit equal to the rectangular area P_MECB. To induce capital investment in the industry under these circumstances, public subsidies may be required. But the taxes out of which subsidies come can cause new and more subtle allocative distortions, and the political barriers to such subsidization are frequently potent. An alternative may be to permit price discrimination as in Figure 11.4. One block of output OX_1 is sold to customers with high reservation prices at the price OP_1, while a second block X_1X_2 moves at the marginal cost price OP_2. On the second block, accounting losses shown by the lightly shaded rectangle occur, but these are more than offset by the profits earned from the first block (darker rectangle). The result of such price discrimination, often used in public utility industries, is the simultaneous attainment of allocatively efficient output levels and financial self-sufficiency.

The special case of multiproduct job shops

Some important special problems arise in the case of multiproduct firms, and particularly for firms with an array of equipment and skills readily adaptable to the production of numerous products. Job shops in the fabricated metal products, machinery, plastics, electrical apparatus, and printing industries fit the pattern well.[19]

What such enterprises offer in a sense is not unique products, but their capacity to produce. And when they sell different blocks of capacity at varying price-cost margins, they are engaging in a subtle form of price discrimination.

The standard analysis of this problem has been developed by Eli Clemens.[20] Here we summarize his geometric treatment, appending an algebraic proof in a footnote. The multiproduct job shop surveys its opportunities and defines for each market a peculiar kind of demand function, relating the price received to the number of units of capacity devoted to satisfying demand in that market. It supplies first those markets with the lowest demand elasticities, charging in them the highest prices (presumably exceeding cost by a substantial margin). However, it will continue to invade markets of higher and higher demand elasticity until there are no markets remaining in which the potential contribution to revenue exceeds the marginal cost of allocating a block of capacity. If any such market remains untapped, the most profitable strategy is to reduce the amount of capacity employed in markets already served, increasing the prices charged there in order to commit at least one unit of capacity to the untapped market.[21]

Now if the last market served has a high price elasticity, which is entirely plausible, the gap

---

F 11.3 Marginal cost pricing with falling long-run costs

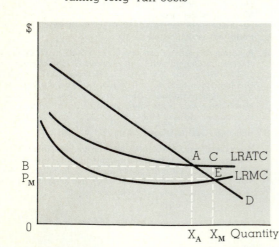

F 11.4 Discriminatory marginal cost pricing with falling long-run costs

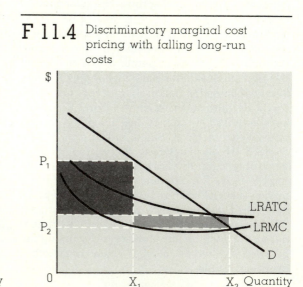

between marginal revenue and price will be small in that line, and since marginal revenue is equated to marginal cost, the gap between price and marginal cost will also be small. Thus the discriminating multiproduct firm approaches full (competitive) utilization of its capacity (where marginal cost is equal to price). Indeed, the firm may be only a competitive fringe member in its marginal market, in which case output is expanded until price and marginal cost are equalized. This result reflects a kind of efficiency in resource use and is clearly a point in favor of multiproduct price discrimination.

Viewed in a different light, however, the efficiency implications are more ambiguous. Only in the marginal product line is price approximately equal to marginal cost. Consumers of the firm's other products pay a price exceeding marginal cost. Buyers are willing to give up more dollars for an additional unit of these products than the cost of producing the additional unit, and hence the firm's output of these inframarginal products is inefficiently low. If this were the whole story, we should have to conclude that misallocation in the accepted sense persists. Still it is conceivable that what to one multiproduct firm is an inframarginal product line (because the firm has a dominant position in the market and/or enjoys special product differentiation advantages) is a marginal line to other multiproduct firms specializing in different fields. Each firm or group of firms might then penetrate the others' markets, granting discriminatory concessions in product lines considered marginal.[22] In the resulting equilibrium, price would approximate marginal cost for at least some producers in virtually every product line.

This result bears a superficial resemblance to the equilibrium of pure competition. Nevertheless, it is not clear that it approaches the allocative efficiency of competition, since price exceeds marginal cost on the inframarginal sales of all firms. If this merely reflects efficiency differences in producing for inframarginal as compared to marginal markets, a tolerably close approximation to the competitive equilibrium may result. But if it reflects higher prices paid by some consumers for comparable products (or slightly differentiated variants) produced at similar costs, allocation is likely to be efficient only if con-

sumers just on the margin between buying and not buying happen to be served by firms offering the lowest prices. There is no reason to believe this will necessarily occur, and so there is also no reason to expect substantially improved resource allocation under the postulated conditions. Still, the problem is so complex that no unequivocal generalizations are warranted.

The effects of discrimination on competition

Price discrimination can be practiced profitably only if the discriminator possesses some monopoly power. The practice of discrimination can in turn have feedback effects on market structure and the vigor of competition. It may strengthen competition or weaken it, depending upon the type of discrimination and how successful it is.

Discrimination can enhance competition by facilitating experimentation in pricing. The best way to determine whether the demand for one's products is price elastic is to try out selected price changes. Recognizing that it is often more difficult

19. The analysis has little applicability to firms using specialized equipment suitable for producing only a narrow line of outputs. Examples include aluminum smelters, breweries, cigarette plants, cement mills, and automobile assembly lines.

20. Eli W. Clemens, "Price Discrimination and the Multiple-Product Firm," *Review of Economic Studies* 19, No. 1 (1951): 1–11. For an extension to retail and wholesale distribution, see Bruce Yandle, Jr., "Monopoly-Induced Third-Degree Price Discrimination," *Quarterly Review of Economics and Business* 11 (Spring 1971): 71–75. For pharmaceuticals, see W. Duncan Reekie, "Price and Quality Competition in the United States Drug Industry," *Journal of Industrial Economics* 26 (March 1978): 223–37.

21. This rearrangement of the product line is profitable for the following reason. Before the new line is taken on, profit maximization requires that marginal revenue in each line be equal to the marginal cost of the last capacity unit utilized. Let MR_i be the marginal revenue of the ith (typical) line in the original equilibrium product array and let MC be the marginal cost of the last capacity unit utilized. Now suppose a new opportunity is found, offering an addition to revenue MR_n exceeding MC. (MR_n will be less than the price in line n, if the market is monopolistic, or equal to it, if the market is perceived to be competitive by the firm in question.) Since $MR_n > MC$ and $MC = MR_i$, $MR_n > MR_i$. The last unit of capacity adds more to revenue when devoted to product line n than to product line i (or any of the other original lines). Therefore it is profitable to take line n on. Output in each previous line should be reduced until marginal revenue in each of these lines rises to equality with MR_n.

22. Certainly, such tendencies are observed in many fields. See J. F. Wright, "Some Reflections on the Place of Discrimination in the Theory of Monopolistic Competition," *Oxford Economic Papers* 17 n.s. (July 1965): 185.

to raise prices than to lower them, sellers may be reluctant to engage in such experimentation if the changes must be implemented across the board—e.g., in every geographic market. They will be much more willing if changes can be tried only in restricted test markets, so that the consequences of an adverse rival or consumer reaction are less serious.

Another important procompetitive effect is the tendency of unsystematic price discrimination to undermine oligopolistic discipline. The dynamics of this process have already been described in Chapters 7 and 10. In order to utilize capacity more fully, producers grant secret, discriminatory price concessions to a few aggressive buyers. Sooner or later the word leaks out, often through the efforts of buyers to extract similar concessions from additional suppliers, and others match or undercut the cuts. As the price concessions spread, list prices become increasingly unrealistic and eventually they are reduced, benefitting all buyers and not just the favored few. When secret price shading of this sort occurs frequently, sellers may lose all confidence in their rivals' willingness to cooperate toward a common price policy, and the resulting loss of discipline makes joint profit maximization impossible.[23]

For price discrimination to enhance competition, it is vital that the discriminatory concessions be *unsystematic*. Systematic price discrimination is likely to have the opposite effect, weakening competition. This it does in several ways.

For one, it may entrench firms in their positions of power by creating strong buyer-seller ties and raising barriers to the entry of new competitors. The tin can industry illustrates this point.[24] American Can's dominant position was bolstered both by the discriminatory price concessions it received from suppliers of tin-plated steel and the discriminatory price reductions it granted to large canners. As a buyer, American received discounts on the order of 7.5 percent from tin plate manufacturers until the practice became illegal in 1936. Smaller tin can makers, denied these discounts on an input accounting for roughly 70 percent of their costs, were at an obvious disadvantage. Other things being equal, American could set prices yielding excess profits as high as 5 percent of costs before smaller competitors could enter and earn a normal return. As

a seller, American granted discounts of up to 14 percent to large customers. These were usually tied in with long-term contracts covering a larger annual volume of cans than smaller can makers could supply. By making it difficult for small producers to secure can orders from large packers, this combination of discriminatory discounts with long-term, high-volume requirements contracts turned "what would have been a fairly innocuous practice into a rather formidable obstacle to open competition."[25]

A different sort of systematic discriminatory pricing was practiced in the shoe machinery industry.[26] United Shoe Machinery Corporation successfully defended its 85 percent market share in part by accepting much lower rates of return on machines that faced competition than on those it supplied exclusively. In this way it could take full advantage of its monopoly power in lines it dominated, while the low prices in lines with competition made it difficult for rivals to maintain a foothold. By discouraging the entry and expansion of rivals, United in turn was able to remain the only shoe machinery manufacturer offering a full line—an advantage that strengthened its position with customers.

Accepting lower rates of return on product lines facing competition shades into more predatory kill-the-rival types of price discrimination. In actual situations the line between meeting competition and destroying it is seldom sharp, since a great deal depends upon intent, which is hard to pin down, and since unsuccessful kill-the-rival discrimination may cause nothing more than an interlude of intensified competition.

A spectrum of cases, some tending clearly toward the kill-the-rival type, came to light through antitrust actions waged against IBM during the 1970s. Unlike United Shoe Machinery, IBM faced *some* competition on each of its main computer lines. But like USM, IBM accepted slimmer profit margins or even losses on computers facing particularly effective competition—e.g, on its 360/90 superpower machine (with Control Data Corporation as prime competitor) and the 360/67 time-sharing machine (aimed especially at General Electric).[27] Even sharper were its reactions to competitive threats from certain plug-compatible peripheral equipment manufacturers (PCMs). Thus, when the Telex and Memorex Corporations began capturing a significant share of IBM's disk drive business in 1970, IBM repackaged an existing disk drive and offered it at a 26 percent discount to price-conscious customers. Meanwhile, it continued to lease the functionally equivalent original machine at the higher price to customers reluctant to effect a physical change.[28] A half year later IBM announced a revised pricing policy for peripheral devices, offering 16 percent discounts to customers accepting two-year term leases instead of the traditional leases, which could be cancelled on a month's notice. Since competing peripheral device manufacturers could not achieve technical compatibility with new IBM computer mainframes until after the mainframes had been delivered, this in effect locked computer users into IBM peripheral leases for the first two years of a new computer model's life. And since technological change in computer designs and their related peripheral device designs was rapid, the two-year lease left too short a remaining peripheral device life span for competing PCMs to recoup their investment. The result of the two-year lease discount strategy, in the words of an IBM staff analysis, was therefore expected to be "PCM corporate revenues lower—no funds for [manufacturing, engineering]—dying company!"[29]

In sum, systematic price discrimination can preserve and strengthen monopoly positions by permitting large firms to enjoy input costs lower than their smaller rivals, by tying buyers together with sellers giving discounts for concentrated purchases, and by making entry into narrow segments of a market difficult or impossible. On the other hand, unsystematic price discrimination can have a procompetitive effect by undermining oligopolistic discipline.

Geographic price discrimination and the basing point system

Another link between price discrimination and competition is so important that it warrants a more extended analysis. This is the whole set of freight pricing practices arising in response to differences in the geographic distance separating producers from their customers.

Approaches to the spatial differentiation problem Even when firms produce physically identical commodities, complete homogeneity is not likely to be attained because of differences in location. From the viewpoint of a consumer in Indianapolis, a ton of hot-rolled steel in Pittsburgh is not the same as a ton of the same hot-rolled steel in Chicago. When producers are located at different points on the map, their products are said to be *spatially differentiated*.[30] Differences in shipping distance imply differences in transportation cost and delivery time. For certain commodities—notably, those of low value relative to their weight—spatial differentiation is of considerable practical significance. In 1966, for example, the freight charges for transporting steel mill products in carload lots from Chicago to Toledo amounted to approximately 5.2 percent of the steel's Chicago mill price. For shipments to Pittsburgh, the freight cost from Chicago was 10 percent of the mill price, and to New York City, 17

23. Conversely, MacAvoy concluded that the price discrimination prohibitions of the Interstate Commerce Act of 1887 provided the necessary foundations for successful collusive pricing among railroads. Paul W. MacAvoy, *The Economic Effects of Regulation: The Trunkline Railroad Cartels and the ICC Before 1900* (Cambridge, Mass.: M.I.T. Press, 1965), p. 204.

24. James W. McKie, *Tin Cans and Tin Plate* (Cambridge, Mass.: Harvard University Press, 1959), pp. 58–64, 160–82.

25. McKie, *Tins Cans and Tin Plate*, p. 175. For similar examples from ocean shipping and the West German electric light bulb industry, see the United Nations Conference on Trade and Development interim report, *Restrictive Business Practices* (New York: United Nations, 1971), pp. 11–13.

26. Carl Kaysen, *United States v. United Shoe Machinery Corporation* (Cambridge, Mass.: Harvard University Press, 1956), especially pp. 126–34.

27. *U.S. v. International Business Machines Corporation*, Pretrial Brief for the United States (October 1974), pp. 242–54.

28. See Gerald W. Brock, *The U.S. Computer Industry* (Cambridge, Mass.: Ballinger, 1975), pp. 114–24.

29. Brock, *U.S. Computer Industry*, p. 121.

30. For an introduction to the theory of spatial differentiation and competition, see Martin Beckmann, *Location Theory* (New York: Random House, 1968), Chapter 3. For extensions, see Melvin L. Greenhut, *A Theory of the Firm in Economic Space* (New York: Appleton-Century-Croft, 1970), especially Chapters 4, 6, 7, and 12.

percent. On shipments of cement, with a considerably lower value per pound, the comparable percentages were even higher—by four to six times.[31] To the producer of a spatially differentiated product, the problem is to determine how to handle freight costs in setting prices. For the economist, the problem is to assess the impact of diverse geographic pricing policies on competition and efficiency.

There are several alternative freight pricing methods. One is the so-called postage stamp system, under which a uniform delivered price is charged to every buyer, regardless of distance from the production source. Or in a variant, buyers in a particular zone—e.g., west of the Mississippi—all pay the same delivered price. In each case, the producer absorbs higher freight costs on shipments to distant customers than on shipments to customers near its plant. It therefore discriminates in favor of distant customers. Postage stamp pricing is used most frequently with commodities whose value is high relative to transportation costs. But some curious exceptions are also encountered. For example, since 1921 aluminum ingots have been sold on a uniform delivered price basis throughout the United States.

An approach better suited to bulky, low-value commodities is uniform F.O.B. mill pricing.[32] Here producers announce a mill price at which customers may buy, paying their own freight bills. Or if delivery by the producer is preferred, the actual charges for transportation from the producing mill to the buyer's destination will be added onto the mill price. This is the only system that entails no geographic price discrimination, since the price paid by buyers increases in direct relation to shipping costs, while (barring other discriminatory concessions) the seller receives a uniform *mill net price* after outbound freight expenses are covered.

Some important properties of uniform F.O.B. mill pricing can be illustrated with a simple diagram. In Figure 11.5, the horizontal axis represents geographic distance between points. One mill is assumed to be located at point C (Chicago), selling at the announced F.O.B. mill price CA. As it sells to customers located to the east, the delivered price rises (somewhat exaggeratedly) along the path AR, reflecting increasing freight costs for shipment over greater distances. Another mill is located at point P (Pittsburgh), selling at the F.O.B. mill price PB, with delivered prices rising along the line BT. Given these assumptions, customers from Dayton westward enjoy lower delivered prices buying from the Chicago mill, and so (if the product is otherwise homogeneous) they will give all their orders to Chicago. The spatial market segment CX is Chicago's *freight advantage territory*, while in the segment XP Pittsburgh enjoys a delivered price advantage, capturing all the orders. If each mill adheres strictly to its F.O.B. mill pricing policy, neither can sell in the other's territory.

This seems a curious kind of competition, in which the two mills quote matching prices and vie directly for orders only in Xenia, Ohio (point X), 1970 population 25,373. How can the Chicago mill increase its sales, say, by capturing some orders in Columbus?

If a uniform F.O.B. mill pricing system is to be maintained, there is only one way—cutting the mill price, e.g., to CA'. Then the delivered price locus shifts downward to A'R', the Chicago mill's freight advantage territory is expanded through Columbus, and the Pittsburgh mill's territory contracts accordingly. But this approach has two obvious disadvantages. First, the Chicago mill is

F 11.5 F.O.B. mill pricing

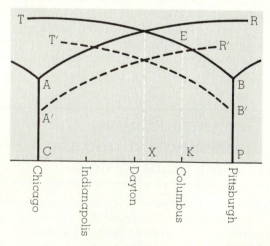

not apt to be very enthusiastic about cutting price to all the customers between Chicago and Xenia, to whom it can otherwise sell at mill net price *CA*, merely to expand sales between Xenia and Columbus. Second, the Pittsburgh mill will be even less enthusiastic about losing its customers between Columbus and Xenia to the rival in Chicago. If Chicago reduces its mill price to *CA'*, Pittsburgh will probably respond with a matching cut in its own price to *PB'*. With the new F.O.B. Pittsburgh delivered price function *B'T'*, the market division point is once again Xenia. Each seller finds itself serving the same market territory as before the round of price cuts, but at a lower mill net price. And each will soon recognize that they will not endow many libraries through such uncooperative tactics.

One way around this problem is to shift to a system of F.O.B. mill pricing coupled with unsystematic discrimination through freight absorption. Each mill then quotes its F.O.B. mill price: *CA* for Chicago and *PB* for Pittsburgh. Normally each delivers output at this mill price plus freight, but if an especially attractive sales opportunity arises in Columbus, Chicago may choose to absorb freight and meet or even undercut the Pittsburgh delivered price *KE*. This is discrimination on Chicago's part, since a lower mill net price (after deduction of freight) is realized on the Columbus order than on Chicago, Indianapolis, and Dayton orders. Yet such discriminatory freight absorption may be attractive to Chicago, since if marginal production costs are less than or equal to *CA'*, Chicago can add to its profits by picking up an occasional Columbus order without having to cut prices to local customers. Of course, two or more can play at this game, and so Pittsburgh is likely to meet or undercut Chicago's prices in Indianapolis and Dayton through its own freight absorption. If the discrimination is unsystematic, both mills will be uncertain how low a price they must quote to win an order in their home territories. As we have seen earlier, such uncertainty can precipitate a breakdown in oligopoly discipline, culminating in a general erosion of the price structure, cuts in the announced F.O.B. mill price, and perhaps even outright price warfare.

Once again, this is not the way to endow libraries and symphony halls. To minimize the temptation toward independent pricing initiatives, the firms may adopt some sort of *basing point system*, as the steel, cement, lead, corn oil, plywood, wood pulp, automobile, sugar, and many other industries have at one time or another.[33] Basing point pricing has been used most frequently by oligopolists selling physically standardized products whose transportation costs are high relative to product value and whose marginal production cost is low relative to total unit cost at less than capacity operation. Under these conditions competitive price cutting through unsystematic freight absorption is probable, unless a collusive disposition of the freight cost problem is worked out.

The most striking variety is the *single basing point system*—e.g., the Pittsburgh-plus system used in the steel industry until 1924, when it was abandoned following an antitrust order, and the Portland-plus system used for plywood into the 1970s. One production point is accepted by common consent as the basing point, and *all* prices are quoted as the announced mill price at that point plus freight (usually rail freight) to destination.

Although the geometry is similar, a new diagram (Figure 11.6) will illustrate the system. Pittsburgh is the basing point, at which the announced mill price is *PB*. Delivered prices are quoted according to the Pittsburgh-plus-freight line *BT* not only by Pittsburgh mills, but also by

31. F. M. Scherer, Alan Beckenstein, Erich Kaufer, and R. D. Murphy, *The Economics of Multi-Plant Operation: An International Comparisons Study* (Cambridge, Mass.: Harvard University Press, 1975), pp. 361–65, 430–31.

32. F.O.B. means free on board; that is, the price quoted to load a product on board the transporting vehicle, after which the buyer becomes responsible for all freight charges.

33. For a more extensive list of industries, see Fritz Machlup, *The Basing Point System* (Philadelphia: Blakiston, 1949), p. 17. Other standard references on basing point pricing include Carl Kaysen, "Basing Point Pricing and Public Policy," *Quarterly Journal of Economics* 63 (August 1949): 289–314; Arthur Smithies, "Aspects of the Basing Point System," *American Economic Review* 32 (December 1942): 705–26; and J. M. Clark, "Basing Point Methods of Price Quoting," *Canadian Journal of Economics and Political Science* 4 (November 1938): 477–89.

Chicago (as well as Birmingham, Los Angeles, and all other) mills. Thus, the Chicago mill will quote the price *CG* to its local customers, *IL* to Indianapolis customers, and *KE* to Columbus customers—a clearly discriminatory pattern. The farther from Chicago and the nearer Pittsburgh the Chicago mill's customers are, the higher Chicago's freight costs are, but the lower is the price at which it sells. On nearby shipments, Chicago charges customers the high freight from Pittsburgh, whereas its actual freight costs (rising along the path *AR*) are modest. The surplus of billed over actual freight under basing point pricing is called *phantom freight*. At Indianapolis, customers pay phantom freight of *DL* if they buy from a Chicago mill (although no phantom freight emerges if they buy from Pittsburgh, whose mills incur the actual freight costs from Pittsburgh).[34] The Chicago mill's phantom freight in selling to local customers is *AG*. Only when it sells in the territory east of Xenia does Chicago receive no phantom freight. Then its actual freight costs exceed billed freight charges, so that in selling to Columbus customers it absorbs freight equal to *EN* dollars per unit. It will be willing to do this if its marginal cost of producing the units for Columbus is less than *CA* minus *NE*. With sufficiently low marginal costs, Chicago

may find it worthwhile to absorb freight and penetrate all the way to Pittsburgh or even farther east. Pittsburgh at the same time receives full compensation for its freight when selling at the Pittsburgh-plus price in Chicago and farther west. Obtaining the same mill net price on such sales as those at home, it has every incentive to seek a share of the Chicago business. Each mill may therefore ship products into the other's home territory, incurring freight charges higher than those required if the order were filled locally. This practice is known as *cross-hauling*.

The incidence of phantom freight is reduced, perhaps greatly, under a *multiple basing point system*. Here more than one producing mill is designated as a basing point, and the delivered price quoted to any given customer reflects the lowest applicable basing point price plus freight to destination. In the steel industry after 1924 there were several basing points (typically including Pittsburgh, Chicago, and Birmingham) for most products. The cement industry had 79 basing point mills and 86 nonbasing point mills during 1937.[35] To illustrate the system's operation, suppose in Figure 11.6 that both Chicago and Pittsburgh are designated as basing points, and that *CA* is the Chicago base price and *PB* the Pittsburgh base price. Then the delivered price *ID* will be quoted on *all* sales to Indianapolis customers, whether made by Pittsburgh or Chicago mills, and *KE* will be quoted to all Columbus buyers. When Chicago sells to Indianapolis it receives no phantom freight if it is its own basing point, and when it sells to Columbus it must absorb freight equal to *EN* dollars per unit. Phantom freight is gained only by nonbase mills—e.g., by a mill located at Dayton and selling in its home territory at the delivered price quoted by Pittsburgh or Chicago.

Superficially, the multiple basing point system is similar to F.O.B. mill pricing with discriminatory freight absorption, and it is sometimes difficult to classify actual borderline cases into one category or the other. There are several important differences in principle, however. For one, buyers under any form of F.O.B. pricing have the option of paying only the mill price, taking delivery at the producing mill, and then providing their own transportation. This is seldom advantageous

F 11.6 Basing point pricing

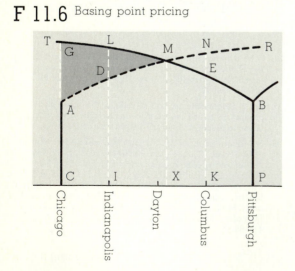

under strict basing point systems, since all prices quoted are *delivered* prices. Second, freight absorption may be unsystematic under discriminatory F.O.B. mill pricing. Producers do not necessarily match the rival mill's delivered price to the penny when they seek orders in the rival's home territory; they may match it, undercut it, or try to gain an order at their full list F.O.B. mill price plus freight. But under multiple basing point pricing, producers *systematically* adhere precisely to pricing rules that enable each to quote identical delivered prices to buyers at every destination. Through such adherence, they avoid independent initiatives that could threaten pricing discipline. Third, to achieve uniformity of price quotations, the delivered price quoted under basing point systems nearly always assumes rail freight charges, whereas the delivered price quoted under an F.O.B. mill system is usually the mill price plus most economical freight costs to destination (or the costs of transportation using a mode specified by the buyer), whether the medium be rail, highway, air, or water.

Basing point systems and competition We have seen that basing point pricing, and especially the single basing point variant, is discriminatory. This may be objectionable in its own right, but even more significant are the effects on competition and efficiency.

Competition is impaired because basing point pricing systems reduce what would be an incredibly complicated price quotation problem, if executed independently, to a relatively simple matter of applying the right formula. As we observed in Chapter 7, cooperation on a joint profit-maximizing policy becomes more difficult, the more heterogeneous the product is. If each producer independently and unsystematically quoted prices to the thousands of destinations it might serve, it would almost surely undercut rivals on some orders, perhaps touching off retaliatory price cuts. But common adherence to basing point formulas in effect eliminates discretion and uncertainty, and if each firm plays the game and sticks to the formulas, price competition is avoided. Identical prices are quoted to a given customer by every producer, leaving the division of orders to chance or nonprice variables (such as deliv-

ery time, special service, the dryness of martinis provided by salespeople at business luncheons, and so on—bases on which oligopolists often prefer to compete). By following the basing point rules, for example, 11 manufacturers were all able to submit quotations of $3.286854 per barrel in response to a government request for bids on cement delivered to Tucumcari, New Mexico.[36]

This is not to say that determining the right basing-point-plus-freight price is easy. Far from it. Freight rate classifications are maddeningly complex, with dozens of exceptions and considerable room for discretion. But discretion is exactly what one wishes to avoid in a system designed to suppress price competition. Consequently, industry trade associations (such as the American Iron and Steel Institute or the Cement Institute) published elaborate freight rate books listing the rail freight charges between every basing point and every conceivable destination point. Member firms were then expected dutifully to add the listed freight charges to the well-known base price (usually published by a price leader) in computing their delivered price quotations, even when they knew the rate book figure was obsolete or when the shipment would travel by water or truck instead of rail.

To be sure, the collusive purpose of basing point systems might be frustrated if producers chose not to adhere to the formulas. There are always incentives to chisel, especially when business is slack and departures from the formula

---

34. There is a certain amount of ambiguity in defining the amount of phantom freight, since the Chicago mill has no announced mill price. To make phantom freight represent the surplus of quoted over actual freight charges, we assume in drawing AR that the price CA if Chicago were a base equals the Pittsburgh base price PB, and that westbound and eastbound freight rate schedules are symmetric. Other writers (e.g., Smithies) have defined CA as the marginal cost in Chicago.

35. See Machlup, *The Basing Point System*, p. 80.

36. Machlup, *Basing Point System*, p. 2. It should be stressed that adherence to basing point formulas is not the only possible explanation for identical price quotations. Prebid meetings or focal point pricing are alternative possibilities. However, in the example cited, there is little doubt concerning the key coordinating role of the basing point system.

price can be kept secret. Examples of nonadherence can be found in virtually every industry following a basing point system.[37] Yet in some industries such as steel (at least in the United States), primary lead, and cement, adherence to formula prices has been remarkably consistent. A survey of cement producers' invoices for the depression year 1938, for example, showed that in only 6 of the 40 states covered did prices depart from identity in more than 10 percent of all dealer transactions. On bids to government agencies, nearly perfect uniformity of quotations was maintained.[38] To encourage such strong adherence to cement basing point prices, other firms imposed upon producers who were caught shading price on even a single transaction a punitive base price equivalent to the mill net realized in that transaction. All quotations for orders in the offender's home territory were then computed at the punitive base price. In effect, a price cut made to one customer, if discovered, became the ruling basis for quotations to every customer in the future. Not surprisingly, Loescher found that "the usual result of an imposition of a punitive base was the cessation of further price cutting by the offending mill. And the awareness that certain mills were being thus disciplined served to deter other competitors from selective cutting of prices."[39]

Assuming that a more competitive solution to the spatial pricing problem is desired, how attractive are the alternatives to basing point pricing? It is doubtful whether uniform F.O.B. mill pricing would induce more competition when the number of sellers is small. As we have seen, such a system makes producers at each shipping point the sole suppliers of customers within their freight advantage territories.[40] Unless several rivals are located at a single shipping point, there is little interfirm competitive contact, except in the zones where mill prices plus freight costs are equalized (e.g., Xenia in Figure 11.5). If these zones are densely populated with potential customers, producers may try to extend their territories and win additional sales by reducing mill prices. Small firms are often in an especially favorable position to gain through mill price reductions, since their inroads into the territory of a large rival (or group of rivals) may be so small that the rival will seldom consider an across-the-board retaliatory response, which would affect sales in other markets as well.[41] But when most sellers are of appreciable size, each firm will expect attempts to extend the area in which it has a delivered price advantage to provoke offsetting price cuts from rivals. If so, it is likely to refrain from aggressive price moves and accept the established distribution of territorial advantage—or at least, until it is modified by plant location actions.

Both single and multiple basing point systems bring producers at different locations into rivalrous contact with one another over a much broader geographic area than they would experience under uniform F.O.B. mill pricing. However, the rules of the game discourage using price as a competitive weapon, and so the greater interfirm contact leads mainly to more intense nonprice rivalry—at best, diligence in providing good service; at worst, inflated customer entertainment outlays.[42]

F.O.B. mill pricing with unsystematic discriminatory freight absorption appears to be the best compromise between the available extremes when market structures are oligopolistic.[43] Unlike uniform F.O.B. mill pricing, it permits sellers to shade mill net prices and invade each others' territories in search of additional business, thereby imparting added flexibility to the price structure and raising the probability that oligopoly discipline will be broken. And unlike multiple basing point pricing, this market interpenetration is achieved through explicit price rivalry, not passive acceptance of prices ordained by the system.

Spatial pricing and efficiency We turn now to the efficiency implications of alternative spatial pricing methods. One problem is excessive transportation—e.g., through cross-hauling. On theoretical grounds we should expect single basing point systems to be the worst offender, since mills located at the basing point incur no mill net price disadvantage even when they serve customers located next door to a distant rival's plant. Also, nonbase mills can be expected to focus their sales efforts on customers located to the far side of the basing point (e.g., west of Chicago in Figure 11.6) rather than toward it, where increasing freight absorption is necessary. Such a non-optimal delivery pattern was observed in the plywood industry.[44] Some cross-hauling is also expected under multiple basing point and discriminatory F.O.B. mill pricing. Only a uniform F.O.B. mill pricing approach has negligible cross-hauling.

Excessive transportation is also encouraged by postage stamp delivered price systems (under which distant customers are offered no incentive to purchase from the nearest mill) and a system of discriminatory freight pricing under which delivered prices rise with distance from the mill, but by less than the amount of increase in shipping costs. Beckmann has shown that when demand at any point on the map is choked off by higher freight charges and shipping costs rise linearly with distance, a monopolist supplying a market of given size realizes higher profits letting prices vary with distance by only one-half the increase in shipping costs than with either straight F.O.B. mill pricing or postage stamp pricing.[45] Such a scheme is the spatial analogue of optimal third-degree price discrimination with richly segregatable markets. However, transportation costs are lower with F.O.B. mill pricing, and the sum of producers' surplus (i.e., profits) plus consumers' surplus is higher, making the F.O.B. mill approach superior in terms of overall economic efficiency.

Evidence on the quantitative magnitude of cross-hauling costs under basing point systems is sparse. One study of the steel industry estimated that in February 1939 freight absorption, which in a multiple basing point system is a rough indicator of cross-hauling, amounted to between 3 and 5 percent of delivered prices.[46] Since demand was slack at the time, encouraging high interpenetration of markets, and since some freight absorption would probably occur under alternative pricing systems, this sets an upper limit on the amount of inefficient cross hauling costs. Two later company estimates that may have been self-serving put the magnitude of cross-hauling costs in the neighborhood of 1 percent.[47] A study of the cement industry found that unnecessary cross-hauling costs during prosperous 1927 approximated 15 percent of total revenue, although there is reason to believe that this estimate may

overstate the true magnitude by as much as a factor of two.[48] In any event, it is clear that cross-hauling costs have not been insignificant.

Another inefficiency fostered by the basing point system is the tendency to employ non-optimal transportation media. As we have observed, basing point prices were normally quoted

37. On the U.S. maple flooring industry, see Almarin Phillips, *Market Structure, Organization and Performance* (Cambridge, Mass.: Harvard University Press, 1962), pp. 153–60. On plywood, see the initial decision of the Federal Trade Commission administrative law judge, *in re Boise Cascade Corporation et al.*, docket no. 8958, November 29, 1976, para. 92, 101, 110–12, 141–49. On the western European steel industry, see Klaus Stegemann, "The Functions of Basing Point Pricing and Article 60 of the E. C. S. C. Treaty," *Antitrust Bulletin* 13 (Summer 1968): 411–21.

38. Samuel M. Loescher, *Imperfect Collusion in the Cement Industry* (Cambridge, Mass.: Harvard University Press, 1959), pp. 162–63. The cement and steel industry basing point systems were declared illegal in 1948.

39. Loescher, *Imperfect Collusion*, pp. 125–26.

40. The actual situation may, however, be more complicated than Figure 11.5 suggests if different transportation methods are used for shipments of varying sizes or to diverse destinations. Under uniform F.O.B. mill pricing a Chicago shipper might, for example, be able to compete effectively for large orders in distant Buffalo by Great Lakes freighter, but not for small orders in nearby Dayton by rail.

41. This point is stressed by Machlup in *The Basing Point System*, pp. 187–88.

42. Sixteen percent of the revenues received by 47 cement manufacturers in 1939 went into distribution and selling costs other than outbound freight. This is extremely high, considering the standardized character of the commodity and the well-informed customers buying it. Cf. Loescher, *Imperfect Collusion*, p. 213.

43. This view is held by Kaysen, "Basing Point Pricing," pp. 313–14. For a dissenting opinion, see Machlup, *The Basing Point System*, pp. 249–51, who favors uniform F.O.B. mill pricing in concentrated industries.

44. *In re Boise Cascade*, para. 113.

45. Martin J. Beckmann, "Spatial Price Policies Revisited," *Bell Journal of Economics* 7 (Autumn 1976): 619–29. See also M. L. Greenhut and H. Ohta, "Monopoly Output Under Alternative Spatial Pricing Techniques," *American Economic Review* 62 (September 1972): 705–13. Unlike Beckmann, Greenhut and Ohta do not assume the market to be of fixed size, and because discrimination enhances the likelihood that distant customers will be served, they infer that output will be higher with the 50 percent freight cost pass-on scheme than with F.O.B. pricing.

46. Cited in Kaysen, "Basing Point Pricing," p. 299. See also McKie, *Tin Cans and Tin Plate*, p. 71; and Machlup, *The Basing Point System*, pp. 56–57, 72, 82–83.

47. United States Steel and Jones & Laughlin estimates cited in Simon N. Whitney, *Antitrust Policies*, vol. I (New York: Twentieth Century Fund, 1958), p. 283.

under the assumption of rail haulage. This in fact encouraged the use of rail transportation, even when truck or water routings would have been cheaper or more convenient. There were several reasons for this anomaly.

If, say, a steel producer shipped by water and saved money, its customers might insist that the savings be shared. Any such concession could disrupt the whole identical price maintenance system. When customers were required to pay full rail costs in any case, they demanded rapid delivery, which placed water transport at a disadvantage. For shipments moved relatively short distances, trucking was usually cheaper and more convenient, but it too was shunned, partly because the lack of any simple, complete published trucking rate tariff rendered mutual adherence to identical delivered price quotations virtually impossible.

Recognizing that delivered prices under the basing point system assumed the use of inefficient transportation methods, some cement and steel buyers asked to take delivery at the producer's plant, paying the rail-delivered price minus rail freight and providing their own trucking services. This too was resisted by sellers because it introduced complications and uncertainty into the calculation of prices on shipments for which freight was to be absorbed, and also because it encouraged a kind of arbitrage. We return to Figure 11.6 to illustrate the arbitrage phenomenon under Pittsburgh-plus pricing. A customer might give a Chicago mill an order allegedly for Indianapolis, ask a freight rebate equal to the delivered price IL less the base price PB, and then pick up the order in Chicago with its own trucks and deliver it (at a cost much lower than the rebate) to its own plants or those of third parties in Chicago rather than in Indianapolis. To discourage such practices, firms using the basing point system collectively refused to ship orders via customers' trucks, refunded only a fraction of the rail freight component of delivered prices on orders picked up at the mill, or charged a punitive extra fee for loading buyers' trucks. As a result, relatively little use was made of trucks, despite their advantages. When the steel industry shifted from basing point to F.O.B. mill pricing, the share of trucks increased from almost nothing

in 1953 to 44 percent of total shipment tonnage in 1963 and 51 percent in 1972.[49]

Similar problems arise under postage stamp pricing systems. If sellers refuse to permit customer pickups, more efficient shipping methods may be shunned, especially when customers have a backhauling truck rolling empty by the shipping point on its way to the delivery point. But if pickups are allowed at an F.O.B. price appreciably below the uniform delivered price, near-in customers have a strong incentive to pick up their own shipments while distant customers continue to let the seller deliver and absorb freight. Deprived of its more lucrative near-in deliveries, the seller must raise its delivered price to break even on freight. This stimulates more distant customers to make their own pickups, inducing further price increases that ultimately undermine the delivered price system. If instead the seller refunds to customers making pickups the actual freight charges it would incur effecting delivery, this distortion is avoided, but customers have an incentive to misrepresent their shipments' destinations in order to collect freight for more distant points. Recognizing these complications, sellers practicing postage stamp pricing typically refuse to grant pickup rebates, and so the efficiencies of backhauling are lost.

Under basing point pricing a more subtle kind of misallocation—the distortion of industrial location decisions—can also occur. Industries heavily dependent upon an input supplied by sellers adhering to basing point pricing may build too much of their capacity near basing points and too little near supply nodes not designated as basing points. This problem is especially serious under the single basing point system. To illustrate, suppose in Figure 11.6 that steel mills in Pittsburgh and Chicago have roughly equal production costs, but that Pittsburgh is designated as the sole basing point. Although steel could be supplied in the Chicago area at a price of approximately CA, the actual Pittsburgh-plus price is CG. Because they must pay an artificially inflated price for steel in the Chicago area, fabricators to whom steel is an important input have an incentive to locate a disproportionate share of their capacity in the Pittsburgh area, where the delivered price is only PB. The Pittsburgh-plus system is said to have retarded the development of steel fabricating industries in the South and West, though it is difficult to isolate conclusively the effect of the geographic price structure from a variety of other elements affecting industry location decisions.[50] In the cement industry no similar effect was observed, partially because a multiple basing point system was employed and partly because decisions to locate, say, a highway or parking structure are not very sensitive to spatial differences in input costs.

It is also asserted that basing point pricing biases producers' locational decisions. A firm planning to build new capacity in an industry operating under the basing point system must weigh the advantages of building at a basing point against those of a nonbase location. Favoring the basing point location is the possibility of serving all customers in the relevant territory without having to absorb freight. Nonbase mills benefit from their ability to realize phantom freight on sales near home, but they suffer an increasing freight absorption burden as they try to expand and serve more distant customers. How this tradeoff is resolved depends upon the facts of each case with respect to such variables as the geographic distribution of customers and basing points, the structure of freight rates, the nonprice advantages (such as more rapid delivery) of greater proximity to customers, and the costs of producing at alternative locations. The consensus of most analysts is that the advantage lies more frequently in favor of concentrating production at basing points, although exceptions certainly exist.[51]

It is clear that basing point pricing also retards the adjustment of capacity in response to secular demand shifts, for mills located at basing points where demand is declining can, at no cost disadvantage, ship their output into growing nonbase areas whose prices are quoted from the same basing point. Recognizing this threat from afar, producers in rapidly growing nonbase areas are likely to expand their capacity at a rate falling short of the local demand growth rate. In support of these generalizations, Loescher found that basing point pricing retarded a desirable shift of cement production capacity during the late 1930s toward the South, where consumption

was increasing more rapidly than in other parts of the country.[52] In steel, there was a distinct acceleration in the rate of capacity growth at Chicago, Birmingham, and California as the industry gradually moved away from Pittsburgh-plus pricing and established new basing points in those areas.[53]

(48) See Loescher, *Imperfect Collusion*, pp. 208–13; and J. M. Clark, "Basing Point Methods of Price Quoting," p. 482. To keep cross-hauling costs from rising further, cement firms sometimes swapped orders. For example, a central Ohio producer would have a Cleveland producer fill its orders in northern Ohio and vice versa. In this way both increased their mill nets. See Loescher, pp. 139–41.

49. See Louis Marengo, "The Basing Point Decisions and the Steel Industry," *American Economic Review* 45 (May 1955): 521; U.S., Bureau of the Census, *Census of Transportation: 1963*, vol. III, Part 2 (Washington, D.C.: Government Printing Office), p. 301; and *Census of Transportation: 1972*, vol. III, Part 1 (Washington, D.C.: Government Printing Office).

In one case known to the author, the basing point system had a much more enduring impact on a cement producer's transportation media choices. The firm's plant was built in the heyday of basing point pricing to take advantage of limestone deposits and rail transportation. When the cement basing point system was declared illegal, the company began considering alternate shipping media and found that water transportation could conceivably yield major savings, but its plant lacked convenient access to a nearby major waterway. Had shipping by water been considered earlier, minor plant location adjustments could have been made to ensure access. But once the plant capital was sunk, such changes became prohibitively costly and so shipment only by rail or truck continued.

50. See Leonard W. Weiss, *Economics and American Industry* (New York: Wiley, 1961), pp. 300–303; Machlup, *The Basing Point System*, pp. 237–47; Kaysen, "Basing Point Pricing," pp. 304–305; and John S. Hekman, "An Analysis of the Changing Location of Iron and Steel Production in the Twentieth Century," *American Economic Review* 68 (March 1978): 123–33.

51. See Smithies, "Aspects of the Basing Point System," p. 723; Machlup, *The Basing Point System*, pp. 233–37; Kaysen, "Basing Point Pricing," pp. 300–306; and M. L. Greenhut, *Microeconomics and the Space Economy* (Chicago: Scott, Foresman, 1963), pp. 130–58. For a slightly dissenting view, see Loescher, *Imperfect Collusion*, p. 151n.

52. Loescher, *Imperfect Collusion*, pp. 199–208. For perspective, it is worth noting that the Soviet Union apparently experienced even worse inefficiencies in locating its cement production units through central planning. See A. Abouchar, "Rationality in the Pre-War Soviet Cement Industry," *Soviet Studies* 19 (October 1967): 211–31.

53. Cf. A. R. Burns, *The Decline of Competition* (New York: McGraw-Hill, 1936), pp. 340–45; Weiss, *Economics and American Industry*, pp. 302–303; and "Billions Build Chicago into a Steel Titan," *Business Week*, 19 November 1966, p. 68. For a more skeptical view, see Walter Isard and W. M. Capron, "The Future Locational Pattern of Iron and Steel Production in the United States," *Journal of Political Economy* 57 (April 1949), especially pp. 131–33.

Overall assessment To sum up, rigid adherence to a basing point system of pricing has several undesirable effects: the virtual elimination of price competition; inefficiencies with respect to costs, prices, and the choice of locations; and discrimination against customers located near nonbase mills. Some of its disadvantages can be avoided by legal proscription. Still it is doubtful whether any completely satisfactory solution to the spatial differentiation problem can be reached, at least for concentrated industries. Firms are adaptive, and where there is a will to avoid competition, ways will be found even when the most direct route is blocked. In the steel industry, for example, a shift from multiple basing point to F.O.B. mill pricing with (not very) unsystematic freight absorption did not precipitate a breakdown in pricing discipline, though it made the avoidance of independent pricing more difficult.[54] Conversely, the nominal employment of basing point formulas need not have serious anticompetitive consequences if industry members disregard them regularly because other structural conditions encourage independent behavior. Nevertheless, from the standpoint of public policy there is much to be said in favor of raising barriers to explicit and tacit collusion in pricing. For this reason, and to minimize the ancillary inefficiencies, legal prohibitions against the use of rigid basing point systems appear warranted. The most favorable solution to the spatial pricing problem when transportation costs are appreciable is without doubt F.O.B. mill pricing with unsystematic but not far-flung freight absorption.

Conclusion

There are so many kinds of price discrimination, with such diverse consequences, that simple generalizations about the economic effects and desirability of discrimination are apt to be misleading. Discrimination always causes a redistribution of income whose merits cannot be assessed without invoking value judgments. Some forms of discrimination increase the efficiency of resource allocation compared to simple monopoly, others are essentially neutral, while still other types such as single basing point systems lead to serious inefficiencies. Unsystematic discrimination can increase the vigor of competition, while systematic discrimination may bolster the market power of already powerful firms and facilitate adherence to a collusive price structure. Given these complexities, it is necessary to judge particular cases of discrimination on their individual merits.

54. See Marengo, "The Basing Point Decisions," p. 521.

12 Conglomerate size and pricing behavior

Our emphasis thus far has been on the relationship between *relative* size—i.e., power in specific markets—and pricing behavior. This is the conventional focus of economic analysis. But absolute size might also matter. The pricing actions of a large multiproduct, multimarket enterprise may differ from those of dispersed independent specialists, each holding in its particular market a share equivalent to the large firm's. Power in narrowly defined markets may interact with overall corporate size to evoke a different outcome than if the absolute size factor were lacking. In this chapter we explore some of the principal hypotheses: that conglomerate size is especially conducive to predatory pricing, spheres of influence agreements among giant rivals, reciprocal dealing, and nonmaximization of profits.[1]

Predatory pricing

One purported trait of large, financially powerful conglomerate firms is their greater ability and willingness to engage in sustained price cutting with the intent of disciplining smaller competitors or even driving them out of the market. This so-called "deep pocket" hypothesis has been stated most forcefully by Corwin Edwards:

> An enterprise that is big in this sense obtains from its bigness a special kind of power, based upon the fact that it can spend money in large amounts. If such a concern finds itself matching expenditures or losses, dollar for dollar, with a substantially smaller firm, the length of its purse assures it of victory. . . . The large company is in a position to hurt without being hurt.[2]

Although there is some disagreement among scholars over semantics, predatory pricing is said to occur when a seller cuts price below the level of its rivals' costs and perhaps also its own costs for protracted periods, until the rivals either close down operations altogether or sell out on favorable terms. The predator's motivation is presumably to secure a monopoly position once rivals

---

1. We limit our analysis to pricing behavior and will not try to cover the whole waterfront of the conglomerate size issue—e.g., with respect to economies of absolute scale, advantages in the exercise of political power, or the loss of economic information resulting when operations in many different industries are lumped together in the consolidated financial reports of a conglomerate. For studies with a broader sweep, see Corwin D. Edwards, "Conglomerate Bigness As a Source of Power," in the National Bureau of Economic Research conference report, *Business Concentration and Price Policy* (Princeton: Princeton University Press, 1955), pp. 331–59; John M. Blair, "The Conglomerate Merger in Economics and Law," *Georgetown Law Journal* 46 (Summer 1958): 672–700; Donald F. Turner, "Conglomerate Mergers and Section 7 of the Clayton Act," *Harvard Law Review* 78 (May 1965): 1313–95; and the Federal Trade Commission staff report, *Conglomerate Merger Performance* (Washington, D.C.: Government Printing Office, November 1972), Chapter 5.

2. Edwards, "Conglomerate Bigness," pp. 334–35.

have been driven from the arena, enjoying long-run profits higher than they would be if the rivals were permitted to survive. If it must itself sustain losses during the price war, the predator's ability to do so may be bolstered if it can draw upon profits gained selling the same product in other geographic territories or from selling different products. In other words, it subsidizes its predatory operations with profits from other markets until the predation creates conditions that will repay the original subsidy.

The most famous case of alleged predatory pricing is that of the old Standard Oil Company. Under the leadership of John D. Rockefeller, the Standard Oil trust between 1870 and 1899 attained and maintained a 90 percent share of the U.S. petroleum refining industry through a vigorous program of mergers, combined with various sharp practices that supposedly increased the willingness of independent refiners to sell out. These included the securing of discriminatory rail freight rates and rebates, foreclosing supplies of crude oil through the control of pipelines, business espionage, price warfare waged both overtly and secretly through bogus independent distributors, and (although never proved) astute placement of an occasional stick of dynamite. Regarding predatory price warfare—our main concern here—the conventional wisdom, handed down from generation to generation of economists, tells us that Standard cut prices sharply in specific local markets where there was competition while holding prices at much higher levels in markets lacking competition. Thereby it presumably softened up its rivals until they were receptive to merger offers. In a precedent-setting opinion, Supreme Court Chief Justice Edward White enumerated the predatory practices of which Standard was accused and cited approvingly the prosecution's contention that "the pathway of the combination . . . is strewn with the wrecks resulting from crushing out, without regard to law, the individual rights of others."[3]

This interpretation stood virtually unchallenged until 1958, when it was attacked by Professor McGee on two main grounds: (1) that there was little evidence to support the contention that Standard achieved its monopoly position through predatory price cutting, and (2) that such a strategy by Standard would have been irrational because it demanded an excessive sacrifice of profits.[4]

McGee's criticism of the supporting evidence was based solely upon an analysis of the voluminous Standard Oil antitrust case record. It is not convincing, since antitrust investigations labor under such severe evidentiary difficulties that they frequently fail to elicit proof of the main points at issue. Had McGee bothered to cast his net further into historical works drawing upon the Rockefeller papers, he would have found that Standard tried in some instances to drive out its rivals through price cutting. As Rockefeller wrote to an associate in 1881, "We want to watch, and when our volume of business is to be cut down by the increase of competition to fifty percent, or less, it may be a very serious question whether we had not better make an important reduction, with a view of taking substantially all the business there is."[5]

McGee's second point is better taken, for the independent evidence suggests that Rockefeller recognized the limitations of local price warfare, only infrequently engaged in it for the explicit purpose of driving rivals to the wall, and instead pursued a much more complex and sophisticated pricing strategy.[6] One problem was that Standard, controlling or attempting to control the lion's share of the markets in which it sold, had to accept profit sacrifices disproportionate to the harm it inflicted upon small rivals when it resorted to price warfare. In the words of another Rockefeller associate, Standard "gained or lost on a titan's scale while its opponents did so on a pygmy's."[7] The profit sacrifices of a sustained local price war were worthwhile only if the postwar situation would be much more favorable once competitors were gone.

Yet this was by no means assured. Except for the difficulty of securing crude oil supplies, barriers to new entry were modest. A refinery of substantial size by 1880s standards could be erected for less than $50,000.[8] Consequently, any attempt by Standard to elevate prices in areas with adequate rail or water transportation from crude oil producing centers could stimulate an influx of new entry. To be sure, the threat of renewed price warfare might deter some potential entrants, but unless Standard repeatedly accepted the profit sacrifices associated with carrying out this threat, it soon lost its credibility. In addition, small-scale refineries closed down during a price war were typically put back into operation when prices were raised unless the facilities were purchased by Standard. And in taking such capacity off the market through acquisition, Standard occasionally created additional troubles for itself, since some entrepreneurs to whom it had paid a handsome liquidation price broke their agreements not to compete in the future, reinvesting the proceeds in new refining capacity![9]

Price warfare to eliminate rivals might also be unprofitable if the liquidation prices at which the victims sold out were not much less than they would have been in a merger agreement entered under less coercive conditions.[10] McGee argues that this was so in the Standard Oil case, that Standard could have acquired rival facilities in any event by paying only a modest premium over their competitive value. But this is doubtful. A successful price war could spell the difference between paying the nuisance value of a firm, which most entrepreneurs opposing Standard believed to be high, and the distress price, which for narrowly based specialists suffering a liquidity crisis would be appreciably lower.

Nevertheless, largely because of the new entry and dormant capacity problem, Rockefeller apparently recognized the futility of trying to drive rivals out of business through predatory pricing in all but exceptional cases. He turned instead to a classic entry-deterring strategy: holding price-cost margins to a value not exceeding Standard's cost advantage, which was modest in territories where Standard's control over low-cost crude oil transportation media was weak. Under this policy efficient competitors were not driven out, but undercutting Standard's price to achieve market share gains at Standard's expense was rendered unattractive, and outsiders' incentives to invest in new refining capacity were weakened. Only where rivals were having trouble getting crude oil supplies—that is, where substantial barriers to entry existed—did Standard price its products to maintain high profit margins.

Several additional studies—e.g., of the gunpowder, sugar refining, and ready-mix concrete industries[11]—have followed McGee in concluding that what was widely believed to be predatory pricing was in fact rare, ineffective, or the symptom of a competitive struggle desired as little by the alleged predators as by its victims. The evidence is persuasive, although it is not completely clear whether this reflects the rarity of hard-core predation or the barrenness of historical records. A more widesweeping examination of 26 antitrust case records reached similarly negative conclusions, but suffers from inadequate factual underpinning and perhaps also inconsistency in examining the information available.[12] Certainly, other cases have been identified in which an inference of predation, even under the strictest definition of the term, appears indisputable.[13] And if one defines predation more expansively to

3. *Standard Oil Company of New Jersey v. U.S.*, 221 U.S. 1, 47, 76 (1911).

4. John S. McGee, "Predatory Price Cutting: The Standard Oil (N.J.) Case," *Journal of Law and Economics* 1 (October 1958): 137–69.

5. Letter to H. A. Hutchins, quoted in Allan Nevins, *Study in Power: John D. Rockefeller*, vol. II (New York: Scribner's, 1953), p. 65.

6. Nevins, *Study in Power*, pp. 62–67.

7. Nevins, *Study in Power*, p. 66.

8. Nevins, *Study in Power*, p. 54.

9. See Wayne A. Leeman, "The Limitations of Local Price-Cutting as a Barrier to Entry," *Journal of Political Economy* 64 (August 1956): 329–32. For evidence on similar reentries into the sugar refining industry, see Richard Zerbe, "The American Sugar Refinery Company, 1887–1914: The Story of a Monopoly," *Journal of Law and Economics* 12 (October 1969): 355–56.

10. See Lester G. Telser, "Cutthroat Competition and the Long Purse," *Journal of Law and Economics* 9 (October 1966): 259–77, for an algebraic statement of this argument.

11. See Kenneth G. Elzinga, "Predatory Pricing: The Case of the Gunpowder Trust," *Journal of Law and Economics* 13 (April 1970): 223–40; Zerbe, "The American Sugar Refinery Company," pp. 351–75; and David R. Kamerschen, "Predatory Pricing, Vertical Integration and Market Foreclosure: The Case of Ready Mix Cement in Memphis," *Industrial Organization Review* 2, No. 3 (1974): 143–68.

12. Roland H. Koller II, "The Myth of Predatory Pricing," *Antitrust Law and Economics Review* 4 (Summer 1971): 105–23. Koller concludes, for example, that old Standard Oil exhibited no predatory intent in its pricing. His findings on the powder trust also diverge substantially from those of Elzinga, even though both authors used the same source materials. But see Bjarke Fog, *Industrial Pricing Policies* (Amsterdam: North-Holland, 1960), pp. 147–51, who found through a survey of 139 Danish companies that large enterprises did not try to cut prices to the bone because they believed that attempts permanently to drive out small rivals were unlikely to succeed.

include situations in which price reductions aimed at driving back newcomers not yet well established in a market, and hence not requiring the presumptive predator to undercut its own (possibly lower) average variable costs,[14] many more illustrations can be found—e.g., IBM's counterattack against plug-compatible peripheral equipment manufacturers[15] and Borden's price warfare against firms selling reconstituted lemon juice in competition with its ReaLemon brand.[16] Still other examples concern attempts not to eliminate rivals, but to discipline them—e.g., when Safeway Stores cut prices below cost in Texas during 1954, evidently to discourage the use of trading stamps by rivals.[17]

Theoretical analysis confirms that pricing below one's own cost to drive out rivals can under some conditions maximize long-run profits. Assume that the output Q_F of fringe rivals increases or contracts according to the differential equation $dQ_F/dt = k[P(t) - P_o]$, where $P(t)$ is the price set and P_o fringe firms' unit cost. Using this model, Gaskins demonstrates that a dominant firm may initially set $P(t)$ below its own unit cost when it enjoys a substantial cost advantage over rivals; rivals exit rapidly in response to its price cuts (i.e., k has a sizeable value); its initial market share is relatively small (i.e., Q_F is relatively large); and its time discount rate is low.[18] This result, it should be noted, is largely independent of whether the dominant firm is big in a conglomerate sense. Below-cost pricing can be "rational" even when the dominant firm is a single-market specialist if its cost advantage and the fringe response coefficient are large enough. Under the Gaskins model assumptions, conglomerate size might matter only by permitting the dominant firm to enjoy a lower cost of capital, and hence to discount future earnings less severely.[19]

In assuming an essentially mechanistic rival response, however, the Gaskins model excludes what may be a more important consequence of conglomerate size—the demonstration effect that sharp price cutting in one market can have on the behavior of actual or would-be rivals in other markets. If rivals come to fear from a multimarket seller's actions in Market A that entry or expansion in Markets B and C will be met by sharp price cuts or other rapacious responses, they may

be deterred from taking aggressive actions there. Then the conglomerate's expected benefit from predation in Market A will be supplemented by the discounted present value of the competition-inhibiting effects its example has in Markets B and C.[20] This view of the payoffs from predation is consistent with events in the coffee industry during the early 1970s.[21] Through its Maxwell House and related brands, General Foods controlled approximately 45 percent of regular coffee sales in the Eastern United States. Folger's, the leading brand in Chicago and points west, but little known in the East, began a campaign to expand eastward. Maxwell House countered the invasion with sharp (possibly below-cost) price reductions and increased promotional spending in selected key cities, evidently with the intent of persuading Folger's that its inroads would be vigorously resisted. The counterattack seems to have been at least partly successful, for although Folger's remained in the cities it entered and continued expanding into the Southeast, it drew back for at least several years from its original plan to move aggressively into New York City and other densely populated Northeast seaboard markets.

For predation to have a deterrent effect in such instances, it is important that conditions in the multiple markets served by the conglomerate be sufficiently similar that potential entrants into, say, Market B believe that the conduct observed in Market A is apt to recur. This seems more likely when the predator's size comes from selling the same product in multiple geographic markets, as in the Maxwell House case, or closely related products in a national market (such as the various types of peripheral equipment plug-compatible with IBM's computers), than with supplying quite unrelated products (like those a "pure" conglomerate would offer). Even when the intermarket similarities are strong, however, bluff and counterbluff problems, analogous to those considered in Chapter 8, appear. If the anticipated future benefits in Market A alone are insufficient to warrant predatory pricing in that market unless supplemented by demonstration effect benefits in Market B, potential rivals in comparable Market B may recognize that a predatory response by the conglomerate in B would be unprofitable, and so they will not be deterred. Much depends upon the extent to which business managers extrapolate from past events rather than sizing up the probabilities in each new situation. On this crucial point we know very little. It may well be, as McGee and others have argued, that the short-run profit sacrifices associated with predatory pricing typically outweigh the prospective longer term rewards from successfully excluding or deterring competitors, and therefore that rational, calculated predation is rare. Much deeper mining of available and unorthodox data sources is necessary before more confident generalizations can be supported.

A variant on the conglomerate size-pricing interaction theme deserves brief mention. It occurs when firms move into a new product line or market, charging a price that fails to cover cost or (more commonly) incurring promotional and other costs exceeding sales revenue in the hope of building a strong market presence, and subsidizing the losses with profits derived from other lines. Many cases of this sort can be observed. Folger's expansion into the East fits the mold, as does Philip Morris's channelling of cigarette profits to support an aggressive expansion program by PM's Miller Brewing subsidiary, acquired in 1970.[22] As in classic predation situations, temporary losses are incurred as an investment in future market position and profits. The differentiating feature is that the firm making the investment is either a newcomer or a previously marginal participant in the relevant market, and its expansion presumably intensifies the competitive challenge to leading sellers, even though weaker industry members may fail as a by-product of the struggle. How meaningful this distinction is depends upon whether rivalry among the surviving firms is likely to be more or less vigorous than under the *status quo ante*—a question to which no simple, general answer can be offered. From our present perspective, the critical issue is again the role of conglomerate size in facilitating such behavior. Size may indeed matter if conglomerates can obtain capital at lower costs, or in larger quantities, than small specialist firms. This was almost surely true in the Miller expansion. It seems improbable that a medium-sized, stagnant brewing company, as

Miller was before its acquisition, could have raised the $30 million Philip Morris lost before its Miller operation turned the corner to profitability and the $850 million PM planned to invest by 1980 in new brewing plant and equipment.

It is sometimes implied that when temporary losses, predatory or not, in one line of business are covered by profits from another line, prices in the subsidizing line may be elevated to generate the subsidies. This view is most likely incorrect, at

(13) Basic S. Yamey, "Predatory Price Cutting: Notes and Comments," *Journal of Law and Economics* 15 (April 1972): 137–47 (on the China steamship trade in the 1880s); "4 Steamship Conferences Face Antitrust Suits for $68.4 Million," *New York Times*, 21 November 1966, p. 89 (on cement shipments to Indochina); and Robert T. Masson and Philip Eisenstat, "A Stochastic Rationale for Predatory Pricing" (paper presented at the meetings of the Econometric Society, December 1975).

14. On various approaches to the definitional problem, see Yamey, "Predatory Price Cutting," pp. 129–37; Roland H. Koller II, "On the Definition of Predatory Pricing," *Antitrust Bulletin* 20 (Summer 1975): 329–38; Phillip Areeda and Donald F. Turner, "Predatory Pricing and Related Practices under Section 2 of the Sherman Act," *Harvard Law Review* 88 (February 1975): 697–733; and the comment by F. M. Scherer and reply by Areeda and Turner, *Harvard Law Review* 89 (March 1976): 869–903.

15. See pp. 324–25 *supra*.

16. *In the Matter of Borden, Inc.*, Federal Trade Commission docket no. 8978, Initial Decision, August 19, 1976.

17. See the Federal Trade Commission staff report, *Economic Report on the Structure and Competitive Behavior of Food Retailing* (Washington, D.C.: Government Printing Office, January 1966), pp. 121–42. A case related to this example, it should be noted, is included in Koller's list.

18. Darius W. Gaskins, Jr., "Optimal Pricing by Dominant Firms" (Ph.D. diss., University of Michigan, 1970), especially pp. 12–22.

19. Fringe rivals' *lack* of conglomerate size might also matter indirectly by making them less able to withstand losses, so that the value of *k* is elevated.

20. See Masson and Eisenstat, "A Stochastic Rationale," who apply similar logic to explain the predatory behavior of the multimarket Associated Milk Producers cooperative.

21. One consequence of the events was the filing of antitrust suits not settled at the time this was written. *In the Matter of General Foods Corp.*, Federal Trade Commission docket no. 9085, July 1976; and *Indian Coffee Corp. et al. v. Procter & Gamble et al.* (W. D. Pennsylvania, October 1976).

22. See "Miller's Fast Growth Upsets the Beer Industry," *Business Week*, 8 November 1976, pp. 58–67. For a more comprehensive but inconclusive analysis of postmerger promotional outlay escalation in 47 food products lines, see Peter C. Riesz, "Conglomerate Subsidization of Advertising Expenditures: Some Empirical Evidence," *Antitrust Bulletin* 19 (Winter 1974): 761–82.

least for enterprises not subjected to some kind of externally imposed profit ceiling. For if the firm is indeed attempting to maximize profits without external constraint, one would expect it to set prices at profit-maximizing levels in high-profit lines, whether or not there are low-profit lines to be subsidized.[23] To do otherwise would be to accept needless profit sacrifices. However, subsidization of losing operations *can* lead to price increases in other lines if a multimarket company is subject to an overall profitability constraint because it is a regulated public utility,[24] because of governmental price controls linked to aggregate corporate profitability,[25] or because it fears a public outcry or governmental intervention if its overall profits exceed some "reasonable" level. Then incremental losses in one line will be offset through price increases on other products whose prices had not previously been raised to the profit-maximizing level.

To sum up, conglomerate size can under at least some plausible circumstances facilitate pricing behavior that undermines the viability of smaller rivals. Yet "predatory" pricing may be both feasible and rational for narrow-line enterprises too, and extremely diversified companies are probably less likely to engage in predation than firms serving multiple but functionally related markets, all else being equal. What remains uncertain is how much difference multimarket size makes, that is, how much more likely predation is when capital-raising economies of scale are enjoyed or demonstration effects spill over into related markets. On this, as on so many points, more evidence of better quality is needed.

The spheres of influence hypothesis

Thus far we have been concerned with whether rapacious rivalry is more apt to emerge when a conglomerate giant faces a group of small specialists in some market than when specialists alone occupy the market. Now we reverse our field, examining the hypothesis that when conglomerate giants face other conglomerates in a web of markets, they will compete *less* sharply than would specialists occupying the same markets. Putting the two propositions together, when there is an asymmetry of conglomerate power, rivalry is said to be more severe, whereas symmetry blunts the incentives for rivalry. This hypothesis was first advanced by Corwin Edwards, who merits quoting at length:

> When one large conglomerate enterprise competes with another, the two are likely to encounter each other in a considerable number of markets. The multiplicity of their contacts may blunt the edge of their competition. A prospect of advantage from vigorous competition in one market may be weighed against the danger of retaliatory forays by the competitor in other markets. Each conglomerate competitor may adopt a live-and-let-live policy designed to stabilize the whole structure of the competitive relationship. Each may informally recognize the other's primacy of interest in markets important to the other, in the expectation that its own important interests will be similarly respected. Like national states, the great conglomerates may come to have recognized spheres of influence and may hesitate to fight local wars vigorously because the prospect[s] of local gain are not worth the risk of general warfare.[26]

Edwards's observations on live-and-let-live attitudes among conglomerate giants were influenced by his experience as director of a U.S. mission to investigate Japanese combines following World War II. Before the war, a substantial share of all Japanese business activity was concentrated in the hands of a few giant conglomerate *Zaibatsu* groups. The four largest Zaibatsu—Mitsui, Mitsubishi, Sumitomo, and Yasuda—controlled a fourth of all paid-up capital in prewar Japanese industry and finance.[27] They were far more diversified than any American corporation. Even after a postwar Zaibatsu dissolution program, Mitsui interests ranged into shipbuilding, coal mining, copper mining, iron and aluminum production, synthetic fibers, plastics, fertilizers, basic chemicals, cameras, banking, insurance, and real estate.[28] Each Zaibatsu group was strong in some lines and relatively weak in others. They came into contact in dozens of markets, especially in the heavy industrial sector. In addition, there were frequent social and matrimonial ties among members of the several families dominating the principal Zaibatsu.

Students of Japanese industrial history disagree on the effect this widespread interpenetration of markets had on competitive behavior. Some concur with Edwards that a live-and-let-live attitude was encouraged by the fear that aggressive action in a market where one had an edge would be countered by aggression in markets where rivals had the advantage.[29] Others found that the principal Zaibatsu were "keen rivals," and that they often refused to cooperate with one another in cartel agreements because of confidence in their own superiority, clique rivalries, prejudice and ignorance, the desire to guard private secrets, and dissatisfaction with prices and output quotas.[30] Perhaps the most balanced view of this complex and conflicting picture is given by Lockwood, who described prewar Japanese enterprise as

> a rather indeterminate blend of sharp jealousy and mutual solidarity, of rugged individualism and collusive action. If rivalries were keen, they yet operated in a setting characterized by a propensity among the rivals to cooperate in abating the rigors of the free market.[31]

Examining the postwar performance of 243 large Japanese manufacturing enterprises, Caves and Uekusa found no evidence that Zaibatsu or similar major bank affiliations raised 1961–70 profitability.[32] In fact, firms with strong bank group affiliations reported slightly lower profits, all else being equal. They also paid somewhat higher rates for borrowed capital, suggesting that if group affiliation did yield supranormal returns, it was the coordinating banks that captured them. In an analysis of market share changes experienced by Zaibatsu and their successor firms, Caves and Uekusa observed a tendency after 1955 for companies weak in particular markets to give ground, perhaps out of conscious deference, to high-share rivals. The evidence is sufficiently tenuous, however, that the authors are led to conclude that "no systematic relations among the groups have been revealed."[33]

Do proclivities toward mutual forebearance exist among Western conglomerate giants, with traditions and (until recently) compass quite different from those of the Zaibatsu? One fragment of qualitative evidence comes from Professor Alfred Kahn's study of interfirm relations in the international chemicals industry.[34] Among the most conglomerate of Western firms prior to World

23. For a special and perhaps unrealistic case in which divisional profit differences interact to affect diverse lines' pricing strategies, see Robert A. Meyer, "Risk-Efficient Monopoly Pricing for Multiproduct Firms," *Quarterly Journal of Economics* 90 (August 1976): 461–74.

24. See Harvey Averch and Leland L. Johnson, "Behavior of the Firm under Regulatory Constraint," *American Economic Review* 52 (December 1962): 1058–59; and Ronald Braeutigam, "The Regulation of Multi-product Firms: Decisions on Entry and Rate Structure," (Ph.D. diss., Stanford University, 1976), pp. 52–58.

25. For a striking case resulting from the imposition of an overall profit ceiling through the renegotiation of defense contractor profits, see *Pacific Engineering & Production Co. v. Kerr-McGee Corp. et al.,* 551 F. 2d 790 (1977), *cert. den.* 434 U.S. 879 (1977). The role of renegotiation is brought out in *Pacific Engineering's Petition for a Writ of Certiorari,* 1977, p. 8.

26. From Edwards's testimony in the U.S., Congress, Senate, Subcommittee on Antitrust and Monopoly hearings, *Economic Concentration,* Part 1, 89th Cong., 1st sess., 1965, p. 45. His original statement of the hypothesis is in "Conglomerate Bigness," p. 335.

27. William W. Lockwood, "Japan's 'New Capitalism,'" in William W. Lockwood, ed., *The State and Economic Enterprise in Japan* (Princeton: Princeton University Press, 1965), pp. 495–500. See also T. A. Bisson, *Zaibatsu Dissolution in Japan* (Berkeley: University of California Press, 1954), pp. 6–32.

28. For analyses of postwar Zaibatsu structure and control, see Eugene Rotwein, "Economic Concentration and Monopoly in Japan," *Journal of Political Economy* 72 (June 1964): 265–72; and Richard E. Caves and Masu Uekusa, *Industrial Organization in Japan* (Washington, D.C.: Brookings Institution, 1976), Chapter 4. See also Chapter 3, pp. 51–52 *supra.*

29. This is Rotwein's view, based on Eleanor M. Hadley, "Concentrated Business Power in Japan" (Ph.D. diss., Radcliffe College, 1949), pp. 7, 13–14.

30. G. C. Allen, *A Short Economic History of Modern Japan: 1867–1937* (New York: Praeger, 1963), p. 135; and William W. Lockwood, *The Economic Development of Japan* (Princeton: Princeton University Press, 1954), pp. 228–30.

31. Lockwood, *Economic Development of Japan,* p. 231.

32. Allen, *Industrial Organization in Japan,* pp. 72–83.

33. Allen, *Industrial Organization in Japan,* pp. 85–86.

34. Alfred E. Kahn, "The Chemical Industry," in Walter Adams, ed., *The Structure of American Industry,* 3rd ed. (New York: Macmillan, 1961), pp. 246–52. See also G. W. Stocking and M. W. Watkins, *Cartels in Action: Case Studies in International Business Diplomacy* (New York: Twentieth Century Fund, 1946), Chapters 9 to 11.

War II were I. G. Farben in Germany, Imperial Chemical Industries in England, and du Pont in the United States. Their interests touched in hundreds of product lines, and they unquestionably adopted a live-and-let-live policy towards one another, negotiating explicit geographic spheres of influence agreements for products on which they had exclusive patent protection and avoiding aggressive price competition where they did compete directly. The relationship between du Pont and Farben was summarized as follows:

> Both companies gave heed to strategic considerations favoring some kind of understanding; each either had something the other wanted or could at least harm the other's interests. Both realized the hazards of seriously antagonizing each other, and, above all, the folly of upsetting the market. This was the nature of their gentlemen's agreement: they would cooperate wherever possible, and in any event they would act like gentlemen.[35]

There is reason to believe competition among the three chemical giants intensified in the postwar period after the Farben combine was broken up, du Pont's spheres of influence agreements were attacked by the American antitrust authorities, and other chemical firms began to diversify and expand into product lines formerly dominated by the Big Three.[36] Still, competition among chemical makers continues to have a mild quality except in lines where severe overcapacity exists, and it may well be that mutual interpenetration of markets is one of the factors inhibiting aggressive instincts.[37]

Respect for spheres of influence also appears to be a prominent characteristic of pricing relationships among the various international merchant marine cartels. According to an individual connected with one of the conferences, particular ship lines and groups of lines strive to negotiate advantageous freight rate agreements covering the routes they dominate by threatening rival groups with rate warfare over routes in which the rivals' profit stake is greatest.[38]

Two studies have attempted to ascertain statistically whether the performance of U.S. companies has been affected by respect for overlapping spheres of influence. Strickland constructed an index of multimarket interdependence for 195 large manufacturing corporations, counting the number of mutual contacts those firms experienced in 408 four-digit manufacturing industries, with each contact weighted by the encountered rival's market share.[39] Introducing this index into multiple regressions of 1963 price-cost margins on an array of more traditional structural variables, he found that margins were *negatively* but weakly related to the richness of multimarket contacts, all else being equal. This is the opposite of what one would expect if price rivalry were dulled by respect for spheres of influence. Arnold Heggestad and Stephen Rhoades developed similar measures of contact frequencies among the top five banks in 187 metropolitan areas.[40] They found that market shares for the three leading banks in those areas were more stable on average between 1968 and 1974, the more frequently the banks encountered each other as rivals in other cities. From this they conclude that rivalry in banking was inhibited by respect for spheres of influence.

To sum up, the evidence on how market interpenetration and respect for spheres of influence affects business behavior is fragmentary and to some extent conflicting. The spheres of influence hypotheses are intuitively plausible, and they find at least some qualitative and quantitative support. But the last word on them surely remains to be heard.

Reciprocal buying

Another business practice with a potentially close connection to conglomerate size is reciprocal buying, that is, giving preference in purchasing decisions to firms that are good customers for one's own products. Even though a majority of company executives responding to a 1953 survey expressed dislike for the practice, most of their firms engaged in it to some extent.[41] A later survey reveals that larger firms are more likely to base purchasing decisions on reciprocity considerations than small firms.[42]

Reciprocal buying is normally associated with the existence of several conditions.[43] First is an oligopolistic market structure, leading industry members to engage in nonprice rivalry when price competition is stalemated. Second, producers must have excess capacity they would like to utilize by filling orders won on nonprice grounds. Surveys show, for instance, that pressures to engage in reciprocal buying are stronger during recessions than in booms.[44] Third, there must be a two-way flow of transactions between companies, with Firm A both buying from and selling to Firm B in significant quantities. This is a fairly restrictive condition in many cases, for a survey of some 300 firms disclosed that the median firm made only from 1 to 3 percent of its sales to suppliers, and only 6 percent of the companies sold more than 30 percent of their output to suppliers.[45] Finally, it is said that asymmetry in size among the firms involved favors reciprocal purchasing, especially when a conglomerate giant towers over rival sellers specializing in one or two narrow lines.[46]

The advantages of conglomerate size are best shown by some examples. One of the most striking, which ultimately provoked an antitrust suit, involved the exercise of power not through direct conglomerate diversification, but through the interlocking of financial interests by individual company executives.[47] Two traffic department (i.e., freight routing) officials of the Armour Company bought stock in a small firm manufacturing special draft gears for the railroad industry. They gave preference in routing Armour's huge meat shipment volume to railroads that purchased gears from their company. As a result, the gear-making firm indirectly exploiting Armour's power moved from seventh place in its field, with a 1 percent market share, to industry sales leadership and a 35 percent market share in only six years.

In 1957 General Dynamics, a leading defense contractor, acquired the Liquid Carbonic Corporation, the largest U.S. seller of carbon dioxide and other industrial gases. The acquisition was motivated in significant measure by the belief that exerting reciprocal purchasing leverage on General Dynamics' thousands of subcontractors could increase the sales and profits of LC, which at the time was losing market share and operating at only 65 percent of capacity. Larger GD subcontractors typically bought quantities of industrial gas (e.g., for cryogenic and inert atmosphere uses) that were small in relation to the volume of sales they made to GD. Subcontracts were often awarded by General Dynamics on the basis of technical evaluations in which price played only a minor role. Emphasizing to its subcontractors the importance of "doing business with friends," the General Dynamics/Liquid Carbonic sales organization recorded reciprocity account sales of nearly $8 million in 1962 (i.e., more than a fifth of total premerger sales). The reciprocal dealing program appears to have been a material factor in reversing LC's market

35. Stocking and Watkins, *Cartels in Action*, p. 489.

36. See the testimony of Joel Dirlam in U.S., Congress, Senate, Subcommittee on Antitrust and Monopoly hearings, *Economic Concentration*, Part 2, 89th Cong., 1st sess., 1965, pp. 755–58; and M. J. Gart, "The British Company That Found a Way Out," *Fortune*, August 1966, pp. 104 ff.

37. See "Air Liquide Protects Its 80%," *Business Week*, 16 May 1977, pp. 170–77, describing how the company that monopolized the French industrial gas industry until an American firm entered sought in response to increase its 6 percent share of the U.S. market. As its chairman said, "If they attack us here, it's important to carry on the counterattack there."

38. For related background, see the report of the U.S., Congress, House, Committee on the Judiciary, Subcommittee on Antitrust, *The Ocean Freight Industry*, 87th Cong., 2nd sess., 1962, especially pp. 223–48.

39. Allyn D. Strickland, "Conglomerate Mergers, Mutual Forebearance Behavior and Price Competition" (processed, University of Delaware, 1977).

40. Arnold A. Heggestad and Stephen A. Rhoades, "Multi-Market Interdependence and Local Market Competition in Banking," *Review of Economics and Statistics* 60 (November 1978): 523–32.

41. M. C. Neuhoff and G. G. Thompson, "Reciprocity: Many Practice, Few Favor," *Business Record* (March 1954): 106–109.

42. Leonard Sloane, "Reciprocity: Where Does the P. A. Stand?," *Purchasing*, 20 November 1961, pp. 70–77.

43. See G. W. Stocking and W. F. Mueller, "Business Reciprocity and the Size of Firms," *Journal of Business* 30 (April 1957): 73–95; Joel Dean, "Economic Aspects of Reciprocity, Competition and Mergers," *Antitrust Bulletin* 8 (September-December 1963): 843–52; and Richard E. Caves, "The Economics of Reciprocity: Theory and Evidence on Bilateral Trading Arrangements," in Willy Sellekaerts, ed., *International Trade and Finance* (London: Macmillan, 1974), pp. 17–54.

44. Sloane, "Reciprocity," pp. 70–77.

45. Sloane, "Reciprocity," p. 77.

46. But see Jesse W. Markham, *Conglomerate Enterprise and Public Policy* (Boston: Harvard Business School Division of Research, 1973), pp. 77–82, who found in a survey of 195 corporations that firms with "trade relations departments" (a euphemism for organizational units seeking out reciprocal buying opportunities) tended to be less diversified on average than firms denying that they maintained such a unit.

47. *In re Waugh Equipment Company et al.*, 15 F.T.C. 232, 242–43 (1931).

Conglomerate size and pricing behavior 343

share decline before the merger was successfully challenged in an antitrust suit.[48]

One limitation on conglomerate size as a bargaining weapon arises when the conglomerate enterprise sells a variety of products to suppliers in a particular industry. The du Pont Company, for instance, is said to have placed special stress on reciprocal buying.[49] To win dynamite orders from steel makers vertically integrated into iron ore mining, it allegedly held out as a bargaining counter substantial steel purchases not only for its explosives divisions, but also for its basic chemical, plastics, synthetic fiber, and other divisions. This practice was disadvantageous to specialists Hercules Powder and Atlas Powder, who (at least until they undertook their own diversification programs) could place on the balance only the steel requirements of their explosives operations. Still, du Pont's reciprocal buying advantage might be attenuated if steel producers dispersed the purchase of their various chemical inputs. If, say, Bethlehem Steel bought all of its explosives from Hercules and Atlas, but purchased a substantial portion of the acid for its pickling baths from du Pont, the latter could scarcely reduce its steel purchases from Bethlehem without risking a loss of acid orders. In general, conglomerate leverage is strongest when the giant firm sells only one or a very few narrow segments of its product line to a supplier who in turn is anxious to satisfy the demand for an input employed by all of the conglomerate's divisions. To the extent that this generalization holds, significant examples of conglomerate leverage are likely to be limited to a small proportion of the typical giant firm's total sales.

The exercise of conglomerate power through reciprocal buying also tends to be less successful when smaller firms offer more attractive sales terms. Most of the 163 corporation executives responding to a 1963 survey stated that their firms' purchases were awarded on the basis of reciprocity only when price, quality, and delivery conditions were equal.[50] A paramount reason for the emphasis on reciprocal purchasing in the railroad and common motor carrier field was the fact that freight rates were equal under the binding scheme of public regulation, and so the distribution of patronage necessarily depended upon nonprice factors.[51] One known exception to the customary *ceteris paribus* rule was the policy of U.S. Rubber Company (now Uniroyal), which permitted its sales department to absorb any excess costs caused by awarding a purchase order to a good customer quoting other than the lowest price.[52] How frequently this latitude was exercised is not known. Another apparent exception is found in the precedent-setting *Consolidated Foods* antitrust case.[53] Consolidated, with extensive food wholesaling operations, acquired Gentry, a manufacturer of dehydrated onion and garlic. It tried to exert leverage from its position as a leading soup wholesaler to induce the purchase of Gentry products by soup makers. In a few instances soup producers yielded to this pressure despite their belief that the Gentry products were qualitatively inferior to rivals' offerings. But these seem to have been exceptional. For the most part the Consolidated-Gentry amalgamation either failed in its efforts to secure reciprocal favors or gave up trying, and during the seven years following the merger, Gentry's share of the dehydrated garlic market fell from 51 to 39 percent.

To the extent that reciprocity affects purchasing decisions only when price, quality, service, and the like are all equal, the main effect of the practice may be merely to redistribute sales among the members of an industry, with no adverse incremental effect on allocative efficiency.[54] Nevertheless, several potentially undesirable side effects may arise, especially when the *ceteris paribus* condition is violated or when power is asymmetrically held.

For one, reciprocity may have an indirect impact on the price structure. On the negative side, when firms get into the habit of basing purchasing decisions on reciprocity considerations, their purchasing agents may become less aggressive in searching out and bargaining for price reductions. Consequently, competitive price shading is inhibited. On the other hand, firms in an oligopolistic industry normally unconducive to price competition might combat a loss of sales to rivals with greater reciprocal leverage by cutting prices. If so, reciprocal purchasing could actually invigorate competition.[55] No satisfactory evidence on the relative strength of these opposing possibilities exists.

Second, when companies do buy at above-minimum prices or accept inferior quality in order to secure reciprocal favors, the functioning of the price mechanism as an allocative guide is thwarted, and society is almost surely the loser. Third, when price, quality, and other conditions of sale are identical but bargaining power is asymmetrically distributed, reciprocal buying enables large firms to increase their market shares at the expense of smaller specialists. It also aggravates barriers to entry for new firms lacking substantial purchase orders to trade for a share of potential customers' patronage. The long-run result is increased concentration.

Finally, the manipulation of purchasing decisions to influence sales may deaden price competition when firms are simultaneously competitors in some markets and trading partners in others. The experience of Consolidated Foods—this time on the short end of the purchasing leverage stick—illustrates the dangers. In 1965, Consolidated's seven subsidiary retail supermarkets in the Chicago area launched a price-cutting and advertising campaign to expand their market shares. This effort bit into the sales and profits of National Tea, a nationwide retailing chain with 237 stores in the Chicago area. In retaliation, National ceased purchasing the baked goods of Consolidated's Sara Lee manufacturing subsidiary for a week. Consolidated's supermarkets shortly thereafter abandoned their price reduction program, and later Consolidated announced a decision to leave the supermarketing field altogether because of the "adverse effect on its processing operations."[56]

How typical such cases are is unknown. In all probability, the situations in which reciprocal purchasing is innocuous outnumber those in which appreciable anticompetitive effects occur. Still the practice offers few advantages to compensate for its drawbacks, and so it should undoubtedly be discouraged by appropriate public policies.

Nonmaximization of profits

Giant conglomerate firms have also been accused, at first by Professor Edwards and more recently by others, of being inordinately slow in responding to changes in demand and in eliminating inefficient or wasteful operations.[57] They may, for example, continue certain lines of business long after profits disappear, subsidizing losses with funds earned in other, more profitable branches. They may become sluggish, failing to introduce the most efficient production methods or lay off unnecessary overhead personnel.

Obviously, such conduct conflicts with profit maximization. According to Edwards, conglomerates depart from the profit-maximizing norm partly because their accounting systems provide inadequate information to top management on actual conditions and potentialities in the operating divisions, and partly because operating level managers resist changes incompatible with pursuing their narrow goals (such as plant or divisional survival) even though such changes may benefit the corporation as a whole.

Although these conjectures are not implausible, they are open to several qualifications and objections. For one, the chiefs of most modern conglomerate enterprises are acutely aware of their information problem and devote extra at-

48. *U.S.* v. *General Dynamics Corp.*, 258 F. Supp. 36 (1966). See also Erwin A. Blackstone, "Monopsony Power, Reciprocal Buying, and Government Contracts: The General Dynamics Case," *Antitrust Bulletin* 17 (Summer 1972): 445–66.

49. Cf. Stocking and Mueller, "Business Reciprocity," pp. 80–85.

50. Neuhoff and Thompson, "Reciprocity," p. 107.

51. Stocking and Mueller, "Business Reciprocity," pp. 80–85.

52. Stocking and Mueller, "Business Reciprocity," p. 87.

53. *Federal Trade Commission* v. *Consolidated Foods Corporation*, 329 F. 2d 623 (1964), 380 U.S. 592 (1965). See also Blackstone, "Monopsony Power," p. 461, on Raytheon's purchase of carbon dioxide from Liquid Carbonic despite an 8 percent price premium.

54. Business managers sometimes argue that reciprocity is a sales-increasing device. But this is true only myopically. As long as price, quality, and the like remain constant, one firm's sales gains must be offset by some other firm's losses, and the net industrywide gain is zero.

55. This is the view of Joel Dean in "Economic Aspects of Reciprocity," p. 851.

56. See the testimony of Willard Mueller in U.S., Congress, Senate, Subcommittee on Antitrust and Monopoly hearings, *Economic Concentration*, Part 5, 89th Cong., 2nd sess., 1966, pp. 1874–75; and *Moody's Industrial Manual*, June 1966, p. 1930.

57. See Edwards's testimony in *Economic Concentration*, Part 1, pp. 43–44.

tention to developing information systems with built-in checks against concealment and distortion. Whether the effort is effective in overcoming the dilemmas of bureaucracy depends in part upon the quality of management. As the widespread incidence of inefficiencies and out-of-control subsidiaries following the conglomerate merger wave of the 1960s attests, success is plainly not assured.[58]

Second, prolonged subsidization of unprofitable lines is hardly possible without some degree of monopoly power in profitable lines. Thus, monopoly power must be linked with conglomerate size for nonmaximizing behavior to persist. When the two structural conditions coexist, it is conceivable that they interact to make profit-maximizing responses more sluggish than if either condition existed in isolation. In this sense conglomerateness could contribute at least marginally to deficient performance.

But finally, it can be argued that conglomerate enterprises allocate capital *more* efficiently than specialists, not less. As long as they avoid becoming locked into an excessively inflexible debt structure, they are able quickly to raise new capital for investment in promising opportunities. The managerial orientation that led to their conglomerate growth may make them peculiarly alert to such opportunities. And since neither the health of the corporation nor the status of top management is likely to be impaired when one or two operations out of many are abandoned, conglomerates may be in a particularly favorable position to reallocate capital out of declining fields and into existing or wholly new ventures with more attractive growth prospects.[59]

Statistical evidence

The behavioral hypotheses advanced in this chapter have diverse and conflicting implications for market performance. The alleged propensity of conglomerate enterprises to respect each others' spheres of influence and win sales through the exercise of reciprocity should enhance profits in particular lines of business, all else being equal. So should conglomerates' superior capital

reallocation opportunities. On the other hand, greater susceptibility to managerial control loss and sluggishness should impair profitability. The effect of any stronger tendency toward predatory pricing is ambiguous, since profits are sacrificed in the short run to achieve higher returns later.

As Chapter 4 brought out, studies of conglomerate firms' overall profitability reveal rising but not superior returns through the mid-1960s as relatively profitable companies were acquired. There followed a period of subaverage profits clearly attributable to loss of managerial control over the acquired entities. The longer run prognosis, when and if these teething problems disappear, remains uncertain.

Another analytic approach to the profitability question has been taken by Rhoades. His focus was the price-cost margins of relatively narrowly defined industries. Using 1963 Census statistics for 241 four-digit manufacturing industries and controlling for a variety of other structural characteristics, he found price-cost margins in industry i to be significantly higher, the more firms with the plurality of their sales in industry i were diversified into other four-digit industries.[60] However, applying similar tests to 117 more broadly defined (i.e., two- or three-digit) industries for 1967, he found an industry's price-cost margin to be *lower*, the more diversified were the firms calling that industry their home base.[61] Rhoades attributes the change in results to the difference in industry definition breadth, with diversification into less closely related activities (i.e., across the broader industry bounds staked out for 1967) leading to managerial inefficiencies. It is also possible, however, that his 1967 observations reflect the widespread postmerger indigestion just beginning to materialize in that period. Neither Rhoades's nor others' results for 1967 and later provide support for hypotheses linking *enhanced* profits to conglomerate power. Somewhat more support might be inferred from Rhoades's findings for 1963, before the conglomerate merger boom reached its peak and when, therefore, more stable diversification relationships predominated. Nevertheless, alternative causal links involving industry definition peculiarities or other factors with less behavioral significance cannot be ruled out completely.

A still different quantitative approach to assessing the impact of conglomeration was taken by Lawrence Goldberg.[62] He isolated a sample of 211 manufacturing industries, one or more of whose sizeable member firms had been acquired in conglomerate mergers between 1954 and 1963. If conglomerate size conferred predatory, reciprocal dealing, or similar advantages, he reasoned, this should be manifested in significant postmerger concentration increases. In fact, four- and eight-firm concentration ratios in the conglomerate merger-impacted industries did rise on the average over the period studied, but the observed average increase was neither statistically significant nor as large as the average concentration increase across all manufacturing industries. This led Goldberg to conclude that conglomerate mergers had a negligible effect on concentration. Interpretation of his results would be facilitated if there were comparable (and ideally, better controlled) evidence covering the period after 1963, when the conglomerate merger wave accelerated. But no updated analysis appears to be available.

Conclusion

To sum up, there are some theoretical grounds for apprehension concerning the economic consequences of conglomerate size. Yet the links between conglomerateness and deficient performance are tenuous and uncertain; and except for appreciable but possibly transient inefficiencies owing to managerial control loss, relatively few serious problems can be traced directly to giant size unaccompanied by more conventional market imperfections. For this reason, conglomerate size has tended to receive relatively low priority as a public policy issue. At the same time, there is also little evidence of significant public benefit from increases in conglomerateness—e.g., through mergers. We shall return to the problem of weighing benefits against costs when U.S. merger policy is examined in Chapter 20.

58. Cf. Chapter 4, p. 138 *supra*.

59. Cf. Chapter 2, p. 40 and Chapter 4, pp. 132–33 *supra*.

60. Stephen A. Rhoades, "The Effect of Diversification on Industry Profit Performance in 241 Manufacturing Industries," *Review of Economics and Statistics* 55 (May 1973): 146–55. For similar results from an analysis of 1963 profit returns on stockholders' equity for 374 large companies, see John R. Carter, "In Search of Synergy: A Structure-Performance Test," *Review of Economics and Statistics* 59 (August 1977): 279–89.

61. Rhoades, "A Further Evaluation of the Effect of Diversification on Industry Profit Performance," *Review of Economics and Statistics* 56 (November 1974): 557–59.

62. Lawrence G. Goldberg, "Conglomerate Mergers and Concentration Ratios," *Review of Economics and Statistics* 55 (August 1974): 303–309.

13 Market structure, administered prices, and macroeconomic stability

In this chapter we replace our microscopic lens with one sweeping a much wider field. Specifically, we ask whether the pricing practices of business enterprises with monopoly power have any noteworthy impact on such macroeconomic phenomena as the rate of inflation and the stability of aggregate employment.

An historical overview

As Figure 13.1 (on p. 350) reveals, there has been a dramatic change over time in the behavior of wholesale prices. The year 1940 stands out as a watershed. Before then, the index of wholesale prices for the United States fluctuated up and down: sometimes it trended or (in war years) shot upward, but at other times it sustained sizeable declines of considerable duration. Since 1940, however, decreases have at best been small and fleeting, and the preponderant pattern has been one of inflation interrupted by two interludes of stability (during the mid-1950s and the early 1960s).[1]

What explains the apparent disappearance of significant downward price level movements? One prime candidate is the Keynesian revolution, commencing with the publication of the *General Theory* in 1936 and continuing with the

adoption of numerous macroeconomic stabilization measures. Also relevant may be a shift toward the consumption of more highly processed goods whose prices are less volatile than those of raw materials. However, such demand mix changes have been gradual and can hardly account for the abrupt behavioral transition after 1940. A more momentous change was the spread of unionization during the 1930s—from 3.4 million union members in 1930, or 6.8 percent of the nonagricultural work force, to 8.7 million in 1940.[2] Much of the increase occurred in such key manufacturing industries as autos, steel, and rubber goods. The kinds of seller market structure and conduct variables emphasized in this book seem a less likely candidate, since seller market concentration in manufacturing has risen at a glacial pace during the 20th century and changes in antitrust law enforcement have if anything made monopolistic conduct riskier. Yet there is reason

---

1. See also Phillip Cagan, "Changes in the Recession Behavior of Wholesale Prices in the 1920's and Post-World War II," *Explorations in Economic Research* 2 (Winter 1975): 54–104.

2. U.S., Bureau of the Census, *Historical Statistics of the United States, Colonial Times to 1970* (Washington, D.C.: Government Printing Office, 1975), p. 178.

to believe that sellers' monopoly power may in fact be part of the explanation, perhaps interacting with unionization or the maturing and professionalization of business management. In this chapter we attempt to determine whether, or to what extent, the pricing practices of monopolistic enterprises have contributed to macroeconomic instability.

The administered price hypothesis

That monopoly power does matter macroeconomically was first argued forcefully by Gardiner C. Means during the Great Depression of the 1930s.[3] He observed that in some industries such as grain farming, dairying, and crude oil extraction, prices fell by 40 to 60 percent between 1929 and 1932 while in other industries they fell very little or even rose. Thus, as we learned in Chapter 6, the Big Three of the cigarette industry actually raised their prices by 7 percent in 1931 while cigarette demand was declining and leaf tobacco prices were falling to their lowest level since 1905. Likewise, the International Nickel Company, controlling at the time 90 percent of

world production, held its refined nickel price constant at 35 cents per pound while its output fell by 80 percent. Despite high fixed costs and low marginal costs similar to those of wheat farmers (whose prices fell 62 percent), the Aluminum Company of America reduced its aluminum ingot price by only 4 percent between 1929 and 1932. This and similar disparities in pricing behavior were attributed by Means to differences in methods of price formation, which he grouped into two broad categories: administered prices and market prices. Administered prices were defined as prices "set by administrative action and held constant for a period of time," whereas market prices were said to be "made in the market as the result of the interaction of buyers and sellers."[4] A prominent reason for the depression insensitivity of administered prices, Means later wrote, was "the relatively small number of concerns dominating particular markets."[5]

Why prices might remain rigid or rise in a depression can be illuminated in part by elementary theory. Under pure competition, one would expect the price to *fall* when an industry's demand function shifts to the left and the supply function is upward sloping, assuming that input costs do not rise, i.e., that the supply function does not shift upward. Under pure monopoly,

F 13.1 U.S. wholesale price movements: 1860–1978

Ratio scale

Source: U.S., Department of Commerce, Bureau of Economic Analysis, Long-Term Economic Growth: 1860–1970 (Washington, D.C.: Government Printing Office, June 1973), p. 52; and Economic Report of the President, January 1978, p. 319.

however, price stability or even an increase in price is compatible with the absence of cost increases under certain recession conditions. Specifically, if marginal costs are constant over a wide range of outputs and the elasticity of demand is unaltered by a leftward demand function shift, the short-run profit-maximizing price remains the same.[6] If marginal costs are constant and the elasticity of demand *falls* owing to recession, or if marginal costs are higher at low outputs than at high outputs (e.g., because of scale economies) and demand shifts leftward with no change in elasticity, the profit-maximizing reaction is in fact a price increase.

Under oligopoly, additional reasons for rigid or increasing prices in the face of declining demand can materialize. A kinked demand curve mentality may prevail, or price leaders may fear that downward adjustments will endanger industry discipline, or sellers may be pricing to maximize long-run profits and see no reason to infer that the optimal entry-impeding price level has changed, or (perhaps in conjunction with a limit pricing strategy) full-cost pricing rules may be in use. Several responses are possible in the simple full-cost pricing case, depending upon the type of rule used. If a standard volume rule like General Motors' is employed, with price set to yield a predetermined rate of return on existing investment at a 'normal' rate of capacity utilization, the price will be invariant, assuming as before that input prices do not change.[7] If a constant dollar margin is added to actual unit costs, the unit profit margin will be invariant, but at reduced outputs the price will be higher (since prorated unit overhead costs are higher). If a constant percentage margin is added to actual unit costs, including prorated overhead, both the dollar margin and the price will be higher at low outputs than at full employment levels. If the firm attempts to maintain a specified percentage return on its invested capital (fixed in the short run), it must seek higher dollar margins at low outputs than at high; and unless it is prevented from doing so by competition and/or highly elastic demand, it will attempt to raise its price during a recession.

Whatever the reason, it was widely believed during the 1930s that the rigid price responses of some industries contributed to the severity and duration of the Great Depression. We shall return to this issue later in the chapter.

Concern over administered prices faded as World War II commenced, substituting inflation of a conventional sort for depression. However, the administered price hypothesis reappeared in new garb during the 1950s when the prices in certain industries continued to rise and contribute to creeping inflation despite two moderately severe recessions.[8] Most striking was the behavior of the steel industry, which among other things effected across-the-board price increases in 1958 while operating at only 61 percent of rated capacity. Using input-output methods to estimate the secondary effects of steel price increases on the costs and prices of products incorporating steel as an input, Eckstein and Fromm found that the U.S. wholesale price index would have risen by 40 percent less over the 1947–58 period had steel prices risen no more rapidly than the wholesale prices of all other goods.[9] Thus, the post-World War II progeny of the administered price hypothesis maintained that the prices of certain sellers with monopoly power

3. *Industrial Prices and Their Relative Inflexibility*, report to the Secretary of Agriculture published as Senate Document no. 13 (January 1935). The body of the report is reproduced in Gardiner Means, *The Corporate Revolution in America* (New York: Crowell-Collier, 1962), pp. 77–96.

4. Means, *The Corporate Revolution*, p. 78.

5. National Resources Committee, *The Structure of the American Economy*, Part I (Washington, D.C.: Government Printing Office, 1939), p. 143.

6. Cf. Chapter 5, p. 158 and Chapter 6, p. 187 *supra*. See also R. F. Harrod, "Imperfect Competition and the Trade Cycle," *Review of Economic Statistics* 18 (February 1936): 84–88; and Richard B. Heflebower, "The Effect of Dynamic Forces on the Elasticity of Revenue Curves," *Quarterly Journal of Economics* 55 (August 1941): 652–66.

7. Cf. Chapter 6, pp. 185–87 *supra*.

8. See U.S., Congress, Senate, Committee on the Judiciary, Subcommittee on Antitrust and Monopoly hearings, *Administered Prices*, Part I, "Opening Phase-Economists' Views," 85th Cong., 1st sess., 1957; and Jesse W. Markham, "Administered Prices and the Recent Inflation," in the Commission on Money and Credit compendium, *Inflation, Growth, and Employment* (Englewood Cliffs, N.J.: Prentice-Hall, 1964), pp. 144–73.

tended to be inflexible downward in depressed times, but disconcertingly flexible upward when business conditions were normal or even slack. Apprehension continued into the mid-1970s, when it was feared that administered pricing might have something to do with the unprecedented stagflation, or inflation coupled with recession, experienced then. This variant of the administered price hypothesis will be our immediate concern.

The theory of administered price inflation

A useful introductory dichotomy distinguishes two broad types of inflation: demand-pull and cost-push. Each has many possible variants and (frequently conflicting) theoretical rationales; and real-world inflations often exhibit aspects of each type, interacting with and feeding upon one another, so that attempts to force actual cases into a single mold run the risk of oversimplification. With this caveat in mind, let us briefly survey the principal variants, devoting special attention to the cost-push types, with which so-called administered price inflation corresponds most closely.[10]

Until the 1950s, demand-pull theories dominated economic thought, and most recorded inflations of any moment conform more closely to the demand-pull model than to any other. To oversimplify, demand-pull inflation is experienced when too much money chases too few goods. In the classical view, this occurs when the stock of money is expanded more rapidly than real output, with no offsetting change in the velocity of monetary circulation, so that the price level P in the quantity theory equation $MV = PQ$ must rise. Or in Keynesian terms, the price level rises when aggregate demand exceeds aggregate supply at the full employment level. The standard illustration of how demand-pull inflation gets under way is the case in which, under full employment conditions, the government attempts to increase defense or social welfare expenditures using funds borrowed from the central banking system, without withdrawing equivalent purchasing power from the private sector, e.g., by credit restraints or taxation.

Cost-push inflation arises when, under conditions of less than full employment, some group tries to raise its real income by securing higher money income; and other groups successfully defend their prior positions in the real income distribution by winning comparable money income gains. For the cost-push inflationary effect to take hold, it is necessary in addition that national authorities pursue fiscal and monetary policies validating the contending groups' money income-raising efforts.

The most important cost-push subcase is wage-push inflation. Here labor is presumed to exercise the initiative, winning through collective bargaining wage increases in excess of productivity gains despite the persistence of some aggregate unemployment. If employers then pass along their higher labor costs by raising end product prices in an attempt to defend their profit share, inflation follows, among other things nullifying much of the workers' hoped-for real income gains. For labor to initiate this wage-push process, it must possess some monopoly power—usually through a strong union. However, monopoly power in the employers' product markets may facilitate the process in several ways.[11]

First, union bargaining power is apt to be stronger in oligopolistic industries. When sellers are few, it is easier to organize the whole industry, at least within the institutional environment that has existed in the United States since the 1930s. And when significant barriers to entry exist, as is often the case in industries that retain oligopolistic structures, it is more difficult for new nonunion producers to enter and undermine labor's united front. Second, wage increases are more readily passed along to consumers when the product market structure is monopolistic or oligopolistic, especially in the case of firm-by-firm (as compared to industrywide) collective bargaining. A purely competitive enterprise cannot expect a price increase following a wage increase unless most other members of its industry are in a symmetric position with respect to labor cost changes. The firm possessing monopoly power (and particularly one filling a price leadership role) is better able to exercise pricing initiatives, even if rivals do not reach exactly the same labor bargain, and recognizing this, it may be more willing to yield wage concessions. Third, sellers in monopolistic industries tend to earn higher profits than competitive producers; and these profits serve as a bargaining target out of which unions strive, alleging "ability to pay," to win above-average wage gains.

Thus, power possessed by labor unions interacts with power in sellers' markets to trigger an upward push on wages and costs. Once substantial wage increases have been won in key industries and the prices of industry products have risen, inflationary pressures spread as other unions attempt to emulate the initial example and as all employee groups try to compensate for increased costs of living by demanding still higher incomes.

The product market analogue of wage-push inflation is profit-push inflation, where producers raise prices in order to increase profit margins, even though there has been no increase in demand or costs. Without doubt the most spectacular example was OPEC's increase in crude oil prices from $2.90 per barrel in mid-1973 to $11.50 in early 1974, touching off a chain of further energy resource and product price changes with a marked inflationary impact throughout the world. A less dramatic case was the U.S. steel industry's attempt in the mid-1950s to alter its pricing formulas so as to raise after-tax profit returns on stockholders' equity from 8 to 12 percent at 80 percent capacity utilization—ostensibly to generate a higher cash flow for use in anticipated modernization programs.[12] Most economists believe that, with rare exceptions of the OPEC genre, pure profit-push stimuli are less likely to cause significant inflation than are wage-push pressures for three main reasons: profits constitute a much smaller share than wages in the national income; the political and social compulsion to emulate a peer group's gain is less potent among business firms than in organized labor; and the opportunity for making profit-push gains vanishes once price-cost margins have been raised to the profit-maximizing level.

It is also said that, by using full-cost rules of thumb, producers with monopoly power facilitate the spread of inflation even when they do not initiate it. Under the standard assumptions of short-run profit maximization by both monopolists

and (assuming rising supply functions) pure competitors, an increase in costs (e.g., following a new wage bargain) normally leads to a rise in price less than the unit cost increase. Part of the higher costs are borne by the seller and only part by buyers. But when full-cost rules are rigidly applied (and also when a limit pricing strategy is adopted and cost increases fall upon potential entrants to the same degree as existing firms), the added costs are transmitted in their entirety to customers.

A hybrid theory synthesizing elements of both the demand-pull and cost-push models has been advanced by Charles L. Schultze.[13] In his view, unionization makes money wages inflexible downward when demand is weak, but flexible upward when the derived demand for labor is strong. Concern over oligopolistic interdependence and full-cost pricing practices in product markets combine to make product prices relatively inflexible downward, but flexible upward in response to cost and perhaps also strong demand increases. Even when the economy as a whole is operating somewhat below the full employment level, demand is apt to be outracing

(9) Otto Eckstein and Gary Fromm, *Steel and the Postwar Inflation*, U.S., Congress, Joint Economic Committee, Study paper no. 2 in the Study of Employment, Growth, and Price Levels, 85th Cong., 2nd sess., 1958, pp. 1–38. For a criticism, see Martin Bronfenbrenner and F. D. Holzman, "Survey of Inflation Theory," *American Economic Review* 53 (September 1963): 636–37.

10. For more comprehensive surveys, see Bronfenbrenner and Holzman, pp. 593–653; and David E. W. Laidler and J. M. Parkin, "Inflation: A Survey," *Economic Journal* 85 (December 1975): 741–809.

11. For various views, see Harold M. Levinson, "Unionism, Concentration, and Wage Changes: Toward a Unified Theory," *Industrial and Labor Relations Review* 20 (January 1967): 198–205; Martin Segal, "Union Wage Impact and Market Structure," *Quarterly Journal of Economics* 78 (February 1964): 96–114; Albert Rees, "Union Wage Gains and Enterprise Monopoly," in *Essays on Industrial Relations Research* (Ann Arbor: University of Michigan-Wayne State University Institute of Labor and Industrial Relations, 1961), pp. 125–39; and Charles C. Holt, "Job Search, Phillips' Wage Relation, and Union Influence: Theory and Evidence," in Edmund S. Phelps, ed., *Microeconomic Foundations of Employment and Inflation Theory* (New York: Norton, 1970), pp. 53–124.

12. See John M. Blair, "Administered Prices: A Phenomenon in Search of a Theory," *American Economic Review* 49 (May 1959): 442–43. Within a decade, the effort to maintain higher profit margins proved unsuccessful as a consequence of the import competition the price increases stimulated.

Market structure, administered prices, and macroeconomic stability

capacity in some sectors while growing slowly in others. Prices will tend to rise in the high demand sectors. But if prices are generally more rigid downward than upward, these price increases will not be offset by equivalent decreases in the sectors experiencing slack demand. As a result, the average price level creeps upward. The more pronounced and frequent the intersectoral demand shifts are, the more rapidly this 'ratchet effect' inflationary process proceeds. Furthermore, the inflationary pressures originating in booming sectors tend after a lag to diffuse throughout the economy as labor unions in the declining sectors seek to match the wage increases offered to attract additional workers to the booming sectors, and as the price increases of overheated sectors raise the cost of living to all employment groups, spurring further demands for wage increases. The end result is a new and higher price-wage plateau from which additional ratchet effects exert their upward leverage.

In concluding this reader's guide to inflation theories, it is worthwhile repeating that unambiguous classification of actual cases is difficult. Elements of several models may coexist and interact. In particular, no type of cost-push inflation can be sustained unless validated by government policies maintaining aggregate demand at some more or less constant employment level. Both union pressures for higher wages and producer efforts to secure higher profits can be choked off by a recession or persistent underemployment equilibrium of sufficient severity. What this means is that persistent cost-push pressures can confront government fiscal policymakers with an agonizing choice between more inflation or more unemployment—the kind of choice that has become epitomized in the so-called Phillips curve.[14]

The evidence on administered price inflation

In the literature on administered prices, anecdotal evidence—e.g., on strange happenings in specific industries—has played a prominent role. But as one might expect of questions involving such eminently quantifiable phenomena as price changes, statistical analysis occupies center stage. There have been scores of quantitative studies—far too many to recount in detail here.[15] And in any event, an overview of the principal findings, disagreements, and methodological pitfalls is a better way of getting to the heart of the issues.

Methodological problems Despite the abundance of price data, testing the administered price hypothesis statistically has not been easy. There are several well-known limitations in the Bureau of Labor Statistics Wholesale Price Index (WPI) series (in 1979 renamed the Producer Price Index), the statistics used most frequently to measure U.S. producers' price levels and price changes. Product quality changes are reflected only imperfectly by the index.[16] The number of sellers surveyed per commodity is typically small, and the frequency of observed changes in a specific product's price index over a given time interval tends to vary directly with the number of surveyed firms. In addition, it is often argued that the *list* or *quoted* prices reported in the WPI are not always a faithful representation of reality because many sales entail unreported discounts, secret concessions, advertising allowances, the supply of free goods, and so on. Comparisons of pricing behavior over the business cycle under differing market structures may be biased, since oligopolists are more inclined than pure competitors to make *sub rosa* price concessions when demand is weak.

Insight into the severity of this last problem is provided by Kindahl and Stigler's ambitious survey of the prices actually paid between 1957 and 1966 by 179 government purchasing agencies and industrial companies for a considerable number of commodities.[17] The Stigler-Kindahl transaction price indices tended to show somewhat more downward flexibility than the most closely corresponding WPI indices during the 1957–58 and 1960–61 recessions, especially for commodities whose quoted WPI prices changed by less than 5 percent.[18] However, over a longer period such as 1958–63, changes in the WPI and

Stigler-Kindahl indices are fairly highly correlated with one another and also with price indices developed from *Census of Manufactures* data, leading Weiss to conclude that all three indices contained similar information and could be used interchangeably for longer run analyses without important bias.[19] As a practical matter, one often has no alternative but to employ WPI statistics because, despite their limitations, no better price data are available.

Another set of difficulties involves stating the administered price hypothesis in testable form. The original approach pursued by Gardiner Means—identifying administered price industries by the observed infrequency of price changes during the 1926–33 period—was circular, since the distinguishing characteristic was either identical or definitionally similar to the phenomenon under investigation. In later analyses of administered price inflation, Means sometimes identified administered price commodities on the basis of judgmental criteria difficult to replicate objectively.[20] Such choices could be influenced by observation of the pricing behavior under study, leading again to circularity. To circumvent this problem, most analyses, including some by Means, have linked the likelihood of perverse pricing behavior to seller market concentration and used industry concentration ratios as their discriminating variable.

Even then, however, problems intrude. As we have seen in Chapters 3 and 9, the concentration ratios available in Census publications are often quite imperfect measures of monopoly power. Scholars sensitive to this limitation have either adjusted their concentration ratios to reflect true structural conditions more meaningfully or discarded the data for industries whose raw concentration measures were perceived to be defective. On the other hand, economists skeptical of any link between concentration and price dynamics are seldom inclined to bother with such refinements, and so they typically throw into their computer the unadjusted data for all industries. One likely consequence of this less selective approach is a statistical bias toward failure to observe relationships that might actually exist. And more generally, with different samples and/or different approaches to measuring concentration,

divergent results can be expected. Indeed, the administered price literature abounds with conflicting conclusions derived from ostensibly similar data bases. It seems almost certain that the methodological differences identified here are responsible for a good deal of the disagreement.

Concentration and short-run price reactions

In view of all this, any attempt to summarize *the* state of knowledge is risky, for virtually every conclusion has been contradicted somewhere. Yet the job must be done, and so we proceed.

One quite general result is that if there is indeed a direct systematic relationship between seller concentration and short-run price changes, it is statistically very weak—that is, it is accompanied by much unexplained variance or noise. To "explain" with some index of concentration for a

13. Charles L. Schultze, *Recent Inflation in the United States*, U.S. Congress, Joint Economic Committee, Study paper No. 1 in the Study of Employment, Growth, and Price Levels, 86th Cong., 2nd sess., 1959, especially pp. 46–59 and 95. See also Richard W. Parks, "Inflation and Relative Price Variability," *Journal of Political Economy* 86 (February 1978): 79–95.

14. See A. W. Phillips, "The Relationship between Unemployment and the Rate of Change of Money Wage Rates in the United Kingdom, 1861–1957," *Economica* 25 (November 1958): 283–99; and for a broad-ranging critique, the papers in Phelps, ed., *Microeconomic Foundations of Employment and Inflation Theory*.

15. For surveys, see John M. Blair, *Economic Concentration* (New York: Harcourt Brace Jovanovich, 1972), Chapters 16 and 17; Ralph E. Beals, "Concentrated Industries, Administered Prices and Inflation: A Survey of Recent Research," U.S., Council on Wage and Price Stability, June 1975; and James A. Dalton and P. David Qualls, "Market Structure and Inflation," *Antitrust Bulletin* 24 (Spring 1979).

16. See Robert J. Gordon, *The Measurement of Durable Goods Prices* (New York: National Bureau of Economic Research, 1980), Chapter 2; and Frank Kottke, "Statistical Tests of the Administered Price Thesis," *Southern Economic Journal* 49 (April 1978): 873–82.

17. George J. Stigler and James K. Kindahl, *The Behavior of Industrial Prices* (New York: Columbia University Press, 1970).

18. Stigler and Kindahl, *The Behavior of Industrial Prices*, pp. 8–9, 60–70; and Cagan, "Changes in the Recession Behavior of Wholesale Prices," pp. 78–79.

19. Leonard W. Weiss, "Stigler, Kindahl, and Means on Administered Prices," *American Economic Review* 67 (September 1977): 610–19.

20. See Gardiner Means "The Administered Price Thesis Reconfirmed," *American Economic Review* 62 (June 1972): 292–306; and Beals, "Concentrated Industries, Administered Prices and Inflation," pp. 24–30.

broad and representative sample of industries 5 percent or more of the variance in price index changes within a single business cycle or phase thereof (i.e., to achieve an r^2 value of 0.05 or more) is extraordinary. If one is willing to draw inferences on the basis of such weak relationships, there are grounds for concluding that industrial wholesale price indices tended to fall more slowly in concentrated industries during the depression years 1929–33 and rise more rapidly during the sluggish 1953–59 period.[21] These were the intervals provoking the most insistent charges that administered prices posed special problems.

Price change-concentration relationships are weak in part because changes in input costs matter greatly but vary erratically. It is entirely possible that, in either a concentrated or atomistically structured industry, the cost of some important input could rise significantly even though business is slack. This can push prices up in seeming defiance of demand conditions. It is equally possible for unit costs to fall during a period of booming demand, pulling prices down in tandem. The steady decline between 1960 and 1966 of plate glass prices owing to the adoption of the more efficient float production technique is an example.[22]

The most widely accepted method of taking cost changes into account has been multiple regression analysis, with price changes as the dependent variable and estimated unit labor and materials cost changes, along with concentration and demand change indices, as independent or explanatory variables.[23] Such analyses support two main conclusions. For one, the prices of more concentrated industries appear to respond somewhat differently to unanticipated changes in business conditions, all else (such as costs) being equal. When demand is declining, concentrated industries' prices tend to fall less or rise more than those of more atomistically structured industries. In business upswings, on the other hand, concentrated industries' prices rise less rapidly. Thus, cyclical pricing responses tend to be more sluggish under oligopoly, and perhaps especially under middling oligopoly, than in more atomistic markets.[24] Second, there is reason to believe that, at least since 1960, this price change sluggishness may have come from a

tendency for concentrated industries to pass on, in the year they occurred, a smaller fraction of cost increases, and especially labor cost increases, than atomistically structured industries.[25] Although the evidence is not as well developed as it might be, this does not necessarily mean that such cost increases are not *eventually* reflected in higher prices; it only means that transmission lags may be longer in concentrated industries. The transmission lag phenomenon became increasingly important during the late 1960s and early 1970s as the general rate of inflation rose. Analyzing it is complicated by the government's use of price "jawboning" during the early 1960s and formal price controls from 1971 to 1974—both of which were targeted disproportionately toward larger corporations and more concentrated industries. It is also possible, though not tested quantitatively when this was written, that concentrated industries' greater cost insensitivity dwindled and perhaps even reversed as continuing inflation became built into producers' expectations during the late 1970s.

An alternate means of holding constant the effects of input cost changes is to examine the behavior over time of price-cost margins—i.e., industry sales less payroll and materials costs, divided by sales.[26] That price-cost margins fell less in the more concentrated manufacturing industries during the business collapse of 1929–33 seems firmly established.[27] Similarly, in a sample of 103 consistently defined manufacturing industries, price-cost margins fell by 17 percent on average from boom year 1947 to recession year 1954 when the four-firm concentration ratio was less than 40, but by only 2 percent with concentration ratios of 40 or more.[28] From recession years 1954 to 1958, price-cost margins rose by 2 percent on average in the less concentrated industries and 9 percent in the more concentrated industries. This suggests that the pricing responses of concentrated industries tended to stabilize margins against recession shocks. However, a behavioral change may have occurred since then. Analyzing annual data for 79 manufacturing industries from 1958 to 1970, Qualls found that price-cost margins tended to be significantly *more* variable over time, the more concentrated the industries were.[29] His interpretation is that the most highly concentrated industries had superior pricing coordination mechanisms and were better able than atomistic competitors and middling oligopolies to fine tune price changes to the unusually mild demand fluctuations occurring over that interval. An alternative explanation consistent with the price response studies cited earlier is that by reacting more slowly to the input cost inflation that gained increasing momentum during the late 1960s, highly concentrated industries permitted their price-cost margins to vary more widely than those of less concentrated industries, for whom generally strong demand facilitated rapid cost pass-on and hence margin maintenance.[30] Whether similar relationships will be found to have persisted for the sharp raw materials cost inflation of 1973–74, the unusually severe recession of 1975, and the open inflation of the late 1970s remains to be seen.

Long-run dynamics The weight of the available statistical evidence suggests that concentrated industries do exhibit somewhat different pricing propensities over time than their more atomistic counterparts. They reduce prices and (perhaps more importantly) price-cost margins by less in response to a demand slump and increase them by less in the boom phase. They may also pass on unit cost changes more slowly. These two phenomena may be related, for it is at least arguable that the relatively more rapid concentrated industry price increases during the recessions of 1953–54, 1957–58, and 1969–70 occurred because those industries had not yet fully passed along to their customers unit cost increases that had accumulated in previous booms. The crucial remaining question is, Does this differential timing have any broader macroeconomic significance—e.g., by affecting the overall pace at which inflation occurs?

One's first inclination is to say that it does not, for if concentrated industries advance their prices relatively more rapidly during some phases of the business cycle, they advance them less rapidly at others, and over the long run the effects should be expected to wash out. Support for this supposition comes from the fact that profit margins are at most a small fraction of price and

21. Cf. Jules Backman, "Economic Concentration and Price Inflexibility," *Review of Economics and Statistics* 40 (November 1958): 404; H. J. de Podwin and R. T. Selten, "Business Pricing Policies and Inflation," *Journal of Political Economy* 71 (April 1963): 116–27; and Leonard W. Weiss, "Business Pricing Policies and Inflation Reconsidered," *Journal of Political Economy* 74 (April 1966): 177–78. See also P. David Qualls, "Price Stability in Concentrated Industries," *Southern Economic Journal* 24 (October 1975): 294–98, who found much less year-to-year variability in wholesale price index changes over the 1957–70 period in highly concentrated industries.

22. Stigler and Kindahl, *The Behavior of Industrial Prices*, p. 166. Note that the flat glass industry is unusually highly concentrated, with a four-firm concentration ratio of 94 in 1963.

23. The first analysis of this type was Weiss, "Business Pricing Policies and Inflation Reconsidered." For a survey of subsequent works, see Beals, "Concentrated Industries, Administered Prices and Inflation," pp. 30–44. For a critique bringing to light possible econometric biases, see Steven Garber and Steven Klepper, "'Administered Pricing' or Competition Coupled with Errors of Measurement?" (Discussion paper no. 430, State University of New York at Buffalo Economic Research Group, March 1978).

24. See P. David Qualls, "Market Structure and Price Behavior in U.S. Manufacturing, 1967–1972," *Quarterly Review of Economics and Business* 18 (Winter 1978): 35–58, who argues that the pricing response relationship may be nonlinear. Qualls predicts the *least* price flexibility in middling oligopolies, where the coordination problem is said to be most acute. Greater flexibility is predicted both for atomistically structured and tightly oligopolistic industries—the latter because of well-developed price change coordination institutions. Weak supporting evidence is found for the 1967–69 expansion and 1969–70 recession.

25. See especially Frank C. Ripley and Lydia Segal, "Price Determination in 395 Manufacturing Industries," *Review of Economics and Statistics* 55 (August 1973): 263–71; Phillip Cagan, "Inflation and Market Structure, 1967–1973," *Explorations in Economic Research* 2 (Spring 1975): 203–16; and Ronald P. Wilder, C. G. Williams, and Davinder Singh, "The Price Equation: A Cross-Sectional Approach," *American Economic Review* 67 (September 1977): 732–40.

26. See also Chapter 9, pp. 271–72 *supra*.

27. See especially Alfred C. Neal, *Industrial Concentration and Price Inflexibility* (Washington, D.C.: American Council on Public Affairs, 1942), pp. 90–140; and Howard N. Ross, "The Determination of Industrial Price Flexibility," *Industrial Organization Review* 3, No. 3 (1975): 115–29.

28. For details, see the first edition of *Industrial Market Structure and Economic Performance*, pp. 311–13.

29. P. David Qualls, "Market Structure and the Cyclical Flexibility of Price-Cost Margins," *Journal of Business* 52 (April 1979): 305–25.

30. Compare Ripley and Segal, "Price Determination," p. 268; with Qualls, "Cyclical Wage Flexibility, Inflation, and Industrial Structure," in the *Journal of Industrial Economics* 28 (1980). Qualls found 1958–70 cyclical wage patterns inconsistent with the hypothesis that concentrated industries underadjusted in booms and overadjusted in slumps.

from the absence of any evidence that the profit returns of concentrated industries, though higher on the average, have either risen or fallen secularly in relation to the returns of atomistically structured industries. If profit relationships have remained pretty much the same, prices must have changed over the long run only enough to track cost changes.

Statistical studies of price movements over the longer span of several business cycles confirm that concentrated industries have not increased their prices abnormally rapidly. If anything, the opposite appears to be true, at least in the United States. In a bivariate regression analysis covering 224 manufacturing industries, J. Fred Weston and S. H. Lustgarten found that wholesale prices rose significantly *less* rapidly on average between 1954 and 1970, the higher the (unadjusted) four-firm concentration ratio was.[31] Or when materials and wage costs and output change variables were also taken into account through multiple regression, the effect of higher concentration on price changes was negative but statistically insignificant. Further analysis led them to conclude that unit costs rose less rapidly over time in the more concentrated industries, resulting in a slower rate of price advance. This occurred despite the fact that wages rose *more* rapidly in the more concentrated industries because output per worker also increased more rapidly, permitting the concentrated industries to pay relatively high wages without raising their prices commensurately.[32]

To the extent that these findings are correct, they suggest a partial answer to the puzzle with which this chapter began. It might seem both natural and just that industries experiencing rapid productivity gains reward their workers with correspondingly high rates of wage increase. But whether such behavior is in fact natural is debatable. The long trend of falling wholesale price levels from 1865 to 1895 observable in Figure 13.1 was almost certainly the result of an interaction between rising productivity and vigorous product market competition—perhaps the most vigorous in American economic history.[33] Technological progress in that era appears to have benefitted the working population primarily by reducing product prices and hence,

to the extent that money wages remained constant, raising real wages.[34] In the second half of the 20th century, the benefits from progress are still spread to some extent in that manner; but apparently there has been a striking quantitative change, with a much higher share of productivity gains going in the form of higher wages to the workers directly involved, and a lower share to the mass of consumers through lower product prices. The reasons for this change are unclear. They could plausibly include the great wave of product market concentration that took place in the 1890s, the surge of unionization in the 1930s and 1940s, the more expansive monetary policies of the 20th century, or some interaction of those developments plus others. Whatever the reasons, a shift from product price-oriented to wage-oriented diffusion of productivity gains must have had a profound impact on overall price level trends.

Concentration, unionization, and wage-price dynamics As noted already, Weston and Lustgarten reported that wages rose more rapidly on average between 1954 and 1970 in the more concentrated manufacturing industries. This is not unprecedented historically. The rate of wage increase appears rather generally to be higher in concentrated industries during times of slack economic activity and perhaps also, but less clearly, in normal times. With booming demand and open or suppressed inflation, however, the relationship reverses. Thus, diverse studies reveal no statistical relationship between manufacturing industry wage increase rates and seller concentration during the generally prosperous 1920s, strong positive correlations during the depression from 1929 to 1937, a strong negative correlation in the booming 1940–47 World War II period, a weak positive correlation from 1947 to 1952, a strong positive correlation in the increasingly slack economy of 1952 to 1958, a continuing positive correlation in the gradually improving economy of 1958 to 1965, and a negative relationship during the 1966–69 Vietnam War boom.[35]

Exactly why this pattern emerged must be explained a step at a time. There are several reasons why wages might rise more rapidly in more highly concentrated industries, at least at times: possibly higher productivity growth (stressed by Weston and Lustgarten); greater capital intensity or its more rapid growth; a deeper pool of profits to be tapped (especially, compared to atomistically structured industries, in periods of slack or normal demand); and (also in the business cycle's slack phase) greater ability to pass on cost increases in the form of price increases. Also relevant may be a higher degree of unionization. William Bowen found, for example, a +0.46 correlation between the percentage of workers employed in establishments operating under collective bargaining agreements and weighted average four-firm concentration ratios for 19 two-digit manufacturing industry groups.[36]

To see whether the positive correlation between wage changes and concentration actually followed from the higher degree of unionization in concentrated industries, nonlinear regression equations of the form

$$(13.1) \quad \Delta W = a + b_1 C4 + b_2 U + b_3 C4 \times U$$

were estimated for three extended time intervals, where ΔW is the percentage change in wages, C4 the four-firm concentration ratio (in percentage scaling), and U the estimated percentage of the work force unionized in an industry sector. Inserting into the resulting equations a value of 30 percent for *low unionization*, 90 percent for *high unionization*, 20 percent for *low seller concentration*, and 75 percent for *high seller concentration*, the computed average wage change rates are shown in Table 13.1. In all three periods, concentration makes a substantial positive difference when the degree of unionization is low and a much smaller, more erratic difference when unionization is high. Unionization appears to be conducive to rapid wage increases when concentration is low, but has a puzzling negative effect in highly concentrated industry groups.

The continuing more rapid rise of wages in the more concentrated industries since 1960 is also surprising. Studies emphasizing late 1950s and early 1960s conditions revealed that average wage *levels* tended even then to be appreciably higher in the more concentrated industries.[37] Presumably (although, in view of possible aggregation effects, not surely), the differential widened in the ensuing decade. This growing divergence could lead to disequilibrium in labor markets.

The relevant dynamics are both subtle and imperfectly understood. All else being equal, a rising wage premium in concentrated industries should imply a net flow of workers to those industries. But unless the concentrated industries are expanding unusually rapidly—and there is no reason to believe they were—that flow could not be actualized. Some sort of nonprice job rationing (e.g., by queue) must take place.[38] But all else is not equal. There is evidence that their higher wages permitted the more highly concentrated and unionized industries to attract workers

31. J. Fred Weston and Steven H. Lustgarten, "Concentration and Wage-Price Changes," in Harvey J. Goldschmid et al., eds., *Industrial Concentration: The New Learning* (Boston: Little, Brown, 1974), p. 322. See also Lustgarten, "Administered Inflation: A Reappraisal," *Economic Inquiry* 13 (June 1975): 191–206.

32. Weston and Lustgarten, "Concentration and Wage-Price Changes," pp. 309, 322–23. More will be said about the concentration-productivity link in Chapter 15. It should be noted, however, that grave data quality problems are encountered in attempting to measure productivity growth for such a broad sample of industries. Also, the authors' indiscriminate use of concentration ratios without adjustment leaves much to be desired.

33. Cf. Chapter 3, pp. 46–47 *supra*.

34. Actually, money wages in industry varied cyclically, rising from 1865 to 1869, falling gradually from then to 1880, rising in the next decade, and maintaining a roughly constant average level in the last decade of the century. See U.S., Bureau of the Census, *Historical Statistics of the United States, Colonial Times to 1957* (Washington, D.C.: Government Printing Office, 1960), p. 90. The average continuously compounded change between 1865 and 1890 was +0.5 percent per annum. In contrast, the wholesale price index graphed in Figure 13.1 fell at a rate of 3.4 percent per annum.

35. See Joseph W. Garbarino, "A Theory of Interindustry Wage Structure Variation," *Quarterly Journal of Economics* 64 (May 1950): 282–305; David Schwartzman, "Monopoly and Wages," *Canadian Journal of Economics and Political Science* 26 (August 1960): 428–38; H. Gregg Lewis, *Unionism and Relative Wages in the United States* (Chicago: University of Chicago Press, 1963), pp. 159–60; Harold M. Levinson, *Postwar Movement of Prices and Wages in Manufacturing*, U.S., Congress, Joint Economic Committee, Study paper no. 21 in the Study of Employment, Growth, and Price Levels, 86th Cong., 2nd sess., 1960, pp. 3–13; the first edition of *Industrial Market Structure and Economic Performance*, p. 299 n. 49; and Weston and Lustgarten, "Concentration and Wage-Price Changes," pp. 309, 322.

36. William G. Bowen, *Wage Behavior in the Postwar Period* (Princeton: Princeton University Industrial Relations Section, 1960), p. 70.

37. See for example Leonard W. Weiss, "Concentration and Labor Earnings," *American Economic Review* 56 (March 1966): 96–117.

Market structure, administered prices, and macroeconomic stability **359**

of higher average quality—where "quality" here encompasses variables such as education, experience, and skill type with a plausible link to productivity as well as variables like family size, geographic location, race, and sex whose relevance to productivity is less clear.[39] When such quality variables are incorporated in multiple regressions with annual earnings or the wage level as dependent variable, the explanatory power of the concentration variable falls—and in earlier studies, dwindled to insignificance.[40] Thus, concentrated industries pay more, but they get more in the bargain. And even though a rising wage differential may precipitate no net quantitative flow of workers from low-wage (i.e., atomistic and/or nonunionized) to high-wage industries, it may encourage a *qualitative* movement as the high-wage industries pick and choose the best qualified workers from their queue.

The key question persists, Is this state of affairs dynamically stable? It might not be if low-wage industries find themselves increasingly deprived of high-quality workers and struggle to reverse the trend whenever market conditions permit— e.g., when demand is booming, prices can be raised, and the value of the marginal product of both high- and low-quality workers rises. Such a reversal evidently did occur during World War II and the boom that followed it and during the Vietnam war boom of the late 1960s. However, those reversals can also be rationalized on strictly quantitative grounds: With rising prices and profits, atomistic and nonunionized industries sought to expand and raised their wages to attract workers from higher wage industries, which reacted more slowly because of long-run-oriented pricing policies, sticky wage bargains, and an accumulated queue of workers.

For a growing *qualitative* differential not to be a source of dynamic instability, the fates would have to load the technological dice so that the more concentrated industries gravitate toward production and marketing methods in which the marginal productivity of better qualified workers tends to be significantly higher than in atomistic industries. This is conceivable, but it is also possible that the higher quality labor hiring bias of concentrated industries stems from those industries' choice of capital-intensive, skill-demanding production techniques *because* such choices were the optimal reaction to high wages conferred as a result of greater ability to pay and/or tougher union bargaining. In other words, the question is whether the more concentrated industries' high-quality labor bias is exogenous or endogenous.[41] On this, our ignorance is vast. If the hypothesis of exogeneity is valid, quality-linked wage differentials need pose no particular dynamic stability problems. The differentials might even continue to increase over time, leading the United States toward a "dual" labor market structure widely considered plausible only for underdeveloped nations.[42] If on the other hand the endogeneity hypothesis holds or if the economy continues to alternate between periods of

T 13.1 Percentage changes in wages by degree of unionization and concentration

Time period	Low unionization		High unionization	
	Seller concentration		Seller concentration	
	Low	High	Low	High
1923–40	+20.1	+70.4	+22.7	+31.4
1948–58	+38.2	+72.7	+69.1	+67.9
1960–74	+79.6	+127.4	+94.6	+103.1

Sources: The 1923–40 and 1948–58 data are from J. W. Garbarino, "A Theory of Interindustry Wage Structure Variation," Quarterly Journal of Economics (May 1950): 282–305; and H. M. Levinson, "Postwar Movement of Prices and Wages in Manufacturing," U.S., Congress, Joint Economic Committee, Study paper no. 21 in the Study of Employment, Growth, and Price Levels, 86th Cong., 2nd sess., 1960, pp. 3–13. The regression equations were reported in the first edition of *Industrial Market Structure and Economic Performance*, p. 300. The 1960–74 estimates are from Steven Rice and A. H. Studenmund, "Relative Wage Changes, Unionism, and Concentration: An Update," (manuscript, Harvard University and Occidental College, November 1977).

slack and boom, with low-wage industries striving to raise their quantitative employment shares during boom phases through wage increases that will be sticky downward, the attempt by concentrated and/or highly unionized industries to maintain substantial and growing wage differentials imparts an overall ratchet-effect inflationary bias.

As suggested earlier, ratchet-effect inflation might also result from workers trying to emulate the wage settlements reached in certain key pattern-setting industries. Historically, these pattern-setters have included such large, highly unionized, more or less highly concentrated industries as automobiles, steel, and chemicals. There is statistical evidence that key manufacturing industry wage bargains are in fact emulated by other industries, but recent research suggests that the pattern does not spread quickly and inexorably to more atomistic, less unionized sectors.[43] In this sense, the hypothesis of a pervasive ratchet effect receives only qualified support beyond what has emerged already in our analysis of wage differential dynamics. It is also probable that the locus of key bargains has become more complex in recent years as truckers, government employees, medical care technicians, and other well-paid groups have joined the auto and steel workers as pattern-setters. For these newer groups, the bases of employers' ability to pay are rather different from those observed in manufacturing industries.

Interpretation Does aberrant price and wage-setting behavior in concentrated industries cause inflation? In a superficial sense, the answer depends upon one's point of view. There is now widespread agreement that there are differences in the dynamics of price and wage setting between the 'typical' concentrated industry and its atomistic counterpart and, in particular, that concentrated industries tend to adjust more sluggishly to unanticipated demand and cost changes. What varies is the interpretation drawn. One school of thought emphasizes that although concentrated industries may lag in their adjustments, they do catch up, so that in the long run it makes no difference. And in the short run, their lags may actually reduce the sting of inflationary shocks. Another school argues that even though

concentrated industries may appear to be lagging chronologically, they lead cost-push inflationary developments in a different sense. That is, with more generous profit margins in normal and depressed times, they have the wherewithal to grant wage increases that would otherwise not occur. This widens their already positive wage level differentials, setting the stage for atomistic industries to try and catch up when strong demand provides the necessary support.

(38) See Michael Wachter, "Cyclical Variation in the Interindustry Wage Structure," *American Economic Review* 60 (March 1970): 75–84; and Stephen A. Ross and Michael Wachter, "Wage Determination, Inflation, and the Industrial Structure," *American Economic Review* 63 (September 1973): 675–92.

39. Studies showing little or no significant residual concentration impact include Weiss, "Concentration and Labor Earnings," pp. 105–16; C. T. Haworth and D. W. Rasmussen, "Human Capital and Inter-Industry Wages in Manufacturing," *Review of Economics and Statistics* 53 (November 1971): 376–80; Orley Ashenfelter and George E. Johnson, "Unionism, Relative Wages, and Labor Quality in U.S. Manufacturing," *International Economic Review* 13 (October 1972): 488–508; and C. T. Haworth and Carol J. Reuther, "Industrial Concentration and Interindustry Wage Determination," *Review of Economics and Statistics* 60 (February 1978): 85–95. Studies revealing a significant residual concentration effect—in each case, using more recent and better quality data—are James A. Dalton and E. J. Ford, Jr., "Concentration and Labor Earnings in Manufacturing and Utilities," *Industrial and Labor Relations Review* 31 (October 1977): 45–60; idem, "Concentration and Professional Earnings in Manufacturing," *Industrial and Labor Relations Review* 31 (April 1978): 379–84; and Frederic Jenny, "Wage Rates, Concentration and Unionization in French Manufacturing Industries," *Journal of Industrial Economics* 26 (June 1978): 315–27.

40. An exception is Jenny, "Wage Rates," who found a positive concentration effect for low-unionization but not high-unionization industries in France even after an impressive battery of labor quality variables was taken into account.

41. Compare Robert D. Brogan and Edward W. Erickson, "Capital-Skill Complementarity and Labor Earnings," *Southern Economic Journal* 42 (July 1975): 83–88; and Lawrence W. Kahn, "Union Impact: A Reduced Form Approach," *Review of Economics and Statistics* 59 (November 1977): 503–507.

42. See Edward Mason, "Has the United States a Dual Economy?," in Robert T. Masson and P. D. Qualls, eds., *Essays on Industrial Organization in Honor of Joe S. Bain* (Cambridge, Mass.: Ballinger, 1976), pp. 19–38. Compare in the same volume F. M. Scherer, "Industrial Structure, Scale Economies, and Worker Alienation," especially pp. 113–16. For a different view, see Gerry Oster, "A Factor Analytic Test of the Dual Economy," *Review of Economics and Statistics* 61 (December 1978): 33–39.

43. See especially Otto Eckstein and Thomas A. Wilson, "The Determination of Money Wages in American Industry," *Quarterly Journal of Economics* 76 (August 1962): 379–414; and Y. P. Mehra, "Spillovers in Wage Determination in U.S. Manufacturing Industries," *Review of Economics and Statistics* 58 (August 1976): 300–12.

Which view of the world is more nearly correct is at bottom a factual question: specifically, whether the slack-period wage increases by industries enjoying sellers' market power do no more than restore a dynamically stable wage equilibrium, or whether they upset it and make subsequent reactions by other producers inevitable in the absence of chronically slack business conditions. Unfortunately, the evidence on this key point is far from adequate.[44] The author's best judgment is that the wage and price behavior of concentrated industries does sometimes create nontrivial dynamic instabilities with a net inflationary bias, but this view is held with less than overwhelming confidence.

It must be recognized too that the relationships between market structure and potentially destabilizing wage-price behavior are weak statistically. Therefore, unless the whole economy can be pulled along through actions by a relatively few large industries like steel (which raised its average hourly wage cost from 1.36 times the all-manufacturing average in 1967 to 1.60 times it in 1975 despite excess capacity and a severe import threat), the inflationary pressure generated by administered wage and price behavior is apt to be modest compared to orthodox demand-pull influences. And to repeat, cost-push inflation cannot be sustained without demand side validation from the fiscal and monetary authorities. The most that can be said with confidence is that the administered price inflation hypothesis cannot be dismissed out-of-hand. The exercise of monopoly power by producers and labor unions can indeed, at least under certain conditions, set off complex dynamic reactions complicating the task of simultaneously maintaining acceptably high aggregate employment and reasonable price stability.

Inflexible prices and business recession

Although there was a time not long ago when most economists believed governments could mitigate and control business fluctuations through the astute use of fiscal and monetary tools, the maladies of recession and unemployment have proved unexpectedly difficult to cure. It is therefore desirable for firms and industries to pursue pricing policies that do not precipitate recessions or aggravate them if they get under way. What pricing policy is best in this regard? And, if a recession does begin, is it better for prices to fall flexibly or remain relatively rigid?[45]

Monopolistic pricing may be a *cause* of recession if it reinforces tendencies toward the stagnation of demand—e.g., by transferring too much income into the hands of individuals or groups with high marginal propensities to save. This possibility was of serious concern to economists during the 1930s, but under normal circumstances it can be counteracted through appropriate tax measures. A major exception was the rapid increase in crude oil prices by the OPEC cartel during the 1970s. Because Saudi Arabia and some of the other more sparsely populated OPEC nations were unable or unwilling to spend their enormously expanded revenues on consumption or real investment, OPEC's annual balance of payments current account surplus rose from $6 billion in 1973 to $67 billion in 1974, precipitating a worldwide recession from which full recovery occurred only slowly.

It is sometimes said that monopolies, by producing less output and hiring fewer workers than competitive industries facing identical demand schedules, cause unemployment. But this view is largely fallacious. The restriction of output in monopolistic industries frees resources for use in other sectors. As we saw in Chapter 2, it is entirely possible to have full employment equilibrium in a world shot through with monopolies. That individual monopolies restrict employment by no means implies that aggregate unemployment results.[46] The critical consideration is how aggregate *demand* is affected.

Should a recession begin for reasons essentially unrelated to the exercise of monopoly power, and should the price in a monopolistic industry remain rigid despite the leftward shift of demand, output in that industry will be cut back more than it would have been had the price been reduced. But it does not necessarily follow that output in general will be lower than it otherwise would have been. The lower output of the monopolistic industry may be offset by higher output in other industries. Whether the monopolist's rigid price reaction contributes *incrementally* to aggregate unemployment depends again upon how aggregate demand is affected. To probe for possible aggregate demand ramifications, we must examine with some care how price inflexibility influences consumption and investment spending.

Price rigidity and aggregate consumption

The link between prices and aggregate consumption stressed most heavily in the literature of macroeconomic theory is the so-called Pigou effect, also known as the real balance effect or the net claims effect.[47] If, after the onset of a recession, prices fall, the real purchasing power of consumers' cash balances and net fixed claims to future cash payments (e.g., the surplus of fixed-interest securities held less outstanding debts) increases. Consumers may therefore consider themselves to be wealthier in a real sense. As a result they may be inclined to consume more and save less, raising aggregate demand. The failure of monopolistic or oligopolistic prices to fall thwarts operation of the Pigou effect and thus chokes off one potential stimulant to economic recovery. In this respect, price rigidity is detrimental to macroeconomic stability. Nevertheless, what evidence we have on the matter suggests that consumption decisions are not much affected by changes in the real value of cash balances and fixed claims within the range of potential price level variation associated with all but the most severe recessions.[48] It is generally believed, therefore, that the Pigou effect consequences of oligopolistic and monopolistic price rigidity are not very serious.

The failure of prices to fall in industries with monopoly power also has an incremental effect on the distribution of income. As we have observed earlier, during the Great Depression of the early 1930s and also in the milder but still significant recessions of the 1950s, profit margins fell by less on average in concentrated than in unconcentrated industries. To the extent that the higher profits and cash flow associated with price rigidity are paid out as dividends to stockholders or as salaries and bonuses to top management,

aggregate consumption will be lower than it would be under flexible competitive pricing, since stockholders and top managers as a group are wealthier and have lower marginal propensities to consume than the average consumer.[49] If corporate earnings are retained rather than paid out, corporate saving rises at the expense of private consumption. This latter adverse effect could be offset if the additional saving is matched by a concomitant increase in corporate investment,

44. The most pertinent statistical analysis finds support for a pervasive ratchet effect in wage bargains, but the data used are too weak to bear the weight of the elaborate model tested. See Douglas F. Greer, "Market Power and Wage Inflation: A Further Analysis," *Southern Economic Journal* 41 (January 1975): 466–79; extending Daniel S. Hamermesh, "Market Power and Wage Inflation," *Southern Economic Journal* 39 (October 1972): 204–12. See also Marvin H. Kosters, "Wage Behavior and Inflation in the 1970s," *Contemporary Economic Problems* series (Washington, D.C.: American Enterprise Institute, 1978).

45. For various views, see Oscar Lange, *Price Flexibility and Employment* (Bloomington, Ind.: Principia, 1944); the review of Lange's book by Milton Friedman, "Lange on Price Flexibility and Employment: A Methodological Criticism," *American Economic Review* 36 (September 1946): 613–31; Kenneth Boulding, "In Defense of Monopoly," *Quarterly Journal of Economics* 59 (August 1945): 524–42, with comments and a reply in the August 1946 issue, pp. 612–21; Alfred Neal, *Industrial Concentration and Price Inflexibility*, especially pp. 141–62; J. A. Schumpeter, *Capitalism, Socialism, and Democracy* (New York: Harper, 1942), especially pp. 90–91; E. A. G. Robinson, *Monopoly* (London: Nisbet, 1941), Chapter 7; Edward S. Mason, *Economic Concentration and the Monopoly Problem* (Cambridge, Mass.: Harvard University Press, 1957), pp. 159–66; Fritz Machlup, "Monopoly and the Problem of Economic Stability," in E. H. Chamberlin, ed., *Monopoly and Competition and Their Regulation* (London: Macmillan, 1954), pp. 385–97; and Emile Despres, Milton Friedman, Albert G. Hart, Paul A. Samuelson, and D. H. Wallace, "The Problem of Economic Instability," *American Economic Review* 40 (September 1950), especially pp. 534–38.

46. Monopolistic distortions may also affect wage rates in such a way as to induce workers to choose more leisure and less work. Cf. Chapter 2, p. 26 *supra*. But this is not unemployment in the customary sense, since the labor supply restriction is voluntary, in response to distorted price signals.

47. See Arthur C. Pigou, "The Classical Stationary State," *Economic Journal* 53 (December 1943): 343–51; and Don Patinkin, *Money, Interest, and Prices*, 2nd ed., (New York: Harper & Row, 1965).

48. See Patinkin, *Money, Interest, and Prices*, pp. 651–64; his "Price Flexibility and Full Employment," *American Economic Review* 38 (September 1948): 543–64; and Thomas Mayer, "The Empirical Significance of the Real Balance Effect," *Quarterly Journal of Economics* 73 (May 1959): 275–91.

49. Cf. Chapter 4, p. 107 *supra*.

but it seems at least as probable that when rigid prices prevent the redistribution of income away from corporations and toward consumers during a recession, hoarding of cash will increase and aggregate demand will be diminished. Thus, the redistributive effects of monopolistic and oligopolistic price rigidity appear to be distinctly unfavorable.

Although it would be misleading to say that policy decisions at the time were guided by anything like a coherent body of theory, the passage of the National Industrial Recovery Act in 1933 was clearly influenced by a belief that recovery from the Great Depression might be hastened through a redistribution of income in favor of wage earners as consumers.[50] Price increases were expected to follow from the Act's provisions legalizing competition-restricting agreements among producers, but it was hoped that wage increases would be implemented even more rapidly. One reason for the subsequent disenchantment with NIRA was the fact that prices actually rose in advance of wages, partly because of speculation and partly because the price-fixing actions of cartelized sellers were more successful in the short run than the wage-raising efforts of labor organizations encouraged under NIRA and concurrent legislation. Thus, the desired redistribution did not ensue. Whether this outcome contributed to the unprecedented persistence of depressed conditions during the 1930s has never been determined conclusively.

A third link among market structure, pricing behavior, and aggregate consumption involves the dynamics of output and employment reallocation. If prices fall less in concentrated or cartelized industries, output must be reallocated so that the relative shares of output supplied by the concentrated industries fall, other things (such as income elasticities of demand) being equal. If this reallocation took place instantaneously and without friction, or if the recession encroached gradually enough to permit smooth readjustment, the reallocation process per se should cause no further downward spiraling of aggregate demand. But the adjustment process is not frictionless. Labor in particular does not flow easily from one occupation into another, especially at the onset of a recession. Usually workers are at least temporarily unemployed before finding new jobs. Some unemployment is an unavoidable direct effect of the recession. But in addition, the amount of frictional unemployment is likely to be larger, the more reallocation there must be owing to divergent price behavior in concentrated as opposed to atomistic industries. If incomes are not fully replaced by unemployment compensation, the marginally displaced workers will reduce their consumption, and this decline in consumption implies an incremental fall in aggregate demand, intensifying the recession. In this sense layoffs by price-maintaining, output-restricting industries aggravate the recession problem.

Nevertheless, a possible qualification must be raised. If rigid-price industries reduce employment in proportion to output, they will tend to lay off relatively more workers during recessions than flexible-price industries, ceteris paribus. But the proportionality assumption may be invalid. Statistical studies show that output per worker and output per man-hour decline during economic downturns and rise in upturns because employers do not adjust their work forces in strict proportion to output changes over short periods of one or two years.[51] During a slump they hold on to workers whose services are not immediately needed. They do this partly to avoid the costs of rehiring and retraining when business conditions improve in the future and perhaps also on humanitarian grounds or to preserve work force morale. Some of a recession's shock is therefore absorbed through underemployment or disguised unemployment, rather than direct unemployment, reducing the drag on aggregate consumption. Only when demand recovers are the workers fully utilized again; and because the expansion of output is accomplished in part by working long-term employees harder, new hirings rise less than proportionately and output per worker increases.

This suggests the question, Is it possible that concentrated rigid-price industries accept more disguised unemployment during a recession than do atomistic, flexible-price industries? A behavioral difference could materialize because firms with monopoly power are less likely to experience a liquidity crisis compelling urgent cost reduction measures. They can afford to maintain more organizational slack; or they may discount the future at a lower rate, placing more weight on avoiding future rehiring and retraining costs.

Market structure and employment variability

To test these conflicting hypotheses, the author carried out a statistical analysis of the cyclical variability of employment in 70 manufacturing industries for which consistent annual data spanning the 1954–72 interval were available. Sample industries accounted for 29 percent of total 1963 value added in manufacturing. To measure the variability of employment, the logarithms of annual employment values were regressed on a simple time trend; and the standard error after the time trend was removed—i.e., the standard error of estimate—was computed. This was done for two main employment variables: production worker man-hours and in-plant staff—that is, the difference between total in-plant employment and the number of production workers. Let these employment variability indices be denoted VMH and VS respectively.

Two indices of seller market concentration were also compiled. One, $C4$, was the simple average of the four-firm concentration ratios for the five Census years 1954, 1958, 1963, 1967, and 1972. The other, $C4A$, incorporated adjustments to the average ratios for 36 industries to compensate for excessively broad or narrow Census product market definitions, the existence of meaningful regional or local markets, and especially high import volumes. The simple correlation between the unadjusted and adjusted ratios was +0.86; the mean values of the ratios were 0.53 and 0.57, respectively.

Other explanatory variables introduced to take into account potentially relevant technological and demand conditions included the following:

Dur A class variable distinguishing durable from nondurable goods

$Cons$ A class variable distinguishing consumer goods from all other goods

K/VA An index of capital intensity, given by the ratio of December 1962 plant investment at book value to 1963 value added

S An index of industry size, given by the simple average of the logarithms of value added for five Census years

Table 13.2 presents the simple correlations between the two indices of employment variability and the two market concentration indices. All of the correlations are positive, contrary to the concentration - organizational slack hypothesis, but consistent with the concentration - rigid price - employment instability hypothesis. However, only the $VS - C4$ correlation is statistically significant at the 95 percent confidence level. This is paradoxical, since one might have expected the organizational slack hypothesis to apply more strongly for in-plant staff than for production workers. Another surprising result is that the correlations for the adjusted index $C4A$, which presumably is a better measure of structural monopoly, are much weaker than those with the naive index $C4$.

When the effects of all relevant independent variables are taken into account through multiple regression, and using the theoretically preferable adjusted concentration index, the estimated relationship for the trend-adjusted variability of

50. For diverse contemporary analyses, see L. S. Lyon, P. T. Homan et al., *The National Recovery Administration* (Washington, D.C.: Brookings Institution, 1935); J. M. Clark, "Economics and the National Recovery Administration," *American Economic Review* 24 (March 1934): 11–25; Karl Pribam, "Controlled Competition and the Organization of American Industry," *Quarterly Journal of Economics* 49 (May 1935): 371–93; and Leonard Kuvin, "Effects of N.R.A. on the Physical Volume of Production," *Journal of the American Statistical Association* 31 (March 1936): 58–60. For a balanced retrospective survey, see Ellis W. Hawley, *The New Deal and the Problem of Monopoly: A Study in Economic Ambivalence* (Princeton: Princeton University Press, 1966).

51. See Edwin Kuh, "Cyclical and Secular Labor Productivity in United States Manufacturing," *Review of Economics and Statistics* 47 (February 1965): 1–12; Stanley H. Masters, "The Behavior of Output per Man During Recessions," *Southern Economic Journal* 33 (March 1967): 383–94; and Thor Hultgren and M. R. Pech, *Cost, Prices, and Profits: Their Cyclical Relations* (New York: Columbia University Press, 1965).

production worker man-hours is:

(13.2) $VMH = .059 + .0055\ C4A + .0223\ Dur$
$\qquad\qquad\ \ (.0095)\qquad\ (.0049)$

$\qquad\qquad - .0048\ Cons - .0063\ K/VA$
$\qquad\qquad\ \ \ (.0054)\qquad\quad (.0038)$

$\qquad\qquad - .0096\ S;\ R^2 = .363,\ N = 70$
$\qquad\qquad\ \ \ (.0047)$

(Standard errors of the regression coefficients are given in parentheses.) For the variability of in-plant staff employment, the regression is:

(13.3) $VS = .079 + .0083\ C4A + .0057\ Dur$
$\qquad\qquad\ \ \ (.0080)\qquad\ (.0042)$

$\qquad\qquad + .0044\ Cons + .0030\ K/VA$
$\qquad\qquad\ \ \ \ (.0045)\qquad\quad (.0032)$

$\qquad\qquad - .0204\ S;\ R^2 = .319,\ N = 70$
$\qquad\qquad\ \ \ (.0040)$

In both regressions concentration continues to have a positive impact on employment variability, but neither coefficient comes anywhere near statistical significance. As in the simple correlations, the positive effect of a naive concentration index in multiple regressions (not shown) is stronger, but in no case was the concentration coefficient statistically significant at the 95 percent confidence level in the two-tail test appropriate for ambiguous theoretical predictions. By far the most powerful explanatory variable in production worker man-hours regression (13.2) is the durable goods class variable, reflecting the greater inherent instability of demand for durable goods. Somewhat surprisingly, in-plant staff employment is not significantly more variable over time in durable goods industries. The principal (and only statistically significant) explanatory variable in equation (13.3) is industry size, which may reflect working of the law of large

numbers as in-plant staff hiring and layoff decisions average out over larger volumes of production activity.

Although the *average* variability of employment is evidently not systematically associated with concentration, *unsystematic* deviations across industries in the staff employment variability index *VS* may be. An *F*-ratio test revealed that the industry observations on *VS* had a significantly higher variance—that is, they varied more widely between high and low values—in industries with *C4A* values of 55 or more than in industries with *C4A* values of 39 or less.[52] This could mean that producers in the more highly concentrated industries enjoy more discretion, which they *sometimes* exercise to cushion sudden changes in staff employment. But this discretion is exercised less uniformly than in atomistic industries, where competitive pressures leave only a slim margin for increasing organizational slack. For production workers, the results of similar tests were more complex. Unsystematic variability of the *VMH* index was somewhat greater in nondurable goods industries with four-firm concentration ratios of 55 or more, although the level of statistical significance was marginal.[53] In durable goods, an opposite but clearly insignificant relationship emerged.

Three other studies of employment variability yielded somewhat different but reconcilable conclusions. D. S. Smith investigated monthly employment variability in 73 manufacturing industries between 1958 and 1966, and Harold Demsetz analyzed annual variation in 375 industries for the 1958–70 period.[54] Both found statistically significant positive associations between employment variability and concentration after removing time trends and taking into account other variables. Their use of unadjusted concentration ratios, their focus on shorter time spans, differing sample coverage, and (in Smith's study) the use of more volatile monthly data may explain the greater strength of their relationships as compared to those reported above. Douglas Greer and Stephen Rhoades discovered preponderantly negative but uniformly insignificant partial correlations between concentration and the degree to which employment in 51 three-digit manufacturing industries varied with physical output

---

T 13.2 Concentration and employment variability correlations

	C4	C4A
VMH	+0.185	+0.033
VS	+0.367	+0.182

between 1954 and 1971.[55] The sign difference no doubt reflects the fact that their data explicitly took into account output variations, focusing in effect only on organizational slack effects, whereas the employment variability data of Smith, Demsetz, and the author embodied both slack and output influences (the output effects in turn presumably stemming *inter alia* from differential pricing behavior).

Summing up, the available evidence reveals that concentration does not have a *stabilizing* impact on manufacturing industry employment. If anything, the tendency is for employment to be somewhat less stable over time in more concentrated industries, although the observed relationships are quite weak statistically. The reason for this tendency—to the extent it exists—is not completely understood: i.e., more rigid price responses as compared to greater inherent demand instability. Whatever the cause, it seems fair to say that concentration and the pricing behavior associated with it do not make much of a difference. Here, as with the adverse Pigou and income redistribution effects associated with price inflexibility, the drag imposed upon the recovery of aggregate consumption from macroeconomic shocks appears at worst to be modest.

The direct effects of price rigidity on investment Most business cycle theories emphasize the role of capital investment as both a triggering element in downturns and (when it recovers) a stimulant to the upturn. In this section we address the question: Does the pricing behavior of monopolistic and oligopolistic industries cushion the fall of aggregate investment when a recession begins and hasten its resurgence as the recession matures, or does it exert a net destabilizing influence? The possibility that differences in market structure affect investment in other ways will be examined in a later section.

It is useful to assume that investment decisions of both individual firms and the economy as a whole are determined by the interaction of two functions: the marginal efficiency of investment schedule (*MEI* in Figure 13.2) and the marginal cost of capital schedule (*MCC* in Figure 13.2). Both may be affected by pricing responses to an economic downturn.

Consider first the capital cost side of the picture.[56] The typical business enterprise consciously or unconsciously estimates its *MCC* schedule by arraying all potential sources of investable funds in the order of their cost, from least to most costly. Many firms apparently view the cost of funds generated by depreciation and (after some customary level of dividends has been paid out) retained earnings to be either zero or (with somewhat better theoretical justification) to be the return attainable by using the funds to buy risk-free securities. These considerations dictate the location of the segment *AB* in Figure 13.2. If additional funds are to be invested, the firm turns first to relatively low-cost borrowing (segment *BD*), whose cost rises with the amount borrowed because of increasing risk, and then to relatively high-cost new equity issues (segment *D-MCC*).

For monopolistic enterprises able to hold their profits up during a recession, the quantity of low-cost internally generated funds is higher than it would be under flexible competitive pricing, *ceteris paribus*, and so the *AB* segment of the *MCC* function is extended to the right. The cost of external funds and the opportunity cost of investing internally generated funds in the securities market may also be affected by pricing responses, but in a more complicated way. If rigid-price firms are able to pay out higher dividends than they would in a flexible-price regime, in-

52. $F = [(1.699/39)/(0.302/18)] = 2.60$, with the 5 percent significance point being 2.07.

53. $F = [(0.583/21)/(0.151/11)] = 2.02$, with a 10 percent significance point of 2.11.

54. D. Stanton Smith, "Concentration and Employment Fluctuations," *Western Economic Journal* 9 (September 1971): 267–77; and Harold Demsetz, "Where Is the New Industrial State?," *Economic Inquiry* 12 (March 1974): 1–12.

55. Douglas F. Greer and Stephen A. Rhoades, "A Test of the Reserve Labour Hypothesis," *Economic Journal* 87 (June 1977): 290–99. More precisely, the dependent variable in their cross-industry analysis was an elasticity of employment with respect to changes in output, computed from individual industry time series.

56. The approach taken here follows James S. Duesenberry, *Business Cycles and Economic Growth* (New York: McGraw-Hill, 1958), Chapter 5.

come is redistributed in favor of wealthy stockholders. Because stockholders have a high marginal propensity to save, they will channel a substantial fraction of these funds back into the securities market, driving interest rates down and pushing the MCC schedules of all companies downward and to the right. Also, the prices of stock issued by monopolistic firms able to maintain strong price discipline will continue to be relatively high, permitting the flotation of new issues at relatively low future earnings costs. This too implies a downward shift in the MCC schedule relative to the flexible price situation, although only in the D-MCC region, which producers may be reluctant to enter during a recession. On the other hand, the failure of product prices to fall makes it necessary for consumers to hold larger cash balances than they would need if price levels declined, thus preventing a release of funds from transactions motive holdings into security markets. This implies a general leftward shift in the MCC schedule. How these countervailing influences affecting the upper reaches of the MCC function net out is uncertain. Perhaps most important, however, is the relative increase in internally generated liquidity associated with

rigid prices, suggesting that on balance the effect of price rigidity is to place the MCC function farther to the right (as shown by the dotted function MCC* in Figure 13.2) than it would be with competitive flexible pricing.

The position of the MEI schedule is also affected by pricing behavior. If the prices of capital goods fail to fall owing to the exercise of market power by suppliers, the MEI schedule for all firms will lie farther to the left than it would under flexible capital goods pricing, since some projects that would have passed a profitability test at bargain machinery and construction price levels will not do so. However, most economists believe that this effect would not be very strong, or that it would be swamped by other effects to be considered in a moment. More important, firms maintaining prices and profit margins in a recession are likely to do so only by operating well below capacity. Under these circumstances, they will hardly be enthusiastic about adding still more capacity or even replacing existing semi-obsolescent but idle equipment. This too implies a leftward displacement of the MEI schedule, and probably also substantial inelasticity of the curves with respect to changes in expected yields. From the considerations examined thus far, the impact of price rigidity on the marginal efficiency schedule appears to be unambiguously adverse.

With the MCC schedule farther to the right and the MEI schedule farther to the left under rigid than under flexible recession pricing, what is the net outcome? Unfortunately, we cannot be sure; the answer depends upon the relative magnitudes of the displacements and on the elasticities of the curves. It does not seem too unreasonable to suppose the result will be a 'damned if we do, damned if we don't' dilemma. Investment is choked off by excess capacity in industries whose high prices generate ample investable funds while it is discouraged by poor profits in industries that maintain output by letting prices drop.

Conditions in European steel markets during the early 1960s illustrate this kind of dilemma.[57] The industry found itself in the throes of a recession as the growth of capacity caught up with and then overtook demand. In the well-disciplined United Kingdom branch, prices held firm,

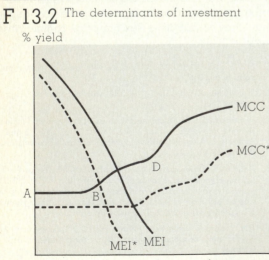

F 13.2 The determinants of investment

% yield

Amount of investment

Solid lines denote the situation with flexible prices; dotted lines, the rigid price case.

368

but producers found themselves with considerable excess capacity. On the Continent, prices fell by 25 to 30 percent while the rate of capacity utilization remained fairly high (mainly because lower prices permitted the successful penetration of overseas markets), but investment was discouraged by the increased intensity of competition and (in 1963) the erosion of profits. The net result was a 93 percent decline in investment between 1960 and 1963 in *both* the British and Continental industries.

Price rigidity and expectations Expectations about the future are another important component of the aggregate investment and consumption pictures. The behavior of prices in the early stages of a recession can affect expectations, and through them both investment and consumption decisions, in a number of ways. Consider first the investment side. If capital goods prices slide continuously downhill when a recession begins, the inclination of producers to defer expansion and replacement expenditures because of excess capacity and/or poor profits will be reinforced by the expectation that if they wait until the price decline has run its full course, they can gain the advantage of lower investment costs and higher returns. This implies a sharp leftward shift in the marginal efficiency of investment function. The resulting decline in investment intensifies the downward spiral through its multiplier effects. Similarly, if raw material and intermediate goods prices are steadily falling, users will draw down their inventories, delaying replacement until the last minute in order to buy at lower prices. Output and employment in the intermediate goods industries will drop sharply, with further adverse multiplier effects.

These unfavorable expectational effects are much less likely to arise when prices are held rigid, e.g., through the exercise of monopoly power. They can also be avoided when price reductions inspired by the recession are implemented in such a way as to convey a once-and-for-all impression, so buyers come to believe that prices will fall no farther and that the time is ripe for taking advantage of bargains. Creating this impression is exactly what strong price leaders seek when they announce across-the-board list price reductions in a time of deteriorating *sub rosa* prices as a means of reestablishing industry discipline around a new rallying point.[58] If buyers are convinced the tactic will succeed, the adverse expectational effect of price erosion is again mitigated.

Rigid prices may be favorable from an expectational standpoint in still another way. A severe recession accompanied by sharply falling prices is apt to precipitate a wave of bankruptcies, with an extremely unsettling effect on business confidence. Loss of confidence in turn means pronounced leftward shifts in marginal efficiency of investment schedules. Nevertheless, to keep the rate of business failure at normal levels during a recession, it might be necessary to accept such widespread cartelization that serious side effects would appear on other dimensions of aggregate demand (e.g., as under the National Industrial Recovery Act). It is not clear that the cure is preferable to the disease.

Similar relationships between pricing reactions and expectations exist in the consumer durables sector, although perhaps in attenuated form, since consumers have less information on current economic conditions and trends. If the prices of durable goods such as automobiles, new housing, cameras, and so forth are sliding downward conspicuously, consumers may choose to defer planned purchases to a more propitious moment. Price rigidity can undermine this basis for delay.

All in all, the impact of price rigidity on entrepreneurial and consumer expectations during the opening phases of a recession appears to be almost unambiguously favorable. On this score at least, the exercise of monopoly power rates high marks.

Other links between market structure and investment stability To the extent that monop-

---

57. Dennis Swann and D. L. McLachlan, "Steel Pricing in a Recession," *Scottish Journal of Political Economy* 12 (February 1965): 95–98.

58. Cf. Chapter 6, p. 184 *supra*.

oly power and the ability to maintain prices in recession stabilize a company's own cash flow and expectations, the effect on the firm's investment should be directly observable. Before we discuss the evidence, however, certain further possible links between market structure and cyclical variations in investment must be considered.

One is suggested by G. B. Richardson's provocative reexamination of the theory of pure competition.[59] Richardson's thesis can be stated succinctly as follows. Suppose a purely competitive industry is in long-run equilibrium when the industry demand curve shifts unexpectedly to the right, say, by 10 percent. In the short run, prices will rise to clear the market, and each producer will be earning positive economic profits. These profits signal the need for additional investment. But how much investment? And by whom? If each producer is operating one plant of minimum optimal scale, and if each attempts to take advantage of the expansion opportunity by building a second plant, the addition to industry capacity will far exceed what is called for by the demand shift. Indeed, if every producer responds to the opportunity, the expansion of capacity will be precisely what is needed to restore a new long-run competitive equilibrium only by the sheerest accident. The result of a demand increase may therefore be a massive investment wave that sows the seeds of later recession. Or alternatively (as Richardson believes will be more likely), if producers recognize this dilemma, they may hold back in a kind of Alphonse and Gaston reaction sustaining too little investment to attain long-run equilibrium. As Richardson argues, a purely and perfectly competitive market structure has no built-in mechanism conveying the information needed to nominate some firms to invest and others to refrain from investing:

[A] general profit potential, which is known to all, and equally exploitable by all, is, for this reason, available to no one in particular. . . . [T]he conditions supposed to ensure allocative efficiency are in fact such as would prevent purposive economic activity of any kind, for they are incompatible with the availability to entrepreneurs of the necessary market information.[60]

From these premises, Richardson goes on to argue that market imperfections are essential if the economy is to respond to demand changes with the correct amount of investment. These can include information asymmetries, so that some producers recognize profit-making opportunities sooner than others; or capital market imperfections may prevent some companies from obtaining investable funds; or when products are differentiated, firms may restrict their investments because they know it will be difficult to win away customers loyal to competitors. Other means of proportioning investment correctly to demand, according to Richardson, are such "contrived restraints" as price-fixing agreements and market-sharing cartels.

Here, however, his analysis is questionable. Collusive arrangements seem as apt to destabilize investment as to stabilize it. If prices are set above the entry-deterring level, as is likely when the colluding sellers have little or no cost advantage over outsiders, instability of investment will follow.[61] In his study of German cartels, Voigt found that price-fixing schemes caused a "peculiar rhythm" of investment with a significant bearing on the growth rate of the overall economy.[62] When the cartels were working successfully, prices were raised to high levels, outsiders began investing heavily to take advantage of lucrative entry opportunities, and insiders invested in efficiency-increasing techniques to prepare for a forthcoming competitive struggle. Then, as the cartel collapsed because members were no longer willing to bear an increasingly onerous burden of output restriction to compensate for the growing supply of outsiders, prices plummeted and investment declined drastically.

Richardson suggests also that market-sharing agreements are conducive to rational investment planning. But the *sine qua non* of such arrangements is a meeting of minds on how the market will be divided. In Germany during the 1920s and 1930s, shares were allocated on the basis of production capacity. Cartel members therefore raced to increase their sales quotas by building more capacity. In the Rhineland-Westphalian coal cartel, for example, production capacity exceeded *peak* demand levels by 25 percent because of the competition in investment.[63] Even when market shares are not linked formally to capacity, a cartel member's bargaining power depends upon its fighting reserves—the amount of output it can dump on the market, depressing the price, if others hold out for unacceptably high quotas. Recognizing this, companies participating in market-sharing cartels will be tempted to invest in more capacity than they need to serve foreseeable demands at anticipated collusive price levels.

A similar bias toward unstable or excessive capital investment may exist when oligopolists collude only tacitly on price. If price competition is shunned, the distribution of orders among sellers will depend largely upon such nonprice considerations as the reliability of service and personal buyer-seller ties. The firm with reserve capacity to serve customers in times of peak demand stands a good chance of retaining their loyalty permanently, and this motivates each enterprise to try raising its market share through competition in production capacity.[64] Also, fear of losing market share to more aggressive rivals spurs oligopolists to invest heavily in additional capacity when demand is growing rapidly—frequently at a collective rate exceeding demand growth, so that new investment must be cut back abruptly when excess capacity begins to disrupt pricing discipline. This is what happened in the plastics and aluminum industries during the late 1950s and in synthetic fibers and nitrogenous fertilizers during the 1960s.[65] The tendency toward overshooting may be particularly strong when investments must be made in large indivisible chunks in order to exploit economies of scale.

We find then that the investment nomination mechanism may be defective, signalling too much or too little investment in response to a demand increase, in collusive and/or oligopolistic markets as well as under pure competition. And as we have seen earlier, it is unclear on a priori grounds whether the ability to exercise monopoly power mitigates investment cutbacks in a demand downturn. The empirical question therefore arises, What market structures are most conducive to the cyclical stability of investment?

Statistical evidence on investment instability

To progress toward an answer, the author collected annual data on capital investment outlays between 1954 and 1972 for 70 U.S. manufacturing industries.[66] Both the sample and the methodology are essentially the same as for the analysis of intertemporal employment variability reported earlier. To measure the degree of investment instability, we use the standard error of estimate obtained after regressing the logarithms of annual new capital investment outlays for each industry on a simple time trend variable. Let us call this index of investment instability VI. The higher VI is, the more unstable observed investment outlays are relative to a smooth exponential growth trend.[67]

59. G. B. Richardson, *Information and Investment* (Oxford: Oxford University Press, 1960). An earlier version of the argument appeared under the title "Equilibrium, Expectations and Information," *Economic Journal* 69 (June 1959): 223–37. For an analysis anticipating Richardson's in some respects, see Tibor Scitovsky, *Welfare and Competition* (Homewood, Ill.: Irwin, 1951), pp. 233–41, 365–67. See also David McCord Wright, "Some Notes on Ideal Output," *Quarterly Journal of Economics* 76 (May 1962), especially pp. 176–78.

60. Richardson, *Information and Investment*, pp. 14, 124.

61. On the relationship between entry barriers, pricing choices, and investment instability, see Joe S. Bain, *Barriers to New Competition* (Cambridge, Mass.: Harvard University Press, 1956), pp. 36–41, 189–90.

62. Fritz Voigt, "German Experience with Cartels and Their Control During Pre-War and Post-War Periods," in John P. Miller, ed., *Competition, Cartels, and Their Regulation* (Amsterdam: North-Holland, 1962), pp. 171–72, 184.

63. See Kurt Bloch, "On German Cartels," *Journal of Business* 5 (July 1932): 213–22.

64. For a seminal discussion, see Duesenberry, *Business Cycles and Economic Growth*, pp. 113–33. See also Donald H. Wallace, *Market Control in the Aluminum Industry* (Cambridge, Mass.: Harvard University Press, 1937), pp. 336–43.

65. M. J. Peck, *Competition in the Aluminum Industry, 1945–1958* (Cambridge, Mass.: Harvard University Press, 1961), pp. 146–47, 162–64, 208; "Too Many Fibers Spoil the Miracle," *Business Week*, 29 October 1966, pp. 165–70; "Oil Companies Bail Out of Fertilizer Surplus," *Business Week*, 13 December 1969, pp. 35–36; and "A Glut of Chemicals in Europe," *Business Week*, 17 March 1973, pp. 78–82.

66. The analysis here is an updating of F. M. Scherer, "Market Structure and the Stability of Investment," *American Economic Review* 59 (May 1969): 72–79; and "Investment Variability, Seller Concentration, and Plant Scale Economies," *Journal of Industrial Economics* 22 (December 1973): 157–60. Increasing the time span covered from 10 to 19 years and dropping five industries from the sample because of data continuity problems caused no material change in the results.

67. As one might expect, investment is much more unstable over time than employment. The average value of VI was 0.155, compared to 0.039 for both production worker man-hours VMH and in-plant staff S.

As in the employment analysis, two concentration variables C4 and C4A—the former unadjusted and the latter adjusted for regional and product market definition problems—were used. Other independent variables incorporated without change from the employment analysis are the durable goods class variable *Dur*, the consumer goods class variable *Cons*, the capital intensity variable *K/VA*, and the industry size variable (in logarithmic scaling) *S*. To take into account the indivisibility effect associated with economies of scale, we introduce still another variable *Top* 50. This is defined as the share of total 1963 industry employment contributed by the average plant among those plants which, when arrayed in descending size order, account for the top 50 percent of an industry's plant employment size distribution. The higher the value of *Top* 50, the larger a minimum optimal scale plant tends to be in proportion to total industry employment.[68]

The simple correlations between the index of investment variability *VI* and the explanatory variables are as follows:

Variable	Correlation coefficient
C4	+0.475
C4A	+0.321
Dur	+0.287
Cons	−0.225
K/VA	+0.342
Top 50	+0.318
S	−0.412

All but the consumer goods correlations are significantly different from zero at the 95 percent confidence level. The relatively strong positive correlations between *VI* and the concentration indices (especially *C4*) offer preliminary support for the hypothesis that concentration destabilizes investment. As one would expect, investment was more unstable in cyclically sensitive durable goods industries, capital-intensive industries, and industries in which an MOS plant tends to involve a relatively large lump of total employment. Investment was more stable in the larger industries, probably because such industries have more highly diversified product lines and face steeper short-run capital goods supply func-

tions in boom times, and possibly also because the larger industries tend to be less concentrated.

To isolate the net effect of concentration among these several influences, multiple regression is used. With adjusted concentration ratios, the estimated regression equation is:

$$(13.4) \quad VI = .244 + \underset{(.029)}{.054\,C4A} + \underset{(.014)}{.041\,Dur}$$
$$- \underset{(.015)}{.009\,Cons} + \underset{(.010)}{.040\,K/VA}$$
$$- \underset{(.068)}{.010\,Top\,50} - \underset{(.014)}{.069\,S;}$$
$$R^2 = .485, N = 70$$

Nearly half the variance in *VI* is explained, with the strongest explanatory variables being industry size, capital intensity, and product durability. The MOS plant lumpiness variable *Top* 50 has an unexpected negative sign but is far from statistically significant. The concentration coefficient is positive, implying a destabilizing role, but with a *t*-ratio of 1.84, it is statistically significant in a two-tail test only at the 90 percent confidence level.[69] With the unadjusted concentration variable used in place of *C4A*, the regression is:

$$(13.5) \quad VI = .221 + \underset{(.028)}{.080\,C4} + \underset{(.013)}{.037\,Dur}$$
$$+ \underset{(.014)}{.007\,Cons} + \underset{(.010)}{.038\,K/VA}$$
$$- \underset{(.068)}{.052\,Top\,50} - \underset{(.014)}{.062\,S;}$$
$$R^2 = .518, N = 70$$

Here the effect of concentration, with a *t*-ratio of 2.82, is significant at the 99 percent confidence level. When all other variables are held at their mean values with equation (13.5), increasing the unadjusted four-firm concentration ratio from 0.20 to 0.80—that is, moving from an essentially atomistic structure to a tight oligopoly—implies a 43 percent average increase in the investment variability index. Or when equation (13.4) is used, increasing adjusted concentration over a similar range implies a 28 percent increase in investment variability.

Why the unadjusted concentration ratios are more closely associated with investment instability warrants further consideration. A plausible rationalization is that the unadjusted ratio better takes into account the dispersion of investment decision-making centers, and with greater dispersion, surges in spending by one firm tend to be offset (i.e., under the law of large numbers) more fully by other firms' reductions. To illustrate, the most extreme concentration ratio adjustment made—from 0.12 to 0.87—was for the soft drink bottling industry. This adjustment reflects the strong localization of markets because of high transportation costs along with franchise provisions restricting bottlers from selling outside their assigned territories.[70] A Coca-Cola bottler in Richmond, Virginia, is apt to have considerable monopoly power in its home territory, as does its counterpart in Minneapolis or Tucson. But as long as those "independent" bottlers do not increase and decrease their investment outlays on common cue from Coca-Cola headquarters in Atlanta—and there is no reason to believe they do—the wide dispersion of decision making across hundreds of bottlers can lead to a considerable averaging out of individual firm investment fluctuations. The unadjusted concentration ratios discriminate more accurately between such industries and those in which national investment aggregates are indeed controlled by a very few hands (or heads)

A related question of critical importance is whether market structure affects the sensitivity of producers' reactions to cyclical demand changes. Cyclical instability could result if oligopolists sharply increase their capital outlays in response to demand spurts, cutting back with equal vigor during slumps. An alternative hypothesis is that concentrated industry outlays, though more unstable owing to the paucity of decision-making centers, are scattered more or less randomly across the business cycle. To shed light on these alternatives, Durbin-Watson autocorrelation coefficients were computed from the time trend adjustment regressions of 53 industries on which complete investment data were available for the 1954–63 subperiod. The Durbin-Watson coefficient can vary from a value of zero, when each trend deviation is positively related to the next

period's deviation, revealing a regular cyclical pattern, to 4.0, when each deviation is negatively related to the next year's deviation, implying annual oscillations. The computed Durbin-Watson coefficients were negatively correlated with concentration, suggesting that the degree of cyclical variability rises with concentration. However, the correlation coefficient of -0.13 is not significantly different from zero by standard statistical tests. Similarly negative but statistically insignificant partial correlations appeared in multiple regression analyses taking the Durbin-Watson coefficient as the dependent variable and concentration as one of several potentially relevant independent variables. This indicates that investment was at worst only slightly more volatile cyclically in the more concentrated industries. The observed instability associated with concentration appears instead to have been preponderantly unsystematic or random, with less averaging-out across firms under the law of large numbers because concentrated industries have relatively few independent decision-making centers.[71]

Differing reactions to demand changes might also affect the level of excess capacity carried by diversely structured industries at various stages

68. Cf. Chapter 9, p. 275 *supra*.

69. When *VMH* is introduced as an additional index of demand instability, the *t*-ratio for *C4A* rises to 1.98. In this respect the results for 19 years of data differ from those for data covering only 1954 through 1963. The *VMH* variable also captures away most of the explanatory power of the durable goods class variable, with which it is collinear ($r = 0.53$).

70. See the initial decision of the administrative law judge in the Federal Trade Commission antitrust case *in the matter of Coca Cola Co. et al.*, Docket no. 8885, October 3, 1975.

71. For further supporting evidence, see Scherer, "Market Structure and the Stability of Investment," pp. 76–77. See also Allen Sinai and Mildred B. Levy, "Industry Structure and Investment Behavior," (manuscript, University of Illinois at Chicago Circle, March 1970), who discovered that rational distributed lag investment models left much lower unexplained variance for three atomistically structured industries—men's suits, sawmills, and nuts and bolts—than in three highly concentrated industries (cereals, flat glass, and hard surface floor coverings). Sinai and Levy found also that the concentrated industries adjusted more rapidly to output and (especially) relative price changes than did atomistic industries.

of the business cycle. On this point the evidence is fragmentary. For a sample of 35 3-digit manufacturing industries, Frances and Louis Esposito found that middling oligopolies reported more excess capacity on average as they emerged from the generally slack business conditions of the late 1950s than either highly concentrated or atomistically structured industries.[72] The least excess capacity was held by industries with four-firm concentration ratios of 70 or more. Using essentially the same data, Mann and associates discovered that during the 1960s, when business conditions were generally improving, the most concentrated industries moved their actual levels of capacity utilization toward preferred levels more rapidly than did less concentrated industries.[73] Whether similar propensities hold at other stages of the business cycle has not been tested for any sizeable statistical sample.

Although these last results provoke doubts about the hypothesized tendency of oligopolies to sustain excess capacity, the available evidence for the most part supports a conclusion that investment is less stable, not more stable, in concentrated industries. But the greater observed variability over time of concentrated industry capital spending may contribute little to macroeconomic instability, at least to the extent that it is largely unsystematic and not synchronized with overall business cycle movements. For although statistical averaging-out does not operate fully *within* specific concentrated industries, there is likely to be further averaging-out *among* industries. What we know on this point suggests a moderately favorable verdict, although, as always, more remains to be learned.

Conclusion

Bringing together the pieces of our macroeconomic stability analysis, we conclude that monopoly and oligopoly are almost surely detrimental to the recovery of aggregate consumption in a slump through the Pigou and income distri-

bution effects associated with downward price rigidity. Certain aspects of oligopolistic market structure and conduct appear to increase the observed instability of investment within industries, but it is unclear whether this greater variability has much of a destabilizing impact at the macroeconomic level. The effects of price rigidity on expectations are probably favorable to aggregate investment and (less clearly) consumption at the start of a downturn. Since the effects are not all in one direction, we cannot demonstrate conclusively whether on balance concentration and the conduct that flows from it intensify or mitigate tendencies toward recession. We are left with an appreciable margin of uncertainty. The case for concentration is strongest if one believes that the expectational effects of price rigidity are what really matter in taming the business cycle. Yet within the range of variation encountered in ordinary experience, the differences in pricing behavior associated with market structure are probably not great enough to have a decisive impact. And it is clear that the intelligent application of fiscal and monetary correctives is more important to overall stability than industrial pricing policies. Therefore, if a bias toward price rigidity is a desirable trait of monopolistic and oligopolistic industries, the benefit to society is surely not great enough to override all other considerations.

---

72. Frances F. Esposito and Louis Esposito, "Excess Capacity and Market Structure," *Review of Economics and Statistics* 56 (May 1974): 188–94. In a more qualitative study, James W. Meehan found that capacity expansion in response to demand increases overshot the levels consistent with long-run equilibrium in two atomistically structured industries—soft coal mining and flour milling—and also in two oligopolistic industries—steel and cement manufacturing. Only in the monopolized prewar aluminum industry was there no evidence of overshooting. "Market Structure and Excess Capacity: A Theoretical and Empirical Analysis" (Ph.D. diss., Boston College, 1967). See also André-Paul Weber, *Capacité Excedentaire et Concurrence* (Paris: Marcel Bon, 1971), especially empirical Part Two.

73. H. Michael Mann, James W. Meehan, and G. A. Ramsey, "Market Structure and Excess Capacity: A Look at Theory and Some Evidence," *Review of Economics and Statistics* 61 (February 1978): 156–60.

14 Product differentiation, market structure, and competition

After being concerned in the past nine chapters primarily with pricing behavior, we shift our attention now to firms' product policies—i.e., the methods by which they strive to differentiate their goods and services from rival offerings. The objective in both pricing and product differentiation decisions is presumably to maximize profits. But there is a difference in timing. It is not hard to change a pricing decision once it has been made. Companies can move from a high-profit-margin, entry-encouraging price posture to a low-margin position virtually overnight. This is not nearly as true of product differentiation decisions. Once the firm has committed itself to a set of physical and subjective product attributes, months or even years may be required before it can escape that commitment. Although each involves both short-run and long-run considerations, it is not too severe an oversimplification to suggest that pricing decisions epitomize the tactical problems of business enterprise, while product differentiation decisions fall more heavily in the realm of strategy.

Sellers differentiate their products in four main ways. First, they may select plant or store locations more convenient (in terms of travel time and/or transportation costs) than rival locations. The locational advantages of the corner drug store and the local gravel quarry are illustrations. Second, they may offer exceptionally good (or bad) service. Some retailers maintain large and well-trained staffs to provide prompt, intelli-gent, and courteous service; others are better known for long checkout lines and grumbling cashiers, mollifying the effect with rock-bottom prices. Some computer manufacturers contribute an array of free programming services to those who use their machines; others do no applications programming; and so on. Third, there are physical differences in the products supplied. Paints may be more or less mildew resistant; a suit may incorporate the most finely woven wool worsted or a coarser substitute; the design of an appliance may be mundane or reflect the genius of a Henry Dreyfuss; an automobile may navigate curves surefootedly or clumsily; beer may be hops laden or bland; a television receiver may project vivid or muddy color; and so forth. Finally, products are differentiated in terms of the subjective image they impress on the consumer's mind. Sellers attempt to enhance the image of their products through brand labelling, advertising, direct word-of-mouth sales promotion, and the design of attractive packages.

Much and perhaps most of the product differentiation effort observed in a modern private enterprise economy represents little more than a natural and healthy response to legitimate demands. Peoples' wants are diverse, and consumers plainly desire a varied menu of consumption opportunities. It is a rare consumer who doesn't value convenience in the location of suppliers, and many will pay a price premium for a certain amount of locational convenience. Nearly every consumer prefers good service over poor, though the prices individuals are willing to pay for extra service vary widely. The diversity of preferences with respect to physical design and performance characteristics is especially great. Some men prefer cotton shirts, some silk shirts, some hair shirts, and some no shirt at all. Some want to fly supersonically; others would just as soon walk in the woods. Likewise, different consumers place varying weights on the subjective aura or image accompanying the products they buy.

The relevant issue for economic analysis is not, therefore, whether product differentiation is a good thing, but rather, how much product differentiation there should be and whether certain market conditions might lead to excessive or inadequate differentiation, or to the "wrong" kinds of differentiation. In this chapter we shall probe the bounds to which economic analysis can carry us in answering such questions and identify the factual assumptions and value judgments that underlie differing points of view.

Image differentiation and its social benefits

The facet of product differentiation singled out most frequently for criticism is image differentiation, and especially the image differentiation created or reinforced through intensive advertising.[1] In 1977, it is estimated, $38 billion were spent on advertising in the United States.[2] Expenditures on advertising per capita in 1974 were approximately $126 in the United States, $114 in Switzerland, $76 in Canada, $41 in West Germany, $40 in the United Kingdom, and $38 in Japan.[3] Does the United States' preeminence reflect only enlightened marketing methods or a set of economic institutions outrunning the bounds of reasonableness?

No careful observer could deny that the costs of advertising are mirrored at least in part by substantial social benefits. For one, advertising serves an informative function, letting buyers know the available product alternatives and permitting them to make better choices than they might if they had to ferret out information from a host of geographically dispersed sellers. A stock question in the debate over advertising is, How much advertising is beneficially informative, and how much merely persuasive? No clear-cut answer can be given, since it is difficult to draw a sharp line between informing and persuading. Much advertising exhibits some of each trait. Nevertheless, a crude impression can be obtained by considering the distribution of advertising expenditures by media in 1977, summarized in Table 14.1 Newspaper advertising, accounting for nearly 30 percent of total outlays, is preponderantly of an informative character, although (as any erstwhile home seller knows) even classified ads are written in persuasive fashion. However unwelcome it may be to the deluged recipient, direct mail advertising plays a largely informative role, as do many of the advertisements in business and farm periodicals. The information content of television commercials is also not zero, despite a seemingly magnetic attraction toward that value. At the very least, they say "I exist—try me." And according to Phillip Nelson, they also tell the potential buyer of goods evaluated best through actual consumption experience, "We believe you will find our product so good that we are spending a lot of money advertising it in the hope of winning your repeat purchases; and from the fact of our high expenditures you can infer that the product is indeed a good risk."[4] Even outdoor billboards sometimes supply wanted information, as travelers who sought gasoline or lodging in the early sign-less days of the U.S. interstate highways can attest.

Another benefit often attributed to advertising is that, by making a firm's products known and broadening their market appeal, it facilitates sales growth and the realization of production scale economies that would otherwise be unattainable.[5] A convincingly documented case concerns the retailing of eyeglasses.[6] In some states all advertising by prescription eyeglass dispensers is prohibited; in other states (and in the District of Columbia) there are no advertising restrictions. Significant economies can evidently be realized by achieving high sales volume in an eyeglass dispensing operation, but attaining that volume is difficult if sellers are constrained by advertising bans and other restrictive provisions found in optometrists' codes of ethics. Where such bans have been given the force of law, the entry of high-volume, low-price retailers has been discouraged.[7] For a sample of 154 purchases, Benham found that prices were 25 to 30 percent higher in states with total advertising bans than in states with no restrictions or only weak restrictions.[8] How typical the eyeglass case is remains unknown. In an early but unusually comprehensive survey of the available evidence, Borden was forced to conclude that "it is impossible from cost data to trace a clear causal relationship between decreased production cost and advertising."[9] The impact on costs and prices depends upon the shapes of cost functions, price elasticities of demand, and the response of demand to advertising outlays. Without detailed quantita-

---

T 14.1 Estimated U.S. advertising expenditures by media in 1977

Medium	Millions of dollars
Newspapers	$11,132
Magazines	2,162
Business and trade publications	1,221
Farm publications	90
Network television	3,460
Spot and local television	4,152
Radio	2,586
Direct mail	5,333
Outdoor	418
Miscellaneous	7,506
Total	$38,060

Source: *Advertising Age*, September 4, 1978, p. 33, drawing upon McCann-Erickson estimates. The miscellaneous category includes the estimated cost of corporate advertising departments, art work, subsidized signs and advertising novelties, and perhaps such true miscellanea as the Goodyear Blimp (of which there were four in 1976, each costing roughly $1.5 million per year to operate).

Reprinted with permission from the September 4, 1978 issue of *Advertising Age*. Copyright 1978 by Crain Communications, Inc.

1. For a synopsis of economists' differing views on advertising and monopoly power, see the papers by Yale Brozen and H. Michael Mann in Harvey J. Goldschmid et al., eds., *Industrial Concentration: The New Learning* (Boston: Little-Brown, 1974), pp. 115–56. See also William S. Comanor and Thomas A. Wilson, "The Effect of Advertising on Competition: A Survey," *Journal of Economic Literature* 17 (June 1979): 453–76.

2. "Estimated Annual U.S. Ad Expenditures: 1959–1977," *Advertising Age*, 4 September 1978, p. 33. On measurement methodology and historical trends, see Neil H. Borden, *The Economic Effects of Advertising* (Chicago: Irwin, 1942), pp. 52–58; Jules Backman, *Advertising and Competition* (New York: New York University Press, 1967), pp. 161–79; and Julian L. Simon, *Issues in the Economics of Advertising* (Urbana: University of Illinois Press, 1970), pp. 187–92, 255–57.

3. "World Ad Total for '74 at $49 Billion," *Advertising Age*, 29 November 1976, p. 71, quoting Starch INRA Hooper estimates.

4. Phillip Nelson, "Advertising as Information," *Journal of Political Economy* 82 (July/August 1974): 729–54; and "The Economic Consequences of Advertising," *Journal of Business* 48 (April 1975): 213–41. Arguing that businesses will advertise most when their product is sufficiently good that it will be repetitively purchased after advertising-induced trial, Nelson concludes that heavily advertised goods are therefore the best buys. From this he infers that even when consumers are induced by deceptive endorsements to purchase a heavily advertised brand, the deception is benign because consumers "are deceived into doing what they should do anyway." "Advertising as Information," p. 751.

    The behavior postulated by Nelson is demonstrably not rational under certain plausible circumstances. The more consumers come to believe that highly advertised brands are superior and act according to that belief, the more incentive there is for the producers of low-quality goods to advertise intensely, especially when prices rise less rapidly than production costs with increasing quality and when consumers have difficulty, even after experimentation, in assessing quality levels. See Richard Schmalensee, "A Model of Advertising and Product Quality," *Journal of Political Economy* 86 (June 1978): 485–503; and George A. Akerlof, "The Market for 'Lemons': Quality Uncertainty and the Market Mechanism," *Quarterly Journal of Economics* 84 (August 1970): 488–500.

5. For an interesting but not altogether convincing dynamic conjecture in this vein, stating that in the late 19th century advertising freed British manufacturers from dependence upon wholesalers, permitting them to tap a mass consumer market, see Nicholas Kaldor, "The Economic Aspects of Advertising," *Review of Economic Studies* 18 (1949–50): 17–21.

6. See Lee Benham, "The Effect of Advertising on the Price of Eyeglasses," *Journal of Law and Economics* 15 (October 1972): 337–52; and Lee Benham and Alexandra Benham, "Regulating through the Professions: A Perspective on Information Control," *Journal of Law and Economics* 18 (October 1975): 421–47. See also "Dentists, Other Professionals, Finding It Pays To Advertise," *New York Times*, 16 January 1978, p. 31.

7. Benham, "The Effect of Advertising," p. 346. In two decades of perennial exploitation by opticians, the most price-competitive source encountered by the author of the present work was a subsidiary of the Giant food chain in Washington, D.C.

8. Benham, "The Effect of Advertising," pp. 340–44. For a larger sample permitting the measurement only of combined examination plus eyeglass prices, Benham found similar but smaller differentials.

Product differentiation, market structure, and competition   **377**

tive information on these relationships, economic theory cannot predict unambiguously whether advertising will lead to output increases or, when it does, whether the increases are sufficient to reduce prices or production costs to minimum feasible levels.[10]

A related conjecture is that advertising, by making known the availability of new products, enables innovators to tap larger markets more rapidly, enhancing the profits from innovation and hence strengthening incentives for investment in innovation. This is consistent with the theory of optimal research and development scheduling,[11] and there is considerable evidence that advertising expenditures tend to be higher when the pace of new product introduction is accelerated.[12] However, the fields in which the introduction of new products has been accompanied by especially high promotional outlays—e.g., proprietary drugs, deodorants, frozen dinners, cosmetics, soaps, hair bleaches, ready-to-eat breakfast cereals, cake mixes, dog foods, and oleomargarine—hardly seem to be those in which human welfare has taken giant strides through technological change.[13] On innovations rooted more solidly in substantial technological achievement we shall have much more to say in Chapters 15 and 16.

A certain amount of image differentiation also helps consumers select products of high quality and reliability and motivates producers to maintain adequate quality standards. If there were no brand names and trademarks, the consumer might never be sure who made a product and would have difficulty rewarding through repeat purchases manufacturers who achieve high quality or cater to his or her special tastes. This is a lesson that dawned late but forcefully upon Soviet Union economic planners, who found that requiring consumer goods manufacturers to imprint their individual 'production marks' on products helped guard against deteriorating quality standards.[14] Trademarking and brand labelling also contribute in a subtle way to distributional efficiency. Without them, the conscientious shopper would have to make repeated inquiries about products susceptible to quality or taste variations, asking whether a particular product was good, what its distinguishing characteristics were, and perhaps (as in the almost bygone days of the pickle barrel) whether he or she might try a sample. This takes a great deal of time for both merchants and shoppers, increasing transaction costs significantly. The existence of branded goods whose characteristics vary little from week to week makes it possible to have convenient self-service shopping and hence to realize the efficiencies of supermarkets.

The crucial question is, How far must image differentiation go to achieve these benefits? Is mere trademarking sufficient, or must there also be advertising to bolster the supplier's or the product's image? The answer depends upon the nature of the product. For industrial goods, even trademarking is usually unnecessary, since industrial buyers are skilled at evaluating the products they receive, and they keep records permitting them to trace responsibility for quality deficiencies to specific suppliers. For consumer goods purchased repetitively, trademarking or labelling with a unique company logotype is probably sufficient, since a bad experience with one brand will induce a prompt shift to another, and this process of experimentation will continue until some brand proves persistently satisfactory.[15] The best case for additional image differentiation exists for consumer durables complex enough to prevent the buyer from distinguishing through inspection whether they will function effectively, and purchased so infrequently that past experience is insufficient or obsolete as a guide. Here many consumers base their decisions on the manufacturer's reputation for quality and reliability—a reputation built up through advertising as well as actual performance.

However, does proclaiming to the world that one's quality is superior make it true? Not necessarily, but there may be some beneficial spillover from image creation to actual behavior. As Borden observed in his massive study of the economic effects of advertising, the advertised brand usually represents a goodwill asset built up at considerable expense, and injury to it would mean a business loss.[16] The link between image and behavior is perhaps strongest for firms selling a broad line of consumer durable goods. Companies like General Electric and Sunbeam are acutely aware that the poor performance of any single appliance series can, through its adverse effect on their reputation, impair the sales of other lines. Though this does not guarantee good performance, it at least increases the probability that the image-conscious producer will try hard to maintain adequate quality standards. This assurance in turn has some value to the consumer, who by purchasing a well-known brand can reduce the risk of being fleeced by a fly-by-night operation—a species unfortunately not yet extinct. Since the majority of all smaller, less diversified enterprises strive as diligently as the large to preserve their reputations for quality, this may be a modest benefit, but it is surely not insignificant.

Advertising is also credited with subsidizing the mass communications media. In recent years the sale of advertising space or time has provided roughly 70 percent of the gross revenues of American newspapers, more than half of general periodicals' revenues, and (excluding educational stations) virtually all the revenue of radio and television broadcasters.[17] Of course, if there were no advertising, newspapers and magazines would be much thinner and publication costs would be lower. Still the best available evidence indicates that advertising revenues yield a net publication subsidy after deducting incremental costs.[18] It is not certain, however, that such subsidies are an unmixed blessing. Subsidies tend to distort the allocation of resources unless the subsidized commodity generates external economies or is produced under conditions of declining long-run unit cost (in which case it could not be sold profitably if priced at marginal cost).[19] Both rationalizations for subsidy apply to some extent in the mass media industries. Yet the very nature of the subsidization process may undermine what might otherwise be an important external benefit of the mass media—the cultivation of a sensitive, informed public. Consumer goods advertisers generally favor media that will transmit their message to the largest relevant audience, and the media respond by attempting to maximize audience size through an appeal to the lowest common denominator. The result is the scandal sheet and television's "vast wasteland," as Federal Communications Commission chairman Newton Minow described it in 1961. Indeed, many TV programs are of such low intellectual caliber that the commercials stand out as a refreshingly sophisticated interlude.

(9) Borden, *The Economic Effects of Advertising*, p. 854. Compare Brozen in *Industrial Concentration*, pp. 121–23.

10. There is an extensive literature on this point, and particularly on Professor Chamberlin's contention that as a cause of product differentiation, advertising leads firms into equilibrium on the falling segment of their long-run average total cost function. Significant contributions include Edward H. Chamberlin, *The Theory of Monopolistic Competition*, 6th ed. (Cambridge, Mass.: Harvard University Press, 1950), Chapter 7; Harold Demsetz, "The Nature of Equilibrium in Monopolistic Competition," *Journal of Political Economy* 67 (February 1959): 21–30; *idem*, "The Welfare and Empirical Implications of Monopolistic Competition," *Economic Journal* 74 (September 1964): 623–41; G. C. Archibald, "Chamberlin versus Chicago," *Review of Economic Studies* 29 (1961–62): 2–28, with comments and a reply in volume 30 (1962–63): 68–71; Donald Dewey, *The Theory of Imperfect Competition* (New York: Columbia University Press, 1969); Yoram Barzel, "Excess Capacity in Monopolistic Competition," *Journal of Political Economy* 78 (September/October 1970): 1142–49; Richard Schmalensee, "A Note on Monopolistic Competition and Excess Capacity," with a reply by Demsetz, *Journal of Political Economy* 82 (May/June 1972): 586–97; H. Ohta, "On Efficiency of Production under Conditions of Imperfect Competition" (summarizing *inter alia* the contributions of Melvin Greenhut), *Southern Economic Journal* 43 (October 1976): 1124–35; and Robert L. Steiner, "Marketing Productivity in Consumer Goods Industries," *Journal of Marketing* 42 (January 1978): 60–70.

   In a survey of 2,700 *Harvard Business Review* subscribers, 82 percent of them business managers, 49 percent believed that on balance advertising led to higher prices, while 35 percent believed it led to lower prices. Stephen A. Greyser and Bonnie B. Reece, "Businessmen Look Hard at Advertising," *Harvard Business Review* 49 (May–June 1971): 26.

11. See F. M. Scherer, "Research and Development Resource Allocation under Rivalry," *Quarterly Journal of Economics* 81 (August 1967), especially pp. 368, 388.

12. See Jean Jacques Lambin, *Advertising, Competition and Market Conduct in Oligopoly over Time* (Amsterdam: North-Holland, 1976), p. 123; W. Duncan Reekie, "Some Problems Associated with the Marketing of Ethical Pharmaceutical Products," *Journal of Industrial Economics* 19 (November 1970): 40–41; and Brozen in *Industrial Concentration*, pp. 115–16, 128.

13. Cf. Backman, *Advertising and Competition*, pp. 23–27.

14. See Marshall I. Goldman, "Product Differentiation and Advertising: Some Lessons from Soviet Experience," *Journal of Political Economy* 68 (August 1960): 346–57; and "Russia Discovers Madison Avenue," *Business Week*, 8 September 1975, pp. 41–42. For more skeptical views, see Philip Hanson, *The Consumer in the Soviet Economy* (London: Macmillan, 1969), pp. 204–206; and "Advertising: A Soviet Comeback," *Washington Post*, 11 April 1976. Soviet expenditures on media advertising of consumer goods increased from roughly $18 million in 1966 to $500 million in 1975.

15. Compare Nelson, "Advertising as Information," pp. 732–34, who argues that advertising makes brand names more memorable, helping consumers remember which products best satisfied their wants and hence merit repeated purchase. Nelson believes that the profitability of advertising is greatest for such repetitively purchased "experience goods."

16. Borden, *The Economic Effects of Advertising*, pp. 631–32, 866.

17. U.S., Bureau of the Census, *Statistical Abstract of the United States: 1976* (Washington, D.C.: Government Printing Office, 1976), p. 540.

This last point suggests still another benefit of advertising and image differentiation. Advertising is art, and some of it is good art, with cultural or entertainment value in its own right. In addition, it can be argued that consumers derive pleasure from the image advertising imparts to products, above and beyond the satisfaction flowing in some organic sense from the physical attributes of the products. There is no simple case in logic for distinguishing between the utility people obtain from what they think they are getting and what they actually receive. As Galbraith observed, "The New York housewife who was forced to do without Macy's advertising would have a sense of loss second only to that from doing without Macy's."[20]

Finally, it is sometimes said that advertising has the desirable effect of mitigating the business cycle and stabilizing the economy. On closer scrutiny, this claim can be divided into two propositions: (1) that business enterprises hasten recovery from recessions by redoubling their promotional efforts to stimulate lagging sales; and (2) that advertising has a long-run stabilizing effect on aspirations, making people less willing to reduce consumption when income falls, thereby minimizing the danger of recessions owing to cyclical or secular stagnation of demand. On the first point, the evidence is uniformly unfavorable. Advertising expenditures exhibit a definite procyclical pattern, rising in booms and falling in recessions, contrary to what is required for stabilization.[21] The second hypothesis has not been tested directly, but tests of the hypothesis that advertising increases aggregate consumption have yielded inconsistent results, and no confident conclusion seems supportable.[22] Whatever the merits of the case may be, advertising is not uniquely effective in stabilizing consumption, since the same job can be done through fiscal and monetary policy measures.

The social costs of image differentiation

Against these benefits, demonstrated and conjectural, we must weigh the social costs of adver-

tising and other image differentiation activities. The most obvious is the cost of the resources used—as noted earlier, some $38 billion, or 2 percent of gross national product, for advertising in 1977, plus uncountable billions for packaging gimmicks and the like.

Second, much of the 'information' conveyed in advertisements is something less than a faithful depiction of reality. Blatant deception, although once common, is now kept in check reasonably well by a voluntary industry self-regulatory group, the National Advertising Review Board, and in the last resort through the enforcement of laws against deceptive practices by the Federal Trade Commission, the Food and Drug Administration, and analogous state agencies. But persuasion through partial disclosure and innuendo persists. The consumer is told, for instance, that Anacin contains 23 percent more pain reliever than other leading headache remedies, but not that the pain reliever is plain aspirin. Or a savings and loan bank proclaims that no other bank offers higher savings account interest rates without mentioning that virtually all of its rivals pay *the same* ceiling rates. When the regulators move in on such practices, advertisers invent new and more subtle ways of "puffing" their products' merits. To be sure, most consumers are sophisticated enough, or have been made sufficiently cynical, to avoid being taken in by such half-truths. Indeed, 46 percent of the 1,510 persons surveyed in a 1976 Harris poll believed that all or most television advertisements are seriously misleading.[23] Some must be gulled, however, for advertisers would not try to mislead if they thought they were convincing no one.

Another possible cost of advertising is the contribution it makes toward instilling or entrenching hedonistic values. How much advertising is responsible for whatever ascendance hedonism has enjoyed in Western society is impossible to say. Certainly, other forces have made independent contributions. And to impute any social cost at all is to make a moral judgment over which reasonable persons can disagree. We shall therefore not belabor the question, leaving the debate to philosophers, who have comparative advantage at it.

We are on only slightly firmer ground chalking up a negative score for image differentiation on a related ethical dimension. The approach of much advertising and style differentiation is to lead consumers into making introspective comparisons between their own well-being and that of people they admire or would like to emulate. They are told they stand a better chance of attaining the status to which they aspire if they follow the example of consumption pacesetters or become pacesetters themselves and, in the more blatant assaults, that their current status is endangered by not consuming what the "right" people consume. Translated into economic jargon, advertising seeks to make the utility of individual consumers depend not merely upon the goods and services they themselves consume, but also upon the consumption decisions of their peers. It renders utility functions interdependent, generating external diseconomies in consumption. To the extent that it is successful in doing this, advertising can destroy utility along with creating it. To be sure, by responding to the stimulus and buying an advertised product, consumers may feel they are gaining something worthwhile. But it is not clear they have done any more than return to the satisfaction level they would have maintained without the persuasive assault on their preference structures.

Finally, to descend to a less esoteric plane, advertising and other forms of image differentiation can confer monopoly power upon the firms using them. They permit the seller to choose within a more or less restricted range whether to charge a higher or lower price for its product. Presumably, if the differentiation effort has been successful, the price will be higher than it would have been under undifferentiated competition, other things (such as costs and "real" product quality) being equal.

This assertion is difficult to substantiate because it is seldom possible to hold all cost and (especially) quality variables constant in analyzing price relationships. One of the clearest cases involves liquid household laundry bleach, which is offered in highly standardized form as a 5.25 percent sodium hypochlorite solution. Visiting five retail food stores in north Chicago area neighborhoods of widely differing socioeconomic characteristics during August of 1977, the author compared the prices of such bleach in two-quart plastic containers. Clorox, the leading nationally advertised brand, sold at $.63 in each of four supermarkets and $.75 at a "Mom and Pop" store located in an affluent residential section. Purex, the second best selling national brand, sold for $.57 in supermarkets, while supermarket chains' own house brands were priced at $.43 to $.48—24 to 32 percent less than the Clorox shelved nearby.[24] Clearly, the price premium associated

18. See Borden, *The Economic Effects of Advertising*, pp. 68–71, 923–33; and Kaldor, "The Economic Aspects of Advertising," p. 6. When the principal New York City newspapers were closed by a strike from December 1962 to March 1963, the *Washington Post*, a company official indicated, chose not to expand its print run and fill the gap because a temporary circulation gain could not justify an increase in advertising rates, and without the increase, the revenue from additional sales would not cover marginal printing costs.

19. Cf. Chapter 11, pp. 321–22 *supra*.

20. J. K. Galbraith, *American Capitalism: The Concept of Countervailing Power*, Rev. ed. (Boston: Houghton Mifflin, 1956), p. 98. For diverse views on the metaphysics of image differentiation, see Jules Henry, *Culture Against Man* (New York: Random House, 1963), Chapters 2 and 3; Walter Taplin, *Advertising: A New Approach* (Boston: Little, Brown, 1963); and Simon, *Issues in the Economics of Advertising*, Chapter 11.

21. See Borden, *The Economic Effects of Advertising*, pp. 725–36, 865–66; Simon, *Issues in the Economics of Advertising*, pp. 67–74; and Richard Schmalensee, *The Economics of Advertising* (Amsterdam: North-Holland, 1972), pp. 58–75.

22. Compare Lester D. Taylor and Daniel Weiserbs, "Advertising and the Aggregate Consumption Function," *American Economic Review* 62 (September 1972): 642–55; and William S. Comanor and Thomas A. Wilson, *Advertising and Market Power* (Cambridge, Mass.: Harvard University Press, 1974), Chapter 5, who find that advertising affected the balance between consumption and savings and the allocation of sales among industries, with the negative conclusions of Schmalensee, *The Economics of Advertising*, pp. 48–86; Simon, *Issues in the Economics of Advertising*, pp. 193–206; Lambin, *Advertising, Competition and Market Conduct*, pp. 136–38; and Ronald P. Wilder, "Advertising and Inter-Industry Competition: Testing a Galbraithian Hypothesis," *Journal of Industrial Economics* 22 (March 1974): 215–26.

23. "Business, Public Out of Sync," *Advertising Age*, 23 May 1977, p. 102. Similarly, 60 percent of surveyed *Harvard Business Review* subscribers indicated that advertisements do not present a true picture of the products advertised. Roughly half believed that advertising often persuaded people to buy things they don't want. Greyser and Reece, "Businessmen Look Hard at Advertising," p. 158.

24. In two Jewel food chain outlets, one-gallon containers of Clorox were on sale at a special price of 75 cents—two to four cents below less-advertised brands. Jewel in turn offered a special 59-cent price on its house brand in the gallon size.

Product differentiation, market structure, and competition   381

with Clorox's long-established 'image' was substantial.

Another unusually well-documented example is reconstituted lemon juice. The product is easy to make and the diverse producers' offerings were in a technical sense essentially identical. As the leading seller's 1971 marketing plan observed:

> Although reconstituted lemon juice is virtually indistinguishable one brand from another, heavy emphasis on the ReaLemon brand through its media effort should create such memorability for the brand, that an almost imaginary superiority would exist in the mind of the consumer, a justification for paying the higher price we are asking.[25]

Recognizing the ReaLemon name as "one of the greatest brand names in the history of the supermarket," the producers of ReaLemon were able in 1973 to command a $.62 retail price for their product and capture 80 percent of all reconstituted lemon juice sales while the price of the principal competitive brand, Golden Crown, was $.46 to $.48.[26]

These cases are apparently not exceptional. Double-blind experiments have repeatedly demonstrated that consumers cannot consistently distinguish premium from popular-priced beer brands, but exhibit definite preferences for the premium brands when labels are affixed—correctly or not.[27] One suspects that this is true for many other products, although it is hard to be certain because unfavorable or equivocal consumer panel results are among consumer goods manufacturers' most closely guarded secrets. According to David Ogilvy, the former head of a leading advertising agency:

> The greater the similarity between brands, the less part reason plays in brand selection. There isn't any significant difference between the various brands of whiskey, or cigarettes, or beer. They are all about the same. And so are the cake mixes and the detergents, and the margarines.[28]

Yet this is not true in all cases. *Some* less advertised brands are definitely inferior, as one who has rushed for the Band-Aid(TM) box after experimenting with private-label razor blades, or

left a store-brand cola drink half full, can attest. Why consumers' experimentation is insufficient to weed out *both* the bad products *and* the prestigious, high-price but objectively mediocre items is without doubt the most important question to be answered in understanding the monopoly power associated with image differentiation. Certainly, the potential rewards for being discriminating are appreciable. The staff of the National Commission on Food Marketing found through a sample survey of ten canned and bottled food products that the price of the most popular nationally advertised brand sold in chain stores was 21.5 percent higher on the average than the price of private-label items of comparable quality. The price premia for nationally advertised goods ranged from 4 to 35 percent.[29] A study of from 46 to 57 products sold by three food chains in 1974 revealed that private-label prices averaged 8 to 13 percent less than national brand prices.[30]

Price differentials between nationally branded and less well-known items appear to be especially large for medicinal products. In the five-store shopping trip described earlier, the author discovered that 100-tablet bottles of Bayer aspirin were typically priced at about $1.09 while store-brand and other generic aspirin could be obtained for $.39 to $.79. The $.39 brand was purchased and found to have a binder inferior to Bayer's; its dissolving time on the tongue was roughly 35 seconds, compared to 22 seconds for Bayer. Whether this difference warrants the substantial price differential is arguable. In Germany, aspirin pricing is affected even more strongly by the fact that Bayer/Leverkusen has exclusive trademark rights to the name "Aspirin"; others must use different trademarks or the generic name acetylsalicylic acid. A survey of German pharmacy prices for August 1977 revealed that Bayer "Aspirin" cost the equivalent of $2.21 for 100 tablets.[31] More generally, Walker found in surveying 217 ethical drugs that the prices of branded, advertised preparations were two-thirds higher on the average than the prices of comparable items sold under their generic chemical names.[32]

The range of cases illustrated here and the fact that drug price differentials are particularly wide suggest three generalizations. First, sellers are likely to be more successful in maintaining elevated prices through image differentiation, the more difficult it is for consumers to determine whether one product is in fact superior to another. Drugs, both prescription and proprietary, are at an extreme here, although dentifrices and laundry products are not far behind. The drug taker typically lacks the knowledge to evaluate therapeutic effects; prescribing physicians only rarely take the time to monitor observable effects; and in many instances there exist no inexpensive means of determining whether one drug is more effective than another, even when the observer is highly trained.[33] Second, especially when the 'objective' characteristics of competing products do not differ widely or when it is difficult to discern whether they do differ, image differentiation is likely to permit wider price differentials, the more prominently status considerations enter into consumption decisions. If consumers are unable to discriminate among American beers by taste, one might suppose that the lowest priced brands would fare best in the market. But this supposition is reversed if a 'premium' image comes to imply sophistication and 'with-it-ness.' Similarly, under the skin Cadillacs differ little from other top-of-the-line General Motors cars, but they command a substantial price premium because they have come to convey a strong "I've made it" image. Third, price differentials linked with image are larger, the greater is the cost of an unfavorable consumption experience in relation to the product's price. Pharmaceuticals are again at an extreme here. A wrong choice could mean prolonged illness or adverse side effects for the patient and a malpractice suit for the prescribing physician. The risk-averse decision maker will almost always choose the best-known product. So also may an uncertain decision maker conscientiously striving to maximize expected utility if there is any evidence that highly advertised drugs are of significantly higher or more uniform quality on the average—a point on which considerable disagreement exists.[34] For razor blades, on the other hand, the risk of a bad choice is only a fleeting pain and perhaps 70 cents wasted on a purchase that will never be repeated. Status connotations are also important in this respect. There are many consumers to whom the risk of disapprobation for using an ineffective mouthwash, displaying the 'wrong' blue jeans label, or

serving the 'wrong' beer is a serious thing. Extended observation by the author suggests that the amount of weight attached to averting risks of this sort has been rising over time. It is unclear whether such a trend is accelerated by image-oriented advertising, or whether it is just the inexorable consequence of rising affluence and the quest for middle-class respectability. That the latter is a stronger causal factor than the former is implied by the image-status link's growing significance in nations with much lower advertising per capita than the United States—e.g., West Germany, England, and even the Soviet Union.

This last point prompts a further remark on

25. Quoted in the initial decision of the administrative law judge *in the matter of Borden, Inc.,* Federal Trade Commission complaint, docket no. 8978, para. 83.

26. *In re Borden, Inc.,* para. 75, 81, and 82.

27. See Simon, *Issues in the Economics of Advertising,* p. 271n; F. M. Scherer, "The Posnerian Harvest: Separating Wheat from Chaff," *Yale Law Review* 86 (April 1977): 997; and editor's note, *Chicago Tribune Magazine,* 24 April 1977, p. 7.

28. David Ogilvy, *Confessions of an Advertising Man* (New York: Atheneum, 1963), p. 102.

29. U.S., National Commission on Food Marketing, *Special Studies in Food Marketing, Technical Study no. 10* (Washington, D.C.: Government Printing Office, June 1966), p. 65.

30. Willard F. Mueller et al., *The Profit and Price Performance of Leading Food Chains, 1970–74,* U.S., Congress, Joint Economic Committee, 95th Cong., 1st sess., April 1977, p. 67.

31. I am indebted to Joachim Schwalbach of the International Institute of Management, Berlin, for providing relevant data. The German tablets are in a 500-mg. dosage size while the American tablets contain only 324 mg. A price adjustment has been made to compare identical dosage sizes.

32. Computed from the median values in Hugh D. Walker, *Market Power and Price Levels in the Ethical Drug Industry* (Bloomington: Indiana University Press, 1971), pp. 94–95.

33. For example, blood absorption levels can be monitored, but the link between blood levels and therapeutic effect is often poorly understood.

34. Compare U.S., Department of Health, Education, and Welfare, Task Force on Prescription Drugs, *Final Report* (Washington, D.C.: Government Printing Office, February 1969), pp. 9, 31–35; and David Schwartzman, *Innovation in the Pharmaceutical Industry* (Baltimore: Johns Hopkins, 1976), Chapters 10 and 11. However rational prescribing physicians' choices might be, given the uncertainty as to which drugs are genuinely superior, it is hard to believe that better choices would not be fostered if the $720 million spent in the United States in 1972 on ethical drug promotion—i.e., $3,600 per prescribing physician—were reallocated toward more objectively informative activities. Cf. Schwartzman, pp. 201–202.

Product differentiation, market structure, and competition

causality. Although advertising clearly reinforces image advantages that in turn support price differentials, it is questionable whether a superior image can be *created* merely by advertising vigorously. Something more is usually needed.[35] The dimensions of that "something more" are complex, but the most important single component is probably an innovative act of some sort. Companies who were the first to offer a new product, or at least the earliest surviving suppliers, appear to enjoy stronger image differentiation than late imitators. A study of two pharmaceutical product groups provides an unusually well-documented illustration.[36]

In the oral diuretic (i.e., body fluid reducing) drug field, Merck and Company made a key technological breakthrough leading to the introduction in 1958 of the product Diuril (i.e., chlorothiazide). Inventing around Merck's patent proved to be easy, and within two years ten other firms were offering therapeutically equivalent substitutes. Yet even in 1971, after further entry had occurred and improved products had been introduced by several competitors, Merck retained a 33 percent share of the oral diuretic market, despite the fact that it spent only three-eighths as much per sales dollar as its rivals on sales promotion and charged a price four times as high as Abbott Laboratories' chemically equivalent brand of hydrochlorothiazide.[37] Among Merck's competitors, those who captured the largest market shares were for the most part those whose products first offered important therapeutic advantages over existing diuretics.

The experience of Warner-Lambert with its pioneering drug Peritrate (i.e., pentaerythritol tetranitrate—PETN) for angina pectoris therapy was remarkably similar. Warner-Lambert introduced Peritrate in 1952, attracted nearly 100 competitors, charged prices averaging five to six times higher than chemically identical substitutes, and spent much less on promotion per sales dollar than rivals; and yet two decades later it retained a 30 percent share of the antianginal drug market.[38] Relative to the oral diuretic case, there were only two noteworthy differences. First, Warner-Lambert was neither the technological inventor nor the first to use PETN in treating angina pectoris. Rather, the sense in which it pioneered was to take that already known and unpatented entity, give it a brand name, and promote it vigorously to physicians for anginal therapy, in which nitroglycerin and various nitrites had previously been the drugs of choice. Second, the promotion of Peritrate and similar nitrates emphasized their use in long-term prophylactic therapy, but from an early date in their history, objective studies cast considerable doubt over whether they were indeed more effective than older entities or even a placebo.[39] Thus, in the case of Peritrate, it was marketing innovation, not technological superiority, that gave Warner-Lambert a highly profitable image advantage.

These two cases bracket the range of circumstances in which advertising and other sales promotion activity interact with innovation to confer image advantages. Sometimes a technological advance exploited vigorously by a firm's marketing staff provides the impetus. Sometimes the advantage may come by chance—e.g., when a particular product variant happens unexpectedly to satisfy untapped consumer wants or capture buyers' imagination. And sometimes the innovative contribution may lie more in the realm of promotion than physical product characteristics—e.g., when Miller Brewing Company discovered that long-established low-calorie beers had a sissy image among heavy drinkers and changed the image for its Lite brand through a massive advertising campaign featuring well-known athletes proclaiming that with Lite they could drink even more beer without feeling filled up.[40] Whatever the combination, if it succeeds, it can give the innovating firm an image advantage sustaining elevated prices and substantial market share retention for a long time to follow. However socially desirable, innocuous, or objectionable the image's source may be, the image itself can be an important basis of monopoly power.

The links between market structure and product differentiation effort

Let us focus more closely now on the relationships between differentiation and monopoly power. The chain of causation can run in two directions. Clearly, differentiation can confer power over price. We have not yet explored the full ramifications of this connection. But also, the structure of the market may affect the character and magnitude of sellers' product differentiation activities. This will be our immediate concern.

The large numbers case Serious thought about product differentiation began with Edward H. Chamberlin's analysis of the case in which numerous firms, each too small to take into account the effect of its price decisions on others, occupied an easily entered market. The analysis is so well known that only two key points need to be summarized. First, cost and demand conditions may be such that sellers find it profitable to differentiate their products. If they do, they will gain some control over price and will set a price that equates marginal cost with marginal revenue. In the short run, monopoly profits may result. But second, these profits lure additional firms into the industry, leaving less market space for the original participants and hence forcing their demand curves to the left. Long-run equilibrium ensues when so much entry has occurred that no further opportunities for making a supranormal profit remain. In the idealized case, each seller ends up with its downward-sloping demand curve tangent to its long-run cost function. For each, average total cost, including promotional costs, is higher than the minimum possible value, and the equilibrium price is correspondingly higher. Whether unit *production* costs are as low as they might be cannot, as we have seen earlier, be determined without additional facts.

An interesting and important variant case arises when the price charged by monopolistic competitors is fixed and beyond their control— e.g., because the government imposes price controls, because sellers have surrendered their price-making discretion to a cartel authority too bureaucratic or unsure of itself to attempt frequent adjustments, or when manufacturers have enforced resale price maintenance upon firms retailing their products. Again, above-normal profits may be earned in the short run. But two kinds of forces will operate to eliminate those profits.

First, existing industry members will strive to increase the sales they make at the fixed price by

F 14.1 Promotional competition with a fixed price

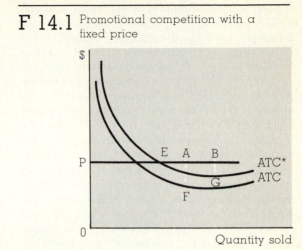

escalating advertising, service, and so on. This is illustrated graphically in Figure 14.1. The unit cost curve without special promotion is given by *ATC*, the fixed price by *OP*, and the quantity sold by a representative firm without special promotion by *PA*. A generous profit margin *AF* is earned. As companies intensify their promotional efforts to increase sales, the cost curve rises, e.g., to *ATC**. Sales expand to *PB*, with the profit margin *BG* resulting. The amount of the sales increase will be greater, the more elastic demand is with respect to promotional expenditures and the less aggressively rival sellers implement offsetting promotions. Unless there are significantly diminishing returns in the winning of additional sales through expanded promotional expendi-

35. See also Lambin, *Advertising, Competition and Market Conduct,* pp. 103–107, 115–18.
36. Ronald S. Bond and David F. Lean, *Sales, Promotion, and Product Differentiation in Two Prescription Drug Markets,* Federal Trade Commission staff report (Washington, D.C.: Government Printing Office, February 1977).
37. Bond and Lean, *Sales,* pp. 20–26.
38. Bond and Lean, *Sales,* pp. 43–56.
39. Bond and Lean, *Sales,* pp. 47–49.
40. See "Let There Be Lite," *Chicago Tribune Magazine,* 24 April 1977, pp. 60–66. See also the discussion of parent firm Philip Morris's marketing strategy in "Philip Morris: The Hot Hands in Cigarettes," *Business Week,* 6 December 1976, pp. 62–64.

Product differentiation, market structure, and competition   **385**

ture, equilibrium profits are likely to be substantially reduced and perhaps even eliminated as a consequence of the promotional rivalry.[41]

Second, if entry is free, new firms will enter the industry to take advantage of the profit-making opportunity. The total quantity demanded will be divided up among more competitors, so that each seller's share of the market shrinks. This process is likely to continue until all opportunities for making a supranormal profit have been exhausted. Equilibrium will then occur at a point like *E* in Figure 14.1, where the sales volume of the representative firm is too small to allow realization of all production and promotional scale economies. The result, then, of monopolistic competition when prices are fixed can be too many firms of too small a size spending appreciable sums on promotion and service.

The liquor retailing trade offers an excellent example of these phenomena.[42] In some U.S. states prices are fixed by a state board, and in others, at least until 1975, manufacturers were permitted by law to prescribe the prices at which their products could be distributed. Given a tendency for retail prices to be set at relatively high levels under these conditions, liquor stores go all out to provide friendly service, offer speedy home delivery, take large advertisements in the yellow pages and local newspapers, and outdo each other in the variety of products offered. The result is a significant increase in promotional and service costs, squeezing profit margins. It is unlikely, however, that margins will be eliminated for this reason alone. Diminishing returns undoubtedly discourage the expansion of promotional efforts before profits disappear altogether. New entry can complete the task if it is allowed to do so. But in certain states and Canadian provinces, entry restrictions are enforced in conjunction with price fixing. Then supranormal profits may persist indefinitely, or at least until they are transformed into rents as established liquor store owners sell out to newcomers at a high price that capitalizes the scarcity value of their operating permits.

The women's dressmaking trades provide a slightly different manifestation of the same phenomenon. Retail dress prices tend to be set at traditional *pricing points* (such as $14.95 and $19.95), and the discount that manufacturers allow retailers is also confined to certain standard percentage values. This leaves manufacturers relatively little pricing discretion. Competition then takes the form primarily of competition in quality, each producer adding increments of quality through better materials, more careful stitching, more liberal cooperative advertising allowances, and so forth so as to make its product as attractive as possible at the anticipated price, subject to the constraint that some target profit margin be realized. With large numbers of firms in the trade and easy entry, this quality competition is frequently so intense that manufacturers find themselves able to realize profit margins yielding on the average no more than a normal return on invested capital.

Advertising by oligopolists   On a *priori* grounds, there is reason to believe that incentives to advertise will be stronger when the number of sellers is limited than when it is very large. Promotional activity can engender two distinguishable types of demand enhancement. Demand might be shifted in favor of the general product line advertised at the expense of all other products, and it may be shifted in favor of the specific firm doing the advertising at the expense of other enterprises making similar products. The second gain can be realized whether the company advertising is one among many or an oligopolist. But the first type is more apt to be significant for monopolists or oligopolists. One firm among many can expect to reap only a very small fraction of the benefits from an overall expansion of market demand through advertising, whereas for an oligopolist the gain will be roughly proportional to its appreciable market share. In other words, the effect of advertising on overall market demand is an externality to the atomistic seller. It can be internalized completely only by a pure monopolist. Whether the amount of advertising undertaken by atomistic sellers is relatively large or small depends then in part upon the nature of advertising's benefits. Do they accrue predominantly to the industry as a whole or to the specific advertiser? This no doubt varies with the degree to which individual sellers' products can be differentiated.

Thus, no individual orange grower has an incentive to advertise on a nationwide basis, since its share of the increased demand for oranges would be minute; and advertising would probably not shift much business toward one particular firm and away from other growers. (Nor would any one firm profit noticeably from such a shift, since it presumably can sell as much as it pleases at the ruling market price.) But the Florida Citrus Commission, representing many growers, has a definite incentive to promote the sale of oranges generally and Florida oranges (which can be distinguished from the California variety) in particular.[43] Similarly, a small mass producer of dresses has little or no incentive to advertise in national fashion magazines. It may, however, undertake cooperative newspaper advertising with retail establishments featuring its wares, since the spillover effects of such advertising are modest. And a small high-fashion garment house may even buy space in the nationwide media, since it can gear its promotional appeal to unique design features.

Although a pure monopolist has the maximum incentive to undertake advertising with broad market-expanding effects, it lacks any incentive for advertising to win sales away from rival sellers. Here oligopolists selling products that can be differentiated occupy the best (or worst) of both worlds. They have rivals from whom they can capture sales, and they share significantly in the overall expansion of market demand. As George Washington Hill, swashbuckling president of the American Tobacco Company from 1925 to 1946, explained regarding his company's advertising philosophy, "Of course, you benefit yourself more than the other fellow . . . but you help the whole industry if you do a good job."[44]

We might expect, therefore, advertising expenditures per dollar of sales to be higher under differentiated oligopoly than under either pure monopoly or monopolistic competition, *ceteris paribus*. There is only one hitch. Mutual interdependence is the hallmark of oligopoly. If one company advertises to draw sales away from its rivals, what is to prevent the rivals from pursuing the same course, with a stalemate as the end result? And if all perceive this, would they not find it preferable to cooperate in spending on advertising only the amount that maximizes their collective profits—i.e., an amount approximating what would be spent by a pure monopolist?[45]

The static structure of oligopolistic advertising rivalry is similar to that of oligopolistic price rivalry, studied in Chapter 5. For each such rivalry a matrix of payoffs associated with alternative strategy choices can be constructed. Each, within the most interesting range of strategies, is a Prisoners' Dilemma game when the rivals occupy symmetric positions. To illustrate, consider the following hypothetical payoff matrix for an advertising rivalry between companies A and B. We

41. See George J. Stigler, "Price and Non-Price Competition," *Journal of Political Economy* 76 (January-February 1968): 149–54; Robert Dorfman and Peter O. Steiner, "Optimal Advertising and Optimal Quality," *American Economic Review* 44 (December 1954): 835–36; and Lawrence Abbott, *Quality and Competition* (New York: Columbia University Press, 1955), especially pp. 139–70.

42. See Leonard W. Weiss, *Economics and American Industry* (New York: Wiley, 1961), pp. 427–30.

   Although few firms serve any given city-pair market, the airline industry exhibited similar behavior under regulated price fixing. See George W. Douglas and James C. Miller III, *Economic Regulation of Domestic Air Transport: Theory and Policy* (Washington, D.C.: Brookings Institution, 1974); and Mahlon R. Straszheim, "The Determination of Airline Fares and Load Factors: Some Oligopoly Models," *Journal of Transport Economics and Policy* 8 (September 1974): 260–73.

43. See Marc Nerlove and Frederick V. Waugh, "Advertising without Supply Control: Some Implications of a Study of the Advertising of Oranges," *Journal of Farm Economics* 43 (November 1961): 813–37; "Sunkist Oranges Blossom on TV," *Business Week*, 23 December 1972, p. 23; and "Promoting Florida's Golden Harvest," *New York Times*, 11 January 1977, p. 52. Whether the Florida and California orange growers' associations indeed have no significant control over supply, as Nerlove and Waugh assume, is debatable but irrelevant to the immediate point.

44. Quoted in W. H. Nicholls, *Price Policies in the Cigarette Industry* (Nashville: Vanderbilt University Press, 1951), p. 60. See also Borden, *The Economic Effects of Advertising*, pp. 207–49; and Lester G. Telser, "Advertising and Cigarettes," *Journal of Political Economy* 70 (October 1962): 471–99.

45. If each firm executes a part of the campaign, the joint profit-maximizing expenditure on advertising under oligopoly may not coincide exactly with the pure monopolist's optimal expenditure. It will tend to be lower if there are economies of scale in promotion that the oligopolists cannot exploit fully in their separate campaigns. It will tend to be higher if the variety of appeals attainable through separate campaigns has a more potent impact on overall market demand than a monopolist's monolithic campaign.

Product differentiation, market structure, and competition

assume symmetry and for simplicity present only two strategy options for each firm—one connected with the Cournot equilibrium outcome and the other with a joint profit-maximizing outcome. Firm A's net profit payoffs (in millions of dollars per year) are given first, and Firm B's after the commas:

		Firm B spends each year on advertising	
		$4 million	$6 million
Firm A	$4 million	10.0, 10.0	6.0, 12.0
spends	$6 million	12.0, 6.0	8.7, 8.7

If the rivals match one another with outlays of $4 million, each gets profits of $10 million. If they increase the ante to $6 million each, overall sales rise, but these are more than offset by the higher advertising costs, so that each firm realizes net profits of only $8.7 million. If A outspends B, A will increase its take to $12 million, while if it is outspent, it will suffer market share losses and realize profits of only $6 million. The $6 million spending strategy dominates the $4 million strategy—that is, each firm's payoff is higher if it elects to spend $6 million, whether its rival spends $4 million or $6 million. Thus, there is a compulsion for each company to commit the larger sum. But by so doing, the rivals end up with lower profits than they would earn if they cooperated in limiting expenditures to $4 million each.

In duopolistic price rivalry, as we saw in Chapter 5, there is reason to expect, at least as a first approximation, that the sellers will cooperate on joint profit-maximizing strategies. But advertising rivalry appears to be different in several respects.[46] First, price cuts can be matched almost instantaneously unless concessions can be kept secret, whereas it takes weeks or even months to set a retaliatory nationwide advertising campaign in motion. During this interim, the initiator may enjoy market share and profit gains at the laggard's expense. The longer the lag between initiation and matching, the stronger the incentive to spend on image differentiation will be. Second, success in advertising depends at least as much upon the way the appeal is presented as on the amount of money spent. The outcome of an advertising campaign is therefore uncertain. Moreover, any fool can match a price

cut, but counteracting a clever advertising gambit is far from easy. In this unpredictable clash of creative power sellers often tend to overestimate their own ability to make market share gains and underestimate their rivals' ability to retaliate successfully, exhibiting little concern for mutual interdependence. Third, since price competition is unappealing in oligopoly, business managers may seek an outlet for their aggressive instincts on nonprice dimensions such as advertising, where the drawbacks are not so obvious. And if prices are held comfortably above marginal production cost, the quest for additional orders through nonprice rivalry is more lucrative than it would be under competitive pricing.

Exactly where this rivalrous behavior will lead is difficult to predict. Cournot-type reactions do not seem improbable, given the lag structure and uncertainties of advertising rivalry. But expenditures may even be pushed higher. To see this, consider the following extension of our example:

		Firm B spends each year on advertising	
		$6 million	$8 million
Firm A	$6 million	8.7, 8.7	6.0, 7.8
spends	$8 million	7.8, 6.0	7.4, 7.4

Here a dominant strategy no longer exists. If Firm B is expected to maintain its outlays at $6 million (the Cournot assumption), the best strategy for Firm A is to hold its expenditures at $6 million also. A Cournot equilibrium will be established. If on the other hand Firm A fears the worst, it may elect its minimax strategy of $8 million and advertising outlays will continue to increase until choked off by severely diminishing marginal returns.[47] In either event, each firm ends up spending a large amount on advertising messages that merely cancel out rival messages.[48]

There is considerable evidence that oligopolists often fail to coordinate their advertising policies successfully, spending much more than they would under joint profit maximization. In cigarettes, advertising expenditures rose from $4.3 million in 1910 to $13.8 million in 1913 after the American Tobacco Company, with 90 percent of the market, was broken into several pieces under an antitrust judgment.[49] Further escalation followed during the 1920s as American attempted to regain industry leadership through an all-out promotional assault. Advertising spending settled down during the 1930s and 1940s, only to rise sharply during the 1950s as new filter tip and king size brands were introduced, upsetting the prior market share equilibrium.[50] After a new plateau was attained, Congress banned advertising on television (by far the most heavily used medium) and radio effective January 1, 1971. Total cigarette advertising outlays dropped from $315 million in 1970 to $252 million in 1971 while profits rose commensurately.[51] For three years expenditures hovered near that lower figure, but then there was another escalation, accompanied by unusually costly free sample distribution.[52] That repeated rivalrous escalations of cigarette advertising have carried outlays far beyond the short-run profit-maximizing point seems indisputable. It is less certain whether long-run profits have been sacrificed or whether, by stimulating the growth of consumption, higher advertising expenditures have more than paid their way. The weight of evidence suggests that long-run growth effects directly attributable to advertising have been modest, and thus that much of the industry's advertising is self-cancelling and unprofitable even in the long run.[53]

In the soap and detergents industry, it seems clear that the enormous sums spent on advertising (e.g., $275 million in 1967, or roughly 11 percent of sales) do little more than cancel rival messages out, since aggregate consumption can hardly be affected much by advertising.[54] Indeed, the principal savings anticipated by Lord Leverhulme in his 1906 proposal to create a soap monopoly in Great Britain were to be realized by eliminating the "frenzied competitive advertising" undertaken by rival producers.[55] A study of several smalltown motion picture markets found that total display ad lineage fell significantly when the number of theatres was reduced from two to only one.[56] Although cement manufacturers successfully enforced agreements to avoid price and quality competition, they found themselves "helpless in combatting excessive selling costs" during the 1930s, with outlays covering salesmen's compensation, entertainment and gifts for cement buyers, and other nonfreight distribution costs mounting to 16 percent of net

46. See William Fellner, *Competition Among the Few* (New York: Knopf, 1949), pp. 183–91; Nicholls, *Price Policies*, pp. 187–203; Alexander Henderson, "The Theory of Duopoly," *Quarterly Journal of Economics* 69 (November 1954): 580–81; Avinash Dixit and Victor Norman, "Advertising and Welfare," *Bell Journal of Economics* 9 (Spring 1978): 1–17; Simon, *Issues in the Economics of Advertising*, pp. 93–103; and (for a dissenting view) James M. Ferguson, *Advertising and Competition: Theory, Measurement, Fact* (Cambridge, Mass.: Ballinger, 1974), pp. 21–27.

47. The worst outcome if Firm A spends $6 million is a profit of $6.0 million. The worst outcome if Firm A spends $8 million is a profit of $7.4 million. The *maximum minimorum* is to spend $8 million.

48. The dynamics of sales promotion by retailers through the use of trading stamps, premiums, and sweepstakes tickets are similar. For various views, see the first edition of *Industrial Market Structure and Economic Performance*, pp. 337–38; the Federal Trade Commission staff report, *On the Use and Economic Significance of Trading Stamps* (Washington, D.C.: Government Printing Office, January 1966); E. M. Tauber, "The Oligopolistic 'Lock-In'," *Applied Economics* 2, No. 3 (1977): 225–29; B. J. LaLonde and J. Herniter, "The Effect of Trading Stamp Discontinuance on Supermarket Performance," *Journal of Marketing Research* 7 (May 1970): 205–209; G. A. Churchill et al., "The Trading Stamp-Price Relationship," *Journal of Marketing Research* 8 (February 1971): 103–106; and Christina Fulop, *The Role of Trading Stamps on Retail Competition*, 2nd ed. (London: Institute of Economic Affairs, 1973).

49. See Borden, *The Economic Effects of Advertising*, pp. 212–16. Likewise, the entry of a second firm into the Australian cigarette industry in 1956 led to a trebling of advertising expenditures in the first year of entry and 22 to 48 percent increases in each of the next four years. M. A. Alemson, "Advertising and the Nature of Competition in Oligopoly over Time," *Economic Journal* 80 (June 1970): 293. See also Chapter 8, p. 259 *supra* on the twelvefold increase in the Swedish Tobacco Company's advertising outlays when import competition appeared. On the low level of advertising outlays by the Japanese cigarette monopoly, see "Recommendation That Japanese Government Monopoly Need Not Print Cigarette Warning Is Assailed," *New York Times*, 4 March 1971, p. 13.

50. See Telser, "Advertising and Cigarettes," pp. 494–98; and Henry G. Grabowski and Dennis C. Mueller, "Imitative Advertising in the Cigarette Industry," *Antitrust Bulletin* 16 (Summer 1971): 257–92.

51. Federal Trade Commission, *Report to Congress pursuant to Public Health Cigarette Smoking Act* (Washington, D.C.: Government Printing Office, December 31, 1974), Statistical Supplement Table 7. Segmental financial reports for Reynolds, Philip Morris, American Brands, and Liggett & Myers reveal that domestic tobacco subsidiary pretax operating profits rose by $91 million from 1970 to 1971 and by another $257 million from 1971 to 1975, the first year without price controls. The rate of cigarette consumption growth also accelerated in this period—apparently because the television advertising ban also eliminated counter-advertising emphasizing health hazards. See James L. Hamilton, "The Demand for Cigarettes, Advertising, the Health Scare, and the Cigarette Advertising Ban," *Review of Economics and Statistics* 54 (November 1972): 401–11.

52. See "R. J. Reynolds Stops a Slide in Market Share," *Business Week*, 26 January 1976, p. 93; and "Marketing Observer," *Business Week*, 8 August 1977, p. 83.

Product differentiation, market structure, and competition 389

sales in 1939.[57] More generally, from an ambitious econometric analysis of advertising behavior in 16 consumer goods product lines in diverse European national markets, Lambin found that in many cases observed levels of advertising might be consistent with profit maximization, short run or long run. But for others, and particularly for gasoline, coffee, yogurt, insecticides, deodorants, detergents, and (less clearly) soft drinks, he concluded:

> The limited capacity of advertising to increase primary demand, the reciprocal cancellation of brand advertising effects combined with the interdependence of advertising policies leading to an escalation in advertising expenditures constitute a built-in mechanism of advertising competition which has undesirable effects from the consumer point of view. . . . [T]his [advertising] duplication does not benefit the consumer in the long run, as does a price war or technological race. Thus, a form of competition restricted to advertising alone is undesirable in the economy.[58]

Although failure to hold advertising expenditures at joint profit-maximizing levels appears to be common in oligopoly, exceptions can be found. During the 1960s the U.S. cigarette manufacturers collectively implemented an advertising code discouraging such tactics as making claims with respect to product tar and nicotine content. This undoubtedly had some effect in suppressing advertising appeals exploiting the cancer scare. However, when the sales of its Kent cigarettes began falling, P. Lorillard Co. withdrew from participation in the code.[59] In 1957 the U.S. auto producers agreed to deemphasize horsepower in their advertisements and to refrain from direct participation in auto racing, ostensibly as a public service gesture but no doubt also to slow the growth of advertising outlays. The agreement was subsequently honored more in the breach than the keeping. They experienced somewhat greater success in avoiding competitive advertising of safety features.[60] Whether this reflects a spirit of oligopolistic forbearance, or merely the belief (based upon Ford's experience during the 1950s) that advertising safety features didn't pay, is not clear.[61] Except in the 'professions' (such as medicine, law, optometry, accounting, and the like), where threats of disbarment or dismissal could be used to enforce discipline under pre-1976 legal doctrines,[62] agreements to restrain advertising rivalry are apparently rare. As Professor Fellner has suggested, nonrivalrous handling of advertising expenditures is most likely to be seen only in very mature oligopolies, where the strategy options of member firms have been reduced to a matter of routine and demand is fairly stable. And these, he adds, are not very common in the industrial and commercial world.[63]

Numerous statistical tests have been conducted of the hypothesis that incentives to advertise are stronger under oligopoly than with either monopoly or an atomistic market structure.[64] Most have suffered from deficient data, small or arbitrarily selected industry samples, and/or failure to incorporate variables other than concentration that undoubtedly affect advertising levels. The most careful study to date has been done by Stephen Martin.[65] Using two-stage least squares regression techniques to take into account the simultaneous links between advertising, market structure, and profitability, and controlling for several other product market characteristics, he found a ∩-shaped relationship between the ratio of advertising expenditures to sales and industry concentration in both consumer and producer goods industries. The most intense levels of advertising in relation to sales across 209 U.S. manufacturing industries appeared at four-firm concentration ratio values of between 43 and 51. However, in both Martin's analysis and others, the observed relationship is statistically frail. Other variables have a stronger impact on advertising intensity than concentration does, and much of the variation in advertising/sales ratios remains unexplained by interindustry differences in concentration and other measurable independent variables. Thus, the causal nexus from concentration to advertising appears at best only weakly deterministic.

The link from advertising to monopoly power
Whether there are further chains of causation running from intense advertising to increased market concentration, strengthened monopoly

power, and ultimately to elevated price-cost margins is a question we have broached in several contexts already. Here we shall for the most part merely recapitulate the theory and evidence from the special perspective of this chapter.

We saw in Chapter 9 that one of the most consistent, potent variables "explaining" interindustry profitability differences in multiple regression analyses was the ratio of advertising outlays to sales. The higher the advertising/sales ratio was in an industry, the higher industry (or in some cases, firm) profits tended to be. The crucial remaining question is, Why?[66] Do the high rates of return in advertising-intensive industries reflect monopoly power flowing from advertising, or some more subtle set of phenomena, real or statistical?

If there is a monopoly power nexus, it is most apt to involve one or both of two phenomena—the development of brand loyalty, and hence market positions insulated from competition, through advertising; and/or other established-firm advantages associated with high advertising that serve as barriers to the entry of new competitors and the expansion of fringe rivals. The brand loyalty hypothesis might explain isolated short-run profit premia. However, it is far from obvious why, if advertising is an effective instrument for creating brand loyalty, *all* sellers do not advertise to establish their own specialized monopolies, and through their actions fragment markets and drive costs up until a profitless Chamberlinian equilibrium emerges. Something more is needed to explain the *persistence* of supranormal profits where advertising is high. Also, there is reason to question whether high advertising/sales ratios are associated in any simple way with strong brand loyalty. In his careful and wide-ranging econometric study of advertising effects, Lambin found *negative* but weak correlations between a measure of consumers' loyalty to particular brands and three different indices of advertising intensity.[67] If then there is a monopoly nexus, it must entail other entry barrier effects.

The most convincing explanation emphasizes a set of interactions between image advantages and advertising. It seems indisputable that certain brands enjoy image advantages permitting their sellers to charge prices well above costs

(53) Compare Simon, *Issues in the Economics of Advertising*, pp. 104–105; Telser, "Advertising and Cigarettes," pp. 498–99; Schmalensee, *The Economics of Advertising*, pp. 187–215; Hamilton, "The Demand for Cigarettes"; Lambin, *Advertising, Competition and Market Conduct*, pp. 143–47; M. M. Metwally, "Advertising and Competitive Behavior of Selected Australian Firms," *Review of Economics and Statistics* 57 (November 1975): 417–27; and "Where Cigarette Makers Spend Ad Dollars Now," *Business Week*, 25 December 1971, p. 56.

(54) Estimated from Stanley I. Ornstein, *Industrial Concentration and Advertising Intensity* (Washington, D.C.: American Enterprise Institute for Public Policy Research, 1977), p. 81. See also M. M. Metwally, "Profitability of Advertising in Australia: A Case Study," *Journal of Industrial Economics* 24 (March 1976): 221–30.

(55) P. Lesley Cook, *Effects of Mergers* (London: George Allen & Unwin, 1958), p. 233.

(56) Simon, *Issue in the Economics of Advertising*, pp. 108–109.

57. Samuel M. Loescher, *Imperfect Collusion in the Cement Industry* (Cambridge, Mass.: Harvard University Press, 1959), pp. 135–36, 213–16.

58. Lambin, *Advertising, Competition and Market Conduct*, p. 167. See also pp. 107–13, 141–47.

59. "P. Lorillard Co. Withdrawing from Voluntary Code on Ads," *New York Times*, 29 March 1966, p. 53.

60. "The Race for Safety Is On," *Business Week*, 11 June 1966, pp. 186–90. Asked by a reporter whether Ford would capitalize in its advertising on safety features its rivals lacked, president Arjay Miller responded, "Probably not. It wouldn't be fair because the others are not anti-safety. They'll move as fast as they can. But we plan to compete like hell on the safety features themselves."

61. As industry wags put it at the time, "McNamara is selling safety, but Chevy is selling cars." See Dan Cordtz, "The Face in the Mirror at General Motors," *Fortune*, August 1966, p. 208.

62. A turning point in the law concerning such restraints was *Virginia Pharmacy Board* v. *Virginia Consumer Council*, 425 U.S. 748 (1976). See also *Bates et al.* v. *State Bar of Arizona*, 433 U.S. 350 (1977).

63. Fellner, *Competition Among the Few*, pp. 188–89.

64. For surveys from rather different perspectives, see Mann in *Industrial Concentration*, pp. 142–46; and Ornstein, *Industrial Concentration and Advertising Intensity*, pp. 25–38. For a rigorous development of the underlying theory, see John Cable, "Market Structure, Advertising Policy and Intermarket Differences in Advertising Intensity," in Keith Cowling, ed., *Market Structure and Corporate Behaviour* (London: Gray-Mills, 1972), pp. 111–24.

65. Stephen Martin, "Theoretical Issues in the Specification of Models of Industrial Organization" (Workshop Paper no. 7705, Michigan State University Department of Economics, January 1978). Compare Ornstein, *Industrial Concentration and Advertising Intensity*, pp. 39–63, who finds significant positive (but not ∩-shaped) relationships using analogous advertising data without taking variables other than concentration into account. See also the comment by D. Stanton Smith et al. and reply by Ornstein, *Southern Economic Journal* 43 (January 1978): 653–60; Brian C. Brush, "Errors in the Measurement of Concentration and the Advertising-Concentration Controversy," *Southern Economic Journal* 44 (April 1978): 978–86; and John T. Scott, "Nonprice Competition in Banking Markets," *Southern Economic Journal* 43 (January 1978): 594–605.

Product differentiation, market structure,
and competition 391

without experiencing rapid market share erosion. As we have seen earlier in this chapter, the possession of such image advantages may or may not follow causally from intensive advertising. Usually there are other precipitating factors such as having pioneered a field, made an important qualitative innovation, or at least found a new sales pitch uniquely appealing to buyers. But when consumers can be induced to pay price premia to companies enjoying such image differentiation, the favored firms will more often than not find it worthwhile to spend appreciable sums on image reinforcement advertising.[68] Rivals who recognize the value of a premium image may also invest heavily in forms of nonprice competition (including advertising) directed toward securing comparable images or at least reducing the gap between themselves and the leading brands. Thus, strong image differentiation will cause, even if it is not caused by, relatively intensive advertising. Also, when a product line amenable to significant image differentiation and hence intense advertising exists, the firms with well-established images and sizeable market shares may have to spend less on advertising per sales dollar than less well-off rivals because they are building upon a superior goodwill asset[69] and because they may realize advertising scale economies. They therefore derive supranormal profits from both price premia and cost advantages. In this more complex view of the advertising-profitability nexus, intensive advertising per se is not necessarily a cause of monopoly power; but it interacts with and feeds back upon image advantages in a way that reflects and perhaps also sustains the power a well-accepted image confers. This, the author believes, is what underlies the positive advertising intensity coefficients in profitability regressions.

Further support for the barriers to entry hypothesis comes from a study that sought to distinguish the role of advertising in different types of media. Analyzing the 1963–65 profitability of 39 consumer goods industries, Michael Porter found that returns on stockholders' equity were more strongly correlated with the ratio of *network* television advertising outlays to sales than with the ratio of *total* media advertising expenditures to sales.[70] This suggests that the type of consumer goods image differentiation most apt to yield supranormal returns lends itself to peculiarly effective reinforcement through network television advertising in which, among other things, the leading national brands may enjoy scale economies.

Image differentiation, advertising, and/or some interaction of the two also appear to have feedback effects on market structure. During the 1950s and early 1960s there was a marked escalation of advertising expenditures in consumer goods industries. We observed in Chapter 4 that concentration changes have followed quite divergent trends in consumer as compared to producers' goods industries: average concentration rose significantly in the former and fell in the latter.[71] Moreover, for the entire 1947–72 period, although not for the 1963–72 subperiod, there is statistical evidence that concentration ratios rose more rapidly in consumer goods industries with relatively intense advertising than in industries with low advertising/sales ratios. These results suggest that there was something special about advertising-prone industries. The "something special" could have been promotional economies of scale that gave larger consumer goods sellers a cost advantage exploited in part (as Chapter 8 brought out) through market share-enhancing pricing strategies; image advantages similarly exploited and linked to intensive advertising; and/or a general and growing susceptibility of consumers in an increasingly complex, more impersonal marketplace to favor well-known brands, which in turn enhanced firms' incentive to advertise. An alternative hypothesis is that in industries amenable to strong image differentiation, marketing strategies tended to emphasize the introduction of new products and the concomitant heavy advertising of special product features. Since it is harder to match an innovative product design or advertising theme than price cuts, one might expect individual sellers' market shares to be more variable over time in industries characterized by strong product differentiation.[72] Under virtually any variant of Gibrat's law, this in turn should imply more rapidly rising concentration in such industries.[73]

Unfortunately, statistical data rich enough to discriminate among these hypotheses have not been available. When they do become available—e.g., through the Federal Trade Commission's Line of Business financial reporting program—several critical tests can be carried out. For one, it will be possible to determine whether the ratio of advertising and other marketing costs to sales varies inversely with individual firm market shares more strongly in industries of rapidly rising concentration. If so, the promotional economies of scale hypothesis will be supported. Second, under the theory of optimal dynamic limit pricing, one might expect profit margins to rise as an industry emerges from a period of rapidly rising concentration to a period of high and stable concentration. With a sufficient time series of annual industry cross sections, this and related hypotheses can be tested. And third, with market share data for several periods, it should be possible to estimate the parameters of Gibrat-type growth processes and relate them to interindustry concentration change differences. Until these and other analyses are accomplished, details of the links among advertising, monopoly power, and profitability are likely to remain obscure.

Market structure and product variety

We turn now to the very important question of whether other dimensions of product differentiation—e.g., in physical product features, convenience, and service—are systematically affected by differences in market structure. As Professor Chamberlin emphasized long ago, consumers have varied tastes, and to satisfy those tastes more or less fully necessitates variety in the goods and services offered.[74] But variety imposes costs of two main kinds: Product differentiation gives sellers some control over price, and hence leads to monopoly pricing distortions; and perhaps more significant, carrying the quest for variety very far conflicts with the realization of scale economies in production and marketing. Indeed, were it not for scale economies, every street corner would have its own conveniently located grocer, pharmacy, and lumber yard; and every household would brew its own beer to taste and weave its own blue denim in the precisely desired texture and weight. Within certain usually applicable bounds, then, a tradeoff must be struck among variety, cost, and price. The question we explore here is, How do diverse market structures affect the outcome of that tradeoff?

The problem is both complex and difficult. During the 1970s it enjoyed a renaissance of interest, and from impressive mathematical labors along several lines have come a few solid new insights. Our objective here is to pull the threads together and make some sense of them.

One aspect that imparts complexity to the problem is the diversity of behavioral assumptions one might make in comparing market structures. Plausible candidates include monopoly with blockaded entry; monopolists deterring entry through either pricing or investment policy (e.g., as they choose how many product variants to offer and how densely to pack geographic space with plants); oligopolistic nonprice rivalry

(66) For surveys from diverse ideological viewpoints, see Ferguson, *Advertising and Competition*, especially Chapters 2 and 6–9; and the exchange between Yale Brozen and H. Michael Mann in *Industrial Concentration*, especially pp. 123–26, 146–51.

(67) Lambin, *Advertising, Competition and Market Conduct*, pp. 115–18.

68. Exceptions certainly exist—e.g., the Hershey Company's long-standing but now abandoned policy of not advertising its chocolate products in the media. Also, without spending appreciable sums on advertising, IBM apparently enjoyed an image advantage commanding substantial price premia relative to rival computers of comparable data processing capacity. See Brian T. Ratchford and Gary T. Ford, "A Study of Prices and Market Shares in the Computer Mainframe Industry," *Journal of Business* 49 (April 1976): 194–218; and "ITEL's Powerful New Computer," *Business Week*, 25 October 1976, p. 74. Yet when IBM entered the minicomputer field, where it had not been a pioneer, it evidently found itself unable to secure similar price differentials. See "IBM's Challenge in Minicomputers," *Business Week*, 29 November 1976, p. 30.

69. Cf. Chapter 4, pp. 109–10 and Chapter 8, p. 260 *supra*.

70. Michael E. Porter, "Interbrand Choice, Media Mix and Market Performance," *American Economic Review* 66 (May 1976): 398–406.

71. See Chapter 4, p. 114 *supra*.

72. Compare Lambin, *Advertising, Competition and Market Conduct*, pp. 118–21; Lester G. Telser, "Advertising and Competition," *Journal of Political Economy* 72 (December 1964): 547–51; W. D. Reekie, "Advertising and Market Share Mobility," *Scottish Journal of Political Economy* 21 (June 1974): 143–58; and Richard E. Caves and Michael E. Porter, "Market Structure, Oligopoly, and Stability of Market Shares," *Journal of Industrial Economics* 26 (June 1978): 289–313.

73. Cf. Chapter 4, pp. 148–49 *supra*.

74. *The Theory of Monopolistic Competition*. See also Chapter 2, p. 24 *supra*.

with interdependence in pricing; rivalry among firms ignoring their interdependence on both price and quality dimensions, i.e., monopolistic competition; and various "ideal" cases in which monopolists or monopolistic competitors are induced to behave optimally in both price and quality decisions, e.g., through government subsidies or controls. Not all of these cases and their manifold variants have been explored theoretically. Nevertheless, a good deal can be said about several of the more interesting cases.

One of the surest ways to call forth the wrong amount of variety is to set, either through governmental regulation or a rigid cartel mechanism, a uniformly high monopoly price and then let individual producers compete for business on nonprice bases. Two kinds of distortions commonly result, both of which are illustrated by U.S. airline regulation during the 1960s and early 1970s.[75] First, the offering of no-frills flights with high seating density was discouraged, and so consumers who preferred to sacrifice convenience or luxury to save money were badly served. Until the Civil Aeronautics Board began reforming its rules in the mid-1970s, European air travellers were better off than their U.S. counterparts in this respect, for an abundant array of low-priced advance-booking charter flights existed alongside high-priced regularly scheduled service. Second, even for the average consumer, the level of quality provided was often not optimal. Under the regulated, cartelized rate structure prevailing during the 1960s, price-cost margins tended to rise with distance. This encouraged airlines to offer too many flights over long hops and too few on short hauls relative to the flight frequency-fare preferences of the average air traveller.

Quite generally, society is almost always better off when consumers enjoy a wide range of choices between high-quality, high-priced and low-quality, low-priced opportunities than when they face a severely restricted choice set. Something approximating the desired level of variety in this sense is likely to emerge whenever entry is relatively easy, as it is, for example, in most of the retail trades. Thus, if the typical consumer can choose among several well-stocked, price-competitive supermarkets within ten minutes' driving distance of home and friendly but high-priced "Mom and Pop" grocery and drug stores within five blocks' walking distance; or between a low-priced, minimum-service gasoline station and a high-priced station offering advertised brands, accepting credit cards, and washing side windows, the state of welfare can hardly be seriously amiss.

With more difficult entry and high concentration, a desirable range of price-quality choices may also (but less certainly) result if sellers engage in appropriate forms of price discrimination.[76] The automobile industry provides an illustration. Some new car buyers desire only basic transportation and are unable or unwilling to pay more than a bare-bones price for it. Others want luxury, prestige, the feeling of power, and so on and are willing to pay well for them. The auto makers react to this in several ways, of which two are immediately relevant. First, they offer new car models spanning a broad range of prices. The key to the profitability of this strategy lies not in the range of prices per se, but in the fact that the prestigious high-price cars typically yield much higher profit margins than low-priced cars.[77] General Motors' pretax profit on a bottom-of-the-line Chevrolet is at most a few hundred dollars, whereas it is probably several thousand dollars on a Cadillac El Dorado. With the much higher profit margins on top-of-the-line cars, GM is in effect extracting surplus from consumers to whom prestige and luxury have high value. Second, surplus is also extracted from inframarginal consumers through the pricing of optional equipment. A "leaked" company memorandum on the 1966 Ford Galaxie four-door sedan revealed that the wholesale price of the basic car with standard equipment exceeded standard accounting costs by 17 percent.[78] Markups on optional equipment were characteristically much higher—e.g., 293 percent for a more powerful V-8 engine, 123 percent for power steering, and 58 percent for air conditioning. Through such discriminatory pricing, the auto makers respond sensitively to consumers' variegated wants, and at least from the standpoint of allocative efficiency, their responsiveness is laudable. As always, judging whether the income distribution consequences are equitable is more difficult.

A more general perspective on the links be-

Total surplus

Producer's surplus

A	AB	B
Relatively bland		Relatively bitter

tween market structure and product variety can be gained by extending the analogy introduced in Chapter 8 between product characteristics and geographic space.[79] Most products and services have, of course, multidimensional characteristics, but the essence of the matter can be grasped by considering a situation in which there is only one more or less continuously variable characteristic—e.g., the turning radius of a car, or the color of a garment (varying over a spectrum), or the speed of a restaurant's service. Figure 14.2 provides the initial framework. The horizontal axis represents a one-dimensional space over which real or perceived product characteristics can vary. Consumers' preferences are mapped by their location in product characteristics space. If, for example, the relevant dimension is the bitterness of a beer, derived from the amount and type of hops used, consumers whose most favored beers are relatively bitter (e.g., Pilseners) would have their preferences located farther to the right on the diagram, while those preferring blander beers would be located more to the left. We assume without serious loss of generality a uniform distribution and intensity of preferences over the relevant portion of product characteristics space.

Figure 14.2 looks somewhat like the geographic pricing diagrams presented in Chap-

ters 8 and 11, but its vertical dimension is in fact quite different conceptually. It represents not prices, but consumers' and producers' surpluses. Concretely, the upper (solid) tent-shaped line shows at any abscissa point the total surplus,

75. See Lawrence J. White, "Quality Variation When Prices Are Regulated," *Bell Journal of Economics and Management Science* 3 (Autumn 1972): 425–36; idem, "Quality, Competition, and Regulation: Evidence from the Airline Industry," in Richard E. Caves and Marc Roberts, eds., *Regulating the Product: Quality and Variety* (Cambridge, Mass.: Harvard University Press, 1975), pp. 17–35; and Douglas and Miller, *Economic Regulation of Domestic Air Transport*, Chapters 4–6.

76. For a more general analysis of the relationships between optimal product variety and price discrimination, see Michael Spence, "Product Selection, Fixed Costs, and Monopolistic Competition," *Review of Economic Studies* 43 (June 1976): 218–20.

77. See Bernard A. Girod, Joseph Vinso, and H. Paul Root, "Profit Comparisons and Product Mix in the Automobile Industry" (Working Paper no. 60, University of Michigan Bureau of Business Research, May 1972).

78. Testimony of Ralph Nader in U.S., Congress, Senate, Select Committee on Small Business hearings, *Planning, Regulation, and Competition: Automobile Industry—1968*, 90th Cong., 2nd sess., 1968, p. 330.

79. This analysis is drawn with only minor modifications from F. M. Scherer, "The Welfare Economics of Product Variety: An Application to the Ready-To-Eat Cereals Industry," *Journal of Industrial Economics*, forthcoming in 1979.

Product differentiation, market structure, and competition **395**

consumers' plus producer's, realized from sales to consumers with preferences located at the corresponding point in horizontal characteristics space.[80] The lower (dashed) line shows the producer's surplus, and so the vertical distance between the upper and lower functions reveals the total consumers' surplus derived by consumers at any given point in product characteristics space.

In Figure 14.2, the supply of only two product variants, **A** and **B**, is assumed. These products have characteristics exactly matching the preferences of consumers located at points A and B in characteristics space. By assumption, however, consumer preferences are distributed uniformly over space. Those whose preferences are imperfectly satisfied by **A** or **B** must either buy **A** or **B** or spend more of their income on unrepresented (perhaps quite different) products—e.g., wine, or orange juice, or sleeping pills. The loss of utility experienced by a consumer with preferences at, say, boundary point AB from having to make do with imperfect substitutes **A** or **B** leads to a lower quantity demanded. Demand is choked off more, the farther the consumer's preferences lie from the characteristics of available products. This, combined with the assumption of a uniform distribution of preferences over characteristics space, gives rise to the tent shape of the surplus

functions, whose maxima are the points in space where product characteristics exactly match some consumers' preferences.

Let us consider now the introduction of a third product, **C**, at the point in characteristics space intermediate between A and B, as in Figure 14.3. This means that consumers in the neighborhood of C will be satisfied better, leading to an increase in consumption by those consumers, and hence to increases in consumers' and producers' surplus represented by the new tent-shaped functions with maxima above point C. If the prices of the various products are equal, purchases will be divided among products at boundaries (i.e., AC and CB) where the total surplus functions intersect. Assuming uniformly distributed preferences, this implies an equal division of the market.

Whether or not product **C** will be offered depends critically upon the fixed costs of supplying it—that is, the required investment in research, development, plant and equipment, and introductory marketing—and upon market structure. Market structure matters in the following way. If the market is at least locally monopolized and entry by outsiders at C is blockaded, the relevant gross payoff to the producer of **A** and **B** contemplating introducing **C** is the diamond-shaped

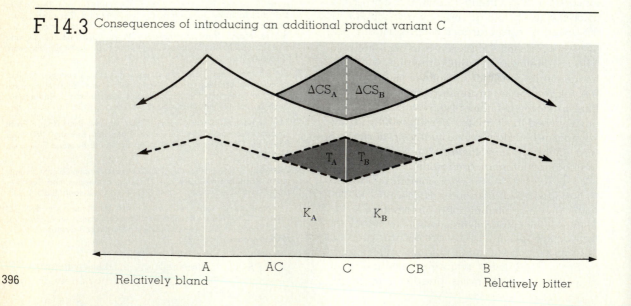

F 14.3 Consequences of introducing an additional product variant C

area consisting of triangles T_A and T_B.[81] Assuming the variable unit production and distribution costs of **C** to be the same as for **A** and **B**, T_A and T_B represent increases in sales revenue from the producer's perspective, although as Figure 14.3 is drawn, they are actually redistributions from what would be consumers' surplus in the absence of **C** to producer's surplus. If the sum of T_A plus T_B exceeds the fixed cost of supplying **C**, our monopolist will offer **C**; if fixed costs exceed $T_A + T_B$, **C** will not be offered, at least under the monopoly conditions postulated.

Let us however relax the assumption that entry is blockaded. A monopolistic competitor considering offering **C** in competition with other sellers' products **A** and **B** and assuming, Cournot-like, that **C** is priced at the same level as the unchanged prices of **A** and **B**, perceives itself as gaining the diamond-shaped surplus $T_A + T_B$ *plus* the surpluses K_A and K_B, which are transfers of producers' surplus from the maker(s) of **A** and **B** to the producer of **C**. Such transfers are sometimes referred to as "cannibalization." The monopolistic competitor unconcerned about whence K_A and K_B come views itself as gaining a larger surplus through product introduction than does the monopolist of **A** and **B**. It is entirely possible that fixed costs exceed $T_A + T_B$, in which case the monopolist enjoying blockaded entry will not launch product **C**, while they are less than $T_A + T_B + K_A + K_B$, in which case a monopolistic competitor *will* offer **C**. Such reasoning lies at the heart of economists' conclusion that a greater variety of substitute products is likely to appear under monopolistic competition, with entry open, than under monopoly with closed entry.[82]

If there is monopoly but entry into C is open, the monopolist may choose also to offer **C** and preempt entry that would otherwise cause it to lose surpluses K_A and K_B. If so, as much product variety may arise under such entry-deterring monopoly (or oligopoly) as under monopolistic competition, other things (such as pre- and postentry prices) being equal.

This seeming virtue of monopolistic competition and entry-deterring monopoly can be carried so far that it becomes a vice. From the standpoint of society as a whole, assuming that a dollar's worth of costs, consumers' surplus, or

producer's surplus are equally valued, a new product should be introduced if its net addition to surplus—i.e., $\Delta CS_A + \Delta CS_B$ in Figure 14.3—exceeds the fixed cost of introduction. (T_A, T_B, K_A, and K_B are irrelevant to the calculation of net social benefit because, as transfers, they cancel out.) That diamond-shaped area may be either larger or smaller than the wall tent-shaped surplus guiding the decisions of monopolistic competitors or entry-deterring monopolists. As Figure 14.3 is drawn, $\Delta CS_A + \Delta CS_B$ is considerably smaller than $T_A + T_B + K_A + K_B$, and so if fixed costs are substantial (i.e., greater than $\Delta CS_A + \Delta CS_B$), but less than the T, K sum, monopolistic competition is likely to lead to *too much* product variety relative to the social welfare-maximizing level.

How can one tell whether the optimal amount of product variety will be overshot in this way? Two sets of considerations provide guidance.

First, the relative flatness or steepness of the surplus functions matters. With relatively flat surplus functions, the net social gain $\Delta CS_A + \Delta CS_B$ is likely to be small relative to the amount of cannibalization $K_A + K_B$, and so excessive product proliferation is apt to be encouraged. The surplus function slopes cannot be measured directly, but they have observable correlates. A

---

80. More exactly, the vertical ordinate for any given point in horizontal product characteristics space measures the integral under the inverse demand function for all consumers whose preferences (or the relevant part of whose preferences) match that point, holding product prices constant and netting out the variable costs of production and distribution.

81. To be more precise, the producer will view as its gross benefit from introducing **C** the discounted present value of the surpluses T_A and T_B over all years in which product **C** is expected to be sold.

82. See Spence, "Product Selection, Fixed Costs, and Monopolistic Competition," pp. 217–35; Michael C. Lovell, "Product Differentiation and Market Structure," *Western Economic Journal* 8 (June 1970): 137–39; Kelvin Lancaster, "Socially Optimal Product Differentiation," *American Economic Review* 65 (September 1975): 580–85; J. E. Meade, "The Optimal Balance Between Economies of Scale and Variety of Products: An Illustrative Model," *Economica* 41 (November 1974): 359–67; and Lawrence J. White, "Market Structure and Product Varieties," *American Economic Review* 67 (March 1977): 179–87. Compare Hayne E. Leland, "Quality Choices and Competition," *American Economic Review* 67 (March 1977): 135–36.

Product differentiation, market structure, and competition **397**

steep surplus function slope means that people shun products located some distance from their most preferred characteristics; a flat slope means that consumers readily substitute a product of less than ideal characteristics if they cannot get exactly what they want. Strong qualitative preferences imply steep slopes and sizeable consumers' surplus gains; fickleness among consumers toward substitutes implies small gains. Also, with steep surplus function slopes, the net noncannibalized sales (or more exactly, gross margin) increase $T_A + T_B$ that results from introducing a new product is likely to be relatively large.

Second, cannibalization will be greater, all else held equal, the higher the elevation of the producers' surplus functions (dashed lines) is in relation to the total surplus functions (solid lines), or more simply, the greater is the ratio of producers' surplus to consumers' surplus. This in turn depends upon two factors. If producers maximize profit in the short-run sense, setting marginal cost equal to marginal revenue, the ratio of producer's to consumers' surplus will be higher when the inverse demand function for an individual product is concave downward (i.e., with a relatively flat top) than when it is convex downward.[83] With concave-downward demand functions, it should be noted, the quantity of a product demanded falls off sharply as the product's price is increased, holding the prices of substitute products constant, which is another manifestation of the tendency for cannibalization to be relatively extensive when products are close substitutes for one another. Producers' surplus is also apt to be relatively high when the oligopolistic sellers of substitute products respect their mutual interdependence in pricing, cooperating in a joint profit-maximizing policy, as compared to behaving in the Cournot-like manner of monopolistic competitors.

In sum, excessive product variety is most likely to be forthcoming when there is open entry or the threat of entry that insiders choose to preempt, high substitutability among product variants, relatively high gross profit margins (i.e., before the deduction of fixed costs); modest sales growth as a consequence of adding an additional product to the existing set; and fixed product introduc-

tion costs that are substantial but less than the amount of potential producers' surplus cannibalization. There is little systematic evidence on how frequently this constellation of conditions occurs. It is certainly possible to find cases in which an inference seems well supported that product proliferation has been carried beyond the point at which marginal social benefits equal social costs. The U.S. ready-to-eat cereal industry during the 1960s, with close respect for mutual interdependence in pricing, price-manufacturing cost margins in excess of 50 percent, fickle consumers, and modest real (noncannibalized) growth despite intensive new product launching, is a probable example.[84] Exploring a wide range of parameters with a simple partial equilibrium simulation model, Michael Spence found a tendency for the number of product variants under monopolistic competition to exceed the social optimum in all cases but those with both high fixed product launching costs and low cross elasticities of demand (i.e., poor substitutability).[85] How realistic or general his results are is unclear. On this important issue, more theoretical and (especially) empirical research is badly needed.

The dynamics of automobile styling rivalry

Further perspective on the nature of product 'quality' choices under oligopoly can be gleaned by considering the dynamics of model style changes in the automobile industry.[86] In this facet of their operations, the leading American producers exhibit a complex blend of rivalry and respect for acknowledged rules of the game (such as the avoidance of daring departures with uncertain mass consumption appeal). After pent-up World War II demands were satisfied, a three-year model cycle became the industry norm. Typically, grille, molding, and other details were altered in a minor facelift a year after some completely new model was introduced; in the second year more extensive changes were made; and after three years the cycle began again as most of the major body parts—fenders, hoods, rear decks, doors, and the like—were totally restyled. Adherence to this three-year cycle was not inviolate, however. On numerous occasions some firm has broken to a two-year cycle in the hope of increasing its market penetration, and wholly new lines (such as the Thunderbird, Edsel, Corvair, Mustang, Dart, Nova, Vega, and Omni) have been introduced at irregular intervals.

Although in some respects the Big Three have been vigorously independent in their styling rivalry, in others their behavior has been conditioned by clear respect for interdependence. One manifestation was their response to the demand for small cars. During the 1950s foreign compact cars began making rapidly increasing inroads into the U.S. market. All three U.S. industry leaders hesitated in introducing the small car models they had already engineered for two reasons. First, profit margins rise with car size, and it was feared that U.S.-made compacts would cannibalize sales away from the more profitable standard domestic models. Second, according to White, because they recognized that if one Big Three member introduced a small car, all would do so, they therefore wanted to be sure that the market was large enough to accommodate all three profitably.[87] All three ultimately unveiled their compacts in the fall of 1959. As those compacts gradually picked up length and weight, leaving a void again filled by imports during the 1960s, reluctance by the Big Three to create additional competition in the low-price range became evident again.

Changes in the industry's competitive and regulatory environment have also acted to slow down the model change cycle from its three-year norm. In 1970 and 1971 General Motors and Ford announced their intent to introduce major changes less frequently, mainly as a consequence of cost pressures resulting from the government-mandated introduction of pollution control and safety devices and intensified price competition from imports. Some deceleration may have occurred,[88] but analysis of the subsequent events is complicated by the impact of government pressures to design smaller, more energy-efficient vehicles. Another significant change in the industry's behavior was the increasingly apparent tendency for Chrysler to follow General Motors' styling lead, supposedly because several of its more daring styling innovations were received poorly by consumers.[89]

Within these restricted bounds, the auto makers have tried hard to secure market advantage through the introduction of new styles. As a result, the number of distinct American-made models increased from 205 in 1949 to 239 in 1959 and 370 in 1967.[90] Three factors energize the process of styling competition. First, consumers are highly sensitive to design differences. The company that comes up with a winning design can make heavy inroads into rival market shares. Second, it takes from 15 to 24 months to produce a new model after a final design commitment has been made. The firm caught in a position of styling inferiority for such a long interval suffers considerably. Therefore, auto producers believe they cannot afford not to cover themselves against rival thrusts. Knowledge that others are preparing new models, coupled with uncertainty over the exact

83. See Spence, "Product Selection, Fixed Costs, and Monopolistic Competition," pp. 224–25. If demand functions are linear and marginal cost is constant, consumers' surplus is a constant one-half of producer's surplus regardless of the specific parameter values influencing the profit-maximizing price.

84. See Scherer, "The Welfare Economics of Product Variety"; and Richard Schmalensee, "Entry Deterrence in the Ready-To-Eat Breakfast Cereal Industry," *Bell Journal of Economics* 9 (Autumn 1978): 305–27.

85. Michael Spence, "Product Differentiation and Welfare," *American Economic Review* 66 (May 1976): 407–14.

86. For various views, see Lawrence J. White, *The Automobile Industry Since 1945* (Cambridge, Mass.: Harvard University Press, 1971), Chapters 11 and 12; Weiss, *Economics and American Industry*, pp. 357–71; Hans Brems, "Response Lags and Nonprice Competition with Special Reference to the Automobile Industry," in Mary Jean Bowman, ed., *Expectations, Uncertainty, and Business Behavior* (New York: Social Science Research Council, 1958), pp. 134–43; Roger Sherman and George Hoffer, "Does Automobile Style Change Pay Off?," *Applied Economics* 3 (September 1971): 153–65; U.S., Congress, Senate, Committee on the Judiciary, Subcommittee on Antitrust and Monopoly report, *Administered Prices: Automobiles*, 85th Cong., 2nd sess., 1958, pp. 77–94; and the Senate Select Committee on Small Business hearings, *Planning, Regulation, and Competition, passim*.

87. White, *The Automobile Industry*, pp. 182–85.

88. But see "Detroit's Dilemma on Prices," *Business Week*, 20 January 1975, p. 83, on the problems encountered in slowing down the cycle when "someone is always trying to get out ahead." See also "GM Bucks New Trend: Will Restyle Big Cars for '80," *Chicago Tribune*, 7 May 1978, on the reappearance of a three-year cycle.

89. See "The Small Car Blues at General Motors," *Business Week*, 16 March 1974, p. 77.

90. White, *The Automobile Industry*, p. 203.

Product differentiation, market structure, and competition 399

character of their plans, compels each firm to sustain its own style change effort and also to engage in such James Bondian tactics as flying observation planes over rival testing grounds to obtain intelligence on new style developments. Third, the difficulty of predicting how consumers will respond to new designs interacts with the self-confidence auto executives develop from climbing above the pack to a top management position, leading each decision-making group to take an optimistic view of its chances for making market share gains through styling innovation.

The game played in this styling arena is not an inexpensive one. Using 1949 as a benchmark year of normal design modification, Fisher, Griliches, and Kaysen estimated that the extra cost of new dies and tooling attributable to the acceleration of auto styling rivalry in the 1950s averaged $560 million per year between 1956 and 1960, or $102 per automobile produced.[91] White found tooling costs in the 1960s to have averaged approximately $92 per car sold by the Big Three.[92]

Although the style changes put forward by one auto maker tend on the average to be offset by rival countermoves, it is not clear that the leading producers are worse off as a result of their competition, since the costs added by rapid change have been passed along to consumers in the form of higher prices. A profit sacrifice would result only if significantly fewer cars were purchased because of the higher unit costs and prices. One's first impulse is to suspect that the opposite is true: Overall car demand has been strengthened by a pace of styling change that makes three-year-old models passé. This is probably correct, but for rather subtle reasons. Ignoring short-run variations, the flow of new cars sold each year depends upon the *stock* of autos consumers wish to hold and on the average life of autos comprising that stock. Does rapid styling change affect either of these magnitudes?

No obvious link between style change and average life is evident, for a visit to any junkyard reveals that the vast majority of all autos there are scrapped for other than aesthetic reasons. To this point, however, we shall return later. There is more reason to believe that the size of the equilibrium stock is affected by style changes. Used car prices fall more rapidly in an environment of rapid styling obsolescence. Outmoded cars are therefore sold at relatively low prices long before their physical utility is spent. With large numbers of stylistically obsolescent automobiles available at low prices, many persons (e.g., teenagers, college students, and other indigents) are able to become car owners when they could not afford to do so if used car prices fell more slowly. Thus, rapid styling change has an output-expanding effect analogous to first- or second-degree price discrimination. The auto makers extract consumers' surplus from buyers affluent and eager enough to pay a high price every two or three years for a vehicle with the latest style gimmicks. Buyers with low ability or willingness to pay are reached through the used car market. At least up to some point, therefore, styling competition probably increases aggregate industry profits. Whether it is carried only to the point of joint profit maximization or beyond is difficult to judge. In view of the evident lack of restraint during the 1950s and 1960s and the auto makers' attempt to lengthen the model change cycle in the 1970s, it is not unreasonable to infer that the maximum-profit point was overstepped.

For auto producers whose weaker image or limited dealer networks lead to lower average sales of any given model, a rapid rate of styling change is generally disadvantageous.[93] If they match the giants in frequency of change, they must amortize the fixed costs of redesign and retooling over a smaller volume, suffering substantially higher unit costs. If they change models less frequently, they run the risk of even greater market penetration sacrifices. For them, the styling rivalry game offers little but negative payoffs. And there is no way for them to escape other than leaving the industry (as the smaller companies have done, one by one), since the rules are dictated by producers willing, at least up to 1971, to sustain a rapid style change pace.

Finally, how about the consumer? Does the buyer benefit or lose from frequent style changes? Clearly, new car buyers pay more than if model changes were effected less often. Equally clearly, they freely elect to do so, for they have the option of holding on to their present auto longer or buying last year's model or an import restyled less frequently. By the stern criterion of consumer sovereignty, styling rivalry would seem to emerge with only minor scars. Still this is not completely convincing. The interdependence of consumer preferences complicates matters. Smith may buy a new model only because he fears that if he does not and neighbor Jones does, his utility will be reduced. Jones perceives the situation symmetrically, and both end up buying new models, though neither might if they could find some way to enforce mutual (and more widespread) buying restraint. This gloomy view may be wrong, imputing to the consuming public values held only by academicians and other malcontents. But it is not necessarily wrong, and therefore one may well harbor qualms about the social desirability of frenetic style change rivalry.

Monopoly, competition, and product durability

In choosing product quality policies, the sellers of durable goods must among other things decide how much durability they will build in. As a rule, it costs more to produce a more durable product, but the product then yields its services to buyers over a longer period of time, which means that the seller must wait longer for replacement sales. Does market structure affect the tradeoff sellers make on this point? The question has been explored in a number of theoretical works. For the most part, only the polar alternatives of pure nondiscriminating monopoly and pure competition have been considered, and all the relevant analyses assume *inter alia* perfect expectations,[94] including perfect foreknowledge by buyers of how long a durable good will last or what its rate of physical deterioration will be. This of course is quite unrealistic. Ordinary consumers are likely to have only a foggy notion of how long the durable goods they purchase will hold up. Knowledgeable purchasers of producer's durables commonly exercise close control through design or performance specifications, thereby minimizing the seller's discretion (on which the theoretical analyses focus). The reader may therefore be sympathetic (or even grateful) if only a bare summary of the principal analytic findings is presented.

Perhaps the most useful and interesting point of departure is the work of Peter Swan, who, after correcting important omissions in earlier analyses, concluded that with perfect foresight, perfect capital markets, and the absence of either economies or diseconomies of scale in production, monopolists and competitors would choose identical durability parameters.[95] The essence of his logic is best captured by considering separately the cases in which durable goods are leased or rented out by the producer, as compared to selling them outright.

In the leasing case, how often the good wears out and has to be replaced is mainly a concern of the lessor. Ignoring possible disruptions associated with installation, durability should be a matter of indifference to the lessee. A monopolistic lessor will of course restrict the supply of its durable good's services more than a set of competitive lessors would, but that classic monopoly restriction is effected by setting the rental rate higher than the competitive rate. Given the choice of price and service levels over time, both the monopolist and the competitor maximize their profits by choosing the degree of durability (and hence rate of replacement) that minimizes the discounted cost of providing the chosen stream of durable good services. And with unit production costs not dependent upon the scale of production, that cost-minimizing durability level will be the same for either monopolist or competitor.

Results for the sales case follow from the leasing logic. With perfect capital markets and fore-

91. Franklin M. Fisher, Zvi Griliches, and Carl Kaysen, "The Costs of Automobile Model Changes Since 1949," *Journal of Political Economy* 70 (October 1962): 433–51.

92. This weighted average was computed from the data in White, *The Automobile Industry*, p. 204.

93. See Chapter 4, pp. 112–13 *supra* and John A. Menge, "Style Change Costs as a Market Weapon," *Quarterly Journal of Economics* 76 (November 1962): 632–47.

94. On some complications that can arise from imperfect expectations, see Ronald H. Coase, "Durability and Monopoly," *Journal of Law and Economics* 15 (April 1972): 143–49; Richard Schmalensee, "Market Structure, Durability, and Maintenance Effort," *Review of Economic Studies* 41 (April 1974): 281; and Wolfhard Ramm, "On the Durability of Capital Goods under Imperfect Market Conditions," *American Economic Review* 64 (September 1974): 794–95.

95. Peter L. Swan, "Durability of Consumption Goods," *American Economic Review* 60 (December 1970): 884–94; *idem*, "The Durability of Goods and Regulation of Monopoly," *Bell Journal of Economics and Management Science* 2 (Spring 1971): 347–57; and E. Sieper and P. L. Swan, "Monopoly and Competition in the Market for Durable Goods," *Review of Economic Studies* 40 (July 1973): 333–51.

sight, the profit-maximizing sales price for a durable good will be exactly equal to the discounted present value of the benefits to marginal users under an optimally priced leasing policy.[96] Neglecting differences in incentives to maintain the durable good conscientiously, the producer under any given market structure should therefore be indifferent between selling and leasing, and the optimal level of durability is consequently the same as under the leasing approach. Since it is invariant with respect to market structure under leasing, it must also be invariant under a sales policy. Even if selling were preferred to leasing, the monopolist's incentive to restrict output can be accommodated by setting the sales price at an appropriately high level. Given the profit-maximizing amount of output restriction, the monopolist's profits are maximized by choosing the least-cost means of 'producing' the services ultimately consumed. This is achieved by offering goods with the cost-minimizing degree of durability.

These conclusions do not always survive the modification of important assumptions.[97] For three sets of modifications, the choice of durabilities continues to be invariant with respect to market structure under a leasing policy, but not under a sales policy. First, when capital markets are imperfect and buyers have a higher interest (i.e., discount) rate than durable good producers, durability will be lower under monopoly than under competition.[98] This is so because future replacement outlays are discounted more heavily by buyers than by sellers, and a monopolist will take advantage of this imbalance by reducing durability to stimulate replacement sales relatively more heavily than it would as a lessor or competitive seller. Second, the Swan analysis ignores the possibility that buyers may incur maintenance costs to prolong the life of their equipment. If the cost of maintenance is beyond the durable good supplier's control, the ratio of the cost of an hour's maintenance effort to the cost of the good will be lower under monopoly (with elevated goods sale prices) than under competition. Thus, relatively more maintenance will be done under monopoly and the good's life will be extended, *ceteris paribus*. Taking this into account, the monopolist is likely to adjust its choices in the direction of reduced durability

(and also reduced prices).[99] Third, it is quite common for the costs of using a durable good to rise over time as the good gradually deteriorates. The more frequently the durable good is replaced, the lower average operating costs will be, but the higher capital (i.e., replacement purchase) costs will be. Under a high-price monopoly policy, this tradeoff will be biased toward later replacement than under competitive pricing.[100] Recognizing this, the monopolist seller of a durable good will adjust its durability choice, although the direction of the change cannot be predicted unambiguously without additional information on the pattern of operating costs.

Enough unexplored variations on the optimal durability theme exist to occupy mathematically inclined economists for some time to come. However, we complete our survey now by returning to an issue with more real-world content: the durability practices of American automobile manufacturers.

There is clear evidence that the durability of American-made automobiles fell appreciably during the 1950s and 1960s. White reports, for example, that 71 percent of the cars manufactured by the Big Three in 1948 were still registered nine years later, but only 55 percent of their 1958 models survived for nine years.[101] Why this occurred is disputed. White found that the pattern of declining durability persisted even after taking into account income levels, scrap metal prices, and the rising cost of repairs. He proposed that the change could have resulted from U.S. auto makers' recognition that reduced durability diminished the stock of used cars, and (assuming price-inelastic demand for used cars in the aggregate) raised used car prices, thereby increasing the attractiveness of early trade-ins by new car owners.[102] However, using a more elaborate econometric model, Parks found that after the tendency for rising repair costs to induce earlier scrapping was taken into account, there was a weak tendency for 1960s vintage cars to last longer, not shorter, than their 1950s counterparts.[103] Independent evidence from auto rental company records suggests a gradual decline in the cost of maintaining and repairing the cars in their fleets.[104] At least for the early years of the typical car's life during which rental companies hold their vehicles, this is consistent with a trend

402

toward rising durability and/or mechanical quality.

A facet of U.S. auto makers' behavior meriting less favorable marks was their selection in the late 1960s of "eggshell" front and rear end designs susceptible to substantial, costly damage in minor collisions.[105] One possible rationalization is that the designs were just what consumers wanted. On this, it is difficult to restrain one's skepticism. A second explanation is that bumpers receded and grilles and trunk trim protruded because auto makers were attempting to maximize useable room within length constraints. This does not, however, explain the recession of bumpers *within* the limiting dimensions of crash-sensitive parts. It is also difficult to reconcile with U.S. auto producers' acknowledged failure to emulate their European counterparts in squeezing more interior body room out of given dimensions.[106] A third possibility is that the eggshell design approach was profitable, given the differing degrees of competition in original equipment as compared to replacement parts sales.[107] As suggested earlier, the manufacturer's profit margin on new cars with standard equipment is typically slim, and margins may have been declining during the 1960s owing to increasing price competition from European and Japanese producers enjoying *inter alia* the advantage of undervalued currencies. But once a car is sold, the manufacturer has a near monopoly on the sale of replacement "crash parts"; and there is reason to believe that the profit margins on such sales are very high. It is at least conceivable that U.S. producers chose crash-vulnerable designs to compensate through higher replacement part sales for the profits lost as a result of increasing competition on original vehicle sales.[108] No direct evidence of such a strategy choice is known, nor is it likely that the auto makers would willingly let such evidence become available. Yet one wonders.

Conclusion

Product differentiation is both desirable and inescapable. Even the most questionable form—image differentiation—confers social benefits. Yet

96. Among other things, a kind of arbitrage by firms buying durable goods and then leasing them competitively will help ensure this result. For instance, when IBM reduced the sales prices of its System 360 computers by 6 percent relative to lease prices in 1966, it precipitated the rapid expansion of computer leasing companies who ultimately brought competitive pressure to bear on IBM's lease rates.

97. In his seminal articles, Swan accepted restrictive assumptions concerning the nature of short- and long-run production cost functions and the dynamic process by means of which an equilibrium stock of durable goods is accumulated. On the modification of Swan's original constant production cost assumption in a comparative statics framework, see Sieper and Swan, "Monopoly and Competition," pp. 347–51; David Levhari and Yoram Peles, "Market Structure and Durability," *Bell Journal of Economics and Management Science* 4 (Spring 1973): 244–48; and Richard W. Parks, "The Demand and Supply of Durable Goods and Durability," *American Economic Review* 64 (March 1974): 45. Such analyses indicate that the monopolist may supply less durable products than competitive firms when unit production costs rise with the scale of operation and more durable products in the opposite case. Intuitively, lower durability implies more production of the durable good to supply a given flow of services. The monopolist is more (less) inclined to reduce durability and increase production when marginal costs are lower (higher) as a consequence of its high prices and monopolistically restricted production volume. However, especially in the diseconomies of scale case, much depends upon whether the monopolist is assumed to have the same number of plants, each smaller, as the number operated by a competitive industry.

For analyses that imply identical durability under monopoly and competition in steady-state dynamic equilibrium, see Leonardo Auernheimer and Thomas R. Saving, "Market Organization and the Durability of Durable Goods," *Econometrica* 45 (January 1977): 219–28; and Peter L. Swan, "Product Durability under Monopoly and Competition: Comment," *Econometrica* 45 (January 1977): 229–35.

98. See Robert J. Barro, "Monopoly and Contrived Depreciation," *Journal of Political Economy* 80 (May/June 1972): 598–602; and Ramm, "On the Durability of Capital Goods," pp. 787–96.

99. Schmalensee, "Market Structure, Durability, and Maintenance Effort," pp. 277–86. It is worth noting that in this and the next case discussed in the text, the monopolist would prefer to lease, all else equal. The problems here are analogous to those under which vertical integration yields efficiency gains. Cf. Chapter 10, pp. 300–303 *supra*.

100. Teddy T. Su, "Durability of Consumption Goods Reconsidered," *American Economic Review* 65 (March 1975): 148–57.

101. White, *The Automobile Industry*, p. 194.

102. White, *The Automobile Industry*, pp. 190–98. On the applicable theory, compare Peter L. Swan, "Optimum Durability, Second-Hand Markets, and Planned Obsolescence," *Journal of Political Economy* 80 (May/June 1972): 575–85.

103. Richard W. Parks, "Determinants of Scrapping Rates for Postwar Vintage Automobiles," *Econometrica* 45 (July 1977): 1099–1115.

104. "Technology: Rising Reliability of American Cars," *New York Times*, 7 September 1977, Sec. IV, p. 1.

105. See "Personal Finance: Insurance Industry Blames Car Designs for Much of Rise in Auto Policy Rates," *New York Times*, 15 March 1971, p. 55.

advertising and product proliferation can be overdone, and that is cause for concern. Advertising campaigns can be carried far beyond the point where they are informative or add spice to consumption, serving merely to barrage the consumer with mutually conflicting or even misleading claims. Prime offenders in this respect include the soap, proprietary drug, cosmetic and toilet goods, cigarette, cereal, beverage, and automobile industries. Image differentiation reinforced through intensive advertising can also be an important barrier to entry, permitting the sustained realization of monopoly profits. Product varieties can be proliferated until scale economy losses outweigh gains from the more complete satisfaction of consumer demands. Thus, high prices, waste, resource misallocation, and income redistribution are the consequences of excessive product differentiation.

The market system as such has no fully satisfactory mechanism for curbing advertising abuses, which are probably the most egregious manifestation of product differentiation run amok. If the problems are considered grievous enough to warrant corrective action, much of the burden must fall upon government. The Federal Trade Commission is already charged, as backstop to a voluntary private group, with detecting and enjoining misleading practices in advertising. The job is not an easy one, for the line between misleading and merely persuading is fuzzy, and too heavy a hand at the controls could suppress desirable initiative and creativity.

In cases where advertising is patently excessive, the government might intervene to induce a reduction. The ban on cigarette advertising over television and radio is an example, but not a successful one. A considerable volume of expenditures was deflected into other media, and the balance flowed (at least in the short run) into profits rather than price reductions. There is little reason to believe that cigarette consumption fell as intended. Another example was set in 1966 when the British Monopolies Commission recommended a 40 percent cut in advertising by Unilever and Procter & Gamble accompanied by a 20 percent reduction in household detergent prices.[109] However, the government settled for a milder compromise under which the two companies agreed to introduce new, less heavily promoted products priced 20 percent lower than existing brands. The effort is said to have accomplished little, largely because the companies refused to admit that the unadvertised products' quality was equivalent to that of existing brands. As a result, consumers showed little interest in purchasing the new products. Other expenditure-discouraging policy alternatives include imposing a progressive excise tax on advertising, perhaps (to avoid a bias against more diversified firms) for outlays within any given four-digit product line; or attacking under the price discrimination laws unwarranted quantity discounts received by large advertisers. All such policies run the risk of evasion and evoking undesirable side effects. It is difficult to be sanguine about the ability of government staff charged with policy enforcement to outwit their business counterparts and ensure that after companies have taken adaptive steps, the situation is significantly improved.

The adverse effects of advertising can be mitigated by making available to consumers objective information on the relative qualities of competing products. Much is already done along these lines; part of the problem is simply to do it better. The government might subsidize the activities of such organizations as the Consumers Union, permitting them to conduct more frequent and extensive product tests and to disseminate reports to a broader audience. The wider implementation of uniform quality grading systems, enforced through inspection and supplemented by programs to inform the consumer, can be encouraged. Reports of quality and suitability tests conducted on thousands of consumer items by federal procurement agencies could be published and distributed on a massive scale. And finally, appropriate government agencies might take the more radical step of subpoenaing the extensive consumer panel test information in company files and making it available to the public in comprehensible form.

Whether problems of excessive product proliferation or insufficient product durability can be corrected through governmental action is arguable. As we have seen, market processes can lead to too much, too little, or the right amount of product variety. Product durability can be optimal or biased under monopoly. The key question is, Can government agencies or courts outperform the market in determining how much variety or durability is enough? Considerable skepticism seems warranted. Intervention is best saved for severe and unambiguous market failures—e.g., as in the government's effort during the early 1970s to require sensible automobile bumper designs.

(106) See "Has Detroit Learned Its Lesson?" *Business Week*, 5 October 1974, pp. 64–72.

(107) See Robert Crandall, "Vertical Integration and the Market for Repair Parts in the United States Automobile Industry," *Journal of Industrial Economics* 16 (July 1968): 212–34; and "The Decline of the Franchised Dealer in the Automobile Repair Market," *Journal of Business* 43 (January 1970): 19–30. The high prices set by manufacturers on crash parts also encourage the formation of "chop shops"—operations that disassemble stolen cars (often, especially in the case of new models, stolen to order) for replacement parts.

(108) The compensation cannot have been complete because crash parts *sales* are only a modest fraction—probably less than a fourth—of automobile company *profits*.

109. Monopolies Commission report, *Household Detergents* (London: HMSO, 1966). See also "Britain and 2 Soap Makers End Price Battle with Compromise," *New York Times*, 2 April 1967, p. 65.

15 Market structure and technological innovation

Making the best use of resources at any moment in time is important. But in the long run, it is dynamic performance that counts. As we observed in Chapter 2, an output handicap amounting to 10 percent of gross national product owing to static inefficiency is surmounted in just five years if the output growth rate can be raised through more rapid technological progress from 3 to 5 percent per annum, or in 20 years if the growth rate can be increased from 3 to 3.5 percent.

From the time of David Ricardo until well into the 20th century, the main stream of bourgeois (non-Marxian) economic theory exhibited remarkably little sensitivity to this possibility. Emphasis was on the result of combining labor and capital with production functions of an essentially static character. Not until the 1950s did technological change become more than a sideshow attraction. Although there had been earlier, equally well-aimed volleys, the shot that signaled a revolution in economic thought is commonly attributed to Robert M. Solow.[1] He set out to measure the extent to which increases in the amount of capital employed were responsible for the rise of U.S. nonfarm output per man-hour of work between 1909 and 1949. To the surprise of economists mired in static modes of analysis, Solow found that increased capital intensity accounted for only 12.5 percent (later corrected to 19 percent) of the measured growth in output

per man-hour. The rest of the 1.5 percent annual average productivity advance was evidently attributable to improvements in production practices and equipment (technological change in the strictest sense) and to increased quality of the labor force. In a subsequent extension, Edward Denison estimated that 22 percent of the rise in output per worker between 1929 and 1969 could be credited to improved work force education, 48 percent to the advance of scientific and technological knowledge, and only 12 percent to increased capital intensity.[2] Some of the assumptions used in reaching these estimates are arbitrary, but it is hard to dispute the main thrust of Solow's and Denison's conclusion: that the growth of output per worker in the United States has come predominantly from the application of new, superior production techniques by an increasingly well-trained work force. Much the

1. Robert M. Solow, "Technical Change and the Aggregate Production Function," *Review of Economics and Statistics* 39 (August 1957): 312–20. Earlier works reaching similar conclusions include Jacob Schmookler, "The Changing Efficiency of the American Economy, 1869–1938," *Review of Economics and Statistics* 34 (August 1952): 214–31; and Solomon Fabricant, "Economic Progress and Economic Change," *34th Annual Report of the National Bureau of Economic Research* (New York: National Bureau of Economic Research, 1954).

2. Denison, *Accounting for United States Economic Growth, 1929–1969* (Washington, D.C.: Brookings Institution, 1974), pp. 131–37.

same conclusion holds for other industrialized nations.[3]

The introduction of new production methods that raise productivity—i.e., process innovation—is one main arm of technological advance. Another is consumer product innovation—the creation of better things for better living, as the advertisement proclaims. The estimates by Solow, Denison, and others take into account only the effects of process innovation on national output, since no satisfactory way of measuring changes in the quality of consumption has been devised. As a result, the overall impact of technological change on consumer well-being is presumably understated by their estimates.

The principal consequences of technological change, then, are increases in productivity and in the quality of consumption. Several subsidiary effects can also be identified. For one, process innovation may alter the structure of labor demands, most likely strengthening demand for skilled workers and weakening demand for the unskilled, with possibly troublesome income distribution repercussions. Second, international differences in the ability to develop and apply modern technology have an impact on the balance of military and political power. Third, it has been discovered that such differences also affect international trade flows, with the most technologically advanced nations enjoying comparative advantage in the export of sophisticated products such as aircraft, machine tools, drugs, and computers.[4] Finally, technological change has effects on market structure, for major innovation often brings new firms to the fore and displaces laggards, defining the structural conditions within which price and other more static forms of rivalry are conducted for decades to come.

Here we shall be concerned largely with a possible causal flow in the opposite direction: from market structure to technological innovation. Is progress faster or slower under monopolistic conditions, or does it make no difference? One of the few influential bourgeois economic theorists who consistently stressed the important role technological change plays in a capitalistic economy was Joseph A. Schumpeter. In a widely read and controversial work, he argued that market struc-

ture does make a difference. Despite the restrictive pricing behavior in which they indulge, he asserted, large monopolistic firms are ideally suited for introducing technological innovations that benefit society:

> What we have got to accept is that [the large-scale establishment or unit of control] has come to be the most powerful engine of [economic] progress. . . . In this respect, perfect competition is not only impossible but inferior, and has no title to being set up as a model of ideal efficiency.[5]

Whether or not this is true is the question we tackle in this chapter. More precisely, we shall explore three narrower issues: Are large firms more adept at making technological innovations than small firms, other things being equal? Are highly diversified firms more vigorous engines of technical progress than companies operating in only one or a few product lines? And is monopoly power—i.e., as manifested in high market concentration—a favorable climate for innovation and technical progress?

Industrial research and development

Before we address these questions, it is useful to pause and examine more carefully what the process of technological change is all about.

Technical innovations do not fall like manna from heaven. They require effort—the creative labor of invention, development, testing, and introduction into the stream of economic life. To some extent innovative effort is a haphazard thing, conducted by individuals or firms as a digression from routine workaday activities. But to an increasing degree, the task of creating and developing new products and processes has been institutionalized through the establishment of formal research and development laboratories. It is not clear exactly when this trend began. We know that in the 1770s and 1780s the firm of Boulton & Watt had the equivalent of a research and development laboratory for work on steam engines.[6] The genesis of the modern R & D laboratory in America is commonly traced to 1876, when Thomas Edison opened his famed laboratory in Menlo Park and Alexander Graham Bell established an analogous facility in Boston. Wherever the starting point is placed, the idea spread rapidly until research and development came to be big business. In 1976, approximately 11,000 U.S. companies expended $25.5 billion on activities formally designated as research and development. Industrial expenditures on R & D grew at a compounded rate of 9 percent per year between 1953 and 1966, tapering off to a 5.4 percent growth rate (not much above the rate of inflation) in the 1967–76 decade.

Total outlays on R & D conducted by all organizations, private and public, in the United States during 1976 amounted to $37.4 billion, or 2.2 percent of the gross national product. Private industry performed the lion's share of this total—roughly 68 percent. The remaining expenditures were divided among federal government laboratories (16 percent), universities and colleges (13 percent), and nonprofit institutions (3 percent).[7]

Of the $25.5 billion spent for R & D conducted by profit-oriented firms in 1976, 63 percent was financed by the performing companies. The remaining financial burden was assumed by the federal government, mostly in connection with contracts for goods and services supplied by private industry to the Department of Defense, the Space Administration, the Department of Energy, and other agencies. Under such contracts the government usually accepts most of the financial risk and exercises more or less detailed control over the decisions and actions of its contractor. This contract work is rather far removed from the conventional functioning of the market mechanism. It is only with respect to the 63 percent privately financed share of industrial R & D effort, amounting to $16.1 billion in 1976, that the links between market structure and performance analyzed in this chapter are directly relevant.[8]

Within industry, research and development spending is heavily concentrated in a few manufacturing groups enjoying a rich scientific base and/or serving the military-space colossus. Table 15.1 presents data on total R & D spending, federal government sponsorship, and private

spending by industry sector (typically at the two-digit level) for 1975. From it, we can see that nearly half of all industrial R & D activity occurred in the electrical equipment and aircraft-missile sectors, which are deeply involved in meeting the government's defense and space demands. Only 3.1 percent of total expenditures took place in nonmanufacturing industries—a catchall including mining, public utilities, transportation, retailing, and others. Privately supported spending as a fraction of sales ranged from 4.4 percent in the instruments sector (which includes measuring devices, optics, photographic equipment, and surgical instruments) down to 0.4 percent in the food products group. The mean level for all industries was 1.9 percent.

A McGraw-Hill survey reveals that the principal goal of industrial firms in conducting R & D is the development of new and improved products. Twenty-eight percent of their 1977 R & D effort went into the development of new products, 59 percent into the improvement of existing products, and 13 percent into new manufacturing processes.[9] However, these estimates do not bring out clearly the impact of industrial R & D on the economy, since what is a new product to the developing firm may be a new production process to another company purchasing it. From the laboratories of General Electric, for example, have come new and improved products such as

3. Edward F. Denison, *Why Growth Rates Differ* (Washington, D.C.: Brookings Institution, 1967).

4. See Raymond Vernon, ed., *The Technology Factor in International Trade* (New York: Columbia University Press, 1970).

5. Joseph A. Schumpeter, *Capitalism, Socialism, and Democracy*, 3rd ed. (New York: Harper, 1950), p. 106.

6. F. M. Scherer, "Invention and Innovation in the Watt-Boulton Steam-Engine Venture," *Technology and Culture* 6 (Spring 1965), especially p. 180.

7. U.S. National Science Foundation, *Science Resource Studies: Highlights*, 31 March 1977.

8. On structure-performance relationships in federally supported R & D programs, see F. M. Scherer, "The Aerospace Industry," in Walter Adams, ed., *The Structure of American Industry*, 4th ed. (New York: Macmillan, 1970), pp. 335–79.

9. "What 600 Companies Spend for Research," *Business Week*, 27 June 1977, p. 63.

electrical generators and turbofan engines. These are sold to electrical utilities and airlines, for whom they are processes that raise productivity. The fraction of industrial research laboratory output flowing to other industries to increase productivity, as opposed to enhancing the quality of consumption for the public, is uncertain. It is undoubtedly large.

The process of research, development, invention, and innovation

Raw data on research and development spending do not reveal much about what actually goes on. To gain additional insight we must view the process from several additional perspectives.[10]

One approach is to break the expenditure totals into three conventional (but not always easily distinguished) categories. *Basic research*, defined as investigation to gain knowledge for its own sake, consumed 3 percent of all industrial R & D outlays in 1975. *Applied research*, investigation directed toward obtaining knowledge with specific commercial implications, accounted for 19 percent of total spending. The remaining 78 percent went into *development*, that is, the translation of technical and scientific knowledge into concrete new products and processes. Private industry accounts for roughly 17 percent of all basic research conducted in the United States, 55 percent of all applied research, and 85 percent of all development. From these figures it is evident

T 15.1 U.S. industrial research and development expenditures in 1975

Industry group	Total 1975 expenditures (millions)	Percentage government supported	Private spending as a percent of sales
Food and tobacco products	$ 367	<1	0.4
Textiles and apparel	64	small	0.4
Lumber, wood products, and furniture	68	small	0.7
Paper and allied products	253	<1	0.9
Chemicals and drugs	2,650	9	3.3
Petroleum refining and extraction	700	4	0.6
Rubber products	283	13	1.5
Stone, clay, and glass products	186	1	1.5
Primary metals	365	3	0.7
Fabricated metal products	311	5	1.2
Machinery	2,658	14	3.5
Electrical equipment and communications	5,530	45	3.9
Motor vehicles and other transportation equipment	2,367	14	3.0
Aircraft and missiles	5,729	79	2.9
Instruments	1,034	18	4.4
Nonmanufacturing industries	739	67	n.a.
All industries	$23,540	37	1.9

Source: U.S. National Science Foundation, *Research and Development in Industry, 1975* (Washington, D.C.: Government Printing Office, 1977), pp. 29–31, 60. Only companies with some R & D activity are included in calculating the third-column percentages.

that industry's forte is applications—specific new products and processes—while pure science remains predominantly the domain of the universities and federal government laboratories.

Schumpeter's writings provide another viewpoint.[11] He visualized technological change as occurring in three steps: invention, innovation, and imitation or diffusion. Invention to him was the act of conceiving a new product or process and solving the purely technical problems associated with its application. Innovation comprised the entrepreneurial functions required to carry a new technical possibility into economic practice for the first time—identifying the market, raising the necessary funds, building a new organization, cultivating the market, and so on. Imitation or diffusion is the stage at which a new product or process comes into widespread use as one producer after another follows the innovating firm's lead.

The trouble with this schema is that it leaves in an ambiguous state the costly technical activities representing the heart of modern research and development programs. It seems more useful to describe the pre-imitation, or innovative, process in terms of four essential functions: invention, entrepreneurship, investment, and development.[12] Invention then is the act of insight by which a new and promising technical possibility is recognized and worked out (at least mentally and perhaps also physically) in its essential, most rudimentary form.[13] Development is the lengthy sequence of detail-oriented technical activities, including trial-and-error testing, through which the original concept is modified and perfected until it is ready for commercial utilization. The entrepreneurial function involves deciding to go forward with the effort, organizing it, and obtaining financial support for it. Investment is the act of risking funds for the venture. These functions need not be performed by the same person or even by the same organization; in many cases, we shall see, they are organizationally separate.

All such attempts at conceptualization are little more than empty words until fitted into a meaningful real-world context. Therefore, it is helpful to consider two brief examples. No case is completely typical; the illustrations presented here were chosen because they reflect unusually

important and ambitious technical changes and because the stages and functions stand out with particular clarity. One, the Watt-Boulton steam engine venture of the 1770s, is ancient; the other, xerography, quite new.

It is generally accepted that James Watt "invented" his steam engine in 1765, when he repaired a Newcomen steam engine model owned by Glasgow University and perceived that its efficiency could be greatly enhanced by condensing the steam outside the operating cylinder. He wrote later that "In three days, I had a model at work nearly as perfect . . . as any which have been made since that time."[14] But much remained to be done before he could supply a machine useful in industrial practice. Full-scale models had to be built, condenser concepts had to be devised and tested, valves designed, methods of machining and sealing the operating cylinder perfected, and so forth. All this required time and money, and for want of both financial support and entrepreneurial initiative Watt twice abandoned the venture to work as a salaried engineer. Not until Matthew Boulton appeared to provide these missing ingredients was a full-scale model completed, and the first commer-

10. For other views, see Edwin Mansfield, *The Economics of Technological Change* (New York: Norton, 1968), Chapters 2, 3, and 4; Richard R. Nelson, M. J. Peck, and E. D. Kalachek, *Technology, Economic Growth, and Public Policy* (Washington, D.C.: Brookings Institution, 1967), Chapters 2, 3, 4, and 5; and John Jewkes, David Sawers, and Richard Stillerman, *The Sources of Invention*, 2nd ed. (New York: Norton, 1969).

11. Joseph A. Schumpeter, *The Theory of Economic Development*, trans. Redvers Opie (Cambridge, Mass.: Harvard University Press, 1934), Chapter 2; and, *Business Cycles* (New York: McGraw-Hill, 1939), especially Chapter 3. See also Carolyn Solo, "Innovation in the Capitalist Process: A Critique of the Schumpeterian Theory," *Quarterly Journal of Economics* 65 (August 1951): 417–28; and Vernon W. Ruttan, "Usher and Schumpeter on Invention, Innovation, and Technological Change," *Quarterly Journal of Economics* 73 (November 1959): 596–606.

12. See Scherer, "Invention and Innovation."

13. "Invention" as used here must be distinguished most emphatically from the mass of trivia that sometimes pass for inventions under the patent system. A higher standard of novelty and insight is implied in this discussion.

14. Quoted in Scherer, "Invention and Innovation," from which this summary is taken.

cially useful Watt-Boulton steam engine was installed only in 1776, 11 years after the original invention. Expenditures preparing the way for operating the first full-scale engine amounted to the equivalent of at least 60 man-years of skilled labor.

While working as a patent attorney, Chester Carlson was impressed by the difficulty of copying documents efficiently.[15] For several years he spent a good deal of his spare time after work mulling over the problem and browsing in potentially relevant technical literature, eventually (in 1938) conceiving the central idea of xerography. With the assistance of an unemployed physicist, he successfully tested his concept with an extremely crude model. After several fruitless attempts to interest industrial firms in helping him develop a commercially practical copying system, in 1944 he enlisted the cooperation of the Battelle Development Company, a subsidiary of the Battelle Institute. From two years' labor by a Battelle research physicist and his aides came two key inventions building upon Carlson's original principle: the use of a selenium-coated plate to store the electrostatic image, and the corona discharge method for sensitizing the plate and applying ink to the copying paper. With these inventions, the xerography concept began to show distinct signs of practical promise.

At this point the Haloid Corporation (later renamed the Xerox Corporation) took over developmental responsibility. By 1950 its engineers had completed a prototype system useful primarily for making offset lithography masters. This was a cumbersome, three-machine contraption, however, with limited market potential. The company then devoted its resources to developing a single-unit console copier—a task that required surmounting a difficult lens design problem along with numerous lesser engineering challenges. The result was the 914 copier, which took the world by storm after its introduction in 1959.

During the more than two decades preceding this event, formulation of the basic xerographic copying concept consumed the inventor's energies part time for a very few years. The selenium plate and corona discharge inventions came from an only slightly greater increment of effort. After Haloid entered the picture, it expended

roughly $4 million on research and development up to 1953, when it redirected attention to developing a console model. To attain that goal, further R & D outlays estimated at $16 million, severely straining the company's financial resources, were committed.

Several generalizations can be extracted from these and the many other case studies now available. First, the initial invention that precipitates a major innovative effort is typically inexpensive, both relatively and absolutely. Its money cost is often so modest that almost any well-prepared imaginative individuals thrown into contact with the problem is in a position potentially to achieve the essential insight. The inventive challenge may be recognized as a result of formal work assignments, as a by-product of work or leisure pursuits, or from any of the hundred-and-one experiences a person has each day. If industrial research and development laboratories enjoy some comparative advantage in generating inventions, it is because they are more likely to put together the critical combination of a fertile mind, a challenging problem, and the will to solve it.

Second, there is a substantial random component in fundamental invention. Thousands of persons may recognize an unsolved problem or unmet need, but only a fraction will be sufficiently intrigued to devote serious thought to it, and an even smaller fraction will have the ingenuity and good luck to gain a correct insight by viewing the problem in exactly the right way—that is, in the proper gestalt.[16] After the insight is achieved, the solution may seem obvious, but before the fact invention is largely unpredictable. If this were not so, every problem, once recognized, would be solved quickly.

Third, supporting inventions of greater or lesser creative magnitude may be required before the innovation begins to look technically and economically viable. Once the original insight is attained, however, it forms a gestalt within which these supporting inventions will tend inevitably to emerge if good minds are focused on the problem.

Fourth, when the necessary conceptual advances have occurred and when their essential correctness has been demonstrated, typically

412

through crude model tests requiring only a modest resource investment, the uncertainties associated with innovation are transformed qualitatively and quantitatively. The question, Is there something interesting and technically feasible here? is no longer a serious issue. Uncertainty centers on such questions as: What will the detailed configuration of the mechanism be? How well can it be made to work? How much will perfecting it cost? How long will it take? At what price can it be sold? What will be the market demand at that price? These are not negligible uncertainties, but usually they are also not overwhelming or outside the bounds of entrepreneurial experience. The vast majority of all industrial R & D projects, it should be noted, begin at this stage, since they either embody no fundamental new concepts or build upon insights achieved elsewhere.

Finally, once the sequence has progressed this far, outlays much greater than those incurred during the early conceptual stages are necessary before an innovation is brought to the point of commercial utility. The investment decision at this juncture entails committing possibly substantial quantities of resources in the face of moderate technological uncertainties. It is quite different from the earlier decision, where the amounts of money involved are small, but the technical uncertainties are great. If inexpensive conceptual work has not reduced the degree of technical uncertainty to tolerable levels, a decision to move into full-scale development will be taken only under the most unusual pressures (as in the atomic and hydrogen bomb programs).[17] Normally, conceptual work will be continued at a low spending level until the main technical uncertainties have been resolved.

Firm size, invention, and innovation

With this background in mind, let us return to our principal theme. We begin by exploring the links between firm size and technological progressiveness. It is important to recall that size and monopoly power are by no means synonymous.

Although the two attributes *may* coincide, we shall try here to preserve a sharp distinction. The central issue can be stated as follows: Are large firms in general more effective than small firms in making technological inventions and introducing them into commercial practice?

A number of a priori hypotheses favorable to big business exist. One of the best known is Professor Galbraith's assertion that the costs of technological innovation in modern times are so great that they can be borne only by large corporations:

> There is no more pleasant fiction than that technical change is the product of the matchless ingenuity of the small man forced by competition to employ his wits to better his neighbor. Unhappily, it is a fiction. Technical development has long since become the preserve of the scientist and engineer. Most of the cheap and simple inventions, have, to put it bluntly and unpersuasively, been made. . . . Because development is costly, it follows that it can be carried on only by a firm that has the resources which are associated with considerable size.[18]

Furthermore, it is argued, research and development projects are risky as well as expensive. Small firms place themselves in a dangerous position when they invest all their resources in a

15. This example is drawn from Jewkes et al., *The Sources of Invention*, pp. 321–23; and Erwin Blackstone, "The Economics of the Copying Machine Industry" (Ph.D. diss., University of Michigan, 1968).

16. This interpretation of the inventive act is based upon Abbott P. Usher, *A History of Mechanical Inventions*, Rev. ed. (Cambridge, Mass.: Harvard University Press, 1954), Chapter 4; N. R. Hanson, *Patterns of Discovery* (Cambridge, England: Cambridge University Press, 1958); and Thomas S. Kuhn, *The Structure of Scientific Revolutions* (Chicago: University of Chicago Press, 1962).

17. See R. G. Hewlett and O. E. Anderson, Jr., *The New World: 1939/1946* (University Park, Pa.: Pennsylvania State University Press, 1962), Chapters 4 through 7; R. G. Hewlett and Francis Duncan, *Atomic Shield, 1947/1952* (University Park, Pa.: Pennsylvania State University Press, 1969), Chapters 12, 13, and 16; and F. M. Scherer, "Was the Nuclear Arms Race Inevitable?," *Co-existence*, January 1966, pp. 59–69.

18. John Kenneth Galbraith, *American Capitalism*, Rev. ed. (Boston: Houghton Mifflin, 1956), pp. 86–87.

single innovative project whose prospects for technical and commercial success are far from guaranteed. This, combined with the risk aversion to which business managers and investors are supposedly prone, is said to discourage technical pioneering by small companies. The large corporation, on the other hand, can afford to maintain a balanced portfolio of R & D projects, letting the profits from successes more than counterbalance the losses from those that fail. The ability to average out losses and gains may lead large firms to consider innovative opportunities on their 'best guess' merits, without being constrained unduly by risk aversion.

Third, there may be economies of scale in the conduct of research and development. A big laboratory can justify purchasing all sorts of specialized equipment—wind tunnels, electron microscopes, heavy-duty strain gauges, and the like—making experimentation easier. It can employ specialists in many disciplines to cross-fertilize one another and to lend temporary assistance when a team working on some development project becomes bogged down by a technical problem outside its regular sphere of competence. This latter advantage might be minimized if small firms could call freely upon outside specialists (such as university engineering professors) when they run into unfamiliar problems, but it is not clear that outside expertise is tapped as willingly and speedily as internal expertise.

Fourth, research and development projects may benefit from scale economies realized in other parts of the large firm's operations. As we have seen in Chapter 4, large corporations can attract additional capital at lower cost and in larger quantities than their smaller cousins, and thus may be better able to finance ambitious R & D undertakings. They have well-established marketing channels and may enjoy certain economies of scale in promotion and physical distribution. Their promotional advantages often permit them to penetrate markets more rapidly with new products, and this affects the profitability of developing a product. Being able to reach 50 percent of a new product's market potential in two years instead of five may make the difference between profit and loss.

Finally, large producers have an advantage in making process innovations. A new process that reduces costs by a given percentage margin yields larger total savings to the company producing a large volume of output than to the firm whose output is small. As a result, the large firm presumably has stronger incentives to develop such improvements.

Against this impressive array of actual and conjectured advantages, the disadvantages of size must be weighed.[19] For one, decisions to bear the risks of R & D projects are made by individual managers, not by impersonal organizations, and so the argument on risk spreading may not hold water. In a small firm, the decision to go ahead with an ambitious project typically involves a small number of people who know one another well. In a large corporation, the decision must filter through a whole chain of command— the person with the idea, his or her section chief, the laboratory manager, the vice president for research, and if substantial financial commitments are required, several members of top management. Each participant is risking his or her reputation, if not money, in backing the project. Under these circumstances there is a distressingly high probability that some member of the chain will prove to be what C. Northcote Parkinson has called "an abominable no-man," and that the idea will die from lack of support or from the objections that can always be raised to an untried proposition.[20]

A direct consequence of this problem, which has been noted time and again in case histories and treatises on research management, is a bias away from really imaginative innovations in the laboratories of large firms. But more important, inability to get ideas approved by higher management drives many of the most creative individuals out of large corporation laboratories to go it alone in their own ventures. Thousands of research-based new enterprises have been founded by frustrated fugitives from the laboratories of such U.S. giants as IBM, Sperry-Rand, Western Electric, Hughes Aircraft, and Texas Instruments.[21]

A related malady is the propensity for research in large laboratories to become overorganized. If too many people are involved in a project, they spend a disproportionate amount of their time writing memoranda to each other at the expense of more creative endeavor. Also, the quickest and surest path to higher status and pay in a large firm's R & D establishment often lies in giving up work at the bench and becoming a member of the management team. Although some companies have tried to combat this tendency by creating well-paid positions for senior research fellows, it is still commonplace to find the most able people in a laboratory devoting nearly all their time to supervising a swarm of drones. This is not the way truly creative work gets done.

The costs and risks of industrial research

How these disadvantages and advantages of bigness balance out cannot be resolved through a priori reasoning; the question is an empirical one. Before we turn to the evidence, however, a further comment on the costs and risks of industrial research and development projects is in order.

In his statement on technical change and the small man, Professor Galbraith is guilty of out-fictionalizing the fiction writers. The costs of technical development cannot be characterized so simply. To be sure, there are projects whose financial burden is beyond the capacity of any but large corporations. But there are also many opportunities that can be exploited on a small scale. At one extreme is the case of a production engineer known to the author who returned at night to the transistor plant where he worked to devise new transistor designs, producing them in experimental quantities the next day when his production operatives had spare time. Many simple mechanical and electromechanical device developments fit this pattern. At the other extreme is the development of unusually complex systems—electronic telephone message switching centrals, reconnaissance satellites, long-range ballistic missiles, and fast breeder reactors—where R & D costs may mount into the hundreds of millions or even billions of dollars. Because of the limited uses for weapon systems and because it may be the only consumer able to afford such products as a trip to the moon, the U.S. federal government subsidizes and frequently pays the full cost of many projects necessitating multimillion dollar R & D commitments, and in such cases the financial advantages of large company size are less relevant. Still, some ambitious projects remain squarely within the private sector. As we saw earlier, the Xerox Corporation invested more than $16 million in perfecting its 914 copier. RCA is said to have spent more than $65 million on color television R & D before anything resembling a mass market materialized. And private investment in the design and development of civilian jet airliners has exceeded the $100 million mark on numerous occasions.

A more fruitful way of considering the technical opportunities confronting small and large firms is to visualize a frequency distribution of development projects, ordered according to their cost. A census would undoubtedly reveal the distribution to be highly skewed. The spectacularly costly projects that receive the most attention in newspapers and trade journals are few in number, forming the distribution's long thin tail. Smaller projects are much more numerous, giving rise to a peak or mode in a spending range somewhere between $250,000 and $400,000 at 1976 price levels.[22] The parameters of this distribution have been shifting over time; that is, the modal R & D project today is more expensive than its counterpart 30 years ago. But firm sizes have also been rising secularly, and so there

19. See Jewkes et al., *The Sources of Invention*, Chapter VI; Dan Hamberg, "Invention in the Industrial Research Laboratory," *Journal of Political Economy* 71 (April 1963): 95–115; Arnold C. Cooper, "R & D Is More Efficient in Small Companies," *Harvard Business Review* 42 (May/June 1964): 75–83; and "The Breakdown of U.S. Innovation," *Business Week*, 16 February 1976, pp. 56–67, 106. For an excellent survey of the issues examined in this chapter, see Morton I. Kamien and Nancy L. Schwartz, "Market Structure and Innovation: A Survey," *Journal of Economic Literature* 13 (March 1975): 1–37.

20. On the bureaucratization and growing risk aversion of erstwhile technical pioneers du Pont and RCA, see "Lighting a Fire under the Sleeping Giant," *Business Week*, 12 September 1970, pp. 40–41; and "RCA's New Vista: The Bottom Line," *Business Week*, 4 July 1977, pp. 38–44.

21. See Edward B. Roberts, "Entrepreneurship and Technology," *Research Management* (July 1968): 249–66; "How the High-Fliers Take Off," *Business Week*, 22 November 1969, pp. 112–16; "Control Data Loses a Genius," *Business Week*, 18 March 1972, p. 24; and "Gene Amdahl Takes Aim at I.B.M.," *Fortune*, September 1977, pp. 106–109.

continue to be many technical challenges that can be met successfully by firms defined as small under current standards. If large firms have an advantage, it is primarily in their ability to select among both modest and ambitious projects in building up their R & D project portfolios.[23] Yet small firms are by no means barred from the game, especially if they are willing to bear the risks of incomplete hedging.

It is also likely that the risks and uncertainties of industrial research and development are less formidable than corporate publicists and proponents of the hero theory of invention would have us believe. Analyzing 70 projects carried out in the central R & D laboratories of a leading electrical equipment manufacturing company, Mansfield and Brandenburg found that in more than three-fourths of the cases, the *ex ante* probability of technical success had been estimated at 0.80 or higher, and only 2 projects had predicted success probabilities of less than 0.50. After the projects were completed, 44 percent turned out to be fully successful technically, and only 16 percent were unsuccessful owing to unanticipated technical difficulties.[24] In a broader survey, Mansfield and associates learned that of all the projects carried out during 1963 to 1965 in 19 company laboratories, the average proportion fulfilling their technical objectives was 70 percent for seven chemical organizations, 32 percent for five drug firms, 73 percent for three electronics firms, and 50 percent for four petroleum companies.[25] The reason for this characteristically high technical success rate has been brought out earlier: Business enterprises do not as a rule begin new product or process development projects until the principal technical uncertainties have been whittled down through inexpensive research, conducted either by their own personnel or by outsiders.

The sequential character of modern research and development also makes it possible for small enterprises to play a creative role in major technological achievements. As we have seen, the earliest, most imaginative steps in the innovative process normally entail only modest resource commitments. The heaviest expenditures do not fall due until full-scale development begins. Neither inadequate size nor insufficient financial capacity necessarily bars small firms from the early stages. Creative thinking power is a scarce resource, but it comes in fairly inexpensive person-sized lumps that can be attracted as easily (and often more easily) by small companies as by large. Also, crude test models are usually not so costly that they cannot be financed by entrepreneurs of modest means, if the will is present. Where trouble may intrude is at the development stage, once creative thought and small-scale testing have pointed the way. Here the small enterprise may find its resources taxed beyond the breaking point, and it may be compelled to yield its position in the race to a larger firm through patent licensing, merger, or default. The chief disadvantage of small firms in the early creative stages is the prospect of deficient bargaining power when and if a transition becomes necessary. They may lack the financial and legal resources to pursue their patent rights against well-heeled infringers, or their inventions may be easily circumvented, rendering patent protection ineffective. But this handicap does not appear seriously to discourage small research-oriented companies from testing their luck, and the combination of a good idea with the zeal and creative talent to develop it has proved an attractive asset in literally hundreds of merger negotiations.

These characteristics of industrial innovation go a long way toward explaining the findings of several recent empirical studies. Jewkes, Sawers, and Stillerman compiled case histories of 70 important 20th century inventions and learned that only 24 had their origin in industrial research laboratories. More than half were pioneered by individuals working either completely independent of any formal research organization or as independent investigators in an academic environment.[26] Hamberg investigated 27 major inventions introduced during the 1946–55 decade. Only 7 were originally conceived in large industrial laboratories, while 12 were traced to independent inventors.[27] Using a more selective approach, Mueller studied the 25 most important product and process innovations pioneered in the United States by the du Pont Company between 1920 and 1950. He found that only 10 or at most 11 were initially discovered in du Pont's laboratories; the rest came from other firms or independent researchers.[28]

These and other studies show that small firms,

academicians, and even the totally independent inventor continue to contribute significantly toward the creation of new products and processes. To stop at this conclusion, however, and by inference to denigrate the role of corporate R & D laboratories, would be to miss an important part of the whole point. For while a seeming preponderance of the original inventions studied by Jewkes, Hamberg, and Mueller originated outside corporate laboratories, in most cases corporations ended up shouldering the burden of developing the inventions for commercial utilization. Thus, in exploding the myth of du Pont's creative genius, Mueller fails to put du Pont's developmental contributions in perspective. He ignores, for instance, the fact that the Calico Printers' Association of England, which sponsored the small-scale research producing the idea for Dacron, found itself unable or unwilling to undertake the long and expensive job of developing the fiber for consumer use, licensing development rights instead to Imperial Chemical Industries, Ltd., and to du Pont. Or to cite a non-du Pont example, major increases in the efficiency of diesel engines were made after General Motors bought out two small companies that had pioneered the technology, assigning the engine problem to a development team led by Charles Kettering. And the Eastman Kodak Co. supported work by the originally independent inventors of Kodachrome for ten years before the new color film was ready for the market. Invention and development are necessary complements in the process of technological advance; neither is sufficient alone if major changes are to be wrought. As Jewkes, Sawers, and Stillerman concede after devoting most of their analysis to the inventive step alone:

> Although when this work was started it was not intended to say anything in detail about the development of inventions, it subsequently became increasingly apparent that some comment on it was unavoidable. For even those who are prepared to accept the description and analysis of invention as given in the foregoing pages might well protest that this is, after all, the less important part of the story of technical progress and that the real determinants of the rate of advance will be

the scale and the speed of the efforts made to perfect new commodities and devices and to contrive ways of producing them cheaply and in quantity.[29]

In any such attempt to clear up popular misconceptions, we must be wary of overcompensating. From the evidence presented thus far, three main generalizations appear warranted. First, small firms and independent inventors play a prominent and perhaps even disproportionate role in generating the new ideas and concepts upon which technological advances rest. Second,

(22) See F. M. Scherer, *The Economic Effects of Compulsory Patent Licensing* (Monograph 1977–2, New York University Graduate School of Business Administration, 1977), p. 15, pulling together the results of several surveys by Edwin Mansfield and associates. The work by Mansfield emphasized research-intensive industries. Average R & D costs may be considerably lower in industries with a weaker research orientation. Thus, Robert D. Buzzell and Robert Nourse found the average R & D cost of 111 new food products developed during the early 1960s to have been $68,000. *Product Innovation, the Product Life Cycle, and Competitive Behavior in Selected Food Processing Industries* (Cambridge, Mass.: Arthur D. Little, Inc., February 1966), Table 8.

23. The 500th firm on *Fortune*'s list of the 500 largest industrial corporations for 1976 had sales of $328 million. Assuming the average R & D/sales ratio for all manufacturing corporations of 1.9 percent, its R & D budget would have been approximately $6.2 million. Assuming an average project cost of $500,000 (i.e., the mean is above the mode) and an average project life of three years, the firm's R & D portfolio could include 37 projects. This suggests considerable opportunity for risk spreading even by medium-sized corporations.

24. Edwin Mansfield, *Industrial Research and Technological Innovation* (New York: Norton, 1968), pp. 56–61.

25. Edwin Mansfield et al., *Research and Innovation in the Modern Corporation* (New York: Norton, 1971), pp. 34–35. See also Edwin Mansfield and Samuel Wagner, "Organizational and Strategic Factors Associated with Probabilities of Success in Industrial R and D," *Journal of Business* 48 (April 1975): 179–98; and (on development risks in the 19th Century) W. Paul Strassmann, *Risk and Technological Innovation* (Ithaca, N.Y.: Cornell University Press, 1959).

26. Jewkes et al., *The Sources of Invention*, pp. 65–78. The authors use a loose and sometimes curious definition of invention. Many of the cases studied are better described as systems or conglomerations of inventions.

27. Hamberg, "Invention in the Industrial Research Laboratory," p. 96. Hamberg began with a sample of 45 inventions. Why he stopped his research after exploring only 27 is not made clear.

28. Willard F. Mueller, "The Origins of the Basic Inventions Underlying du Pont's Major Product and Process Innovations, 1920 to 1950," in the National Bureau of Economic Research conference report, *The Rate and Direction of Inventive Activity* (Princeton: Princeton University Press, 1962), pp. 323–46.

29. Jewkes et al., *The Sources of Invention*, p. 152.

Market structure and technological innovation   417

developing these ideas to the point of practical utility normally requires a significant investment of resources. Usually, however, the costs of development are not so high that they cannot be borne by medium-sized and small companies. Third, there remain a relatively few advances demanding such heavy private developmental investment that they can be undertaken with something approaching equanimity only by very large corporations, or with less than equanimity by medium-sized firms possessing an especially high tolerance for risk.

One conclusion relevant to public policy follows immediately. No single firm size is uniquely conducive to technological progress. There is room for firms of all sizes. What we want, therefore, may be a diversity of sizes, each with its own special advantages and disadvantages.

Firm size and the intensity of R & D efforts
Granted then, the search for a firm size uniquely and unambiguously optimal for invention and innovation is misguided. Nevertheless, are there broad statistical tendencies for companies in some size categories to be more vigorous than others in advancing technology, even though the pattern may not hold in all cases?

To address this question, quantitative evidence is needed. Unfortunately, it is not easy to measure the vigor of firms' inventive and innovative efforts. In attempts to do so, several measures have been used: expenditures on research and development, the number of personnel engaged in formal R & D activities, a count of invention patents received, a count of significant innovations pioneered, and estimates of the sales associated with new products introduced. None is completely satisfactory, and the relative merits of alternative approaches are debated.[30] We shall not prolong that debate here. It suffices to say that each approach has its own peculiar merits, and so the best strategy is undoubtedly to employ a variety of approaches, testing one's conclusions for their sensitivity to the choice of measures.

One salient relationship is the high concentration of formal R & D effort among the largest manufacturing companies. In 1972, U.S. corporations with 5,000 or more employees accounted for 53 percent of all manufacturing industry employment. At the same time they made 89 percent of all expenditures on R & D performed by manufacturing companies, including 91 percent of expenditures on federally supported R & D programs and 87 percent of the privately financed effort.[31] Federally supported expenditures were more highly concentrated than private spending in part because government agencies apparently prefer the convenience of dealing with large firms, but mainly because key tasks in the weapons system development programs contracted out by the federal government were so large that they could be handled only by sizeable enterprises, even when diligent efforts were exerted to disintegrate the work vertically through subcontracting.

A different pattern emerges when one uses a count of invention patents received to assess the relative contributions of large and small producers. A complete count was made of patents issued in 1959 to 463 manufacturing corporations included on *Fortune*'s list of the 500 largest U.S. industrials for 1955. This sample, closely overlapping the population of companies with 5,000 or more employees, received 56 percent of the U.S. invention patents issued to domestic manufacturing corporations in 1959 and accounted for approximately 57 percent of the 1955 sales of U.S. manufacturing corporations.[32] Thus, the largest firms barely held their own in the receipt of invention patents despite their disproportionate share of both government and private R & D spending.

A possible explanation for this disparity might be that the patented inventions of large firms are in some sense of higher quality than those of smaller companies, reflecting a more intensive technical resource input. However, there is no empirical support for this hypothesis, and what evidence we have points in the opposite direction. Notably, the percentage of patented inventions actually brought into commercial utilization—one indicator of quality—is higher for small firms than for large. Interview studies also reveal that large corporations with an active staff of patent attorneys are less discriminating in their choice of inventions on which patent protection is sought.[33] Two alternative hypotheses appear more plausible. First, the division of labor has not progressed far enough in many smaller firms to permit the establishment of formal research and development programs. Their efforts to advance technology tend more often to be a casual, part-time endeavor not detected in statistics on formal R & D spending. This is consistent with Jacob Schmookler's estimate from a random sample of 1953 patented inventions that for every eight inventions flowing from full-time R & D employees, companies obtained five inventions from employees engaged only part time in innovative activity.[34] Second, as suggested in the previous section, small firms may be at their best in the early, most inventive stages of the process of technical advance, while large corporations enjoy a comparative advantage at those types of detailed development generating relatively few patentable inventions.

That formally organized R & D is disproportionately the domain of the larger corporation is shown by additional data from the U.S. National Science Foundation. In 1972 there were approximately 263,000 manufacturing firms with fewer than 1,000 employees, including 32,000 with from 50 to 999 employees. A formal R & D effort was maintained by roughly 10,000 of those firms.[35] Of the 1,315 manufacturing companies with from 1,000 to 4,999 employees, 47 percent had R & D programs. Of the 540 with 5,000 or more employees, 487, or 90 percent, had formal programs. Thus, most of the largest manufacturing enterprises engage in some formal R & D, while only a small fraction of the smallest companies do.

Table 15.2 provides further perspective on the 1975 company-financed R & D spending of 679 corporations large enough to have their securities traded on exchanges regulated by the Securities and Exchange Commission. The companies were ranked on the basis of sales. Except for the 20 very largest, companies in the diverse size tiers accounted for virtually identical fractions of sales and R & D outlays.[36] It appears then that even though the smallest manufacturers did little formal R & D, medium-sized manufacturers supported a volume of research and development proportional to their sales.

Aggregated analyses of this sort could conceivably mask significant deviations from pro-

portionality in narrower industry groups. To explore this possibility, there have been numerous studies of the relationship between R & D effort and firm size within individual industry categories. This has typically been done by using nonlinear regression techniques and testing to see whether significant nonlinearities existed.[37]

30. See Simon Kuznets, "Inventive Activity: Problems of Definition and Measurement," and Barkev S. Sanders, "Some Difficulties in Measuring Inventive Activity," both in *The Rate and Direction of Inventive Activity*, pp. 19–90; U.S. National Science Foundation, *Methodology of Statistics on Research and Development* (Washington, D.C.: Government Printing Office, 1959); and C. Freeman and A. Young, *The Research and Development Effort in Western Europe, North America and the Soviet Union* (Paris: Organisation for Economic Co-operation and Development, 1965).

31. U.S. National Science Foundation, *Research and Development in Industry: 1973* (Washington, D.C.: Government Printing Office, 1975), pp. 26, 28, 31; and U.S., Bureau of the Census, *1972 Enterprise Statistics*, Part I, "General Report on Industrial Organization" (Washington, D.C.: Government Printing Office, 1977), p. 148.

32. See F. M. Scherer, "Firm Size, Market Structure, Opportunity, and the Output of Patented Inventions," *American Economic Review* 55 (December 1965): 1104–1105; and the testimony in U.S., Congress, Senate, Committee on the Judiciary, Subcommittee on Antitrust and Monopoly hearings, *Economic Concentration*, Part 3, 89th Cong., 1st sess., 1965, pp. 1198–99.

33. See Barkev Sanders et al., "Patent Acquisition by Corporations," *Patent, Trademark, and Copyright Journal of Research and Education* 3 (Fall 1959): 238; Richard L. Sandor, "Some Empirical Findings on the Legal Costs of Patenting," *Journal of Business* 45 (July 1972): 375–78; and U.S. Federal Council for Science and Technology, Committee on Government Patent Policy, *Government Patent Policy Study*, vol. IV, "Effect of Government Patent Policy on Commercial Utilization and Business Competition," Part I (Boston: Harbridge House, June 1968), pp. 31, 43.

34. Jacob Schmookler, "Bigness, Fewness, and Research," *Journal of Political Economy* 67 (December 1959): 630.

35. U.S. National Science Foundation, *Research and Development in Industry: 1972* (Washington, D.C.: Government Printing Office, 1974), p. 37; and U.S., Bureau of the Census, *1972 Enterprise Statistics*, Part 1, p. 148.

36. A bias could conceivably intrude because companies whose R & D outlays were less than 1 percent of sales were not *required* to report. However, any such bias is believed to be small. Of the reporting companies, 37 percent had R & D/sales ratios of less than 1 percent. The weighted average R & D/sales ratio for all reporting companies was 1.89 percent. The comparable figure for all manufacturing companies covered by the National Science Foundation survey for 1975 was 1.9 percent.

For an analysis of the concentration of 1955 R & D employment and 1959 patenting by 352 large corporations, see the first edition of *Industrial Market Structure and Economic Performance*, p. 360. There it is shown that the largest 50 corporations had shares of R & D employment and patenting *lower* than their sales shares.

By far the most common finding for U.S. industries has been that research and development employment or spending rose either just proportionately or less than proportionately (i.e., exhibiting diminishing returns) with firm size, especially after some size threshold near the bottom range of *Fortune*'s 500 industrials listing was reached.[38] This means that the largest firms in any given industry group did not support R & D more intensively relative to their size than did smaller counterparts, and in many instances they provided less intensive support. Chemicals may have been an exception, with the largest companies, and du Pont in particular, spending more in relation to sales than small and medium-sized chemical producers. However, this difference appears to have faded over time, for in 1975 there was no indication of a positive correlation between R & D/sales ratios and firm size among the 54 industrial and specialty chemicals producers covered by Table 15.2.[39]

Similar R & D intensity-firm size analyses have been carried out for a number of other industrialized nations, including Japan, West Germany, France, Canada, and Belgium.[40] The findings are more variable than, but generally consistent with, U.S. results: The very largest companies do no better than smaller rivals, and frequently they support a share of R & D effort less than their sales or total employment share. Exceptions do exist, however. Thus, the largest Japanese chemical and electrical producers spent proportionately more on R & D than did medium-sized enterprises. And in Belgium, whose corporations are much smaller on average than those in the United States, the threshold at which diminishing R & D effort returns take hold seems to be comparable in absolute company size to that found in the United States. Hence, the number of Belgian firms whose size lies above the threshold is much smaller.[41]

Even though the very largest corporations characteristically do not support a share of R & D effort more than proportionate to their size, they might nevertheless contribute disproportionately to innovative *output* because, for example, they enjoy R & D scale economies and can generate more output per unit of input.[42] This hypothesis has also attracted a fair amount of research. The most comprehensive statistical analyses have related patents as a measure of output to various measures of R & D input. For the United States, a linear homogeneous relationship has been found: that is, the patenting of larger corporations varies proportionately with R & D employment.[43] Since R & D employment tends to rise less than proportionately with firm size once some sales threshold has been passed, one might expect patenting to rise less than proportionately with firm size too. This has been verified for the United States, England, and Sweden, although the chemicals industry stands as an exception to the rule for all three.[44]

Using trade association and other informed sources, other studies have attempted to identify the most significant innovations made by industrial firms. Since this is a relatively costly procedure, the number of industries covered is rather small. The most comprehensive survey is for the United Kingdom, where 1,102 innovations introduced between 1945 and 1970 were traced to originating enterprises. Although the results vary somewhat by industry, the central tendency was for companies with fewer than 1,000 employees to

T 15.2 Concentration of sales and company-financed R & D outlays in 679 U.S. manufacturing corporations, 1975

Number of firms, ranked by sales	Percentage of total for all 679 firms	
	Sales	R & D outlays
First 8	25.3	24.5
First 20	38.1	38.1
First 50	55.4	55.6
First 100	70.7	70.3
First 200	86.2	86.0
First 300	93.0	93.0
First 500	98.5	98.2
All 679	100.0	100.0

Computed from data appearing in "Where Private Industry Puts Its Research Money," *Business Week*, 28 June 1976, pp. 64–84. Companies in the publishing, restaurant, and services categories were excluded, and the sales of Western Electric rather than its parent AT&T were used.

contribute a share of innovations lower than their share of industrial employment—i.e., 21 percent of innovations vs. 35 percent of 1963 employment.[45]

Most other systematic research on this point has focused on the innovative contributions of larger enterprises in specific industries. Brock identified 21 major computer industry innovations and found that IBM was responsible for only 28 percent of them, even though its share of the market during the period covered ranged between 66 and 78 percent.[46] Mansfield found that the four largest firms accounted for a share of innovations between 1919 and 1958 larger than their share of capacity in the petroleum and coal industries, but that the obverse was true in the steel industry. Further analysis revealed that firms with the *highest* innovation outputs relative to their size were of medium size (i.e., roughly sixth in rank within the industry) in coal and petroleum refining and of quite small relative size in steel.[47] A parallel study by Mansfield showed that the output of significant innovations in steel, petroleum, and chemicals per dollar of R & D tended to fall as firm size increased.[48] Still another Mansfield study linked 89 important pharmaceutical preparations introduced into the United States market between 1934 and 1962 to the companies responsible for their introduction. For both the 1934–49 and 1950–62 subperiods, the share of innovations contributed by the four largest ethical drug companies was lower than those firms' share of all U.S. pharmaceutical sales, and the most vigorous innovators again turned out to be companies of intermediate size.[49] However, for a subset of 30 innovations weighted by a panel of experts according to medical importance, the four leading firms' 1950–62 weighted innovation share was larger than their sales share—48 percent as compared to 33 percent.[50]

Analyzing less selective counts of virtually all new pharmaceutical chemical entities introduced in the U.S., Grabowski discovered that from 1957 to 1966, the four leading companies' share of drug innovations was approximately consistent with their ethical drug sales share.[51] After that, with drug development and testing costs soaring from $534,000 per new chemical entity in the 1950s to more than $10 million in the late 1960s, in part because of more stringent governmental regula-

(37) It is important that one avoid biases associated with the exclusion of atypical nonreporting firms, nonmonotonicity of the R & D-size relationship, and differential weights assigned to the relatively many small firms as compared to the few large enterprises. See F. M. Scherer, "Size of Firm, Oligopoly, and Research: A Comment," *Canadian Journal of Economics and Political Science* 31 (May 1965): 256–66.

38. See J. S. Worley, "Industrial Research and the New Competition," *Journal of Political Economy* 69 (April 1961): 183–86; Edwin Mansfield, "Industrial Research and Development Expenditures," *Journal of Political Economy* 72 (August 1964): 319–40; Dan Hamberg, "Size of Firm, Oligopoly, and Research: The Evidence," *Canadian Journal of Economics and Political Science* 30 (February 1964): 62–75; W. S. Comanor, "Market Structure, Product Differentiation, and Industrial Research," *Quarterly Journal of Economics* 85 (November 1967): 639–57; Thomas M. Kelly, "The Influences of Size and Market Structure on the Research Efforts of Large Multiple-Product Firms" (Ph.D. diss., Oklahoma State University, 1969), pp. 81–82; Scherer, *The Economic Effects of Compulsory Patent Licensing*, pp. 73–74; Ronald E. Shrieves, "Firm Size and Innovation: Further Evidence," *Industrial Organization Review* 4, No. 1 (1976): 26–33; and David J. Teece and H. O. Armour, "Innovation and Divestiture in the U.S. Oil Industry," in Teece, ed., *R and D in Energy* (Stanford: Stanford University Institute for Energy Studies, 1977), pp. 11–35.

39. Scherer, *The Economic Effects of Compulsory Patent Licensing*, p. 74.

40. Richard E. Caves and Masu Uekusa, *Industrial Organization in Japan* (Washington, D.C.: Brookings Institution, 1976), pp. 127–28; Jörg Tabbert, *Unternehmensgrösse, Marktstruktur und technischer Fortschritt* (Göttingen: Vandenhoeck & Ruprecht, 1975), pp. 56–108; W. J. Adams, "Firm Size and Research Activity: France and the United States," *Quarterly Journal of Economics* 84 (August 1970): 386–409; J. D. Howe and D. G. McFetridge, "The Determinants of R & D Expenditures," *Canadian Journal of Economics* 9 (February 1976): 57–71; Alexis P. Jacquemin and Henry W. de Jong, *European Industrial Organisation* (London: Macmillan, 1977), pp. 152–54; and Louis Phlips, *Effects of Industrial Concentration: A Cross-Section Analysis for the Common Market* (Amsterdam: North-Holland, 1971), pp. 121–32.

41. Phlips, *Effects of Industrial Concentration*, p. 137.

42. Franklin M. Fisher and Peter Temin, "Returns to Scale in Research and Development: What Does the Schumpeterian Hypothesis Imply?," *Journal of Political Economy* 81 (January-February 1973): 56–70.

43. F. M. Scherer, "Research and Development Returns to Scale and the Schumpeterian Hypothesis: Comment" (Berlin: International Institute of Management Preprint I/73–34, July 1973), pp. 7–9; *idem*, "Firm Size, Market Structure, Opportunity, and the Output of Patented Inventions," *American Economic Review* 55 (December 1965): 1113; Dennis Mueller, "Patents, Research and Development, and the Measurement of Inventive Activity," *Journal of Industrial Economics* 15 (November 1966): 26–37; and W. S. Comanor and F. M. Scherer, "Patent Statistics as a Measure of Technical Change," *Journal of Political Economy* 77 (May-June 1969): 392–98.

In *The Semiconductor Industry*, Federal Trade Commission staff report, January 1977, pp. 108–12, Douglas Webbink reports results by John Tilton showing patents rising less than proportionately with semiconductor R & D expenditures. Similarly diminishing returns in the patent output-R & D input relationship were found by J. C. Morand for eight out of ten French industry groups. See Jacquemin and de Jong, *European Industrial Organisation*, p. 155. A possible reconciliation could be that larger firms pay a higher average salary

tion, the structural relationships changed radically.[52] From 1967 to 1971, Grabowski reported, the top four U.S. pharmaceutical companies accounted for 26 percent of industry sales, but 49 percent of the new chemical entities receiving Food and Drug Administration approval.

Implications What we find from analyzing the qualitative and quantitative evidence is a kind of threshold effect.[53] A little bit of bigness—up to sales levels of $250 to $400 million at 1978 price levels—is good for invention and innovation. But beyond the threshold further bigness adds little or nothing, and it carries the danger of diminishing the effectiveness of inventive and innovative performance. This conclusion naturally bears all the limitations of a statistical generalization. Exceptions certainly exist. Companies far below the suggested threshold may be extraordinarily prolific in generating new ideas, and they may suffer no handicap in developing relatively uncomplicated new products and processes. Firms above the threshold have an advantage in developing extremely complicated and costly systems or chemical products, but a tiny firm (as Control Data Corporation was when it led the way to very high speed digital computers for scientific applications) can overcome its inherent disadvantage through a combination of genius, pluck, and luck.[54] Giants may escape the stultifying effects of size through unusually enlightened management, but this too is not easy or even probable. All things considered, the most favorable industrial environment for rapid technological progress would appear to be a firm size distribution that includes a preponderance of companies with sales below $500 million, pressed on one side by a horde of small, technology-oriented enterprises bubbling over with bright new ideas and on the other by a few larger corporations with the capacity to undertake exceptionally ambitious developments.

Diversification, research, and invention

Another dimension of market structure with possible relevance to the rate of progress is diversification. The leading hypothesis imputing a potentially beneficial role to diversification has been advanced by Richard R. Nelson.[55] In his view, research, and especially basic research, is a venture into the world of uncertainty, yielding inventions and discoveries in unexpected areas. The company with interests in a diversity of fields generally will be able to produce and market a higher proportion of these unanticipated inventions than will an enterprise whose product line is narrow. Therefore, the profitability of speculative research is greater for highly diversified firms, and such firms will tend to support more of it. Diversified enterprises may also have an advantage in research and development because the very breadth of their interests allows particularly effective hedging against the risks of failure on any single R & D project or group of projects.

The Nelson hypothesis applies most directly to the support of basic research. Unfortunately, only limited company size breakdowns are available from National Science Foundation surveys.[56] What evidence on basic research spending we do have lends little support to the hypothesis. Companies with fewer than 5,000 employees are much less diversified than those of larger size. Yet they performed 14 percent of all U.S. basic industrial research between 1970 and 1974—a contribution exceeding their 11 percent share of total R & D outlays.

Several statistical analyses of total research and development spending, employment, or patenting by companies have included *inter alia* a test of diversification effects.[57] The results have been mixed and to some extent contradictory. There is evidence that diversification beyond a very narrow focus—e.g., beyond a single five-digit product line or four-digit industry—is associated with somewhat more intensive research and development effort. However, variables measuring very broad diversification—e.g., across two-digit industry groups—reveal little or no clear positive behavioral effect. Interpretation of the available statistical evidence is complicated by the fact that diversification variables appear in part to be compensating for biases caused by classifying multiproduct firms to a single principal industry. Thus, a company whose home base is the relatively unprogressive food products group but which operates also in chemicals is likely to exhibit a higher average R & D/sales ratio than a corporation producing only food products.[58] Yet it does not necessarily follow that the chemicals operations of the diversified company are more vigorous technically than specialized chemicals producers of comparable size. To disentangle behavioral from industry locus consequences of diversification, one needs data linking company applied research and development expenditures to particular lines of business. Then the effect of diversification on R & D spending relative to appropriate industry benchmarks can be identified. A definitive exploration of this nexus and of the links between basic research spending (which may not be industry specific) and diversification awaits the availability of data being gathered through the Federal Trade Commission's Line of Business reporting program.

Another form of diversification with a possible impact on innovation is the extension of domestic operations to foreign markets. Multinational operation broadens the markets to which a firm's new products and processes have direct access. To the extent that licensing the use of innovations abroad is an imperfect substitute for on-site production and marketing, the profitability of R & D is enhanced. Indeed, in a survey of U.S. multinational enterprises, Mansfield and associates found that on average, 29 to 34 percent of the profit returns from R & D projects came from overseas exploitation.[59] Chemical companies covered by the survey estimated that their R & D budgets would be reduced by 12 percent if they were unable to pass innovations on to foreign subsidiaries. For other multinational firms (e.g., in machinery, instruments, and rubber tires), the average estimated R & D reduction was 15 per cent.

Monopoly, concentration, and innovation

Monopoly power is the final variable whose impact on technical progress must be ascertained. There are two ways it might operate. First, the *expectation of achieving a monopoly*, with accompanying supranormal profits, through successful invention and innovation may induce firms to invest in creating new products and proc-

per R & D employee, so that even though the patent-R & D employment relationship is linear, the patent-R & D expenditure relationship exhibits diminishing returns.

(44) Scherer, "Firm Size . . . and the Output of Patented Inventions," pp. 1103–13; D. J. Smyth, J. M. Samuels, and J. Tzoanos, "Patents, Profitability, Liquidity and Firm Size," *Applied Economics* 4 (June 1972): 77–86; and Bengt Johansson and Christian Lindström, "Firm Size and Inventive Activity," *Swedish Journal of Economics* 73 (December 1971): 427–42.

(45) Christopher Freeman, *The Role of Small Firms in Innovation in the United Kingdom since 1945*, Research Report no. 6, Committee of Inquiry on Small Firms (London: HMSO, 1971), p. 10. Employment shares are from the U.K. *Report on the Census of Production: 1968*, Part no. 158.

(46) Gerald W. Brock, *The U.S. Computer Industry* (Cambridge, Mass.: Ballinger, 1975), pp. 185–207.

(47) Mansfield, *Industrial Research and Technological Innovation*, pp. 83–100. It should be noted that in both the Freeman and Mansfield studies, companies credited with an innovation were not necessarily its developer. Particularly in the coal mining industry, new machinery is typically developed by specialist machinery makers, not by mining firms.

(48) Mansfield, *Industrial Research*, pp. 40–42.

(49) Mansfield et al., *Research and Innovation in the Modern Corporation*, pp. 157–72.

(50) See also John M. Vernon and Peter Gusin, "Technical Change and Firm Size: The Pharmaceutical Industry," *Review of Economics and Statistics* 56 (August 1974): 294–301, who found that larger companies achieved higher average sales on new chemical entities introduced during the 1965–70 period. Mansfield also reported a tendency for the largest firms' new drugs to have higher sales in their first five years on the market. The tendency was just strong enough to equalize the four leaders' total sales and sales-weighted innovation shares.

(51) Henry G. Grabowski, *Drug Regulation and Innovation* (Washington, D.C.: American Enterprise Institute for Public Policy Research, 1976), p. 57. An analogous study showed the four leading *United Kingdom* pharmaceutical companies to have an overall sales share of 27 percent and new product sales share of 40 percent from 1962 to 1966, with a reversal to 30 percent and 15 percent, respectively, from 1967 to 1971.

52. The 1950s development cost estimate is from Mansfield et al., *Research and Innovation in the Modern Corporation*, p. 67. The late 1960s estimate is from Harold A. Clymer, "The Changing Costs and Risks of Pharmaceutical Innovation," in Joseph D. Cooper, ed., *The Economics of Drug Innovation* (Washington, D.C.: American University Center for the Study of Private Enterprise, 1970), pp. 109–24.

53. Cf. Jesse W. Markham, "Market Structure, Business Conduct, and Innovation," *American Economic Review* 55 (May 1965): 325.

54. See "Small, Smart, Sharp," *Business Week*, 25 May 1963, pp. 154–66; and "Control Data's Magnificent Fumble," *Fortune*, April 1966, pp. 165ff.

55. Nelson, "The Simple Economics of Basic Scientific Research," *Journal of Political Economy* 67 (June 1959): 297–306.

56. U.S. National Science Foundation, *Research and Development in Industry: 1974*, pp. 62–64.

57. See especially Scherer, "Firm Size . . . and the Output of Patented Inventions," pp. 1114–16; Henry G. Grabowski, "The Determinants of

esses. Here innovation leads to monopoly, and the belief that such a link exists is what provides the incentive to innovate. This hypothesis is at the heart of the theory of patent protection, which we shall defer for extended analysis in Chapter 16. Second, the *possession of monopoly power* might provide conditions that make business managers more willing and able to undertake the burdens of innovation. Here a quite different causal connection is implied: monopoly power already in existence leads to innovation. It reflects a more uniquely Schumpeterian *Weltanschauung*, and to it we shall devote the balance of this chapter.

Innovation and the availability of funds

There are a number of subhypotheses to the conjecture that a monopolistic market structure favors innovation. One suggested directly by Schumpeter[60] begins with the notion that innovation is costly and risky. Through the profitable exploitation of monopoly power, firms may assemble a pool of funds they are disposed to invest in advancing technology—an investment they would be afraid or unable to make if fresh outside capital had to be tapped.[61] Or to put the proposition in more general form, enterprises with monopoly power are more apt to possess financial and organizational slack that can be used in a variety of discretionary ways, including investment in research and development.

In opposition to this view is the contention that innovation is the result of a conscious search for new and better solutions to pressing problems, and that such search activity is triggered by stress—e.g., by the sort of pressure on profits a competitive market applies.[62] Affluence, on the other hand, might breed complacency and disinterest in change.

It is conceivable that organizational slack favors certain kinds of innovations while pressure induces a different kind. Still one might hope to discern which influence is dominant statistically. Sundry studies addressing this issue have yielded contradictory conclusions.[63] One evident source of difficulty is that two distinct temporal chains of causation could plausibly be at work: High profits might lead to increased spending on research and development, but the latter, if successful, may with a lag lead to new products and

processes that enhance profits. Since companies' R & D budgets do not as a rule change dramatically from year to year, observations on a cross section of companies over a single time interval can confound the effects of profit on R & D with the effects of R & D on profits. We therefore emphasize here the study that probed most carefully into the alternative lag structures.

Ben S. Branch assembled consistent data series on patenting and annual 1950–65 profitability for 111 manufacturing corporations operating in the chemicals, drugs, petroleum refining, paper products, nonferrous metals, machinery, and electrical industries—in all of which appreciable amounts of privately supported R & D were performed.[64] Estimating distributed lag functions for the pooled company-time series data by industry, he found support for *both* hypothesized causal flows—from profitability to patenting (implicitly, by way of R & D spending) *and* from patents to subsequently increased profits. Of the two, the chain from profitability to patenting was less consistent and statistically weaker. Using average values for the relevant variables and parameters, Branch estimated that an extra dollar of profit led at most to about 6.5 cents of additional R & D spending.[65] To the extent that his estimate is valid, encouraging monopoly profits willy-nilly would appear to be a clumsy, low-yield means of stimulating R & D, if indeed further stimulus is desired. More precise, less leak-prone targeting could be achieved by granting special income tax credits (in addition to standard cost deduction status) for some fraction of company R & D outlays, or for increases in R & D above some benchmark period average.

Other hypotheses This by no means exhausts the list of ways monopoly might affect the pace of invention and innovation.[66] Organizational slack may be associated less with higher profits, cash flow, or liquidity than with ample R & D staffs and high salaries that attract the superior brains.[67] Or companies insulated from short-run competitive pressures may be better able to make long-range plans concerning research projects that must be supported for several years and perhaps even a decade before bearing fruit. And by steadying the ship, monopolistic restrictions may establish a more stable platform for shooting at the rapidly and jerkily moving targets of new technology, to use Schumpeter's metaphor.[68] Producers dominating their markets may be able to internalize most of the benefits from innovations they make, whereas some benefits elude the atomistic innovator, who confers external economies upon competitive imitators learning both the technical shortcuts and the blind alleys from its example. On the other hand, critics charge that a monopoly position breeds lethargy and complacency toward technological pioneering.

These global assertions make no distinction between product and process innovations. From the orthodox profit-maximizing theory of firm behavior it can be deduced that pure competitors often have an edge over monopolistic sellers in developing and installing new production processes, other things (such as the volume of pre-innovation output) being equal. This is illustrated in Figure 15.1, which is adapted from a more complex analysis by Professor William Fellner.[69] Suppose the short-run marginal cost function (excluding investment costs) before innovation is MC_1 and after innovation MC_2. To facilitate comparison, we assume in all cases a preinnovation output of OX_1. The competitive firm equates MC_1 with its horizontal marginal revenue function MR_c; the monopolistic producer equates MC_1 with its downward-sloping function MR_M. Each then weighs the profitability of introducing a new process characterized by cost function MC_2. After

Industrial Research and Development: A Study of the Chemical, Drug, and Petroleum Industries," *Journal of Political Economy* 76 (March/April 1968): 292–305; William S. Comanor, "Research and Technical Change in the Pharmaceutical Industry," *Review of Economics and Statistics* 47 (May 1965): 182–91; Kelly, "The Influences of Size and Market Structure," pp. 91–93; and William A. McEachern and Anthony A. Romeo, "Stockholder Control, Uncertainty and the Allocation of Resources to Research and Development," *Journal of Industrial Economics* 26 (June 1978): 349–59.

(58) See the Federal Trade Commission staff report, *Annual Line of Business Report: 1973* (Washington, D.C.: Government Printing Office, March 1979), pp. 29–31.

(59) Edwin Mansfield, Anthony Romeo, and Samuel Wagner, "Foreign Trade and U.S. Research and Development," *Review of Economics and Statistics* 61 (February 1979): 50–52.

60. Schumpeter, *Capitalism, Socialism, and Democracy*, p. 101.

61. For a theoretical analysis, see Nancy L. Schwartz and Morton I. Kamien, "Self-Financing of an R & D Project," *American Economic Review* 68 (June 1978): 252–61. See also Ralph G. M. Sultan, *Pricing in the Electrical Oligopoly*, vol. 2 (Boston: Harvard Business School Division of Research, 1975), pp. 215–25, who argues that General Electric's technological leadership in turbogenerators was directly attributable to the cash flow stemming from its dominant market position, lower unit costs, and control over the price structure.

62. See Richard M. Cyert and James G. March, *A Behavioral Theory of the Firm* (Englewood Cliffs, N.J.: Prentice-Hall, 1963), pp. 278–97.

63. See Jora R. Minasian, "The Economics of Research and Development," in *The Rate and Direction of Inventive Activity*, especially pp. 118–22; Scherer, "Firm Size . . . and the Output of Patented Inventions," p. 1117; idem, "Corporate Inventive Output, Profits, and Growth," *Journal of Political Economy* 73 (June 1965): 290–97; Grabowski, "The Determinants of Industrial Research and Development," pp. 292–305; and Dennis C. Mueller, "The Firm Decision Process: An Econometric Investigation," *Quarterly Journal of Economics* 81 (February 1967), especially pp. 71–73.

64. Ben S. Branch, "Research and Development Activity and Profitability: A Distributed Lag Analysis," *Journal of Political Economy* 82 (September/October 1974): 999–1011. For another distributed lag analysis that found a link of unclear causal direction between R & D spending and profitability, see J. Walter Elliott, "Funds Flow vs. Expectational Theories of Research and Development Expenditures in the Firm," *Southern Economic Journal* 37 (April 1971): 409–22. Elliott's interpretation is that R & D is stimulated by the expectation, rather than the receipt, of profits.

65. Ben S. Branch, "Research and Development, Profits, and Sales Growth" (Ph.D. diss., University of Michigan, 1970), pp. 65–67.

66. For a masterful early survey of the a priori arguments, see P. Hennipman, "Monopoly: Impediment or Stimulus to Economic Progress?," in E. H. Chamberlin, ed., *Monopoly and Competition and Their Regulation* (London: Macmillan, 1954), pp. 421–56.

67. Cf. Schumpeter, *Capitalism, Socialism, and Democracy*, p. 101.

68. Schumpeter, *Capitalism*, pp. 87–88, 103.

69. William Fellner, "The Influence of Market Structure on Technological Progress," *Quarterly Journal of Economics* 65 (November 1951): 560–67.

For another view of process innovation incentives that has experienced elaborate theoretical development despite questionable realism, see Kenneth J. Arrow, "Economic Welfare and the

F 15.1 Process innovation by a monopolist and a pure competitor

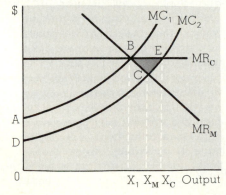

innovation, the monopolist will equate MC_2 with MR_M, producing output OX_M. It realizes an incremental quasi-rent contribution to profits and the recoupment of R & D and capital equipment outlays of $ABCD$ per period. The competitive firm after innovation expands its output to OX_C, realizing the incremental quasi-rent contribution $ABED$ per unit of time. Because the competitor has an incentive to expand output further following a cost reduction, its quasi-rent increment exceeds that of the monopolistic firm by the shaded area BEC per period, *ceteris paribus*.[70] This extra margin might just tip the balance between innovating and not innovating, and so we should expect competitive producers to adopt new cost-reducing processes somewhat more readily than firms with monopoly power, other things being equal.

With respect to product innovations, it is often argued that progress will be especially rapid under oligopoly for reasons similar to those adduced in explaining the vigor of oligopolistic advertising rivalry.[71] Oligopolists have most of the advantages attributed to a monopolist. Their ability to suppress price competition increases organizational slack and permits a longer run decision-making horizon. They are large enough relative to their markets to internalize a significant share of the benefits from innovations subsequently imitated. In addition, because sales at tacitly collusive prices are profitable, oligopolists have an incentive to try increasing their market shares by maneuvering on nonprice dimensions—e.g., through product innovation. Nonprice rivalry may also provide a needed outlet for ingrained aggressive instincts.

Normally, oligopolists find it difficult to establish a cooperative solution to the game of product innovation. Like price rivalry, new product rivalry often has a static payoff structure of the Prisoners' Dilemma type. But each R & D project differs in numerous respects from all previous undertakings, so opportunities for tacit learning, the development of quantitative precedents, and the dynamic use of threats to elicit cooperation are minimal. The sensitivity of outcomes to variations in the participants' skill, creativity, and luck is much higher than in price rivalry, complicating the problem of reaching mutual accommoda-

tion.[72] During the early stages of a research and development project, so few persons are typically employed that plans can be kept secret; and uncertainty about what its rivals are brewing in their laboratories compels each firm to fear the worst. Even more important, several years of development may be required to bring a complex new product from the concept stage to a point where it is ready for the market. The enterprise caught off guard by a rival innovation is condemned to a position of inferiority during this catching-up period. Recognizing this danger, each firm has an incentive to begin development of any important, threatening new product possibility in which rivals have shown interest. For all these reasons, we should not expect oligopolists to be very successful in handling product innovation collusively, though it is possible to find some apparent exceptions to the rule.[73]

A model of oligopolistic product R & D rivalry Further insight into the structural conditions favoring a rapid pace of innovation can be gained by formulating the problem of new product rivalry more rigorously.[74] We start from the standard profit maximization premise: Firms seek to conduct their research and development projects in such a way as to maximize the surplus of expected revenues over expected costs. For simplicity, we assume that imitation in kind is feasible, i.e., that patent barriers can be surmounted; that rivalry takes the form of matching each others' improved qualitative features; and that each participant in the process must carry out its own R & D to market its improved product.

The potential innovator's problem is to decide how rapidly it will proceed in developing its product and introducing it into the market. Development can be carried out at a leisurely pace, as a crash program, or at various speeds in between. Accelerating the pace of development is costly for three reasons. First, errors are made when one overlaps development steps instead of waiting for the information early experiments supply. Second, it may be necessary to support parallel experimental approaches to hedge against uncertainty. Third, there are conventional diminishing returns in the application of additional scientific and engineering manpower to a given technical assignment. The possibilities for saving time by spending more money to develop a given new product starting at time 0 are specified by the time-cost tradeoff function C in Figure 15.2. The shorter the development schedule, the more the effort costs, *ceteris paribus*. This represents the cost side of the firm's R & D scheduling problem.

Against the costs of accelerated development, a potential innovator must weigh the benefits of proceeding more rapidly. These are reflected in a benefits function like V_1 in Figure 15.2, which indicates the discounted total quasi-rents (i.e., the surplus of sales revenues over production and distribution costs) expected from having the new product ready for commercial introduction at varying dates. It is negatively sloped for two main reasons: Completing the development effort earlier allows the firm to tap the market's profit potential over a longer time span, and earlier completion improves the firm's competitive position relative to rivals, with possibly lasting implications for its market share and hence its share of the market's total profit potential.

Now the firm's problem is to choose the development schedule that maximizes the surplus of benefits V_1 over costs C. The optimum is found

F 15.2 Optimizing the speed of new product development

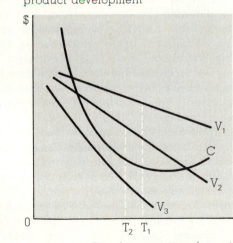

Development time (years)

Allocation of Resources for Invention," in *The Rate and Direction of Inventive Activity*, pp. 609–25; Harold Demsetz, "Information and Efficiency: Another Viewpoint," *Journal of Law and Economics* 12 (April 1969): 1–22; Morton I. Kamien and Nancy L. Schwartz, "Market Structure, Elasticity of Demand and Incentive To Invent," *Journal of Law and Economics* 13 (April 1970): 241–52; Sheng Cheng Hu, "On the Incentive To Invent: A Clarificatory Note," *Journal of Law and Economics* 16 (April 1973): 169–78; Douglas Needham, "Market Structure and Firms' R & D Behavior," *Journal of Industrial Economics* 23 (June 1975): 241–55; Ward Bowman, "The Incentive To Invent in Competitive as Contrasted to Monopolistic Industries," *Journal of Law and Economics* 20 (April 1977): 227–28; and Kevin Sontheimer, "Some Further Considerations Regarding Market Structure and the Incentive To Invent" (Discussion paper, State University of New York at Buffalo, September 1976).

70. An oligopolist subject to the kinked demand curve mentality will not increase output at all unless the cost reduction owing to innovation is sufficiently large to jump the marginal revenue function's gap. See Oscar Lange, "A Note on Innovations," *Review of Economic Statistics* 25 (February 1943): 23–24.

71. See especially Galbraith, *American Capitalism*, pp. 88–90; Henry Villard, "Competition, Oligopoly, and Research," *Journal of Political Economy* 66 (December 1958): 483–97; and James W. McKie, *Tin Cans and Tin Plate* (Cambridge, Mass.: Harvard University Press, 1959), pp. 253–54.

72. See William Fellner, *Competition Among the Few* (New York: Knopf, 1949), pp. 185, 220–21.

73. The U.S. automobile industry's record in resisting the development of small cars, pollution control devices, and electric propulsion are probable illustrations. On these and other delayed innovations, see Lawrence J. White, *The Automobile Industry Since 1945* (Cambridge, Mass.: Harvard University Press, 1971), Chapters 11 and 14. White argues that the Big Three delayed the introduction of small cars both to avoid the loss of higher profit margins on their large cars and to ensure that the demand for small cars was large enough for all three to sell such cars profitably.

74. The analysis presented here is developed more fully in F. M. Scherer, "Research and Development Resource Allocation under Rivalry," *Quarterly Journal of Economics* 81 (August 1967): 359–94; and W. L. Baldwin and G. L. Childs, "The Fast Second and Rivalry in Research and Development," *Southern Economic Journal* 36 (July 1969): 18–24. Generally similar conclusions flow from a much richer model that incorporates uncertainty concerning rivals' time of innovation, development cost changes associated with learning from or being blocked by rival developments, the possibility of complete foreclosure by preempting rivals, and a variety of complex strategy options. See Morton I. Kamien and Nancy L. Schwartz, "Potential Rivalry, Monopoly Profits and the Pace of Inventive Activity," *Review of Economic Studies* 45 (October 1978): 547–57. Earlier contributions by Kamien and Schwartz in the same framework include "Timing of Innovations under Rivalry," *Econometrica* 40 (January 1972): 43–60; and "On the Degree of Rivalry for Maximum Innovative Activity," *Quarterly Journal of Economics* 90 (May 1976): 245–60. See also Raymond R. de Bondt, "Innovative Activity and Barriers to Entry," *European Economic Review*, October 1977, pp. 95–109.

where the slope of the benefits function equals the slope of the time-cost tradeoff function, i.e., at development time OT_1. At the optimum, the marginal benefit from schedule acceleration (i.e., the increase in discounted quasi-rents from compressing the development period by one more unit of time) is equal to the marginal cost of acceleration (the increase in cost from reducing development time by one more unit).

At any given moment, the shape and position of the time-cost tradeoff function C is largely determined by the state of technology. But the shape of the benefits function depends *inter alia* upon market structure. That is the core of our concern. From the conditions for profit maximization, we know that the pace of innovation will be faster, the steeper the slope of the innovator's benefits function is. Is the slope steeper when the number of firms is large or small? And is it steeper for small firms or relatively large (e.g., dominant) enterprises?

There is no absolutely general, unambiguous answer; it depends upon a number of conditions. There are, however, some most probable answers. If we accept the Cournot-like assumption that firms consider themselves unable to influence rival schedule decisions by their own decisions—an assumption compatible with the many obstacles preventing collusive handling of new product rivalry—and if innovators are not restrained from penetrating into the new product's market by capacity bottlenecks, then an increase in the number of rivals or a reduction in the relative size of the innovator accelerates the pace of development.

Concretely, when the number of evenly matched rivals increases from, say, two to three, *ceteris paribus*, the benefits function faced by a potential innovator will undergo a shift, as from V_1 to V_2, and the optimal time of development will be compressed from OT_1 to OT_2. This is so because by introducing its new product ahead of the others, the innovator enjoys temporarily what would otherwise be the market domain of its rivals. The more evenly matched rivals there are with a stake in the market, the larger will be the portion (which would otherwise go to rivals) the innovator gets to enjoy during its term of leadership. Moreover, by leading the way, the innovator

may also be able to gain an image or reputation advantage, enabling it permanently to increase its market share at the expense of rivals.[75] The larger the share of the market rivals would command if they exactly matched its new product introduction date, the more the innovator has to gain by being first and permanently capturing some of that share, *ceteris paribus*. Or to put the point the other way around, the smaller a company's share of some new product market will be if it *fails* to lead, the more it has to gain by leading, and hence the more rapidly it will be inclined to proceed in its R & D effort.

It follows obversely that a monopolist or a company that already dominates the market it supplies has little to gain by speeding up the introduction of product improvements as long as other firms refrain from doing so, since there is not much it can take away from others.[76] Dominant firms are not likely to be vigorous innovators. But if their market position is threatened by the intrusion of a smaller innovator, they have a great deal to lose from running a poor second: the larger share they would otherwise enjoy. The theory predicts then that profit-maximizing dominant firms will be potent imitators when their market shares are endangered. They may even accelerate their development efforts so strongly in response to a challenge that they induce the challenger to relax its development pace and settle for the smaller market share associated with being second. Still, in this more complex "fast second" case, it is the small firm that wins honors for hastening technological progress, since without its initial challenge, the dominant firm would not have moved so quickly.

We conclude from the analysis thus far that the rapidity of innovation increases with the number of firms, and that sellers with small market shares are more likely to trigger a rapid pace of innovation than dominant firms, though the latter may retaliate vigorously. This suggests that tight oligopoly is less conducive to progress than loose oligopoly and that both are better than pure monopoly. Reinforcing this inference is a point heretofore neglected. The more rivals an industry includes, the more independent centers of initiative there are, and the more likely it is that some entrepreneur will consider the development of a potential new product worthwhile. Once he does so, he threatens the market shares of other industry members, precipitating a spiral of reactions that ends with each seller introducing its countervailing new product at an earlier date than would have been the case in the absence of rivalry.

These conclusions rest solely upon analyzing how market structure affects the *slopes* of the benefit functions confronting would-be innovators. There is another side to the picture, however. While an increase in the number of rivals steepens the slope of the benefits function, it also shifts the function down and to the left, reducing the total discounted profit an innovator can expect to realize. This occurs because after imitation takes place, and especially if it comes fairly rapidly, the innovator will find itself dividing up the market's total profit potential with more rivals and enjoying a smaller share itself, all else being equal. Also, if the number of imitating rivals becomes large, pricing discipline may break down, causing not only the innovator's *share* of the profit pie, but the pie itself, to shrink. If the number of likely imitators is sufficiently large, the benefits function confronting a would-be innovator may lie as far to the left as V_3 in Figure 15.2. Here pioneering a new product development is expected to be downright unprofitable; and if all sellers have similar expectations, none will be willing to take the first step. A kind of Alphonse-and-Gaston dynamics will ensue, each industry member holding back initiating its R & D effort in the fear that rapid imitation by others will be encouraged, more than wiping out its innovative profits. Whether or not this happens depends largely upon the interrelationship of five variables: the size of the overall market profit potential, the number of actual or potential rivals vying to share that potential, the speed at which rivals are expected to react and imitate, the degree to which being first confers a permanent product differentiation advantage, and the magnitude of anticipated R & D costs. The smaller the new product market's total profit potential is in relation to any single firm's development costs, *ceteris paribus*, the more the presence of a significant number of rivals is apt to discourage early innovation.

What we find then is a clash of structural propensities. In terms of the marginal conditions for profit maximization, an increase in the number of sellers is conducive to more rapid innovation. This influence can be called the *stimulus factor*. But in terms of the requirement that expected profits from innovation be non-negative, an increase in the number of firms can, beyond some point, discourage rapid innovation. This influence might appropriately be called the *market room factor.*[77]

To carry the analysis further we need a broader dynamic conception of the process of technological advance. The profitability of innovation depends in the most fundamental sense upon supply and demand conditions. On the supply side, the costs of carrying out a research and development project are influenced by changes in the stock of knowledge. As scientific and technological knowledge advances, what may be impossible today will be feasible but costly tomorrow and easy the day after tomorrow. That is, there is a tendency for time-cost tradeoff functions, recalibrated periodically in current time, to shift toward the origin of Figure 15.2 (i.e., in a southwesterly direction) as time passes and knowledge accumulates. The benefits function is concurrently affected by changing demand conditions. As population grows, per capita incomes rise, and (less certainly) input cost ratios vary, the benefits function for a potential innovation may shift in a northeasterly direction. An innovation becomes profitable when, as a result of changes in knowledge and/or demand, the benefits function comes to lie at least partially above the time-cost tradeoff function. Innovations induced primarily by advances in knowledge are called technology-push innovations. Those ren-

75. On the image advantages of being first with a new product, see Chapter 8, p. 260 and Chapter 14, p. 384 *supra*.

76. Concerning the theory of similar drags on innovation by IBM as a dominant firm lessor of computers, see Brock, *The U.S. Computer Industry*, pp. 211–15.

77. For similar views, see Jewkes et al., *The Sources of Invention*, pp. 133–36 of the second edition; and Hennipman, "Monopoly: Impediment or Stimulus?," p. 449.

dered attractive by rising demand are called demand-pull innovations. Usually both supply and demand conditions are changing, and innovation may be induced by a combination of the two forces.[78]

Suppose now that the advance of knowledge and increases in demand take place smoothly and continuously. At some moment in time, an innovation that was not profitable before will suddenly become profitable for a pure monopolist as the shifting benefits and time-cost tradeoff functions fleetingly become tangent with one another. At this same moment, the development would not yet have become profitable if the market were divided among oligopolists, each anticipating having to share the new product's sales with rivals, and hence unable completely to monopolize the fruits of its R & D effort. If innovation is to occur as rapidly as is profitably feasible under the conditions postulated, monopoly is essential!

Of course, a monopolist may choose not to innovate at this first profitable moment. If it can foresee continuing cost and benefit function shifts, it will prefer to wait until it can earn more than a bare normal profit on its development investment.[79] Indeed, even when cost and benefit function shifts are smooth and continuous, it may delay so long that innovation is also profitable by oligopolists. And when the functions have shifted discontinuously, as in the case of technological breakthroughs, or when there have been lags in the recognition of profitable innovation opportunities, it is likely that there will be ample room in the market for the new products of multiple firms. These conditions may be satisfied frequently in practice, since many innovations do follow from breakthroughs, and since evidence of generous prevailing profit returns to R & D investment suggests that the profit potential of new product markets is by no means spread too thinly.[80]

We emerge, as is often our lot, with ambiguous theoretical predictions. Monopoly and high concentration are conducive to rapid innovation in certain respects—e.g., through the market room and organizational slack effects. But rivalry among numerous sellers is beneficial in others, notably, in terms of its stimulus effects. Which tendencies dominate in the real world is an empirical question to which we now turn.

Qualitative evidence Like the predictions from theory, the qualitative evidence from case studies of technological progress in specific industries presents a mixed picture. One theme that appears repeatedly is the apparent inhospitality of an atomistic market structure to research, development, and innovation. The paucity of significant innovations conceived and developed within the home construction industry, with its thousands of small producers, is well known.[81] A chronicle of the snail's pace at which automated brick-making equipment was developed reveals deficient incentives to innovate when the leading four producers together account for only 12 percent of nationwide production, even when substitute materials are eroding industry sales.[82] In the fertilizer industry, with 85 bulk producers in 1967 and a four-firm concentration ratio of 35, vigorous innovative activity was conspicuously absent. Many of the leading new developments had to be pioneered and demonstrated by the Tennessee Valley Authority—an arm of the federal government.[83] Two book-length studies of the radio industry in the United States and Great Britain reached the common conclusion that small manufacturers did little to advance the underlying technology during the 1920s and 1930s. Instead they concentrated on producing attractively styled products at low cost. Most of the significant research and development contributions came either from powerful firms like AT&T, General Electric, and RCA or from independent inventors.[84]

Nevertheless, there are some exceptions to this pattern. Since World War II an impressive R & D effort has been sustained in both unconcentrated and concentrated product lines of the electronics industry, with small competitors bearing at least their share of the load.[85] Peck found that most of the innovations in aluminum end product applications came from the 24,000-odd firms engaged in fabricating such products, not from the oligopolistic primary metal refiners. He observed also that the general pace of innovation was accelerated when Alcoa's monopoly position in ingot production was dissolved through the government-sponsored entry of several rivals.[86] And in petroleum refining, where the leading four firms, although very large in an absolute sense, originate only a third of total national output, active R & D programs are supported by both the industry leaders and numerous smaller producers. Phillips, one of the most technically progressive refiners, commands a national market share of only 3 percent.

Certain case studies demonstrate too that innovation was retarded when competition was suppressed. Maclaurin concludes, for example, that technical progress would have been faster in the radio field during the 1920s and 1930s if AT&T, General Electric, and Westinghouse had not agreed to limit competition among themselves by defining spheres of influence and by forming the Radio Corporation of America to coordinate their patent portfolios.[87] Bright and Maclaurin observed that cartelization of the U.S. electric lamp industry during the same period slowed down the development of fluorescent lighting and other advances.[88] And the general sluggishness that led to a gradual deterioration of Imperial Chemical Industries' position in world markets has been traced to its participation in elaborate cartel and spheres of influence agreements with international rivals.[89]

There is also considerable evidence to support our earlier prediction that companies dominating their markets will be slow innovators but aggressive followers. Examples include Gillette's experience in bringing out a stainless steel razor blade during the 1960s,[90] IBM's slow start and fast finish in developing digital electronic computing equipment and time-sharing computers,[91] AT&T's record in the development of microwave radio relay systems and communications satellites,[92] National Cash Register's "fast second" role in the shift to electronic point-of-sale devices,[93] the reaction of Kellogg and General Mills to small firms' success in selling granola-type cereals,[94] the United Shoe Machinery Corporation's response to Compo's sole-cementing device innovations,[95] and General Electric's move to join forces with the small company that led the way to experimental hydrogen fusion using laser techniques.[96] Even here, however, the record is not completely uniform. RCA's almost single-handed struggle to develop and promote color television after the Federal Communications Commission approved its dot-sequential system as the national standard (rejecting the Columbia field-sequential system) suggests that technical pio-

78. For a brilliant theoretical and empirical investigation of the demand and supply influences inducing technological advance, see Jacob Schmookler, *Invention and Economic Growth* (Cambridge, Mass.: Harvard University Press, 1966). See also Nathan Rosenberg, "Science, Invention and Economic Growth," *Economic Journal* 100 (March 1974): 90–108.

79. To see this, let b be the dollar quasi-rent realized each year once an innovation is commercially introduced, T the date of introduction, t a running time variable, r the discount rate, and C_o the cost of development (assumed for simplicity to take place instantaneously, without the kind of time-cost tradeoff implied by Figure 15.2) at time $t = 0$. The assumed constancy of b implies that demand-pull influences are absent. However, development costs are assumed to fall as a result of exogenous technological progress at a rate of $100\,\alpha$ percent per annum. Thus, the cost of development at year T is $C_o\,e^{-\alpha T}$. The monopolist's problem is to choose an introduction date T so as to maximize the discounted present value of quasi-rents less development cost:

$$(1) \qquad \int_T^\infty b\,e^{-rt}dt - C_o e^{-(\alpha+r)T} = \frac{b\,e^{-rT}}{r} - C_o e^{-(\alpha+r)T}$$

Setting the derivative of this expression equal to zero for a local maximum, we obtain:

$$(2) \qquad b\,e^{-rT} = (\alpha + r)C_o e^{-(\alpha+r)T}$$

Discounted quasi-rents equal development cost—i.e., the break even point is fleetingly attained—when the first term in equation (1) equals the second term. Rearranging, we have:

$$(3) \qquad b\,e^{-rT} = (r)C_o e^{-(\alpha+r)T}$$

which differs from equation (2) only in the absence of α in the first parenthesized term on the right-hand side. To satisfy the equality with a lower value of the first right-hand side parenthesis term, and since the right-hand side exponent is more heavily discounted than the left-hand side, equation (3) must have a lower value of T than equation (2). Thus, the break even date for innovation occurs earlier than the monopolist's profit-maximizing date unless immediate introduction maximizes the monopolist's profits.

On this and related issues, see Yoram Barzel, "Optimal Timing of Innovations," *Review of Economics and Statistics* 50 (August 1968): 348–55. For an ambitious extension, see Carole Kitti, "Patent Policy and the Optimal Timing of Innovations" (Ph.D. diss., University of Chicago, 1973). Cf. also Scherer, *The Economic Effects of Patent Licensing*, pp. 31–34; and Glenn C. Loury, "Market Structure and Innovation," *Quarterly Journal of Economics* 93 (August 1979).

Barzel and Kitti make the important point that innovation might occur *too soon* when rivalry accelerates the introduction date to the break even point [eq. (3)]. If R & D investments are not duplicated, break even point introduction is socially optimal only when $(\alpha + r)/r$ equals the ratio of discounted social benefits to the innovator's (i.e., private) discounted quasi-rents. If the social/private benefit ratio exceeds $(\alpha + r)/r$, innovation comes too late under break even rivalry; if the obverse, too soon. For a sample of 17 innovations, Mansfield and colleagues found the median social/private benefit ratio to be on the order of 2.25. "Social and Private Rates of Return from Industrial Innovations," *Quarterly Journal of Economics* 91 (May 1977): 221–40. Since it is likely that $\alpha < r$, it seems improbable that $(\alpha + r)/r \geq 2.25$, so competitive acceleration of development is likely on average to serve the social interest.

Kitti also observes that a decision maker with perfect foresight and market control would never choose a development schedule accelerated in the sense that one operates to the left of the minimum-cost point on Figure 15.2. Rather, by starting development earlier and proceeding more slowly, resources would be conserved and profits or consumers' surplus enhanced. This is of course difficult

neering is not a virtue totally foreign to industry leaders. Equally impressive was the invention and development of the float glass technique by Pilkington Brothers, Ltd., who supplied 90 percent of all British flat glass requirements.[97] The Aluminum Company of America spent $25 million developing a new energy-efficient smelting method using aluminum chloride.[98] And before World War II the I. G. Farben combine, which dominated Germany's chemical industry, is said to have been one of the most research-intensive firms in the world.[99]

The main lesson to be drawn from a review of the qualitative evidence is that no simple, one-to-one relationship between market structure and technological progressiveness is discernible. Indeed, it seems reasonable to infer that market structure has less influence on the pace at which innovation occurs than certain other variables.

The most important determinant is undoubtedly the richness of opportunities opened up by advances in science and technical knowledge. It would be myopic to suggest that there are no attractive opportunities for improving fire bricks or the way they are made. But companies producing electronic circuit modules, synthetic hormones, peripheral input and output devices for computers, nuclear reactors, artificial kidneys, numerically controlled milling machines, and color film surely face a much more bountiful array of unexploited technical possibilities. The richness of technological opportunity varies widely from one product area to another, giving rise to extensive interindustry variation in R & D spending, patenting, and the like.[100] Furthermore, some industries are in a better position than others to take advantage of new opportunities. To extend a homely example, the brick-making industry might benefit from computer control of its production processes, but economies of specialization dictate that the computer be designed by and acquired from an electronics producer. Such specialization is a prominent feature of every industrialized economy. Because of it, companies at home in the electrical and chemical fields, blessed with rich and growing funds of scientific knowledge, have enjoyed a distinct advantage in developing and producing new processes and intermediate materials used by a host

of other sectors.[101] For firms surrounded by a more meager knowledge base, progressiveness may demand no more than the ability to recognize their own needs and the willingness to utilize products and processes others develop to satisfy those needs.

A second, more illusive prerequisite for rapid progress is an attitude of receptiveness on the part of entrepreneurs to harness science for industrial purposes. Opportunities created by the advance of knowledge may not even be recognized unless resources are devoted to identifying them and unless business managers listen to the people able to identify them. This "research conception," as Maclaurin put it, is much stronger in some U.S. industries than in others.[102] Likewise, Hohenberg observed that differences in technological progressiveness among the German, French, British, and Swiss chemical industries from 1850 to 1914 resulted more from differences in entrepreneurial attitudes than from disparities in scientific opportunity, raw material endowments, or market structure.[103]

Why a research conception appears in some industries or nations and not in others is unclear. The only conceivable way market structure might affect the process is through a kind of demonstration effect, e.g., when some monopolistic firm with organizational slack decides to dabble in research, as du Pont did during the 1920s, and has such good luck that others are inspired to follow suit. But this is only one of many possible precipitating factors. The strikingly successful application of science to warfare during World War II undoubtedly had a much more potent demonstration effect on the electrical, instruments, chemicals, and drug industries in the United States, and this in turn may explain the rapid spread of formal R & D program sponsorship to smaller firms in those industries.[104] For our present purposes, it does not seem too great an oversimplification to assume that industries acquire a research conception largely by historical accident. To the extent that this is true, it adds random variation or 'noise' to the relationships observed between market structure and technical progressiveness. If such relationships exist, therefore, we should not expect them to be powerful statistically, and certainly not to explain all the interindustry variation in progressiveness indices.

Quantitative evidence

Cautioned against expecting too much, let us see whether any general statistical relationships can be detected.

One measure of technological progress is the growth over time of productivity—that is, output per worker (ideally, adjusted for differences in capital intensity). Early attempts to relate productivity change to some index of market concentration yielded equivocal or contradictory results[105]—in part, it would appear, because of differently defined variables or sample coverage, failure to take into account variables other than concentration associated with productivity growth, and the formidable difficulty of measuring productivity growth when product characteristics are complex and changing. Perhaps the most carefully conducted study to date is one by Douglas Greer and Stephen Rhoades.[106] They correlated indices of productivity growth with concentration ratios, taking into account also such variables as industry growth and capital/output ratios, for three samples of manufacturing industries and time spans—35 narrowly defined industries on which physical quantity-based productivity data were available over the 1919–40 period, 80 three-digit industries (with somewhat less carefully controlled productivity data) for 1954–71, and 394 industries with catch-as-catch-can data for 1958–69. For all three samples, seller concentration ratios were positively and significantly correlated with the productivity growth indices, other relevant variables being equal. The results for the two post-World War II samples imply that a difference in the four-firm concentration ratio of 40 points (e.g., from 40 to 80) was associated on average with a half percentage point difference in the annual productivity growth rate.

Why concentration should make this sort of a difference is somewhat perplexing. As we have seen earlier, less than 20 percent of U.S. enterprises' R & D is directed toward improving internal production processes; most is devoted to new or improved *products*. There is also extensive specialization by certain industries in supplying machines or raw and intermediate materials to

to achieve, and the desirability of leisurely development is less clear in a world of technological discontinuities and recognition lags.

(80) See Mansfield, *Industrial Research and Technological Innovation*, pp. 57, 65, 75–76.

(81) See Charles Foster, "Competition and Organization in Building," *Journal of Industrial Economics* 12 (July 1964): 163–74.

(82) "Brick Kiln Builds Up Its Speed," *Business Week*, 15 July 1967, pp. 72–74.

(83) See Jesse W. Markham, *The Fertilizer Industry* (Nashville: Vanderbilt University Press, 1958), pp. 164–68, 212–14; and U.S., Federal Council for Science and Technology, Committee on Government Patent Policy, *Government Patent Policy*, vol. III, "Government Promotion of Federally Sponsored Inventions," Section VIII (Boston: Harbridge House, June 1968). Perhaps the most dramatic innovation of recent decades—large-scale centrifugal compressor-driven plants for synthetic ammonia production—was pioneered in 1965 by Monsanto Chemical Co., which was not listed by Markham as one of the top 22 nitrogen producers in 1955. See Markham, p. 103; and "Ammonia's New World: More Plant, Less Crew," *Business Week*, 13 November 1965, pp. 134–39.

(84) W. R. Maclaurin, *Invention and Innovation in the Radio Industry* (New York: Macmillan, 1949), pp. 153–224, 251–56; and S. G. Sturmey, *The Economic Development of Radio* (London: Duckworth, 1958), pp. 155, 162, 233.

(85) See Webbink, *The Semiconductor Industry*, pp. 103–12, 130–35.

(86) M. J. Peck, "Inventions in the Postwar American Aluminum Industry," in *The Rate and Direction of Inventive Activity*, pp. 291–98.

(87) Maclaurin, *Invention and Innovation in the Radio Industry*, p. 254.

(88) Arthur A. Bright, Jr., and W. R. Maclaurin, "Economic Factors Influencing the Development and Introduction of the Fluorescent Lamp," *Journal of Political Economy* 51 (October 1943): 449.

(89) "The British Company That Found a Way Out," *Fortune*, August 1966, pp. 104ff.

(90) "How Gillette Has Put on a New Face," *Business Week*, 1 April 1967, pp. 58–60; and "Gillette Hones Its Edge," *Business Week*, 23 October 1965, p. 143.

(91) Brock, *The U.S. Computer Industry*, pp. 11–21, 102–106, 187–207.

(92) F. M. Scherer, "The Development of the TD-X and TD-2 Microwave Radio Relay Systems in Bell Telephone Laboratories" (Case study, Harvard University Graduate School of Business Administration, October 1960).

(93) "The Battle of the Cash Registers," *Business Week*, 10 April 1971, pp. 67–68.

(94) "Kellogg Moves Out with Own Natural Entry," *Advertising Age*, 15 October 1973, pp. 1, 98.

(95) Carl Kaysen, *United States v. United Shoe Machinery Corporation*, pp. 77, 184–89.

(96) See "KMS Industries Bets Its Life on Laser Fusion," *Fortune*, December 1974, pp. 149ff.; and "Versatile Laser," *Barron's*, 2 June 1975, p. 3.

97. Monopolies Commission, *Report on the Supply of Flat Glass* (London: HMSO, February 1968).

98. "A Revolutionary Alcoa Process," *Business Week*, 20 January 1973, p. 92.

99. C. Freeman, "The Plastics Industry: A Comparative Study of Re-

other industries. To the extent that process technology is imported from other industries, productivity growth shortfalls over such long periods as 1919–40 or even 17 years, if indeed causally linked to concentration, would have to reflect producers' unwillingness to cooperate with process improvement specialists or reluctance to replace worn-out equipment with the best new techniques available on the market. While pathological cases of refusal to accept what is practically a free lunch may exist, it seems improbable that this is what the Greer-Rhoades results reveal. More plausibly, there may be a tendency for concentrated industries to enjoy richer opportunities to improve productivity—e.g., because labor-saving technical change is biased in favor of industries for which minimum optimal scales are large in relation to market size.

Other investigations, proceeding from the premise that new machines or materials are in fact widely available, have explored the rate at which the adoption of innovations diffuses through the population of potential users. Comparisons of adoption rates across several industries—in one case, with the specific innovation (numerically controlled machine tools) the same for ten different using industries—suggest that diffusion occurs more quickly with many sellers and a low variance of firm sizes in the using industry.[107] Without insights or facts that currently elude us, it is difficult to reconcile this finding with the productivity relationships observed by Greer and Rhoades.

Still other studies of the market structure-progressiveness nexus have focused on some measure of efforts directly to advance technology, such as R & D employment or spending. The pioneering analyses of this genre sought to ascertain the correlation between the ratio of R & D expenditures to sales, obtained for a sample of from 13 to 20 highly aggregated U.S. industry groups, and an index of market concentration.[108] In every such instance, a positive correlation coefficient ranging in magnitude from 0.29 to 0.54 was obtained. Consistent with Schumpeter's conjectures, the more concentrated markets were, the more intensely R & D was supported.

An important shortcoming of these early analyses is that they failed to take into account interindustry differences in technological opportunity. Some industries tap a rich and growing knowledge base; others do not. More light is shed on this problem by statistical investigations that have tried to adjust for something corresponding to differences in the potential for making innovations. Although the data and statistical models are quite heterogeneous, the conclusions tend to be similar, at least for those analyses focusing on patterns in the United States.[109]

One finding common to all such analyses is that the intensity of industry or company R & D efforts is strongly correlated with the indices of technological opportunity, whether they reflect subjective categorizations of the industry science base, a factor analysis of company scientists' and engineers' disciplinary specialities, or a more conventional division according to consumers' versus producers' goods and durables versus nondurables. After differences in opportunity were taken into account, the correlation between R & D intensity continued in most cases (with Wilson's results as the principal exception) to be positive but much weaker.[110] In the author's own study of 56 industries, for instance, a simple correlation of $+0.46$ was obtained between the ratio of scientific and engineering to total employment and the concentration index. However, when differences in product technology were taken into account, the partial correlation between the technological employment index and concentration fell to $+0.20$. This occurred because concentration was higher on the average in fields of high technological opportunity (notably, electrical equipment and industrial chemicals) than in the traditional technology groups; and the intensity of scientific and engineering employment, while correlated with both differences in opportunity and concentration, was more strongly correlated with the former than the latter.

This raises a delicate question of cause and effect. Is technological opportunity independent of concentration, or is there some causal connection? And if the latter, in what direction does the chain of causation flow: from high opportunity to high concentration, or from high concentration to high opportunity? Observation leads us to believe that the greater progressiveness of the chemicals, electrical, and (in Phillips's and

Shrieves's samples) aircraft industries is not attributable primarily to high concentration, since the advance of scientific knowledge has been exceptionally generous to these fields during the past century. Some support can, however, be mustered for the hypothesis that technological innovation associated with opportunity has led to concentration. The high concentration in such fields as synthetic fibers, organic chemicals, telephone equipment, electric lamps, and photographic equipment was built in part upon patent and know-how barriers to entry. Also, a rapid pace of technological change in high opportunity industries is likely to have increased the variance of member firms' growth rates, with successful innovators growing rapidly and unsuccessful ones being displaced. This would have the effect of raising concentration levels over time under some variant of Gibrat's law.[111] It appears more plausible, therefore, that technological opportunity and concentration are either independent or that the observed correlation between them reflects a causal flow from opportunity to concentration. In either event, the inclusion of opportunity indices helps avoid imputing to concentration a stimulative effect that is not warranted.

Yet even after differences in opportunity were taken into account, a positive association between intensity of R & D effort and concentration tended to persist. This suggests that the climate for innovation is more favorable in concentrated than in atomistic industries, other things being equal. To this a vital qualification must be added. Three of the studies attempted to proceed further and analyze the correlation between R & D vigor and concentration *within* opportunity classes. In all three, the strongest positive correlations emerged for industries facing relatively sparse innovative opportunities.[112] For my own analysis of 56 industries, the correlation between scientists and engineers per 1,000 employees and concentration was $+0.47$ among the "traditional" products industries, which on the average employed by far the fewest technical personnel. It was $+0.30$ for the general and mechanical products group and *negative* for the five industries in the chemicals class. The mean level of scientific and engineering employment predicted by the tradi-

search and Innovation," *National Institute Economic Review* No. 26 (November 1963): 33.

(100) See Scherer, "Firm Size . . . and the Output of Patented Inventions," pp. 1099–1103, in which it is estimated that some 30 percent of the observed interfirm differences in patenting can be attributed to interindustry differences in technological opportunity.

(101) See Schmookler, *Invention and Economic Growth*, pp. 165–78.

(102) W. R. Maclaurin, "Technological Progress in Some American Industries," *American Economic Review* 44 (May 1954): 178–89.

(103) Paul M. Hohenberg, *Chemicals in Western Europe: 1850–1914* (Chicago: Rand McNally, 1967), especially pp. 67–84.

(104) It is conceivable that before World War II had its demonstration effect, the organizational slack associated with monopoly power was a more important basis of technological leadership. This could explain why the performance of such firms as du Pont, I.C.I., I. G. Farben, RCA, and AT&T was more impressive relative to that of smaller concerns before the war than after.

(105) See George J. Stigler, "Industrial Organization and Economic Progress," in L. D. White, ed., *The State of the Social Sciences* (Chicago: University of Chicago Press, 1956), pp. 269–82; Almarin Phillips, "Concentration, Scale, and Technological Change in Selected Manufacturing Industries, 1899–1939," *Journal of Industrial Economics* 4 (June 1956): 179–93; Leonard W. Weiss, "Average Concentration Ratios and Industrial Performance," *Journal of Industrial Economics* 11 (July 1963): 250–52; and Bruce T. Allen, "Concentration and Economic Progress: Note," *American Economic Review* 59 (September 1969): 600–604.

(106) Douglas F. Greer and Stephen A. Rhoades, "Concentration and Productivity Changes in the Long and Short Run," *Southern Economic Journal* 43 (October 1976): 1031–44.

107. See Mansfield, *Industrial Research and Technological Innovation*, pp. 136–44 (on the diffusion of 12 innovations in the coal, brewing, steel, and railroad industries); Anthony A. Romeo, "Interindustry and Interfirm Differences in the Rate of Diffusion of an Innovation," *Review of Economics and Statistics* 57 (August 1975): 311–19; and idem, "The Rate of Imitation of a Capital-Embodied Process Innovation," *Economica* 44 (February 1977): 63–69.

108. Ira Horowitz, "Firm Size and Research Activity," *Southern Economic Journal* 28 (January 1962): 298–301; D. Hamberg, "Size of Firm, Oligopoly, and Research: The Evidence," *Canadian Journal of Economics and Political Science* 30 (February 1964): 74–75; and Yale Brozen, "R & D Differences Among Industries," in Richard A. Tybout, ed., *Economics of Research and Development* (Columbus: Ohio State University Press, 1965), pp. 90, 128.

109. See Almarin Phillips, "Patents, Potential Competition, and Technical Progress," *American Economic Review* 56 (May 1966): 301–10 (using highly aggregated R & D spending data for 11 industry groups); F. M. Scherer, "Market Structure and the Employment of Scientists and Engineers," *American Economic Review* 57 (June 1967) (using Census of Population employment statistics for 56 diversely defined manufacturing categories); Comanor, "Market Structure, Product Differentiation, and Industrial Research," pp. 524–31 (using R & D employment data on 387 companies classified into 33 two- and three-digit industry groups); Kelly, "The Influences of Size and Market Structure," pp. 78–90 (using R & D data for 111 companies similar to Comanor's, but with weighted average concentration ratios for the multiple industries in which companies operated); Joel P. Rosenberg, "Research and Market Share: A Reappraisal of the Schumpeter Hypothesis," *Journal of Industrial Economics* 25 (December 1976): 133–42 (using R & D data similar to Comanor's for 100

tional product class regression equation was 110 percent higher in industries with a four-firm concentration ratio of 60 than in those with a four-firm ratio of 25; while in the general and mechanical products group, it was only 50 percent higher in the more concentrated industries. Similarly, Comanor found that size-adjusted R & D employment was roughly twice as high in concentrated as in unconcentrated industries when the opportunities for product differentiation through innovation were meager, but only 10 to 20 percent higher for the more concentrated industries in high opportunity fields. And Shrieves observed a significantly negative concentration coefficient only for companies at home in his "specialized durable equipment" industries, which included computers, electronic communications equipment, aircraft, and optical instruments.

This last set of results is extraordinarily important, for it permits us to tie theory and evidence together in a coherent, though still empirically fragile, explanatory framework. The class variables used to measure technological opportunity presumably take into account differences in the rate at which the stock of scientific knowledge and technical concepts is growing. This in turn manifests itself in the rate at which the time-cost tradeoff function C moves toward the origin of Figure 15.2. In high opportunity industries, the C function shifts more rapidly than in low opportunity industries, ceteris paribus. These shifts may occur either smoothly and continuously or in discrete breakthroughs. A breakthrough suddenly opens up room for numerous firms to exploit a new product opportunity profitably, and so consideration of the benefits function's slope dominates firms' development scheduling decisions. Under these circumstances, technological progress is more rapid with many sellers (i.e., low concentration) than with few. The same holds true for smooth and continuous changes if there are more or less uniform lags in the recognition of new opportunities. Suppose it takes five years on the average between the moment when a new R & D effort first becomes potentially profitable under monopolized conditions and the moment when some entrepreneur first recognizes that opportunity.[113] Meanwhile the C function is steadily shifting. It will have shifted more in high opportu-

nity fields than in low opportunity fields, and so more room will have been created for profitable development by numerous companies. With either continuous or discontinuous change in the knowledge base, then, fear of market overcrowding is less likely to deter vigorous innovative effort when the knowledge base grows rapidly, as in high opportunity fields. It follows that high concentration is less essential for heavy R & D investment in high opportunity, rapid shift industries than it is in low opportunity fields. Or to put the proposition negatively, when the overall profit potential for a recognized new product opportunity is modest in relation to contemplated development costs, investment in development may not take place unless the number of rivals, and hence the number of likely imitators, is low—that is, unless concentration is high. And this is exactly what the empirical evidence suggests.[114]

Nevertheless, there could be another explanation for the results. In low opportunity fields, technological pioneering may appear to be relatively unprofitable, or it may have only a modest impact on market positions, so that companies come to view innovation as a relatively unimportant strategy option. In this case only firms with considerable organizational slack—e.g., those in the more concentrated industries—will undertake significant R & D programs. In high opportunity industries, on the other hand, firms learn through experience that success in the market comes from innovative leadership; and an attempt by some to move ahead of the pack forces other industry members to mount their own R & D programs. Competition then leads to a high equilibrium level of R & D spending, whether concentration is high or low. By way of empirical support, an analysis of 463 large corporations' 1959 patenting revealed that companies in industries characterized by high technological opportunity matched each others' innovative efforts closely, receiving similar numbers of patents per billion dollars of sales, whereas patenting intensity varied widely from firm to firm in low opportunity fields.[115] This conjecture, it should be noted, is not necessarily incompatible with the market room hypothesis. They may complement one another in describing the complexities of real-world behavior.

It seems clear in any event that market concentration has a favorable impact on technological innovation in certain situations. *How much concentration is advantageous* remains to be determined. Obviously, there is no general answer; the optimum depends upon the size of the overall market profit potential in relation to the cost of development in any given case. Still, the available empirical evidence suggests a very crude generalization. In the study of 56 manufacturing industries, tests were conducted to determine whether there was a nonlinear pattern in the ratio of scientific and engineering effort to total employment in the low (traditional) and intermediate (general and mechanical) technological opportunity fields. Each revealed that below a four-firm concentration ratio of 10 to 14, virtually no scientific and engineering effort takes place. The maximum intensity of scientific and engineering employment occurred between concentration ratios of 50 and 55, implying that a modest degree of oligopoly is beneficial in fields of limited technological opportunity.[116] Concentration in excess of this magnitude appears on average to be unnecessary for, and perhaps even detrimental to, the vigorous exploitation of opportunities for technical advance.

The role of new entry and entry barriers

One further facet must be explored. In his analysis of structural variables affecting research and development, Comanor discovered that industries with moderate barriers to new entry—i.e., those with minimum optimal plant scales requiring production of from 4 to 7 percent of total industry output, and/or a capital investment of from $20 million to $70 million—had much higher R & D employment relative to their size than industries with either high or low entry barriers, *ceteris paribus*.[117] The comparative unprogressiveness of industries with low entry barriers, he speculated, might be associated with fear that when entry is easy, rapid imitation would quickly erode the profits from an innovation. In industries with high entry barriers, on the other hand, insulation from the threat of new competition could dull producers' incentive to conduct research and development.

There is abundant evidence from case studies to support the view that actual and potential new

companies chosen to reflect either high or low technological opportunity); Robert W. Wilson, "The Effect of Technological Environment and Product Rivalry on R & D Effort and Licensing of Inventions," *Review of Economics and Statistics* 59 (May 1977): 171–78 (using 1971 R & D expenditure data for 350 large companies); and Ronald Shrieves, "Market Structure and Innovation: A New Perspective," *Journal of Industrial Economics* 26 (June 1978): 329–47 (using updated R & D employment data similar to Comanor's for 411 companies, along with a particularly sophisticated method of assessing technological opportunity).

(110) Kelly's study is also a partial exception. But see note 115 *infra*.

(111) Cf. Chapter 4, pp. 147–49 *supra*; Almarin Phillips, *Technology and Market Structure: A Study of the Aircraft Industry* (Lexington, Mass.: Heath Lexington, 1971); and Richard R. Nelson and Sidney G. Winter, "Forces Generating and Limiting Concentration under Schumpeterian Competition," *Bell Journal of Economics* 9 (Autumn 1978): 524–48.

(112) Similar results were found in analyses of data for Canada and (less clearly) France. See Adams, "Firm Size and Research Activity," pp. 401–402; and Steven Globerman, "Market Structure and R & D in Canadian Manufacturing Industries," *Quarterly Review of Economics and Business* 13 (Summer 1973): 59–67. On the other hand, exactly the opposite results were obtained for Belgium: the strongest positive correlations between R & D intensity and concentration were for chemical and electrical industry members. Phlips, *Effects of Industrial Concentration*, pp. 134–36. Compare Jacquemin and de Jong, *European Industrial Organisation*, p. 148.

113. Of course, speed of recognition may be correlated with market structure. Recognition of opportunities might be faster in atomistic industries because there are more independent centers of initiative, or in monopolistic industries if monopolists alone maintain staffs of researchers to keep track of outside scientific advances.

114. Whether this interpretation is completely consistent with Comanor's results is less clear. His classification scheme emphasizes opportunities for differentiation more than opportunities opened up by changes in knowledge, although it is possible the two are associated. Also, if a strong product differentiation advantage can be gained by being first on the market with a new product, the force of imitation is blunted, and so the innovator's profit potential is greater than it would be with weak differentiation and easy imitation.

115. Scherer, "Firm Size . . . and the Output of Patented Inventions," p. 1100, note 6. See also Henry G. Grabowski and Nevins D. Baxter, "Rivalry in Industrial Research and Development: An Empirical Study," *Journal of Industrial Economics* 21 (July 1973): 228–33, who found the *variability* of R & D employment intensity among companies to be inversely correlated with both the *average* industry R & D/total employment ratio and industry concentration.

116. Scherer, "Market Structure and the Employment of Scientists and Engineers," pp. 529–30. Using quite different data, Kelly found a similar ∩-shaped relationship, with maximum company R & D/total employment ratios occurring at a weighted average four-firm concentration ratio of 56. "The Influences of Size and Market Structure," pp. 85–86.

117. "Market Structure, Product Differentiation, and Industrial Research," pp. 652–56. Compare Rosenberg, "Research and Market Share," who used a dichotomous entry barrier variable and found R & D employment intensity to be greater in the high barriers category.

118. Maclaurin, *Invention and Innovation in the Radio Industry*, pp. 255–56.

119. Sturmey, *The Economic Development of Radio*, p. 277.

entrants play a crucial role in stimulating technical progress, both as direct sources of innovation and as spurs to existing industry members. Established producers often develop physical and psychological commitments to the customary way of doing things. Because they lack such commitments, new entrants contribute a disproportionately high share of all really revolutionary new industrial products and processes. The illustrations are numerous: arc lighting (Brush), the incandescent lamp (Edison), alternating current (Westinghouse), electric traction for street cars (Sprague), radio telegraphy (Marconi), radio telephony (Fessenden and de Forest), FM radio (Armstrong), the transistorized radio (Sony), the photoflash lamp (Wabash), the dial telephone (Automatic Electric), the synchronous orbit communications satellite (Hughes), the turbojet engine (Whittle in England, Heinkel and Junkers Flugzeugwerk in Germany), sound motion pictures (Western Electric and Warner Brothers), catalytic cracking of petroleum (Houdry), the electric typewriter (IBM), self-developing photography (Polaroid), electrostatic copying (Haloid), the electronic calculator (Sharp and Texas Instruments), and laser-actuated hydrogen fusion (KMS Industries), to name only a few. In several of these cases, well-established firms flatly rejected invitations to collaborate with the inventor of a concept that later revolutionized their industry. Many other cases can be found in which the threat of entry through innovation by a newcomer stimulated existing members to pursue well-known technical possibilities more aggressively. Examples include General Electric's handling of the fluorescent lamp; AT&T's development of microwave radio relay systems, ornamental handsets, and electronic office switchboards; IBM's response to the electronic computer innovations of Sperry Rand, Control Data Corporation, and Digital Equipment Company; and the sudden awakening of old-line aircraft makers' interest in basic research and systems engineering in 1955 when the U.S. Air Force chose the infant Ramo-Wooldridge Corporation to oversee its Atlas ICBM development program.

All in all, the record of invention and innovation by new entrants is an impressive one, lending support to Maclaurin's conclusion (from a study of the radio industry before 1940) that "although some degree of monopoly is desirable, it is equally important to have new firms and rising firms searching for technical developments that may have been overlooked or not pressed by the large companies."[118] Or as Sturmey concluded from a similar study:

> The major economic force leading to innovation is not any particular structural form in the industry, but the conditions regarding entry to that industry. . . . Where the entry of significant competitors appears to be impossible, innovation will be slow; when the entry of significant competitors is possible, innovation will be much faster.[119]

Conclusion

We emerge again with a threshold concept of the most favorable industrial climate for rapid technological change. A bit of monopoly power in the form of structural concentration is conducive to invention and innovation, particularly when advances in the relevant knowledge base occur slowly. But very high concentration has a favorable effect only in rare cases, and more often it is apt to retard progress by restricting the number of independent sources of initiative and by dampening firms' incentive to gain market position through accelerated research and development. Likewise, it seems important that barriers to new entry be kept at modest levels, and that established industry members be exposed continually to the threat of entry by technically audacious newcomers. Schumpeter was right in asserting that perfect competition has no title to being established as the model of dynamic efficiency. But his less cautious disciples are wrong when they imply that powerful monopolies and tightly knit cartels have any stronger claim to that title. What is needed for rapid technical progress is a subtle blend of competition and monopoly, with more emphasis in general on the former than the latter, and with the role of monopolistic elements diminishing when rich technological opportunities exist.

16 The economics of the patent system

Few economic institutions have stirred as much controversy for such a long time as the patent system. Debate over the granting of patent monopolies on inventions has continued ever since the practice was formalized by the Republic of Venice in 1474.[1] In the United States, an interminable procession of blue-ribbon commissions and special legislative committees has been constituted, but from their labors no major substantive reforms have followed. Every attempt to change the system has been drowned in a sea of argument and special pleading. Here we shall explore the logic and paradoxes of the system, seeking to shed light where too frequently there has been only heat.[2]

Some background on the system

An invention patent is an exclusive right to one's invention, including the derivative right to prevent others from using it. Patents are issued in the United States under the broad authority of Article I, Section 8 of the Constitution, which gives Congress the power "to promote the progress of science and useful arts, by securing for limited times to authors and inventors the exclusive right to their respective writings and discoveries." The term of a U.S. patent grant is 17 years from the date of issue.

Under the applicable U.S. laws, as amended in 1952, a patent can be issued to cover "any new and useful process, machine, manufacture, or composition of matter, or any new and useful improvement thereof."[3] Before a patent can be granted, the application is examined in the Patent Office to ensure that the invention is new and nonobvious, that it was not commercialized or known to the public for more than a year before the date of application, and that it has practical utility.

The test for utility has in most instances been perfunctory, requiring nothing more than the barest suggestion that some practical use might ensue. However, more stringent standards have been applied to chemical inventions. For example, in 1966 the U.S. Supreme Court held that the test could not be satisfied for a chemical com-

---

1. For a survey of the early history of patent grants and the controversy that attended them, see Fritz Machlup, *An Economic Review of the Patent System*, Study no. 15 of U.S., Congress, Senate, Subcommittee on Patents, Trademarks, and Copyrights, 85th Cong., 2nd sess., 1958, pp. 1–5, 22–44.

2. There is an enormous literature on patent systems in the United States and abroad. The most comprehensive compact source is the series of studies commissioned by the Senate Subcommittee on Patents, Trademarks, and Copyrights during the late 1950s. Contemporary U.S. developments are followed in two journals, the *Journal of the Patent Office Society* and *Idea*.

3. 35 U.S. Code 101.

pound simply by showing that molecularly related compounds inhibited tumors in mice.[4]

A more critical hurdle in determining patentability is often the test for nonobviousness. The basic rule is that an invention is not patentable if "the subject matter as a whole would have been obvious at the time the invention was made to a person having ordinary skill in the art."[5] More stringent tests have been applied in certain Supreme Court decisions, e.g., that an invention must reveal "the flash of creative genius," and not merely crystallize gradually through trial and error.[6] In an apparent effort to neutralize such precedents, Congress specified in 1952 that "patentability shall not be negatived by the manner in which the invention was made."[7] Nevertheless, in 1966 the Supreme Court declared that it would continue to impose strict criteria of nonobviousness in contested cases and noted disparagingly the "notorious difference between the standards applied by the Patent Office and by the courts."[8]

The criteria implemented by the Patent Office have not in fact been very restrictive, since many gadgets and minute improvements receive patent protection. Picking up at random an issue of the weekly *Official Gazette*, one can find patents covering a hand-operated nutcracker (No. 4,009,651), a bird perch (No. 4,009,686), and a coin-holding pocket comb (No. 4,009,725), along with such impressive contributions as a method for removing radioactive contaminants from nuclear reactor coolants (No. 4,010,068). Roughly three-fourths of the applications filed with the U.S. Patent Office eventually lead to the issuance of invention patents, and during the 1970s the number of patents issued (excluding design and plant patents) ranged between 70,000 and 81,000 per year. Most covered inventions of slight technological and economic significance, but in any given year there are likely to be a thousand or so moderately to extremely important inventions patented.

In principle, a patent goes to the person making the invention, but scientists, engineers, and technicians employed by corporations normally assign all rights in their work-related inventions to their employer. Of the U.S. invention patents issued between 1971 and 1975, 51 percent were assigned to domestic corporations, 23 percent to foreign corporations and governments, 2 percent to the U.S. federal government, and 23 percent were issued to individual inventors. As one might suppose, the role of the unaffiliated inventor has been declining both relatively and absolutely over time, while corporate patenting has been on the ascendancy. The share of all U.S. patents issued to individual inventors was 81 percent in 1901, 72 percent in 1921, 42 percent in 1940, and 25 percent during the 1960s. Individual inventors received their largest absolute number of patents (30,332) in 1925. From 1971 through 1975, they averaged 17,607 patents per year.

The purposes of the patent grant

Governments have chosen to grant exclusive patent rights on inventions for three main reasons: to promote invention, to encourage the development and commercial utilization of inventions, and to encourage inventors to disclose their inventions to the public.

Early writers on the patent system seldom defined the term invention carefully, and as a result they were vague about how they perceived the role patents played in fostering invention. This has led to considerable confusion, for many scholars have assumed that the patent laws were enacted primarily to promote invention, construed narrowly to include only conception and crude proof testing. Some then infer that the traditional justification has lost most of its relevance to the modern industrial world, where inventive and developmental activities are often divorced from one another organizationally and where development outlays constitute more than three-fourths of all industrial R & D expenditures. Critics seize upon this interpretation by insisting that the system should be abolished; defenders argue in return that the system's rationale has changed over time.

It is questionable whether such a sharp historical dichotomy is empirically tenable. In England, from which U.S. patent precedents stem, patent rights were granted both before and after the 1624 Statute of Monopolies to protect the domestic exploitation of inventions made abroad as well as to encourage invention. One of the most famous English patents covered James Watt's separate condenser principle for steam engines. In extending that patent's life, Parliament in 1775 recognized that the central invention had already been made, and that what it was doing was encouraging further work by Watt to perfect the engine and to "render the same of the highest utility to the publick of which it is capable." Its decree implied furthermore that this was not an unusual case, calling attention to "the many difficulties which always arise in the execution of such large and complex machines . . . and the long time requisite to make the necessary trials."[9] From this and other cases, it would appear that when early patent grants were made ostensibly to encourage invention, what was meant was the complete spectrum of invention, investment, and development—that is, the whole process of innovating.

At any rate, encouraging developmental investment is clearly not an inherently inappropriate function of the patent grant. It might even carry more weight as a public policy objective than merely fostering invention. As Judge Jerome Frank observed in an *obiter dictum* on the conventional rationale:

> The controversy between the defenders and assailants of our patent system may be about a false issue—the stimulus to invention. The real issue may be the stimulus to investment. On that assumption, a statutory revision of our patent system should not be too drastic. We should not throw out the baby with the bathwater.[10]

Yet to state the issue in this way is not to resolve it. On whether patent protection is actually necessary and desirable to stimulate investment in development, we must for the moment retain an open mind.

The third purpose of the patent system—encouraging disclosure—can be dealt with more briefly. Supposedly, the prospect of patent protection leads inventors to make public what they otherwise would keep secret. This view has numerous critics, who argue that inventors will conceal whatever they can, with or without a patent system, and that only the inventions that would be found out anyway will be patented.[11] Inventions affecting internal production processes are especially susceptible to secrecy while product inventions are not, since a product can be purchased and inspected by any would-be imitator. The assertion that patent rights make no difference at all in the choice between secrecy and disclosure is nevertheless an oversimplification. Relying on secrecy is always risky. Business espionage is common, and engineers migrate frequently from one job to another, carrying knowledge of trade secrets with them.[12] If there were no patent system, producers would have no alternative to accepting the risk of trying to maintain secrecy. But patent protection *is* an alternative, and it can be sufficiently attractive to tip the decision toward disclosure in borderline cases. This interpretation draws support from a statistical study of corporate patenting, which showed that firms deprived of patent rights through antitrust judgments reduced their patenting relative to that of unaffected firms.[13] Thus, the patent system probably does encourage more disclosure than there otherwise would be. How great the difference is,

4. *Brenner* v. *Manson*, 383 U.S. 519 (1966).

5. 35 U.S. Code 103, in effect codifying the rule stated in *Hotchkiss* v. *Greenwood*, 11 Howard's Reports 248, 267 (1851).

6. *Cuno Engineering Corp.* v. *Automatic Devices Corp.*, 314 U.S. 84, 91 (1941).

7. 35 U.S.C. 103.

8. *Graham et al.* v. *John Deere Co. et al.*, 383 U.S. 1, 18 (1966).

9. 15 George III, c. 61 (1775), cited in F. M. Scherer, "Invention and Innovation in the Watt-Boulton Steam-Engine Venture," *Technology and Culture* 6 (Spring 1965): 184, 187.

10. *Picard* v. *United Aircraft Corp.*, 128 F. 2d 632, 643 (1942).

11. Cf. Machlup, *An Economic Review of the Patent System*, p. 76; and Alfred E. Kahn, "The Role of Patents," in J. P. Miller, ed., *Competition, Cartels and Their Regulation* (Amsterdam: North-Holland, 1962), p. 317.

12. On the legal protection accorded trade secrets, see *Kewanee Oil Co.* v. *Bicron Corp. et al.*, 416 U.S. 470 (1974).

13. F. M. Scherer, S. E. Herzstein, A. W. Dreyfoos et al., *Patents and the Corporation*, 2nd ed. (Boston: Galvin, 1959), pp. 137–46, 153–55. Further support was drawn from interviews and a questionnaire survey.

and how it affects the rate at which new technology diffuses throughout industry, is uncertain.

The costs and benefits of the patent system

Stimulating the invention and development of new products and processes is without doubt the most important benefit expected of the patent system. For it society pays a price: the monopoly power conferred by patent grants. In simplest terms, the overriding issue of patent policy is whether the benefits of the system outweigh the costs. Or on a more sophisticated plane, the problem is to design a system—e.g., by adjusting the length or strength of patent grants—that will yield the maximum surplus of benefits over costs.

Inventions and innovations bestow benefits upon society. How beneficial they are depends upon how fully they are utilized. Here one of the patent system's many paradoxes appears. Under the system, inventors are given the right to control and restrict utilization of their inventions, so outputs may be lower and prices higher than they would be if the inventions were utilized under purely competitive conditions. Normally, patent holders can choose between alternative methods of controlling utilization. They can reserve exploitation of the invention exclusively to themselves, calling upon the courts to enjoin anyone who attempts to infringe upon that right. In this way, the profit-maximizing price can be set directly. Or they can license as few or as many firms as they please to exploit the invention, charging royalties for the privilege. Through astute determination of the royalty rate, the patentees can in theory achieve the same price-quantity outcome and profits as they could retaining exclusive exploitation, other things (such as the costs of internal versus licensed production) being equal.[14] In many nations, patent holders can also solidify their control over licensees by prescribing prices at which the product can be sold, imposing output quotas, and limiting licensees to particular markets or fields of use. Such restrictions have come under increasing attack in the United States, but they have not yet been ruled illegal when enforced unilaterally by the patentee.[15]

That patent owners exercise their power to set prices exploiting whatever monopoly power their patents confer does not mean that society is denied the benefits stemming from invention and innovation. On the contrary, it gains at the very least from the resources that cost-saving innovations release for alternative uses, less the research and development cost of achieving that saving. In addition, consumers other than the patentee benefit directly in two ways. First, after the patent has expired, the patent holder should in principle have no further power to restrict output, competitive pricing will prevail, and consumers will reap the full benefits of the invention. Ideally, the life of a patent should be no longer than it needs to be to encourage the optimal amount of invention, so that monopolistic restrictions are terminated as soon as possible.[16] Second, consumers may also realize immediate gains even when innovations are exploited monopolistically. Several theoretical cases must be distinguished:

Case 1 A new and superior consumer product is introduced. Although the proof is too elaborate to reproduce here, it can be shown that the innovation necessarily increases consumers' surplus unless the innovator is able to practice perfect first-degree price discrimination.[17] Consumers therefore benefit directly even when the product is priced monopolistically. Whether overall social welfare is enhanced depends upon the innovation's cost, the impact of the innovation on substitute products, and other considerations analyzed in Chapter 14.[18]

Case 2 A new and more efficient production process is introduced by a firm already exercising monopoly power. Here the effect is to shift the monopolist's marginal cost curve downward, inducing a decrease in price if the marginal revenue curve is continuous. Consumers enjoy lower prices and higher consumers' surplus. An exception occurs if the kinked demand curve mentality prevails.

Case 3 A substantially more efficient production process is introduced under patent protection into a previously competitive industry. This is illustrated by the cost curve C_2 in Figure 16.1, where C_1 was the preinnovation cost function and OP_1 the preinnovation price. The firm controlling the new process will find it worthwhile to monopolize the industry, computing its marginal revenue MR and setting a price OP_2 that drives existing producers out of business. Or alternatively, it will license the invention at a per-unit royalty equal to the difference between the cost of production with C_2 and price OP_2. In either case, consumers benefit from the lower price. This result is more likely, the greater the reduction in cost is and the more elastic demand is at outputs exceeding the preinnovation output, *ceteris paribus*.[19]

Case 4 A slightly more efficient production process is introduced under patent protection into a competitive industry. This is illustrated by cost curve C_3 in Figure 16.1. If the patent holder could monopolize the industry without restraint by virtue of its patent, it would like to set price OP_3. But it cannot do this because of competition from the preinnovation process C_1. It must therefore either set a price slightly below OP_1 and drive others out, or license others at a per-unit royalty slightly less than the difference between C_3 and C_1. Here the reduction in price will be insignificantly small, and consumers at large will benefit little from the innovation until its patent protection has expired and competitive pricing commences. Then the innovator's profits are redistributed to consumers and, in addition, the dead-weight welfare loss triangle *EFG* is transformed into consumers' surplus.

In three cases out of the four, consumers gain immediately to some extent from the introduction of a patented invention, though they enjoy the full price reduction benefits only after its patent protection has expired. And except when innovators' profits come largely from cannibalization of the profits that would otherwise be enjoyed by the producers of substitute products, it is likely that society as a whole (i.e., including both consumers and producers) gains from inventions and innovations induced or hastened by the grant of patent rights.

Alternative incentives to invent and innovate

There is a rub, however. Patents are granted upon all inventions meeting the established standards of novelty and utility. But the exclusionary power conferred by patents may not be necessary to induce invention and/or innovation in all cases. There are alternative inducements that could render the patent incentive redundant. If an invention would be conceived and developed without patent protection, no social benefit can be attributed to that particular patent grant. Yet the inventor is likely to take advantage of the opportunity to secure patent protection, and so the restrictive aspects of the system take their toll. On such inventions, the social benefits from patent rights are zero but the social costs may be positive. In assessing the patent system's overall value, we must weigh the net benefits associated with inventions that would not have been availa-

14. This point is stressed, and a partial proof is provided, in John S. McGee, "Patent Exploitation: Some Economic and Legal Problems," *Journal of Law and Economics* 9 (October 1966): 135–62.

15. The governing precedent is *U.S.* v. *General Electric Co.*, 272 U.S. 476 (1926). Two attempts to overturn the doctrine were held back by a 4–4 split among the participating Supreme Court justices. *U.S.* v. *Line Material Co. et al.*, 333 U.S. 287, 315 (1948); and *U.S.* v. *Huck Mfg. Co. et al.*, 382 U.S. 197 (1965).

16. For a path-breaking treatment of this problem, see William D. Nordhaus, *Invention, Growth, and Welfare* (Cambridge, Mass.: M.I.T. Press, 1969), pp. 70–90. See also Carole Kitti, "Patent Policy and the Optimal Timing of Innovations" (Ph.D. diss., University of Chicago, 1973).

17. See Dan Usher, "The Welfare Economics of Invention," *Economica* 31 (August 1964): 279–87.

18. See Chapter 14, pp. 395–98 *supra*.

19. See also McGee, "Patent Exploitation," pp. 143–44; Kenneth J. Arrow, "Economic Welfare and the Allocation of Resources for Invention," in the National Bureau of Economic Research conference report, *The Rate and Direction of Inventive Activity* (Princeton: Princeton University Press, 1962), pp. 619–22; and S. C. Hu, "On the Incentive To Invent: A Clarificatory Note," *Journal of Law and Economics* 16 (April 1973): 169–77.

ble without patent protection against the net social losses associated with patented inventions that would be introduced even if no patent rights were offered. This is a difficult and perhaps impossible task. Our insight into the problem can nevertheless be sharpened by trying to determine what kinds of inventions fall into each of these two categories.

If pure and perfect competition in the strictest sense prevailed continuously—i.e., if sellers and buyers were numerous, products homogeneous, resources highly mobile, entry easy, and knowledge perfect—incentives for invention and innovation would be fatally defective without a patent system or some equivalent substitute. Developing an invention to the point of commercial applicability is costly. The risks of development, though often exaggerated, are also appreciable. To be willing to bear these costs and risks, potential innovators must have some hope of being able to sell their product at a price exceeding the cost of production so that they can recoup their development costs plus a premium for risk. But if imitators can swarm in to copy the invention as soon as it has been introduced, postinnovation prices will fall rapidly to the level of production cost, wiping out supranormal profits for innovators and imitators alike. One would have to be a fool or a philanthropist to invest heavily in invention and development when the imitative steamroller is expected to eliminate divergences between price

and production cost so quickly and relentlessly. The fundamental argument for a patent system is that patent protection permits the innovator (or inventor) to retard competitive imitation, and hence to anticipate earning supranormal profits if its contribution proves technically and commercially successful.

However, real-world markets are almost never purely and perfectly competitive. Therefore, the crucial question is, Does imitation actually eliminate innovative profits so rapidly? It may not because of three phenomena: natural imitation lags, the advantages of competitive product leadership, and the existence of nonpatent barriers to the emergence of a competitive market structure.

There are several reasons why imitation naturally lags behind the profitable introduction of new products and processes, often by a substantial interval. Secrecy is one. Even when patent protection is sought in exchange for disclosure, the details of an invention may with luck be kept secret until the patent is issued—in the United States, nearly two years on the average after an application is filed.[20] During this interim, the invention's sponsor may be able to secure a significant head start preparing its production facilities and marketing channels. According to a 1957 statistical survey, roughly 90 percent of the sampled inventions used commercially were first put into use before the covering patent was issued and thus before patent disclosure hoisted a tell-tale flag to potential imitators.[21]

Second, knowledge is almost never perfect. It takes time for entrepreneurs to learn about a new and promising invention, even after its existence has been publicized, and it takes even longer for them to decide it is worth imitating. Some are quicker than others in this regard, but imitation must be widespread in order to eliminate the innovator's profits, and for nontrivial inventions the diffusion process often proceeds slowly. For example, the approximate intervals elapsing between first use in the United States and the date when 60 percent of all relevant producers had imitated for seven innovations studied by Edwin Mansfield were as follows:[22]

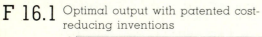

F 16.1 Optimal output with patented cost-reducing inventions

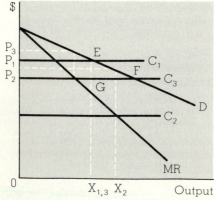

| Packaging beer in tin cans | 1 year |
| High speed beer bottle filler | 7 years |

Continuous wide strip steel mill	9 years
By-product coke oven for steel mills	18 years
Continuous annealing of tin-plated steel	20 years
Continuous coal mining machinery	4 years
Diesel locomotives	11 years

In a statistical analysis of these and other innovations, Mansfield found that the speed of imitation was positively correlated with the profitability of the new process or product and inversely related to the magnitude of the investment required. For product innovations in particular, this implies among other things that the speed of imitation depends upon the innovator's pricing policy. Companies pricing their new products to make a quick killing will encourage rapid imitation, while those pursuing a limit pricing strategy will experience slow imitation. Depending upon the circumstances, either strategy may suffice to yield substantial profits.

Third, merely knowing that an attractive new product or process exists and examining the patent specifications is often an inadequate basis for imitating successfully. Know-how that can come only from carrying out one's own R & D effort, receiving generous technical assistance from the innovator, or hiring away several of the innovator's key engineers may also be required. The importance of know-how as a barrier to rapid imitation varies widely from field to field. A new garment design or a children's toy can be copied in hours, while it may take years to develop independently the know-how required to produce rayon or high-quality color film.[23] Moreover, there is probably a positive correlation between the complexity of the original development job and the difficulty of acquiring sufficient know-how to imitate it. As a result, those developments that entail the highest risks tend to be the least rapidly imitated.[24] For all these reasons, innovators often enjoy freedom from competitive imitation for a sufficiently long time to recoup their original investment manyfold even without patent protection.

Competition, product differentiation, and natural lags interact to form a second set of incentives for investment in research and innovation. Frequently a company's image is enhanced by being first on the market with a new product, and through this product differentiation advantage it may be able to maintain a favorable price differential or retain a sufficiently large share of the market to earn supranormal profits for some time.[25] The expectation of gaining such a position is a tempting carrot for investment in R & D. There is also a complementary stick. Firms that lag in the innovative race may find their differentiation advantages and market positions eroding, and to avoid this fate they invest in defensive research and development. Competition to be

20. In many foreign jurisdictions publication is more rapid, sometimes following shortly after application and before the patent issues. In the 1950s and 1960s, U.S. application issuance lags averaged three to four years.

21. Barkev Sanders, "Speedy Entry of Patented Inventions into Commercial Use," *Patent, Trademark, and Copyright Journal* 6 (Spring 1962): 87–116. With the acceleration of processing by the U.S. Patent Office more recently, the percentage used before patent issue has undoubtedly fallen.

22. Estimated (with assistance from the author) from Edwin Mansfield, *Industrial Research and Technological Innovation: An Econometric Analysis* (New York: Norton, 1968), pp. 134–35. Mansfield's figures cover any use, however small, by industry members. Much longer average imitation lags are found when the percentage of industry output produced with a new process is analyzed. See Bela Gold, W. S. Peirce, and Gerhard Rosegger, "Diffusion of Major Technological Innovations in U.S. Iron and Steel Manufacturing," *Journal of Industrial Economics* 18 (July 1970): 219–22.

23. See Jesse W. Markham, *Competition in the Rayon Industry* (Cambridge, Mass.: Harvard University Press, 1952), pp. 20–24, 56–57; and George E. Frost and S. Chesterfield Oppenheim, "A Study of the Professional Color Motion Picture Antitrust Decrees and Their Effects," *Patent, Trademark, and Copyright Journal* 4 (Summer 1960): 126–27.

24. An exception might occur when protracted research is required to identify a workable solution, but once that solution is known, it becomes easy to find slightly different but equally effective inventions. Trial-and-error search for chemical compounds with desired new therapeutic effects, where there was no theory to guide the search toward specific molecular configurations, was an example before changes in the U.S. drug laws imposed heavy clinical test burdens on imitators as well as innovators.

25. See especially Ronald Bond and David Lean, *Sales, Promotion, and Product Differentiation in Two Prescription Drug Markets*, Federal Trade Commission staff report (Washington, D. C.: Government Printing Office, February 1977), Chapters 3–6.

first or at least not to be left behind thus acquires a self-sustaining momentum that needs little or no extra boost from patent rights. That this is commonly the case in American industry is suggested by the results of a questionnaire and interview survey covering 91 large corporations holding approximately 30 percent of all U.S. corporate patents in 1956. When asked what factors played an important role in their R & D investment decisions, only 7 companies selected "patent protection to be secured" as first or second most important of five factors. The majority indicated that patent protection was least important, emphasizing instead the necessity of maintaining competitive leadership or remaining competitively viable.[26]

Here, however, we must be wary of oversimplifying complex relationships. The patent system may affect the competitive struggle for innovative superiority in subtle but important ways. If there were no patents, the advantages of being first and the disadvantages of being a poor second might be less pronounced, though not vanishingly small. It is also conceivable that the prospect of gaining patent protection serves as a primer in igniting an innovation rivalry which then becomes self-sustaining. That is, some firm decides to pioneer a new field of technology because it believes *inter alia* that patent barriers to rapid imitation will help make the venture profitable. Others react after a lag with countervailing programs to protect their flanks. The threat each firm's program poses to the market positions of rivals becomes in and of itself a sufficient incentive to induce continued R & D investment. Whether there are many cases of innovative rivalries that would not have been triggered without an initial patent stimulus, or that would have begun much later, is hard to tell. The development of television is one plausible candidate; the development of xerography another; and the race to introduce new products in the pharmaceuticals industry following World War II may be a third.[27] But innovative rivalry can and does get under way for reasons unrelated to the expectation of patent rights in many instances, and once it does, it generates its own incentives for continuation.

Another patent-related reason why companies conduct R & D is to guard against being foreclosed from some field of technology by another concern exercising parallel patent rights. By making and patenting appropriate inventions, a firm stakes out its own independent claim in the field and obtains a bargaining counter to deal with others holding complementary inventions. However, few patents are sufficiently basic and broad to 'fence in' a field altogether. Most can be invented around, and an appreciable amount of industrial R & D is motivated by a desire to avoid infringing or paying royalties upon other firms' patented inventions. The fact that patent rights stimulate this search, and that sometimes the search yields an unambiguously superior new product or process, is frequently cited as a major benefit of the patent system. Yet the sword cuts both ways, for the resources devoted to circumventing patents might, if inventions were made freely available, be allocated instead to alternative activities with higher incremental social payoffs. For instance, Comanor found that while a number of important pharmaceutical improvements were discovered in this manner, competitive research also led to a great many products with therapeutic effects quite similar to drugs already available. He concluded that society would lose relatively little if fewer resources were devoted to duplicative "molecule manipulation" R & D.[28] S. G. Sturmey observed that British radio manufacturers wasted "a lot of ingenuity" during the 1920s devising circuit arrangements that reduced royalties paid to the Marconi Company, even though radio tube technology advanced in the process.[29] On the other hand, the pace of advance in petroleum cracking technology was almost certainly accelerated by the vigorous efforts of companies to invent around rival processes.[30] All we have to go by at present are examples and counterexamples, and so it is impossible to determine whether, on balance, the benefits of R & D motivated by the hope of circumventing patents exceed the costs of duplication.[31]

The third major reason why firms may find investment in innovation profitable despite the absence of patent protection is the existence of nonpatent barriers to the emergence of a competitive market structure. Here we tie into the analysis of the previous chapter. For all but those innovations that define a completely new field, the most likely early imitators are companies already operating in the industry to which the innovation pertains. Lack of production facilities, managerial experience, and distribution channels impedes the entry of outsiders. When in addition the market is moderately or heavily concentrated, postimitation pricing discipline is apt to remain fairly firm. Even for innovations requiring substantial development outlays there may be sufficient room for all industry members to imitate without preventing the leader from recovering its development investment. It follows obversely that patent protection will be most important as an inducement to progress when there are large numbers of probable imitators or when development costs are expected to be high in relation to the stream of quasi-rents the innovation could support under favorable (e.g., oligopolistic) pricing conditions.[32]

We find then that business firms may invest in innovation without patent protection if natural imitation lags are substantial, if there are major competitive differentiation advantages from being first in the market with a new product, and/or if the relevant market is oligopolistic. All three characteristics are widespread in a modern industrialized economy. Any one of the three can provide a sufficient incentive if the invention is economically important—that is, if it has the potential of yielding marketwide cost savings or premium profits large in relation to the innovator's development costs. In such instances, the prospect of a relatively short lead over imitators—e.g., as little as two or three years—may be attractive enough to induce investment. To cite an extreme example, the Reynolds International Pen Co. earned back its original investment a hundredfold during the 18 months it enjoyed an almost exclusive position, before a host of firms imitated its ball point pen.[33] It is only when the barriers to widespread and rapid imitation are weak, or when the advantages of competitive leadership are modest, or when the profit potential of the innovation is small, or when there is some adverse combination of the three, that patent protection becomes an important incremental stimulus.

A similar conclusion emerges when one attempts to determine, assuming that no other incentives for innovation exist, how long the life of a patent must be to induce the amount of cost-saving innovation that maximizes the surplus of discounted consumers' plus producer's surplus less R & D costs. William Nordhaus has shown that the more important a process innovation

26. Scherer, Herzstein, Dreyfoos et al., *Patents and the Corporation*, pp. 107, 118, 149.

27. See W. R. Maclaurin, "Patents and Technical Progress: A Study of Television," *Journal of Political Economy* 58 (April 1950): 152; and William S. Comanor, "Research and Competitive Product Differentiation in the Pharmaceutical Industry," *Economica* 31 (November 1964): 372–84. On the other hand, in *Sales, Promotion, and Product Differentiation*, p. 45, Bond and Lean show that innovative rivalry in the anti-anginal drug field emerged without significant patent protection.

28. Comanor, "Research and Competitive Product Differentiation," pp. 381–84.

29. S. G. Sturmey, *The Economic Development of Radio* (London: Duckworth, 1958), p. 223.

30. See McGee, "Patent Exploitation," p. 151; John L. Enos, "Invention and Innovation in the Petroleum Refining Industry," in *The Rate and Direction of Inventive Activity*, pp. 302–303; Roger L. Beck, "Patents, Property Rights, and Social Welfare," *Southern Economic Journal* 43 (October 1976): 1050–54; and Daniel L. Landau, "Patents and Over-Investment in Process Inventions? Comment," *Southern Economic Journal* 45 (July 1978): 285–88, with a reply by Beck, pp. 289–92.

   In xerographic copying and float glass production, competitive research was apparently inhibited by decisions of the dominant patent holders to license at least some of their patents on favorable terms. See G. H. Wierzynski, "The Eccentric Lords of Float Glass," *Fortune*, July 1968, p. 123; and Erwin Blackstone, "The Copying Machine Industry: A Case Study" (Ph.D. diss., University of Michigan, 1968, pp. 98–112).

   For a different view of the "inventing around" problem that seems little influenced by any concern for reality, see Edmund W. Kitch, "The Nature and Function of the Patent System," *Journal of Law and Economics* 20 (October 1977): 265–90. Compare the *Report to the Federal Trade Commission on Federal Energy Land Policy*, Senate Committee on Interior and Insular Affairs print (Washington, D.C.: Government Printing Office, 1976), pp. 657–74.

31. See also C. T. Taylor and Z. A. Silberston, *The Economic Impact of the Patent System* (Cambridge, England: Cambridge University Press, 1973), pp. 199–201, who found in a survey of British companies relatively little wastefully duplicative R & D spurred by the desire to invent around competitors' patents.

32. Along analogous lines, Jesse Markham suggests that the patent system has its strongest incentive value when all other means of obtaining a monopoly are foreclosed by law, since then innovation will be the main open route to supranormal profits. "The Joint Effect of Antitrust and Patent Laws Upon Innovation," *American Economic Review* 56 (May 1966): 293.

33. See Thomas Whiteside, "Where Are They Now?," *New Yorker*, 17 February 1951, pp. 39–58.

is—that is, the more it reduces unit production costs—the shorter the socially optimal patent life will be.[34] This is so for two reasons. An R & D effort that facilitates large cost savings before running into the stage of severely diminishing returns pays for itself quickly. And, secondly, the incremental resource misallocation losses attributable to extended patent lives soon begin to outweigh the added induced cost-reduction gains. Making arbitrary but plausible estimates for the parameters of his model, Nordhaus discovered that the optimal life of a patent for process inventions reducing unit production costs by roughly 10 percent ranges between three and seven years for end product demand elasticities in the neighborhood of 0.7 to 4.0. Only when research yields cost savings grudgingly and in modest amounts—e.g., 1 percent of unit production costs—and when demand is of unit elasticity or less are patent lives of 15 to 20 years optimal.

This perspective on incentives for innovation has profound implications for judging the patent system's value. In most situations, to repeat, natural lags and other advantages permit sponsors to tap an innovation's full profit potential without experiencing substantial competition for at least a couple of years, if not more. For the most part, it would appear, only those innovations that offer potentially exploitable benefits small in relation to development costs need the extra lure of patent protection before entrepreneurs will choose to plunge. Important contributions, on the other hand, should pay for themselves in short order. We are led then to ask, Would society really lose much at the margin if, by abolishing the patent system, it sacrifices mainly innovations with low benefit/cost ratios? The answer implied by the analysis thus far is negative. A negative answer is also suggested by the detailed interviews Taylor and Silberston conducted with 27 British companies operating in research-oriented industries. They found that without effective patent protection, R & D expenditures would be reduced negligibly in the electrical industries, by 5 percent on average in the machinery and mechanical components industries, by 5 percent also in basic chemicals, by 25 percent in such specialty chemicals as pesticides and adhesives, but by 64 percent in pharmaceuticals (where imitation in the absence of patents was expected to be especially swift and effective).[35]

Despite this sanguine prognosis (except for drugs), it is conceivable that without a patent system certain spectacular technical contributions—those effecting a genuine revolution in production or consumption patterns—might be lost or (more plausibly) seriously delayed because their support lends itself poorly to rational benefit/cost calculation. Such innovations may lie off the beaten paths of industrial technology, where no firm or group of companies has a natural advantage; and the innovator may be forced to develop completely new marketing channels and production facilities to exploit them. They may entail greater technological and market uncertainties, higher development costs, and longer inception-to-commercialization lags than the vast bulk of all industrial innovation. Entrepreneurs may be willing to accept their challenge only under highly favorable circumstances—notably, when it is anticipated that if success is achieved, it can be exploited to the fullest, among other things through the exercise of exclusive patent rights.

That such cases exist is virtually certain. Black-and-white television and the early development of xerographic concepts are probable examples.[36] Both would undoubtedly have come to fruition eventually, but patent protection evidently speeded up the process. The most important single gap in our knowledge of patent system economics is how many inventions and innovations fit this pattern, and how long their introduction would have been delayed if there were no patent system. It is the kind of gap that could be narrowed by spending on research sums small in relation to the cost of maintaining the patent system or the social losses incurred when an innovation as important as xerography is delayed by only a single year. The author's best guess is that such cases are rare, occurring perhaps a few times per decade. But this is no more than a stab in the dark.

A related question is what kind of reward structure best encourages work in such unexplored, uncertain new technologies. A structure that satisfies orthodox notions of equity, proportioning gains to the investments made, might be the wrong answer. Under the patent system, enormous gains out of all proportion to original investments are occasionally realized. Edwin Land of Polaroid camera fame amassed a fortune estimated at $500 million from his numerous inventive contributions; the market value of securities received by Chester Carlson for his xerography patent rights had mounted to $160 million in 1968; Pilkington Brothers, Ltd., was expected to collect $100 million in royalties alone for the use of its float glass patents; and Hoffmann-La Roche of Switzerland must have realized profits in the multibillion dollar range from the worldwide sales of its Valium and Librium tranquilizers.[37] Occasional success stories like these may be what best energizes technical risk bearing, as Schumpeter observed more generally of the capitalist reward system:

> Spectacular prizes much greater than would have been necessary to call forth the particular effort are thrown to a small minority of winners, thus propelling much more efficaciously than a more equal and more "just" distribution would, the activity of that large majority of businessmen who receive in return very modest compensation or nothing or less than nothing, and yet do their utmost because they have the big prizes before their eyes and overrate their chances of doing equally well.[38]

Whether the largest prizes need to be as large as some of those cited here is doubtful, but too close a proportioning of gains to costs is sure to discourage investment in the most uncertain technical ventures.

Within this overall incentive framework, is the patent system of more value in stimulating invention and innovation by large firms, small firms, or by independent inventors? In general, it appears to be the small firm and the independent inventor who are affected the most. Small companies commonly lack the distribution channels and market acceptance of their larger rivals. As a result, their rate of penetration into new markets through innovation is likely to be slower and the profit they realize in the first years after innovation lower.[39] Also, their market positions are more vulnerable when large, well-entrenched rivals retaliate with imitative products. The independ-

ent inventor occupies an even less tenable position. Patent protection should in principle help offset these disadvantages, permitting the small entrepreneur to compete in the innovation game on a more equal footing with the giants, who enjoy adequate (or perhaps even excessive) protection against premature imitation by virtue of their established market positions.

Nevertheless, the real-world patent system does not always operate in this ideal fashion. Size confers an advantage not only in promoting new products, but also in waging harassment campaigns. The grant of rights conferred by a patent is not a certain thing. The validity of a patent can be challenged in court, and among the scores of lawsuits fought to completion each year, more than 60 percent have ended in invalidation decisions.[40] As one jurist remarked, "A patent is merely a license to bring a lawsuit."[41] In such contests the odds are weighted in favor of the large corporation, which has superior legal

34. *Invention, Growth, and Welfare*, pp. 76–82. See also F. M. Scherer, "Nordhaus' Theory of Optimal Patent Life: A Geometric Reinterpretation," and the reply by Nordhaus, *American Economic Review* 62 (June 1972): 422–31.

35. Taylor and Silberston, *The Economic Impact of the Patent System*, pp. 194–208, especially p. 199. The figure for pharmaceuticals may be biased upward because two of the three drug makers interviewed were newcomers to the industry who might not have entered without patent protection. See also note 27 *supra*.

36. Cf. Maclaurin, "Patents and Technical Progress"; and Blackstone, "The Copying Machine Industry," pp. 7–23, 75–80.

37. See Arthur M. Louis, "America's Centimillionaires," *Fortune*, May 1968, pp. 152–53; Wierzynski, "The Eccentric Lords," p. 91; Robert Ball, "The Secret Life of Hoffmann-LaRoche," *Fortune*, August 1971, p. 134; and F. M. Scherer, *The Economic Effects of Compulsory Patent Licensing* (New York University Monograph Series in Finance and Economics, 1977), pp. 43–47.

38. Joseph A. Schumpeter, *Capitalism, Socialism, and Democracy*, 3rd ed. (New York: Harper, 1950), pp. 73–74.

39. F. M. Scherer, "Research and Development Resource Allocation Under Rivalry," *Quarterly Journal of Economics* 81 (August 1967): 385, 388–89.

40. See Charles L. Trozzo and Carole E. Kitti, *The Effects of Patent and Antitrust Laws, Regulations, and Practices on Innovation* (Washington, D.C.: Institute for Defense Analyses Paper P-1075, February 1976), Chapter 9; and Lawrence Baum, "The Federal Courts and Patent Validity," *Journal of the Patent Office Society* 56 (December 1974): 758–87.

41. *Guide* v. *Desperak et al.*, 144 F. Supp. 182, 186 (1956).

The economics of the patent system   **449**

and financial resources. Therefore, small enterprises whose patents are challenged by powerful rivals on either good or spurious grounds often choose to settle out of court, giving up their exclusive position and licensing the challenger to avoid the cost and uncertainty of protracted litigation. Or they may sell out altogether to the challenger. The ability of well-heeled companies to harass smaller patent holders in this way has been curbed considerably by unsympathetic antitrust judgments. But to the extent that patent validity contests persist, apprehension about them diminishes the incentive value of the patent system for small firms and independent inventors. Yet on balance, the system probably does more to stimulate invention and innovation by small entrepreneurs than by the large corporation, and this is a telling argument in its favor.[42]

One final comment on the benefits of a patent system is appropriate. Our discussion thus far has been from the perspective of industrialized nations. But what role should patent grants play in less developed lands? Newly emerging nations seldom sustain much of a domestic R & D effort, partly because they lack the necessary human resources and partly because they can tap into the reservoir of technology available in other nations.

An indication of this dependence upon external technology sources is given by statistics on the percentage of patents granted to foreigners by various nations during 1970 through 1972. In Argentina, foreigners received 76 percent of all patents issued; for Venezuela, the figure was 94 percent; for Iran, 92 percent; and for Portugal, 94 percent. This can be compared with 29 percent in the United States, 31 percent in Japan, and 53 percent in West Germany.[43]

Since the amount of domestic inventive activity is modest in underdeveloped countries, one might expect the benefits of a patent system to be particularly small relative to the social costs of granting foreigners patent protection. Indeed, it is somewhat surprising that such countries offer conventional patent rights. Professor Machlup attributes many emerging nations' membership in the International Union for the Protection of Industrial Property to pressures from industrialized nations and to prestige motives, suggesting

that newly independent nations seem irrationally eager to "have the honor of paying higher prices for imported products."[44] An alternative rationalization is that foreign firms are more willing to establish a base of operations in underdeveloped lands or license their know-how to domestic firms if they can protect their position through patents.[45] But this is not completely convincing, since know-how is often sold in packages independent of patent licenses, and since emerging nation markets are so imperfect and imitation is so sluggish that an efficient producer should usually be in a favorable position to realize normal and quite possibly even supranormal profits without the fringe benefit of patent protection.[46]

The social costs of the patent system

While encouraging some inventions and innovations that would not otherwise be made and hastening the introduction of others, the patent system simultaneously generates social costs. The most obvious cost is the resource misallocation attributable to monopolistic pricing of patented inventions that would have been available without patent protection. How much power over price a patent confers varies widely from case to case, depending upon the availability of substitutes and consumers' knowledge of their availability. Some of the most extreme cases concern the pricing of patented pharmaceutical items, for which demand is typically quite inelastic over a considerable price range. From 1956 through the mid-1960s, the Pfizer Company and its four licensees sold the antibiotic tetracycline to druggists at a wholesale price of $30.60 per bottle of 100 capsules. Total sales at wholesale to drug stores exceeded $1 billion during this period. Production costs ranged between $1.60 and $3.80 per bottle; and when doubts about the validity of Pfizer's patent began to mount, several unlicensed firms began producing and selling tetracycline at approximately $2.50 per bottle wholesale. Many similar cases of price-cost margins on the order of 90 percent for patented drug products have been identified.[47] They are, to repeat, extreme, but it is not at all rare for patent holders to charge prices substantially in excess of full production and distribution costs and to earn handsome profits as a result of their protected market position.

Furthermore, companies have managed through various legitimate and shady practices to extend and pyramid the monopoly power derived from their patents.[48] One way they do this is by fencing in a field of technology. As we have seen earlier, it is usually possible to invent around a single patent, and so the amount of monopoly power conferred by any but the most basic and sweeping patents is constrained, perhaps severely, by the possibility of substitution. However, by accumulating an extensive portfolio of patents, producers can solidify their monopolistic domination of a field. When du Pont scientists "invented" nylon, for instance, they did not rest content with patenting the basic superpolymer's composition and processes for producing it. They systematically investigated the whole array of molecular variations with properties potentially similar to nylon, blanketing their findings with hundreds of patent applications to prevent other firms from developing an effective substitute. Similar tactics have been pursued by du Pont and many other corporations in such fields as cellophane, plastics, synthetic leather, synthetic rubber, photo supplies, tranquilizers, radio, television, shoe machinery, data processing equipment, electric lamps, telephone equipment, copying processes, and can-closing machinery, to name just a few. When one company comes to dominate a field by accumulating a massive patent portfolio, it not only prevents rivals from operating except on its acquiescence, but also becomes the logical buyer for related new concepts patented by independent inventors. Thus, at some point the process of patent accumulation may take on a "snowball effect."[49]

Under current U.S. judicial interpretations, this is perfectly legal when it is achieved through one's own internal research and development efforts unaccompanied by abusive practices. As the Supreme Court commented in one leading case, "The mere accumulation of patents, no matter how many, is not in and of itself illegal."[50] However, companies run the risk of antitrust vio-lation if they build up an impregnable patent portfolio by systematically buying out rival patents, especially when coercive tactics are employed to soften up the sellers.

A dynamic ramification of the pyramiding phenomenon is the extension of one's monopoly power over time by prolonging the effective life of basic patents and by amassing improvement patents once basic patents expire. Since the grant of U.S. patent rights continues for 17 years from the date of issue, applicants have been known to delay a patent's ultimate expiration date by dragging their heels on Patent Office procedural matters while the application is pending. No doubt more important is the prolongation of control achieved through improvement patenting. Electric lighting is the classic illustra-

42. See also John Jewkes, David Sawers, and Richard Stillerman, *The Sources of Invention* (New York: St. Martin's, 1959), p. 251, for a similar conclusion.

43. *Industrial Property*, Statistical Annexes, December 1971, December 1972, and December 1973.

44. Fritz Machlup, "Patents," *International Encyclopedia of the Social Sciences*, vol. 11 (London: Macmillan, 1968), p. 465.

45. See Raymond Vernon, *The International Patent System and Foreign Policy*, Study no. 5 of U.S., Congress, Senate, Subcommittee on Patents, Trademarks, and Copyrights, 85th Cong., 2nd sess., 1958; Edith Penrose, "International Patenting and the Less Developed Countries," *Economic Journal* 83 (September 1973): 768–86; Douglas Greer, "The Case Against the Patent System in Less-Developed Countries," *Journal of International Law and Economics* 8 (December 1973): 223–66; and the articles by S. J. Patel, Pedro Roffe, and Peter O'Brien in *World Development* 2 (September 1974): 223–66.

46. On the costs of transferring know-how abroad, see David J. Teece, "Technology Transfer by Multinational Firms: The Resource Cost of Transferring Technological Know-how," *Economic Journal* 87 (June 1977): 241–61.

47. See Henry Steele, "Monopoly and Competition in the Ethical Drugs Market," *Journal of Law and Economics* 5 (October 1962): 131–63; idem, "Patent Restrictions and Price Competition in the Ethical Drugs Industry," *Journal of Industrial Economics* 12 (July 1964):198–223; and (on Valium and Librium) Scherer, *The Economic Effects of Compulsory Patent Licensing*, pp. 44–45.

48. For a comprehensive catalogue, see Floyd L. Vaughan, *The United States Patent System* (Norman: University of Oklahoma Press, 1956).

49. See Carl Kaysen, *United States v. United Shoe Machinery Corporation* (Cambridge, Mass.: Harvard University Press, 1956), p. 90; and Carl Kaysen and Donald F. Turner, *Antitrust Policy* (Cambridge, Mass.: Harvard University Press, 1959), p. 166.

50. *Automatic Radio Mfg. Co. v. Hazeltine Research, Inc.*, 339 U.S. 827, 834 (1950).

tion. General Electric virtually regimented the domestic incandescent lamp industry from 1892 through the 1930s, first by acquiring the basic Edison patents; then through patents on the argon-filled lamp and tungsten filaments; and finally through patents on such features as tipless bulbs, internally frosted bulbs, and nonsag filaments.[51]

A further charge against the patent system is that it permits the suppression of inventions from which the public might otherwise benefit. Nearly everyone has heard the recurrent rumor that some shadowy power in the automobile or petroleum industry has obtained and suppressed patents on a carburetor that would let full-sized autos travel 50 miles per gallon of gasoline. Most such rumors, including the present example, prove on investigation to have little or no substance.[52] Yet some valid complaints remain. When corporations assemble huge patent portfolios to bolster their market positions, they inevitably include many inventions they do not intend to use directly, patenting them only to prevent others from using them. If decision makers choose rationally, the inventions left unused will normally be those that are economically inferior to, or at least not superior to, those that are used.[53] Whether this should be called suppression is an empty semantic question. Despite their inferiority, such inventions might well be commercialized profitably by other firms if the superior invention is priced monopolistically and if the inferior inventions are at least better than the freely available technology. It is also possible that patent holders make mistakes, utilizing inventions inferior to others in their portfolios because they misjudge costs or demand. Abstracting from such situations, there are very few convincingly documented cases of the deliberate suppression of clearly superior inventions. The least ambiguous instances typically involve products which for various reasons could not be priced as profitably as available inferior variants, or inventions whose use could upset the status quo in a delicately coordinated price-fixing scheme.[54]

As noted previously, companies may spend substantial sums inventing around the patent positions of rivals. This cost is offset to an unknown extent by the benefits of superior inventions resulting from the circumventing effort. One firm's patent position may also block another producer from introducing improvements complementary to the original invention. An early example was James Watt's steam engine patent. Access to it was essential if one were to develop high-pressure engines, in which Watt saw little value. Watt's refusal to grant licenses impeded the work of Jonathan Hornblower, Richard Trevithick, and others on high-pressure engines until the patent expired in 1800, and this may in turn have had some small effect in delaying the introduction of steam locomotives and steamboats.[55] Similar blockages occur frequently in modern times—e.g., when the Pfizer Company found that it had to produce aureomycin, patented by the American Cyanamid Company, as an intermediate step in making tetracycline. In more cases than not, such problems are resolved through purchase of the improvement patents or through a cross-licensing agreement under which each party permits the other to utilize its patents, usually with provisions for the payment of royalties proportionate to the parties' respective patent contributions.

Cross-licensing is a constructive means of avoiding stalemates between complementary patent portfolios. However, it also has considerable potential for abuse. Some of the most egregious price-fixing schemes in American economic history were erected on a foundation of agreements to cross-license complementary and competing patents. Industries cartelized at one time or another in this way include electric lights, glass bottles, parking meters, eyeglasses, magnesium, synthetic rubber, titanium paint pigments, radio broadcasting equipment, motion picture production, gypsum board, hardboard, machine tools, bathtubs, and a host of other electrical and chemical products.[56] Typically, such arrangements have been implemented by adding to the patent exchange agreement provisions specifying prices, market quotas, membership in the industry, and other aspects of conduct and structure. All attempts reciprocally (i.e., not unilaterally by a single patentee) to extend patent licensing agreements into the realm of price and output determination have been ruled illegal by the American courts, but restrictions of this sort continue to be legal in most other nations. Where they persist, the restrictive effects of a patent system are magnified.

A more subtle practice in the grey area of U.S. law concerns the settlement of patent ownership and validity disputes.[57] It is not unusual for two or more corporations to have conflicting claims to the priority of their employees in making an invention, or they may possess evidence that an invention did not satisfy the criteria for patentability, unknown to the responsible Patent Office examiner. They can fight out their case before the Patent Office and in the courts, but this is costly and it also risks invalidation of the patent, so that no one is able to bar entry into the field. Fearing this, they may simply agree to live and let live, permitting the most advantageously situated firm to receive the patent without opposition and then to license the potential challengers. If there is an explicit agreement that no other producers are to be licensed, a violation of the antitrust laws exists. But it is difficult to prove this in court, and in any event it may be unnecessary for the companies involved to reach an outright agreement. Recognizing where its interests lie, the patent recipient merely elects unilaterally to license only rivals able to endanger its patent position, restricting the size of the 'club' to sufficiently few sellers that awareness of mutual interdependence makes tacitly collusive pricing likely. Thus, results similar to what would obtain under overt price fixing are secured. Still it is possible to be tripped up playing this game of legal brinkmanship, as the makers of tetracycline discovered in a series of antitrust cases in which they ultimately achieved substantial acquittal, but only after paying damages of some $120 million.[58]

We observed earlier that the patent system permits powerful corporations to harass financially weak firms and independent inventors through protracted litigation. This causes obvious inequities, and the legal costs can be significant. Between 1900 and 1941, 684 radio patents were entangled in a total of 1,567 infringement suits.[59] Inventors like Lee de Forest and Edwin Armstrong were forced to sell out their rights in key patents because, as Armstrong later lamented, he was "in danger of being litigated to death."[60] A single lawsuit over petroleum cracking patents lasted 15 years, piling up court costs and legal fees exceeding $3 million.[61]

An additional source of inequity arises from the priority system, under which (in the United States) the first person to invent a device or process receives full patent rights, while those who finish second in the race get nothing.[62] Invention

51. See Arthur A. Bright, *The Electric Lamp Industry* (New York: Macmillan, 1949), pp. 84–104, 235–302; and G. W. Stocking and M. W. Watkins, *Cartels in Action* (New York: Twentieth Century Fund, 1946), pp. 304–12.

52. But see "The Culprit: Carburetion," *Business Week*, 7 April 1973, p. 5, which provokes continuing apprehension.

53. See Machlup, *An Economic Review of the Patent System*, pp. 12, 41; McGee, "Patent Exploitation," pp. 145–48; and Beck, "Patents, Property Rights, and Social Welfare," pp. 1047–55.

54. One of the best-documented cases is New Jersey Standard Oil's suppression of the Santopour pour-point depressant for lubricating oils. See Stocking and Watkins, *Cartels in Action*, pp. 497–98. For a more extensive list, see Vaughan, *The United States Patent System*, pp. 231–38; and for a list that errs on the side of including doubtful cases, U.S., Senate, Committee on the Judiciary, Subcommittee on Antitrust and Monopoly hearings, *Economic Concentration*, Part 6, 90th Cong., 1st sess., 1967, pp. 3271–74. On Romanoff's apparent suppression of low-cost synthetic caviar, see "Marketing Observer," *Business Week*, 28 June 1976, p. 51.

55. See Charles Singer, E. J. Holmyard et al., *A History of Technology*, vol. IV, "The Industrial Revolution" (London: Oxford University Press, 1958), pp. 188–97.

56. For a summary of the leading cases, see Vaughan, *The United States Patent System*, pp. 105–67. For an attempt to develop criteria for identifying cross-licensing agreements of a primarily restrictive character, see George L. Priest, "Cartels and Patent License Agreements," *Journal of Law and Economics* 20 (October 1977): 309–78.

57. Vaughan, *The United States Patent System*, pp. 203–10.

58. *Federal Trade Commission* v. *American Cyanamid Co. et al.*, 363 F. 2d 756 (1966), 72 F.T.C. 623 (1967); *U.S.* v. *Charles Pfizer and Co., Inc., et al.*, 281 F. Supp. 837 (1968), reversed 426 F. 2d 32 (1970), 404 U.S. 548 (1972), and 367 F. Supp. 91 (1973); and "5 Drug Makers Will Settle Price Suits for 120 Million," *New York Times*, 7 February 1969, p. 1. See also *U.S.* v. *Singer Manufacturing Co. et al.*, 374 U.S. 174 (1973).

59. W. R. Maclaurin, *Invention and Innovation in the Radio Industry* (New York: Macmillan, 1949), p. 273.

60. Maclaurin, *Invention and Innovation*, pp. 256–57.

61. McGee, "Patent Exploitation," p. 153.

62. Section 102 (g) of the Patent Code mentions three distinct and potentially conflicting criteria for deciding priority contests: "In determining priority of invention there shall be considered not only the respective dates of conception and reduction to practice of the invention, but also the reasonable diligence of one who was first to conceive and last to reduce to practice." Many other nations such as West Germany, Japan, and France award priority to the first person who files a patent application.

is responsive to changes in the state of knowledge and demand; and since new opportunities may become evident to many persons at about the same time, it is quite common for two or more inventors to arrive at the same result independently and almost simultaneously. When a priority contest subsequently materializes in the Patent Office, the odds favor the inventor backed by ample resources.[63]

Finally, we must take into account the direct costs of administering a patent system. The budget of the U.S. Patent Office for fiscal year 1978 was $90 million, including salaries for 2,945 authorized employees plus sundry other expenses. The American Patent Bar Association has nearly 3,000 members, most of whom work outside the Patent Office. Assuming salary, clerical support, transportation, and office maintenance costs of roughly $80,000 per practicing patent attorney, we estimate total annual patent system administration costs of roughly $330 million at 1978 prices.

The costs and benefits on balance

Only in this last category are we able to hazard anything like a numerical estimate of the patent system's costs. The monopolistic restrictions facilitated by the system add costs that are no doubt higher but unmeasurable. On the opposite side of the balance, the system allows society to enjoy the benefits of some inventions that would not otherwise be made or that would become available at a later date without the patent incentive. These benefits are probably confined largely to two categories of inventions: those whose economic value is modest in relation to development costs, and those that represent unusually bold, risky departures from known technology. The social gain forgone through losing an invention in the first category because no patent protection is offered would by definition be slight. How the ledger would stand when all such gains are accumulated—on hundreds or perhaps even thousands of borderline inventions per year—is hard to say. The author's best guess is that the total would still not be enormous. Inventions in

the second category represent a horse of a different color. They are few and far between, but even a few can make a big difference in the efficiency of production or the quality of life. For instance, the introduction of xerographic copying processes permitted business enterprises and government agencies to realize savings of at least a quarter billion dollars per year at 1967 levels of utilization.[64] Without a patent system, the American economy would probably have been forced to wait at least several years longer for xerography. Recognition that a few such cases exist, offsetting the patent system's substantial costs, is what deters governments from scrapping the system altogether. As Jewkes, Sawers, and Stillerman observed:

> It is almost impossible to conceive of any existing social institution so faulty in so many ways. It survives only because there seems to be nothing better.[65]

Proposals for reform

This is perhaps too complacent a stance. Even if we concur that the basic system should be preserved, we can try to improve it by making major or peripheral adjustments. Several substantive proposals for reform deserve consideration.

One possibility is to reduce the life of a patent. Obviously, any decision on the duration of the patent grant must be a compromise.[66] Some inventions will be made even if the term of protection is a year, others only if the term runs for 30 years. An ideal patent system would hand-tailor the life of each patent to the peculiar circumstances of the invention it covers, but this is administratively infeasible. Debate centers, therefore, on the optimal average life. For a special case Nordhaus has shown that terms longer than 15 years are optimal only for inventions yielding very modest cost savings or facing unusually inelastic demand, but his analysis ignores such elements as uncertainty, risk aversion, and alternative incentives to invent and innovate.[67] Making horseback assumptions about relevant but highly aggregated variables, Professor Machlup concluded that the marginal benefits of the patent system fall short of the marginal costs for terms longer than 15 years.[68] Here again, however, the impact of longer protection on rare but spectacularly novel and ambitious developments is ignored. In the absence of more conclusive support for a shorter term, policymakers have been reluctant to move away from the status quo.

A different way of coping with the optimal life problem is to draw a dichotomy, as the Germans do, granting full-term patents on significant inventions but only petty patents (*Gebrauchsmuster*), with a term of three years, on minor inventions and improvements.[69] This proposal has considerable appeal, especially as a means of preventing the extension of monopoly power for decades on end, as in the incandescent lamp industry. Of course, if companies seek full-term rather than petty patent protection and succeed, the most a petty patent system will accomplish is the weeding out of nuisance patents with little entry-blocking power.

There are also alternative or complementary ways to prevent patents on minor inventions from clogging the arteries of technological advance. More rigorous standards might be imposed in deciding whether an invention is patentable, so that trivial contributions receive no protection. The American courts have waged a continuing campaign on this front without striking success. And at the administrative level, the proportion of patent applications approved by the Patent Office increased from roughly 60 percent in the 1950s to more than 70 percent in the 1970s, suggesting a possible reduction of standards. Second, to discourage purely defensive patenting, provision can be made for the mere registration of inventions, after which the inventions are rendered unpatentable unless another inventor proves priority within a limited period of time. Such a procedure was instituted by the U.S. Patent Office in 1968. It appears to have met with little success, for in contrast to the hundred-thousand-odd regular patent applications filed each year, there have only been one to two hundred defensive registrations. Third, patents in force could be subjected to an annual tax or renewal fee and cancelled in the event of non-payment, so that patent holders are forced each year to reassess whether it is worthwhile main-

taining their exclusive rights. This is done in many countries outside the United States. In Germany, the annual renewal fee in 1976 was DM 50 (about $21) for the third and fourth years, escalating to DM 1,700 ($720) for the terminal eighteenth year. In order to retain exclusive rights over the full 18-year term, a German patent holder must pay a cumulative total exceeding DM 10,000. Under this scheme fewer than 5 percent of all German patents remain in force for the full term, and the average life of a patent is less than eight years.[70] The system is highly effective in weeding out patents with nothing but minor nuisance value. However, neither a defensive registration system nor a renewal fee system can encourage voluntary abandonment of patents that protect important inventions in use or play a key role in fencing off some area of technology. Thus, they would not do much to reduce the amount of monopoly power based upon patents.

In many nations no patent protection is given for drug entities, other chemical compounds, and foodstuffs. This is ostensibly done to protect the public from monopolistic exploitation on the pur-

63. For a possible exception to the rule, in which an erstwhile graduate student inventor appears to have won rights to basic laser patents following an 18-year legal struggle against Bell Telephone Laboratories and others, see "A Laser Patent That Upsets the Industry," *Business Week*, 24 October 1977, pp. 122–23. Compare "Who Invented the Laser?," *Business Week*, 27 November 1965, pp. 132–37; and *Gould* v. *Schawlow and Townes*, 363 F. 2d 908 (1966).

64. Estimated from cost and demand data in Blackstone, "The Copying Machine Industry."

65. Stillerman, *The Sources of Invention*, p. 253.

66. The 17-year term of United States patents was a compromise between following the British precedent of a 14-year term (originally, time to train two sets of apprentices) and permitting special exceptions to allow a 21-year term.

67. Nordhaus, *Invention, Growth, and Welfare*, pp. 81–82.

68. Machlup, *An Economic Review of the Patent System*, pp. 66–73; and Machlup, "Patents," p. 471.

69. See Alfred F. Crotti, "The German *Gebrauchsmuster*," *Journal of the Patent Office Society* 39 (August 1957): 566ff. Other nations with similar systems include Japan, Italy, Spain, and Venezuela.

70. See P. J. Federico, "Renewal Fees and Other Patent Fees in Foreign Countries," Study no. 17 of U.S., Congress, Senate, Subcommittee on Patents, Trademarks, and Copyrights, 85th Cong., 2nd sess., 1958; and Thomas Dernburg and Norman Gharrity, "A Statistical Analysis of Patent Renewal Data for Three Countries," *Patent, Trademark, and Copyright Journal* 5 (Winter 1961–62): 340–60.

chase of vital staples. The notion has an element of paradox. If the patent system is justified at all as a means of encouraging technological progress, one might think the case for patent rights should be at its strongest in fields like medicine, where the public stands to gain the most from innovation. One can logically favor both the patent system generally and medical exemptions from it only if there are peculiar extenuating circumstances—e.g., if pharmaceutical research would be almost as vigorous without patents as with them because it is concentrated in universities and government laboratories, or for smaller or less developed countries that have little hope of stimulating significant domestic research but can benefit from the unimpeded importation of foreign medical technology.[71]

A more fundamental reform—the introduction of general compulsory licensing provisions—has been proposed numerous times by commissions and congressional committees, but every attempt to alter the U.S. law in this direction has been beaten down as a result of determined opposition from industrial groups and the patent bar.[72] Compulsory licensing is an accepted feature of patent laws abroad.[73] Typically, it can be invoked when a patent recipient fails to utilize an invention in the domestic market within a specified period of time, when licensing is essential to bring a complementary invention into use, or when the patent owner abuses a patent position—e.g., by restricting supply excessively. If a potential licensee has been refused a license but can prove that one of the applicable criteria is met, the courts will compel the patent holder to issue the license, intervening further to set a "reasonable royalty" when the parties are unable to come to mutually satisfactory terms. Curiously, these sanctions are not invoked very frequently. In West Germany and Japan, for example, a number of compulsory license applications were filed under post-World War II patent laws, but as of 1975 no licenses had been mandated.[74] Sixteen applications were filed between 1959 and 1968 under the British provisions governing general compulsory licensing, but only two license grants were compelled.[75] The number of applications and grants might be small because inventions worth the cost of a legal battle are too valuable

not to be utilized, because the criteria that must be satisfied before licensing is ordered are stringent, and/or because the very existence of compulsory licensing procedures encourages patent holders and would-be licensees to settle out of court. That stringency of the criteria is an important factor is suggested by the British and Canadian experience with compulsory licensing of pharmaceutical patents, for which special and more permissive legal provisions have been adopted. Between 1950 and 1971, there were 56 drug patent compulsory license applications in the U.K., 20 culminating in Comptroller of Patents decisions favoring the applicant.[76] Similarly, 15 licenses were granted during the 1960s under the Canadian drug patent provisions.[77] There is also reason to believe that compulsory licensing provisions do encourage voluntary agreements to license.[78]

Although the U.S. Congress has not seen fit to enact general compulsory licensing laws, compulsory licensing has been specified as a remedy in more than 125 antitrust cases, making available tens of thousands of patents at "reasonable" royalties or (in a few instances) royalty free.[79] In this respect the United States has outdistanced its European neighbors, whose antitrust and patent bureaucracies have for the most part been chary about intervening in patent matters. By vigorously prosecuting predatory practices and attempts to extend monopoly power beyond the limited bounds of specific patent grants, the U.S. antitrust authorities have managed materially to limit the social costs of the patent system.[80] This has been achieved without doing serious damage on the benefits side of the equation, for most of the corporations subjected to compulsory licensing orders had alternative incentives to innovate by virtue of natural lags, competitive differentiation, and established market positions. To them the prospect of profits gained by abusing the patent grant apparently had little incremental incentive value, for the effect of compulsory licensing on their R & D efforts appears to have been minute. Thus, an analysis of 1975 research and development expenditures data revealed that 42 companies subjected to compulsory licensing decrees of appreciable scope spent no less on R & D relative to sales than nonimpacted corporations of comparable size and industrial orientation.[81] The only observable adverse consequences entailed a likely propensity for decree-impacted firms to patent fewer of their inventions, resorting to secrecy more often.[82]

All in all, the substantial amount of evidence now available suggests that compulsory patent licensing, judiciously confined to cases in which patent-based monopoly power has been abused or extended far beyond levels needed to provide adequate incentive, would have little or no adverse impact on the rate of technological progress and would on occasion mitigate significant monopoly burdens.[83]

Finally, if one despairs of reforming the patent system through halfway measures, there remains the possibility of abolishing it. This is not an alternative favored by the author, but that should scarcely bar considering it seriously. We have no reason to fear that such a step would bring all inventive and innovative activity to a halt, since there are many alternative incentives. Yet some contributions would undoubtedly be lost, unless substitute incentives were created. There are two main alternatives.

First, the government might assume an increasingly active role in sponsoring and subsidizing innovation where private initiative proves inadequate. As Chapter 15 brought out, the U.S. federal government already supplies funds to support 37 percent of all industrial R & D activity plus considerable work in government and university laboratories. Most of this support is directed toward meeting unique governmental needs, as in the defense and space fields, but approximately 30 percent of federal expenditures go for R & D in such civilian areas as agriculture, food products, mining techniques, energy technology, water desalination, civil aviation, and the full spectrum of medical and medicinal technologies. Extension of the government's role would therefore not be a radical departure. Still, it has certain drawbacks. A centralized R & D resource allocation process could hardly avoid overlooking promising new opportunities, backing the wrong concept, neglecting unknown young people at the peak of their creative powers, and in general bogging down in red tape. A steady diet of research at the government trough can also

71. On India, see Sanjaya Lall, "The International Pharmaceutical Industry and Less-Developed Countries, with Special Reference to India," *Oxford Bulletin of Economics and Statistics* 36 (August 1974): 143–69.

72. See Catherine S. Corry, *Compulsory Licensing of Patents—A Legislative History*, Study no. 12 of U.S., Congress, Senate, Subcommittee on Patents, Trademarks, and Copyrights, 85th Cong., 2nd sess., 1958.

73. See Fredrik Neumeyer, *Compulsory Licensing of Patents Under Some Non-American Systems*, Study no. 19 of U.S., Congress, Senate, Subcommittee on Patents, Trademarks, and Copyrights, 85th Cong., 2nd sess., 1959; and P. J. Federico, "Compulsory Licensing in Other Countries," *Law and Contemporary Problems* 13 (Spring 1948): 295–309.

74. See David J. Henry, "Multi-National Practice in Determining Provisions in Compulsory Patent Licenses," *Journal of International Law and Economics* 11 (March 1977): 325–51.

75. Committee to Examine the Patent System and Patent Law, *The British Patent System* (London: HMSO, July 1970), p. 214.

76. *The British Patent System*, p. 214; and Scherer, *The Economic Effects of Compulsory Patent Licensing*, pp. 40–43.

77. O. J. Firestone, *Economic Implications of Patents* (Ottawa: University of Ottawa Press, 1971), p. 38. For an analysis of royalty setting in several cases, see Scherer, *The Economic Effects of Compulsory Patent Licensing*, pp. 43–50.

78. See Taylor and Silberston, *The Economic Impact of the Patent System*, pp. 16, 111–40.

79. U.S., Congress, Senate, Committee on the Judiciary, Subcommittee on Patents, Trademarks, and Copyrights, staff report, *Compulsory Patent Licensing Under Antitrust Judgments*, 90th Cong., 1st sess., 1960; and Scherer, *The Economic Effects of Compulsory Patent Licensing*, pp. 62–66.

80. For a quite different view, see Ward S. Bowman, Jr., *Patent and Antitrust Law* (Chicago: University of Chicago Press, 1973). Bowman argues that many of the so-called patent abuses subjected to antitrust attack were in fact desirable because they enhanced the patent-holding firm's profits and hence added incentive for investment in innovation. He largely ignores competitive stimuli and other nonpatent inducements to such investment and hence bases his case upon an unrealistically narrow view of the innovative process. Bowman is on sounder ground in arguing that certain patent "abuses"—e.g., discriminatory royalty rates—contribute to economic efficiency.

81. Scherer, *The Economic Effects of Compulsory Patent Licensing*, pp. 67–75.

82. Scherer, *The Economic Effects*, pp. 64–67; and Scherer et al., *Patents and the Corporation*, pp. 137–46, 153–54.

83. Cf. Taylor and Silberston, *The Economic Impact of the Patent System*, who conclude at p. 350 that "the balance of economic advantage for the [United Kingdom] lies narrowly with the existing patent system" rather than a worldwide system of compulsory licensing at "reasonable" royalties for all patents, without any required showing of abuse or excessive monopoly power.

dull incentives for efficiency, encouraging those who are subsidized to substitute money for ingenuity. Therefore, while government sponsorship will continue to be a valuable supplement, it holds little promise as a complete alternative to incentive systems that rely as much as possible on private initiative.

The other possibility is to institute a system of governmental awards or bonuses for individuals and firms making significant technological contributions. Such a system was proposed by James Madison at the Constitutional Convention of 1787 as an explicit alternative to the patent system.[84] Something like it was written into the U.S. Atomic Energy Act of 1946, establishing a Patent Compensation Board to confer monetary awards upon individuals making inventions related to military uses of atomic energy, which under the law could not be patented. The award approach is also a standard method of motivating invention by individuals in the Soviet Union, where inventors can apply for certificates of invention. When a certificated invention has been introduced into industrial practice, the inventor is entitled to a 2 percent share of the cost savings during the first five years of use up to a ceiling of 20,000 rubles.[85] Despite their evident attractions, award systems of this genre suffer from three main drawbacks. First, estimating the value of inventive contributions is a difficult task, and any bureaucratic council entrusted with the job is bound to make mistakes and perpetrate inequities. When inequity is inevitable, one might prefer that it be the result of a more impersonal income distribution mechanism. Second, as the approach has been traditionally interpreted, it pertains only to inventions in the narrow sense. If no provision were made to reward developmental contributions, and if in addition alternative incentive structures were deficient, there might be some danger, to reiterate Judge Frank's caveat, of throwing out the baby with the bathwater. It is worth noting that a chronic complaint of Soviet inventors is

that all too frequently their inventions are not accepted or put into practice by unsympathetic managers.

Third, there is an inherent conservative bias in the prizes granted by administrative and quasi-judicial bodies. Munificence is a rare committee virtue. For example, the Atomic Energy Commission's Patent Compensation Board awarded the assignee of Enrico Fermi's basic patent on the production of radioactive isotopes—forerunner of the methods for producing plutonium—a sum of $300,000 when the patent was dedicated to the public. In an analogous case, the federal government agreed to pay $1 million as compensation for utilizing Robert H. Goddard's basic liquid rocket engine patents. During the life of the Goddard patents, U.S. expenditures on liquid-propelled rockets amounted to roughly $10 billion. Compared to the value of the inventions and the profits that might have been earned if exclusive patent rights could have been enforced, the Fermi and Goddard awards were miserly. They were certainly not what Schumpeter had in mind in describing "spectacular prizes . . . thrown to a small minority of winners." It is doubtful whether a generalized reward system administered in this conservative tradition would motivate as much risk bearing as the patent system presently does. Still, the crucial policy question is how serious the loss of inventions and innovations owing to lessened risk bearing would be. And that, unfortunately, is a subject on which much more remains to be learned.

84. See Machlup, *An Economic Review of the Patent System*, pp. 15–16.

85. See Francis Hughes, "Soviet Invention Awards," *Economic Journal* 55 (June–September 1945): 291–97; *idem*, "Incentive for Soviet Initiative," *Economic Journal* 56 (September 1946): 415–25; E. Artemiev, "The New Soviet Law on Inventive Activity," *Industrial Property* (July 1974): 320–25; and (for details of the reward determination system), the "Laws and Treaties" section of *Industrial Property* (February 1977).

17 Market structure and performance: overall appraisal

It is time to stand back now and assess what we have learned about the dependence of industrial performance on market structure and conduct. This is best accomplished by addressing the question introduced at the end of Chapter 2, Is competition workable? Or more concretely, How serious are the performance deficiencies resulting from monopolistic structure and conduct in the United States?

No sublime analytic vision is required to discern that industrial performance, viewed broadly and generally, is not at all bad. Professor Galbraith has likened the American economy to the bumblebee.[1] According to aerodynamic theory (as interpreted by Galbraith), the bumblebee cannot fly. Yet it does. Similarly, even though the American economy is shot through with monopolistic and oligopolistic elements that might lead one to predict the direst consequences, performance is in fact rather good.

This exhausts our complacency quota. While performance is good, it is far from perfect. How large are the social losses associated with monopolistic structure and conduct? What keeps performance from departing further from the norm of workability? What can be done to make it still better? These are the questions to which we shall devote the balance of our attention. We must consider several dimensions of performance in our appraisal: allocative efficiency, efficiency of resource use, equity of income distribution, progressiveness, and macroeconomic stability.

The welfare losses attributable to resource misallocation

One adverse consequence of monopoly, the theory of welfare economics instructs, is the misallocation of resources. By raising price above marginal cost, monopolists restrict output, divert resources to less pressing demands, and reduce consumer welfare.

By making a number of simplifying assumptions it is possible to obtain a foothold for estimating the social losses associated with the resource misallocation owing to elevated monopoly prices. Figure 17.1 provides a frame of reference. Suppose that in the neighborhood of output levels attainable by sellers of moderate size there are neither economies nor diseconomies of scale. Suppose also, as is common in manufacturing, inputs are supplied at more or less constant prices, so that the long-run marginal (and average) cost function for an industry is the horizontal line *LRC*. The equilibrium price under pure

1. J. K. Galbraith, *American Capitalism* (Boston: Houghton Mifflin, 1952), p. 1.

competition would be OP_C, the output OX_C, and the total realized consumers' surplus the triangular area FEP_C. If the industry were monopolized but without blockaded entry, the price would be raised, say, to OP_M, and output would be restricted to OX_M. (We assume that entry-limiting considerations or imperfections in collusion among oligopolists preclude the elevation of prices all the way to the short-run monopoly profit-maximizing level.) Consumers' surplus is reduced to the triangular area FBP_M, and what was consumers' surplus given by the rectangular area P_MBAP_C is transformed into monopoly profit or producer's surplus. If the marginal utility of income to consumers and the industry's stockholders is identical, or if one has no basis for determining which group has higher marginal utility, the redistribution P_MBAP_C may be regarded as a 'washout' without significance for economic efficiency. There remains, however, the triangle BEA whose area was consumers' surplus under competition, but which is lost to consumers under monopoly pricing and not captured by (nondiscriminating) monopolists. In effect it vanishes into thin air and therefore represents the *dead-weight welfare loss* attributable to the misallocation of resources under monopolistic pricing and output restriction.

A bit of algebra will help put these geometric results in more useful form. Let ΔP denote the dollar amount by which the monopoly price deviates from the competitive price P and ΔQ the amount (in units of output) by which the monopoly output differs from the competitive output. Since the area of a triangle equals one-half its base times its height, we measure the dead-weight welfare loss W by:

(17.1) $W = 1/2\,\Delta P\,\Delta Q$

The *relative price distortion* under monopoly, or the ratio by which the monopoly price deviates from the competitive price, is defined as $d = \Delta P/P$. Ignoring signs and assuming ΔP and ΔQ to be small, we define the elasticity of demand to be approximately:

(17.2) $e = \dfrac{\Delta Q/Q}{\Delta P/P} = \dfrac{\Delta Q/Q}{d}$

which can be rearranged to:

(17.3) $\Delta Q = e\,d\,Q$

Substituting $Pd = \Delta P$ and equation (17.3) into equation (17.1), we obtain:

(17.4) $W = (1/2)P\,Q\,e\,d^2$

Thus, the dead-weight welfare loss from monopoly rises as a quadratic function of the relative price distortion d and as a linear function of the demand elasticity e.

All of the variables in equation (17.4) are potentially measurable. The first to seize upon the measurement possibilities was Arnold Harberger.[2] His wedge into the problem was a study of profit returns on capital in 73 manufacturing industries, originating 45 percent of all manufacturing output, for the more or less normal years 1924–28. Assuming that equating price with long-run unit cost implied earning a profit return neither greater nor less than the full sample's average return, he took individual industry deviations from the sample profit mean as an estimate of the relative monopoly price distortion d. Using available industry sales (PQ) data, and accepting the further assumption that demand was of unit elasticity in every instance, he had all the variables contained in equation (17.4), plugging them in to arrive at an estimated dead-weight welfare loss of $26.5 million for the industries sampled. Expanding this estimate to cover the

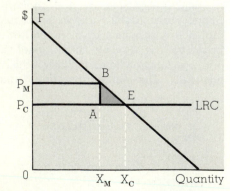

F 17.1 The welfare loss attributable to monopolistic resource misallocation

whole of manufacturing industry raised the estimated welfare loss to $59 million—about 0.06 percent of gross national product at the time. Further adjustments to compensate for inadequacies in his data led to a final judgment that eliminating monopolistic resource misallocation in manufacturing during the 1924–28 period would have increased social welfare by slightly less than 0.1 percent of GNP. At 1978 levels of output, this implies a dead-weight loss of about $2 billion per year, or roughly nine dollars per capita—enough to treat everyone in the land to a steak dinner at a good (monopolistically competitive) restaurant.

Not surprisingly, Harberger's article, with its implication that economists were wasting their time (and that of students) studying quantitatively insignificant phenomena, stimulated a considerable amount of methodological criticism[3] and attempts to reassess the extent of monopolistic allocative inefficiency using different data sets and conceptual assumptions. Several empirical studies yielded figures in the same general range as Harberger's.[4] At least two others, however, came up with much larger estimates of the dead-weight welfare loss triangle's magnitude—i.e., in the range of 4 to 7 percent of U.S. GNP.[5] It repays some effort to explore the principal grounds for disagreement.

Harberger's study was limited to the manufacturing sector. This introduces two biases. For one, the average return on capital tends to be lower in agriculture and many divisions of the retail and service trades than in manufacturing. Consequently, using the average return in manufacturing alone as a proxy for 'normal profits' leads to an understatement of monopoly price distortions. Also, Harberger's welfare loss estimate for manufacturing was ultimately related to national income. Distortions attributable to monopoly also exist in other sectors, although they are more difficult to isolate because data are scarcer and because profit figures do not necessarily reflect the magnitude of price/marginal cost deviations in monopolistically competitive markets. The manufacturing sector originated about a fourth of total U.S. GNP in the period studied by Harberger and also during the 1970s. To arrive at an economywide welfare loss estimate, figures derived for manufacturing alone must be inflated—perhaps by as much as a factor of three or four.

The profit data available to Harberger were mostly for quite broadly defined industries. Aggregation biases dead-weight loss estimates downward by submerging the high monopoly returns of narrow product lines within broad industry averages. Also, some monopoly gains may have been capitalized as costs rather than profits when, for example, assets changed hands through merger. And as we shall see in a moment, there is reason to believe that some of what might have been monopoly profit was actually exploited as cost, so that the departure between price and true marginal social cost was greater than available profit data imply. On the other hand, not all the profit deviations observed in the Harberger study (or similar studies) were necessarily the result of monopoly; some may reflect transient influences or special risks or superiority rents. Harberger made crude adjustments in his

2. Arnold C. Harberger, "Monopoly and Resource Allocation," *American Economic Review* 44 (May 1954): 77–87.

3. See for example George J. Stigler, "The Statistics of Monopoly and Merger," *Journal of Political Economy* 64 (February 1956): 33–35; Dean A. Worcester, Jr., *Monopoly, Big Business, and Welfare in the Postwar United States* (Seattle: University of Washington Press, 1967), pp. 210–27; Charles K. Rowley, *Antitrust and Economic Efficiency* (London: Macmillan, 1973); Abram Bergson, "On Monopoly Welfare Losses," *American Economic Review* 63 (December 1973): 853–70; and the exchange among R. Carson, Worcester, and Bergson in the *American Economic Review* 65 (December 1975): 1008–31.

4. See for example David Schwartzman, "The Burden of Monopoly," *Journal of Political Economy* 58 (December 1960): 627–30; Dean A. Worcester, Jr., "New Estimates of the Welfare Loss to Monopoly, United States, 1956–1969," *Southern Economic Journal* 40 (October 1973): 234–45; and John J. Siegfried and Thomas K. Tiemann, "The Welfare Cost of Monopoly: An Inter-Industry Analysis," *Economic Inquiry* 12 (June 1974): 190–202. It is worth noting that Siegfried and Tiemann find by far the largest single share of welfare losses to have originated in the automobile industry, where extensive price discrimination makes it unclear that the conventional Figure 17.1 analysis applies. Cf. Chapter 14, pp. 394, 400 *supra*.

5. David R. Kamerschen, "An Estimation of the "Welfare Losses from Monopoly in the American Economy," *Western Economic Journal* 4 (Summer 1966): 221–36; and Keith Cowling and Dennis C. Mueller, "The Social Costs of Monopoly Power," *Economic Journal* 88 (December 1978): 724–48. Note that the numbers in the text are confined to the dead-weight loss triangle only and not other possible loss components included in the Cowling-Mueller analysis, among others.

estimates to compensate for all but the excessive cost problem, but it is doubtful whether he eliminated what was undoubtedly a net downward bias. Thus, using methodology generally similar to Harberger's, Cowling and Mueller found that aggregating from the individual firm to the three-digit industry level led to a 47 percent reduction in the indicated welfare loss.[6]

A key assumption, differences in which account for much of the variation in diverse scholars' welfare loss estimates, is the value given the demand elasticity coefficient e. Harberger rather arbitrarily assumed a constant unit elasticity. At the other extreme, Kamerschen and Cowling and Mueller attempted to estimate elasticities for individual industries or firms by invoking a mathematical relationship that holds when monopolists maximize profits in the conventional (presumably short-run) sense:[7]

$$(17.5) \qquad e = \frac{P}{P - MC}$$

When, for example, price is 10 percent higher than unit cost, the estimated value of e is $1.1/(1.1 - 1) = 11$. The smaller the observed deviation is between price and cost, the larger the imputed demand elasticity must be. Since the accounting data used in monopoly misallocation studies rarely show price-cost deviations in excess of 15 to 20 percent, this method gives rise to much larger elasticities and hence much larger welfare loss estimates than the Harberger method. Indeed, the imputed elasticities appear inconsistent with reality in at least two major ways. First, respect for mutual interdependence in oligopoly is often imperfect, leading to prices below the monopoly profit-maximizing level. The less successful oligopolists are at achieving joint profit maximization, the more they will fall short of satisfying equation (17.5), and yet the larger will be the imputed elasticity (and consequent welfare loss) derived by the unjustified application of (17.5). Second, even when coordination among oligopolistic insiders is perfect, optimal dynamic limit pricing leads to a price below the level satisfying equation (17.5) except when entry is blockaded. Firms seeking to maximize their long-run profits may even set prices in the range of *inelastic* industry demand—a result totally in-

consistent with the application of equation (17.5) either as a prescription for pricing or as a means of estimating demand elasticities.[8] Consequently, the welfare loss estimates by Kamerschen and Cowling and Mueller must be regarded with skepticism.

A point emphasized by Professor Bergson suggests that relatively high demand elasticities might nonetheless be relevant in at least some cases.[9] When the products of an industry are moderately differentiated, each product's individual *ceteris paribus* demand function is likely to be quite elastic, and pricing behavior that distorts consumer choices could lead to large intra-industry output shifts and hence sizeable welfare losses. There are, however, important limiting factors. Confronted with high demand elasticities, monopolistic competitors selling close substitute products are apt to pursue similar pricing policies. If no close substitute's price is much higher in relation to marginal cost than that of other substitutes, the misallocation of resources *within* the industry will be small. In a collusive differentiated oligopoly protected by appreciable entry barriers, this state of affairs could conceivably coexist with relatively high (but uniform) price/marginal cost disparities for the whole range of the industry's products, while *inter*industry misallocation losses are held down by low *industry* (as distinguished from individual product) demand elasticities. These relationships are clearly quite complex, and little is known about their real-world significance. The most one can say with confidence is that Harberger-type welfare loss estimates assuming unit demand elasticities are biased downward more, the more important misallocation among relatively close substitute products tends to be.

An equally complicated problem overlooked by most authors concerns the transmission of monopoly distortions through successive vertical stages.[10] To illustrate, suppose there are two industries, A and B, each with sales of $1 billion per year and constant long-run marginal costs (including a normal return on capital) of $900 million. With $d = 100/900 = 0.11$ in each, and assuming unit demand elasticity, we obtain by applying equation (17.4) a combined welfare loss estimate of $12 million. However, suppose Industry A supplies some of its output as a raw material to Industry B—e.g., that half of Industry B's $900 million costs are for purchases from A. Then the long-run marginal social cost of B's output is not $900 million, but $450 million + .9($450 million) = $855 million. With B's relative price distortion raised to 145/855 = 0.17, our estimate of the total dead-weight loss increases to $17.9 million ($3.4 million on final goods sales by A plus $14.5 million on sales by B).

Since every dollar's worth of final output sales by business enterprises is supported on average by an additional dollar or more of intermediate transactions, one might suppose on a priori grounds that welfare loss estimates derived using equation (17.4) should at least be doubled to take this bias into account. However, this is probably not a correct approximation. Michael Klass has estimated the direct impact of vertical pricing distortions on allocative efficiency by computing price distortion ratios for both intermediate and final goods industries and then flowing those distortions through an input-output matrix of the U.S. economy for 1958.[11] It turns out that some major industries with exceptionally low and perhaps even subnormal returns, such as coal mining, transmitted a disproportionate share of their output ultimately to final goods industries like automobile manufacturing with unusually high returns, mitigating to some extent misallocations at the later stages. When price distortion estimation techniques similar to Harberger's were employed, taking vertical distortion effects into account actually *reduced* the final estimate of total welfare losses attributable to monopoly, given the 1958 structure of the economy. When an alternative distortion measurement technique "smoothing" unsystematic inter-industry pricing behavior was used, taking vertical distortions into account *raised* welfare loss estimates by roughly 40 percent compared to the figure obtained with a model assuming that all outputs satisfied final consumer demands.

Labor is also an intermediate input, and its pricing poses analogous difficulties. As Chapter 13 brought out, wage levels tend to be higher in the more concentrated industries.[12] If these higher wages are not offset by higher productivity—a point on which the evidence is inconclu-

sive—there will be further resource misallocations in both the labor and product markets undetected by the Harberger measurement technique. This compels an additional upward adjustment but the size of the effect, if indeed it exists, is too conjectural to permit any informed guess on how large the adjustment should be.[13]

One more complication lurks in the shadows. Any attempt to measure the dead-weight loss attributable to monopolistic resource misallocation by estimating the size of the triangle *BEA* in Figure 17.1 rests ultimately upon an assumption that resources are worth no more (and no less) in alternate uses than their marginal cost in the monopolistic industries scrutinized. This implies a partial equilibrium context in which, among other things, second-best considerations are irrelevant.[14] But in a world of oligopolies and monopolistic competition, the theory of second best *is* relevant, even if nonoperational, and so in the strictest sense we operate with a measuring rod (or triangle) of distressingly elastic rubber. In principle we cannot even tell the direction of measurement error imparted by neglecting second best and other general equilibrium repercussions, but it seems more likely to be on the

6. Cowling and Mueller, "The Social Costs of Monopoly Power," Table 3.

7. For the derivation, see Chapter 6, p. 187 *supra*.

8. See Chapter 8, pp. 237, 242 *supra*.

9. Bergson, "On Monopoly Welfare Losses," p. 860; and his reply in the *American Economic Review* 65 (December 1965): 1024–31.

10. See Chapter 2, pp. 26–27 and Chapter 11, pp. 300–303 *supra*.

11. Michael Klass, "Inter-Industry Relations and the Impact of Monopoly" (Ph.D. diss., University of Wisconsin, Madison, 1970).

12. See Chapter 13, pp. 359–61 *supra*.

13. Compare Frederick W. Bell, "The Effect of Monopoly Profits and Wages on Prices and Consumers' Surplus in U.S. Manufacturing," *Western Economic Journal* 6 (June 1968): 233–41.

14. Cf. Chapter 2, pp. 27–29 *supra*. For a simulation analysis suggesting that partial equilibrium analyses significantly overestimate the welfare losses caused by monopoly, even with no second-best relationships, see Thomas S. Friedland, "The Estimation of Welfare Gains from Demonopolization," *Southern Economic Journal* 45 (July 1978): 116–23. See also John Whalley, "How Reliable Is Partial Equilibrium Analysis?," *Review of Economics and Statistics* 56 (August 1975): 299–310.

side of exaggerating monopoly welfare losses.

Faced with this disconcerting observation, we have two options. We can give up trying to measure the allocative burden of monopoly, or we can cross our fingers and hope the errors from proceeding in a partial equilibrium framework are not too serious. Leaning toward the second alternative more on faith than with strong logical support, we conclude that Harberger's estimate was biased downward. Applying the multiplicative correction factors suggested in our critique of Harberger's results, it appears that the dead-weight welfare loss attributable to monopolistic resource misallocation in the United States lies somewhere between 0.5 and 2 percent of gross national product, with estimates nearer the lower bound inspiring more confidence than those on the high side.[15]

Other inefficiencies

Thus far we may have glimpsed only the tip of the iceberg. It is hard to think of realistic circumstances under which the dead-weight loss triangle *BEA* would be really sizeable, for it involves the square of the relative price distortion ratio *d*, whose average value was only 0.036 in the Harberger sample and 0.084 (calculated on a supranormal return basis) in seven industries with high barriers to entry analyzed by Qualls.[16] More serious consequences follow if monopoly affects costs as well as prices. Then the welfare loss has as its major dimension the whole output of the monopolized industry, not just the *change* in output associated with an elevated price. Inefficiencies might proliferate to fill or perhaps even overflow the trapezoidal area $P_M BEP_C$ in Figure 17.1 instead of its triangular right-hand extremity.

There are two broad sets of reasons why costs under monopoly might be excessive. First, in the absence of competitive pressure on profit margins, cost controls may become lax. Adam Smith recognized this danger two centuries ago: "monopoly . . . is a great enemy to good management."[17] More recently the refrain has been taken up and refined by Professor Leibenstein, who argues that when competitive pressure is weak, business organizations may tolerate and maintain what he called "X-inefficiency."[18] Second, the lure of monopoly profits can induce firms to incur substantial and possibly wasteful expenditures to obtain, strengthen, and defend monopoly positions.[19] Included here are certain outlays on product differentiation, the maintenance of excess capacity, and political lobbying and litigation, among others.

X-inefficiencies Whether business enterprises actually indulge in so-called X-inefficiency has been debated on various theoretical and semantic grounds, but those who oppose the concept in general terms have by far the poorer case.[20] Anyone with the remotest knowledge of real-world organizations must recognize that something resembling X-inefficiency exists. The important questions are, To what extent is there a systematic relationship between monopoly power and X-inefficiency, and of what general magnitude is the monopoly-correlated component? On this we have little broad-ranging quantitative evidence because it is so difficult to measure what unit costs would be if all firms in a cross section of industries ran tight ships.[21] There is, however, persuasive evidence from a sprinkling of individual industry studies.

Great Britain in the 1950s and 1960s provided a unique laboratory for observing the effects of a transition from monopoly to competition. Up to 1956, there were no effective legal barriers to price-fixing arrangements, and cartelization was widespread. But by 1960, strong judicial decisions interpreting a new antitrust law undercut the bases of most cartels. Many cartels found other ways to maintain price discipline.[22] But some did not, and significant price competition emerged. It in turn triggered a search for ways to reduce cost. The glass bottle industry exemplifies the latter reaction.[23] After price competition wiped out previously comfortable profit margins, a cost-cutting drive was implemented by the leading producers, outmoded plants were closed down, and modern bottle-making equipment (long available on the market) was introduced, making it possible to produce with 750 to 900 employees the same output that had previously occupied 1,400 workers. Similar reactions were observed in the transformer, automobile battery, galvanized tank, surgical dressings, and sanitary ware industries, among others. Likewise, Britain's Imperial Chemical Industries Ltd. reacted to new domestic and import competition with a strenuous effort to reduce its patently excessive costs. As its chairman explained the situation in 1966:

We had been in existence thirty-four years and had been having a comfortable time. We were doing well without too much exertion and had been favored by a good deal of scientific discovery. Then we ran into competition and had to learn to deal with it.[24]

Still, one must not make too much of these examples. There are many other U.K. industries that failed significantly to improve their efficiency in response to new antitrust laws and the challenge of Common Market competition, and "the British sickness" continues to be a generic term characterizing low industrial productivity. It is unclear whether efficiency was improved only sporadically because effective competition failed to materialize in many fields, because obsolete work practices were too deeply entrenched, or because there is only a weak correlation between competition and attempts to root out inefficiency.

Further evidence of cartelization's effects on costs exists for a handful of industries in other nations. Erickson studied illegal price-fixing conspiracies in three U.S. industries and found signs of deficient cost controls in all three. When, for instance, the gymnasium bleacher price-fixing agreement broke down in 1959, newly initiated cost reduction efforts led to a decline of approximately 23 percent in manufacturing costs.[25] The U.S. steel industry stands out for its chronic avoidance of price competition and also for the sluggishness of its leading firm. Thus, the report of a management consulting firm hired during the 1930s to study the United States Steel Corporation's operations has been summarized as follows:[26]

[T]he report of the industrial engineers . . . pictured the Steel Corporation as a big sprawling inert giant whose production operations were improperly coordinated; suffering

15. A best-guess partial equilibrium estimate is derived as follows. Raise Harberger's estimate of 0.06 percent to 0.12 to take into account excessive aggregation and the use of too high a normal profit return. Inflate this by a multiplier of 3 to cover the entire economy, by a multiplier of 2 to reflect more plausible demand elasticities, and by a multiplier of 1.2 to take into account vertical distortions. The resulting estimate is 0.86 percent of GNP.

16. P. David Qualls, "Stability and Persistence of Economic Profit Margins in Highly Concentrated Industries," *Southern Economic Journal* 40 (April 1974): 608.

17. Adam Smith, *The Wealth of Nations* (New York: Modern Library, 1937), p. 147. See also E. G. West, "The Burdens of Monopoly: Classical versus Neoclassical," *Southern Economic Journal* 44 (April 1978): 829–45.

18. See especially Harvey Leibenstein, "Allocative Efficiency vs. 'X-Efficiency,'" *American Economic Review* 56 (June 1966): 392–415; and *Beyond Economic Man: A New Foundation for Microeconomics* (Cambridge, Mass.: Harvard University Press, 1976).

19. For articles generalizing this hoary notion, see Gordon Tullock, "The Welfare Costs of Tariffs, Monopolies, and Theft," *Western Economic Journal* 5 (June 1967): 224–32; and Richard A. Posner, "The Social Costs of Monopoly and Regulation," *Journal of Political Economy* 83 (August 1975): 807–27.

20. See for example Ross M. Parish and Y. K. Ng, "Monopoly, X-Efficiency, and the Measurement of Welfare Loss," *Economica* 39 (August 1972): 301–308; George J. Stigler, "The Xistence of X-Efficiency," *American Economic Review* 66 (March 1976): 213–16; and Leibenstein's reply, "X-Inefficiency Xists—Reply to an Xorcist," *American Economic Review* 68 (March 1978): 203–11.

21. The closest thing to a systematic interindustry study is by Bo Carlsson, "The Measurement of Efficiency in Production: An Application to Swedish Manufacturing Industries 1968," *Swedish Journal of Economics* 74 (December 1972): 468–85. He finds a positive correlation between seller concentration and the extent to which the output of 26 Swedish industries approached maximum feasible output, given the mix of inputs. However, his measure of output, value added, includes profits and advertising outlays, confounding efficiency and monopoly price-raising effects. See also Lawrence J. White, "Appropriate Technology, X-Inefficiency, and a Competitive Environment: Some Evidence from Pakistan," *Quarterly Journal of Economics* 90 (November 1976): 575–89, who finds that Pakistani industries had higher capital/labor ratios in relation to their U.S. counterparts, the higher seller concentration was. White's interpretation is that monopoly power permitted firms to indulge a possibly uneconomic preference for capital-intensive processes.

22. Dennis Swann et al., *Competition in British Industry* (London: George Allen & Unwin, 1974), Chapter 4.

23. This discussion is based upon Swann et al., pp. 167, 185–86; supplemented by the author's own interviews with British glass bottle company executives.

24. "The British Company That Found a Way Out," *Fortune*, August 1966, pp. 104–105; and "Reshaping a Chemical Giant for Common Market Competition," *Business Week*, 2 December 1972, pp. 58–60.

25. W. Bruce Erickson, "Price-Fixing Conspiracies: Their Long-Term Impact," *Journal of Industrial Economics* 24 (March 1976): 189–202.

26. Statement of George Stocking in U.S., Congress, House, Committee on the Judiciary hearings, *Study of Monopoly Power*, 81st Cong., 2nd sess., 1950, pp. 966–67.

from a lack of a long-run planning agency; relying on an antiquated system of cost accounting; with inadequate knowledge of the costs or of the relative profitability of the many thousands of items it sold; with production and cost standards generally below those considered every day practice in other industries; with inadequate knowledge of its domestic market and no clear appreciation of its opportunities in foreign markets; with less efficient production facilities than its rivals had; slow in introducing new processes and new products.

It is significant that United States Steel began visibly to improve its operations and approach the profitability levels of other steel makers during the late 1960s, after it was exposed to increasingly severe import competition and it relaxed its efforts to maintain strong price leadership. In Sweden, significant behavioral changes followed 1961 legislation ending the Swedish Tobacco Company's exclusive control over wholesale distribution of imported cigarettes. One reaction was the closure of small, obsolete plants and the construction of a modern plant. The explicit goal was to minimize Swedish Tobacco's cost disadvantage relative to newly emerging competitors in other European Free Trade Association nations.[27] An interview revealed company managers' belief that they could no longer sustain the quiet life that characterized their earlier legal monopoly era.

Statistical evidence that competition matters comes from a study of electric power costs in the 49 U.S. cities where there were two competing companies. Primeaux found significantly lower unit costs—by about 11 percent on average—in municipally owned firms facing such competition than in an otherwise matched sample of monopoly municipal electric utilities.[28] In a statistical study covering 34 U.S. metropolitan areas, Edwards discovered that banks maintained larger staffs and incurred higher labor expenses when they operated in highly concentrated markets, taking into account also a variety of urban size, bank demand, and bank branching variables.[29] This "expense preference" behavior, he surmised, explains a tendency for banks' prices (i.e.,

interest rates on loans) but not net profits to be positively correlated with concentration. And to add one more industry, the author and several colleagues observed through detailed case studies of 12 aircraft and guided missile programs that efforts to reduce production costs were more vigorous when aerospace firms operated under contracts imposing a significant threat of losses than when the main consequence of incremental cost reduction was expected to be an increase in already satisfactory profits.[30] That is to say, incentives for cost reduction under a pressure theory of motivation had more powerful behavioral effects than incentives under a reward theory alone.

The evidence is fragmentary, but it is persuasive. "X-inefficiency" exists, and it is more apt to be reduced when competitive pressures are strong than when firms enjoy insulated market positions. What we do not know is how large are the differences systematically correlated with monopoly power. That X-inefficiencies attributable to monopoly are at least as large as the welfare losses from resource misallocation seems eminently plausible. And they may well be considerably larger.

Monopoly-induced waste Other relevant inefficiencies are those induced by the attempt to gain, extend, and defend monopoly positions. Advertising and similar product differentiation provide an important example, although here we must tread warily for reasons articulated in Chapter 14. Some advertising is clearly informative or otherwise beneficial, some is conducted in the hope of enhancing product differentiation and securing monopoly profits, and some results from producers' attempts to increase sales through nonprice rivalry when the suppression of price competition has left price-cost margins at temptingly high levels. An illustration of the inverse link between price and nonprice competition comes from the experience of the Kellogg Company.[31] During much of the 1960s there was little price competition among American breakfast cereal manufacturers, and the margin between price and unit production costs averaged roughly 50 percent. This stimulated intensive spending on advertising. Kellogg's Corn Flakes was no exception; advertising outlays ranged from 16 to 22 percent of sales between 1965 and 1967. But then growing private-label corn flake sales began bringing competitive pressure to bear on prices, at first squeezing margins and then provoking Kellogg in 1971 to announce a sizeable list price reduction. As its margins were reduced, Kellogg lowered its corn flakes advertising to 11 percent of sales in 1968 and then, after the list price reduction, to 6 percent in 1972. Similar advertising cuts were effected by rival General Foods on its Post Toasties corn flakes.

Considering the mutually cancelling nature of much advertising by oligopolists, the inducement provided by high price-cost margins, and the fact that producers in nations such as West Germany, Japan, and the United Kingdom manage to sell their wares despite much lower advertising outlays per capita than their U.S. counterparts, it does not seem too extreme to propose that roughly a fourth of the $38 billion spent on advertising in the United States during 1977, or about 0.5 percent of GNP, represented a waste more or less directly attributable to monopoly. To this sum must be added the amounts spent on disfunctionally elaborate packaging, personal sales calls unsolicited and unwanted by buyers, administering premium giveaway programs and sweepstakes, and accelerated styling changes that do nothing more than render last year's model obsolete. The sum of these items is unknown and, because tastes differ, unknowable. In the author's opinion, the total annual expenditure on wasteful sales promotion could not be less than 1.0 percent of gross national product.

It is natural to proceed another step and ask whether product differentiation efforts might lead to an excessive proliferation of product variants. "Excessive" here means that the costs of development, product launching, and the sacrifice of product-specific economies owing to small-lot production outweigh the surplus consumers undoubtedly derive from variegated product offerings catering to special tastes.[32] Judging whether the right balance has been struck is extremely difficult. Social losses from excessive product variety are most likely when a cartel or tight-knit oligopoly maintains uniformly high price-cost margins, thereby stimulating efforts to capture additional business through nonprice rivalry, and when it refrains from offering low-price options of lower "real" quality or with less prestigious images. A further symptom of wasteful product proliferation is the absence of strong consumer preferences for one product variant over others, as manifested in frequent brand switching or high price elasticities of demand, holding the prices of close substitutes constant.[33] It is certainly possible to find industries exemplifying these conditions.[34] It is unclear, however, how widespread they are, and since a certain amount of monopoly power (i.e., in the form of monopolistic competition) is surely necessary to call forth sufficient product variety, no general conclusions seem possible.

Price-fixing agreements, tacit oligopolistic collusion, and monopoly pricing can also stimulate the wasteful accumulation of excess capacity. There are four main mechanisms.

27. Based upon an interview reported in F. M. Scherer et al., *The Economics of Multi-Plant Operation: An International Comparisons Study* (Cambridge, Mass.: Harvard University Press, 1975), especially p. 157. On other aspects of Swedish Tobacco's response to new competition, see Chapter 8, pp. 258–59 *supra*.

28. Walter J. Primeaux, "An Assessment of X-Efficiency Gained through Competition," *Review of Economics and Statistics* 59 (February 1977): 105–108.

29. Franklin R. Edwards, "Managerial Objectives in Regulated Industries: Expense-Preference Behavior in Banking," *Journal of Political Economy* 85 (February 1977): 147–62.

30. F. M. Scherer, *The Weapons Acquisition Process: Economic Incentives* (Boston: Harvard Business School Division of Research, 1964), pp. 229–36.

31. Drawn from the author's testimony *in re Kellogg Company et al.*, Federal Trade Commission docket no. 8883, December 1977, pp. 28,013–28,018.

32. See Chapter 14, pp. 395–99 *supra*.

33. Note the link to our earlier discussion of allocative efficiency and demand elasticities. When intra-industry demand elasticities are high, interindustry elasticities are low, and producers pursue uniformly high markup policies, the welfare losses associated with conventional allocative inefficiency may, as we have seen, be small. But these conditions are precisely the ones under which product proliferation is most likely to be socially wasteful.

34. F. M. Scherer, "The Welfare Economics of Product Variety: An Application to the Ready-to-Eat Cereals Industry," *Journal of Industrial Economics* 28, forthcoming in 1979.

First, offering ample reserve capacity provides another kind of nonprice rivalry advantage—e.g., as travellers patronize airlines with the most flights and seats available at the last moment, or as industrial buyers favor suppliers who were able to meet their demands in unusually tight grey markets. Second, when cartel sales quotas are allocated in proportion to capacity, as they were under the U.S. crude oil prorationing system up to the early 1970s, investment in excess capacity to get a higher quota is encouraged. Third, excess capacity may be carried to strengthen the credibility of a monopolist's entry deterrent. And fourth, monopolistic pricing cushions the survival of capacity in secularly declining industries.

There is reason to believe that the relationship between monopoly power and certain of these propensities is nonlinear. Thus, ocean shipping cartels that perfected their monopoly through controls over entry, investment, and scheduling were less prone toward costly excess capacity or "overtonnaging" than the looser "open" cartels serving U.S. routes. Two studies revealed unit cost elevations on the order of 38 percent as a result of excess capacity on U.S. routes.[35] Similarly, cement producers using the basing point system as a collusive device were unable to control the tendency toward excess investment stimulated by their high prices. Between 1909 and 1946, the fraction of practical production capacity utilized by the U.S. industry averaged 68 percent; and in only three years out of 38 did the level of capacity utilization climb above 90 percent.[36] More generally, Frances and Louis Esposito found excess capacity levels in loosely oligopolistic U.S. industries (i.e., with four-firm concentration ratios of 40 to 69) to be 5 to 6 percentage points higher than in either atomistically structured or tightly oligopolistic industries.[37] Some excess capacity, it should be recognized, serves a socially useful purpose by enhancing producers' ability to meet peak demands.[38] But the optimal level can be overshot, and there appears to be a tendency toward overshooting, at least in loose oligopolies and cartels. Excessive costs are the consequence.

Other social costs of the basing point system and similar methods of handling the spatial pricing problem collusively include excessive cross-hauling and nonoptimal industrial location decisions. Counting only a dozen major industries (such as cement, steel, aluminum, and tin cans) whose pricing systems foster wasteful cross-hauling, and assuming conservatively from the data presented in Chapter 11 that cross-hauling costs amounted to 2.0 percent of sales, the costs of cross-hauling are estimated to have been roughly 0.1 percent of GNP in 1963. The additional losses associated with nonoptimal location choices under basing point pricing cannot readily be estimated. They have undoubtedly declined since formal basing point pricing systems were declared illegal, but in such industries as fluid milk production (where geographic pricing relations have been distorted collusively with express government approval) they continue to be appreciable.[39]

At least as difficult to assess are the costs associated with and resulting from the regulation of industries in which, for good reasons or bad, lawmakers have concluded that market forces cannot be counted upon to operate unfettered. Three rather different sources of waste should be distinguished. For one, classic public utility industries such as electric power, telecommunications, and (less clearly) some branches of transportation gravitate toward natural monopoly, causing market failures that motivate the imposition of various governmental controls. As we shall point out at somewhat greater length in the next chapter, the controls in turn distort producers' incentives, leading *inter alia* to deficient cost control, excessive investment, and arbitrary market divisions that misallocate resources. Second, companies spend substantial sums attempting to use political and judicial processes to erect artificial barriers to entry, impose other limitations on competition, and defend themselves when their monopolistic conduct or structure runs afoul of antitrust or similar laws. Third, even when markets would function well if left alone, business firms often succeed in securing protective and/or regulatory laws that simultaneously restrict competition and distort incentives in waste-inducing directions. Not all the costs associated with these phenomena can be attributed directly to monopoly. Indeed, distortions of the third type stem more from a failure of government than from market failure. It is widely believed that the total social costs imposed by all such forms of governmental regulation are very large—probably larger than the costs traceable to monopolistic market failures unprovoked by government intervention.[40] Even if the tally is confined, as it should be in the context of this chapter, to inefficiencies of the first and second type—i.e., resulting from natural monopoly regulation and attempts to secure legal monopolies—significant costs must be recognized. An extremely rough estimate would place them at 1 percent of GNP, give or take half a percentage point.[41]

Finally, it must be recognized that monopoly can reduce costs as well as impose them—notably, when high concentration is conducive or necessary to the full realization of scale economies. A number of complex considerations must again be integrated. Monopolistic competition makes it inevitable that some plants will be smaller than what appears from a technological standpoint to be the minimum optimal scale of production. Small geographic markets will be served at lowest total cost by small plants when transportation costs are high, and highly specialized products and services can often be supplied at lower cost by firms below the MOS of general-line producers. No social cost can properly be counted for such cases of sub-MOS operation. Second, when prices are elevated well above minimum unit costs through monopoly, cartels, or tacit oligopolistic collusion, an umbrella is held up to attract and sustain small, high-cost fringe producers. Similar results have been evident in abundance in such trades as retail pharmacies, liquor stores, and gasoline distribution when prices were held at generous levels through the formal (but increasingly rare) or informal imposition of resale price maintenance by manufacturers. But third, holding technology, product mix, and geographic variables constant, sellers with large market shares appear better able to capture sufficient demand to justify building large-scale least-cost plants.[42]

How these conflicting second and third influences balance out is an empirical question. We have systematic evidence only for manufacturing industry. It appears clearly established that average plant sizes tend to be larger, and the incidence of suboptimal scale capacity lower, when seller concentration is high than when it is low.[43]

In this respect, concentration is cost saving. A crude estimate of the potential magnitudes involved can be derived from research by Weiss and the author. On average in U.S. manufacturing during the 1960s, between 48 and 58 percent of all capacity was less than the general-line plant minimum optimal scale. For the median of 12 industries on which consistent estimates were available, plants one-third the MOS incurred a 5 to 6 percent unit cost penalty. A percentage point

35. J. W. Devanney III, V. M. Livanos, and R. J. Stewart, "Conference Ratemaking and the West Coast of South America," *Journal of Transportation Economics and Policy* 9 (May 1975): 154–77; and University of Wales, Institute of Science and Technology, *Liner Shipping in the U.S. Trades* (April 1978), pp. 46–50, 251.

36. Samuel M. Loescher, *Imperfect Collusion in the Cement Industry* (Cambridge, Mass.: Harvard University Press, 1959), pp. 168–69.

37. Frances F. Esposito and Louis Esposito, "Excess Capacity and Market Structure," *Review of Economics and Statistics* 56 (May 1974): 188–94.

38. See Arthur S. de Vany, "Capacity Utilization under Alternative Regulatory Restraints: An Analysis of Taxi Markets," *Journal of Political Economy* 83 (February 1975): 83–94; and "Uncertainty, Waiting Time, and Capacity Utilization: A Stochastic Theory of Product Quality," *Journal of Political Economy* 84 (June 1976): 523–41.

39. See Reuben A. Kessel, "Economic Effects of Federal Regulation of Milk Prices," *Journal of Law and Economics* 10 (October 1967): 51–78; Floyd Lasley, *Geographic Structure of Milk Prices, 1964–65* (Washington, D.C.: U.S. Department of Agriculture Economic Research Service, 1965); and, for loss estimates said to be conservative, Richard A. Ippolito and Robert T. Masson, "The Social Cost of Government Regulation of Milk," *Journal of Law and Economics* 21 (April 1978): 56–59.

40. For various views, see Posner, "The Social Costs of Monopoly and Regulation," pp. 818–21; Almarin Phillips, ed., *Promoting Competition in Regulated Markets* (Washington, D.C.: Brookings Institution, 1975), especially Chapters 2, 3, 8, and 9; Murray Weidenbaum and Robert De Fina, *The Cost of Federal Regulation of Economic Activity* (Washington, D.C.: American Enterprise Institute for Public Policy Research, 1978); and B. Peter Pashigian, "The Number and Earnings of Lawyers: Some Recent Evidence," *American Bar Foundation Research Journal* (Winter 1978): 77–81.

41. For supporting evidence now outdated in some respects, see the first edition of *Industrial Market Structure and Economic Performance*, Chapter 22.

42. See Chapter 4, pp. 100–3, *supra*.

43. Scherer et al., *The Economics of Multi-Plant Operation*, Chapter 3; and Leonard W. Weiss, "Optimal Plant Size and the Extent of Suboptimal Capacity," in Robert T. Masson and P. D. Qualls, eds., *Essays on Industrial Organization in Honor of Joe S. Bain* (Cambridge, Mass.: Ballinger, 1976), pp. 123–41. See also D. K. Round, "Monopoly Power and Inefficiency in United Kingdom Manufacturing Industries: A Note," *Bulletin of Economic Research* 26 (November 1974): 130–32.

increase in the average industry's four-firm concentration ratio appears to be accompanied by a decrease of 0.56 to 0.95 points in the percentage of sub-MOS capacity. In estimating the consequences of higher concentration, one must recognize also that cost functions are nonlinear, that some sub-MOS plants would surely survive in small spatial and specialized product niches, that plant size distributions tend to be approximately log normal in shape, and that many of the shifts would involve plants already close to minimum optimal scale. Given all these assumptions, it seems reasonable to infer that a doubling of average four-firm industry concentration ratios in manufacturing—i.e., from 40 to 80—would over the long run cause about one-third of total capacity to move from the sub-MOS into the MOS category, with an average unit cost reduction of 1.5 to 2.5 percent for the shifted plants. The average cost reduction relative to total manufacturing sector costs would be on the order of 0.50 to 0.85 percent.[44] This is, of course, about as extreme a structural change as can reasonably be imagined. Whether unit cost reductions of equal magnitude would result from comparable structural changes in nonmanufacturing industries is less certain. Since economies of scale are probably less compelling on the average outside manufacturing, the overall economywide unit cost reduction would most likely be somewhat smaller in percentage terms.

Considerations similar in principle apply to the relationship between concentration and the realization of product-specific scale economies. On one hand, cartelization and rigid oligopolistic pricing undermine firms' incentives to specialize and achieve long production runs. Respect for mutual interdependence inhibits price cutting to win a large share of a product variant's production, and buyers confronted with uniform oligopoly prices have a natural tendency to split their orders rather than concentrate them with a single low-price supplier.[45] On the other hand, it is conceivable that sellers with large market shares in concentrated industries manage to aggregate orders in such a way as to realize larger lot sizes and longer production runs than they would if concentration were lower, all else being equal.[46] There is very little evidence on this point, and

as a result it is impossible to tell whether on balance monopolistic market structures worsen or improve the attainment of product-specific scale economies.

Economies of scale in advertising and sales promotion pose equally difficult problems. They surely exist. For a given pattern of conduct, increasing concentration undoubtedly brings savings. The trouble is, conduct does not remain constant, and if price-cost margins rise, expenditures on advertising and other forms of nonprice competition will also tend to rise, perhaps overwhelming the savings associated with scale economies. Again, our knowledge is too meager to estimate the net cost effect.

Overall assessment In the first edition of this work, estimates of the diverse social costs attributable to monopoly were brought together into a single composite total. The combined estimate was roughly 6 percent of gross national product, with a range of uncertainty running from 3 to 12 percent of GNP. No attempt is made here to present a similar revised estimate. In addition to the caution that comes with age, there are two main reasons. The composite estimate in the first edition was surrounded by appropriate caveats, yet these were assiduously ignored by journalists and politicians seeking to enliven an article or speech with a seemingly precise magic number. Truth was not well served. Also, no cost reductions stemming from monopoly were netted out, largely because the negative association between concentration and the incidence of suboptimal scale plant capacity had not yet been discovered. It seems certain now that partly offsetting benefits do exist. The author's best estimate is that they are a good deal smaller than the burdens imposed by monopolistic conduct, but there is considerable uncertainty on this point, and truth is better served by shunning a spuriously precise net social cost figure.

The most that can be said with reasonable confidence is that the social costs directly ascribable to monopoly power are modest. It is appropriate to inquire why this is so. From our analysis in foregoing chapters, several explanations emerge. First, a large fraction of the American economy—perhaps as much as half—consists

470

of industries whose structures, although seldom atomistically competitive, include enough sellers to sustain a vigorous, workable species of competition as long as outright collusion is neither tolerated nor encouraged by the government. Second, many of the industries with oligopolistic structures possess little or no collective power to hold prices substantially above costs for extended periods because barriers to new entry are modest. Obversely, pricing performance is *least* satisfactory in those concentrated industries sealed off by very high scale economy, product differentiation, resource control, or patent barriers to entry. Third, high long-run price elasticities of demand reflecting the threat of product substitution frequently discourage maximum exploitation of short-run monopoly power, even when new entry with a perfect substitute is blockaded. This constraint has become increasingly important with industrial firms' growing sophistication in harnessing science to create new and superior synthetic materials. Uncertainty enhances the effect as professional managers strive to protect their market positions against feared but indistinct future threats by avoiding pricing strategies that encourage substitution through innovation. Fourth, the exercise of power by large buyers may countervail the pricing power of sellers, preventing the pyramiding of price distortions through a chain of vertical transactions and often (but not always) transmitting the savings to consumers. Finally, public policy has played a role. Except in some 'special case' industries, the United States has since the late 1930s maintained a fairly vigorous antitrust program, striking down restrictive agreements, punishing abuses of monopoly power, preventing the consolidation of power, and raising legal and financial obstacles in the path of countless monopolistic arrangements.

Other effects of monopoly power

To round out our assessment, we must consider the impact of monopoly power on other dimensions of performance.

One is income distribution. Monopoly profits represent a redistribution of income from the consuming public at large to the owners—usually, the stockholders—of monopolistic enterprises. From diverse industry and firm data samples and a variety of methodological assumptions, after-tax monopoly profits in U.S. manufacturing industry have been estimated at between 3 and 4 percent of manufacturers' contribution to gross national product.[47] Since profit returns in other sectors are lower on average than those in manufacturing, it seems plausible to extrapolate that the redistribution associated with monopoly for the entire economy is at a somewhat lower rate—probably between 2 and 3 percent of GNP.

Economists traditionally refrain from imposing their own value judgments concerning the equity of such redistributions. Nevertheless, several implications merit discussion. Many fortunes have been gained through monopoly positions, although monopoly in the orthodox sense is by no means the sole path to immense riches. On *Fortune's* list of the 13 richest Americans in 1968 were

44. This estimate might have to be doubled if the steeper but arguably less representative and reliable cost curve slope estimates of Weiss and Pratten are substituted. Pratten's sample was biased toward industries with relatively compelling scale economies. See Aubrey Silberston, "Economies of Scale in Theory and Practice," *Economic Journal* 82 (March 1972) Supplement, 379.

    If instead of being doubled, concentration ratios were *halved* on average, an increase in unit costs of somewhat larger relative magnitude would be expected, since the shift in plant scales would be toward more steeply ascending cost curve ranges. Cost curve nonlinearities make it more difficult to predict the size of the change. Cost increases would be significantly attenuated if concentration were reduced only in industries with either meager scale economies or plants whose sizes are characteristically well above the minimum optimal scale. Whether such changes might be accomplished by feasible antitrust policy measures will be considered in Chapter 20.

45. See Martin Howe, "Competition and the Multiplication of Products," *Yorkshire Bulletin of Economic and Social Research* 12 (November 1960): 57–72; *idem*, "A Study of Trade Association Price Fixing," *Journal of Industrial Economics* 21 (July 1973): 250; and Scherer et al., *The Economics of Multi-Plant Operation*, pp. 311–16.

46. See Chapter 4, pp. 103–4 *supra*.

47. See Schwartzman, "The Burden of Monopoly"; Bell, "The Effect of Monopoly Profits," p. 236; and Cowling and Mueller, "The Social Costs of Monopoly Power" (whose monopoly profit estimates are given in before-tax terms).

four men who rose to the top through oil wildcatting, where shrewdness and luck were, at least in an earlier and simpler era, as important as government-sponsored output restrictions.[48] The others were three members of the Mellon family, with long-standing interests in the Aluminum Company of America, Gulf Oil (an early challenger to the Standard Oil trust), and Pittsburgh's dominant bank; Howard Hughes, whose fortune was based on patented oil well drilling equipment and extended in defense contracting, motion pictures, and the regulated airline industry; Edwin Land of Polaroid camera fame; the former president and dominant spirit of Minnesota Mining & Manufacturing, with strong patent positions in Scotch tape and other heavily differentiated products; an early stockholder and executive of General Motors; a shipping and shipbuilding tycoon; and an insurance entrepreneur.

Typically, those who gained their fortunes at least in part through monopoly power have long since diversified their portfolios and may no longer dominate the corporations from which they profited. Subsequent stockholders often earn little or no supranormal profit on their investments, for the expectation of monopoly gains is likely to have been capitalized into the price they paid for their shares. Even so, those who receive most of the profits from corporations with monopolistic market positions occupy a higher stratum in the income distribution than the average American. It is estimated that the wealthiest 1 percent of all individuals in the United States owned approximately 57 percent of all personally held corporate securities in 1972; the wealthiest 6 percent owned more than 72 percent.[49] Thus, monopoly profits realized by corporations transfer income from the average consumer to the relatively rich. If one accepts the arguable premise that the marginal utility of income is lower to a rich person than to a poor person, it follows that aggregate social welfare is reduced by such transfers.

Moreover, the reinvestment of monopoly profits can have an important influence on the distribution of wealth. Over most of the 20th century, average rates of return on corporate common stock have been considerably higher than the rate of growth of personal income per capita. If wealthy corporate stockholders invest their income in an average portfolio and avoid excessive dissipation of monopoly gains through consumption, inheritance taxes, and the proliferation of heirs, they can increase their share of the total wealth distribution. Making what appear to be plausible assumptions about savings and dissipation rates, Comanor and Smiley found that in the absence of monopoly profits amounting to 3 percent of GNP between 1890 and 1962, the share of total personal wealth controlled by the wealthiest 2.4 percent of all U.S. families in 1962 would have been reduced from 41 percent to somewhere between 17 and 27 percent.[50] Or if the eliminated monopoly profits amounted to only 2 percent of GNP, the same families' share of personal wealth would have been reduced to between 31 and 34 percent.

There is evidence that the compensation of corporate executives is more generous in companies whose home base is a concentrated industry.[51] This is another transfer of income to the relatively affluent. Also, the wage income of rank and file employees appears to be higher in concentrated than in atomistic industries. Whether such redistributions among workers pose significant equity problems is arguable. Another possible inequity arouses greater concern. It has been suggested that one way business firms might indulge the discretion they enjoy when competitive pressures are weak is by practicing racial or religious discrimination in hiring—e.g., by not hiring or promoting up to the profit-maximizing point blacks or other minorities against whom prejudice exists. Statistical tests of this hypothesis, mostly covering periods before federal government efforts to enforce equal employment opportunity gained full momentum, reveal no clear discriminatory pattern for wages among manufacturing industries of varying structure. However, there was evidence of somewhat more favorable wage levels for blacks in government and nonprofit organizations than in profit-oriented enterprises.[52] Other studies indicate that for given worker characteristics and wage levels, more highly concentrated and/or profitable industries tended to hire a disproportionately small number of black workers, especially for upper level jobs.[53]

Turning to the effects of market structure on

the rate of technological progress, we confine ourselves to four summary observations. First, concentration is much higher and leading firm sizes are much larger in many industries than they need to be to support the most vigorous rate of progress. Second, in some atomistic industries, concentration is too low and representative firm sizes are too small for ambitious research and innovation efforts to thrive. Whether the technological needs of these industries are adequately served by materials and equipment suppliers operating under structural conditions more conducive to innovation is not certain. Third, some of the most strikingly profitable monopoly positions were the result, not the cause, of successful innovation attended by strong patent protection. The rewards realized in these instances serve an indirect incentive function. However, much corporate inventive and innovative effort does not require a patent stimulus, and abuses and extensions over time of patent positions appear to be unambiguously disfunctional. Fourth, our knowledge is too limited to predict confidently whether the rate of technical progress could be accelerated significantly by structural reforms— e.g., by forcing the deconcentration of highly concentrated industries and permitting a movement toward concentration of atomistic industries. The author's best guess is that such measures, taking the current structure of American industry as a point of departure, would make very little difference.

A similar conclusion applies regarding the effects of market structure on macroeconomic stability. Capital investment may be somewhat more volatile in concentrated than in unconcentrated industries, but business expectations are probably affected favorably by the price stability flowing from monopoly power. Given the fiscal and monetary tools available to combat business fluctuations, the consequences of these and other industrial organization variables appear to be of only a second or third order of relative importance.

On the goal of preventing inflation, a less sanguine verdict is required. The principal culprit in inflation is indisputably fiscal and monetary imbalance. Yet two features of concentrated industries—the tendency for their prices to be more flexible upward than downward, and their vulnerability to wage increase demands rationalized on grounds of ability to pay—probably contribute modestly to creeping inflation. This can create a dilemma for economic policymakers, forcing them to choose between lower, more acceptable unemployment rates on the one hand and less inflation on the other. Our knowledge is still too imperfect to be certain that monopoly power in product markets definitely affects the inflationary process in this way. If, however, a judgment must be rendered on the basis of the available evidence, it will have to be an unfavorable one.

Finally, there are implications of concentration and monopoly we must dismiss summarily because they lie outside the conventional domain of economics or because we have failed to

48. "The Richest of the Rich," *Fortune*, May 1968, p. 156.

49. See U.S., Bureau of the Census, *Statistical Abstract of the United States, 1976* (Washington, D.C.: Government Printing Office, 1976), p. 427, citing studies by and unpublished data from James D. Smith and Stephen D. Franklin; and "Distribution of Personal Wealth in the United States," *New York Times*, 30 July 1976, sec. IV, p. 11. See also Robert J. Lampman, *The Share of Top Wealth-Holders in National Wealth* (Princeton: Princeton University Press, 1962).

50. William S. Comanor and Robert H. Smiley, "Monopoly and the Distribution of Wealth," *Quarterly Journal of Economics* 89 (May 1975): 177–94. On the crucial role of dissipation in limiting tendencies toward rising concentration of wealth, see Stanley Lebergott, "Are the Rich Getting Richer? Trends in U.S. Wealth Concentration," *Journal of Economic History* 36 (March 1976): 147–62.

51. See Oliver E. Williamson, "Managerial Discretion and Business Behavior," *American Economic Review* 53 (December 1963): 1040–47.

52. See William R. Johnson, "Racial Wage Discrimination and Industrial Structure," *Bell Journal of Economics* 9 (Spring 1978): 70–81; and Edwin T. Fujii and John M. Trapani, "On Estimating the Relationship between Discrimination and Market Structure," *Southern Economic Journal* 26 (January 1978): 556–67. Compare Leonard W. Weiss, "Concentration and Labor Earnings," *American Economic Review* 56 (March 1966), especially pp. 105–108, 115.

53. See William J. Shepherd, *Market Power & Economic Welfare* (New York: Random House, 1970), pp. 213–21; Shepherd and Sharon G. Levin, "Managerial Discrimination in Large Firms," *Review of Economics and Statistics* 55 (November 1973): 412–22; William S. Comanor, "Racial Discrimination in American Industry," *Economica* 40 (November 1973): 363–78; and Walter Haessel and John Palmer, "Market Power, Discretionary Authority, and Employment Discrimination" (Research report 7607, University of Western Ontario Department of Economics, April 1976). None of the papers on market structure and racial discrimination takes into account fully the simultaneous relationships determining wages and employment levels.

Market structure and performance overall appraisal   473

find anything perceptive to say about them in previous chapters. For instance, one may condemn the concentration of economic power because it allows decisions to be made personally by an elite rather than impersonally by market forces, or because it slants political processes in favor of affluent and well-organized groups.[54] Or large-scale plants and firms may be faulted because they contribute to worker alienation.[55] Or the sensitivity of oligopolists to the adverse effects of output expansion in their home markets may drive them to search not only for domestic diversification opportunities, but also for investment outlets abroad. However beneficial or harmless this modern brand of imperialism may seem to Americans, it is a cause of concern in other nations—all the more so when it is coupled with CIA subversion or the exercise of overt military power.[56] On these and other neglected dimensions of industrial performance, the reader must make his or her evaluations from a broader base of evidence.

Conclusion

We return to our original question, Is competition workable? The simpleminded reply must be, If it is results that count, the performance of American industry is remarkably good, though far from perfect. Nevertheless, this is not a very constructive answer. A more operational approach is to apply Professor Markham's test of workability: Competition is workable when there is no clearly indicated change attainable through public policy measures leading to greater social gains than social losses.[57] From this two further conclusions follow. First, as noted earlier, the standard of performance achieved by U.S. industry is at least in part a result of the public policy measures already adopted to encourage (or suppress) competition. And second, things are not so good that they cannot be improved by adding or deleting policy measures or applying existing policies more intelligently.

Our assignment in the remaining chapters will be to explore the principal policy alternatives, determining where they have succeeded and where their chief weaknesses lie. The ultimate goal is to find a set of policy measures that best channels the energy of industry to serve the public interest. To this task we now turn.

54. See R. W. Pitman, "The Effects of Industry Concentration and Regulation on Contributions in Three 1972 U.S. Senate Campaigns," *Public Choice* 27 (Fall 1976): pp. 71–80; and Lester M. Salamon and John J. Siegfried, "Economic Power and Political Influence," *American Political Science Review* 67 (September 1977): 1026–43.

55. See F. M. Scherer, "Industrial Structure, Scale Economies, and Worker Alienation," in Masson and Qualls, eds., *Essays on Industrial Organization in Honor of Joe S. Bain*, pp. 105–21.

56. For various views, see K. W. Rothschild, "Price Theory and Oligopoly," *Economic Journal* 57 (September 1947): 318–19; Paul A. Baran and Paul M. Sweezy, *Monopoly Capital* (New York: Monthly Review Press, 1966), pp. 178–217; Stephen Hymer and Robert Rowthorn, "Multinational Corporations and International Oligopoly: The Non-American Challenge," in Charles P. Kindleberger, ed., *The International Corporation: A Symposium* (Cambridge, Mass.: MIT Press, 1970), pp. 57–91; United Nations Department of Economic and Social Affairs, *Multinational Corporations in World Development* (New York: United Nations, 1973), especially Chapter 3; Bertrand Russell Peace Foundation, *Subversion in Chile: A Case Study in U.S. Corporate Intrigue in the Third World* (Nottingham: Spokesman Press, 1972); "I.T.T. Elaborates on Funds in Chile," *New York Times*, 13 May 1976, pp. 51, 54; and "I.T.T.—Chile Case Closed," *New York Times*, 8 March 1979, p. D-1.

57. Jesse W. Markham, "An Alternative Approach to the Concept of Workable Competition," *American Economic Review* 40 (June 1950): 349–61.

18 Policy approaches to the monopoly problem

That government should intervene when the market fails is widely, though not universally, accepted. Among those who accept at least the principle of intervention, debate centers on when the government should step in, how vigorous its involvement should be, and what specific policy instruments it should use. In this chapter, we survey some of the principal policy alternatives. They include taxation, price controls, moral suasion, public regulation, public ownership, policies to enhance the stock of consumer and investor information, and antitrust policy. Then, in Chapters 19 through 21, we shall focus more intensively on one set of instruments—antitrust policy.

Taxation policy

The powers of the government to tax and subsidize might be employed to combat monopoly and its effects, although as a practical matter, taxation is generally too blunt an instrument to rely on heavily.

Monopolists restrict output unduly because marginal revenue to them is less than price. One way to remedy this condition is to pay the monopolist a per-unit subsidy equal to the difference between marginal revenue and price at the output that would prevail under pure competition. This subsidy will be just sufficient to induce an expansion of production to the competitive level. Of course, the adverse income distribution effects associated with monopoly are compounded. In principle, a lump-sum tax equal to the subsidy could be imposed to take back with the left hand what has been given with the right. However, it is extraordinarily difficult to levy lump-sum taxes with the desired neutral effect on output, and it would also be hard to obain the data needed to set the proper per-unit subsidy rate. Therefore, we must concur with Joan Robinson's judgment that this approach is only "an ingenious though unpractical scheme."[1]

By levying graduated excise taxes whose rates rise with the price charged, it may also be possible to induce monopolists to expand their output.[2] However, achieving a favorable output effect depends upon getting the right rate of tax progression in relation to the elasticity of demand, and gaining sufficient information to implement such a tax without making matters worse rather than better is apt to be difficult or prohibitively costly.

A corporation profits tax acts to channel prof-

---

1. Joan Robinson, *The Economics of Imperfect Competition* (London: Macmillan, 1933), pp. 163–64.
2. See Ned Shilling, *Excise Taxation of Monopoly* (New York: Columbia University Press, 1969).

its away from relatively wealthy shareholders into lower strata of the income distribution. As a device for combating the effects of monopoly, however, it has two main limitations. First, empirical research suggests that firms with monopoly power may be more likely than competitive producers to pass on all or part of a profits tax to consumers by raising prices.[3] If true, the incidence of a profits tax falls relatively more heavily upon competitive than monopolistic firms—the opposite of what is desired. Second, even if this were not true, the corporate profits tax as presently administered in the United States has no special potency with respect to monopoly profits. An enterprise earning 30 percent before taxes on its invested capital pays the same percentage tax rate as a company earning only 8 percent, at least after some modest absolute profit threshold is crossed, and therefore ends up about as well off relative to the less profitable firm after taxes as it was before.

When the capture of monopoly profits is a primary goal, it is necessary to implement some kind of excess profits tax that applies especially high marginal rates to income exceeding a normal return on invested capital. Such an approach was pursued in the United States during World Wars I and II and the Korean war, though more as a means of curbing wartime profiteering in general than as an antimonopoly measure. As the wartime experiences showed, formidable accounting problems arise in administering an excess profits tax, and it is impossible to avoid inequities, whether loopholes are opened up liberally (as has been the case historically) or through a strict, no exceptions policy.[4] Business decisions may also be distorted. For instance, if the tax is applied to profit returns in relation to common stockholders' equity, it can discourage the use of low-cost bonds. More important, it can induce enterprises with monopoly power to make excessively capital-intensive investment choices or to spend more on advertising or managerial amenities than they otherwise would. Because of these drawbacks, there has been little enthusiasm in the United States for maintaining peacetime excess profits taxation instruments.

During the 1960s an increasingly popular method of financing mergers was for the acquiring firm to issue new interest-bearing debt in exchange for the common stock of companies it acquired. Although this increased the riskiness of the merged corporation's capital structure, it had significant tax advantages, since income paid out to investors in the form of interest was tax-deductible to the corporation, whereas earnings on common stock were not. To narrow this tax loophole and discourage speculative or empire-building mergers, Congress in 1969 abolished the tax deduction privilege for interest on convertible debentures issued expressly to consummate a merger.

The structure of tariffs might also be manipulated to deal with monopoly—e.g., by denying tariff protection to monopolistic industries, thereby intensifying the threat of import competition as a constraint on their pricing freedom. President Grover Cleveland recommended in 1887 that Congress deal with the emerging trust problem in this fashion, and an unsuccessful amendment to the Sherman Antitrust Act of 1890 would have stripped violators of their tariff protection. The Canadian antitrust laws do incorporate such a penalty, honored more in disuse than implementation. The main difficulty is that if pricing performance fails to improve after tariff barriers are lowered, imports will rise without any direct assurance of compensating export growth. For nations concerned, as most are, with their exchange rate and balance of payments position, this may seem too high a risk to run for the sake of promoting competitive domestic pricing. Indeed, the United States has on occasion gone to the opposite extreme—e.g., implementing in 1978 a system of cost-linked tariff barriers to protect American steel makers from importers who, unlike their U.S. counterparts, exhibited little oligopolistic restraint and cut prices when business was slack.[5]

Price controls

A second general policy option is to enforce price controls, placing binding ceilings on the prices producers can charge. This approach has been used on a broad scale by the U.S. government during wartime and in a modified form during the early 1970s. Its permanent use to counter the alleged inflationary propensities of administered price industries has been advocated by some economists.

Under the orthodox assumptions of monopoly profit maximization, an astute program of price controls can bring about salutary results. To see this, consider Figure 18.1. We assume a monopolist in long-run equilibrium before price controls, charging the price OP_M and operating a plant described by the short-run average total cost curve $SRATC$ best suited to producing output OX_M. Now the government steps in to impose a ceiling price lower than the monopolist's preferred price. This, in effect, renders that portion of the demand curve above the ceiling price, along with its corresponding marginal revenue segment, inaccessible. The monopolist's new marginal revenue function is a horizontal line at the level of the ceiling price, at least to the left of the ceiling price line's intersection with the demand function. It follows that by setting the ceiling price OP_S, the government can induce the monopolist to expand its output all the way to OX_S, where price equals short-run marginal cost. Thus, price controls can lead simultaneously to lower prices and increased output—the best of both worlds!

There are, however, some practical hitches.

Starting from the assumed cost conditions, a ceiling price of OP_S still permits the firm to earn supranormal profits. This is sure to upset government price fixers and the legislators who review their accomplishments, so there will be pressure to lower the ceiling. Also, the price controllers never have sufficient knowledge to locate precisely the point E, where the short-run marginal cost function intersects the demand function. In their ignorance, they will be inclined to set a price commensurate with observed unit costs, which again implies undercutting OP_S. Suppose they set the price OC equal to minimum unit costs. Then the firm's optimal response will be to produce the output OX_M—the same as under unconstrained monopoly pricing. At price OC, however, the quantity demanded is OX_L. There will be a shortage of $X_M X_L$ units that can be resolved only by drawing down inventories (at best a temporary expedient), arbitrary customer quota allocations, rationing by queue, the appearance of a black market, or some form of quantity rationing by the government. Any such rationing scheme is likely to be inefficient in the sense that it puts output in the hands of consumers with low reservation prices—i.e., below OP_S—at the expense of high reservation price consumers who would have derived greater consumers' surplus from having an extra unit of output. For a given total output, therefore, the sum of consumers' plus producers' surplus is not maximized. At ceiling prices intermediate between OP_S and OC there will also be shortages, but they will be smaller than at price OC.

In the long run, the monopolist can probably be persuaded to expand its production capacity along the long-run cost function $LRATC$ if the price ceiling is held slightly above OC, and so eventually the shortage problem will disappear.

3. See Robert J. Gordon, "The Incidence of the Corporation Income Tax in U.S. Manufacturing, 1925–62," *American Economic Review* 57 (September 1967), especially pp. 751–53.

4. See George Lent, "Excess Profits Taxation in the United States," *Journal of Political Economy* 59 (December 1951): 481–97.

5. "Steel-Price 'Dumping' Guide Issued," *New York Times*, 4 January 1978, p. 1.

F 18.1 Influencing monopoly output through price controls

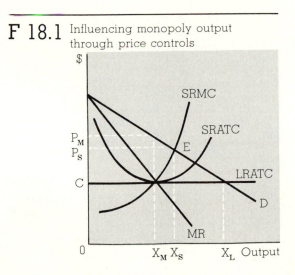

Its place may be taken, however, by another problem. Given their limited knowledge of cost and demand conditions, government price controllers have little practical alternative but to set a price that covers the observed unit costs of the monopolistic producer or, if the industry has more than one seller producing identical items, of those suppliers who account for the bulk of output. Some sort of cost-plus pricing rule will probably be adopted. This can have debilitating effects on cost control incentives, for if producers recognize that any industrywide cost increase will compel an upward ceiling price revision, they may strive less vigorously to hold the line against wage concessions exceeding productivity gains, to introduce new and more efficient processes, and so on.

Theoretical reasoning suggests, then, that price controls *may* have a favorable impact on the performance of monopolistic industries, but that inevitable mistakes by the price controllers can lead to shortages and disequilibrium in the short run and operating inefficiencies in the long run. Is this consistent with the evidence?

The experience with price controls in monopolistic and oligopolistic industries during World War II is generally considered to have been fairly successful. One reason was that American industry emerged from the depression of the 1930s into the wartime period with considerable unutilized capacity, and this provided favorable conditions for price controls to have their predicted output-expanding effect.

Other contributing factors have been identified by Professor Galbraith, a veteran World War II price controller.[6] It was much easier administratively to deal with oligopolistic industries, whose chief executives could be assembled conveniently around a small conference table. Product differentiation facilitated the allocation of scarce supplies expediently, though not always equitably, as sellers gave preference in shortage situations to buyers with whom they had traditional ties, rationing their output among those buyers on the basis of historical purchasing patterns. Letting prices be unresponsive to short-run changes in demand was a familiar *modus operandi* for oligopolistic producers. Under these circumstances, the functioning of wartime price controls in monopolistic industries surpassed the expectations of economists responsible for their administration.

On the other hand, the Office of Price Administration experienced its "most dismal failures" in the more competitive markets, where direct administrative control was impossibly cumbersome and producers responded to distorted price signals in unexpected ways.[7] For example, the price ceilings initially set for clothing permitted higher profit margins to be earned on high-priced items, and so resources surged into expensive clothing lines while shortages of work clothes appeared. To correct this imbalance, the OPA increased the prices of low-end items, but this merely diverted more demand toward high-priced items. Similarly, miscalculations in setting meat and grain prices channelled excessive resources toward producing meat, considerable portions of which flowed into black markets; and this eventually forced the government to supplement its food price control program with an elaborate quantity rationing scheme.

A more bitter aftertaste followed the United States' experience with comprehensive price controls (or more accurately, wage and profit margin controls) during the early 1970s—a period of less than full wartime mobilization.[8] At first the three-month price freeze and subsequent Phase II controls of 1971 and 1972 worked rather well. As at the beginning of World War II, the economy was emerging from a recession and had appreciable slack. The nub of the problem was to dampen inflationary expectations underlying cost-push pressures and put the economy on a noninflationary growth path. Progress toward this objective was made initially with only a few accompanying distortions—e.g., when heating oil prices were frozen at their summer low point, discouraging refiners' autumnal shift to an output mix entailing relatively less gasoline.

Nevertheless, the situation deteriorated in 1973. The most fundamental reason for the change was that many key industries reached the point at which they had insufficient capacity to meet growing demands at the controlled prices. Bad luck also played a role: A series of agricultural setbacks throughout the world pushed raw food prices up sharply; and in contrast to prior history, virtually all the world's industrial nations simultaneously experienced boom conditions, precipitating an upsurge in raw material prices ultimately aggravated by OPEC's unprecedented price increases in late 1973. This concatenation of pressures was too much for the U.S. control system to contain. Shortages appeared in many product lines; and with a less compelling mandate than in wartime, the Nixon government chose to intervene as little as possible in helping solve rationing problems. This minimal intervention policy also had adverse psychological effects, for with government officials openly proclaiming their distaste for even the limited controls in force, it was impossible to inculcate the kind of public-spirited "muddling through" attitude among business firms and consumers that helped make wartime controls work.

Neither their hypothetical output expansibility (whose short-run potential had largely been tapped) nor the susceptibility of oligopolistic industries to across-the-table confrontation and guidance contributed much toward alleviating the shortage problems of 1973. In fertilizers, for example, U.S. prices were held below both domestic market-clearing and world market levels. Exports thereupon rose, aggravating the domestic shortage. When this was recognized, leaders of the loosely concentrated industry met with government officials and bargained for freedom from price controls in exchange for a pledge of lower exports, moderation in price increases, and the expansion of capacity. The fertilizer makers evidently kept their promise to limit price increases, but their widely scattered, atomistic distributors failed to follow suit, reaping large windfall profits as the prices paid by farmers for fertilizer soared. In other industries, controls aggravated propensities of long standing toward market failure. Thus, during the 1960s, growing imports curbed the price-raising instincts of the domestic steel oligopoly. In 1973 foreign steel prices rose to exceed controlled U.S. prices; severe shortages materialized domestically; and American steel producers allocated short supplies on the basis of historical purchase volume, making no attempt to conceal the implicit lesson that buyers who had defected in the past to for-

eign sources were now being punished for their infidelity by low allocations. This experience made steel buyers more cautious in subsequent years about becoming dependent upon low-price foreign sources, thereby blunting to some extent the disciplining force of import competition on domestic pricing. And in petroleum, vertically integrated companies favored their captive retail outlets in allocating scarce gasoline supplies, subjecting independent marketers to shortfalls that jeopardized the independents' continued ability to provide motorists with a low-priced alternative. To preserve this competition from the independents, the federal government introduced a series of increasingly elaborate price and crude oil allocation controls that obliterated most vestiges of a free market in petroleum and its products.[9]

These and many other problems largely unrelated to market structure led to the dismantling of the Nixon wage and price control system in 1974, touching off a surge of price increases and inventory speculation that sowed the seeds for a sharp recession at the end of the year. Whether worldwide macroeconomic forces conspired to make the 1971-74 controls an inevitable disappointment, or whether the program might have been more successful if implemented more ag-

6. J. K. Galbraith, "Reflections on Price Control," *Quarterly Journal of Economics* 50 (August 1946): 475–89; and "The Disequilibrium System," *American Economic Review* 37 (June 1947): 287–302.

7. Galbraith, "The Disequilibrium System," p. 300; Seymour E. Harris, *Price and Related Controls in the United States* (New York: McGraw-Hill, 1945); and Harvey C. Mansfield, *A Short History of OPA* (Washington, D.C.: Office of Price Administration, 1947).

8. For various views, see D. Quinn Mills, "Some Lessons of Price Controls in 1971–1973," *Bell Journal of Economics* 6 (Spring 1975): 3–49; Marvin H. Kosters, *Controls and Inflation: The Economic Stabilization Program in Retrospect* (Washington, D.C.: American Enterprise Institute for Public Policy Research, 1975): Robert F. Lanzillotti et al., *Phase II in Review: The Price Commission Experience* (Washington, D.C.: Brookings Institution, 1975); John Kraft and Blaine Roberts, eds., *Wage and Price Controls: The U.S. Experiment* (New York: Praeger, 1975); and A. Bradley Askin and John Kraft, *Econometric Wage and Price Models: Assessing the Impact of the Economic Stabilization Program* (Lexington, Mass.: Heath, 1974).

9. See Calvin T. Roush, Jr., *Effects of Federal Price and Allocation Regulations on the Petroleum Industry*, Federal Trade Commission staff report (Washington, D.C.: Government Printing Office, 1976).

Policy approaches to the monopoly problem   **479**

gressively and consistently, continues to be debated. How much the 1971-74 experience reveals about the feasibility of a more limited price control program aimed only at monopolistic enterprises is also arguable. The incentive and inter-industry interdependence problems encountered even in concentrated industries during the 1970s suggest little basis for optimism. Neither does the experience of other industrialized nations with more or less selective peacetime price controls.[10] All things considered, the case for price controls appears to be sufficiently tenuous that one is inclined to search for a better alternative, holding the control option in reserve as a last resort.[11]

Moral suasion

An approach short of formal price controls employed on occasion by the U.S. government is "jawboning"—that is, attempting to persuade producers that both the public interest and their self-interest would be served by holding prices down.[12] The most active use of this suasion instrument was from 1962 to 1968 under the Kennedy-Johnson "Guideposts" program and, with more aggressive exercise of ancillary government powers, under the Carter Administration beginning in 1978.

During the 1960s an attempt was made to curb cost-push inflation by issuing nonbinding guideposts spelling out desired patterns of wage and price behavior. Price reductions were called for when an industry's productivity growth rate exceeded the economywide trend rate, estimated at 3.2 percent per annum, while price increases could be tolerated in industries whose productivity growth rate fell short of the overall average. Exceptions to take into account special capital needs, the existence of excess capacity, the behavior of material input prices, and excessive monopoly returns were spelled out in broad terms. For wage settlements, a target growth rate equal to the economywide productivity growth rate was stated, with deviations from the target being permitted if they reflected unusual labor market conditions. Adherence to the guideposts was encouraged through publicity, conferences

between government and business leaders, gentle and sometimes trenchant persuasion by the President and his cabinet, threatened sales from government stockpiles or the withdrawal of government contracts and subsidies, and (in the steel price confrontation of 1962) thinly veiled threats of antitrust action.

Although there are, as always, dissenting views, the weight of the statistical evidence supports a conclusion that the guidepost program did help suppress latent inflationary pressures, particularly during 1964 and 1965.[13] Its influence was especially noticeable in tightly concentrated and strongly unionized industries such as aluminum, steel, copper, and automobiles, which presented compact, highly visible targets for governmental suasion. However, after 1966, efforts to secure adherence collapsed as a result of the strong demand-pull forces generated by inflationary financing of the Vietnam war. As under formal price control programs, once the slack was taken up, concentrated industries were like their atomistic cousins in either having little discretion to exercise in the public interest or facing the necessity of extensive nonprice rationing with prices held below market-clearing levels.

Nonbinding wage and price guidelines were announced in late 1978 in an attempt to slow down 6 to 9 percent inflation that persisted despite appreciable unemployment rates.[14] An effort to create incentives for compliance was made through presidential jawboning, the denial of government contracts to companies breaking the guidelines, publicity, and the threat of diminished import and regulatory protection, among others. At the time this book went to print, the program showed few signs of success in curbing potent inflationary forces.

Proposals are advanced with some regularity to establish more formal institutions for injecting suasion into the price and wage-setting processes of organizations possessing monopoly power. Typically, they would require prenotification of price increases by corporations exceeding some size threshold and/or in industries of high concentration. Hearings to explore the rationale for the increases could be called by an appropriate commission with power to delay the increases—e.g., for 30 days from the announcement date—and make its views known to the public, but not to issue an outright prohibition. No such proposal has been implemented in the United States, at least in part because of the very large number of price changes that could conceivably be subject to review and the difficulty of determining whether particular pricing actions are in fact justified.[15]

Public regulation

Government price control is one form of what has come to be called the public regulation of business. Yet the scope of public regulation is much broader. For industries that are regarded as public utilities, control by a regulatory authority often extends not only to prices, but also to entry and exit, service standards, financial structure, accounting methods, and a host of other elements. In other instances government regulators may leave business firms' price making untouched, but attempt to control entry into the industry, product quality, the disclosure of information, labor-management relations, access to scarce resources imperfectly rationed by the price mechanism, health and safety standards, and/or effects on the environment. The extent to which government, and in particular the federal government, has intervened to guide and control the actions of ostensibly private enterprises has increased enormously since the first modern federal regulatory agency, the Interstate Commerce Commission, was established in 1887. There was a time when scholars conventionally distinguished between the traditional regulated industries—e.g., transportation; the electrical, gas, and water utilities; telecommunications, banking, and insurance—and everything else, also called the unregulated sector. Perhaps the line was always drawn too sharply. Yet the division has become increasingly blurred with the growth of old-line regulatory agencies' mandates, the extension of pervasive federal regulation to the energy sector, and the creation since World War II of new federal agencies with broad authority to regulate in such areas as product safety, occupational health and safety, pension funding, equal employment opportunity, and environmental pollution. It is fair to say that federal regulation has been one of the United States' more prominent growth industries.[16]

Economic analysis of public regulation has proceeded apace. When the first edition of this book was written in the late 1960s, a renaissance of interest in the economics of regulation was under way. A single chapter of moderate length seemed sufficient to capture the essence of what economists had to say. Since then, there has been an explosion of theoretical and empirical work, confronting the author with a dilemma: one

10. See for example D. H. Aldcroft, "The Effectiveness of Direct Controls in the British Economy, 1946–1950," *Scottish Journal of Political Economy* 10 (June 1963): 226–42; Allan Fels, *The British Prices and Incomes Board* (Cambridge, England: Cambridge University Press, 1972); John Sheahan, "Problems and Possibilities of Industrial Price Control: Postwar French Experience," *American Economic Review* 51 (June 1961): 345–59; Michael Walker, ed., *The Illusion of Wage and Price Control* (Vancouver: Fraser Institute, 1976); Bela Csikos-Nagy, *Socialist Price Theory and Price Policy* (Budapest: Akademiai Kiado, 1975); and "Guidelines: The British Experience," *Dun's Review*, November 1978, pp. 77–79.

11. For an exploration of alternative instruments such as tax-based incentives, see Arthur M. Okun and George L. Perry, eds., *Curing Chronic Inflation* (Washington, D.C.: Brookings Institution, 1978).

12. For a longer historical view, see Craufurd D. Goodwin, *Exhortation and Controls* (Washington, D.C.: Brookings Institution, 1975).

13. See John Sheahan, *The Wage-Price Guideposts* (Washington, D.C.: Brookings Institution, 1967), pp. 79–95; George L. Perry, "Wages and the Guideposts," *American Economic Review* 58 (June 1968): 456–67; Arthur J. Alexander, "Prices and the Guideposts," *Review of Economics and Statistics* 53 (February 1971): 67–75; and James L. Cochrane and Gary L. Griepentrog, "Cotton Textile Prices, 1965–66: The Microeconomics of Moral Suasion," *Southern Economic Journal* 44 (July 1977): 74–84. For more skeptical views, see the comments of Paul S. Anderson, Michael L. Wachter, and A. W. Throop in the *American Economic Review* 59 (June 1969): 351–69; and Richard Mancke, "The Determinants of Steel Prices in the U.S.: 1947–65," *Journal of Industrial Economics* 16 (April 1968): 147–60.

14. See the Council of Economic Advisers white paper, *The President's Anti-Inflation Program*, 24 October 1978.

15. On European nations' experiences with such notification schemes, see M. A. G. van Meerhaeghe, "Prior Notification of Price Increases as an Instrument of Price-Stabilization Policy," *Kyklos* 21, No. 1 (1968): 26–42; and "The Belgian Prices Commission," *Weltwirtschaftliches Archiv* 99 (December 1967): 257–70.

16. Thus, James C. Miller III has calculated that there was a trebling between 1970 and 1975 in the number of pages contained per year in the *Federal Register*—the daily journal in which new regulatory plans and rules are published. See "Trends in Regulation," *Regulation* (July/August 1977): 43.

chapter on the economics of regulation was patently inadequate; multiple chapters would break the reading camel's back. The decision taken was to provide only the briefest overview of the central issues here and refer the reader to the excellent general and specialized works on regulation now available.[17]

We begin with the question, Why regulate? There are several explanations, each mirroring a facet of reality. One is that market failure occurs and regulation is required to correct matters and serve the public interest better. The most traditional economic case for regulation assumes the existence of natural monopoly—that is, where economies of scale are so persistent that a single firm can serve the market at lower unit cost than two or more firms. Reasonably clear examples include electric power and gas distribution, local telephone service, railroading between pairs of small to medium-sized metropolitan areas, and the long-distance transportation of petroleum and gas in pipelines. Regulation is said to be necessary in such instances to protect consumers from the monopoly pricing behavior that achieving all scale economies renders virtually inevitable.[18] External economies and diseconomies are the perceived cause of market failure motivating some of the newer forms of regulation—e.g., when automobiles, chemical plants, and steel furnaces pollute the environment. Or regulation may avert market failure owing to informational disparities—e.g., when companies withhold information that might cause investors to value their securities less highly or when consumers lack the technical expertise required to recognize health or safety hazards in the products they buy.

Regulation may also be imposed because, no matter how efficiently the market is working, those who hold political power are displeased with the results or consider some good or service too important to be priced and allocated by market processes. This "governmental habit," Professor Hughes documents, has deep roots in American traditions.[19] (However, the historical propensity to have government override the market is even stronger in Europe, from which the U.S. tradition was drawn and adapted to an expanding geographic frontier following a revolution against central authority.) Sometimes intervention by the government is rationalized on trumped-up claims

of monopoly, as when regulation was extended to the wellhead prices of natural gas in 1954.[20] More often, the outcome of any free market process, monopolistic or competitive, would fail to satisfy those who hold the policy reins. An example was the bitter debate over natural gas deregulation between 1973 and 1978, when depletion, rising marginal costs, and the pull of demand combined to ensure that gas producers would realize large rents (i.e., windfall profits) at consumers' expense in an unregulated market.

A third hypothesis states that regulation occurs because there are well-organized vested interests expecting to benefit. It goes on to observe that the producers subjected to regulation are usually much better organized and able to manipulate political levers than consumers. Therefore, the principal beneficiaries of much regulation are not consumers, but producers.[21] This can happen in two main ways. First, producers may work through their legislators to have laws passed that correct what they perceive to be a pressing problem. Sometimes the problem is alleged cutthroat competition. In 1887, for example, the desire to lessen competition drew industry support and legislative drafting help for federal railroad regulation, which was subsequently extended to trucks and inland water shipping.[22] Or it may reflect producers' desire to avoid spoiling the market through excessive new entry—a motive behind many state occupational licensure laws passed ostensibly to perpetuate high standards of professional competence. Second, even when legislators have only the public interest at heart in passing regulatory laws, those who are regulated end up as important beneficiaries by "capturing" the agency regulating them. This happens *inter alia* because the regulated firms use their political influence to have friendly regulators appointed, because the regulated enterprise has superior technical knowledge upon which regulatory agency staffs come to depend, and because regulators, like most people, seek identification and approval and are more likely to find them by cultivating a community of interest with the well-organized firms they regulate than with a remote and unresponsive public.

Whatever their motivation, overt or subconscious, those who oversee the fortunes of the traditional regulated industries such as electric power, natural gas, railroads, common carrier trucking, taxicabs, and telephony must determine what prices may be charged. This in turn has two main components: setting the average level of prices and fashioning a proper price structure.

In price level determination, the ruling principle has been that of conferring "a fair return upon . . . the fair value of the property being used."[23] Concretely, this entails establishing a *rate base* reflecting the value of the regulated firm's (or industry's) assets and authorizing prices sufficient, after noncapital costs are covered, to let the firm expect to realize some specified *allowed rate of return* on its assets. An effort is normally made to set the allowed rate of return high enough so that the regulated firm can raise additional funds, if they are needed, in capital markets.[24] From this essentially cost-plus-profit orientation flow some important problems. For one, utilities failing to keep their costs at minimum feasible levels can be reasonably confident that prices will nevertheless be set high enough to cover their costs and provide a return on capital. Also, when the allowed rate of return exceeds the market cost of new capital, certain theoretical analyses predict, profit-maximizing regulated enterprises may have a systematic incentive to invest inefficiently large sums in capital equipment—e.g., by choosing excessively capital-intensive production processes or building peak-load capacity whose unit cost exceeds the probable value of the services provided to consumers.[25] These incentive breakdowns may be corrected to some extent by "regulatory lag"— that is, by the tendency for regulatory price setting to lag behind changing cost conditions, so that unexpectedly rapid cost reduction by a regulated firm enhances profits temporarily while overly rapid cost escalation squeezes them, in both instances generating an inducement for cost control. Regulators might also engage in "incentive regulation," awarding higher allowed rates of return to firms operating efficiently than to those that do not. But this is seldom done, largely because of the difficulty of setting absolute or comparative efficiency standards and, perhaps more important, a natural human instinct to avoid the unpleasant task of punishing laggards. The desire to run a tight ship and serve consumers economically may also affect regulated enterprises'

17. A definitive treatise reflecting the state of knowledge in the late 1960s and anticipating many new developments is Alfred Kahn, *The Economics of Regulation*, 2 vols. (New York: Wiley, 1970). Newer developments are surveyed admirably in Paul L. Joskow and Roger G. Noll, "Regulation in Theory and Practice: An Overview," in the National Bureau of Economic Research conference volume, *The Economics of Regulation*, forthcoming in 1980; and Richard Schmalensee, *The Control of Natural Monopolies* (Lexington, Mass.: Heath, 1979). Case studies of how regulation affects specific industries are collected in Almarin Phillips, ed., *Promoting Competition in Regulated Markets* (Washington, D.C.: Brookings Institution, 1975); U.S., Congress, Senate, Committee on Government Operations, *Study on Federal Regulation*, vol. 6, "Case Studies," 95th Cong., 2nd sess., 1978; and Bruce Owen and Ronald Braeutigam, *The Regulation Game: Strategic Use of the Administrative Process* (Cambridge, Mass.: Ballinger, 1978).

18. For an argument that the problem can be largely solved by auctioning off monopoly franchises, see Harold Demsetz, "Why Regulate Utilities?," *Journal of Law and Economics* 11 (April 1968): 55–66. Compare Oliver E. Williamson, "Franchise Bidding for Natural Monopolies," *Bell Journal of Economics* 7 (Spring 1976): 73–104.

19. Jonathan R. T. Hughes, *The Governmental Habit: Economic Controls from Colonial Times to the Present* (New York: Basic Books, 1977), especially Chapter 2.

20. On the history, see Paul W. MacAvoy, "The Reasons and Results in Natural Gas Field Price Regulation," in MacAvoy, ed., *The Crisis of the Regulatory Commissions* (New York: Norton, 1970), especially pp. 153–57.

21. See George Stigler, "The Theory of Economic Regulation," *Bell Journal of Economics and Management Science* 2 (Spring 1971): 3–21; Richard A. Posner, "Theories of Economic Regulation," *Bell Journal of Economics and Management Science* 5 (Autumn 1974): 335–58; and Sam Peltzman, "Toward a More General Theory of Regulation," *Journal of Law and Economics* 19 (August 1976): 211–40.

22. This cynical view of what underlay the Interstate Commerce Act is supported in Gabriel Kolko, *Railroads and Regulation, 1877–1916* (Princeton: Princeton University Press, 1965); Paul W. MacAvoy, *The Economic Effects of Regulation: The Trunkline Railroad Cartels and the Interstate Commerce Commission Before 1900* (Cambridge, Mass.: MIT Press, 1965); and George W. Hilton, "The Consistency of the Interstate Commerce Act," *Journal of Law and Economics* 9 (October 1966): 87–113. The standard more roseate history of the act and the early years of railroad regulation is I. Leo Sharfman's five-volume work, *The Interstate Commerce Commission* (New York: Commonwealth Fund, 1931–37).

23. *Smyth v. Ames et al.*, 169 U.S. 466, 546–547 (1898).

24. See *Federal Power Commission et al. v. Hope Natural Gas Co.*, 320 U.S. 591, 605 (1944), which clarified and in effect overturned *Smyth v. Ames*.

25. Seminal articles demonstrating these points rigorously were Harvey A. Averch and L. L. Johnson, "Behavior of the Firm Under Regulatory Constraint," *American Economic Review* 52 (December 1962): 1052–69; and Stanislaw H. Wellisz, "Regulation of Natural Gas Pipeline Companies: An Economic Analysis," *Journal of Political Economy* 71 (February 1963): 30–43. For a survey of subsequent developments, see Elizabeth Bailey, *Economic Theory of Regulatory Constraint* (Lexington, Mass.: Lexington, 1973). See also John T. Wenders, "Peak Load Pricing in the Electric Utility Industry," *Bell Journal of Economics* 7 (Spring 1976): 232–41.

Policy approaches to the monopoly problem **483**

behavior positively, but there is reason to believe that on balance, regulated monopolists' incentives for cost control are not all they should be or would be in a more competitive environment. The incentive situation is somewhat different when regulators set prices for whole groups of firms in one action, as in most transportation industry regulation. Then any single company that surpasses industry efficiency norms may have a sufficiently small impact on overall industry profitability that no general price reduction will be ordered, and so the firm may be able to retain the profit benefits of its superior performance.

Regulators are commonly concerned not only with the level of prices but also with the price structure—that is, how prices charged for different services and to diverse customers relate one to another. This task becomes especially important under natural monopoly, for if average total cost falls persistently with increased scale, marginal cost must be continuously less than average cost, and if the regulated monopoly is forced to charge a single market-clearing price equal to marginal cost, it will run at a loss.[26] Authorizing a uniform price equal to average total cost allows the firm to break even, but it causes allocative inefficiency as marginal consumers who would buy at a price covering marginal cost choose not to consume at the higher average-cost price. The standard escape from this dilemma is some system of multiple and usually discriminatory prices. Thus, electricity customers may be charged a high price for the first hundred kilowatt hours of output consumed each month and a lower price for additional blocks, or they may pay a fixed connection charge plus a price per unit consumed more closely tailored to marginal cost. Or when market segmentation by classes of customers with different elasticities of demand is feasible, the regulated monopoly may set prices to satisfy the Ramsey-Baumol-Bradford conditions—that is, with the average level of prices sufficient to ensure break-even, and the price quoted a given customer class being higher, the lower that group's price elasticity of demand is.[27]

Complex multipart price structures may be authorized not only to reconcile marginal cost pricing with covering full costs under natural monopoly, but also to subsidize certain classes of customers deemed by the regulatory agency or its legislative sponsors worthy of special treatment. In either case, a price structure that solves one set of problems can create others. Customers paying discriminatorily high prices are likely to search for ways of easing their burden. Time and again, they have found a solution by turning to firms—often called "cream skimmers"—who specialize in supplying the high-priced product or service segments. Thus, common carrier trucks took away from the railroads the finished goods freight on which high rates had been charged, leaving the railroads to carry low-rated bulk commodities. Private unregulated trucks in turn captured steady, high-volume hauls from common carrier trucks, leaving the latter to carry irregular and smaller shipments. Independent companies such as Microwave Communications, Inc., have offered specialized intercity telephone and data transmission service to business users, leaving to the Bell System the low-volume traffic and, after a furious legal battle, the task of providing local connections between the independent transmission companies' terminals and customer offices. Industrial firms build their own electricity generators to supply their base-line demands and turn to regulated public utilities for emergency or peak-period power. And so on.

What should a regulatory agency do when such cream-skimming entry is imminent or has occurred? Should it allow the regulated firm to reduce its prices and combat the threatened loss of business? If the firm loses orders that would, if retained, add more to revenues than to cost, prices may have to be raised to other customers—i.e., those with no competitive alternatives—in order to keep the enterprise at the break-even level. If price reductions are permitted, to what floor should they fall: Short-run marginal cost? Long-run marginal cost? Any sales retained by the regulated firm at a price exceeding short-run marginal cost makes some contribution, at least temporarily, to covering other costs, and hence lessens the magnitude of required price increases on other services. However, as equipment wears out or demand grows, prices that barely cover short-run marginal cost will not cover long-run marginal cost, and so letting the regulated enterprise reduce its prices to short-run marginal cost may over the longer run be unremunerative. Also, should the regulated monopoly be permitted to raise its prices again after a competitive threat has been repelled through marginal cost pricing? Allowing on-again, off-again pricing tactics by the regulated firm might be considered unfair to competitors entering in good faith and also to consumers, who enjoy low prices only when the competitive pressure is on. And equally important, such pricing may effectively exclude competitors who, if given a chance to become established in the market and grow, might be able to provide a specialized service at unit costs lower than the regulated utility's long-run incremental cost.[28]

An alternative approach is for the regulatory agency simply to prohibit or curtail new entry into the fields it regulates—if need be, as in the Interstate Commerce Commission's history, by securing a legislative extension of its regulatory domain. But this poses further dilemmas. The power to exclude is a power likely to be used, especially when the companies already regulated come to be veiwed as "us" and potential entrants as "them." There is a risk that firms will be excluded which could, if allowed to enter, offer innovative services at lower costs or otherwise transform the industry and improve its performance. And when regulators are "captured" by the regulatees, suppression of competition for its own sake may come to be the dominant criterion in entry control decisions. Few regulatory agency decisions are more difficult than determining how the public interest is best served when new entry threatens what is believed to be a natural monopoly. And few regulatory agency powers lend themselves so readily to abuse.

When complex regulated price structures evolve, it is probable that the gap between price and marginal cost will be much wider on some services than on others. If there are multiple sellers (that is, when natural monopoly imperatives are absent) and price competition is controlled but other forms of competition are not, nonprice competition may emerge, driving costs up on the more lucrative products or services until supranormal returns erode. Airline regulation provides an illustration. Until reforms were introduced during the late 1970s, prices were higher relative to costs on long flights than on short hops (where bus, train, and private auto competition had a restraining influence). The ample margins on long flights stimulated competitive escalation in the number of flights offered, leaving what appears to have been an inefficiently large number of seats unfilled on the average flight.[29] Meanwhile, on shorter hops and between small cities, there were complaints of inadequate flight frequency. The Civil Aeronautics Board found itself pressed to demand more frequent service in some cases and to rescue airlines from their alleged excessive competition (e.g., by authorizing collusive flight scheduling) in others. Similarly, in railroading, the regulated price structure made no provision for seasonal variations in demand, and as a result the Interstate Commerce Commission repeatedly had to order the diversion of boxcars to farming states at harvest times. Had the price mechanism's working not been suppressed by regulation, prices would have risen during peak seasons and fallen (at least relatively) in slack times, inducing farmers and grain elevator operators to build more local storage capacity and hence to lessen their peak demands on the railroad network.

The problems in regulating product quality, safety, and the like are different but no less difficult.[30] Rather than dwelling on them, we advance to our conclusion. It is not easy to regulate an industry well. The cost-plus orientation toward which pricing methods gravitate weakens incentives for efficiency. Price structures can become

26. Cf. Chapter 11, pp. 321–22 supra.

27. Frank P. Ramsey, "A Contribution to the Theory of Taxation," Economic Journal 37 (March 1927): 47–61; and William J. Baumol and David Bradford, "Optimal Departures from Marginal Cost Pricing," American Economic Review 60 (June 1970): 265–83.

28. On the difficulties of determining whether natural monopoly exists in a multiproduct situation and setting prices that sustain the cost advantages of natural monopoly when it does exist, see John C. Panzar and Robert D. Willig, "Free Entry and the Sustainability of Natural Monopoly," Bell Journal of Economics 8 (Spring 1977): 1–22; William J. Baumol, Elizabeth Bailey, and R. D. Willig, "Weak Invisible Hand Theorems on Pricing and Entry in a Multiproduct Natural Monopoly," American Economic Review 67 (June 1977): 350–65; and Ronald Braeutigam, "Optimal Pricing with Intermodal Competition," American Economic Review 69 (March 1979): 38–49.

29. See George W. Douglas and James C. Miller III, Economic Regulation of Domestic Air Transport (Washington, D.C.: Brookings Institution, 1974), Chapters 6 and 7; and George C. Eads, "Competition in the Domestic Trunk Airline Industry," in Phillips, ed., Promoting Competition in Regulated Markets, pp. 16–39.

Policy approaches to the monopoly problem   **485**

extremely complex and have unexpected service level biases and entry-stimulating effects. Regulatory agencies characteristically suffer from severe information handicaps relative to the businesses they are regulating, leading to mistakes and capture. The opportunities for abuse are abundant. There are situations in which the alternatives to regulation are sufficiently unattractive that, despite its flaws, some form of regulation is a sensible choice, especially when there is reason to believe the job can be done by a competent agency that avoids industry capture. It has become increasingly clear, however, that in many instances the benefits of regulation, however well intentioned, are less than its costs, and that the public would be better off relying upon unfettered competitive market forces as a regulator even though they function a good deal less than perfectly. In a subset of those cases, regulation is little more than a producer-dominated scheme to suppress competition and enhance profits or wages.

Unfortunately, it is not easy to measure the balance between benefits and costs, particularly when regulation causes extensive income redistribution on whose desirability a clear public consensus is lacking or when, for good reasons or bad, legislators place high weight on what to the skeptical economist may seem to be minor or dubious benefits. In a rare show of near unanimity, economists during the 1970s led a movement toward the systematic lessening of regulatory controls in the American economy. Frequent glances in the rearview mirror suggested that public opinion was not far behind. But the staying power of vested interests is considerable, and with the major exception of the airlines, on which unusually persuasive economic research had been done, progress was slow. Where the new equilibrium will ultimately rest is hard to predict.

Public ownership of industry

Public ownership and operation of industry is an option chosen more frequently abroad than in the United States when unfettered private market

processes fail to function satisfactorily. It has many variants. It can entail government monopolization of a whole market, or government operations may coexist and compete with private firms. It can be achieved through the nationalization of existing private firms or the establishment of new government facilities. Its organization can take myriad forms, ranging from operations fully integrated into conventional government departments to public corporations autonomous except with respect to top management appointments. We cannot possibly do justice to the full range of issues in this brief survey, but let us try to highlight some of the principal fields, objectives, opportunities, and limitations of public ownership.[31]

Activities undertaken extensively by governmental units in the United States include the supply of water, electricity, local transit service, garbage collection service, public housing, and postal service; the operation of hospitals and clinics; the maintenance of schools, universities, and laboratories; the conduct of bank and crop failure insurance programs; the retailing of liquor; and various minor manufacturing endeavors, such as running the Government Printing Office. Professor Pryor has estimated that publicly owned enterprises accounted for 2 percent of U.S. manufacturing and mining employment in 1970; 21 percent of transportation and communications employment; 32 percent of employment in electric, gas, water, and sanitation utilities; 2 percent of commerce and finance; and 3 percent of agricultural, forestry, and fisheries employment.[32] In most other industrialized nations, the railroads, airlines, broadcasting networks, electric and gas utilities, and telephone and telegraph services are typically owned and operated by the government. Public ownership abroad frequently extends also into such important manufacturing industries as steel, automobiles, and aircraft, and into the extraction of crude oil, coal, and other basic minerals.

Three broad strategies can be pursued in attempting to improve industrial performance through public ownership. The first is the *yardstick approach*. Under it, only part of an industry's capacity is government owned. The cost and pricing performance of that segment is held out as a standard for evaluating the comparative performance of privately owned producers. A good example is the Tennessee Valley Authority, the largest U.S. electrical utility, whose exceptionally low costs presented a challenge for private utilities, and which demonstrated to traditionally conservative private firms the advantages of probing the lower reaches of consumer demand curves by reducing prices. Other government yardstick operations include the naval shipyards and the army arsenals, but these have been withering away as a result of ideological attacks and pressures from private weapons producers. Aside from their vulnerability to political undermining, the chief disadvantage of publicly owned yardstick operations is the difficulty of making direct comparisons in dissimilar situations. Citing TVA's costs as a standard, for instance, is criticized by private power interests because the Authority obtains its capital at favorable interest rates, pays no income taxes, and enjoys special cost advantages from using dams built for navigation and conservation purposes. These complaints are well founded, but valid comparisons can be made if appropriate analytic adjustments are introduced.[33]

A second strategy, also requiring only partial government ownership, is to have government enterprises pursue aggressive policies calculated to compel desired behavioral changes on the part of private operators. This is essentially a second-best approach. Given the market position of the private producers and their probable responses to alternative public enterprise price and output choices, the public firms adopt the pricing policy that induces the most favorable attainable overall industry performance. Richard Harris and Elmer Wiens show that under particularly favorable conditions (including full information and homogeneity of products), a government enterprise can induce oligopolistic producers to behave competitively by announcing credibly that it will react to their output restrictions by increasing its output or investment and driving price to the competitive level.[34] A variant occasionally employed by the U.S. government is the sale of defense stockpile materials to depress inflated prices, although the long-run leverage attainable with this tactic is limited if the stockpiles must

eventually be replenished by purchases from colluding private sellers. Competition may also be waged on nonprice dimensions. For example, the government-owned Renault Company is said to have had a beneficial impact on the French automobile industry's performance by leading the way to low-cost compact car lines in a calculated attempt to facilitate automobile ownership by citizens occupying lower income strata.[35] In general, however, vigorous competition between public and private enterprises has not been widespread. Political opposition by private firms is one reason, at least in the United States. Also, public enterprise heads frequently display even

(30) On product quality, see for example Henry G. Grabowski, *Drug Regulation and Innovation* (Washington, D.C.: American Enterprise Institute for Public Policy Research, 1976); and Richard L. Landau, ed., *Regulating New Drugs* (Chicago: University of Chicago Center for Policy Study, 1973).

31. For more extensive surveys, see Ralph Turvey, ed., *Public Enterprise* (Baltimore: Penguin, 1968); W. G. Shepherd, ed., *Public Enterprise: Economic Analysis of Theory and Practice* (Lexington, Mass.: Heath, 1974); and (from the perspective of lawyers) Wolfgang G. Friedmann and J. F. Garner, *Government Enterprise* (New York: Columbia University Press, 1970).

32. Frederic L. Pryor, "Public Ownership: Some Quantitative Dimensions," in Shepherd, ed., *Public Enterprise*, pp. 3–22. Pryor also presents extensive data on publicly owned enterprise employment shares in a number of other capitalistic and socialistic nations.

33. See for example Richard Hellman, *Government Competition in the Electrical Utility Industry* (New York: Praeger, 1972), who shows that TVA had both favorable yardstick effects and direct competitive effects on private utilities adjoining its network; and Robert A. Meyer, "Publicly Owned Versus Privately Owned Utilities," *Review of Economics and Statistics* 57 (November 1975): 391–99 (whose analysis suffers from not taking into account the possibly greater use of hydroelectric energy by government utilities). Compare Sam Peltzman, "Pricing in Public and Private Enterprises: Electric Utilities in the United States," *Journal of Law and Economics* 14 (April 1971): 109–47, who finds more use of output-expanding price discrimination by privately owned companies and an average government utility rate advantage that may only reflect lower tax burdens.

34. Richard G. Harris and Elmer G. Wiens, "Government Enterprise: An Instrument for the Internal Regulation of Industry" (Ottawa, Canada, Carleton Economic Paper 77–05, July 1977); and "Dynamic Oligopoly, Investment in Capacity and Government Firms" (Kingston, Ontario, Queens University Discussion Paper No. 266, June 1977). The pioneering work of this genre was W. C. Merrill and Norman Schneider, "Government Firms in Oligopoly Industries," *Quarterly Journal of Economics* 80 (August 1966): 400–12.

35. John Sheahan, "Government Competition and the Performance of the French Automobile Industry," *Journal of Industrial Economics* 8 (June 1960): 197–215.

Policy approaches to the monopoly problem **487**

less zest for the competitive struggle than private entrepreneurs. To avoid complaints about subsidization and to prove their managerial mettle, they may be anxious to show a profit, and vigorous competition could frustrate that ambition. Thus, Lord Melchett, the first chairman of the renationalized British Steel Corporation, announced his opposition to letting the individual constituent steel mills compete with one another because "that would be giving the profits to the consumers."[36]

The third main strategy is that of total or virtual public monopoly. It is the dominant approach in all but the service trades and agriculture in communist nations, and it is a common feature of the mass transportation, electric power, and communications sectors of most other industrialized countries outside the United States. A spectrum of operating philosophies can be identified. At one extreme is the classic Soviet approach, under which detailed output plans, labor allocations, capital allowances, raw materials quotas, prices, wages, and the like are assigned to each operating unit by central planners. At the other extreme is the approach conceived by "market socialists" during the 1920s and 1930s, under which prices are set by central planners to reflect supply and demand conditions and then individual enterprise managers expand the output of their products until marginal cost rises into equality with price.[37] In principle, the latter scheme approximates the operation of a purely competitive economy while avoiding such problems as monopoly pricing and inequitable income distribution. In practice, governments representing the various ideological colorations have strayed widely from these pure models, sometimes by design and sometimes inadvertently to achieve the results they seek.

Numerous advantages are claimed by the proponents of public monopoly. Perhaps most important from an economic standpoint, it is a way to secure the benefits of size in industries with large minimum optimal scales without suffering the disadvantages of monopolistic pricing. Other alleged advantages include the channelling of returns on capital to the commonwealth rather than to private individuals, the ability to raise capital at no risk premium through governmental risk pooling, and the reduction of alienation by convincing workers that they ultimately own and control the main branches of industry.

It is hardly necessary to add that certain of these advantages are often more conjectural than real. Moreover, public enterprises face real problems devising operational criteria to guide and motivate decision makers and workers—something the market system does automatically. Merely telling enterprise managers to act in the public interest is distinctly nonoperational, for such a rule is so vague it could have a dozen plausible interpretations in any given situation. To ensure that the "correct" interpretation is chosen and to prevent line managers from advancing their own selfish interests under the discretion a broad criterion allows, countless decisions would have to be passed up the ladder for review and resolution. But this can overload management, causing decision-making breakdowns. Also, excessive centralization of decision making stifles initiative and responsibility. To make a large organization work at all well, some criterion is needed that is sufficiently tangible and specific to permit decentralized decision making and to provide a standard against which accomplishments can be judged. Under the traditional Soviet approach the detailed plan attempts to serve this function. However, as an economy becomes more complex, difficulties multiply because of the plan's rigidity and its frequent failure to reflect operating level realities. The rule "expand until marginal cost equals price" is better in theory, but higher echelons may be unable to ensure that operating units are following it because marginal cost is so hard to measure. Moreover, adherence to the rule under natural monopoly conditions can lead, as we have seen, to losses that upset legislators and treasury officials.

Because of these problems, it has become commonplace in Western nations and (more recently) in Soviet satellites to prescribe a profit maximization criterion as the primary guide to decentralized decision making and accountability. However, government monopolies can increase profits not only by improving their operating efficiency, but also by raising prices or persuading central authorities to raise them. This often happens. Indeed, prices may be raised sufficiently to let the firm pay excessive wages and absorb considerable outright waste while earning what appears to be a satisfactory profit. It is said, for instance, that the worker representatives directing some Yugoslavian industrial collectives quickly learned that by restricting output and exercising what power they had over prices, they could enhance total revenues and the incomes of collective members.[38] So we come full circle. The very pricing distortions that lead nations to embrace public ownership may reappear as a result of attempts to make public enterprise function more efficiently.

To be sure, the incentive to raise prices and restrict output is probably not as strong in public enterprises as it is in private monopolies. Altruism serves as a check, as do controls by the central government, the absence of stock options and other ownership motives, and, to the extent that it exists, interenterprise competition. However, the pressure to reduce costs and innovate is probably weaker than in private firms exposed to significant competition. Political intervention and rigidities introduced by government accountability standards and civil service procedures may impose a further drag on public enterprise efficiency.

How these virtues and drawbacks of public enterprise balance out is an empirical question. The evidence is mixed. It is possible in the United States to find examples of vigorous, efficient, enlightened public enterprises like the Tennessee Valley Authority and also operations like the Postal Service bogged down in a morass of inefficiency and resistance to change. Likewise, in Great Britain, the nationalized coal and electric power industries have apparently performed rather well,[39] while mismanagement and political resistance to needed plant closures caused British Steel Corporation to fall woefully short of its plan to build a modern, efficient operation out of the mostly outdated facilities it acquired through nationalization.[40] The best-controlled "experiment" on the relative merits of nationalized versus private enterprise is the domestic airline industry of Australia, where there is one firm of each type, each with virtually the same route structure, schedules, equipment, tariffs, and wage rates. That output per employee is higher for the privately owned airline appears conclusively demonstrated.[41] On the other hand, there is evidence that the Canadian airline industry, with a nationalized firm playing a key role, operated more efficiently—i.e., with higher load factors and lower price-cost markups—than its privately owned but publicly regulated United States counterpart.[42] There is also reason to believe that publicly owned electric power companies in the United States operate at lower unit costs on average than regulated private utilities, although water rights differences and other disparities cloud the comparison.[43] And even though plant closure decisions were significantly retarded by political considerations, the state-owned French and Swedish tobacco monopolies achieved

36. "Britain's Steel Debate," *New York Times*, 25 March 1967, pp. 31ff. See also "Government Halves Rise in Prices by British Steel," *New York Times*, 3 April 1971, pp. 39 ff.; and Aubrey Silberston, "Surveys of Applied Economics: Price Behaviour of Firms," *Economic Journal* 80 (September 1970): 554–56.

37. See Oskar Lange and Fred M. Taylor, in B. E. Lippincott, ed., *On the Economic Theory of Socialism* (Minneapolis: University of Minnesota Press, 1938).

38. See the testimony of Joel Dirlam, U.S., Congress, Senate, Committee on the Judiciary, Subcommittee on Antitrust and Monopoly hearings, *Economic Concentration*, Part 7, "Concentration Outside the United States," 90th Cong., 2nd sess., 1968, pp. 3758–74. On the relevent theory, compare Jaroslav Vanek, "Decentralization Under Workers' Management: A Theoretical Appraisal," *American Economic Review* 59 (December 1969): 1006–14; and J. E. Meade, "Labour-Managed Firms in Conditions of Imperfect Competition," *Economic Journal* 84 (December 1974): 817–24.

39. See William G. Shepherd, *Economic Performance under Public Ownership* (New Haven: Yale University Press, 1965); and Richard Pryke, *Public Enterprise in Practice* (London: Macmillan, 1971).

40. See "British Steel Is Struggling To Compete," *New York Times*, 22 August 1977, pp. 39–40. It is worth noting that nationalized enterprises, not unlike private firms, sometimes resist the disclosure of information that could subject them to effective public (i.e., legislative) control. On British Steel Corporation, see "House Group Issues Order," *New York Times*, 18 January 1978, Sec. IV, p. 1.

41. David G. Davies, "The Efficiency of Public Versus Private Firms, the Case of Australia's Two Airlines," *Journal of Law and Economics* 14 (April 1971): 149–65; and "Property Rights and Economic Efficiency—The Australian Airlines Revisited," *Journal of Law and Economics* 20 (April 1977): 223–26.

42. See John R. Baldwin, *The Regulatory Agency and the Public Corporation: The Canadian Air Transport Industry* (Cambridge, Mass.: Ballinger, 1975), pp. 200–205.

43. Cf. note 33 *supra*.

Policy approaches to the monopoly problem   489

higher output per worker during the late 1960s than the privately owned, oligopolistic West German, British, and Canadian industries.[44] It seems clear that public enterprises *can* perform well, although (like private organizations) they do not do so consistently. What remains unknown is the average difference and variance in performance over a wide array of cases. Partly to provide a basis for better-informed judgment and partly because yardstick and direct competition between public and private enterprises appears to have generally desirable effects in monopolistic or tightly oligopolistic industries, additional experimentation with various forms of public ownership seems desirable.

Informational programs

Some of the most serious market performance problems in the contemporary American economy are attributable more to inadequate knowledge on the consumer's part than to structural imperfections of a traditional sort. Two deficiencies stand out. First, consumers pay unnecessarily high prices for heavily advertised and otherwise differentiated products because they lack the technical knowledge to tell whether a particular gasoline, dentifrice, detergent, pain remedy, vacuum cleaner, or weed killer is actually better than less expensive, unadvertised substitutes. Second, in such fields as home building and repair services, the consumer can be cheated or exploited because he or she cannot readily distinguish honest from dishonest workmanship and because, once a contract is signed or a wheezing automobile is left with a particular vendor, the consumer is in effect locked into a bilateral monopoly relationship conferring considerable pricing power upon the better informed party. In home construction, builders frequently turn over shoddy workmanship or fail to complete details of a job, leaving the buyer in a typically weak position to take legal action. Or they set inflated prices for contract changes once the buyer has signed on the dotted line and cannot secure outside competitive bids.[45] Repairmen charge for work they have not done and/or fail,

through incompetence or deceit, to remedy the problem originally troubling the consumer. The hapless consumer may never find out he or she has been duped, or may learn only when the item repaired fails again to work properly.

The best strategy for attacking the first set of problems is undoubtedly to provide the consumer with more information on what he or she is buying. For goods whose purchase is significantly influenced by advertising, this can be done by developing uniform grading systems, combatting plainly deceptive advertising, encouraging seller disclosure of relevant product quality information, publishing reports on government product tests, and subsidizing the testing and disclosure activities of such independent consumer research organizations as the Consumers Union.[46]

Improving the performance of the repair services and home construction trades demands a different approach. What the consumer in effect buys in hiring a particular repair person or (to a lesser degree) building contractor is reputation. The key to improvement lies in perfecting the consumer's knowledge of how well alternative suppliers have served their customers in the past. This is especially important in large cities, where word-of-mouth communication operates least effectively. A space age solution might function along the following lines. Each service and building trades person would be assigned an identification number, which would be published in telephone directory advertising. After every job exceeding a specified dollar value, the vendor would be required by law to give the customer two computer cards prepunched with this identification number. These would be imprinted with questions calling for multiple-choice answers characterizing the consumer's satisfaction with the job done. One would be completed and mailed to a central collection point immediately, the other after a time interval sufficient to let the consumer judge in hindsight how well the job was done. The central data bank's computer would process the information received and store it in summary form. When electronic telephone switching comes into widespread use, consumers could dial the data bank's telephone number plus the identification numbers of prospective vendors, receiving in return an oral summary of the vendors' performance records compared to the average for all vendors in the relevant service category. To be sure, such a system would not be perfect; the information it supplies could be no better than the information originating with fallible consumers. But random aberrations in individual consumer evaluations would average out under the law of large numbers, and the system would surely offer a better foundation for rational consumer choice than the present system, based as it is on total ignorance or fragmentary hearsay.

Consumers are not the only ones for whom the unavailability of information can lead to misguided purchases. Securities investors could be in the same boat were it not for the company financial data disclosure requirements enforced in the United States by the Securities and Exchange Commission. How important a role such mandatory disclosure plays in perfecting the working of financial markets is a matter of some dispute.[47] It may do little to help institutional investors and others who have access to inside information and whose actions suggest foreknowledge of what published reports will say. But it probably narrows to some extent the gap between the "smart money" and the large number of small investors, who are less apt to be gulled as a result.

Securities investors need information on companies. Entrepreneurs making real investments, on the other hand, need information on what is happening in particular product lines or industries. The better the information is on sales, costs, profits, and new investment in individual product lines, the more effectively market processes can work in guiding investment and new entry into those areas where demand is inadequately satisfied. One consequence of conglomerate mergers is a loss of financial information on what before the mergers were more narrowly specialized enterprises, whose accounts become aggregated for public reporting purposes with the accounts of many other activities within a conglomerate corporation's compass. To reverse this "information loss" was one purpose of the Federal Trade Commission's Line of Business financial reporting program, requiring large corporations to segment income statement and bal-

ance sheet information according to some 275 industrial categories.[48] In this way, it was hoped, important pockets of monopoly profit could be identified more rapidly and eroded away through competitive entry.

Antitrust policy

Finally, we come to antitrust policy. In the United States, and to an increasing degree in other industrialized nations of the Western world, the enforcement of antitrust laws is one of the more important weapons wielded by government in its effort to harmonize the profit-seeking behavior of private enterprises with the public interest. Antitrust performs this function in two ways: by inhibiting or prohibiting certain undesirable kinds of *business conduct*, and by channelling and shaping *market structure* along competitive lines so as to increase the likelihood that desirable conduct and performance will emerge more or less automatically. Because of its prominence, antitrust policy will be the concern of the next three chap-

44. See F. M. Scherer et al., *The Economics of Multi-Plant Operation: An International Comparisons Study* (Cambridge, Mass.: Harvard University Press, 1975), pp. 73, 157, 231.

45. Cf. Charles Foster, "Competition and Organization in Building," *Journal of Industrial Economics* 12 (July 1964): 163–74.

46. Cf. Chapter 14, pp. 404–5 *supra*. For differing views of the efficacy of government controls on consumer product advertising, see Robert Pitovsky, "Mandated Disclosure in the Advertising of Consumer Products," and Richard A. Posner, "The Federal Trade Commission's Mandated Disclosure Program: A Critical Analysis," in Harvey Goldschmid, ed., *Business Disclosure: Government's Need To Know* (New York: McGraw-Hill, 1979), pp. 311–66. See also Pitovsky, "Beyond Nader: Consumer Protection and the Regulation of Advertising," *Harvard Law Review* 90 (February 1977): 661–99.

47. For divergent views, see George J. Benston, "Required Disclosure and the Stock Market: An Evaluation of the Securities Exchange Act of 1934," *American Economic Review* 63 (March 1973): 132–55; and Irwin Friend, "The Economic Consequences of the Stock Market," *American Economic Review* 62 (May 1972): 212–19.

48. See also Chapter 9, p. 271 *supra*. On the pros and cons of the FTC's and similar programs, see F. M. Scherer, "Segmental Financial Reporting: Needs and Tradeoffs," and George J. Benston, "The Segment Reporting Debate," in Goldschmid, ed., *Business Disclosure*, pp. 3–118.

ters. We will review the substantive content of the principal U.S. antitrust laws, identify significant differences between American laws and their counterparts in other lands, and explore unsettled policy issues. The remaining pages of the present chapter provide a general introduction and historical backdrop.[49]

Early background Almost the entire edifice of U.S. federal antitrust law rests upon three foundation statutes—the Sherman Act of 1890, the Clayton Act of 1914, and the Federal Trade Commission Act of 1914. These three were virtually the first of their kind in the modern world; they were preceded only by an 1889 addition to the Canadian criminal code similar to the Sherman Act. The legislation establishing antitrust rules in Canada and the United States during the brief span of 25 years represented the reaction of New World dwellers to a concatenation of profound changes in the character of industrial capitalism.

Several things happened during the latter half of the 19th century to set the stage for antitrust. For one, capital-intensive production on a large scale, although by no means unknown previously, spread rapidly in the manufacturing industries. This occurred partly because of technological innovations in metallurgy, industrial chemistry, energy generation and utilization, and the use of interchangeable parts. Also, transportation costs fell, reducing the physical distribution constraint on optimal plant scales. The quest for economies of scale was facilitated by the ascendance of new managerial methods[50] and the development of modern capital markets able to supply large quantities of venture capital to a single firm. Liberalization of state incorporation laws also contributed, permitting the acquisition of other firms' stock (e.g., in mergers) and the delegation of stockholders' decision-making power to full-time managers.

While production operations were growing in size, so also were markets. The rapid extension of rail networks created for the first time a "common market" in the United States, with an accompanying intensification of competition. Producers once isolated spatially found their markets penetrated by outsiders. International competition also increased as transatlantic shipping rates fell sharply with the introduction of iron vessels propelled by efficient compound steam engines.

Two severe business depressions—one international in scope commencing in 1873 and persisting in the United States for six years, the other beginning in 1883 and lasting until 1886, added ferment to the economic broth. The first reaction of large manufacturers, carrying a heavy burden of fixed costs and faced with increasingly intense competition, was to cut prices. This course was viewed with scant enthusiasm by business leaders, whose second reaction was an effort to subdue the forces of competition by entering into restrictive agreements and by consolidating former competitors into a single monolithic enterprise with control over prices.

In Europe, cartel formation was the prevalent means of coping with the turbulent conditions of the 1870s and 1880s. Fritz Voigt reports that in Germany there were 4 cartels in 1865, 8 in 1875, 70 in 1887, 106 in 1889, and 250 in 1896.[51] American producers also entered into formal and informal price-fixing agreements with their rivals. But the more striking American response—striking both in absolute magnitude and its contrast with what happened in Europe—was the large-scale merger, consummated at first through trust devices.[52] The pacemaker was the Standard Oil Company. It had many imitators, and the 1880s and 1890s witnessed a wave of horizontal mergers and corporate consolidations unequalled in subsequent U.S. history.

Why the U.S. merger wave was so distinctly American, while European business managers were generally satisfied with their cartel arrangements, is not altogether clear. One possible explanation is that American entrepreneurs, reflecting the expansive frontier spirit of their times, were more inclined toward corporate empire building, while Europeans preferred operating small, closely held enterprises in restrictive fashion. Another is that American business managers, poured from a melting pot of ethnic and economic backgrounds, held such diverse attitudes and goals that they were psychologically unable to cooperate in maintaining nonbinding cartel agreements. Only through a complete surrender of decision-making power to a monolithic consolidation could their maverick impulses be

492

leashed. Europeans, on the other hand, may have shared sufficiently homogeneous cultural traditions to work together amicably in their national markets. Third, mergers tend to be the product of boom times, while cartels are the children of depression. The depressions of the 1870s and 1880s were milder in America than in Europe. The more buoyant expectations of American entrepreneurs may have been conducive to consolidation, while Europeans, troubled by the perplexing new forms the business cycle had taken, were propelled toward loose confederations. Finally, differences in the legal environment had some bearing. In Germany, at one extreme, cartel agreements were held to be binding contracts.[53] Recalcitrant members could be compelled under the law to honor their restrictive promises. Under American common law and also (with a few qualifications) in England, price-fixing agreements were generally considered unlawful and unenforceable at law. This made it difficult to maintain industry discipline in the face of dissident members' actions, and so, at least in the United States, business managers turned to the more certain control of trustification.

Although the common law in America took a generally dim view of agreements to restrain trade, it was impotent as a positive preventive force. Restrictive agreements could only be challenged by parties to the agreement, who had little incentive to do so, or by injured private persons, who seldom could sustain the evidentiary and financial burden of proving their case. The pricing practices of trusts lay almost completely beyond the law's grasp. As a result, monopolistic restraints and abuses flourished, stirring in their wake a public hue and cry for corrective action.

Several alleged misdeeds of big business provoked widespread resentment. Through predatory pricing, the trusts were said to have driven many small firms out of business, and it was with these small entrepreneurs that the public's sentiments lay. The trusts engaged in local and personal price discrimination, angering the communities and individuals who lacked competitive alternatives and paid high prices. The fortunes built upon monopoly profits increased the inequality of income distribution, evoking reactions

especially bitter because of the way wealth was flaunted at that time by those who possessed it. And farmers, comprising a majority of the voting population in the Midwest, joined in protest as the industrial consolidations raised manufactured goods prices while farm product prices declined.

About the only group in America other than big business outspokenly unconcerned about the trust problem were the professional economists. Many were captivated by Darwin's theory of biological selection. They saw the growth of big business as a natural evolutionary response consistent with economies of scale, or when scale economies were patently absent from mergers, as a step necessary to eliminate cutthroat competition. But in that unenlightened era, the views of economists concerning big business had little influence on public policy.

The public clamor reached a crescendo during the late 1880s. Between 1889 and 1891, no fewer than 18 states (beginning with Kansas) enacted antitrust laws. These, however, were not particularly effective against monopolistic consolidations operating in interstate commerce. At the national level, all the major political parties engaged in the presidential election of 1888 in-

49. For insight into the early background, see Hans B. Thorelli, *The Federal Antitrust Policy* (Stockholm: Stockholms Högskola, 1954); and William Letwin, *Law and Economic Policy in America* (New York: Random House, 1965). The most thorough legal analysis of the substance of antitrust is the multivolume treatise by Phillip Areeda and Donald F. Turner, *Antitrust Law* (Boston: Little, Brown, 1978 et seq.).

50. See Alfred D. Chandler, Jr., *The Visible Hand: The Managerial Revolution in American Business* (Cambridge, Mass.: Harvard University Press, 1977).

51. Fritz Voigt, "German Experience with Cartels and Their Control during Pre-War and Post-War Periods," in John Perry Miller, ed., *Competition, Cartels, and Their Regulation* (Amsterdam: North-Holland, 1962), p. 170.

52. England also experienced a merger wave at the same time, but it was of much more modest proportions. See Ralph L. Nelson, *Merger Movements in American Industry, 1895–1956* (Princeton: Princeton University Press, 1959), pp. 129–38; P. L. Payne, "The Emergence of the Large-Scale Company in Great Britain, 1870–1914," *Economic History Review* 20 (December 1967): 519–42; and Leslie Hannah, "Mergers in British Manufacturing Industry, 1880–1918," *Oxford Economic Papers* 24 n.s. (March 1974): 1–17.

53. See Fritz Blaich, "Der 'Standard-Oil-Fall' vor dem Reichstag," *Zeitschrift für die gesamte Staatswissenschaft* 26 (October 1970): 663–82.

Policy approaches to the monopoly problem   **493**

cluded antitrust planks in their platforms. The initiative in Congress was exercised by Senator John Sherman (Rep.-Ohio), who introduced antitrust bills during the 1888, 1889, and, finally with greater success, 1890 terms. His 1890 bill was debated warmly, subjected to a plethora of amendments, referred to the Judiciary Committee for extensive rewriting, and returned to the Senate to be passed by a 52-1 vote. After House of Representatives concurrence, it was signed into law by President Harrison on July 2, 1890.

Substance of the basic statutes The resulting statute, bearing little resemblance to Senator Sherman's original proposal, contained two main substantive sections. Section 1 prohibits contracts, combinations, and conspiracies in restraint of trade, prescribing penalties for violators of imprisonment and/or a fine up to $5,000 (raised over time to a maximum of $1 million by 1974). Section 2 prohibits monopolization, attempts to monopolize, and combinations or conspiracies to monopolize "any part of the trade or commerce among the several States, or with foreign nations," specifying criminal penalties for violation similar to those of Section 1. Of the procedural sections, the most important were Section 4, permitting the Attorney General to institute suits in equity to enjoin illegal practices, and Section 7 (since superseded), permitting private persons injured by actions illegal under Sections 1 or 2 to sue for recovery of three times the amount of actual damages sustained.

Enforcement of the Sherman Act during its first ten years was unspectacular, to say the least. Several attorneys general entrusted with enforcing the law lacked not only funds and personnel but also enthusiasm, partly because of prior affiliations as private counsel to leading corporations. The government also suffered significant legal defeats in cases brought against the whiskey and sugar trusts—setbacks traceable in no small measure to careless preparation and unimaginative argumentation. However, government test case victories in 1897 and 1899 set the stage for an invigorated enforcement program after Theodore Roosevelt took office as president in 1901. Roosevelt secured new legislation providing streamlined judicial procedures for civil

antitrust cases and creating a special antitrust enforcement division in the Department of Justice. A series of important case decisions (discussed in subsequent chapters) followed, establishing for decades to come the rules by which businesses obtaining and exercising monopoly power were required to live.

The remaining two horses of the U.S. antitrust troika were put in place at the urging of President Woodrow Wilson. The Clayton Act was designed to outlaw specific practices not covered by the Sherman Act and to restrain the growth of monopoly "in its incipiency," before full-blown Sherman Act violations could develop. Section 2, heavily amended in 1936, prohibited price discrimination that substantially lessened competition or tended to create a monopoly. Section 3 outlaws tying clauses and exclusive dealing agreements adversely affecting competition. Section 4 supersedes Sherman Act Section 7 in authorizing treble damages suits, and Section 5 eases the burden of proving antitrust violation for parties suing to recover treble damages. Section 7, amended in 1950, prohibited certain mergers tending substantially to lessen competition; and Section 8 forbids interlocking directorates among competing firms.

For some time prior to 1914, both critics and advocates of antitrust saw the need for an agency performing both investigatory and adjudicative functions and possessing special competence in business affairs. To create such an agency was the purpose of the Federal Trade Commission Act, which established a panel of five full-time commissioners invested with substantial quasi-judicial powers and aided by a staff of professional personnel. The FTC Act also, in substantive Section 5, outlawed "unfair methods of competition," leaving to the Commission and ultimately the Supreme Court the task of determining what practices were to be included under this blanket prohibition.[54]

With the passage of the Clayton and Federal Trade Commission Acts, the substantive framework of American antitrust law was basically complete, to be rounded out only by a series of amendments closing loopholes and clarifying exceptions; and the enforcement machinery used ever since 1914 was assembled. Responsibility for enforcing the antitrust laws is currently shared primarily by the Antitrust Division of the Justice Department, which in 1978 spent $31 million for the task; and the Federal Trade Commission, whose 1978 budget for antitrust activities (as distinguished from such additional responsibilities as combatting misleading advertising and other deceptive practices) was $29 million. The Antitrust Division is predominantly an investigative and enforcement agency. Cases it initiates are adjudicated before a federal district court, whose decisions in particularly important civil (i.e., noncriminal) cases may be appealed on matters of law by either the government or the defendant directly to the Supreme Court. The Federal Trade Commission, on the other hand, does economic and financial research along with collaborating in case investigations through its Bureau of Economics, investigates and prosecutes complaints in its Bureau of Competition, and adjudicates cases through a separate group of administrative law judges, who can recommend that the five-member Commission issue a cease-and-desist order against corporations found to be violating the law. Commission decisions can be appealed (primarily on matters of law) to a federal appellate court and from there to the Supreme Court. The FTC's legal procedures, originally intended to provide streamlined antitrust enforcement, are actually more cumbersome than those of the Justice Department; and full adjudication of FTC cases takes longer on the average.[55] As the jurisdictional provisions of the various statutes have come to be interpreted, both the Justice Department and the FTC may institute civil actions against violations of the Sherman Act and the Clayton Act.[56] This overlapping of responsibilities poses coordination problems that are not always solved successfully. A positive attribute of the dual enforcement approach is a tendency for one agency's oversights to be corrected by actions of the other agency.[57]

Exemptions from antitrust Over the course of time, a number of exemptions have been written into the antitrust laws and related statutes. Some of the most important relate to labor unions, agricultural cooperatives, export associations, and regulated industries.[58]

Several of the earliest attempts to enforce the Sherman Act were directed against labor unions, including railroad union supporters of the famous 1894 Pullman strike.[59] However, Section 6 of the Clayton Act exempted from antitrust the activities of labor and agricultural or horticultural organizations whose objective was the mutual help of members. The efforts of laborers to secure higher wages through unionization received further support under the Norris-LaGuardia Act of 1932 and the National Labor Relations Act (Wagner Act) of 1935. There is a certain inconsistency in permitting sellers of labor services but not the sellers of goods or more complex services to join together in a common effort to enhance their economic rewards.[60] However, the exemption for collective bargaining has strong political support as a means of balancing more equally the power of employers and employees. The currently binding judicial interpretations have not permitted the exemption to be extended beyond the bounds

54. A series of Supreme Court decisions expanding Section 5's scope culminated in *FTC* v. *Sperry & Hutchinson Co.*, 405 U.S. 233, 244–245 (1972), to include practices that, without necessarily having been previously considered unlawful, offend public policy or cause substantial injury to consumers.

55. See Richard A. Posner, "A Statistical Study of Antitrust Enforcement," *Journal of Law and Economics* 13 (October 1970): 374–81.

56. More precisely, Sherman Act violations can be attacked as unfair trade practices under Section 5 of the Federal Trade Commission Act. However, only the Justice Department can institute criminal complaints.

57. For comprehensive but somewhat dated critical analyses of the two agencies' antitrust functioning, see American Bar Association, *Report of the ABA Commission To Study the Federal Trade Commission* (Washington, D.C.: American Bar Association, 1969); and Mark J. Green et al., *The Closed Enterprise System* (New York: Grossman, 1972).

58. For a survey, see U.S. Department of Justice, *Report of the Task Group on Antitrust Immunities* (Washington, D.C.: Government Printing Office, 1977).

59. *U.S.* v. *Debs et al.*, 64 Fed. 724 (1894).

60. For a strong statement of the case for limiting union power, see H. Gregg Lewis, "The Labor-Monopoly Problem: A Positive Program," *Journal of Political Economy* 59 (August 1951): 277–87. For more moderate statements, see Edward S. Mason, *Economic Concentration and the Monopoly Problem* (Cambridge, Mass.: Harvard University Press, 1957), pp. 196–208; and G. H. Hildebrand, "Economics By Negotiation," *American Economic Review* 49 (May 1959): 399–411.

of particular employer-employee wage and working conditions bargains. Attempts by labor unions to collude with unionized employers in fixing end product prices or driving nonunion firms out of business have been deemed violations of the Sherman Act.[61]

In addition to the exempting language of Clayton Act Section 6, joint activities by agricultural cooperatives were further shielded from antitrust through the Capper-Volstead Act of 1922 as long as they do not "unduly" enhance farm product prices. Responsibility for enforcing the Act was assigned to the Department of Agriculture, which during the 1930s also acquired the power to issue *marketing orders* binding farm goods handlers and processors to abide by farm cooperative programs. The Department exhibited little concern about the price-raising activities of such powerful cooperatives as the cranberry growers, the California (i.e., Sunkist) citrus growers, and Associated Milk Producers, Inc. A 1976 meeting with the Secretary of Agriculture brought an embarrassed admission that the Department had not even considered how one ascertained whether prices had been enhanced "unduly." There is reason to believe that this gaping loophole may be tightened despite strong political pressure from the cooperative groups.[62]

The 1918 Webb-Pomerene Act exemption from antitrust of price fixing and other agreements pertaining solely to export sales is a mercantilist throwback common to the antitrust policies of most industrialized nations.[63] Although its intent was partly to permit small domestic firms to penetrate foreign markets more effectively and to secure economies of scale through coordinated marketing, a more fundamental objective has been to alter the terms of trade and to enhance payments balances by allowing domestic producers to exploit whatever power over export prices they might collectively possess. Under Webb-Pomerene, American companies are permitted to form and operate associations that restrain the export trade as long as prices of commodities covered are not intentionally or artificially affected in the United States market. Agreements must be registered with the Federal Trade Commission, which is charged with a con-tinuing supervisory role. The FTC's position is a difficult one, for the mere establishment of a cooperative arrangement affecting overseas markets may facilitate virtually undetectable tacit or explicit collusion with respect to domestic prices. Despite the opportunities it affords, extensive advantage has not been taken of the Webb-Pomerene loophole. In 1965 only 32 Webb-Pomerene associations, originating about 4 percent by value of U.S. exports, were registered. Most involved concentrated industries, and several had histories of perceptibly inhibited competition in the United States and active cooperation with cartelized rivals abroad.[64]

In the early years of American antitrust, Sherman Act bans on price-fixing agreements and monopolization applied with equal force to regulated and unregulated industries. Gradually, grants of immunity were written into the principal statutes governing regulated industries. However, the wheel has been turning as the antitrust agencies have won court injunctions against mergers, price fixing, and other restrictive practices in a number of industries previously assumed to be exempt by virtue of being regulated. Although it is traditional for regulated firms to seek refuge following such defeats by gaining new and more explicit legislative exemptions, an increasingly skeptical Congress has in recent years been more inclined to let the procompetitive judicial interpretations stand.

---

61. An important Supreme Court decision was *Pennington* v. *United Mine Workers et al.*, 381 U.S. 657 (1965); with the subsequent district court opinion, 257 F. Supp. 815 (1966). It is analyzed by Oliver E. Williamson in "Wage Rates as a Barrier to Entry: The Pennington Case in Perspective," *Quarterly Journal of Economics* 82 (February 1968): 85–116. See also *U.S.* v. *Hutcheson*, 312 U.S. 219 (1941).

62. See U.S., Department of Agriculture, Capper-Volstead Committee, *The Question of Undue Price Enhancement* (Washington, D.C.: Department of Agriculture, 1976).

63. For a survey of international export cartel activity throughout the world, see the United Nations Conference on Trade and Development interim report, *Restrictive Business Practices* (New York: United Nations, 1971), Chapter 3.

64. See the testimony of Willard F. Mueller in U.S., Congress, Senate, Committee on the Judiciary, Subcommittee on Antitrust and Monopoly hearings, *International Aspects of Antitrust*, 90th Cong., 1st sess., 1967, pp. 31–60; and David A. Larson, "An Economic Analysis of the Webb-Pomerene Act," *Journal of Law and Economics* 13 (October 1970): 461–500.

19 Antitrust policy: price-fixing agreements

The Sherman Act, wrote Chief Justice Charles Evans Hughes in 1933, "as a charter of freedom . . . has a generality and adaptability comparable to that found to be desirable in constitutional provisions."[1] Only by studying the trend of actual judicial interpretations can we attach specific meaning to its broad prohibitions. In this chapter we begin the task, focusing on the legal status of price-fixing agreements and similar agreements in restraint of trade.

The *per se* illegality of explicit restraints

Section 1 of the Sherman Act proscribes "every contract, combination . . . or conspiracy in restraint of trade or commerce among the several States." An extended series of court decisions has interpreted this language as making illegal *per se* all agreements among competing firms to fix prices, to restrict or pool output, to share markets on a predetermined basis, or otherwise directly to restrict the force of competition. Such agreements have been singled out for judicial treatment different from the *rule of reason* approach taken with respect to a variety of other practices under U.S. antitrust law. Under a *per se* rule, it is only necessary for the complainant (i.e., the Justice Department) to prove that certain conduct occurred and that it fell within the class of practices

"so plainly anticompetitive" that they are subject to *per se* prohibition.[2] No detailed inquiry into its economic rationale and consequences is required. Under the rule of reason, on the other hand, the courts undertake a broader inquiry into facts peculiar to the contested practices, their history, the reasons why they were implemented, and their competitive significance.[3]

The *per se* rule against overt agreements in restraint of trade was initially articulated in the *Trans-Missouri Freight Association* decision—the first price-fixing case to be appealed to the U.S. Supreme Court. In an effort to eliminate the freight rate wars toward which they were inclined, 18 railroads operating west of the Missouri River entered into formal agreements establishing the rates each line would charge. The U.S. district attorney in Topeka brought suit in 1892 to dissolve the agreements. The railroads advanced two main defenses: that they were exempt from Sherman Act prohibitions by virtue of their status as carriers regulated under the Interstate Commerce Act of 1887, and that the rates they fixed by agreement were in any event legal because they

---

1. *Appalachian Coals, Inc.* v. *U.S.*, 288 U.S. 344, 359–360 (1933).
2. *National Society of Professional Engineers* v. *U.S.*, 98 S. Ct. 1355, 1365 (1978).
3. 98 S. Ct. 1355, 1365 (1978).

were reasonable. Both defenses were sustained by the lower courts. As the district court judge observed, finding the agreements reasonable and hence not in violation of the Sherman Act:

> When contracts go to the extent only of preventing unhealthy competition, and yet at the same time furnish the public with adequate facilities at fixed and reasonable prices, and are made only for the purpose of averting personal ruin, the contract is lawful.[4]

However, this interpretation, as well as the ruling exempting regulated railroads from Sherman Act jurisdiction, was rejected by the Supreme Court in a 5–4 decision. Speaking for the majority, Justice Peckham found that the language Congress used in the Sherman Act could not be construed to admit a test of reasonableness:

> When . . . the body of an act pronounces as illegal every contract or combination in restraint of trade or commerce among the several states, etc., the plain and ordinary meaning of such language is not limited to that kind of contract alone which is in unreasonable restraint of trade, but all contracts are included in such language, and no exception or limitation can be added without placing in the act that which has been omitted by Congress.[5]

He went on to note that while preventing ruinous competition among the railroads might be socially desirable, it would be impossible for the courts to determine whether the rates set through interfirm agreements were reasonable, and that recognition of this difficulty might have prompted Congress to prohibit *all* agreements in restraint of trade and not just unreasonable ones. His view of the judiciary's role in carrying out the stated intent of Congress is revealed most clearly in this passage:

> It may be that the policy evidenced by the passage of the act itself will, if carried out, result in disaster to the roads. . . . These considerations are, however, not for us.[6]

Through a decision the following year the *per se* prohibition's sweep was limited to contracts "whose direct and immediate effect" was to restrain commerce.[7] In another concurrent case involving six midwestern and southern producers of cast-iron water and gas pipe, the rule was reiterated on a new and different logical plane. The six, accounting for about two-thirds of total output in the Middle West and West, operated in an industry that gravitated toward price warfare because of sharp fluctuations in orders, the large size of individual orders, and a cost structure characterized by high overhead and low marginal costs at less than full capacity operation. They formed a bidding cartel that rigged the prices quoted to buyers in certain cities, reserved other cities as the exclusive domain of a single seller, and pooled contributions made to a central fund in implementing the scheme. Hearing the case for the Circuit Court of Appeals, Judge (later President and Supreme Court Chief Justice) William Howard Taft went beyond a literal reading of the words used by Congress in Sherman Act Section 1, attempting to build a *per se* prohibition upon the common law prevailing in America and England at the time. He argued that the common law permitted restraints of trade which were merely ancillary to some legitimate cause, but that it voided those contracts whose main object was to restrict competition. Taft insisted that past decisions inconsistent with this view had been erroneous, "set[ting] sail on a sea of doubt" in their attempt to determine how much restraint of competition was in the public interest.[8] Ruling that the pipe producers' agreements were clearly not ancillary, Taft concluded that the reasonableness of the agreements was irrelevant:

> It has been earnestly pressed upon us that the prices at which the cast-iron pipe was sold . . . were reasonable. . . . We do not think the issue an important one, because . . . we do not think that at common law there is any question of reasonableness open to the courts with reference to such a contract. Its tendency was certainly to give the defendants the power to charge unreasonable prices, had they chosen to do so.[9]

He added in the next line that "if it were important, we should unhesitatingly find that the prices charged in the instances which were in evidence were unreasonable." This afterthought muted the force of Taft's decision as a precedent, for while citing the material quoted here approvingly, the Supreme Court on appeal placed more emphasis on the unreasonableness of the prices charged than on Taft's harmonization of the common and statutory law.[10]

The scope of the *per se* prohibition against price fixing was attenuated and muddied somewhat during the next three decades as the Supreme Court applied a rule of reason to Sherman Act monopolization cases (considered in the next chapter) and as decisions were rendered in borderline areas such as patent license restrictions and trade association activities falling short of clear-cut price fixing. A forceful restatement had to await the *Trenton Potteries* decision in 1927. The defendants, some 23 manufacturers controlling roughly 82 percent of the bathroom bowl market, published standardized price lists through a trade association committee, discussed prices at frequent association meetings, and exhorted one another not to sell at off-list prices. Evidence compiled through a criminal trial suggested that the exhortations were not very successful. Pricing discipline of the association members was weak, and for many members adherence to list prices was apparently more the exception than the rule. Hearing the case on appeal, the Supreme Court directly addressed the question of whether reasonableness of the prices actually charged was a relevant consideration in determining the defendants' guilt or innocence. It first distinguished price-fixing cases from other cases in which a rule of reason had been applied, observing that the meaning of reasonableness "necessarily varies in the different fields of the law." It then went on to conclude:

> The aim and result of every price-fixing agreement, if effective, is the elimination of one form of competition. The power to fix prices, whether reasonably exercised or not, involves power to control the market and to fix arbitrary and unreasonable prices. The reasonable price fixed today may through economic and business changes become the unreasonable price of tomorrow. . . . Agreements which create such potential power may well be held to be in themselves unreasonable or unlawful restraints, without the necessity of minute inquiry whether a particular price is reasonable or unreasonable as fixed and without placing on the Government in enforcing the Sherman Law the burden of ascertaining from day to day whether it has become unreasonable through the mere variation of economic conditions.[11]

The Court's decision has been criticized for neglecting the constraints on the pottery makers' willingness to carry out the agreements they reached, and hence for failing to see that the defendants may well have lacked the very power it condemned.[12] The decision nevertheless represents a clear *per se* prohibition of explicit price-fixing conspiracies, whether carried into effect or not, and it is generally viewed as the basic precedent in price-fixing cases.

Still the courts, like other human organizations, do not always hew faithfully to the rules they have enunciated. A significant break from the *Trenton Potteries* precepts took place only six years later when the economy was in the trough of the Great Depression. An industry hit especially hard by the slump was coal mining. Prices of bituminous coal fell by 25 percent from 1929 to

4. *U.S.* v. *Trans-Missouri Freight Association et al.*, 53 Fed. 440, 451 (1892).

5. *U.S.* v. *Trans-Missouri Freight Association*, 166 U.S. 290, 328 (1897).

6. 166 U.S. 290, 340 (1897).

7. *Hopkins* v. *United States*, 171 U.S. 578, 592 (1898). See also *U.S.* v. *Joint Traffic Association*, 171 U.S. 505, 568 (1898).

8. *U.S.* v. *Addyston Pipe & Steel Co. et al.*, 85 Fed. 271, 284 (1898). Taft's decision has been criticized for reading things into the common law that were not there. See Almarin Phillips, *Market Structure, Organization and Performance* (Cambridge, Mass.: Harvard University Press, 1962), p. 114.

9. *U.S.* v. *Addyston Pipe & Steel Co. et al.*, 85 Fed. 271, 293 (1898).

10. *Addyston Pipe & Steel Co. et al.* v. *U.S.*, 175 U.S. 211, 235–238 (1899).

11. *U.S.* v. *Trenton Potteries Co. et al.*, 273 U.S. 392, 396–398 (1927).

12. See Phillips, *Market Structure, Organization and Performance*, pp. 171–76. See also Richard A. Posner, *Antitrust Law: An Economic Perspective* (Chicago: University of Chicago Press, 1976), Chapter 4, who criticizes the courts' failure to examine the actual consequences of attempted price fixing as a "cops and robbers" approach to antitrust.

1933, while output was reduced by 38 percent. More coal mining firms reported losses than profits. To cope with these conditions, 137 producers in the Appalachian Mountain region formed in 1931 a new company, Appalachian Coals, Inc., to serve as exclusive selling agent for member firms. Its members accounted for 12 percent of all soft coal production east of the Mississippi River and 54 percent of production in the Appalachian territory and immediately surrounding states. The agency was instructed to get the "best prices obtainable" for member output, and if all output could not be sold, to allocate orders among the member mines. In effect, it served as a kind of sales cartel, but with far from complete control over the relevant market. The government brought suit to dissolve the agency. A district court found Appalachian Coals in violation of Sherman Act Section 1, citing the *Trenton Potteries* decision as a precedent.[13] But on appeal the Supreme Court reversed the decision. Chief Justice Hughes, speaking for an eight-member majority of the Court, pointed to the "deplorable" economic condition of the industry; stated that the purpose of the Sherman Act was to prevent *undue* restraints of interstate commerce; and called for the judiciary to engage in "close and objective scrutiny of particular conditions and purposes . . . in each case" to determine whether or not defendants were merely adopting reasonable measures to protect commerce from injurious and destructive practices.[14] He concluded that Appalachian Coals would not be able to fix the price of coal in consuming markets because of competition from nonmembers, and that in any event, abuse-correcting measures with the effect of stabilizing trade and making prices more reasonable were not necessarily an unreasonable restraint of trade. Hughes suggested further that the Appalachian Coals type of selling agency was clearly no worse than a full-blown consolidation of coal producers through merger, which was not likely to be declared illegal under prevailing antitrust law interpretations, and toward which the mines might be driven if not allowed to pursue the less drastic selling agency alternative. As a result, the injunction against Appalachian Coals was quashed. But since no concrete experience under the proposed scheme had been accumulated, the Supreme Court ordered the District Court to retain jurisdiction and to take remedial action if Appalachian's operations should in fact prove to impose an undue restraint upon interstate commerce. No review of the association's activities was actually made, since Congress subsequently authorized explicit price restoration measures under the National Industrial Recovery Act of 1933, the Bituminous Coal Conservation Act of 1935, and the Bituminous Coal Act of 1937.

The *Appalachian Coals* decision is widely regarded as an anomaly in antitrust law with no status as a precedent. After disillusionment with cartelization as an antidepression weapon set in during the mid-1930s and after President Roosevelt "packed" the Supreme Court with five new and more liberal justices during the late 1930s, the Court returned to a clear *per se* rule against explicit price-fixing arrangements. The return came in another case covering depression-inspired pricing practices, this time in the gasoline industry. Independent refiners had been dumping gasoline in the midwestern market at panic prices, demoralizing the whole price structure. During 1935 and 1936, some 12 to 18 major refining companies organized themselves into a committee and agreed to take surplus gasoline from the independents, disposing of it in a more orderly manner so as not to depress prices. Each major firm chose one or more independent "dancing partners," whose surplus it was to acquire. In a subsequent antitrust trial, the defendant firms admitted that their scheme contributed to a rise in prices, but argued that the surplus disposal program's influence on prices was minor compared to the effect of general economic recovery, and that the increase in prices was reasonable in view of the excessively low levels to which prices had fallen during the depression. They were found guilty by a jury; and after review by an appellate court, the Supreme Court on appeal sustained the jury's verdict with respect to 12 corporate defendants. Following an unconvincing attempt to rationalize its *Appalachian Coals* opinion, the Court said that:

for over forty years this Court has consistently and without deviation adhered to the principle that price-fixing agreements are unlawful *per se* under the Sherman Act and that no showing of so-called competitive abuses or evils which those agreements were designed to eliminate or alleviate may be interpreted as a defense. . . . If the so-called competitive abuses were to be appraised here, the reasonableness of prices would necessarily become an issue in every price-fixing case. In that event the Sherman Act would soon be emasculated; its philosophy would be supplanted by one which is wholly alien to a system of free competition; it would not be the charter of freedom which its framers intended. . . . Any combination which tampers with price structures is engaged in an unlawful activity. . . . Congress . . . has not permitted the age-old cry of ruinous competition and competitive evils to be a defense to price-fixing conspiracies.[15]

Since 1940, the Supreme Court's blanket condemnation in the gasoline case of all combinations tampering with price structures has been followed consistently. Included under the *per se* prohibition have been not only express price-fixing agreements but also conspiracies seeking indirectly to limit price competition, such as agreements to restrict output, to divide up the market into exclusive spheres of influence, to allocate customers by seller, to follow standardized pricing formulas or methods, and to boycott or exclude from the market firms declining to abide by industry pricing norms.[16] The courts have also gone far toward declaring illegal all bilateral or multilateral patent licensing agreements with provisions governing prices to be charged, markets to be served, and outputs to be produced by parties to the agreement.[17] However, under current interpretations, the owner of a valid patent may legitimately include restrictions with respect to price, output, and markets served in the licenses it unilaterally grants to other firms.[18]

Despite the acceptance of *per se* rules against explicit price fixing, there remain certain grey areas in which a rule of reason has been applied. We will explore two of the main exceptions a few pages hence. Here another borderline case

deserves brief mention. In 1918, the Supreme Court found that the Chicago Board of Trade was not violating the Sherman Act when it passed a rule requiring that members buy or sell grain when the exchange was not in session (e.g., at night) only at the closing price of the last previous session. Declaring the rule not inconsistent with the Sherman Act, the Supreme Court stated:

> The legality of an agreement or regulation cannot be determined by so simple a test as whether it restrains competition. Every agreement concerning trade, every regulation of trade, restrains. To bind, to restrain, is of their very essence. The true test of legality is whether the restraint imposed is such as merely regulates and perhaps thereby promotes competition, or whether it is such as may suppress or even destroy competition. To determine that question the Court must ordinarily consider the facts peculiar to the business to which the restraint is applied; . . . the nature of the restraint and its effect, actual or probable.[19]

At face value this opinion implies a willingness to apply a rule of reason in borderline cases, where it is not obvious whether an agreement merely establishes conditions conducive to competitive trading or actually suppresses competition. However, subsequent criticism has shown that the

13. *U.S.* v. *Appalachian Coals, Inc., et al.*, 1 F. Supp. 339 (1932).

14. *Appalachian Coals, Inc.* v. *U.S.*, 288 U.S. 344, 359–360 (1933).

15. *U.S.* v. *Socony-Vacuum Oil Co. et al.*, 310 U.S. 150, 218–221 (1940).

16. For an admirable survey of the cases, see A. D. Neale, *The Antitrust Laws of the United States of America* (Cambridge, England: Cambridge University Press, 1966), pp. 65–80.

17. Neale, *The Antitrust Laws*, pp. 261–86.

18. The governing decision is *U.S.* v. *General Electric* Co., 272 U.S. 476 (1926). Two attempts to overturn the doctrine were frustrated by 4-4 divisions of opinion among the participating Supreme Court justices. *U.S.* v. *Line Material Co. et al.*, 333 U.S. 287, 315 (1948); and *U.S.* v. *Huck Mfg. Co. et al.*, 382 U.S. 197 (1965).

19. *Board of Trade of the City of Chicago* v. *U.S.*, 246 U.S. 231, 238 (1918). See also the Supreme Court's restatement and affirmation in *National Society of Professional Engineers* v. *U.S.*, 98 S. Ct. 1355 (1978).

Court failed to distinguish adequately between the rule's effect on grain prices, which at worst was small, and its much more significant effect in protecting Board member dealers from the competition of off-exchange transactions on which they received no commissions.[20] In so doing the Court may unwittingly have set the stage for a presumption that dealers on an organized exchange were somehow different from others engaged in the hurly-burly of trade, meriting special antitrust immunity that has to some extent persisted even to the present.[21] Similar opportunities to set fees collectively without antitrust prosecution were enjoyed for a long time by members of such professions as medicine, dentistry, law, architecture, and civil engineering. Only during the 1960s and 1970s did these immunities come under significant and largely successful attack.[22]

For restrictive business conduct lying in the grey area where a rule of reason approach is adopted, the wider scope of judicial inquiry does not mean that the courts will consider any and all conceivable defenses. As Sherman Act Section 1 has come to be interpreted, the central concern is whether conduct is anticompetitive.[23] The courts do not have an open mandate to weigh, say, the sacrifices in allocative efficiency or equitable income distribution resulting from lessened competition against any benefits that might accrue— e.g., as the National Society of Professional Engineers argued in defending its rules prohibiting competitive price bidding, the encouragement of high-quality engineering and hence public safety.[24] Although actual judicial implementation is messier, the basic conceptual difference between the rule of reason approach and *per se* rules under U.S. law is that with the former, the courts will embark upon a careful factual inquiry to determine whether on balance competition is suppressed, whereas suppression of competition is automatically presumed for practices falling clearly within the bounds of *per se* proscriptions. This poses among other things a semantic problem, for the words "rule of reason" are preempted to describe a rather limited span of judicial inquiry. No generally accepted terminology is left to characterize antitrust procedures under which the reasonableness of practices is judged by weighing the benefits of competition against other potentially conflicting social goals, or even procedures that attempt to determine whether collusively established prices are not "unreasonably high." For want of a better alternative, we shall call that more far-ranging adjudication approach an "expanded rule of reason."

Remedies and penalties in price-fixing cases

Under the Sherman Act the Justice Department possesses two weapons for attacking price-fixing violations. It can institute a civil suit (i.e., a suit in equity), the end result of which may be a court injunction against illegal practices; or it can seek a criminal indictment leading to punitive fines and/or prison sentences. Because the legal proscriptions against express price-fixing agreements are so clear, and because business managers engaging in price fixing cannot help but know they are violating the law, the Justice Department has tended to seek criminal rather than civil sanctions against pricing conspiracies. It may also proceed in tandem, prosecuting a criminal action for punitive purposes and a civil action to secure an injunctive remedy. Between 1955 and 1969, an average of 15 criminal cases per year were initiated against alleged Sherman Act violations, nearly all involving price-fixing and related restrictive practices prohibited under Section 1.[25]

Until 1955, the maximum fine assessable for Sherman Act violations was $5,000 per count. This was so low that it was often more profitable to violate the law and risk being caught than to refrain from violations, although the costs of presenting a defense and the odium of criminal conviction constituted an additional deterrent. In 1955 Congress raised the maximum fine to $50,000 per count. In 1974 the ceiling was raised again to $100,000 for individuals and $1 million for corporations, and price-fixing violations were made a felony (rather than a misdemeanor, as they had been until then). Both individual and corporate fines, it should be noted, are not tax deductible. However, the courts have seldom taken full advantage of either the earlier upper limits or the increased limits set in 1974. Thus, for an uncontested conspiracy involving electrical switch and outlet sales of $200 million per year, the highest individual fine was $40,000 and the highest company fine $300,000.[26] Total corporate fines in all cases concluded during 1977 were $2.6 million, increasing to $11 million for cases ending in 1978.[27] The threat of such penalties has evidently been insufficient to deter many violations, as the continuing stream of convictions demonstrates.

A more potent deterrent may be the imposition of prison sentences. This approach was used infrequently at first. Between 1890 and 1940, jail sentences were imposed in only 24 cases, 13 involving trade union leaders and 11 businessmen. All the businessmen imprisoned during this period had perpetrated acts of racketeering accompanied by overt threats, intimidation, and violence.[28] Only since the late 1950s have business officials been incarcerated for simple price fixing. Even then, judges have traditionally been reluctant to treat white-collar antitrust violators as harshly as, say, forgers, burglars, and other nonviolent garden variety criminals.[29] As a result, the longest price-fixing sentence up to 1974 was 90 days, and more often than not, suspended sentences were imposed. However, in extending the maximum Sherman Act violation sentence from one to three years in 1974, Congress made clear its intent to escalate the stakes; and the Justice Department began urging significant jail terms as a regular matter in hard-core collusion cases. In the accounting year ending September 30, 1978, 29 individuals were sentenced to a total of 2,921 days in prison for antitrust violations.[30]

Another relatively recent development may have an even more potent impact. Clayton Act Section 4 (which amended Section 7 of the original Sherman Act) permits persons injured by antitrust law violations to sue for the recovery of three times the amount of damages sustained. Clayton Act Section 5 permits treble damage plaintiffs to draw upon prior antitrust judgments resulting from government-initiated cases in proving that a violation has occurred. However, these provisions were used infrequently and without much success until after World War II. Then a series of favorable Supreme Court decisions simplified the problems of obtaining evidence, forming classes of aggrieved plaintiffs, and proving damages; and the number of treble damage suits rose sharply.[31] During the decade of the 1950s, it is estimated, more than 2,100 treble damage antitrust suits were initiated.[32] In the 1960s the number was 6,500, including 2,333 connected with one massive conspiracy—that of the heavy electrical equipment manufacturers. By 1976, the number of private antitrust suits commenced in a single year had risen to 1,504.[33] Payments resulting from the electrical equipment suits alone were somewhere between $400 and $600 million, all tax deductible.[34]

The tendency for the courts to view treble damage suits kindly and the ensuing rush of private litigants to take advantage are such new phenomena that their full effect on business be-

20. See Richard O. Zerbe, Jr., "The Chicago Board of Trade Case (1918)" (Manuscript, University of Washington, 1977).

21. In 1974 the scope of Chicago Board of Trade members' collective commission fixing was narrowed in a consent decree. Antitrust and congressional attack on the practices of New York Stock Exchange brokers led to the phased elimination of fixed commissions beginning in 1972. See H. Michael Mann, "The New York Stock Exchange: A Cartel at the End of Its Reign," in Almarin Phillips, ed., *Promoting Competition in the Regulated Markets* (Washington, D.C.: Brookings Institution, 1975), pp. 301–27.

22. A key decision was *Goldfarb* v. *Virginia State Bar Association*, 421 U.S. 773 (1975).

23. See James A. Rahl, "Price Competition and the Price-Fixing Rule—Preface and Perspective," *Northwestern University Law Review* 57 (May–June 1962), especially pp. 139–43.

24. *National Society of Engineers* v. *U.S.*, 98 S. Ct. 1355 (1978).

25. See Richard A. Posner, "A Statistical Study of Antitrust Enforcement," *Journal of Law and Economics* 13 (October 1970): 385.

26. "Antitrust Penalties," *Business Week*, 20 February 1978, p. 38. See also "Gulf Is Fined on Uranium Price Fixing," *New York Times*, 3 June 1978, p. C-27.

27. "A Dramatic Rise in Lawsuits and Costs Concerns U.S. Bar," *New York Times*, 18 May 1977, p. B-9.

28. James M. Clabault and John F. Burton, Jr., *Sherman Act Indictments, 1955–1965* (New York: Federal Legal Publications, 1966), p. 104. See also Posner, "A Statistical Study," p. 391.

29. See the statement of Judge Parsons in *U.S.* v. *Alton Box Board Co. et al.* (N.D. Illinois), 15 February 1977, ordering community service work by executives in place of extended prison terms.

30. "Antitrust Violators May Get Leniency," *Washington Post*, 5 October 1978. See also "Washington & Business: Tougher Penalties in Antitrust Cases," *New York Times*, 16 March 1978, p. 61.

31. For a compendium of papers analyzing the legal developments and issues, see the *Journal of Reprints for Antitrust Law and Economics* 2 (Winter 1970).

32. Posner, "A Statistical Study," pp. 370–72.

33. "A Dramatic Rise in Lawsuits," *New York Times*, 18 May 1977, p. B-9.

havior remains unclear. The stakes of the antitrust game have been raised substantially, and sellers are likely to become more scrupulous in abiding by the law. This is in many respects a good thing, at least insofar as Sherman Act Section 1 is concerned. However, treble damage suits have also proliferated in connection with alleged violations of other antitrust laws, and the effect in some such cases (especially in price discrimination and monopolization cases) may be to encourage generally more conservative, less aggressive business behavior. There is also a strong temptation for nuisance suits to be filed in the expectation that the target companies will offer an out-of-court settlement (including an appreciable fee for the plaintiff attorneys, who often act as entrepreneurs in initiating the case) rather than bear the costs and risks of litigation. And in the 1976 debate over *parens patriae* legislation permitting state attorneys general to sue for treble damages on behalf of all state residents affected by an alleged collusive scheme, it was argued that poorly grounded suits might be brought by ambitious, publicity seeking politicians.[35]

These dangers are real. Proposals for reform include requiring unsuccessful plaintiffs to pay all litigation costs, the award of only single damages for nonhard-core violations, and complete elimination of antitrust damage suits and substitution of fines commensurate with the monopoly profits realized by lawbreaking corporations.[36] Yet the damages approach also has compelling advantages—e.g., decentralizing initiative to buyer groups and private law firms with superior access to information and more legal talent than a government enforcement agency can normally command. Certainly, the treble damages approach has added a potent weapon against monopolistic practices. Whether the right balance has been struck is likely to remain controversial for some time to come.

Antitrust abroad: a comparison

The *per se* prohibition of price-fixing and related agreements in the United States stands in contrast to the situation overseas. While the *per se* rule was emerging in America during the early part of the 20th century, most European nations had no statutory antitrust laws at all, and cartels flourished. The few laws that did exist related only to abuses of individual or collective monopoly power, and they were seldom enforced. Following World War II, there was an international antitrust legislation boom. Now nearly every industrialized Western nation (and many a developing nation) has some kind of antitrust law or, to use a name accentuating the positive, competition policy.[37] None, however, adopts a strict *per se* rule against price-fixing conspiracies; all tolerate pricing agreements within more or less narrowly circumscribed boundaries.

Examining the approach adopted toward antitrust abroad puts the U.S. laws in perspective and brings out more clearly the underlying philosophy, advantages, and drawbacks of the American system. No nation's laws are completely typical, and a superficial survey of all would be of little value. We shall therefore focus mainly on the British system, which represents one of the tougher, more thoroughgoing codes adopted by a Western nation thus far. The laws of several other leading nations will then be summarized much more briefly to indicate the range of approaches taken.

Prior to World War II, the British had no significant statutory law concerning price-fixing arrangements and cartels. The applicable rules were those of common law which, in the *laissez faire* spirit of the 19th century, had gradually given increasing weight to the principle of free contract, permitting businesses to enter freely into contracts with one another, including contracts and agreements restricting competition. In emphasizing this right, the courts implicitly sacrificed another: of individual citizens to enjoy the benefits of free and unrestricted competition. Recognizing the antisocial potential of restrictive agreements, the British courts refused to provide positive support by enforcing such contracts against parties who breached them. But they also would not intervene to overturn restrictive agreements or award damages to an injured third party unless some explicitly unlawful act of violence, intimidation, molestation, or fraud was perpetrated in connection with the restriction.[38] It was on this question of balancing producers' rights against the rights of consumers that the U.S. Congress chose a quite different path when it passed the Sherman Act.

Reconciliation of the British and American philosophies did not begin in earnest until 1956, when Parliament approved the Restrictive Trade Practices Act.[39] The act required all agreements in restraint of trade among suppliers of goods to be registered with a Registrar of Restrictive Practices;[40] it authorized the Registrar to challenge any agreements that appear contrary to the public interest; and it established a special Restrictive Practices Court, with streamlined procedures and a membership including both judges and laypeople, to determine whether challenged agreements should be prohibited.[41] Parties to a challenged agreement bear the burden of proving to the Court that their agreement provides positive benefits covered under one or more of eight "gateways" and of showing in addition that the benefits from the agreement outweigh the harm. The gateways include such defenses as the following: The agreement is necessary to protect the public against injury; it is necessary to counteract measures taken by competitors not party to the agreement; it is necessary to negotiate fair prices with powerful suppliers; it is necessary to sustain the level of export earnings; its removal would have serious and persistent adverse effects on local employment and unemployment; it does not materially restrict competition and is unlikely to do so; and its removal would deny the public substantial benefits or advantages. This is clearly an expanded rule of reason approach. The Restrictive Practices Court has broad discretion to determine whether or not an agreement is, on balance, socially desirable or undesirable.

Despite the breadth of certain gateways and legal traditions far from hostile to cooperation among business enterprises, the Restrictive Practices Court demonstrated its willingness to adopt a hard line. By the end of 1964, more than 2,400 agreements had been registered and 32 cases had been contested before the Court. Of these 32, only 9 led to decisions in favor of the companies; the other 23 agreements had to be discontinued or substantially revamped. In more than 75 other cases the Court rendered uncontested decisions, typically against the restrictions in

question. In its very first contested price-fixing case, the Court accepted as a valid defense the contention of the British Cotton Yarn Spinners Association that theirs was a declining industry and that painful pockets of localized unemployment would develop if their pricing scheme were rejected. But the Court held that the benefits of the agreement were outweighed by the harm— notably, the retention of inefficient and unnecessary capacity in the industry.[42] This ringing (and to most observers unexpected) declaration of faith in competitive market processes, supplemented by hard-line decisions in several subse-

(34) Charles A. Bane, *The Electrical Equipment Conspiracies: The Treble Damage Actions* (New York: Federal Legal Publications, 1973), especially pp. 250–65. Exact damage figures are not available, since many of the suits were settled quietly out of court.

35. To discourage ill-founded suits, the *parens patriae* law ultimately enacted gave the courts discretion to award attorney fees to respondents who defended themselves successfully against suits brought in bad faith or for oppressive reasons.

Such moral hazards are not unique to state-initiated litigation. Federal government enforcement agency lawyers often view bringing and litigating a complaint as their best chance to prove their mettle and obtain a high-paying partnership in private practice. The case screening procedures used by the Federal Trade Commission and Justice Department are not always effective in weeding out inadequately grounded complaints urged by eager legal staff members.

36. See William Breit and Kenneth G. Elzinga, "Antitrust Enforcement and Economic Efficiency: The Uneasy Case for Treble Damages," *Journal of Law and Economics* 17 (October 1974): 329–56.

37. There is now a vast comparative literature. Perhaps the most useful single source is the multivolume, periodically updated Organisation for Economic Cooperation and Development compendium, *Guide to Legislation on Restrictive Business Practices*. New developments are also summarized in biannual OECD publications, *Annual Reports on Competition Policy in OECD Member Countries*.

38. A key decision was *Mogul Steamship Co.* v. *McGregor, Gow, and Co.*, 21 Q. B. D. 544 (1888), 23 Q. B. D. 598 (1889).

39. An extensive literature on the Act and its interpretation exists. Especially valuable surveys include R. S. Stevens and B. S. Yamey, *The Restrictive Practices Court* (London: Weidenfeld, 1965); the Symposium on Restrictive Practices in *Oxford Economic Papers* 17 n.s. (November 1965); and Dennis Swann, Denis P. O'Brien, W. P. Maunder, and W. S. Howe, *Competition in British Industry* (London: George Allen & Unwin, 1974).

40. Under 1973 amendments, the Registrar's office was taken over by an Office of Fair Trading with expanded jurisdiction. The registration of agreements concerning services (but not professional services) as well as goods was also required beginning in 1973.

41. In 1968 the law was amended to make clear that agreements not registered within the allowed time limit were void without any action by the Court.

quent cases, led to the voluntary abandonment of more than a thousand other restrictive agreements and the modification of hundreds more.

Nevertheless, in at least a few cases the Restrictive Practices Court has been willing to accept price-fixing arrangements as reasonable. These decisions are of special interest because they show how far the Court can go in weighing benefits against costs. They therefore provide a valuable contrast to the American scene. The first involved a bidding cartel among six steam boiler manufacturers, with facts similar to the *Addyston Pipe & Steel* case of U.S. fame.[43] Overhead costs were high; demand was cyclical; orders often came in substantial chunks; and a single customer (the government's Electricity Generating Board) placed 83 percent of all domestic orders. One attempted defense, pleading that price fixing was necessary to maintain industry capacity and support research and development during recessions, was rejected by the Court after an analysis of the facts. Another, emphasizing the necessity of creating countervailing power to deal with the monopsonistic Electricity Generating Board, was struck down on a technicality, although there is reason to believe it influenced the Court's ultimate decision. The Court's approval was formally premised on its acceptance of a defense argument that cooperation was required in order to compete more effectively in export markets. The decision, applying to both domestic and overseas transactions, is consistent with the approach of the U.S. Webb-Pomerene Act toward export cartels, except that American law prohibits extension of a cartel's influence to the domestic market.

Price fixing by nut and bolt manufacturers was approved in order to save small-lot purchasers the trouble of shopping around, after a finding that the prices fixed were reasonable.[44] A cement industry agreement was authorized when the Court concluded that the industry was charging reasonable prices and that it would be able to attract capital at lower costs (and hence charge lower prices) if the uncertainties created by substantial cyclical fluctuations in an environment of high overhead costs were ameliorated through collusion.[45] It is worth noting that the American cement industry, advancing similar

arguments in defense of less extensive collusive arrangements, was found to be violating the U.S. antitrust laws.[46] An agreement among magnet manufacturers was endorsed when the Court concluded that desirable cooperation in research and development would be inhibited unless the firms could also cooperate in pricing.[47] A purchasing cartel among sulphuric acid producers was approved in order to countervail the power of the American sulphur export cartel.[48] Price fixing by ceramic tile makers was sanctioned to enforce standardization of tile sizes, allowing alleged economies in production.[49] And as one last example, an agreement among steel manufacturers and scrap dealers stabilizing scrap prices was authorized because of its presumed effect in reducing the price of finished steel.[50]

Several of the price-fixing agreements approved by the British Restrictive Practices Court would never have survived an American antitrust challenge. Some of the Court's permissive decisions have been sharply criticized for defective economic reasoning; and commentators have argued that the benefits claimed were dubious at best, so that a *per se* prohibition against all price-fixing arrangements would have caused no serious social losses while saving substantial legal costs.[51] The Court's procedures, too, have been criticized as inefficient, slow and unnecessarily expensive, with too much duplication of testimony, failure to define issues clearly, and boring cross-examination.[52] A major lacuna is the lack of subpoena and grand jury powers to detect the apparently numerous informal agreements driven underground by the law's registration mandates.[53] Still the British have tried harder than most nations to implement an ambitious procompetitive policy without shutting the door on restrictions that might conceivably yield net social benefits. And the special adjudication procedures devised to deal with restrictive practices, making it possible to record all the evidence and arguments for a case in from 6 to 35 hearing days, are clearly more efficient than comparable U.S. procedures.

We turn now much more briefly to the laws in several other jurisdictions. The Canadian antitrust code dating back to 1889 has from the beginning included provisions authorizing criminal penalties (i.e., fines and/or imprisonment) for any one who "conspires, combines, agrees or arranges with another person . . . to prevent, limit or lessen, unduly, the manufacture or production of a product, or to enhance unreasonably the price thereof." The words "unduly" and "unreasonably" suggest an expanded rule of reason approach. But in leading cases the courts held that the public has a vested interest in the maintenance of competition and that every agreement which "materially interferes with competition in a substantial sector of trade" is detrimental to the public interest.[54] This comes close to the U.S. philosophy. Amendments effective in 1976 stipulated that proof of violation does not require a showing that complete or virtual elimination of competition is likely, and bid-rigging agreements were singled out as per se illegal.[55] At the same time antitrust coverage was extended to services as well as goods; and civil remedies such as injunctions, the reduction of tariffs on offending products, and suits for damages were made available as substitutes for, or complements to, criminal sanctions. Public support for invigorated antitrust measures was evident in the extended debates preceding enactment of the 1976 amendments, and it seems likely that relatively tough-minded enforcement will replace the loophole-strewn record of earlier decades.

The original West German antitrust statute, passed in 1957, generally outlawed price-fixing agreements but permitted exceptions to ease the adjustment problems of secularly stagnating industries; to reduce costs through joint research and development, marketing, or production specialization arrangements; to promote exports or facilitate imports; and to cope with "exceptional circumstances" in the economic situation. In 1973 the law was amended to exempt agreements promoting the efficiency of small and medium-sized firms (e.g., with a combined market share of less than 15 percent).[56] Other amendments at the same time made clear that in nonexempt areas, "concerted actions" as well as restrictive agreements of a contractual nature were prohibited. Enforcement of the law was initially inhibited by divisions of opinion within the government concerning the efficacy of antitrust and resulting stringencies in the Federal Cartel Office's

(42) In re Yarn Spinners' Agreement, L. R., 1 R. P. 118 (1959). Shortly after the decision, the Conservative government passed a law providing compensation for yarn spinning firms required to close down plants because of price competition. There was also a wave of horizontal and vertical mergers among textile makers.

43. In re Water-Tube Boilermakers' Agreement, L. R., 1 R. P. 285 (1959).

44. In re Black Bolt and Nut Association's Agreement, L. R., 2 R. P. 50 (1960).

45. In re Cement Makers' Federation Agreement, L. R., 2 R. P. 241 (1961). For various critical views, see Arthur Beacham, "Some Thoughts on the Cement Judgment," Economic Journal 72 (June 1962): 335–43; the comment by J. B. Heath and J. R. Gould and reply by Beacham, Economic Journal 73 (June 1963): 350–55; and Alister Sutherland, "Economics in the Restrictive Practices Court," Oxford Economic Papers 17 n.s. (November 1965): 386–98. An executive of one U.K. cement firm told the author in a 1970 interview that the cartel rules introduced so many inflexibilities that it was questionable whether even the cement producers really benefitted from it. Nevertheless, an attempt by the Registrar to overturn the agreement's approval because of changed circumstances was unsuccessful. See Beacham, "Cement Revisited," Bulletin of Economic Research 27 (November 1975): 104–108.

46. Federal Trade Commission v. Cement Institute et al., 333 U.S. 683 (1948).

47. In re Permanent Magnet Association's Agreement, L. R., 3 R. P. 119 and 392 (1962).

48. In re National Sulphuric Acid Association's Agreement, L. R., 4 R. P. 169 (1963).

49. In re Glazed and Floor Tile Home Trade Association's Agreement, L. R., 4 R. P. 239 (1963).

50. In re British Iron and Steel Federation and National Federation of Scrap Iron, Steel, and Metal Merchants' Agreement, L. R., 4 R. P. 299 (1963).

51. See Sutherland, "Economics in the Restrictive Practices Court," pp. 422–23; J. P. Cairns, "Benefits from Restrictive Agreements: The British Experience," Canadian Journal of Economics and Political Science 30 (May 1964): 228–40; and Warren Pengilley, "Comments on Arguments in Justification of Agreements in Restraint of Trade—The United Kingdom, Australian and New Zealand Experience," Antitrust Bulletin 19 (Summer 1974): 257–81.

52. See I. A. MacDonald, "The Restrictive Practices Court: A Lawyer's View," Oxford Economic Papers 17 n.s. (November 1965): 372–75.

53. See Swann et al., Competition in British Industry, pp. 85–87, 169–70, 199–200.

54. See the Organisation for Economic Cooperation and Development compendium, Guide to Legislation on Restrictive Business Practices in Europe and North America, 2nd ed. (Paris: OECD, 1962), Canada, "Explanatory Notes on Legislation," pp. 2–3, and the selection of court decision excerpts in section 3.0.

55. Ministry of Consumer and Corporate Affairs, Proposals for a New Competition Policy for Canada: Second Stage (Ottawa: Consumer and Corporate Affairs Canada, March 1977), pp. 202 (sec. 32. (1.1)) and 207 (sec. 32.2).

56. See Kurt E. Markert, "The New German Antitrust Reform Law," Antitrust Bulletin 19 (Spring 1974): 147–48.

budget. But support for a procompetition policy has grown to the point that, even though numerous expanded rule of reason exceptions have been made, West German antitrust enforcement has probably come to be second only to that of the United States in stringency. Unlike their British counterparts, the German antitrust authorities are armed with abundant subpoena powers so that, for example, their staff was able in September 1971 to burst in upon cement industry executives *in flagrante delicto*—using a slide projector to display sales quotas for upcoming months. Amendments in 1968 authorized fines commensurate with the excess profits gained through violations. Early applications included a fine of DM 5.6 million (later reduced by an appeals court to DM 1.1 million) against two colluding linoleum makers; fines totalling DM 48 million (i.e., roughly $15 million at the time) against nine synthetic fiber producers; and fines of DM 7 million against seven breweries fixing prices in the Dortmund area.

Japan's postwar antitrust laws provide exemptions from price-fixing prohibitions on a number of grounds. They have been used liberally so that, for example, in 1972 there were 9 authorized depression cartels, 10 rationalization cartels, 175 export and 2 import cartels, and 604 small business cartels in existence.[57] How far to go in preventing cartelization has been a question of sustained tension between the Japanese Fair Trade Commission, which is responsible for antitrust enforcement, and the Ministry of International Trade and Industry. Characteristically, the FTC acquiesced in a watered-down policy, but in 1973 it became more assertive, among other things indicting 12 petroleum refiners for price-fixing agreements apparently carried out under MITI's approval and guidance.

France had a law curbing price fixing and other restrictive practices as early as 1791, but it was undermined by 19th century procartel legislation. Ordinances issued following World War II prohibit agreements, express or tacit, that encourage the artificial increase of prices. Exemptions are allowed when producers can show that gains in efficiency or technical progress will be achieved as a by-product. Because there was little enthusiasm in the French government-

business establishment for the systematic promotion of competitive market processes, enforcement was sporadic and lackadaisical.[58] In 1977 the law was amended to provide stronger, more expeditious enforcement. What will come of it remains to be seen.

As a final stop on this Cook's tour of antitrust laws abroad, we consider the policies of a supranational entity, the European Community. Its predecessor, the European Coal and Steel Community, had an article in its 1951 treaty prohibiting restrictive practices that distorted the normal operation of competition. However, the High Authority of ECSC seldom perceived competitive conditions to be "normal," so it stepped in frequently to set minimum and maximum prices, assign output quotas for individual firms, and in other ways to make private price-fixing redundant.[59]

Article 85, Section 1, of the 1957 Treaty of Rome (which established the European Community) prohibits all interfirm agreements that have the effect of preventing, restraining, or distorting competition within the Common Market. Among the offenses explicitly mentioned are agreements fixing prices and restricting output. Section 3 of the same article then provides an escape hatch permitting the exemption of agreements that contribute toward improving the production or distribution of goods or promoting technical progress, as long as consumers receive a fair share of the resulting benefits and competition is not substantially eliminated. Interpretation of this expanded rule of reason was delegated to the EC Commission and the Court of Justice. In 1962 the Commission set up a system for the registration of restrictive agreements and was soon buried under an avalanche of some 37,000 filings (the majority of which covered such vertical restrictions as exclusive dealerships, as contrasted to horizontal agreements).[60] A decade later its staff had still not dealt with all the registrations, but a clear policy had begun to emerge.[61]

A generally tough line was taken toward straightforward price-fixing and market-sharing agreements covering a significant share of Community output, and beginning with a cartel among quinine sellers in 1969, fines of growing severity were imposed upon violators. The Commission has been more tolerant of specialization agreements—e.g., when one firm supplies the combined market demand for certain product variants and yields the market for other variants to rivals—as long as the number of suppliers is not reduced unduly. Specialization agreements among small and medium-sized firms with a combined national market share of 10 percent or less were given block exemptions in a 1972 ruling. And in what appeared to be a significant reversal of position, the Commission concluded in 1977 and 1978 that depressed conditions in the steel, shipbuilding, and synthetic fiber industries warranted the establishment of company-by-company production quotas and various coordinated measures for shutting down excess and obsolete capacity.[62] However, the Commission subsequently withdrew its approval of specific provisions governing the fiber cartel; and at the time this was written, the thrust of the EC's policy toward such cartels was unusually uncertain.[63]

The EC competition policy has evolved out of a continuing ferment, with the French most sympathetic to monopolistic restraints and the West Germans leading the procompetitive forces. In the compromise that prevailed at the end of its second decade, the Community appears to have taken a generally unsympathetic stance toward unvarnished price-fixing cartels of appreciable scope; but it is willing to consider exceptions when a plausible case on efficiency grounds can be argued or when unfettered competition may impose unacceptable pain.

The *per se* vs. rule of reason question revisited

We find then that the United States stands virtually alone in applying a *per se* prohibition against price fixing and related restraints of trade. Being a minority of one is always unsettling. Has the U.S. made the best policy choice, or are there superior alternatives?

Given the complexity of the links between market structure, conduct, and performance, it seems almost certain that there are at least some market conditions under which agreements to fix

"reasonable" prices will permit better economic performance than unfettered competition. Leading candidates include high overhead cost industries subjected to severe random or cyclical business fluctuations, and industries that would be unable to cooperate in desirable cost-saving programs without some mitigation of price competition. The key question is not whether such cases exist, but how frequently they occur and whether the social benefits realizable through a policy that seeks to allow restrictive agreements only in those cases exceed the social costs of the policy. Obviously, we have no good quantitative estimates of either benefits or costs; we must resort to rough intuitive judgments. The author's personal assessment, based upon a detailed study of 12 industries in six nations[64] and reading the standard works on such "cutthroat competition" industries as railroading before 1887 and soft coal mining, is that the social gains from permitting restrictive agreements on a selective basis would be quite modest. Or to put the point negatively, sharp price competition does not

57. Richard E. Caves and Masu Uekusa, *Industrial Organization in Japan* (Washington, D.C.: Brookings Institution, 1976), pp. 141–48.

58. See B. Clement, "An Appraisal of French Antitrust Policy," *Antitrust Bulletin* 19 (Fall 1974): 587–603; and Frederic Jenny and Andre Paul Weber, "French Antitrust Legislation: An Exercise in Futility?," *Antitrust Bulletin* 20 (Fall 1975): 597–639.

59. See Corwin D. Edwards, *Cartelization in Western Europe* (Washington, D.C.: U.S., Department of State, 1964), pp. 61–82; and Klaus Stegemann, *Price Competition and Output Adjustment in the European Steel Market* (Tübingen: Mohr, 1977), pp. 4–11, 239–89.

60. See "Judging the Nine by the Companies They Keep," *The Economist*, 20 January 1973, p. 57.

61. For a survey, see Alexis P. Jacquemin and Henry W. de Jong, *European Industrial Organisation* (London: Macmillan, 1977), pp. 206–27. For details, see the Community's *First Report on Competition Policy* (Brussels: EEC Office for Official Publications, April 1972) and subsequent annual reports.

62. See "The Common Market's Rush into Cartels," *Business Week*, 27 March 1978, p. 107; "Competition Within the EC," *Business Week*, 15 May 1978, p. 4; and "The European Fibers Cartel," *New York Times*, 17 May 1978, p. D-5.

63. "Cartel To Cut Excess Fiber Output Held Illegal by Common Market Body," *New York Times*, 10 November 1978, p. D-9.

64. F. M. Scherer, Alan Beckenstein, Erich Kaufer, and R. D. Murphy, *The Economics of Multi-Plant Operation: An International Comparisons Study* (Cambridge, Mass.: Harvard University Press, 1975).

Antitrust policy: price-fixing agreements   509

seem to have impaired performance appreciably; and the chief rationale for assertions to the contrary appears to be the natural propensity for those whose oxen are gored to raise the loudest, most persuasive possible cries of distress. It is also doubtful whether the gains from full-blown "rationalization" cartels would be large, for vigorous competition is often as effective an inducement to production specialization as cartelization; and if pooling indivisible resources or cooperating in research and development is genuinely advantageous, it is usually worth doing without the additional encumbrance of price-fixing or market-sharing agreements. The need for cartelized cooperation is especially small in a market as vast as the United States, where the conflict between scale economies and competition is seldom acute.[65]

Let us nevertheless grant for the sake of argument that the benefits of a selective restriction policy would be finite and positive. If the expanded rule of reason approach required to implement this policy were itself costless, it should be adopted. But it is not costless. There are definite costs in the form of added uncertainty, more complex adjudication, and an enhanced probability of irrational and erroneous choices.

A relatively unimportant cost would be the increased uncertainty business firms would face as to which agreements are illegal. At least in borderline areas, it would be impossible to proceed with confidence until the enforcement agencies or judiciary has rendered an opinion. This is not a serious problem, however, for companies could always avoid legal uncertainty by refraining from brinkmanship. In so doing, they would be no worse off than under a *per se* rule prohibiting all clear-cut restrictions.

Much more impressive would be the costs of adjudicating and enforcing the policy, for each case would become, in the jargon of the antitrust law firms and economic consultants who would be its principal financial beneficiaries, "the big case." Even with relatively simple *per se* rules, elaborate proceedings are often needed merely to establish whether or not a prohibited act was perpetrated. An expanded rule of reason case would surely have to go further, examining economic and social variables connected with the agreement in question and perhaps analyzing both past industry performance and projecting future trends to reach a balanced judgment on the agreement's reasonableness. A thorough investigation of this sort conducted under traditional antitrust procedures would be so costly in terms of money and, more important, high-level talent that the enforcement agencies would find the number of cases they could initiate sharply limited. As Professor Mason has argued, "The demand for a full investigation of the consequences of a market situation or a course of business conduct is a demand for nonenforcement of the antitrust laws."[66]

If approval of price-fixing arrangements were made contingent upon the reasonableness of the prices fixed, the antitrust agencies would run squarely into the dilemma perceived by the Supreme Court in its *Trenton Potteries* opinion: "The reasonable price fixed today may through economic and business changes become the unreasonable price of tomorrow."[67] To place upon the enforcement agencies and courts "the burden of ascertaining from day to day whether [the price] has become unreasonable through the mere variation of economic conditions"[68] would be exorbitantly costly, and it might well break the back of an already bowed and groaning camel.

Yet these problems are in part only symptoms of a more fundamental deficiency: the unsuitability of the U.S. judicial process for making balanced judgments on issues as technical and complex as the reasonableness of a price-fixing scheme. This is in turn the consequence of several specific peculiarities and flaws. First, the rules of evidence applied in antitrust cases are cumbersome in the extreme. If delay is deemed advantageous, as it often is, counsel can stretch out proceedings to prodigious lengths by challenging the authenticity and materiality of each document and nit-picking the testimony of expert witnesses. Company witnesses called by the government are frequently well coached by their lawyers in techniques for "stonewalling" substantive discovery. Second, jurists are seldom trained in economics, and many lack the knowledge to separate sense from nonsense in the contending parties' briefs or to get a firm analytic handle on the conduct and performance variables at issue. The brightest judges do amazingly well, but the middle ranks turn in performances that could merit no more than a low C on an undergraduate theory examination. Third, the whole adversary process on which the courts operate was designed and is best suited for reaching "either-or" decisions: Is the defendant guilty, or not? It is much less effective in ascertaining, say, how much competition is optimal out of a continuous spectrum of possibilities.[69] Nor is it well suited for weighing many conflicting considerations to reach a decision that, say, on balance, it appears X best serves the public interest. Indeed, the facts and arguments in antitrust cases are often so complex that they swamp a judge's ability to comprehend and integrate them logically. He or she may then arrive at a decision on the basis of raw instinct, working backward from that point to develop a line of reasoning which, however strained, supports the predetermined conclusion. It is for this reason, Professor Bok suggests, that one frequently encounters antitrust decisions that hold *all* the arguments in a case to support the conclusion taken, though industrial conduct problems are seldom so simple.[70] Decisions reached in this manner by overtaxed jurists will almost surely be erroneous a significant fraction of the time. And those decisions approving a restrictive agreement when it is, if an accurate balance were to be struck, socially undesirable, constitute an additional cost of the expanded rule of reason approach.

Difficult though the task may be, costs and benefits must be assessed in formulating rational public policies. The author's opinion, shared by most American economists concerned with antitrust policy, is that in the present legal framework the costs of implementing an expanded rule of reason would exceed the benefits derived from considering each restrictive agreement on its merits and prohibiting only those that appear unreasonable.

Nevertheless, the art of policy design calls for more than merely comparing well-known possibilities in the context of existing institutions. It is equally important to try inventing new, dominant alternatives. Three main alternatives to the conventional dichotomy can be identified.

For one, Almarin Phillips has proposed that the antitrust authorities concern themselves not with whether prices are fixed at reasonable levels—the approach rejected in *Trenton Potteries*, *Socony-Vacuum*, and other decisions—but with whether the organizational characteristics of an industry are such that price fixing would improve economic performance.[71] This approach would require the courts to examine industry structure and conduct, as they relate to performance, but not to exercise continuing surveillance over prices charged and profits realized. On purely logical grounds the Phillips proposal is appealing. But it would demand far more economic sophistication from jurists than even an expanded rule of reason, for they would be required to *predict* the efficacy of performance from observed structural and conduct variables. Even if the theoretical knowledge required to specify all relevant structure-conduct-performance links were available—and it is clear we have not yet reached that utopian state—it is doubtful whether the judiciary, as presently constituted, could exercise the requisite skill in applying those tools.

A second proposal is credited to Professor S. Chesterfield Oppenheim. He has suggested that instead of holding price-fixing agreements *per se* illegal, they be considered *prima facie* illegal. In order to escape censure, price fixers would then

65. Scherer et al., *The Economics of Multi-Plant Operation*, pp. 388–92. On the utility of specialization agreements in a much smaller economy such as Canada, see Klaus Stegemann, "The Exemption of Specialization Agreements: As Proposed for Stage II Amendments to the Combines Investigation Act," *Canadian Public Policy* 3 (Autumn 1977): 533–45.

66. Edward S. Mason, *Economic Concentration and the Monopoly Problem* (Cambridge, Mass.: Harvard University Press, 1957), p. 398. He goes on to concede that many rule of reason cases might not have to be quite so thorough.

67. *U.S.* v. *Trenton Potteries Co. et al.*, 273 U.S. 392, 397 (1927).

68. 273 U.S. 392, 398.

69. For a superb discussion of this problem, see Derek C. Bok, "Section 7 of the Clayton Act and the Merging of Law and Economics," *Harvard Law Review* 74 (December 1960): 291–99.

70. Bok, "Section 7," p. 270.

71. Phillips, *Market Structure, Organization and Performance*, pp. 235–40.

bear the burden of proving that their agreements do not constitute an unreasonable restraint of trade.[72] This approach has the merit of forcing the parties with the closest knowledge of internal industry workings to carry forward most of the positive economic analysis. If there is information that might vindicate their conduct, the members of an industry are in a position to supply it. Conversely, it is much more difficult for a government enforcement agency to obtain evidence needed to prove an agreement's unreasonableness. Yet despite its advantages from an enforcement standpoint, a *prima facie* rule does not solve the problem of continuing surveillance, nor does it overcome the judiciary's inability to deal analytically with the evidence, once it has been assembled.

A third alternative, which could be integrated with either the Phillips or Oppenheim proposals, is to reform the judicial system, perhaps along lines similar to the British Restrictive Practices Court. A special antitrust court would be established with streamlined procedures, rules of evidence suitable to economic investigations, and a membership that includes judges competent in economics, qualified laypeople, or both. The procedures would be designed to get to the heart of the economic issues without tedious quibbling over the admissibility of evidence, argumentative and evidentiary shotgun blasts aimed at covering all conceivable allegations and defenses, and so forth. One approach, suggested by N. H. Leyland as a means of expediting British restrictive practices cases, would be to have a panel of experts representing the contending parties prepare a common document that defines the issues, advances and criticizes the arguments and counterarguments, and analyzes relevant factual and statistical evidence, going as far as possible toward the point where an intelligent decision on the disputed matters can be rendered.[73] Even without this last feature, impressive gains in adjudicative efficiency might be achieved by streamlining procedures. As an admittedly extreme example, the trial record in the Federal Trade Commission case charging illegal price fixing by cement manufacturers required three years of hearings to compile and ran to some 49,000 pages of testimony plus 50,000 pages of exhibits.[74] The case dragged on for 11 years between the filing of a complaint in 1937 and resolution by the Supreme Court in 1948. A similar case involving the British cement industry was dispatched after 16 days of hearings before the Restrictive Practices Court. The lag between initial complaint and final judgment was just three and one half years.[75]

To be sure, some sacrifices have to be accepted to reduce the cost of implementing a rule of reason, conventional or expanded. As noted earlier, it is apparent from the record of the British Restrictive Practices Court that cold economic logic does not always carry the day. But the incidence of mistakes is probably not any higher than it would be under more thorough yet cumbersome (and hence confusing) procedures. More important, the British Restrictive Practices procedures sacrifice certain safeguards by abandoning traditional rules of evidence and by placing strict limits on what can be appealed to higher courts. To make the system work efficiently, a substantial amount of discretion is allowed the court of primary jurisdiction. A rule of men is to some extent substituted for the more plodding rule of law. It is here that U.S. traditions depart most strongly from those dominating European antitrust.

The difference between nations is summarized perceptively by A. D. Neale, a British observer, in his treatise on American antitrust laws:

> One of the profoundest institutional differences between the two countries is the absence in the United States of anything corresponding to the amorphous but recognizable assemblage of public bodies and personages that we know in Britain as 'the Establishment'; and this has much to do, both as cause and effect, with American distrust of authority *per se*. In general the possession of power by established authorities arouses a much lesser degree of anxiety or resentment in Britain, where the emphasis is much more on the use of power. Whereas American institutions often appear to be designed to hamper the exercise of power, ours are designed on the whole to facilitate it, though great importance is attached to protecting minorities against its abuse. . . . It is in line with the same general

attitude to power that, if regulation is required, British opinion tends to be more open-minded than American about the choice between judicial enforcement of rules of law and some form of administrative supervision. . . . In the United States administrative decisions (the "government of men") tend to be unpopular as such, and the search is always for a "government of laws." In Britain the choice is more open.[76]

A similar but more complex historical view of the differences in antitrust attitudes on the European Continent is presented by Corwin Edwards:

Whereas American political institutions were formulated after overthrowing colonial status, under the influence of a philosophy that distrusted concentrated governmental power, and in a setting affected by the individualism of the frontier, European political institutions have evolved gradually from origins of monarchy in the state and hierarchy in the church. . . . The European libertarian movements that expressed distrust of state power and sought to curtail state functions found their program in guarantees of freedom of contract and freedom of association. . . . But as the market economy developed, free association came to mean that businessmen were free to form cartels, and free contract came to include the right to make agreements by which the parties impaired free trade and free competition. Thus the programs that challenged the power of the state tended to strengthen rather than to challenge the power of cartels. It is understandable that as programs to curb cartels developed they tended to accept and rely upon a broad exercise of the regulatory power of the state as a major instrument of control. [These] inherited attitudes . . . have resulted in cartel laws which characteristically grant broad discretion to public officials to amend cartel practices in accord with their own views of the public interest.[77]

The reluctance of the American Congress to discard its cumbersome judicial approach to antitrust problems is undoubtedly the result of a more fundamental unwillingness to place great discretionary power in the hands of a few officials whose decisions are not controlled by rules of law and judicial review. And because the rule of law is cumbersome, a rule of reason approach to price-fixing cases shows up unfavorably in benefit/cost analyses. The policy debate between *per se* rules and the rule of reason turns, therefore, on important questions of political as well as economic philosophy. On such political issues the economist has no special license to prescribe the "correct" public policy.

Oligopoly pricing and the conscious parallelism doctrine

American law on express agreements to fix prices and restrict output is crystal clear: They are illegal *per se*. But what if no definite proof of meetings, discussions, and agreements can be established? What if there is in fact no explicit agreement among rivals in the strict sense of the word, but only an implicitly accepted policy of cooperating to avoid price competition?

Collusion without outright agreement is not very likely when market concentration is low, for sellers producing only a small fraction of a standardized item's total output have strong incentives to secure additional orders by undercutting the established price whenever that price significantly exceeds marginal cost. This must sooner or later pull prices down to the competi-

---

72. S. Chesterfield Oppenheim, "Federal Antitrust Legislation: Guideposts to a Revised National Antitrust Policy," *Michigan Law Review* 50 (June 1952): 1158–61.

73. N. H. Leyland, "Competition in the Court," *Oxford Economic Papers* 17 n.s. (November 1965): 465. See also Posner, *Antitrust Law*, pp. 232–36.

74. *Federal Trade Commission v. Cement Institute et al.*, 333 U.S. 683, 687 (1948).

75. *In re Cement Makers' Federation Agreement*, L. R., 2 R. P. 241 (1961).

76. Neale, *The Antitrust Laws of the United States*, pp. 475–76.

77. Edwards, *Cartelization in Western Europe*, pp. 46–47.

tive level. The only effective way to eliminate such undercutting is to impose penalties upon price cutters, and this is hardly possible without some kind of formal agreement. But in oligopoly the incentives are different. When the number of sellers is small, each firm recognizes that aggressive actions such as price cutting will induce counteractions from rivals which, in the end, leave all members of the industry worse off. All may therefore exercise mutual restraint and prevent prices from falling to the competitive level. And they can do this independently, in the sense that each firm makes its own price and output decisions without consulting the others in a smoke-filled room. Although product heterogeneity, financial pressures during a slump, opportunities for secret price cutting, low entry barriers, and plain human cantankerousness may prevent oligopolists from playing the Chamberlinian joint profit maximization game with complete success, it is clear that collusion without formal agreement is both feasible and tempting in many oligopolistically structured industries. Its status under the antitrust laws is therefore an important issue.

The relevant principle is the so-called *conscious parallelism* doctrine, whose implications are best discovered by analyzing the key decisions through which it evolved.[78] To keep what is a messy development in clearer perspective, it must be pointed out immediately that the doctrine has at various times been related to two rather different problems: first, with the behavioral problem of oligopolists acting noncompetitively; and second, with the evidentiary problem of proving illegal collusion where only circumstantial evidence, and not hard direct evidence, can be offered.

In the earliest applicable cases, the emphasis was on evidentiary matters. One of the first involved a retail lumber dealers' trade association that published a list of wholesalers who sold at retail (and hence competed with members of the association).[79] Once the list was issued, many retail dealers ceased purchasing from those wholesalers. The Justice Department, charging the retailers with an illegal conspiracy, could produce no evidence of an explicit agreement to boycott the blacklisted wholesalers. Nevertheless, the Supreme Court upheld the charge, observing,

[I]t is said that in order to show a combination or conspiracy within the Sherman Act some agreement must be shown under which the concerted action is taken. It is elementary, however, that conspiracies are seldom capable of proof by direct testimony and may be inferred from the things actually done, and when in this case, by concerted action the names of wholesalers . . . were periodically reported to the other members of the associations, the conspiracy to accomplish that which was the natural consequence of such action may be readily inferred.[80]

A reiteration and modest extension occurred in another boycott case 25 years later.[81] The manager of the Interstate Circuit and another motion picture exhibition chain with a large share of the Texas market wrote identical letters to eight motion picture distributors (e.g., Paramount, Metro-Goldwyn-Mayer, and RKO), each letter naming all eight distributors, and each demanding that the distributors not release their first-run films to theaters competitive with Interstate charging less than 25 cents admission or using the films in double features. Interstate's motive was obviously to reduce competition with its own theaters. The eight distributors could also benefit by realizing higher exhibition fees as long as all eight adhered to the Interstate plan. After the letter was sent out, independent low-price exhibitors in fact found it impossible to secure first-run films, and many reacted by raising their prices to the 25-cent minimum. When a district court ordered an end to the boycott, the defendants appealed to the Supreme Court, arguing *inter alia* that no evidence was presented to show an agreement or conspiracy among the eight distributors. The Supreme Court rejected the appeal, noting the "singular unanimity of action on the part of the distributors" in carrying out the proposed restraint:

It taxes credulity to believe that the several distributors would . . . have accepted and put into operation with substantial unanimity such far-reaching changes in their business methods without some understanding that all were to join, and we reject as beyond the range of probability that it was the result of mere chance.[82]

As proof of illegal conspiracy, the Court said,

> It was enough that, knowing that concerted action was contemplated and invited, the distributors gave their adherence to the scheme and participated in it.[83]

Thus, the distributors (along with the two exhibition chains) were found to have violated Sherman Act Section 1 without proof of express agreement, and without even initiating the message that brought about their behavioral change. Yet it is important to see that in both this and the lumber dealers' case, there was an overt act (the publication of a blacklist or the receipt of a letter) to which the restraint of trade could be traced.

This requisite seemed to disappear in the 1946 *Tobacco* decision, which was said by one observer to constitute "a legal milestone in the social control of oligopoly" by "permitting the inference of illegal conspiracy from detailed similarity of behavior" and nothing more.[84] To recapitulate the well-known facts briefly, the Big Three of the cigarette industry—American Tobacco, Reynolds, and Liggett & Myers—for two decades manifested a pattern of strikingly parallel pricing. Especially noteworthy were the prompt matching of Reynolds's price increase in June 1931, in the depths of the depression, when tobacco leaf prices and labor costs were falling, and the sharp concerted price cuts effected 18 months later to recapture the ground gained by smaller rivals after the 1931 action permitted "ten cent" brands to sell at an attractive price differential. In addition, the Big Three brought pressure to bear on retailers to ensure that their products sold at the same price; they declined to participate in leaf tobacco auctions unless buyers from all three were present; they conducted their bidding so that all ended up paying the same price per pound; and each refrained from buying tobacco grades in which the others had a special interest. Although some suspicious incidents came to light,[85] the Justice Department was unable to present any concrete evidence of meetings, messages, or explicit agreements among members of the Big Three. The evidence was entirely circumstantial, centering on the parallelism in pricing and purchasing behavior. Nevertheless, a jury found the defendants guilty of price fixing and other Sherman Act violations; and in reviewing the case, the Sixth Circuit Court of Appeals found the purely circumstantial evidence sufficient to sustain the criminal charges.[86] On appeal, the Supreme Court declined to review the Appellate Court's decision on the price-fixing count, thereby approving it implicitly. It also issued a more general pronouncement on the problem of proving guilt in Sherman Act conspiracy cases:

> No formal agreement is necessary to constitute an unlawful conspiracy. Often crimes are a matter of inference deduced from the acts of the person accused and done in pursuance of a criminal purpose. . . . The essential combination or conspiracy in violation of the Sherman Act may be found in a course of dealings or other circumstances as well as in an exchange of words. . . . Where the circumstances are such as to warrant a jury in finding that the conspirators had a unity of purpose or a common design and understanding, or a meeting of minds in an unlawful ar-

78. For analyses of additional cases, see Phillips, *Market Structure, Organization and Performance*, pp. 47–73; Neale, *The Antitrust Laws of the United States*, pp. 81–94; Richard Posner, "Oligopoly and the Antitrust Laws: A Suggested Approach," *Stanford Law Review* 21 (June 1969): 1562–1606; and Stephen Nye, "Can Conduct-Oriented Enforcement Inhibit Conscious Parallelism?," *Antitrust Law Journal* 44, No. 2 (1975): 206–30.

79. *Eastern States Retail Lumber Dealers' Association* v. *U.S.*, 234 U.S. 600 (1914).

80. 234 U.S. 600, 612 (1914).

81. *Interstate Circuit, Inc., et al.* v. *U.S.*, 306 U.S. 208 (1939).

82. 306 U.S. 208, 223 (1939).

83. 306 U.S. 208, 226 (1939).

84. William H. Nicholls, "The Tobacco Case of 1946," *American Economic Review* 39 (May 1949): 296.

85. On the circumstantial evidence that all three had advance notice of the February 1933 price cut, see note 39, Chapter 6, p. 179 *supra*.

86. *American Tobacco Co. et al.* v. *U.S.*, 147 F. 2d 93 (1944).

rangement, the conclusion that a conspiracy is established is justified.[87]

The *Tobacco* decision was viewed by many antitrust aficionados as a dramatic new precedent bringing, as Nicholls speculated, "wholly tacit, nonaggressive oligopoly fully within the reach of the conspiracy provisions of the Sherman Act."[88] From a more distant perspective, it appears that the courts were not going quite as far as Nicholls believed, but were only extending the possibilities of finding guilt on the basis of circumstantial evidence where there was good reason to believe that outright collusion occurred. It is likely also that the *Tobacco* decision implicitly applied a rule of reason to oligopoly behavior: The firms were found guilty despite weak evidence because their conduct during the 1930s was so flagrantly inconsistent with economic conditions at the time.[89]

Were the law against tacitly collusive oligopoly pricing to follow as strict a line as many persons saw in the *Tobacco* decision, a dilemma would arise. How should oligopolists change their behavior so as to avoid breaking the law? Must they begin ignoring their interdependence in pricing decisions, when to do so would be irrational? As Liggett & Myers attorneys asked rhetorically in their brief before the Court of Appeals, "Is everything the appellants do illegal, or evidence of illegality, if done by more than one of them?" When restraint in pricing is the natural consequence of high concentration, legal injunctions against such behavior are virtually impossible to enforce. To be effective, the remedy may have to deal with the basic cause—market structure—and not just with its behavioral symptoms. The dilemma is a real one, but we must leave it unresolved until we address other aspects of antitrust policy in the next chapter. It suffices here to note that after fines totalling $255,000 were levied upon the tobacco firms and their executives, there was little observable change in their conduct.

Following the *Tobacco* case, additional decisions involving the cement and steel industries carried the conscious parallelism doctrine further, outlawing adherence by mutual tacit consent to a *common system* of pricing—the basing point system.[90] The problem in both cases was characterized succinctly in the Court of Appeals' rigid steel conduit decision:

> [E]ach conduit seller knows that each of the other sellers is using the basing point formula; each knows that by using it he will be able to quote identical delivered prices and thus present a condition of matched prices under which purchasers are isolated and deprived of choice among sellers so far as price advantage is concerned. . . . Each seller . . . in effect invites the others to share the available business at matched prices in his natural market in return for a reciprocal invitation.[91]

And this, the court said, was a violation of Federal Trade Commission Act Section 5, which had been stretched in the prior *Cement Institute* decision to cover combinations in restraint of trade as unfair methods of competition. In a subsequent staff memorandum, the Federal Trade Commission pointedly expressed its belief that parallel pricing had become fair game for attack:

> [W]hen a number of enterprises follow a parallel course of action in the knowledge and contemplation of the fact that all are acting alike they have, in effect, formed an agreement. . . . The obvious fact [is] that the economic effect of identical prices achieved through conscious parallel action is the same as that of similar prices achieved through overt collusion, and, for this reason, the Commission treated the conscious parallelism of action as a violation of the Federal Trade Commission Act.[92]

As events transpired, 1948 proved to be a high-water mark in the legal construction of conscious parallelism. Erosion took place in still another boycott case.[93] Nine film distributors all refused to grant first-run status to a new theater in a suburban Baltimore shopping center, giving preference instead to established downtown theaters, three of which were owned by distributors. No evidence was adduced to prove express agreement among the distributors. Judgment was rendered for the distributors in a jury trial. In its sustaining decision, the Supreme Court found that the distributors' decisions to deny first-run status could have been taken independently and based upon "individual business judgment motivated by the desire for maximum revenue"[94]—e.g., because of the suburban theater's inadequate drawing power, the paucity of its newspaper display advertising compared to downtown theaters, and the fact that giving it first-run status would adversely affect rentals to existing customers. The Court went on to administer a rude jolt to those who had construed its *Tobacco* decision broadly:

> The crucial question is whether respondents' conduct toward petitioner stemmed from independent decision or from an agreement, tacit or express. To be sure, business behavior is admissible circumstantial evidence from which the fact finder may infer agreement. . . . But this Court has never held that proof of parallel business behavior conclusively establishes agreement or, phrased differently, that such behavior itself constitutes a Sherman Act offense. Circumstantial evidence of consciously parallel behavior may have made heavy inroads into the traditional judicial attitude toward conspiracy; but 'conscious parallelism' has not yet read conspiracy out of the Sherman Act entirely.[95]

Additional setbacks came in two drug industry cases. In 1954, the National Foundation for Infantile Paralysis licensed six pharmaceutical firms to produce the Salk polio vaccine.[96] During a two-and-one-half-year period beginning in March of 1955, there were only two significant price changes. Each was matched promptly, with virtual identity of price quotations prevailing in the sealed bids submitted to state and local government purchasing offices at almost all times. There was no direct evidence of price-fixing agreements, but the Justice Department alleged that there was "a continuing agreement, understanding, plan and concert of action" to "submit uniform price quotations" and to "adopt uniform and noncompetitive terms and conditions" on sales to public authorities. After the government had presented its case, defense attorney (and former presidential nominee) Thomas E. Dewey made an eloquent plea for acquittal. The court accepted his motion and dismissed the case. It held

that a reasonable alternative hypothesis existed for explaining the defendants' pricing behavior on the basis of "independent business considerations only." Notably, the firms had accepted "most favored customer" clauses in their contracts with government agencies, requiring them in effect to reduce the price of vaccine to all customers if they reduced it for one. This disincentive to price cutting was deemed sufficient to cause the observed price identity and stability without collusion.

A further test of the conscious parallelism doctrine came in a second major drug industry case—one of the most closely contested actions in antitrust history. The facts are complex. Essentially, however, there were two main charges: that the defendants (Pfizer, American Cyanamid, and Bristol-Myers) had during the mid-1950s settled conflicting claims over rights to the tetracycline antibiotic patent by entering a cross-licensing agreement with the explicit or implicit understanding that further entry into the field would be restricted; and that from 1953 to 1961 the three defendants plus two licensees conspired to fix identical and noncompetitive prices. No direct

87. *American Tobacco Co. et al.* v. *U.S.*, 328 U.S. 781, 809–810 (1946).

88. "The Tobacco Case of 1946," p. 285.

89. *American Tobacco Co. et al.* v. *U.S.*, 147 F. 2d 93, 103.

90. *Federal Trade Commission* v. *Cement Institute et al.*, 333 U.S. 683, 712–721 (1948); and *Triangle Conduit and Cable Co. et al.* v. *Federal Trade Commission*, 168 F. 2d 175 (1948).

91. 168 F. 2d 175, 181 (1948). The appellate court's decision was upheld only by a 4-4 tie vote in the Supreme Court. 336 U.S. 956 (1949).

92. "Notice to the Staff: In Re: Commission Policy Toward Geographic Pricing Practices," October 1948, cited in U.S., Department of Justice, *Report of the Attorney General's National Committee To Study the Antitrust Laws* (Washington, D.C.: Government Printing Office, 1955), p. 38.

93. *Theatre Enterprises, Inc.* v. *Paramount Film Distributing Corp. et al.*, 346 U.S. 537 (1954). See also *Peveley Dairy Co.* v. *U.S.*, 178 F. 2d 363 (1949), cert. den. 339 U.S. 942 (1950), in which two St. Louis dairies pursuing parallel pricing policies were found innocent of criminal conspiracy, since the Circuit Court of Appeals was convinced that their behavior could be explained as the result of uniform changes in fluid milk and labor input costs.

94. 346 U.S. 537, 542.

95. 346 U.S. 537, 540–541.

96. *U.S.* v. *Eli Lilly & Co. et al.*, CCH 1959 Trade Cases, para. 69, 536.

evidence of illegal agreements was produced, and on the witness stand company executives vehemently denied any wrongdoing. However, contemporary memoranda revealed American Cyanamid's keen awareness and concern that failure to settle their patent dispute might encourage a flood of new competitive entry, with adverse effects on price. The government also showed that prices were stabilized for several years at $30.60 per bottle of 100 capsules to druggists and $19.1884 per bottle to the Veterans Administration, despite unit production costs of only $3.00 per bottle. In his instructions to the jury, District Judge Frankel observed that the evidence was entirely circumstantial, and that:

> whether the prosecution has sustained its burden of proving a conspiracy must frequently be judged by what the jury finds the parties actually did rather than from the words they used. The unlawful agreement may be shown if the proof establishes a concert of action, with all the parties working together understandingly with a single design for the accomplishment of a common purpose. . . . It is not sufficient to show that the parties acted uniformly or similarly or in ways that may seem to have been mutually beneficial. If such actions were taken independently as a matter of individual business judgment, without any agreement or arrangement or understanding among the parties, then there would be no conspiracy.[97]

A key point of contention was the large disparity between prices and production costs. Judge Frankel repeatedly cautioned the jury that the reasonableness or unreasonableness of prices charged was irrelevant in a direct sense. But it was relevant indirectly as part of the circumstantial evidence:

> I think you will find it helpful to translate the word "unreasonable" to mean "unusual" or "artificial" or "extraordinary." By these suggested definitions I am trying to convey the thought that the idea of unreasonableness in the present context is meaningful only if it is understood to refer to kinds of price behavior or price levels which appear to be divorced from variations and differences in available supply or demand or cost or other economic factors that may normally be expected to cause variations or changes in the prices charged in a competitive market. To put the thought in another and slightly shorter way, the charge of unreasonableness in this case is material only insofar as it poses the issue whether the prices involved exhibited qualities or peculiarities of a type that could be deemed evidence that such prices resulted from agreement rather than from competition. . . . Unreasonably or extraordinarily high prices or profits charged uniformly by competing sellers over a substantial period of time may be evidence, taken with all the other circumstances of the case, supporting an inference that the parties had an agreement rather than a competitive situation with respect to prices.[98]

The jury found the defendants guilty on all counts, and maximum fines were imposed.

On appeal, however, the conviction was reversed and a new trial was ordered in a 2–1 split decision of the reviewing judges.[99] The majority stressed the government's claim in its bill of particulars that a conspiracy came into being at certain patent rights settlement meetings between Pfizer, American Cyanamid, and Bristol-Myers executives. Company witnesses denied under oath that they had reached any agreement to limit entry or fix prices at those meetings. Much of the government's evidence related to pricing, profits, and the disposition of entry-barring patent claims both before and after the meetings; and in his charge to the jury, Judge Frankel had dealt at length with that conduct and performance evidence as well as with the testimonial evidence on what happened at the meetings. Noting that its finding might have been different had the government framed its bill of particulars more broadly, the appellate court majority concluded *inter alia* that in devoting substantial attention to such "inflammatory issues" as patents, pricing, and profits, Judge Frankel had failed to focus the jury's attention on the key issue of what happened at the meetings, and he may indeed have diverted it from that issue.[100] A 2–1 majority of other Second Circuit Court judges denied a petition for rehearing *in banc;* and on further appeal, the reversal was upheld when the Supreme Court divided 3–3 on the merits.[101] The matter was thereupon returned to the district court for retrial. Nearly 6 years after the first trial and 12 years after the indictment had been filed, Judge Cannella ruled in favor of the companies.[102] In a brief opinion looking beyond what had happened at the meetings, he stated that the Justice Department had not conclusively shown Pfizer's decisions to limit the number of tetracycline patent licensees and the firms' parallel pricing to have resulted from conspiracy, since they might alternatively have stemmed from Pfizer's independent business judgment and a natural tendency toward uniform pricing in the highly concentrated, prescription-oriented market for antibiotics.

In view of the apparent mismatch between the government's bill of particulars and the broader, more interesting conduct patterns at issue, it is difficult to say whether the tetracycline decisions represent an even tighter constriction of the conscious parallelism doctrine. It is quite clear that recent decisions have moved far from the mere parallelism of behavior emphasized in cases of the late 1940s. What is not clear is where one draws the line in determining what circumstantial evidence warrants an inference of conspiracy. It seems accurate to say that the accumulated precedents call for "parallelism plus."[103] The key question remains, Of what can the "plus" consist? From the early cases, chain letters and blacklists qualify. A careful reading of the *Tobacco* case facts suggests that when firms have advance knowledge of impending rival actions that could hardly have been gained without covert communications, the necessary plus can be inferred. Other sufficient plus factors might be the mutual adoption of "price protection" plans discouraging price cutting and the publication of books simplifying the computation of uniform bid prices, as General Electric and Westinghouse did following their 1960 conviction for outright collusion in turbogenerator pricing.[104] Less settled is whether tacit conspiracy can be found when there is no circumstantial evidence of meetings or similar communications, but when the conduct

and performance of sellers are strikingly different from what one would expect if the firms were independently seeking to maximize their individual profits.[105]

An important subissue is how much weight the courts should give to extraordinarily high profits as an indication that sellers' actual (but imper-

97. *U.S.* v. *Charles Pfizer & Co., Inc. et al.,* S. D. New York, from pp. 6200–6201 of the trial record. See also the District Court's denial of motions in 281 F. Supp. 837 (1968).

98. From pp. 6270–71 and 6275–76 of the trial record.

99. *Charles Pfizer & Co., Inc. et al.* v. *U.S.,* 426 F. 2d 32 (1970).

100. 426 F. 2d 32, 39–43. A speculative alternative explanation of the court's reversal is that it was strengthening procedural safeguards in the use of circumstantial evidence to infer conspiracy, following apparent abuse of a directly analogous conspiracy doctrine to prosecute Vietnam war opponents. See Herbert L. Packer, "The Conspiracy Weapon," *New York Review of Books,* 6 Nov. 1969, pp. 24–30.

101. 437 F. 2d 957 (1970); 404 U.S. 548 (1972).

102. 367 F. Supp. 91 (1973). Parallel to the criminal proceedings was a Federal Trade Commission action that began in 1958 and ended in 1967 with a finding of illegality on the patent and entry-limiting allegations but not the price-fixing allegations. See 63 F.T.C. 1747 (1963) and 72 F.T.C. 623 (1967). Reversals were again the order of the day; e.g., the first hearing examiner's dismissal was reversed on all counts by the Commission, whose decision in turn was reversed by the Appellate Court and remanded for rehearing. See *American Cyanamid Co. et al.* v. *F.T.C.,* 363 F. 2d 757 (1966).

103. *Naumkeag Theatres Co.* v. *New England Theatres, Inc. et al.,* 345 F. 2d 910, 912 (1965).

104. See Chapter 5, pp. 163–64 and Chapter 6, p. 182 *supra,* citing *U.S.* v. *General Electric Co. et al.,* E. D. Pennsylvania, "Plaintiff's Memorandum in Support of a Proposed Modification to the Final Judgment Entered on October 1, 1962, Against Each Defendant" (December 1976). Because the matter was settled by consent decree, no clear precedent was established. It is worth noting that the turbogenerator price protection plan, although similar in substance and effect to the "most favored customer" clauses in Salk vaccine contracts, is distinguishable in having been instituted at General Electric's initiative, and not in response to customer demands.

105. This seems to have been a critical consideration in the finding by the Court of Justice of the European Communities that ten aniline dye manufacturers had engaged in illegal "concerted pricing practices." Also, the producers regularly discussed forthcoming price changes at meetings. See the text of the opinion, *Imperial Chemical Industries Ltd.* v. *Commission of the European Communities,* in the *Antitrust Bulletin* 18 (Spring 1973): 117–38.

    Amendment of the German antitrust laws in 1973 to include "concerted actions" as a violation was apparently motivated by a judicial decision overturning a similar national action against the dye producers' parallel pricing. See Markert, "The New German Antitrust Reform Law," p. 147.

    On the (absence of a) British policy, see the Monopolies Commission report, *Parallel Pricing* (London: HMSO, July 1973).

fectly observed) conduct is incompatible with the hypothesis of independent competition. Departing from Judge Frankel's position, both the Second Circuit Appellate Court and (on retrial) Judge Canella took a dim view of inferring anything about conduct from the tetracycline profit and price-manufacturing cost margin evidence. However, in its *Tobacco* decision, the Supreme Court referred to the Big Three's "tremendous profits" in 1932 as one component of the circumstantial evidence of conspiracy.[106] And in an opinion delivered only a year after the tetracycline reversal, the Ninth Circuit Court of Appeals, in a case involving the pricing of a herbicide used by rice growers, ruled that:

> [i]t may be true that in a two-seller market of fungible products, the products are likely to be priced at the same levels in any given market, and thus no inference of price fixing could be drawn therefrom. . . . However, evidence that pricing schedules were identical for both products warrants a scrutiny of profit margins. Competition could be inferred from a low profit margin in such a market. Similarly, evidence of high profit margins is probative of the existence of a conspiracy.[107]

Nevertheless, retrial on the profit issue came to naught, for the district court found the problems of ascertaining individual product profitability in multiproduct enterprises to be so complex that introducing such evidence, it believed, would do more to confuse than to clarify the issues.[108] Thus, a definitive test of how profits enter into the conscious parallelism doctrine must await some future case important enough to compel the Supreme Court's attention.

A final grey area concerns the common business practice of cultivating a favorable climate for parallel price increases through statesmanlike laments at trade association meetings or to the trade press that industry profits are unsatisfactory and that relief from cost pressures is badly needed. Executives who make such exhortations are plainly doing so to influence their competitors' attitudes, and those who listen and utter an audible amen are completing a chain of communication that facilitates pricing decisions based upon something more than "independent business considerations only." How one reconciles the plus such "signalling" behavior contributes to conscious parallelism with First Amendment guarantees of free speech is a difficult open issue. In 1978, the Federal Trade Commission initiated a test case alleging price signalling by the four producers of tetraethyl lead anti-knock compounds.[109]

Price leadership

One of the most important institutions facilitating tacitly collusive pricing behavior is the existence of a well-established system of price leadership. The legality of price leadership was considered by the Supreme Court in cases involving United States Steel Corp. and the International Harvester Co. The most succinct statement of the Court's viewpoint is found in its *Harvester* decision:

> [International Harvester] has not . . . attempted to dominate or in fact controlled or dominated the harvesting machinery industry by the compulsory regulation of prices. The most that can be said as to this, is that many of its competitors have been accustomed, independently and as a matter of business expediency, to follow approximately the prices at which it has sold its harvesting machines; but one of its competitors has habitually sold its machines at somewhat higher prices. The law, however, does not make the mere size of a corporation, however impressive, or the existence of unexerted power on its part, an offense, when unaccompanied by unlawful conduct in the exercise of its power. . . . And the fact that competitors may see proper, in the exercise of their own judgment, to follow the prices of another manufacturer, does not establish any suppression of competition or show any sinister domination.[110]

This has continued to be the basic law on price leadership, though other points of the *U.S. Steel* and *Harvester* decisions have since been overturned. Price leadership is not apt to be found contrary to the antitrust laws unless the leader attempts to coerce other producers into following its lead, or unless there is evidence of an agreement among members of the industry to use the leadership device as the basis of a price-fixing scheme. As long as sellers exercise their own independent judgment in choosing to follow the leader, e.g., "because they ma[k]e money by the imitation,"[111] they remain on relatively safe ground.

There is a certain logic in this rule, which avoids making one party's guilt (the price leader's) hang on the autonomous actions of other parties (the followers). Still the rule, in combination with limits written into the conscious parallelism doctrine since 1950, makes it difficult for the antitrust agencies to deal effectively with oligopolists quietly but firmly refraining from price competition. We shall be concerned with this problem further in the next chapter.

Trade association price and cost reporting activities

Trade associations have often performed functions that run afoul of the antitrust laws. Their meetings are superb vehicles for getting together and agreeing on prices, outputs, market shares, and the like. This is *per se* illegal, however difficult it may be to detect, and need not detain us further. But what if the trade association, through its central office staff, merely collects and then distributes to members detailed information on the prices quoted in recent sales transactions, or detailed comparative breakdowns of member production costs?

It might seem paradoxical that there could be anything harmful about information dissemination activities, which at first glance appear only to perfect the market. However, perfect information is unambiguously beneficial only in the context of purely competitive markets. When the market is oligopolistic, it may impair rather than invigorate rivalry. As we have learned in Chapter 7, one important hindrance to collusive oligopoly pricing is secret price shading. If price cuts can be kept secret, a firm may be able to capture additional orders while avoiding the adverse repercussions—retaliatory price cuts—at least for a while. Yet when many sellers begin behaving in this way, *sub rosa* competition can become fierce, and it will be difficult to hold prices at anything approximating monopolistic levels. If, on the other hand, every transaction is publicized immediately, all members of the industry will know when one has made a price cut; and each therefore can retaliate on the next transaction. Knowledge that retaliation will be swift serves as a powerful deterrent to price cutting and therefore facilitates the maintenance of a tacitly collusive price structure.

One of the first persons to recognize this and do something about it was Arthur Jerome Eddy. His solution to the secret price-shading problem, advocated in *The New Competition*,[112] was the formation of "open price associations" that would rapidly supply complete information on all sales transactions to all members of an industry. A few quotations convey the flavor of his approach. On the book's frontispiece is the theme, "Competition Is War, and War Is Hell." The analysis runs along the following lines:

> Of all the rivalries in which man engages, brute competition in the production and distribution of wealth is the most contemptible, since it is the most sordid, a mere money-making proposition, unrelieved by a single higher consideration. . . . Cooperation, whether voluntary or involuntary, . . . is the only regulator of prices. Competition, free and

106. *American Tobacco Co. et al.* v. *U.S.*, 328 U.S. 781 at 805–806.

107. *Estate of LeBaron* v. *Rohm and Haas Co. et al.*, 441 F. 2d 575, 578 (1971).

108. 506 F. 2d 1261 (1974).

109. *In re Ethyl Corp. et al.*, docket no. 9128, complaint filed May 1978. See also "U.S. Seeks Steel Data in Inquiry on Prices," *New York Times*, 14 July 1977, p. 29.

110. *U.S.* v. *International Harvester Co.*, 274 U.S. 693, 708–709 (1927).

111. *U.S.* v. *United States Steel Corp. et al.*, 251 U.S. 417, 447 (1920).

112. A. J. Eddy, *The New Competition*, 1st ed. (Chicago: McClury, 1912). Subsequent references are to the fourth (1917) edition.

unfettered, is absolutely destructive to all stability of prices.[113]

And now the essence of his message:

> The theoretical proposition at the basis of the open price policy is that, Knowledge regarding bids and prices actually made is all that is necessary to keep prices at reasonably stable and normal levels.[114]

Eddy preached his open price gospel widely and persuasively, and soon open price associations became a prominent feature of the American industrial landscape. In 1921, there were at least 150 open price associations in operation, and possibly as many as 450.[115] After a sharp decline during the late 1920s, the movement thrived again under federal government auspices between 1933 and 1935, when 422 industrial "fair competition" codes including open price reporting provisions were approved by the National Recovery Administration.

Eddy was an able corporation lawyer. He designed his open price system to stay within the bounds of antitrust law, as he perceived them at the time. On this he was at least partly successful. The law on trade association price and cost reporting activities is one of the most subtle (and some would add the most confused) branches of antitrust doctrine. The courts have adopted a rule of reason approach, examining each set of industry practices on its merits.[116] Typically the cases cover such a complex admixture of activities that case-by-case comparison breaks down, and on specific practices some of the judicial pronouncements are downright contradictory.

The first test case to reach the Supreme Court was a defeat for advocates of "the new competition."[117] The American Hardwood Manufacturers' Association, whose members produced roughly a third of the nation's hardwood lumber, instituted an open price scheme that required each member firm to submit to a central office price lists, a detailed daily report on all sales and shipments (with copies of each invoice), monthly production and stock reports, and various other documents. The central office in turn forwarded to members weekly reports listing each transaction, the price at which it was made, the buyer, the seller, and so on. Special attention was drawn to list price departures. In addition, meetings were held fre-

quently to discuss market conditions, and at both the meetings and in newsletters the association's Manager of Statistics exhorted members to restrict their output and maintain prices. The Supreme Court, finding the system an illegal conspiracy in restraint of trade, observed in its opinion that:

> [g]enuine competitors do not make daily, weekly, and monthly reports of the minutest details of their business to their rivals, as the defendants did; they do not contract . . . to submit their books to the discretionary audit . . . of their rivals for the purpose of successfully competing with them; and they do not submit the details of their business to the analysis of an expert, jointly employed, and obtain from him a "harmonized" estimate of the market as it is and as, in his specially and confidently informed judgment, it promises to be. This is not the conduct of competitors, but is so clearly that of men united in an agreement, express or implied, to act together and pursue a common purpose under a common guide. . . .[118]

Nevertheless, the seeds of subsequent dilution were sown in dissenting opinions by three members of the Court, including Justice Brandeis's suggestion that the Sherman Act did not require business rivals to compete blindly and without the aid of relevant trade information.

Following a second decision striking down an open price plan in the linseed oil industry,[119] the Supreme Court seemingly reversed its field in a case involving the Maple Flooring Manufacturers' Association.[120] Disposition of the case may have been affected by inadequate preparation on the Justice Department's part, but there were also certain characteristics distinguishing the facts from those of previous cases. In particular, evidence of relatively low and nonuniform prices charged by association members was presented; the members supposedly ceased discussing prices in their association meetings after the Supreme Court found the Hardwood Lumber and Linseed Oil operations illegal; the association's weekly report to members stopped linking transactions with specific sellers after the government filed a complaint; and in general, the association made an obvious effort to stay within the letter, if not the spirit, of the antitrust laws. Given these apparent differences, the Supreme Court countermanded a district court decision, showing its willingness to permit trade association activities that went little further than the dissemination of detailed information:

> We decide only that trade associations . . . which openly and fairly gather and disseminate information as to the cost of their product, the volume of production, the actual price which the product has brought in past transactions, stocks of merchandise on hand, approximate cost of transportation from the principal point of shipment to the points of consumption [i.e., a basing-point system freight rate book], as did these defendants, and who, as they did, meet and discuss such information and statistics without however reaching or attempting to reach any agreement or any concerted action with respect to prices or production or restraining competition, do not thereby engage in unlawful restraint of commerce.[121]

In another decision handed down on the same day, the Court lent its seal of approval to price-reporting activities of a cement industry trade association, despite its recognition that they tended to bring about uniformity of prices.[122]

The next major case involving open price policies was a victory for the antitrust enforcement agencies, but only because the defendants—15 sugar refining companies—had entered into an explicit agreement to adhere to the prices they quoted until they publicly announced changes.[123] While condemning this agreement, the Supreme Court went on to observe that:

> competition does not become less free merely because of the distribution of knowledge of the essential factors entering into commercial transactions. The natural effect of the acquisition of the wider and more scientific knowledge of business conditions on the minds of those engaged in commerce, and the consequent stabilizing of production and price, cannot be said to be an unreasonable restraint or in any respect unlawful.[124]

During the late 1930s and 1940s the Federal Trade Commission launched a series of attacks against open price associations that had continued reporting programs originated under National Industrial Recovery Act auspices. All but one led to cease-and-desist orders. However, in most of the cases, the trade associations had gone further than merely disseminating price information—for example, by hiring a consultant who contacted individual firms and lectured them on the irrationality of price cutting,[125] or by encouraging and facilitating rigid adherence to a basing point pricing system.[126] The sole defeat came in a case against the Tag Manufacturers Institute.[127] The 31 companies who formed the Institute accounted for 95 percent of the output of price tags, pin tickets, and similar devices used to mark consumer goods. Member firms agreed to file their price lists with the Institute, to submit duplicate copies of every shipment invoice, and to report within 24 hours any sales that deviated

113. A. J. Eddy, *The New Competition*, 4th ed., pp. 18, 29.

114. A. J. Eddy, *The New Competition*, 4th ed., p. 126.

115. See L. S. Lyon and Victor Abramson, *The Economics of Open Price Associations* (Washington, D.C.: Brookings Institution, 1936), pp. 15–23, for an historical analysis of the movement.

116. For a more thorough review of the leading cases, see George W. Stocking, "The Rule of Reason, Workable Competition, and the Legality of Trade Association Activities," *University of Chicago Law Review* 21 (Summer 1954): 527–619.

117. *American Column and Lumber Co. et al. v. U.S.*, 257 U.S. 377 (1921). See also the discussion in Phillips, *Market Structure, Organization and Performance*, pp. 138–60.

118. 257 U.S. 377, 410 (1921).

119. *U.S. v. American Linseed Oil Co. et al.*, 262 U.S. 371 (1923).

120. *Maple Flooring Manufacturers' Association v. U.S.*, 268 U.S. 563 (1925).

121. 268 U.S. 563, 586 (1925).

122. *Cement Manufacturers Protective Association v. U.S.*, 268 U.S. 588 (1925).

123. *Sugar Institute v. U.S.*, 297 U.S. 553 (1936).

124. 297 U.S. 553, 598.

125. *Salt Producers' Association v. Federal Trade Commission*, 34 F.T.C. 38 (1941), 134 F. 2d 354 (1943); and *United States Maltsters Association v. Federal Trade Commission*, 35 F.T.C. 797 (1942), 152 F. 2d 161 (1945).

126. *Federal Trade Commission v. Cement Institute et al.*, 333 U.S. 683 (1948).

127. *Tag Manufacturers Institute et al. v. Federal Trade Commission*, 43 F.T.C. 499 (1947), 174 F. 2d 452 (1949).

from the list price. Financial penalties were assessed against members who failed to submit the agreed-upon information on time. The Institute in turn circulated to all members copies of each member's price lists, periodic summaries of the invoice data (which did not identify specific sellers), and daily reports listing each off-list transaction, the name of the seller, the state in which the buyer operated, the seller's list price, and the price actually quoted. There was no express agreement among Institute members to adhere to list prices, and the Institute's director scrupulously avoided encouraging members to respect their list prices. Emphasizing the absence of such agreements or encouragement, and noting that 25 percent of the tag manufacturers' sales were made at off-list prices, the Court of Appeals reversed a prior FTC decision and found that the tag makers had not acted illegally. The decision was not appealed to the Supreme Court, apparently because of the tag industry's diminutive size.

In 1969 the Supreme Court returned to the open price battlefield, reversing a district court decision that had absolved the price reporting activities of 18 companies supplying 90 percent of the cardboard cartons used in southeastern United States.[128] No systematic centralized price reporting organization had been formed. Instead, the producers supplied to one another upon request (as often as a dozen times per month, for one firm that kept records) information on prices currently or last quoted to particular customers. Once a company received this information from a rival, it usually quoted the same price to that customer; and it was common for buyers to divide orders among producers offering identical quotations. Sometimes, however, lower prices were quoted, and there was evidence of considerable shifting by purchasers from one supplier to others. Although entry into carton production was easy, the market structure was oligopolistic, with six producers contributing 60 percent of total sales. The industry showed signs of excess capacity despite rapidly growing demand. Prices were said to be trending downward between 1955 and 1963, but only gradually and within a narrow band of fluctuation. Speaking for a majority of the Supreme Court, Justice Douglas observed that the facts fit none of the earlier precedents readily. In a brief opinion addressed only to the immediate circumstances, he concluded that the defendants' information exchange practices had tended to stabilize prices and that this was an anticompetitive effect illegal under Sherman Act Section 1. Three members of the Court dissented, arguing that the government had not provided sufficient evidence of intent to restrain competition or actual anticompetitive effect to support the majority's conclusion.

The majority position in the cardboard carton case appears to take a somewhat tougher line than earlier decisions, but it was too narrowly drawn to offer clean guidelines for future cases. More generally, it is possible to extract from the leading decisions only a statement of probabilities concerning the legality of price reporting practices. Few certainties exist, except where express agreements to adhere to reported prices have been made. With caution and a bit of luck, producers may be able to stay within the law in maintaining a reporting system sufficiently elaborate to reduce, if not to eliminate altogether, the temptation toward price shading in an oligopolistic market. However, an open price arrangement is less likely to pass legal muster if it provides that extra margin of active encouragement needed to establish well-disciplined pricing when the industry structure is ill-suited to tacit collusion—e.g., when there is only loose oligopoly or the product is not homogeneous. The chances of withstanding antitrust attack are also impaired when price reporting is carried to extremes of detail.

This is not the worst of all possible worlds, but it is also not the best. Tacitly collusive oligopoly pricing could be combatted more effectively if the law on trade association information dissemination activities were strengthened. Specifically, competition would be enhanced if, in addition to prohibitions commonly applied in the past, the courts were to take a uniformly dim view of price reporting schemes that identify the buyers and/or sellers in individual transactions, have elaborate auditing provisions,[129] or impose penalties for failure to report transactions.[130] It would also be desirable to limit the frequency with which detailed market condition reports are issued, but here a rule of reason is definitely needed. Weekly reports are probably harmless when transactions are small and occur with great frequency, but they may enhance collusion significantly in industries with large, infrequent transactions.

One final comparative note is in order. Price reporting schemes are by no means a uniquely American phenomenon. When the British Restrictive Practices Court handed down its first decisions prohibiting overt price-fixing arrangements, there was a rush to adopt open price agreements, which did not have to be registered under the 1956 Restrictive Practices Act. According to one observer, more than 150 such agreements had already been put into effect by 1960.[131] In 1968 the Act was amended to close the loophole, making information agreements subject to registration and challenge. The number of agreements registered is said, however, to have been small.

Conclusion

In sum, the United States, unlike other industrialized Western nations, has adopted an antitrust policy that holds explicit price-fixing and market-dividing agreements to be *per se* illegal without regard to their reasonableness. But the law is more permissive with respect to subtler forms of conduct that could have the same effect as explicit agreements. Oligopolists refraining from price competition merely because they recognize the likelihood of rival retaliation do not violate the law as long as their decisions are taken independently. And by avoiding any suggestion of encouraging or compelling rivals to cooperate, they may also facilitate uniform and nonaggressive pricing through such devices as price leadership and open price-reporting systems. These limitations in the law permit the survival of potentially significant departures from competitive pricing.

128. *U.S. v. Container Corporation of America et al.*, 273 F. Supp. 18 (1967), 393 U.S. 333 (1969). See also *U.S. v. United States Gypsum Co. et al.*, 98 S. Ct. 2864 (1978), which will be considered further in Chapter 21.

129. Here again the turbogenerator pricing practices of General Electric and Westinghouse during the 1960s and early 1970s are relevant. An important prop to their price protection plan was allowing buyer representatives to audit their records to ensure that no secret price concessions had been granted. Cf. note 104 *supra*.

130. For a further discussion of possible criteria, see Carl Kaysen and Donald F. Turner, *Antitrust Policy* (Cambridge, Mass.: Harvard University Press, 1959), pp. 150–52.

131. J. B. Heath, "Some Economic Consequences," *Economic Journal* 70 (September 1960): 74–84. See also Swann et al., *Competition in British Industry*, pp. 74–80, 158–63. For a broader survey of open price activities and laws in Europe, see the OECD report, "Report by the Committee of Experts on Restrictive Business Practices on Information Agreements," excerpted in the *Antitrust Bulletin* 13 (Spring 1968): 225–60.

20 Antitrust policy: the control of market structures

In addition to rules governing pricing behavior, the antitrust arsenal contains substantive provisions designed to channel industrial structure in competitive directions. The main weapons are Section 2 of the Sherman Act and Section 7 of the Clayton Act.

Monopoly and monopolization

Sherman Act Section 2 reads in part:

> Every person who shall monopolize, or attempt to monopolize, or combine or conspire with any other person or persons, to monopolize any part of the trade or commerce among the several states, or with foreign nations, shall be deemed guilty of a felony . . .

The language suggests concern primarily with structural conditions rather than conduct. But why did Congress choose the word "monopolize" to describe what it condemned, and not some more conventional phrase such as "obtain or possess monopoly power"? When does a firm monopolize? How large a share of the market must it control? Is it illegal to dominate an industry merely because one is so much more efficient than rivals that they all disappear in the face of one's competitive efforts? These are questions that cannot be answered merely by reading the statute. We must analyze the intent of Congress and interpretations rendered by the courts.

Unfortunately, the historical record provides only limited insight into what Congress had in mind in enacting Section 2.[1] The original bill proposed by Senator Sherman was debated briskly on the Senate floor; but it was changed in major respects by the Judiciary Committee, and passage of the amended bill was preceded by only a cursory debate. It appears probable, however, that the choice of the unorthodox word "monopolize" reflected the mixed emotions of legislators toward big business. They were acutely aware of abuses by the "trusts." But they also believed that many combinations brought economies of large-scale production, benefitting the consumer. This ambiguity is reflected superbly in Finley Peter Dunne's characterization, through the voice of Mr. Dooley, of Theodore Roosevelt's attitude a decade later:

> "Th' trusts," says [T. R.], "are heejous

---

1. For various views see Hans B. Thorelli, *The Federal Antitrust Policy* (Stockholm: Stockholms Högskola, 1954), pp. 166–210; William Letwin, *Law and Economic Policy in America* (New York: Random House, 1965), pp. 88–99; Harlan M. Blake and William K. Jones, "Toward a Three-Dimensional Antitrust Policy," *Columbia Law Review* 65 (March 1955): 423–25; and Robert H. Bork, "Legislative Intent and the Policy of the Sherman Act," *Journal of Law and Economics* 9 (October 1966): 7–48.

monsthers built up be th' enlightened inther-
prise iv th' men that have done so much to
advance progress in our beloved country. . . .
On wan hand I wud stamp thim undher fut; on
th' other hand not so fast."[2]

As a way out of this dilemma, the Sherman Act
draftsmen wrote into the law a prohibition only of
monopolizing, which they apparently intended to
mean an active process of securing to oneself a
monopoly, going beyond the mere possession of
monopoly power as a consequence of superior
efficiency.

Early litigation The executive branch and the
judiciary did not in fact proceed very rapidly to
stamp the monopolistic trusts under foot. An early
action against the Whiskey Trust was dismissed
at the district court level, first because of a procedural error and then on various substantive
grounds.[3] A case involving the sugar refining
trust was fought all the way to the Supreme
Court, only to be thrown out on the technical
question of what constituted interstate commerce.[4] An indictment against the notorious cash
register trust was sustained by a district court on
4 out of 18 counts, but then the case was dropped
by the government.[5]

The first real government victory over a
close-knit combination came in 1904, when the
Supreme Court struck down the Northern Securities Co., formed in 1901 to consolidate the joint
control of J. P. Morgan, James Hill, and other
contemporary tycoons over the Northern Pacific
and Great Northern railroads.[6] The government's
attack was based both on Sherman Act Section 1,
alleging an illegal combination in restraint of
trade, and Section 2, charging an attempt and
conspiracy to monopolize rail transportation in
northern states west of the Mississippi River. Its
relevance as a judicial precedent has been confined mainly to merger cases, on which we shall
have more to say later. It is also not a paragon of
legal consensus, with four Supreme Court justices
dissenting in two separate opinions from the majority's decision. As newly appointed Justice Oliver Wendell Holmes prefaced his dissent, implicitly objecting to the grandstand tactics pursued
by President Roosevelt and his attorney general

in focusing public attention on the case's all-star
cast of entrepreneurs:

> Great cases like hard cases make bad law.
> For great cases are called great, not by rea-
> son of their real importance in shaping the
> law of the future, but because of some acci-
> dent of immediate overwhelming interest
> which appeals to the feelings and distorts
> judgment.[7]

Emergence of a rule of reason A more important step followed in 1911, when the Supreme
Court held that the Standard Oil Company of
New Jersey had illegally monopolized the petroleum refining industry.[8] "The Standard" had
been organized as an Ohio corporation in 1870
by the Rockefeller brothers. It pioneered the trust
form of consolidation during the 1880s and then,
after a skirmish with the Ohio antitrust laws, was
incorporated as a New Jersey holding company
in 1899. From its inception, it seemed determined
to dominate the refining and sale of petroleum
products—notably, in that prehorseless carriage
era, kerosene and lubricating oil. It managed to
maintain a 90 percent share of those markets
throughout most of the 1880s and 1890s. This it
accomplished by acquiring more than 120 former
rival companies, securing discriminatory rail
freight rates and rebates, foreclosing crude oil
supplies to competitors by buying up pipelines,
conducting business espionage, and allegedly
waging predatory price warfare to drive rivals
out of business or soften them up for a takeover.
Whether Standard actually cut prices deeply to
destroy or discipline rivals on any widespread
scale has been disputed. Careful analysis suggests that more frequently it pursued a sophisticated region-by-region limit pricing strategy.[9]
This subtlety, however, eluded contemporary jurists and economists.

Sustaining a district court's finding of guilt,
the Supreme Court stated that the crime of monopolization involves two elements: the acquisition of a monopoly position, and the intent to
acquire that position and exclude rivals from the
industry. The Court went on to articulate a rule of
reason for ascertaining whether or not actions by
accused firms exhibited the essential element of

intent: If the acts unduly restrained competition, going beyond normal business practice, intent could be inferred. Specifically, it ruled that Standard's

> intent and purpose to exclude others . . . was frequently manifested by acts and dealings wholly inconsistent with the theory that they were made with the single conception of advancing the development of business power by usual methods, but which on the contrary necessarily involved the intent to drive others from the field and to exclude them from their right to trade and thus accomplish the mastery which was the end in view.[10]

To remedy matters, the courts ordered that the Standard Oil holding company be dissolved, its controlling shares in 33 geographically dispersed operating subsidiaries to be distributed on a pro rata basis to Standard Oil of New Jersey stockholders. At first this led to no appreciable increase in competition, for a controlling interest in the 33 fragments remained in the hands of John D. Rockefeller and associates who had managed the original Standard Oil trust.[11] But as the dominant stockholders distributed their shares among numerous heirs and gave substantial blocks to nonvoting philanthropic institutions, as expansion to meet growing gasoline demands necessitated issuing new stock to a broader base of investors, and as some of the fragments merged with Standard competitors, competition among the surviving entities gradually developed, and each interpenetrated markets dominated by its former affiliates.

Two weeks after the Supreme Court handed down its *Standard Oil* opinion, it reinforced the rule of reason doctrine in a decision against the American Tobacco Company, also called the Tobacco Trust.[12] American was found guilty of monopolizing the cigarette trade through such unreasonable business practices as excluding rivals from access to wholesalers, engrossing supplies of leaf tobacco, buying out some 250 former rivals, and predatory pricing. In the cold light of hindsight, its pricing behavior appears more swashbuckling than Standard Oil's. It frequently established ''fighting brands'' that were sold in rivals' local markets at less than cost and

on at least one occasion at an effective after-tax price of zero, forcing the hapless competitors to sell out. In many cases the acquired plants were promptly closed down. The Supreme Court found these practices to be clear evidence of illegal monopolistic intent. A district court subsequently ordered that the Tobacco Trust be split into 16 pieces, including a successor American Tobacco Company, Liggett & Myers, P. Lorillard, Reynolds (which at the time had no cigarette brand), and the American Snuff Co. (which even today dominates its declining field).

During the next few years, the government scored further but less spectacular victories against the Powder Trust,[13] the glucose and cornstarch trust,[14] Eastman Kodak Company,[15] the Thread Trust,[16] and a group of railroads dominating the anthracite coal industry.[17] The next important step by way of precedent oc-

---

2. Cited in Letwin, *Law and Economic Policy*, p. 205.

3. *U.S.* v. *Greenhut et al.*, 50 Fed. 469 (1892); 51 Fed. 205 (1892); 51 Fed. 213 (1892); and *In re Greene*, 52 Fed. 104 (1892). See also Letwin, *Law and Economic Policy*, pp. 111–13, 145–49.

4. *U.S.* v. *E. C. Knight Co. et al.*, 60 Fed. 306 (1894); 60 Fed. 934 (1894); 156 U.S. 1 (1895).

5. *U.S.* v. *Patterson et al.*, 55 Fed. 605 (1893).

6. *U.S.* v. *Northern Securities Co. et al.*, 120 Fed. 721 (1903); 193 U.S. 197 (1904). In 1970 a merger between the two was approved. *U.S.* v. *Interstate Commerce Commission et al.*, 396 U.S. 491 (1970).

7. 193 U.S. 197, 400 (1904).

8. *U.S.* v. *Standard Oil Co. of New Jersey et al.*, 173 Fed. 177 (1909); 221 U.S. 1 (1911).

9. Cf. Chapter 12, pp. 336–37 *supra*.

10. *U.S.* v. *Standard Oil Co. of New Jersey et al.*, 221 U.S. 1, 76 (1911).

11. On the absence of an adverse stock market reaction to Standard's dissolution, see M. R. Burns, ''The Competitive Effects of Trust-Busting: A Portfolio Analysis,'' *Journal of Political Economy* 85 (August 1977): 717–39.

12. *U.S.* v. *American Tobacco Co.*, 221 U.S. 106 (1911). See also P. C. Porter, ''Origins of the American Tobacco Company,'' *Business History Review* 43 (Spring 1969): 59–76.

13. *U.S.* v. *E. I. du Pont de Nemours & Co. et al.*, 188 Fed. 127 (1911).

14. *U.S.* v. *Corn Products Refining Co. et al.*, 234 Fed. 964 (1916).

15. *U.S.* v. *Eastman Kodak Co. et al.*, 226 Fed. 62 (1915).

16. *U.S.* v. *American Thread Co.*, settled by consent decree in 1913.

17. *U.S.* v. *Reading Co. et al.*, 253 U.S. 26 (1920); and *U.S.* v. *Lehigh Valley Railroad Co. et al.*, 254 U.S. 255 (1920).

curred, however, when the government was defeated in its suit against the United States Steel Corporation.[18]

U.S. Steel was formed through a billion-dollar merger in 1901, consolidating control over 65 percent of domestic iron and steel output. It added to its holdings in 1907 by acquiring, with the express permission of President Roosevelt, the Tennessee Coal and Iron Corporation. In that same recession-impacted year Judge E. H. Gary, its chairman, initiated the four-year series of dinners with rival company leaders that did much to solidify the industry's pricing discipline. Unlike Standard Oil and American Tobacco, U.S. Steel was not accused of trying to drive rivals from the industry through cutthroat pricing and other predatory practices. Instead, it exercised price leadership in setting prices sufficiently high to encourage the entry and growth of other steel makers. Partly because of this, its share of the market had fallen to 52 percent in 1915, despite the sizeable Tennessee Coal and Iron merger, and was continuing to fall into 1920.

After winning the *Standard Oil* case, the government brought suit in 1911 to dissolve U.S. Steel. A district court, applying the *Standard Oil* rule of reason, found in favor of the steel company in 1915. The Justice Department appealed to higher authority. With two justices abstaining because they had criticized or prosecuted U.S. Steel in the past, a four-member majority of the Supreme Court ruled for the corporation. They argued that since Judge Gary felt compelled to meet with competitors in order to fix and control steel prices (a practice discontinued before the suit was initiated), and in view of the decline in its market share, U.S. Steel had not in fact attained monopoly power. They noted further that a multitude of witnesses representing competitors, dealers, and customers had paraded before the district court, and none had anything but good to say about U.S. Steel's conduct. Competitors in particular had testified that they were in no way restrained by the corporation's pricing policies. From this evidence, the majority concluded that U.S. Steel had not monopolized in the Sherman Act sense, and that even if the corporation did possess monopoly power, it had certainly not exercised that power. There followed the famous *obiter dictum* that:

> the law does not make mere size an offense or the existence of unexerted power an offense. It . . . requires overt acts . . . It does not compel competition nor require all that is possible.[19]

Thus, despite the vigorous dissent of a three-justice minority, the greatest consolidation in contemporary U.S. industrial history escaped antitrust censure. Moreover, it became settled that dominant firms would subject themselves to telling antitrust attack only if they behaved in a predatory or aggressive manner toward rivals. And the first seeds were sown for a cynical view that Sherman Act Section 2 protects competitors, not competition.

The *United States Steel* precedent was cemented in three parallel cases. Two years earlier, the Supreme Court held in a similar 4–3 decision that the United Shoe Machinery Corporation was innocent of monopolization.[20] It found *inter alia* that the five-company merger underlying United's formation in 1899 involved producers of complementary and hence noncompeting machines, that 59 subsequent acquisitions were "justified by exigencies or conveniences of the situation," and that United's 80 to 95 percent share of the relevant markets had been maintained largely through superior efficiency and the legitimate exploitation of valid patent rights. The government also suffered a 1916 defeat at the district court level in its suit against the American Can Company. The facts were strikingly similar to those of the *Steel* case. American Can had been formed through a 1901 merger of some 120 independent entities; but competitors thrived under the umbrella of its high prices, eroding its market share from 90 percent in 1901 to roughly 50 percent in 1913. The district court observed that American "had done nothing of which any competitor or any consumer of cans complains, or anything which strikes a disinterested outsider as unfair or unethical," adding that it was "frankly reluctant to destroy so finely adjusted an industrial machine."[21] After the Supreme Court rendered its *Steel* decision, the Justice Department dropped its appeal of the *American Can* judgment along with a number of other pending and planned monopolization suits. It persevered in prosecuting only one other major monopolization case, seeking to extend the modest divestiture program ordered in an earlier court judgment against the International Harvester Company.[22] Here again it was rebuked by the Supreme Court, which reiterated its *U.S. Steel* rule that mere size unaccompanied by unlawful conduct was not illegal.[23] Discouraged by these defeats, the Justice Department for more than a decade gave up trying to attack consolidations of monopoly power under Sherman Act Section 2.

The Alcoa case and its aftermath The next important development came in the *Alcoa* case, resolved 25 years after the *Steel* decision.[24] The Aluminum Company of America, or Alcoa, was formed in 1888 to exploit the Hall electrolytic reduction patents. It bought out the competing Bradley patents in 1903. There were several attempts to enter the industry after the basic patents expired in 1909, but none was successful until 1940. Reasons for the dearth of new entry included the difficulty of obtaining conveniently located high-grade bauxite reserves, most of which Alcoa controlled; plain bad luck by two would-be entrants; and the general unattractiveness of entering at a cost disadvantage while Alcoa practiced moderation in pricing.

Over the years Alcoa had been in and out of the courts frequently in patent disputes and on antitrust charges concerning mergers, international cartel agreements, and price discrimination, but it was never seriously discommoded. However, as interest in antitrust revived following disenchantment with the depression-born National Recovery Administration, the Justice Department in 1937 charged the company with illegal monopolization. Culminating a district court trial lasting 358 hearing days, Alcoa was absolved on all counts, with the *U.S. Steel* and *International Harvester* cases stressed as precedents. The government appealed, but because four Supreme Court justices had been associated with the earlier litigation, a quorum could not be obtained. Consequently, the case was heard by a three-member panel of Circuit Court judges, with Learned Hand presiding, as a court of last resort. Its decision in 1945 reversed the lower court and found Alcoa guilty of monopolization. The opin-

ion focused on two central issues: whether Alcoa possessed a monopoly, and whether it had exhibited the intent essential to find monopolization.

The first question turned on how the market in which Alcoa operated was defined. As we have seen in Chapter 3, it is not always easy to identify meaningful market boundaries. In the *Alcoa* case, unlike most of its Section 2 predecessors, this proved to be so. There was no problem of local versus national market definitions, for aluminum was sold nationally on a uniform delivered price basis. Substitution on the production side—i.e., the possibility that companies producing other materials might convert their plants to produce aluminum—was also of no concern, since aluminum refining facilities are highly specialized and durable. The key issue was, What substitutes on the demand side should be included as part of the relevant market?

Because of aluminum's unique properties, other metals such as steel, copper, and magnesium were summarily excluded, despite the fact that aluminum and other metals are viewed by users as feasible substitutes in many applications, and although aluminum's cross elasticity of demand was apparently on the order of 2.0 with respect to steel and even higher with respect to copper.[25] The court limited its analysis to the following three alternative definitions of Alcoa's

---

18. *U.S. v. United States Steel Corporation et al.*, 223 Fed. 55 (1915), 251 U.S. 417 (1920).

19. 251 U.S. 417, 451 (1920).

20. *U.S. v. United Shoe Machinery Co. of New Jersey et al.*, 247 U.S. 32 (1918). An earlier criminal case against United's officers was also unsuccessful. *U.S. v. Winslow et al.*, 195 Fed. 578 (1912), 227 U.S. 202 (1913).

21. *U.S. v. American Can Company et al.*, 230 Fed. 859, 861, 903 (1916).

22. *U.S. v. International Harvester Co. et al.*, 214 Fed. 987 (1914), with settlement effected in a 1918 consent decree.

23. *U.S. v. International Harvester Co.*, 10 F. 2d 827 (1925), 274 U.S. 693 (1927).

24. *U.S. v. Aluminum Co. of America et al.*, 44 F. Supp. 97 (1941), 148 F. 2d 416 (1945).

25. M. J. Peck, *Competition in the Aluminum Industry* (Cambridge, Mass.: Harvard University Press, 1961), pp. 31–34.

aluminum ingot market share, where the numerator denotes the output credited to Alcoa and the denominator the output attributed to all sources of supply in the market:

$$S_1 = \frac{\text{Alcoa's output of primary ingots less the primary metal Alcoa used internally to fabricate end products}}{\text{All primary ingot production plus all secondary ingot production plus aluminum ingot imports}}$$

$$S_2 = \frac{\text{Alcoa's output of primary ingots}}{\text{All primary ingot production plus all secondary ingot production plus aluminum ingot imports}}$$

$$S_3 = \frac{\text{Alcoa's output of primary ingots}}{\text{All primary ingot production plus aluminum ingot imports}}$$

Under the first definition, which was accepted as correct by the district court, Alcoa is found to have possessed only a 33 percent share of the market during the 1930s; under the second, its share would be calculated at 64 percent; and under the third, 90 percent. The appellate panel rejected the first definition, which deducts from the ingot production of Alcoa the metal used internally by Alcoa to fabricate aluminum sheets, panels, pots and pans, and the like, because "all intermediate, or end, products which 'Alcoa' fabricates and sells, *pro tanto* reduce the demand for ingot itself."[26] This makes good analytic sense, although one might have nagging doubts, given evidence that Alcoa found it desirable to stimulate the demand for aluminum by pioneering many fabricated product applications. The only difference between definitions S_2 and S_3 is the inclusion of secondary (i.e., reprocessed scrap) metal, accounting for roughly 40 percent of all domestic aluminum metal supplies, in the denominator of S_2 but not S_3. Judge Hand favored the third definition, arguing that since Alcoa had produced the metal reappearing as reprocessed scrap, it would have taken into account in its output decisions the effect of scrap reclamation on future prices; hence, it exerted effective monopolistic control over the supply of secondary metal.

Here again, economic analysis supports the Appellate Court's choice, especially when one recognizes that a considerable fraction of the secondary metal, as defined by the court, came from "factory scrap" melted down only a short time after it left Alcoa's primary reduction works.[27]

How the court decided these market definition issues had a crucial bearing on the case's outcome, for Judge Hand went on to observe that 90 percent "is enough to constitute a monopoly; it is doubtful whether sixty or sixty-four percent would be enough; and certainly thirty-three percent is not."[28]

Having concluded that Alcoa did possess a monopoly of the aluminum market, the court had to determine whether it had exhibited the intent to achieve its position that proof of monopolization under Section 2 demands. In his opinion, Judge Hand acknowledged that Alcoa's profits had not been extortionate; but he added that whether or not profits were "fair" was irrelevant to proving monopolization. He admitted also that Alcoa would be within the bounds of legality if its monopoly position had merely been "thrust upon" it by the failure of rivals to enter the market, or because it had outlasted its rivals owing to superior skill, foresight, and industry. "The successful competitor," he warned, "having been urged to compete, must not be turned upon when he wins."[29] But he found that Alcoa had gone further. He pointed to Alcoa's building up of ore reserves and electric power sources and production capacity in advance of demand:

> It was not inevitable that it should always anticipate increases in the demand for ingot and be prepared to supply them. Nothing compelled it to keep doubling and redoubling its capacity before others entered the field. It insists that it never excluded competitors; but we can think of no more effective exclusion than progressively to embrace each new opportunity as it opened and to face every newcomer with new capacity already geared into a great organization, having the advantage of experience, trade connections and the elite of personnel.[30]

And this, said the court, was sufficient to show the intent to maintain a monopoly position:

"Alcoa" meant to keep, and did keep, that complete and exclusive hold upon the ingot market with which it started. That was to "monopolize" that market, however innocently it otherwise proceeded.[31]

This decision, broadly endorsed by the Supreme Court a year later in the latter-day *American Tobacco* case,[32] in effect overthrew the *Standard Oil* and *U.S. Steel* precedents, making it possible to infer illegal monopolization without evidence of unreasonable practices driving competitors from the market. It did not exactly make the possession of monopoly power by means other than the receipt of valid patents *per se* illegal, but it came close. And it is possible to read into the decision, with its references to "fair" profits and expanding capacity to meet demand, a condemnation of dominant market positions maintained merely through limit pricing.

Remedial action was deferred until the disposition of war plants built with government funds and operated by Alcoa could be settled. Alcoa was barred from bidding to buy the plants, and as a result the primary ingot supply industry was transformed from a monopoly to a triopoly through the sale of integrated facilities to Reynolds Metals and Kaiser Aluminum. This, a district court later concluded, was almost sufficient, so Alcoa was not fragmented.[33] The principal additional remedy ordered was the divestiture of joint stockholdings in Alcoa and Aluminium, Ltd., of Canada by the Davis, Hunt, and Mellon families, removing the possibility that these potential competitors would be jointly controlled.

A series of cases following on the heels of the *Alcoa* decision contributed to the strengthening of Section 2. Three deserve special mention.

Shortly after bringing suit against Alcoa, the Justice Department also moved against several motion picture exhibition chains, charging them with monopolizing first-run film exhibition. Some were said to have threatened not to exhibit certain producers' films in towns where they operated the only theaters unless the producers gave them first-run preference in cities where they faced competition. In every such instance the Supreme Court found that illegal monopolization existed.[34] This was no large step beyond *Stand-*

ard Oil of 1911. However, speaking for a 6–1 majority upholding the government's case against a chain absolved of making such threats, Justice Douglas stated that specific intent to achieve monopoly need not be proved if monopoly has in fact resulted from the defendant's conduct, and that "monopoly power, whether lawfully or unlawfully acquired, may itself constitute an evil and stand condemned under Section 2 even though it remains unexercised."[35] That the old *U.S. Steel* doctrine had now been overturned could scarcely have been reaffirmed more pointedly.

In 1946 the A&P Company, several subsidiaries, and various company executives were convicted on criminal charges of conspiracy to monopolize the food retailing industry; and in 1949 the conviction was upheld by a circuit court of appeals.[36] The prosecution charged, and the courts accepted, that A&P had engaged in abusive practices—notably, by refusing to purchase

26. *U.S.* v. *Aluminum Co. of America et al.,* 148 F. 2d 416, 424 (1945).

27. See Darius W. Gaskins, Jr., "Alcoa Revisited: The Welfare Implications of a Secondhand Market," *Journal of Economic Theory* 7 (March 1974): 254–71. Compare the comment by Franklin M. Fisher in the *Journal of Economic Theory* 9 (November 1974): 357–59, who emphasizes that in a less rapidly growing market, even an 'old scrap' supply originally restricted by Alcoa to maximize long-run profits would eventually have had significant price-constraining effects. See also Peter L. Swan, "Alcoa: The Influence of Recycling on Monopoly Power" (Australian National University Working paper no. 56, November 1977).

28. *U.S.* v. *Aluminum Co. of America et al.,* 148 F. 2d 416, 424 (1945).

29. 148 F. 2d 416, 430.

30. 148 F. 2d 416, 431. There is reason to believe that the court's conclusion on this crucial issue of fact was incorrect. In his definitive study of the aluminum industry, Professor Donald H. Wallace found to the contrary that Alcoa's capacity had *lagged behind demand* on numerous occasions. *Market Control in the Aluminum Industry* (Cambridge, Mass.: Harvard University Press, 1937), pp. 252, 259–60, 291–92, 307–308, 331.

31. 148 F. 2d 416, 432 (1945).

32. *American Tobacco Co. et al.* v. *U.S.,* 328 U.S. 781, 813–814 (1946).

33. *U.S.* v. *Aluminum Co. of America et al.,* 91 F. Supp. 333 (1950).

34. *U.S.* v. *Crescent Amusement Co.,* 323 U.S. 173 (1944); *U.S.* v. *Griffith Amusement Co.,* 334 U.S. 100 (1948); and *Schine Chain Theatres* v. *U.S.,* 334 U.S. 110 (1948).

35. *U.S.* v. *Griffith Amusement Co.,* 334 U.S. 100, 105, 107 (1948).

from suppliers who would offer no special preferential discounts, by threatening to extend its own internal manufacturing operations and compete with recalcitrant suppliers, and by reducing retail grocery prices in cities where it faced "rough competition" while retaining high prices (or supposedly, although implausibly, even raising prices) in those markets where competition was less intense. These conclusions have been severely criticized, mainly on two grounds: that A&P's conduct did not go beyond what one would expect of a vigorous rival seeking to minimize costs and maintain its market position, and that consumers benefited from the purchasing methods pioneered by A&P and imitated by other grocery chains.[37] Alcoa and A&P seemingly share the dubious distinction of having been found guilty of competing too vigorously and successfully. The A&P case is different, however, in the sense that only conspiracy to monopolize and not outright monopolization was inferred, since A&P's share of nationwide retail grocery sales was less than 10 percent, and its share of local markets exceeded 40 percent in only 23 relatively small cities. As a result of its conviction, A&P was fined $175,000 and subsequently was required to dissolve its food brokerage subsidiary.

A third decision paralleling *Alcoa* came in a renewed attack against the United Shoe Machinery Corporation. This time United was found guilty of monopolization because certain of its business policies, although not objectionable *per se*, tended to prevent new entry and to perpetuate United's dominance.[38] These included the refusal to sell machines, which were instead only leased for long (e.g., 10-year) terms; a price structure that accepted lower profit margins on machines exposed to competition than on those shielded by United's formidable patent portfolio; and pricing, service, and machine replacement provisions that made it advantageous for shoe manufacturers to employ the full line of United machines. This array of practices appears to stray further from orthodox business conduct than Alcoa's "embracing each new opportunity," and so the *United Shoe Machinery* decision cannot be considered as daring a departure from earlier precedents.

The decline and renaissance The *Alcoa, A&P,* and motion picture exhibition chain decisions of the late 1940s appear to have been a high-water mark in judicial willingness to infer monopolization without proof of oppressive business practices, just as the conscious parallelism doctrine under Sherman Act Section 1 reached its zenith in nearly contemporaneous decisions. Any illusion that the courts had shifted to a uniformly hard line against dominant firms was shattered in 1956, when the Supreme Court found du Pont innocent of monopolizing cellophane production.[39] Once again, the crucial issue was definition of the relevant market. The Justice Department, emphasizing cellophane's unique properties, the substantial price differences between cellophane and other packaging materials, and the unusually high profits realized, argued for a narrow definition embracing only cellophane sales. These du Pont clearly dominated by virtue of patents it acquired from a French company, patents it secured on its own improvement inventions, and licensing arrangements it worked out with an American company challenging its patent claims.[40] Attorneys for du Pont argued that there was a high cross elasticity of demand between cellophane and other flexible packaging materials, and therefore that cellophane ought to be considered only a part of that broader market, in which its share was roughly 18 percent. A Wilmington, Delaware, district court accepted the broader market definition, acquitting du Pont. In a 4–3 split decision, the Supreme Court affirmed the lower court's judgment, concluding that:

> While the application of the [market definition] tests remains uncertain, it seems to us that du Pont should not be found to monopolize cellophane when that product has the competition and interchangeability with other wrappings that this record shows.[41]

During the late 1950s and through the 1960s there was little judicial action on the Section 2 front involving charges of horizontal market domination untainted by other prohibited practices.[42] Several potentially spectacular actions were initiated by the Department of Justice, but these were settled not with a bang but a whimper through *consent decrees*—remedial agreements negotiated out of court by the adversaries in a case. A consent decree leaves unresolved the question of guilt versus innocence, but it is binding upon the parties once the decree has been approved by a federal court. A suit alleging monopolization of color film processing by Eastman Kodak Company, for example, was settled with an agreement that Eastman would "unbundle" processing services from the price of film and that it would reduce its share of the processing market to below 50 percent within seven years, helping new firms enter the industry by licensing its patents and conveying its know-how to them.[43] A consent decree with similar provisions affecting tabulating card production ended the suit against IBM charging monopolization of the key punch and related mechanical (but not electronic) data processing equipment industry.[44] The Radio Corporation of America emerged from a suit challenging its domination of television technology by agreeing to license large numbers of patents on a royalty-free basis.[45] Western Electric, the manufacturing arm of AT&T, consented to a program of patent licensing and the divestiture of minor subsidiary operations, escaping the three-way structural breakup originally sought by the government.[46] In 1958 the United Fruit Corporation agreed to relinquish a part of its banana barony by establishing and spinning off a new firm capable of handling 35 percent of all U.S. banana imports.[47] And in an action attacking General Motors' 85 percent share of the domestic intercity bus manufacturing industry, the consent settlement specified several actions by GM to enhance the viability of existing competitors, plus the possibility of future divestiture if any existing rival failed or if GM retained its dominant share despite market growth.[48]

A pronounced upsurge in structural antitrust action—this time marked by contending party decisions to fight their battles out to the bitter end in court—began in the late 1960s. After preliminary skirmishes, the salvo that signalled a new era was a Justice Department complaint concerning IBM's dominance of the computer industry, filed on the last day of the Johnson administration in 1969.[49] It was followed by Justice Department

(36) *U.S.* v. *the New York Great Atlantic and Pacific Tea Co. et al.*, 67 F. Supp. 626 (1946); 173 F. 2d 79 (1949). The case was not appealed to the Supreme Court.

37. See especially M. A. Adelman, *A & P: A Study in Price-Cost Behavior and Public Policy* (Cambridge, Mass.: Harvard University Press, 1959); and Donald F. Turner, "Trouble Begins in the 'New' Sherman Act," *Yale Law Journal* 58 (May 1949): 969–82.

38. *U.S.* v. *United Shoe Machinery Corporation*, 110 F. Supp. 295 (1953), affirmed by the Supreme Court in 347 U.S. 521 (1954). Later the case was reopened when the Justice Department insisted that the remedies ordered in 1954—compulsory licensing of patents and divestiture of minor subsidiary operations—had been insufficient to restore competition. After a Supreme Court decision approving further action, a divestiture program to reduce United Shoe Machinery's market share to 33 percent was agreed upon in a consent decree. 391 U.S. 244 (1968); and CCH 1969 Trade Cases Para. 72,688. On the aftermath, see "USM's Hard Life as an Ex-Monopoly," *Fortune*, October 1972, pp. 124–30.

39. *U.S.* v. *E. I. du Pont de Nemours and Co.*, 118 F. Supp. 41 (1953), 351 U.S. 377 (1956). See also the critical article by G. W. Stocking and W. F. Mueller, "The Cellophane Case and the New Competition," *American Economic Review* 45 (March 1955): 29–63.

40. Also at issue was the question of whether the patent practices through which du Pont maintained its dominance justified an inference of illegal intent to monopolize. The district court thought not, but the Supreme Court, having concluded that du Pont had no monopoly, did not consider the question.

41. *U.S.* v. *E. I. du Pont de Nemours and Co.*, 351 U.S. 377, 404 (1956).

42. The principal government victories were *U.S.* v. *International Boxing Club of New York*, 358 U.S. 242 (1959), 171 F. Supp. 841 (1959); and *U.S.* v. *Grinnell Corporation et al.*, 236 F. Supp. 244 (1964); 384 U.S. 563 (1966). The *Grinnell* case is noteworthy both for its strained definition of a national market for fire and burglar alarm services monitored by local central stations, and for a restatement of what is required to constitute monopolization under Section 2, viz: "the possession of monopoly power in the relevant market and . . . the willful acquisition or maintenance of that power as distinguished from growth or development as a consequence of a superior product, business acumen, or historic accident." 384 U.S. 563, 570–571 (1966). Significant defeats included *U.S.* v. *National Malleable & Steel Castings Co. et al.*, CCH 1957 Trade Cases, Para. 68,890; and *U.S.* v. *General Motors Corporation* (the diesel locomotive case), dropped by the Justice Department in 1967 owing to insufficient evidence. On the locomotive case, see Thomas G. Marx, "Economic Theory and Judicial Process: A Case Study," *Antitrust Bulletin* 20 (Winter 1975): 775–802.

43. *U.S.* v. *Eastman Kodak Co.*, CCH 1954 Trade Cases, Para. 67,920; CCH 1961 Trade Cases, Para. 70,100. Although the *Kodak* case was a probable exception, compulsory patent licensing decrees appear in general to have had little discernible impact on market structure. See F. M. Scherer, *The Economic Effects of Compulsory Patent Licensing* (New York: New York University Graduate School of Business Administration Monograph Series in Finance and Economics, 1977), pp. 75–78.

44. *U.S.* v. *International Business Machines Corp.*, CCH 1956 Trade Cases, Para. 68,245; CCH 1963 Trade Cases, Para. 70,628.

45. *U.S.* v. *Radio Corporation of America*, CCH 1958 Trade Cases, Para. 69,164.

46. *U.S.* v. *Western Electric, Inc., et al.*, CCH 1956 Trade Cases, Para.

monopolization suits against the leading rubber tire makers[50] (dropped for lack of proof before trial began) and another (apparently more determined) try to sever Western Electric from AT&T.[51] A new development was the effort by a revitalized Federal Trade Commission to order reorganization of monopolistic industries under its broad mandate to combat "unfair methods of competition."[52] An FTC complaint against the Xerox Corporation was settled through a consent decree making Xerox's extensive portfolio of copying machine patents available for licensing at a royalty rate not exceeding 1.5 percent.[53] Other more ambitious FTC actions sought structural fragmentation of the three leading ready-to-eat breakfast cereal manufacturers,[54] the eight largest petroleum refining companies,[55] and the titanium dioxide pigment manufacturing operations of du Pont.[56] During the late 1960s and early 1970s there was also a surge of private suits—far too many to survey here—charging monopolization under Sherman Act Section 2. Most were geared toward recovering treble damages and enjoining alleged abusive practices, but a few also attempted (thus far unsuccessfully) to have market-dominating enterprises broken up.[57]

The two recent government-initiated cases that had gone to trial at the time this book was written illustrate the kinds of economic issues contested in the new structural antitrust wave. In both, as usual, market definition was a focus of dispute. IBM argued for a broad definition of the computer industry, including special purpose process control, message switching, and military computers; programmable hand-held calculators; and computer leasing and service activities. Such a definition would place its indicated share of the 'market' at roughly 32 percent in 1972. The government emphasized "general purpose electronic digital computer systems," in which IBM's share ranged from 82 percent in 1962 to 72 percent in 1972. In the cereal industry case, the FTC staff defined the relevant market as ready-to-eat (i.e., cold) cereal breakfast foods, in which the leading four sellers had 90 percent of total sales during the late 1960s. The cereal makers urged a much broader definition encompassing other breakfast foods such as hot cereals, toast, frozen waffles, liquid instant breakfasts, and bacon and eggs.

The more interesting questions in the computer and cereal cases were whether the companies had engaged in conduct warranting an inference that they had willfully monopolized in the Sherman Act Section 2 sense. It appears indisputable that IBM vaulted to a dominant position in the infant computer industry during the 1950s by recognizing the potentialities of electronic business data processing, providing superior applications engineering to tap that potential, and offering machines that, although no more advanced technically than those of rivals, performed well.[58] It also seems clear that the first computer maker to win an organization's data processing business—in more cases than not, IBM—had an advantage in placing its next generation of machines because of both the close working relationships established and the frequent difficulty of rewriting programs to run on other manufacturers' machines.

Where observers of the industry could and did disagree is on whether IBM's continued dominance merely reflected these advantages plus sustained good performance, or whether IBM went out of its way to erect obstacles to the entry and growth of rivals. Was IBM's policy of "bundled" pricing—i.e., offering computer hardware, applications programming, and maintenance at a single package price—a natural choice, or did it make entry by independent programming and service firms (who might have to compete against an effective price of zero) needlessly difficult? Was an IBM price structure that usually encouraged short-term leasing rather than the purchase of computers merely a boon to risk-averse computer users, or was it deliberately structured to maximize the amount of capital would-be competitors needed to compete with IBM? Was it normal business practice for IBM, seeing Control Data Corporation take the lead in large-scale scientific computers, to price its counterpart 360/90 machine with the expectation of making a much thinner profit margin than models facing less competition, and in fact to lose $100 million on the project? Was it lawful for IBM to set a sale versus lease price ratio on its System 360 line that spurred the growth of companies purchasing IBM computers and leasing them to users, and then consciously to readjust the ratio on its System 370 line five years later so as to render those firms' continued purchase and lease business unprofitable? Did IBM carry its compulsion for winning too far in the early 1970s when it commissioned detailed studies of rapidly growing plug-compatible tape and disc drive manufacturers, discerned from those studies that the PCM firms would have great difficulty securing continued financing if IBM adopted certain new pricing strategies, and implemented those strategies by introducing repackaged 'fighting machines' at sharply reduced, discriminatory lease prices?[59] Did it step across the line in designing peripheral equipment control unit interfaces that made interconnection of plug-compatible manufacturers' devices as difficult as possible? These are questions on which IBM's ultimate guilt or innocence of monopolization charges is likely to turn.

The computer industry has been extraordinarily dynamic. Abundant opportunities for technological innovation interacted with IBM's practice of seeking generous profit margins to trigger much new competitive entry in IBM program-compatible computer systems, central processing units, add-on memories, and input-output equipment, among others. A recurrent theme in the government's monopolization case and numerous private suits was how IBM reacted to such entry.

The general issue underlying this theme is very important. How *should* a dominant firm behave when confronted by a competitive challenge? Should it maintain high prices, as United States Steel Corporation did, letting rivals enter and nibble away at its market share? Should it be permitted to pursue a limit pricing strategy, holding prices persistently at or below the level consistent with its cost or brand image advantage and thus discouraging rival entry and expansion? IBM's behavior during the 1960s and early 1970s is not well characterized by either of these "pure" models, although there is reason to believe it moved toward a more straightforward limit pricing strategy in the mid-1970s. But during the period addressed in its monopolization suits, it tended to charge high prices when and where it could, effecting strategic price reductions when significant competitive entry appeared. These reactions were challenged as predatory. Yet confusion permeated the IBM (and other) cases because, despite 80 years of Sherman Act history, there were no well-defined rules for determining

what constituted a predatory pricing reaction.

One possible approach is to consider direct evidence of the dominant firm's intent, as manifested in testimony and subpoenaed decision-making documents. A difficulty is that courts might read too much into executive memoranda written in the spirit of a coach's pregame locker room exhortations. Also, companies spending liberally to have their lawyers clean out their files periodically can greatly reduce the risk of incrimination. Some scholars have urged instead that predation be inferred only if the dominant firm cuts its price below cost, variously defined in average total, short-run marginal, long-run marginal, or short-run average variable terms.[60] Though intuitively appealing, such cost-based rules have severe drawbacks, including cost ac-

68,246. On the high-pressure tactics by which AT&T played off the Department of Defense against the Justice Department to secure an innocuous settlement, see U.S., Congress, House, Committee on the Judiciary, Antitrust Subcommittee report, *Consent Decree Program of the Department of Justice*, 86th Cong., 1st sess., 1959, pp. 29–120.

(47) *U.S.* v. *United Fruit Corporation*, CCH 1958 Trade Cases, Para. 68,941.

(48) *U.S.* v. *General Motors Corporation*, CCH 1965 Trade Cases, Para. 71,624.

(49) *U.S.* v. *International Business Machines Corporation*, S.D. New York, complaint filed January 17, 1969. The author was a witness for the government in the ensuing trial.

50. *U.S.* v. *Goodyear Tire & Rubber Co. et al.*, N.D. Ohio, complaint filed August 9, 1973.

51. *U.S.* v. *American Telephone & Telegraph Co. et al.*, District of Columbia, complaint filed November 20, 1975.

52. Federal Trade Commission Act Sec. 5, 15 U.S.C. 45. Structural reorganization was also approved as part of the remedy in an earlier FTC case charging monopolization of the fraternity and sorority jewelry market. See *L. G. Balfour Co. et al.* v. *FTC*, 74 FTC 345 (1968), 442 F. 2d 1 (1971).

53. *In the matter of Xerox Corporation*, decision and order, 86 F. T. C. 364 (1975).

54. *In the matter of Kellogg Co. et al.*, docket no. 8883, complaint filed January 24, 1972.

55. *In the matter of Exxon Corporation et al.*, docket no. 8934, complaint filed July 18, 1973.

56. *In the matter of E. I. du Pont de Nemours & Co.*, docket no. 9108, complaint filed April 10, 1978.

57. See *International Telephone & Telegraph Corp.* v. *General Telephone & Electronics Corp. et al.*, 351 F. Supp. 1153 (1972), reversed 518 F. 2d 913 (1975).

58. Cf. Chapter 15, p. 421 *supra*.

59. Cf. Chapter 12, pp. 336–37 *supra*.

counting perplexities, the encouragement of inefficient capacity building and utilization by would-be deterrers, and a bias toward permitting successful exclusionary price cutting against capital-short newcomers who need some time in the market to learn by doing and to achieve scale economies.[61] An alternative rule proposed by Professor Williamson is that dominant firms be permitted to follow the Bain-Sylos limit pricing postulate, maintaining but not increasing their output in the face of new entry.[62] Such a rule, he shows, is easier to enforce and has superior efficiency properties in comparison with cost-based approaches. Yet if monopolistic enterprises are permitted to behave in this way, their limit pricing may freeze industries into persistently deficient performance molds, especially when demand is price-inelastic in the neighborhood of the limit price and scale economies are appreciable but not so overwhelming as to compel natural monopoly.[63] In other words, there may be situations in which long-run industry performance would be much better if entry were not deterred, and one might wish to see the courts analyze dominant firms' pricing and other responses in a way that takes such special circumstances into account.[64] The problem of setting appropriate conduct standards for firms dominating the markets they serve is as challenging as it is important.

However difficult judicial decision making may have been, the IBM case was very much in the mainstream of U.S. monopolization precedents. IBM left a trail of badly bruised and complaining rivals, and the courts had to decide *inter alia* whether the injury it inflicted upon *competitors* significantly lessened *competition* by maintaining a concentrated market structure and discouraging other would-be entrants. The FTC's *Kellogg et al.* (cereal) case was radically different in this regard.[65] No rivals came forward to air grievances in court, and indeed, the closest thing to aggressive pricing was an isolated price cut to contain (but not eliminate) private-label corn flake competition. Rather, the cereal makers maintained persistently high prices—twice the level of their manufacturing costs, and high enough to let them spend 16 cents per sales dollar on advertising and still realize an after-tax return on assets between 1958 and 1970 roughly twice the average for all manufacturing corporations. If there was injury, it was to consumers, not competitors.

The case was unorthodox in other respects. For one, the charge of monopolization was levied not against a single dominant firm, but against four (later three) companies who together controlled 90 (or 81) percent of ready-to-eat (RTE) cereal sales.[66] Charges of collective monopolization were not entirely new to antitrust. They were, for example, an important component of the tetracycline and the 1946 *American Tobacco* cases, analyzed in Chapter 19.[67] But in only one prior case, involving the five leading motion picture producers, had multifirm structural reorganization been ordered. The five controlled 70 percent of the first-run theaters in cities with population exceeding 100,000, and they were required to sever their vertical ownership ties for 1,197 theaters.[68]

With its cereal case, the FTC sought for the first time horizontal fragmentation of collectively monopolizing sellers. In this it was attempting to advance antitrust law beyond the unsatisfactory state in which it was left following the 1946 *American Tobacco* decision. That is, if oligopolists behave noncompetitively because of the very market structure in which they operate, punishing them without altering the underlying structural conditions may do little to improve economic performance.[69]

The behavior of the three leading RTE cereal makers was similar in many respects to that of the cigarette oligopoly. There was an unusually high degree of parallelism and respect for mutual interdependence. Kellogg exercised price leadership, and although price matching was less close than in cigarettes owing to greater product differentiation, discipline was strong, list price reductions were rare, and *sub rosa* price cutting was essentially unknown.[70] As a matter of policy Kellogg and General Mills refused to engage in private-label cereal production, which was recognized as a threat to branded product price levels. Post acquired one of the leading private-label producers in 1943 and let its operations atrophy, choosing during the 1960s not to compete actively for additional business even though it had substantial excess capacity and internal analyses showed sizeable private-label accounts to be quite profitable. There was circumstantial evidence that the Big Three reached an agreement in 1957 to limit stringently the use of in-pack premiums, which they considered a potent but mutually cancelling marketing tool. At the same time, but for unexplained reasons, the granting of "trade deal" cash discounts to retailers—one of the most common forms of price competition among food processors—declined sharply and indeed dried up except with respect to new products. During the late 1960s the Big Three mutually shunned the extension of vitamin fortification to most of their standard products. When criticized before a congressional committee for the low nutritional content of their offerings, they discussed concerted action at a Cereal Institute meeting, reportedly without reaching a conclusion. Yet afterwards all implemented nearly simultaneous fortification programs.

Although the leading cereal producers, like the United States Steel Corporation early in the century, charged high prices and realized supranormal profits, their collective market share did not decline. To the contrary, it rose slightly between 1950 and 1970. The explanation of how new entry and the expansion of fringe firms were restrained without the kinds of exclusionary practices condemned in earlier monopolization cases was another unorthodox facet of the cereal case. Economies of scale were no answer, for the minimum optimal scale appeared to entail a market share of only 4 to 6 percent. The FTC staff's principal theory was that opportunities for profitable new entry had been largely preempted by existing sellers' proliferation of product variants, with the number of brands distributed nationally by the six leading firms rising from 27 in 1950 to 74 in 1971. The logic of this entry deterrence mechanism has been spelled out in Chapter 8. There was little direct evidence that the cereal makers channelled their rivalry into product proliferation with the explicit intent of precluding new entry, but the entry-deterring effects of brand proliferation were certainly known to marketing managers during the 1960s, if not earlier.[71] And as Judge Hand wrote in his *Alcoa* opinion, "no monopolist monopolizes unconscious of what he is doing."[72] It remains to be seen whether the evidence of parallel noncompetitive behavior, monopolistic profits and innovative performance, persistently high concentration, and a plausible mechanism of collective market share maintenance will be deemed sufficient to conclude that there was illegal monopolization.

Still another unorthodox feature was the FTC staff's plea for a remedy. Structural reorganization—splitting three new competitors off from

(60) See Phillip Areeda and Donald F. Turner, "Predatory Pricing and Related Practices under Section 2 of the Sherman Act," *Harvard Law Review* 88 (February 1975): 697–733.

61. F. M. Scherer, "Predatory Pricing and the Sherman Act: A Comment," with reply by Areeda and Turner and counter-rejoinder by Scherer, *Harvard Law Review* 89 (March 1976): 869–903; Oliver E. Williamson, "Predatory Pricing: A Strategic and Welfare Analysis," *Yale Law Journal*, (December 1977): 284–340; Areeda and Turner, "Williamson on Predatory Pricing," with a response by Williamson, *Yale Law Journal* 87 (June 1978): 1337–53; and Williamson, "Commentary: Williamson on Predatory Pricing II," *Yale Law Journal* 88 (May 1979): 1183–1200.

62. Williamson, "Predatory Pricing." Cf. Chapter 8, p. 244 *supra*.

63. See the generalizations in Chapter 8, pp. 245–46 *supra*.

64. If competitive entry would substantially change industry conduct and performance, dominant firms weighing their strategy options are likely to be acutely aware of the probable changes. Unfortunately, whether this awareness shows up in memoranda and testimony depends in part upon how well the dominant firm's lawyers have done their job.

65. Again, full disclosure requires noting that the author was a witness for the government.

66. Quaker was dropped after the government completed its case in 1978, leaving respondents Kellogg, with 45 percent of 1970 sales, General Mills, with 21 percent, and General Foods (Post), with 15 percent.

67. Cf. Chapter 19, pp. 515–16 and 517–19 *supra*.

68. *U.S.* v. *Paramount Pictures, Inc., et al.*, 334 U.S. 131, 167–175 (1948), 85 F. Supp. 881 (1949). In its finding that the five had collectively monopolized, the district court concluded: "In respect to monopoly power, we think it existed in this case. As we have shown, the defendants were all working together. There was a horizontal conspiracy as to price fixing, runs, and clearances. The vertical integrations aided such a conspiracy at every point. In these circumstances, the defendants must be viewed *collectively* rather than independently as to the power which they exercised over the market by their theatre holdings." 85 F. Supp. 881, 894 (emphasis added).

69. Cf. Chapter 19, p. 516 *supra*.

70. See Chapter 6, pp. 181–82 *supra*.

71. Cf. Chapter 8, pp. 258–60. See also Chapter 14, pp. 395–98 *supra*.

72. *U.S.* v. *Aluminum Co. of America et al.*, 148 F. 2d 416, 432 (1945).

Kellogg, one from General Mills, and one from General Foods—was not new. But the staff also asked that many of the Big Three's cereal formulas and trademarks—e.g., for Rice Krispies, Cheerios, and Grape Nuts—be made available for licensing to the newly created firms and other rivals, thereby encouraging new price-oriented competition analogous to private-label competition.[73] Licensees would be able to use, say, the name Cheerios and indicate that they had followed the original formula under rigorous quality control standards; but they would have to distinguish their product with a prominent company name identification—viz., Smith's Cheerios as contrasted to General Mills' Cheerios. The cereal case was uncommonly innovative in its juxtaposition of alleging monopolization by oligopolists rather than by a dominant firm, the theory of entry preclusion invoked, and the request for a trademark licensing remedy.

Proposals to reform Sherman Act Section 2

At the time this book was written, the reach of Sherman Act Section 2 and its Federal Trade Commission Act Section 5 counterpart was unusually uncertain. Decisions in fairly traditional cases like *IBM* would determine whether the law retained its sting toward dominant market positions maintained through business policies adopted with a conscious eye to their entrenchment effects. Decisions in more novel cases like *Kellogg* would indicate whether the law encompassed competitive punch-pulling oligopolies using *inter alia* the more sophisticated, less rapacious entry-deterring methods of Madison Avenue. These decisions will be made by a Supreme Court generally considered to be much more conservative than the assemblage responsible for the *Paramount Pictures*, *Griffith*, and 1946 *American Tobacco* precedents and for affirming *United Shoe Machinery*. Among those who favored a tough structural antitrust policy, there was hope, but hardly unbounded optimism. It is difficult to tell how much impact the exist-

ing monopolization doctrines have had on American industry. It seems reasonable to suppose that they discourage such conduct as localized price warfare and harassment through protracted patent litigation by enterprises with substantial market positions. Yet the large number of suits litigated during the 1970s alleging various types of predation cause one to wonder how potent the deterrent has been.[74] Fear of Section 2 and related treble damage suits may also have induced some leading sellers to restrain their competitive efforts so as not to exceed that magic 60 to 64 percent market share identified by Judge Hand as the threshold of monopoly. That General Motors is so inhibited in selling its automobiles has been claimed repeatedly, though the charge is denied with equal frequency by GM's management.[75] Kaplan and associates heard officials of several large corporations report in interviews that they prefer to concentrate their energy on invading new markets rather than building legally vulnerable positions in traditional markets.[76] To the extent that such statements are true, they lend support to the adage, "The ghost of Senator Sherman sits at the board table of every large corporation."

Apart from indirect behavioral effects, the *direct* impact of Sherman Act Section 2 in lessening market concentration has been modest. Between 1890 and 1970, the courts have ordered structural reorganization in only 32 Section 2 cases—all but 7 of them before 1950.[77] A few of the orders were drastic, such as the division of New Jersey Standard Oil into 33 pieces, the dissolution of the Tobacco Trust, the splitting of du Pont into three separate powder manufacturing enterprises, and the requirement that United Shoe Machinery Corporation spin off sufficient business to reduce its market share to 33 percent. But most have been mild, such as the order requiring du Pont to end its joint venture with Imperial Chemical Industries, Ltd., and the dissolution of A&P's food brokerage subsidiary. One reason for the relative paucity of major reorganization actions is a natural reticence by the federal courts to impose what are considered to be harsh remedial measures without compelling cause. As Judge Wyzanski cautioned in his first *United Shoe Machinery* decision:

In the anti-trust field the courts have been accorded . . . an authority they have in no other branch of enacted law. . . . They would not have been given, or allowed to keep, such authority in the anti-trust field, and they would not so freely have altered from time to time the interpretation of its substantive provisions, if courts were in the habit of proceeding with the surgical ruthlessness that might commend itself to those seeking absolute assurances that there will be workable competition.[78]

Because of this judicial reticence and the preoccupation of Section 2 restructuring precedents with dominant firms (which are rare) to the exclusion of tight-knit oligopolies (which are much more common), enforcement of the law on monopolization has fallen short of the more ardent trustbusters' aspirations. (Others, needless to say, insist that it has nonetheless gone too far.)

A further limiting factor has been the prodigious complexity and cost of major monopolization suits. Section 2 actions have always tended to be "big cases," but in recent years there has been noticeable escalation. Record holder at the time this book was written was *U.S.* v. *IBM*. Presentation of the government's case alone—that is, before IBM began its lengthy defense—took nearly three years and filled 72,000 pages of trial transcript. IBM is believed to have spent close to $100 million on legal fees and related expenses defending itself in that action and half a dozen treble damage suits alleging similar and overlapping violations. The Justice Department's costs in *U.S.* v. *IBM* were expected to exceed the $10 million mark.

Responsibility for such vast costs is multisided. Attorneys, including government lawyers, tend to be risk averters. When they represent plaintiffs, they strive to support every conceivable allegation, maximizing the likelihood that at least some charges will be decided in their favor. They also try to enhance the credibility of documentary evidence by linking it to the live testimony of respondent company witnesses, who are well-coached by defense attorneys and testify for hours without saying anything substantive. With potentially enormous stakes in the balance, defense attorneys do everything in their power to block or delay the discovery and introduction of prejudicial documents, to pick apart or obscure the testimony of opposing witnesses through protracted cross examination, and to present a thoroughly hedged case in defense. Judges often contribute by failing to force attorneys to focus on the central issues. And at bottom, the system is at fault for providing rules that do more to advance the income of antitrust practitioners than the quest for truth.

Widespread dissatisfaction with the status quo has inspired numerous proposals for reform. There have, of course, been suggestions that Sherman Act Section 2 be scrapped without replacement.[79] Strengthening the law substantively and streamlining procedures have commanded more serious and widespread attention.[80] Among

73. Trademark licensing had been recommended by an administrative law judge in an earlier FTC case, when the Borden Company, maker of ReaLemon, was found to have monopolized the reconstituted lemon juice market through more orthodox exclusionary tactics. *In the matter of Borden, Inc.*, docket no. 8978, initial decision, August 19, 1976. However, in November 1978 the Commission as a whole denied the licensing order, deeming it unnecessary to curb Borden's monopoly power. The Commission instead enjoined Borden from selling juice "below its cost or at unreasonably low prices" with the effect of eliminating competition. See also Richard Schmalensee, "On the Use of Economic Models in Antitrust: The ReaLemon Case," *University of Pennsylvania Law Review* 128 (forthcoming in 1979).

74. The reasons for an apparent surge of predatory pricing cases are mysterious. Was it because of procedural changes improving the odds for a more or less constant stock of potential treble damages claimants? Or did sizeable producers become more inclined to pursue exclusionary tactics—e.g., because of changes in the intensity of profit maximization stimuli, the increased importance of brand image barriers to entry, a more sophisticated understanding of entry deterrent pricing strategies, or the belief that antitrust was less of a threat?

75. See, for example, Simon Whitney, *Antitrust Policies*, vol. 1 (New York: Twentieth Century Fund, 1958), pp. 482–83; and Martin Shubik, *Strategy and Market Structure* (New York: Wiley, 1959), pp. 304–307.

76. A. D. H. Kaplan, J. B. Dirlam, and R. F. Lanzillotti, *Pricing in Big Business* (Washington, D.C.: Brookings Institution, 1958), p. 268.

77. See Richard A. Posner, "A Statistical Study of Antitrust Enforcement," *Journal of Law and Economics* 13 (October 1970): 406; and U.S., Department of Justice, *Report of the Attorney General's National Committee To Study the Antitrust Laws* (Washington, D.C.: Government Printing Office, 1955), p. 354n.

78. *U.S.* v. *United Shoe Machinery Corporation*, 110 F. Supp. 295, 348 (1953). See also *Timken Roller Bearing Co.* v. *U.S.*, 341 U.S. 593, 603 (1951).

proposals of the latter sort, three warrant elaboration. A task force established by President Johnson recommended in 1968 a new "Concentrated Industries Act" under which the leading sellers in "oligopoly industries" meeting certain structural criteria would be subjected to reorganization before a specially constituted court.[81] Companies singled out for fragmentation would be those with a 15 percent or greater market share in an industry with sales of $500 million or more and a four-firm concentration ratio persistently in excess of 70 percent. The special court would order divestiture so that no seller had more than a 12 percent market share *unless* a substantial loss of scale economies would result. In 1972 and 1973 Senator Philip A. Hart introduced a proposed Industrial Reorganization Act under which the existence of monopoly power would be presumed if a company's after-tax returns on stockholders' equity exceeded 15 percent for five consecutive years, or if there were no substantial price competition among two or more corporations in an industry for three years running, or if the four-firm concentration ratio exceeded 50 percent.[82] If monopoly power were found, divestiture would be required unless the firm or firms showed that the monopoly power resulted from lawfully acquired and utilized patents or that divestiture would cause a loss of substantial economies. The law would be enforced by a specially constituted Industrial Reorganization Commission, which would also be given a specific mandate to conduct studies pointing toward structural reorganization in the chemical, drug, electrical equipment, computer, communications equipment, energy, steel, motor vehicle, and nonferrous metal industries. In 1976 Senator Hart proposed an alternative "no-fault" monopolization bill under which Sherman Act Section 2 enforcement proceedings would be simplified by eliminating the government's need to prove intent to monopolize.[83] Companies shown to possess monopoly power could escape fragmentation only by demonstrating that their power came solely from legally acquired and used patents or that divestiture would cause a loss of substantial scale economies. None of these or similar proposals gained sufficient congressional support to be voted out of committee. However, a much more narrowly focused natural gas bill amendment that would have required vertical dismemberment of the largest U.S. petroleum companies was defeated in 1975 by only a narrow margin in a Senate roll call vote.[84]

Senator Hart, sponsor of the two broad monopolization law reform bills, was highly respected by his Senate colleagues—sufficiently so that they named the third Senate office building for him shortly after his death. This suggests that the desire for a strengthened monopolization law reflects something more than the maunderings of a radical fringe. Yet the failure of Congress to support such legislation reveals widespread doubts concerning likely costs and benefits. The issues have both economic and sociopolitical ramifications. The economic aspects alone extend to virtually everything we have considered in this book. Nevertheless, certain central points merit renewed emphasis.

A key question is whether economies of scale are sufficiently pervasive that significant efficiency losses would occur if structural fragmentation were pursued vigorously. This question of costs also has a benefits dimension, for if scale economies and high concentration tend to coincide, many firms would escape reorganization under the scale economies defense included in virtually every proposal for strengthening Sherman Act Section 2. And if little reorganization occurred, the new law's benefits would be small.

We saw in Chapter 4 that the leading sellers in most American manufacturing industries owe their size to the operation of multiple plants, and not simply to having large plants.[85] We observed that the reduction in unit production, distribution, and management costs associated with multi-plant operation tended more often than not to be small or even negligible. We also found that for a sample of 12 important manufacturing industries, Big Three members were typically much larger than they needed to be to take advantage of all but slight residual advantages of multi-plant size.[86] All this suggests that a considerable amount of fragmentation could take place without appreciably impairing industrial efficiency. However, the statistical analysis of PIMS data discussed in Chapter 9 raises doubts whether the advantages of size are indeed exhausted at modest market shares. Exceptions certainly exist. In some highly concentrated industries that might stand out as prime targets for antitrust action, single-plant scale economies are compelling and the extent of multi-plant operation is low. Concentration of all production in a single-plant complex complicated divestiture efforts in the shoe machinery and bus industries, and low levels of multi-plant operation would make it difficult to reorganize the turbogenerator, cigarette, and outboard motor boat engine industries, among others. It should be recognized too that there may be a tendency for compelling scale economies and deficient pricing performance to coincide, for as we have seen in Chapter 8, if small-scale entry at equivalent unit costs is feasible, the leading sellers in a concentrated industry are unlikely, in the absence of other entry barriers, to be able to hold prices persistently above costs.

There are, of course, other entry barriers. Considering one of them sheds further light on the possibilities for monopolization law reform. Having a well-received nationwide brand image was one of the more important advantages pulling companies toward multi-plant operation, the author's research on 12 industries revealed.[87] The advantages of size in exploiting a favorable image are different from other economies of scale: They accrue primarily in the form of higher prices rather than lower unit costs, although there may also be interaction effects.

Image differentiation appears to underlie much of the observed correlation between high advertising/sales ratios and supranormal profitability.[88] Divestiture actions that fail to cope with entrenched image differentiation are apt to leave the sources of monopoly power undisturbed, create nonviable firms (i.e., those deprived of access to well-accepted brand names), or both. However, divestiture coupled with trademark licensing and assurance of quality control, as sought in the breakfast cereal case, could do much to reduce monopoly distortions.[89]

Despite these reassurances, one must be wary of overestimating the benefits from a strengthened deconcentration law. One limitation on benefits is the fact that pricing behavior in some highly concentrated industries conforms tolerably closely to competitive norms. If performance is already good, not much will be gained by imposing a more competitive market structure. Second, economies of scale might constrain the amount of reorganization attainable, which in turn will affect benefits. It is doubtful, for example, whether more than two new automobile manufacturers could be carved out of the existing U.S. industry without sacrificing significant efficiencies; and it is improbable that the creation of two additional rivals would do much to alter auto industry conduct and performance. Third, transportation costs could limit the amount of competition achieved following structural reorganization. The U.S. cement industry, for instance, is highly concen-

(79) For one of the better argued proposals in this vein, see Richard A. Posner, *Antitrust Law: An Economic Perspective* (Chicago: University of Chicago Press, 1976), especially Chapters 1, 5, and 8. See also Robert Bork, *The Antitrust Paradox* (New York: Basic Books, 1978), Chapters 7 and 8.

(80) Early proposals included one by the Twentieth Century Fund's Committee on Cartels and Monopolies, described in G. W. Stocking and M. W. Watkins, *Monopoly and Free Enterprise* (New York: Twentieth Century Fund, 1951), pp. 553, 563–64; and Carl Kaysen and Donald F. Turner, *Antitrust Policy: An Economic and Legal Analysis* (Cambridge, Mass.: Harvard University Press, 1959), especially Chapters 3 and 4.

81. *Report of the White House Task Force on Antitrust Policy,* July 5, 1968, Section II and Appendix A, reprinted in the *Journal of Reprints for Antitrust Law and Economics* 1 (Winter 1969). A more conservative Task Force on Productivity and Competition appointed by President Nixon concluded in 1969 that it could not endorse strengthened deconcentration legislation. See the same issue of the *Journal of Reprints*, pp. 845–46.

82. S. 1167, 93rd Cong., 1st sess. (1973). For the text, see Appendix B of Harvey J. Goldschmid et al., eds., *Industrial Concentration: The New Learning* (Boston: Little, Brown, 1974), pp. 444–48. See also in the same volume Harlan M. Blake, "Legislative Proposals for Industrial Deconcentration," pp. 340–60, and the ensuing debate among Walter Adams, Phil Neal, Almarin Phillips, Richard Posner, Senator Hart, and Senator Roman Hruska.

83. S. 3429, 94th Cong., 2nd sess., introduced May 13, 1976.

84. See "Ford Gas Program Backed in Senate," *New York Times,* 9 October 1975, p. 21. In 1976 a bill calling for vertical divestiture of petroleum companies was approved by the Senate Judiciary Committee but failed to come to a floor vote.

85. Cf. Chapter 4, pp. 100–1 *supra.*

86. Cf. Chapter 4, pp. 118–19 *supra.*

87. Cf. Table 4.10, pp. 118–19 *supra.*

88. See Chapters 9 and 14 *supra.*

89. See also the author's analysis in "The Posnerian Harvest: Separating Wheat from Chaff," *Yale Law Journal* 86 (April 1977): 995–1000.

trated in most meaningfully drawn regional markets; its economic performance has historically been poor; the leading companies operated in 1970 an average of 13 plants each; and economies of multiplant operation are slight.[90] One might consider cement a prime candidate for reorganization. But plants are typically so widely scattered geographically, and shipping costs are so high, that not much competitive interpenetration of newly independent plants' natural market territories could be expected.

For all these reasons, the subset of industries in which structural fragmentation would lead to significantly enhanced price and other competition without appreciable scale economy losses is a good deal smaller than the set of all highly concentrated industries. There is no reason to believe that the subset is empty; important opportunities for improving performance through invigorated structural antitrust undoubtedly remain untapped. But excessive optimism about the payoff potential is unwarranted.

These and other economic factors must be weighed carefully in deciding whether to strengthen and expand the law on monopolization. In addition, noneconomic considerations are relevant. The dispersion of power as an end in itself has from the beginning been an objective of antitrust, as it was in the drafting of the U.S. Constitution. As Senator Sherman said in his principal speech supporting his 1890 bill:

> If the concentrated powers of [a trust] are intrusted to a single man, it is a kingly prerogative, inconsistent with our form of government, and should be subject to the strong resistance of the State and national authorities. If anything is wrong this is wrong. If we will not endure a king as a political power we should not endure a king over the production, transportation, and sale of any of the necessaries of life.[91]

Whether this is what the people of the United States continue to desire, and if so, how vigorously they wish to see the dispersion of economic power pursued, has become increasingly unclear as the size and complexity of the economy have grown and the accumulation of power, private and governmental, has been taken for granted.

One might suppose that attitudinal survey research methods could be employed to inform Congress about the direction and strength of public preferences. A Congress armed with such insights plus what has been learned about the economic benefits and costs might rationally debate whether the substantive reform of monopolization law should in fact be carried out.

Even without a broad social consensus, procedural reform is clearly needed. A revised approach might work as follows. Following the discovery of evidence, the contending parties would submit polished briefs documenting their views on both the mandate for structural reorganization and the probable consequences. The presiding judge, assisted by a court-appointed panel of impartial economic experts subject to questioning by the contending parties, would then narrow the issues and allow testimony covering only those relevant disputed issues on which further useful illumination is deemed probable. Counselled in open court by the panel of experts, the judge would then hear final arguments and render a decision. In addition to costing less, such a procedure would almost surely lead to decisions that better satisfy the important goals of truth and equity.

Merger policy

Besides breaking up consolidations of monopoly power already in existence, there is another way to help maintain competitive market structures: by curbing the dynamic process of concentration before it goes too far. This is the task of merger policy.

Formulating an optimal policy A sensible policy must take into account the costs and benefits of mergers and the ability of enforcement agencies to weigh those costs and benefits. As we have seen in Chapter 4, mergers are consummated for complex motives and have many effects, intended and unintended. Some mergers, and especially the vast wave of mergers at the turn of the century, have been inspired by the desire to achieve monopoly power, and although many fell short of their aspirations, increased concentration and elevated prices were a frequent consequence. Others stem from less overtly monopolistic motives but entail a competition opportunity loss—e.g., when firms seek to "expand" by merger rather than build new capacity whose presence would move prices nearer competitive levels. Mergers can have unambiguously beneficial consequences when new possibilities for achieving production and distributional scale economies are created; when complementary managerial, technical, and/or marketing resources can be utilized more effectively; or when for one reason or another coordinated planning proves more effective than competitive pressure in weeding out redundant resources. They may also have what appear to some parties to be benefits but from a broader perspective are mere redistributions—e.g., when some shareholders or financial brokers realize speculative gains, when capacity changes hands at bargain prices, when tax laws permit stockholders to gain at the Treasury's expense, and when resulting monopsony power permits purely pecuniary gains in purchasing. Still other apparent benefits of merger are of unclear or doubtful value from a social perspective—for instance, when the pooling of risks reduces capital costs only because financial markets have failed to make available optimally diversified portfolio instruments, or when promotional economies permit a seller to reinforce brand images and as a result elevate prices. And finally, mergers can have unambiguously undesirable but unintended consequences, as when diseconomies of large-scale management ensue or overextended chains of command sap employees' incentive.

An ideal public policy would be one weighing the social (not private) benefits and costs of mergers and letting pass only those mergers that are on balance benign or beneficial or, if noneconomic considerations motivate a presumption against enhanced economic concentration, only those mergers with significant net benefits. Professor Williamson has shown that if the focus in such benefit-cost analyses is confined to possible cost reductions and the dead-weight welfare losses flowing from monopolistic price raising,

modest unit cost savings tend rather quickly to outweigh appreciable price effects.[92] Thus, Williamson calculates that with a market demand elasticity of unity, a unit cost reduction of less than .5 percent would be sufficient to offset the allocative inefficiency resulting from a 5 percent price increase. An implausibly high price increase of 20 percent would be offset by 3 percent unit cost savings. His analysis assumes *inter alia* that the merger reduces costs rather than enhances them and that society is unconcerned about redistributions of income from consumers to monopolists as a result of merger. To the extent that these and other assumptions are accepted, the implication is that the identification of cost savings flowing from a merger should be an important component of the merger scrutiny process.

Unfortunately, it is difficult to enforce merger policy in anything approaching an ideal manner. Identifying probable social benefits and costs is the key problem. Business executives called into court to explain their motives and plans may have incentives to be less than candid. Nor is faulty testimony necessarily the result of deliberate dissembling. Because of the inherent uncertainties pervading business decisions and the frequently muddled state of business thinking on mergers, executives may not foresee clearly the effects of alternative actions. Thus, the New York Central-Pennsylvania Railroad merger was expected to generate cost savings of roughly 4 percent after a five-year shakedown period.[93] The actual result was organizational confusion, costs rising without control, bankruptcy, and ulti-

90. F. M. Scherer et al., *The Economics of Multi-Plant Operation: An International Comparisons Study* (Cambridge, Mass.: Harvard University Press, 1975), pp. 208, 334–36, 394.

91. *Congressional Record*, vol. 21, p. 2457 (1890). See also James Madison's *Federalist Paper* no. 51 on "opposite and rival interests" in private affairs.

92. Oliver E. Williamson, "Economies as an Antitrust Defense: The Welfare Tradeoffs," *American Economic Review* 58 (March 1968): 18–36; augmented and corrected in the *American Economic Review* 58 (December 1968): 1372–76, and *American Economic Review* 59 (December 1969): 954–59. See also Raymond Jackson, "The Consideration of Economies in Merger Cases," *Journal of Business* 43 (October 1970): 439–47. Williamson's approach is illustrated in the analysis accompanying Figure 2.4, p. 22 *supra*.

mate quasi-nationalization. Similarly, a high Bethlehem Steel Corporation official, explaining his company's motives for acquiring the Youngstown Sheet and Tube Co. in 1956, testified that Bethlehem (whose capacity was concentrated in the East) could not develop integrated steel-making operations in the Midwest, where aggregate capacity was insufficient to satisfy demand, unless it was permitted to take advantage of Youngstown's existing position in the Chicago area.[94] Four years after the merger was prohibited, Bethlehem began constructing its Burns Harbor, Indiana, complex—the *only* integrated green-field blast furnace-oxygen converter-rolling mill complex built during the 1960s and 1970s to provide a U.S. counterpart to the modern steel-making capacity growing by leaps and bounds abroad. Meanwhile, Youngstown undertook a $450 million program to modernize and expand its old Indiana Harbor facility.[95]

Deluged with such misinformation, courts attempting to weigh merger benefits and costs under a rule of reason would make many faulty decisions. Especially if the antitrust enforcement agencies were required to bear the burden of proving unreasonableness, the bias in decisions would probably fall on the side of permitting questionable acquisitions, since government economists and attorneys rarely have as much information about the effects of a proposed merger as the merging companies. Recognizing this, many students of antitrust policy have urged the adoption of tougher rules.[96] One might be to establish a *prima facie* case against certain mergers—viz., those involving substantial shares of the relevant market—to be rebutted only if the prospective partners can offer convincing evidence that the social benefits of the merger outweigh the injury to competition. Or still tougher, all mergers entailing a substantial share of the market might be declared *per se* illegal, without regard to benefits. Several arguments for taking a hard line can be advanced.

First, antitrust prohibitions affect only a small but important proportion of all actual and potential mergers—notably, those in which an adverse impact on competition is especially likely. From 1969 through 1974, the number of government suits challenging mergers averaged 22 per year—less than 1 percent of all recorded mergers, but roughly 15 to 20 percent of all acquisitions of companies with assets of $10 million or more.[97] To be sure, an unknown number of mergers were thwarted by the recognition that they would be challenged if consummated. Still the fact remains that relatively few mergers would come under attack even with stringent rules.

Second, as we have seen in Chapter 4, an impressive accumulation of evidence points to the conclusion that mergers seldom yield substantial cost savings, real or pecuniary. Indeed, the weight of the postmerger profitability evidence for an assortment of nations suggests that on average, the private gains from mergers were either negative or insignificantly different from zero.[98] Since social benefits are seldom large, and since firms would be free alternatively to expand through internal building and market development, the net balance of benefits versus costs under a strict policy is hardly apt to be decisively unfavorable, and it seems more likely to be favorable.

Third, it is much easier to nip the growth of market concentration in the bud through a hard line against mergers than it is to correct abuses or atomize market structures once monopoly or tight oligopoly has emerged. To stop a merger before it is consummated means at most quenching an opportunity, while tampering with an already integrated monopolistic organization is sure to cause considerable pain and might even lessen efficiency. Once the eggs are scrambled, it is hard to unscramble them.

For these and perhaps also for sociopolitical reasons, there is much to be said for a policy that errs on the side of a hard line against mergers, accepting the risk that occasionally mergers offering substantial efficiency benefits will be barred because the judicial system is such an imperfect screen. On this more will be said when a fuller historical foundation has been laid.

The evolution of statutory law In the early years of U.S. antitrust, mergers were challenged as illegal combinations in restraint of trade under Sherman Act Section 1 and as attempts to monopolize or (when carried far enough) as outright

546

monopolization under Section 2. The first government victory came in 1904, in the *Northern Securities* decision discussed earlier. It was followed by successful attacks on other railroad consolidations, including the Union Pacific's acquisition of a dominant stock interest in the Southern Pacific and the Southern Pacific's control of the Central Pacific. During the 1920s and 1930s, however, Sherman Act suits against mergers were attempted only infrequently. Whether this was because there were few mergers deemed to have restrained competition sufficiently, because the 1920 *U.S. Steel* rule was so permissive, or because of a general lack of interest and enthusiasm within the enforcement agencies, is not entirely clear. A noteworthy defeat occurred in 1948 when the Justice Department attempted to stop another United States Steel Corporation acquisition, this time vertical, of the Consolidated Steel Corporation. Consolidated accounted for 11 percent of structural steel and plate fabrication activity in the Pacific and Mountain states, where U.S. Steel controlled 39 percent of all raw steel ingot capacity.[99] New life was breathed into the law when a merger between two Lexington, Kentucky, banks—one with 40 percent of local banking assets and the other with 13 percent—was successfully challenged in 1964. In that case the Supreme Court summarized its position as follows:

> [W]here merging companies are major competitive factors in a relevant market, the elimination of significant competition between them, by merger or consolidation, itself constitutes a violation of Section 1 of the Sherman Act. That standard was met in the present case in view of the fact that the two banks in question had such a large share of the relevant market.[100]

As the precedents have evolved, the Sherman Act has no bite unless the merging firms are on the verge of attaining substantial monopoly power, and this may already be too late if the objective is to maintain competitive market structures. To remedy this and related deficiencies, Congress in 1914 passed the Clayton Act, whose stated purpose was "to arrest the creation of trusts, conspiracies and monopolies in their incipiency and before consummation."[101] The

principal provision concerning mergers was Section 7, which read in part:

> That no corporation engaged in commerce shall acquire, directly or indirectly, the whole or any part of the stock or other share capital of another corporation engaged also in commerce where the effect of such acquisition may be to substantially lessen competition between [the two firms] or to restrain such commerce in any section or community or tend to create a monopoly of any line of commerce.

This choice of language left a gaping loophole through which able corporation lawyers could navigate their clients. It banned only *stock* acquisitions—the dominant large-scale consolidation method of the times. By shifting to the outright purchase of a competitor's *assets*, com-

(93) Compare "The Big Merger Begins To Click," *Business Week*, 4 May 1968, p. 104; "Penn Central Sees a Light in the Tunnel," *Business Week*, 22 November 1969, p. 44; and "The Penn Central Bankruptcy Express," *Fortune*, August 1970, pp. 104 ff.

94. See Willard F. Mueller, *The Celler-Kefauver Act: Sixteen Years of Enforcement*, Federal Trade Commission staff report to the Antitrust Subcommittee, House Committee on the Judiciary (Washington, D.C.: Government Printing Office, 1967), p. 17; and *U.S.* v. *Bethlehem Steel Corporation et al.*, 168 F. Supp. 576, 615–616 (1958).

95. For citations to numerous similar cases in which company predictions turned out to be false, see Joseph F. Brodley, "Potential Competition Mergers: A Structural Synthesis," *Yale Law Journal* 87 (November 1977): 64n.

96. See, for example, George J. Stigler, "Mergers and Preventive Antitrust Policy," *University of Pennsylvania Law Review* 104 (November 1955): 176–84; Kaysen and Turner, *Antitrust Policy*, pp. 132–33; Derek C. Bok, "Section Seven of the Clayton Act and the Merging of Law and Economics," *Harvard Law Review* 74 (December 1960): 271–74, 299–321; and Richard B. Heflebower, "Corporate Mergers: Policy and Economic Analysis," *Quarterly Journal of Economics* 77 (November 1963): 537–38.

97. Estimated from annual Federal Trade Commission reports on the number of mergers in all fields and the value of manufacturing and mining firm assets acquired.

98. See Chapter 4, pp. 138–41 *supra* and Dennis C. Mueller, ed., *The Determinants and Effects of Mergers: An International Comparison*, (forthcoming in 1980).

99. *U.S.* v. *Columbia Steel Company et al.*, 334 U.S. 495 (1948).

100. *U.S.* v. *First National Bank & Trust Co. of Lexington et al.*, 376 U.S. 665, 671–672 (1964).

101. Senate Report no. 698, to accompany H. R. 15,657, 63rd Cong., 2nd sess., 1914, p. 1.

panies could escape the law's reach. Direct asset acquisition is not always easy, but the loophole was opened even wider through subsequent Supreme Court interpretations. In three 1926 cases the Court ruled that a merger could not be dissolved if the acquiring firm first bought its rival's stock, but liquidated the stock and transformed its position to one of asset ownership before the antitrust enforcement agencies brought suit.[102] Then, in 1934, the Court found that a merger was safe if converted to the asset ownership form before a Federal Trade Commission order barring the merger was *issued*.[103] These decisions left Section 7 with few teeth. Moreover, the Supreme Court decided in 1930 that in proving a Section 7 violation, the government had to show nearly as substantial a lessening of competition as in Sherman Act cases.[104] The cumulative effect of these decisions was complete emasculation. Altogether, only 15 mergers were ordered dissolved as a result of antitrust actions initiated between 1914 and 1950, and 10 of the dissolutions were accomplished through the Sherman Act rather than Clayton Act proceedings.

Passage of a strengthened Section 7 Two events provoked Congress to take corrective action. One was the government's defeat in its attempt to stop the U.S. Steel-Consolidated Steel merger. The other was publication of a report by the Federal Trade Commission viewing with alarm the increase in merger activity following World War II and suggesting that if nothing were done, "the giant corporations will ultimately take over the country."[105] The report was criticized for making inferences unsupported by the evidence, but Congress nevertheless passed the Celler-Kefauver Act of 1950. The Act amended original Clayton Act Section 7, removing the asset acquisition loophole and making several changes in wording to bring nonhorizontal mergers within the reach of the law, to eliminate a previously split infinitive, and to make clear Congress' desire to see a more vigorous antimerger program implemented. Its principal substantive paragraph provides:

[t]hat no corporation engaged in commerce shall acquire, directly or indirectly, the whole or any part of the stock or other share capital and no corporation subject to the jurisdiction of the Federal Trade Commission shall acquire the whole or any part of the assets of another corporation engaged also in commerce, where in any line of commerce in any section of the country, the effect of such acquisition may be substantially to lessen competition, or to tend to create a monopoly.

This new mandate was taken seriously by the enforcement agencies and the courts. From late 1950, when the Celler-Kefauver amendment was signed, through 1965, the Justice Department and Federal Trade Commission initiated some 173 antimerger complaints under the new law—more than twice as many as they had attempted during the 36-year life of old Section 7. By 1976, the cumulative number of new Section 7 suits had climbed to 329.[106] Moreover, as we shall see, the enforcement agencies' efforts were rewarded this time with an impressive string of victories in appeals to the Supreme Court. These judgments communicated in the strongest possible way that a tough line was to be taken.

Further actions strengthened the enforcement agencies' antimerger weapons. A rider to a 1973 bill gave the Federal Trade Commission authority to seek preliminary injunctions against mergers—a power the Justice Department already possessed. In 1969 the FTC instituted a premerger notification program under which companies agreeing to mergers of appreciable size had to file information on their sales broken down to the Census seven-digit product level. This program was sanctioned and extended in a 1976 statute that required *inter alia* a 15- to 30-day waiting period following initial notification before the merger could be consummated.[107] An attempt to begin the waiting period only when the requirements were fulfilled to the enforcement agencies' satisfaction was defeated as a result of vigorous opposition from industry and financial community leaders, who claimed that the government might effect much longer delays by insisting that the information submitted was incomplete.

Judicial rulings: horizontal and vertical mergers To see what principles have been applied by the courts in interpreting the new Section 7, we must examine the leading decisions. Before beginning, however, we digress briefly to consider one more case brought under old Section 7. To the surprise of nearly everyone concerned, the government in 1957 was sustained by the Supreme Court on a 1949 suit to require divestiture of du Pont's 23 percent stock interest in General Motors.[108] The Court found that the financial ties between du Pont and GM foreclosed du Pont's competitors from the opportunity to serve a substantial portion of the automobile industry's demand for synthetic lacquers and fabrics. Besides breaking a long chain of government defeats, the case was distinctive in three respects: It was the first successful Section 7 action against a vertical acquisition; there was a delay of 32 years between the challenged stock acquisition and the initiation of a suit; and the case posed considerable divestiture problems. On the last point, Congress in 1962 passed a special act allowing du Pont stockholders to pay only capital gains tax rates on the General Motors shares distributed to them under the divestiture decree, instead of the higher regular income tax rates normally applicable.[109]

The first major government victory under new Section 7 came, fittingly enough, in another steel industry merger case.[110] Bethlehem Steel Corporation, the nation's second largest producer, with 16.3 percent of total U.S. ingot capacity, sought to acquire the Youngstown Sheet & Tube Co., the sixth largest producer, with 4.6 percent of ingot capacity. The companies argued that the merger did not substantially lessen competition because Bethlehem sold most of its output in the East, while Youngstown was primarily active in the Midwest, so that only about 10 percent of their combined output was shipped to customers in overlapping geographic territories. This defense was rejected by the district court, which held that freight cost barriers to interpenetration of regional markets were overcome sufficiently to view the market as nationwide in scope,[111] and that a merger combining 16.3 and 4.6 percent of national capacity exemplified the substantial lessening of competition Congress sought to outlaw under new Section 7. It also found the combined market shares excessive for several narrowly de-

fined product lines (such as cold-rolled sheet) and in certain geographic submarkets (such as the Ohio-Michigan territory). The court was unimpressed by the defendants' argument that through the merger they could compete more effectively with United States Steel Corporation. It concluded to the contrary that the merger would make "even more remote than at present the possibility of any real competition from the smaller members of the industry who follow the leadership of United States Steel."[112] The respondents

102. *Thatcher Mfg. Co. v. Federal Trade Commission, Swift & Co. v. Federal Trade Commission,* and *Federal Trade Commission v. Western Meat Co.,* 272 U.S. 554 (1926).

103. *Arrow-Hart & Hegeman Electric Co. v. Federal Trade Commission,* 291 U.S. 587 (1934).

104. *International Shoe Co. v. Federal Trade Commission,* 280 U.S. 291 (1930). On the development of Clayton Act Section 7 interpretations during this period, see David Dale Martin, *Mergers and the Clayton Act* (Berkeley: University of California Press, 1959), especially pp. 104–47.

105. U.S., Federal Trade Commission, *The Merger Movement: A Summary Report* (Washington: Federal Trade Commission, 1948), p. 68. Historical perspective reveals that the supposed merger wave was of quite modest proportions. See Figure 4.5, Chapter 4, p. 120 *supra.*

106. See the testimony of Willard F. Mueller in U.S., Congress, House, Committee on the Judiciary, Subcommittee on Monopolies and Commercial Law, *Merger Oversight and H. R. 13131,* 94th Cong., 2nd sess., 1976, p. 100.

107. Public Law 94–435, 15 U.S.C. Sec. 18A. For the implementing rules, see the *Federal Register,* 31 July 1978, pp. 33450–557.

108. *U.S. v. E. I. du Pont de Nemours and Co. et al.,* 353 U.S. 586 (1957); 366 U.S. 316 (1961).

109. For a more general analysis of the stock price effects of divestiture orders, see Kenneth J. Boudreaux, "Divestiture and Share Price," *Journal of Financial and Quantitative Analysis* 10 (November 1975): 619–26.

110. *U.S. v. Bethlehem Steel Corp. et al.,* 168 F. Supp. 576 (1958).

111. The court's reasoning on this point is perceptive but not entirely persuasive. Freight costs from Baltimore (where Bethlehem's largest plant was located) to Chicago were roughly 15 percent of product value, which means that midwestern prices could be elevated substantially above long-run unit costs before an East Coast plant operating near capacity would find it profitable to supply Chicago customers. See Scherer et al., *The Economics of Multi-Plant Operation,* pp. 90, 365. In the vast body of Celler-Kefauver Act opinions, there is conspicuous inattention to the key question of *how much* prices can be elevated before drawing supplies from other points included at the margin of the relevant market. In other words, how broadly a market is defined is really a question of how much elevation of prices is to be tolerated before inferring that unacceptable monopoly power exists.

112. *U.S. v. Bethlehem Steel Corp. et al.,* 168 F. Supp. 576, 604 (1958).

chose not to appeal, and as we have seen earlier, Bethlehem soon launched an ambitious program of building its own independent capacity to serve the midwestern market.

New Section 7 withstood its first substantive Supreme Court test in 1962, when a lower court decision against the Brown Shoe Company's merger with the G. R. Kinney Co. was affirmed.[113] The merger had both horizontal and vertical ramifications. Brown was the fourth largest U.S. shoe manufacturer in 1955, producing approximately 4 percent of national output. Kinney was the twelfth largest manufacturer, with 0.5 percent of output. Brown was vertically integrated into shoe retailing, directly operating some 313 to 470 of the nation's 22,000 retail shoe outlets along with selling at wholesale to 760 independently owned retailers who accepted Brown franchises cancellable on 30 days' notice. Kinney owned and operated more than 350 stores, selling 1.6 percent of all nonrubber shoes in the United States.

There was no contention that the merger posed a threat to horizontal competition in shoe manufacturing. Debate centered on competition in shoe retailing. The Supreme Court supported the lower court's finding that the relevant markets were individual cities with a population exceeding 10,000 and their environs, rejecting Brown's plea for detailed analysis of spatial buying patterns in particular cities. The combined unit sales shares of the two firms exceeded 20 percent of the local market in 32 cities for women's shoes and in 31 cities for children's shoes.[114] This, said the Court, was sufficient to find a substantial lessening of competition under new Section 7.

On the merger's vertical dimension, the relevant market was said to be nationwide in scope. No distinction was made as to price ranges within which manufacturers and retailers specialized. The Court noted a trend in the shoe industry toward increasing vertical integration, with manufacturers becoming increasingly important sources of supply to their captive retail outlets. In the two years following the merger, Brown moved from supplying no shoes to Kinney stores to producing 8 percent of their needs. The tendency of the merger was thus to foreclose other shoe manufacturers from a substantial share of the market,

the Court concluded. And so the merger was struck down for its probable effects on competition both horizontally and vertically.

Subsequent decisions reinforced the impression that a hard line was to be taken. The Von's-Shopping Bag case is particularly significant.[115] Von's Grocery Co., third largest retail grocery chain in the Los Angeles area, with a 4.7 percent share of the market in 1958, acquired Shopping Bag Food Stores, the sixth largest retailer, whose elderly president and principal stockholder sought a merger to ensure managerial continuity of the chain he had built. Together they accounted for 7.5 percent of all grocery sales in the area, second only to Safeway Stores, with 8 percent of the market. Between 1950 and 1961 the number of independent single-unit grocery stores in the area had declined from 5,365 to 3,818. The market share of the top 20 chains had risen from 44 percent in 1948 to 57 percent in 1958, although the combined share of the leading five chains had fallen. A 6–2 majority of the Supreme Court reversed a lower court decision in favor of the merger. They stressed the trend toward increasing concentration in grocery retailing and the contribution the Von's-Shopping Bag merger made toward further concentration:

> It is enough for us that Congress feared that a market marked at the same time by both a continuous decline in the number of small businesses and a large number of mergers would slowly but inevitably gravitate from a market of many small competitors to one dominated by one or a few giants, and competition would thereby be destroyed. Congress passed the Celler-Kefauver Act to prevent such a destruction of competition.[116]

In a dissenting opinion, Justices Stewart and Harlan argued that the decline in the number of single-unit stores was the result of "transcending social and technological changes" and that competition in Los Angeles grocery retailing remained "pugnacious," with successful new entry at modest initial investment levels perceptibly eroding the market shares of leading firms.[117] Still, as usual, the majority carried the day, providing a powerful precedent for future enforcement actions.

With the basic precedents concerning horizontal and vertical mergers established, the Department of Justice published in 1968 formal "guidelines" it expected to apply in deciding whether to challenge acquisitions.[118] For horizontal mergers in industries with four-firm concentration ratios of 75 percent or more, the Department announced that ordinarily it would challenge mergers involving the following market shares:

Acquiring firm	Acquired firm
4%	4% or more
10%	2% or more
15% or more	1% or more

In industries with four-firm concentration ratios of less than 75 percent, its challenges would be directed toward mergers with the following market shares:

Acquiring firm	Acquired firm
5%	5% or more
10%	4% or more
15%	3% or more
20%	2% or more
25% or more	1% or more

And in industries displaying a trend toward increasing concentration, it planned to challenge any merger in which one of the leading eight producers acquired a company with 2 percent or more of the market. For vertical mergers, a 10 percent share of the market for the supplying firm and purchases of 6 percent or more by the buyer were identified as danger points.

Market definition precedents As in Sherman Act monopolization cases, merger case decisions often hinge on how the relevant market is defined. There are two main subproblems: defining the relevant geographic market and defining the product line.

The Celler-Kefauver Act allows considerable scope for defining geographic markets, since it prohibits mergers that may "in any section of the country" substantially lessen competition. Given this broad mandate, the courts have been inclined to strike down mergers whenever a reasonable argument (and sometimes even a tortured argument) could be supported for delimiting markets in such a way as to show substantial anticompetitive effects. In the *Bethlehem-Youngstown* case, for example, both national and single-state definitions were accepted. In the *Brown Shoe-Kinney* case, a national definition was chosen for the vertical facets and a single-city definition for the horizontal effects. The Supreme Court found the State of Wisconsin and also the three-state Wisconsin-Michigan-Illinois territory to be relevant markets in considering the merger of Pabst Brewing Company with the Blatz Brewing Co. The two firms together accounted for 24 percent of Wisconsin beer sales—enough to hold the merger illegal, if one accepts the dubious single-state definition—but only 4.5 percent of sales in the United States as a whole.[119] And in a bank merger decision, the Supreme Court concluded that even though certain large potential customers reached out hundreds of miles to secure banking services, a local definition was appropriate because:

[i]ndividuals and corporations typically confer the bulk of their patronage on banks in their

---

113. *Brown Shoe Co.* v. *U.S.*, 370 U.S. 294 (1962).

114. There is reason to believe that these figures, which include Brown sales through independently owned retailers operating under cancellable franchises, exaggerate Brown's true control of *retail* markets. See John L. Peterman, "The Brown Shoe Case," *Journal of Law and Economics* 18 (April 1975), especially pp. 93–106.

115. *U.S.* v. *Von's Grocery Co. et al.*, 384 U.S. 270 (1966).

116. 384 U.S. 270, 278 (1966).

117. 384 U.S. 270, 300 (1966). Los Angeles was in 1958 and continued to be in 1972 one of the least concentrated retail grocery markets. See the Joint Economic Committee study, *The Profit and Price Performance of Leading Food Chains, 1970–74* (Washington, D.C.: Government Printing Office, 1977), pp. 126–32.

118. U.S., Department of Justice, *Merger Guidelines*, May 30, 1968, reprinted in the *Journal of Reprints for Antitrust Law and Economics* 1 (Summer 1969): 181–200. The Federal Trade Commission published analogous guidelines for particular industries such as grocery products, textiles, and cement, but many of them were rescinded during the 1970s.

119. *U.S.* v. *Pabst Brewing Co. et al.*, 384 U.S. 546 (1966). The case was remanded to a district court for rehearing on other issues. For a critique of the market definition reasoning, see Kenneth G. Elzinga and Thomas F. Hogarty, "The Problem of Geographic Market Delineation in Antimerger Suits," *Antitrust Bulletin* 18 (Spring 1973): 45–81.

local community; they find it impractical to conduct their banking business at a distance. . . . The factor of inconvenience localizes banking competition as effectively as high transportation costs in other industries. . . . [T]hat in banking the relevant geographical market is a function of each separate customer's economic scale means simply that a workable compromise must be found: some fair intermediate delineation which avoids the indefensible extremes of drawing the market so expansively as to make the effect of the merger upon competition seem insignificant, because only the very largest bank customers are taken into account . . . or so narrowly as to place appellees in different markets, because only the smallest customers are considered.[120]

Similarly broad scope has been allowed in defining the relevant product line or "line of commerce." The seeds for an eclectic (and many economists would say confused) approach were sown by the Supreme Court in its *Brown Shoe* opinion:

The outer boundaries of a product market are determined by the reasonable interchangeability of use or the cross-elasticity of demand between the product itself and substitutes for it. . . . However, within this broad market, well-defined submarkets may exist, which, in themselves, constitute product markets for antitrust purposes. . . . The boundaries of such a submarket may be determined by examining such practical indicia as industry or public recognition of the submarket as a separate economic entity, the product's peculiar characteristics and uses, unique production facilities, distinct customers, distinct prices, sensitivity to price changes, and specialized vendors.[121]

How the law has been interpreted is best seen by comparing two cases decided by the Supreme Court in the Spring of 1964.

One concerned acquisition of the Rome Cable Corporation by the Aluminum Company of America.[122] Alcoa produced various types of aluminum electrical conductor cable—a product line it pioneered and in which it was still the U.S. sales leader, though its share of the market had declined owing to the entry of new competitors.

T 20.1 Market shares of Alcoa and Rome under alternate market definitions

	Alcoa	Rome
Bare aluminum conductor wire and cable	32.5%	0.3%
Insulated aluminum conductor wire and cable	11.6%	4.7%
Combined aluminum conductor wire and cable	27.8%	1.3%
All bare conductor wire and cable, including both aluminum and copper	10.3%	2.0%
All insulated conductor wire and cable	0.3%	1.3%
Combined insulated and bare wire and cable, all metals	1.8%	1.4%

Source: *U.S.* v. *Aluminum Co. of America et al.*, 214 F. Supp. 501, 514 (1963).

Rome specialized in copper conductor cable, but about 10 percent of its cable output was of aluminum. In defining the relevant market, the courts had to decide whether to view aluminum and copper conductors separately or in common, and whether or not to break down the market into narrower insulated and uninsulated cable subclasses. Estimates of Alcoa's and Rome's 1958 market shares for six alternative definitions are presented in Table 20.1. In choosing among these six possibilities, many facts had to be weighed. The use of aluminum was clearly on the ascendancy, especially for overhead utility lines, in part because copper prices had risen more rapidly than aluminum prices in the postwar period. Between 1950 and 1959, aluminum's share of new bare high-voltage transmission line installations rose from 74 to 94 percent, and its share of all new overhead transmission and distribution line installations rose from 25 to 80 percent. Copper fared better in insulated than in bare applications, although insulating machines could coat either aluminum or copper wire interchangeably.

The litigants agreed that bare aluminum cable was a distinct line of commerce, but the district court found Rome's share (0.3 percent) under this definition to be too small to threaten any substantial lessening of competition when added to Alcoa's 32.5 percent share. The Justice Department conceded that combined insulated and bare aluminum and copper wire and cable represented a relevant market, but there again the market shares were too small to impute illegality. Reversing a district court decision permitting the merger to stand, a 6–3 majority of the Supreme Court held that the combined (insulated plus bare) aluminum wire and cable market definition, with all copper products excluded, could also be applied. It defended this choice by observing that the price of aluminum conductors was generally lower than the price of comparable copper conductors, and that copper conductor prices had not changed over time in response to changes in aluminum conductor prices or vice versa. Having reached this judgment, the Court went on to find that the addition of Rome's 1.3 percent share to Alcoa's 27.8 percent share constituted a substantial lessening of competition, since Rome served as an important source of independent action in an otherwise oligopolistic industry:

> The record shows indeed that Rome was an aggressive competitor. It was a pioneer in aluminum insulation and developed one of the most widely used insulated conductors. . . . Preservation of Rome, rather than its absorption by one of the giants, will keep it "as an important competitive factor," to use the words of S. Rep. No. 1775. . . . Rome seems to us the prototype of the small independent that Congress aimed to preserve by Section 7.[123]

In the second case, the Supreme Court struck down a merger between the Continental Can Company, second largest maker of tin cans in the United States, and the Hazel-Atlas Glass Co., the third largest bottle manufacturer.[124] Continental sold roughly 33 percent of all tin cans; Hazel-Atlas 10 percent of all glass bottles. A district court found cans and bottles to be separate lines of commerce and hence concluded that competition was not substantially reduced by the merger. But on appeal, the Supreme Court emphasized that tin cans and glass bottles were closely competitive in such applications as beer, soft drink, and baby food packaging, each product challenging and sometimes winning away trade from the other. Representing a majority of the Court, Justice White wrote that:

> In defining the product market . . . we must recognize meaningful competition where it is found to exist. . . . [T]hough the interchangeability of use may not be so complete and the cross-elasticity of demand not so immediate as in the case of most intraindustry mergers, there is over the long run the kind of customer response to innovation and other competitive

120. *U.S. v. Philadelphia National Bank et al.*, 374 U.S. 321, 358, 361 (1963).

121. *Brown Shoe Co.* v. *U.S.*, 370 U.S. 294, 325 (1962).

122. *U.S. v. Aluminum Co. of America et al.*, 214 F. Supp. 501 (1963), 377 U.S. 271 (1964).

123. 377 U.S. 271, 281 (1964).

124. *U.S. v. Continental Can Co. et al.*, 217 F. Supp. 761 (1963); 378 U.S. 441 (1964).

Antitrust policy: the control of market structures   553

stimuli that brings the competition between these two industries within Section 7's competition-preserving proscriptions. . . . That there are price differentials between the two products or that the demand for one is not particularly or immediately responsive to changes in the price of the other are relevant matters but not determinative of the product market issue. . . . Where the area of effective competition cuts across industry lines, so must the relevant line of commerce.[125]

The Court therefore defined the relevant market as metal cans and glass bottles combined. In this market, Continental occupied second place with a 22 percent share, and Hazel-Atlas sixth place with a 3 percent share. This, the Court ruled, was too much; the merger had to be undone.

These two decisions are logically inconsistent. The long-run cross elasticity of demand between aluminum and copper in cable applications is undeniably high, just as it is between bottles and cans. If anything, copper cable and aluminum cable are more perfect substitutes within an appropriate price range, as the massive market share shifts between 1950 and 1959 testify. Only by assuming that copper prices would never again come close enough to aluminum prices to challenge aluminum in overhead conductor cable applications could one reconcile the Supreme Court's *Alcoa-Rome* decision with its *Continental-Hazel-Atlas* opinion. While this was possible and perhaps likely, it was not inevitable. Even then, an opportunity cost check on aluminum prices would remain, for by reducing the aluminum/copper price ratio, the aluminum cable producers could make further inroads into the many electrical conductor applications still dominated by copper. Nevertheless, the *Alcoa-Rome* and *Continental-Hazel-Atlas* decisions exhibit a different sort of consistency: the consistent willingness of the courts to accept market definitions that resolve inherent doubts on the side of preventing mergers with possible anticompetitive effects. This in turn may have been no more than faithful stewardship to the will of Congress.

There is, however, another possible explanation. No matter what civics texts may say, decisions on matters as complex as mergers represent a rule of men, not laws. The Supreme Court that handed down *Alcoa-Rome Cable*, *Continental-Hazel-Atlas*, and other key merger decisions was inclined toward overriding laissez faire presumptions to stem the concentration of economic power, which a majority perceived as undesirable. By 1974, with new and more conservative appointments to the Court, the balance changed. One manifestation was the Justice Department's first defeat at the Supreme Court level on a merger market definition issue.

The case involved General Dynamics' acquisition of the United Electric Coal Companies.[126] Through a previous merger General Dynamics had come to own the Freeman Coal Mining Co., one of the largest deep mine operators in the Midwest. At the time General Dynamics acquired control of United (although not earlier), United was exclusively a strip miner. Following a district court ruling in favor of the merger, the central issue on appeal was whether emphasis should be placed on the merger partners' shares of recent coal production, which the Supreme Court majority conceded were sufficiently high to support a finding of "undue concentration" under past precedents, or whether "other pertinent factors affecting the coal industry and the business of the appellees" could be allowed to override the historical market share analysis.[127] Speaking for the majority, Justice Stewart, a frequent dissenter in previous merger cases, found that most coal sales were made on long-term contracts, that competition in the industry turned on the ability to commit blocks of coal reserves in seeking such contracts, that at the time of the trial (but not when General Dynamics first assumed control) United had committed virtually all of its strip-mineable reserves, and that appreciable new midwestern strip mine reserves could not be found. Concluding that from the perspective of uncommitted reserves United was "a far less significant factor in the coal market . . . than the production statistics seemed to indicate," the majority ruled General Dynamics' acquisition of United to be legal. Especially in view of the revolution in coal industry economics wrought by the OPEC oil price increases of 1973 and by increasingly stringent sulphur emission standards (making Rocky Mountain coal competitive in the Midwest), there is much to criticize in both the majority's opinion and the vigorous dissent of four Supreme Court members. The case's primary significance, however, may lie in its demonstration that the new Supreme Court was no longer willing consistently to define markets in a way that gave the benefit of the doubt to the antimerger forces. Its long-term impact remains to be seen.

Merging firms' defenses Under a strict *per se* approach to merger law, merging firms would have no defense if adverse structural effects were demonstrated. To what extent has this been so under the Celler-Kefauver Act? What defenses have been permitted?

One accepted loophole is the so-called failing firm defense, invoked when the acquired company is unlikely to survive as a viable competitor in the absence of a merger. It has been construed narrowly by the courts to cover only *acquired* entities as failing firms, to require that they face "a grave probability of business failure," and to insist that there be no other merger prospect with a less severe concentration-increasing effect.[128] Managerial weaknesses that could be solved through an infusion of new talent rather than merger have not been found sufficient to warrant its application.[129] In practice, however, the enforcement agencies have enjoyed considerable discretion to invoke a failing firm rationale for not suing in borderline cases—e.g., in the massive 1967 merger between McDonnell Aircraft Co. and Douglas Aircraft Co. or the 1978 merger between the parents of Jones & Laughlin Steel and Youngstown Steel.

The prospect of cost savings or other economies resulting from merger might also be considered as a defense. But the courts have expressed a consistent reluctance to attempt a weighing of potential benefits against adverse structural consequences. Thus, addressing the argument that merged banks could make larger loans and thereby stimulate Philadelphia's economic development, the Supreme Court said:

> We are clear . . . that a merger the effect of which "may be substantially to lessen competition" is not saved because, on some ultimate reckoning of social or economic debits and

credits, it may be deemed beneficial. A value choice of such magnitude is beyond the ordinary limits of judicial competence, and in any event has been made for us already, by Congress when it enacted the amended Section 7. Congress determined to preserve our traditionally competitive economy. It therefore proscribed anticompetitive mergers, the benign and the malignant alike, fully aware, we must assume, that some price might have to be paid.[130]

Similarly, in its *Brown Shoe* opinion, the Court conceded that vertical integration of Brown with Kinney would yield certain economies:

> Of course, some of the results of large integrated or chain operations are beneficial to consumers. Their expansion is not rendered unlawful by the mere fact that small independent stores may be adversely affected. It is competition, not competitors, which the Act protects. But we cannot fail to recognize Congress' desire to promote competition through the protection of viable, small, locally owned businesses. Congress appreciated that occasional higher costs and prices might result from the maintenance of fragmented industries and markets. It resolved these competing considerations in favor of decentralization. We must give effect to that decision.[131]

Or as it stated flatly in its *Clorox* opinion, "Possi-

125. 378 U.S. 441, 449, 455, 457 (1964).

126. *U.S.* v. *General Dynamics Corp. et al.*, 415 U.S. 486 (1974).

127. 415 U.S. 486, 498 (1974).

128. See *International Shoe Co.* v. *F.T.C.*, 280 U.S. 291 (1930); *Citizen Publishing Co.* v. *U.S.*, 394 U.S. 131, 136–139 (1969); and *U.S.* v. *Pabst Brewing Co. et al.*, 296 F. Supp. 994, 1002 (1969).

129. *U.S.* v. *Third National Bank of Nashville*, 390 U.S. 171, 189 (1968).

130. *U.S.* v. *Philadelphia National Bank et al.*, 374 U.S. 321, 371 (1963). See also (on Ford Motor Company's acquisition of the Autolite spark plug operations, thereby allegedly making Autolite a more effective competitor against General Motors) *Ford Motor Co.* v. *U.S.*, 405 U.S. 562, 569–570 (1972).

131. *Brown Shoe Co.* v. *U.S.*, 370 U.S. 294, 344 (1962).

ble economies cannot be used as a defense to illegality."[132]

If these statements mean only that the courts are unable confidently to assess merger benefits in the highly imperfect milieu of litigation and weigh them against costs, the circumstances are sad but understandable. One might prefer a more insightful decision-making process; but if the social benefits from challengeable mergers are small on average, not much is lost owing to judicial frailty. However, there is a more disturbing alternative view. It is possible to interpret the rather muddled *Brown Shoe* opinion as saying that the merger was illegal *because* it would yield economies and hence lead to the competitive attrition of small retailers.[133] To virtually all economists, such a rule seems unwise public policy, posing among other things a direct conflict with the efficiency goals of antitrust. The *Clorox* case raises similar questions, but with a different flavor. Both the Federal Trade Commission and the Supreme Court believed, probably erroneously,[134] that the Clorox Company would realize substantial discounts in purchasing television advertising as a result of being integrated into Procter & Gamble's much larger media budget. The Supreme Court circumspectly avoided singling out any particular savings as undesirable, but the FTC was more assertive:

> [T]here does come a point "at which product differentiation ceases to promote welfare and becomes wasteful, or mass advertising loses its informative aspect and merely entrenches market leaders." We think that point has been reached in the household liquid bleach industry. . . . Price competition, beneficial to the consumer, has given way to brand competition in a form beneficial only to the seller. . . . [C]ost advantages that enable still more intensive advertising only impair price competition further; they do not benefit the consumer.[135]

Since the alleged cost savings were almost exclusively pecuniary while strengthened differentiation could have real social costs, this position is not unreasonable. However, in other opinions the Commission was less discriminating, suggesting that *any* economies realized through merger in an industry harboring small, vulnerable firms should be regarded unfavorably. This attitude emerges most clearly in a dairy products chain merger decision not appealed to the Supreme Court:

> [T]he necessary proof of violation of [Section 7] consists of . . . evidence showing that the acquiring firm possesses significant power in some markets or that its over-all organization gives it a decisive advantage in efficiency over its smaller rivals.[136]

Those who, like the author, view this antiefficiency bias with alarm can derive some solace from its evident attenuation as the FTC and Supreme Court rosters changed in the late 1960s and early 1970s.

The problem of relief Having established strong legal precedents, the Department of Justice and Federal Trade Commission have "won" more than three-fourths of the antimerger suits they initiated under the Celler-Kefauver Act, where "won" is taken to mean that the merger was abandoned or ruled illegal following a challenge or that a consent decree settlement was negotiated.[137] However, a government victory in this sense does not mean that the structural status quo ante is restored. In fact, the more prevalent experience has been to the contrary. Elzinga investigated in detail 39 merger cases filed through 1960 and settled under a litigated judgment favoring the government, or a consent decree, by 1965.[138] He found that in only ten of the cases was the remedy either "successful" or "sufficient" in the sense that all or most of the acquired assets were divested and reestablished as a viable, essentially independent competitor. Twenty-one of the cases ended in a remedy characterized as "unsuccessful" because there was no divestiture, insignificant divestiture, transfer of the assets to a significant horizontal competitor or vertically linked buyer posing vertical foreclosure risks, divestiture of a nonviable entity, and/or the imposition of "marketing orders" that required continuing government surveillance of pricing or other business conduct. Furthermore, even in the cases with relatively successful remedies, there were long delays before something approximating the status quo was achieved—five and one-half years on average from acquisition to divestiture. Celler-Kefauver Act enforcement history provides much support for the Washington adage that the government usually wins antitrust cases but loses the relief.

A few illustrations must suffice to show the remedial disappointments following government victory. When Continental Can was required to divest itself of Hazel-Atlas Glass, most of the Hazel-Atlas plants went to Brockway Glass Co., catapulting Brockway from fourth to second rank in glass bottle sales, with a market share of roughly 18 percent. Given the bottle industry's tightly oligopolistic structure, a direct merger of Brockway and Hazel-Atlas would surely have been challenged as illegal. The Kinney Company was sold by Brown Shoe to the F. W. Woolworth Co., which operated shoe departments in many of its stores and hence was a competitor at retail to Kinney—perhaps even more so than Brown, whose outlets emphasized higher priced items. While the Pabst-Blatz merger case was in litigation, Pabst closed down the old Blatz brewery in Milwaukee and shifted its production to Pabst plants. Therefore, when divestiture finally occurred in 1969, all that was left for the G. W. Heilemann Brewing Co. to acquire was a triangle (the Blatz trademark), 32 trucks, and the Blatz marching band.[139] Also, in the period of transition to divestiture, Pabst withdrew most of its advertising support for Blatz and quietly urged its distributors to push Pabst rather than Blatz, leaving Heilemann with a problem of rapid sales erosion on its newly acquired brand. And to assure the viability of Autolite spark plug operations when they were divested from Ford Motor Company in 1972, Ford was ordered *inter alia* to stay out of the spark plug business for ten years and to buy half its requirements from Autolite for five years—a remedy hardly apt to encourage the development of *new* competition in a market dominated by three domestic firms.

There are numerous reasons why restoration of the status quo proves difficult in merger cases. The passage of time during negotiations and litigation is accompanied by mounting complexities. The eggs become scrambled, new investments are made, production assignments are reallocated, and top managers leave. There are also perverse incentive problems. Acquiring companies naturally want to give up as little as possible and, in horizontal mergers, are seldom eager to spin off new entities that will inject new and vigorous competition. Their attorneys are well motivated to bargain hard for a favorable settlement. Government enforcement agencies on the other hand are dominated by trial-oriented lawyers to whom the sweet smell of victory (which, to be sure, may significantly deter similar future mergers) is often more important than the economic substance of what follows. Negotiation of remedial details is commonly passed on to an overworked, poorly informed second team. The remedial contest is an uneven one in which an outcome significantly enhancing competition is more the exception than the rule.

Stung by the criticisms of Professor Elzinga and

132. *Federal Trade Commission* v. *Procter & Gamble* Co. *et al.*, 386 U.S. 568, 580 (1967).

133. See for example Peterman, "The Brown Shoe Case," pp. 138–41. At pp. 106–17 Peterman shows there was virtually no evidence that the merger would yield efficiencies—conceivably because Brown believed any such evidence would be used against it. An alternate explanation is that the merger did not in fact promise appreciable economies. See Scherer, "The Posnerian Harvest," p. 986.

The "efficiency as a bad" argument was carried to perhaps ludicrous extremes when the Carrier Corporation tried to avert being taken over by United Technologies Corp., asserting *inter alia* in an antitrust suit that the merger would make Carrier a more technologically progressive, potent competitor. See "Carrier Case: Question of Size," *New York Times*, 27 November 1978, p. D-6.

134. See note 103, Chapter 4, p. 111 *supra*.

135. *In re Procter & Gamble* Co., 63 F.T.C. 1465, 1581–1582 (1963). The internal quotation is from Joel B. Dirlam, "The Celler-Kefauver Act: A Review of Enforcement Policy," in Senate, Committee on the Judiciary, Subcommittee on Antitrust and Monopoly, *Administered Prices: A Compendium on Public Policy* (Washington, D.C.: Government Printing Office, 1963), p. 103.

136. *In the matter of Foremost Dairies, Inc.*, 60 F.T.C. 944, 1084 (1962) (emphasis added).

137. See the compilations of cases in Mueller, *The Celler-Kefauver Act*, pp. 44–67; Betty Bock, *Mergers and Markets*, 5th ed. (New York: National Industrial Conference Board, 1966); and U.S., Congress, House, Monopolies Subcommittee hearings, *Merger Oversight*, 96th Cong., 1st sess., pp. 148–50, 155–58.

138. Kenneth G. Elzinga, "The Antimerger Law: Pyrrhic Victories," *Journal of Law and Economics* 12 (April 1969): 43–78.

139. See Chapter 4, p. 135 *supra*.

Antitrust policy: the control of market structures   557

others, the antitrust enforcement agencies attempted during the 1970s to improve their remedial record. They have three main lines of attack. First, they can seek preliminary injunctions against consummation of the merger or orders to hold the merging organizations separate until the substantive disputes are settled. When such an order is issued, effective divestiture is greatly facilitated, but the agencies have had only limited success in satisfying the stringent legal criteria for a preliminary injunction. Out of some 60 instances between 1955 and 1976 in which preliminary injunctions were requested and a court decision was rendered, the government's plea was granted wholly or partially in slightly more than half.[140] As we have seen earlier, an attempt to strengthen the agencies' bargaining position by tying a waiting period to the completion of premerger information submissions was rebuffed by Congress in 1976. Second, the agencies can "hang tough" and insist upon full divestiture despite company cries of pain. By so doing, they show merging firms that it is contrary to their own best interests to scramble assets and increase the pain when and if divestiture eventually occurs. This was the course pursued, amidst much criticism, by the Federal Trade Commission when Kennecott Copper Company resisted the divestiture of Peabody Coal Company.[141] Kennecott's will to resist was buttressed by the fact that it paid a half billion dollars for Peabody in a booming stock market, doubled its commitment

through subsequent capital outlays, and was ordered to divest during a stock market slump that made it impossible to recover much more than half its investment. Its reluctance was overcome by an FTC plea for fines of $100,000 per day of additional delay along with a partial stock market recovery. Finally, the antitrust agencies can seek "spin-off" of a freestanding enterprise when sale of acquired assets to a third party would create as many competitive problems as it would solve. Since stock in the divested company would be distributed pro rata to the acquiring firm's stockholders, managers of the acquiring firm would normally be well motivated to ensure the new entity's viability.

Conglomerate merger policy The U.S. merger laws have evolved into a potent deterrent against sizeable horizontal and vertical mergers. It is doubtful, however, whether they have had much impact on the overall level of merger activity, which has continued at high levels, reaching an all-time peak in 1968.[142] Rather, their main effect appears to have been reallocative, channelling companies' urge to merge in directions less likely to provoke an antitrust challenge.

In its statistical analyses, the Federal Trade Commission divides mergers into five categories: horizontal, where the merging firms are actual competitors in some relevant market; vertical, where the merging firms occupy adjacent stages in some vertical chain of production and distri-

T 20.2 Distribution of manufacturing and mining merger activity by type, 1948–77

Type of merger	Percentage of all assets acquired in period			
	1948–53	1956–63	1963–72	1973–77
Horizontal	37%	19%	12%	15%
Vertical	13	22	8	6
Product extension	45	36	39	24
Market extension	2	7	7	6
Pure conglomerage	3	16	33	49

Source: Federal Trade Commission, *Statistical Report on Mergers and Acquisitions*, (Washington, D.C.: Government Printing Office, various years).

bution; product extension, where the merging firms, though not direct competitors, sell products functionally related in terms of manufacturing processes or channels of distribution; market extension, where the merging firms sell the same products in geographically distinct markets; and pure conglomerates, involving essentially unrelated enterprises. Recapitulating Table 4.11, we see in Table 20.2 that as the Celler-Kefauver Act took hold and was interpreted stringently by the courts, there was a marked decline in the proportion of manufacturing and mining corporation assets acquired in horizontal and vertical mergers and a corresponding increase in pure conglomerate mergers. Especially in view of the fact that merger activity in industrialized nations without statutes analogous to Celler-Kefauver continued to be preponderantly horizontal, it seems unmistakable that the U.S. law had a strong rechannelling effect.[143]

From the standpoint of antitrust policy, product extension, market extension, and "pure" conglomerate mergers are all viewed as conglomerate—i.e., not directly horizontal or vertical. Concurrent with the development of the law on horizontal and vertical mergers, precedents have emerged permitting the antitrust agencies successfully to challenge at least some conglomerate mergers, particularly of the product extension and market extension types.[144]

One line of attack is opened up when a merger leads to the creation and exercise of reciprocal purchasing leverage.[145] A key case concerned the acquisition of Gentry, Inc., a specialist in the manufacture of dehydrated onion and garlic, by the Consolidated Foods Corporation, which had far-flung interests in food products wholesaling, manufacturing, and retailing.[146] The record shows that Consolidated brought reciprocal buying pressure to bear on some of its suppliers, especially those making soups and related products on which Consolidated affixed its own brand labels for retail distribution, to use Gentry onion and garlic. Although the Gentry products were qualitatively inferior to those of a leading competitor, the reciprocal buying campaign had modest success; and Gentry's average share of the combined onion and garlic market rose from 32 to 35 per-

cent in the ten years following the merger, increasing in onions while falling in garlic. Climaxing eight years of litigation, the Supreme Court rejected the decision of an appellate court that the reciprocity program had no substantial effect on competition, and it ordered that Consolidated divest itself of Gentry. It went on to assert that it was neither necessary nor desirable to wait many years until evidence on the actual effects of a merger become available before rendering judgment; rather, mergers should be judged by their *probable* effects. Framing a general rule for reciprocal buying cases, the Court stated that not all mergers offering reciprocity opportunities should be prohibited, but where "the acquisition is of a company that commands a substantial share of a market, a finding of probability of reciprocal buying . . . should be honored, if there is substantial evidence to support it." Proving that reciprocal buying is a probable consequence of mergers has generally been difficult; as a result, few mergers have been struck down on reciprocal purchasing grounds, and the government has experienced several noteworthy defeats.[147]

Another argument advanced in several Federal Trade Commission actions during the 1960s is that the intrusion of a well-heeled conglomer-

---

140. House, Monopolies Subcommittee hearings, *Merger Oversight*, pp. 43–44, 145–47.

141. See "Down the Chute with Peabody Coal," *Fortune*, May 1977, pp. 228–48.

142. Cf. Figure 4.5, p. 120 *supra*.

143. However, there is evidence of an upturn in British and West German conglomerate mergers during the late 1960s. See the Organisation for Economic Co-Operation and Development report, *Mergers and Competition Policy* (Paris: OECD, 1974), Chapter 1.

144. For an important early analysis, see Donald F. Turner, "Conglomerate Mergers and Section 7 of the Clayton Act," *Harvard Law Review* 78 (May 1965): 1313–95. For a more recent survey, see Peter O. Steiner, *Mergers* (Ann Arbor: University of Michigan Press, 1975), Chapters 9–12.

145. On the relevant economic analysis, see Chapter 12, pp. 342–44 *supra*.

146. *Federal Trade Commission* v. *Consolidated Foods Corp. et al.*, 380 U.S. 592 (1965).

147. See Steiner, *Mergers*, pp. 244–48.

ate into a market previously populated by small independent sellers increases the likelihood of predatory conduct, which in turn could drive small firms out of business or make them more docile because they fear punishment. This was a major point in an appellate court opinion affirming the Federal Trade Commission's order that Reynolds Metals Co., the nation's leading producer of aluminum foil, disgorge its merger with a small firm specializing in florists' foil (a decorative wrapping for flowers):

> The power of the "deep pocket" or "rich parent" for one of the . . . suppliers in a competitive group where previously no company was very large and all were relatively small opened the possibility and power to sell at prices approximating cost or below and thus to undercut and ravage the less affluent competition.[148]

Similarly, the Commission found in a decision establishing guidelines for dairy product industry mergers that:

> [a] firm strongly entrenched in a number of markets may thereby be able to engage in deep, sustained, and discriminatory price cutting in selected markets to the detriment of weaker competitors.[149]

While such conduct is forbidden by the price discrimination laws, the Commission continued, a conglomerate could legally meet the equally low price of a rival, and:

> [i]n the hands of a powerful firm, able to sustain selective price cuts for so long as may be necessary to ensure against a loss of trade, such price cutting may be a potent weapon for repulsing new competition and preventing entry into concentrated markets.[150]

This view was reiterated in a Supreme Court decision concerning Procter & Gamble's acquisition of the Clorox Co. "There is every reason to assume," the Court said, "that the smaller firms would become more cautious in competing due to their fear of retaliation by Procter."[151]

Whether conglomerate size materially increases the likelihood of predatory conduct is, as we have seen in Chapter 12, a matter of consid-

erable uncertainty and debate.[152] Perhaps because it enjoyed such frail intellectual support, the "deep pocket" theory received much less emphasis in conglomerate merger cases of the 1970s.

By far the most important argument invoked against conglomerate mergers is that they eliminate *potential competition* that would have existed or materialized in the absence of merger. The doctrine has undergone a complex evolution. One of the earliest cases concerned acquisition of the Pacific Northwest Pipeline Corporation, a company tapping extensive natural gas reserves in New Mexico and western Canada, by the El Paso Natural Gas Co., which supplied gas to California users.[153] Pacific Northwest had no pipeline into California and had never sold its gas in that state, but the trial record showed that it had repeatedly considered entering the California market and had in fact bid unsuccessfully to supply California electrical utilities. The Supreme Court ordered the merger dissolved because it eliminated a substantial competitive factor, noting that "[w]e would have to wear blinders not to see that the mere efforts of Pacific Northwest to get into the California market, though unsuccessful, had a powerful influence on El Paso's business attitudes within the state."[154] Nine more years of litigation, political maneuvering, and further appeals to the highest court followed before divestiture actually took place.

The fact that Pacific Northwest had actually tried to enter the California market made its status as a source of competition clear. Most potential entry cases are not so simple. Thus, in the *Clorox* case, attorneys for Procter & Gamble insisted, and an appellate court agreed, that there was no evidence Procter & Gamble intended to enter the liquid household bleach market on its own, and hence that without its acquisition of the Clorox Company, Procter & Gamble could not have been considered a potential competitor. The Supreme Court disagreed, finding that Procter & Gamble had all the resources needed to enter on its own, had entered similar markets that way, was indeed the most likely entrant into liquid bleach distribution, and chose not to enter as an independent competitor because it could capture a larger market share by acquiring Clorox, which enjoyed 49 percent of all liquid bleach sales.[155]

Similar difficulties attended the protracted litigation over a joint venture between Pennsalt Chemicals and Olin Mathieson Corp. to manufacture sodium chlorate, another bleaching agent, for southeastern United States paper pulp processors. A district court decided that competition was not lessened by the joint venture (in effect, a partial merger) because it was extremely unlikely *both* firms would have entered the market independently.[156] The Supreme Court vacated this judgment, ruling that the relevant question was whether *one* of the two firms would have entered independently, with the other remaining "at the edge of the market, continually threatening to enter," and hence keeping pressure on the oligopolists actually operating sodium chlorate plants.[157] Reconsidering the evidence under these new instructions, the district court found that independent entry by either of the two firms was improbable, among other things, because the rates of return projected in go-it-alone plant investment studies, though in the range of 11 to 16 percent for Pennsalt, did not meet the firms' aspirations.[158] This conclusion seems doubtful in view of several facts: The market was growing rapidly and there was an apparent capacity deficit larger than the scale of the Penn-Olin joint venture plant; the joint venture plant was nearly twice as large as the initial sizes of plants built by three other producers in the southeastern market and by Pennsalt in Oregon; such smaller plants had projected returns nearly as high as (or for Olin Mathieson, higher than) the joint venture plant; and both firms had shown intense interest in entering the market. Nevertheless, when the Justice Department appealed a second time, the Supreme Court divided 4–4, and so the lower court's decision stood.[159]

The Supreme Court's position evolved further in a brewing industry merger case.[160] In 1965 the Falstaff Brewing Corp., at the time the fourth largest producer of beer in the United States, acquired the Narragansett Brewing Co., the leading seller in New England, with a market share of 20 percent. Falstaff's business strategy emphasized attaining nationwide distribution,

and the Narragansett acquisition was a part of that expansion effort. When the merger was challenged, Falstaff executives testified that they would not have built a brewery on their own in New England. The district court ruled *inter alia* that Falstaff had no intent to enter New England except through acquisition and therefore did not eliminate itself as a potential competitor by merging. On appeal, the Supreme Court said it was not enough to consider acquiring company evidence as to whether entry would or would not occur without merger. Rather, how firms already in the market might reasonably perceive Falstaff as an entry threat was also relevant:

> The specific question . . . is not what Falstaff's internal company decisions were but whether, given its financial capabilities and conditions in the New England market, it would be reasonable to consider it a potential entrant into that market. . . . [I]f it would appear to rational beer merchants in New England that Falstaff might well build a new brewery . . . then its entry by merger becomes suspect. . . .

148. *Reynolds Metals Co.* v. *Federal Trade Commission*, 309 F. 2d 223, 229 (1962), affirming 56 F.T.C. 743 (1960). The opinion was delivered by Judge (and later Supreme Court Chief Justice) Warren Burger.

149. *In re Beatrice Foods Co.*, CCH Trade Regulation Reporter, Federal Trade Commission Complaints and Orders, Para. 17,244, p. 22,334 (1965).

150. *In re Beatrice Foods Co.*, Para. 17,244, p. 22,334 (1965).

151. *Federal Trade Commission* v. *Procter & Gamble Co. et al.*, 386 U.S. 568, 578 (1967).

152. Cf. Chapter 12, pp. 335–40 *supra*.

153. *U.S.* v. *El Paso Natural Gas Co. et al.*, 376 U.S. 651 (1964).

154. 376 U.S. 651, 659 (1964).

155. *Federal Trade Commission* v. *Procter & Gamble*, 386 U.S. 568, 574, 580–581 (1967).

156. *U.S.* v. *Penn-Olin Chemical Co. et al.*, 217 F. Supp. 110 (1963).

157. *U.S.* v. *Penn-Olin Chemical Co. et al.*, 378 U.S. 158 (1964).

158. *U.S.* v. *Penn-Olin Chemical Co. et al.*, 246 F. Supp. 917 (1965). See also James W. Meehan, Jr., "Joint Venture Entry in Perspective," *Antitrust Bulletin* 15 (Winter 1970): 693–711, for a different interpretation of the facts.

159. *U.S.* v. *Penn-Olin Chemical Co. et al.*, 389 U.S. 308 (1967).

160. *U.S.* v. *Falstaff Brewing Corp. et al.*, 332 F. Supp. 970 (1971), 410 U.S. 526 (1973).

The District Court should therefore have appraised the economic facts about Falstaff and the New England market in order to determine whether in any realistic sense Falstaff could be said to be a potential competitor . . . so positioned on the edge of the market that it exerted beneficial influence on competitive conditions in that market.[161]

Reconsidering the evidence on remand, the district court concluded that Falstaff was not a perceived potential entrant in the sense specified by the Supreme Court, and so the merger was allowed to stand.[162] Among other things, the court noted that competition among brewers in New England was, and continued to be, intense, and so sellers in the market had too little control over their prices to be influenced by Falstaff's remote threat. An irony of the case is that after the acquisition, Falstaff's profitability deteriorated—in part because Falstaff had, as with Narrangansett, bought up old breweries whose high unit costs and insusceptibility to modernization left it in an unfavorable position relative to Anheuser-Busch and Schlitz, who expanded by building new, highly automated, decentralized plants.

In 1974, a year after its *Falstaff* decision, the Supreme Court returned to the potential competition issue in a bank merger case. It restated its view of how the pieces of the potential competition doctrine fit together:

Unequivocal proof that an acquiring firm actually would have entered *de novo* but for a merger is rarely available. . . . Thus, . . . the principal focus of the doctrine is on the likely effects of the premerger position of the acquiring firm on the fringe of the target market. . . . [A] market extension merger may be unlawful if the target market is substantially concentrated, if the acquiring firm has the characteristics, capabilities, and economic incentive to render it a perceived potential *de novo* entrant, and if the acquiring firm's premerger presence on the fringe of the target market in fact tempered oligopolistic behavior on the part of existing participants in that market.[163]

562 The last phrase in this guideline is crucial. Unlike the rules developed for horizontal and vertical mergers, it clearly implies an inquiry into whether the *behavior* of sellers in the market entered by merger is oligopolistic in the pejorative sense and whether the acquiring firm's premerger posture as a possible entrant constrained insiders' pricing discretion. In the case it was reviewing, the Supreme Court found that when a large Seattle bank acquired the third largest Spokane bank, there was no substantial lessening of competition because State of Washington branch banking laws severely limited the Seattle bank's ability to become a significant presence in Spokane by any means other than large-scale merger and because Spokane banks could not help but recognize the Seattle bank's limited potential as a *de novo* entrant. But the *Marine Bancorporation* decision is important not so much for the specific set of facts under which the merger survived government challenge as for the difficult burden of proof imposed upon antitrust enforcers invoking the potential competition doctrine to stop market extension and product extension mergers.[164] And along with the nearly contemporaneous *General Dynamics—United Electric Coal* decision, it appeared to signal the reluctance of a new and more conservative Supreme Court to continue resolving the benefit of the doubt against sizeable mergers. Since lower court judges generally dislike being reversed, it is hardly surprising that the *Marine Bancorporation* decision was followed by a string of government defeats in potential competition merger cases.[165]

One facet of the potential competition approach to mergers had not yet been subjected to direct Supreme Court consideration at the time this book was written. This is the so-called "toehold acquisition" theory. Under it, a large conglomerate's acquisition of a leading seller in a concentrated industry is challenged by claiming that competition could have been stimulated more had the conglomerate acquired a smaller industry participant and invested resources in building up its acquisition to full fighting weight.[166] That society benefits under all but rare circumstances by channelling large corporations' energies into building rather than merely buying seems clear. The problem, as always, comes in determining whether, denied the opportunity to take over a market leader, a potential acquirer would plausibly have entered by toehold and sustained the desired developmental effort.

Other theories advanced in suits opposing conglomerate mergers—e.g., that such mergers could encourage mutual forebearance among sellers encountering one another in many markets and that the aggregate economic concentration they enhance is undesirable in its own right—have been rejected summarily by lower courts as going beyond the express intent of Congress in passing the Celler-Kefauver Act.[167] This no doubt reflects an admirable judicial reluctance to intrude where legislators have feared to tread. Still the question remains, Should Congress amend the law to create a stronger presumption against conglomerate mergers? In the absence of legislative change, several things seem clear. First, most sizeable conglomerate mergers, and especially the relatively "pure" ones, are sufficiently inoffensive on traditional competitive grounds that they will slip more or less easily through the antitrust net. Second, in the absence of conglomerate mergers, aggregate concentration would almost surely have increased a good deal less than it did during the 1960s and 1970s, and by some measures it might even have fallen.[168] Third, there is scant evidence that conglomerate mergers have done much on average to enhance industrial efficiency—certainly less than the average horizontal or vertical merger. Indeed, by leading to losses of managerial incentive and control, they may have had a negative net efficiency effect.[169] Many have been consummated primarily for speculative reasons or as a kind of ego trip for prestige and power-hungry managers. To the extent that these characterizations are approximately accurate, a case can be made for congressional intervention to stop or at least retard this game that confers little social benefit but conflicts with the goal of decentralizing economic power to the maximum practical extent. The antitrust laws might be amended to prohibit the acquisition of any company with sales or assets exceeding, say, $50 million by any of the 250 largest industrial corporations, the 100 largest financial corporations, the 50 largest retailers, and so on *unless* the

merger partners sustain the burden of proving that substantial efficiency gains or other public benefits were likely to flow from the merger.[170] Adjudicating future efficiency claims would undoubtedly be difficult, and mistakes would be made. But if the American public attaches appreciable weight to the goal of maintaining an industrial structure that decentralizes economic decision making, it may over the long run prove to be an even more serious mistake to permit the essentially unfettered growth by merger of conglomerate enterprises. The question at bottom is what kind of society people want. And on that, only the people, speaking through their elected representatives, can make the ultimate choice.

Structural antitrust abroad: a comparison

To put American structural antitrust policy in perspective, it is useful to compare it with analogous policies in other industrialized nations.

For quite some time structural antitrust was one of the United States' less successful postwar exports. At the end of World War II the U.S. occupation forces imposed upon defeated Germany and Japan stringent antitrust laws, including deconcentration measures directed toward breaking up such consolidations as the Krupp and I. G.

161. 410 U.S. 526, 533–534, 532 (1973).

162. *U.S.* v. *Falstaff Brewing Corp. et al.*, 383 F. Supp. 1020 (1974).

163. *U.S.* v. *Marine Bancorporation et al.*, 418 U.S. 602, 624–625 (1974).

164. See Brodley, "Potential Competition Mergers," pp. 17–25.

165. Brodley, "Potential Competition Mergers," p. 19.

166. See for example, *in the matter of the Bendix Corporation et al.*, 77 F.T.C. 731 (1970), reversed on procedural grounds at 450 F. 2d 534 (1971).

167. See *U.S.* v. *International Telephone and Telegraph Corp. et al.*, 306 F. Supp. 766, 796–797 (1969); 324 F. Supp. 19, 51–54 (1970); and *U.S.* v. *Northwest Industries, Inc. et al.*, 301 F. Supp. 1066, 1092–1096 (1969).

168. See Chapter 4, p. 126 *supra*.

169. See Chapter 4, pp. 138–41 *supra*. Conglomerate mergers appear much less likely than horizontal and vertical mergers to yield substantial real efficiency gains.

Farben empires and the Japanese Zaibatsu. The deconcentration program had two purported objectives: to punish the leading industrial groups for their complicity in the war, and to weaken the industrial bases of Germany and Japan so they would be less able to pursue militaristic adventures again.[171] The second objective, although not universally accepted as logically valid, implies a curious contradiction of the conventional American wisdom. If one breaks up monopolistic concentrations to weaken industrial might, what should be done to strengthen it? Contributing to the paradox was the fact that when the United States reversed its field and resolved to build up West German and Japanese industry as bulwarks against communism, one of the first occupation policies to be relaxed was the deconcentration program. These developments did not escape the attention of business managers eager to effect monopolistic restrictions, who drew support for their views from the U.S. policies. More generally, the postwar structural antitrust serum inoculations engendered a reaction of hostility to such measures after the occupation pressures were relaxed.

This, of course, is not the whole story, since a belief that big business and monopoly can contribute to national economic strength extends far beyond the borders of Germany and Japan. In part, there are objective reasons for such views. Many national markets are quite small, and if all economies of scale are to be realized, appreciable seller concentration—often extending into the range of tight oligopoly or even natural monopoly—is essential.[172] Also, there is a tendency for individual plants to fall below the minimum optimal scale more, the smaller a national market is. In nations such as France, Italy, the United Kingdom, Sweden, Canada, and Japan (but not in West Germany) one finds a relatively high incidence of suboptimal scale plants.[173] Recognizing this, policymakers abroad have tended to look kindly toward mergers and other measures that increase firm sizes and supposedly (though with more tenuous empirical support) plant sizes. Also, in the first two decades following World War II, the United States led all other nations in most fields of industrial technology. It likewise harbored a preponderance of the free world's largest industrial enterprises. Putting two and two together, economic policymakers abroad concluded that their nations could achieve equivalent proficiency at technological innovation only by encouraging domestic corporations greatly to increase their size—typically through mergers. Gradually such beliefs have been eroded by research showing little correlation between the intensity of research and development effort and firm size in nations abroad as well as in the United States.[174] It has also been recognized that mergers have often led to little or no rationalization of production operations. But this change in perceptions has occurred only slowly, and in the meantime, there was rather little support for structural antitrust measures.

Other than divestitures imposed by the occupying forces upon Japanese and German enterprises following World War II, there are no known counterparts outside the United States to U.S. cases in which market-dominating firms were broken up because of their monopoly power. Indeed, there is considerable opposition even to including the possibility of such remedies in foreign antitrust law. Giving Japan's Fair Trade Commission divestiture powers was vigorously debated during the mid-1970s; but at the time this was written, the proposal had been deleted from the pending Anti-Monopoly Act and had little chance of being restored. A similar strengthening of Canada's antitrust law, under consideration during 1978, had uncertain prospects.[175] Unlike most Continental European antitrust agencies, the British Monopolies Commission has since 1965 had the power to recommend structural reorganization, but it has shown no inclination to do so, choosing instead in some cases conduct remedies aimed *inter alia* at reducing barriers to new entry.[176]

Outside the United States one finds much less of a philosophical bias toward reliance upon impersonal competitive market forces and (although the U.S. is moving to close the gap) more willingness to entrust regulatory functions to some governmental authority. The emphasis abroad is therefore on preventing *abusive conduct* by firms or groups of firms possessing monopoly power. This "abuse doctrine" permeates the antitrust laws of every non-American nation with any provisions at all concerning concentrations of economic power.

The difference between nations is illustrated well by considering how the U.K. Monopolies Commission handled a problem that also commanded the attention of U.S. antitrust authorities: monopolistic pricing in the cereal industry. In the United States, we saw earlier, the Federal Trade Commission sought to undermine the bases of the three leading cereal makers' monopoly power through divestiture of plants and the compulsory licensing of formulas and trademarks. In the United Kingdom, the Monopolies Commission found in 1972 that an evident reluctance to compete on the basis of price, along with 1967–71 profit returns on the Kellogg Company's capital ranging between 37 and 58 percent before taxes, were "largely attributable to the [highly concentrated] structure of the industry."[177] Concluding that structural change was infeasible, at least in part because industry leader Kellogg operated only one factory, but overlooking the possibility of trademark licensing, the Commission recommended, and the Ministry of Trade ordered, that Kellogg be required to seek government approval before effecting any further breakfast cereal price increases.[178] Continuing governmental surveillance of Kellogg prices, costs, and profit rates followed.

Similarly, the Commission recommended a 20 percent reduction in the prices of household detergents sold by Procter & Gamble and Unilever, but the government settled after negotiations for a remedy under which the two companies introduced new unadvertised detergents priced 20 percent lower than existing products.[179] Finding prices and profits of the tranquilizers Valium and Librium excessive, the Commission recommended 75 and 60 percent price reductions.[180] Price cuts averaging 40 percent were recommended following a Monopolies Commission investigation of the contraceptive sheath monopoly.[181]

There are two obvious difficulties in this abuse-oriented approach to monopoly power. For one, determining whether or not prices are excessive and what price level is reasonable calls for judgments in which the antitrust enforcers are invariably at an information disadvantage vis-à-vis those whose prices they seek to control. It is hard to avoid arbitrary judgments, as the round percentage reductions recommended by the U.K. Monopolies Commission strongly suggest. Distorted resource allocation can result; and as firms with monopoly power come to recognize the level of profit margins considered acceptable, they may find it preferable, rather than to constrain prices, to let costs rise until a "safe" margin is maintained. Second and perhaps more important, as the U.S. Supreme Court recognized long ago, today's reasonable price may through economic changes become the unreasonable

(170) Legislation along these lines was under consideration in 1979, but strong business and financial community opposition made passage unlikely.

171. The German ordinance stated explicitly that its objective was in part "to destroy Germany's economic potential to wage war." Gesetz Nr. 56, "Verbot der uebermaessigen Konzentration deutscher Wirtschaftskraft," February 1947.

172. Scherer et al., *The Economics of Multi-Plant Operation*, pp. 93–94.

173. Scherer et al., *The Economics of Multi-Plant Operation*, pp. 63–87, 103–108, 133–36; Joe S. Bain, *International Differences in Industrial Structure* (New Haven: Yale University Press, 1966), pp. 55–66, 144–48; and (on a broader array of nations) Frederic L. Pryor, "The Size of Production Establishments in Manufacturing," *Economic Journal* 82 (June 1972): 547–66.

174. See Chapter 15, pp. 419–22 *supra*.

175. See the Ministry of Consumer and Corporate Affairs white paper, *Proposals for a New Competition Policy for Canada: Second Stage* (Ottawa: Consumer and Corporate Affairs Canada, March 1977), pp. 45–49. The only significant government victory in earlier attempts to enforce the Canadian monopolization law involved predatory discrimination, fighting brands, business espionage, mergers, and other practices strongly reminiscent of the U.S. 1911 *Standard Oil* and *American Tobacco* cases. A fine of $85,000 plus costs was levied. *Rex v. Eddy Match Co., Ltd.*, 104 C.C.C. 39 (1951), 109 C.C.C. 1 (1953).

176. See Alister Sutherland, *The Monopolies Commission in Action* (Cambridge, England: Cambridge University Press, 1969), especially pp. 74–75.

177. Monopolies Commission, *Report on the Supply of Ready Cooked Breakfast Cereal Foods* (London: HMSO, 1973), p. 25.

178. *Breakfast Cereal Foods* report, p. 30; and "Britain: A Chill on Kellogg's Pricing Policies," *Business Week*, 3 March 1973, p. 35.

179. See Sutherland, *The Monopolies Commission in Action*, pp. 48–49. Few consumers bought the new unadvertised products.

180. Monopolies Commission, *Chlordiazepoxide and Diazepam* (London: HMSO, 1973), p. 70: See also "A Drug Giant's Pricing under International Attack," *Business Week*, 16 June 1975, pp. 50–51.

181. See "A Classic in the History of Monopoly," London *Financial Times*, 7 February 1975. The decreases ultimately negotiated by the Office of Fair Trading were in the range of 2 to 11 percent.

Antitrust policy: the control of market structures   565

price of tomorrow.[182] Therefore, an abuse-oriented approach requires, if it is to be anything more than an occasional lightning bolt, continuous monitoring of monopolists' behavior. Intervention of this sort is inconsistent with the principles (although not always with the practice) of U.S. antitrust. It is better, runs the logic of Sherman Act Section 2, to take once and (one hopes) for all whatever structural actions are needed to restore effective competition and then stand back and let market processes do their job. Europeans appear much more willing to involve government authorities in a more or less permanent price controller's role.

Armed with new statutory powers, the West German Federal Cartel Office began in 1974 a series of actions to force price reductions or rollbacks by "market-dominating" enterprises. Early targets included Merck, the dominant producer of vitamin B-12; the leading petroleum refiners; Hoffmann-La Roche of Valium fame; and the automobile industry.[183] The Cartel Office's power to control prices as part of its responsibilities under the abuse concept was confirmed in 1976 Federal Supreme Court decisions on appeals from Merck and Hoffmann-La Roche. However, its specific price reduction orders—60 to 70 percent for vitamin B-12, 40 percent for Valium, and 35 percent for Librium—were reversed and remanded for reconsideration on the basis of reasonableness principles whose practical implementation seems likely to engender manifold difficulties.[184] Undaunted, the Cartel Office pushed the abuse concept even further in 1977 by warning the three largest automobile companies that it considered their contemplated (i.e., not yet announced) price increases excessive and thereby forced a rollback.[185]

Article 86 of the European Economic Community treaty prohibits "any improper exploiting . . . of a dominant position" affecting Common Market trade. In a precedent-setting 1975 decision, the European Commission fined the United Brands Co. $1.2 million and ordered it to reduce banana prices in Germany by 15 percent. United was said to have abused its dominant position by charging substantially higher prices in some Common Market nations than in others and by preventing its national distributors from reselling

green bananas (which in effect segmented markets on a national basis).[186] The fine was upheld by the European Court of Justice in 1978, but the Commission's claim that United Brands had charged excessive prices in Germany was overruled for lack of proof. Where this leaves the Commission's power as a controller of monopolistic firms' prices remains to be determined in additional cases.

The scope of Article 86 was also clarified in a 1974 Court of Justice opinion sustaining the Commission's judgment against the Italian subsidiary of the Commercial Solvents Corporation.[187] CSC was the sole commercial-scale supplier in the Common Market of a raw material used to produce a drug effective against tuberculosis. When CSC's Italian subsidiary began producing the drug itself, it ceased supplying the raw material to other Common Market firms. This was ruled an abuse of CSC's dominant position, and in addition to paying a $215,000 fine, CSC was ordered to resume supplying independent would-be buyers. Using the antitrust laws to attack such "refusals to deal" has for the most part been avoided by U.S. courts, although there have been significant deviations in the case of public markets, railroad terminal facilities, and most recently, the transmission of electric power.[188] The fundamental difficulty is that a monopolist who chooses to sell to no one else can do so either by proclaiming its refusal to deal or by setting its announced price so high that no one will buy. To police such abuses effectively, therefore, the courts may once again have to play a continuing role as price controllers.

Only slightly more convergence between U.S. and foreign policies is found in the realm of mergers. Among European nations, the United Kingdom was the first to adopt merger control laws as a part of its competition policy. The 1965 Monopolies and Mergers Act assigned to the Monopolies Commission responsibility for reviewing certain mergers—notably, those involving market shares of 33 percent or greater. Special, tougher criteria were established for newspaper mergers. Up to 1973, the law was enforced sparingly. Of the nearly 800 nonnewspaper mergers registered with the Board of Trade under the act, only 20 were referred to the Monopolies Commission for review. Seven of these were abandoned before the Commission could begin its investigation, and six more were judged by the Commission to be contrary to the public interest.[189]

One reason for the paucity of references was ambiguity in high government circles over the desirability of retarding concentration-increasing mergers. Indeed, in 1966 the Labour Government created an Industrial Reorganisation Corporation to encourage and help finance mergers that might build enterprises better able to hold their own in international trade. Its record included acting as broker in the merger of Britain's two largest domestic auto manufacturers (British Motor Holdings and Leyland); aiding the formation of Europe's third largest electrical equipment manufacturer through the merger of English Electric and Elliott Automation; and arranging a merger of three firms (including the most prominent price cutter) with a combined 35 percent share of the U.K. ball and roller bearing market.[190] The IRC was allowed to lapse during the 1970s, in part because the Conservative government briefly in power was less inclined to view mergers as a means of forming enterprises large enough to be susceptible to central government control and partly out of disappointment over how few palpable efficiencies had materialized through major consolidations. The extent to which its promerger advocacy role was preserved by the industry "working parties" established under the National Economic Development Council's wing was uncertain at the time this was written.

In 1973 the U.K. merger law was toughened by reducing the actionable market share threshold to 25 percent. However, no pronounced escalation of antimerger activity was discernible. In the first four years after the amendment, the Monopolies Commission ruled against four additional mergers. It is difficult for an outsider (and quite possibly also for insiders) to see clear differences in probable competitive consequences between sizeable mergers that the responsible ministers chose not to refer to the Monopolies Commission for scrutiny, those that the Commission approved, and those few that it opposed during the initial decade of the 1965 Merger Act's existence.[191]

The first merger formally approved by the Commission illustrates the differences between British and American policy. British Motor Corporation, the leading auto producer, with a 25 to 30 percent share of total passenger car output, sought in 1965 to acquire Pressed Steel Co., Ltd., the largest British body stampings specialist. At the time, Pressed Steel sold 60 percent of its output to BMC, which lacked internal stamping capacity, and the remainder to BMC's competitors. Such a merger creates vertical foreclosure dangers. A price squeeze might be imposed upon outsiders, or supplies might be denied to rivals during periods of peak demand, when each forgone body stamping means the loss of a car sale. However, BMC management assured the Com-

182. See Chapter 19, p. 499 *supra,* quoting *U.S.* v. *Trenton Potteries Co. et al.,* 273 U.S. 392, 397 (1927).

183. In 1975 the German Monopolies Commission, an advisory panel, published a report criticizing this line of antitrust law development. See "Price Control Is Not the Answer," London *Financial Times,* 20 March 1975, p. 7. There is reason to believe that deemphasis of pricing abuse actions was under consideration in 1978.

184. See the OECD. *Annual Reports on Competition Policy in OECD Member Countries, 1977,* No. 2 (Paris: OECD, 1977), pp. 30–31.

185. See "Preemptive Jawboning Astonishes Business," *Business Week,* 28 March 1977, p. 36.

186. See the OECD. *Annual Reports on Competition Policy, 1976,* No. 2, pp. 167–69.

187. The European Court's opinion is excerpted in "Refusal by a Dominant Firm To Sell Raw Materials," *Antitrust Bulletin* 19 (Fall 1974): 605–18.

188. *U.S.* v. *Terminal Railroad Association,* 224 U.S. 383 (1912); *Gamco, Inc.* v. *Providence Fruit and Produce Bldg. et al.,* 194 F. 2d 484 (1952), cert. den. 344 U.S. 817 (1952); and *Ottertail Power Co.* v. *U.S.,* 410 U.S. 366 (1973). See also Peter D. Byrnes et al., "Product Shortages, Allocation and the Antitrust Laws," *Antitrust Bulletin* 20 (Winter 1975): 713–30.

189. See J. D. Gribbin, "Recent Antitrust Developments in the United Kingdom," *Antitrust Bulletin* 20 (Summer 1975), especially pp. 382–83.

190. See the three documents on the Industrial Reorganisation Corporation reprinted in the *Antitrust Bulletin* 15 (Winter 1970): 829–57. On economies resulting from the bearing industry merger—one of IRC's most successful ventures—see Chapter 4, pp. 133–34 *supra.*

191. See also Sutherland, *The Monopolies Commission in Action,* pp. 69–70; C. L. Pass, "Horizontal Mergers and the Control of Market Power in the U.K.," *Antitrust Bulletin* 17 (Fall 1972): 811–34; and Geoffrey Meeks, *Disappointing Marriage: A Study of the Gains from Merger* (Cambridge, England: Cambridge University Press, 1977), pp. 66–67.

mission that outside customers would continue to be served on a nondiscriminatory basis. Satisfied that this promise would be honored throughout the foreseeable future, the Monopolies Commission approved the merger. Under U.S. law, the merger would in all probability have been struck down to maintain structural conditions that impersonally minimize the risk of foreclosure. In Britain, the authorities were willing to rely upon *personal* assurances that the same end would be achieved.[192]

On the European Continent, the European Coal and Steel Community treaty of 1951 required that mergers be expressly authorized by the Community's High Authority if they might bring about concentration. During the ECSC's first decade some 136 cases were considered. None resulted in outright disapproval, although three mergers may have been abandoned voluntarily owing to the High Authority's display of reticence.[193] The coal and steel merger control function was subsumed by the European Community Commission in later years, and after 1962 a number of very large mergers were approved. One joined Thyssen Huette (with 1966 sales of $1.7 billion) and Huettenwerk Oberhausen (with sales of $252 million), creating the world's fourth largest steel-making concern, with more than 10 percent of total ECSC capacity. In 1973 the Commission approved a joint venture between the two largest French producers, whose combined 67 percent French market share was the result of numerous earlier mergers, to operate a massive new steel works at Marseilles. The Commission's published statements placed no emphasis on the likelihood that the joint venture would augment the coordination of business policies by the two firms, whose price-fixing agreements were one of the worst-kept secrets in Europe.[194] Sixteen months later, leading German producer Thyssen was permitted to join the Marseilles venture.

In 1971 the European Commission moved outside the coal and steel arena to challenge acquisitions by the Continental Can Company's Belgian subsidiary of the largest German and Dutch metal container producers.[195] This decision was overturned in 1973 by the European Court of Justice because of inadequacies in market definition. But the Court confirmed the Commission's

authority under EEC treaty Article 86 to prohibit as an abuse of power horizontal acquisitions by already dominant enterprises. With its new power established, the Commission began informally reviewing major mergers. At the time this was written, several had received the Commission's blessing, sometimes subject to promises of good conduct or prior consultation on future merger plans. None had been disapproved. Although there was considerable disagreement among member nations over what policy the Commission should pursue toward mergers, the threat of a blocking action by the Commission was widely considered to be real, especially for large transnational mergers.

Strong opposition to the European Commission's merger control policy, and especially on mergers among two companies of the same nationality exporting to other EEC nations, was expressed by France. French domestic policy during the 1960s actively encouraged large-scale mergers. In 1977, however, partly because of disillusion over the fruits of that policy but mainly to preempt the Common Market authorities, France passed its own law creating a new Commission on Competition to review domestic mergers entailing market shares exceeding 40 percent. Previously, in 1973, West Germany passed merger control amendments to its basic antitrust law. Several of the German Federal Cartel Office's early rulings against mergers were reversed by the Ministry of Economics or appellate courts, but by 1978 it had successfully opposed four mergers, including one between large British and German auto component makers that had been approved by Common Market authorities.[196] Four other mergers were permitted subject to partial divestiture or other modifications.

Since 1923 Canadian law prohibited mergers that operate to the detriment of the public. However, a series of adverse higher court rulings left the law unable to cope with any mergers other than those from which unregulated enterprises secured a virtual monopoly that they exploited against the public interest.[197] No contested antimerger action over a period of 54 years ended in conviction. In 1978, the Canadian Parliament was considering amendments that would substantially toughen the law, permitting a weighing of costs against benefits on mergers leading to combined market shares exceeding 20 percent.

Under the remnants of the Anti-Monopolies Law imposed upon Japan by the occupying forces following World War II, sizeable mergers must be registered with the Fair Trade Commission for review to ensure that a "controlling position" does not result. The first test came in 1969 when Yawata Iron and Steel and Fuji Iron and Steel, broken apart after the war, proposed to merge and form Nippon Steel Corporation. Yawata had 18.5 percent of Japanese steel ingot capacity at the time, Fuji 17.0 percent. The Fair Trade Commission opposed the merger, angering other government agencies, who threatened to have the FTC stripped of its powers. A compromise was eventually worked out under which the duly merged Nippon Steel would supply rival steel makers with rails and pig iron until they established their own facilities, provide know-how to a competitor entering the sheet pile business, and spin off its stockholdings in a tin can maker to a rival tin-plated steel producer.[198] In this way, it was said, alternate sources of supply would be assured in the most highly concentrated product lines affected. Since then through 1978, the Fair Trade Commission did not challenge another merger, even though roughly a thousand were registered with it yearly during the mid-1970s.

This virtually exhausts the list of nations with more or less active merger control laws as a part of their competition policies.[199] Although a start has been made abroad, there is still a considerable difference between the United States and its industrialized world counterparts. Indeed, in the sweep and toughness of its antimerger policy, the United States stands virtually alone. Being so isolated often leads to feelings of self-consciousness and doubt. Yet there is little evidence that appreciable costs have been imposed by the U.S. policy, and the trend overseas suggests gradual recognition that the benefits of mergers have been badly overestimated in the past. An important part of wisdom is knowing that solitude does not necessarily imply error.

192. It is conceivable that in Britain the sense of fair play is so finely cultivated and Establishment ties are so strong that harmful foreclosure would be unlikely, despite the pull of profit incentives. But one cannot avoid entertaining doubts. On the role of such assurances in other U.K. merger decisions, see the OECD committee of experts report, *Mergers and Competition Policy*, p. 35.

193. See Corwin D. Edwards, *Cartelization in Western Europe* (Washington, D.C.: U.S. Department of State, 1964), pp. 76–79; Hans Mueller, "The Policy of the European Coal and Steel Community Towards Mergers and Agreements by Steel Companies," *Antitrust Bulletin* 14 (Summer 1969): 413–48; and Klaus Stegemann, *Price Competition and Output Adjustment in the European Steel Market* (Tübingen: Mohr, 1977), pp. 272–76.

194. See the European Economic Community Commission's *Third Report on Competition Policy* (Brussels: European Economic Commission, 1974), pp. 64–65.

195. See the EEC Commission's *First Report on Competition Policy* (Brussels: European Economic Commission, 1971), pp. 78–83; and the *Third Report on Competition Policy* (1974), pp. 15, 28–38.

196. See the OECD's *Annual Reports on Competition Policy in OECD Member Countries*, especially no. 2, 1977, pp. 39–44.

197. See D. G. McFetridge, "The Emergence of a Canadian Merger Policy: The ERCO Case," *Antitrust Bulletin* 19 (Spring 1974): 1–11; Ministry of Consumer and Corporate Affairs, *Proposals for a New Competition Policy*, pp. 38–41; and G. B. Reschenthaler and W. T. Stanbury, "A Clarification of Canadian Merger Policy," *Antitrust Bulletin* 22 (Fall 1977): 673–85.

198. See "Japan Forges a Colossus in Steel," *Business Week*, 5 April 1969, pp. 92–96; "Japan's Steel: Easing the Merger Rules," *Business Week*, 14 June 1969, p. 92; and "Japanese Fair Trade Commission Decision on the Yawata-Fuji Steel Merger," *Antitrust Bulletin* 15 (Winter 1970): 803–27.

199. Australia enacted merger control provisions in 1974. At the time of writing, similar legislation was under consideration in Belgium, Holland, and Ireland, among others.

21 Antitrust policy: other restrictions on conduct

We return now to some further aspects of business conduct and their status under the antitrust laws. In this final chapter we explore the law on price discrimination, tying contracts, requirements contracts, exclusive dealing, and resale price maintenance. All but the last fall primarily under the jurisdiction of Clayton Act provisions originally framed by Congress to "arrest the creation of . . . monopolies in their incipiency." Whole books have been written on each of these practices. Here we can do no more than hit the highlights, overlooking many intricacies that delight antitrust aficionados.

Price discrimination

In simplest terms, price discrimination is the sale (or purchase) of different units of a good or service at price differentials not directly related to differences in the cost of supply. There are many varieties of price discrimination, and the diversity of economic effects is equally great. Discrimination can affect allocative efficiency, the equity of income distribution, and the vigor of competition. It may improve the efficiency of resource allocation by permitting monopolistic producers to serve, at prices approaching marginal cost, certain markets they would shun if forced to charge a uniform price; or it can have adverse allocative effects. Some forms of discrimination permit the

poor to pay lower prices than the rich—an income redistribution of which many observers might approve. Nearly all forms tend to increase the incomes of producers with monopoly power, and some benefit large firms more than small—effects eliciting widespread disapproval. Systematic discrimination and predatory discrimination can raise barriers to new entry and entrench established sellers in positions of power. Unsystematic discrimination can undermine oligopoly discipline and contribute to the emergence of competitive price-cost relationships.

With such a complex array of effects, a suitable price discrimination law must be sophisticated and discerning to encourage desirable practices and discourage undesirable ones. Unfortunately, as we shall see, the principal antidiscrimination provisions currently applicable in the United States fall visibly short of this ideal.

The first statutory pronouncement on price discrimination for U.S. industries other than railroading was Section 2 of the 1914 Clayton Act. It outlawed price discrimination between different purchasers where the effect "may be to substantially lessen competition or tend to create a monopoly." However, discrimination on account of differences in the grade, quality, or quantity of the commodity sold was exempted, as was discrimination that merely made due allowance for differences in cost or that was carried out in good faith to meet competitive pressures. The quantity loophole proved to be a gaping one, for many discriminatory price structures could be rationalized in terms of quantity differences. Because of this flaw and others, enforcement of the law was not particularly successful. Between 1914 and 1936 the Federal Trade Commission, with primary enforcement responsibility, initiated 43 complaints charging illegal price discrimination. Only 8 of these led ultimately to cease-and-desist orders not overturned on appeal to the courts.[1]

Recognition of these problems played some role in stimulating enactment of a much tougher law. However, other considerations had a more direct and potent influence. During the 1920s and 1930s, chain stores like A&P began to rise to the forefront of retail distribution, displacing small independent retailers. A 1934 Federal Trade Commission report on the chain store movement stated that one reason for the decline of independent retailers was the ability of giant chains to wrest discriminatory price concessions from their suppliers. These savings were then passed along to consumers; and because of the chains' low prices, sales were drawn away from smaller retailers. The investigation also revealed that pecuniary gains from induced price discrimination accounted for only about 15 percent of the chains' selling price advantage over independents; the rest could be traced to direct operating cost efficiencies.[2] But to eliminate whatever advantage the chains derived from exerting purchasing leverage, the Commission's report recommended that Clayton Act Section 2 be strengthened.

Congress was receptive. Under heavy pressure from independent grocer and drug store lobbies and expressing special concern over the buying power allegedly wielded by A&P, it passed the Robinson-Patman Act, substantially amending Clayton Act Section 2, in 1936.[3] The attendant reports and debates made it clear that Congress was anxious to protect small independent enterprises from the price competition of large firms discriminating in both their sales and purchasing functions. As Representative Wright Patman, the bill's cosponsor, later observed, the law was designed "to give the little business

fellows a square deal."[4] There is virtual unanimity among students of the Act that, in sharp contrast to the other antitrust laws, its motivation was a desire to limit competition, not to enhance it. In this respect the Robinson-Patman Act was not inconsistent with the spirit of the times, for in 1936, with recovery from the Great Depression not yet in sight, there were serious doubts afoot concerning the efficacy of unfettered competitive market processes.

The Robinson-Patman Act was enforced much more vigorously and with greater prosecutorial success than the original Section 2. Between 1936 and December 1957, the Federal Trade Commission decided 429 cases in which price discrimination had been challenged under the new law. In 311, or 72 percent, cease-and-desist orders were issued.[5] Only 4 of the 23 Commission decisions appealed to higher courts during this 21-year period were reversed. Between 1960 and 1972, 758 cease-and-desist orders were issued by the Commission.[6]

The core of the Robinson-Patman Act is embodied in Sections 2(a) and 2(b). They prohibit charging different prices to different purchasers of "goods of like grade and quality" where the effect "may be substantially to lessen competition or tend to create a monopoly in any line of commerce, or to injure, destroy, or prevent competition with any person who either grants or knowingly receives the benefit of such discrimination, or with customers of either of them." Three potential escape routes are then specified. Discrimination may be justified if (1) it is carried out to dispose of perishable or obsolescent goods, or under a closeout or bankruptcy sale; (2) it merely makes due allowance for differences in "the cost of manufacture, sale, or delivery resulting from the differing methods or quantities" in which the commodity is sold or delivered; or (3) it is effected "in good faith to meet an equally low price of a competitor." The most prominent change in language from old Section 2 was the provision specifying the requisite character of injury to competition. It seemed to embrace a wider class of cases than the clause "where the effect . . . may be to substantially lessen competition or tend to create a monopoly" contained in old Section 2 and two other substantive sections of the original Clayton

Act. We shall return shortly to analyze its interpretation and the construction of other especially controversial provisions.

The Robinson-Patman Act also reached out to deal with a number of practices ignored in the original Section 2. Section 2(c) of the newer law flatly prohibits the receipt (or payment) of brokerage commissions or any allowance or discount in lieu thereof except by (or to) middlemen actually performing services as independent brokers. No defenses—e.g., on the basis of cost differences or good faith meeting of competition—are permitted. Some historical background is essential to understand its significance. During the 1920s and 1930s, and to a lesser degree more recently, many small manufacturers and processors marketed their output through independent sales brokers who contacted potential customers, solicited orders, dispatched the orders to the producer, and collected a commission for their services. Companies like A&P, large enough to seek out producers and deal with them directly, insisted that they be paid the customary brokerage fee or given a commensurate price discount for eliminating the brokerage function. Through Section 2(c) Congress sought to thwart this practice. The prohibition has been stringently enforced; 145 of the 311 cease-and-desist orders issued by the FTC between 1936 and 1958 hinged solely on violations of Section 2(c). Between 1960 and 1972, 133 additional Section 2(c) orders were issued.

The brokerage payment provisions are open to objection on both economic and legal grounds. For one, Section 2(c) implicitly encourages either the preservation of possibly uneconomic brokerage functions or the retention by producers of savings ("phantom brokerage") from eliminating such middlemen, since buyers may not under the letter of the law take advantage of any savings effected from streamlining this aspect of the distribution system. Indeed, the law appears to enforce price discrimination *against* direct buyers, who might have to pay for services not rendered, even when they incur internal costs carrying out tasks otherwise performed by brokers.[7] Second, to enforce the section it is necessary to make delicate distinctions between brokerage commissions, which are illegal if received by a company buying for its own needs, and wholesalers' functional discounts, which in certain instances can be justified under Robinson-Patman Sections 2(a) and 2(b).[8] In the early days of Robinson-Patman Act enforcement, the distinction was often obvious from industry traditions. But as marketing institutions changed, it became increasingly vague, particularly with respect to firms serving as agents for buyers as well as for sellers and for enterprises simultaneously purchasing goods to be distributed through their own retail outlets and performing middleman services for other retailers. Some of the most intricate hair splitting in antitrust law has occurred in Section 2(c) contests of this type.[9] As the interpretations have

1. See Corwin D. Edwards, *The Price Discrimination Law* (Washington, D.C.: Brookings Institution, 1959), p. 6.

2. U.S., Federal Trade Commission, *Final Report on the Chain Store Investigation* (Washington, D.C.: Government Printing Office, 1934), p. 55.

3. For further background, see Edwards, *The Price Discrimination Law*, Chapter 2; and Frederick M. Rowe, *Price Discrimination Under the Robinson-Patman Act* (Boston: Little, Brown, 1962), Chapter 1. Many of the criticisms of A&P have since been shown to have been distorted or erroneous. See M. A. Adelman, *A&P: A Study in Price-Cost Behavior and Public Policy* (Cambridge, Mass.: Harvard University Press, 1959).

4. "Robinson-Patman: Dodo or Golden Rule?," *Business Week*, 12 November 1966, p. 66.

5. See Edwards, *The Price Discrimination Law*, pp. 66–91. Nearly 60 percent of these cease-and-desist orders pertained to firms operating in the food products industry, with which Congress has been particularly concerned.

6. U.S., Congress, House, Committee on Small Business, Ad Hoc Subcommittee on Antitrust, the Robinson-Patman Act, and Related Matters hearings, *Recent Efforts To Amend or Repeal the Robinson-Patman Act*, Part 2, 94th Cong., 1st sess., 1976, pp. 186–91.

7. See Adelman, *A&P*, especially pp. 160–61.

8. See *Federal Trade Commission v. Standard Oil Co. of Indiana et al.*, 355 U.S. 396 (1958). At an earlier stage in this and other cases, companies performing both wholesaling and retailing functions were allowed by the FTC to secure a wholesaler's discount on goods they purchased for sale to independent retailers, but not on purchases made for resale in their own outlets. For an analysis of the contradictions and distortions to which this policy led, see Edwards, *The Price Discrimination Law*, pp. 286–348; and U.S., Department of Justice, *Report of the Attorney General's National Committee To Study the Antitrust Laws* (Washington, D.C.: Government Printing Office, 1955), pp. 202–209.

9. *Central Retailer-Owned Grocers, Inc. v. Federal Trade Commission*, 319 F. 2d 410 (1963); *in re E. J. Hruby*, 61 F.T.C. 1437 (1962); and *Empire Rayon Yarn Co. v. American Viscose Corp. et al.*, 354 F. 2d 182 (1965), superseded in 364 F. 2d 491 (1966).

evolved, middlemen are likely to be classified as wholesalers if they customarily take title over the goods being distributed, assume the risks of price fluctuations and granting credit, and maintain warehouses and inventories. If they perform none of these functions, a payment for a middleman's services is apt to be called a brokerage fee. But the line between these poles is hard to draw, and there is certainly no compelling case in logic for drawing it at one point rather than another. Finally, large companies have managed to escape Section 2(c) by purchasing the entire output of their suppliers, or by purchasing only from suppliers who employ no brokers, or through other such dodges. In this respect Section 2(c) may operate to the disadvantage of medium-sized buyers who have less flexibility in choosing sources of supply. Because of these and other shortcomings, there is widespread sentiment for the repeal of Section 2(c).

Section 2(d) of the Robinson-Patman Act prevents sellers from making payments (such as advertising allowances) to buyers for promotional and other services rendered by the buyer, unless the payment is available to all buyers "on proportionally equal terms." Section 2(e) prohibits sellers from providing services (such as the use of special display racks, or the supply of inventories on a consignment basis) unless the service is made available to all customers on proportionally equal terms. These rules were intended to prevent discrimination on nonprice as well as price dimensions. In enforcing them it has not always been easy to determine when buyers of widely varying characteristics have in fact been accorded "proportionally equal" treatment.[10]

Section 2(f) makes it illegal for a buyer "knowingly to induce or receive a discrimination in price" prohibited by other parts of the law. It reflects the belief of Congress that powerful buyers were mainly to blame for the discriminatory practices inspiring the Robinson-Patman Act's passage. Its enforcement has not mirrored this apportioning of responsibility. Out of the more than 1,100 Robinson-Patman cease-and-desist orders issued by the Federal Trade Commission between 1936 and 1966, only 30 were brought under Section 2(f).[11] One reason was the stringent standard of proof demanded by the Su-

preme Court in a key case.[12] The phrase "knowingly to induce" requires, said the Court, proof not only that the buyer received illegal price concessions, but that it had good reason to believe the concessions were illegal.

Whether such knowledge was present was one of the many questions addressed in a case that nearly ensnared the A&P Company, whose purchasing practices had been a prime target of the Robinson-Patman Act's passage 40 years earlier.[13] Bargaining hard over the procurement of private-label milk for its Chicago area stores, A&P told its supplier, Borden, that a price offer from rival dairy Bowman was sufficiently attractive that "you [Borden] people . . . are not even in the ball park." Needing the A&P business to keep its new plant operating at satisfactory levels, Borden thereupon submitted a new offer that increased A&P's annual saving through milk discounts from $410,000 to $820,000, or roughly 15 percent of the total value of A&P's Chicago area purchases from Borden. Borden informed A&P that it was offering the large discount solely to meet the competitive bid described in vague terms by A&P, implying that the discount was discriminatory and could not be cost justified. Emphasizing A&P's knowledge of Borden's probable discrimination and its knowledge (which Borden lacked) that Borden's bid not only met, but undercut, Bowman's quotation, the Federal Trade Commission found that A&P had illegally induced discrimination.[14] However, A&P was exonerated when the Supreme Court ruled that seller Borden had a valid defense to charges of price discrimination because of the imprecise competitive threat with which it was confronted.[15] The Court concluded further that buyers (i.e., A&P) could not be held liable for violating Section 2(f) unless their suppliers' discriminatory prices were illegal, having no valid defense under other sections of the Robinson-Patman Act.

Some interpretations of Section 2(a) We return now to Section 2(a), under which many of the most important Robinson-Patman Act cases have been brought. The basic prohibition covers charging different prices to different customers. Quoting the same price to different customers served at diverse unit costs—e.g., when there are differences in order processing or delivery costs between customers—is generally not illegal, even though it is discriminatory in a meaningful economic sense.

Actionable discrimination can be inferred only if the goods sold at different prices are of "like grade and quality." The principal point of contention under this clause concerns price differentials between products unlike only in terms of brand name or some other aspect of image differentiation. The issue came to a head in 1966, when the Supreme Court ruled that the Borden Company had engaged in price discrimination by selling physically homogeneous canned evaporated milk at two prices, one for cans sold under the Borden label and a lower price for milk to which buyers affixed their own brand labels.[16] This opinion provoked a cry of protest from those who feared that the competitive challenge of low-priced, high-quality unbranded consumer products might be blunted. However, the case was shorn of its potentially revolutionary impact when an appellate court ruled on remand that no injury to competition resulted if "a price differential between a premium and nonpremium brand reflects no more than a consumer preference for the premium brand," since it merely represents "a rough equivalent of the benefit by way of the seller's national advertising and promotion which the purchaser of the more expensive branded product enjoys."[17]

One of the most complex and controversial features of the Robinson-Patman Act is the Section 2(a) condition that price discrimination, to be declared illegal, must injure competition in some manner. There are two main issues: upon whom the burden of proving injury rests, and what constitutes the requisite injury. On the first, the Second Circuit Court of Appeals held in early decisions that a *prima facie* presumption of injury existed when the mere presence of price discrimination had been shown.[18] This placed upon respondents the difficult burden of proving that competition had *not* been injured. However, appellate courts for the other circuits adopted the opposite rule, requiring the enforcement agency or party seeking damages to present affirmative evidence of competitive injury before the burden of defending itself passed to the discriminator.

This view has been accepted by the Federal Trade Commission, so the controversy has faded.[19]

Injury to competition under Robinson-Patman Act Section 2(a) may be shown at any of three levels: the primary line, the secondary line, and the tertiary line. A primary line injury involves competition among firms that are direct rivals to the seller practicing discrimination. A secondary line injury involves firms competing with buyers to whom a discriminatory price has been granted. A tertiary line injury involves firms competing with customers of the buyer to whom a

10. See for example *Fred Meyer, Inc. v. Federal Trade Commission*, 390 U.S. 341 (1968); *in re Marpos Network, Inc.*, advisory opinion 88, 3 September 1971, withdrawn 29 June 1972, reinstatement refused, 6 February 1976; and *in re Dan Odessky, Inc.*, advisory opinion dated 6 February 1976, revoked 1 February 1979.

11. See "Robinson-Patman: Dodo or Golden Rule?," *Business Week*, 12 November 1966, p. 66; and Edwards, *The Price Discrimination Law*, p. 72.

12. *Automatic Canteen Co. v. Federal Trade Commission* 346 U.S. 61 (1953).

13. *In the matter of the Great Atlantic & Pacific Tea Co. et al.*, 87 F.T.C. 962 (1976).

14. An irony of the case is that the net price at which A&P ultimately bought its milk from Borden was apparently not appreciably lower than the unit cost at which Jewel, the leading food retailer in the Chicago area, obtained milk from its own vertically integrated dairy. In 1976, A&P had only the fifth largest Chicago area market share.

15. *Great Atlantic & Pacific Tea Co., Inc. v. F.T.C.*, 99 S.Ct. 925 (1979).

16. *Federal Trade Commission v. Borden Co.*, 383 U.S. 637 (1966).

17. *Borden Co. v. Federal Trade Commission*, 381 F. 2d 175, 181 (1967). The appellate court also noted approvingly that Borden offered all buyers the opportunity to buy unlabeled milk at the lower price. Some evidently chose not to do so only because the differential was not sufficiently large to overcome consumers' preference for branded milk. This emphasis on the efficacy of subjective consumer preferences molded through advertising as a justification for price differentials, it might be added, appears logically inconsistent with the Supreme Court's condemnation of such differentials in the Clorox merger case. *Federal Trade Commission v. Procter & Gamble Co. et al.*, 386 U. S. 568 (1967). But Robinson-Patman Act interpretations have never been distinguished for their consistency with the other antitrust laws.

18. See especially *Samuel H. Moss, Inc. v. Federal Trade Commission*, 148 F. 2d 378 (1945); and *Federal Trade Commission v. Standard Brands, Inc.*, 189 F. 2d 510 (1951).

19. *Minneapolis-Honeywell Regulator Co. v. Federal Trade Commission*, 191 F. 2d 786 (1951), cert. den. 344 U.S. 206 (1952); and *in re General Foods Co.*, 50 FTC 885 (1954).

discriminatory price has been granted. Somewhat different standards have evolved for handling primary as opposed to secondary and tertiary line injuries. We will focus on the leading primary and secondary line rulings.

The central issue is whether the injury essential for a violation is injury to the *vigor of competition* or to particular *competitors*. These are usually not synonymous, although they might be, e.g., when individual competitors have been injured so lethally that they withdraw from the market, leaving fewer firms competing more cautiously. In primary line decisions something more than incidental injury to competitors has been required, but the courts have been willing to infer actionable injury when rivals were not literally driven from the market. Two cases reviewed by the Supreme Court illustrate the distinctions drawn.

Through sequential price reductions in January and June of 1954, the Anheuser-Busch Co. (AB) completely eliminated the price differential that had customarily prevailed in the St. Louis area between its Budweiser beer and other locally brewed beers. Prices were not reduced in other markets, and as a result the St. Louis price of Budweiser was considerably below prices AB charged elsewhere. AB's share of St. Louis beer sales rose from 12.5 percent in December 1953 to 39.3 percent in February of 1955. Then, in March of 1955, AB raised its St. Louis wholesale price $0.45 per case to $2.80, restoring a substantial price differential relative to competing local beers. Its share of the market dropped to 21 percent within four months and to 17 percent in 1956. Testimony revealed that AB had initiated its price-cutting program in response to severe midwestern market sales losses during 1953; that its St. Louis rivals continued to earn positive profits during the period of reduced Budweiser prices; and that part of the market share gain by AB was attributable to rival quality control and merchandising difficulties. After the Supreme Court found that AB had in fact engaged in price discrimination as defined under the Robinson-Patman Act, the Seventh Circuit Court of Appeals ruled that competition had not been injured sufficiently to find a violation; since the Budweiser price cuts were experimental, temporary, and necessitated by competitive conditions; and since

the shift in sales volume among competitors was only temporary.[20] It observed that the Robinson-Patman Act is "not concerned with mere shifts of business between competitors" and that "AB used restraint in its competitive efforts," refraining from "the predatory misconduct" condemned in other cases.

In late 1957 the Utah Pie Company, a tiny family-owned and -operated firm, began producing and marketing frozen dessert pies in the Salt Lake City area. Its principal rivals were three large nationwide concerns—Continental Baking, Pet Milk, and the Carnation Company. All had entered the frozen pie business before Utah, shipping their products into Salt Lake City from plants in California. Utah enjoyed a significant transportation cost advantage over the three, and through aggressive price competition it was able to build its Salt Lake City area market share to 67 percent in 1958. Each of the three cut prices sharply in response to Utah's gains, selling pies in Salt Lake City at prices below average total cost (including overhead allowances) and (at least occasionally) below the levels quoted in markets nearer their production sources. Utah's share of the market thereupon fell to 34 percent in 1959, rising to 45 percent in 1961. Its absolute volume of frozen pie sales expanded steadily in the rapidly growing market, however, and it operated profitably throughout the period. Utah sued the three rivals for damages resulting from their alleged price discrimination. After Utah appealed an appellate court decision overturning a jury verdict for Utah, the Supreme Court found that the jury could rationally have inferred the requisite injury to competition.[21] It stressed the sales of the three rivals below cost, the fact that Pet Milk management had identified Utah Pie as an "unfavorable factor" that "dug holes in our operation," and the fact that Pet had sent a spy into Utah's plant to seek evidence of quality deficiencies. Recognizing in a footnote the possible claim that Pet, Continental, and Carnation were only displaying "fierce competitive instincts," the Court nevertheless pointed to the evidence of predatory intent and argued that:

[a]ctual intent to injure another competitor does not . . . fall into that category, and neither . . . do persistent sales below cost and

radical price cuts themselves discriminatory. . . . We believe that the Act reaches price discrimination that erodes competition as much as it does price discrimination that is intended to have immediate destructive impact.[22]

The *Utah Pie* decision has been criticized for excessively protecting a seller whose cost advantage made it quite able to fend for itself.[23] Since the decision, there has been continuing controversy over the circumstances under which injury to primary line competition can reasonably be found, and over the closely related question of what constitutes predatory pricing under both the Robinson-Patman Act and Sherman Act Section 2.[24] Two appellate court decisions during the 1970s rejected Robinson-Patman primary line injury claims, stressing *inter alia* that prices had not been cut below marginal or average variable cost—the test of predation urged by Harvard Law School professors Areeda and Turner.[25] The Areeda-Turner tests have in turn been criticized for focusing on short-run allocative efficiency and ignoring the longer run strategic considerations governing the pricing decisions of sellers with substantial monopoly power.[26] A return to the question by the Supreme Court—augmented, one hopes, by appropriate economic analysis—seems needed before anything resembling a coherent policy can be discerned.

In secondary line cases a clearer and perceptibly tougher stance has been adopted. This presumably reflects the desire of the courts to respect Congress' avowed goal of discouraging discrimination adversely affecting the fortunes of small buyers. The Supreme Court's 1948 opinion in the *Morton Salt* case set the standard. Morton systematically sold its table salt at $1.60 per case in less-than-carload lots, at $1.50 per case for carload purchases, and at still lower prices when larger quantities were purchased over the span of a year. Observing that the discounts permitted large buyers to set retail prices below those of smaller rivals, the Court found an illegal injury to competition, supporting its conclusion as follows:

The legislative history of the Robinson-Patman Act makes it abundantly clear that Congress considered it to be an evil that a large buyer could secure a competitive advantage over a small buyer solely because of the large buyer's quantity purchasing ability. . . . [I]n enacting the Robinson-Patman Act Congress was especially concerned with protecting small businesses which were unable to buy in quantities, such as the merchants here who purchased in less-than-carload lots. . . . That respondent's quantity discounts did result in price differentials between competing purchasers sufficient in amount to influence their resale price of salt was shown by evidence. This showing in itself is adequate to support the Commission's appropriate findings that the effect of such discriminations "may be substantially to lessen competition . . . and to injure, destroy and prevent competition. . ."

Congress intended to protect a merchant from competitive injury attributable to discriminatory prices on any or all goods sold in interstate commerce, whether the particular goods constituted a major or minor portion of his stock.[27]

20. *Federal Trade Commission v. Anheuser-Busch, Inc.*, 363 U.S. 536 (1960), 289 F. 2d 835 (1961).

21. *Utah Pie Co. v. Continental Baking Co. et al.*, 386 U.S. 685, 697 (1967).

22. 386 U.S. 685, 702–703 (1967).

23. See Ward S. Bowman, "Restraint of Trade by the Supreme Court: The *Utah Pie* Case," *Yale Law Journal* 77 (November 1967): 70–85; "Note: Unlawful Primary Line Price Discriminations: Predatory Intent and Competitive Injury," *Columbia Law Review* 68 (January 1968): 137–54; and the *Report of the White House Task Force on Antitrust Policy*, July 1968, Appendix C, reprinted in the *Journal of Reprints for Antitrust Law and Economics* 1 (Winter 1969): 753–65.

24. See especially Phillip Areeda and Donald F. Turner, "Predatory Pricing and Related Practices under Section 2 of the Sherman Act," *Harvard Law Review* 88 (February 1975): 697–733.

25. *International Air Industries, Inc. v. American Excelsior Co.*, 517 F. 2d 714 (1975); and *Pacific Engineering & Production Co. of Nevada v. Kerr-McGee Corp. et al.*, 551 F. 2d 790 (1977), cert. den. 434 U.S. 879 (1977). On the latter, see also Chapter 12, p. 341 *supra*. Compare *Holleb & Co. v. Produce Terminal Cold Storage Co. et al.*, 532 F. 2d 29, 35–36 (1976), in which the Seventh Circuit Appellate Court held that a jury could infer primary line injury to competition on the basis of evidence that there was price discrimination, the companies were competing for the same customers, and the discriminator *undersold* a new entrant when customers expressed interest in purchasing from the entrant.

26. See Chapter 20, pp. 537–38 *supra*.

27. *Federal Trade Commission v. Morton Salt Co.*, 334 U.S. 37, 43, 47, 49 (1948).

This statement of the law was amplified in subsequent secondary line cases to indicate that actionable injury will not be inferred when the price differentials are too small to have any significant effect on sales and market shares, or when they exist for too short a period to affect industry member positions significantly. Still the general emphasis on possible injury to specific competitors or classes of competitors remains, as a 1965 appellate court opinion reveals:

[I]t seems well-established that where the record indicates a price differential substantial enough to cut into the purchaser's profit margin and discloses a reduction which would afford the favored buyer a significant aggregate saving that, if reflected in a resale price cut, would have a noticeable effect on the decisions of customers in the retail market, an inference of injury may properly be indulged.[28]

From these and related decisions it seems clear that the courts and the Federal Trade Commission are more inclined to err on the side of protecting competitors than protecting competition when the two goals are not congruent. And in this respect, the criteria applied in enforcing the Robinson-Patman Act are at odds with the broader procompetitive objectives of antitrust.

The discriminator's defenses Affirmation that competition has been injured through price discrimination does not complete a Robinson-Patman Section 2(a) proceeding. The burden of proving that its prices were legally justifiable then shifts to the discriminator. This is normally attempted under either the cost justification or "good faith meeting of competition" defenses.

Price differentials that merely reflect differences in the costs of serving particular customers are clearly unobjectionable, and to forbid them would be to encourage reverse discrimination. The Robinson-Patman Act permits companies to justify such differentials by showing that they "only make due allowance for differences in the cost of manufacture, sale, or delivery resulting from the differing methods or quantities in which . . . commodities are . . . sold or delivered." However, attempts to sustain a cost defense have

encountered several obstacles. For one, the FTC and the courts have insisted that the differential be justified in terms of *full costs*, including prorated overhead, and not merely the marginal costs upon which rational decision makers base their price structures. This approach has the debatable advantage of setting high standards for legality. If price differentials could be justified on marginal cost bases, only the most aggressive discrimination would fail to pass the test. Still, the imposition of a full-cost rule leads to inherently arbitrary judgments, since there is no uniquely correct way of prorating fixed and joint costs; and any convention adopted necessarily affects the cost comparison and perhaps the case outcome. Second, the FTC and courts have imposed heavy documentation demands upon sellers attempting to sustain a cost defense. Informed guesstimates have not been accepted, and the kinds of data generated routinely under normal accounting procedures have typically been found wanting. Rather, companies have been forced to conduct special cost studies, pinpointing the amount of order taking, packaging, delivery, maintenance, and other effort associated with serving specific classes of customers. General Electric is said to have spent $100,000 developing the data needed to justify its radio and television tube discount structure, and this sum (in 1960 dollars) is apparently not atypical.[29] Even when special cost studies have been made, firms' customer classifications have been rejected—sometimes for valid reasons, but in other cases because the FTC staff or judge lacked an adequate understanding of the underlying statistical methodology.[30] Finally, the FTC has insisted that price differentials be *fully* cost justified before it will accept the defense as valid. If a respondent shows that 90 percent of a price discount can be traced to cost savings, but cannot account for the remaining 10 percent, its cost defense fails completely. Partly because of these problems, but also because the cost defense is inapplicable in many price discrimination situations, only 11 attempts were made to employ the cost defense in cases contested before the Federal Trade Commission between 1936 and 1954. Of these, only 2 were fully successful.[31] However, companies have been able more frequently to head off impending FTC complaints at the informal investigation stage by presenting convincing cost data to justify their price differentials.[32]

When discrimination injurious to competition has been found, Section 2(b) of the Robinson-Patman Act permits a seller to rebut the *prima facie* presumption of illegality by showing that its lower price was "made in good faith to meet an equally low price of a competitor." Interpretation of this "good faith meeting" defense presents a tangle of legal and economic problems. For the most part, the Federal Trade Commission has taken a skeptical view of discriminators' attempts to use the defense. Some of its decisions have been rebuffed by higher courts, but many issues remain unsettled and controversial.[33]

A few of the earlier contested decisions involved the use of basing point pricing systems. In the leading case, A. E. Staley Co., a central Illinois producer of glucose and corn syrup, systematically matched the delivered prices set from a Chicago basing point by its principal rival. For sales in the Chicago area Staley quoted lower delivered prices than in downstate Illinois, even though its shipping costs were higher on Chicago orders. Staley argued that its discrimination was justifiable, since it merely met in good faith the prices of its Chicago rival. Sustaining an FTC cease-and-desist order, the Supreme Court ruled that the good faith meeting of competition defense could not apply when the prices met were themselves illegal, stemming from an illegal discriminatory system.[34]

In a related case appealed twice to the Supreme Court, the FTC argued that the Standard Oil Company of Indiana could not plead good faith meeting of competition when it granted 1.5 cent per gallon functional discounts to four Detroit gasoline jobbers who took delivery in rail carload lots (instead of the much smaller truckload lots accepted by retailers) and then sold the gasoline in their own retail outlets as well as to independent retail gas stations. Stressing the *Staley* precedent, the Commission insisted that Standard's functional discounts to jobbers were made pursuant to a discriminatory pricing system, and therefore did not qualify as a good faith meeting of "individual competitive situations." The Supreme Court rejected this inference, not-

ing that Standard had lost three of its jobbers by not meeting competitors' discounts during a price war and that it granted the jobber's discount to one distributor only after prolonged haggling. It found that "Standard's use of . . . two prices, the lower of which could be obtained under the spur of threats to switch to pirating competitors, is a competitive deterrent far short of the discriminatory pricing of Staley," and that Standard's good faith meeting of competition could therefore serve as an absolute defense to the charge of illegal discrimination.[35] This "Detroit Gas" case is distinctive in two main respects: It demonstrated that the "good faith meeting of competition" defense could be used successfully despite the FTC's reticence; and it required 17 years of litigation to acquit a practice that reflected nothing more than a rational competitive response to secure the valuable services of gasoline jobbers.

28. *Foremost Dairies, Inc.* v. *Federal Trade Commission,* 348 F. 2d 674, 680 (1965).

29. "Robinson-Patman: Dodo or Golden Rule?," *Business Week*, 12 November 1966, p. 68. See also R. A. Lynn, "Is the Cost Defense Workable?," *Journal of Marketing* 29 (January 1965): 39, citing a half-million dollar expenditure in another case.

30. Compare *U.S.* v. *Borden Co.*, 370 U.S. 460 (1962), with *Federal Trade Commission* v. *Standard Motor Products, Inc.*, 371 F. 2d 613 (1967). In the latter case, the Second Circuit Court of Appeals displayed considerable statistical sophistication in overturning an FTC decision.

31. See the *Report of the Attorney General's National Committee To Study the Antitrust Laws*, p. 171.

32. Edwards, *The Price Discrimination Law*, pp. 587–91.

33. For surveys of recent decisions, see Robert W. Steele, "Section 2(b) of the Robinson-Patman Act—Rules for Meeting Competition in the Past and Present," *Antitrust Bulletin* 13 (Winter 1968): 1223–69; and Michael M. Eaton, "The Robinson-Patman Act: Reconciling the Meeting Competition Defense with the Sherman Act," *Antitrust Bulletin* 18 (Fall 1973): 411–30.

34. *Federal Trade Commission* v. *A. E. Staley Mfg. Co. et al.*, 324 U.S. 746 (1945). See also *Corn Products Refining Co.* v. *Federal Trade Commission*, 324 U.S. 726 (1945); *Federal Trade Commission* v. *Cement Institute et al.*, 333 U.S. 683 (1948); and (on plywood) *in re Boise Cascade Corp. et al.*, decision and final order, Federal Trade Commission docket no. 8958 (February 1978). In *Safeway Stores, Inc.* v. *Oklahoma Retail Grocers Association, Inc.*, 360 U.S. 334 (1959), the Supreme Court held that a firm cannot in good faith discriminate to meet competitor prices which it believes violate state laws prohibiting sales below cost.

35. *Federal Trade Commission* v. *Standard Oil Co.*, 355 U.S. 396, 404 (1958). See also the earlier opinion at 340 U.S. 231 (1951).

Antitrust policy: other restrictions on conduct **579**

Some of the more exotic Section 2(b) deliberations have focused on the discriminator's knowledge of the existence and legality of rival prices. When sellers vie for orders through secret price shading, it is not always clear to the would-be discriminator whose prices it must meet, nor can one always be sure that a customer is telling the truth in reporting competitive offers. Also, the rival price a seller must meet to secure some order may itself be illegally discriminatory—e.g., because it cannot be justified on the basis of cost savings. The Federal Trade Commission has demanded that respondents show diligence in ascertaining the existence and even the cost justification of rival price offers.[36] Although extreme versions of this doctrine have been rejected by higher courts, there is a dilemma in the whole approach. For buyers, a certain amount of secrecy may be essential to extract the best possible bargain. This limits the seller's ability to verify rival offers through its contacts with buyers. And if a salesperson checks with rivals alleged to have offered a concession, he or she runs the risk of violating the Sherman Act Section 1 prohibition against price-fixing conspiracies.[37]

Equally baffling questions arise in determining what it means to "meet" a competitor's price. A literal reading of the statutory language suggests that firms practicing discrimination may match rival prices exactly but not undercut them. Widespread seller adherence to such a rule, which has been embraced in several decisions,[38] could smother the forces that undermine oligopoly price structures. Matters become even more complicated when one firm's product customarily commands a premium price because of image differentiation. In gasoline retailing, for instance, the lesser known brands must charge several cents less per gallon than nationally advertised brands to maintain their market positions, though tacit agreement on the "correct" differential is difficult to obtain, and price wars often have begun when some company has tried to alter the differential. Against this circumstantial background, the Federal Trade Commission and the courts have in certain cases ruled that "good faith meeting" of competition for nationally branded gasoline sellers consists of maintaining the traditional price differential, and that the

defense cannot be sustained when a refiner squeezes the differential.[39] While this position can be defended as a matter of logic, rigid adherence to it could discourage innovation in marketing and freeze price structures into increasingly archaic molds.

One further illustration completes our survey. The Federal Trade Commission has held in some decisions that sellers can escape under the "good faith meeting" clause only when they discriminate in self-defense to retain existing customers but not to attract new ones. This interpretation was rejected by the Seventh Circuit Court of Appeals in a case concerning the pricing of Sunshine Biscuit's Krun-Chee potato chips in Cleveland. The court noted that the Robinson-Patman Act permits sellers to meet rival price offers to "any purchaser," and not just to old customers. It observed further that the FTC approach was unworkable, since it is hard to distinguish in practice between new and old customers, and economically unsound, since "competition for new customers would be stifled and monopoly would be fostered."[40] However, two other circuit courts of appeal have approved the FTC position,[41] and so in this respect as well the question of how aggressively sellers can compete for patronage remains uncertain.

Conclusion The Robinson-Patman Act is an extremely imperfect instrument. It is questionable whether the circle of its beneficiaries extends much wider than the attorneys who earn sizeable fees interpreting its complex provisions. In many ways it conflicts with both the spirit and the letter of other antitrust laws. It certainly has the potential of encouraging competitors to pull their punches. That potential has been aggravated through unenlightened enforcement by the Federal Trade Commission—e.g., in letting its attorneys sweep down New York's Seventh Avenue and secure from 298 garment manufacturers virtually identical consent agreements that they will refrain from offering advertising allowances to customers on other than proportionally equal terms.[42] The impetus came from the garment makers themselves, who were unhappy about the use of advertising allowances as a form of *sub rosa* price shading. Whether the law has actually had substantial anticompetitive effects is unclear, in part because it is difficult to amass persuasive evidence on what business behavior would be in the absence of Robinson-Patman orders or the threat of enforcement.[43] If adverse effects have been minimal, as Professor Brooks argues,[44] credit must go more to the resilience of the forces of competition than to the Act itself or its administration. And there is surely much to criticize about a law that requires business decision makers regularly to consult their attorneys before making price moves.[45]

There is a further irony in the FTC's enforcement record. As we have seen, the Robinson-Patman Act was passed to help small businesses. Nevertheless, of the 564 companies named in FTC Robinson-Patman complaints between 1961 and 1974, only 36, or 6.4 percent, had annual sales of $100 million or more at the time of complaint.[46] More than 60 percent had sales below $5 million. Thus, the brunt of the Commission's enforcement effort fell upon the small businesses Congress sought to protect. Moreover, when large companies were caught in the net, their greater incentive and financial resources allowed them to resist the Commission's efforts more vigorously and with greater success. Consent settlements were accepted without any litigation by between 84 and 95 percent of the respondents with sales of less than $10 million, but only 37 percent of the $100 million companies.[47] And 23 percent of the corporations with sales exceeding $100 million ultimately succeeded in having complaints against themselves dismissed, whereas none of the companies with sales of less than $10 million did. FTC Robinson-Patman Act lawyers, the statistics suggest and the author's personal experience reinforces, prefer to run up their success tallies bullying small companies unlikely to fight back vigorously.

Most of this record of law enforcement run amok was compiled during the early 1960s. With a change in membership, the FTC reduced the number of companies named in Robinson-Patman Act complaints from an average of 74 per year in 1960–65 to 5.6 in 1966–70.[48] A further drop followed in the early 1970s as attempts were made to reform the Commission's case selection procedures and screen out specious or downright

36. See *Forster Mfg. Co. et al. v. Federal Trade Commission*, 355 F. 2d 47 (1964), cert. den. 380 U.S. 906 (1965); 361 F. 2d 340 (1966); *in re Tri-Valley Packing Association*, 60 F.T.C. 1134 (1962); *Standard Oil Co. v. Brown*, 238 F. 2d 54 (1956); and *in re A&P*, 87 F.T.C. 962, 1057–1066 (1976).

37. In *U.S. v. United States Gypsum Co. et al.*, 98 S. Ct. 2864 (1978), the Supreme Court held that such contacts could successfully be defended against price-fixing charges only in those relatively few situations where "the veracity of the buyer seeking the matching discount was legitimately in doubt, other means of corroboration were unavailable to the seller, and the interseller communication was for the sole purpose of complying with the Robinson-Patman Act."

38. *Samuel H. Moss, Inc. v. Federal Trade Commission*, 148 F. 2d 378, 379 (1945); *in re Champion Spark Plug Co.*, 50 F.T.C. 30 (1953); and *A&P v. Federal Trade Commission*, 87 F.T.C. 962, 1056 (1976); 557 F. 2d 971, 982 (1978). Compare *Callaway Mills Co. et al. v. Federal Trade Commission*, 362 F. 2d 435, 443 (1966); and *National Dairy Products Corp. v. Federal Trade Commission*, 395 F. 2d 517, 523 (1968), cert. den. 393 U.S. 977 (1968), in which special factual circumstances were considered to be extenuating.

39. *In re American Oil Co.*, 60 F.T.C. 1786 (1962), set aside on other grounds at 325 F. 2d 101 (1963); and *Continental Oil Co. v. Frontier Refining Co.*, 338 F. 2d 780 (1964).

40. *Sunshine Biscuits, Inc. v. Federal Trade Commission*, 306 F. 2d 48, 52 (1962). See also *Hanson v. Pittsburgh Plate Glass Industries, Inc.*, 482 F. 2d 220, 227 (1973); and *Cadigan v. Texaco, Inc., et al.*, 492 F. 2d 383, 387 (1974).

41. *Standard Motor Products, Inc. v. Federal Trade Commission*, 265 F. 2d 674, 677 (1959), cert. den. 361 U.S. 826 (1959); and *Viviano Macaroni Co. v. Federal Trade Commission*, 411 F. 2d 255, 258 (1969) (where a distinction was drawn between obtaining additional business and defending oneself against the inroads of rapacious competitors).

42. *In re Abby Kent Co. et al.*, 68 F.T.C. 393 (1965). For contrasting views on the impact of that action, see "Note: Eine kleine juristische Schlummergeschichte," *Harvard Law Review* 79 (March 1966): 926–28; and Robert C. Brooks, Jr., "Report of Pilot Field Survey on Market Effects of Robinson-Patman Orders," in *Recent Efforts To Amend*, Part 1, pp. 313–54.

43. The only known systematic study is by Brooks, "Report of Pilot Field Study," which was based upon superficial and poorly controlled interviews. See *Recent Efforts To Amend*, Part 1, pp. 276–82, 421.

44. *Recent Efforts To Amend*, p. 423.

45. See for example the initial decision *in re A&P*, reprinted in *Recent Efforts To Amend*, Part 1, p. 75. In a Robinson-Patman action in which the author participated, a small business was driven to the point of bankruptcy while FTC attorneys debated interminably the legality of a merchandising scheme the firm offered to food retailers.

46. See the testimony of F. M. Scherer in *Recent Efforts To Amend*, Part 2, pp. 145–48, and Part 3, pp. 19–22. Section 2(c) complaints were excluded from the count.

47. *Recent Efforts To Amend*, Part 3, p. 18.

48. *Recent Efforts To Amend*, Part 2, p. 147. Section 2(c) brokerage commission cases, whose incidence also declined sharply, are excluded because comparable statistics were unavailable.

Antitrust policy: other restrictions on conduct   **581**

anticompetitive actions. Under this new policy, the Act's social cost has undoubtedly been lessened. However, treble damages litigation initiated by aggrieved private parties continues unabated.

There have been many proposals to amend the Robinson-Patman Act and eliminate its less-desirable provisions.[49] However, such efforts have been vigorously opposed by small business interest groups, who evidently believe (although, in view of the FTC's enforcement history, not necessarily correctly) that they have been benefitted by the Act. Congress has continued to be responsive to such small business pressures. The best hope, therefore, for a rational public policy toward price discrimination may lie in the higher courts' willingness (granted, with less than perfect consistency) to overturn Robinson-Patman Act interpretations patently inconsistent with competition, efficiency, or plain common sense.

Tying contracts, requirements contracts, and exclusive dealing

Section 3 of the Clayton Act prohibits contracts for the sale or lease of commodities imposing a condition that the purchaser or lessee "shall not use or deal in the goods, . . . supplies, or other commodities of a competitor . . . of the lessor or seller" where the effect "may be to substantially lessen competition or tend to create a monopoly." It applies to three main types of practices: tying contracts, requirements contracts, and exclusive dealing arrangements. A common feature of most such arrangements is some restriction on competition spanning different (and usually adjacent) vertical stages in the chain of production and distribution—e.g., an agreement between manufacturers and their distributors or between the makers and users of a product. As such, they are often referred to as vertical restrictions.

Under a tying contract, the purchaser of some article—e.g., a machine—agrees as a condition of purchase to buy the seller's supplies of some other commodity, such as raw materials processed by the machine. The agreement in effect forecloses competing materials sellers from the opportunity of selling the 'tied' commodity to that purchaser. A requirements contract is an agreement by the buyer to purchase all its requirements of some commodity from a particular seller. Here again, competing sellers are foreclosed for the duration of the contract. Exclusive dealing is a special subcase under which some firm (typically a retailer or wholesaler) agrees to sell only the products of a particular manufacturer, and thus implicitly or explicitly agrees not to handle the products of competing producers. The law on these practices has developed along divergent lines, so we shall examine each separately.

Tying contracts Businesses have diverse reasons for attempting to tie the sale of one product to that of another. First, a firm may have monopoly power over one product by virtue of patent protection, strong product differentiation, or scale economies; and it may try to exploit this leverage in a second market where, without the tie, it could earn no more than a normal return.[50] Thus, it adds to its monopoly profits in the tying good market the profits it can realize by exercising power over price in at least part of the tied good market. The economics of such ties are similar to those of downstream integration by a firm to obtain control over the purchase of inputs complementary in production to the input on which the firm enjoys monopoly power.[51] Second and closely related, the profits attainable from coordinated monopoly pricing of two goods which, for example, are complements in use, will generally be higher than those realized by setting a monopoly price for each commodity separately.[52] This is so because, by ignoring interdependence between the demand functions of complementary products, a producer in effect fails to adjust for all the variables affecting its profit maximum, just as oligopolists producing the same product maximize joint profits only when they take into account fully the interdependence of their demand functions. Third, tying is sometimes a convenient way of discriminating in price according to intensity of demand. Suppose, for instance, that one copying machine user makes 3,000 copies per month, while another makes 10,000 copies per month. It would be difficult for a company selling

582

only copying machines to price its machines in such a way as to extract more revenue from the more intensive user. But if the machine maker can tie the purchase of special copying paper to the purchase of its machine, and if it can wield sufficient leverage in the paper market to realize a supranormal profit margin there, it will be able to secure additional profits from the high-volume user. An analogous but more complex variant occurs when firms sell related but separable products only at a single package or "bundled" price.[53] Fourth, the producer of a technically complex machine may engage in tying to control the quality of materials and supplies used with its machine, so that the reputation of its product is not sullied by breakdowns caused through the use of faulty supplies. Fifth, certain economies may be realized by producing or distributing the tied and tying goods together. For example, supplies of special copying machine paper or ink may be delivered by maintenance personnel in the course of routine service visits, saving separate delivery costs. It is doubtful, however, whether the savings realized in this way could be very substantial. Finally, tying contracts may be employed to evade governmental price controls—e.g., when a firm supplying some commodity such as gas or telephone service whose price is regulated requires customers to buy from it fixtures and attachments whose prices are not effectively controlled.

In early tying case decisions, companies requiring purchasers of their patented machines also to purchase unpatented supplies were allowed to enforce their tying contracts and secure injunctions against the use of competing supplies.[54] However, these precedents were overturned after the Clayton Act was passed.[55] From then on, tying arrangements have been dealt with severely not only in Clayton Act Section 3 cases, but also in Sherman Act Section 1 and patent infringement actions.[56] In a decision setting forth general guidelines for the interpretation of Clayton Act Section 3, the Supreme Court observed that "[t]ying agreements serve hardly any purpose beyond the suppression of competition."[57] In a nearly contemporaneous case tried under both Clayton and Sherman Act charges, the Court ruled that it is "unreasonable, *per se*, to

foreclose competitors from any substantial market" by means of tying contracts.[58]

These statements have the ring of a flat *per se* prohibition, but the presumption against tying arrangements is not quite as strong as the *per se* rule against price-fixing conspiracies. Violation will not be found unless there is appreciable monopoly power in the tying good market or unless a substantial volume of sales is foreclosed in the tied good market.[59] For relatively small sellers of unpatented products, these conditions are not likely to be satisfied. Small companies attempting to break into a new market under the protection of tying contracts may also escape censure.[60] And the courts have been willing to consider extenuating circumstances such as the need to exercise control over complementary

49. See for instance Carl Kaysen and Donald F. Turner, *Antitrust Policy* (Cambridge, Mass.: Harvard University Press, 1959), pp. 184–85; *Report of the White House Task Force on Antitrust Policy*, Appendix C; and *Recent Efforts To Amend*, Part 1, pp. 243–50, 538–39, 590–93.

50. For varying views, see Ward S. Bowman, Jr., "Tying Arrangements and the Leverage Problem," *Yale Law Journal* 67 (November 1957): 19–36; M. L. Burstein, "A Theory of Full-Line Forcing," *Northwestern University Law Review* 55 (March–April 1960): 62–95; and W. L. Baldwin and David McFarland, "Tying Arrangements in Law and Economics," *Antitrust Bulletin* 8 (September–October 1963): 743–80.

51. See Chapter 10, pp. 300–2 *supra* and Roger D. Blair and David Kaserman, "Vertical Integration, Tying, and Antitrust Policy," *American Economic Review* 68 (June 1978): 397–402.

52. For a proof, see Martin J. Bailey, "Price and Output Determination by a Firm Selling Related Products," *American Economic Review* 44 (March 1954): 82–93.

53. See W. J. Adams and Janet L. Yellen, "Commodity Bundling and the Burden of Monopoly," *Quarterly Journal of Economics* 90 (August 1976): 475–98.

54. *Heaton Peninsular Button-Fastener Co.* v. *Eureka Specialty Co.*, 77 F. 288 (1896); and *Henry* v. *A. B. Dick Co.*, 224 U.S. 1 (1912).

55. The turning point was *Motion Picture Patents Co.* v. *Universal Film Manufacturing Co.*, 243 U.S. 502 (1917). An important Section 3 decision outlawing tying agreements imposed by firms dominating some market was *United Shoe Machinery Corp.* v. *U.S.*, 258 U.S. 451 (1922).

56. Key patent infringement decisions include *Carbice Corp.* v. *American Patent Development Corp.*, 283 U.S. 27 (1931); and *Morton Salt Co.* v. *G. S. Suppiger Co.*, 314 U.S. 488 (1942).

57. *Standard Oil Co. of California et al.* v. *U.S.*, 337 U.S. 293, 305–306 (1949).

58. *International Salt Co.* v. *U.S.*, 322 U.S. 392, 396 (1947). See also *Northern Pacific Railway Co.* v. *U.S.*, 356 U.S. 1, 5–6 (1958).

goods or services to ensure satisfactory operation of the tying product. This was a central issue in a case involving the International Business Machines Corporation's requirement that its unpatented tabulating cards be used exclusively in the key punch, card sorting, and other mechanical data processing equipment it leased. IBM argued that the use of faulty cards could cause machine jams and processing errors, damaging its reputation. The Supreme Court rejected this contention after studying the evidence. It found that other suppliers were capable of manufacturing cards conforming to IBM's specifications and that IBM was not prevented under the law from "proclaiming the virtues of its own cards" or even from making its leases conditional upon the use of cards meeting the necessary quality standards.[61] In a later case, a slightly more tolerant judgment was rendered. The Jerrold Electronics Corporation, a pioneer in the development and installation of community antenna television systems, required purchasers of its system also to accept five-year maintenance contracts. This was done to avoid breakdowns that could result if the complex, delicate equipment were serviced by inadequately trained personnel. In a decision broadly endorsed by the Supreme Court, a district court ruled that the service tying arrangement was not unreasonable at the time of its inception, but that it came to violate Sherman Act Section 1 as the "industry took root and grew."[62]

The law also does not reach tying arrangements that are purely voluntary and informal— e.g., when customers habitually buy a machine producer's special supplies in the belief that the machine will thereby function more effectively, or because it is more convenient, and not because the machine maker refuses to sell or lease machines without a supplies contract. There were many informal ties of this type on electrostatic copying machines requiring specially coated paper during the early 1960s.[63] However, the ties were gradually weakened as newcomers entered the paper-coating trade, offering their products at substantially reduced prices. Some machine suppliers reacted to this emerging competitive challenge by attempting to formalize their ties, but they were soon dissuaded by the threat of

antitrust suits. They then accepted their fate stoically, raising the price of their machines because machine sales could no longer be counted upon to generate a profitable stream of subsequent paper sales. Such a pricing reaction is common when a tie between complementary products is severed.

The effects of a legal ban against tying contracts on market structure and conduct vary from field to field, depending upon the degree to which producers can sustain informal ties through product differentiation. On one hand, the 1936 decree requiring IBM to end its tying contracts had very little effect, for data processing machine users continued to buy their tabulating cards from IBM. Twenty years later IBM still accounted for roughly 90 percent of greatly expanded tabulating card production.[64] On the other hand, an attack on tying practices appears to have had a major impact in the tin can industry. Prior to 1950, the American Can Company tied the sale of tin cans to the lease of its patented can-closing machines by arranging to have the expiration dates of machine leases and long-term can requirements contracts coincide, and by refusing to conclude new machine lease contracts unless the canner also accepted a can requirements contract. After the courts found this subterfuge illegal, American was required to offer its machines for sale at attractive prices and to limit the life of its can supply contracts to one year.[65] Similar injunctions bound Continental Can, its leading rival. Within four years, customers responsible for 75 percent of the two firms' machine leases had taken advantage of the opportunity to own their can-closing machines. Price competition in the industry has intensified, and the market share of can sellers outside the Big Four increased from 20 percent in 1954 to 34 percent in 1972.[66]

Requirements contracts Under a requirements contract, the buyer agrees to purchase all of its requirements for some commodity or group of commodities from a particular seller. Such arrangements have the possibly undesirable effect of foreclosing a market to competing sellers during the life of the contract. They also offer a number of potential advantages, however, as the

Supreme Court acknowledged in its 1949 *Standard Stations* opinion:

In the case of the buyer, they may assure supply, afford protection against rises in price, enable long-term planning on the basis of known costs, and obviate the expense and risk of storage in the quantity necessary for a commodity having a fluctuating demand. From the seller's point of view, requirements contracts may make possible the substantial reduction of selling expenses, given protection against price fluctuations, and—of particular advantage to a newcomer to the field to whom it is important to know what capital expenditures are justified—offer the possibility of a predictable market. . . . They may be useful, moreover, to a seller trying to establish a foothold against the counterattacks of entrenched competitors.[67]

After listing these possibilities, the Court went on to observe that jurists are seldom in a good position to weigh the anticompetitive effects of specific requirements contracts against their economic advantages. It therefore ruled that contested contracts should be judged primarily in terms of their structural impact, and that a violation of Clayton Act Section 3 should be found when there is proof "that competition has been foreclosed in a substantial share of the line of commerce affected."[68] In the case at bar, the Standard Oil Company of California had entered into requirements contracts with 5,937 independent franchised Standard gasoline retailers, comprising 16 percent by number of all gas stations in a seven-state western United States area and making 6.7 percent of all 1946 gasoline sales in that area. Some contracts required the stations to purchase only their gasoline supplies exclusively from Standard; others covered tires, batteries, and other products in addition to gasoline. Emphasizing the 6.7 percent market share and the fact that annual gasoline sales of roughly $58 million were at issue, the Supreme Court held that a substantial share of commerce had in fact been foreclosed and that the contracts were therefore illegal.[69] This decision served not only to constrain the use of requirements contracts in many fields, but also established a tough structural test of anticompetitive effects upon which subsequent merger decisions were based.

Requirements contracts negotiated by sellers possessing a very small share of the relevant market do stand a good chance of escaping

(59) The courts may also strain economic logic beyond the breaking point to acquit reasonable practices by finding that the necessary structural tests are not satisfied. This is apparently what happened in *Times-Picayune Publishing Co.* v. *U.S.*, 345 U.S. 594 (1953). The Supreme Court found New Orleans's largest newspaper publisher innocent of violating Sherman Act Section 1 when it required persons desiring to advertise in the morning *Times-Picayune* also to take identical insertions in its evening paper, *The States*. Notwithstanding the Supreme Court's arguments to the contrary, this was a clear-cut tying arrangement. But it did have the merit of permitting typesetting and composition cost savings.

(60) See especially the *dictum* in *Brown Shoe Co.* v. *U.S.*, 370 U.S. 294, 330 (1962).

61. *International Business Machines Corp.* v. *U.S.*, 298 U.S. 131, 139–140 (1936).

62. *U.S.* v. *Jerrold Electronics Corp.*, 187 F. Supp. 545, 557 (1960); affirmed per curiam 363 U.S. 567 (1961).

63. See Erwin A. Blackstone, "Restrictive Practices in the Marketing of Electrofax Copying Machines and Supplies," *Journal of Industrial Economics* 23 (March 1975): 189–202. Similarly, the toner (ink) for Xerox machines, tied informally to the lease of copying machines, was called "black gold" by persons familiar with its price-cost relationships.

64. *U.S.* v. *International Business Machines Corp.*, CCH 1956 Trade Cases, Para. 68,245. On subsequent developments in *IBM* and similar cases, see William L. Baldwin, "The Feedback Effect of Business Conduct on Industry Structure," *Journal of Law and Economics* 12 (April 1969): 123–53.

65. *U.S.* v. *American Can Co. et al.*, 87 F. Supp. 18 (1949).

66. See James W. McKie, "The Decline of Monopoly in the Metal Container Industry," *American Economic Review* 45 (May 1955): 499–508; and Charles H. Hession, "The Metal Container Industry," in Walter Adams, ed., *The Structure of American Industry*, 3rd ed. (New York: Macmillan, 1961), pp. 430–67.

67. *Standard Oil Co. of California et al.* v. *U.S.*, 337 U.S. 293, 306–307 (1949).

68. 377 U.S. 293, 314 (1949).

69. See also *Richfield Oil Corp.* v. *U.S.*, 343 U.S. 922 (1952), in which a similar arrangement involving even smaller market shares was struck down. In "Exclusive Dealing in the Petroleum Industry: The Refiner-Lessee Dealer Relationship," *Yale Economic Essays* 3 (Spring 1963): 223–47, Richard A. Miller argues that the elimination of formal requirements contracts in gasoline retailing has had little effect on industry conduct, since refiners can bring to bear a number of informal pressures to induce retail outlets to stock their products. These range from the threat of cancelling station leases to negligence in refilling a station's storage tanks. Prohibiting such vertical restrictions may also induce producers to integrate vertically downstream, establishing outlets whose purchasing and other policies they can control directly.

challenge, and not all challenged contracts have been found illegal. In another case carried to the Supreme Court, the Nashville Coal Company contracted to supply at predetermined prices the total coal requirements of a new Tampa Electric Co. generating station for a period of 20 years. Nashville then tried to back out of the agreement. When Tampa sued for breach of contract, Nashville defended itself by arguing that the contract violated Clayton Act Section 3 and was therefore unenforceable. Specifically, the contract was said to foreclose a substantial market, since Tampa's requirements equalled the total volume of coal purchased in the state of Florida before the contract's inception. After two lower courts accepted this defense, the Supreme Court reversed and ruled in favor of Tampa.[70] It defined the relevant market as the *supply* market in an eight-state area, noting that mines in that coal-producing region were eager to sell more coal in Florida. When the market was so defined, the share foreclosed by the Tampa-Nashville contract amounted to less than 1 percent. And this, the Supreme Court said, was not enough to find a Section 3 violation.

Exclusive dealing and exclusive dealer franchises Somewhat more extensive treatment is merited for two special classes of restrictions promulgated by manufacturers in association with the retailers or wholesalers who distribute their products. They are quite distinct legally; but since they are often used in tandem, they are best analyzed together.

An exclusive dealing agreement, which falls under the coverage of Clayton Act Section 3, is a special type of requirements contract. The wholesaler or retailer agrees to devote its efforts exclusively to distributing the product line of a particular manufacturer. Handling the products of competing manufacturers is explicitly or implicitly disavowed, and so the dealer in effect agrees to purchase from the manufacturer its full requirements.

As a *quid pro quo* for an outlet's willingness to deal exclusively and sometimes without any such pledge, manufacturers may grant their dealers *exclusive franchises*. These generally place some limit on the amount of competition the franchised dealer will have to face from other concerns distributing the manufacturer's line—e.g., by restricting the number of dealers franchised in a particular area, or by confining dealers to specific territories or customer classes. The legality of such arrangements is governed by Sherman Act Section 1.

Three main sets of interests are affected by the restrictions connected with exclusive dealing and exclusive franchise agreements: the dealer's, the manufacturer's, and the public's. The dealer given an exclusive franchise presumably derives some benefit from having to face less competition from other dealers handling the same product line, especially when the line enjoys a product differentiation advantage. This will be reflected in price/wholesale cost margins higher than they would be under an unrestricted entry policy. The dealer may also find it advantageous to deal exclusively in the products of a single manufacturer, although the benefit from contract provisions *compelling* it to specialize is dubious, since more freedom of action is almost always preferable to less if other dimensions of the arrangement are unaffected. Indeed, the fact that dealers occasionally have sued to recover damages attributed to such restrictions suggests that exclusivity is not always desirable from the dealer's standpoint.

For manufacturers, exclusive dealing arrangements are often appealing, because they ensure that their products will be merchandised with maximum energy and enthusiasm. The dealer confined to a single manufacturer's line can scarcely be indifferent as to whose brand consumers purchase.[71] By granting exclusive franchises and restricting competition among its dealers, the manufacturer may benefit in several ways, all related to the possibility of letting dealers secure a generous margin between price and operating cost. Offering the prospect of supranormal returns may permit manufacturers to attract dealers of superior ability. Also, once a business manager has taken on a profitable dealership, he or she will be reluctant to lose the franchise, and will therefore be responsive when the manufacturer suggests changes in methods of operation. If the margin between price and wholesale cost is ample, dealers have an incentive to carry larger inventories, and they can spend more money on advertising and other promotional activities, enhancing the manufacturer's market penetration. The dealer with a profitable franchise may also be better able and more willing to provide high-quality maintenance and repair services. This is especially important in the sale of complex durable goods, for shoddy service by some distributor out to make a quick killing can permanently damage the manufacturer's reputation.

From the viewpoint of the consuming public, the effects of restrictions on dealer activities are mixed. Exclusive franchising can limit competition among the dealers handling a particular brand or line and stimulate product differentiation activities. Strengthened product differentiation can be good, bad, or neutral, depending upon its responsiveness to consumer wants. An escalation of uninformative advertising that merely cancels out rival messages does consumers little good and raises costs; informative advertising (which is more the rule than the exception in retailing) helps consumers make better decisions.[72] High-quality service is presumably desirable, especially when consumers retain the option of buying the same brand or equivalent products with less service at lower prices. Distribution costs may be reduced, with lower retail prices as a less certain consequence, if dealers can achieve economies of scale and specialization or avoid the duplication of marketing efforts. On the other hand, costs may be increased if distributors are confined, as they were in the U.S. soft drink bottling industry, to exclusive territories much too small to support operations of minimum optimal scale.[73] The blunting of intrabrand price competition does not necessarily arouse concern as long as interbrand competition remains vigorous. Whether this condition is satisfied depends mainly upon how entry opportunities are affected. The use of exclusive franchises can invigorate competition if it facilitates the entry of small, struggling manufacturers by permitting them to secure the services of capable dealers and to build a favorable image. But when franchising and exclusive dealing together raise barriers to new entry, significant anticompetitive effects can follow.

The automobile industry provides the clearest example of this last case.[74] There are moderate economies of scale in automobile retailing. Established manufacturers with substantial market penetration are able to have a good-sized exclusive dealership even in relatively small towns, and the opportunity to sell a well-accepted make is attractive to would-be dealers. Therefore the largest producers have first pick among candidates and can engage the most able ones. This in turn gives General Motors and Ford a lasting product differentiation advantage, for auto buyers flock in disproportionate numbers to the better or more aggressive dealers. Also, the prospect of obtaining factory-authorized parts and service in both large cities and small may influence the car purchase decisions of mobile consumers. Lack of an extensive first-rate sales and service network is one of the reasons why Studebaker-Packard was forced to discontinue passenger automobile production, why foreign cars have had a difficult time penetrating the U.S. market, and why American Motors and to a lesser degree Chrysler have not found it easy to build up and sustain their sales volume. If all formal and informal pressures

---

70. *Tampa Electric Co.* v. *Nashville Coal Co. et al.*, 365 U.S. 320 (1961).

71. Obviously, distribution through exclusive dealers is attractive only for specialty and shopping goods. For convenience goods, the manufacturer's best strategy is to get its product into as many retail outlets as it can, even though competing brands are also carried. See Chapter 1, p. 5 *supra* for definitions.

72. For a more skeptical view, see William S. Comanor, "Vertical Territorial and Customer Restrictions: White Motor and Its Aftermath," *Harvard Law Review* 81 (May 1968): 1419–38.

73. For various views, compare Robert Larner, "The Economics of Territorial Restrictions in the Soft Drink Industry," *Antitrust Bulletin* 22 (Spring 1977): 145–55; Richard A. Posner, "The Rule of Reason and the Economic Approach: Reflections on the *Sylvania* Decision," *University of Chicago Law Review* 45 (Fall 1977), especially p. 6; Barbara G. Katz, "Territorial Exclusivity in the Soft Drink Industry," *Journal of Industrial Economics* 27 (September 1978): 85–96; and "Cola Maker Taking on Pepsi and Coke," *Washington Post*, 6 November 1978, p. A-10 (emphasizing the high cost and obsolescence of the leading cola makers' distribution systems). In 1978, the Federal Trade Commission ruled the territorial restrictions in soft drink bottling to be illegal. *In re Coca Cola Co. et al.*, docket no. 8885. Appeals were pending at the time this was written.

74. See Chapter 4, p. 112 and B. P. Pashigian, *The Distribution of Automobiles: An Economic Analysis of the Franchise System* (Englewood Cliffs, N.J.: Prentice-Hall, 1961).

toward exclusive dealing in autos could be eliminated and if a sufficient number of dealers were willing to take on additional makes, competition from smaller and foreign automobile producers would be stimulated.[75]

The limits to which sellers may legally go in using exclusive dealing agreements have been progressively narrowed through a series of court decisions. In a 1922 opinion, the Supreme Court found an exclusive dealership arrangement illegal under Clayton Act Section 3 when it encompassed 40 percent of all dress pattern outlets in the United States.[76] Subsequent pronouncements in related requirements contract cases such as *Standard Stations* shifted the margin of structural tolerance to much lower levels. However, manufacturers with modest market shares are not likely to run afoul of the law when they urge exclusive dealing without actually coercing their dealers to eschew competitive products. For instance, the J. I. Case Company, selling roughly 7 percent of all U.S. farm machinery in 1948, avoided censure when a district court found that it had not made exclusive dealing an inviolable condition of its franchises, that 2,600 of its 3,738 dealers handled at least some competitive products, and that other farm machinery manufacturers experienced no demonstrated difficulty obtaining outlets for their products.[77] Similarly, an appellate court found that the Hudson Motor Company was within its rights in refusing to renew a dealer's contract because the dealer diffused its efforts over too many competing automobile makes.[78] It is doubtful whether the domestic Big Three would emerge as favorably from such a test, and they studiously avoid treading too close to the brink. Still they can and do apply many informal pressures to encourage exclusive dealer loyalty, and the antitrust agencies have taken no noteworthy steps to foster the spread of multimake auto retailing.

Frequently, the manufacturers of complex vehicles and equipment have insisted that their dealers refrain from selling or installing repair parts produced by competing firms. This practice is essentially a tying arrangement, since it makes the dealer's ability to buy complete vehicles or machines for resale contingent upon buying only the franchisor's spare parts. Unlike most tying

contracts, it has withstood antitrust attack with fair success, though the defenses have shown signs of erosion. In a 1936 decision, the Supreme Court affirmed a lower court opinion approving General Motors' requirement that GM dealers install only GM replacement parts. It accepted the argument that installation of inappropriate or defective parts could impair an automobile's functioning and thereby damage the manufacturer's reputation.[79] Five years later the Federal Trade Commission ordered General Motors to cease insisting that dealers stock and sell only GM supplies and accessories. However, it permitted exclusive dealing agreements for "parts necessary to the mechanical operation of an automobile, and which are not available, in like quality and design, from other sources of supply."[80] Following the tightening of Clayton Act Section 3 criteria in the *Standard Stations* decision, the early General Motors parts decisions were criticized by some courts.[81] And in 1959 the Sixth Circuit Court of Appeals ruled that attempts by Ford Motor Company to force its dealers to deal exclusively in Ford-made or approved parts might be found illegal if they substantially lessened competition.[82] In the absence of a definitive Supreme Court reinterpretation, the limits to which producers can safely probe are not completely clear.

Franchise agreements that restrict competition among a manufacturer's outlets are not covered by Clayton Act Section 3. They can, however, be challenged in some situations as illegal contracts in restraint of trade under Sherman Act Section 1. At present a manufacturer is fully within the law in limiting the number and location of outlets to which franchises are granted, and this may be sufficient to protect dealer price-cost margins when the product line enjoys significant differentiation advantages. But in some cases manufacturers have gone further, delineating the territories within which particular dealers might sell and the customers they might serve. In so doing they run a risk of violating the Sherman Act. There are two main subcases, depending upon whether the limitations are imposed horizontally or vertically.

When the dealers agree *among themselves* not to interpenetrate each other's markets or to solicit the same customers, or when they induce the manufacturer to impose upon them such restrictions, the law is clearly violated. Indeed, in a case concerning a collective attempt by Los Angeles Chevrolet dealers and GM officials to prevent some dealers from bootlegging cars to unfranchised automobile supermarkets, the Supreme Court ruled that such horizontal agreements constitute "a classic conspiracy" in restraint of trade.[83]

Nearer the borderline, but still ruled *per se* illegal by the Supreme Court, were the territorial restrictions implemented by Topco Associates, a cooperative association that procured private-label grocery items for 25 small and medium-sized regional supermarket chains.[84] Association members argued that exclusive use of Topco-label products in their home territories significantly enhanced their ability to compete effectively against nationwide chains large enough to have their own private-label lines. Members enjoyed an effective veto power over new applicants whose geographic proximity might threaten territorial exclusivity, and this, said the Court, was an illegal horizontal restraint. Recognizing that the Topco arrangement might have desirable economic effects, the Supreme Court insisted nonetheless that *per se* rules had been prescribed for such situations to shield the courts from "ramb[ling] through the wilds of economic theory."[85] As in many antitrust cases, once the Department of Justice won its symbolic victory, a lower court fashioned an order that eliminated Topco's formal power to maintain exclusivity, but left the cooperative considerable flexibility in assigning members "areas of primary responsibility."[86] Many members continued to have *de facto* exclusivity in their home markets; and by all accounts, the cooperative's ability to provide a worthwhile and important service remained basically unimpaired.

Purely vertical restrictions—those imposed unilaterally by the manufacturer upon its dealers—have experienced a more turbulent history, but are now viewed with greater sympathy than horizontal restrictions. In 1963, a 5–3 majority of the Supreme Court refused to condemn out of hand the territorial and customer restrictions placed in dealer franchise contracts by the White

Motor Company, a truck manufacturer with sales exceeding half a billion dollars at the time. The Court acknowledged that it did not "know enough of the economic and business stuff out of which these arrangements emerge" to be certain whether they merely stifle competition, or whether they may be "the only practicable means a small company has for breaking into or staying in business."[87] It therefore remanded the action to the district court for a thorough exploration of the facts, i.e., for the application of a rule of reason. The case was settled through a negotiated consent decree in which White agreed to terminate the restrictive provisions in its dealer franchises.[88]

75. Automobile distribution is not completely exclusive in the United States. Many U.S. dealers carry more than one brand of the same manufacturer, and during the early 1950s, about 7 percent of General Motors' dealers also sold non-GM cars. See Pashigian, *The Distribution of Automobiles*, pp. 118–23; and U.S., Congress, Senate, Committee on Small Business hearings, *Planning, Regulation, and Competition in the Automobile Industry—1968*, 90th Cong., 2nd sess., 1968, pp. 627, 712.

76. *Standard Fashion Co. v. Magrane-Houston Co.*, 258 U.S. 346 (1922).

77. *U.S. v. J. I. Case Co.*, 101 F. Supp. 856 (1951). Compare *Federal Trade Commission v. Brown Shoe Co.*, 384 U.S. 316 (1966), in which less than completely exclusive franchise arrangements of seemingly innocuous scope were condemned. See the critique by John L. Peterman in the *Journal of Law and Economics* 18 (October 1975): 361–419.

78. *Hudson Sales Corporation v. Waldrip*, 211 F. 2d 268 (1954).

79. *Pick Manufacturing Co. v. General Motors Corp. et al.*, 80 F. 2d 641 (1935), affirmed *per curiam*, 299 U.S. 3 (1936).

80. *In re General Motors Corp. and General Motors Sales Corp.*, 34 F.T.C. 58, 86 (1941).

81. *Dictograph Products, Inc. v. Federal Trade Commission*, 217 F. 2d 821, 828 (1954).

82. *Englander Motors, Inc. v. Ford Motor Corp.*, 267 F. 2d 11 (1959). The case was remanded to the district court for a finding as to whether the facts warranted a conclusion that competition was lessened, but apparently the suit was settled out of court. See also *Alles Corp. v. Senco Products, Inc.*, 329 F. 2d 567 (1964).

83. *U.S. v. General Motors Corp. et al.*, 384 U.S. 127 (1966). See also *U.S. v. Sealy, Inc., et al.*, 388 U.S. 350 (1967).

84. *U.S. v. Topco Associates, Inc.*, 405 U.S. 596 (1972). This account relies in part upon a term paper written at Northwestern University by Ms. Lee Sheppard in 1978.

85. 405 U.S. 596, 610.

86. See the order at CCH 1973 Trade Cases Para. 74,485; affirmed on appeal at 414 U.S. 801 (1973).

87. *White Motor Co. v. U.S.*, 372 U.S. 253, 263 (1963).

88. *White Motor Co. v. U.S.*, CCH 1964 Trade Cases Para. 71,195.

In 1967 the Court tightened the screws, ruling, with no coherent attempt to rationalize its change, that manufacturers selling their products subject to territorial and other restrictions upon resale committed *per se* violations of the Sherman Act.[89] Withering criticism by legal scholars, economists, and even lower courts followed.

A decade later, the Court returned to the problem and admitted its error.[90] At issue were certain actions following from franchise contracts limiting selected retailers of Sylvania television sets to store locations specified by the manufacturer. Sylvania had initiated the program of winnowing out weak retailers and concentrating its distribution efforts on a limited number of aggressive franchised outlets after a decline in its national market share into the 1 to 2 percent range. The Court articulated its newly acquired belief that vertical restrictions can promote interbrand competition by allowing the manufacturer to achieve distributional efficiencies.[91] It observed further that there had been no showing, either generally or in the specific case of Sylvania, that vertical restrictions have or are likely to have "a pernicious effect on competition" or that they lack "any redeeming value."[92] It therefore concluded that although particular vertical restrictions might well be anticompetitive, vertical restrictions in general should be judged under a rule of reason. A more reasonable rule could scarcely have been asked. How well the courts will do in implementing it—i.e., "rambling through the wilds of economic theory"—remains to be seen.

Resale price maintenance

Resale price maintenance—the specification by manufacturers of prices below which retailers may not sell their products—is in some respects analogous in motivation and effect to vertical territorial restrictions. However, it has had a different and even more checkered legal history. It is useful to begin by recounting the principal developments into the 1950s.

Legal background In the early days of Ameri-

can antitrust, vertical price-fixing agreements were condemned in a series of decisions from which the *Schwinn* opinion was a lineal descendant.[93] In response, retailer and some manufacturer groups banded together for a lobbying campaign they euphemistically entitled the "Fair Trade Movement." They received intellectual support from such eminent figures as Supreme Court Justice Louis Brandeis, an arch-foe of big business but friend of the small merchant.[94] Bills were introduced in every session of Congress from 1914 to 1936, but none was enacted. The movement experienced its first legislative success in 1931, when the State of California passed a statute authorizing "fair trade." By 1935 nine other states had enacted resale price maintenance laws; and within five years after a 1936 Supreme Court decision upholding the California and Illinois statutes, every state but Texas, Missouri, and Vermont had climbed aboard the fair trade bandwagon.

The state laws, however, were effective only with respect to goods sold in intrastate commerce. The retail merchants' lobby, led by the druggists, continued to exert pressure; and in 1937 Congress passed the Miller-Tydings Resale Price Maintenance Act, appending it as a rider to the District of Columbia appropriations bill in order to avert a presidential veto. It amended Section 1 of the Sherman Act, exempting from antitrust prohibition contracts prescribing minimum prices for the resale of trademarked or branded commodities "in free and open competition with commodities of the same general class produced or distributed by others" where such contracts were authorized under state laws.

Given this permissive mandate, vertical price fixing thrived in the consumer goods industries. Nevertheless, there was one loophole in the law. Not all retailers were interested in adhering to the manufacturer's specified minimum prices. Those who preferred to seek high sales volume through rock-bottom markup policies refused to sign "R.P.M." contracts with their suppliers. To bring these intransigents into line, most states added "nonsigner clauses" to their "fair trade" laws, making adherence to a manufacturer's price floors binding upon *all* retailers in the state if *any single* retailer signed a resale price maintenance contract with the manufacturer. However, the Supreme Court ruled in 1951 that the Miller-Tydings Act exempted only express contracts to maintain minimum prices on goods in interstate commerce and that the exemption did not cover nonsigning retailers.[95] The retail lobby again went to work; and in the following year Congress passed by overwhelming majorities the McGuire Act, amending Section 5 of the Federal Trade Commission Act. It reiterated the Miller-Tydings policy and extended it to permit the enforcement of resale price maintenance upon nonsigning sellers where state laws permit. A challenge to the constitutionality of the new law was rejected by two of the three judges on a Fifth Circuit Court of Appeals panel; and the Supreme Court, reluctant to interfere when Congress had expressed its intent so forcefully, chose not to review the decision.[96] As a result, resale price maintenance enforced unilaterally by manufacturers on both willing and nonsigning retailers was immune from federal antitrust attack in states with nonsigner clauses. On the other hand, any attempt by retailers collectively to enforce price maintenance among themselves continued to be strictly illegal, like all other horizontal price-fixing conspiracies.

The policy adopted toward resale price maintenance in the United States was considerably more permissive than that of other leading industrialized nations whose antitrust laws were in other respects much weaker.[97] Canada passed an unconditional ban on R.P.M. in 1951, although it was amended in 1960 to allow exceptions when 'loss leader' pricing or other abuses can be proved. France has had a law against R.P.M. since 1953, but there is some question about how vigorously it has been enforced. In 1964 the British, after extended debate, passed a Resale Prices Act. It adopted a *prima facie* presumption that vertical price fixing is illegal, to be relaxed only if the producer can bear the burden of proving before the Restrictive Practices Court that the benefits of resale price maintenance outweigh the detriments. The Court's decisions took a generally tough line, with only proprietary drugs and books receiving exemptions.[98] In 1973 West Germany joined the ranks of nations with strong R.P.M. prohibitions, though nonbinding "recom-

mended prices" (*Empfehlungspreise*) continue to be legal and widely used. At the time the German law was strengthened, 810 companies had resale price maintenance stipulations covering 174,000 branded articles registered with the Federal Cartel Office.[99] In Japan, R.P.M. agreements are inconsistent with several provisions of the 1947 and 1953 antitrust laws, but antitrust enforcers have the power to exempt certain commodities and have done so on a blanket basis for cosmetics, drugs, toothpaste, soaps, and synthetic detergents.

The economic case for and against 'fair trade' With this legal backdrop in view, let us turn to the economic issues in the resale price maintenance debate. The arguments for R.P.M.

89. *U.S.* v. *Arnold, Schwinn & Co. et al.*, 388 U.S. 365 (1967). Following the decision, Schwinn terminated the contracts with its 22 independent wholesale distributors and established a vertically integrated wholesaling subsidiary.

90. *Continental T. V., Inc., et al.* v. *GTE Sylvania, Inc.*, 433 U.S. 36 (1977).

91. 433 U.S. 36, 54 (1977).

92. 433 U.S. 36, 58 (1977).

93. The first was *Dr. Miles Medical Co.* v. *John D. Park and Sons Co.*, 220 U.S. 373 (1911). For an excellent survey of subsequent extensions, see A. D. Neale, *The Antitrust Laws of the United States of America*, 2nd ed. (Cambridge, England: Cambridge University Press, 1970), pp. 272–99. Authoritative works on resale price maintenance include B. S. Yamey, *Economics of Resale Price Maintenance* (London: Pitman, 1954); and a symposium edited by Yamey, *Resale Price Maintenance* (Chicago: Aldine, 1966).

94. See his article (written before he ascended the bench), "Cut-Throat Prices: The Competition That Kills," *Harper's Weekly*, 15 November 1913.

95. *Schwegmann Bros. et al.* v. *Calvert Distillers Corp.*, 341 U.S. 384 (1951).

96. *Schwegmann Bros. Giant Super Markets et al.* v. *Eli Lilly & Co.*, 205 F. 2d 788 (1953), cert. den. 346 U.S. 856 (1953). See also *Hudson Distributors, Inc.* v. *Eli Lilly & Co.*, 377 U.S. 386 (1964), in which the Supreme Court did explicitly review the legality of nonsigner clauses and bowed to the will of Congress.

97. For somewhat outdated surveys of the various national and supranational policies, see Yamey, ed., *Resale Price Maintenance*; and René Joliet, "Resale Price Maintenance under EEC Antitrust Law," *Antitrust Bulletin* 6 (Fall 1971): 589–632.

98. See J. F. Pickering, "The Abolition of Resale Price Maintenance in Britain," *Oxford Economic Papers* 26 n.s. (March 1974): 120–46.

99. "Vor dem endgültigen 'Aus' für die Preisbindung," Berlin *Tagesspiegel*, 13 June 1973.

boil down to three main propositions.[100] First, resale price maintenance protects the margin between retail and wholesale prices from being eroded by competition (or by cutthroat competition, as the fair trade lobby puts it). In this respect it is analogous to franchising restrictions. The effects are also similar. The retailers are supposedly better off economically—a fate to which they can hardly be unsympathetic. The manufacturer may also benefit, since dealers have more funds to spend on advertising and service, which in turn can have a favorable impact on the manufacturer's brand acceptance. Second, resale price maintenance prevents the use of a manufacturer's products as "loss leaders"—items sold by a retailer at sharply reduced prices, and perhaps even below cost, in order to attract customers who, once they have entered the store, will buy other goods at standard prices. Loss leader sales are said to injure the manufacturer by detracting from its reputation for quality (since consumers allegedly judge quality from price) and limiting its access to the market (since many retailers will be reluctant to stock an item being sold at much lower prices by others). They may also endanger the survival of small retailers who specialize in an item diversified stores use as a loss leader. Third, and no doubt most important in the Washington political equation, resale price maintenance tends to protect the small, locally owned retail establishment from the competition of big, more efficient chain stores and discount houses seeking to achieve high volume at low markups. Survival of small retail businesses is valued both as a derivative of the populist ideology and as an important source of political support.

It is impossible to quarrel analytically with this last argument, for it rests largely on value judgments over which reasonable persons may disagree. Against it and other tenets of the case for fair trade, however, several objections can be counterpoised.

For one, the loss leader conjecture is neither convincing nor firmly supported by the evidence.[101] It is hard to believe that many consumers are gullible enough to downgrade their estimates of a product's quality simply because some merchant is selling the item at a reduced price, or that they are bamboozled into switching their patronage to a particular store because it offers a few items as loss leaders. It is also doubtful whether manufacturers suffer reduced access to retail outlets because their product is used as a loss leader. Sales below wholesale cost—the most extreme though less common form of loss leader pricing—are likely to be only temporary, and even if other retailers reduce their stocks of the affected commodity temporarily, they bounce back rapidly when the price cutting ends.

To be sure, specialty shops find survival more difficult when the merchandise they stock is offered permanently at positive but thin profit margins by supermarkets, discount houses, and other diversified outlets. The same is true more generally of small, high-service retail establishments. But here the sword cuts two ways. If consumers flock to the low-margin discount houses and shun the small, high-margin shops, they must do so because that is what they prefer. To prevent large retailers from pursuing a low-margin strategy, which at bottom is what the fair trade laws seek, is to frustrate the adaptation of distribution channels to meaningful changes in consumer wants and to encourage the perpetuation of obsolete, inefficient channels. Indeed, the experience of European countries suggests that resale price maintenance retarded the spread of supermarketing; and the pace of innovation in retailing accelerated perceptibly when legalized R.P.M. was abolished.[102]

Moreover, the widespread adoption of resale price maintenance tends to deprive consumers of a choice between buying on the basis of service and buying at the lowest possible price. The latter alternative is eliminated unless a substantial segment of the output in each industry is not fair-traded. If there is a genuine consumer demand for service and the other amenities accompanying a high-margin policy, the market will normally support without the coercion of R.P.M. the survival of retailers who satisfy that demand, coexisting with other retailers who cater to the (no doubt much larger) mass of price-conscious consumers.[103]

Three further drawbacks of resale price maintenance can be treated more briefly. First, as the discussion thus far has implied throughout, when

R.P.M. attains its primary goals, it tends in all but special cases to raise retail margins and prices.[104] This has sometimes been denied by advocates, but the weight of the available evidence supports a conclusion that R.P.M. does raise prices.[105] For instance, a 1956 Justice Department survey revealed that the prices of 132 widely fair-traded products were 19 percent lower than the fair trade minimum on the average in eight cities not bound by R.P.M. laws.[106] Second, vertical price fixing not only eliminates price competition among retailers selling a particular manufacturer's product, but may also dampen interbrand price competition. It gives oligopolistic producers firmer control over the prices at which their products are ultimately sold, thereby permitting them to prevent retail price shading that might induce retaliatory wholesale price cuts by rival manufacturers. Finally, it is doubtful whether R.P.M. really benefits the small retailer as much as one might at first suppose. Unlike the situation under restrictive franchising, entry into the retailing of specific fair-traded goods is usually easy. If retailers are earning supranormal profits because of R.P.M., additional sellers will enter and/or stock the fair-traded items, squeezing the sales volume of the original outlets until unit merchandising costs have risen to wipe out the surplus. The representative retailer ends up operating at a smaller than optimal scale, but earning no more than a normal profit return.

Abolition and its effects The federal fair trade law was born during the Great Depression of the 1930s. It died in the recession of 1975—the sharpest since the 1930s. With unusually severe price inflation persisting despite rapidly rising unemployment, the balance of power beween consumer and retail business interests shifted in Congress; and in December of 1975, a bill repealing the Miller-Tydings and McGuire acts was signed. After the bill took effect 90 days later, manufacturers risked violating Sherman Act Section 1 if they attempted to enforce resale price maintenance on goods moving in interstate commerce.

Although death came swiftly and unexpectedly, it was preceded by a long illness. Two main

forces—legal setbacks at the state level and the pressures of competition—had been slowly sapping fair trade's vitality.

R.P.M. laws were never passed in Texas, Missouri, Vermont, and the strategically located District of Columbia. In several additional states, including Alabama, Utah, Montana, Wyoming, Virginia, and Ohio, state courts ruled the applicable fair trade statutes inconsistent with state constitutions and/or legally unenforceable. In more than a dozen other jurisdictions, the nonsigner provisions of state laws were declared unconstitutional within 15 years of the McGuire Act's passage, typically on the ground that they deprived nonsigners of property without due process of law. These developments created a number of islands where it was possible to ignore manufacturers' prescribed minimum prices. Entrepreneurs took advantage by locating mail order houses in nonfair trade areas, building a lively business of shipping branded merchandise at reduced prices to customers in fair trade states. This practice was encouraged by federal court decisions in 1957 holding that such shipments

100. See P. W. S. Andrews and Frank A. Friday, *Fair Trade: Resale Price Maintenance Re-Examined* (London: Macmillan, 1960); Andrews, *On Competition in Economic Theory* (London: Macmillan, 1964), pp. 127–38; and Lester Telser, "Why Should Manufacturers Want Fair Trade?," *Journal of Law and Economics* 3 (October 1960): 86–105.

101. See especially the contribution by L. A. Skeoch in Yamey, ed., *Resale Price Maintenance*, pp. 41–53.

102. See, for example, the analysis of developments in Sweden by U. af Trolle in Yamey, ed., *Resale Price Maintenance*, pp. 134–40.

103. A possible exception occurs when there is a "free-rider" problem—e.g., when consumers inspect a product and secure expert advice at high-priced specialty shops and then buy at discount houses. This can of course happen, jeopardizing specialty shops' survival. But its empirical significance appears modest. Cf. Telser, "Why Should Manufacturers Want Fair Trade?," pp. 91–92.

104. For a theoretical analysis of conditions under which prices might be reduced, see J. R. Gould and L. E. Preston, "Resale Price Maintenance and Retail Outlets," *Economica* 32 (August 1965): 302–12.

105. For a survey of the U.S. evidence, see the contribution by S. C. Hollander in Yamey, ed., *Resale Price Maintenance*, pp. 93–98; and Marvin Frankel, "The Effects of Fair Trade: Fact and Fiction in the Statistical Findings," *Journal of Business* 28 (July 1955): 182–94.

106. See the testimony of Robert Bicks in U.S., Congress, House, Committee on Interstate and Foreign Commerce hearings, *Fair Trade: 1959*, 86th Cong., 1st sess., 1959, pp. 506–507.

could not be enjoined under the fair trade statutes of the states into which the merchandise was shipped.[107] And even where retailers were clearly bound by state R.P.M. laws, some of the more aggressive outlets chose to ignore them. Faced with this challenge, manufacturers often decided not to initiate the legal proceedings available for enforcing compliance, partly because the burden of proving actionable departure from the stipulated price floor was difficult and costly, and partly because producers were reluctant to alienate important high-volume retailers.

When a significant fraction of the transactions in some product line began taking place at prices that undercut the fair trade minimum, the whole R.P.M. system in that line tended to crumble. Manufacturers who did enforce their minima found themselves losing sales to those who did not or who refused altogether to play the fair trade game. Some abandoned R.P.M. completely. Others like the Sunbeam Corporation brought out new product lines to be sold at uncontrolled retail prices alongside their fair-traded items. With enforcement weak and retailers stocking products of comparable quality, some fair-traded and some not, one of the more serious objections to resale price maintenance was defused. Consumers were no longer deprived of the opportunity to choose which mix of price and product differentiation attributes they preferred.

By 1975, the processes of erosion had advanced much farther. Only 13 states had valid nonsigner laws still in effect. And although 23 other states retained fair trade laws without nonsigner provisions, the competition from nonsigning retailers tended to undermine manufacturers' enforcement incentives. The value of fair-traded items fell from an estimated 10 percent of retail sales in 1959 to 4 percent in 1974.[108] Efforts to enforce R.P.M. persisted in only a few lines such as high fidelity equipment, cosmetics, liquor, television sets, glassware, and prescription drugs. In some (but not all) of these lines, price competition at the retail level increased following the end of legally permissible fair trade.[109] But for the most part, the effects of abolition were imperceptible because the forces of competition had already repealed the federal law in their own quiet way.

That happy note seems as good as any for ending our analysis of how real-world market processes operate and what government can do to help them operate better.

107. *Bissell Carpet Sweeper Co.* v. *Masters Mail Order Co. of Washington*, 240 F. 2d 684 (1957); and *General Electric Co.* v. *Masters Mail Order Co. of Washington*, 244 F. 2d 681 (1957), cert. den. 355 U.S. 824 (1957).

108. See "Depression's Fair-Trade Laws May Be Retired By Congress," *Chicago Tribune*, 10 February 1975, citing a Consumers Union estimate.

109. See for example, "Fair-Trade Ban Is No Bonanza," *Atlanta Constitution*, 14 December 1975; and "Few Notice Fair Trade Laws' End," *Washington Post*, 11 March 1976, p. B-13.

Appendix to chapter 2

The purpose of this appendix is to demonstrate some central points in the welfare economics of competition and monopoly. It does not pretend to be an exhaustive exposition of general equilibrium theory or welfare economics. The reader with sufficient mathematical background and a desire to penetrate further is urged to consult one of the more ambitious standard expositions.

For our present purposes the optimal tradeoff between simplicity of notation and richness calls for analyzing an economy with three consumption goods, X, Y, and leisure (which is the difference between the number of hours available per time period and hours worked L); along with one input, homogeneous labor hours L. There can be as many or as few consumers and producing firms as the analysis requires. The total quantity of output consumed or labor supplied is the sum of the quantities consumed or supplied by individual members of society. Thus, where x_i is the quantity of good X consumed by the ith consumer, the total quantity consumed $X = \Sigma i x_i$. Similarly, $Y = \Sigma i y_i$ and $L = \Sigma i l_i$.

We begin with the seemingly innocuous but actually powerful criterion of Pareto optimality in consumption. Social welfare cannot be at a maximum if it is possible through reallocation to make some consumer better off without making any other consumer worse off. To see what this entails, let $U^i(x_i, y_i, l_i)$ be the utility function of the ith consumer and $U^j(x_j, y_j, l_j)$ the utility function of the jth consumer. Where U^i_X is the first derivative of the ith consumer's utility function with respect to X and U^i_{XX} the second derivative, we assume that

$U^i_X > 0$; $U^i_{XX} < 0$; $U^i_Y > 0$; $U^i_{YY} < 0$; $U^i_L < 0$; and $U^i_{LL} < 0$. We maximize U^i subject to the condition that consumer j's utility U^j be held constant at U^{j*}, and subject to the further condition that the two individuals' consumption and labor supplies sum to the amounts X, Y, and L, assumed provisionally to be fixed:

$$(1) \quad \text{Max } \Gamma = U^i(x_i, y_i, l_i) \\ - \gamma_1[U^j(x_j, y_j, l_j) - U^{j*}] - \gamma_2(x_i + x_j - X) \\ - \gamma_3(y_i + y_j - Y) - \gamma_4(l_i + l_j - L)$$

Differentiating with respect to the quantities consumed by individuals i and j, we obtain the following first-order conditions for a maximum:

$$(2a) \quad \frac{\partial \Gamma}{\partial x_i} = U^i_X - \gamma_2 = 0$$

$$(2b) \quad \frac{\partial \Gamma}{\partial y_i} = U^i_Y - \gamma_3 = 0$$

$$(2c) \quad \frac{\partial \Gamma}{\partial l_i} = U^i_L - \gamma_4 = 0$$

$$(2d) \quad \frac{\partial \Gamma}{\partial x_j} = \gamma_1 U^j_X - \gamma_2 = 0$$

$$(2e) \quad \frac{\partial \Gamma}{\partial y_j} = \gamma_1 U^j_Y - \gamma_3 = 0$$

$$(2f) \quad \frac{\partial \Gamma}{\partial l_j} = \gamma_1 U^j_L - \gamma_4 = 0$$

Rearranging and dividing through by the conditions for Y as the numeraire commodity, we obtain.

$$(3a) \qquad \frac{U_X^i}{U_Y^i} = \frac{\gamma_2}{\gamma_3} = \frac{U_X^j}{U_Y^j}, \text{ and}$$

$$(3b) \qquad \frac{U_L^i}{U_Y^i} = \frac{\gamma_4}{\gamma_3} = \frac{U_L^j}{U_Y^j}$$

A Pareto-optimal allocation of consumption goods requires that the ratio of the marginal utilities of any two goods—i.e., the marginal rate of substitution—for any given consumer equal the marginal rates of substitution of the same commodity pair for all consumers and for all commodity pairs. If this set of ratio equalities does not hold, it is possible to make at least one consumer better off (increasing his or her utility) without making any other consumer worse off, and so welfare cannot be at a maximum.

Many different consumption goods allocations will undoubtedly satisfy this set of conditions, although only one may be consistent with a given real income distribution and/or set of initial resource endowments. To go from conditions like (3a) and (3b) to specifying a global welfare optimum, it is necesary somehow to combine the utility functions of individual consumers into an aggregate social welfare function. No useful purpose would be served by plunging into the many difficulties any such attempt involves. We shall simply assume that a social welfare function

$$(4) \qquad U = U(X,Y,L) = \underset{x_i, \, y_i, \, l_i}{\text{Max }} \mathfrak{U}[U^i(x_i, y_i, l_i)]$$

can in fact be defined. The reader may interpret U in any of at least three ways: as reflecting the preferences of some representative consumer with whom we are uniquely concerned; as reflecting the preferences of some central authority, democratically or dictatorially selected; or as reflecting a social consensus approving the existing distribution of income or the distribution with which individuals enter the market after various redistributive measures have been effected. The third approach is most realistic and most closely compatible with the spirit of Chapter 2, but it has no unique claim to scientific or moral validity. What is crucial here is only one point. However the social welfare function is put together, it cannot attain a maximum for society as

a whole unless the Pareto-optimal conditions (3a) and (3b) for individual consumers are satisfied.

The production opportunities open to society with a given state of technological knowledge can be represented by a transformation function defined in implicit form $T(X,Y,L) = 0$. Society's objective is to maximize social welfare $U(X,Y,L)$ subject to the limitations imposed by the transformation function. We define the Lagrangian function:

$$(5) \qquad \text{Max } \Lambda = U(X,Y,L) - \lambda[T(X,Y,L)]$$

First-order conditions for a maximum include:

$$(6a) \qquad \frac{\partial \Lambda}{\partial X} = U_X - \lambda T_X = 0; \quad \frac{U_X}{T_X} = \lambda$$

$$(6b) \qquad \frac{\partial \Lambda}{\partial Y} = U_Y - \lambda T_Y = 0; \quad \frac{U_Y}{T_Y} = \lambda$$

$$(6c) \qquad \frac{\partial \Lambda}{\partial L} = U_L - \lambda T_L = 0; \quad \frac{U_L}{T_L} = \lambda$$

In view of the common equalities wih λ, these can be reduced to:

$$(7a) \qquad \frac{U_X}{T_X} = \frac{U_Y}{T_Y}; \quad \text{so } \frac{U_X}{U_Y} = \frac{T_X}{T_Y}, \text{ and}$$

$$(7b) \qquad \frac{U_L}{T_L} = \frac{U_Y}{T_Y}; \quad \text{so } \frac{U_L}{U_Y} = \frac{T_L}{T_Y}$$

The ratios U_X/U_Y and U_L/U_Y are marginal social rates of substitution directly analogous to the individual marginal rates of substitution in (3a) and (3b). The ratio T_X/T_Y is a marginal rate of transformation, equal except in sign to the slope of a familiar transformation curve like $t\,t'$ in Figure 2A.1, assuming some given quantity of labor and other inputs. To see this, we differentiate the transformation function implicitly to obtain $T_X\,dX + T_Y\,dY + T_L\,dL = 0$. If L is held constant, $dL = 0$. We have then:

$$(8) \qquad T_X\,dX + T_Y\,dY = 0$$

Rearranging, we obtain:

$$(9) \qquad -\frac{T_X}{T_Y} = \frac{dY}{dX}$$

where dY/dX is obviously the slope of the transformation curve.

The social welfare function can be represented by a field of social indifference curves like U_1 and U_2 in Figure 2A.1. By analogous manipulation, it can be seen that their slope at any point is the ratio $-U_X/U_Y$, or the marginal social rate of substitution. For social welfare to be at a maximum (as at point C in Figure 2A.1) a social indifference curve must be tangent to the transformation curve. This means that their slopes must be equal, and so $U_X/U_Y = T_X/T_Y$, as equation (7a) states. The conditions implied by equation (7b) could be represented by a similar though less familiar figure.

All this preliminary groundwork is necessary to specify what conditions an optimal (social welfare-maximizing) allocation of resources must satisfy. Concretely, we look for the satisfaction of global conditions (7a) and (7b) and at a more disaggregated level individual consumer conditions (3a) and (3b). Do competitive and monopolistic market processes in fact meet these standards? To find out, we must investigate the role prices play in the market economy.

Consider first the behavior of any representative consumer i with utility function $U^i(x_i, y_i, l_i)$ confronted with parametric prices P^X, P^Y, and W for good X, good Y, and his or her labor services respectively. The consumer maximizes his or her utility subject to the constraint that expenditures on consumption $P^X x_i + P^Y y_i$ equal income from work $W l_i$. Thus, we have:

(10) $\quad \text{Max } \Theta = U^i(x_i, y_i, l_i)$
$$- \theta(P^X x_i + P^Y y_i - W l_i)$$

Differentiating with respect to x_i, y_i, and l_i and rearranging the necessary first-order conditions for a maximum, we obtain:

(11a) $\quad \dfrac{U_X^i}{U_Y^i} = \dfrac{P^X}{P^Y}$, and

(11b) $\quad \dfrac{U_L^i}{U_Y^i} = \dfrac{-W}{P^Y}$

Since similar conditions must hold for every consumer and since (in an idealized world) each consumer faces the same set of prices P^X, P^Y, and W, it must be true that for any consumers i and j that:

(12a) $\quad \dfrac{U_X^i}{U_Y^i} = \dfrac{P^X}{P^Y} = \dfrac{U_X^j}{U_Y^j}$, and

(12b) $\quad \dfrac{U_L^i}{U_Y^i} = \dfrac{-W}{P^Y} = \dfrac{U_L^j}{U_Y^j}$

Therefore, Pareto optimum conditions (3a) and (3b) are satisfied when all consumers purchase goods and sell their labor services at identical parametric prices. Since each consumer has the same marginal rate of substitution for any commodity pair in utility-maximizing equilibrium, and since the social welfare function is simply some weighted aggregation of all individual utility functions, the marginal social rates of substitution must be equal to the corresponding price ratios in consumer equilibrium. Thus, we have as a condition of equilibrium:

(13a) $\quad \dfrac{U_X}{U_Y} = \dfrac{P^X}{P^Y}$, and

(13b) $\quad -\dfrac{U_L}{U_Y} = \dfrac{W}{P^Y}$

Now suppose the production of X and Y using L as an input is organized competitively. To avoid notational complexity, let us assume that X is produced by a representative competitive firm with the production function $X = \mathcal{X}(L^X)$ and that Y is produced by a representative firm with the production function $Y = \mathcal{Y}(L^Y)$. The firm producing X maximizes:

(14) $\quad \pi^X = P^X \mathcal{X}(L^X) - W L^X$

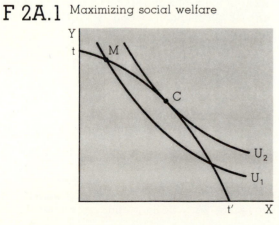

F 2A.1 Maximizing social welfare

Differentiating with respect to L^X, we obtain the first-order maximum condition:

(15) $\quad \dfrac{d\pi^X}{dL^X} = P^X \dfrac{dX}{dL^X} - W = 0$

Likewise, the firm producing Y maximizes:

(16) $\quad \pi^Y = P^Y \mathcal{Y}(L^Y) - W L^Y$

Differentiating, we obtain:

(17) $\quad \dfrac{d\pi^Y}{dL^Y} = P^Y \dfrac{dY}{dL^Y} - W = 0$

Assuming that all producers pay the same wage W, equations (15) and (17) solve to the equilibrium condition:

(18) $\quad \dfrac{P^X}{P^Y} = \dfrac{dY/dL^Y}{dX/dL^X}$

From (17) we have also:

(19) $\quad \dfrac{W}{P^Y} = \dfrac{dY}{dL^Y}$

But as long as there are no external effects in production, the right-hand sides of (18) and (19) are merely microscopic replications of the transformation ratios T_X/T_Y and T_L/T_Y respectively. To see this, we recall that $T_X\, dX + T_Y\, dY + T_L\, dL = 0$. Holding X constant, we have $T_Y\, dY + T_L\, dL = 0$. This solves to:

(20) $\quad -\dfrac{T_L}{T_Y} = \dfrac{dY}{dL}$

which is the aggregate analogue of the right-hand side of (19). Holding Y constant, we obtain $-T_L/T_X = dX/dL$. Using this and (20), it follows that:

(21) $\quad \dfrac{dY/dL}{dX/dL} = \dfrac{-T_L/T_Y}{-T_L/T_X} = \dfrac{T_X}{T_Y}$

which is the societywide analogue of (18).

Introducing into competitive profit maximization conditions (18) and (19) equations (20) and (21) and consumer equilibrium conditions (13a) and (13b), we obtain our final set of competitive equilibrium conditions:

(22a) $\quad \dfrac{dY/dL^Y}{dX/dL^X} = \dfrac{T_X}{T_Y} = \dfrac{P^X}{P^Y} = \dfrac{U_X}{U_Y}$, and

(22b) $\quad \dfrac{dY}{dL^Y} = -\dfrac{T_L}{T_Y} = \dfrac{W}{P^Y} = -\dfrac{U_L}{U_Y}$

Thus, equations (7a) and (7b) necessary for a welfare maximum are satisfied under competition as consumers and producers equate their respective marginal rates of substitution and marginal rates of transformation to the common price ratios P^X/P^Y and W/P^Y. In this way competitive market processes provide the basis for achieving an efficient allocation of resources.[1]

Suppose now that the sector producing good X is monopolized. No longer can the producer of good X consider the price P^X to be a parameter unaffected by its output decisions. Rather, it must take into account its demand function $P^X = D^X(X) = D^X[\mathcal{X}(L^X)]$. Its total revenue $R^X = D^X[\mathcal{X}(L^X)] \cdot \mathcal{X}(L^X)$. It maximizes $\pi^X = R^X - W L^X$, with the first-order maximum condition:

(23) $\quad \dfrac{d\pi^X}{dL^X} = \dfrac{dR^X}{dX} \dfrac{dX}{dL^X} - W = 0$

If Y continues to be produced competitively, equation (17) still holds as the profit maximization condition for sector Y. Combining equations (17) and (23) and introducing transformation relations (20) and (21), we obtain the production equilibrium conditions:

(24a) $\quad \dfrac{dY/dL^Y}{dX/dL^X} = \dfrac{T_X}{T_Y} = \dfrac{dR^X/dX}{P^Y}$, and

(24b) $\quad \dfrac{dY}{dL^Y} = -\dfrac{T_L}{T_Y} = \dfrac{W}{P^Y}$

Note that (24a) differs from the left-hand side of (22a) in the replacement of P^X by dR^X/dX. Since $dR^X/dX < P^X$ under monopoly, $(dR^X/dX)/P^Y$ in (24a) is necessarily less than P^X/P^Y. Consumers meanwhile make the best of the price ratio P^X/P^Y. Equilibrium occurs in a mixed monopolistic and competitive economy where:

(25) $\quad \dfrac{T_X}{T_Y} = \dfrac{dR^X/dX}{P^Y} < \dfrac{P^X}{P^Y} = \dfrac{U_X}{U_Y}$

Clearly, condition (7a) necessary for a welfare maximum is violated. The slope of the social indifference curve attained when X is sold monopolistically and Y competitively exceeds the slope of the transformation curve—e.g., at a point like M in Figure 2A.1. Society ends up on the lower social indifference curve U_1, with relatively less X and relatively more Y produced than at the competitive and optimal equilibrium position C.

One way to try escaping this unhappy state of affairs is to enforce a "world of monopolies" solution, letting industry Y be monopolized too. Suppose that $dR^X/dX = kP^X$ in equilibrium, where $k = (1 - 1/\eta_X) < 1$ when η_X is the price elasticity of demand for good X.[2] If by chance (owing to identical equilibrium price elasticities) or coercion it is possible to make the marginal revenue dR^Y/dY to producers of Y equal kP^Y, equilibrium of the goods markets will occur with the following conditions:

$$(26) \quad \frac{dY/dL^Y}{dX/dL^X} = \frac{T_X}{T_Y} = \frac{dR^X/dX}{dR^Y/dY}$$

$$= \frac{kP^X}{kP^Y} = \frac{P^X}{P^Y} = \frac{U_X}{U_Y}$$

In this case welfare maximum condition (7a) is again satisfied. However, now problems arise in satisfying condition (7b). With production of Y monopolized, the profit-maximizing condition is $(dR^Y/dY)(dY/dL^Y) = W$. We assume as before that $dR^Y/dY = kP^Y$. Rearranging and using (20), we obtain:

$$(27) \quad \frac{dY}{dL^Y} = -\frac{T_L}{T_Y} = \frac{W}{kP^Y}$$

Clearly, $W/kP^Y > W/P^Y$. By (13b) consumers as labor suppliers react to their market environment by setting $-U_L/U_Y = W/P^Y$. Equilibrium occurs where:

$$(28) \quad -\frac{T_L}{T_Y} = \frac{W}{kP^Y} > \frac{W}{P^Y} = -\frac{U_L}{U_Y}$$

which fails to satisfy welfare maximum condition (7b). The ratio of the price of leisure to the price of good Y as perceived by consumers *qua* labor suppliers is lower than the ratio W/kP^Y guiding producer decisions. Unless the labor supply is perfectly inelastic (i.e., $U_L = -\infty$), equilibrium occurs with relatively more leisure and relatively fewer goods being consumed than under the set of choices that maximizes social welfare. In effect, the transformation curve tt' in Figure 2A.1 is shifted inward, though the goods market equilibrium continues to occur at a tangency point like

C. To restore the equality between T_L/T_Y and U_L/U_Y required by (7b), it would be necessary somehow either to reduce the wage producers perceive themselves to pay by the factor k or to increase the wage consumers as labor suppliers perceive themselves to receive by the factor $1/k$. Although this might conceivably be achieved through a system of subsidies, the scheme hardly seems practical.

The other leading alternative is to strive for a second-best optimum. There are various possible formulations. Here we present only the most general approach taken by Lipsey and Lancaster.[3] We assume that monopoly in the production of good X prevents society from satisfying welfare maximization conditions (7a) and/or (7b). To bar the attainment of a first-best world of monopolies solution there must also be some sector—i.e., the labor-leisure market—whose behavior cannot effectively be diverted from competitive rules. Thus, we begin with the assumption that it is impossible to bring the marginal rate of substitution between X and L into equality with their marginal rate of transformation. Concretely,

$$(29) \quad \frac{T_X}{T_L} = k\frac{U_X}{U_L}$$

where $k = (1 - 1/\eta_X) < 1$. This condition acts as a constraint upon society's ability to maximize its welfare. To secure a second-best optimum it is necessary to manipulate outputs and prices in controllable sectors—in this case, in sector Y only—so as to maximize $U(X,Y,L)$ subject to $T(X,Y,L) = 0$ and to (29) as a further constraint. We set up the Lagrangian function:

$$(30) \quad \text{Max } \Phi = U(X,Y,L) - \lambda[T(X,Y,L)]$$

$$- \phi\left[\frac{T_X}{T_L} - k\frac{U_X}{U_L}\right]$$

1. We ignore certain other conditions necessary for a welfare maximum—notably, the absence of corner equilibria in which none of some good is consumed or produced, and the satisfaction of various market-clearing equations. To derive a full set of sufficient conditions for a maximum would carry us beyond the objectives of this appendix.

2. A proof is given in note 78, Chapter 6, p. 187 *supra*.

3. R. G. Lipsey and Kelvin Lancaster, "The General Theory of Second Best," *Review of Economic Studies* 24, No. 1 (1956–57): 26–27.

The first-order conditions for a maximum include:

$$(31a) \quad \frac{\partial \Phi}{\partial X} = U_X - \lambda T_X - \phi \left[\frac{T_L T_{XX} - T_X T_{XL}}{(T_L)^2} \right.$$
$$\left. - k \frac{U_L U_{XX} - U_X U_{XL}}{(U_L)^2} \right] = 0$$

$$(31b) \quad \frac{\partial \Phi}{\partial Y} = U_Y - \lambda T_Y - \phi \left[\frac{T_L T_{XY} - T_X T_{YL}}{(T_L)^2} \right.$$
$$\left. - k \frac{U_L U_{XY} - U_X U_{YL}}{(U_L)^2} \right] = 0$$

$$(31c) \quad \frac{\partial \Phi}{\partial L} = U_L - \lambda T_L - \phi \left[\frac{T_L T_{XL} - T_X T_{LL}}{(T_L)^2} \right.$$
$$\left. - k \frac{U_L U_{XL} - U_X U_{LL}}{(U_L)^2} \right] = 0$$

Rearranging to a form comparable with (7a), this means that the behavior of firms producing Y must be altered so as to satisfy second-best equilibrium conditions like:

$$(32) \quad \frac{U_X}{U_Y} = \frac{p^X}{p^Y}$$

$$= \frac{T_X + \frac{\phi}{\lambda} \left[\frac{T_L T_{XX} - T_X T_{XL}}{(T_L)^2} - k \frac{U_L U_{XX} - U_X U_{XL}}{(U_L)^2} \right]}{T_Y + \frac{\phi}{\lambda} \left[\frac{T_L T_{XY} - T_X T_{YL}}{(T_L)^2} - k \frac{U_L U_{XY} - U_X U_{YL}}{(U_L)^2} \right]}$$

This, as the saying goes, plus a dollar will get you a ride on the New York subway. There is no way short of having detailed information on tastes and technology to evaluate the signs of such cross-partial derivatives as U_{XY} and T_{YL}; and even if the signs of all derivatives were known, the signs of the complete bracketed terms could be determined only if the exact magnitudes of all their components were ascertained.

One possible exception to this impasse was first suggested by Davis and Whinston.[4] If the welfare and transformation functions are *separable*, all cross-partial derivatives such as U_{XY} and T_{YL} equal zero. This occurs when a consumer's marginal utility from good X is unaffected by changes in the amount of good Y consumed, or when the marginal physical product in producing Y is unaffected by changes in the total amount of labor employed. If both the welfare and transformation functions are separable, then for a commodity whose production is susceptible to second-best manipulation, the bracketed expression in its first-order maximum condition (i.e., equation 31b) has a zero value, and first-best behavior rules may (ignoring certain numeraire problems) continue to be optimal.

Absent such separability, practical use of second-best conditions like (32) is barred by the virtual impossibility of observing and measuring derivatives of the transformation and (especially) utility functions. However, second-best problems can also be formulated in the framework of demand and cost function theory, with the analogues of the utility derivatives appearing as more operationally tractable income, own price, and cross price elasticities of compensated demand, and the transformation function analogues emerging as cost functions. This is the approach successfully pursued by Bergson,[5] among others. Because the mathematical derivations are even more complex than those presented here, we commend the interested reader to Bergson's article.

4. Otto A. Davis and Andrew B. Whinston, "Welfare Economics and the Theory of Second Best," *Review of Economic Studies* 33 (January 1965): 2–3.

5. Abram Bergson, "Optimal Pricing for a Public Enterprise," *Quarterly Journal of Economics* 86 (November 1972): 519–44.

Appendix to chapter 3

The purpose of this appendix is to explain some elementary concepts of regression and correlation analysis—tools used often by industrial organization economists. We do so through an extended analysis of actual industry data drawn from an article by Leonard W. Weiss.[1] He gathered statistics on profit returns after taxes as a percentage of stockholders' equity averaged over the years 1949–58 for 22 broadly defined manufacturing industry groups. The data are arrayed in column (2) of Table 3A.1. Note that profits range from a low of 5.9 percent in the textile products sector to a high of 16.1 percent in motor vehicles. The question is, Are there variables that help "explain" or "predict" the observed variations in industry profitability? And in particular, do market structure variables have such explanatory power? To find out, Weiss computed for each industry group weighted average four-firm seller concentration ratios adjusted for excessively broad or narrow industry definitions, shown in column (3) of Table 3A.1. Profitability here is the *dependent variable*, or the variable whose variation is to be explained. Seller concentration is an *independent variable* believed on the basis of industrial organization theory to influence profitability. The problem is to measure that influence and the influence of other independent variables such as the average annual output growth rates given in column (1). Let us, however, temporarily ignore the role of output growth and view the numbers in column (1) merely as means of tagging and keeping track of the various industry groups.

The simplest possible hypothesis about the influence of seller concentration (call it C4) on profitability (i.e., π) is that π varies positively in a linear or straight-line relationship with C4. That such a relationship exists is suggested by Figure 3A.1, which is called a scatter diagram. It plots as small circles the conjunction of π and C4 values for each industry group, with profitability measured on the vertical axis and seller concentration on the horizontal axis. Thus, the circle for the furniture industry (identified by the industry's Table 3A.1, column (1) value of 3.5 inscribed within the circle) is located vertically above the 17 percent concentration value and horizontally across from the 9.3 percent value on the profitability axis. Other industry groups' profit-concentration pair values are plotted similarly. We see at once that profits tend to rise with concentration. Assuming that the relationship is linear, an upward-sloping straight line has been drawn in Figure 3A.1 to characterize it.

That line is in a certain sense the straight line that best fits the observations on industry profitability and concentration. Specifically, the line, called a least squares regression line, has been fitted in such a way as to minimize the sum of squares of the vertical distances between each of the actual observations (i.e., circles) and the line.

1. Leonard W. Weiss, "Average Concentration Ratios and Industrial Performance," *Journal of Industrial Economics* 11 (July 1963): 233–54. The detailed data were kindly provided by Professor Weiss.

Industry	(1) 1947–59 growth rate (GR)	(2) Profit return (π)	(3) Seller concentration (C4)	(4) Profit deviations from mean	(5) Seller concentration deviations from mean
Food products	2.0	9.2	42	−1.53	−1.14
Tobacco products	1.6	9.8	68	−0.93	+24.86
Textile products	1.3	5.9	27	−4.83	−16.14
Apparel	2.8	6.2	14	−4.53	−29.14
Lumber and wood products	1.4	9.1	15	−1.63	−28.14
Furniture	3.5	9.3	17	−1.43	−26.14
Paper	3.8	11.2	37	+0.47	−6.14
Printing and publishing	2.8	10.5	22	−0.23	−21.14
Chemicals	5.6	13.1	51	+2.37	+7.86
Petroleum products	3.5	12.9	63	+2.17	+19.86
Rubber products	4.5	12.0	55	+1.27	+11.86
Leather products	1.3	6.6	29	−4.13	−14.14
Stone, clay, glass products	3.1	13.4	52	+2.67	+8.86
Primary iron and steel	0.7	10.4	60	−0.33	+16.86
Primary nonferrous metals	3.4	11.8	67	+1.07	+23.86
Fabricated metal products	2.4	10.4	38	−0.33	−5.14
Machinery	2.4	10.9	38	+0.17	−5.14
Electrical equip.	4.9	13.5	51	+2.77	+7.86
Motor vehicles	2.5	16.1	75	+5.37	+31.86
Other transportation equipment	7.3	12.6	50	+1.87	+6.86
Instruments	4.9	12.4	54	+1.67	+10.86
Miscellaneous manufacturing	2.1	8.8	24	−1.93	−19.14
Sum	67.8	236.1	949	+0.04	−0.08
Mean	3.08	10.73	43.14		
Sum of squares				136.07	7078.59
Sum of cross products					714.21

Consider again the furniture industry. The actual profit value is 9.3 percent. Reading vertically down to the regression line at the appropriate seller concentration level of 17 percent and then horizontally across to the vertical axis, one can by careful measurement ascertain that the linear ordinate value is 8.1. The line says in effect that an industry like furniture with a four-firm seller concentration ratio of 17 should on average have a profit return of 8.1 percent. But actually observed profits are 9.3 percent. There is a deviation, a prediction error. It is the actual profit value less the value predicted by the regression line for the observed concentration value, or

9.3 − 8.1 = +1.2. We square it and get $1.20^2 = 1.44$. The regression line is fitted mathematically so as to minimize the sum of all such squared prediction error values. This "least squares" line-fitting criterion is employed in part because of its mathematical convenience and sometimes also because squaring the prediction errors puts relatively heavy weight on the larger errors, which we may want especially to avoid.

Any straight line can be characterized by an equation of the form $Y = a + bX$, where a is the vertical intercept term and b is the slope. The least squares regression equation fitted to the data in Figure 3A.1 has the specific parameters:[2]

(6) Predicted profit	(7) Deviation from prediction
10.62	−1.42
13.24	−3.44
9.10	−3.20
7.79	−1.59
7.89	+1.21
8.10	+1.20
10.11	+1.09
8.60	+1.90
11.53	+1.57
12.74	+0.16
11.93	+0.07
9.31	−2.71
11.63	+1.77
12.43	−2.03
13.14	−1.34
10.21	+0.19
10.21	+0.69
11.53	+1.97
13.95	+2.15
11.43	+1.17
11.83	+0.57
8.80	0.00
236.12	−0.02
10.73	
	63.92

predictor of industry group profitability is this regression equation? There are two means of approaching such a question. One involves the notion of correlation. To understand it, let us begin by assuming we have no regression equation like (3A.1). In its absence, about the best global characterization we could make of profit tendencies would be to cite the *mean* or average level of profits—i.e., 10.73 percent, as found at the bottom of column (2) in Table 3A.1. This 'one parameter' characterization will be subject to errors, often substantial, for any specific industry group's case. We measure those errors by the sum of squares of deviations between *observed* and *mean* profits, i.e., by the sum of the squared values in column (4), or 136.07. Call this sum *SSDM*. Now, if our regression analysis is successful, we can do a better job of predicting profits, where "better" is taken to mean having a lower sum of squared deviations. Our predictor is the fitted regression equation. We plug into equation (3A.1) the observed values of seller concentration to calculate a predicted profit value. Thus, for the furniture industry group, our predictor is $6.38 + 0.1009 \times 17 = 8.1$, as before. These predicted values are given in column (6) of Table 3A.1. They deviate, sometimes appreciably, from the actual profit values. The deviations (i.e., of the actually observed profit values minus the predicted values) are given in column (7). We square them and take the sum of the squares, which we shall call *SSDR* (sum of squared deviations from regression). (It was this sum that was

$$(3A.1) \qquad \pi = 6.38 + 0.1009\ C4$$

where profitability π is said to be *regressed* on the seller concentration variable $C4$. The intercept value of 6.38 says that if one could properly extrapolate to a situation of zero concentration (e.g., approximated by wheat farming), the average level of profits is predicted to be 6.38 percent. The slope value of 0.1009 says that with each percentage point increase in the four-firm concentration ratio (the independent variable), profits rise on average by 0.1009 percentage points, or about a tenth of a point.

One might ask, How powerful and reliable a

2. There are simple computational methods for obtaining the numerical values. One means (though not the easiest for hand calculations) is to deduct from each industry observation the mean value for all industries. This is done in columns (4) and (5) of Table 3A.1. Call these values *the deviations*. The slope is then computed by the formula:

$$\text{Slope} = \frac{\text{Sum of } (\pi \text{ deviations} \times C4 \text{ deviations})}{\text{Sum of squared } C4 \text{ deviations}}$$

The term in the numerator of this expression is called the sum of cross products. Having calculated the slope, we then find the intercept by the formula *Intercept = Mean π − (Slope) × (Mean C4)*. For other problems, π here should be taken to represent the dependent variable and $C4$ the independent variable.

F 3A.1 Concentration-profits scatter diagram

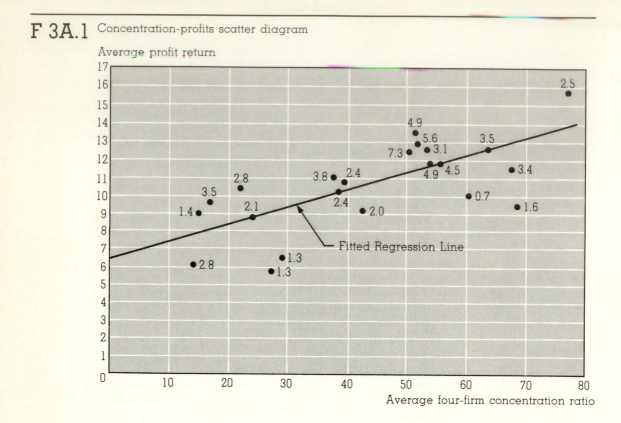

Average profit return

Average four-firm concentration ratio

Fitted Regression Line

minimized in fitting the regression equation.) The value of *SSDR*, we see at the bottom of column (7), is 63.92.[3] Again, this is a measure of prediction errors, or the variation in actual profitability values we have failed to predict or explain with regression equation (3A.1). But note that this *SSDR* value is a good deal less than the *SSDM* value obtained using only the mean of profits as a predictor. Specifically, using the mean, our *SSDM* is 136.07, whereas using equation (3A.1), *SSDR* is 63.92. We say then that through regression we have "explained" 136.07 − 63.92 = 72.15

F 3A.2 Perfect positive correlation

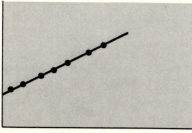

π

C4

F 3A.3 Negative correlation

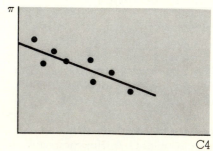

π

C4

of the *SSDM*, or $(72.15/136.07) \times 100 = 53.0$ percent of the *SSDM*. The latter value in ratio form (i.e., 0.530) is uniformly called r^2 (pronounced *r*-square), or in analyses with additional explanatory variables, R^2. Quite generally, $r^2 = (SSDM - SSDR)/SSDM$. It is, again, the fraction of the sum of squared deviations about the dependent variable's mean that no longer remains as prediction error when the regression equation is used in place of the mean as a predictor. The maximum possible value of r^2 is 1.0, which would result if all observed dependent variables exactly coincided with the regression line, so that there are no prediction errors at all, as shown in Figure 3A.2. The minimum possible value of r^2 is 0, which would occur if the observed values were in essentially random disarray so that the regression does no better in explaining the pattern (or lack of it) in the observations than does the mean profit value. Our computed r^2 value of 0.530 is intermediate between these extremes, indicating predictions that are far from perfect, but still fairly good by the standards of industry cross-section analysis.

This r^2 value is the square of the simple correlation coefficient r (sometimes called the bivariate correlation coefficient or the zero-order correlation). The unsquared correlation coefficient, which can also be calculated more directly,[4] can take on either positive or negative values ranging from $+1.0$ to -1.0. A negative correlation reveals that the variables under investigation vary inversely: as one increases, the other goes down, as shown in Figure 3A.3. The nearer the extremes of $+1.0$ or -1.0 the correlation coefficient comes, the stronger the correlation is said to be, which in turn reflects the preponderance of systematic (i.e., linear) relationships between the variables over unsystematic prediction errors.

Another approach to assessing the power and reliability of the relationships revealed by a regression equation is to test for the statistical significance of estimated values such as the slope coefficient. We have seen that the "fit" between equation (3A.1) and the actual profit and concentration data is not perfect; there are prediction errors. Those errors may have some important unascertained cause such as the neglect of other relevant explanatory variables; or they may

have occurred because there were genuinely random forces influencing actual profits, our measurement of profits, or the particular sample we drew. If indeed there were random influences, the scatter of points might conceivably have turned out differently, leading to a fitted regression line with either a steeper or less steep slope. We assess the degree to which some other value of the slope might have resulted by analyzing the magnitude of the observed prediction errors. This was the basis on which we computed r^2, but the same procedure can be extended to compute a variable reflecting the statistical reliability of a slope coefficient:

(3A.2)   Standard error of the slope $=$
$$\sqrt{\frac{SSDR/(N-2)}{\text{Sum of the squared C4 deviations}}}$$

which is $\sqrt{(63.92/20)/7078.59}$ in the example at hand. (In equation 3A.2, N is the number of observations—i.e., industry groups—in our sample.) What matters is the size of this parameter in relation to the size of the computed slope coefficient. From equation (3A.1), the slope coefficient is 0.1009; its standard error is 0.0213. Their ratio, called the *t*-ratio, is $0.1009/0.0213 = 4.74$. Thus, the slope is nearly five times as large as its standard error. This plus reference to standard statistical tables tells us that there is a very low probability—indeed, less than one chance in a thousand—that we would have observed such a sizeable positive association between profitability and seller concentration purely as a result of chance elements in sampling or measurement when in truth there was *no* systematic relationship (or a negative relationship) between the

---

3. If one does one's computations accurately, the sum of the unsquared deviations should be zero. Our computations are a bit off owing to rounding errors.

4. Specifically, the correlation coefficient is calculated by the formula:
$$r = \frac{\text{Sum of } (\pi \text{ deviations} \times \text{C4 deviations})}{\sqrt{(\text{sum of squared } \pi \text{ deviations}) \times (\text{sum of squared C4 deviations})}}$$
For π and C4, it is $714.21/\sqrt{136.07 \times 7078.59} = +0.728$, which is identical to $r^2 = \sqrt{.530} = 0.728$. The correlation coefficient always has the same sign as the regression coefficient.

two. In effect, the ratio of a slope coefficient to its standard error gives us information about the probability of wrongly inferring the existence of relationships that owe their appearance in data samples more to chance than to some link of genuine economic significance.[5] As a crude rule of thumb, economists conclude that observed relationships are "statistically significant" when a coefficient exceeds its standard error by two times or more. A t-ratio of 2.0 means that one can be 94 to 98 percent confident that a positive (or negative) regression slope coefficient is the result of something more than chance. The exact level of confidence depends upon the size of the sample and the nature of the behavioral hypothesis being tested.

With a relatively large t-ratio of 4.74, the slope coefficient in equation (3A.1) provides strong support for the hypothesis that high seller concentration leads to high profitability. However, equation (3A.1) is too simple to be a full representation of real-world structure-performance relationships. There are surely variables other than seller concentration that also influence profitability. How should they be taken into account? A common solution is *multiple regression analysis*—that is, statistical analysis in which there is not just one independent or explanatory variable, as in equation (3A.1), but multiple variables. Quite generally, where Y is the dependent variable to be explained and $X_1, X_2, \ldots, X_k$ are k different independent variables, linear multiple regression analysis computes explanatory equations of the form:

$$(3A.3) \quad Y = a + b_1 X_1 + b_2 X_2 + \cdots + b_k X_k$$

where the elements $b_1, b_2, \ldots, b_k$ are multiple regression coefficients analogous to the single slope coefficient b in equation (3A.1). Each reflects the influence on Y of the explanatory variable to which it relates, *given* the values of the other explanatory variables, or as we sometimes say, holding the values of the other explanatory variables constant.

To see this in terms of a concrete application, let us focus more closely now on the data in column (1) of Table 3A.1. These indicate the average annual percentage rate at which an industry's output grew between 1947 and 1959. It

might be argued (and indeed is in Chapter 9) that the more rapidly an industry is growing, the more likely it is that the industry is in disequilibrium, with investment not having caught up to demand and hence with profits at supranormal levels. A crude way to take into account the additional influence of growth on profits is to compute the average growth index values for the ten observations (i.e., circles) clearly *above* the regression line in Figure 3A.1 and compare it with the average for the seven observations clearly below the line. The averages are 3.73 and 1.87 respectively. Evidently, rapidly growing industry groups had profits higher than one would predict on the basis of seller concentration alone, while slowly growing industries had profits less than predicted.

A more general means of testing the growth hypothesis is to introduce the growth indices as a second explanatory variable and compute the multiple regression of profitability on both seller concentration and growth variables. When this is done, the resulting least squares regression equation is:

$$(3A.4) \quad \pi = 4.99 + 0.088\ C4 + 0.637\ GR;$$
$$ (.018) (.211)$$

$$R^2 = 0.682$$

Here 4.99 is the intercept value—now the profit level predicted when *both* seller concentration and growth are effectively zero. Profits rise by 0.088 percentage points for every percentage point increase in seller concentration and by 0.637 for every percentage point increase in the annual output growth rate. What has been fitted in equation (3A.4) is not an upward-sloping straight line, as in equation (3A.1), but a flat plane whose third dimension, output growth, can be visualized as perpendicular to the surface of Figure 3A.1. The plane slopes upward from left to right, reflecting the impact of seller concentration, and is elevated off the Figure 3A.1 surface more (reflecting high growth rates) at high levels of profitability than at low levels. Note now the value of R^2. It is conceptually identical to the r^2 value computed for simple equation (3A.1). It reveals the proportion of *SSDM* "explained" by the independent variables. But it is considerably higher than the r^2 of equation (3A.1)—0.682 vs. 0.530. This tells us that with two explanatory variables, we have been able to "explain" 15.2 percentage points more of the variation in industry profitability from its mean than with a concentration variable alone. Finally, note the values given in parentheses in equation (3A.4). These are the standard errors of the regression coefficients. Each regression coefficient has its own standard error. Both standard errors are less than a third of the coefficient values (i.e., the t-ratios are above 3.0), suggesting that concentration and output growth *each* have a statistically significant influence on profitability.

Although there are various limiting factors, it is often possible to compute multiple regression equations with numerous independent or explanatory variables, in which case one is fitting not a straight line or flat plane to the data, but a linear hyperplane. Here geometric intuition acquired in a three-dimensional world falters and algebra must take over. Nonlinearities, interactions among independent variables, multiequation relationships, and many other complications consistent with real-world complexities can also be taken into account. Space limitations and economists' union jurisdictional rules preclude a fuller treatment. The elementary concepts described here should be sufficient to understand most of the statistical results presented in this volume. We conclude therefore with a caveat. Multiple regression is a sharp, powerful tool. It is easy to hurt oneself playing with it carelessly or without sufficient knowledge of its intricacies. For those who wish to use it beyond merely fathoming the results of statistical research, solid training in econometrics is essential.

(5) It is important to recognize that high t-ratios do not necessarily mean one has found a relationship reflecting some genuine chain of causation running from X to Y. It is possible to have spurious correlation—e.g., because both X and Y are correlated with some third variable Z. Good theory and common sense are important to avoiding the inference of causation from high t-ratios or correlation coefficients when no such inference is truly warranted.

Law Case Index*

610

Author Index

Subject Index